*f*P

ALSO BY RANDALL B. WOODS

Vietnam and the American Political Tradition:
The Politics of Dissent (editor)

J. William Fulbright, Vietnam, and the Search
for a Cold War Foreign Policy

Fulbright: A Biography

The Dawning of the Cold War:
America's Quest for Order, 1945–1950

A Changing of the Guard:
Anglo-American Relations, 1941–1946

A Black Odyssey:
John Lewis Waller and the Promise
of American Life, 1878–1900

The Roosevelt Foreign Policy Establishment and the Good Neighbor:
Argentina and the U.S., 1941–1945

LBJ

ARCHITECT OF
AMERICAN AMBITION

Randall B. Woods

FREE PRESS

NEW YORK LONDON TORONTO SYDNEY

FREE PRESS
A Division of Simon & Schuster, Inc.
1230 Avenue of the Americas
New York, NY 10020

For information regarding special discounts for bulk purchases,
please contact Simon & Schuster Special Sales:
1-800-456-6798 or business@simonandschuster.com

Book design by Ellen R. Sasahara

Manufactured in the United States of America

1   3   5   7   9   10   8   6   4   2

Library of Congress Control Number: 2006041259

ISBN-13: 978-0-684-83458-0
ISBN-10: 0-684-83458-8

For Darcy, Cullen, Avery, and Abigail

CONTENTS

x

Contents

In those days John the Baptist appeared in the wilderness of Judea, proclaiming, "Repent, for the kingdom of heaven has come near." This is the one of whom the prophet Isaiah spoke when he said, "The voice of one crying out in the wilderness: 'Prepare the way of the Lord, make his paths straight.' " Now John wore clothing of camel's hair with a leather belt around his waist, and his food was locusts and wild honey.

MATTHEW 3:1–12

PROLOGUE

T HE TALL MAN WEARING THE STETSON SITTING IN the back of an open convertible was as unhappy as he had ever been in his life. Three years earlier, Lyndon Johnson had reluctantly agreed to serve as John F. Kennedy's running mate in the 1960 election. The Kennedys had not really wanted him, but the Democrats had to have Texas to win the presidency, and LBJ, the Lone Star State's most famous contemporary politician, could carry Texas. Johnson reasoned at the time that his position as majority leader would be meaningless if Richard Nixon and the Republicans won. The thirty-four months he had served as vice president had been excruciating. The "Irish Mafia" surrounding the president, and the liberal intellectuals that JFK had brought to Washington, snubbed Lyndon and Lady Bird at every opportunity. Portrayed as hayseed, a rube with coarse language and coarser looks, he was the constant butt of jokes on the Georgetown cocktail circuit and at Hickory Hill, Bobby and Ethel Kennedy's country home. The president had been outwardly respectful but had shunted LBJ aside to oversee the Space Program and the Committee on Equal Opportunity. As a consolation prize, the Johnsons had been sent on numerous overseas junkets where the vice president invariably responded to the warnings of pretentious U.S. diplomats by deliberately offending local customs. He had grown heavy, looked slovenly, and drank too much, Johnson thought ruefully. He was disgusted with his life and himself. Goddamn the Kennedys and goddamn his political luck!

Beside him in the car were his wife, Lady Bird, and the senior senator from Texas, Ralph Yarborough. Lady Bird was his only spouse but just one of a number of lovers. Throughout their marriage, she had simultaneously supported, reassured, and disappointed him. His volatility craved her stoicism, but at times it infuriated him.

Johnson and Yarborough shared similar values. Yet, LBJ thought, he could not look at the senior senator without a degree of unease. He was a liberal who had won in a state dominated by John Connally, the governor and conservative protégé of LBJ. Yarborough and Connally, like the two wings of the Democratic party in Texas, were continually at each other's throats, and the Kennedys were constantly after Johnson to clean up the mess. He had hoped that national office would free him from the prejudices and ignorance of the Texas oil and land barons, but it had not. Connally and Yarborough could both go to hell.

But then Johnson roused from his depressing reverie and looked up; it was a beautiful day, crisp and clear with the sun shining brightly out of the huge Texas sky. He noted with relief that the crowds lining the route being taken by the presidential motorcade were large and receptive. Dallas was a notorious hotbed of right-wing fanaticism. Lyndon and Lady Bird had been jostled, cursed, and spat upon by a hostile crowd outside the Adolphus Hotel during the 1960 campaign, a memory burned into their brains. But there were no signs of protesters. Perhaps the day would go well after all. There were already signs that Connally and Yarborough were, for appearances' sake, going to paper over their differences, at least for the time being.

With one hand holding his hat in the air and the other waving to the crowd, LBJ felt himself beginning to relax when he heard the crack of a rifle. Time stopped moving; the crowd seemed to hold its collective breath. Then another shot, and another. Rufus Youngblood, the Secret Service agent assigned to the Johnsons, was sitting in the front seat. He reached back with one arm and forced LBJ to the floor. As Lady Bird and Senator Yarborough ducked, Youngblood vaulted over the seat, covering the vice president's body with his. The Secret Service's radio crackled as snippets of information came over the air. By now it was clear to all concerned that they were in the midst of an assassination attempt.

As the motorcade raced off to Parkland Hospital, Johnson, weighed down by Youngblood's two hundred pounds, began to consider his situation. Before their departure for Texas, Washington had been full of rumors that JFK was going to drop him from the ticket. Now there was a possibility that he would become, temporarily at least, president of the United States. The sudden reversal of fortune, if it came, would be stunning. He was both exhilarated and apprehensive. Then his thoughts turned from the personal to the public. Johnson, who could become hysterical over life's most trivial disruptions but who was given to calm deliberation in a major crisis, began to compose his thoughts. The country, the world, must be reassured, no matter what the origins of the conspiracy against the president or how vast the scope. He let his mind wander briefly to possible perpetrators. The Russians? Unlikely. Since Khrushchev's ascension to power, the Soviet Union had acted more and more like a conventional, status quo power, Marxist rhetoric notwithstanding. Right-wing true believers? Possibly. But most likely it was Castro. Bobby had been trying to kill the Cuban leader ever since the Missile Crisis. Hopefully, the culprit was some deranged American acting alone. God forbid that it turn out to be a Negro and the motive racial. Whoever the shooter was and whatever forces were behind him, the deed was done. He must bind the Union and its people tightly together until the crisis eased.

At Parkland, Lyndon and Lady Bird were hustled into a brightly lit room, the windows covered with sheets. Would-be assassins must be denied a shot at the vice president. The emergency room at the hospital seemed a maze of self-contained compartments, one housing Secret Service personnel, another the Dallas police, and others various medical teams, grieving Kennedy aides, and members of the Johnson entourage. While Lyndon conferred with Youngblood and his colleagues, Lady Bird went to console Jacqueline Kennedy and Nellie Connally, whose husband had also been shot.

Finally, LBJ was informed that Kennedy was dead. Lyndon Johnson was president of the United States. He was tempted to give in to the awe of the moment, but he resisted. Every second was crucial. The way he handled the assassination and its aftermath would do much to determine his success or failure as president, Johnson sensed. It was decided that he and his staff would return on Air Force One rather than Air Force Two because of the former's superior communication equipment. During the ensuing mad dash to Dallas Love Field, LBJ informed Kennedy aide Kenneth O'Donnell that he was not leaving without Jackie and the president's body. They had come together, and they would return together.

Aboard Air Force One, while Johnson gathered his aides and the Kennedy people waited in shock for the presidential coffin to arrive, LBJ decided for symbolic reasons to be sworn in as president. The country was subsequently treated to the famous picture of LBJ, hand on Bible, standing before Judge Sarah T. Hughes, flanked by Lady Bird and Jackie, her green suit still splattered with her husband's blood. During the flight back, LBJ holed up in the state room, leaving Jackie the bedroom and personal quarters. From the front of the plane, LBJ could hear O'Donnell and his comrades, who were drinking steadily and growing more boisterous in the process. The new president knew that they were talking about him and what they were saying, how unfit he was to follow their fallen hero, how the trip to Texas would have been unnecessary if he had done his job, how difficult it was going to be to stomach his coarseness after JFK's elegant grace. He was tempted to get rid of the whole lot, cabinet and all, but he quickly rejected the idea. Unlike duly elected presidents, he would not have the time intervening between election and inauguration to vet and choose members of his government. Though Johnson knew that he could not trust most of the Kennedy team and that many of them would actively conspire against him, he would have to rely on them—at least for a time.

The accidental president's mind drifted to his past, to the Hill Country, his mother and father, his choice of politics as a life. She had played the role of genteel, literate Baptist, he of a carousing populist politician. A respect, almost adulation, for public service had been one of the few things that had bound Rebekah and Sam Ealy Johnson together. Both looked to their eldest son to fulfill their unrealized dreams. His father had lived to see him elected to Congress, his mother to see him chosen Senate majority leader. Now he was leader of the free world. Perhaps now their ambition for him would be sated.

Air Force One landed at Andrews Air Force Base. Bobby Kennedy boarded the plane, brushing past the Johnsons without acknowledgment, rushing to join

Jackie and the coffin containing his brother's body. The Kennedys deplaned first and then, separately, Johnson and his aides. LBJ spoke a few words to the small crowd that had gathered in the rain and darkness. Accompanied by National Security Adviser McGeorge Bundy and Secretary of Defense Robert McNamara, LBJ flew by marine helicopter to the White House. After greeting those of the staff who were on hand and receiving selected congressional leaders, the new chief executive departed for The Elms, the modest estate he and Lady Bird had chosen as their vice presidential residence. Selected friends and staff were there. So was daughter Lucy, who was then attending high school in Washington. Lynda, the Johnsons' older daughter, was a student at the University of Texas in Austin. There was supper and conversation. LBJ watched television footage of the assassination until he could stand it no longer. He went to bed. With aide Horace Busby and his wife holding his hands, he drifted off to sleep.

The next two days were filled with funeral preparations and meetings with cabinet members. LBJ at first intended to leave the investigation of the assassination to the Texas attorney general's office but was then persuaded to constitute a national commission; the stakes were too high to leave the matter to state authorities. In the midst of the national outpouring of grief that accompanied JFK's murder, Johnson realized that he would be spending the rest of his days as president living and acting in the shadow of a martyr. He could either be overwhelmed by Kennedy's death, or he could use it to advance his personal and political agenda.

Elected repeatedly from a state dominated by conservatives, LBJ had dreamed liberal dreams. So closely had he aligned himself with FDR that, during the late 1940s, some New Dealers had looked to him as Roosevelt's natural successor. But his Texas origins, his need to trim his sails before the winds generated by the oil and gas lobby, and his provincial image had seemed to doom whatever chances he had to become president and bring the New Deal–Fair Deal to fruition. But now, having acceded to the highest office in the land, perhaps Johnson could use the Kennedy mystique to realize the social justice agenda of Medicare, federal aid to education, environmental protection, immigration reform, an end to poverty, and equal rights for all.

In the days that followed, LBJ stayed up night after night at The Elms filling one legal pad after another with ideas for legislation that would comfort the afflicted and reassure the comfortable. Above all, he aspired to redeem the white South by shaming it into granting black Americans equal rights and equal opportunity. The shadow of Vietnam was barely visible, a mere spot on the horizon.

CHAPTER I

ROOTS

TEXAS AND LYNDON JOHNSON ARE INSEPARABLE. Both have been caricatured beyond recognition by historians. Texas stereotypes are legion, yet absurd for such a vast land, comprising 266,807 square miles, one-twelfth of the land area of the United States. One can travel eight hundred miles in a straight line without ever leaving the state. Texas is so diverse that it is the only member of the Union with a constitutional provision allowing it to divide into as many as five states (with, of course, the permission of the federal government). East Texas, with its coastal plain, piney woods, temperate climate, and high rainfall, is physically and culturally a westward extension of Louisiana. The north-central portion of the state, featuring rolling hills and numerous rivers, resembles Oklahoma and Kansas. The western portion of the state includes the Llano Estacado, or Staked Plain, a grassy, treeless, semiarid extension of the High Plains that rises to the Davis Mountains. South-central Texas is dominated by the Edwards Plateau, an area of low, angular hills, narrow valleys and thin, rocky soil, the eastern portion of which is known as the Hill Country.

The people of the Lone Star State are as diverse and unpredictable as its topography and climate. There are cowboys and Indians. There are also African Americans, Hispanics, Czechs, Jews, Chinese, Poles, Bohemians, Germans, Japanese, Italians, Moravians, and French Creoles, all of whom have interbred if not intermarried. Most famously, Texans are oilmen, cattle ranchers, farmers, and agribusinessmen. But they are also intellectuals, artists, social activists, scientists, and communitarians. The state boasts culturally active population centers that predate the founding of Jamestown. Texas is the birthplace of the Farmers' Alliance and for a time, at the turn of the nineteenth century, host to a vigorous Socialist Party. Its people have embraced religion, but generally on Sunday and less frequently on Wednesday. God is to be worshipped but not nec-

5

essarily strictly emulated. Texas is a land with a violent hand and an empathetic heart. Politically, the state is famed for its pragmatism and lack of ideology; this is true not because of too few values and ideas, however, but too many.

In its relationship with the federal government, Texas exhibited, in its first years as a state, attitudes that would prevail for the next hundred years. Much like the stereotypical welfare cheat that Texans would rail against in the mid-twentieth century, the Lone Star State looked to the federal government to provide largesse without expecting to exert any authority or control in return. Texans were states righters to the core. The Anglo-Celts who had migrated from Appalachia and Missouri had in some ways never left the eighteenth century behind. For them the Union was an association of sovereign states. The national authority existed to shoulder the burden of tasks the states could not or would not take on for themselves—defend the Texas frontier against the twenty thousand hostile Amerindians who continually threatened it, for example. When Washington failed to live up to its perceived responsibilities, Texans developed and nurtured a burning resentment against it and its denizens.

In many ways, mid-nineteenth-century Texans were an anomaly. For those yeomen not defeated by the frontier, literacy was an obsession, the most important badge of civilization. When two or three gathered together, they invariably pooled their resources to start a community school, one-roomed enterprises that taught the equivalent of the first eight grades. Approximately 95 percent of the white population could read and write. In 1859 Baylor University, a Baptist institution, granted twenty-two bachelor degrees. In that year, Texas boasted forty academies, thirty-seven colleges, including Blum's College for Males and Females, twenty-seven institutes, seven universities, two seminaries, and one medical college—some of these institutions more loosely defined than others. In 1860, there were seventy-one newspapers being published in Texas with a total circulation of about one hundred thousand. Politics, local and national, was a Texan preoccupation. Even on the frontier, families followed with great interest the impending crisis that would eventually split the union. The cultural and educational mother lode in virtually every region was the King James Version of the English Bible. It was not only the guide to Christian worship but also the principal work of literature. Texans learned of good and evil, power and corruption, hope and salvation from the Bible, absorbing a bit of Greek philosophy and Jewish mysticism along the way. The God of the Old Testament threatened the wayward with eternal damnation while the God of the New Testament promised them salvation. Not surprisingly, churches were even more important than schools to the communal life of the yeoman farmer. Their social significance was as great as their religious. Members congregated to worship, converse, eat, and court. Because there was little else to compete for the farmers' attention, the churches, increasingly evangelical in nature, played a huge role in shaping value systems. They augmented already strong tendencies toward fundamentalism, temperance, and social democracy.

The true planter aristocracy in Texas was numerically minuscule, no more than two thousand families. To qualify one had to possess enough chattel to employ an overseer. Freed from the restraints of labor, the planting class dabbled in politics, worshipped their Episcopalian God, raced horses, fought duels, gambled, drank, and tolerated lesser mortals. The planter was gracious, hospitable, charitable, and decent, rather than puritanically moral. The slave aristocracy was accorded deference in Texas, but it was grudging, and though politically influential, it was not the force it was in Mississippi or South Carolina. Slaves were relatively well treated, not because planters and their overseers were kindhearted; rather, they were practical men who refused to damage a prized commodity except under the most extreme circumstances. Ironically, but not atypically, this class would lead the way in Texas in opposing secession.

But Texas did secede—states rights was better than federal submission—and suffered the fate of the other members of the Confederacy. What happened after the Civil War did much to revive Texas's dominant political culture. Reconstruction and all things associated with it—blacks, federal troops, carpetbaggers, and scalawags—were reviled. The denouement of Reconstruction in Texas came in 1874, when Richard Coke and a band of ecstatic Democrats seized control of the political machinery. A new constitution virtually emasculated central authority in the state. The terms of state officers, including the governor, were set at two years. With virtually all state offices elective, the governor was no more than a peer among equals. At the polls, conservative Republicans deserted en masse to the Democrats. In this one-party atmosphere, virtually devoid of ideology, politics consisted of a continual grab for power. Participation in the rebellion became an enduring status symbol. The Texas Rangers were resurrected, and a Frontier Battalion organized. Between 1874 and 1880, the Rangers policed the Indian and Mexican frontiers, earning their reputation as fearless, ruthless, and sometimes lawless restorers and maintainers of order.

The order that the Rangers compelled made possible the coming of the Cattle Kingdom, the Anglo-Celt's economic and cultural response to the Great Plains. The cattle ranchers and drovers were in reality small businessmen who turned their enterprise into a legend. The Texas cowhand was neither northern nor southern, and cowherding was in many ways the first economic and cultural step reuniting North and South following the Civil War. The longhorn frontier, with its reverence for the horse and rifle, its buckskin, bunkhouses, dusters, and ten-gallon hats, bred certain characteristics. The cattle culture called for Darwinian efficiency. There was no room for waste, for mistakes, for wishful thinking. Those who prayed for rain rather than anticipating drought failed. Those who wished for peace and trusted Indians and Mexicans lost their cattle, if not their lives. Ideas and notions were valid in the West only if they worked. Natives, like wolves and bobcats, were beasts to be kept at bay or exterminated. Brave and generous to their fellows, residents of the cattle frontier were contemptuous of those who could not stand alone. Next to cattle thieving, the worst crime on the frontier was ineptitude. The cattle culture was the purview of the young because the old could not go west and survive. Women suffered disproportionately. Love and romance took a backseat to sexual gratification and utility in relations between the sexes. Frontier wives were immensely respected, if not understood; prostitutes and dancehall girls were valued, if not respected. In this male-dominated culture, reverence for fair play and for the principle of equality of opportunity took precedence over complicated legal codes imported from the East. Until the turn of the century, the penalty for killing another individual in a fair fight was less than that imposed for burglary, if any sentence was imposed at all.

The land into which Lyndon Johnson's immediate ancestors came marked an intersection between the farming and cattle frontiers. The Hill Country of Texas lies along the eastern edge of the Edwards Plateau as it begins its ascent to the great Staked Plain. The first settlers found a land of big sky, abundant sunlight, violent storms, flash floods, and bone-chilling northers. The soil was generally thin, covering the limestone base rock that extended westward to constitute the foundation of the Edwards Plateau. The richest land was to be found in the river bottoms, in this case, the Pedernales and Blanco, western tributaries of the Colorado that paralleled each other. The landscape was gently rolling, covered by live oak, mesquite, and cedar, punctuated by picturesque limestone springs.

The first white men to take up permanent residence in the Hill Country were German immigrants. In late 1845 Henry Fisher and Burchard Miller sold their original land grant of some 3 million acres obtained from the Spanish to a group of German noblemen who hoped to extend the fatherland to Texas. The first German settlers arrived at Galveston, and after some indecision settled in New Braunfels. Following completion of the Fisher-Miller deal, John Meusbach led a wagon train of 120 families and established the community of Fredericksburg thirty miles northwest of New Braunfels on Barron's Creek. Eclipsing the weather as a threat to the newcomers were the Comanche. Having mastered the horses first imported by the Spanish, these Native Americans, guided by the light of the moon, rode two hundred miles or more across New Mexico and West Texas to kill, kidnap, steal, and burn and then backtrack across the plains at breakneck speed. Eventually, Meusbach concluded his famous treaty with the Comanche, and the Germans lived in relative peace with that people, if not the Lipan Apache, thereafter. In 1848 German settlers organized Gillespie County with Fredericksburg as its county seat. The booming village then boasted more than a dozen commercial structures, including the Nimitz Hotel. Shortly after the Germans came to the Hill Country, other frontier farmers began building dog-run cabins along the picturesque Blanco River, whose valley was rich with fish and game.[1] The Pittsburgh Land Company, owned by Captain James Callahan and John D. Pitts, established a small community, and in 1858 Blanco County was organized. It was at this point that the Johnsons arrived on the scene.[2]

Lyndon's great-great-grandfather, John Johnson, was an Anglo-Celt immigrant whose parents settled in colonial Georgia. A veteran of the Revolutionary

War, John was a successful farmer and the owner of two slaves.[3] His fourth son, Jesse, Lyndon's great-grandfather, was one of those frontier farmers who stayed ahead of the expanding plantation system and behind the Indian-fighting frontier. The year Texas became a state, Jesse gathered up his slaves, eight of his ten children, his wife, and four grandchildren, and in covered wagons made the nine hundred–mile trek from Alabama to Lockhart, some twenty-five miles south of Austin.[4] It turned out to be an economic mistake. Despite the fertility of the black, waxy soil, Jesse Johnson did not prosper. At his death in 1857, his estate was in arrears.

Thus, Jesse's sons, Andrew Jackson (Jack) Johnson, Jesse Thomas (Tom) Johnson, and Samuel Ealy Johnson (Sam), Lyndon's grandfather, had to start virtually from scratch.[5] In 1859, attracted by the endless acres of shimmering prairie grass, Jack settled on the north bank of the Pedernales River, some twelve miles north of Blanco. He built a double-room, dog-run cabin and began raising sheep, horses, and cattle. Shortly thereafter, Tom and Sam followed. They constructed a rock cabin and pens and began gathering cattle in anticipation of a profitable drive north to Sedalia or Abilene. The Civil War intervened, however. Sam, the youngest, enlisted in the Confederate Army, Company B, DeBray's regiment, in the fall of 1861. Tom would later join the Texas State Troops headquartered at Blanco, but he spent most of the war with his brother Jack raising stock for sale to the Confederacy.[6]

When Union occupying forces landed at Galveston, Sam Johnson returned to the Hill Country, but he found it difficult to leave the Civil War behind. German Unionists living between New Braunfels and Fredericksburg had been hunted and harassed throughout the war. Some fifty were hanged by Confederate state militia in Gillespie County alone.[7] During Reconstruction, the limestone hills witnessed numerous armed clashes between loyalists and warriors of the Lost Cause. "Bushwacking" became a common occurrence.[8]

The Johnson brothers had better things to do. Between 1867 and 1870, Tom and Sam made four six hundred–mile trips along the Chisholm Trail to Kansas. By 1871, they headed the largest cattle operation in Blanco County, their corrals occupying several dozen acres. In 1870 alone, Tom and Sam drove seven thousand head north, grossing nearly $100,000.[9] "I got my best experience," reported one drover, "joining the 'roundup' for Sam and Thomas Johnson . . . with headquarter pens and branding stall at the mouth of Williamson's Creek in Blanco County and headquarters at Johnson's ranch on the Pedernales . . . The roundup of range hands and range boss usually gathered, road branded and delivered a herd of from 2,500 to 3,000 head of cattle, which a trail boss and his outfit received at headquarters ranch, but sometimes we delivered them at the Seven Live Oaks on the prairie west of Austin."[10] The drives were long and arduous, featuring blistering heat, violent thunderstorms, dangerous river crossings, frigid northers, and occasional raids by hostile Indians.[11]

The Johnson brothers were one of the best-known outfits in Kansas. "I am in

Johnson's camp now, out at the cattle pens," Horace Hall wrote his father in November 1871. "The boys have sold all of their cattle and tomorrow they will commence 'outfitting' and then go to Texas." The following spring Hall reported, "We have been gathering cattle for the past month and now they have two herds about ready to start . . . This is a beautiful country through here: mountains, clear rocky streams, live oaks, mesquite with rich valley and bottom lands for farming . . . abundance of game & Indians once a year." [12]

In December 1867 Sam Johnson married Eliza Bunton. Sam and Eliza set up housekeeping in the cabin that the Johnson brothers had occupied as bachelors. Eliza was one of those Texas women who fought the frontier and won. With the black hair, black eyes, and ivory skin of her father, she cut a striking figure. Intensely proud of her family's accomplishments, Eliza held up her ancestors, Joseph Bunton, a Revolutionary war hero, and Joseph Desha, who had served in Congress and as governor of Kentucky, as examples to her children. [13] In the early years, she accompanied Sam and Tom on their drives up the Chisholm Trail. After children came, she lived the more conventional and, in some ways, harder life of the frontier wife, toiling over a wood fire, hauling water, sewing, nurturing, and persevering. [14] One of the characteristics that Sam and Eliza shared, according to those who knew them, was their patrician bearing. "He was an aristocrat . . . Just natural," recalled Ida Felsted, who knew the Johnsons as a child. [15] Patricians or not, the couple could not escape the dangers of the frontier. Well into the 1870s, Sam, Eliza, and their neighbors had to deal with the marauding Lipan Apache and renegade Comanche.

In the summer of 1869, Tom and Eliza Phelps of Blanco County were cut off by a band of Comanche while fishing in a creek near their house. Both were stabbed, bludgeoned, stripped, and scalped. Both died of their wounds. Sam joined the party of armed men organized to hunt down the Indians and avenge the Phelpses' murder. Some of the war party doubled back, however, and Eliza Johnson and her infant daughter, Mary, were nearly caught at their well. Alerted by the war whoops, Eliza, with baby in arms, ran to the house. For hours the two hid in a space under the cabin, she stifling Mary's cries with a dirty rag, while the Comanche ransacked the house. Eventually, the Indians rounded up their booty, including horses, and rode off. Eliza dared not move until, hours later, she heard her husband's voice as he searched through the remains of their possessions. [16] In 1872, a force of Rangers met and defeated a band of Comanche at Deer Creek. Several of the wounded Texans were carried to the Johnson ranch for medical attention. It would be the last pitched battle between Indians and whites that the Hill Country witnessed.

The cattle business was boom or bust. From 1867 through 1871, Tom and Sam Johnson flourished. Flush with the profits from their drives, they bought thousands of acres in Blanco and Gillespie Counties, plus property in Austin. In late 1871, together with sixteen cowboys, the brothers drove several thousand head north to Kansas, only to find that the bottom had dropped out of the cattle market. Hoping that prices would rise, the Johnsons wintered their herd on the plains. Many of the animals froze to death, prices refused to rise, and upon their return to Texas, Sam and Tom had to sell much of their property to pay their debts.[17] The following year brought no relief. They drove smaller herds to market but found prices still depressed. A Comanche raid cost the brothers their remuda of horses and broke them. County tax rolls showed Tom worth a mere $180 in 1873; Sam was not listed at all. In 1872 Sam, Eliza, and their children decided to abandon the frontier and, with her father's help, bought a farm near Buda, a community southeast of Austin. Tom Johnson died in 1877.[18]

Sam Johnson could never reconcile himself to the flat land and tame existence that he found in east-central Texas. He and Eliza owned an eight hundred–acre spread but cultivated only a hundred. What income the family had—there were six children by 1880—came from the sale of a few bushels of wheat and a bale or so of cotton each year. The Johnsons lived off the pigs, goats, chickens, and milk cows that populated their barnyard and the vegetables they could grow. They were certainly no worse off than any of their neighbors, however. The Panic of 1873 had plunged the entire country into a depression from which it took more than a decade to recover. Sam longed to return to his "mountains," however, and in 1882 persuaded Eliza to allow him to sell their most elegant possession, a silver-mounted carriage with matched horses, to purchase a 950-acre spread on the Pedernales near Stonewall in Gillespie County. It was only twelve miles from the old Johnson ranch that by then had become the site of the tiny community of Johnson City. Tom and Sam's spread had been bought by James Polk (Jim) Johnson, a nephew who had emigrated from Alabama. In 1889, Sam, Eliza, and eight of their nine children left Buda and returned to the Hill Country.[19]

Life on the Pedernales was more picturesque, perhaps, than life near Buda, but it differed little in substance. The Johnson property was beautiful. The grassy acres studded with live oaks and pecan groves sloped down to the limestone-bedded river. Like their neighbors, Sam and Eliza lived as subsistence farmers, raising wheat, some cotton, and living off their livestock and vegetables. By selling some of their land, the Johnsons were able to raise enough money to build a house, barn, smokehouse, and corral. Their home was a typical dog-run cabin with precarious porch in front and lean-to in back. Barbed wire fencing kept the chickens and children from wandering too far. The Johnsons refused to be impoverished by their lack of material wealth. Both read as widely as the availability of books allowed them, and Sam followed politics and civic events, for which he had a passion, in the newspaper. Avid conversationalists, Sam and Eliza raised their children to be aware of the world around them and not to live on received wisdom. After a traveling Christadelphian minister won an all-day debate with the local Baptist minister on the meaning of the Bible, Sam converted.

Christadelphianism seemed a strange choice for Sam Johnson. The Christadelphians (Greek for "brethren of God") were a small Christian sect introduced into America in 1848 by an English physician named John Thomas. It was both democratic and judgmental. All brethren were equal in the sight of God. Institutional structure was weak to nonexistent; worship services, when they were held, were lay-initiated and -dominated. Smoking, drinking, and dancing were discouraged. Converts were required to study the New Testament and pass a test before being baptized by immersion. "Basic to Christadelphian social teaching and practice is the exhortation to be separate from the world, to love not the world nor the things which are in the world," writes one of the sect's historians.[20] The brethren had little faith in political or legislative prescriptions for society's ills because both were the work of men and not God.[21] They studied politics and civic life intensely, however, in search of signs of the coming Millennium.

Sam Johnson was by all accounts a friendly, gregarious man who enjoyed conversation and the company of his fellow human beings. He had been in battle, endured the dangers of the cattle drive, and prowled the streets of Abilene—hardly a Puritan. The Christadelphian sect had originated among the working poor of London, who were attracted by Christ's promise that the last shall be first and the first last. Sam embraced Christadelphianism during the Populist revolt, attracted, no doubt, by its emphasis on brotherhood and social justice. He was also taken by the emphasis on the relationship of salvation to service to one's fellow man, to the Christadelphians' contempt for the institutional church, and by its near mystical reverence for nature.[22] Because of his interest in politics, Sam Johnson chose to serve his Maker by running for public office.

Sam and Eliza may have struggled, but they did not, like so many other southern and midwestern farmers, lose their property during the prolonged agricultural depression that marred the last decades of the nineteenth century. The late 1880s and early 1890s saw falling grain and cotton prices and an epidemic of farm mortgage foreclosures. The principal problem facing American agriculturalists was overproduction, but as rugged individualists, they resisted the notion of involuntary or even voluntary limits on the amount and kinds of crops they raised. Increasingly, farmers blamed their woes on the railroads, grain warehousers, meatpackers, and the refusal of the federal government to inflate the currency. In 1877 in Lampasas, Texas, a group of farm activists created the Texas Farmers' Alliance, which in turn formed cooperatives and pushed for state regulation of rail rates. The agricultural revolt produced a panoply of colorful grassroots politicians, "Sockless" Jerry Simpson, for example, and Mary E. Lease, who urged Kansas farmers to "raise more hell and less corn." Harried and harassed, farmers decided that there was no option but establishment of a third national political party. In 1891, Texans formed a state People's Party, which the following year became part of a national Populist Party. Among other things, the Populists advocated government ownership of the railroads and telephone and telegraph lines and government control of the financial system. In the fall of 1892, Sam Ealy Johnson Sr. offered himself as the Populist candidate for Blanco and Gillespie County's seat in the state legislature. His Democratic opponent, bizarrely, was his son-in-law, Clarence Martin. Indeed, Clarence and his wife,

Frank Johnson Martin, lived in a house not five hundred yards west of Sam and Eliza. Clarence Martin and Sam Johnson frequently rode in the same buggy to address political gatherings at Blanco City and in the rural pecan groves that dotted the countryside. After calling each other a wild-eyed radical and a soulless reactionary, the two would remount their buggy and head for home or the next meeting. Sam warned the voters that if something was not done about the moneylenders and middlemen who were sucking the farmers dry, there would be civil war. "Cleveland [Democratic President Grover, who favored hard money and the status quo] ought to be hung," he told his neighbors. The Populist candidates made a respectable showing, but that was all. The Democratic party had moved leftward just far enough, embracing government regulation of rails and trusts, to co-opt the political middle. Sam lost to Clarence two to one, but he hardly overestimated the passions aroused by the Populist moment. "Clarence Martin defeated his father-in-law," the *Dallas Morning News* reported, "but suffered a serious stab wound at a public speaking at Twin Sisters, Blanco County."[23]

Of Sam and Eliza's nine children, the first four were girls. Sam loved them all but longed for a son, resenting the nickname, "Gal Johnson," that some of his friends gave him. So frustrated was he that he named his second daughter, Clarence Martin's future wife, Frank. Thus was the birth of Sam Ealy Jr. on October 11, 1877, an occasion of great joy in the Johnson household.

Little Sammie's parents doted on him. Eliza insisted that his ivory skin and black curls linked him most strongly with the Buntons, and she constantly regaled her son with the exploits and achievements of the Buntons and Deshas. Sam Jr. was his father's son, however; he dressed like him, walked and talked like him. He accompanied his father on some of his speaking trips when the latter ran for state legislature. A relatively unattractive youth, with huge ears and lips so thin as to be nonexistent, Little Sam was possessed of a dominating personality. Intense, active, ambitious, and gregarious, he made an impression on those he encountered. And he was self-made. According to some accounts, his parents were so poor, Sam Jr. had to pay his own way through public school in Johnson City. (In those virtually taxless days, public schools charged tuition.) The younger Johnson borrowed his father's wagon for a time, slaughtered three steers his father had given him, and sold beef and soup bones in and around Stonewall. When the Johnson City barber retired, Sam bought his chair and tools, and after practicing on friends, began giving haircuts on Saturdays and after school.[24]

The strain of having to grow up too young soon took its toll; Sam Jr. was felled with an attack of nervous stomach and forced to drop out of high school. His mother sent him to recuperate with her younger brother, Lucius Desha Bunton, and his family, who lived on a ranch near Marfa. His stay with his uncle, together with years of labor on his parents' hardscrabble farm on the Pedernales, convinced Sam that there was a better way to live one's life than being a tiller of the soil or raiser of livestock.[25]

Physically rejuvenated by his months in west Texas, Sam returned to Johnson City determined to be a teacher. He had not completed high school however, and even if he had, there was no money for him to attend one of Texas's new teachers colleges. In that day, however, degrees were not required to teach; one merely had to pass an exam. He borrowed the books necessary to prepare and moved in with his grandmother, Jane Bunton, herself a former schoolteacher. Living primarily on antacids and dried fruit, Sam crammed. He not only passed the Texas state teacher's exam, but earned perfect scores on the Texas and American history tests. His first assignment was in 1896 at the White Oak School near Sandy, a one-room institution featuring grades one through eight. Some of the students, Sam recalled, were older and larger than he. Sam Johnson was then nineteen. Like most teachers in Texas, he was forced to live with a family in the community. It was a life of isolation, poverty, and hard work. The winter term following found him at Hye, a German hamlet just a few miles from Stonewall. There he made the acquaintance of a fellow boarder, Captain Rufus Perry, a famous Indian fighter whose tales of derring-do made a lasting impression. Disgusted and disillusioned, Sam finished his teaching career in the spring of 1898 in a school near Rocky.[26]

Ready for a fresh start, Sam Ealy Johnson Jr. made arrangements to lease a portion of his father's farm. He moved into the first house Sam Sr. and Eliza had built on the property when they moved from Buda in 1889. His parents lived several hundred yards to the west, and beyond them was Clarence and Frank Martin's house. For farmers, the years 1898 to 1906 were relatively prosperous, with commodity prices rising at home and abroad. Sam Jr. managed to live the life of gentleman farmer, working his place with hired hands. According to contemporaries, he could often be seen in Johnson City dressed in a suit and polished boots and riding a groomed horse. The very idea of bib overalls was anathema. He never changed from his "money spending into money making clothes," as Ida Felton put it.[27] Simple though his cabin was, it became something of a salon for those interested in politics and public affairs. His best friends, according to future wife Rebekah, were "W. C. Linden and Dayton Moses, lawyers of statewide repute; and Kay Alexander, teacher and engineer."[28]

Influenced, no doubt, by Linden, Moses, and his brother-in-law, Clarence Martin, who would become a district court judge for Gillespie County, Sam Jr. was strongly drawn to a career in the law. He decided, however, to delay law school and run for local office and was elected justice of the peace in 1902. The office was not the most challenging. "In those days they had dance halls in Stonewall and Albert and elsewhere," according to Otto Lindig. "And if there wasn't two or three fights in the dance hall that night, why the people didn't enjoy themselves . . . They went to the Justice of the Peace and filed a complaint. Then the other man had to pay a fine."[29] Two years later, Martin persuaded Sam to stand for the seat in the state legislature that he had held. According to tradition, the position was rotated among the four counties in the district; in 1904 it was Gillespie's turn. Sam campaigned on a platform that straddled the positions of his father and his brother-in-law. His speeches were somewhat apocalyptic, insisting that the very future of the republic depended on the struggle then being waged between the people and monopolistic corporations. When he got down to specifics, he hardly proved a socialist, however, favoring regulation of the railroads, taxation of the insurance industry and utilities, and a franchise tax on corporations. It was pure Theodore Roosevelt. Somewhat to Sam's surprise, he won.

In Austin, Johnson soon earned a reputation for diligence and astuteness. In addition to regulation and taxation measures, he supported an eight-hour day for rail workers, a pure food bill, and state regulation of lobbyists. Most of these measures failed, but his Hill Country constituents, many of them former Populists, applauded their representative's stands. Sam was at his best working the corridors of power behind the scenes, trading votes on bread-and-butter issues that would benefit the residents of Gillespie and Blanco counties in an immediate and material way. In 1906 the twenty-nine-year-old politician challenged the rotation tradition and was elected to a second consecutive term. Both the *Blanco News* and the *San Antonio Express* supported him. That same year, financial disaster struck when the bottom fell out of the cotton market, and Sam was nearly wiped out. "My daddy went busted waiting for cotton to go up to twenty-one cents a pound and the market fell apart when it hit twenty," Lyndon later recalled.[30] His pay as legislator was $3.00 a day for the regular session and $5 for special sessions.[31] Aware of his neighbor's plight, Rob Crider, who operated a grocery store near Hye, persuaded the stubbornly proud Sam to accept a $300 loan. His constituents deserved to have their man go to Austin "in style," Crider remarked.[32] At times, Sam had to borrow gas money to make the trip back and forth to Austin.

Still, vulnerable as he was, Sam Ealy Johnson remained notoriously independent. The legislature was dominated by lobbyists who brazenly bought and sold votes and entertained lavishly. The young man from the Hill Country was not a Puritan; he was no stranger to Austin's saloons and brothels. He simply hated to be beholden. He "will bear gentle reproof, but will kick like a mule at any attempted domination," the house chaplain remarked of Sam.[33]

In 1906 a young reporter from the *Blanco News* interviewed Representative Sam Johnson in Austin. She was Rebekah Baines, the daughter of Joseph Baines, the man Sam had replaced in the legislature, and the future mother of Lyndon Johnson. The interview did not go well. Rebekah remembered being "awfully provoked" with the outspoken young lawmaker.[34] Sam was taken with the young woman, with her interest in politics, and particularly with her education and family credentials. Indeed, Rebekah Baines was as proud of her ancestry as Eliza Bunton was of hers. Her forefathers had trekked to America in the eighteenth century from Scotland and her great-grandfather was something of a legend. Born in North Carolina in 1809, George W. Baines Sr. moved with his family first to Georgia, and then to Alabama, where he earned a B.A. from the state college at Tuscaloosa. After being ordained a Baptist minister, G. W. Baines served a stint in the Alabama legislature, but in 1850 he migrated to Texas, settling near Huntsville. His flock eventually included Sam Houston, who, out of gratitude for his conversion, loaned Reverend Baines $300 to help with his ministry.[35] A rising star in the Baptist State Convention, Baines was elected president of Baylor University in 1861.[36]

Joseph Wilson Baines, the Baineses' third son and father of Rebekah, was born in Louisiana in 1846 and moved with his family to Texas in 1850. Joe Baines attended Baylor and served two years in the Confederate Army. Following Appomattox, he taught for a brief period, found it as impoverishing as did Sam Johnson Jr., but unlike him proceeded with the study of the law. Joe subsequently passed the state bar exam and joined the firm of Throckmorton and Brown in McKinney, Texas. Young Baines prospered, practicing law and editing the *McKinney Advocate,* an influential Democratic newspaper. After campaigning hard for Governor John "Oxcart John" Ireland, Joe was appointed secretary of state, serving from 1883 to 1887. While teaching at Rowlett, he had married fifteen-year-old Ruth Huffman, one of his students. Ruth's mother was a struggling widow with several children; despite her daughter's tender years, she agreed to the union with the young Baptist teacher. The marriage lasted forty years.[37]

Rebekah was born in Austin in 1881, twelve years into her parents' marriage. In 1887, Joe Baines moved his family to the town of Blanco. For the next fifteen years he practiced law, served as an elder in the Baptist church, and accumulated a minor fortune in real estate. He somehow found time to serve a term in the state legislature. Rebekah remembered growing up in Blanco as idyllic. "I love to think of our home, a two-story rock house with a fruitful orchard of perfectly spaced trees, terraced flower beds, broad walks, purple plumed wisteria climbing to the roof, fragrant honeysuckle at the dining room window whose broad sills were seats for us children," she later wrote of her youth.[38] The house was filled with books and music, the hallmarks of an educated Baptist family. "At an incredibly early age, my father taught me to read," she later recalled. "He taught me how to study, to think and to endure, the principles of mathematics, the beauty of simple things."[39] Rebekah loved Browning and Tennyson and, in fact, spent much of her imagining life in the world of the British romantics. Josepha Saunders, Rebekah's sister, remembered, "I had such a happy childhood. Rode horseback, and went swimmin', and . . . rode calves—everything else that was lots of fun. But now, sister never did that. She was more of a lady . . . I've seen her standin' at the window, at the kitchen window, washing dishes, with the book up in the window."[40] The center of the girl's life, apparently, was her father, "the dominant force in my life as well as my adored parent, reverenced mentor, and most interesting companion."[41] "Most interesting companion" is an unusual term to use for a father when in one's adolescence, but it seems to have been the truth. Wilton Woods remembered that Joe Baines had run for Congress and lost. Rebekah was devastated, unable to understand why voters had not turned out overwhelmingly for her father. According to Woods, however, "He seldom got out of the house . . . kind of a recluse . . . a very intelligent person and a most, most religious person."[42] There was no doubt about Joe Baines's piety. "We had such a wonderful Christian home," Josepha said.[43] Not priggish, however. The girls were allowed to attend dances, a somewhat unusual departure for a turn-of-the-century Baptist family. But Joe abhorred alcohol and instilled that dislike into Rebekah.[44] Not only was alcohol "an abomination to the Lord," its use by an individual was an indication of his lack of discipline and general worthlessness. The father and his adoring daughter prized order, predictability. "He taught me obedience and self-control," Rebekah recalled, "saying that without them no one is worthy of responsibility or trust."[45]

Like Sam Johnson Sr. and Sam Johnson Jr., Joe Baines crashed on the rocks of market fortunes. In 1903 he went broke, victimized by falling cotton prices and a real estate deal gone bad. It was a humiliating experience for a proud family. Rebekah, who was at the time attending Baylor, had to take a job in the bookstore to enable her to finish, and her brother, Huffman, had to drop out of the agricultural college to return home and help support his family. Or so Rebekah claimed. The record indicates that cotton prices fluctuated during this period, but not abnormally. More likely, health or personal scandal were responsible for the turmoil in the Baineses' family. Joseph Wilson Baines moved his family to Fredericksburg, designed and built a modest house, was elected to the legislature, and made a desultory effort to practice law. Nothing seemed to lift his spirits, however; he fell ill and died a lingering death in 1906. Rebekah, meanwhile, had finished college and moved to Fredericksburg to rejoin her family. She taught elocution and wrote columns for several area newspapers.[46] Her father's death bore hard on her. "This was the first great sorrow of my life and it required all my determination and strength of will to adjust myself to life without my father."[47] She was being somewhat melodramatic. In fact, Joe Baines had quickly rebuilt his fortune; his decline was physical and mental, not economic. At the time she met Sam Ealy Johnson Jr., Rebekah was a self-confident, relatively affluent young woman in the unusual position of being free to choose marriage or a professional career.[48] It was at this point that Rebekah began her courtship with Sam Ealy Johnson Jr.

During 1906 Sam Johnson made the seventeen-mile, three-hour horseback trip from Stonewall to Fredericksburg as frequently as he could. The couple was particularly drawn to political gatherings. Sam's coup was a date to hear the famed William Jennings Bryan address the state legislature. Both were entranced by the great orator.[49] When Sam proposed, Rebekah hesitated; the young politician could be rough and aggressive; he lacked formal education and was sometimes drawn to the wrong crowd. But he was dynamic and ambitious; he was also a Christian, having taken up his father's Christadelphianism. Sam, she believed, had the makings of her sainted father in him; under her influence, he would continue to grow. The picture she conjured in her mind that persuaded her to accept marriage was compelling, "a personable young man, slender and graceful, immaculately groomed, agreeable and affable in manner and with great personal magnetism."[50] Moreover, at age twenty-five, Rebekah believed this might be her last, best chance. The couple married on August 20, 1907. Both would live to regret the decision.

There was no money for a honeymoon. The newlyweds made the trip from Fredericksburg to Stonewall and immediately settled in Sam's house, the now somewhat improved cabin he had grown up in.[51] There were two bedrooms, each twelve feet square, with one a living room–bedroom and the other a bedroom opening to the kitchen–dining room in the rear. The Johnson cabin still boasted a rambling front porch covered by a slanting roof, with another porch and lean-to in the rear. The house was guarded in front by a barbed wire fence with a gate and in the rear by a rail fence. There was no yard to speak of, but from the front porch a grassy slope, dotted with oak and pecan trees, unfolded across two hundred yards to the Pedernales. To the rear of the house were cistern, pump, outhouse, smokehouse, and barn. The farm consisted of approximately five hundred acres, one hundred in cultivation and four hundred in pasture to support fifty or so head of cattle. According to Rebekah, the first year was trying in the extreme. "I was confronted not only by the problem of adjustment to a completely opposite personality, but alas to a strange and new way of life," the new bride later wrote. "I shuddered over chickens and wrestled with a mammoth iron stove." Thus began Rebekah Baines Johnson's existence as a self-appointed martyr.

Life on the Johnson ranch was tough. Rebekah's husband was in Austin part of the year. Her brother, Huffman, temporarily jobless, helped out for most of 1907. "They were busy on the farm and needed help . . . milking, feeding, hoeing, plowing, cutting wood," he later explained. "We, like all farmers, were up early but late in getting the farm work done."[52] But what did Rebekah expect? After a year's courtship, certainly she had visited the farm and Sam's house. She had seen the rudimentary kitchen, the constant stream of chores. Perhaps in her imagination, her most frequent abode, others always took responsibility for life's more mundane matters. During those early years she struggled with work—and with Sam. "She'd hear Sam coming home," a girl who worked for them at the time remembered. "Her face would light up like a little kid's, and out she'd go flying down to the gate to meet him."[53] But Sam Ealy Johnson Jr. was not a particularly easy man to love. Not unkind, just emotionally calloused. He liked to drink with his brother-in-law and his lawyer pals. "His idea of pleasure was to sit up half the night with his friends, drinking beer, telling stories, and playing dominoes," Lyndon later told historian Doris Kearns Goodwin.[54] He loved to dance, and she did not despite her parent's tolerance of the practice. "I don't think Rebekah ever went to a dance," Otto Lindig recalled.[55] Sam however, was dynamic, public-spirited, and Rebekah's contact with the fascinating world of politics. Like her, Sam's sense of family and its importance was intense.[56]

The Hill Country was a hardscrabble existence, but the world was changing.

A new century had begun, a progressive, activist, president sat in the White House, and a newly wed couple in central Texas believed that they could make a difference.

For Sam Ealy Johnson Jr., 1907–1908 were the most eventful years of his young political life. When Rebekah interviewed Sam in 1906, she had asked him his opinion of Texas's charismatic, corrupt senator, Joseph W. Bailey, and he had pleased her by saying that he disliked and distrusted him. The Seventeenth Amendment providing for the direct election of senators not yet being in effect, the Texas legislature had elected Bailey, a long-time congressman, to a term in the Senate. He had campaigned as a champion of the common man against Wall Street, the railroads, and the trusts, but rumors began to drift back from Washington that Bailey was on the take from the very interests he had promised to police. The senator was a man of powerful personality, dramatically attired in black frock coat and black slouch hat, skilled at the histrionics that turn-of-the-century politicians so dearly loved. With Bailey up for reelection in 1907, the Texas legislature was forced to confront the charges concerning his misconduct. The oil and lumber interests that the senator had so dutifully represented and Bailey himself descended on Austin to lobby on his behalf. Sam Johnson was one of those called to the great man's hotel room, but despite the pressure, he remained noncommittal.[57] The house voted to conduct an official investigation but refused to put off the senatorial election. Bailey won a second term by a vote of eighty-nine to thirty-six. Seven members were listed as present but not voting, one of them was Sam Johnson. "It is a well known fact," he explained, "that I have been for a full investigation of his conduct, and it would not be consistent for me to vote for him at this time."[58] It was a courageous act. Following his victory, Bailey promised to bury his enemies "face down so that the harder they scratch to get out, the deeper they will go toward their eternal resting place."[59]

CHAPTER 2

GROWING UP

L YNDON WAS BORN ON AUGUST 27, 1908, A YEAR AND A week after Sam and Rebekah had spoken their wedding vows. The night Rebekah went into labor was stormy. It had rained all day, and the Pedernales was out of its banks. Fortunately, Sam was home. The nearest doctor was some twenty miles away. As soon as Rebekah's contractions began, Sam sent for him, but she declared that the baby would not wait. The family decided that Sam Sr. should fetch the nearest midwife. He forded the Pedernales at a point several hundred yards upstream from his house and brought Mrs. Christian Lindig, a neighbor and experienced midwife, to Rebekah.[1] The young mother's imagination and displaced ambition would turn the birth of her firstborn into a near mystical experience: "Now the light came in from the east, bringing a deep stillness, a stillness so profound and so pervasive that it seemed as if the earth itself were listening . . . And then there came a sharp compelling cry."[2] Thus did Rebekah Johnson give birth that day to both a man-child and a messiah complex.

The original birth document listed the child simply as "un-named Johnson." Sam and Rebekah had not settled on a name and were not able to do so for weeks thereafter. It was the custom in the Johnson household for Sam to rise first, dress, build a fire, and warm the house before Rebekah got up to cook breakfast. One morning two months or so after the baby's birth, Sam got up, tended to his chores, and pronounced the room warm. Rebekah rebelled: "Sam, I'm not getting up to cook breakfast until this baby is named. He is nearly three months old . . . I've submitted all the names I know and you always turn them down." Taken aback, Sam thought while he laced up his boots. He suggested Clarence for his brother-in-law and Dayton for his longtime friend. She rejected both. Finally they settled on Linden (for W. C. Linden), with the stipulation that Rebekah could spell it Lyndon. Thereupon she rose and made the brown biscuits that were Sam's favorite.[3] "The reason Mother didn't want him named Clarence, didn't want him named Dayton, didn't want him named after Judge Linden," Sam Houston, Lyndon's brother, recalled, was that "they were all three judges, and district attorneys, you know, and famous people, but they all drank."[4]

Lyndon Baines Johnson was immediately and forever his parents' favorite. His cousin Ava remembered him as a beautiful little boy with flashing brown eyes and golden curls, even if his ears were a bit prominent.[5] In the spring of 1909, Sam and Rebekah took him to a community picnic. According to his mother, Lyndon smiled and reached for every adult admirer. "Eddie Hahn . . . a leading citizen of the community exclaimed: 'Sam, you've got a politician there. I've never afore seen such a friendly baby,' " a family member remembered.[6] Lyndon's mother showered attention on him. Before he was two, he learned the alphabet from ABC blocks. At three, he could recite not only Mother Goose rhymes but snippets of poems by Tennyson, Longfellow, and others of his mother's favorites. "I'll never forget how much my mother loved me when I recited those poems," he told an interviewer. "The minute I finished she'd take me in her arms and hug me so hard I sometimes thought I'd be strangled to death."[7] Sam was no less attentive. He would give words for Lyndon to spell from Noah Webster's speller; by four the child had acquired a small reading vocabulary. As he got older, Rebekah read him history and Bible stories. Reminding her that he was his father's child, too, he always wanted to know if the stories were true.[8]

Lyndon's grandfather's house was just several hundred yards away, and the boy frequently listened to him tell tales of cattle drives and Indian skirmishes. As with all children there was mischief. "Lyndon and I was tired of riding that old puller mare," Ava Johnson, a cousin, told an interviewer, "and we were going to get her fattened up and both of us took one of Aunt Rebekah's wash tubs and we filled it full of oats . . . and pulled it out of that big barn out there . . . under the shed where old Coofy [the mare] was, and fed her that tub full of oats. Well we had a dead horse the next morning."[9]

Grandmother Baines spent long stretches with the family and made most of their clothes on a treadle sewing machine. There was a party telephone line to Johnson City that Rebekah could use to order dry goods and staples from the general store, including, on one memorable occasion, a brand-new Garland stove. One of the men in the family would pick up orders in town, or occasionally a wagon would deliver. Ava Johnson remembered a Jewish peddler coming through the Stonewall area periodically. He would trade his finished goods for butter, vegetables, and meat. "I can well remember . . . the very same peddler . . . came by, stopped at Uncle Sam's and sold them a pair of shoes for Lyndon. We went down and we had to compare shoes. Mine was black patent leather with a little red top. His was plain black. And Lord he thought those shoes of mine were the prettiest things, so we swapped shoes. When we got to the house, and Aunt Rebekah saw that—she just had a fit."[10]

There were Fourth of July and Christmas celebrations at Uncle Clarence and Aunt Frank's larger house further up river.[11] The Lutheran church, situated across the Pedernales from the Johnson spread, was the center of life in Stonewall. "They had church in the mornings, on Sundays," Byron Crider, a Johnson City resident, recalled, "and then they had dinner on the ground, and they'd bring their own food . . . and we'd all eat. Then the men would get out and they'd have shootin' matches and play horseshoes and washers. That evening, they'd bust out the keg beer . . . and they had a German band. The women would sit around on the benches, around the edge of the dance hall and the men would go up and ask 'em to dance."[12] One of Lyndon's prize possessions was a stereopticon, an early version of the Viewmaster. He would sit for hours exploring the wider world by holding the black instrument and its slides up to the light.[13]

From the beginning, Lyndon and Rebekah Johnson formed a special relationship, according to both, one of mutual dependency that to a degree shut out Sam Ealy. LBJ recalled that his first memory of his mother was dramatic. "I was three or four years old," he told writer Ronnie Dugger. "She was crying, it was nine or ten o'clock. Now father was a cotton buyer. He had to stay at the gin till twelve or one at night till the cotton was ginned. She was frightened, afraid. I told her I'd protect her. I remember standing there by the well."[14] In later years Rebekah recalled to Virginia Durr that her eldest son constantly dreamed of rescuing her. "You know, I'm always so embarrassed and ashamed about my hands," she confided. "Where we lived at down in the country when I was young, I had to do so much hard work, and my hands never recovered. Even as a little boy Lyndon used to say to me, 'Oh, Mama, when I get big I'm going to see that you don't have to do any of this hard work so you can have pretty white hands.' "[15] He later told an interviewer, "She never wanted me to be alone . . . She kept me constantly amused. I remember playing games with her that only the two of us could play. And she always let me win even if to do so we had to change the rules. I knew how much she needed me . . . I liked that . . . It made me feel big and important."[16]

But the greatest source of Lyndon's security was also the greatest source of his insecurity. If Rebekah became displeased with her son, if he disappointed her, she refused to touch him, talk to him, to acknowledge his existence. When he was seven or eight and the family had moved to Johnson City, Rebekah arranged dance and then violin lessons for her son. He eventually abandoned both, the violin after only eight months. "For days after I quit those lessons," Lyndon remembered, "she walked around the house pretending I was dead. And then to make it worse, I had to watch her being especially warm and nice to my father and sisters."[17] Who had the upper hand in the relationship was a matter of debate. According to Wilton Woods, it was mother: "She recognized early that he had more than an average share of brains, energy, and she wanted to keep control and she did it very cleverly. He almost concealed nothing from her, and I do mean nothing."[18] Sam Houston Johnson disagreed. "They say . . . Lyndon was a mama's boy, but I don't think that's so," he observed. "More often than not our mother was doing Lyndon's bidding, rather than the other way around."[19]

Other children soon followed Lyndon, Rebekah Luruth in 1910 and Josefa Hermine in 1912. The apple of his parents' eyes was not pleased. At four he began running away. "He wanted attention," observed Jesse Lambert, the family maid at the time. "He would run away, and run away, and the minute his mother's back was turned he would run away again, and it was all to get attention."[20] Lyndon's escapades kept the family in turmoil. Rebekah feared he would fall into the river and drown or be bitten by one of the numerous Hill Country rattlesnakes. She had a toddler and a baby and couldn't leave the house. Sam or a hired hand would search during one of Lyndon's disappearing acts while she stood anxiously on the porch with babe in arms. Sometimes the runaway could be found hanging around Junction School, the community one-room facility adjacent to the Johnson property. Ava Johnson and her sister Margaret were already there and frequently encouraged Lyndon.[21] After repeatedly punishing her son, Rebekah decided to make a virtue out of a vice. She and the teacher at Junction School, Miss Katie Deadrich, agreed to petition the school's trustees to admit Lyndon even though he was not yet five. When they concurred, he began accompanying Ava and Margaret to school—this time with his parents' approval.

Junction School and its solitary teacher were typical of rural Hill Country, Texas. The one-room structure on the banks of the Pedernales housed the first eight grades and counted thirty-five students. At first, Miss Katie couldn't understand the strapping four-year-old—"We had the Texas mingle accent, and I think he was more on the rolling of his r's and things like that that made him an exception"—but with a little coaching from "Miss Rebekah," Lyndon soon proved comprehensible. Junction's youngest student invariably showed up in costume: cowboy outfit complete with his father's Stetson and a toy gun or the classic Buster Brown uniform. He never strayed far from his teacher's side, frequently clinging to her skirts. When it was time for his work, that is, for him to recite his lesson, Lyndon would "come up . . . stand here but he wouldn't say a word until I took him on my lap . . . he had to sit on my lap . . . he would show the other kids what he could do."[22]

Rebekah Johnson was not one to suffer in silence. She did not like life on the farm and made no bones about it. If the truth be known, Sam Ealy wasn't all that fond of it either. Whenever possible, he left the heavy work to hired hands.[23] In September 1913, when Lyndon was five, Sam moved his family fourteen miles east to Johnson City. The term "city" was a misnomer. Lyndon's new home was a community of 323 souls living on ten north-south numbered streets and eight east-west lettered avenues. To Stella Glidden, who moved from Fredericksburg, "a town where you could almost eat off the streets," Johnson City was a wasteland. "I thought I had come to the end of the world," she recalled.[24] There were no paved streets, electric lights, or indoor toilets. Only two houses had bathtubs and running water.[25] The roads connecting Johnson City to Austin, fifty miles to the east, and Fredericksburg, thirty miles to the west, were dusty and potted in the dry season and nearly impassable quagmires during wet spells.[26] But compared to Stonewall, Johnson City was a thriving metropolis.

Sam bought Rebekah one of the finest houses in town, a six-room double-ell frame structure with flowerbeds and a white picket fence. Newcomers to the town quickly became aware of a friendly populace and an intense sense of community. "I wondered just why people would like a town like Johnson City, but it wasn't long before I, too, liked it, because I found the people so warm and so friendly," remembered Glidden. "It seemed after a period of about three months that I had lived in this little town all my life."[27] There were three churches: Methodist, Baptist, and Christian. None had a permanent pastor, and the members of all three attended the Sunday services of the church that happened to have clergy visiting that day. The frequent tent revivals attracted virtually everybody in town. These week-long affairs featured two services daily. Children would go swimming in the river after the last service, and then everyone would settle in for an evening picnic. "One thing about it is the cooperative spirit of the town—it was all one, you couldn't tell one from the other," Mamie Klett, a classmate of Lyndon's, remembered. "Everybody cooperated and they had what they called Union Revivals, all the churches got in together and that happened each summer."[28] "In those days," Otto Lindig said, "when a house was built all the neighbors helped. Maybe they had one carpenter, but all the neighbors helped . . . If one man worked two days and another man worked only half a day, they forgot about it."[29]

There were dance halls in neighboring German communities like Hye. "Everybody went to the dance, mothers, daddies, kids, and the babies would be put in the back on a pallet, and they danced till 4 o'clock in the morning," remembered Gene Waugh, a local merchant.[30]

Freight was brought in from Austin, first by mule team or horse-drawn wagon, and then by truck. In the summer, families imported ice in two to three hundred–pound blocks from the state capital for their sawdust-lined iceboxes.[31] At the center of the town's life was the school. Germans had always valued education; Fredericksburg, Blanco, and Johnson City were exemplary in this regard. During the first quarter of the twentieth century, central Texas furnished the state with a disproportionate number of public school teachers.[32] Johnson City's institution of learning was a two-story, six-room structure that employed six teachers. Elementary classes were held in the three rooms downstairs; two of the upstairs rooms housed secondary students. The middle room featured a stage, and the classroom walls could be folded back to convert the upper floor into a theater-auditorium. Here the students and community members gathered for plays, declamations, interscholastic league contests, and commencements.[33]

In Johnson City, Rebekah began leading what basically was a double life. First there was Rebekah the delicate, reclusive, martyr. She would later portray herself as the oppressed sophisticate, exiled to a rural hell, washing, drawing water, cooking, scrubbing the floors virtually alone while her husband rambled. Her health did suffer. The births of Sam Houston in 1914 and Lucia Huffman in 1916 were difficult and required long periods of convalescence. Two minor operations in 1917 added to her problems. Some neighbors did recall her as sickly and somewhat of a recluse during this period. She even failed to show up regularly for church. Sam hired maids, took in poverty-stricken girls in return for their keeping house, and induced relatives to come and help out. When there was no one to do the cleaning, the chores backed up. The children remembered the sink piled high with dirty dishes for days on end. At times, the Johnson brood ran wild. Rebekah depended on Sam to administer discipline. When he was gone, which was frequently, she would sometimes call on the neighbors to give spankings.[34]

Then there was Rebekah the cultural and literary doyen of Johnson City. "The fellow that mowed my lawn up there . . . his mother used to do all the washing and ironing for my mama," Sam Houston recalled. "I never saw mama do any washing nor ironing in my life that I know of. Now, Grandmother made the kids [clothes], sewed and that, but Mother had an extremely wonderful education."[35] Indeed she did, and she was not going to let anyone forget it. Sam Johnson's bride was a stubborn woman, determined to live the life she had imagined for herself. She struggled to maintain the trappings of genteel society the best she could under the circumstances. To those few neighbors who dropped by she served tea in paper shell china cups, always on a tablecloth, never on oilskin. "I was determined to overcome circumstances instead of letting them overwhelm me," she later recalled.[36] But Rebekah Johnson was no shrinking violet, no delicate flower. "His mother was actually hard," George Reedy, an LBJ aide, later recalled. "She was awfully hard."[37] She was by training and avocation a teacher, a journalist, and an aspiring intellectual. "She had aristocratic manners and bearing and had been an elocution teacher . . . in her younger years," said Fritz Koeniger.[38] Lyndon remembered his mother's bed always piled high with books. To appease his wife, Sam bought her a Victrola, and then the local weekly newspaper, the *Record-Courier,* which she edited for a year. Rebekah also served as Hill Country correspondent for the *Dallas Morning News,* the *Austin American-Statesman,* and the *San Antonio Express,* signing her columns RBJ. Sam Houston remembered clipping the columns for his mother, who had to send them in to the home newspaper to receive payment.

Sam Johnson was one of the first men in Johnson City to own an automobile, a Ford Model T. He subsequently bought Rebekah a Hudson, in which she was chauffeured by Guy Arrington, the typesetter at her newspaper.[39] Rebekah Luruth remembered that her father didn't want her mother to learn how to drive. She badgered Arrington to teach her until he was forced to confess that Sam had made him promise not to.[40]

By the time Lyndon was ten, Rebekah's health had recovered somewhat, and she began to take an intense interest in community education and culture, offering elocution lessons to children who would come to the house after school. "She was quiet, soft-spoken, and quite a lady," recalled Kitty Clyde Leonard, another of Lyndon's classmates. "She helped the youngsters with all of their schoolwork and interscholastic league. She helped Lyndon with debate."[41] After her oldest son reached high school, Rebekah worked with the teachers to put on plays, including the traditional senior play. She would select a script, hold auditions for parts, drill the young actors and actresses, and generally supervise the production. The commuity paid a nominal sum to see *Wild Oats Boy, Jethro's Daughter,* and *Diamond in the Rough.*[42]

There were things that Sam and Rebekah agreed on. Johnson City may have been a small pond, but the Sam Johnsons were going to be among the biggest fish in it. Even more than money, education was the badge of rural aristocracy. Truman Fawcett, who owned the drug store, denied that the Johnsons were poor. "I mean they were poor, but everyone was poor," he observed. "We were all poor but not poverty stricken. But some families had more culture and more education than others, you know. Even my father's family had some college education and other families did, too. They were poor, but they had what their standard of culture called for."[43] The Johnsons were educated, and they had the first bathtub in town. "They were the equivalent of the banker's family," Charles Boatner, a family friend, recalled, "the first family of Johnson City. They were the ones who got all the way to Austin and saw the world, and consequently they were the style setters."[44] Both Sam and Rebekah were determined that their children be seen as educated, cultured—witness Lyndon's abortive dance and violin lessons. For Rebekah, the emphasis was on literature and history. "She'd just sit up in bed and read all day and all night, and try to make everybody else read all day and all night," Lyndon told Isabelle Shelton. "Largely she was a great Browning woman, a great Tennyson woman, and she liked biographies because all the children liked biographies . . . and didn't make any difference whether it was about [Texas governor] Jim Hogg . . . or Andrew Jackson, [or] Abraham Lincoln."[45]

Sam's focus was on current events and politics. "He was a fella that thought that a child should read—read the newspaper—keep up with the current events," cousin Ava Johnson remembered. "He would drill you on what was really happening." On one occasion Sam asked her what the Socialist Party was. When she replied that she did not know, he gave her a copy of the *Pathfinder* magazine with an article on Eugene V. Debs, a past and future presidential candidate. "Sure enough, the next evenin' he asked." As a teacher, Sam was as impatient as Rebekah was patient. "If he asked you what 7 x 9 was—you didn't say 7 x 9? You said 63—by the time he got it out of his mouth—or you went to the end of the class. It was almost a disgrace to be at the end of the class."[46] The entire family dressed well. "The first time I ever saw Lyndon," recalled Stella Johnson Luxcon, "he was in Wither's store down here about four years old. He had on a little white linen suit."[47] The legislator–real estate dealer and his journalist-teacher wife also shared an extreme competitiveness. There was Sam's famous early morning instruction to Lyndon: "Get up, Lyndon, every boy in town already has a thirty-minute head start on you."[48] As a coach of boys and girls participating in interscholastic league events, Rebekah was legendarily tough. "She taught me speech for the county meet, and I won my little school," Lyndon said. "[I] had a little playmate that went to another school . . . he was the son of a Lutheran minister, and he had quite a brogue . . . he spoke German . . . I felt so sorry for him because you could hardly understand him." Lyndon persuaded Rebekah to give the child elocution lessons. On the day of the county contest, the boys rode with Rebekah together in the same car. Lo and behold, the judges turned out to be German and were engaged rather than offended by the playmate's accent. He defeated Lyndon. Rebekah cried all the way home in anger and frustration.[49]

Both Rebekah and Sam believed in the God of the New Testament. She was a Baptist, but a particular sort of southern Baptist. She and her father embraced science, education, and the arts. Both were committed to the Social Gospel. They might have been paternalistic, but they were a far cry from the Reverend J. Frank Norris of Fort Worth, who preached hell and damnation, led the anti-evolution crusade, and conducted a reign of terror against science teachers at Baylor.[50] From Christadelphianism, Sam had taken its emphasis on equality, compassion, and community spirit. He was also attracted by its anti-institutionalism. "Dr. Shelton of Dripping Springs . . . he was the legislator of Hays County while Sam was representing Blanco County . . . [They] were friends and the two smartest men in the Hill Country when I lived there," Ruth Goddard, a family friend, remembered. "There was always the heavy spiritual feeling. They had—I guess it is the mystical—but they were men of faith."[51]

Sam cared about the land and its people. Rebekah cared about service and sacrifice as noble abstractions. The mix produced a potent commitment to social justice. Indeed, visitors to the Johnson household frequently were treated to the oratory of William Jennings Bryan playing on the Victrola. For the Johnsons, social justice, public service, and community building were unquestioned values.[52] Sam agreed with Rebekah's contention that there were only three things a son of hers could do to fulfill himself: teach, preach, or go into politics.[53]

But there were more differences than agreements in the marriage. Increasingly, those schisms centered on lifestyle and on Lyndon. Sam bought and sold real estate in and around Johnson City, traded in cotton futures, and invested in various schemes. He was able to purchase the Withers Opera House and set up his offices in the ground floor rooms. "I make a specialty of handling Farm and Ranch Lands," his ad in a 1916 edition of the *Record-Courier* ran. "Yours for a square deal."[54] On a typical day, Sam would rise, have his breakfast, go down to the local barbershop for his shave, and check in with his office.[55] Then he would be out in the country in his Model T, inspecting property and visiting. By all accounts he was a charming, gregarious man. "When I was quite young, to me, he seemed the most elegant man," said Ruth Goddard. She remembered Rebekah coming with him one time and not saying a word, unsmiling and aloof.[56] Ruth

Goddard considered Rebekah a prig. Sam Johnson was a real man, and his drinking did not make him any less so in her eyes. Lyndon recalled one Thanksgiving when his mother had cooked a turkey, set the table with the best dishes, and put on "her fancy lace dress and big wide sleeve." She was saying the dinner prayer when a knock came at the door. It was a Mexican family who lived on the edge of town and whom Sam had befriended. They bore a large green cake as a gift. Instinctively, Sam invited the family, which included five children, for Thanksgiving dinner. "The dinner was loud. There was a lot of laughing and yelling. I liked it. But then I looked at my mother. Her face was bent toward her plate and she said nothing . . . After the meal, she stood up and went to her room. I followed a little behind her and heard her crying in her room."[57] "Sam Johnson was a good man," Ruth Byers, a neighbor, declared. "Mrs. Johnson was a different person. She never would get close to anyone."[58]

There was another reason for Rebekah's coolness. "The one thing that I remember about his father was he had the reputation of being the slowest driver in the whole country," John Koeniger related. "He was known to drink and drive, but it was agreed that he was never in any danger because he drove so slowly. He liked to come through town and motion to some boy to come and go with him and open the gates for him, for which he paid a reward, maybe fifty cents or something like that."[59] In the evenings, Sam would go to town, play dominoes, visit with his cronies, drink beer at King Casparis's, or go to a dance with Clarence, who was a champion square dance caller.[60] As Sam's economic circumstances deteriorated, he would degenerate into an episodic drunk.

Nevertheless, Sam was the man of the family and a self-conscious role model. According to Lyndon's sister Rebekah, he spoiled the girls in the family. He would never return from an out-of-town trip without a doll or some other gift for them. "Now Mr. Johnson was great with the girls," Charles Boatner said. "They all remember how he would come to their bed in the morning and, especially Lucia, carry her in by the stove to dress so she wouldn't get her feet cold."[61] He was determined that his eldest son be a man's man. When Lyndon was five, Rebekah had still not cut his hair. Sam became increasingly upset at the child's shoulder-length blond curls and at the Buster Brown, Little Lord Fauntleroy costumes his wife dressed him in. One Sunday, while Rebekah was away at church, Sam got out the scissors and cut Lyndon's hair. When Rebekah returned she was so mad that she did not speak to her husband for a week.[62]

Apparently, the degree of Sam's harshness with his son depended on his alcohol consumption and the price of cotton. "When he had too much to drink, he'd lose control of himself," Lyndon recalled. "He used bad language. He squandered the little money we had on the cotton and real estate markets."[63] Sam was particularly concerned that his son not embarrass him in public. One day, some of the men in the barbershop pulled a prank on Lyndon. He was in the habit of sauntering in and plopping himself down in the shoeshine chair. Seeing him coming, they filled the tin bottom that held the chair together with oil and mustard seed. Lyndon had no sooner seated himself than he jumped up yelling in pain from his rapidly blistering butt. He ran toward his father's office on the bottom floor of the opera house, pulling his pants down. Some of Sam's friends had gathered and were kibitzing. Instead of consoling the wailing Lyndon, Sam pulled a board off an apple crate and whipped him until he stopped crying. Rebekah, of course, was furious.[64]

To compensate, she played the role of ostentatious nurturer, especially with Lyndon. In the evenings after dinner, Rebekah would assemble the children at the table and by the light of the kerosene lamp go over their lessons with them. All too frequently her eldest son was absent or inattentive. She would recall of Lyndon: "I would not catch up with the fact that [he] was not prepared on a lesson until breakfast time of a school day. Then I would get the book and put it on the table in front of his father and devote the whole breakfast period to a discussion with my husband of what my son should have learned the night before . . . That way and by following him to the front gate nearly every morning and telling him tales of history, geography, and algebra, I could see that he was ready for the work of the day."[65] Like many southern women of the period, Rebekah attempted to rule her family through guilt. There were frequent tears. Some of Lyndon's earliest memories are of his mother crying, of her waiting anxiously late at night for his father's return, of the frustrations of trying to lead a cultured life in rural central Texas, or of some perceived personal slight. Most of Rebekah's emotional outbursts were designed to get people to do what she wanted them to do or to feel sorry for her. Tears of empathy were rare. "Oh, she'd see your leg broken in two, or she'd see your face cut open, and she'd look at it, and she'd never cry," Lyndon told an interviewer.[66] "My father loved to dance and loved the people much more than mother did," Rebekah Johnson Bobbitt recalled. "She liked her few people . . . She was very reserved and she didn't like any form of intimacy."[67] "He [Sam] was I believe more involved with other people perhaps than so much involved with his own family," Truman Fawcett observed. "She was more involved with her family and he was more involved with other people."[68] Lyndon agreed: "She was a little bit too selfish as far as her children were concerned . . . She put them ahead of anything . . . even her own husband."[69]

Increasingly, Sam and Rebekah led separate lives. She had her books, plays, students, newspapers, and children. He had his cronies, business, dominoes, dancing, and politics. In time, the house on Ninth Street came to reflect the compartmentalization of their conjugal existence. "She had her front porch and he had his front porch," Charles Boatner noted. "They were even decorated different. She had spools on her side of the porch and his was plain . . . He had his friends; she had hers."[70] "If you'd come in Daddy's entrance, you could go in there and talk politics and drink and you wouldn't be bothered about your language," Sam Houston said. "But if you crossed over that line, not like the David Crockett line at the Alamo but it was damn near as bad, go over in the other part, why, there was no drinking in the other part and no cussing."[71] The house in Johnson City featured two bedrooms, a living room–dining room with a large fireplace, a kitchen with a wood-burning stove, a screened-in back porch, and a front porch. By 1916 the family had grown to include Sam, Rebekah, Lyndon, little Rebekah, Josefa, Sam Houston, and Lucia. Sometimes the girls slept on the back porch, the boys in one bedroom, and the parents in another. More often, the females occupied one end of the house and the males the other. Sam Houston recalled that when he was about three and Lyndon was nine, he would spend cold nights moving back and forth from Lyndon's to Sam Ealy's bed in an effort to keep his father and older brother warm.[72]

There were playmates galore and fascinating places to play. Ava and Margaret Johnson had moved to town. There was Kitty Leonard and Louise Edwards. The Crider and Redford boys were among Lyndon's closest friends. They would wander down to the gin, watch the bales come tumbling out, and when there was a lull jump off the loading platform. "The man that ran the gin was Mr. Stanford," Gerrard Casparis, a local businessman recalled. "He had a big negra fella working for him there—he was a big jolly fella. He'd stand on the ground and we'd get on that platform and jump off and he'd catch us!"[73] From April through September the kids could swim and fish in the river. "We carried watermelons and cantaloupes down and threw them in the creek so that they'd be very cool," Truman Fawcett's wife recounted. "Then we swam at dinnertime and along about three-thirty we went down and ate watermelons and came back. The boys, if they got there first, went in swimming without bathing suits and we couldn't go in swimming. And we quite often took their clothes off and tied them in knots because we were mad."[74] In the late summer and early fall, families would take turns throwing harvest parties for Johnson City's children. The family vehicle would collect them, and they would spend part of the day picking cotton or gathering corn and the rest swimming and picnicking.[75]

The large barn behind Sam and Rebekah's house was a favorite playhouse. "I'll tell ya one of the best things that we did in that in-town barn," Ava Johnson recalled. "We had cob fights. We'd take the white cobs and the red cobs and we'd choose sides . . . And whenever they hit you with that cob you was supposed to fall . . . we always chose sides and Lyndon would always have to the be leader."[76] During one game Lyndon fell out of the hay door and broke his leg. "Oh, I'm killed, I'm killed," he screamed. Emmette Redford ran and got Dr. Barnwell, who set Lyndon's leg on Rebekah's kitchen table. Lyndon demanded and got his mother's wooden bed to convalesce in. "Margaret and I went by to see him, and gave him his lessons, and he wanted to play mumble peg (a game in which contestants try to throw and stick a knife in a target)," said Ava. "I said, well Lyndon, there's no place to play mumble peg in here. He said, that's what you think, and he . . . took that knife and stuck it in that bed—in the beadboard of that wooden bed."[77]

The willful little boy who ran away in bids for attention grew only more spoiled and turbulent. When he was six, his mother arranged for him to deliver a recitation at a Confederate reunion. He showed up at home the morning of the big day with his head shaved. Furious and humiliated, Rebekah canceled the performance. Stella Gliddon, who attempted to teach Lyndon violin and dance, found him arrogant and difficult, the "kind of little boy that his mother had to tell him three or four times to get in the stove wood."[78] Luiza Casparis, who taught the elder Johnson boy in elementary school, remembered him as "a little tart, a real hellion." On one ocassion, she told him he would have to stay in from recess and make up work he had missed. Instead of obeying, he stalked out and, as he passed Casparis's window, spat at her. As punishment, she locked him in the ice house in back of the school. He screamed, hollered, and pushed so hard on the door that when she opened it, he fell out and bloodied his nose.[79]

At times, Lyndon's need for attention and affection seemed overwhelming. He was constantly drawing attention to himself, playing practical jokes on his classmates and acting the clown. "He was very sensitive . . . and wanted so much for people to like him," Georgia Cammack, a classmate, recalled. In dance class, he spent most of his time poking, pinching, and tormenting the little girls. He sometimes ran around with Joe Payne, a rough boy from Austin whose stepfather Sam knew. "It's hard to remember who was meanest, cause we both like to get in trouble, some kind of devilment," Payne remembered. They threw rocks at black kids and chased them. When Joe visited Johnson City, the two boys stayed out most of the night. "We got a couple of horses out, run 'em up and down the street, and like they got the town Marshal on us about it."[80]

Lyndon's taste for costuming continued into adolescence. Where most boys wore overalls, jeans, and, at most, khakis to school, he frequently dressed in slacks, white shirt, and bow tie. He reportedly possessed the only Palm Beach suit and straw boater in town.[81] But he was a joiner, not a loner. In the fall and spring, young males spent many nights hunting coon, possum, or virtually any nocturnal animal they could find. They'd hunt at night for varmints," Othello Tanner recalled. "And when they'd get out there they'd hear another hunting party off down the ways, and they'd holler and meet each other somewhere, and probably would be 10 to 15 little boys and they'd wrestle the rest of the night. They'd get back in home 4 or 5 o'clock the next morning—time to get a little nap before daddy called 'em out."[82]

Frequently Lyndon had to be spanked to persuade him to go to class. School records for 1920 show him missing 50 of 180 school days. When he did attend, he often did not complete his written work. Rebekah would take his texts, read them, and orally prepare Lyndon for his exams. He cajoled the brighter girls in his class to "help" him with his homework, which frequently meant doing it for him. "He never would have got through high school, if it hadn't been for Kitty Clyde to do his math and for me to write his book reports for him," Louise Edwards recalled.[83] Contemporaries remember that Lyndon was always drawn to the older boys because they had the power. "Most of the [Crider] boys were older because they had been held out of school to work on the farm and they kind of ran the school," Truman Fawcett remembered. "We didn't have any coaches and they'd say who could play baseball and basketball and who couldn't. Lyndon got in with that bunch of boys."[84]

Among male schoolchildren at the turn of the century, bullying was almost a given. Lyndon could be found on both sides. "I can remember that Lyndon and Louie Rountree and one of the Crider boys had been teasing a boy in school that rode a horse to school," Kitty Leonard said. He was big, rough, and crude, a real hayseed, even by Johnson City standards. "They had been tormenting him and one day he came to school prepared for them. He took his knife—took them all together and set them down . . . back of Gene Stevenson's store—and had them eating peanut butter and crackers without any water until they couldn't eat any-more . . . He was threatening them with his knife if they didn't go on and eat it . . . So they ate, and ate, and ate, and ate, peanut butter and crackers, 'til they were almost choked to death—without having anything to drink."[85]

A number of his teachers remembered Lyndon as affectionate, compassion-ate, and loyal. He was aggressive with his fellow students, but never cruel or un-kind, one recalled. "He would crawl up on my lap and pet and pat me," reported another. Lyndon, the Crider boys, and the Redford brothers were inseparable. One or more slept over with him or he with them virtually every night. "I was the closest friend Lyndon ever had," Ben Crider said. "We were so poor that Lyndon would give me half of anything he had," Otto recalled.[86] On Sam Hous-ton Johnson's first day in school, he was writing on the blackboard when the urge to urinate seized him. The first-grade teacher had neglected to tell her class the routine for asking to go to the outhouse. The little boy wet himself and burst into tears. The teacher summoned Lyndon, then in the sixth grade, who came in, cleaned up Sam, consoled him, and led him home without a sign of embar-rassment or annoyance.[87]

No doubt Lyndon's behavior reflected the amount of turmoil at home at any given time. His mother's tears of frustration and loneliness, his father's ab-sences and bouts with both the bottle and the market provoked rebelliousness and defiance. There was also the specter of his grandmothers. Eliza Johnson, the frontier wife of Sam Sr., suffered a stroke when Lyndon was four or five. She became a constant presence in his life, paralyzed, withering, increasingly in-comprehensible, until she died five years later. Eliza had to be carried to a wheelchair when visitors came, where she sat mute and drooling. "Her skin was brown and wrinkled," Lyndon remembered. "Her body was twisted. I was afraid that I was meant to kiss her. I tried to imagine her as the strong pioneer woman she had once been. I remembered the amazing stories I had heard about her staggering courage . . . But age and illness had taken all life out of her face . . . She sat perfectly still. And I was terrified to sit beside her."[88] His other grandmother, Ruth Baines, was physically unimpaired but menacing in her own way, judgmental, humorless, disapproving. Lyndon remembered her as "very conservative, very Baptist, anti-boys."[89]

There is another explanation for Lyndon's mercurial behavior as a child, his defiance, rebelliousness, his disdain for schoolwork, and his fits of temper. He was the classic gifted and talented child. He had reached the third grade by age seven. His mind "seized upon learning," one of his teachers recalled. "Lyndon

Johnson was the most intelligent man I ever met," McGeorge Bundy would later say. (This from the dean of the College at Harvard.) School bored him, especially the endless recitations by other students; the waiting and patience that the multigrade, one- or two-room school experience required drove him to distraction. Ben Crider believed that the reason Lyndon sought the company of older boys and men was that "he was a very brilliant young man and the boys his age wasn't his class mentally."[90] According to Luiza Casparis, "If there were some boys playing ball out in the yard and some men sittin' around whittlin' and talkin', you wouldn't find Lyndon out there with the boys. No, he'd be right in the middle of those men listenin' and talkin'."[91] At an early age he began to display the almost frantic energy that characterized the rest of his life.

When he was eight, Lyndon helped his mother at the offices of the *Record-Courier* as a printer's assistant and gopher. He got a job shining shoes at the local barbershop and persuaded Rebekah to run an ad in the paper touting his services. Shoe shining allowed the boy to earn money and simultaneously be privy to the gossip and political talk that he would love all of his life.[92] Tom Crider remembered that when Lyndon was ten, a candidate for state office came to town to speak. "Ol' Lyndon went right up on the platform and shook his hand."[93] Throughout his childhood, the family had a dog of one sort or another. When one gave birth, he put up a sign in the barbershop window: "See me first for hound pups. Lyndon B. Johnson." He sold all of them.[94] When he got older, Lyndon chopped cotton with the Redford boys and herded goats for twenty-five cents a day.

Somewhat to his mother's chagrin, Lyndon came increasingly to identify with his father, especially after his Grandfather Johnson died in 1915. The years between 1914 and 1920 were the best of Sam Johnson's life. He was one of the leading citizens of Johnson City, the owner of two automobiles, the opera house, and large tracts of real estate in and out of town. He dressed well—suit, Stetson hat, and four-in-hand tie framed by a stiff celluloid collar—and sported an educated, cultured wife.[95] At his gregarious best, Sam became active in politics once again. In 1914 and 1916 Sam Ealy and his brother-in-law, Clarence Martin, were instrumental in helping Governor James E. Ferguson carry Blanco, Gillespie, Kendall, and Llano Counties. It should be noted that although Sam may have been, like Ferguson, a champion of the tenant farmer, he was not one of them. The Johnsons and Martins were part of a rural aristocracy that formed an integral part of virtually every community under five thousand in Texas: businessmen, lawyers, and doctors. They could be found in Copeland, Granger, Bartlett, and Belton. They owned automobiles, and their women dressed in the fashions of the day, purchased not at the local dry goods store but through the Sears and Roebuck catalogue.

After the United States entered World War I, Sam was appointed head of the Blanco County draft board. When the sitting state representative from his district resigned his seat in the legislature to enlist, Sam announced for the now open position. Such was his reputation that no one opposed him in the special election held in February 1918. He subsequently won a two-year regular term in November of that year.[96] As the second phase of Sam Johnson's political career got into full swing, Lyndon began to accompany his father everywhere—to the office, to political rallies, to country stores, post offices, and voters' homes. At the barbershop, Lyndon insisted on sitting in the chair adjacent to his father's and receiving a mock shave. "I wanted to copy my father always, emulate him, do the things he did," Lyndon said later. "He loved the outdoors and I grew to love the outdoors. He loved political life and public service. I followed him as a child and participated in it."[97]

At six Lyndon was handing out campaign pamphlets at a rally for Ferguson's first run at office. He would sit for hours on his father's end of the front porch and listen to the political talk. Among his fondest memories was being on the campaign trail with Sam: "We drove in the Model T Ford from farm to farm, up and down the valley, stopping at every door. My father would do most of the talking. He would bring the neighbors up to date on local gossip, talk about the crops and about the bills he'd introduced into the legislature, and always he'd bring along an enormous crust of homemade bread and a large jar of homemade jam. When we got tired or hungry, we'd stop by the side of the road . . . I'd never seen him happier . . . Christ, sometimes I wished it could go on forever."[98]

Sam Johnson was an outspoken supporter of women's suffrage and an equally outspoken opponent of the Anti-Saloon League and its allies. But it was on the nativist issue that he distinguished himself. The legislative session that began in the spring of 1918 was dubbed "Burn the Germans" by one newspaper. And, in fact, the night skies in and around Austin were frequently alight with flames from German homes and businesses set afire by Texan super patriots aroused by the wartime rhetoric of George Creel, Woodrow Wilson's propaganda chief, and his minions. The state legislature responded to nativist pressure by passing House Bill 15, a measure that made it a felony punishable by a term of two to twenty years in prison for "uttering in the hearing of another person . . . disloyal or abusive language . . . concerning the entry of the United States of America into or continuation of the war."[99] Representative Johnson rose on the floor of the House to oppose the bill that would bear heavily on his German American constituents. He denounced the measure as an unconstitutional violation of every American's civil liberties, and he pled with his fellow citizens to temper their patriotism with reason and compassion. The bill passed, but Sam and other liberals did succeed in eliminating from it a provision that would have granted the right of arrest to every Texas citizen.[100]

His stand against Prohibition was almost as unpopular with his colleagues as his position on free speech, but they both endeared him to his beer-drinking German constituents. "Although sentiment ran high during this session," declared the *Fredericksburg Standard,* "Johnson stood by his promises and voted against prohibition and kindred measures. He knew from the start that the small bunch of liberals would lose out in the maelstrom of fanatical propaganda, but he stood by his promise and voted accordingly, notwithstanding unfounded and vicious attacks on his character as a loyal American citizen." [101]

It was during the 1918 special session that Sam began taking Lyndon to Austin with him. For a nine-year-old boy, life in the state capital with his legislator father was intoxicating. Little did he know that from then on, his life and that of Austin would be forever intertwined.

LYNDON JOHNSON recalled that as a nine-year-old he would sit in the gallery of the state House of Representatives for hours watching the proceedings on the floor and then would wander around the halls trying to figure out what was behind all the activity. Growing bolder, he would sit or stand by his father on the floor of the House. Though not officially a page, he would run errands for Sam and nearby legislators, who always tipped. One of Sam's seatmates remembered Lyndon as a bright, energetic, friendly boy, a bit too aggressive, but overall, pleasing. [102] As a legislator, a drinking man, and, no doubt, an admirer of the ladies, Sam Johnson moved in interesting crowds. Texas solons entertained and were entertained by lobbyists in the elegant Driskill Hotel on Sixth Street, a Victorian edifice completed in 1886 whose marble floors, arched columns, and walnut paneling were famous throughout the South. [103] Lyndon saw it all.

A year after the end of the Great War, in November 1919, Sam Johnson mortgaged everything he owned to purchase the entire 433-acre farm his grandfather and granduncles had carved out on the Pedernales. Stimulated by wartime government purchasing, cotton prices had risen to unheard of levels—forty cents a pound—and Sam saw a chance to make his fortune. To his family's dismay, he decided to rent out the house in Johnson City and move back to the Pedernales where he (or they) could oversee farming operations. Suddenly, Lyndon found himself in the eighth grade in Albert School, a one-room enterprise near Hye. One of his classmates remembered the eleven-year-old Lyndon riding to school on a donkey, with his long legs trailing in the dust. The students, as many as sixty, were taught in one room. They were predominantly German, and there was some fighting and name-calling between the German and non-German children, an aftertaste of the prejudices generated by the Great War. Lyndon shied away from athletics and music (Albert School had a twelve-piece "Ompah" band) and tried to focus on his books. Rebekah helped with declamation and drama contests. [104] During his absences, Sam would leave Lyndon in charge, and he would dutifully organize his brothers and sisters to chop wood, gather eggs, slop the pigs, and tend the other livestock. Rebekah had domestic help to do the washing and cleaning. When Lyndon turned thirteen, plans had to be made for him to attend high school. The nearest was in Johnson City, so he moved in with his Uncle Tom and Aunt Kitty Johnson, who lived on a ranch near town.

Meanwhile, Sam Johnson was going broke. The year 1920 brought searing heat and drought; the land yielded only a fraction of its normal production of cotton. Then, in 1921 the bottom dropped out of the market. With the stimulus of the war gone, the European economy in shambles, and a surplus glutting the market, prices fell to seven cents a pound and rose only slightly throughout the remainder of the decade.[105] Sam couldn't pay his mortgages and had to sell the farm for a few cents on the dollar. In a matter of three years, according to Lyndon, his father lost $100,000 and was forced to carry a debt of some $40,000 for the rest of his life. In 1922, the family, humiliated, moved back into the house in Johnson City.[106] Sam refused to let the second great financial crisis of his life drive him out of politics, however. In the fall of 1920 he announced for a second full term in the Texas House of Representatives. He again enjoyed the support of the *Blanco County Record* and the *Fredericksburg Standard.* During the previous session he had helped push through the legislature a bill appropriating $2 million for the relief of drought-stricken farmers. In addition, he had pressured the state department of education to increase subsidies to rural schools to the point where every student was eligible for seven months of free education. Sam won easily in 1920 and again in 1922.

Sam was a progressive legislator, working to protect the public from fraudulent stock sales, for example. But his real claim to fame was his opposition to the KKK. The second Ku Klux Klan was founded in Atlanta in 1915 by a former Methodist minister-turned-huckster named William Joseph Simmons. In 1920, Simmons joined with a shrewd publicity expert, Edward Clarke, in a scheme to sell the organization. Agents tried first to convert the leading citizens of a given community on the theory that lesser mortals would follow. Clarke and Simmons hoped to grow rich by collecting from each new member a $10 initiation fee known as a "klectoken." The Klan was a self-styled superpatriotic organization dedicated to protecting white womanhood, Protestantism, and the purity of the white race. It was anti-Catholic, anti-Semitic, anti-Negro (although in this, the heyday of Jim Crow, there was little left to do to further degrade African Americans), anti-immigration, and anti-alcohol. From September 1921 to December 1922, national membership in the new KKK grew from one hundred thousand to seven hundred thousand.[107]

The Klan was immensely, if briefly, popular in Texas, where it was welcomed by the silk stocking set as a means to better control working-class whites, by working-class whites as a source of excitement and a means of escape from their social and economic plight ("A Knight of the Invisible Empire for the small sum of ten dollars," H. L. Mencken observed. "Surely Knighthood was never offered at such a bargain."), and by Protestant clergymen as a means to restore moral authority. According to one historian, it was the appeal to moral authority that was most important in the formation and growth of the Texas Klan, whose membership numbered between seventy-five thousand and ninety thousand by the close of 1921. The state recorded over eighty whippings administered by various Klaverns in that year alone. Among the victims were a Houston lawyer accused of fraternizing with blacks, a Beaumont doctor charged with performing abortions, a Houston attorney accused of annoying young girls, and a Bay City banker allegedly guilty of domestic abuse and infidelity. In Dallas a black bellboy suspected of pandering for white prostitutes was whipped and the letters KKK burned into his forehead with acid.[108]

During the regular session of the legislature in 1922, Wright Patman, Sam Ealy's deskmate, introduced a resolution putting the House on record as condemning the Klan by name and labeling it "un-American." When that proposal failed, Patman offered a bill to make it an offense "for two or more persons to conspire together for the purpose of injuring, oppressing, threatening or intimidating any person" and to "go in disguise upon the public highways." It died in committee.[109] Sam spoke forthrightly and publicly for both measures. His stand was popular with his German constituents, but not with others. "The Ku Klux Klan had threatened to kill him on numerous occasions after he had made a widely publicized speech on racial tolerance before the state legislature," Sam Houston recalled. "His words were quoted in newspapers all over the state, mostly in articles and editorials that condemned his stand, and almost immediately he started receiving anonymous phone calls and unsigned letters that threatened his entire family."[110]

On one occasion, when Sam Ealy received a particularly offensive call, he exploded. "Now, listen here, you kukluxsonofa bitch," he shouted into the receiver, "if you and your goddamned gang think you're man enough to shoot me, you come on ahead." Throughout the night, Sam, together with his brothers George and Tom, sat on the porch with their shotguns, waiting. Nobody came. From that day until he left the legislature in 1924, Sam always carried a pistol.[111]

The Klan's star declined as rapidly as it had risen. When some of its members in Tenaha kidnapped from a hotel a young woman whom they suspected of being a bigamist, stripped her to the waist, beat her with a wet rope, and tarred and feathered her, a wave of revulsion swept the state. Both the Texas Chamber of Commerce and the Texas Bar Association, led by a young San Antonio lawyer named Maury Maverick, voted to denounce the organization.[112] Lyndon later attributed his lack of bigotry to his father, citing his stand on the Klan.[113] But it was the hooded brotherhood's hypocrisy and holier-than-thou attitude rather than race that moved Sam Ealy. When the *Houston Chronicle* asked various legislators to give their view of the Klan, Sam responded, "I am for the old Ku Klux Klan, but not the new." Patman contended that Johnson was remembering the organization's struggle against northern radicalism in the wake of the Civil War, but he also acknowledged that his deskmate was not in favor of giving blacks the right to vote.[114]

The Johnson family's attitude toward African Americans during the teens and twenties is largely a matter of speculation. There were only one or two blacks living in Johnson City, but near Fredericksburg a community of some forty African Americans resided on land they had acquired after the Civil War. Apparently several of them were successful farmers and stock raisers. Judge Baines, Rebekah's father, did considerable business in "the Peyton Colony," as it was called.[115] More than likely, Sam and Rebekah supported Jim Crow, but not the cruder forms of racism so evident in the South, including parts of Texas. They would have agreed with Booker T. Washington that in return for giving up the vote temporarily and accepting segregation, African Americans ought to enjoy every economic and educational opportunity and be allowed to climb white society's ladder of civilization.

Lyndon could recall only one story from his childhood in any way touching black-white relations. One day Melvin Winters, a road crew boss for a private construction company, brought a gang of some forty black construction laborers to Johnson City to work on a road project. In the saloon, a local redneck and bully confronted Winters and warned him to get his charges out of town by sundown. Winters refused and a mammoth fight broke out. It spilled out into the streets, attracting a crowd of townspeople, including Lyndon, who cheered for Winters. Finally, the road crew boss managed to get on top and began beating the man's head against the sidewalk, yelling, "Do my niggers stay? Do my niggers stay?" "Yes," replied the bully. "Yes."[116] Sam Ealy may have once supported Joe Bailey, an avowed segregationist, but his personal beliefs made it impossible for him to be a thoroughgoing racist. "Though not exactly an atheist or agnostic, he never seemed to give much thought to a formal religion," Sam Houston said. "Still, he was deeply committed to certain ideas that you might consider religious. He was certainly a believer in the dignity of all human beings regardless of race or creed, and some of that rubbed off on all of us."[117]

During these years Sam's financial problems bore heavily upon him. Visitors to the legislature noted that the once dapper, poised legislator from Johnson City seemed gaunt and stooped, "a cadaverish looking fellow with a [large] Adam's apple."[118] To save money, Sam began sleeping on a cot in a large tent with other impecunious lawmakers; they hired a cook and attempted to survive on a dollar a day. After the family moved back to Johnson City, he was stricken with an unknown illness that caused him to waste and suffer outbreaks of boils. He was so sick that he had to drop out of the legislature before it finished its term in 1923 and take to his bed.[119] Residents of Johnson City remember calling on Sam Johnson at home; he was so weak that he could not rise for days at a time and had the family put his bed on the porch, where he could receive visitors.

Sam retired from the legislature in 1924 at age forty-six. In the short run, the best job he could land was as a $2.00-a-day game warden. He could never get politics out of his blood, however. When his health allowed, he spent as much time as possible in Austin, mostly drinking at the Driskill bar. To his family's intense embarrassment, Sam could sometimes be found sleeping off his binges in the wagon yard at Second and Congress.[120] "When things went really bad," a family friend observed, "he did start drinking too much. He didn't do that always, but when things got too bad, you know, when the depression was at its worst, and the cattle market and the cotton market was really gone, his means of livelihood just vanished. And he had a wife and five children. Then he did get depressed, but other times he was an energetic, vital kind of man, like Lyndon."[121]

In 1922, at age thirteen, Lyndon moved upstairs into Johnson City High School. The next three years were typical and relatively pleasant. Although not studious, Lyndon was a quick learner, and with his mother's and girlfriends' assistance, a successful student. The curricular emphasis was on English, history, math, and languages—Spanish and German. Science instruction was purely theoretical; laboratories were nonexistent. There was poetry memorization— "Evangeline" and "The Ancient Mariner"—and themes. "We had math assignments nearly every night of the world to do at home," remembered classmate Louise Edwards. "We had two years of Algebra, then we had Plane Geometry, and Solid Geometry and Trigonometry."[122] Contemporaries remember young Johnson and the Redford brothers, Emmette and Cecil, continually preoccupied with politics and current events. Emmette, who would later become a professor of government at the University of Texas and president of the American Political Science Association, could usually be seen with a copy of the *Congressional Record* protruding from his back pocket.[123] The Redford boys and Lyndon spent much of their free time at the courthouse when a trial was under way, listening to Clarence Martin or some other colorful country lawyer. "Well, there wasn't anything in town except three churches and a courthouse," Emmette later observed, "and although Lyndon and I gave some attention to what was going on in the churches . . . we were more interested in what happened at the courthouse."[124]

Sports were a prominent part of the lives of Johnson City High School students and, in fact, a focus for the entire community. "Down here at the three points where you come into town, where the highway comes this way and goes out that way was part of the Fawcett farm," Truman Fawcett remembered, "and we had a big relay track out there with baseball rounds. It was under the auspices of the school. Both boys and girls ran track and relay and played ball."[125] Volleyball and tennis were available for Lyndon's last two years. "Albert Morrison [a high school teacher] took a great interest in us," Louise Edwards said. "He put up a tennis court, and of course, he had the one arm, but he got out there and trained us to play tennis."[126] Lyndon's specialty was baseball, which he had played since he was six. Tall and rangy, he was a solid first baseman for the Johnson City nine. In basketball he was more successful as a cheerleader than as a player.

Lyndon's real skill, however, lay in debate. He won his first contest in 1921 at Klaerner's Opera House in Fredericksburg. The question of the day was whether to divide Texas into five states, as provided for in the state constitution. When he was a senior, he and John Casparis, a tenth-grader, won first in the Blanco County meet and finished third in the district at San Marcos.[127] The topic for the county meet was the pros and cons of U.S. participation in the League of Nations, and for the district meet the relative merits of the Monroe Doctrine.[128]

Lyndon graduated in 1924 at age fifteen. He was one of six students, including Louise Edwards, Emmette Redford, Kitty Clyde Leonard, and his cousin

Margaret. It was an elite and unusually small group. When Principal Scott Klett came to Johnson City, he had found a wide discrepancy in the abilities and accomplishments of students within a given grade. He decided to do something about it. "I'm thinking some twenty-five or thirty children always in our group," Louise Edwards recalled. "When we got into high school, we had a little shake-up. A new principal came . . . He decided that some children were too far advanced. [The others] were not doing the work that they should do for that particular grade. Our class was divided and a number of our classmates stayed behind and a few of us went on. I'm thinking there were just about ten of us out of the thirty that went on into the next grade. Then when we finished school in 1924, there were just six of us to graduate." [129]

Lyndon dated in high school, most frequently Kitty Clyde Leonard, a pretty girl whose classmates predicted a future as a model for her. Dating in that day and time usually meant walking together to church, to the opera house for a once-a-month showing of a movie, or to a "snap" party. "Some young fellas would come, ask the mother—'Can we have a party tonight?' And—yes," remembered Mamie Klett. "Well then, they'd go out and spread the word around . . . There's gonna be a party at such and such a house." [130] The girls would station themselves around the outside walls of the parlor. A boy would approach one and snap his fingers. The couple, holding hands, would go outside and station themselves under a tree. When the next couple came out, they would chase the pair around the house until they caught them, at which point they exchanged partners. [131]

But there was another social realm in which Lyndon moved, a rougher, more dangerous male world. When Principal Klett began dating Dena Meyer, one of the new young teachers at the high school, Lyndon and the Crider boys began spying on them. They would cling to the rear bumper of Klett's car when he and his girl were on their way to park and then harass them. The boys would peer in the principal's window in hopes of catching a glimpse of his love life. The young teacher he was dating did not last the year. [132] Bootleg liquor was readily available; on more than one night Lyndon and the Criders failed to return home. Christian Lindig recalled that a group of Johnson City boys was constantly stealing his homemade wine. "I'm not calling any names," Lindig said, "but one of them is the son of a representative." [133] Then there were the dance halls. Reingold, a tiny German community near Willow City, boasted a huge hall that featured beer, whiskey, and dancing at least once a month. "I know Myrtle [Shelly Crawl] . . . she was a real good dancer . . . the boys would come up there. She was married, but then she still danced with all the boys. And she said she remembered helpin' teach Lyndon how to dance." [134] And the boys fought. According to Louise Edwards's brother, he and Lyndon joined battle every Friday afternoon. "He wanted my girl friend and I wanted his, and we'd fight." [135] Apparently, Lyndon had a terrible temper. He rarely lost it, but when he did, he was completely out of control. An argument with another boy at the blacksmith's shop degenerated into a fistfight. Lyndon picked up a small anvil and would have brained his opponent if one of the men present had not intervened.[136]

When Lyndon was fifteen, he joined the Christian (Disciples of Christ) church. Explanations vary. His mother recalled that he was dating a girl who was a Disciple. Accompanying her to a revival, he became so caught up in the evangelical fervor that he allowed himself to be baptized. According to other sources, it was his cousins, Ava and Margaret, that attracted him to the Christian church. But there was more to it than that. Put off by the fire-and-brimstone sermons of his mother's Baptist ministers, Lyndon began to look around for a kinder, gentler religion. The preachers, Lyndon later recalled, were "the Billy Graham type" who would get people to thinking they were "goin' to hell in a hack . . . I got to believing it pretty deep."[137] "And they told me that the devil was going to get the whole outfit of us, real hell fire and damnation stuff."[138] Moreover, he had attended his father's occasional Christadelphian camp meetings and was exposed continually to his father's railing's against Baptist preachers as teetotaling hypocrites who pandered to the guilt and prejudices of their congregations. Joining the more liberal Christian church seemed the answer to his dilemma. The inclusiveness and tolerance of the denomination, with its emphasis on good works, was to have a lasting impact on Lyndon. Rebekah was not pleased, however. "I marched right home and told Momma," Lyndon said, "and she cried. She said that all of us were Baptists, and I was the only one that joined the Christian Church."[139]

A continual nagging sidebar to Lyndon's life as a high school student was the conflict between his mother's and father's lifestyles, a conflict that he could not help but internalize. Rebekah joined a temperance society and continued to make no secret of her abhorrence of alcohol. Sam would periodically attempt to dry out; his neighbors recalled his constant, almost frenzied gardening. When Sam fell off the wagon, which was fairly often, he fell hard. John Casparis remembers that when Sam was still in the legislature, he would sometimes speak to the assembled student body in the upstairs auditorium of the Johnson City School. On more than one occasion, he was so intoxicated that he stumbled and fell going up and down the stairs. "Several times I've seen Sam come to the school just lit up like a country church and have to climb up the steps on his all fours."[140] Lyndon was mortified. There is the famous story of his standing outside the Johnson City saloon calling in a loud voice for his father to come home to his family.[141]

Sam Ealy and Lyndon's relationship was complex: loving, fearful, competitive, protective. Later in life, Lyndon recalled for an interviewer that he frequently went hunting with his friends but did not like to kill the small animals, the squirrels and rabbits, that abounded in the Hill Country. Noticing that he never brought any game home, Sam challenged his son. Was he a coward who could not shed blood? Lyndon recalled that he took his .22, went into the hills, shot a rabbit, and proceeded to throw up. When his father was away, Lyndon would refuse to do his chores, disobeyed his mother, and got into his father's personal things. When he returned, Sam would take a strap to the boy, but the pattern would only repeat itself. Later, after he was out of high school, Lyndon borrowed his father's car for a blind date. When the girl in question realized that she was three years older than her escort, she refused to go out with him. Thereupon, Lyndon gathered up a few of his friends for beer and joy riding. The luckless youth hit a bridge and overturned the car. No one was hurt, but Lyndon was terrified. Instead of going home to face his father, he bought a bus ticket for New Braunfels, intending to hide out for a few days with an uncle who lived there. By the second day, Sam had tracked his son down. He phoned: "Lyndon, I traded in that old car of ours this morning for a brand-new one and it's in the store right now needing someone to pick it up . . . I was wondering if you could come back, pick it up, and drive it home for me . . . I want you to drive it around the courthouse square, five times, ten times, fifty times, nice and slow. You see there's some talk around town this morning that my son's a coward, that he couldn't face up to what he had done." [142] Lyndon dutifully returned and picked up the car.

The tension between his parents, his father's unpredictability, his mother's lofty expectations, spoken and unspoken, continued to produce rebelliousness and defiance. Lyndon's table manners were atrocious. He would eat with loud slurping noises until his mother burst into tears and left the table. When his father was out of town, Lyndon would refuse to do his chores and boss the other children. He would use and abuse his parents' personal possessions. "No one could boss him or persuade him to do anything he didn't want to do," Sam Houston recalled. [143]

Parental conflict and mixed signals aside, Lyndon was able to live the life of a fairly normal teenager in rural Texas. His parents and siblings loved him, and he them. They wanted the best for him, and he knew it. He was part of a close-knit community that "cared when you were sick and knew when you died," as Sam Ealy put it. [144] Despite his ups and downs, Lyndon performed satisfactorily in school. He was extremely bright, as were the select group of classmates who survived together to enter the eleventh grade (the final grade in the Johnson City School). All of Lyndon's contemporaries remarked on his confidence and social skills. "He had a very pleasing personality and a very lovable personality," Georgia Edgeworth recalled. "If he wanted something, he could usually get it through persuasion. He was especially good with the elderly, remembering their names, visiting them when they were sick." [145] He seemed to have a confidence beyond his years, particularly in public venues.

One of the highlights of the school year was the senior play. Lyndon acted the lead in both the tenth and eleventh grades. The production his senior year was *The Thread of Destiny*, a plantation melodrama. "Lyndon was the hero, and I was the heroine," Louise Edwards remembered. To earn money for a senior trip, the class took the production on the road. "The people at Cyprus Mills though—they thought it was right out of New York," Edwards said. [146] At the commencement exercises held in the Johnson City High auditorium, Lyndon, six feet tall, rail thin, with his curly black hair cropped short, read the class poem. The senior motto was "Give to the world the best that you have and the best will come back to you."[147] The official prophecy predicted that Lyndon Johnson would become governor of Texas.

CHAPTER 3

COLLEGE

Throughout the summer of 1924, Lyndon's parents continued to send him mixed messages. He must go to college like his fellow graduates or face a life of poverty and hardship. Education was the ultimate status symbol. His mother talked of little else. At the same time, his father made it clear that there was no money to pay for college. Indeed, his father owed hundreds of dollars to local merchants as well as thousands to the bank for back mortgage payments, debts that would be settled by Lyndon after his father's death. The Johnsons were proud but poor, an unfortunate combination.

Reluctantly, Lyndon agreed to take the first step. He enrolled in the subcollege in San Marcos run by Southwest Texas State Teachers College for children from rural schools like Johnson City that did not have a twelfth grade. "Lyndon is very young [he was then sixteen], and has been considerably indulged," Rebekah wrote one of her son's teachers, "[and] so finds the present situation very trying . . . To be away from home and to be compelled to really study are great hardships to him. Your sympathy and encouragement will help him keep up his interest and enthusiasm." [1]

In fact, the whole experience proved too much for him; after a few weeks, he was back in Johnson City. [2] Lyndon's stint at the subcollege was more traumatic than his family realized. He felt trapped, stifled. Johnson later told Doris Kearns Goodwin of a recurrent dream that originated during this period. He was sitting alone in a cage, bare except for a stone bench and a pile of books. As he bent down to pick up one of the books, an elderly woman passed by carrying a mirror. Glancing up, Lyndon caught sight of himself reflected; the image was not that of a healthy adolescent but of an old man with tangled hair and gnarled skin. He pled with the woman to let him out, but she refused and turned away. [3]

• • •

THE SUMMER OF 1924 was one of the most difficult the Hill Country had experienced. It was hot and dry; farmers were mired in a five-year-long agricultural depression. There was little work for anyone, especially a sixteen-year-old recent graduate of Johnson City High. Lyndon learned that three of his older friends, Tom Crider, Payne Roundtree, and Otho Summy, and his contemporary, Otto Crider, were planning a trip to California. The word around central Texas was that California was the promised land. Money grew on trees, Otho said; all you had to do was reach up and pluck off the bills. Two Johnson City boys, Ben Crider and John Koeniger, were already there working in a plant owned by the Monolith Portland Cement Company.[4] Lyndon was intrigued. He longed to see the wider world, to escape his domestic dilemma.

Tom Martin, Clarence's son and Lyndon's cousin, was then practicing law in San Bernardino and reportedly making a small fortune representing movie stars. The boys bought a 1918 Model T from Walter Crider for $50 and began modifying it in Crider's garage, where Payne Roundtree worked part time as a mechanic. The back seat was converted to a bed so that one of the boys could drive during the night when it was cooler while the others slept. The Model T had a windshield but no roof, so the adventurers fashioned one out of barrel staves and canvas. Johnson City's response to Horace Greeley's invocation, "Go West, young man," was the talk of the town. Sam Ealy was not pleased. No son of his was going to become a wandering vagabond. According to Sam Houston, his father told one and all that "the minute he sees Lyndon gittin' in that car to take off, he's going to yank him out by his britches and carry him off home."[5] Lyndon tried to muster the courage to tell his parents that he was going but could never face them. When the appointed day arrived, Sam was conveniently out of town on real estate business. Lyndon simply gathered up his belongings, left the house, and jumped into the car with the other boys. They drove out of Johnson City at full throttle, waving to pedestrians. It was July 3, 1925, the day before Independence Day.

Sam and Rebekah reacted differently. Noting that Lyndon had forgotten to take his pillow, Rebekah called his Aunt Josefa in Fredericksburg and asked her to intercept the boys and give him one of hers. When Sam got home he exploded. Cursing, he called every sheriff he could think of between Fredericksburg and El Paso, asking them to stop the runaways and return them home. Neither Aunt Josefa nor the law was able to locate Lyndon and his friends, however.[6]

The trip to California took ten days over potholed dirt or gravel roads, or in the desert over plank highways. To escape the worst of the desert heat, the boys traveled mostly at night and slept or lounged around a town on the route during the day. Each expeditioner had about $25 in his pocket. It cost forty cents to fill up the Model T. To save money they camped out along the way. "We lived entirely on fatback and bacon, cornbread and homemade molasses," Otho Summy recalled. They also carried five-gallon jugs of water and a single-shot .22 rifle, which was fortunate, as they were forced to shoot a rattlesnake on their first camping stop. When Lyndon and his mates halted for sleep, they buried their money in a common hole to protect against thieves. The largest slept on top of the hole. "I'm burying my money, but I'm savin' a little change," Otho told the others. "I've heard they'll kill you if you don't have a little change."[7]

The five made their way to El Paso and across New Mexico. The mesas and towers were awe-inspiring even in the withering heat. "It was the most beautiful trip I ever made," Otto remembered, "five of us boys . . . because I was young, and everything was new to me."[8] In Arizona they took a wrong turn, got lost, and had to ask directions in Tombstone. The biggest problem in that state, however, was the blowing sand, which sometimes covered the planked highway. If ever they got off the beaten track, the Johnson City five would become so mired in the sand that they could never dig out. The boys encountered four female schoolteachers from Minnesota who were touring the Southwest, helped them fix a broken spring on their car, and accompanied them briefly northward to see the "Garden of the Gods," as the Grand Canyon was sometimes then called. Lyndon and his friends made the crossing into California at Blythe, paying fifty cents to be ferried across the river. They could count $8 among them.

Having entered the promised land, the boys from Johnson City proceeded directly to San Bernardino, where Lyndon's cousin lived. Tom Martin immediately invited Lyndon to stay with him. After dropping off their friend, the Crider boys, Payne, and Otho drove on to Tehachapai, where Ben Crider and John Koeniger were working. Martin took Lyndon out, bought him some clothes, and offered to teach him the law if he would work as office boy.[9] He could offer room, board, and nominal pay. Lyndon accepted and shortly thereafter began working in his cousin's law offices in downtown San Bernardino, a thriving suburb of Los Angeles. Lyndon subsequently persuaded Tom to take John Koeniger in as well.

LIKE HIS FATHER, CLARENCE, Sam Ealy's best friend and Rebekah's nemesis, Tom Martin was a character. Before coming to California, he had served as chief of police in San Antonio. Twenty-eight when he was elected, Tom Martin was reputed to be the youngest chief of police in the country. In the years before and after Prohibition, San Antonio was a wide-open town. Like his father, Tom was a drinking man. For a small fee, the chief would allow certain bootleggers to operate openly in the city. Periodically, the police would sweep the city for prostitutes. Tom and a couple of his friends from the Hill Country got into the dangerous habit of selecting two or three of the most attractive, freeing them from jail, and taking them on trips to Mexico. When the political faction opposed to Tom's came to power, the district attorney brought a seventeen-count indictment against the chief. He thereupon decided that the better part of valor was to migrate to California.[10]

Tom Martin's California was a new and wonderful world for Lyndon. Talkies were just making their appearance, and Hollywood was finding its place in American culture. The major studios were beginning to make melodramas with Clara Bow and westerns with Tom Mix. Tom Martin's clientele was diverse. He was a Democrat and a labor lawyer. San Bernardino was a major railhead, and the rail workers were in the process of unionizing. But he had also worked for a time for Cornelius Vanderbilt Jr., who had settled in Los Angeles and established the *Los Angeles Illustrated News*. Tom also specialized in divorce. Lyndon recalled that his cousin-boss could make from $2,000 to $5,000 a case handling broken celebrity unions. He was married to the former Olga Priess, a Fredericksburg beauty queen, and the couple had one child. Lyndon and John Koeniger were able to gawk at and even meet the rich and famous. One of Tom's clients, who was also his mistress, had been married to Jack Dempsey's father. The famous fighter once came to the house, where the boys were introduced.[11] Tom Martin also had a pretty young secretary. She would frequently call a friend and they would go dining and dancing with Lyndon and John Koeniger in Tom's Model A coupe.

Tom told Lyndon and John that if they worked in his office, read law, and accompanied him to court, they could qualify to take the California Bar exam and become lawyers without ever having to go to college. For several months, they ran his errands, filed court papers, and did whatever needed to be done. They soon learned, however, that California required three years of experience before a novice could even apply to take the bar exam.

Tom spent much of his time partying. He would be gone for days and sometimes weeks at a time. The boys' pay came so intermittently that at one point, Lyndon had to take a second job as an elevator operator in the Platt Building, where the law offices were located.[12] The last straw came in the summer of 1925. Olga and her son returned to Texas for a month's vacation in Fredericksburg. "Tom got in the car and drove to Hollywood and was back . . . that same evening with his girlfriend . . . who was named Lottie Dexter Dempsey," John Koeniger recalled. She was a cowgirl from Idaho whose beauty and ability to ride horses had landed her minor roles in the movies. Tom had met her while handling her divorce from Jack Dempsey's father. Tom called up his favorite bootlegger, who delivered a case of gin. There began a three-week party. It was left to Lyndon and John to run the law practice. "Tom said it was a rule of his to never talk to his clients while he had liquor on his breath, and that was so much of the time that he almost never went to the office," John Koeniger recalled. The tryst ended when Tom received a telegram from Olga that she was arriving on the evening train. John drove Lottie back to Hollywood while Tom and Lyndon labored to eradicate any sign of her presence. Lyndon decided that he had had enough. Among other things, he and John were afraid they were going to get into trouble for practicing law without a license.[13]

For a time, Lyndon tried to make it on his own. His job as elevator operator paid $90 a month. Other odd jobs came and went but failed to make ends meet. "I found at the end of the month, after I paid for three meals and paid for my room and my laundry, that I was probably better off back there eating mama's food than I was in California," Lyndon subsequently told journalist Ronnie

Dugger.[14] Lyndon later claimed that he hitchhiked back to Texas—his memory of his early years was sometimes exaggeratedly harsh—but the best evidence is that he drove back with his Uncle Clarence, who had come to San Bernardino to help Tom with a difficult murder case.[15]

Lyndon's parents were glad to see him, and he them. The pressure to go to college began almost immediately, but still he resisted. "I was too young to go to college and at that time I wasn't interested," Lyndon remembered. "A lot of people thought I was grown up because I was tall, but I wasn't grown up."[16] His friends were relentless. He came back, as he recalled, with "empty hands and empty pockets." "We teased him that he didn't come through and we kidded him about being an elevator boy," his cousin Ava recalled.[17]

Although Jim Ferguson had been impeached, he and his political philosophy were still popular in Texas. He could not run again, but in 1924 the citizens of the Lone Star State elected his wife, Miriam "Ma" Ferguson, governor. One of her first acts was to toss her Hill Country supporter, Sam Johnson, a small plum. The Texas Highway Department hired him to a supervisory post. From this lofty position, Sam was able to get Lyndon a job on the road gang then building a highway from Johnson City to Austin. He and Ben Crider, who had also returned from California, worked from sunup to sundown six days a week for $92.50 a month. Lyndon drove a tractor, wielded a pickax, and managed a dirt-scraper, called a "Fresno," pulled by a team of mules. It was hot, dirty, monotonous work. The soil, caliche, would dry to a fine powder in the summer and when mixed with water or human sweat would form an alkaline solution that could cause major skin irritations.[18] Lyndon and some of his coworkers traveled to and from the job in a gravel truck. One of the men on the road crew recalled that Lyndon "always talked big, he had big ideas . . . and he wanted to do something big with his life."[19] Another remembered how stubborn he was: "He's the hardest-headed thing I ever tried to work with. He could do better if he'd let you tell him something, but he won't listen."[20]

At night, Lyndon lived the life of a day laborer with no future, drinking bootleg liquor, hanging out at dance halls, and getting into fights. He borrowed a hundred dollars from his Aunt Jessie Hatcher to buy a stripped-down Model A.[21] "Lyndon wasn't afraid of nothin'," Otto Crider recalled. "He'd stand up toe to toe with them. He had a lot of fist fights around Johnson City over any damn thing."[22] If they were really bored, the boys were not above stealing a few sticks of dynamite from the Highway Department and setting them off just to keep the local authorities off balance.[23] Once Lyndon and his mates burned down a barn, and they carried on a running feud with a young deputy sheriff who was constantly trying to rein them in.[24] There was more than one wrecked automobile. On the way back from a dance in Fredericksburg where Lyndon and his friends had been drinking heavily, they rolled their car. Lyndon was thrown some fifty feet into a pasture, from which he emerged scratched and bleeding, but with no broken bones.[25]

All through this period, Sam and Rebekah kept picking at Lyndon. "He said

I'd never be more than a day laborer and that if I had the brains of the rest of the family I'd be making something of myself," Lyndon remembered. "I used to resent the hell out of it."[26] His mother made no bones about her disapproval of his chosen lifestyle and never missed a chance to regale him with the achievements of her illustrious ancestors, emphasizing particularly the role that education had played in their lives. Lyndon's cousin Margaret and her boyfriend Alfred "Boody" Johnson were then attending Southwest Texas State in San Marcos; on their visits home they, too, urged Lyndon to give up the laboring life for college.[27] "He was at this time running the county grader there in Johnson City, out there about two or three miles out on the road there," Boody Johnson related. "It had rained that morning and then the sun came out, and it was really hot, steaming hot. We all chatted around there a while . . . and I told Lyndon, 'My goodness, is that all you're going to do, just sit up there and run a grader the rest of your life? You ought to get an education and use your brain.' He said, 'Well, I don't know. I tried that and got kicked out of school.' "[28] The low point came one Saturday night in January 1927. He picked a fight with a German boy who turned out to have fists like pile drivers. He beat Lyndon until blood from his mouth and nose soaked his white silk shirtfront. The next morning Rebekah found him in bed hung over and caked in blood, his nose broken.[29] She began to cry. It was incredible to her that "my eldest son would be satisfied with a life like this." Lyndon gave in. He would enroll for the spring semester at Southwest Texas State Teachers College. An overjoyed Rebekah immediately had her husband get on the phone with the president of SWT, Dr. Cecil Evans, to get the process started. Sam had met Evans in the legislature when the latter came to Austin to lobby in behalf of his institution.[30]

LYNDON JOHNSON GREW UP with people determined above all to make a difference—to educate, to inform, to reform, to uplift—despite Sam's drinking and business failures. Not to go to college, not to connect to the larger world would mean a kind of self-loathing that would be intolerable. Six months experiencing the corrosive effect of being an underachiever in a family of achievers was more than enough. But there were ways to connect to the larger world and there were ways. Lyndon had experienced the larger life led by people like Clarence and Tom Martin, exciting, worldly, somewhat dissolute. It was seductive, but in the end it seemed to lack substance, as Lyndon confided to his Aunt Jessie Hatcher on his return from California.[31] The Martins, like other trial lawyers, seemed merely interested in manipulating the system for their own advantage rather than acting with any larger good in mind. Increasingly, Lyndon was drawn to the notion of living the life of a principled politician closely connected to his people. In 1928, still in college, he would venture to Houston to attend the Democratic National Convention. He was dazzled and moved. "He came back," Vernon Whiteside, a college friend, remembered, "and that was when he began to say that he wanted to live such a life that after he'd been dead a hundred years somebody would know that he had lived on this earth, and that was his prime purpose in life, not to become a great . . . or a wealthy man or anything of that nature."[32]

SOUTHWEST TEXAS STATE TEACHER'S COLLEGE began as one of the state's normal schools dedicated solely to the preparation of public school teachers. Established in 1903, it consisted when Lyndon entered of some ten buildings situated on and around Chautauqua Hill overlooking the San Marcos River. At the center of campus on the crest of the hill was "Old Main," a multi-storied neo-Gothic building whose red roof and spires were visible for miles around. By the time Lyndon entered, SWT had become a true regional institution. It remained primarily a teachers college, but students came and earned degrees who also became businesspeople, lawyers, and doctors. Tuition in the 1920s was $17 a semester; there were no dormitories for men, but rooms were available at private homes for between $30 and $40 a month. The base cost for attending Southwest Texas State Teachers College, between $40 and $50 a month, was a bargain. Two degrees were available, the bachelor of arts and the bachelor of science, plus a sophomore diploma after successful completion of two years. The institution included fifty-six instructors scattered across twenty departments comprising not only the arts and sciences but agriculture, business, and physical education. The largest faculty was English with eight. Most instructors had a master's degree, several from the Peabody School at Columbia University. SWT operated on a quarter system: three three-month terms plus a summer term. Both the BA and BS required 180 credit hours; those who earned a BA had to complete twenty-seven hours of foreign language.[33] The library contained a respectable twenty-one thousand volumes.

The student body at SWT, some seven hundred strong, was white, predominantly Protestant, and rural, the vast majority having grown up within fifty miles of the campus. Blanco County, with only twenty-five hundred citizens, had twenty-two students enrolled in 1927. Anglo-Saxons, Germans, Poles, and an occasional Latino passed for diversity at the institution. SWT was a southern college in an age in which Jim Crow still prevailed. Racism was sometimes overt. A picture that appeared in *Pedagog,* the student annual, featured Lyndon and several of his friends with a composite of a black girl wedged in. "There's an old favorite saying back in that time that said, 'Wait a minute, there's a nigger in the woodpile someplace,' " Vernon Whiteside said. "That's what that was meant to be."[34]

San Marcos was a bustling town, and SWT offered an active social life, especially for one who had grown up in Johnson City. Women, who outnumbered men by three to one, were allowed three dates a week, although it was against the rules for female students to ride with males in an automobile. Curfew was 10:30 on weeknights and midnight on weekends. Couples attended dances at the women's dormitories or went to the Palace Theater to see Charlie Chaplin or Bebe Daniels in the latest silent film. Afterward there were sodas at Williams's Drug Store downtown.

Though Dean of Women Mary Brogdon fought to keep hemlines down, most women adopted the prevailing "flapper" style, featuring short, low-waisted, straight-lined dresses. Men wore khakis and sports shirts, or, as did Lyndon, khakis, white shirt, and tie.[35] SWT prohibited fraternities and sororities, but there were literary clubs that served the same function. Women joined the Idyllics, the Philosophians, the Pennybackers, and the Shakespeares; men the Harris-Blairs and Jeffersonians. Books were reviewed and issues debated, but the societies' main preoccupations were dinners and dances. Student publications were the *Pedagog* and a newspaper, the *College Star.* A speaker's program featured such figures as Carl Sandburg and Alexander Kerensky. Attendance at weekly assembly held in the auditorium in Old Main was mandatory. President Evans opened with the same prayer every week, and the dean of men closed with "Let's get that Bobcat spirit!"[36]

Athletics had become an important part of college life at SWT by the late 1920s. Coach Oscar Strahan's basketball teams had begun the decade playing on outdoor courts, but by 1927 there was a gymnasium and football stadium as well as tennis courts and a track facility on campus. Strahan's basketball teams won several conference championships during the decade. When the football team played neighboring institutions, it was customary for the whole student body, together with faculty chaperones, to travel to the game on a chartered train.[37]

Because it catered to public school teachers, SWT's enrollment almost doubled during the summer sessions. Classes began at 7 A.M. and were over by noon. Students and faculty spent their afternoons along the banks of the tree-shaded San Marcos River, just a stone's throw from Old Main. The stretch along the border of SWT featured pavilions and promenades and was known as "Riverside." Each summer, student organizations constructed elaborate floats, adorned them with campus beauties attired in "modern" bathing suits, and paraded down the river to the cheers of students and townspeople. Riverside was also the stage for College Nights, welcoming parties for new students held each semester. President Evans would address the newcomers, music faculty and students would perform, and dancing would ensue.[38] There were, of course, extra-extracurricular activities. The clubs would hold unofficial and unchaperoned beer busts at campgrounds in nearby Seguin and New Braunfels. In these German communities, Prohibition was observed principally in the breach. "Where we went to drink the beer was over at Hunter, right out of San Marcos," Horace Richards, one of Lyndon's classmates, remembered. "And halfway to Seguin over there—I can't remember the name of the place but you would go over there, and there would be fifty or a hundred students every night sitting out under the trees drinking beer, the college professors, and all of them."[39] Austin was just thirty miles to the north, and a few of the male students possessed cars. A truly wild time was a trip to Boystown in Nuevo Laredo across the border in Mexico. There the men of SWT could find saloons and brothels that catered even to the most immature.

• • •

AT THE TIME LYNDON JOHNSON ENTERED COLLEGE, America was experiencing profound cultural change. The twenties is a period famed for its revolution in morals and manners. The postwar rebellion was first evidenced by a revolt among young people, especially among the so-called flaming youth on college and university campuses, against the rules governing sexual behavior. The automobile extended the possibilities of lovemaking far beyond the sitting room. Increased drinking, despite Prohibition, among women and middle-class young people weakened inhibitions. But most important was the phenomenal spread of the teachings of Sigmund Freud, whose writings were popularly misinterpreted to mean that the main cause of maladjusted personality was the suppression of sexual desire, and that a free expression of the libido promoted mental health.

Women achieved political equality with the adoption of the Nineteenth Amendment in 1920, and the twenties saw women not only voting but also holding offices. Masculine supremacy had been based on the male's economic primacy in the family. It rapidly deteriorated as spinster sisters moved into apartments of their own, unmarried daughters went into schoolteaching or office work, and wives gained independence either by going to work or threatening to do so.

President Evans had promised Rebekah and Sam that their son could have a job, but the best on campus paid only $30 a month. The most Sam could rake up to help Lyndon launch his college career was $25. The bank at Johnson City turned down Lyndon's request for a loan, but a Fredericksburg banker who had been an admirer of Joe Baines loaned him $75.[40] It was enough to get started. Sam Ealy offered to drive Lyndon to San Marcos, but he refused, telling his father in a show of independence that he would rather hitchhike. But instead of standing on the side of the road and holding out his thumb, he positioned himself in the middle of the road, holding up both hands. He simply refused to be passed by. He arrived on campus in early February 1927. Once in San Marcos, Lyndon moved in with Boody Johnson, bought a meal contract at the Gates Boarding House, and then turned his attention to school.

As Lyndon well knew, he would not be able to enroll immediately for regular spring classes. He had completed only eleven grades and would have to attend the subcollege run by SWT. The professor who evaluated his transcript for the preparatory program was impressed with the individual, if not his academic record. Lyndon "sat down there and talked to me for thirty or forty minutes and there was absolutely no fear," he recalled. Lyndon described the course of action he hoped to follow not only during his college years, but for the rest of his life. He wanted, he said, to learn all he could about government, politics, and society so that he could improve the world.[41] Even at this point the young man from Johnson City seemed to realize that how well he learned to work the machinery would determine how effectively he would be able to implement his ideals.

• • •

FOR THE NEXT SIX WEEKS Lyndon wrote themes, studied, and took exams. His performance was exemplary, except in geometry. Rebekah came down to help him prepare for the exam, yet he barely passed. One of his English papers that dealt with current politics was so good that the teacher who graded it suspected its authorship—and probably with good reason.[42] Where Lyndon's composition ended and Rebekah's revision began was a fine line. Whatever the case, Lyndon graduated from subcollege on March 21 and enrolled for the regular spring term.

Money would always be a problem for Lyndon while he was in college, which is why he had taken Boody Johnson's offer to share his garage apartment. The flat, which belonged to President Evans, was a two-room affair divided by a narrow hallway, at the end of which was a toilet and lavatory. An outside staircase connected the apartment to the ground. Boody was a starter on the basketball and football teams, who, together with another athlete, Clayton Stribling, was allowed to live above Evans's automobiles rent-free.[43] Stribling, who had to share the larger room and a bed with Lyndon, did not approve of the new arrangement. He regarded Lyndon as loudmouthed, overbearing, and inconsiderate. "I had a job in the Power Plant and I went to work at 3:30 and I went to bed regular at 9 o'clock, so I could go to work," he recalled. "It was a little aggravatin', 'cause he was comin' in at 9, 10, 11 o'clock at night."[44] After a month, Stribling had had enough; he forced Lyndon to move out. A family crisis soon forced Stribling to leave school, however, and Lyndon moved back in with Boody. Vernon Whiteside subsequently joined them.[45] Whiteside, who worked in the college business office, made sure that the quarters above President Evans's garage continued to be marked vacant so that the boys would not have to pay rent.[46]

Academically, Lyndon's first semester in college was a struggle. He received two Ds, one in public speaking and one in English, his strongest subjects, two Cs, and a B. He had to spend more time worrying about where his next meal and next semester's tuition were coming from than he did his studies. The two meals at Gates Boarding House, which he purchased for $16 a month, were not enough to fill him up. He was notorious for always eating, never passing the dishes to others, constantly talking to distract the other boarders. "There were eight or ten of us ate there, just on a table all together," Horace Richards said, "and he stood up most of the time and reached all the way across the table. Never passed anything, never. He was just pouring it down while he was talking."[47] The venerable Mrs. Gates had a rule that her boarders had to keep one foot on the floor while reaching for dishes, a rule that gave the six-foot-two Lyndon something of an advantage. "I'd call my mother and tell her I was bringing Lyndon home with me for Sunday dinner," Vernon Whiteside recalled. "She always killed an extra chicken because she knew that Lyndon could eat an entire fried chicken."[48]

The garage apartment that the Johnson boys occupied did not come with a bathtub, so they were forced to settle for a twice-a-week shower after gym class.[49] Discouraged by his poverty, Lyndon thought of dropping out of school. He wrote Ben Crider. "Lyndon said it was embarrassing to go to class with the seat of his pants worn," Crider later recalled. "He said he didn't have any money to operate on . . . He wanted to come out there [California] and go to work."[50] Ben, who was in communication with Rebekah, wrote back, telling his friend that life in a cement plant was no life at all and sending him $80. Cecil Evans had promised Sam and Rebekah that Lyndon would have the opportunity to work, not work itself. Employment was available, but student applicants had to pay a price. "Every morning for one week I saw that man [President Evans] at seven o'clock," Boody Johnson recalled. "Finally the last morning I went he said, 'You've been very faithful. I believe you want to go to school. You have a job.' " The $15-a-month job consisted of picking up trash on campus. Like his roommate, Lyndon began his working career stabbing errant cups and paper, but he soon landed a spot as a janitor's assistant cleaning the science building for $30 a month.[51] Within a matter of weeks he had secured the prize position of assistant to Tom Nichols, President Evans's secretary, complete with a desk in the president's outer office. The position paid $37.50 a month.[52]

Finally, Lyndon was able to devote at least part of his attention to scholastic matters. He would attend SWT continuously, with the exception of a six-month teaching stint at Cotulla, until he graduated with a BS in education in August 1930. He took the courses in education necessary to earn a secondary school teaching certificate. Years later, he confided to an interviewer that his grade point average in college was a low B. Transcripts reveal eleven As, twenty-two Bs, fourteen Cs, four Ds, and one F, in physical education, an enterprise in which, like all athletics in general, Sam Ealy's boy showed almost no interest. As had been the case in high school, Lyndon chose to learn through conversation rather than by reading. His mother and cousins, Ava and Margaret, continued to help him with his written work and his math assignments.

YOUNG JOHNSON PROVED SKILLED at cultivating his instructors. In class and in informal discussions around campus, he was deferential, respectful, attentive, not so much to earn high marks, but to learn about life, society, psychology, anything that would better prepare him for a career in politics. Those of his contemporaries who did not particularly like Lyndon regarded him as a "kiss-ass" or "brown-noser,"[53] but others noted that he was respectful and deferential to those older than he from whom he had nothing to gain. "My parents loved Lyndon," Ella Porter said, "because he paid attention to them and showed them respect always."[54] Moreover, many of the relationships he forged with instructors at SWT endured well past his college years. Lyndon's favorite subjects were history, civics, and various social sciences. He took all the basic and advanced courses in history and government, especially diplomatic history and politics.[55] To those instructors who taught subjects in which he was not interested—generally math and science—Lyndon was indifferent, and they resented it. "He had a peculiar effect on both the faculty and the students,"

English instructor Mattie Allison remembered. "You either liked him or you didn't."[56]

Lyndon's favorite faculty member was Professor H. M. "Harry" Greene of the government department. Greene was a small, disheveled, tobacco-chewing iconoclast who had earned a master's degree at the University of Texas and had a year toward his doctorate at the University of Illinois. Like Lyndon, he preferred to gain knowledge through conversation and reading newspapers. He frequently taught using the Socratic method, the classic dodge of the unprepared. Frequently appearing in class unwashed and unshaven, he punctuated his dialogues by spitting tobacco juice in a sand-filled coffee can in his desk drawer.[57] He related particularly well to the needy students because he was poor himself. He lived with his wife and nine children, the last named Hambone, in a cabin in the beautiful Hill Country resort village of Wimberly. Greene's political philosophy was something of a cross between Thomas Jefferson and Robert LaFollette. He was a great respecter of democracy and the Bill of Rights, a self-appointed champion of the common man. He taught his students to be devoted to the American form of government but suspicious of those who held authority. The temptation to pervert the machinery, to exploit and oppress was ever present.

Lyndon Johnson was Harry Greene's kind of student, and he did not hesitate to show his favoritism. Lyndon would readily join in the political debates that Greene loved to provoke, and the professor would allow the young man from Johnson City to follow him around campus, pumping him for his views on current events. Lyndon would walk downtown to listen in person as Greene gave the news and his latest political prediction over a contraband radio station operated by Horace Richards, another student and admirer, out of the Ford Motor Co. showroom. A staunch Democrat, Greene would lambast the pro–big business, do-nothing policies of the Coolidge administration and hinted more than once that they would in the end produce a massive depression. Lyndon's contemporaries remember the government instructor singling him out in class: "Son, if I were headed for the political arena, I would bear in mind that the United States Senate is one spot where a man of integrity has a real opportunity to serve his country."[58]

PREVIOUS BIOGRAPHERS have made much of the "simple" patriotism that characterized the environment in which LBJ grew up. There were certainly the trappings of patriotism: the Pledge of Allegiance in school, the Fourth of July celebrations, the reverence for the landmarks of American history: the Constitution, the Revolution, the western frontier, the sense of exceptionalism. Yet patriotic though the ethos was, simple it was not. Even at nineteen Lyndon realized that the American political system was a process, not a state, that it contained the seeds of social good but also of social evil. Interests must be accommodated but not at the expense of the common good. American democracy would not in and of itself guarantee social justice and national cohesion; only men and women with the higher good in mind who were willing to get their hands dirty in the day-to-day workings of politics could do that. The Johnson family's patriotism was the patriotism of Woodrow Wilson and Theodore Roosevelt, not Warren Harding and Calvin Coolidge. Their liberalism was the "positive" liberalism of the Progressive Era presidents, who saw the federal government as an active agent dedicated to conserving natural resources, regulating big business to ensure a modicum of social justice, and doing its best to ensure equality of opportunity to the white citizenry of the country. The Johnsons saw the passive, laissez-faire "negative" liberalism of the modern Republican party, which envisioned the role of government as almost exclusively limited to protecting the rights of the individual, for what it was: a throwback to the nineteenth century, unsuited to the needs of a modern age or the imperatives of New Testament Christianity. Unlike William Jennings Bryan and Robert LaFollette, however, the Johnsons' idealism did not stop at America's borders. Lyndon (or Rebekah) would write an editorial for the SWT student newspaper accepting and defending the notion that America had entered the Great War to make the world safe for democracy.

In addition to politics, Lyndon and Harry Greene shared a passion for debate. Greene was the debate coach at SWT, and Lyndon became one of his star performers. In 1928, Greene paired Lyndon with Elmer Graham, a bright and pious young man who would go on to become a Baptist minister in San Antonio. The trio traveled around the state competing with comparable institutions and winning most of their matches. The topics assigned were current: Should the United States participate in the League of Nations? Should the United States send troops to Nicaragua? Should the United States continue "to protect, by armed force, capital invested in foreign countries except after formal declaration of war"?[59] Teams did not know whether they would be assigned the affirmative or the negative until right before the debate started. Typically, the organized and logical Graham would lay out SWT's position, leaving it to Lyndon to attack the weaknesses in the opponents' argument. According to Graham, his teammate could be ruthless once he had the advantage. He never lost his temper, however, and never took the matches personally. Greene provided motivation and an occasional offbeat fact. Graham was both repelled and attracted by Greene and Johnson. He found their active minds and conversation stimulating but was repulsed by their swearing, off-color jokes, tobacco chewing, and occasional drinking.[60]

FOR LYNDON JOHNSON, college was not just a place to learn about the theory of politics and government but a laboratory to conduct experiments in them. He was interested in the job in President Evans's office as much because of its potential for power as for personal income. He also appreciated the crucial role that apprenticeship played in the political world. Indeed, if ever anyone understood the word *protégé,* it was Lyndon. Cecil Evans found the young man compelling. His ambition, his deference, his willingness to serve, his obvious intelligence and energy attracted the president, a man known for keeping his social distance from students and faculty alike. "I was tremendously fond of him," Evans said. "We promoted him to increasingly responsible positions. He could handle people extremely well." [61] Though he was Tom Nichols's assistant, most people on the SWT campus came to think of Lyndon as President Evans's secretary—frequently to Nichols's irritation. "Tom liked Lyndon," Vernon Whiteside observed, "but he thought he was too pushy, and he was always trying to do something for Dr. Evans. He knew which buttons to press, all right . . . Tom would try to embarrass him by [saying], Lyndon, empty that wastebasket over there . . . Tom tried to put him in his place. But he was pretty hard to put in his place." [62] And his power grew. Within a year, Lyndon was a frequent companion of Evans on his trips to the capitol in Austin to lobby for the college. By 1928, he was in a position to influence, if not control, the life-sustaining jobs that were handed out to students. [63]

President Evans's protégé Lyndon might have been, but he was still a second-class citizen on the SWT campus because he was not an athlete. As was the case on virtually every other college and university campus in Texas, athletes were a privileged class. Coach Strahan's basketball and football players were allowed to register early, miss assembly without punishment, and go to the head of the line in the cafeteria. They had their choice of coeds for dates. The social event of the season was a dinner given every winter in honor of the football players by the women of the Shakespeare Literary Society. To show their respect, President Evans and the deans as well as the coaches attended. In 1920, to better control campus life, student athletes created a secret society, Beta Sigma, or, as it was more popularly known, the Black Stars. Virtually all lettermen belonged to the organization initially, but by the late 1920s its self-selecting policies excluded some. A nominee had to receive unanimous support in a secret ballot of the existing membership. The organization dominated student government, and through it controlled the blanket activity tax that every student was compelled to pay. The Black Stars determined selections for Gallardians, the most popular and beautiful women who subsequently had their picture published in the *Pedagog*. Through the student council, which it dominated, the fraternity of athletes was able to control selection of the editors of the *College Star* and *Pedagog* as well as of the business manager of the *Pedagog*, prized positions because they paid $30 a month. Inevitably, this athletocracy created a groundswell of resentment and opposition among lesser male mortals—"The Brains vs. The Beef," as one outsider put it. [64]

As the fall 1928 term opened, a number of students in a variety of settings began to discuss formation of an organization to counter the Black Stars. One of the instigators was Harry Greene, who believed that the campus ought to be controlled by the brightest, most politically savvy students on campus, not the strongest. "We were all about nineteen years old, and we went up to Wimberly," Horace Richards, one of Greene's students, remembered. "Just boys. We had a keg of beer . . . And the next time we took our girls and this thing just kind of grew and grew." [65] When several athletes kept cutting in on Richards and White-side as they danced with their dates at a campus function, the dye was cast. Richards, Vernon Whiteside, Hollis Frazer, Wilton Woods, Willard Deason, and several other boys anted up $2 for a room on the fourth floor of the Hofheinz Hotel in downtown San Marcos to plan strategy. They were afraid to meet in any of the boarding houses for fear the administration or the athletes would become privy to their schemes. The conspirators hammered out a constitution and devised an initiation ceremony, both of which were to be kept absolutely secret. They selected the unoriginal name Alpha Omega, but became known, not surprisingly, as the White Stars. "Walter Grady from Tennessee seemed to be the only one that had prior knowledge of how fraternities operated," Wilton Woods remembered, and so he guided the founders. Several days later, the anti-athletes gathered at midnight on the banks of the San Marcos and by candlelight swore the necessary oaths on Horace Richards's Bible (a large dictionary, as it later turned out). [66]

After Lyndon became assistant to Tom Nichols and purveyor of student jobs, Boody Johnson put him up for membership in the Black Stars, but he was blackballed. Allegedly he had aroused the ire of one of the athletes by courting his girlfriend, but he probably did not get in because he did not play football, baseball, or basketball. Lyndon naturally came to the attention of the White Stars following their founding. Despite his later claims to the contrary, he was not one of the originators but was brought in later because of his position and his political savvy. [67] Even then, the founders had their doubts. "He tried a couple of times to get in," Horace Richards said. "He'd been turned down by the Black Stars, and we didn't want him because he talked too much. We called it flapping . . . He'd tell our secrets. We were afraid." [68] But eventually, the membership relented. The first year there were only about ten White Stars. The organization had a rule that no more than two of them could be seen together on campus. There were no officers and no dues. The membership met frequently, usually late at night, in one of the student's rooms to plot their strategy. The focus initially was on alliances with other groups: women students, YMCA members, the Harris-Blair Literary Society. [69] They were bright, resourceful, iconoclastic.

The first issue over which The Brains challenged The Beef was allocation of the student activity fee. Instead of pep rallies and athletic equipment, the White Stars wanted the money to go toward support of the debate team, the drama club, the choir, and special speakers. They insisted that the Gallardians be elected by the entire student body rather than chosen by the student council. The struggle went to the heart of what SWT was about, its importance underscored by Greene and other faculty's active support of the White Star position and Strahan and the coaches' backing of the Black Stars. The insurgents pitched the fight in terms of whether or not democracy was to prevail at San Marcos. In the dead of night, Osler Dunn, a White Star clad in long black coat and floppy hat, passed out subversive material. One pamphlet was entitled "Democracy and Equality."[70] In this first great battle, the White Stars prevailed, and funds were gradually shifted to cultural activities.[71] Unbeknown to the Black Star leadership, the White Stars, with Lyndon's help, had recruited several athletes— Boody Johnson and Sub Pyland the most prominent—who were also members of the Black Stars.[72]

The ultimate challenge for the White Stars was to capture the presidency of the student body. The athletes put up the handsome, popular Dick Spinn of Brenham, who was also a member of the YMCA group. The Brains nominated Willard Deason. Both sides campaigned vigorously for the votes of the two hundred seniors. The night before the election, Deason's managers conducted a head count and found that their man was some twenty votes shy of a majority. Discouraged and resigned, they went to bed—all except Lyndon. Into the early hours of the morning he made the rounds of the boarding houses, knocking on doors, pleading and cajoling with those who would listen. When the final tally was in the next day, Deason had won by twenty votes.[73] Eventually the White Stars gained control of the student council, which enabled them to appoint the staffs of the *College Star* and the *Pedagog*. One student who remained nonaligned remembered that it was easy to tell that the pendulum of power had shifted at SWT; all the White Stars were inside working in offices and the library, all the Black Stars outside picking up trash and painting.[74]

VERNON WHITESIDE did not remember Lyndon as being particularly popular or unpopular. "He wasn't trying to be popular. He was busy. He was so busy, like I say, his coattail was on fire all the time."[75] His contemporaries remember seeing him on campus perpetually in motion, his long stride hurried, always focused on the next task: a class, delivering messages for the president, organizing a meeting, going to a debate, hustling some little money-making scheme. Boarders at the Gates House knew him only as "Bull" Johnson. The meaning of the term differed with the person. Some said the nickname stemmed from his aggressive nature, his willfulness, his impatience. Others blamed it on their classmate's tendency to exaggerate, to overemphasize his woes, to inflate his dreams and accomplishments, to "bullshit," in short.[76] "Hell, if the sun shone, Lyndon would have remembered the day as the day it snowed eight feet," Sam Houston observed of his brother.[77] Athletes like Clayton Stribling and Joe Berry didn't like him, for obvious reasons. "When he was destroying the Black Stars," Berry said, "he was never visible. He manipulated his friends and pulled the strings from behind the scenes . . . Down inside I just didn't have very high regard for him."[78] Lyndon's loquaciousness irritated even his closest friends. "I remember one time . . . he was living over the President's garage and we were playing poker up there," Horace Richards said. "Two of us was on the bed and then two or three more were sitting in chairs around a little table . . . Old Dr. Evans would have died if he had known a big poker game was going on in his garage . . . [Mylton 'Babe'] Kennedy was a pretty good sized guy, and I never will forget. He said, 'Lyndon, if you open your mouth one more time, I'll knock every tooth you've got plumb down your throat.' "[79] Lyndon was respectful of authority, but not that respectful. "Well, the first time we made beer," Richards recalled, "the President went off on a trip with his wife, and the old boy that was his caretaker let us go in the President's kitchen to heat the water on his electric stove, and after we got the beer all made, we put it down in the basement. Then as we needed a dozen bottles, we'd slip down in the basement at night and get it out."[80] "I can recall Lyndon getting up on the stage in the auditorium for the assembly and giving the best imitation of Prexy [Dr. Evans] that you can imagine, imitating him, mocking him."[81]

Lyndon's contemporaries at SWT noted a characteristic that was to mark the man for the rest of his life: aggressiveness to the point of personal offense, followed by feelings of regret and efforts at atonement. "My first encounter with him was a little bit unpleasant," Willard Deason recalled. "We were taking a math course and I having been a teacher thought I knew all the answers, and he thought he knew some of the answers, too, and we got in a little dispute right in the classroom . . . I kind of got in a huff and turned away from him. When the class was over I walked out ahead of him, he walked up and dropped his long arm down on my shoulder and said, 'Now, that's nothing to be mad about. That's just all in the day's work. No use you and I being mad at one another, might as well be friends.' "[82] But Lyndon did not apologize. Lyndon Johnson never apologized.

ACCOUNTS OF LYNDON'S DATING HABITS DIFFER. One of his roommates, Barton Gill, recalled that he had dates two or three nights a week. He was vain of his appearance. Gill remembered him standing before the mirror endlessly grooming, smoothing down his curly hair, "drawing his neck down into his collar so that it would not look so long."[83] Following those first desperate, penniless weeks when he had to cover worn spots in the seat of his pants with a newspaper tucked in his back pocket, he dressed as well as he could on a limited budget. A bow tie was his trademark. According to others, Lyndon dated only intermittently. In fact, the young man from Johnson City fell in love in the spring of 1927 with Carol Davis, the daughter of a well-to-do businessman and former mayor of San Marcos. She was, he recalled, "very beautiful, tall and blond with dark blue eyes. Her skin was pale and very soft. She was very clever and everyone admired her. I fell in love with her the first moment we met."[84] Carol played the violin, wrote poetry, and sang. Johnson City residents recall her coming home with Lyndon and performing at various venues. "I still remember the summer evenings we spent together, lying next to the river in a waist-high mass of weeds talking about our future," Lyndon later recalled. "I had never been happier. After a while we began to talk about marriage."[85]

It was not to be. Lyndon became temporarily obsessed with national politics in 1928, a presidential election year. Early in the summer Governor Dan Moody and State Senator Alvin Wirtz came to campus and delivered speeches at Riverside. Lyndon, of course, was on hand and introduced himself to both men.[86] According to a fellow student, he bored his classmates silly with "marathon talk about political personalities and how he would run a campaign if he were a candidate."[87] The Democratic Convention was scheduled for Houston in August. Lyndon decided to go; he had been named summer editor of the *College Star* and could pass himself off as a representative of the press. "All during the months before the Democratic national convention that summer in Houston, Lyndon ran great headlines about it in the *Star*," Tom Nichols remembered. "Later I saw his motive when he carried a bundle of his *College Stars* down there to the convention chairman and laid them on the table and asked for a ticket to the press box."[88] He persuaded Carol and her father to accompany him. Lyndon stayed with his Uncle George, while Carol and Mr. Davis made their own arrangements.

COMPARED TO THE 1924 DEMOCRATIC CONVENTION in New York, which had lasted sixteen days and cast 104 ballots, the gathering in Houston was a tame affair. Nevertheless, the convention proved to be the most memorable event of Johnson's young life. He not only got onto the floor but also secured gallery passes for the Davises. Once inside, Lyndon refused to leave. "He had stayed in the convention hall because they didn't have enough places for reporters," Vernon Whiteside said. "He slept on the table . . . and these other reporters, him being a young buck, brought him sandwiches and so forth."[89] The Democrats nominated Governor Alfred E. Smith of New York, a Catholic and a wet, over the objections of most southerners and westerners who tended to be Protestant and dry. The KKK, which embodied the ethos of the South and West, was an issue but not as important as it had been in 1924.[90]

The Houston experience was exhilarating for the young man from Johnson City, but it marked the beginning of the end of his relationship with Carol Davis. Her father was very conservative and a member of the KKK. He regarded Sam Ealy, Lyndon's father, as liberal to radical in his views. Contrasting political philosophies created strains in the young couple's relationship that were exacerbated by differences in tastes and by a long separation in 1928 and 1929, when Lyndon taught public school at Cotulla and Carol at Pearsall. Her hobbies were music, poetry, and motion pictures; politics bored her. "Miss Sarah," Lyndon told his landlady in Cotulla, "this girl loves opera. But I'd rather sit down on an old log with a farmer and talk."[91] Nevertheless, Lyndon was not only physically attracted to Carol; her family's high social standing and relative wealth made her the perfect marriage partner for an up-and-coming young politician. Matters came to a head over dinner one evening at the Evans home. According to Lyndon, he had had several glasses of wine and began talking freely about his experiences in California, his relatively liberal views on government and society, and his family's involvement in politics. The atmosphere tensed. Mr. Davis defended the Klan and denounced Jim Ferguson and all he stood for. Everyone in Blanco County knew, he said, that Sam Ealy Sr. had been "nothing but an old cattle rustler."[92] Infuriated, Lyndon stalked out. Carol later told him that her father had forbidden her to marry into "that no-account Johnson family . . . one generation after another of shiftless dirt farmers and grubby politicians."[93] According to Ronnie Dugger and Sam Houston, Carol came to Lyndon crying, indicating that she was willing to defy her father and marry him. He would have none of it. Family pride and cohesiveness were too important; the Johnsons had been insulted and there could be no thought of any union with the Davises. Johnson biographer Robert Dallek writes that Carol dumped Lyndon in the spring of 1929 for another suitor. Whatever the case, the love affair was over.[94]

During the 1927–1928 terms, Lyndon had been sure to take the five education courses that qualified him for an elementary school teaching certificate. With the help of President Evans, he secured a job as principal and teacher at the Welhausen School in Cotulla, Texas. If he saved most of his princely salary of $125 a month, he could pay for his final year of college and afford to buy some sort of automobile, his earlier acquisition having lasted only a couple of months.[95]

COTULLA WAS SITUATED in the middle of the Brush Country, a flat, dry, ranching region stretching from south of San Antonio to Laredo. In 1928, the town of three thousand was 75 percent Mexican American, most of whom lived in one-room, dirt-floored shacks in the *colonia,* or rural ghetto, on the south side of the Missouri-Pacific train line that divided the town east to west. Founded in the years after the Texas Revolution, Cotulla sported a violent past. Before and after the Civil War, marauding bands of Hispanics and Anglos roamed the territory, raiding cattle ranches and waging low-level warfare. When the Rangers came to clean up La Salle County, of which Cotulla was the county seat, they directed most of their attention to the brown-skinned banditos. "The killing of Mexicans [in Texas] without provocation is so common as to pass unnoticed," the *New York Times* editorialized in 1921.[96] By the 1890s, Anglos had gained control of almost all of the land in the region by means of high taxes, purchase, and a legal system heavily weighted in their favor. The vast majority of Mexican Americans became day laborers, many on land they had previously owned. At the time Lyndon came to Cotulla, most Mexicans worked for large agribusinesses, made possible by modern irrigation methods, but some still worked on family farms.

Prejudice against Hispanics was deeply embedded in the culture of the state. Indeed, it was implicit in Texan nationalism. The Mexicans who remained after the Alamo were generally regarded as uncivilized trespassers, dirty, lazy, and priest-ridden. They were fit only in the view of most Anglos, to serve as beasts of burden. "Ranch culture [was] like a feudal system," remembered Rita Binkley Worthy, whose father managed the giant Callaghan ranch south of Cotulla. Ranchers demanded total obedience and racial deference. No Mexican dared question the long, backbreaking hours of work at subsistence wages or rebel at the crop-lien system.[97] At lunch counters, in movie theaters, in parks, and on trains, Texans of Mexican descent were segregated and excluded. In the 1920s, nativists in the KKK pressed for legislation banning further immigration, but Mexicans were too valuable a labor source for ranchers and farmers, and the movement foundered. Thus did Lyndon Johnson come to teach and inspire in a community in which it was considered dangerously subversive to lead Mexican children to hope.

The twenty-year-old college junior was profoundly affected by what he found at Welhausen School, and it aroused all of his missionary sensibilities. The children of Mexican Americans were discouraged from attending school at all. State funds were distributed on the basis of the total school-age population; Anglo authorities quickly realized that the fewer Mexican children who went to school, the more funds would be available for white facilities. Some Mexican families insisted, however, and so schools like Welhausen were built, but they were intended to be dead ends, where children learned basic English and other minimal skills that would make them good workers. Lyndon found this institutionalized hopelessness intolerable: "They knew in their youth the pain of prejudice," he recalled later in a speech in behalf of the Voting Rights Act. "They never seemed to know why people disliked them. But they knew it was so, because I saw it in their eyes. I often walked home late in the afternoon, after classes were finished, wishing there was more that I could do. But all I knew was to teach them the little I knew, hoping that it might help them against the hardships that lay ahead . . . Somehow you never forget what poverty and hatred can do when you see the scars on the hopeful face of a young child." [98] Privately, Lyndon was appalled by the attitude of the Anglo population of Cotulla: they treated Mexicans "just worse than you'd treat a dog," he later remarked, and he remembered "the Mexican children going through a garbage pile, shaking the coffee grounds from the grapefruit rinds and sucking the rinds for the juice that was left." [99] He meant to teach the thirty-odd children in his charge more than English; he was determined to convince them that they were human beings who could learn, strive, and live the American dream. But he would do it without confronting authority. He would use the ideals that underlay the system to defeat the flaws that threatened to corrupt it. It would become a pattern.

Lyndon arrived in Cotulla, rented a room at a local boarding house, and checked in with his boss, Superintendent W. T. Donoho, who would prove to be an ally. Young Johnson would be the fourth teacher at Welhausen School and the principal. He would tutor the sixth-, seventh-, and eighth-graders while the other members of the staff, Elizabeth Woolls Johnson, Twila Kerr, and Mary (Mamie) Wildenthal, taught the other grades. The new principal, dressed in a blue serge suit with bow or four-in-hand tie, cut a dashing figure. One of the high school teachers at the time remembered thinking that he was the handsomest young man he had ever seen. As a classroom instructor, Lyndon was typical of his times. A strict disciplinarian, he brooked no disrespect or disorderly conduct, not hesitating to spank male students who transgressed. In conformity with school policy, he allowed no Spanish to be spoken in the classroom or on the playground. Fifth-grade boys who came to school unprepared had their ears pinched. Yet once his authority was established, he was kind, solicitous, and even affectionate.

The new principal was astounded to find that there were no extracurricular activities, which he regarded just as important as classroom instruction. Recess consisted of scuffling in the dust.[100] "I took my first paycheck," he said, "and bought them a volleyball net, singing books for the choir, second-hand musical instruments."[101] He compelled the other teachers, who usually spent recess smoking in the bathroom, to organize and supervise volleyball, baseball, and other games. And, of course, he organized a debate team. There were no buses for Welhausen, and so Lyndon drafted several Mexican families with automobiles to transport his debaters and athletes to competitions with other schools. With the janitor, Thomas Coronado, he planted the grounds with flowers and shrubs. He had his mother send him toothpaste for the children and began daily hygiene checks. Lyndon had his students greet him each day with a ditty he had set to a popular vaudeville tune:

> *How do you do, Mr. Johnson,*
> *How do you do?*
> *Is there anything that we can do for you?*
> *We will do it if we can,*
> *We'll stand by you to a man.*
> *How do you do, Mr. Johnson,*
> *How do you do, do, do?*[102]

Lyndon's three grades of twenty-eight students and their parents found him exhilarating. "He put us to work," one of his pupils said. "But he was the kind of teacher you wanted to work for." The Mexican parents were astonished that an Anglo teacher would take such an interest in their children, particularly one who encouraged them to dream of becoming a doctor, lawyer, or even president of the United States. "We wanted to take advantage of his being there," Dan Garcia remembered. "It was like a blessing from the clear sky."[103] Lyndon wasn't much into cultural relativity. He did not lead his charges and their families to believe that their heritage was superior or equal to Anglo culture. Rather, he taught them that the United States was a nation of immigrants, and that they had as much right to the American dream as German, Polish, or Italian Americans. To whites in Cotulla, in Texas in the 1920s, his was a profoundly repugnant notion.

Initially, Lyndon's fellow teachers resented his sometimes coercive approach, and they were not used to having to spend time outside the classroom on the extracurricular activities of mere Mexicans. One Friday, when their boss was out of town, they went to the superintendent to complain. "Our traces are down and we have balked," the spokeswoman for the group said. "The teachers went out on strike on me," Lyndon later related. "They said they weren't supervising any recesses with those kids; and they were some of the best-connected people in town, the daughter of a banker and another was a sister of the mayor, and another the sister of the postmaster."[104] But the principal had his allies. One of the most prominent members of the school board was Rebecca Knaggs, a graduate of Randolph Macon and scion of one of the wealthiest families in Cotulla. The Knaggses had a reputation as progressives, frequently speaking out for fair treatment of the Mexican labor force and equal educational opportunity for their children. Evenings would frequently find Lyndon on the Knaggses' front porch, for example, discussing national issues. "The brightest man we've ever had in Cotulla," Rebecca told her daughter.[105] When Mamie Wildenthal offered her resignation and those of her colleagues, Ms. Knaggs suggested that they be accepted.[106] "Just accept their resignations," Lyndon remembered her saying, "and go back to San Marcos and get replacements for them, replacements that will come here and supervise during recess."[107] The teachers withdrew their resignations and accepted Mr. Johnson's authority.

SO PLEASED WAS THE COTULLA SCHOOL DISTRICT with Lyndon that they offered him another contract. Superintendent Donoho remembered him as "one of the very best men that I have ever had with me . . . more than willing to carry out the policies of the school regardless of personal opinion."[108] But the young man from Johnson City had no intention of remaining in the Brush Country of south Texas. While performing all of his duties as teacher and missionary for Americanism, Lyndon had managed to take five extension courses, including one entitled "Race Relations," all taught by Donoho. "I wanted to finish my college work, and in June of '29 I went back to San Marcos and continued right straight through until August of 1930 when I got a bachelor of science degree," Lyndon said.[109]

The final fourteen months of Lyndon's college life were a blur of activity. He quickly reestablished contact with his friends, moving into Mrs. Miller's Rooming House on North Comanche with Boody Johnson and purchasing a meal contract with Mrs. Gates. "We were rooming together in that room on the right as you enter the Miller house," Boody later recalled. "Of course, [there were] no fans or nothing, and it was hot. So we'd tie a sheet down the middle of the bed, and you better not get over on his side and he better not get over on my side."[110] Meanwhile, things had gone from bad to worse for Sam and Rebekah. Lyndon's friends had noted that whenever he had a little extra cash, he would stuff a dollar or two in an envelope and send it to his mother, but it wasn't until Vernon Whiteside went home with Lyndon for a visit that they realized how bad things were. "I went up there one time on a weekend," Whiteside later recalled. "And they had two old poor cows just grazing out there . . . You didn't have to ask what the weather was, you could see through [the walls] where the piece of the batting was off . . . So we're out there that evening, and his daddy hollers at us, said, 'Lyndon, draw us some water and milk them cows.' I remember Josefa . . . and Sam Houston. His younger sister [Lucia], she was still in diapers almost . . . What we had for supper that night was cornbread and milk." He remembered Lyndon looking at his mother cooking over a wood stove and swearing that someday he would bring electricity to the Hill Country.[111]

Things between Lyndon and Sam Ealy were not good. "The next morning, about five-thirty, Mr. Sam came in our room, and we were sleeping in an old iron bed that had an old cotton mattress on it. He kicked that bed and it really shook us up. I opened my eyes and looked up at him . . . and he had a water glass that was about half-full of whiskey and water . . . He said, 'Lyndon, get up from there. Every boy in Giles County has got an hour's start on you already.' Where Giles County is I don't know; I thought Giles County was over in East Texas somewhere . . . So we got up and got out of there and we went on back to San Marcos pretty quick."[112]

While he was living in the Miller house, Lyndon got the idea of renting a house in San Marcos so that his mother could come down and take in boarders. It would give her some independent income, and Sam Houston and Josefa would have a place to live when they went to college. He found an eight-room, single-story house west of campus at 542 Burleson that he rented for $30 a month.[113] The family did not immediately move, so he and Vernon Whiteside occupied the house. They slept on a mattress Vernon brought from home in Lockhart. Lighting was a single bare bulb. "It was a pretty crummy place, really," Vernon remembered. "We stayed about forty days, and we changed the bedroom three different times because we didn't have a broom to sweep out."[114] Eventually, Rebekah, Sam, and the children moved in; Lyndon went back to the Miller house. In the fall, when Boody finished school, Lyndon relocated to Mrs. Hopper's Boarding House on West Hopkins, where he shared a large screened-in porch with three other men.[115] He resumed working in President Evans's office, signed up for a full load of courses, and plunged into a series of extracurricular activities. He was elected secretary of the Schoolmasters Club, an organization of present and future teachers, and he rejoined the Harris-Blair Literary Society. Many of his contemporaries thought at this point that "Bull" Johnson would become a public school teacher. He did his practice teaching at the Demonstration High School in San Marcos and seemed to glory in it. His students remembered how animated and involved he was. "He was very vivid," one said. "He walked around and slung his big, old long arms out and pointed and gestured." Another remembered that all the girls had a crush on him because he was so handsome.[116] He managed to have himself appointed summer editor of the *College Star* again, and editorials under his byline appeared throughout the 1929–1930 school year. The paper's offices were situated on the first floor of Old Main directly across the hall from President Evans's suite. Tom Nichols, Lyndon's boss, was the faculty sponsor.[117]

Initially, Lyndon's editorials were set pieces on such flaccid subjects as "Fatherhood," "Independence Day," and "Thanksgiving," or flattering biographies of administrators and faculty. Nearly all his editorials were written by his mother or a member of the staff he could command. "He'd say, 'Now, next week is the paper that comes out the day before Thanksgiving,' " Wilton Woods recalled. " 'You write an article about the origin of Thanksgiving and the whole story,' and I'd usually say, 'Where am I going to get the stuff?' He said, 'From an encyclopedia.' " [118] One article on Charles Lindbergh's transatlantic flight dwelt unoriginally on "the independence of spirit" that the feat symbolized. After a time, however, Lyndon began to put some of himself in his writing. After he returned from Cotulla, he penned a tribute to teaching: "To lead inquiring and impressionable minds into the great treasure house of the knowledge that the world has accumulated is of itself a priceless privilege. To be of service to humanity is recompense for struggling years and patient study." [119] Gradually the themes and goals that would characterize Lyndon's adult life would emerge: the value of public service, the nobility of duty, the virtues of a disciplined, self-controlled life.

Character, he said, comes from the "perfectly educated will." [120] "There are no tyrannies like those human passions and weaknesses exercise . . . No master is so cruelly exacting as an indulged appetite." [121] Joe and Rebekah Baines could not have said it better. One of Lyndon's favorite scriptural quotes when he became president was "Without vision, the people perish." In a 1928 editorial, he applauded the vision that gave inspiration to artists, architects, but particularly statesmen, as they sought to frame laws for the general good. [122] Even as a college student, Lyndon seemed profoundly counterrevolutionary. He lauded Benjamin Franklin as a reluctant rebel more interested in building a new government after the fighting was over than in tearing down the existing regime. He saw danger, the edge of chaos, in professional revolutionaries like Patrick Henry. The 1920s produced some of America's great iconoclasts: Sinclair Lewis, H. L. Mencken, F. Scott Fitzgerald. Although he was a person of biting satirical wit himself, Lyndon distrusted critics, or "cynics," as he labeled them. To him they seemed profoundly subversive, especially those who attacked America and its institutions. In an editorial denouncing the then current genre of debunking biographies, he pointed out that hero worship was a "tremendous force in uplifting and strengthening humanity." [123]

Lyndon's utopia was an inclusive society dedicated to orderly growth. He was certainly a nationalist. Knit more and more closely together, the American people would bring forth and sustain a government that would act positively not only to protect individual rights but to advance the cause of social justice. His notion of the ideal public servant was quite Confucian: selfless, disinterested, humble, introspective, and yet dynamic in his dedication to the common good. Respect your elders, your laws, your ideals, and above all, be responsible. Young Lyndon Johnson was a natural mandarin with an affinity for democracy. Above all, he seemed an individual determined to make his mark, to make a difference in the lives of others for the better, to earn a place in the books of Whig historians. [124]

Though a somewhat naïve exponent of the Horatio Alger myth and the American dream, Johnson as a collegiate was not one of the rural "hayseeds, hillbillies, and boobs" that H. L. Mencken continually derided in the *American*

Mercury. Like his father, he was an outspoken opponent of the Klan and Prohibition. He certainly believed in the equality of the sexes insofar as the culture of the 1920s defined it. Technology was not a threat to traditional values, but the pathway to a brave new world. Lyndon applauded science and rationalism for their promise to create a safer, more prosperous, more just world. He was the quintessential hustler, but not of the Babbitt genre. In the first place, Lyndon and his father did not dream of $50,000 a year; they dreamed of $2,500 a year. Financial disaster, a lifetime of debt were just one bad deal, just one commodity price collapse away. Materialism was not a matter of choice for the struggling middle class of central Texas, it was a necessity. Success in providing the fundamentals of life plus a few extras was the ultimate badge of manhood. As he wrote in one of his editorials, fatherhood was an exercise in stoic responsibility. A mature man was above all the "producer, provider, and protector." [125] A mature public servant was one who worked to make tangible the ideals implicit in the Constitution, the Declaration of Independence, and the machinery of republican government. In that sense, Lyndon was profoundly conservative, but no more so than Theodore Roosevelt or Woodrow Wilson or, for that matter, Samuel Gompers or Robert LaFollette.

It should also be noted that for Lyndon Johnson, the press existed to serve the people and the responsible officials who watched over them. In the summer of 1930 Mylton Kennedy was the editor of the *Star*. He did a satirical piece on the relationship between Lyndon and President Evans. At that time, the *Star* was printed in the offices of the town paper, the *San Marcos Record*. "This particular Thursday morning we had put it [the issue] to bed the night before," Kennedy explained. "I guess that I had stayed down there all night that night, because this particular time we were running the paper on the presses . . . I had written a story about Lyndon in a satirical approach . . . Someway, somehow, Lyndon got wind of it . . . The *Record* got a telephone call . . . my inclination would be to say that it was from Dean [H. E.] Speck. But they were told to stop the paper. Then I was told to bring up all of the copies of that paper that had been run off . . . And when I got up to the top of the hill, the remains were seized and I had to get some filler to put in for that particular column." [126]

Though he was writing editorials, taking an overload of classes, working for the president's office, and generally playing the big man on campus, Lyndon still had time for politics: 1930 was an election year, and a political gathering was scheduled at Henly, a wide spot in the road near Dripping Springs. Some two hundred people gathered at the campground to eat a picnic lunch and listen to the candidates for various offices stand in the back of a flatbed truck and extol their virtues. One of those speaking was Welly Hopkins, who was running for the state senate seat held by the retiring Alvin Wirtz. Hopkins recalled that he made his pitch and stepped down. The master of ceremonies then asked if Pat Neff, who was making a bid for a place on the Railroad Commission, was there. He was not. Would anyone make a speech in his behalf? As it turned out, Sam Ealy, who had gotten a patronage job from Neff, was supposed to speak, but he was not in attendance. Hopkins recalled that after some delay, a voice called out of the crowd, " 'Well, I'll make a speech for Pat Neff.' And here through the crowd came this tall, brown haired, bright-eyed boy, kind of, with a bushy-tail attitude of vigor . . . He spoke maybe five to ten minutes in a typical fashion, a little bit of the oratorical effect, and a good one, some of the arm waving that I guess I'd indulged in some too. But he showed pretty good cause why Pat Neff should be reelected, and was favorably received." [127]

It had all been a set-up. Sam Ealy and Neff had been in regular correspondence. Neff's opponents had already criticized him for using public employees for political purpose. Thus was it decided that the twenty-two-year-old Lyndon, already a seasoned campaigner, would speak, rather than Sam. [128]

Back in San Marcos Lyndon enlisted the help of Wilton Woods, Willard Deason, and others of his more politically inclined friends. In the weeks that followed, he accompanied Hopkins on campaign swings throughout Blanco and Hays Counties. "I rode all the byways in Blanco County with Lyndon," Hopkins recalled, "and followed his judgment in Hays County almost completely because he had a favorable standing with the local people in San Marcos." On the night before the election, the student politician organized mass meetings for his candidate in both New Braunfels and San Marcos. Hopkins won going away. [129]

CHAPTER 4

THE SECRETARY

L YNDON DREAMED OF A LIFE IN POLITICS, BUT IN THE
meantime, he had to have a job. He had to support himself, and his
siblings as well. In 1930, the year his son officially entered the working world, Sam Ealy was employed by the Railroad Commission.
Sam never made more than $150 a month, yet he and Rebekah were deter-
mined that each of their children would attend college. "During those years . . .
all of us children got through college by helping each other," Lyndon recalled.
"When I graduated and started teaching, I helped the younger ones. When my
sister graduated and began teaching, she helped the younger ones."[1] Sam and
Rebekah continued to live in the house on Burleson Street, taking in boarders,
while Rebekah and Josefa attended Southwest Texas State Teachers College.[2]

Other than his mother and father, perhaps the relative Lyndon was closest to
was Sam Ealy's brother, George Desha Johnson, who was chair of the history
and government department at Sam Houston High School in Houston. In visits and letters, nephew and uncle had discussed history and politics over the
years. In the spring of 1930, Lyndon's last term in college, George used his considerable influence with Superintendent E. E. Oberholtzer to have Lyndon appointed to a position teaching public speaking and business arithmetic at a salary
of $160 a month. Unfortunately, the Great Depression, then beginning its sec-
ond year, had caused a hiring freeze, and the job in Houston was contingent on
a vacancy opening up. None did, so Lyndon persuaded his old friend George
Barron, superintendent of schools at Pearsall, to give him a job teaching speech
and government at $1,530 a year.[3] Pearsall, where Carol Davis had taught, was a
small town some thirty-five miles north of Cotulla.

Lyndon had not been in Pearsall a month when he got a call from his Uncle
George. The position at Sam Houston High had opened up. He promptly
marched into George Barron's office, perched himself on the corner of the su-

perintendent's desk, and said, "George, I look upon you as an older brother. I feel somehow that you have a kindred feeling toward me. If I didn't feel that way toward you, I wouldn't make this request."[4] He wanted out of his contract in order to take a job in the state's largest, most exciting city. "I don't want to leave you," he told Barron, "but what I am looking for in life will not be found in Pearsall."[5] The indulgent Barron agreed to release his new teacher on the condition that he find a replacement. Lyndon had already thought of that. His sister Rebekah and a friend took the job, splitting the salary between them.

DESPITE THE DEPRESSION, Houston in 1930 was a dynamic city. During the previous decade, the population had nearly doubled to three hundred thousand. The federally funded Houston ship channel, connecting the city to the Gulf of Mexico, had been completed just prior to World War I, ensuring Houston's future as a major port. The first of the east Texas oil wells, Spindletop, had come in in 1901. The 1920 census reported oil as the leading industry in the state, responsible for $240 million in products for the preceding year. Houston was at the geographic and economic center of that industry.[6] In addition to oil storage and refining plants and shipbuilding yards, the thriving metropolis boasted oil field equipment manufacturing concerns, cotton warehouses, and numerous financial institutions. The Depression had had an impact. The jobless loitered on city street corners or stood in line waiting for bread and soup, but there was a sense in the city that the downturn was temporary and that the future held great promise.[7]

Lyndon moved in with George Johnson and his extended family in their two-story, white frame house in downtown Houston some ten blocks from the high school. Occupying the house with George, a bachelor, were Jessie Johnson Hatcher, a widow, and her daughter and son-in-law, Ava and John Bright, and their two daughters. Bright coached football and taught math at Sam Houston High. Lyndon shared a room with his Uncle George. The two rode to work together virtually every day of the year that Lyndon lived in Houston.[8] He augmented his income by taking a job teaching speech in night school for the Houston Independent District.

The newest faculty member was delighted to learn that Sam Houston High had a debate team and that it had not fared well in recent competitions. Here was a chance for a twenty-two-year-old novice teacher to make his mark. As the speech instructor, Lyndon was the ex officio debate coach. The goal that he set for himself and his team was nothing less than a state championship in interscholastic league competition. Gene Latimer, one of the team members, recalled his initial experience with "the Chief," as he came to be called: "Let's say it is an October day in 1930 at Sam Houston High School as I enter my speech class. A few things become quickly apparent. If I am to continue on the debate team, my outside activities will be confined to after-school practice and visits to the city library in search of arcane references to the jury system, which is the subject selected for this year's high school debates."[9]

Lyndon immediately held a series of class competitions to select his team; the male winners were Gene Latimer and Luther Jones, the females Margaret Epley and Evelyn Lee. From December to April, when the ISL competitions were held, Coach Johnson arranged for more than fifty practice debates, beginning with archrival San Jacinto High, and extending to schools throughout east and central Texas.[10] "I never will forget—the principal of the school was W. J. Moyes, and I can recall two or three discussions where I was present and heard rather vigorous arguments by Mr. Johnson," Luther Jones recalled. "He'd be asking for money, for example, to take the debaters on trips, and he would be informed that it had never been done. Mr. Johnson would say, 'Yes, but you've never had a teacher like me.' "[11] Lyndon recruited other teachers to judge practice sessions. When they would whisper criticisms to him, he would yell at the offending speaker, cutting him or her off. He would roam the room, sit, watch, wait, criticize, his arms flailing, and walk again. "If they would take one side of the question, I would take the other, and I would just try to run them underground, just almost stomp them," he later said. "But always make it clear that I loved them, so they never ran completely off. But I'd humiliate them and embarrass them, and I would make fun of them and everything until they got to where they could take care of themselves, which they did."[12] He also kidded his team, encouraged them, and made them feel valued. He had his students stand up in front of class and act silly, making animal noises, for example, until they felt comfortable. He once challenged his class to debate the virtues of string or the proposition "Spit is a horrid word." When no one accepted, he delivered a fifteen-minute oration on string.[13]

During competitions, the Chief would sit in the back of the auditorium making eye contact with his debaters. Gene Latimer reconstructed the scene: "Once in a while he opens his mouth in amazement at how clearly I am making a point. He sits up straight and looks around in wonderment at the audience to make sure they're not missing this. And it is then that he makes me think I . . . am in the process of improving on the Sermon on the Mount."[14] Reflecting his mother's passion for poetry, Lyndon displayed a penchant for romantic, sentimental language. "Bob Ingersoll was a great speaker of 75 years ago," Luther Jones said. "One of these was a speech at his brother's grave. Lyndon used to read that because it's filled with beautiful language."[15] On April 1, the Sam Houston debaters defeated Milby High for the right to represent Houston in the county competition. The debates took place before a packed house. "I used to have pep rallies before debating contests," Lyndon said. "I'd have people get up and sing songs, and I'd have people hurrah for Jones and Latimer, just like you would at a football game. And we had them running out of seats at the final debate and you couldn't get in. Every place was taken in the balcony, every one on the floor, and they were sitting in the windows to hear the debate."[16] The Sam Houston debaters went on to win the district and to earn a place in the state finals in Austin. The girls were defeated in the first round; Latimer and Jones lost in the finals by a vote of three to two. After congratulating the winners, Lyndon went into the bathroom and threw up.[17] By the time the Chief was done, "we were more important than the football team," Latimer recalled.[18]

LYNDON LATER REMEMBERED 1930–31 as one of the best years of his life. One of the reasons was Uncle George Johnson. A tall, balding, gracious man, he seemed to have none of the demons that tormented Sam Ealy. Childless, he lavished his attention on his nieces and nephews, but particularly Lyndon, probably because of his interest in politics and history. George was a "yellow dog" Democrat (meaning that he would have voted for "an old yellow dog" if it were running on the ticket), whose principal historical interest was the age of Andrew Jackson. He talked often to his young protégé of the life and times of Old Hickory.[19] The president who had been Sam Houston's friend made no secret of his attachment to the great republican principles of Thomas Jefferson, which assumed continual conflict between liberty and power and between virtue and corruption. Public virtue, which required a willingness to subordinate private interests to the common good, was essential to preserving the precarious balance between liberty and power, Jackson (and Uncle George) believed. The best means of combating corruption in a society undergoing rapid and profound change, Jackson argued, was to hold fast to majority rule, limited federal power, and government protection of the interests of ordinary citizens. Jackson's ability to blend his idealism with practical politics captured Uncle George's and Lyndon's imagination. "The first president I really loved was Jackson," Lyndon later told an interviewer.[20]

Both SWT President Cecil Evans and George Johnson were passionate about politics and no doubt fantasized about running for office, but they would not leave the security of academia. Instead, they projected their dreams onto Lyndon. "I was never disinterested in politics," he later recalled. "But I did think about teaching. Dr. Evans . . . and my Uncle George both had the same idea, that teaching was a wonderful profession and gave a man a satisfaction that he could never get out of just making money, but it did have one drawback . . . The teacher was a law unto himself in the classroom, and it wasn't the competitive operation that either the law or politics would bring out. They bring out more of what is in you than teaching."[21] "I never heard him [George] tell Lyndon to get into politics," one of George's colleagues said, "but I did hear him say that 'if I were a young man like you, I'd run for Congress.' "[22]

Lyndon's opportunity came when Congressman Harry M. Wurzbach, the lone Republican representing Texas in the House of Representatives, died suddenly on November 6, 1931. The governor called a special election to be held twelve days thence to fill the vacancy. The Fourteenth District that Wurzbach represented stretched north from Corpus Christi on the coast to San Antonio and from there northwestward into the Hill Country. The cattle and oil interests that dominated the district were determined to control the seat. To this end, Roy Miller, chief lobbyist for Texas Gulf Sulphur, persuaded Richard Kleberg to become one of eight candidates for the position. Kleberg was heir to the famous

King Ranch that stretched more than one hundred miles from Corpus south to Brownsville.[23]

The upper part of the congressional district included Sam Ealy's old legislative district, so it was natural for Miller to enlist his aid in the campaign. There was another connection with the Johnsons as well. Kleberg's father had been president of the Texas Cattle Raisers Association when Sam's friend, Dayton Moses, had served as its chief counsel. Finally, Kleberg remembered that as a young law student in Austin, he had been in the galleries when Sam had made his famous speech defending the liberties of German Americans. Sam readily agreed to help and even managed to draft Lyndon for a few days' service.[24]

Kleberg won by several thousand votes over his nearest opponent and, inexperienced as he was, began searching immediately for an administrative assistant (then called simply "secretary"). He offered the job to Felix McKnight, a Houston journalist, who accepted, but he had not reckoned on Sam Johnson. Secretary to the newly elected congressman would be the perfect entrée into politics for Lyndon, Sam Ealy decided. He immediately enlisted the aid of Welly Hopkins and Dayton Moses. Both called Roy Miller, who was impressed with descriptions of Lyndon's energy and political instincts and with the notion of gaining a political foothold in the area between San Marcos and Fredericksburg for Kleberg's run at a regular term in 1932. "Lyndon knows almost every man, woman and child in Blanco County," Hopkins told him, "and has a wide acquaintance in Comal, Kendall and Guadalupe counties."[25] Helen Weinberg, a history teacher, was in the office when Lyndon was summoned to take a long distance call: "He was so excited he didn't know what to say," she remembered. "When he hung up, he turned to me and said with great excitement, 'Mr. Kleberg wants me to be his private secretary. I'll have to go up and tell Uncle George.' "[26] George was as excited as his nephew, of course. Lyndon called Kleberg back and arranged a meeting for the 29th. Driving to Gonzales the day before, he rendevouzed with his mother and father at Welly Hopkins's house. The next day, the four drove to Corpus, where Lyndon met first with Miller and then with Kleberg. Hopkins remembered that the young high school teacher made a very favorable impression as a likeable, hard-working individual who would be devoted to his boss's interests. He got the job, and Miller arranged for McKnight to return to his paper.[27]

Lyndon persuaded the administration to grant him a leave of absence from his teaching job at Sam Houston. Willard Deason recalled that he wanted to make a good impression when he arrived in Washington, but "like the rest of us . . . he never had a dollar ahead on anything." So he borrowed his Uncle George's overcoat and Deason's new leather suitcase.[28] The train carrying Lyndon and his new boss was scheduled to leave Houston at four in the afternoon on December 2. "All that day I'd gone about feeling excited, nervous, and sad," he later recalled. "I was about to leave home to meet the adventure of my future. I felt grown-up, but my mind kept ranging backward in time. I saw myself as a boy skipping down the road to my granddaddy's house. I remembered the many nights I had stood in the doorway listening to my father's political talks. I remembered the evenings with my mother when my daddy was away. Now all that was behind me. On the platform more than two dozen people, relatives and friends, waited about to say goodbye. I tried to say something important to my mother, but I couldn't think of anything to say. When the train came, I felt relieved. I kissed my parents and climbed aboard." [29] His recollection seems maudlin, even contrived, but it was not. "He was inclined to be emotional," Luther Jones recalled. "He was fiercely loyal to those he loved. He loved people and they loved him." [30]

The appointment as Kleberg's secretary introduced Lyndon not only to the nation's capital, but also to the congressman's opulent lifestyle. Kleberg and his assistant rode first-class aboard the sleek Bluebonnet Express that provided a direct connection between Houston and Washington. Once there, the two shared a red-carpeted room at the Mayflower Hotel—"Washington's finest," Lyndon wrote a former student—shared early morning coffee brought by room service, and took daily cab rides to and from the House Office Building. [31] The new secretary went with his boss to pay his respects to Congressman John Nance Garner from Uvalde, Texas, who, it was rumored, would be the next speaker of the House. Lyndon remembered the future vice president as a close-mouthed man with "cold blue eyes." [32] His second evening in Washington, Lyndon and Kleberg had dinner with Senator Morris Sheppard at the Occidental, which Lyndon subsequently described in a letter to Luther Jones as "an exclusive Washington eating place where they advertise: 'Where Statesmen Dine.' " [33] "You just had to look around, and it was very exciting to me to realize that the people, many of them that you were passing, were probably congressmen at least, maybe senators, members of the cabinet," he later recalled his first impressions. "And there was the smell of power. It's got an odor, you know, power, I mean." [34]

THERE WAS NO WAY, of course, that Lyndon could match Richard Kleberg's lifestyle. Although he made $3,900 a year, a princely sum in the Depression era, his family obligations and his decision to supplement the salaries of a staff to help him run Kleberg's office meant that he would have to live as frugally as possible. Besides, he had a lot to learn and he wanted to get as close to his peers—other congressional secretaries—as possible.

Kleberg's election had helped tip the scales in favor of a Democratic majority in the House. John Nance Garner was indeed elected speaker. As a Texan, Lyndon was able to take a seat in the speaker's box at the front of the chamber to witness Garner's swearing in. There he met another young secretary, Robert Jackson. No sooner had he settled in for the ceremony, Jackson later recalled, then he was aware of this "tall, countrified boy, talking loud, embarrassing me," squeezing into the box. There was a tapping on his shoulder. It was Lyndon, who extended his hand and introduced himself. Abashed, Jackson rose and responded in kind. After some initial patter, Lyndon asked his fellow Texan where he lived. The Dodge Hotel, he replied, which was also home to some twenty other congressional aides. "I'll move there," Lyndon said.[35]

The Dodge was a relatively elegant establishment that had traditionally catered to upper-class women. The dining room, complete with maître d'and white-jacketed stewards, was one of the best in Washington. To cope with the cash shortfall brought about by the Depression, the Dodge began renting rooms on its two basement-level floors to congressional staffers. The B floor, the first floor down, featured large, well-furnished rooms with semiprivate baths. Lyndon would later occupy one of these, but to save money he moved into one of the twelve cubicles on the men's side of the A floor where Robert Jackson resided. Each enclosure included two cots, a wash basin, and a table and chair. The twenty or so occupants shared a common shower and toilet facility at the end of the hall. Rent was $20 a month. A duplicate row of cubicles occupied by women employees of Congress composed the other half of the floor. There was, of course, no entryway connecting the two. Occupants came and went by separate outside doorways. The facilities were clean and well-lighted, but the steam pipes hammered loudly and relentlessly in the winter. Lyndon and his fellow secretaries could afford to eat in the hotel dining room only once a month, and then they purchased the cheapest course available for a dollar. When the young staffers were not taking advantage of the House cafeteria, they ate at the lunch counter at the neighboring Continental Hotel, the All States Cafeteria on Massachusetts where a meal could be purchased for fifty cents, or at Child's Restaurant across from Union Station.[36]

Although Lyndon was Richard Kleberg's chief lieutenant, he knew absolutely nothing about a secretary's duties or how Congress worked behind the scenes. His move to the Dodge was designed not only to save money but also to alleviate his ignorance. By his own account, he took four separate showers his first night there and brushed his teeth five different times the next morning in order to meet as many people as possible. At Child's he would rush to the head of the line, buy his food, and wolf it down as quickly as he could to be able to question the other staffers while they ate. He organized bull sessions at the Dodge that went long into the night. Living in the basement of that hotel, recalled Arthur Perry, another congressional staffer, "was like living in a permanent debating society, with Lyndon as the focal point."[37] Lyndon had to learn quickly because he was thrust into a situation in which he had to be follower and leader, the captain of a team of which he was one of two members.

Richard Kleberg had little or no interest in being a congressman. He had run to represent his class and his vested interests in the national legislature and for the prestige of living large in the nation's capital. Kleberg was a handsome, athletic man who stood five feet, seven inches and weighed 157 pounds. He loved to ride horses—polo ponies, not quarter horses—and to play golf, which he did as frequently as possible at Burning Tree Country Club in nearby Maryland. Fluent in Spanish, he took frequent trips to Mexico to hobnob with wealthy friends there. In Washington he lived with his wife, Mamie, in a suite at the elegant Shoreham Hotel on Rock Creek Park. He quickly made it clear that he was going to leave all the work to Lyndon. Kleberg's routine brought him into the office in the late morning, when he would check with Lyndon to see if there were any important visitors with whom he had to spend a few minutes. He would make the noon roll call vote in the House and then depart for Burning Tree and an afternoon of golf. What else could be expected of a man who lived on a ranch that was larger than the state of Rhode Island and whose cattle and oil operations brought in millions each year.[38]

Initially it was only Kleberg, Lyndon, and a House stenographer who occupied Room 258, a single office facing the inner courtyard of the old House Office Building (now the Cannon Building). In January, Lyndon hired Estelle Harbin, a young woman from Corpus Christi who had been recommended by Roy Miller.[39] Kleberg's district included some five hundred thousand souls, making it almost twice as populous as the next largest Texas district. The mail arrived three times a day; soon the office was full to overflowing with letters from veterans asking the congressman's help in obtaining early payment on bonuses promised at the close of the Great War, from cotton and vegetable farmers asking for legislation guaranteeing crop prices or for help in refinancing their farm mortgages, from small businessmen and bankers asking for low-interest loans. Neither Lyndon nor Estelle had any idea initially in which order to answer the letters or how to meet the needs of the correspondents. They quickly learned. Lyndon continued to hound his contemporaries for information and even had the temerity to approach congressmen themselves. "He'd come across [the hall] and talk to me and want to know just how everything was done," Marvin Jones, a Texas congressman who was also chair of the House Agriculture Committee, remembered. "He wanted to find out how that big piece of machine operated. And he'd talk to all the other chairmen . . . And he learned more in six months than the average [novice] learned in twice that length of time."[40]

The twenty-three-year-old Lyndon was a young man of immense, almost frantic energy, but even working seven days a week, he and Estelle found it difficult to keep up. "I don't know when I've been so tired as I am tonight," he wrote his mother. "To start to tell you how I've worked since I came here would require more time and effort than I feel like expending. I get up at 6 o'clock and go to the office by 7:30, take off 30 minutes sometime during the day for lunch and leave the office about six or seven depending on the correspondence. I run the office force. Mr. Kleberg doesn't spend an hour a day there and then only signing letters. Frequently I go back at night to finish so I won't get behind . . . Am afraid I can't come home Xmas. You don't know how I want to."[41]

Lyndon decided to answer personally every letter that came into the office. He would dictate and Estelle would type. More important, he decided to get results for the district's constituents. Quickly he learned who to call in the Department of Agriculture or Veterans Administration. If the bureaucrat were a woman, particularly an elderly woman, he would sweet-talk; the men he would alternately cajole and threaten. Because "Mr. Dick," as he called Kleberg, was rarely in the office, Lyndon sometimes posed as the congressman himself. "He was as persuasive on the telephone as he was in person," Estelle Harbin said. Typically, he refused to take no for an answer, and the office soon acquired a reputation for efficiency and effectiveness throughout the district.

The routine took its toll. Though constantly busy and among people, Lyndon grew lonely and discontented that first winter. He seemed to survive on his mother's twice-a-week letters. One of his roommates remembered that one morning while reading the latest missive from Rebekah, the Texan started weeping and said, "I love my Mother so much." [42] "Haven't been out of the office all day," he wrote Luther Jones. "Didn't get up until late this morning so I was forced to rush to work and have been at it until only a few minutes [ago]. I never get time to do anything but try to push the mail out to the people back home. Received over 100 telegrams today . . . You are a real boy. I love you and Gene [Latimer] as if you were my own. I know you are going places and I'm going to help you get there." [43]

As it turned out, Lyndon's promise to help his protégés get ahead was more than just hyperbole. Typically, however, he tended to view their welfare in terms of his own. He persuaded first Latimer and then Jones to come to Washington and go to work in Kleberg's office. Latimer, a short, good-natured Irish kid, full of life and energy, came first, in December 1932. His fiancée had moved to Washington, and he was looking for something exciting to do in the capital. After two years of college at Rice University in Houston, Jones, the more serious and studious of the two, decided he needed a job and took Lyndon's offer in August 1933. The most immediate problem the secretary faced was how to pay his two new employees. A congressman was allotted $5,000 a year to pay for office expenses. As $3,900 of that went for Lyndon's salary, only $1,100 was left for all the rest. He succeeded in getting Gene a $130-a-month patronage job in the House post office. Because he could get most of his deliveries in before noon, Latimer was free to type for Lyndon in the afternoons and evenings. Jones was more of a problem. Finally, Lyndon decided to reduce his own salary to pay Jones the $1,200 a year he asked for. He moved them into his basement cubicle in the Dodge, where they paid $15 a month each.

By the fall of 1934, Lyndon had moved upstairs to the B level, with its relatively spacious rooms and semiprivate baths. [44] With his new staff in place, he felt he had time to take on an extra job, as assistant doorkeeper on the Democratic side. Tending the door and carrying messages from staff and constituents into the chamber, he quickly got to know most of the members. He was able to listen to debates and familiarize himself with the arcane parliamentary procedures that were so crucial to the flow of legislation. More important, perhaps, he was witness to the whispered conversations and cloakroom deals that revealed the formal and informal power structure in the House. The experience brought home to the young man from the Hill Country that the exercise of power in Washington involved not only what state you represented, what committee assignment you were able to secure, but how strong your personality was, how much you drank, whom you slept with. "He'd say, 'But how did he do it?' " Russ Brown, a friend, remembered his asking in regard to some legislative coup. " 'Did he know somebody? Is he a nice guy? What's his secret of getting ahead . . . Well, I tell you one thing, it isn't any accident . . . I don't believe in luck.' " [45]

"At first, Lyndon Johnson was a hard man to work for," Jones said in a mastery of understatement. He drove himself and his staff relentlessly.[46] Robert Jackson remembered being struck by Johnson's "absolutely incredibly restless energy." If he and his staff took time to go to a movie, which was rare, Lyndon would nearly always get up before the end to return to the office or to his room to read mail or the *Congressional Record.*[47] Estelle Harbin recalled occasionally persuading him to take a walk around the Capitol grounds on a sunny day. By the time they finished, she was running to keep up as he loped to get back to the office.[48]

It was nothing for Latimer and Jones to work seven days a week, twelve or more hours a day. On the way to the office Lyndon would "issue enough instructions to put ten people to work for a month."[49] Coffee and cigarette breaks were forbidden, and if he could, Lyndon would make his staff eat their lunch at their desk. He was a perfectionist. Latimer remembers having to retype literally hundreds of letters when he first came. The secretary sometimes compared members of his staff unfavorably with one another to instill competition. He could be abusive toward Jones, who was the more aloof and self-contained of the two. He would ridicule his work, tongue-lashing him in front of the rest of the staff. It was with Jones that Lyndon began the repulsive habit of giving instructions or dictating while defecating in the bathroom. And he could be incredibly intrusive. Johnson found out that Latimer had run up bills with the local cleaner, tailor, and other merchants. He summoned the young man and demanded all of the cash he had on him. Stunned, Latimer gave it to him. Lyndon handed back a dollar and said, "Now I'm going to pay your rent over there at the Hotel, and I'm going to give you a dollar a day to eat on . . . When your checks come in, you're going to endorse them over to me and I'm going to pay your bills. I'm going to give you twenty-four hours to get me a list of all your bills." Gene, who enjoyed his drinks, replied tearfully, "You mean I'm not going to get any money for whiskey?" Not one nickel until the bills were paid, his boss replied.[50]

His staff sometimes thought about quitting, but they never followed through. Lyndon did not ask anything of them that he did not ask of himself. He was incredibly loyal to his boss and obviously dedicated to the interests of Kleberg's constituents. And he was loyal to his staff. When Latimer got married in 1935, Lyndon arranged for a $100 bonus from Kleberg, secured the use of an automobile, and arranged a $2,600-a-year job at the Federal Housing Administration. When Jones and Latimer began attending law school, Johnson gave both a raise and saw that they got two to three hours a day off from work to study. He wrote the two young men's parents frequently to report on their progress.[51] There would be innumerable tales in the future of Lyndon learning of an illness or misfortune suffered by an employee or an employee's close relative and his paying off debts or hospital bills. Both Jones and Latimer recall that when all was said and done, they liked, even loved Lyndon Johnson. "A reasonable statement is that Lyndon Johnson is hard and he is tough," Latimer said, "but far from being ruthless to his employees, their welfare was very important to him."[52]

AT AGE TWENTY-THREE Lyndon Johnson was a tall—six feet, two or three inches—slender young man with a broad forehead, fair skin, and dark, wavy hair. He was always neatly dressed in suit and tie, as expensive as his limited funds allowed. He smoked Camels and ate sporadically, consuming strange combinations of food, chile and steak, for example, in large amounts. He drank socially, almost as an afterthought. And he read voraciously: all the Washington newspapers plus the *New York Times, Wall Street Journal, Time Life,* and of course, the *Congressional Record.* But not books. He had no time for information that was not absolutely, immediately useful. There was a social life of sorts. Russell Brown, who would later work for Lyndon, remembered galas put on by the Texas Society, frequently at the Dodge. Lyndon would come and dance the night away, but not with the young, pretty, single girls—with the wives of congressmen and senators. There was sex, but in these early frantic months, it was hurried, almost a biological response. "When I think of Child's [restaurant]," Latimer recalled, "I think of a little discussed side of the Chief, and that is that prior to his marriage . . . he had an eye for girls with pretty faces and figures and did not regard too much what was behind those faces. One of the beauteous young ladies at Child's succumbed almost instantly, at least after two or three nights, and I was not to see the Chief until the early hours of the morning."[53]

Within six months, Lyndon had established his dominance over Richard Kleberg, personally as well as politically. He was always deferential to Mr. Dick and mindful of his interests, but one did not come into Lyndon's sphere with any sort of vulnerability without being subsumed. And Kleberg had vulnerabilities. He was not a person of ambition, but of tastes and appetites. He was a student of classical Spanish, a connoisseur of horses and fine whiskey, an avid sportsman. He sent his four children to private schools and lived with his wife, "Miss Mamie," in the city's most expensive hotel. Though rich, Kleberg was constantly cash-strapped because most of his wealth was tied up in land, cattle, and oil rigs. "He got five thousand dollars a year as chairman of the King Ranch corporation and ten thousand dollars a year as congressman," recalled Sam Houston, who would replace Lyndon as Kleberg's secretary. His mother was secretary-treasurer of the corporation and would provide funds when approached, but Kleberg frequently did not want to ask or simply forgot. As a result, creditors were constantly knocking at his door, or rather, the door of House office 258. As with Gene Latimer, Lyndon took over. He would sit down periodically with his boss, go over the bills, and tell Kleberg how much money he needed. Eventually, the congressman gave his secretary the authority to sign his personal checks.[54]

When Miss Mamie initially attempted to make personal use of Lyndon and the staff, she was rebuffed. One time she called and asked Johnson to pick up her daughter, Mary Etta, at the train station; he replied simply, "Mrs. Kleberg . . . we don't have any chauffeurs here."[55] She was at first offended, but Mamie Kleberg, like her husband, soon came to place her trust in the young man from Johnson City. Hailing from Brenham, Mamie Searcy had attended the University of Texas, where she had been a beauty queen. "She was quite a handsome-looking woman," Russ Brown recalled, "and she had real grace and charm."[56] In 1932, Mr. Dick had an affair with another woman. Mamie got wind of it and fled in tears to Corpus Christi. Lyndon intervened to try to patch things up, and from the beginning she treated him as a confidant. "It tore my heart out . . . to leave him," she wrote, "but I knew I would never get myself straightened out up there . . . I am so thankful that you are with him."[57] Kleberg attempted a reconciliation but to no avail. Upset and exhausted, the congressman followed his wife to Corpus, but she would not see him.

Lyndon arrived on the scene and informed Mamie that he was going to camp out on her front porch until she relented. Eventually she did, and the couple was reunited. "Mr. Kleberg was on the edge of a nervous breakdown," she subsequently wrote Lyndon. "He is so appreciative of all you have done and could not love you more if you were his own son, and I feel just like he does, Lyndon. If you had not been in Corpus the night I went all to pieces, I know I would have done something desperate . . . Love from us both—your other Mother."[58] Mamie suspected that the other woman was Estelle Harbin. She was not, but Lyndon and Mr. Dick decided that it would be better if Estelle left. Lyndon got her a job with the Texas Railroad Commission. According to Sam Houston, the ever suspicious Mamie intermittently rifled through her husband's and even Lyndon's mail. Sometime in 1934 or 1935 she came across a letter from Estelle to Johnson: "Lyndon, you don't know how much I appreciate you getting me out of that mess." Mamie interpreted this to mean that Estelle had been her husband's lover and that Lyndon had been an accomplice. She never forgave him.[59]

MAMIE AND RICHARD KLEBERG were not the only Americans on the verge of a nervous breakdown in 1932; hundreds of thousands of others were suffering. The country was entering the depths of its unprecedented Depression. The Republican presidential candidate in 1928 was Herbert Hoover, a wealthy mining engineer with a distinguished record of public service, who easily defeated Alfred E. Smith. Hoover was the high priest of free regulated capitalism. It was to society's benefit for the rich to get richer, he argued, because the wealth would "trickle down" to even those occupying the lowest rungs on the socioeconomic ladder. His philosophy rested on two principles: individual self-help and voluntary cooperation. Enlightened self-interest would presumably motivate businessmen to pursue self-regulation to achieve economic stability and prosperity. Described by his public relations team in 1928 as the great engineer, an efficiency expert, able administrator, humanitarian, and even "miracle man," Hoover appeared to be precisely the individual needed to perpetuate the prosperity of the 1920s. He proclaimed the arrival of a new day in his inaugural address and predicted that the free enterprise system would end poverty in America in his lifetime.

Less than six months after his inauguration, in the fall of 1929, the Hooverian vision collapsed with a resounding stock market crash that heralded the onset of the Great Depression. By midsummer 1932, the gross national product had declined by more than 50 percent. Unemployment grew from 4 million in October 1930 to between 12 and 14 million during the first months of 1933. National income declined from $87 million in 1929 to $40 million in 1933. Adjusted for the cost of living, per capita income declined from $681 to $495 per year. Some two hundred thousand residents of Chicago converged on the Loop in a hunger march, chanting "We want bread." Everywhere, unemployed men by the thousands simply stood on street corners waiting futilely for something to happen. In rural areas, farmers suffered from the twin tragedies of drought and depression. During the early part of the 1930s rain simply disappeared from certain parts of the country. Huge dust storms rolled across the plains, darkening the sky and depositing silt over a vast area of the United States. In the Midwest, Milo Reno's National Farm Holiday Association set up armed roadblocks in an effort to call attention to the farmer's plight by stopping the flow of milk and food to the nation's urban dwellers. Young men and women stopped going to college, and families disintegrated. In many cases, rural dwellers were forced to resort to barter to survive.

By experience, temperament, and philosophy, Herbert Hoover was unprepared to deal with the Depression. He was no laissez-faire economist of the classical school. He approved of friendly regulation of businesses clothed with public interest, and he championed order and efficiency in finance and industry rather than destructive competition. At the same time, he believed that under almost no circumstance should the government provide jobs to citizens to combat unemployment. And he was convinced that relief activities were a duty of private charities and local governments rather than the federal authority. Eventually, under intense pressure from Congress and the states, Hoover would initiate a federal public works program and would secure from Congress the legislation necessary to create the Reconstruction Finance Corporation (1932) to extend federal credit to banks, insurance companies, and various industries, but all major economic indices continued to decline.

Dick Kleberg did not care for the president any more than the common man did, but it was because he considered him too liberal, not too conservative. Like his friend and patron, Roy Miller, Kleberg "was a democrat in name only," Russ Brown said. "He was a wealthy man, and he associated with wealthy people and he had no feeling for the needs of the economically underprivileged in the community. This was not part of his background and he hadn't trained himself to think about it or to worry about it at all."[60] Kleberg and Miller, who flew back and forth from Washington to Corpus Christi in Kleberg's private plane, were in fact reactionaries who embraced the notion of the divine right of wealth. Well-dressed, well-groomed, and well-fed, they were as insensitive as rocks. Miller treated Kleberg's office as his own, occupying the congressman's desk during his frequent absences and conducting Gulf Sulphur's business. They believed that workers had no right to organize and were in fact economic units whose labor was to be bought or sold at whatever rate the market dictated. The only action they wanted from the government was help to maintain the prices of cattle, oil, and cotton. Indeed, Kleberg and his sponsors were about as far removed as could be in temperament, philosophy, and experience from the Hill Country Johnsons.

"His [Lyndon's] thinking, if you could call it that, was Populist," Robert Jackson recalled.[61] His father's life, in practice, and his mother's life, in theory, had been built on the notion of helping other people. During Lyndon's months in Washington, virtually all of his waking hours had been devoted to taking care of the needs of others. "When I first went to work for Mr. Kleberg," Luther Jones recalled, "a large part of the work of the office consisted of helping veterans of World War I get their claims for service compensation to show that any ailment they then had was connected with some injury they sustained in the war. Lyndon spent an enormous amount of time on this . . . His service [provided relief for] hundreds of them."[62]

Lyndon was also exposed to legislators who were very different from Kleberg. He left standing orders with the doorman of the House to call him whenever the newly elected senator from Louisiana, Huey Long, was making a speech. Dressed in iridescent suits that ran from maroon to lime green and two-toned shoes, the short, wavy-haired demagogue quickly earned a reputation as the new champion of the common man. Both quoting the Bible and spouting racist anecdotes, Long attacked monopoly capitalism and proposed a massive redistribution of wealth through confiscatory taxation. Campaigning for Hattie Carraway, who was running for governor of Arkansas, he told the citizens of that state that 540 men on Wall Street made more money each year than all the farmers in the country and that he wasn't going to allow the situation to continue. Criticized back in the Senate by Democratic Majority Leader Joe T. Robinson for interfering in the politics of his native Arkansas, Long counterattacked in an incident Lyndon would never forget. "He had this chocolate silk suit on," he later recalled, "and his bright-toned brown-and-white shoes, and he was just marching back and forth." He marched over to Robinson, a very conservative and very portly man, and put his hand on the majority leader's shoulder. Almost affectionately, Long told the galleries, "I wasn't in Arkansas to dictate to any human being. All I went to Arkansas for was to pull these big, potbellied politicians off this poor little woman's neck."[63]

In 1935, while making a bid for the Democratic nomination for president, Long would promulgate his "Share Our Wealth" program. It promised every American family a homestead worth $5,000 and an annual income of $2,500 to be paid for by expropriating the holdings of the nation's wealthiest citizens. "He hated poverty with all his soul and he spoke against it until his voice was hoarse," Lyndon later told an interviewer. "For leading the masses and illustrating your point humanly, Huey Long couldn't be beat."[64] To the young secretary from the Hill Country, Hoover was the opposite: a do-nothing president, the tool of Wall Street who thought that "constitutional government gave every man, woman, and child the right to starve."[65] "Giving a man a chance to work and feed his family and provide for his children does not destroy his initiative," Lyndon would later say. "Hunger destroys initiative. Hopelessness destroys initiative. Ignorance destroys initiative. A cold and an indifferent government destroys initiative."[66] The task facing Lyndon Johnson, one that had confronted him in Cotulla and that would reappear throughout his career, was how to finesse the conservatives. His double-pronged strategy was to cultivate them personally and then, if necessary, invoke the Jeffersonian-Jacksonian ideology of representative democracy to justify government activism in behalf of the underprivileged.

In May and June 1932, twelve to fourteen thousand unemployed and destitute veterans descended on Washington to lobby for passage of a $2.4 billion soldiers' bonus bill. Congress had passed such a measure immediately following the Great War, but it was in the form of a paid-up insurance policy that would come due in 1945. The veterans wanted their money now, when they needed it. After marching down Pennsylvania Avenue, the tattered Bonus Expeditionary Force, as the media dubbed the group, built a shantytown on Anacostia Flats on the edge of the capital. Hoover denounced the bonus bill as an unnecessary raid on the treasury that would unbalance the budget. With the gaunt veterans, who had risked their lives for their country and who represented the ultimate injustice of the Depression, vowing to sit it out all summer if necessary, the House took up the measure.

When Lyndon learned that his boss intended to vote against the bonus bill, he rebelled. Confronting Kleberg, he pounded on his desk, shouting, "Mr. Kleberg, Mr. Kleberg, you can't do this!" Congressmen and senators were elected to represent their constituents, Lyndon said, and mail from the district was running fifteen to twenty to one in favor. He knew what was best for his people, Mr. Dick replied, and an unbalanced budget was not in their interest. Maybe not, but there were a huge number of veterans in the Fourteenth District, and if Kleberg voted no he would not be representing their or anybody's interests after the fall elections.[67] Lyndon's boss voted for the bonus; it passed the House only to fail in the Senate.

When some six thousand veterans still refused to go home, Hoover called on the military, which dispatched a contingent of troops under the command of a young brigadier general named Douglas MacArthur. Declaring that the very "institutions of our Government" were being threatened, he led a small army equipped with tanks and machine guns, clearing the veterans from Anacostia and burning down their shantytown. Lyndon was appalled. He would never forget seeing "the Bonus Army being driven down Pennsylvania Avenue by quirts like sheep by a man on a white horse."[68]

AS A NUMBER of his contemporaries have observed, Lyndon Johnson tended to absorb people, particularly people who were weaker willed than he and who were useful to his larger ends. Thus it was with Richard Kleberg. Lyndon placed his desk strategically in the office so that anyone wanting to see the congressman had to go through him. He prepared memoranda for his boss on the major issues of the day, cultivated other congressmen and their staffs on his behalf, and saw that he got full credit with the people of the Fourteenth District for everything positive that the office did. The individual services—veterans' benefits, green cards, Reconstruction Finance Corporation loans, agricultural aid—ran into the thousands. Once a full staff was in place, Lyndon decided that every boy and girl in the district graduating from high school should get a letter of congratulation from the congressman. "When he was Kleberg's secretary," recalled Sam Fore, a Floresville newspaper editor and mentor of Lyndon's, "he made a number of trips back to our county—Wilson County—and he'd have those farmers and ranchers meet him at the courthouse and give him their troubles. He'd take them in his car even to Houston to try to save their farms through the Federal Land Bank . . . I think he stayed about two or three weeks one time just on jobs like that, doing things for people in distress."[69] As Robert Montgomery, a young UT economist who had gone to work for the Department of Agriculture, said, being secretary to Congressman Kleberg was excellent training for Lyndon because he could be Congressman Kleberg, or rather Congressman Johnson using Kleberg's name.[70]

It never crossed Lyndon's mind to run against Kleberg. Loyalty, Russ Brown recalled his friend saying, was the most important of all human virtues. "If a fellow is brilliant and energetic and smart and he's not loyal, then I don't know who he's being brilliant and energetic and smart for," he said, "and I haven't got room for him around me."[71] Lyndon and his boss returned to Texas and stumped the Fourteenth District as if there were no tomorrow. Kleberg's secretary and campaign manager linked up with Fore, the 275-pound Seguin newspaper editor and Democratic activist who had contacts throughout the district. Typically, Lyndon covered more territory and saw more people in a shorter time than any advance man in the district's memory. He "wasn't one of those who walked into the office and sat down and wasted a lot of time," a Seguin attorney remembered. "He covered not only the area around the office but all of Seguin in a whirlwind fashion and yet he saw everybody and talked to everybody."[72] Kleberg won the nomination, capturing ten of eleven counties in the Fourteenth District and winning the general election easily.[73]

While campaigning for Kleberg, Lyndon followed the contest for the Demo-

cratic nomination for president with rapt attention. Even as a congressional secretary, he acquired a reputation for political prescience. That reputation was
based in part on instinct and in part on a never-ending search for political information. "Lyndon dropped by my office almost every day," Texas Congressman
Wright Patman remembered. "He wanted to talk politics—who was doing what
and what the probable outcome would be."[74] He did the same thing with Sam
Rayburn from Bonham, Martin Dies of Lufkin, and even John Nance Garner.
He read all of the political pundits, including Raymond Clapper, whom he
liked, and Walter Lippmann, whom he did not (smart but too theoretical—and
pretentious).[75] As a result, Johnson's political intelligence was among the best in
the capital. Treated to a Lyndon tour de force on the upcoming House elections,
a dazzled Robert Montgomery remarked to his wife that Johnson was a savant,
one of Plato's political animals who "just knew."[76] In the presidential race, Lyndon was putting his money on a young man from New York named Franklin D.
Roosevelt. "Very quickly after I met [Lyndon], the campaign of 1932 started,"
Robert Jackson said, "and he was just terribly stirred up about the Roosevelt
campaign and Franklin Roosevelt. Radios were not very common then. Car radios were especially unusual, but Arthur Perry [another congressional aide] had
a little Chevy coupe with a radio in it. Every time Roosevelt talked, and it was
broadcast we would get in this little coupe and drive around."[77]

BY 1932 FDR HAD EMERGED as the leading contender for the Democratic nomination, but he was by no means a shoo-in. By promising the vice
presidency to John Nance Garner of Texas, speaker of the House and a presidential hopeful, the New Yorker survived a serious "Stop Roosevelt" movement
and won the nomination. Shattering precedent, he flew to Chicago to accept in
person and promised the American people "a new deal." The ensuing campaign
between Roosevelt and Hoover was a rather dull affair. Although Roosevelt
traveled extensively, his radiant smile and air of self-confidence on constant display, he took few risks and spoke primarily in general, even vague terms about
how he intended to combat the economic crisis. He did, however, lay the blame
for the Depression at the feet of Hoover and the Republican party. Because
Americans tended to share this view, they elected Roosevelt in a landslide. Although the Socialist and Communist Parties were convinced that the severity of
the economic crisis would expose the bankruptcy of capitalism and prompt a
massive shift in popular support to their causes, American voters proved to be
less radical than the left hoped and the right feared. They rejected the revolutionary alternatives offered by socialist and communist candidates and opted for
a capitalist system shorn of its defects.

   Inauguration day in Washington was cold and rainy, so Lyndon and his friend
Robert Jackson watched the proceedings from the shelter of John Nance
Garner's office in the Capitol. It was a striking scene. Despite the weather, a
huge crowd gathered, anxious, fearful, expectant. Soldiers with machine guns
stood guard. Roosevelt was resplendent in cutaway and top hat. Lyndon later re-

called the famous Rooseveltian phrase, "The only thing we have to fear is fear it-self," and his quote from Proverbs: "Where there is no vision the people perish." Those words, he recalled in 1964, would stay with him the rest of his life.[78]

LYNDON JOHNSON WAS MIGHTILY AFFECTED by the New Deal, and it would be slightly affected by him. Roosevelt did not enter office with any mas-ter plan for solving the myriad problems that faced the nation, but his lack of ideological inhibitions meant that he had few qualms about using federal power to alleviate human suffering and to correct what he perceived as grievous flaws in the economic system. Nor was he averse to experimentation to achieve the desired results. The ideological sources of the New Deal were as numerous as they were diverse. The host of economists, former social workers, business-men, young lawyers, and others who converged on Washington to build the new order represented a bewildering array of economic philosophies and policy perspectives. Among them were fiscal conservatives wedded to government economy and balanced budgets, advocates of deficit spending to expand mass purchasing power, and devotees of expensive federal social programs. Some were reformers from Theodore Roosevelt's day; a few were Woodrow Wilson–style progressives; still others represented a younger generation that had come of age in the postwar years. Yet, Franklin Roosevelt stood as the cen-tral figure in the New Deal, its spokesman and symbol; he was the one who gave it what coherence it possessed and who saw that proposals were enacted into law. Some have argued that Roosevelt was incapable of sustained thought and possessed more style than substance, but no one has questioned his mastery of the art of politics, his skills in communication and public relations, and his fine-tuned sensitivity to the shifting moods of the public and Congress.

During the first two and a half years of the Roosevelt administration, Con-gress, overwhelmingly Democratic in both houses, would pass more than a hun-dred laws creating dozens of new government agencies and programs. They were designed to save American capitalism by providing relief and jobs to the millions of unemployed and then reforming the system to ensure that the Great Depression did not repeat itself. Congress convened on March 9 and passed leg-islation providing government guarantees and funds to the struggling banking system. The Truth in Securities and Securities Exchange Acts aimed at prevent-ing another stock market crash. A host of new public works agencies, the most important of which was the Works Progress Administration (WPA), were cre-ated to provide jobs for the struggling workforce. The Public Utility Holding Company Act sought to bring regulation to an industry manifestly clothed with the public interest. Labor benefited from passage of the Wagner, or National Labor Relations Act that sanctioned, for the first time, the principle of collective bargaining. Two Agricultural Adjustment Acts established a system of payments to farmers, first to destroy some existing crops and livestock and subsequently not to plant a certain portion of their acreage or not to raise a portion of the live-stock they had planned to raise in an effort to limit production and elevate farm prices. A reorganized Farm Credit Administration emerged to provide low-interest loans to farmers. In August 1935, Congress passed the Social Security Act, which set up a system of old-age insurance, compelled employers to contribute to state unemployment programs, and offered federal aid to the states on a matching basis for the care of the nation's crippled, blind, dependent mothers and children, and for the establishment of public health systems.

Like Charles Lindbergh, Herbert Hoover, and most of Wall Street, Richard Kleberg believed that the Roosevelt administration was nothing but a bunch of socialists who were waging war against the free enterprise system. When he announced his intention to vote against legislation creating the Tennessee Valley Authority, the Federal Emergency Relief Corporation, and other New Deal agencies, Lyndon could no longer stand mute. The confrontation came over the first Agricultural Administration Act that, to raise prices, proposed to pay farmers not to plant. Kleberg came into the office one afternoon to find his secretary emptying his desk into cardboard boxes. "What's the matter?" the congressman asked. "I'm going home," Lyndon replied. Seeing his golf game going down the drain, Kleberg pled, "My gosh, Lyndon, you can't go off and leave me." Lyndon said, "Well, Mr. Dick, I feel like the folks back home sent us up here to support the President, and that's what we've got to do. If you don't do that, they're bound to think I'm not supporting him either, and I just can't face them . . . Our people are for this legislation by ten-to-one or more."[79] In fact, Texas farmers hated the Act: it ran counter to their go-it-alone ethos, and it made no sense to be paid not to produce. Kleberg observed that he knew what was best for the people and that he was going to vote his conscience. Fine, said Lyndon. The congressman would have to do without his services—and he would be sure to lose the next election. Kleberg relented and voted for the AAA.

It was a temporary victory. The scion of the King Ranch steadfastly refused to embrace other aspects of the New Deal. In 1935, with the Social Security Act pending, Lyndon had to go through the whole routine again.[80] Johnson was particularly enthusiastic about the Federal Housing Administration. When consumers had to rely solely on private lending institutions, a homebuyer had to agree to pay off the mortgage in five years and put up as much as one-third of the cost as down payment. Banks could or could not renew at the end of five years; if they did, they charged exorbitant refinancing fees. With the establishment of the FHA, it became possible to take out a twenty-five-year mortgage with a 10 percent down payment. Private institutions had to follow suit or lose out completely.[81]

It was in the application of New Deal programs to the citizens of the Fourteenth District that Lyndon proved most effective, however. The object of the AAA was to restore to American farmers the purchasing power they had enjoyed during the peak years 1909–1914. This was to be done by means of a domestic allotment scheme for basic commodities such as cotton, wheat, corn, and pigs. The incentive for farmers to reduce acreage under cultivation was a system of government subsidies, known as "benefit payments." The AAA would pay out $100 million in 1933 to farmers to destroy existing crops and livestock. Lyndon worked furiously to persuade farmers that limits on production were the only answer to the persistent farm depression, and in the end the Fourteenth District had one of the highest percentages of farmers signing up for the program. Similarly, after the administration pushed through Congress legislation creating a Federal Land Bank to refinance farm mortgages, Lyndon saw to it that every struggling farmer in south Texas knew about and took advantage of the low-interest loans.[82]

Lyndon met some of the dozens of young Ivy League lawyers and economists who flocked to Washington during the New Deal; most he did not like. They dressed better than he did, and many did not have to work for money. And they refused to give him his due because he was from Texas.[83] His famous dislike of eastern intellectuals would not stem from any sense of inferiority. "Johnson had awfully strong class feelings," Horace Busby, his friend and future speech writer, recalled. "They were not of someone from the underclass feeling strongly against the upper class; it was the fact that Johnson [felt] . . . that there were an awful lot of people from the upper classes elsewhere who did not understand he was from the upper class in Johnson City. I mean, it was aristocrat against aristocrat."[84] With those young New Dealers who he felt were not condescending, Johnson established close ties. The AAA general counsel Jerome Frank and staffers Adlai E. Stevenson, Abe Fortas, and Alger Hiss all became friends.[85]

During a late-night bull session in the Dodge House involving Lyndon, Arthur Perry, Texas Senator Tom Connally's assistant, and Robert Jackson, the subject of the "Little Congress" came up. In 1919, legislative secretaries had created a model house of representatives, complete with speaker and parliamentary rules. The body quickly degenerated into a closed debating society dominated by a handful of the oldest and most conservative of the secretaries. It was a shame, Perry observed, because the organization could be used to share useful information and bring in speakers of national prominence. "Why don't you run for speaker?" Perry asked Lyndon. "I might just do that," he replied.[86]

The next organizational meeting was scheduled for April 1933. Quietly Lyndon and his friends began to circulate among the congressional staff. Most had not participated in the Little Congress, believing that the $2 yearly dues were not worth it. Lyndon campaigned against the "standpatters," who ran the organization, calling them "dictatorial" and "reactionary" and promising his own new deal: open debate and stimulating speakers. On the evening of the election, the usually half-empty committee room was packed with more than 250 people. "It was quite an occasion," Carroll Keach, who worked in Kleberg's office, recalled. "It was held in the Democratic caucus room . . . the main caucus room in the old House Office Building. It was packed to the rafters and people even standing around the walls . . . They had all the news media of the day there, klieg lights all over the place."[87] The old guard shouted that many in the room were not eligible and that it was only Johnson's second meeting, which was true. Nevertheless, the vote was held, and Lyndon won two to one. Immediately, he moved to placate his defeated foes, promising that his appointments would be nonpartisan and reflect both seniority and membership. The Little Congress coup brought Lyndon his first national publicity. The *Washington Evening Star* ran a two-column story under the heading "Little Congress Upset: Progressives Put Over New Slate in Election."[88]

AT VARIOUS TIMES DURING HIS YOUNG LIFE, Lyndon had been advised by his elders to earn a law degree. Both Sam Ealy and Lyndon had been fascinated by Clarence and Tom Martin's careers. There was power and money in the profession. In 1934, Alvin Wirtz, who had preceded Welly Hopkins in the Texas State Senate and who was an old friend of Sam's, became a member of an up-and-coming law firm in Austin. During one of Lyndon's visits back home, Wirtz urged him to go to law school. He could then come back to Austin, join the firm, and make "a ton of money."[89] Lyndon thought it over and decided to give it a try. Georgetown Law School offered early evening courses, from five o'clock to seven, for federal employees who got off work at 4:30. Lyndon enrolled for classes beginning in September. Russell Brown recalled that first class: "This big tall fellow from Texas sat right beside me. He looked over at me and he said, 'I'm Johnson from Texas.' I said, 'I'm Russell Brown from Rhode Island.' He was cordial in sort of an impersonal way."[90]

After a week or so, Lyndon, Brown, and Luther Jones went to dinner. Lyndon asked Brown why he always seemed to know the answers. Because he did not have a job and could study when he was not pounding the pavement looking for work, Brown said. Lyndon replied that he wished he had that luxury; he usually had to go back to the office and work after class was over. But Luther Jones, who confronted the same routine, found time to study for an hour or two every night after returning to the Dodge. He noticed that his boss neglected to hit the books even when he had the chance. For Lyndon, the law was too abstract and too much of a detour from his chosen profession: politics and public service. When a professor went over the procedure required to pass a law in Congress, he scoffed. He knew more about it than his teacher. He wanted to know why the legal profession insisted on using Latin terms when plain English would do. "I should say that Lyndon's attendance at the law school was, to say the least, sporadic," Brown recalled. "He was probably running congressional errands for the Congressman or meeting with people and setting up arrangements, making political alliances and friends."[91] Still, he could have gotten by. Brown, for whom Lyndon found a job as assistant doorkeeper of the House, took excellent notes. He, Lyndon, and Luther would have intensive study sessions in his room over a meat market. "He had a mind like a sponge, quick and alert and very perceptive," Brown recalled. He was aware of and interested in the great theoretical divide that separated most legal scholars: the traditionalists or "natural law" advocates, who insisted that the Constitution and other legal statutes be read narrowly with a view to what the framers had in mind, legal precedent, and little else, and proponents of "sociological jurisprudence," who agreed that the Constitution and federal law should be interpreted in the social, economic, and political contexts from which the case in question arose. "In the course of our conversation," Philip Kane, another of Lyndon's Georgetown classmates, recalled, "we began to discuss Reverend Francis E. Lucey, S. J., then regent of the Law School and Professor of Jurisprudence. It should be noted that Father Lucey was strictly a Natural Law scholar and did not think much of Justice [Oliver Wendell] Holmes, particularly of Holmes's approach to moral issues. [LBJ's] comments were 'That Father Lucey can certainly talk. He knows his material and puts it over to the students. But I can't go for that Natural Law stuff.'"[92] It did not take Lyndon long to decide that law school was a useless diversion. He did not even bother to take the first-term exams. There was another reason for his neglect of his legal studies. In September 1934, Lyndon had met Claudia Alta Taylor.

CHAPTER 5

LADY BIRD AND THE NYA

THE YOUNG WOMAN WHO WOULD CAPTURE LYNDON'S imagination hailed from a wealthy but troubled east Texas family. Claudia Taylor was born on December 22, 1912, in a seventeen-room southern mansion dubbed "the Brick House," which lay tucked away in the piney woods near the hamlet of Karnack some fifteen miles from the Louisiana border. Her father, Thomas Jefferson "T. J." Taylor, an imposing man, six feet, two inches and well over two hundred pounds, had come to east Texas in 1899 from Alabama. The son of a tenant farmer, T. J. had arrived under a cloud. Rumor had it that he and his brother had robbed a train. In Texas, he paid $500 for a section of land at the intersection of two trails and made plans to open a general store. Living in a boarding house for $5 a week, T. J. managed not only to build a dry goods operation but to establish a small agricultural and business empire.[1]

By the time Claudia was born some thirteen years later, her father owned a fifteen thousand–acre cotton plantation, two general stores, a cotton gin, and a fishing business on nearby Lake Caddo. In fact, as Lady Bird recalled, her father, known to blacks as "Mr. Boss" and to whites as "Mr. Cap'n," ruled Karnack and its environs as a feudal fiefdom. More than half of the residents of Harrison County were black, and many worked as sharecroppers for T. J. Taylor, buying the necessities of life at hugely inflated prices from his general store. "I worked for him sunup to sunset for fifty cents a day," recalled Dorsey Jones, one of the oldest African Americans living in Harrison County.[2]

After establishing himself in Texas, Taylor returned to Alabama to marry Miss Minnie Lee Patillo, daughter of a Confederate officer who was also one of the largest landholders in Autauga County. Her father viewed T. J. as nothing more than a low-life criminal, and no members of the family, including Minnie's beloved sister, Effie, attended the wedding.[3] The couple was married in Taylor's brother's house. Minnie, a bright but physically unattractive girl, stout with thin reddish-blond hair, had had a difficult childhood. Her father, Luke, liked to boast he was "the meanest man in Autauga County." Her mother, Sarah, had been married previously and had two children by a man killed in the Civil War. She never got over him, and Luke resented both the dead man and his children. Sarah died bitter and broken, her family riddled with suicides and alcoholism. After Minnie ran off with T. J. Taylor, Effie took to her bed with migraines and ulcers.

Claudia's past reeked of the Civil War, Reconstruction, slavery, of the burden of history borne by a land torn between cruelty and gentility, education and ignorance, promise and hopelessness. When she was five, a group of white men confronted a local black in the woods near Karnack. They accused him of "some crime," she remembered. "The poor man was so terrified that he just took off running. The white men shot him in the back." The little girl, shivering, heard the story in her father's general store. Claudia's favorite author was William Faulkner. "He describes a South I'm somewhat acquainted with," she later told biographer Jan Jarboe Russell. "It has a dark side. It's shadowy but yet it speaks to a world I know."[4]

Minnie followed national and international affairs and was active in local politics. Not surprisingly, she was a committed suffragist.[5] Contemporaries recall her as somewhat aloof. "I remember that she wore this large hat with a veil and her carriage was excellent," said Lucille McElroy, a Karnack resident.[6] She gave birth to her first son, Thomas J. Taylor Jr., on October 20, 1901, and her second, Antonio J., on August 29, 1904. The pregnancies damaged her health and further strained her relationship with her ever-absent husband.

By all accounts, T. J. Taylor was a shameless womanizer, making little effort to hide his affairs. Rumor had it that he had fathered a son by a local black woman. The child was nicknamed "Sugar" because he would periodically come by the general store and Taylor would give him bags of sugar. He made little effort to hide his faithlessness or his racism. A contemporary, Jack Hayner, remembered dropping in at the general store one morning with his hunting dog. When the dog persisted in sniffing Mr. Boss's groin, he told Hayner, "I've been out with a nigger woman this morning. The dog's got her scent."[7] Shortly after the birth of her second son, Minnie Patillo Taylor took her children and left for Alabama.

Confronted with two ailing daughters, Luke Patillo turned to Dr. John Kellogg, who ran his famous sanitarium out of a six-story building in Battle Creek, Michigan. As the Patillos listened, Kellogg, dressed dramatically in a long white coat, lectured on the physical and psychological benefits of a strict vegetarian diet, exercise, sweat baths, and frequent enemas. Meanwhile, T. J. Taylor was ruthlessly building his business empire, silently, relentlessly competing with "Old Man Patillo." He was rich and wanted people to know it. Mr. Cap'n paid the salary of the Methodist minister, whose sermons he listened to, and half of the Baptist minister's, whose sermons he did not. He loved dependency. "You were nobody in this world without a white man standin' behind you," Dorsey Jones said. "Boss Taylor was a good stand-behind man."[8] As long as you stayed and worked. Many a local black forfeited his land to T. J. Taylor for bad debt. Despite their differences, T. J. and Minnie reconciled briefly in 1910. He bought her the Brick House as a present.

On December 22, 1912, Minnie gave birth to a daughter, Claudia Alta, whom T. J. nicknamed Lady Bird after the nursery rhyme: "Lady Bird, Lady Bird, fly away home, your house is on fire and your children will burn." (Actually, the rhyme T. J. had in mind begins, "Lady bug, Lady bug . . .")[9] The baby was bright-eyed and pretty, with fair skin and dark hair. The prominent Taylor nose, which would inevitably hook, was already evident. Minnie was thirty-nine and did not feel well enough to care for three children, so the two boys were sent away to the Raymond Riordan School for Boys in upstate New York. In 1918, at age forty-four, Minnie Taylor became pregnant again. Two months later, she fell down the circular staircase at the Brick House. Rushed to the hospital in Marshall, Minnie died on September 14, 1918. It was the defining moment of Lady Bird's young life.[10]

There were rumors that T. J. had pushed his wife down the stairs. In 1909, during one of Minnie's trips to Michigan, her husband filed for divorce, claiming that she had abandoned him and that she was mentally unbalanced. Their sons were then seven and five. In 1911, with Minnie still absent, the divorce was granted. At this point she returned, and in a retrial the divorce decree was overturned. Minnie feared the loss of custody of her children and of her inheritance. The reunion was hardly a joyous one.[11]

Lying on her deathbed in Marshall, Minnie Taylor called her daughter to her. Lady Bird remembered, "She looked over at me and said, 'My poor little girl, her face is dirty.' " She called for a washcloth and carefully wiped Lady Bird's face. " 'Nobody at home to care for you but the Black nurse,' she said. 'Poor child.' " Minnie was more right than she knew. T. J., who waited almost a year to tell his two sons in boarding school that their mother had died, was not about to take up the task of raising a little girl. The period from September through December, when tenants brought their cotton to be ginned, was the busiest time of the year for Mr. Boss. A few months after Minnie's death, T. J. put Lady Bird on the train and sent her off to Alabama. She bore with her a suitcase containing her worldly possessions and a sign around her neck that read "Deliver this child to John Will Patillo," who was Minnie's uncle.[12] Lady Bird had in effect become an orphan.

Lady Bird responded to the devastating loss of her mother by withdrawing emotionally. Instead of melting into a pool of self-pity, however, she transformed her pain into feelings of sympathy for her undeserving father and her brothers. After she arrived in Alabama, no one in the Patillo family was allowed to mention Minnie's death. "No one dared say a word about it—including me," Lady Bird later said.[13] A friend of Effie's remembered the first time she saw Lady Bird. On an automobile ride into the country, the little girl, clad in a starched dress, sat silently on the back seat reading a book and munching fruit. The ability to withdraw, to rise above whatever storm threatened her psychological and emotional balance, would remain with her throughout the rest of her life. Both of her daughters, Lynda Bird and Luci Baines, would recall their mother as the most emotionally self-contained person they had ever met.

After a stay of several months in Alabama, it was decided that Effie and Lady Bird would move back to Karnack. Lady Bird could attend elementary school at the one-room Fern School, located on a wooded hill near the Brick House. In theory, Aunt Effie would take care of Lady Bird; in reality, it was the child who cared for the adult. Effie continued to be a self-conscious semi-invalid. Rarely was a trip made to Marshall without a visit to the drug store for a bottle of Lydia Pinkham's Tonic. Nearly 40 percent alcohol by volume, Lydia Pinkham's was the perfect medicine for Effie's aching head and queasy stomach. When she was eleven, Lady Bird accompanied her aunt on one of her periodic visits to Battle Creek. She did calisthenics with Dr. Kellogg and caught a glimpse of the famous senator from Wisconsin, Robert "Fighting Bob" LaFollette. Lady Bird's playmates at the Brick House were the children of Cap'n Taylor's black employees. She even occasionally attended services at the local black church.

When it was time to enter the seventh grade, Lady Bird and Effie moved to nearby Jefferson, an important nineteenth-century inland port that had gone to seed. Jefferson was quintessential Old South, its social life dominated by the local chapter of the Daughters of the Confederacy. It was here that Lady Bird developed her marked southern accent; for the rest of her days, unless making a conscious effort, she would roll her *r*'s and use the short *a* in place of *i*. When she was ready for high school, she and Effie moved back to the Brick House, and Lady Bird was transported to and from Marshall, a town of fifteen thousand, by one of T. J.'s employees.[14]

Two years after Minnie's death, Lady Bird's father married one of his employees, Beulah Wisdom, an attractive young woman with a business degree from a college in Tyler. Lady Bird was simultaneously attracted to and repelled by Beulah. She and Effie resented the intrusion; they were the women of Brick House. Beulah wore short skirts, bobbed her hair, and careened around Karnack and environs in her new car. Married to a rich older man, she made no attempt to hide her sexuality. Lady Bird admitted she was pretty, but "in a coarse and crude sort of way."[15] But there was something about her independence and daring that was attractive. She was so un–Aunt Effie. During one of her trips to Battle Creek, Lady Bird, in a Beulah-like moment, paid $2.50 to ride in a biplane with an aviatrix. "It was the most exciting ride of my young life," she later remembered.[16] In the clouds she was above it all, in control, free.

BY THE TIME SHE REACHED HIGH SCHOOL, Lady Bird had come to see books and learning not as an escape from reality but as a means for living a fuller and freer life. She made excellent grades, graduating third in her class. At Marshall High, she was neither popular nor unpopular. Her best friend, Emma

Boehringer, was also a rival, a pretty girl who sometimes excluded Lady Bird from her clique. Although her father had money, the girl from Karnack did not pay much attention to fashion. She was sensible, self-effacing, down-to-earth. There were boyfriends, J. H. Benefield in Jefferson and later Thomas C. Soloman, but Lady Bird had to be escorted to the senior prom by the boyfriend of a friend whose mother felt sorry for her. Lady Bird's real love was nature. She and her friends spent the summers roaming the woods, swimming in Lake Caddo, collecting the wildflowers to which she would later give so much of her life. She found consolation in her father's power and money. And she realized that the root of his power was money. In 1928, she kept a running tab of monthly sales in Cap'n Taylor's store—down to the penny. The total gross sales for that year alone for one store was $212,127.45. As an adult and successful businesswoman, Lady Bird would earn a reputation as a tight-fisted, no-nonsense manager. Not wealth particularly, but financial security was very important to her.

Graduating from high school at fifteen, Lady Bird enrolled in summer school at the University of Alabama. Her high school friend, Helen Bird, the daughter of the Episcopal priest in Marshall, talked her into attending St. Mary's, an exclusive Episcopal girls' school in Dallas, beginning in the fall. There, she made excellent grades, embraced Episcopalianism, but decided to transfer to the University of Texas for her final two years of college.[17]

When Lady Bird arrived in 1930, Austin was the place to be for a young person. Her friend, Emma Boehringer's sister, Eugenia ("Gene"), picked her up in her car. They drove down Congress Avenue, passing the famous Driskill Hotel on their way to the Texas capitol, built of rose-hued granite and modeled after the national Capitol. Gene drove her west to Zilker Park, which included the cold, clear-blue swimming hole of Barton Springs. Dominating the city was the sprawling UT campus, home to some 6,652 of the state's brightest and most socially ambitious students. Despite paeans to gender equality, men came to UT to get an education that would land them a substantial job, and not a few women came to find a husband. Given the fact that men outnumbered women four to one, those interested in the latter goal could not have come to a better place. UT was typical of many state institutions: students could get an excellent education if they chose, or could graduate without getting much of one at all. Tuition was $25 a year, and for $10.50 students could buy a blanket "tax" that gained entry to all sporting and cultural events.

Lady Bird chose to stay in a boarding house with six other girls rather than in Scottish Rite, Littlefield, or one of the other large dormitories for women. Her roommate was Cecille Harrison, an outgoing blonde from San Antonio. Lady Bird pledged a sorority but was forced to drop out when her father objected to the organization as a waste of money.[18] For the next two years she ran with Gene, who worked as secretary to C. V. Terrell, head of the powerful Texas Railroad Commission. Lady Bird continued to dress down; her friends wore tailored ensembles with high heels, while she sported simple skirts and blouses and loafers. Despite her somewhat dowdy appearance, she had no trouble getting dates. Her companion for most of her last two years at UT was Duncan Dawson, "a handsome, smart man who was absolutely smitten with Lady Bird."[19] Dawson covered the capital for the *Dallas Morning News* and was largely responsible for her decision to major in journalism.

Lady Bird was no prude. One afternoon, she and Wayne Livergood, a wealthy boy from Houston, and another couple drove to Nuevo Laredo. They drank gin and danced all night at a spot called the Bohemian Club. She, Cecille, and another friend became acquainted with Hiram King, a vice president of Sinclair Oil Company. A married man, King owned a large house on Mt. Bonnell. He frequently entertained the young women with cocktails and steaks. Her companions remembered the undue attention King seemed to be paying Lady Bird.[20] Despite a relatively active social life, Lady Bird made As and Bs and graduated with two degrees, in journalism and history.[21] Politically, she and her friends were liberals. They all supported Miriam "Ma" Ferguson, who as governor would oppose the Klan, support repeal of Prohibition, and authorize $20 million in bread bonds to feed the hungry.

As her graduation present to herself, Lady Bird decided on a trip to Washington, D.C. Cecille Harrison agreed to accompany her. Gene Boehringer urged Lady Bird to go by the offices of Congressman Richard Kleberg and meet his handsome, dynamic young secretary, Lyndon Johnson. The two young women had a grand time touring the nation's capital, but the trip did not include Lyndon. Instead, as she had planned, Lady Bird spent time with Victor McRea, a young man from Roby, who had just graduated from law school and taken a job with the postal service. Then, two weeks following her return to Austin, she stopped by Gene's office at the Railroad Commission. Who should appear but Lyndon Johnson. He had a date with Dorothy Muckleroy, Gene's roommate, who was there waiting. Before taking Dorothy to dinner, Lyndon asked all three out for a drink. "He was very, very good-looking." Lady Bird later said. "Lots of hair, quite black and wavy, and the most outspoken, straightforward, determined young man I'd ever met."[22] While Gene and Dorothy were talking, Lyndon leaned over to Lady Bird and asked her to meet him for breakfast the next morning at eight at the Driskill Hotel Coffee Shop. Without really thinking, she agreed.

Lady Bird was attracted to Lyndon, but he had come on a bit strong. She decided to keep an appointment the next morning with Hugo Kuehne, an Austin architect she had hired to remodel the Brick House, and skip the date with young Johnson. In the summer of 1934, Beulah Taylor had taken up with one of her husband's hired hands. Discovering the affair, Boss Taylor kicked both of them off his property. The divorce became final in September, and Taylor had asked Lady Bird to take charge of renovating the family home, which had fallen into disrepair. On her way to Kuehne's office, which was next door to the Driskill, Lady Bird saw Lyndon waiting at a corner table. As she was leaving, he was still there. This time he saw her and waved her down. "I was sitting at the front table waiting for her, when I saw her come out of that office," Lyndon said.

"I've always doubted whether she would ever have found the courage to walk in there otherwise."[23]

For the next hour she sat wedged into the coffee shop booth listening to a nonstop monologue by Lyndon on Lyndon. He related his family history, told her about Kleberg and his job. He was, she recalled, a young man who wanted to rise in the world by helping others. Lyndon seemed intoxicated with Roosevelt and the New Deal and bragged of his ability to maneuver the reactionary Kleberg into supporting legislation to help farmers, workers, small businessmen, and the jobless. "He began to tell me all about his job, his family," she remembered. "And he just kept on asking the most probing questions: 'What did you take in school? What's your family like? What do you want to do?' He was telling me all sorts of things I would never have asked him, certainly on first acquaintance."[24] "It was just like finding yourself in the middle of a whirlwind," remembered Lady Bird of her breakfast. "I just had not met up with that kind of vitality before."[25]

After breakfast, the two got into the automobile Lyndon was driving, a showy Ford convertible complete with hand-tooled leather seats stamped with the King Ranch symbol, and spent the rest of the day driving around the hills of west Austin. Periodically, Lyndon would ask Lady Bird about her life and family, but before she could answer would interrupt with more about himself. He spoke glowingly of Rebekah and her capacity for self-denial. Lady Bird recalled the impression Lyndon's description of his mother made: "I saw her as an absolutely lovely woman, who had given too much to her husband and family."[26] He made no secret that he had dated numerous other women, and he described his failed love affair with Carol Davis. Instead of being offended, Lady Bird was sympathetic and impressed. "My feeling was here was a very attractive man, who had all kinds of women interested in him," she remembered. "I was a little amazed that he was at all interested in me." At the close of the day, Lyndon asked Lady Bird to marry him. "You must be joking," was her altogether appropriate reply, but she agreed to drive to San Marcos with him the next day to meet his parents.[27]

The day with Sam and Rebekah was as strange for Lady Bird as the day before. Everything was so serious. Sam, Lady Bird noted, seemed "pretty much used up." On this, the second day of their relationship, Lady Bird got the feeling Rebekah was evaluating her, judging her, seeing if she measured up. "I just wanted to reassure her that really I had no interest in taking her son away from her," Lady Bird said, "and wasn't at all sure that I wanted any part of him myself, and on the other hand if I did, it wouldn't do her any harm."[28] From San Marcos Lyndon drove the somewhat stunned Lady Bird to Corpus Christi to show off the King Ranch. That night they had dinner with Ben Crider and then checked into separate rooms in a midtown hotel. The next day, Lyndon drove Lady Bird out to meet Alice King Kleberg, the family matriarch. At the close of the visit, she told the young couple that they were perfect for each other and advised them to get married. Back in the car, Lyndon informed Lady Bird that he had to go to San Antonio to pick up Malcolm Bardwell, secretary to newly elected Congressman Maury Maverick, and return to Washington. He again pressed her for a commitment to marry him. It was absurd to make such a momentous decision after such a short time, Lady Bird told him, but she invited him to stop by Karnack and meet her father on the way back to Washington.

Not surprisingly, Lyndon was impressed with the Brick House, the Taylor empire, and the Boss himself. More surprising, given that Lyndon continued to babble about himself and the New Deal throughout dinner, T. J. was impressed with his daughter's suitor. "You've been bringing home a lot of boys," he told Lady Bird after dinner. "This one looks like a man." [29] Taylor may have been impressed with Lyndon, but he also wanted to get his daughter out of the house. By then, Lady Bird's father, sixty years old, had taken up with Ruth Scoggins, two years younger than Lady Bird. She would become his third wife. [30]

As he left, Lyndon gave Lady Bird a book which he told her to think of as an engagement present. It was a collection of essays by a group of German journalists entitled *Nazism: An Assault on Civilization.* "To Bird," he inscribed it, "in the hope within these pages, she may realize some little entertainment and find reiterated here some of the principles in which she believes and which she has been taught to revere and respect." [31] She responded with Voltaire's *Candide,* whose absurdly optimistic protagonist reminded her of Lyndon. Over the next few weeks, the two continued their courtship by long-distance telephone and through the mail. As always, he was impatient when she did not respond to him immediately. "For three days, I've watched and waited for your second letter," he wrote. "Honey, don't be so long between notes." [32]

Lyndon was then enthralled by the dynamic liberal Maury Maverick, who was already beginning to attack some of FDR's lieutenants as too conservative. "Maury Maverick and Malcolm Bardwell have been with me all week and every day has been a busy day for me," he related. "We have visited dozens of departments to bring relief and satisfaction to . . . constituents." Maverick took Lyndon to see the famous black Washington cleric, Elder Michaux, preach. "This was my first time to be in a Negro church," he wrote, "but here I learned the effectiveness of psychology. I heard some of the best singing to be heard anywhere. All of the Negroes [were] laughing, shouting and happy. Why can't we have more enjoyment and happiness?" [33] Lady Bird began to respond. "And whenever do you play, Lyndon?" she wrote back. "There isn't any time left for you to, you poor lamb. But I adore you for being so ambitious and dynamic." [34] In fact, Lyndon always found time to play. He went to the circus with Maverick and Bardwell. "Sunday and until early Monday with Bill & Mrs. White, Helen and Malcolm," he wrote. "I dined, drank and danced. Monday night we drove several miles into Maryland and had dinner and music that almost made me leave for Texas and you that night." [35]

Johnson pressed Lady Bird to agree to marry as soon as possible; to his disappointment and frustration, she suggested they wait a year. Lyndon regaled her with all the adventures they would have, all the sights they would see: Civil War battlefields, New York City, the Smithsonian.[36] She responded with descriptions of long, melancholy walks in the woods. "[Neighbor and friend Doris Powell and I] walked through the woods to the old Haggerty place—site of an old colonial mansion, now quite dilapidated and doleful looking," she wrote. "It always gives me a very poignant feeling to go over there. It must have been a lovely place. There are the tallest magnolias I've ever seen, and great live oaks and myriads of crepe myrtle, and a carpet of jonquils and flags in the spring."[37] She told him of a favorite movie, *The World Moves On:* "The love-making is in the most flawless good taste I've ever seen on the screen. It makes me feel very set up about the human race to watch them."[38] Then later, "There's nothing I like better than being comfortable in a nice cozy place and reading something amusing or well-written or interesting to someone I like."[39] His response: "This morning I'm ambitious, proud, energetic and very madly in love with you. I want to see people. I want to walk through the throngs, want to do things with a drive. If I had a box I would almost make a speech this minute. Plans, ideas, hopes, I'm bubbling over with them."[40] Lyndon continued to accuse her of being distant and aloof, but she was hardly that. "Darling" and "lamb" were some of her favorite appellations for him. There were frequent declarations of love and some teasing. "When I get up to Washington my brain will have reverted to the idiot state!" she wrote, hinting at a commitment. "So I'm going to buy me two or three up-to-the minute books on economics or government . . . And one good one on Russia, which I'm very interested in."[41]

As Lyndon continued his romantic assault, Lady Bird, living in the yet to be remodeled Brick House, reading at night by kerosene lamp, became depressed, then frantic. What if this dynamic young man, her pathway to brave new worlds, found someone else? She got in the car and drove to Alabama to consult the perpetually bedridden Aunt Effie. "If he really loves you as much as he says he does, he'll wait," Effie advised.[42] Oh God, Lady Bird thought, and if he does not, I'll wind up just like you. Another aunt, Ellen Cooper Taylor, told her to follow her heart. During long-distance telephone calls, he kept up the pressure. Perhaps he should go into another line of work, one that was more secure and that paid better. The Klebergs had promised to obtain for him the presidency of Texas A&I College at Kingsville if he wanted it, but the life of an academic, particularly such a provincial one, was not very appealing. He had received an offer from General Electric in New York to work for them as a lobbyist at $10,000 a year, but money was not everything. He was called, he believed, to a life of public service.[43] By this point, Lady Bird was distraught and confused. "Lyndon, please tell me as soon as you can what the deal is . . . I am afraid it's politics. Oh, I know I haven't any business—not any proprietary interest—but I would hate for you to go into politics. Don't let me get things any more muddled for you than they are though, dearest . . . I still love you, Lyndon, I want to say it over and over, goodnight, not goodbye, Bird."[44]

Sensing that he had the object of his desire on the ropes, Lyndon intensified the courtship. "I see something I know I want," he wrote back. "I immediately exert efforts to get it. I do or I don't but I try and do my best . . . You see something you might want. You tear it to pieces in an effort to determine if you should want it . . . and conclude that maybe the desire isn't an 'everlasting' one and that the 'sane' thing to do is to wait a year or so."[45]

While Lady Bird was visiting her relatives in Alabama and Mississippi, Lyndon had to return to Texas on business. They arranged to meet in Marshall and then drive to Karnack for dinner. Aunt Effie had written Lyndon pleading with him to delay marriage until spring at least so that Lady Bird could spend the winter with her in Florida. The next morning T. J. Taylor found Lyndon at the breakfast table, "blue." "Mr. Taylor," he said, "I guess I will be gone when you come from town today as I must be back in Austin tonight. I was so in hopes that I could persuade Bird to marry me [on] Thanksgiving, but her aunt says 'no.' And Bird seems to think she should regard her wishes." Taylor sided with Lyndon, telling him that Effie was old and sick and had no right to require further sacrifice of Lady Bird. When he returned from town, the couple was gone. The maid told him they had left around ten o'clock "with four big grips."[46] Sometime between nine and ten Lady Bird had succumbed. "I'll marry you," she said. "When?" "Tonight," he replied.[47]

They decided to "commit matrimony," as Lady Bird would describe her marriage to a friend, in San Antonio rather than Austin. It would offend her many friends, but this was in essence an elopement, and as such was best executed in an unfamiliar place. On the road, Lyndon pulled over and phoned Dan Quill, the postmaster in San Antonio and a fellow politico who had helped in the Kleberg campaign. Lyndon told his friend of his intention to marry at 8:00 P.M. in Saint Mark's Episcopal Church. Make all the arrangements, he instructed Quill, who was used to Lyndon's habit of treating everyone as a willing coworker in a scheme of which he was the mastermind. While a triumphant Lyndon and an excited but apprehensive Lady Bird traversed the three hundred miles to San Antonio, Quill worked feverishly.[48]

The first task was to persuade the Reverend Arthur R. McKinstry, who oversaw the wealthiest congregation in Bexar County, to perform the ceremony. He refused. The young couple needed counseling, their faith in God affirmed, their understanding of the burdens as well as the joys of marriage confirmed. The congressman's secretary had to get back to Washington, Quill cajoled. McKinstry was mindful of Lyndon's friendship with the powerful Mavericks and his position as assistant to San Antonio's congressman. Reluctantly, he agreed.[49]

Under Texas law, couples applying for a marriage license had to undergo a physical examination. Obviously there would not be time for that, so Quill filled out the marriage license himself and persuaded the deputy clerk at the courthouse to sign it. The breathless couple arrived in the Alamo City around six and checked into adjoining rooms at the Plaza Saint Anthony Hotel; Lyndon, Quill, and two lawyer friends of theirs retired to one and Lady Bird, alone, to the other. She phoned her college friend Cecille Harrison, and asked her if she would "come stand up with me," that is, be her maid of honor, at St. Marks at eight o'clock. She agreed, pulled a black cocktail dress out of her closet, and headed for the hotel. Meanwhile, Lyndon and Dan Quill discovered that neither had procured a ring. Quill rushed off to the local Sears, Roebuck. He persuaded the clerk there to allow him to take ten or so rings of various sizes on approval. Lady Bird tried them on until she found one that fit.[50] Quill returned the rest and paid $2.50 for the symbol of the complicated, famous relationship that would last for nearly forty years. Cecille arrived at the Saint Anthony to find Lady Bird sitting on a window seat looking pensively down at the street. "If you give me a quarter," she told her friend, "I'll jump out of this window."[51]

Perhaps it was a premonition. But she quieted her fears, rose, and put on the lavender sheath she had bought in Corpus several weeks before. Prior to the ceremony, Lady Bird had read the wedding vows carefully, committing them to memory. She asked Lyndon if he had read them. He said yes, and she said she hoped so because "I want to make sure you understand what's in them."[52] There were only twelve guests at the ceremony at Saint Mark's. The wedding party celebrated with a dinner on the roof garden of the Saint Anthony. One of the guests, Henry Hirshberg, had sent for several bottles of wine from his private stock at home, and the group drank and danced until well after midnight. Cecille remembered what a handsome couple Lyndon and Lady Bird made, he at six foot three and she with her head nestled naturally in the hollow of his shoulder.

IN THE YEARS THAT FOLLOWED, Lyndon would love Lady Bird in conventional and unconventional ways. "She was the best piece of ass I ever had," he would confide indelicately to friends. But he meant it, and he loved her. He would buy her clothes, entrust business and political matters to her, solicit and take her advice on public and private questions; she was virtually the only person he was to so trust as president. He also yelled at her, humiliated her in public and private, ignored her emotional needs, and cheated on her. Through it all, she seemed undiminished. Lady Bird attended to his every need, laying out his clothes, waiting dinner until all hours, suffering continual invasions of her privacy, abandoning her daughters to be with him, and acquiescing in his dalliances. "He took her completely for granted," said family friend Virginia Durr, "and he expected her to devote every waking hour to him, which she did."[53]

But Lady Bird reveled in her husband's energy and ambition. She was part of his great mission to serve mankind. She enjoyed the power that he wielded. Lyndon simultaneously provided escape from the world of Aunt Effie and protection from the chaos and destruction that lurked in every brave new world. As a southern woman, she was conditioned by heritage and experience to suffer and to sacrifice with dignity and integrity. "Ours was a compelling love," she told Jan Jarboe Russell. "Lyndon bullied me, coaxed me, at times even ridiculed me, but he made me more than I would have been. I offered him some peace and quiet, maybe a little judgment."[54] To another interviewer. "He needed somebody around him who was soft and gentle and laughed, and who was tough about his or her own priorities and feelings of the right course of action, but perfectly glad to hear him out."[55]

And what was she to him? With her hooked nose and somewhat irregular features, Lady Bird was certainly not the most beautiful woman Lyndon had ever met. She was certainly not the most sophisticated or confident. And yet she was attractive, educated, and unintimidated. He sensed that she could love him like his mother, but without the guilt and emotional manipulation. She was obviously capable of putting his interests and career first, of making them her own. Her calmness was capable of quieting the emotional and psychological storms that frequently swept over him. Lyndon loved her for all of those things but in the end could not keep from subsuming her, treating her as an appendage. "He never paid any attention to Lady Bird when she was around," journalist John Chancellor observed," and when she wasn't around, he seemed to miss her badly."[56] The fact that she was fully aware and accepting of the terms of the relationship did not excuse him, but they both must be given credit for the truth that she was strong enough to have left him at any time. And he knew it.

By mutual agreement, Lyndon and Lady Bird opted for a honeymoon in Mexico. They spent their first night in the Grand Ancira Hotel in Monterrey. The following day, the newlyweds took the train to San Luis Potosí, enjoying the quaint hotel there and the incredible bargains in the marketplace. From Monterrey, they made the long rail trip to Mexico City. Lady Bird tried to interest her mate in the countryside—she was particularly fascinated by the innumerable shrines to the Virgin Mary—but all he could talk about was Washington and what he was going to do to help save the nation from poverty and become the greatest congressional secretary of all time. In Mexico City, they climbed the pyramids and visited the floating garden of Xochimilco, which dated from the time of the Aztecs. There they posed for a photo standing in the prow of a gondola, he in formal double-breasted suit with his arm around her and she in a dark dress holding a bouquet of flowers.[57] What Lyndon seemed to have liked most about the honeymoon was sex. Lady Bird did not complain about her aggressive husband, but on their return to San Antonio before leaving for Washington, she made a hurried appointment with a gynecologist.[58]

Instead of renting an apartment, Lyndon and Lady Bird resided for over a month in the basement of the Dodge. He had lived in close quarters with others all his life, frequently sharing a bed with relatives and roommates. He seemed to have no concept of private space, hating to be alone even when he went to the bathroom. She had grown up at times as an only child. After weeks of sharing a bathroom with others and having to hide under the covers in the early morning while Lyndon and his friends discussed the forthcoming business in their room, she persuaded him to rent a one-bedroom apartment at 1910 Kalorama Road overlooking Rock Creek Park.

Lady Bird learned to be Lyndon Johnson's wife. He expected her to man the home front, to do the cooking and cleaning, to pay the bills, to be ready to entertain at a moment's notice. She knew how to do none of these things at first. Every month, Lyndon kept $100 of his $267 paycheck and gave the rest to Lady Bird to run the household. She had to write checks intermittently to Rebekah and his siblings. Both came to resent this unending drain on their resources. Indeed, Lady Bird's relationship with the Johnson clan was at times strained. She thought the other children resented Lyndon's success and what they thought was their mother's favoritism toward him. She became particularly peeved when Sam Houston, who was attending law school, moved in with them, sleeping on a cot in the living room. To his friends and sometimes to Lyndon, Sam Houston was a weak but lovable playboy who drank too much. To Lady Bird he was a loudmouthed, self-indulgent lush. Typically, she kept her feelings to herself, but a letter from Lyndon to his mother revealed the strain the younger brother was causing: "I don't know what to do—I am borrowing money this month to get by on . . . Sent S. H. $100 in January [he had finally moved out]—$50 in February to school and additional $20 or more spending money . . . and now he is yelling for more . . . I can't continue to bear his expenses when he spends more than I do and apparently can't find time to do more than call for more."[59] With Rebekah, Lady Bird was correct, deferential, but distant. She was aware that her mother-in-law saw her as nothing more or less than a tool to sustain her son and help advance his career.[60]

Lyndon was frequently absent. The trips to Mt. Vernon and Washington-area museums that he had promised during their ten-week courtship did not materialize. When she saw him, it was frequently in the company of staffers or journalists whom he had brought home for a late dinner. "He'd call Bird—I used to hear him—and say, 'get the furniture insured. I'm having the newspapermen out to the house on Friday night!' " Russ Brown recalled. "He'd get several cases of whiskey, and everybody would get crazy with booze."[61] Even within the Texas Society, Lyndon's main social circle, Lady Bird was a virtual unknown. Arthur E. "Tex" Goldschmidt, a fellow Texan who worked in the Department of Interior, wrote his wife in August 1938, "Lyndon and his wife (I never knew there was one before . . .) took me to a curb service place for a late meal after a day that started about 6:30 A.M."[62]

Mainly, Lady Bird later recalled, Lyndon took getting used to. Everything about him was exaggerated. Once, while riding in Rock Creek Park, he helped her mount a young skittish stallion and then slapped him on the rump. The horse bolted, bucking, nearly throwing Lady Bird. When she managed to dismount, she rushed up to him: "Damn you! I could have been killed." He brushed it off as a prank. Lyndon Johnson never apologized. On another occasion, the couple went to see the movie version of John Steinbeck's *The Grapes of Wrath*. In the darkness of the theater, Lady Bird was moved to hear her husband sobbing quietly at the fate of the Joad family. "He had a tender, sentimental side which he didn't show very often," she remembered.[63] He wanted his wife to dress attractively, sexy but respectable, with bold colors and straight skirts. Finding her needing makeup, he would bark, "Put your lipstick on. You don't sell for what you're worth." [64] Lady Bird took comfort in the belief that such outbursts were an indication that she was attractive to her husband.

During those first months in Washington, the couple with whom Lyndon and Lady Bird spent the most time was Maury and Terrell Maverick. The new bride tried out her domestic skills on her fellow Texans, with mixed results. Of a simple dinner of baked ham, rice, and lemon pie, Terrell later recalled of the starch, "It tasted like library paste." [65] Both the Johnsons felt deeply drawn to the charismatic Maury, whose views were to have a major impact on Lyndon.

The Mavericks were one of the first families of Texas. Samuel Maverick had fought in the Texas Revolution and was a signer of the Declaration of Independence. Maury could count on his family tree both James Madison and Meriwether Lewis. After a stint in the American Expeditionary Force during World War I, he studied law and settled down to practice in San Antonio. By the time he was twenty-four, Maury had been elected president of the San Antonio Bar. According to his brother, Maverick was one of the country's leading experts on Erasmus. He was attracted to the writers of the Enlightenment and novelists such as James Joyce and Anatole France. He read everything he could by and about Thomas Jefferson. In his copy of George Bernard Shaw's *Androcles and the Lion,* Maury underlined passages in the preface that linked Christianity with social justice. [66]

That Maverick would opt for a life in politics was, of course, inevitable. His chance came in 1929, when reformers led a revolt against the city machine that controlled San Antonio, a machine, said its critics, beside which Tammany Hall was pale in comparison. In 1930 Maury was elected city tax collector as part of the "clean government" slate. In 1934 he decided to run for Congress as a representative of the Twentieth District, newly carved out of the old Fourteenth. He won the primary over his nearest rival by some three thousand votes, despite being attacked as a communist for belonging to the American Civil Liberties Union. [67]

In Washington, Maverick embraced the New Deal, quickly emerging as the uncrowned head of the left wing of the Democratic party. "As for me I am throwing in with the Yankees and the liberals," he told his constituents in one audacious speech, "the agriculture boys of the West—and the big-city Democrats too. That is the only way the Democratic party can do a good job and serve America." [68] He proved a staunch champion of the Tennessee Valley Authority, which he characterized as an attempt to substitute care and forethought for the wasteful, hit-or-miss methods of rugged individualism. He believed that the state had an obligation to help those who could not help themselves; relief projects like the Works Progress Administration topped his list of legislative priorities. Personally, Maverick was humorous, compassionate, crude, erudite, and combative. Standing a little over five feet, in constant pain from a serious war wound, he had, in the words of a contemporary, "taken a running broad jump onto the nation's front pages."[69] In speech he was tough and blunt; opponents were "bastards" and "sons-of-bitches." He despised pretense and superficiality. Maury Maverick was, in short, Lyndon's kind of politician.

Meanwhile, Mamie Kleberg, convinced that Lyndon had conspired with her husband's lover to keep the affair from her and subsequently to see that she had a soft landing, plotted to get him fired. Lyndon was too active in his own behalf, she told the clueless Richard; he was promoting himself at the expense of his boss and clearly intended to run against him in 1936. For a while, the congressman resisted, but he was no match for his wife, and in the spring of 1935 he told Johnson that he would have to look for another job. In desperation, Lyndon went to see Maverick and another fellow Texan, Sam Rayburn, who was a leading candidate to become speaker of the House in the next session. Both were sympathetic, but neither had positions available on their staffs. Providentially, the Roosevelt administration had just created a new agency, the National Youth Administration, a division of the WPA intended to keep students in school through a system of work study and to provide part-time employment and job training for those who were not students but who were unemployed. The head of the NYA was Aubrey Williams, a southern liberal who was an ardent New Dealer and an early advocate for black civil rights. Rumor had it that DeWitt Kinard, a former state legislator, would head the operation in Texas, but before he could be appointed, Lyndon heard about the job from Malcolm Bardwell and decided that the NYA would be the perfect springboard from which to launch a political career of his own.[70]

LYNDON, Arthur Perry, Senator Morris Sheppard's assistant, and Bardwell met in Maverick's office to plot strategy. Subsequently, Rayburn went to see Senator Tom Connally, who was not exactly enthusiastic about the New Deal and its myriad agencies, but agreed to support Lyndon for a job that was on his patronage list. Meanwhile, Maverick went straight to the top, calling on both FDR and Eleanor Roosevelt about his protégé. Roosevelt at first protested that he was not going to entrust a major state relief agency to an untested twenty-six-year-old. But Maverick listed Lyndon's qualifications and insisted that youth required youth to lead it out of the Depression. Eventually the president relented, and Lyndon was named Texas director of the NYA.[71]

The multibillion-dollar WPA was designed to put heads of households to work, but it wasn't enough. New Dealers like Harry Hopkins and Eleanor Roosevelt had become worried that the Depression would cause the nation to lose the services as well as the interest of an entire generation of young people. As of 1935, 20 percent of America's 22 million youth were out of school, on relief, or, more often, wandering the countryside looking for work. These numbers would continue to grow unless the federal government did something. Texas was typical in its numbers but unique in its sprawl and diversity. When Lyndon was sworn in on July 25, 1935, some 125,000 Texans between sixteen and twenty-five were on relief and many thousands more would have to forgo the 1936–1937 school year if they did not receive aid.[72]

Directing the National Youth Administration was a perfect fit for Johnson. It would allow him to get his name in newspapers throughout Texas as a community builder and benefactor of the state's youth. Through his ferocious energy and organizational skills, he could ensure that the NYA operated efficiently and effectively, thus blunting possible criticism from conservatives. "When I come back to Washington, I'm coming back as a congressman," he had told Malcolm Bardwell before leaving the capital.[73] One of the first things he would tell his staff was to ensure that all letters and publications used his full name, Lyndon B. Johnson, not some abbreviation or variation. "But I don't understand why," one asked. He replied, "Oh, some day you'll understand why."[74] Most important, the NYA job appealed to his idealism.

Throughout his life, Lyndon Johnson was happiest when he was on some kind of crusade for one segment of humankind or another. What greater cause in the eyes of God, mother, country, and state than to help young people stay in school or train for gainful employment? There were a number of options for dealing with needy youth, he told a group of educators in September 1935: "We could starve them to death; we could send them to school; we could kill them through war. Obviously the answer lies in sending some of them to school; giving some of them vocational training; finding work projects for others. That briefly is the work cut out for the NYA."[75]

After attending a White House send-off for state directors, Lyndon and Lady Bird departed for Austin. The day he arrived, the new NYA director called a press conference and delivered his version of Roosevelt's "The only thing we have to fear is fear itself" speech. He called at the capitol, where he secured Governor James V. "Jimmy" Allred's public endorsement and then departed for a whirlwind tour of the state's major cities to publicize his program. Returning to Austin, Lyndon turned his attention to staffing his agency while Lady Bird moved their possessions into the comfortable San Gabriel Street home of Professor Robert Montgomery, the UT economist who was on leave working in Washington. Lyndon first called Willard Deason, who was then employed by the Federal Land Bank in Houston, and asked him to go to work for the NYA. Deason replied that he was not ready to give up his job but that he would come to Austin and help his old friend set up the NYA office. He came and subsequently agreed to take a six-month leave of absence from his Houston position.[76]

With Deason on board, Lyndon called former SWT classmates Jesse Kellam and Sherman Birdwell and asked them to meet him at the Post Office Café in San Marcos at 7:30 the next morning. For an hour and a half he talked nonstop, giving them his vision of what the NYA could do for Texas, for kids "who couldn't buy pencils and paper much less shoes."[77] Birdwell, who agreed to go to work as Lyndon's finance director at $2,200 a year, recalled the experience of being recruited by Johnson: "His intensity made you feel like this is the most important thing in the world, not just to Lyndon Johnson, but the most important thing in the world, and you want to be part of it . . . He [made] helping these young people an accomplishment to be done that would be so important to you that you just felt like, 'I've got to do this for these young people. I mean, I'm the only chance they've got. Me!' "[78] Kellam, a former SWT football player and Black Star who had collaborated with The Brains, was a tougher sell but eventually agreed to leave his post as assistant to State School Superintendent L. E. Woods to go to work as deputy director of the Texas NYA at $3,900 a year. Lyndon's compensation had been set at $7,500 per year, a princely salary in 1935.[79]

To help conceptualize and publicize the program, Lyndon hired Herbert Henderson, a freelance writer and newspaper reporter who had played a key role in Maverick's congressional campaign. To oversee his NYA field representatives, the director hired Charles P. Little, then with the Texas Relief Commission. The Little courtship was typical. "I received a call from a man by the name of Lyndon B. Johnson," Little later recalled,

> about four o'clock on a Friday afternoon . . . He said, "I want to talk to you about a job." I said, "Well, thank you, but I have a job right now and am doing quite well . . ." He said, "Well, I still would like to talk with you." I said, "well, the first time I'm in Austin, sometime next week, why don't I call you and make a date for us to discuss what you have in mind, even though I want you to understand I'm perfectly happy where I am." He said, "No, next week is too late." I said, "Well, how about Monday morning? I could drive in on Sunday and see you the first thing Monday morning." Lyndon said, "Well, Monday morning is not quite good enough either." . . . I said, "Well, what is it you have in mind?" . . . He said, "How long would it take for you to drive in here? . . . I'll be in my office at nine o'clock tonight" . . . Great day! What kind of man was this? I went into Lyndon's office at nine o'clock that night. He was sitting at his desk . . . We sat and talked until midnight . . . He was the first man, I suppose, that I had talked to in these depression years who had hope and vision for the future. Bear in mind the time that we're talking about is the time when there was no hope for anything . . . When I left there, I had accepted a job for a hundred and fifty dollars a month, which was sixteen dollars less than what I was earning."[80]

The headquarters of the Texas NYA were located on the sixth floor of the Littlefield Building in downtown Austin. Lyndon and his staff were crammed into a tiny suite that included rooms 601, 603, and 605. Birdwell and Jones recalled that the sense of urgency was incredible. They worked sixteen hours a day, seven days a week, week after week. Typically, Lyndon would have his employees eat their lunches at their desks and return to work after dinner. Birdwell remembered many a night working by kerosene lantern and then finding his way down six flights of steps in the dark because the electricity in the Littlefield Building went off at 10:30 every evening.[81] Even then, the staff would sometimes retire to the Montgomery house, where Deason and Jones rented rooms, for late-night planning sessions on the living room floor.

In the beginning there were four districts in the state with four men in the field. Within a year there were twelve districts with fifteen to twenty supervisory staff operating out of Austin and another twenty in the field.[82] At the close of one eight-hour Sunday meeting of district representatives, Lyndon put both hands in his pockets. "I carry Ex-Lax in this pocket to get me going . . . and I carry aspirin in this pocket . . . Take both Ex-Lax and aspirin, but we have got to get the job done and we're going to do it."[83] He ranted and raved when he felt the office wasn't keeping up with the workload. He doled out tongue lashings, threats to fire, and ridicule. "Why don't I just fire you," he shouted at one staffer. "Then you can go back to making fifty dollars a month. You know why you were making fifty dollars a month, don't you? Because that's what you were worth."[84] When Herbert Henderson went on a binge and missed a day of work, Lyndon terminated him on the spot.[85] He would drive his workforce to the point of rebellion and then back off. "Maybe once a month he would say, 'Well, now let's play awhile.' Saturday after noon we would take off and all day Sunday and there would be no meetings. We would play golf, ride horseback or go to San Antonio for the weekend."[86] As always, Lyndon led by example. He was the first in the office, and unless he had business in the field, the last to leave. Suffering through repeated colds and flu, he drove himself mercilessly.

At first, there were no clear guidelines for the state youth administrations. Deason recalled that initially, Lyndon and the staff would stay up long into the night at the Montgomery House trying to decipher the changing regulations as they came down from Washington. With the opening of school looming and the threat that thousands of Texas youth would drop out, Lyndon decided to cast caution to the wind and forge ahead. Fundamental to the Texas youth effort was the school aid program, whereby secondary students could earn up to $6 and college students up to $15 a month doing odd jobs around their institutions, emptying trash cans, trimming lawns, grading papers for professors. By the start of the school year, Herbert Henderson and the secretaries had mailed forty-five hundred letters to administrators across the state and placed notices in eight hundred newspapers. The office was inundated with inquiries from every point in Texas. To Johnson's frustration, only 1,266 student applications for part-time jobs had been processed by September 1935.[87]

The sticking point was the WPA and its state offices in San Antonio. In many states, WPA directors insisted that the NYA report to them and act as a WPA subsidiary. Texas was no different. The WPA office was slow to process certifications for students showing that their family was on relief, a prerequisite for receiving student aid, because it felt heads of household were a priority. Lyndon's original annual budget was a half-million dollars, and Harry Drought, the state

WPA director, was determined to see that it not get any larger. "LBJ was a man who could not abide mediocrity," said Willard Deason. "He had a speed which was usually overdrive. He expected everybody else to operate that way, and they didn't."[88] Matters came to a head when Drought tried to have Sherman Birdwell fired for pushing too hard to have district WPA offices grant certificates to prospective NYA applicants. "Mr. Drought called Washington and told them to fire me off the NYA," Birdwell said. "Mr. Johnson had already talked to Washington and a decision was made at that time, for the first time and for the future, that no one hired or fired NYA supervisors except Mr. Johnson."[89] Gradually, then quickly, the logjam began to break. By November, 8,500 students were receiving aid from the NYA; by May 1936, 11,000, and by the end of the first full year of the NYA's operation, 12,342 Texas boys and girls were being helped.[90]

The NYA's college program went more smoothly, in part because there were only eighty-five colleges and universities in Texas, whereas there were more than two thousand high schools. Unlike high school students, college aid recipients had to be certified only by their institutions. Many performed simple clerical or janitorial work for their pay, up to $15 a month, but others toiled in their respective disciplines: chemists and biologists in laboratories, English and history majors in libraries and archives. As of the end of September 1935, the NYA was funneling aid to 5,036 undergraduates. Unfortunately, more than 21,000 had applied for help. At UT alone there were 3,500 applicants for 761 jobs. "I have done the most difficult job I have ever done in my life," the dean of students complained to Jesse Kellam. "In making these selections, I feel that I have blood on my hands."[91] Week after week, Lyndon pressed Washington for more funds, and he had some success. By the end of the 1935–1936 academic year, the number of recipients approached 5,500, but at the same time, the number of applicants had risen to 29,000.[92] An innovation unique to the Texas program was the Freshman College Center. Aimed at high school graduates who had to stay at home and work to support their families, these centers, eventually some twenty in number, allowed down-and-out but ambitious young people to take one or two tuition-free courses from instructors paid with NYA funds. They were the forerunners of community or junior colleges that would prove instrumental in opening up higher education to the American working class.[93]

For those young people who were not interested in college, there were work projects coupled with vocational training. Teams of Texas youths between the ages of sixteen and twenty-one would labor at construction and other jobs of benefit to the community and simultaneously learn how to weld, lay bricks, or sew. The problem with this WPA-style approach was funding. The NYA had only enough money to pay the part-time salaries of the youths so employed. The state or some other agency would actually have to cover materials, equipment, and housing. It was Gladys Montgomery, Robert's wife, who came up with the idea of a statewide system of roadside parks where motorists could safely pull off to rest, picnic, change a tire, or relieve themselves. She got the idea after a family of five was rammed from behind and killed while waiting out a rainstorm on the San Antonio highway.[94]

The idea immediately captured Lyndon's imagination. The state would provide the materials and living arrangements, and the NYA would pay the salaries of young workers. The public welfare would be promoted through a system of parks that would enhance travelers' comfort and safety. The Littlefield staff worked overtime to complete the paperwork, and Johnson managed to obtain approval from Washington days instead of weeks. Governor Allred and the Texas Highway Department, which eventually would become the single largest employer in the state, fell in line. By the summer of 1936, thirty-six hundred young men were at work building 125 permanent roadside parks. This work project in turn led to others. The NYA and the Highway Department put unemployed youth to work planting shrubs, building erosion barriers, and painting guard rails and highway signs. Next to the roadside parks, the most enduring and famous of the NYA projects was La Villita in San Antonio, a restored and operating nineteenth-century Mexican village built in the heart of one of the city's worst slums. The reconstruction and maintenance employed hundreds of Hispanic youths, paid with NYA money.[95]

NO GROUP BENEFITED MORE from New Deal relief projects than African Americans, and this was perhaps truer in Texas than elsewhere. Always "the last hired and the first fired," blacks suffered disproportionately from the Depression. Indeed, as one observer noted, "The Negro was born in depression. It only became official when it hit the white man."[96]

By 1932, black unemployment in the United States had reached 50 percent; those who managed to hold on to their jobs suffered average wage reductions of 40 percent. Approximately 40 percent of those employed were tenant farmers or share croppers with incomes of less than $200 per year. Initially, most New Deal agencies routinely discriminated against African Americans, especially in regard to relief benefits and wages, and virtually all adhered to stringent segregation practices. The president rejected the pleas of the National Association for the Advancement of Colored People (NAACP) and similar organizations to support a federal antilynching bill and in general to exert his influence in behalf of civil rights for blacks. Although Roosevelt was no stalwart champion of racial justice, his refusal to heed such pleas stemmed not so much from a lack of sympathy as from fear that he would antagonize powerful white congressmen from the South and jeopardize his New Deal legislative agenda.

It was Mrs. Roosevelt and key New Dealers such as Secretary of the Interior Harold Ickes and relief czar Harry Hopkins who used their influence to eliminate discrimination and segregation in New Deal agencies and programs. As a result, increasing numbers of African Americans shared in the benefits available from federal work and relief projects; others gained appointment to administrative and judicial posts in New Deal agencies. A group of these administrators, known as the "black cabinet," conferred with and advised the president on issues relating to African Americans. In addition, in 1936, for the first time blacks were accredited as delegates to the Democratic National Convention. By the close of the decade, 11 percent of Civilian Conservation Corps workers were black and the Farm Security Administration was giving 23 percent of its aid to black farmers. Of all the New Deal agencies, the NYA had the best civil rights record; 20 percent of its annual budget went to black youngsters. Although programs and work sites were generally segregated, black projects were supervised by black administrators.

As of 1935, some 855,000 African Americans lived in Texas; nearly a quarter were sixteen to twenty-five years of age. Most resided in decaying ghettos in Houston, Dallas, and San Antonio, in squalid tarpaper shacks on the outskirts of towns, or in rickety farm cabins. In rural areas, indoor plumbing and running water were virtually nonexistent. Ancient maladies like tuberculosis, malaria, and cholera ravaged young and old alike. But like black populations everywhere, Texas Negroes boasted middle and upper classes. Thousands of black high school and college students called out to Lyndon Johnson and the National Youth Administration for help.

If Johnson had had his preference, the Texas NYA would have been completely color-blind. Governor Jimmy Allred recalled that as the NYA was getting under way, he summoned its young director to his office. "Now, Lyndon," he said, "I know what you're about to do. You're passing out this money and you are planning to give some grants to Prairie View [A&M, an all-black institution in Texas] . . . I think, Lyndon, that you possibly have a fine future in politics; you can go far. But I want you to know that Texas is not ready for people to give federal money to Negroes at Negro schools." At that point, Lyndon stood up and came around to the side of Allred's desk. "Well," he said, "you have nothing else to say, Governor?" No, Allred replied. "I want to express my appreciation to you for inviting me in here, calling me in. There were some important things I could have been doing, but I came because you are the governor and you called me. It's just been such an inspiration to me. I'll never forget this moment, this time with you, to be able to see what a man like you, whom I know to be a good practicing Christian, to have this splendid example that you've just given me of the Christian spirit as applied to your fellow human beings. It's very touching." What was he going to do, Allred asked? "I'm going back to my office and I'm going to double the money I'm giving to Prairie View and I'm sending it down there this afternoon."[97]

Shortly thereafter, the NYA director met with local black leaders in the basement of the African Methodist Episcopal Church in Austin and announced that, of course, black youths would be included in all programs. He held similar meetings in Houston and San Antonio. From these contacts he put together a Negro Advisory Committee to help with the operation of student aid, work projects, and freshmen centers.[98] On October 12, 1935, according to a local newspaper account, he chaired a meeting in Dallas "attended by the Colored Advisory Committee and one hundred leaders from all parts of the state . . .

Every phase of the National Youth Administration program as it pertains to the colored people of Texas was discussed thoroughly in a session lasting all day." As of March 1936, the NYA was providing aid to 887 high school students and 473 college students. Of the twenty freshmen centers, fifteen were open to African Americans, 471 of whom were enrolled.[99]

Occasionally, money would be freed up from other programs. "We couldn't have paid our faculty except for Mr. Johnson," recalled O. H. Elliott, bursar of Huston-Tillotson College. "He'd send us our quota of money. Then, off the record, he'd say, 'I've got a little extra change here. Can you find a place for it?' We could always find a place."[100] Robert C. Weaver, later to be the first black cabinet member, recalled that Frank Horne, Lena Horne's uncle, who also worked for the NYA, kept talking about this fellow Lyndon Johnson in Texas. "Johnson didn't think the NYA was for middle-class people, the way a lot of congressmen did," Horne said. "He thought it was for poor people, including Mexican-Americans and Negroes."[101] The year was 1936. It would be eight years before the Supreme Court in *Smith v. Allwright* would invalidate the white primary in Texas.

But the state director realized that there were limits. Initially, National Director, Aubrey Williams and his deputy, John Corson, believed that NYA programs ought to be integrated, and they pressed Johnson and other state directors to put at least one black on their state advisory boards. After due consideration, Lyndon refused. He had consulted with many prominent individuals, both white and black, he wrote Corson. "The racial question during the last 100 years in Texas . . . has resolved itself into a definite system of mores and customs which cannot be upset overnight," he said. "But it is exceedingly difficult to step over lines so long established and to upset customs so deep-rooted, by any act which is so shockingly against precedent as the attempt to mix negros and whites on a common board." If a black were placed on the board, he told Washington, all nine white members would resign, he would have to resign (and "in all probability, be 'run out of Texas' "), and black leaders would refuse to cooperate. "Their leaders," he said, "are interested in the progress of their race and its development, not by such manifestations of force against the will of white leaders, but by harmony and cooperation."[102]

At the same time, many of the work projects around the state were integrated. Black, whites, and Hispanics labored side by side whenever it was feasible. "There was no distinction between them," Sherman Birdwell said. "Your NYA boys and girls at that time were an entirely different breed of cat than you've got now . . . Since they first had to be eligible, they had to be members of a WPA family . . . So these people were used to hard work, and they were used to working on a farm. When you're chopping cotton, you're chopping alongside of a Negro." Sometimes, he said, "we found more literate blacks than we did whites," and they would be made timekeepers who were paid more and had some authority. "Where we would run into trouble would be the Mexicans and the Negroes, particularly if a Negro would try to give orders to the Mexican boy."[103]

• • •

IN 1936, Bob Montgomery returned from his sojourn in Washington, and Lyndon and Lady Bird moved into one side of a two-storey duplex just off 34th Street at No. 4, Happy Hollow Lane.[104] Luther Jones and Willard Deason lived with them for a while, as did Aunt Effie. "She was like a piece of Dresden china," Deason recalled, "something out of a storybook, immaculately dressed with lace around her neck and long, flowing skirts . . . and very well-educated, very refined. She had but one mission, and that was to try to take care of Lady Bird . . . As a matter of fact, Lady Bird was taking care of her."[105]

Occasionally Lady Bird accompanied Lyndon on his innumerable trips across the state to publicize the program. "Bird left with me last week," Lyndon wrote Welly Hopkins, "and we visited El Paso, Lubbock, Amarillo, Abilene, and Brownwood. We really had a very enjoyable trip. Spent two or three days in El Paso and several evenings across in Juarez."[106] There were continual visits from dignitaries, including black leader Mary McLeod Bethune, Eleanor Roosevelt, and the president himself. Lyndon had hoped for a personal meeting with FDR when he came, but there was no time. Instead, the director assembled some fifty NYA workers along the president's route of travel between Dallas and Fort Worth and, with him at their head, had the youths stand at attention and present shovels as the president, thoroughly amused, passed in review.[107]

Friends and acquaintances, admirers and detractors, never failed to comment on young Johnson's behavior. "A tornado," "a whirlwind," "steam engine in pants," were some of the terms journalists used to describe him. Lyndon was never still. Even when lounging in a chair at home he was thinking, planning, giving orders. In social situations, he talked continually, always determined to be the center of attention. If in the presence of a star, he had to orbit as closely as possible. He was never alone; he never seemed to want to be alone. His physical health reflected the stress. There were kidney stones, gall stones, endless colds degenerating into pneumonia at least seven or eight times by the time he was forty. Lyndon Johnson was raised to be responsible—for his mother, for his siblings, for the residents of the Hill Country, for the Tenth Congressional District, for Texas, for the nation, for the world. His mother was relentless. "You have always been one whom others can lean upon in times of trouble and the role of devoted son and strong and protective big brother is yours by nature and inheritance as well as by training . . . I am very proud and fond of my big boy," Rebekah wrote to him in 1938.[108]

Sam Houston continued to drink and run up hotel and other bills, bills that were inevitably presented to Lyndon for settlement. Occasionally, he proved to be more than his brother could bear. One night in 1934, when Sam was living with Lyndon and Lady Bird in their one-bedroom apartment in Washington, Lyndon came home from playing golf. He had had too much to drink, it was raining, and he was soaking wet. As he came through the door, he caught sight of his brother sleeping one off on his cot in the living room. Lady Bird woke to the sound of her husband screaming at Sam. She went in and found a soaking wet Lyndon holding up Sam by his shirt, shaking him: "I want Sam Houston to look at me," he told her. "Yes, by God, I want you to take a damned good look at me, Sam Houston. Open your eyes and look at me. I'm drunk, and I want you to see how you look to me, Sam Houston, when you come home drunk." [109] None of this, however, diverted the director from his appointed tasks.

The NYA's accomplishments made Lyndon a minor celebrity in Texas and in New Deal circles in Washington. Garth Akridge, NYA southern regional director, reported that Johnson "has developed within his organization a spirit, a devotion to duty, and a sense of personal loyalty that is little short of remarkable . . . The public seems to be back of the program and the press is supporting it almost 100%." Aubrey Williams continually held up the Texas program as an example to the rest of the state directors. Both Eleanor Roosevelt and Mary McLeod Bethune sang its praises publicly and privately. As one of Williams's staff put it, Lyndon Johnson was "easily one of the best men directing one of the best staffs in one of the best programs with the most universal and enthusiastic public support of any state in the Union." [110] He was twenty-eight years old.

CHAPTER 6

CONGRESS

I N LATE FEBRUARY 1937, LYNDON HAPPENED TO BE IN Houston on National Youth Administration business. As usual, he stayed with his Uncle George. The morning after he arrived, the two men chatted while George shaved. Lyndon opened the *Houston Post* and, after a stunned silence, read the headline aloud: "Congressman J. P. Buchanan of Brenham Dies." Seventy-year-old James P. "Buck" Buchanan, a twenty-year veteran of the Tenth Congressional District and chair of the House Appropriations Committee, had dropped dead of a heart attack. "Son, I have $400 in the bank, and if you'll announce for Congress, I'll give you the $400," George Johnson told his nephew.[1] The thought had already crossed Lyndon's mind. He had to return to Austin to host visitors from the Kansas NYA, but, as he later recalled, he found it impossible to keep his mind off politics: "I kept thinking that this was my district and this was my chance . . . The day seemed endless . . . I had to pretend total interest in the things we were doing and seeing. There were times when I thought I would explode from the excitement bottled up inside . . . Finally, finally, the tour ended and I went home."[2]

After consulting with Lady Bird and finding her not unalterably opposed, Lyndon got on the phone and called a meeting for the next afternoon at Jesse Kellam's house. Willard Deason, who was in San Antonio on NYA business, and Dan Quill came up. Sam Fore drove in from Floresville. Rebekah and Sam were there. Also in attendance was former state senator and prominent Austin attorney Alvin Wirtz, whom Lyndon had named chair of the state NYA advisory board. They took stock. The race would be all uphill; an article on the 23rd on Buchanan's death and the forthcoming special election in the *Austin American-Statesman* had not even mentioned Lyndon's name. Lyndon and Lady Bird's savings amounted to about $3,900. Wirtz advised that the campaign would cost a minimum of $10,000. His opinion, everyone recognized, was key to making the decision whether or not to run. Indeed, Alvin Wirtz would be one of the most important figures in Lyndon and Lady Bird's lives for the next decade.[3]

The son of a carpenter, Alvin Wirtz had worked his way through the University of Texas and the UT School of Law. Upon graduation in 1917 he had moved to Eagle Lake and opened a practice. Shortly thereafter, he relocated to Seguin, which was a better base for a German American with legal and political ambitions. In 1922, with the help of Sam Ealy Johnson, he was elected to the state senate, where he served until 1930. Wirtz became acutely aware that Texas's future and his future as a politician depended in part on developing better means of water conservation and usage. While living in Seguin, he became involved in an enterprise to build a chain of privately owned dams on the Guadalupe River. But he quickly learned that the real key to the economic development of central Texas was the Colorado River. If its billions of gallons of water could be dammed into reservoirs, the frequent floods that periodically ravaged its watershed could be eliminated. Moreover, hydroelectric plants associated with the dams could provide electricity to homes and attract industry to the region. In 1935, the Texas legislature created the Lower Colorado River Authority and authorized it to create and administer a network of dams and power stations for flood control, power production, water conservation, and irrigation. Wirtz was named general counsel to the LCRA. Without federal money, however, the LCRA and its system of dams would remain a pipe dream. Wirtz had supported both Kleberg and Buchanan because they had promised to work in Washington to make the dream of public power in Texas come true. With Buck Buchanan's death, Wirtz and his associates needed to find a reliable individual to take his place in the House. LBJ was young, but he was well connected on the Hill and there was no question about his commitment to the cause of public power and economic development in central Texas.[4] But there was more to the Wirtz-Johnson relationship than utility.

As he climbed the ladder of political power, Lyndon made excellent and repeated use of surrogate fathers. Indeed, he could almost qualify as a professional protégé; the number of men who "were like a father to him" would make Lyndon look like Abraham in reverse. Alvin Wirtz was one of the first. "You have been more like a father to me than a mere friend and adviser," Johnson would write in 1938. "You are the finest companion in the world, the best sport, the pattern of a man."[5] LBJ had met Wirtz when, as a boy, he had accompanied his father to the legislature. He had visited his offices in both Seguin and Austin while he was at college, and after he became secretary to Kleberg he began consulting Wirtz on a regular basis. Mary Rather, who worked in Wirtz's office and would later become one of LBJ's secretaries, remembered the first time she saw Johnson: "He came in, and he didn't stay long, but he turned the place upside down . . . He was tall and thin, and his hair was black and curly . . . His eyes were dark brown and they had a twinkle." At the time she thought, "He's like a tornado, that young man," recalling Josephine's comment on Napoleon when she first met him.[6] "He . . . had a tremendous influence upon Lyndon through the years," Welly Hopkins said of Wirtz.[7] "He kind of treated Lyndon like a son," Virginia Durr recalled.[8]

Wirtz was a tall, heavy-set man, outgoing, warm, with a cigar continually clenched between his teeth. He and his wife, Kittie Mae, loved to give parties and entertain. He was also possessed of a brilliant legal mind and an iron will. He coveted political influence and wealth, and he managed to acquire a great deal of both. In politics he preferred to stay behind the scenes, attending state and national Democratic conventions and raising money. As a businessman and lawyer, he took the long view of things. Thus did he support the NYA and regional development projects like the Tennessee Valley Authority and the LCRA. But he also cultivated corporate clients, including Humble Oil, and worked assiduously for their interests.[9] "Alvin Wirtz knew how to carry buckets of bubbling acid on both shoulders without spilling a drop," remarked Senator Tom Connally. "He had some of the most reactionary and ignorant Texans as his law clients, and he pursued their interests ruthlessly against a lot of helpless people. On the other hand, he loved Roosevelt and the New Deal."[10]

On matters of race, he was at best a paternalist. It was probably Wirtz who had authored Lyndon's letter to John Corson regarding naming a black to the state advisory board. "I remember Alvin and Lyndon and all of them sitting down at our house on Seminary Hill [in Washington, D.C.,] one Sunday afternoon," Virginia Durr recalled. "I was off on the right to vote [for blacks]. Alvin said, 'Now you know if you do get that through, all the colored people are going to vote, and that's going to really mess things up.' I said, 'Well, why shouldn't they vote?' he said, 'Look, I like mules, but you don't bring mules into the parlor.' "[11]

That fateful day in February 1937, in Jesse Kellam's house, Alvin Wirtz first went over the negatives of Lyndon's running for Buck Buchanan's seat. He would have to give up his job as director of the NYA, and economic times were worse than uncertain. A number of older, more seasoned politicians would certainly seek the seat. And, of course, there was the money. Lady Bird stepped in and declared that she could come up with the $10,000. With that, Wirtz told Lyndon to go ahead and he would do all that he could to help. The rest of the group immediately pledged their meager savings. "I think I gave him around $500 which I had in my savings account," Deason said. "And I had a new Chevrolet automobile that he needed for a campaign car, and I gave him that. Before I did, I took it down to my hometown of Stockdale and borrowed another $500 on the car and gave him that $500 plus the car."[12]

Several days later, Bird got on the phone with her father in Karnack. According to the community property laws that then prevailed, she and her two brothers had been entitled to half of the family estate upon their mother's death in 1918. At the time, the value of T. J. Taylor's real property was estimated to be around $100,000. During the 1920s he had settled with the two boys but not with Lady Bird. What she wanted, Bird told her father on that day in late February, was a $10,000 advance on her inheritance. "Well, Lady Bird, today's Sunday," he told her. "I don't think I could do it before morning, about nine o'clock." That would be fine, she said.[13] "I was on the other end of the phone, my heart pumping the whole time," Johnson later recalled.[14] To his credit, Lyndon never let anyone forget who bankrolled his first campaign. That Sunday evening, even before the money was deposited in the bank, Johnson issued a statement to the press declaring his candidacy.

The urgency stemmed from the possibility that Buchanan's sixty-two-year-old widow would announce for his seat. Wirtz had learned that Governor Allred was pledged to support her if she decided to run, but Mrs. Buchanan had made it clear that if significant opposition materialized, she would not make the race. LBJ's early announcement took her out of the picture.

Members of the Roosevelt administration were at first opposed to Johnson's candidacy. Hearing of his Texas director's plans, Aubrey Williams went to Thomas G. Corcoran, a New Deal whiz kid who had the president's ear. "Tommy, you've got to get the President to make this guy Johnson lay off running for the Congressional seat down in Austin," Corcoran remembered him saying. "He's my whole youth program in Texas, and if he quits I have no program down there." Corcoran went to Roosevelt, but before the White House could act to restrain Johnson, he had announced. The administration's preferred candidate was Bob Montgomery, the Johnsons' close friend and sometime adviser. Montgomery "was the smartest man I ever met," Lyndon said. "He was a man of the people and a populist."[15] Clearly, he would compete with Johnson for the New Deal vote. Montgomery was disappointed, but faced with his friend's candidacy, he, too, decided not to run. The Monday morning after the announcement, Lyndon met first thing with Wirtz at his offices in the Littlefield Building. "So he walked out of the office, we got on the elevator . . . walked out on the street," Luther Jones recalled, "and he immediately, first person we passed, stuck his hand out and said, 'I'm Lyndon Johnson. I'm running for Congress.' I bet he shook hands with fifty people before we got to his car."[16]

IN THE 1937 SPECIAL ELECTION, Johnson would face eight other candidates, several of whom were favored over him. The leading contender was C. N. Avery, a fifty-eight-year-old businessman who had been Buchanan's campaign manager and secretary. He was able to pose as Buck's natural heir. Merton Harris of Smithville, an assistant state's attorney, had nearly defeated Buchanan in 1932 and believed that 1937 was his year. Judge Sam Stone of Williamson County, the second largest county in the district, threw his hat in the ring, too, as did Austin attorney Polk Shelton, who had been a star athlete at Southwest Texas Teachers' College and was a veteran of the Great War.[17] What the twenty-eight-year-old Johnson needed was an issue that would distinguish him from the rest of the pack. That issue, Alvin Wirtz and Sam Fore advised him, should be Franklin Delano Roosevelt.[18] Fore told Johnson that "the important thing about this race is FDR. People like him, and he's in hot water over that Court-packing thing. He needs our help and we are going to come out loud and clear for him."[19]

At first glance, a Texas congressional campaign based on "Franklin D. and Lyndon B." might have seemed risky in the extreme. Texas and the South had embraced the first New Deal because it had provided direct relief to individuals, saving banks, small farms, and businesses; it had poured money into local economies. A July 1933 survey conducted by the Federal Emergency Relief Agency revealed that in seventy southern counties some thirty-seven thousand families, 15 percent of the entire population, had received federal aid.[20] By the end of the 1930s, the federal government had invested more than $2 billion in the region. As of May 1936, the Public Works Administration had completed more than six hundred projects in the Lone Star State alone.[21]

Beginning in 1935, however, the New Deal began emphasizing structural reform. The Wagner Act sought to empower organized labor by endorsing the principle of collective bargaining. Regional development programs like the TVA and LCRA were allegedly competing with privately owned businesses. The Farm Security Administration was seen by agribusiness as a threat to its drive to enclose small farms into large, efficient, corporate entities. Conservatives denounced Social Security as creeping socialism.

Although oil, the Houston ship channel, agribusiness, the insurance industry, and various New Deal initiatives to promote economic development in the South and West had placed Texas on the road to modernization, it resisted. The voters' mind-set was still very rural. Peter Molyneaux, editor of the *Texas Monthly,* described it: "In general it is a habit of thought to which almost anything which transcends a purely agricultural form of society is in some degree alien. In its most narrow form the rural habit of thought is a neighborhood habit of thought, prescribed in its outlook by the interests and horizons of a rural countryside."[22] Southern conservatives supported early New Deal programs like the Agricultural Adjustment Administration and the National Youth Administration because they could control them, ensuring that the federal government subsidized rather than sabotaged the existing social and economic structures.[23]

But as Roosevelt used the WPA, Social Security, the Wagner Act, and the Agricultural Adjustment Administration to build his famous New Deal coalition composed of organized labor, African Americans, big-city political machines, tenant farmers, sharecroppers, and women, old-line southern Democrats felt they were losing control. Southerners were involved in the administration of programs but not in the central planning that gave rise to them. The famous brain trust included not a single prominent son or daughter of Dixie. The three southerners who were members of FDR's cabinet had little or no impact on economic and social policy. Committed to the philosophy of individualism and wedded to a landed aristocracy and the institutions that served it, they came to see Roosevelt and his programs as subversive.[24]

There was, in addition, a broad streak of populism evident in a number of Texas politicians who rose to prominence during the 1930s. Typical was Wright Patman, who would represent his east Texas congressional district in Washington for forty years. He championed the little man without proposing any alterations in existing institutions. Indeed, like the Populists of the 1890s, he depicted the process of modernity as a threat. He condemned large national banks headquartered on the East Coast, high interest rates, and chain stores owned and operated by outsiders. He denounced a national economy in which the industrialists and bankers of the Northeast colonized and exploited the agricultural South and West. During the Depression, Patman voted for most New Deal programs, but the entire enterprise made him uneasy. Unlike other southern liberals such as Frank Porter Graham, Johnathan Daniels, and Aubrey Williams, Patman feared industrialization and urbanization. By 1935, FDR sensed the revolt impending within his own party.[25]

Of particular concern to conservatives in the South was Roosevelt's Judicial Reorganization Bill, or "Court-packing plan." On February 5, 1937, little more than two weeks after his second inauguration, the president forwarded to Congress without warning a judiciary reorganization bill. The measure provided that whenever any federal judge who had served ten years or more failed to retire at age seventy, the president might appoint an additional judge to his court. No more than fifty judges could be named under the Act, and the maximum size of the U.S. Supreme Court was fixed at fifteen. The latter provision was the crux of Roosevelt's plan; it would have allowed him to expand the existing nine-member Supreme Court by six justices. Roosevelt justified his bill on the grounds of crowded dockets and the physical inability of the aged justices on the Supreme Court to perform their duties. In reality, frustrated and angered by the Court's invalidation of so much New Deal legislation, including the Agricultural Administration Act and National Industrial Recovery Act, the president feared that none of his important social and economic reforms would survive the scrutiny of the justices. He was especially concerned about the fate of the Social Security and the National Labor Relations Acts.

FDR's court-packing scheme touched off a storm of controversy in Congress. It gave credence to the charge of "caesarism" hurled at Roosevelt by critics on the right. The anti–New Deal press charged the president with deception and duplicity. Republicans waged a quiet, largely invisible campaign against the court-packing plan, but left the public fracas in Congress to members of the president's own party. Large numbers of Democrats, including some usually reliable New Deal supporters, deserted Roosevelt for the first time.

Given its distrust of central planning, its reverence for existing institutions, and its seeming commitment to the strict constructionist views of the Court's conservative majority, Texas would seem to have been a logical state to lead the charge against Roosevelt and the court-packing plan, despite his carrying the state in 1936. For Johnson to link his fate with that of the New Yorker in the White House was risky at best. But as Wirtz and Fore knew, the Tenth District, which included Austin and Travis County, was not necessarily typical of the rest of the state. Education levels were high throughout the region. Although the Germans of the Hill Country were conservative in their way, they did not have the same fears about modernization that Patman's East Texas constituents did. The state capital was the intellectual and political center of the state. "We comprised a predominately liberal group by yesterday's definition of liberal," said Paul Bolton describing Austin's press corps during the 1930s.[26] FDR had carried the Tenth District nine to one in the 1936 election. Straw polls conducted during the campaign indicated that voters favored the Judicial Reform Act by margins of seven or eight to one.

Johnson was enthusiastic about hitching his star to FDR. Aside from being good politics, throwing his lot in with the president appealed to the idealistic young Texan. Moreover, such a strategy might provide him access to the White House and the corridors of power in Washington if he did indeed win.

THE WEEK FOLLOWING ISSUANCE of the press release, LBJ reannounced his candidacy at public rallies in San Marcos and Johnson City. "San Marcos was exactly the right place to launch the campaign," Lady Bird said. "I sat on the stage behind Lyndon, and I remember his mother and sisters were up there. One of the most reassuring things I saw was the governor . . . sitting there close to the front."[27] In Johnson City, Lyndon read his statement from the front porch of his boyhood home. Sam Ealy, who had suffered a major heart attack in 1935, and Rebekah were living there once again. One reporter estimated that the entire population of Johnson City turned out to hear their candidate. After Lyndon announced, Sam rose to address the crowd. "My father became a young man again," Lyndon said, describing the scene. "He looked out into all those faces he knew so well and then he looked at me and I saw tears in his eyes as he told the crowd how terribly proud he was of me and how much hope he had for his country if only his son could be up there in the nation's capital with Roosevelt and Rayburn and all those good Democrats . . . When he finally sat down, they began applauding and they kept applauding for almost ten minutes."[28]

What Johnson and Wirtz wanted, quite naturally, was the public endorsement of both the Allred and Roosevelt administrations. Allred was sympathetic but unwilling to stick his neck out. The governor said as much to Johnson, but indicated that he would do what he could behind the scenes to help. Noticing that Lyndon was wearing a brand-new snap-brim fedora in the style of Dick Tracy, Allred told him that that would never do and presented him with the Stetson that he had worn during his successful bid for the governorship.[29]

Meanwhile, Wirtz had gone to see Claude Wild, who had managed Allred's campaign, to see if he would do the same for Johnson. "Who the hell is Lyndon Johnson?" Wild is reported to have said. Nonetheless, he signed on for a fee of $5,000 and an agreement by Lyndon to follow his campaign instructions to the letter.[30]

The Johnson campaign also experienced mixed success in Washington. Wirtz, Harry Hopkins, and others wrote various high-ranking members of the administration seeking endorsements. "Since this will be the first election held in any of the states since the President announced his program [of judiciary reorganization] . . . and since the press through all news agencies will 'play up' the result of this race as indicative of public sentiment on the court issue," it would well behoove the administration to lend all support to Lyndon Johnson, Hopkins wrote Charles West of the Interior Department.[31] West did not reply, but Elliot Roosevelt, Franklin and Eleanor's second son, who owned a string of radio stations in Texas, told his listeners that he looked forward to a "glorious victory" by the former NYA state director.[32]

If nothing else, Johnson was determined to outwork his opponents. "Don't ever let me be in the house when there's daylight and keep the screen locked until dark," he told Bird.[33] As he had promised, Sam Fore spent much of the campaign at Lyndon's elbow, giving him advice and handing out introductions. "I know the first few days of the first campaign Sam Fore came up there," recalled campaign worker and friend Wilton Woods, "and he got in the back seat of that Chevrolet, and we'd go down the road and Sam'd see a guy plowing that was going to be close to the fence . . . and he told Lyndon, 'Now, Lyndon, you jump that fence, give him a card and tell him that you're for Roosevelt . . . Now, don't waste a lot of time with one person. We've got too much ground to cover.' " Fore had a strategy for town campaigning as well: " 'Now Lyndon, we're going to stop on this edge of town and Wilton's going to go to the other edge. He's going to order us some hamburgers, and meanwhile we're going to be walking that-a-way . . . Now you go in every place of business between here and there, and you don't stop and shake hands with the guy behind the cash register. Pass him up. Go to the kitchen and talk to the hired help, because there's more of them. They'll listen better and they haven't committed themselves like the guy behind the cash register.' "[34]

The city of Austin, where the Johnson clan was virtually unknown, would be key. "I took him out to South Austin to the end of what we call Main Street, Congress Avenue, which was almost the southern limit of Austin at that time," Sherman Birdwell said. "Another person took our car back toward town five or six blocks, and we would just go in every store, every fire station, every place of business and he would personally meet every person in there all the way to the back door to where the janitor was sitting."[35] Some of his hard work with the NYA began to pay off. "I did all the driving," Carroll Keach, another aide, said. "If he had close friends in the town, they would put us up for the night . . . He had built quite a base there of friendships with the public officials, school people from the college level on down, business leaders, civic leaders at all levels." There was the omnipresent sound truck with loudspeaker playing patriotic songs and announcing that Candidate Johnson would be speaking at the town square at a specified time. "While he was speaking, I'd go around town putting placards in drugstores and tacking up placards and handing out stickers," recounted Keach. "His speeches were all extemporaneous. He carried his stuff in his head."[36] "It seems incredible," Paul Bolton later said, "but LBJ said in effect that he had to exercise all of his will power to campaign as was expected of him in the small towns, walking up and down main street, with a handshake and a smile for every person. He said in substance that he recoiled from offering his hand to a stranger."[37] The will to win would be sufficient to overcome these and any other deficiencies, LBJ was convinced.

In the beginning, the speeches were chiefly about Roosevelt, the New Deal, and even the Judicial Reorganization Plan. "The entire program of social reform instituted under President Roosevelt," Johnson told one audience, depended on the Supreme Court. The people had spoken clearly; they wanted certain economic and social reforms and the conservative majority was trying to thwart the will of the people. Emphasizing the role that the LCRA would play in the economic development of central Texas, he declared that "any candidate who poses as a friend of the Colorado River Authority but is against Court reform is contradicting himself."[38]

LBJ was not the only candidate supporting Roosevelt and the court-packing plan. "C. N. Avery Backs the President of the United States," proclaimed one campaign poster. While promising not to be a mere yes man, Sam Stone declared his support for the New Deal and judicial reform. Attacking his opponents as "eight in the dark," Johnson insisted that this support was half-hearted or feigned entirely: "There is only one who will fight [opponents of the president], who will fight them until the last dog is dead, without a compromise. They know I am that man." When Senator Houghton Brownlee, another candidate, dared condemn court packing, Johnson accused him of "stabbing the president and the people in the back."[39] Leader of the opposition to LBJ's candidacy in San Marcos and environs was none other than Carol Davis's dad, who declared that if that son of a poor dirt farmer were elected, he (Johnson) would support public ownership of all utilities.[40]

Johnson was an enthusiastic but not particularly effective speaker, especially over the radio. Early polls in the *San Antonio Express,* the *San Antonio Light,* and the *Dallas News* put Avery in the lead and predicted that Johnson would come in third.[41] If Lyndon were going to create some separation between himself and the other candidates, his advisers said, he was going to have to sling a little mud. Both he and Lady Bird protested. "Mrs. Johnson," Claude Wild told Lady Bird, "you're going to have to make up your mind whether you want your husband to be a congressman or a gentleman."[42] He did not want the office if it meant he had to get down in the gutter, Johnson declared. But after Wild threatened to resign, he and Lady Bird gave in. He began labeling Avery a Washington lobbyist who lived in an $8,000-a-year hotel suite and spent most of his time in cocktail bars.[43] He dismissed Polk Shelton as an attorney who had "spent his life defending criminals, racketeers, and underworld characters."[44] Brownlee was nothing more than an "economic royalist" who had devoted his career to serving the power companies and special interests.

Suddenly, Johnson began picking up support. Those blacks who could vote in the Tenth District favored him, in part thanks to his NYA work. During the campaign, Johnson met with Austin's black leaders in the same church basement that had served as a meeting ground when he was launching his youth programs. He told them there would be things that he could do and could not do as a congressman but that he would work for change and that he would see that black votes counted in Washington. "He was very favorable [*sic*] disposed toward us, and he was askin' for our help," F. R. "Friendly" Rice, principal of the black high school in Austin, recalled. During one speaking stop in a small central Texas community, Johnson paused to shake hands with a knot of blacks who had gathered, causing an interracial fistfight to break out after he left.[45]

On the night of April 8, two days before the election, Lyndon addressed a rally at the courthouse in Austin. "After the speech was over," Sherman Birdwell recalled, "I went up to where he was and he was covered with perspiration. It wasn't a particularly hot night . . . He was covered with perspiration and he was constantly wiping his brow and he turned to me and said: 'I'm sick. Stand here beside me.' " As soon as the rally was over, he was taken to Seton Hospital where, shortly after midnight, the doctor removed his appendix.[46] The candidate was so afraid of being accused of staging an illness for sympathy that he tried to postpone the operation. When that proved impossible, he insisted that Senator Brownlee's brother, who was a physician, attend in order to certify that his appendix was indeed ready to burst.[47]

Election day brought a surprisingly decisive victory. Although Johnson garnered only slightly less that 28 percent of the vote, he polled almost thirty-two hundred votes more than Merton Harris, his closest opponent. Sam Stone and C. N. Avery, the early favorites, came in fourth and fifth, respectively. Of the ten counties that made up the Tenth District, Lyndon finished third in two, second in two, and first in six, including Travis, where he received nearly 3,000 out of the 10,300 votes cast. A postelection photograph depicts him, wan, disheveled, but happy, his hospital bed covered with congratulatory telegrams.[48]

THE NEW CONGRESSMAN, thirty pounds lighter, was persuaded to put off his departure for Washington until he could recuperate from his surgery. There was another reason for delay. FDR had decided to couple a Gulf Coast fishing trip with a rendezvous with his new champion from Texas. The meeting would highlight popular support for the administration's position and place the New Deal's seal of endorsement on Congressman Johnson. LBJ was, of course, delighted when Governor Allred told him to be prepared to meet Roosevelt in Galveston on May 11. In the early morning hours of May 10, Lyndon drove with Elliot Roosevelt in the president's open touring car from Houston to Galveston. FDR, tanned and relaxed from his nine-day fishing trip aboard the presidential yacht, *Potomac,* rolled down the gangway at Galveston harbor to be greeted by Governor Allred, Mayor Harry Levy, and Congressman Johnson. After the mayor presented FDR with the keys to the city, hailing him as "the Pericles of the West," the president and his new protégé posed for pictures. Observers noted that Johnson's suit hung loosely on him and that his face was still pale and pinched. As expected, Roosevelt asked Johnson to accompany him by train as he traveled to College Station to address the cadet corps of Texas A&M,

where Elliot served on the Board of Trustees. LBJ was now FDR's official champion in Texas, and FDR would be LBJ's official public role model.[49]

Rather brashly, LBJ asked the president during their postelection conversations on the train to see that he received Buchanan's seat on the powerful House Appropriations Committee. Rebuffed, Johnson told the president of a life-long interest in the navy and naval matters in general. It was two years since Hitler had renounced the Versailles Treaty, openly rearming, and one year since he remilitarized the Rhineland. Mussolini had invaded Ethiopia in 1935, and Japan was at war with China. Johnson understood that the Roosevelt administration sympathized with the victims of aggression and wanted to help. Although isolationists would prevent America from entering the war until after Pearl Harbor, Roosevelt intended to do everything in his power to strengthen the military, especially the navy. Johnson knew that the president had an abiding interest in the sea and had served as Wilson's assistant secretary of the navy. The House Naval Affairs Committee would be the perfect thing for the newly elected congressman. This agreed, Johnson outlined plans for a federally funded naval station at Corpus Christi.

Several of LBJ's contemporaries feared that their friend would come on too strong with FDR. Come on strong he did, acting the part of Washington insider, referring to prominent New Dealers by their first names and denouncing Roosevelt's enemies in the harshest terms. The president was far from put off, however. After he returned to Washington, FDR called Harold Ickes to sing Johnson's praises. Ickes recalled the president saying that "if he [Roosevelt] hadn't gone to Harvard, that's the kind of uninhibited young pro he'd like to be—that in the next generation the balance of power would shift south and west, and this boy could well be the first Southern President."[50]

Despite his electoral victory and Roosevelt's seal of approval, Lyndon was as insecure as ever. Charles Little, an NYA staff member, was in Dallas when he heard that FDR was coming to Fort Worth to visit Elliot's family. He booked two rooms at the Worth Hotel and drove to Dallas in hopes of seeing the president and Lyndon. "I met the train and was standing about two or three cars from the end of the train where the President was getting off," Little recalled. "It just so happened Lyndon stepped off of a railroad car about fifty feet from me . . . He came over to visit and we talked while the President was saying a few words at the end of the train. Then Elliot and his dad and all of their party took off for Elliott's home." At this point, the train began pulling out, headed for Fort Worth. A flustered LBJ told Little good-bye and tried to get back on the train. But no one knew him, and the Secret Service would not let him on. Finally, with LBJ trotting behind the last car, a conductor recognized him and hoisted him aboard. Little then drove to the Fort Worth train station and found the presidential train deserted. "Here was Lyndon, sitting in a railroad car that was half dark. He was really dejected. He was all by himself . . . Lyndon was going to sleep on the Pullman by himself. 'It's all I can do,' " he told his friend. Little persuaded him to spend the night instead with him at the Hotel Worth. "Lyndon was despondent for he felt terrible physically," Little said. "One of his remarks then to me was, 'You know, I feel like maybe I made a mistake running for Congress. Here I am'—I think he said seven thousand dollars in debt—'and I don't know any way in the world I'm going to get out of debt.' "[51]

The next day, LBJ left for Austin to say good-bye to his family. It had been decided that the congressman would take the train to Washington in time to be sworn in on May 13. Lady Bird would follow by automobile with assorted staff and household belongings. A sizable crowd, including Sam Ealy and Rebekah, gathered at the train station to see him off. Sam as usual had advice for his eldest. "Son," Lyndon remembered him saying, "measure each vote you cast by this standard: Is this vote in the benefit of people? What does this do for human beings? How have I helped the lame and halt and the ignorant and the diseased?" Sacrifice and the general welfare was much on the old man's mind, for he was dying. He finished by advising Lyndon to follow the two men in Washington he respected most: Wright Patman and Franklin Roosevelt. A photograph taken at the time shows the son, standing on the steps of his train car, leaning down to kiss his father full on the mouth.[52]

Lyndon arrived in Washington, D.C., the evening of the 12th. The Robert Jacksons met him at the station and took him to their apartment to spend the night. "We walked there from the Union Station, and he kept us up practically all night telling us about his campaign," Jackson recalled. "My wife, she had never met him before; she was just amazed by him. 'That man is going to be president of the United States' . . . I remember it because I argued that nobody from Texas could ever be President of the United States."[53] The next day, with House Majority Leader Sam Rayburn at his side, Lyndon Johnson was sworn in by Speaker William Bankhead in the well of the House. Maury Maverick asked permission to address the chamber for thirty seconds: "Mr. Speaker, the gentleman just sworn in, Mr. Lyndon Johnson, supported the president's judiciary plan and was overwhelmingly elected."[54]

AS A NEWLY ELECTED CONGRESSMAN, Lyndon Johnson was as junior as junior could be. He was assigned office 503 in the "attic" of the old House Office Building. Two days later, Carroll Keach and Sherman Birdwell, whom Lyndon had hired to be the core of his staff, arrived in Washington. "It was late in the afternoon and we were driving over to the House Office Building," Birdwell said. "We had not even gone to try to find a place to stay. As we arrived we saw Mr. Johnson walking by the side of the Old House Office Building . . . We went to the office and there were 213 bags of mail waiting to be opened . . . and Carroll Keach and I started on them when we got there that night, opening them up and sorting them, till way after midnight." The two slept on the office floor.[55] Before Lady Bird could arrive with Birdwell's wife and their furniture in tow, Johnson had rented a two-bedroom apartment on Connecticut Avenue. For the next several years, the couple shared their quarters with various staffers, Aunt Effie, and, of course, the ever-present Sam Houston.

• • •

SHORTLY BEFORE THEY PARTED COMPANY in Fort Worth, Roosevelt had given Johnson the name of Thomas "Tommy the Cork" Corcoran, the thirty-six-year-old Harvard Law graduate who, as a member of the brain trust, had helped shape much of the First and Second New Deals. Indeed, just back from Washington, FDR called Corcoran: "I've just met the most remarkable young man," he said. "Now I like this boy and you're going to help him with anything you can." [56]

Johnson did indeed call, and in the days that followed, the ebullient Irishman introduced his charge to Undersecretary of the Navy James Forrestal and Secretary of the Interior Harold Ickes. Roosevelt had Fred Vinson, the chair of the House Ways and Means Committee, to dinner at the White House to put in a good word for the Texan. As head of Ways and Means, Vinson controlled committee assignments, including Naval Affairs. This was just the beginning. At the home of Clifford and Virginia Durr (Clifford was an RFC director; he and Virginia were liberal Alabamians), Lyndon met Senator (and soon to be Supreme Court Justice) Hugo Black; William O. Douglas, a former Yale Law School professor who would ascend to the high court in 1939; Douglas's protégé, the brilliant Abe Fortas, a twenty-six-year-old lawyer with the Public Power Division in the Interior Department; and Fortas's boss, Arthur "Tex" Goldschmidt from San Antonio. [57] He also began a lifelong political and personal friendship with James Rowe, who at twenty-eight had helped write the Securities and Exchange Acts. In 1938 Rowe would become White House assistant to James Roosevelt, the president's son.

"When we first got to Washington," Lady Bird recalled, "we would go out to Aubrey Williams's house, which was, as I recall, a big, rambling frame house. They would be likely to have a very lively bunch of people out there . . . Conversations always got back to politics, but they all had a social-economic bent. There was always a goal to achieve some sort of improvement in agriculture or welfare or building dams or education. Reform and improvement were considered highly possible, and they were the people who were going to do it." [58] From the very beginning, then, LBJ took his place as a member of what Michael Janeway would call "the House of Roosevelt." [59]

BY CHANCE, Lyndon and Lady Bird were in Austin in October, when Sam Ealy took to bed with his last illness. Stricken with a second heart attack, he developed uremic poisoning and was given only days to live. The elder Johnson did not die well. Lyndon complained to other relatives that his father was uncontrollable, yelling and cursing both doctors and nurses. [60] As the end neared, Sam demanded that Lyndon take him home to Johnson City: "I'm going home where they know when you're sick and care when you die and love you when you live." [61] His son refused and instead moved him to the apartment at No. 4 Happy Hollow. Sam Ealy died listening to President Roosevelt on the radio making the case for a national minimum wage. He was buried in the family plot by the Pedernales River, across from Stonewall. A family friend in attendance remembered various men muttering under their breath, "Well there went my $1500" and "Yeah, I've got $1000 in that too."[62]

Russ Brown recalled coming into Johnson's office some days after the funeral: "He was sitting in his office, and it was half dark in there. He was rubbing his forehead, and he said, 'My God, Russ, I'm in debt five thousand dollars and all I make is three thousand a year. [He was actually making $10,000 a year as congressman, but he and Lady Bird were repaying her father $500 a month.][63] . . . I'll never get all my debts paid.' . . . And I told him he would . . . I remember there were tears running down his cheeks, and after I said we'd make it, he said, 'We'd better, buddy. We'd better.' "[64]

THE MAJOR LEGISLATIVE ACHIEVEMENTS of Roosevelt's second term were the second Agricultural Adjustment Act and the Fair Labor Standards Act. But victories for New Dealers were increasingly rare. By 1938, much of the country was in a conservative mood, with the white South positively reactionary. In addition to the repercussions of the bitter court fight and the recession, the growing militancy of labor contributed to a sea of troubles for New Dealers. The occasional outbreaks of violence that accompanied union activities, the passionate rhetoric of union spokesmen, and especially the tactic of the sit-down strike used successfully by the United Auto Workers outraged many middle-class Americans. For them, the strikers' lack of respect for private property smacked of European radicalism and even anarchism. In effect, the aggressiveness of unions tended to lend credence to charges by right-wing conservatives that the labor movement, coupled with the Wagner Act, was a creature of the New Deal and its chief instrument for destroying free enterprise.

Almost as offensive to conservatives was the administration's efforts in behalf of black Americans. "The landlord is always betwixt us, beatin' us and starvin' us and makin' us fight each other," proclaimed a black tenant farmer in Poinsett County, Arkansas, to an integrated audience. "There ain't but one way for us to get him where he can't help himself and that's for us to get together and stay together."[65] Beginning in 1934, Arkansas and Alabama tenants, sharecroppers, and farm laborers joined together to organize the Alabama Sharecroppers Union and the Southern Tenant Farmers Union. Enraged and frightened, southern landlords, with the support of local political and law enforcement officials, retaliated. At the least, union members saw their credit cut off; at the worst, their homes burned down. In Alabama, members of the private police force operated by Tennessee Coal and Iron stomped Joe Gelders, a University of Alabama professor and union activist, nearly to death.[66]

Outraged in turn by the violence and repression that seemed to be sweeping the South, Eleanor Roosevelt presided over the first meeting of the Southern Conference for Human Welfare in Birmingham in the fall of 1938. The gathering included Frank Porter Graham, president of the University of North Carolina, and Hugo Black, among others. They concluded that one of the keys to the liberation of the poor of both races was elimination of the poll tax. Legislation to that effect was subsequently introduced into Congress, but it failed.

As FELLOW TEXANS AND NEW DEALERS, Johnson and Sam Rayburn naturally gravitated toward each other. It would be the start of a famous relationship. Twenty-six years LBJ's senior, Rayburn had first been elected to the House in 1913. He married once, but only for a brief period; Congress became his wife and children. A short, stocky, prematurely balding man, Sam Rayburn stood for honesty, integrity, and intelligence in the halls of power. Hailing from Bonham, he represented a homogeneous district made up overwhelmingly of white, Anglo-Saxon, Protestant farmers. He took care of his constituents and fought off occasional challengers to maintain his seat in the House for more than fifty years. Politically, he was a New Dealer rooted in Populism and Progressivism, a strong conservationist, sympathetic to the goals of organized labor, and a late convert to the cause of civil rights.

Like his friend Harry Truman, Rayburn loved to read American history and revered the nation's institutions and political habits. Indeed, as D. B. Hardeman, his secretary and biographer, observed, Rayburn would have been more comfortable in the nineteenth century than the twentieth. Modern conveniences annoyed him; he was a notoriously bad driver. When dial phones were installed in the Capitol he would not let technicians put one on his desk.[67] His traditionalism was balanced by a compelling sense of justice, the abiding belief that all men had been created equal, and a faith in young people. Rayburn would become speaker in 1940, following the death of William Bankhead, and would occupy that position for the next twenty years. He presided over the House quietly but decisively, holding power meetings in the "Board of Education," a private hideaway office under the speaker's formal office. There, decision makers would gather late most afternoons to "strike a blow for liberty," John Nance Garner's Prohibition-era euphemism for having a drink. Lyndon Johnson was the only man other than Rayburn who had a key to the Board room.[68]

Rayburn and Johnson would become one of the best-known father-son, mentor-student duos in American history, although in reality, the association was more of a partnership. The two men had a number of things in common. Rayburn lived alone in his apartment in the Anchorage just off Connecticut. He was at times desperately lonely, venturing out only occasionally on fishing trips with colleagues or to baseball games or dinner with friends. But he was miserable when Congress was not in session. LBJ was garrulous, never alone, yet, as, he confessed to an interviewer late in life, frequently lonely. Both loved politics, living it, talking about it, reading about it. Both were vain about their achievements; both were proud men who hated pretension. Johnson offered Rayburn the companionship of his family and personal affection. Beginning in the late 1930s, rarely a week went by when Rayburn did not eat a Sunday meal with the

Johnsons. When he would encounter the speaker in a congressional hallway, LBJ would frequently bend down and kiss him on his bald head.

If ever anyone needed a protégé, it was Rayburn, and he early identified the young congressman from the Tenth District as a likely candidate. LBJ recalled that when he was Kleberg's secretary, he had succumbed to one of his frequent bouts of pneumonia. "Some of the kids [who lived in the Dodge] found me there. I was unconscious, and they got me to the hospital . . . When I came to and opened my eyes a little bit, sitting over in the chair was a dumpy, bald-headed man, had a vest on. He was nodding; he'd dropped off to sleep. He had a cigarette in his hands and ashes were all down his vest." It was Rayburn, who had known Sam Ealy and met Lyndon when he was a boy.[69] The two were constantly spatting and making up. Johnson was deferential but not subservient. He began offering advice to the majority leader on how to run the House's business, and ignored Rayburn's frequent advice to talk less, listen more, and defer to his elders. LBJ was, Rayburn observed, "a damn independent boy; independent as a hog on ice."[70]

BY THE END OF 1939, Johnson had assembled a formidable staff, some on his payroll, others compensated by the House or a federal agency. John Singleton came up from Texas to take a job as Capitol policeman and moonlight for Johnson. He and UT graduate Jake Pickle roomed together in the basement of the Dodge. Sherman Birdwell served as secretary, or chief administrative aid. Herbert Henderson, who apparently held no grudge for his previous firing, came to work as a speechwriter. Luther Jones accepted a temporary job in the office while he looked for another full-time position. Gene Latimer, employed during the day by the Federal Housing Administration, came in nights and weekends to help with the mail. Johnson seemed to have lost none of his ability to inspire. "Concerning myself," Lyndon's former student wrote when LBJ contacted him about coming onboard, "I am sure you know that upon your request I will move any place from Houston to Honolulu—at $1.00 per month or anything else you might wish to give me. I have always had the conviction . . . that you would never ask me to do anything which would not redound to my own personal benefit."[71]

Life in House Office Building 508 was no different than it had been under Lyndon in Kleberg's office. He drove his workers mercilessly, demanding perfection.[72] After fifteen months, Birdwell, thirty pounds lighter, resigned. Latimer took over as secretary and lasted exactly one year. "Nature took its toll," he said, "and [I] had what is commonly called a breakdown."[73] In 1939 Lyndon and Lady Bird—she generally had a hand in all hiring decisions, especially those involving women—employed three new staffers, Dorothy Nichols, Walter Jenkins, and John Connally, to run the state office. Henderson joined them. That year was the first and only year that the Texas office was run out of Johnson City.[74]

The principal victim of the Johnson mania, however, was the congressman himself. His ambition, his need to control, his overwhelming sense of responsibility, his perfectionism, and the feeling, continually reinforced by his mother and his own internal voice, that enough was never enough, drove him mercilessly. He was on the go every waking hour, lobbying some federal agency, courting the president or a cabinet member, attending to business in the House, grasping and absorbing every tidbit of political information and gossip he could find, taking care of family, schmoozing, partying. He insisted on reading and signing every letter to every constituent. There was virtually no place nor any situation so intimate that business could not be conducted in its midst. His first congressional office did not include a private bathroom, but there was a sink with running water. Friends and staff remember him going behind a screen and urinating in the sink while continuing to discuss scheduling and the current political situation.[75] "I am in terrible physical condition," he wrote Jesse Kellam in late 1937, "and I need a week or two of rest."[76] Johnson developed a nervous rash that made the skin between his fingers crack and bleed.[77]

IN JOHN CONNALLY, LBJ had finally found a person with the mental toughness, vanity, intelligence, self-assurance, and ambition to work for him without being devoured. Their association would be fundamental to the rest of their lives and to the political history of twentieth-century America. Connally was born on a farm near the south Texas town of Floresville. With a grant from the NYA, he managed to attend the University of Texas, where he spearheaded the UT Independents, a liberal association of ambitious outsiders (including Robert "Bobbie" Strauss, future chair of the Democratic National Committee). With the help of this organization, Jake Pickle would in 1936 become the first nonfraternity president of the student body at Texas. He was succeeded in 1938 by John Connally, who was then in his second year of law school. Meanwhile, the tall, strikingly handsome student from Floresville had become active in university theater, playing the leading role in several productions and assuming the presidency of the Curtain Club, an organization that included such future film luminaries as Zachary Scott and Eli Wallach. It was through the theater that he met his future wife, Nellie Brill, a Tri Delt and campus beauty.

Even during his college days it was clear that Connally saw politics as a means to an end, the end being his own personal advancement. Like Strauss and Joe Kilgore, another classmate and politico, he was not guided by any overriding sense of social justice—the Connallys' Methodism was more form than substance. He wanted to rise above the insecurities and problems of his fellow man, not immerse himself in them and devote his life to their alleviation. What made him attractive, even to such ultraliberals as Maury Maverick, was that he was not hypocritical about it. "I've fought every crazy conservative in this state," Maverick would say, "but John Connally never had the self-righteousness of the normal reactionary. He'd kick the shit out of you and later he would laugh [with you] about it. He would never invoke Jesus. To him, politics was a game, and he meant to win." Johnson hired Connally at Alvin Wirtz's suggestion, who, in turn, had heard about him from a wealthy, liberal oil man and UT regent. Connally reported for duty in the spring of 1939.

When Connally and Jenkins arrived in Washington from Johnson City, they, not surprisingly, took rooms in the basement of the Dodge. Although he immediately demonstrated that he could take what his boss could give and remain absolutely loyal, Connally insisted on maintaining a life for himself. He had a car and that gave him some independence. He never missed the Texas State Society monthly dances and was a frequenter of the Gayety, a scandalous burlesque house owned by Colonel Jimmy Lake. Among his fellow roomers at the Dodge, Connally quickly gained a reputation for vanity. Luther Jones remembered him standing in front of the mirror by the hour brushing his lustrous, wavy hair.[78]

FROM HIS FIRST WEEK in Washington LBJ labored to bring the blessings of public power and rural electricity to Central Texas. "I had visions of damming the Colorado and Pedernales Rivers," he said, "of building a simple, rural electric line out to the farmers that lived in my Hill Country, of flood control, irrigation, cheap power, of conserving the land and putting in new grasses that would prevent excessive wash off and hold the soil. And I knew it was electricity that could do all this."[79]

At his urging, the Lower Colorado River Authority (LCRA) made a survey of the electricity needs of the forty thousand square miles drained by the Colorado and sent out agents to whip up support for the establishment of rural cooperatives. In the meanwhile, he set about persuading the administration to release another $7.35 million to make loans to these cooperatives. The first obstacle to this joint effort in behalf of cheap and available public power was the Rural Electrification Administration (REA) itself and its administrator, John Carmody. The REA had an ironbound rule that it would loan money only to cooperatives that served areas with a population density of three persons a square mile. The Hill Country averaged only about one and a half.

Finding Carmody immovable, LBJ went straight to FDR. The first time, he got the typical Roosevelt runaround. "I started talking to him," Johnson recalled, "and President Roosevelt said, 'Did you ever see a Russian woman naked?' And I said, 'No, but then I never have been in Russia,' and then he started telling me what Harry Hopkins, who had just been to Russia, had told him—how their physique was so different from the American woman because they do the heavy work . . . Well, before I knew it my fifteen minutes was gone, and old Pa Watson [the president's appointments secretary] was tugging at the end of my coattails, and I found myself in the West Lobby without even having made my proposition."[80]

Johnson immediately made another appointment and went to see Tommy Corcoran for advice. "Roosevelt likes pictures, the bigger the better," he told the congressman. So LBJ ordered a series of thirty-six-inch-high photos of the dams and the regions that their power lines would serve.[81] "I had a picture of one of those little old tenant farmer's houses, you know, under the transmission lines," he said. Roosevelt looked at the pictures and called Carmody: "John, I know you've got to have guidelines, and rules and I don't want to upset them, but you just go along with me—just go ahead and approve this loan and charge it to my account. I'll gamble on those folks because I've been down in that country and those folks—they'll catch up to that density problem because they breed pretty fast."[82]

Other obstacles to rural electrification included the private power companies and many of the rural dwellers themselves. Texas Power and Light did not want to supply outlying areas, but it did not want the cooperatives to either. Indeed, private power denounced the very concept of cooperatives as socialistic, communistic, classic cases of governmental entities competing with private enterprises and using tax monies to drive them out of business.[83] "They hated me for these dams," LBJ subsequently told an interviewer. "They called me a communist."[84]

Most farmers and ranchers initially resisted paying the $5 membership fee to join a cooperative and the subsequent $2.45 monthly rate. Many rural-dwelling central Texans were dubious about public condemnation of portions of their property for the construction of power lines. Most tenant farmers could not imagine the benefits that electricity would bring. "In those days," Sim Gideon, an LCRA official, said, "if you built a line out to a rural place, all the man wanted was a drop line in the house [for lighting] . . . Nobody at that time ever thought about air conditioning and feed mills and milling and washing clothes and radios and television and so many other things."[85]

Throughout the summer of 1938, LBJ roamed up and down the countryside making the case for public power. By the fall of that year, twenty-five out of twenty-six cities had voted for public power and enough farmers and ranchers had signed up to make several central Texas cooperatives viable. In October 1939, Johnson reported in his constituent newsletter that the people of central Texas were "now getting the benefits of cheap public power." Previously, consumers had paid one dollar for ten kilowatt hours of power. With the advent of cooperatives, people were receiving fifteen kilowatt hours for seventy-five cents. And this was just the beginning. As recognition for his tireless and successful efforts in behalf of public power, the president offered the post of REA administrator to LBJ. Ickes, Corcoran, and Roosevelt preferred that Johnson, whom Ickes described as the only real liberal in Congress from Texas, stay in the House, and so they breathed a sigh of relief when he respectfully turned down the president's offer.[86]

BY THE MID-1930s FDR had come to identify the South, overwhelmingly rural and poor, as the number one economic problem in the nation. In 1937 he asked a group of southern New Dealers to put together a report and set of recommendations to guide him. During the next year, Aubrey Williams, Cliff and Virginia Durr, Alvin Wirtz, Arthur Goldschmidt, Senator Hugo Black, Congressman Lyndon Johnson, and various southern businessmen gathered regularly at Goldschmidt's house in Washington. The result was *The Report on the Economic Conditions of the South,* published in 1938.[87] That document surveyed the region, describing the rural poverty, racial discrimination, external economic exploitation, and sense of alienation that seemed so pervasive. It looked forward to a time when the South would join the political, economic, and social mainstream. Its findings threatened the landed aristocracy and the white political power structures that controlled life in the South, especially in rural areas, but they garnered limited support among southern and western entrepreneurs. George and Herman Brown, founders of Brown and Root Construction Company, were among them.

In the process of obtaining the contract to build the Marshall Ford dam, the Brown brothers formed a political and financial alliance with Lyndon Johnson that would prove key to their fortunes and his career. In the early 1920s, the Brown Construction Company received a much needed infusion of cash from Dan Root, Herman's brother-in-law; hence the changing of the firm's name to Brown and Root. Like Kaiser and Bechtel, Brown and Root was able to take advantage of the New Deal's penchant for large, multiuse public works projects to grow into a nationally and then internationally competitive enterprise. What emerged in central Texas in the late 1930s was an informal partnership between the LCRA, Brown and Root, and the federal government, with Alvin Wirtz and Lyndon Johnson providing the legal expertise and political clout, respectively.[88]

The payoff for Johnson was the recognition and popularity that came with economic development and a permanent financial angel to fund his political career. "I hope you know, Lyndon," George Brown wrote in May 1939, "how I feel [in] reference to what you have done for me and I am going to try to show my appreciation through the years to come with actions rather than words . . . Remember I am for you, right or wrong and it makes no difference whether I think you are right or wrong. If you want it, I am for it 100%."[89] In 1939 Brown and Root received the contract to lay some nineteen hundred miles of power lines for the Pedernales Electric Cooperative. "They [Lyndon, Wirtz, and the Brown brothers] were a good deal alike," Lady Bird said, "in that they shared a vision of a new Texas and they were going to be part of it. By gosh, they were going to make things happen—bring Texas whatever industry and whatever had made the eastern part of the United States the so-called elite and rich part . . . They were all builders, strong, young, aggressive, determined."[90]

Johnson's relationship with the Brown brothers was not the only liaison that would give him sustenance and bring him controversy in these years. For all his hyperactivity, the congressman cut a dashing figure. A reporter for the *State Observer* caught up with him during one of his visits to Texas, "Lyndon Johnson is six feet three inches tall," he wrote, "dark, and Robert Taylorish–handsome; weighs 198 pounds which he says is 28 pounds too much; has burning brown eyes, deep black hair, a quirkish grin."[91]

Most women he encountered individually found him attractive, and he they.

Monogamy was never part of his life plan. During a political trip to Texas with Walter Jenkins in 1939, the conversation turned to sex. "[He said] he didn't see anything wrong with people having sex outside of marriage," Jenkins recalled. "It kind of shocked me. I said, 'Well, wouldn't that bother you in your own family?' He said, 'Well, not really.' "[92]

Johnson was then in the midst of a seven-year love affair with Alice Glass, the mistress and then wife of Charles Marsh, publishing tycoon and LBJ supporter. "Alice was tall, nearly six feet," John Connally recalled in his memoir, "red-haired, statuesque, beautiful by any man's standard."[93] But the attraction was more than physical. Glass was sophisticated, poised, intelligent, charming; she had read all the best books and was familiar with the finest wines. At Longlea, Marsh's elegant eight hundred–acre horse farm in the Blue Ridge Mountains, she presided over elegant dinner parties replete with stimulating conversation from the nation's political, intellectual, and artistic elite.[94] "Alice had a great presence," said Frank Oltorf, a lobbyist for Brown and Root and a friend of both the Johnsons and the Marshes. "When she walked in a room, everyone looked at her. She was tall, slim, good-looking, and extremely smart. She had a voice that was both sexy and soothing."[95]

There were rendezvous in New York, in Texas, and at Longlea. Shortly after Connally became LBJ's secretary, Johnson left for a trip to New York to meet Alice. He would be staying at the St. Regis Hotel, he told Connally, and gave him the phone number. It was only for emergencies, he told his aide. A couple of days later, Charles Marsh called, looking for Lyndon. "He said he had to talk to Lyndon and 'no one could find him,' " Connally said. Thinking that Johnson surely did not mean to exclude such an important personage as Marsh, Connally proudly gave him the number. Shortly thereafter, a steely voiced LBJ called his aide. "Do you have a brain in your head?" he demanded. "The next time I tell you not to let anyone know where I am, I mean exactly that."[96]

Johnson feared that Marsh had found them out, but he had not. A number of mutual friends insisted that Marsh never knew. More likely, he did and just did not care. In his office, Johnson kept a special telephone in a bottom drawer of his desk. He left orders that no one was to answer that phone but himself. "When that telephone rang, you knew it was the Horse Lady calling," said O. J. Weber, then an aide to Johnson.[97] Johnson was absolutely fascinated by Alice; she loved him and believed for some time that he would eventually leave politics, divorce Lady Bird, and marry her.

Lady Bird denied knowing anything about this or other affairs. "I never saw that side of him," she told an early interviewer. When confronted with proof of the affair, she said, "Lyndon was a people person. It would be strange if he withheld his love from half the people."[98]

But of course she knew. Lady Bird initially attended dinners at Longlea with her husband and could hardly help noticing how he looked at the openly seductive Alice. Their mutual friends believed that she suffered intensely from the knowledge. "Everything about Longlea—Alice, the fine surroundings, the smart talk—all of it made Lady Bird feel real green," said one of her friends.[99] She responded by withdrawing physically and emotionally. When forced to be in a social situation where both Lyndon and Alice were present, Lady Bird reacted with exaggerated graciousness.

Privately, quietly, though, Lady Bird fought to save her marriage. She checked dozens of books out of the library, including *War and Peace*, and started wearing more feminine clothes. She lost weight, getting down to 115 pounds, the weight she would maintain throughout her husband's presidency. She wielded her money, coming up with the $10,000 necessary to enable Lyndon to make his run for Congress. And she tried to become pregnant. The Glass affair depressed her but seemed to increase rather than decrease her attraction to Lyndon.

By any measure, Lyndon could be a boor. James Rowe recalled that during this period, when young New Dealers would gather for a dinner party and Lyndon would be invited, he would inevitably dominate, holding the floor with stories and short lectures until the other guests would drift off and start their own conversations. "When he saw he had lost his audience, he would just go to sleep, just sit there and go to sleep . . . I think it embarrassed Lady Bird at the time."[100] Still, she seemed to think he was grand. She found the 1937 campaign exhilarating. "Lyndon was never so young, never so vigorous, and never so wonderful," Lady Bird recalled.[101]

The Glass affair, like Lyndon's other extramarital liaisons, came as no surprise. It was something that strong men, like her father, T. J. Taylor, did. And her husband did not boast about his dalliances with women to others. He bragged about his sexual prowess in general, yes, but he never mentioned names, discussed circumstances, or described events. Affairs were hurtful and should be challenged if they were marriage-threatening, Lady Bird believed, but certainly not a reason to end a relationship. Thus did two strong personalities work out the ground rules for a marriage that would last more than four decades.

CHAPTER 7

PAPPY

OTHER THAN THE WELFARE OF THE PEOPLE OF THE Tenth District, the fate of the New Deal, and Alice Glass, LBJ's principal preoccupation during his first two terms as congressman was the United States Navy and its role in defending the nation should war with the Axis powers prove inevitable. During this period, the House Naval Affairs Committee under the chairmanship of Georgia Democrat Carl Vinson was one of the islands of preparedness in a sea of congressional indifference.

Vinson was the typical cigar-chewing, good-old-boy southern legislator—or so it seemed. He was "about once removed from the cracker barrel," a member of the Capitol Hill press corps put it. "His collar is two sizes too big, his tie ordinarily has spots blotched on it, and his office spittoon is rimmed with a two-inch circle of ashes, matches, and crumpled cigar-wrappers."[1] He liked to be called "Admiral" by younger committee members, and he referred to them as "Ensign," "Commander," or "Captain," depending on his estimation of their contributions. But he was devoted to the interests of the navy and was no fool. He demanded that the naval brass who came before his committee make their case effectively, and he then moved heaven and earth to see that their needs were met. In this, however, he frequently was stymied by the chair of the Senate Naval Affairs Committee, David Ignatious Walsh, from Massachusetts. The successor to Massachusetts Senator Henry Cabot Lodge, who had stood down Woodrow Wilson over the League of Nations, Walsh was something of an isolationist. Vinson hated him for this and also because Walsh was a homosexual, whom the Georgian accused of preying on Naval Academy cadets.[2]

Johnson and another young member of the House committee, Warren Magnuson, of Washington State and the Puget Sound Naval Base, quickly made it clear to the Admiral that they were enthusiastic supporters of his preparedness crusade. They also proved adept at cultivating him personally. Vinson's wife, "the sweetest woman ever to put on a dress," was an invalid; every day at 4:45 Vinson left for home to attend to her, never emerging until the next morning. Johnson and Magnuson got into the habit of dropping by to pay their respects to Mrs. Vinson and of filling in the Admiral each morning on the previous day's political news and gossip. They became Vinson's pets. "Lyndon and I were very young and very aggressive," Magnuson recalled, "and we were more available than the older members to travel on special chores for Carl Vinson. When a problem arose with the Pacific Fleet or at a Navy yard, Carl would say, 'You two fellows go and find out about it for the committee.' "[3]

Typically, Johnson used his growing influence on the Naval Affairs Committee to benefit his home state. On June 11, 1940, the federal government appropriated $46 million for the construction of a naval air station at Corpus Christi. The contract, negotiated on a cost-plus basis rather than a competitive bid, a first in American history, went to a trio of companies, the chief of which was Brown and Root. Work on the 14,500-acre facility employed over nine thousand men.[4]

LYNDON JOHNSON was one of the relatively few Americans who paid much attention to the anti-Semitic overtones of Nazism and one of only a handful who did anything about Hitler's prewar persecution of the Jews. In the spring of 1938, Charles Marsh brought to Johnson's attention the plight of twenty-five-year-old Austrian conductor Erich Leinsdorf. A brilliant Jewish musician, Leinsdorf was fleeing Nazi persecution and seeking political asylum in the United States. Johnson was bound to do his patron's bidding but was genuinely struck by the young man and his art. With his temporary visa about to expire, Leinsdorf was faced with the prospect of returning to Austria to confront the tender mercies of the Austrian Nazis. LBJ arranged a six-month extension for Leinsdorf and a trip to Cuba, from whence he could apply for permanent residency.[5]

From Leinsdorf and from Jim Novy, one of the leaders of Austin's four hundred–member Jewish community, Johnson learned of the fate facing European Jewry if Hitler had his way. Novy, a contributor to the Democratic party, had known the congressman since his Kleberg days. In the spring of 1938, Novy, his brother, Louis, and LBJ devised a plan. Jim would go to Poland and Germany and "get as many Jewish people as possible out of both countries," while Johnson's office arranged for the necessary paperwork. In all, Novy managed to bring back forty-two Jews, including four relatives.

In the spring of 1940, with France falling and Britain under siege, Johnson worked with the Austin Jewish community and Jesse Kellam, head of the Texas National Youth Administration, in a scheme to funnel as many European Jews as possible through Cuba, Mexico, and other Latin American countries into the United States. Once they had gained temporary entry into Latin America, Johnson and his co-conspirators would arrange through visas, fake passports, and every other possible means to get them into Texas, where Kellam would put them to work on NYA projects or as work trainees. Because it was illegal to house and train noncitizens at NYA facilities, Operation Texas was kept secret for over twenty years.[6] In 1963, Lyndon and Lady Bird attended the dedication of a new synagogue in Austin. She recalled, "Person after person plucked at my sleeve and said, 'I wouldn't be here today if it weren't for him. He helped me get out.' "[7]

JOHNSON'S BUDDING LIBERALISM threatened to put him at odds with the conservative wing of the Democratic party in Texas. Since 1928, when Texas went for Herbert Hoover over Al Smith, the state had featured two parties in fact, if not in name. That the Civil War and Reconstruction made membership in the GOP untenable for most Texans did not keep them from espousing the values of traditional Republicanism: rugged individualism, states' rights, the equation of material success with social and even spiritual validation, fiscal conservatism, distrust of unions, strict construction of the Constitution, and antipathy toward anything that smacked of collectivism, socialism, and, of course, communism.

Constituting the core of Texas conservatism was the upper class, consisting of the wealthiest families, the managers of the largest corporations and agribusinesses, and the great landowners. Conspicuous for their money and the radicalism of their views, if not their numbers, were Texas oilmen. Living in River Oaks and on Memorial Drive in Houston, in Olmos Park, Terrell Hills, and Alamo Heights in San Antonio, in Highland Park in Dallas, and in Westover Hills in Fort Worth, members of the Texas elite were bound together by common lifestyle and common political ideology. They sent their children primarily to the University of Texas, where they enrolled in the best fraternities and sororities, and they used their money and status to control a political system devoted above all else to the preservation of the status quo. The instrument through which they exerted their domination was the legislative lobby, numbering several hundred by 1940 and devoted overwhelmingly to the interests of big business and big agriculture. Contributions from lobbyists frequently approached the total salary of the legislator being supported. Upper-class conservatives controlled most of the state's newspapers. In 1956, when liberal Ralph Yarborough ran for governor, not a single one of the state's 114 dailies endorsed him.[8]

The ostentatious lifestyles of these oil and land barons during the interwar period gave rise to the national caricature of Texans as dandified cowboys with more money than they knew what to do with. Amon Carter and his crowd acted out the stereotype. Carter had made his fortune wildcatting for oil and controlled the political life of Fort Worth and much of west Texas. His retreat and showplace was Shady Oak Farm, which featured an open-fronted saloon and a stuffed horse adorned with signs reading "Texas Horse's Ass, You've met the New York kind," and "the national Bird—Old Crow." Here Carter hosted huge parties through which he rode on his palomino pony clad in ten-gallon hat, sheepskin chaps, and six-guns. He could put on rodeos or have a full-curtained stage erected for more dignified entertainment. Shady Oak became a kind of celebrity trap, and none were immune. "There the dignified Elsa Maxwell fired Amon's sixguns," Carter's biographer writes, "yippeeing like a soiled dove from Hell's Half Acre. It was there FDR, seated in the rear of a Packard open sedan, cast for and caught a five-pound bass, and there one of the world's richest men, banker Otto Kahn, insisted on paying for his grub by mowing the lawn."

For Carter and his guests' entertainment, Lord Sidney Rothermere, chairman of the board of the London *Daily Mail* and owner of seventy other English publications, donned a huge, high-crowned black hat, the kind worn only by enemies of Hopalong Cassidy, and "held up" passing guests.[9] All of this while ordinary Americans were struggling against the ravages of the Depression.

THERE WAS ANOTHER TEXAS, culturally and politically, that outsiders rarely saw. Progressive political activists—teachers, lawyers, ministers, union organizers—attempted to rally the state's manual workers in behalf of populist causes. Their would-be constituents were the people who laid pipelines, put up telephone poles, painted houses, labored in the canneries of south Texas's "Winter Garden," caught shrimp, or rode the range as cowboys. In 1940, the Texas manual workforce was 40 percent of the total, a group larger than either the nonmanual or the farm workforce, and that percentage grew until 1960.

Compared to the upper classes, manual workers were politically disorganized. Residing primarily in hundreds of inner-city enclaves and industrial suburbs, these individuals joined churches and fraternal organizations not primarily concerned with maintaining and advancing class interests. One scholar estimates that fewer than one-third of this group voted in any election at any time. Lower on the socioeconomic ladder were welfare recipients, day laborers, and farm workers. Some three-fifths of Texas's 2 million poor were blacks or Hispanics. They were even less likely to vote.[10]

The upper classes, through the white primary and through a one-party system that often made it impossible to identify candidates with stands on specific issues, helped perpetuate this disorganization and nonparticipation. "The people [of Texas] are as honest, liberal, progressive and wide-awake as the people of any state in the Union," Alvin Wirtz wrote Eliot Janeway in 1945. "But we have had a minority group in this state which has been enriched by oil or other fortuitous circumstances entirely apart from the merit of the individual. These men have used their money to obtain influence out of all proportion to their deserts. The [state] capitol is much worse than the Temple when Jesus had to scourge the money changers."[11]

As Lyndon Johnson, Maury Maverick, and other up-and-coming politicians recognized, there was a strong if latent populist impulse in Texas. In statewide elections in 1912, at the height of the Progressive Era, the Socialists had polled the second largest vote after the Democrats.[12] The driving ethos of frontier farming communities like Johnson City was communitarian. "Whole church congregations, sometimes virtually whole communities where shifting economic conditions brought hard times, came to the plains of Nebraska and Kansas and other western states," one historian has observed. "They came to found communities where they could enjoy a corporate life." Rugged individualism was only part of the frontier story; house raisings, school and church building, community harvesting, and cooperative cattle roundups were important as well.[13]

Cultural conservatism was not to be confused with political conservatism. There was no proven link between a preference for country and western music, pickup trucks, cowboy boots, the phenomenon of the "good old boy," and the Texas two-step on the one hand and antiunion attitudes and a regressive sales tax on the other.[14] Johnson had come to believe by the end of his first year in Congress that if blacks and Hispanics could be enfranchised and empowered and if the white working class could be persuaded to make common cause with them, the balance would shift to progressives. It was, he would come to believe, the only alternative to continued second-class citizenship for not only Texas, but the entire South.

AS THE ELECTION OF 1940 APPROACHED, however, the prospects for a progressive triumph in Texas, indeed, in the nation as a whole, seemed to be fading. The state, like the nation, was increasingly preoccupied with the lingering Depression and the war clouds gathering in Europe and Asia. Union activists were beginning to appear in Texas, and the plutocracy was gripped once again by fears that working-class leaders would seize on economic issues to build an interethnic alliance among whites, blacks, and Mexican Americans. Though they were in principle Republicans, there was no reason for conservatives to abandon the Democratic party; a one-party system continued to be a convenient tool to confuse and subdue the working classes. Rather, the task seemed to be to wean the party away from the New Deal. This effort came to focus on the presidential candidacy of John Nance Garner.

Garner was the archetypal Texas individualist, with boots, cowboy hat, tobacco plug, and Horatio Alger credo.[15] Ambition was more important than ideology to "Black Jack" Garner, however, and he remained quiet as Roosevelt's first-term vice president. With the waning of the New Deal, the court-packing plan, the popular reaction against CIO-led sit-down strikes in the automobile industry, and FDR's unsuccessful effort to purge conservative southern congressmen from the Democratic party in 1938, Garner began to make his move. More and more openly, he spoke against the New Deal. A 1939 article in *Time* termed the dispute between Roosevelt and Garner "an undeclared war" and quoted New Dealers who labeled Garner "the leader of reaction against six years of enlightened reform."[16]

Most observers believed that FDR would not challenge the two-term tradition established by George Washington, but never sanctioned in the Constitution, and run again in 1940. The drubbing he had received in the 1938 midterm elections, when Republicans gained eight seats in the Senate and nearly doubled their numbers in the House from 88 to 170, coupled with the fact that conservative Democrats won throughout the South, seemed to indicate that the New Deal was on the wane and FDR's fortunes with it. In March, the Texas legislature passed a resolution endorsing "that sterling American and outstanding statesman, John N. Garner," for president. Out of gratitude for past favors done, Rayburn announced his support for "Black Jack" for president. In December 1939, Garner officially declared. Shortly thereafter, Roosevelt told a meeting of his cabinet, "I see that the Vice President has thrown his bottle—I mean his hat—into the ring."[17] Thereafter, the president steadfastly refused to take his name out of consideration.

Garner's apostasy created a dilemma for LBJ. "Lyndon and I spent a great deal of time talking about the Senate," said Warren Magnuson, "because we both wanted to be senators."[18] If FDR's star was indeed on the wane, it appeared to be in Johnson's interests to throw in with Garner and Rayburn. His contacts in the White House—Corcoran, Ickes, Hopkins—advised him not to jump ship, however. The old man had not made up his mind, and if he were not assured that his successor would support both his domestic and foreign policies, he would probably run.

LBJ never hesitated. Throughout 1938 and 1939 he demonstrated repeatedly that he was an administration man. In the House he voted against the Hatch Act, a measure prohibiting federal employees from taking an active part in political campaigns. The Garner camp had pushed it, fearing that hundreds of "Roosevelt's employees" would take an active part in the 1940 Democratic Convention, just as they had in 1936. In surveying congressional votes on twenty-three of the most controversial pieces of legislation supported by the administration, the *Dallas Morning News* found that only six congressmen had voted yea every time. LBJ was one of them.[19]

In May 1940, Texas Democrats gathered at Waco in their quadrennial convention to select and instruct delegates to the national nominating convention. As the Roosevelt and Garner forces prepared for a knock-down, drag-out battle, FDR contacted Johnson. "I want you to see the Texas delegation goes for Garner," he said. Johnson: "Mr. President, what are you talking about?" "People are proud of their leaders," he replied. "If I go in there and take the people away from their leader—I don't need those votes. I'd rather John Garner have the votes. I want to be magnanimous."[20]

In April, Roosevelt had decisively beaten Garner in Democratic primaries in Wisconsin and Illinois. More fundamentally, the German blitzkrieg against Belgium, the Netherlands, and France was creating an overwhelming determination among American voters not to change horses in midstream. With FDR's guidance, Johnson and Rayburn drafted a compromise "Harmony Resolution." Under its terms, the delegation would vote for Garner on the first ballot as Texas's favorite son candidate. Members would then be released to vote their choice on subsequent ballots, however. Participation in any "Stop Roosevelt" movement was strictly prohibited.

The delegates who gathered in Waco were not initially in a harmonious mood. Garnerites and Third Termers, led by Maury Maverick, shouted each other down, demonstrated, and engaged in sporadic fisticuffs. After three hours, some semblance of order was restored, and the convention accepted the Harmony Resolution. Rayburn was named head of the delegation, with LBJ chosen as vice chairman.[21]

By 1940, Roosevelt and his advisers had come to see the Johnson-Rayburn faction in Texas as the hope of the future, a progressive counterweight to Garner, Houston business tycoon Jesse Jones, Roy Miller, Amon Carter, and other Republicans masquerading as Democrats. The events of 1940, Tommy Corcoran told FDR, helped "crystallize a new leadership in Texas around your man, Lyndon Johnson. Local control of the Texas situation is desperately important." Mutual acrimonies splitting 'the Texas crowd' presented "an extraordinary opportunity to get control . . . The two growing points in the Texas situation are Rayburn and Johnson, who, with his sponsor, Wirtz, has taken over all the strength Maury Maverick once had on a much more intelligent plane . . . The natural place to build up John-son . . . is as Secretary of the National Democratic Committee."[22]

FDR was tempted. Despite the president's personal popularity, prospects for the 1940 congressional campaign looked bleak. The Democrats enjoyed a large majority in the House, but Roosevelt's political intelligence told him that as many as 101 of the Democratic seats were in jeopardy. If the GOP could win forty-seven, they would have a majority in the lower chamber for the first time in ten years, unseating Rayburn as speaker and threatening the administration's preparedness program. LBJ, who ran unopposed in 1940, was certainly willing. "We may lose fifty close House seats," he wrote Roosevelt on October 1. "Call on me for anything at any time. P.S. We lost eighty-two seats in 1938. The present forty-five margin gives me the night-sweats at three a.m."[23] FDR was reluctant, however, to appoint such a junior person to such an important post. When Rayburn and House Majority Leader John W. McCormack of Massachusetts suggested to him that he name Johnson as the unofficial congressional campaign manager for the House, the president jumped at the idea. "Sold," he told them. "That was my idea, too. That boy has got what's needed."[24] Although he was not so officially designated, Johnson acted as liaison between the Democratic National Committee and the House Congressional Campaign Committee.

There was no time to waste. With five weeks to go in the election, the financial arm of the DNC had raised less than $10,000 of the $100,000 promised. "You could have cut the gloom around Democratic congressional headquarters with a knife," journalist Drew Pearson wrote. "The campaign committee, headed by Representative Pat Drewry, a charming and dawdling Virginian, had collapsed like the minister's one-hoss shay."[25] After huddling with FDR, Johnson rented office space in the Munsey Building in downtown Washington at 1329 E Street, NW. Within hours he had it furnished with desks, chairs, a divan, and telephones. From that evening until the election, he, John and Nellie Connally, and Herbert Henderson began working eighteen-hour days.

In 1940 the average congressional campaign cost around $5,000; in big urban districts, twice that amount. Coordinating with Sam Rayburn, Johnson turned to Texas, seeking money from both friends and enemies of FDR and the New Deal. A few high rollers could have easily provided the entire $100,000 that was needed, but federal law prohibited direct campaign contributions by corporations, and the Hatch Act limited individual contributions to $5,000. Of course, as with all campaign finance laws, there were ways around the restrictions. George and Herman Brown came through immediately, funneling $30,000 to LBJ through business associates.[26]

Ironically, the big strike came when Johnson and Rayburn persuaded oilmen Clint Murchison and Sid Richardson to chip in between $60,000 and $70,000, again through third-party donations of the $5,000 maximum. "Bring in a Republican Congress, with a new Speaker and new committee chairmen," Rayburn warned them, "and they'll tear your depletion allowance and intangible-drilling write-offs to pieces."[27] Finally, Johnson used his entrée with the Jewish community, since 1936 an important element in the New Deal coalition. "I think he got most of the money out of Texas," Jim Rowe recalled, "and then he got some from New York. I remember he went to New York several times and spoke to people, largely to Jewish groups, I believe."[28]

Roosevelt arranged for a direct telephone line from the dining room in his mother's house in Hyde Park, New York, so that he could talk to Johnson and other campaign managers on election night. Just after midnight, LBJ, who was attending a party with Jim Rowe and others in Georgetown, called the Boss. How many seats will we lose, FDR asked his thirty-two-year-old protégé. "We're not going to lose . . . We're going to gain," Johnson told the president.[29]

And gain they did. Although FDR's plurality in 1940 was half what it had been in 1936, and the Democrats lost three seats in the Senate, the party actually enjoyed a net gain of six in the House. Roosevelt was enormously impressed. So were political pundits. "To the boys on the Democratic side of the House of Representatives," wrote Drew Pearson and Robert S. Allen in their widely syndicated "Washington Merry-Go-Round" column, "many of them still nervously mopping their brows over narrow escapes, the hero of the hair-raising campaign was no big shot party figure . . . The Democrats' unknown hero was Representative Lyndon Baines Johnson, a rangy, 32-year-old . . . who . . . has political magic at his finger tips."[30]

GREAT POLITICAL CAREERS are built on hard work, instinct—but also luck. Johnson's longing glances at the Senate had seemed pointless so far; Texas's two senators, Morris Sheppard and Tom Connally, were firmly entrenched. "Connally was in," D. B. Hardeman, recalled, "it looked like he was good for years, and Sheppard looked like he was good for years. And they were both unbeatable."[31]

But just as it had in 1937, fate intervened. On April 4, 1941, Senator Sheppard died suddenly of an intracranial hemorrhage. He was sixty-five.[32] "I happened to have been the first one to tell Mr. Johnson that there was a vacancy in the Senate," Walter Jenkins recalled. "I was on the police desk at the front door of the New House Office Building, and early that morning someone came in and said that Morris Sheppard had just died. I picked up the phone on the desk and called Mr. Johnson. He said, 'Well, I won't be in this morning.'"[33]

Johnson huddled with Wirtz, who urged him to run. There was little to lose, he observed. Sheppard's seat would be filled by a special election, which meant that LBJ would not have to give up his position in the House. A week later, the two met with Charles Marsh and Harold Young, a Texas attorney on Vice President Henry Wallace's staff, to map a campaign strategy.

The first task, all agreed, was to obtain FDR's explicit endorsement of LBJ's candidacy. Fond of Johnson though he was, the president was at first reluctant. Virtually all of the liberal southerners he had endorsed for Congress in the attempted 1938 purge had been defeated. Johnson was young and virtually unknown outside his district. Roosevelt did not need to tie himself to another loser. Corcoran, Rowe, and Ickes all went to bat for LBJ, however. The alternatives to Johnson were "too frightful for contemplation," Rowe told the president.[34]

Roosevelt and his advisers were particularly concerned that the red-baiting chair of the House Un-American Activities Committee, Congressman Martin Dies from east Texas, would replace Sheppard. Roosevelt called his protégé to the White House to confer. He wanted to support him, the president said, but he did not want to lead him down the garden path. Johnson was equally circumspect in the meeting. He wanted to run, he said, but he was young, the field would be strong, and he did not want to embarrass the White House.[35] Both decided that he should return to Texas and test the waters.

During the ensuing whirlwind tour, Johnson addressed a joint session of the state legislature. His speech, urging support for the administration's foreign and defense policies, elicited a standing ovation.[36] In Washington, a reporter asked FDR if he would be willing to endorse Congressman Johnson for Senator Sheppard's seat. "I can't take part in a Texas primary," Roosevelt replied. "If you ask me about Lyndon himself . . . I can only say what is perfectly true—you all know he is a very old and close friend of mine. That's about all. Now don't try to tie those two things together!"[37] The White House press corps erupted with laughter. "F.D.R. Picks Johnson to Defeat Dies," read a *Dallas Morning News* headline.[38] Significantly, however, Governor W. Lee O'Daniel appointed eighty-six-year-old Andrew Jackson Houston, the son of the father of the republic, to be interim senator, an appointment that would leave O'Daniel with all options open.

Despite the president's unofficial endorsement, Johnson's chances appeared bleak. A statewide survey taken by pollster Joe Belden, who would effectively apply George Gallup's techniques to state politics, gave LBJ only 5 percent of the vote. The leaders were Dies with 9 percent, Attorney General Gerald Mann with 26 percent, and the still undeclared O'Daniel with 33 percent. All in all, twenty-nine candidates threw their hats, boots, bottles, aprons, and guns into the ring.[39]

For LBJ, Mann was the most problematic. A handsome former football star at Southern Methodist University who hailed from Sulphur Springs, Mann had a reputation for honesty, integrity, and courage. He had earned a law degree from Harvard while at the same time ministering to a Congregationalist church in Gloucester, Massachusetts. After serving as assistant attorney general and secretary of state, he was elected state attorney general in 1938 at age forty. He compiled an excellent record prosecuting loan sharks and antitrust violators and was offered the post of chief justice of the state supreme court; he turned it down to run for another term as attorney general. A strong supporter of the New Deal, Mann was most likely of all the candidates to cut into Johnson's natural constituency.

Dies was also a threat. As self-anointed superpatriot and chair of HUAC, Martin Dies was set to capture the conservative vote. While endorsing the administration's preparedness programs, he charged repeatedly, to the glee of Garner and his supporters, that New Deal agencies were rife with communist agents. Communists and Nazis were under every bed, some 7 million in the United States alone, he declared; abroad, a "secret" army larger than the entire American armed force plotted invasion.[40]

Within days of Johnson's announcement, his campaign team began to come together. Wirtz resigned his position in the Interior Department to act as LBJ's chief strategist. Although Claude Wild was once again named campaign manager, it was the twenty-four-year-old John Connally who actually oversaw day-to-day operations from his headquarters on the sixteenth floor of the Stephen F. Austin Hotel.[41]

Connally, who had married his college sweetheart, Nellie Brill, in December 1940, had grown increasingly close to Johnson. Fashioning himself after LBJ, he quickly became one of the best-known congressional aides on the Hill and, like LBJ before him, secured the speakership of the Little Congress. Contemporaries remarked on the almost symbiotic relationship that developed. Adopting many of Johnson's mannerisms, Connally did not hesitate to perform the toughest assignments. He was and would be regarded as LBJ's hatchet man. "LBJ," read one cryptic note dated 1939, "delivered $300.00 in cash to Maury on the floor today. Jbc."[42] The 1941 campaign was to be John Connally's baptism of fire. He worked feverishly and effectively, but in the end, his inexperience would cost LBJ the election.

Johnson opened his campaign, as he had in 1937, with a giant rally in San Marcos. The ever loyal President Cecil Evans had SWT alumni bussed in from all over the state. The auditorium was packed with three thousand people when a somewhat overstimulated Johnson strode to the microphone. In a booming voice he read from a prepared script: his campaign theme, he said would be "Roosevelt and Unity." [43] If elected, he would continue to work for full parity payments for farmers, old-age pensions of up to $40 a month for those sixty years of age and over, and state control over conservation of natural resources. He pledged undying support for the administration's military buildup and attempts to confront and contain the Axis powers. "If the day ever comes when my vote must be cast to send your boy to the trenches," he declared prophetically, "that day Lyndon Johnson will leave his Senate seat and go with him." [44]

Between May 3 and 10, the candidate covered two thousand miles and delivered five radio addresses. Virtually all were high-minded appeals to care for those who could not care for themselves, to ensure that all Americans had an equal opportunity to enjoy the fruits of prosperity, and for unity in the face of the international crisis. "For two weeks," he told his listeners, "I waited to announce in the hope some candidate would have the courage to commit himself to all-out support for the President and his foreign policy. This was not done. Therefore, I am in the race . . . National defense is the job. War is near our borders." [45] To his dismay, the crowds proved unresponsive—not to his message, but to his delivery. Johnson was not a gifted orator, particularly when reading from a prepared text. He came across as artificial, forced, a voice completely untethered from the message.

Although he would not officially declare until the third week in May, Governor O'Daniel was already running hard. A new Belden poll taken on May 3 gave him 33.8 percent of the vote, with Mann second at 28.2 and Dies third with 27.9. Lyndon was a distant fourth at 9.3 percent. [46]

Hailing originally from Ohio, where his father worked in a plow factory, Wilburt Lee O'Daniel had graduated from business college at age eighteen. In 1935, O'Daniel started his own firm, the Hill Billy Flour Company. Each sack of his company's product was emblazoned with a goat, beneath which was the slogan "Pass the biscuits, Pappy." From the day the first sack hit the market he was known far and wide as Pappy. By 1938, he had formed his family into a band: Pat on the banjo, Mike on the fiddle, and Molly teaming with Texas Rose on vocals. Within months the cornpone ensemble was reaching hundreds of thousands of Texans over a statewide radio hookup.

While his offspring strummed and hummed in the background, the handsome, beaming Pappy delivered homilies on the virtues of motherhood, Texas, the Ten Commandments, and the Golden Rule. He even composed songs for the program, "Your Own Sweet Darling Wife" and "The Boy Who Never Gets Too Big to Comb His Mother's Hair" being among the most notable. [47] "At twelve-thirty sharp each day," a national publication reported, "a fifteen-minute silence reigned in the state of Texas, broken only by mountain music, and the dulcet voice of W. Lee O'Daniel." [48] A political career was inevitable.

In 1938 Pappy asked his radio audience what they thought of the idea of his running for governor. He subsequently reported that more than fifty thousand voiced their approval. Ignoring his inexperience, O'Daniel campaigned blithely on the teachings of the Bible and a promise of a $30-a-month pension for every Texan over the age of sixty-five. To the disgust of Texas elite—economic, political, and intellectual—Pappy captured 573,000 votes, 51 percent of the total. In 1940 his total climbed to 645,000 or 54 percent of the whole, which made him the most prolific vote getter in the state's history.[49]

WITH O'DANIEL MOPPING UP RURAL VOTES across the state, and polls showing him last, an overwrought Johnson took to his sickbed. The second week in May he succumbed to a bout of severe depression complicated by a throat infection. As his fever rose, Lady Bird and his doctors made arrangements to hospitalize him. Connally; Wirtz; Roy Hofheinz, a Harris County judge; and Everett Looney, an Austin attorney, would fill in for him. As Johnson was preparing to leave for the hospital, Connally and Gordon Fulcher, publicity director for the campaign, tried to persuade him to sign a press release announcing his forthcoming hospitalization. He was upstairs in his bedroom, "nearly out of his head from the fever, not rational, and bellowing that we were not to put out a press release under any circumstances."[50] "Congressman," Connally replied, "you can't hide for a week. You can't check into one of the finest hospitals in Texas and expect people not to notice. You can't cancel out a week's schedule, have a substitute give your speeches, and not have every newsman in the state wondering where you are . . . We are going to tell them where you are." Johnson was unrelenting. "Well, if you do, I'll never speak to you again. And you can get the hell out of my house."[51]

Lady Bird followed Connally and Fulcher down the stairs, asking them to ignore Lyndon's advice. Connally duly issued the press release and refused to have anything to do with Johnson until Charles Marsh intervened. "After a few more days, we began to talk again about the campaign and what needed to be done," Connally said. "But that was one of the first serious encounters we had, and there would be others as the years passed."[52]

Ironically, by the time Lyndon emerged from the hospital some two weeks later and hit the campaign trail, his poll numbers had increased to 17.6 percent. O'Daniel's total had fallen ten points to 22 percent, while Mann and Dies were neck-and-neck at 26 percent.[53] It now appeared that the young man from the Hill Country had a fighting chance.

Marsh decided to step in and take charge of the care and feeding of the candidate. "Personally, I believe that the watching of the physical Lyndon Johnson is the most important single thing to get every ounce into this thing," he wrote Gordon Fulcher. See that he sleeps and get him a rubdown to see that he does, he ordered. Greens, salads, vegetables, and a glass of hot water on rising to prevent constipation. "I don't think you will need to watch alcohol."[54] The candidate's mental development must be attended to as well. "I am hoping for intellectual curiosity which will cause him to substitute an hour of new food daily, not pertaining to the business of government . . . [but] geography, background history, a smattering of science, especially pertaining to agriculture, and possible general thinking called philosophy or psychology, which had nothing to do with an immediate object."[55]

There were style suggestions. "Your voice high-tones under emotion," Marsh advised Johnson. "You can't lose the emotion, but you must lose the high notes. Your gestures should be natural, but you must weed out about 50 percent. You have learned domination of slower and smaller people by pounding the table like a machine gun. When you are speaking, the physical pounding would stop the sense."[56]

Marsh himself was subject to terrible mood swings. Sometime during 1941, he paid several visits to a sanitarium for personal treatment. He had already admitted to drinking too heavily, not exercising, and obsessing. Out of those visits came a remarkable, rambling essay on manic depression which he may or may not have shown to LBJ but certainly wrote with him in mind. "The great actor," Marsh opined, "is always the natural one—the one who, in a delicate shading, merges his own personality in an imperceptible marriage with the character to be acted, so that only one, and not two, is seen and heard by the audience . . . the man who presumes to serve his world in sanity . . . His first business is the truth of it all—his private attitude toward the expression of his truth . . . This double word [manic depressive] should not be thrown away. It defines a person of great force who may have temporarily been out of line in service through a curving, or a stoppage, or a backtracking of sane force in action serving others. A manic-depressive then is merely one of great force out of the line of the universal oneness which is the sane movement of force through human life."[57]

LBJ's physician, J. Willis Hurst, later speculated on the possibility that LBJ suffered from a bipolar disorder. "I think [it is] perfectly normal . . . Extremely interesting people do display many emotions, ranging from anger, to humor, to unpredictability, to all kinds of things: up to a point this of course is entirely normal. Now, whether or not you want to say that his swings in all of this, his emotional swings, reached the abnormal state, would be a very debatable issue. I would be unwilling myself to say that these were outside the normal range."[58]

WITH DIRECTION AND ENCOURAGEMENT FROM WIRTZ, the Roosevelt administration joined the fray in Johnson's behalf. By the end of May, the congressman's office was able to report hundreds of thousands of new WPA dollars to fund public works projects in Texas. Newspapers began to swing into line. LBJ outbid Mann for the support of Houston Harte's extensive chain of publications.[59] O'Daniel, who had several times advocated large tax breaks to draw industry to the state, who steadfastly opposed any type of minimum wage law, and who advocated jail terms for workers who dared strike, enjoyed the support of much of the business community and their mouthpieces, but there were exceptions. Introduced to Amon Carter, publisher of the *Fort Worth Star Telegram,* "Lyndon got right up in his face—talked to him thirty minutes, standing right up next to him," said insurance executive and Johnson supporter Raymond Buck. "At the end of that time, Amon was sold," and the *Telegram* came out for Johnson.[60]

Financial backing was never a problem for LBJ in the 1941 campaign. Grateful for the Marshall Ford and Corpus Christi contracts and poised to take their place as major defense contractors, Herman and George Brown pledged to spend whatever was necessary to secure Johnson's election. "We never were in danger of running out of money," Herman later told Eliot Janeway, "but we damn near ran out of names [i.e., of third parties through whom checks could be funneled]."[61] There was no exact accounting of campaign donations and expenditures. When Alvin Wirtz found that Wilton Woods, who managed the Austin campaign office, was keeping an account, he ordered him to destroy it. In response to numerous complaints of campaign finance fraud, the IRS conducted an investigation from 1942 through 1944. Its tax agents estimated that Brown and Root had contributed some $300,000, much of it illegally.[62] The reason nothing came of the investigation, aside from the fact that it occurred during a Democratic administration, was that "it was rather a customary way of doing business in Texas politics to take money wherever you could get it," as one veteran politico put it. O'Daniel had collected millions of dollars over the years at his many rallies. Following the performances, his children passed small barrels labeled "Flour, not Pork," in which supporters were invited to drop nickels, dimes, and quarters.[63] None of it was reported.

Brown and Root were not Lyndon's only financial angels. Welly Hopkins, who had represented the United Mine Workers, raised several thousand dollars from labor sources.[64] And, of course, there was Charles Marsh and his Fort Worth partner, Sid Richardson. Marsh, an idealistic newspaperman, had financed Richardson's oil ventures during the early years of the Depression and was largely responsible for the latter's financial success. By 1941, the elevation of Lyndon Johnson to high national office had become something of an obsession, even though the candidate was making a cuckold of him. In fact, in 1940, Marsh offered LBJ complete financial independence so that once in office, he could act solely in accordance with his conscience and the public interest. During a conversation in which a run for the Senate was being discussed, Marsh suddenly said, "I want to give you my half of the oil properties that I own with Sid Richardson and you will have the money and you won't be responsible to any special interest."[65] In 1965 that property was worth $100 million. Stunned, LBJ sat for a moment; he realized that Marsh was absolutely serious. With some embarrassment, he refused. Better to be beholden to several interests than just one.

In fact, the strategy and substance of LBJ's 1941 campaign were largely the work of Marsh, a disciple of Henry A. Wallace and his "Century of the Common Man" philosophy. "Johnson will grow more frank, more direct, and I hope more powerful, with each new experience and with age," he wrote an acquaintance. "You and I both know that men grow and men shrink . . . These men (and Rayburn is merely a high-class one) shrink as they pass fifty, as [Senator Tom] Connally has shown, because they are so completely aware of themselves in their later years. They become defensive in holding on to that which they have . . . Johnson won't do this . . . He will drive through Washington . . . The ladies of the evening won't get him as the feminine camp followers of the drawing rooms flatter. On that front to date he is the victor, because he has always, thus far, known what he wants, and when he wants it."[66]

LBJ would be the engine of Marsh's vision. A devout if profane believer in the Christian God, Marsh looked to Johnson to lead the South out of its political and economic bondage and the downtrodden, disadvantaged, and oppressed of all regions to a better life. "We [Johnson and Marsh] agreed that a whole could be no healthier than its parts," he observed to a friend. "We agreed that every small community in the South was in danger of its life. We saw that the North and East had the factories and the brains." The North and East had "looted" the South and Southwest during the Great War; "only weather and space saved Texas until oil came along."[67]

Like Wallace, Marsh looked forward to an American free of domination by a privileged plutocracy, to a countervailing society in which educated farmers and workers cooperated with public-spirited business people. Also like Wallace, Marsh believed that American foreign policy should be aimed in the short run at defending and liberating Western Europe, but in the long run at helping the peoples of Afro-Asia and Latin America with their transition from colonialism to independence.[68]

AS THE CAMPAIGN ENTERED ITS LAST MONTH, LBJ and his team increasingly viewed Pappy O'Daniel as the man to beat. Pappy had announced his candidacy from the Governor's Mansion over a statewide radio hookup. He ridiculed the Roosevelt-Johnson relationship by mimicking the president's endorsement of LBJ as "mah old, old friend." During a news conference that followed, reporters reminded O'Daniel that he had sponsored legislation to force state officeholders who ran for jobs other than the ones they held to resign. Did he plan to give up the governorship? "I should say not," he replied indignantly.[69] On his radio show, he told listeners, his campaign would be based on "one hundred percent approval of the Lord God Jehovah, widows, orphans, low taxes, the Ten Commandments, and the Golden Rule."[70] He put together a traveling show that featured a bus equipped with a special dome in the shape of the state capitol. Pat, Mike, and Molly were accompanied by Leon Huff, the "Texas Songbird." It was a hillbilly spectacle to rival all hillbilly spectacles.

O'Daniel was the archetypal political evangelist offering up the traditional contradictory mix of Christian family values and laissez-faire capitalism spiced with a little social welfare for the elderly. It was frequently said of O'Daniel that his aim in life was to save the soul of the poor man and the wealth of the rich man.[71]

Johnson's response was to wage two separate campaigns, one substantive and one show. The issue, he said in his serious speeches, was "support of Roosevelt against appeasement and in defiance of dictators."[72] He assumed that war was inevitable and declared his backing for a two-ocean navy, a fifty thousand–plane air force, and a 2 million–man army. Supreme Court Justice William O. Douglas happened to be driving through Texas with his family on his way to vacation in his beloved West during the campaign. His car pulled into Big Spring just when LBJ was holding some three thousand in thrall. "Everytime he mentioned your name," Douglas wrote FDR, "the crowd cheered. Every time he mentioned [Charles] Lindbergh the crowd booed."[73] When O'Daniel criticized Roosevelt as a backslapping politician who could not operate a peanut wagon, Johnson commented, "It must have comforted Hitler to hear the governor talk like that."[74]

LBJ's other theme was unity. "We must refuse to elect any man . . . who will in any way lend aid to discord, division, or disunity."[75] Liberals noted with dismay that in his zeal for unity, LBJ came close to labor baiting. "Texas labor has been free of strikes and disturbances," he told his audiences, "free of radical leadership and membership." He was quite ready to use troops to break strikes. "We're going to support the $21-a-month draft boy the president sends to open plane plants where communist agitators and radical labor leaders close them."[76] Still, to the extent that it took an active role in the Texas Senate campaign, organized labor supported LBJ.[77]

Then there was the LBJ version of the "Pass the Biscuits, Pappy" campaign. "We finally decided if you couldn't beat 'em, you might as well join 'em," Lady Bird declared, "so we got ourselves a band and had ourselves a starlet," saying more than she meant. The Johnson campaign hired Houston radio personality Harfield Weedin, paying him $1,000 a week and giving him carte blanche. He put together a two-hour patriotic review designed to link LBJ with FDR, the red-white-and-blue, and democracy's struggle against fascist aggression. The gala, performed repeatedly during the last three weeks of the campaign, began with musical numbers by a twenty-three-piece swing band, the Patriots, dressed in white dinner jackets, red carnations, and blue trousers. Mary Lou Behn, the tour's sex symbol, followed, singing such hits as "San Antonio Rose" and "I Want to Be a Cowboy's Sweetheart." Finishing up the review was Sophia Parker, a 285-pound songstress who labeled herself the "Kate Smith of the South," belting out "I Am an American" and "The Eyes of Texas Are upon You." Weedin then came on stage to narrate a thirty-minute hagiographic history of the Roosevelt administration, featuring FDR as savior of his country, first from the Hoover Depression and then from Nazi aggression. Finally, with the master of ceremonies and company marching in step to the tune of "God Bless America," Lyndon made his appearance. Not even his wooden delivery could dissipate the crowd's enthusiasm.[78]

Polls taken a week before the election showed LBJ in a virtual dead heat with O'Daniel and Mann. Then, on June 22, Hitler invaded the Soviet Union, giving vast reinforcement to Roosevelt and Johnson's claim that Nazi Germany was

bent on world domination and that the surviving democracies must band together to stop it. Belatedly, O'Daniel tried to identify himself with FDR. Not
only had he voted for him in 1936, he said, but he had written a campaign song
for him in 1932 and offered up numerous radio prayers in his behalf. It was too
little, too late; the last poll before the election showed Lyndon clearly in the lead
with 31.2 percent, with O'Daniel second at 26.7 and Mann third at 25.2.[79]

ON ELECTION DAY, Lyndon and Lady Bird drove to Johnson City to vote.
Friends noted that he had not regained the weight he had lost while in the hospital and had again developed a nervous rash. Sleep had come only fitfully during the last stages of the campaign. Back in Austin from Johnson City, he took a
sleeping pill and then awoke around 10 P.M. to catch the first returns. They were
encouraging. When LBJ went to bed in the early morning hours of June 29, he
led O'Daniel by three thousand votes. When he awoke, the margin had increased to five thousand with 96% of the vote in. It seemed impossible with four
major candidates in the field that Johnson would not come out on top. Jubilant,
his staff raised the candidate on their shoulders and paraded him around the
Stephen F. Austin Hotel. "Lyndon Johnson Elected Senator," ran the banner
headline in the *Dallas Morning News*. But, as one Texas sage put it, "It ain't over
'til it's over."[80]

There were quite a number of powerful Texans who wanted to see Pappy
elected to the Senate to get him out of the state. Chief among these were the
liquor, beer, and horse racing interests, who feared a fundamentalist Christian
attack on their livelihoods. If the election could be swung to O'Daniel, Lieutenant Governor Coke Stevenson, no friend of Prohibition, would become
governor. The day after the polls closed, some fifteen state legislators met with
Stevenson and former Governor Jim Ferguson to lay plans to swing the election
to O'Daniel. All had been heavily subsidized in the past by the state's brewers
and distillers.[81] After the Texas Election Bureau declared LBJ the winner, reporters asked O'Daniel if he was going to concede. "Mrs. O'Daniel is in the
Governor's Mansion praying," was his only reply.[82]

As of Monday, eighteen thousand votes, mostly in east Texas, remained un-
counted. The Stevenson-Ferguson forces did not know how many they needed
to put Pappy past Johnson, and in their inexperience John Connally and Lyndon Johnson blundered by telling them. Bloc voting was typical in Texas, and
corruption was a multicandidate sport. The counties from San Antonio to the
Rio Grande, many of them with heavy Hispanic populations, were controlled
by political machines such as those of the Mavericks in San Antonio, George
Parr in Duval County, and Manuel Cuellar in Zapata County.[83] As anticipated,
the region delivered up to 90 percent of the vote for Johnson in some counties.

Anxious to show that they were in the lead, Johnson and Connally told their
managers to report the vote totals to the election bureau as soon as possible.
George Parr, the boss of Duval County, kept telling them when they would call,
"Look, you're children; you don't know what you're doing. You're going to get

all your votes out on the table and they'll come in with however many votes it takes to beat you."[84] By Sunday night, the Stevenson-Ferguson forces had the information they needed. "We . . . intercepted a telegram from Coke Stevenson . . . that went out Sunday to various key county men in East Texas . . . to hold up counting the votes until further notice from W. Lee O'Daniel's campaign head-quarters. Surprisingly enough, the voting trends in those counties showed a very interesting and surprising change beginning Monday morning."[85]

Once it was clear that Martin Dies could not win, Ferguson and Stevenson had persuaded him to allow county judges to shift some of his votes to O'Daniel. By Wednesday the governor had a 1,311-vote lead. Johnson's managers appealed to their south Texas allies to do something. But there was nothing to be done. The county judges could switch votes, but it was more difficult to manufacture them, especially after the fact.

In an effort to block the O'Daniel forces, the Roosevelt administration sent FBI agents into the Piney Woods to investigate electoral wrongdoing. The probe did not begin, however, until July 3, two days after Pappy had been declared the official winner. Joe Belden conducted a postelection survey of east Texas voters that revealed "an amazing change of votes" from the reported count, especially from Dies to O'Daniel.[86] "It is certain that the Texas voters got bilked and lost control of their state again by a merger of stupid drys with smart wets under Ferguson and brewery money who financed the deal and backed by the Senate coronation men who hate Roosevelt and Johnson as the developers of public water power," Marsh grumped in a letter to a friend.[87]

Not surprisingly, Connally and his coworkers wanted to contest the results.[88] H. M. Greene, Lyndon's professor from his SWT days, argued that it would be immoral to allow such a blatant case of political theft to go unchallenged. A surprisingly philosophical LBJ would have none of it, however. "Well boys, I've listened to all the arguments and heard all these figures," he said. "It looks to me like we've been beat. You just don't turn one of these elections over. I don't see how we can do it. We'd better just admit that we're defeated and be a good loser. There might be another time."[89] Without his participation, the Texas legislature on July 3 authorized an investigation, and the chair of the State Democratic Executive Committee wired the U.S. Senate's Committee on Elections asking for a probe. Nothing came of either initiative, thanks largely to Alvin Wirtz. "Hell . . . I hope they don't investigate me," Johnson laughingly remarked to his brother.[90] There had been as much vote buying by the Johnson campaign as the O'Daniel. And there were all those illegal contributions. The best thing to do was take your medicine and wait until the next election.

"LYNDON, apparently you Texans haven't learned one of the first things we learned up in New York state," Roosevelt subsequently told him, "and that is that when the election is over, you sit on the ballot boxes."[91] "Did you ever see a shooting gallery with its circular, rotating discs with lots of pipes and rabbits on the circuit?" Lyndon subsequently asked Tommy Corcoran. "Well, when you miss one the first time, you get a second chance. And the sonofabitch who trimmed you will always come up again." [92] "A memory of Lyndon that I will always cherish," Lady Bird said, "was the way he looked, walking away to catch the plane to Washington after his defeat had been announced. I still see him striding off, looking very jaunty, and putting extra verve into his step." [93] O'Daniel would have to face a contest for a regular six-year term in 1942. "I thought I could be elected the next year as a martyr," LBJ later told Ronnie Dugger. [94]

Viewed in broader terms, LBJ's 1941 Senate campaign was remarkable. Beginning with but 5 percent of the vote and little visibility outside the Tenth District, he had defeated (numerically, if not officially) a football hero turned law enforcer, a red-baiting racist, and a political evangelist. At thirty-three, Lyndon Johnson had become a force to be reckoned with in state and national politics. It was all the more astonishing considering how few signs of progressivism were visible in Texas at the time. Unions were just beginning to gain a foothold in the petrochemical and shipping industries, but were not yet seen as a major institutional magnet for the have-nots. Segregation would not be challenged until *Smith v. Allwright* in 1944. Political machines, urban and rural, still held sway. The rural ethic remained extremely strong in Texas. "The boys at the forks of the creek," declared one observer, "see the cities becoming big and wealthy, commercial and financial interests merging for their own benefit . . . and they doubt the disinterestedness of their political friends and register their disapproval of anything they sponsor . . . on the theory that no good can come out of Nazareth." [95] Yet, a plurality of voters had responded to Johnson's commitment to social justice.

LIKE OTHER PORTIONS of the South and West, Texas was struggling in the late 1930s and 1940s to comprehend the new American nationalism that was then emerging and to identify the state's place in it. Industrialists and financiers like the Brown brothers and Houston banker Jesse Jones wanted the blessings of federal regulation and largesse without federal control. Liberals like Lyndon Johnson and Charles Marsh, however, saw the state becoming part of a larger national community in which a commitment to social justice was an integral part of the patriotic creed. [96]

Indeed, it might be said that, through his support for the New Deal not only in fact but in theory, and for FDR's campaign to defend free world democracies from fascist aggression, LBJ was the voice of American nationalism calling on Texans to abandon their parochialism, their fears, their deliberate ignorance and become part of an emerging consensus in behalf of social justice and internationalism. "One cannot separate the thought of the future of democracy from the continuity of our own country as we know it," Johnson declared in his speech to the Texas legislature. "An American is not born of a certain blood or ancestry. Through the history of our country, there has predominated a common belief in the rights of man. A belief so strong it has welded together into one nation every nationality."[97] Modernization would create the economic capacity for a general prosperity, and a sound social policy would guarantee access to that prosperity. His fellow Texans who thought otherwise, who were in fact modern-day Luddites, deserved pity, not anger. "Because I am of the common people, I say let us be kind and gentle to the backward people who seek to ride the horse and buggy days into our day" he opined to one audience. "They will catch up and their children's children will march down the road to work and self contentment."[98]

CHAPTER 8

WAR

T HE MONTHS FOLLOWING THE FAILED SENATE CON-
test of 1941 were hell for Lyndon, Lady Bird, and his staff. The
prolonged mania of the campaign was followed by a devastating
psychological crash. Fits of depression were punctuated by angry
outbursts in which he blamed anybody and everybody for his loss to the flour
salesman. He was going to quit politics, go home, and make some money, he
told all who would listen. "One day I didn't get a telephone number fast enough
for Mr. Johnson and he threw a book at me," recalled Nellie Connally, who was
then filling in at the office. "I was a little afraid of him after that." He felt he had
embarrassed FDR and that his status as the White House's fair-haired boy was
in jeopardy.[1]

Eventually, Lady Bird and the worsening international situation snapped
him out of it. She told him to count his blessings. He still had his congressional
seat and there would be another opportunity to run for the Senate.[2]

When LBJ returned to Washington from Texas, the year-long battle over the
direction of American foreign policy was reaching its climax. From 1939
through 1941, a debate raged in the United States between those who were convinced that the war in Europe had no bearing on the national interest and those
who believed that America's very survival depended on its indirect and, if necessary, direct participation in the conflict. In the fall of 1940, isolationists formed
the America First Committee that included German and Irish Americans, conservative nationalists such as Republican Senator Robert A. Taft of Ohio, aviator
Charles Lindbergh, and former president Herbert Hoover. Though isolationism was Midwest-centered and made up largely of business-oriented opponents of the New Deal, it included former progressives and elements of the
extreme left. Until Hitler invaded the Soviet Union in 1941, even the Communist Party of the United States mouthed the isolationist line. America Firsters, as

the isolationists were called, argued that the United States was safe and secure within the Western Hemisphere. They likened the Atlantic and Pacific to two great moats and argued that the wars in Europe and the Far East were indigenous and perpetual.

Confronting the isolationists were the interventionists, who organized their own mouthpiece, the Committee to Defend America by Aiding the Allies. Composing this group were Anglo- and Franco-Americans and those who could trace their origins to one or another of the nations victimized by the Axis powers. Ideologically, interventionists tended to be liberal New Dealers; politically, they were generally Democratic, although members of the eastern, liberal wing of the Republican party supported all-out aid to the Allies. Because of lingering disillusionment with Wilsonian internationalism, the interventionists tended to downplay ideology and collective security. Instead, they emphasized national security: once the Axis overwhelmed contiguous areas, the fascist coalition would turn to the Western Hemisphere. In view of the airplane and modern warship, the Atlantic and Pacific were not moats but highways. It was better for the United States to act while it still had allies, argued William Allen White, the Kansas newspaper publisher who had founded the Committee to Defend America, than to wait and face the aggressors alone.

The fall of France had a dramatic impact on American opinion. As the Luftwaffe battered London and other British cities night after night, virtually everyone anticipated a German invasion of the United Kingdom, an undertaking that most feared would succeed. By the spring of 1941, the Roosevelt administration was no longer able to avoid a confrontation with the isolationists in Congress. Churchill, with whom Roosevelt had struck up an almost daily correspondence, wrote thanking the president and his countrymen for the opportunity to purchase the planes, bullets, and guns that were enabling Britain to hold its own against the Axis. Unfortunately, he reported, by the late summer his country would run out of gold and dollars with which to keep the life-giving flow of supplies going. The president and his advisers responded by asking Congress to pass the lend-lease bill. Under this deceptively titled measure, the United States would "lend" or lease munitions, raw materials, machinery, and other items to those nations fighting aggression.

Senator Taft remarked that lending bullets or food to someone was like lending chewing gum; you really did not want it back. His colleague, Senator Burton K. Wheeler, declared lend-lease to be the "administration's triple-A [Agricultural Adjustment Act] in foreign policy." It was designed to "plow under every fourth American boy."[3] Nonetheless, following a vigorous debate, both houses of Congress passed the aid measure by wide margins. Over the course of the war, the United States provided the British Empire with over $25 billion in lend-lease aid and billions more to other nations fighting the Axis.

During his first few weeks back in Washington, Johnson was reluctant to approach FDR. "I felt that I had written too many checks on my rather wobbly account," he wrote former Texas governor Jimmy Allred. "I did not want a check to bounce back in my face."[4] He need not have feared. The O'Daniel defeat did nothing to diminish LBJ in Roosevelt's eyes, and besides, he would need every strong arm in Congress in his ongoing battle with the isolationists.

In 1940, amid great controversy, the administration had persuaded Congress to pass the nation's first peace-time draft law. Opponents had ensured, however, that the legislation included a one-year limit. Unless the measure was repassed and the time of service extended, America's conscript army would evaporate. Reports coming into the White House were that an extension would create open mutiny among the draftees. The most popular graffiti at military camps was said to be "Ohio," for "Over the hill in October."[5] Roosevelt met in early August 1941 with the Democratic congressional leadership, including Rayburn and Johnson, to plot strategy. An unofficial nose count by LBJ indicated that a majority of Democratic congressmen were opposed. Rayburn subsequently learned from his longtime friend, Republican Minority Leader Joe Martin, that the GOP had also decided not to support an extension of the draft law.

The speaker took passage as a personal challenge. With Johnson acting as his chief lieutenant, he spent two weeks buttonholing Democrats and Republicans alike, appealing to their patriotism and promising political favors. LBJ made a rare House speech. Filled with maudlin and chauvinistic references to the Alamo and the fighting spirit of Texas boys, it was a disaster.[6] On the fateful day, the galleries were full of isolationists and soldiers' families waving small American flags. As the roll call began, a tense Rayburn stationed himself behind the clerk of the House to follow the tally. He and Johnson knew that the Republican leadership had ordered several of their congressmen to withhold their vote until the second round, when it would be clear how many nays would be required. When the clerk announced that 203 members had voted yes and 202 no, Rayburn quickly declared the measure passed and the voting closed. Pandemonium erupted in the galleries and on the floor. Martin and his lieutenants demanded that the vote be reopened for revisions and additions. All the speaker would allow was a recapitulation of the original vote. "No correction in the vote," Rayburn declared, "the vote stands, and the bill is passed, and without objection a motion to reconsider is laid on the table."[7] LBJ would later claim that fate had intervened to ensure that he remained in the House in 1941 to cast the deciding vote for the draft renewal bill.

BY THIS POINT, LBJ had decided that, as much as he wanted to run for the Senate again in 1942, it would be unwise. He continued to portray himself not only as the defender of democracy against fascist aggression, but as a herald of a new, more progressive South. His efforts were funneling millions of federal dollars into Texas for the establishment of military camps and the support of war-related industries, industries that he believed would continue to prosper after hostilities had ended, changing the face of the region. Indeed, he and New South leaders such as Claude Pepper of Florida hoped that in the future the white southern power structure would focus more on economic development than on maintaining an antiunion, segregationist status quo.[8]

If he ran for the regular Senate term in 1942, however, Johnson would have to give up his congressional seat and would not have another chance to run until 1944. John Connally and others warned him that O'Daniel would be harder to beat in 1942 than he had been in 1941; the support and the money that had crystallized in the special election could not be expected to reappear such a short time later. The O'Daniel people were already circulating rumors that Lady Bird had made $79,000 from a fraudulent stock deal (a charge that Johnson adamantly denied and that in fact was untrue).[9]

SEVERAL THINGS WERE CONSTANT in Lyndon's life: his mother's gushing, his brother's drinking, and, for each, their constant need for money. By November 1941, Sam Houston's profligate ways—he had not paid his federal taxes for three years and he had run up a huge bill with the Edgewater Beach Hotel in Florida as well as other concerns—was threatening his position as regional director of the National Youth Administration in Memphis. Aubrey Williams turned over copies of the IRS report to Lyndon and summoned Sam Houston to Washington. "If I were you," Lyndon wrote his brother, "I would try to have a complete and accurate statement from all of your creditors when you get here."[10]

Sam Houston, whose wife was then living with her family in Matoon, Illinois, was given a large loan and put on a payment schedule by Lyndon and Lady Bird; only then did Williams agree to let him keep his job. "I have contributed everything I know of," Lyndon wrote Albertine, Sam's wife, "and I was hopeful that when he went to Memphis he would follow a new route. That may still be possible, but from what I gather, it is not probable."[11] She thanked Lyndon profusely and begged him not to abandon his brother.

Rebekah, then living in an apartment in Austin, was meanwhile putting the squeeze on her "darling boy." "Please send me $100 for Nov. rent and other expenses and on the first of every month send the rent $35, direct to First Federal and the $65 allowance for groceries, etc. to me."[12] As usual, Rebekah's missives to her son were full of praise for his "high-mindedness," his "spotless character," his willingness to sacrifice for others. Rather than buoying him, of course, such praise caused deep-seated feelings of inadequacy to surface. "She was very proud of her son," an aide remembered, "but would be critical of him, esp. when she believed he had not lived up to the standards [she] had set for him . . . In a way she felt politics was beneath Lyndon."[13]

Lyndon's struggles with his personal demons and his anxiety over his political future were temporarily eclipsed by the Japanese attack on Pearl Harbor. The thought that he might not wear his nation's uniform never once crossed Johnson's mind. Back in the spring of 1940, while the German armies were rolling across Western Europe, he had joined the Naval Reserve, using his connections to obtain lieutenant commander commissions for both himself and

John Connally. Fulfilling the pledge he had made at San Marcos during the 1941 Senate campaign, LBJ cabled FDR on December 8: "As a member of the Naval Reserve of the United States Navy, I hereby urgently request my Commander-in-Chief to assign me immediately to active duty with the Fleet." [14]

The navy had no intention of giving a thirty-three-year-old congressman with not a shred of military or nautical training a line position where he could endanger men and equipment. Reluctantly, Johnson accepted a position in Undersecretary of the Navy James V. Forrestal's office. He would be overseeing naval training programs and shipbuilding facilities in Texas and on the West Coast. Packing up Lady Bird, Connally, and Willard Deason, he headed to San Francisco for a five-month tour of duty.[15] For the first month, Lady Bird acted as his secretary. "When I left Austin right after Christmas," she wrote relatives, "I went to the West Coast with Lyndon . . . doing some typing and short-hand for him at night and going sightseeing to the local art galleries, museums, China-town, and ocean beach in the day time." [16]

Johnson's task was an important one. Though Congress and the administration had authorized a vast expansion of the navy and merchant marine, American shipyards had actually produced fewer warships and troop transports during the second half of 1941 than during the first half. Inadequate manpower training programs, bottlenecks constricting the movement of labor and materials, bureaucratic wrangling, and lack of a sense of urgency characterized the military-civilian effort.[17] Without transports and the vessels to protect them, America would remain impotent in both Europe and Asia.

Throwing himself into his task with characteristic energy, Johnson virtually lived in the air, meeting with officials from Boeing, Lockheed, the Richmond Shipyard near San Francisco, Ed Weisl of Paramount Pictures, and various NYA directors. He came up with a plan to create a central manpower authority, which would include the NYA and Civilian Conservation Corps, that would train and distribute war industry workers for the navy and all branches of the service. At Lockheed he put on what one executive in attendance described as "a brilliant (I mean it) symposium of the factors in the procurement of an adequate labor supply for defense industries." [18]

In letters to Rayburn and others LBJ bemoaned the lack of focus among industry and government officials, their seeming lack of motivation. "It is time to quit 'conferring' and go to work," he proclaimed. "Decision must replace indecision. Action must replace inaction. The road to hell is paved with indecision and inaction." [19] "Thank God for our grabbing Lyndon Johnson," wrote J. W. Barker, Forrestal's assistant for labor problems. "He's going to be a grand 'goad' stuck into everyone's side, including me." [20]

During this period, Johnson's political future was a subject of intense debate among his friends and advisers. Marsh was desperate for him to challenge O'Daniel and believed that running as a lieutenant commander in the navy would be nothing but a plus. "Johnson has a campaign under his belt," he wrote Roy Hofheinz on March 13, 1942, "and you and I both agree that he was elected. The people may want to complete this election. All the poppycock talk about a man in the army being unavailable as an instrument of Texas people doesn't mean any more to me."[21]

He even went so far as to leak a story to the press that Johnson would run.[22] Wirtz and Connally were absolutely opposed. "I suppose this makes me a life-long enemy of Charlie Marsh," Wirtz wrote Lady Bird, "but I cannot see any merit in his idea of running Lyndon for the Senate against O'Daniel, Allred and [former Governor Dan] Moody . . . If his name were put on the ballot, I do not believe he would get enough votes to be near a run-off and would be out of his Congressional seat . . . I think it would ruin his future political career because the people would have the idea he is trying to make political capital out of his uniform. Furthermore, I think he is under obligation to help Allred, and no man can afford to disregard his obligations."[23] "Wirtz believes a live Congress-man is better than a dead Senator," Marsh observed disgustedly.[24] When Con-nally and Lady Bird sided with Wirtz, however, Marsh threw in the towel.[25]

Wirtz and Connally had no compunction about Lyndon running for reelec-tion to Congress while in uniform, however. Early on, it was decided that the best strategy was for Lady Bird to return to Washington and manage the congres-sional office. Lyndon could claim to be faithfully serving his constituents even though he was on active duty in the navy. To save money, she sublet their spa-cious apartment and moved into the Connallys' much smaller place with Nellie, who, along with O. J. Weber, a twenty-one-year-old lawyer from Beaumont, constituted her office staff. "I've been going to business school ever since I got back to Washington in order to regain my speed (I had already studied typing and short-hand in the University years ago)," she wrote her aunt and uncle, "but the first of this week I 'graduated myself,' because it's so interesting here at the of-fice."[26] She and Nellie would arrive at the office around 8:30 and leave when the work was done.

The office turned out more than sixty letters a day, and Lady Bird proved to be sensitive, diplomatic, and thorough. Alternating between steak and fried chicken, the limit of their repertoire as cooks, Lady Bird and Nellie entertained dinner guests twice a week. "It is a stimulating experience to be here in War-time," she told her friend Ella Powell, "provided you have strong nerves and extra strong feet—you have to stand in line to go to a movie, pay a bill, get gaso-line at a filling station, get a meal in a cafe—everything."[27]

To ensure Lyndon's reelection to Congress, Lady Bird, Wirtz, and Jake Pickle, who took leave from his NYA job, launched a petition drive in the Tenth District requesting that Lyndon have his name placed on the ballot and that Lady Bird "be the acting Congressman while her husband was off at war." Twenty thousand of the forty thousand Democrats registered in the district signed, and, as hoped, Lyndon was able to run unopposed in 1942. "This was another of the three high-adrenalin periods in my life," Lady Bird later recalled. "Everybody was just full of determination, tense, hard-driving, just willing to go to any exertion."[28]

In Lady Bird's absence, Charles Marsh took pains to see that Lyndon was not without female companionship while he was on the West Coast. "I am sending an agent to the West Coast," he wrote a friend in California. "He is Johnson, Congressman from the Austin district . . . He seems to need a bit of the sort of thing you give people . . . He is very fine, but might get some benefit from your person, and from the view from your porch."[29]

After Johnson had spent four months of important but unspectacular work as facilitator of the war effort, Marsh decided that it was time to push him. "Nobody who loves you could be satisfied with you," he wrote his protégé in April. "You haven't gone anywhere. You haven't done anything . . . Get your ass out of this country at once where there is danger, and then get back as soon as you can to do real work."[30]

Johnson was thinking along the same lines. In March 1942, he had written to request meetings with Harry Hopkins and the president. Receiving word at last that Roosevelt would see him on April 26, Lyndon departed the West Coast by train and arrived in Washington on April 17.[31] Johnathan Daniels, a journalist then employed by the Office of Civilian Defense, recalled running into Johnson in the bar of the Carlton Hotel: "Immaculate in blue uniform with the two and a half gold stripes on his sleeves, he seemed still the rangy Texan. He talked slowly with a tone that gave the impression that he was confiding completely to one whose attention he greatly desired. But there was no rest in his dark, bright eyes. His mood altered easily. Slim and curly-haired, joking and laughing, he looked less like the conventional portrait of a congressman than the equally conventional picture of a movie actor in seagoing costume."[32]

Roosevelt knew what Johnson wanted and was sympathetic. The White House and Rayburn were already laying plans to recall congressmen and senators from active duty in July. But the president also recognized the value of combat experience to Johnson and other of his supporters in their future political endeavors. In their meeting at the White House, FDR and Johnson discussed the manpower situation, the forthcoming congressional elections, and the deteriorating military situation in the South Pacific. General Douglas MacArthur had been forced to flee the Philippines by submarine shortly before American forces there had surrendered to the Japanese. In the weeks that followed, the flag of the Rising Sun was raised over Singapore, the Dutch East Indies, and the Solomon Islands. As of April 1942, the Japanese seemed poised to invade Australia and New Guinea. Roosevelt and his military advisers had decided on a Europe-first strategy, and the relative trickle of men and supplies reaching the Southwest Pacific did not sit well with MacArthur, who in March had been named supreme commander of Allied forces in the region. The theatrical MacArthur, adulated by some of his subordinates and despised by others, was already being encouraged by the GOP to think about running against Roosevelt and was becoming openly critical of the administration.

LBJ's mission was to tour the area. "Want you to represent Navy and stand up and fight for me," Roosevelt instructed, according to Johnson's notes of the conversation.[33] On May 1, Johnson scribbled a will on a piece of notebook paper, leaving everything to Lady Bird, and departed by plane for New Orleans en route to Honolulu.[34] On the eve of his departure, Lyndon received a remarkable letter from the eccentric Marsh: "So now it is your place in uniform . . . You are to fight with skill and frankness amid the dull, the frightened, the lazy, the vengeful, the jealous, the sly. St. George of the Dark Ages killed the dragon that ravaged all with his sword of virtue. And so you shall be the victor with your sword of service. The pace and the challenge shall quicken you. . . . Finally, in your love for your country, when in doubt see your natural father and myself at either hand . . . visualize humanity as you think and work for all."[35]

Johnson's orders attached him to the party of Admiral Robert L. Ghormley, who had been assigned the task of retaking the Solomon Islands from the Japanese. Aboard Ghormley's flying boat, LBJ departed Honolulu on May 14 for an eight-day tour that took him through Palmyra Island, Canto Island, Suva in the Fiji Islands, Noumea, New Caledonia, and ended in Auckland, New Zealand.[36] Toward the end of the trip, he met Lieutenant Colonel Francis R. Stevens and Lieutenant Colonel Samuel E. Anderson of the Operations and Plans Division of the War Department General Staff. Their assignment, like his, was to meet with MacArthur and survey the Southwest Pacific theater. From that point on, the three traveled together and acted as a team.

MacArthur was not particularly glad to see the trio when they arrived at his headquarters in Melbourne on May 25. He could understand the two War Department officials, he said, but "God only knows what you're doing here," he told Johnson.[37] He saw the congressman, as he insisted on referring to him, as a political commissar sent out by the White House to spy on him. LBJ spent the next five days persuading MacArthur that he was friend, not foe, and that he was there to gather information on the general's needs, to convey them to Washington, and to use whatever influence he had to see that they were met.

In time, LBJ succeeded in ingratiating himself, not only because he was able to appeal to the general's vanity but also because he was sincere. In a two-hour-and-ten-minute declamation that, according to Johnson, featured "perfect organization, a forceful presentation, and rhetoric most pleasing, colorful, and descriptive," MacArthur pledged to help the three to see everything. The situation was desperate, he told them. The Australians were completely unprepared to defend themselves. They lacked training, equipment, and leadership. He needed heavy warships, particularly aircraft carriers and the fighters to protect them. Johnson scribbled notes furiously.[38]

FOR THE NEXT MONTH, LBJ, Stevens, and Anderson toured Australia, New Zealand, and the adjacent islands that were still in Allied hands. As his navy diary reveals, Johnson was always uncomfortable, frequently sick, and often lonely. On the voyage to Palmyra: "Had terrible night Wednesday night. Fever. Night sweats. Headache. Young Ensign got aspirin at midnight . . . All wet in motor boat . . . Crossed equator. Stood watch." At Canto Island Johnson checked in with the infirmary and received treatment for a nasal infection. He was constipated to boot: "Good dinner at 6:30. Enema at 8. Sleep at 9. Up at 5:30." Morale and army management was bad. The island had no form of radar or radio detection system and almost no anti-aircraft facilities. "Hot as Hell . . . 1100 soldiers on Island . . . not a man on the island that wouldn't leave in a moment." There was only one woman on Canto, the sixty-year-old wife of the U.S. consular officer. As a result, "only intercourse—social." Conditions in Suva were somewhat better. There were women but also many cases of syphilis and clap. On the way from Suva to Auckland, thunderstorms forced Johnson's plane to fly at seven hundred feet. From Auckland he and his colleagues took off on an uneventful flight to Sidney. "Thought of 'Miss Jesus' all day as I traveled the long 1400 miles." The affair between Lyndon and Alice Glass was still on; the Miss Jesus reference, which would appear again and again in his notes, was probably to her but may have been to a woman he had met in the Pacific. There were, he noted, constant problems with black soldiers. "Negroes and constables knife threat," LBJ wrote in his notes. He would express the opinion in his report that black troops should not be sent into areas where indigenous women were not prepared to accept them.[39]

Throughout his stay in Australia, Johnson had been badgering MacArthur's headquarters to allow him to fly on an actual combat bombing mission. The officers there advised against it. The raids then being conducted against the Japanese bases at Rabaul in New Britain and Lae in New Guinea were extremely dangerous. American B-25 and B-26 medium bombers were subjected to constant attack by Japanese Zeros before and after their bombing runs and had to deal with heavy anti-aircraft fire over the targets. The Allies had not yet developed a fighter with the speed and maneuverability capable of dealing with the Zeros. Losses on these bombing raids were frequently 25 percent or higher. Johnson was insistent. If he were to make a credible case for MacArthur and his needs, he would have to have a combat mission to his credit. Finally, the general intervened and personally ordered space to be cleared for Johnson and his two colleagues from the War Plans Division.[40]

Johnson, Anderson, and Stevens arrived at Seven Mile Drome at Port Moresby on the morning of June 9, 1942. They were scheduled to fly with a squadron of B-26 Martin Marauder medium bombers as they attacked the Japanese airfield at Lae in New Guinea. LBJ was assigned to the *Wabash Cannonball*, commanded by Lieutenant Willis G. Bench. He greeted the crew, climbed aboard, and inspected his seat in the cubicle behind the cockpit. He left the plane to relieve himself. When he returned, he found his seat occupied by Stevens. When Johnson told him that he had been there first, Stevens just grinned and told him to find another plane. Johnson shrugged and approached Lieutenant Walter H. Greer, captain of the *Heckling Hare*.

Greer agreed to take Johnson, who then began introducing himself to the crew. "Johnson at that time was thin," recalled Sergeant Claude A. McCredie. "I asked him if he would like to take a look in the bay and see the bombs. We were getting them fused and ready for the mission at the moment—one of the last things we do before climbing aboard and starting to taxi out. He showed close interest in what we were doing. In fact, I was startled at the questions he asked me. We've had the 'wheels' that came poking around before, but it was more for effect than anything else. You can tell at once if a man really is interested or if he's just acting to put on a show. Most of that type would never dream of going along on a combat mission—not against Lae, especially. Down there at the time, the word 'Lae' was almost synonymous with hell, and the odds were about one in four or five that you wouldn't make it back from the mission."[41]

The mission to which LBJ was assigned employed a new strategy designed to trick the Japanese into lowering their defenses. The raid would unfold in three waves: first, three B-17s would drop their loads from thirty thousand feet, causing the Zeros at Lae to scramble. A second wave consisting of twelve B-25s would come in at eighteen thousand feet and engage the enemy fighters. Thinking that this was the extent of the attack, the Zeros were supposed to return to their base and be sitting ducks for the twelve B-26s that would constitute the third wave. Johnson took his seat at the radioman's position just behind the cockpit. Unbeknown to him, he wore tail gunner Harry Baren's parachute. There were no extras, and orders were that all guest VIPs should have a parachute.[42]

The American attack lacked coordination. As the B-26s approached their target, they found not empty skies but the B-25s, which had mistimed their attack, fully engaged with dozens of Zeros. "It was those B-25s and at once, in the same instant that I saw them," Lieutenant Jerry Crosson, the copilot, said, "I knew something or someone had really fouled up this whole mission on us. Because the B-25s were between us and the target instead of far away from the Lae airdrome, and there was a swarm of tiny dots all around the B-25s . . . They were up at eighteen thousand feet, working over the B-25s, and then they came straight for us, coming down to where we were at fourteen thousand feet."[43] Raked by cannon fire, the *Wabash Cannonball* caught fire and crashed into the sea, killing Colonel Stevens and all aboard. Just as it was about to begin its bombing run, the *Heckling Hare* lost one of its two generators, forcing the plane to drop out of formation and making it a sitting duck for the Zeros.

Lieutenant Greer immediately made the decision to jettison the ship's bombs and head for home. With bullets ripping through the plane, Greer dove for temporary safety into cloud cover. Emerging, the *Heckling Hare* engaged in a fifteen-minute battle with a squadron of Zeros. From his vantage point, Johnson could see everything through the Plexiglas nose of the B-26. Several times during the fight, he made his way back to the waist to see if he could assist Lillis Walker, who was on his knees, moving back and forth from left waist gun to right as targets presented themselves. "He—the Navy officer with us—came back to my position a few times when the going was real rough," Walker recorded. "He moved through the plane, trying to see everything that was going on."[44] As Johnson looked on, "cool as a cucumber," according to one crew member, Baren shot down the only Zero destroyed during the mission. Miraculously, the *Heckling Hare* escaped and landed safely.[45]

Johnson's description of the battle in his diary was terse: "I lost my friend Steve—One fighter down. Another lands with wind and only two gallons gas. [Lieutenant Colonel Dwight, II] Divine brings B26 down on belly wonderful— Boys unshaven, breath smells, they haven't bathed but Crockett, Bowie, Bonham and Travis had nothing on them in guts . . . To bed at 8:30 after bath and shave and scotch. Couldn't get my mind off Steve . . . and other fine boys."[46]

What they needed, the crew of the *Hare* told him, was long-range fighters that could take the bombers all the way to their target and back. And they needed parts and supplies for existing aircraft. Maintenance crews were having to hold the B-25s and B-26s together with glue and bailing wire. "I told Johnson," Baren said, "that we couldn't have cared less what the papers were saying about MacArthur back in the States. Out here, where the chips were down, he was probably the most unpopular man we knew of."[47] His bombastic and self-serving accounts of heroic battles fought and won were creating a totally false picture among press and public.

FROM PORT MORESBY Johnson flew with other brass to Darwin on the north coast of Australia to inspect an air facility that had come under repeated attack by the Japanese. After a brief tour, the party, including an Australian air marshal, took off for the long trip to Melbourne. Several hours into the flight the crew of the *Swoose* discovered that the navigational equipment had gone out. For four hours the plane searched the outback for some tell-tale landmark that would indicate to its crew where they were. With fuel running low and the sun setting, the captain decided to make an emergency landing.

Throughout the flight, LBJ and the other officers with him had sat in their compartment reading, chewing gum, or just waiting apprehensively. There were no parachutes on the plane. Finally the captain spied an open space near a farmhouse and brought his plane down for a safe but bumpy landing. The inhabitants of Carris Brook Farm brought some food and water, but the party had to spend the night in the open before someone from the nearby town of Winton could fetch them. Finally, LBJ reached Melbourne and civilization on June 12.[48]

The relative comfort was delicious. "First restful day," Johnson's diary records, "took some pictures. Stayed in room most of day working on notes and reading. Went to Tess's [?] party. Good food not very interesting people. Left at 10 after a couple of dames . . . Home late—slept late Sunday. Luxurious living—coffee in room—called Tess. No answer . . . Had sent cables to Miss Jesus. Hope and pray for answer."[49] That Miss Jesus was not Lady Bird is clear from a letter that she wrote Rebekah Johnson on June 14: "I have no idea where Lyndon is and have heard nothing from him since his cablegram May 29th."[50]

On June 18, Johnson and Anderson got in to see MacArthur. The two gave him a lengthy report emphasizing the valor of the men and inadequacy of the equipment. LBJ reported that the general was appropriately somber, given the loss of Stevens. "Glad to see you two fellows here where three were last," he remarked. "It was a mistake . . . to go on combat mission but it did justice to your heart. It was just what I would have done."[51]

At the close of the interview, he informed them that he was awarding Stevens the Distinguished Service Cross and the two of them the Silver Star.[52] The gesture was political. The other crew members of the *Cannonball* received only Purple Hearts, and no other member of the *Hare* was decorated. Johnson was embarrassed. He drafted a letter declining the Silver Star, the military's second-highest award for valor.[53] "My very brief service with these men and its experience of what they do and sacrifice makes me all the more sensitive that I should not accept a citation of recognition for the little part I played."[54] He left both Tommy Corcoran and Harold Ickes with the impression that he was going to turn the medal in. But he did not.

BY THE END OF HIS TOUR, Johnson had decided to leave the navy, if possible, and return to Congress. He believed he could better serve his country prodding the federal bureaucracy and private industry to new feats of efficiency and production rather than playing a combat or supporting military role for which he was completely unprepared. Lady Bird, Wirtz, and Marsh supported his decision but warned of the political fallout if LBJ were seen to be leaving to others the fighting and dying.

FDR agreed that Lyndon would be more useful in Washington in civilian clothes than in some remote part of the world in uniform. He and Rayburn put their heads together to see how to recall Lyndon and other legislators without doing them political harm. The first directive they framed placed all members of Congress serving in the armed forces "on inactive duty July 1, 1942 . . . except those who wish to remain on active duty for the duration of the war."[55]

Through Lady Bird, Lyndon objected to the phrasing. It could leave him dangling. Rayburn once again trotted off to the White House; he succeeded in persuading FDR to drop the exception. Of the eight congressmen in uniform, four chose to give up their seats and remain in the service.[56] Still worried, Lyndon arranged for a private off-the-record meeting with the Boss on July 15. Out of that conference came an explicit statement from Secretary of the Navy Frank Knox declaring that "the President has determined that your services to the nation in this critical period are more urgently required in the performance of your duties as a member of the House . . . than as an officer on active duty with the Navy."[57]

Back in Washington, Lyndon set about becoming the House's version of Harry S. Truman. In 1941, Truman, the junior senator from Missouri, had succeeded in having himself named chair of a special subcommittee of the Senate Military Affairs Committee. He spearheaded a friendly ongoing investigation of the war effort on the home front, uncovering waste and fraud in government defense contracts and landing him on the cover of *Time. Look* named him one of the ten civilians most useful to the war effort.

In meetings with the president, in press releases, in speeches in Congress and over the radio, LBJ trumpeted the achievements of the common soldier and sailor in the Pacific and the compelling need for more LSTs, aircraft carriers, and fighter planes. He criticized American industry for producing at only 70 percent of capacity and the aircraft industry in particular for not being able to develop a fighter to match the Zero. As was his wont, he succumbed to rhetorical excess. "Some of our high officials have let the President down," he declared. "We must get rid of the indecisive, stupid, selfish and incompetents among our Generals, Admirals, and others in high military positions," he declared. "We must not be temporarily lulled to sleep by prophetic statements, rosy headlines, and the 'let John do it attitude.' "[58] On August 19, over a national radio hookup, he denounced "selfish groups," especially the steel, aluminum, rubber, and oil industries, "for their 'business as usual' policy" and their obsession with profits.[59]

Johnson wanted FDR to blame everything on the Republicans, but the president had decided to swamp his political enemies, both Republicans and conservative Democrats, in a sea of patriotism. He had already taken GOP luminaries Frank Knox and Henry Stimson into the cabinet as secretaries of the navy and war, respectively. "This is war," he told reporters. "Politics is out." When LBJ went to the White House to discuss strategy for retaining a Democratic majority in the House in the 1942 midterm elections, Roosevelt would not even see him. Even the loss of forty-four seats in the House, cutting the Democratic majority to thirteen, could not move the president. Similarly, Roosevelt had decided to placate rather than confront big business. In financing the war and supplying Allied armies, the administration faced a choice. It could either nationalize banks and defense-related industries, or it could work with them, in essence relying on capitalism to win the war. FDR chose the latter course. Johnson's attacks on selfish industrialists were out of touch with the times. The Boss had traded "Dr. New Deal" for "Dr. Win the War."[60]

DISCOURAGED, LBJ considered abandoning politics for a lucrative business career in Texas. It seemed that the war was making many of his friends and acquaintances millionaires while he was left behind to wallow in a middle-class existence, doling out money to the ne'er-do-wells in his family. To make matters worse, late in 1941, the Internal Revenue Service had launched an investigation of Brown and Root, Lyndon's financial agent, for tax evasion. As IRS agents subpoenaed books and interviewed company employees throughout 1942, Wirtz and Johnson became increasingly worried that investigators would turn up the numerous illegal contributions funneled to Johnson's 1941 Senate campaign through Brown and Root employees. At their behest, Jim Rowe intervened with the White House, charging that the investigation was being spearheaded by anti–third term and anti-Roosevelt conservatives, the same gang that had supported John Nance Garner. Why, he asked rhetorically, were Pappy O'Daniel, Coke Stevenson, and Martin Dies not being investigated for their funding irregularities? Roosevelt appealed to Secretary of the Treasury

Henry Morgenthau, but the politically obtuse and scrupulously honest Morgenthau refused to call off the dogs.

On September 4, the IRS called for a full investigation. Rowe convened a meeting with Wirtz, Johnson, and the Brown Brothers at the Brown and Root condominium on Sheridan Circle in Washington. So worried was he about an IRS bug that he had them confer in the street outside the building. A distraught LBJ asked Rowe to redouble his efforts to kill this "politically inspired" investigation. To no avail.

At the conclusion of its probe in the fall of 1943, the IRS ruled that Brown and Root owed $1,161,000, including $300,000 in fraud penalties. Rumors were that some company officials would go to jail. Not until January 1944, and only after two personal calls on Roosevelt by Johnson and Wirtz, did the government relent. The company agreed to pay all outstanding taxes and penalties. Even then, the principal IRS agent in Texas had to be ordered to abandon an investigation he wanted to continue indefinitely.[61]

Adding to LBJ's woes, Lady Bird was intensely unhappy by the second half of 1942. She was tired of her husband being in love with another woman, or perhaps women. "I remember when we went out to the house after he was back and he showed some movies he'd taken," Jim Rowe said. "One was of a very pretty woman in a bar, and Lady Bird said, 'Who's that, Lyndon, that pretty woman?' and Johnson passed it off. And then he quietly said, 'I'm not going to tell her who it was.' "[62]

Her plans to become pregnant had come to naught. In the fall of 1942, she suffered the second of three miscarriages. Even after his long absence on the West Coast and Australia, LBJ was his usual inattentive self. "One season she had bought tickets for the Theater Guild," Russell Brown said. "But it developed that Lyndon's program was such that he couldn't possibly go to the theater with her. And his disposition is not such as to sit through that sort of thing . . . Anyway, it turned out that I was the one who took Bird to the theater that season . . . He'd probably take her to dinner and then bring her to the theater, and I'd go inside with her. I was always prepared to see her home, but she never would let me do so. She always went home by herself, on the Connecticut Avenue bus."[63]

Lady Bird also wanted a permanent nest. Tired of apartment living, she shopped around and found a white brick colonial in Cleveland Park, with eight rooms. LBJ gave in but continued to haggle with the owner over the price, even though the down payment was to come from Lady Bird's inheritance. With the sale in jeopardy, she blew up at her husband. John Connally remembered her telling Lyndon angrily, "I want that house. Every woman wants a home of her own. I've lived out of a suitcase ever since we've been married. I have no home to look forward to. I have no children to look forward to. I have nothing to look forward to but another election!" As she stormed out of the room the two men stared at each other. "What should I do?" LBJ asked. "I'd buy the house," Connally advised.[64]

To open up a revenue stream and an alternative business career and to find an outlet for Lady Bird's talents and energies, Johnson and his wife decided to purchase either a newspaper or a radio station. By 1942, Lady Bird had collected all $41,000 coming to her from her mother's estate. In addition, her namesake uncle, Claude Patillo, had died the year before and left her around $20,000. Some thirty-eight hundred acres in Alabama deeded to her by Aunt Effie brought in an annual income from tenant farmers and timber sales.[65] A diversion was entirely affordable.

Initially attracted to the newspaper business because of her degree in journalism, Lady Bird looked into buying the *Waco Tribune*. The asking price, and Charles Marsh's opposition to the Johnsons' owning a competing paper, squelched the plan, however. Instead, Lyndon and Lady Bird decided to buy KTBC, an Austin radio station that seemed to be going nowhere. Limited to 250 watts and daytime transmission, KTBC had to compete with the university station at Texas A&M for air time, and owner Wesley West, a rabid anti–New Dealer, could not persuade the FCC to help. For two years, West's application for nighttime permission and relief from the franchise at College Station languished. When he died in 1942, ownership of KTBC passed to his sons, Wesley and James Jr., and E. G. Kingsbery, a conservative Austin businessman.[66]

Wirtz and others of Johnson's friends in Austin urged him and Lady Bird to buy KTBC. Lyndon understood that the station was struggling, but he had reason to believe that he would succeed with the FCC where the Wests had failed. Lady Bird inquired directly of her friend Clifford Durr, an FCC commissioner, whether or not KTBC would be a good investment. "I told her that . . . if she would get that station on its feet and get it well managed, it ought to be a very good investment," Durr later recalled.[67]

To avoid charges that he was using his political office to enrich himself and to pour oil on troubled domestic waters, LBJ insisted that Lady Bird be listed as the sole purchaser. She paid only $17,500 for KTBC, although the station listed assets of $30,000. But it also listed liabilities of $30,000 and had lost $7,500 the previous year. In January 1943, Lady Bird applied to the FCC for approval of the purchase, listing total personal assets of $64,322. In a little less than a month the commission acquiesced.[68]

According to George Reedy, who would later join LBJ's Senate staff, the Johnsons did not have to do anything overt to sway the FCC: "For a man in his position, bringing influence to bear would be utterly and completely irrelevant. But to think that the members of the Federal Communications Commission would be unaware when they were dealing with KTBC that the husband of the woman who owned it was one of the most powerful figures in Washington, anyone that would believe that would believe twenty-two impossible things before breakfast."[69]

Lady Bird embraced KTBC as if it were her longed-for child, and it proved to be a very needy child indeed. Control room, office, studio, and nine-person staff were crowded into two and a half rooms together with "obsolete" and "barely workable" equipment. She descended on the facility with mop and bucket.[70] She also set about the more important tasks of increasing the station's power, moving A&M off its frequency, and securing a bank of reliable, paying advertisers. In May, she and Lyndon persuaded Harfield Weedin, the public relations and advertising whiz from Houston, to take over management of the station, and they moved it into more spacious quarters downtown in the Brown Building. By June, the FCC had approved KTBC's application to go to 1,000 watts and begin nighttime programming. In August, the station turned its first profit: $18.[71]

Lady Bird familiarized herself with every aspect of the business. "She could read a balance sheet the way a truck driver reads a road map," said Leonard Marks, who would later head the USIA.[72] Indeed, despite efforts by LBJ's political handlers to portray Lady Bird as the sweet, dutiful little southern wife immersed in dresses and dinners, she was the brains and will behind what would become a small family broadcasting empire. She quickly acquired a reputation among employees for organization, an eye for detail, and frugality. A not entirely apocryphal story circulated that the staff had to bring their own Kleenex and toilet paper lest the station run out. She paid Weedin the handsome salary of $265 a month but made it clear that she expected results. He put the station on a simple format based on popular music and news, abjuring the pervasive country and western genre in an effort to appeal to what he believed would be more educated listeners.

Lyndon played the role of active if silent partner. KTBC desperately needed network affiliation. Shortly after the FCC approved Lady Bird's purchase of the station, he took the train to New York and presented himself at the corporate headquarters of CBS. William Paley, the president, agreed to see the congressman from Texas. He informed Lyndon that CBS already had affiliates in San Antonio and Dallas but sent him to see his assistant in charge of franchises, Frank Stanton.

After much conversation, Lyndon convinced Stanton and Paley that Austinites were able to pick up neither KTSA nor the Dallas station on their radios. In September, CBS and KTBC signed a contract under which the network committed to providing at least thirty-five hours of programming a week.[73]

From Austin and Washington, Lyndon began badgering Wirtz, Mayor Tom Miller, Austin attorney Ed Clark, and any of his other friends who would listen to push their business associates to advertise with KTBC. In October 1943, Clark sent Johnson the names of key individuals with local and regional banks, hotels, car dealerships, funeral homes, sporting goods stores, and other enterprises. "I am today writing Corpus," Clark reported to Lyndon, "so that Howard Butt [owner of the H.E.B. food store chain] will contact the advertisers whose products he sells at his stores in Austin so that he will have an opportunity to get coverage here."[74] Lyndon drew up a list of forty-seven CBS daytime programs that were being heard on the CBS affiliate in Dallas but not on KTBC. He then pressured Tommy Corcoran to persuade the advertisers of these programs to force CBS into airing them on KTBC.[75]

Gradually but steadily, KTBC's profitability increased. At the end of the first year of the Johnson ownership, the books revealed a $17,000 profit.[76] In 1945, a year in which the FCC approved a power boost to 5,000 kilowatts, the station showed an after-tax profit of $40,000 and boasted a listening audience of 2.5 million.[77]

THE ACQUISITION OF KTBC did not immediately improve Lady Bird's relationship with her husband. For seven weeks, she commuted between Austin and Washington, spending weekends in D.C. and weekdays tending to business. In Austin, she stayed with her mother-in-law, who continued to hold her at emotional arm's length. She in turn cordoned off Lyndon into a smaller and more manageable place in her life. "If you don't start writing me more often," he complained on May 7, "I'm going to have you drafted into the WAC. Then you have to write your next of kin at least twice a month."[78] Once the station was stabilized, however, Lady Bird was able to spend more time in Washington, where she delighted in decorating her new home.

The Johnsons had moved ten times in ten years of marriage; a permanent residence meant more to both of them than they could have imagined. Located at 4912 Thirtieth Place, a few blocks off Connecticut Avenue in northwest Washington, the house was a two-story brick colonial with attic, basement, and large backyard porch that overlooked a modest garden. The Johnsons were surrounded by their peers: congressmen, federal judges, and government officials. J. Edgar Hoover, director of the FBI, lived directly across the street.[79]

In August 1943, Lady Bird once again became pregnant. The previous year Virginia Durr had taken her to a gynecologist in Baltimore who had performed a procedure to prevent miscarriages. Lady Bird believed that this, coupled with her new nest, did the trick. "Lady Bird and I are going to have a baby in March," Lyndon wrote Gene Latimer. "Nothing in the world has ever happened that has made me happier, and I am even going to be elated if it is a girl."[80]

On the afternoon of March 19, 1944, Lady Bird went into labor. She told Lyndon, got dressed, and went to the car. Typically, he first got on the phone but eventually emerged to take her to the hospital. Once he delivered her into the hands of the hospital staff, he spent the next few hours driving around Washington talking with various political friends and then returning to the hospital with Willard Deason to play dominoes and wait. Finally, the labor nurse emerged and announced it was a girl. Lyndon showed no disappointment. It had been a difficult delivery, the nurse told them.[81]

Rebekah came to visit, but Lady Bird made it clear that she was to be treated as a house guest. The care and feeding of the baby she reserved exclusively to herself. Never bashful, Mother Johnson suggested Lynda as a first name—it would have been Lyndon had the child been male—and Bird as a second. Johnson thought the idea brilliant; the family would all have the same initials, a wonderful political gimmick. Lady Bird acquiesced.[82]

JOHNSON'S HOPES to imitate Harry S. Truman came to fruition in January 1943, when Naval Affairs Committee chair Carl Vinson allowed him to head up a subcommittee to examine all aspects of the naval war effort with a view to ensuring that the navy and its contractors were acting "efficiently, expeditiously, and economically" in prosecuting the war.[83] LBJ hired Donald C. Cook, a former assistant director at the Securities and Exchange Commission, as the subcommittee's chief counsel and Gene Latimer as chief of staff. For the next two and a half years, Johnson and his team looked into deferments of civilian employees in the Navy Department, investigated the Procurement Division, and toured shipyards and naval air training stations around the world.[84] It was a highly visible watchdog role, and he played it to the hilt.

As Johnson's national exposure and reputation were growing, his political base in Texas was shifting uncertainly. Johnson's moves to the right were attempts to straddle a growing divide that threatened to stretch him to the breaking point. Since 1940 and the defeat of John Nance Garner, neo-Republicans, calling themselves conservative or "regular" Democrats, had been working quietly but furiously to take control of the party in Texas and return it to its states' rights, free enterprise roots. Led by Jesse Jones, Senator O'Daniel, and Houston cotton broker and Assistant Secretary of State for Economic Affairs Will Clayton, these bankers, oilmen, and insurance executives appealed to the public's frustrations with price controls on gasoline and food, to fears that the ruling party had fallen under the control of Henry Wallace and his fellow travelers, and to white apprehension over the 1944 Supreme Court ruling, *Smith v. Allwright,* that outlawed Texas's white primary law. "The rising groups of individualists . . . special privilege seekers, and personal liberty folks" were ready for a fight to the finish, one of Johnson's constituents wrote him.

In fact, the Texas elite had become a Republican fifth column within the Democratic party. A privately compiled list of the 212 major Texas contributors to national campaign committees in 1944 showed 66 percent (71 percent of the dollars) given to Republicans. The list included H. L. Hunt, Harry Bass, the Cullen family of Houston, Jim and Wesley West, the King Ranch clan, Stanley Marcus of Nieman Marcus, the Brown brothers, and Oveta and William P. Hobby, publishers of the *Houston Post.*[85] The conservatives well realized that if they were to prevail, they would have to prevent the Democratic party from developing a mass base. Hence their profound and assiduous opposition to unions, a primary vehicle for funneling manual laborers into the political life of the state and nation. Taking advantage of the unit rule then governing Texas conventions—a winner-take-all requirement that operated from the precinct conventions up—conservatives discouraged grassroots participation by the less affluent and minorities in party affairs. When liberals did succeed in gaining office, they were ostracized by the leadership.[86]

Opposing the regulars were Roosevelt Democrats, a vast collection of former Populists and Progressives, teachers, small farmers and businessmen, advocates of equality of opportunity if not condition, academics, a handful of public intellectuals, and the ethnic minorities and manual workers who too frequently proved apathetic. Typical were Mr. and Mrs. C. W. Webb of Elgin. "We do not lay much stress upon a movement in the South to decentralize the Government and recentralize a Southern faction," they wrote LBJ. "This movement is stimulated by political desire and expediency . . . The race issue is here to stay . . . The Negro, the Mexican, the foreign stock and all should be treated fairly and without prejudice and should have the result of their labor and of peaceful living as long as deserved . . . Do not worry about the fourth term of Franklin D. Roosevelt. He is the best qualified man in the world today to lead in the program of progress we are in."[87]

JOHNSON ENTERED THE 1944 POLITICAL SEASON running scared. Opinion polls showed that 65 percent of Texans would vote for FDR if given the chance, and he was as much Roosevelt's man as he ever was. But there was the very real possibility of a German backlash in the Hill Country. More important, he had given great offense to the oil industry. In 1943 the petroleum interests had launched a major lobbying campaign in behalf of a thirty-five-cent-a-barrel increase in the price of crude oil. Companies large and small claimed that they simply could not make a profit at the government-mandated $1.35 a barrel.

Secretary of the Interior Harold Ickes supported the measure, as did Sam Rayburn, who descended from his speaker's chair into the well of the House to make a speech in favor. On the other side, Fred Vinson, head of the Office of War Mobilization (OWM), and Chester Bowles, who ran the Office of Price Administration, opposed the price increase, insisting that not only would it add half a billion dollars a year to oil profits, it would lead to price increases on virtually every other product, thus confronting the nation with the specter of runaway inflation.

Congress eventually rejected the measure. Only two representatives from the oil-producing states voted against the raise in oil prices, Mike Monroney of Oklahoma and Lyndon Johnson of Texas. "Johnson told me that he could not conscientiously support this increase while our boys were dying in foxholes," Paul Porter of OWM said. "I remember that many commentators said that here were Lyndon Johnson and Mike Monroney signing their political death warrants."[88]

Told by Alvin Wirtz and Ed Clark that the oil interests were searching for "a worthy opponent" to run against him, Lyndon hurried off to Texas to mend some fences. What he found in the Tenth District reassured him. His constituents seemed solidly for Roosevelt and for him, applauding especially his efforts to bring efficiency and effectiveness to the home front.

The best his opponents could come up with was Buck Taylor, a sixty-year-old World War I veteran and former committee clerk in the legislature. "The kindest thing that could be said of Buck," one of Lyndon's political friends observed, "was that he was a nobody." [89] Yet, when the state party convention met in May to select and instruct delegates to the Democratic National Convention, Wirtz, Johnson, Allred, and the liberals discovered that they had been outworked and outmaneuvered. Although the vast majority of Democrats supported Roosevelt and a fourth term, regulars outnumbered liberals nine to seven. "The 'Regular' convention was dominated by Willkie-ites, Roosevelt haters, and out-right Republicans," Wirtz reported to the White House. "They organized in secret and were heavily financed. They got control of the County Conventions in the four big cities of Houston, Dallas, Fort Worth and San Antonio and refused to let a single friend of the Administration go as a delegate to the State Convention." [90]

Immediately, the regulars introduced a resolution demanding that the Democratic party restore the two-thirds rule that it had abandoned in 1936, the requirement that any successful candidate for the Democratic presidential nomination receive two-thirds of the votes at the nominating convention rather than a simple majority. It would give back to the South its veto over national affairs. According to the resolution backed by the regulars, if the DNC rejected its demand, the Texas delegates would go to Chicago free to vote for the candidate of their choice. At this point, Wirtz introduced a motion requiring Texas electors to vote for the Democratic candidate who won the popular vote in the November general election. When Johnson rose to speak in favor of the proposal, he was jeered off the stage. "Throw that Roosevelt pin-up boy out of there!" and "Get that Goddamn 'Yes-man' off that platform!" were among the less obscene catcalls. [91]

When the Wirtz resolution was voted down 952 to 695, the liberals walked out of the Senate chamber where the convention was being held and reconvened in the House across the rotunda. The rump convention elected Wirtz temporary chair and called on LBJ for a speech. Instead of a rousing condemnation of the self-styled regulars, what they got was a calm appeal to reason. Johnson warned against the dangers of internal warfare. The issue, he said was who was a Republican and who was a Democrat. "When I bolt a convention," he declared, "it's going to be a Hoovercrat convention." [92]

He persuaded Wirtz and the permanent chairman, Tom Miller, to issue a call to the regulars to vote yea or nay as to whether they would support the national ticket. They did, and the answer was a resounding "No!" Those gathered in the Senate chamber voted overwhelmingly to order the twenty-three presidential electors allocated to Texas to vote for any man except Roosevelt. At this point the loyalists decided to send their own delegation to Chicago, selecting Senator Tom Connally and speaker Sam Rayburn as delegates-at-large and naming Mrs. Clara Driscoll, a Johnson financial backer, chair of the delegation. [93]

As he had in 1940, FDR first attempted to work out a compromise that would bring the loyalists and regulars together, but the neo-Republicans would have none of it. Charging Roosevelt with plotting a "bloodless revolution," the Texas regulars joined in a conspiracy with other southern conservative Democrats to withhold their state's electoral votes from Roosevelt in hopes of throwing the election into the House of Representatives.[94]

As usual, FDR was too shrewd for them. At the Chicago convention, he spiked the guns of the reactionaries by dumping Henry Wallace in favor of the much more conventional, less controversial Senator Harry S. Truman of Missouri. The delegates voted to divide the accredited Texas delegation evenly between the loyalists and the regulars.

Because of the Texas Democrats' unusual habit of holding two conventions in a presidential election year, one in May to choose delegates to the national convention and another in September to elect a state party chair and executive committee, Lyndon, Wirtz, Miller, and the loyalists had another chance. This time Wirtz worked hard to mobilize moderates and liberals so that when the Democrats convened in September the loyalists were clearly in charge.

Wirtz was quick to exact revenge. With Allred named chair of the convention, Wirtz then conducted a thorough purge. He removed George Butler, Jesse Jones's nephew, as state Democratic chair, replacing him with one of his friends. He then had fifty of the sixty-two members of the State Executive Committee expelled, replacing them with Rayburn-Johnson-Roosevelt men. The fifteen Texas presidential electors who would not commit to Roosevelt were also removed and replaced with loyalists. When, subsequently, the secretary of state, a Coke Stevenson appointee, refused to certify the new slate of electors, Wirtz successfully appealed to the state supreme court. Frustrated, the regulars attempted to participate in the presidential contest as a separate Democratic party, but when Senator Harry Byrd of Virginia refused their nomination, they were left without a candidate. Neo-Republicanism in Texas was down but hardly out.[95]

JOHNSON WON REELECTION EASILY. Sam Rayburn squeaked by. A few months later, on April 7, 1945, with the Red Army advancing on the outskirts of Berlin, Adolf Hitler committed suicide. Shortly thereafter, General Dwight D. Eisenhower, supreme commander of Allied forces in Europe, accepted the unconditional surrender of all German forces.

CHAPTER 9

TRUMAN AND THE COMING
OF THE COLD WAR

O N APRIL 12, 1945, JOHNSON STRODE INTO SAM
Rayburn's hideaway office hoping to find other members of
the Board of Education and have a drink. What he found was a
somber solitary speaker. FDR had just died of a heart attack in
Warm Springs, Georgia, Rayburn declared.

Like many, LBJ was overwhelmed with grief. Everyone knew that Roosevelt
was desperately ill, so ill that he had to deliver his State of the Union message
seated. But they had always thought of him as somehow immortal. It seemed
impossible that the voice of a new nationalism that had pulled the country out
of Depression and defeated Hitler was gone. Lyndon grieved for himself and for
the people. "He was just like a daddy to me always; he always talked to me just
that way," he said. "I don't know that I'd ever have come to Congress if it hadn't
been for him. But I do know I got my first great desire for public office because
of him."[1] "The people who are going to be crushed by this," he subsequently
told a reporter, "are the little guys—the guy down in my district, say, who makes
$21.50 driving a truck and has a decent house to live in now, cheap, because of
Mr. Roosevelt."[2]

Later, in a speech at the Roosevelt presidential library in Hyde Park, Johnson
would declare, "He was an Easterner and a New Yorker but the second important task he set himself was to bring to the West the electric power, the rural
electrification and the water which it needed to grow. And the West and the
South will forever love him."[3]

For days after the president's passing, Johnson would give way to fits of
weeping and long periods of withdrawal. "The day Roosevelt was buried the
whole town was just immobile, frozen, stunned, almost disbelieving, almost

angry that it could have happened to them," Lady Bird recalled. "Lyndon actually went to bed, and I myself wanted to go down and stand on the street corner and watch the cortege pass by . . . I said, 'Let's go down,' and he turned to me almost with hostility and said something about how he just didn't see why, did I think it was a show . . . I'm still sorry I didn't. So we just sat glued to the radio."[4] Back in the office Dorothy Nichols tearfully asked Lyndon, "Who do we have now?" Johnson said, "Honey, we've got Truman now . . . There is going to be the damnedest scramble for power in this man's town in the next two weeks that anybody ever saw in their lives."[5]

Johnson was right. With FDR's death and the end of the war in sight, the political waters were roiled to a degree the country had not seen since the onset of the Great Depression. The end of the war released pent-up energy and desires. Americans were tired of war, of violence, of rationing, of intrusive government; they wanted to return to normal family life and the pursuit of material gratification. The U.S. military was quickly demobilized, and a conservative coalition in Congress abruptly ended wartime controls on the economy and blocked efforts to expand the New Deal. Women and ethnic minorities, especially African Americans, anticipated that wartime opportunities would extend into the postwar period, but they were mistaken. The white, male-dominated power structure demanded that blacks, Hispanics, and women resume their normal, circumscribed roles in national life.

COMPARED TO EUROPE, life in postwar America was idyllic. As head of a delegation to investigate the status of "naval properties" in the European theater, LBJ toured Britain, the continent, and North Africa in May 1946, where he surveyed entire blocks of London in ruins and witnessed hundreds of Italians lining up for rations of a thick soup made from the garbage from the American enlisted men's mess. He flew over and landed near German cities with endless blocks of neatly bulldozed rubble, beneath which lay the stinking corpses of tens of thousands of bodies. In Rheims, the delegation met the hero of the hour, General Dwight D. Eisenhower, whom they found charming, unassuming, and anxious to please. Lyndon, however, was more impressed by a forty-five-minute audience with the pope.

According to aide Donald Cook's notes of the conversation, the pontiff and the congressman discussed "the sadness of the struggle, the terrible consequences of the war, the necessity for peace and rehabilitation and the drawing together again of mankind to the extent that it was possible." Johnson seemed totally unaware of Pius XII's dalliance with the forces of fascism. There was much sightseeing in Rome and Paris, where Lyndon and a group found time to attend the Follies. "One night we went to the Folies-Bergère and he did not like it," said Virginia "Jerry" English, a Red Cross worker and old friend of Johnson and Connally. "He [LBJ] got up and left: 'I'm going. Any of you want to stay, can.' It's burlesque, and if you don't understand the language, of which I'm not too familiar either, it's kind of dull. If you're not interested in naked women."[6]

In Naples the delegation dined with Admiral William A. Glassford, commander of Allied naval forces in the Mediterranean. He lived in a sumptuous villa overlooking the Bay. While the group feasted on assorted delicacies and the finest wine, which the admiral was having flown in from France, Johnson could see starving women and children begging in the streets. He never forgot the scene, it added a cynicism to his view of high-ranking military officers that would remain with him for the rest of his life.[7]

Before the delegation's departure for home, Lyndon met with U.S. Ambassador Jefferson Caffrey in Paris. The Europe that they had known, he warned, was being threatened by the forces of international communism from within and without. The Red Army was in physical occupation of Eastern Europe, including the eastern third of Germany and Berlin, and there were strong domestic communist parties operating in both France and Germany."[8] It was a warning that was given to the new president of the United States as well, a warning he would quickly take to heart.

BY HIS OWN ADMISSION, Harry Truman was not the best-equipped person in the country to occupy the Oval Office. He was somewhat undereducated, had no experience in foreign affairs, and had been shut out of the decision-making process by Roosevelt. He tended to analogize Kansas City politics to international affairs, seeming always to want to simplify the complex. He was given to clichés but also to plain speech, such as "The buck stops here," and he carefully cultivated the image of a no-nonsense, practical, decisive public leader. He had no sympathy for "intellectual" or "nonpolitical" liberals. As he confided to one aide, he wanted to distance himself from the "crackpots and lunatic fringe" that had unduly influenced FDR and put the country through wasteful and pointless social and economic "experiments."

Truman's emphasis on personal loyalty led to charges, partially true, of cronyism, and he was given to intemperance in public statements, occasionally lapsing into profanity when provoked. Yet, Harry Truman was a man of integrity and courage, devoted to the interests of his country. He was an experienced administrator and a fairly effective politician. He understood budgetary matters and the political process. In foreign affairs he proved, after his first two years in office, a tough-minded defender of the nation's economic and strategic interests as he perceived them.

In the domestic sphere, Truman was a moderate New Dealer, believing that the government had a responsibility to care for those unable to care for themselves and to ensure fair play in the marketplace. He was, moreover, a lifelong crusader against discrimination based on race or religion. Though initially tentative, Truman was always tough in a crisis; he had no intention of giving in to antireformists at home or would-be aggressors abroad.

WITHIN SIX MONTHS OF ROOSEVELT'S DEATH, Truman and Republicans in Congress, joined by conservative, mostly southern, Democrats, were locked in a bitter struggle over aspects of economic and social policy. In September 1945, the president called on the House and Senate to revive the reform program that had been sidetracked by World War II, including the extension of Social Security to cover farm and other workers, an increase in the minimum wage, creation of a national health insurance system, and reorganization of the executive branch. Instead, Congress rejected the president's attempt to extend the New Deal and enacted the most far-reaching antiunion bill ever passed by a national legislature.

Johnson was initially encouraged by Truman's statements and programs, if not by the man. Despite the Republican resurgence in Texas and his longing for statewide office, LBJ clung to the New Deal, continuing to believe that a commitment to social justice was at the heart of both patriotism and liberalism. Like many economists and government officials, LBJ feared that the end of hostilities and reconversion to a peacetime economy would produce a new economic downturn.

In late August 1945, he convened a meeting of businessmen, state officials, and academics in Austin to discuss ways and means for reabsorbing returning servicemen and war workers into the peacetime economy. The best way was for the private enterprise system to do the job, he told the group, but if it could not, public works and other community projects funded by taxpayers must take up the slack. "We're going to try to make our system work," Johnson said, "but we're not going back to 1933. I know that hungry, sick, jobless, illiterate men lead nations into war. I'm for local self-government, but a hungry man can't eat it. I'm for states' rights, but you can't feed that to a starving baby."[9]

Johnson voted for the Employment Act of 1946. As originally envisioned, the measure would have committed the federal government to public works and controlled inflation to hold unemployment to a certain level. To Johnson and Truman's dismay, conservatives watered the measure down, limiting it to establishing a Council of Economic Advisers to make recommendations to the president on measures to combat depression and recession. In the end liberals decided to accept this half-loaf. LBJ was a passionate supporter of the Hill-Burton Act that began with a five-year, $375 million appropriation to assist states in building hospitals. Denying that the measure was part of a nefarious scheme to nationalize the nation's hospitals and doctors, he declared in a rare speech on the floor of the House, "The fly which eats at the open privy of a slum area has no scruples about carrying polio to the child in a silk-stocking area. The health of a community can be no better than the health of those least able to afford medical and hospital care."[10]

By the fall of 1945, Roosevelt New Dealers were being pushed out of power by Truman and his lieutenants. "Truman's line is, 'Let me have men about me not too smart,' " quipped Tommy Corcoran. The last straw for the New Deal crowd was the forced resignation of Secretary of the Interior Harold Ickes. Corcoran again: "It was funny last night. I was out at Bill Douglas' with Hugo [Black], and Ickes . . . and some others and I couldn't help saying to myself,

'Well, here's a bunch of guys . . . that had the world in their hands last year, and now they're just a bunch of political refugees . . . a helpless bunch of sheep.' " Corcoran, of course, should have included himself among their number.[11] From their vantage points in Congress, Rayburn and Johnson were relatively safe from the Truman broom, but they, too, lamented the fall of the house of Roosevelt.

By February 1946, Johnson and Rayburn had become thoroughly disgusted at the administration's failure to confront and control the conservative coalition. Truman's incompetence was going to cost the Democratic party heavily at the forthcoming midterm elections, they believed. "Sam says we've got to have some brains in there," Johnson reported to Corcoran and company. "You know how bad off we are, don't you?" The New Dealers briefly plotted to have William O. Douglas, then a member of the Supreme Court, named to replace Ickes and from that position to rebuild the New Deal coalition from within. But the enigmatic Douglas proved unwilling to leave the Court. Increasingly, Tommy Corcoran, James Rowe, Abe Fortas, and Harold Ickes began to think of Lyndon Johnson as the most likely caretaker of the New Deal flame.[12]

THE BURGEONING POWER STRUGGLE in Washington focused not just on the postwar domestic agenda, but on a new international conflict that most Americans did not, at first, want to join. There was no thought of returning to isolationism; revelations concerning the Holocaust convinced Americans that the Axis powers had constituted a threat not only to Western civilization but to humanity in general. Congress and the Truman administration rejected isolationism and declared their support for a new world order based on collective security and the creation of an interdependent world economy that would bring prosperity to all. The rush to internationalism, the willingness to assume a leading role on the world stage, stemmed from the fact that many Americans believed that the defeat of the Axis signaled the beginning of a long period of peace and tranquility in international affairs. A new, global struggle with Soviet-style communism was not what most had in mind.

The Truman administration itself was initially reluctant to confront the Soviets in Central Europe and the Near East. During the first year after the war, America's 11 million–person armed forces dwindled to 2 million. Four years of propaganda had portrayed the Russians as America's gallant allies and Stalin as friendly old "Uncle Joe." Most Americans found it difficult to make the transition to thinking of the Russian leader as another Hitler bent on world domination. Not only was Truman inexperienced and uninformed concerning world affairs, but he picked as his first secretary of state James F. Byrnes, a man who was better known for his ability to deal with Congress than with experienced foreign diplomats. New Dealers like Secretary of Commerce Henry Wallace insisted that the Soviet Union, devastated by the war, was in no position to conquer Europe, much less the world. The task ahead, he argued, was to disarm Moscow's fears by extending economic aid and distancing America from Great Britain and the other declining imperial powers.

Gradually, however, as the Soviet Union consolidated its power in Eastern Europe, American attitudes began to harden. In the first week of March 1946, Truman arranged for Winston Churchill to deliver a major speech on foreign affairs at Westminster College in Missouri. With Truman on the speaker's stand, Churchill declared that an "iron curtain" had descended across Europe from the Baltic to the Adriatic. Behind that frontier, the forces of communist totalitarianism ruled. The Soviet Union was an inherently expansionist power, and the forces of international communism would sweep over Europe if the United States did not intervene, Churchill declared. In January 1947, Truman replaced Byrnes as secretary of state with General George C. Marshall, the architect of Allied victory over the Axis.

To head the newly formed policy planning staff in the department, the secretary chose George Kennan, a career diplomat and seasoned student of Russian culture and politics. In February 1947, Kennan published an article in the prestigious journal *Foreign Affairs* entitled "The Sources of Soviet Conduct." It was nothing less than a call to arms. Russia's wartime and postwar advance on Europe was simply another chapter in the never-ending story of the effort by the barbaric peoples of the Asiatic heartland to overrun Western civilization, he wrote. Because the United States was part of this civilization and because the Western democracies had been gravely weakened by the war, America would have to act. The best approach would be containment, a policy of less than war itself but of opposing force with force, of drawing a line, establishing a defensive perimeter and telling the Russians, "Thus far you shall go and no farther."

An opportunity to implement the new approach was not long in coming. In late February 1947, Great Britain informed the United States that for financial reasons it was dismantling its outposts in the eastern Mediterranean and cutting off aid to its allies in that area.

Moscow was not slow to take advantage of the resulting power vacuum. Starting in 1944, the pro-Western Greek monarchy had been fighting a bitter civil war against an insurgent force that included a significant contingent of communists and that received aid from communist Yugoslavia. In addition, Turkey was then being pressured by the Soviet Union to grant it permission to build bases on the Bosporus and elsewhere in the country. Stalin had even massed several divisions of the Red Army along the Soviet-Turkish border. Truman and Marshall quickly decided that the United States would have to assume Britain's role in the eastern Mediterranean.

On March 12, 1947, the president addressed a joint session of Congress. He asked for $400 million in emergency aid for Greece and Turkey. More important, he requested approval for Kennan's containment strategy. "It must be the policy of the United States," Truman declared, "to support free peoples who are resisting attempted subjugation by armed minorities or by outside pressure." [13] Within days, Congress had overwhelmingly approved the Truman Doctrine. The civil war in Greece ended in less than two years, and Turkey succeeded in resisting pressure from the Kremlin. America's conflict with communism was only just beginning, however. In the summer of 1947, in the Marshall Plan, Congress approved a multibillion-dollar aid program to stabilize and reconstruct the war-devastated countries of Western Europe.

INITIALLY, LBJ believed that the best approach to the international situation was continued efforts at Soviet-American cooperation. Mounting anticommunist hysteria in the United States alarmed him. Although he had been only thirteen at the time, he could remember the first Red Scare following World War I, when Attorney General A. Mitchell Palmer had led a nationwide witch hunt for "reds" and "subversives." When, in May 1946, Congress voted to convert the House Un-American Activities Committee into a permanent standing committee, LBJ was one of only eighty-one House members voting no. He vigorously supported a plan developed by financier Bernard Baruch for the international control of atomic energy. "We are here to make a choice between the quick and the dead," he said in support of Baruch's scheme.[14]

But as the Truman Administration moved toward a policy of confrontation, so did Johnson. His commitment to preparedness was a given. Between 1945 and 1948 he served on the Naval Affairs Committee, the Armed Services Committee, and the Joint Committee on Atomic Energy. He established a close relationship with Assistant Secretary of War for Air Stuart Symington and became an ardent advocate of a seventy-group air force. He railed against the "budget politicians . . . [who] would give us the second best Army, Navy and Air Force," and quoted Air Force General Ira Eaker's remark that "having the second best air force is just like having the second best poker hand."[15] In 1947 Johnson spoke in behalf of both the Truman Doctrine and the Marshall Plan.[16]

IN EMBRACING THE ROLE of cold warrior, Johnson's motives were several. Most obviously, he believed that keeping in step with rapidly hardening public opinion was crucial to his hopes for winning a seat in the Senate. In addition, preparedness was good not just for the country but for Texas and the New South. Johnson, like Richard Russell, John Sparkman, and others, saw the burgeoning military-industrial complex as a means to continue their native region's economic development.[17] Johnson was also acting on conviction and immediate historical memory. "This 'Truman Doctrine' is very serous business," he wrote in a remarkable letter to Alvin Wirtz,

> and although I regret the necessity of seeing it through I am confident [the president's] hand must be upheld and the alternative would be fatal . . . I personally feel that it is incumbent upon this rich, powerful and still free country to utilize its every resource to help the free peoples of Greece. It is not just a charitable attitude or a maternal feeling that I have toward Greece. It is my own yearning for self-preservation. Marshall very correctly states what I think our viewpoint should be toward Russia—a friendly, reasoned, patient tolerance, but "our action cannot await com-

promise through exhaustion" . . . There is no real difference to me between Nazism and Communism . . . I think, however, we should be very
careful to point out that this is only the first step, that it will continue to
cost much in money, that it is a terrific gamble that can be won only if the
Congress and the people enthusiastically and in unity support the doctrine.[18]

LBJ listened particularly to both Charles Marsh and Alvin Wirtz on domestic
issues. Here his idealism was even stronger, though it was in constant conflict
with the need to appeal to the prejudices of his constituents. His support of rural
electrification, public housing, federally funded health care, and full employment measures fit with both Marsh and Wirtz. His positions on organized labor
and civil rights bowed to the latter. As Johnson well knew, unions were key to
raising the political consciousness of manual laborers in Texas and throughout
the South, and thus to combating creeping Republicanism, bringing forth a liberal majority, and incorporating the region into the national mainstream.[19] But
the New South mix included men like George and Herman Brown and companies like Brown and Root, without whom there would be no workforces to
unionize. Paternalists to the core, George and Herman prided themselves on
being close to their workers and attentive to their needs. The issue for them was
as much control as labor costs. Antiunion they were and to the core.[20] So, too,
was Alvin Wirtz, one of the prime architects of the Lower Colorado River Authority. "The citizen who is prevented by force and violence from going upon,
using and enjoying his property in mass picketing is deprived of his civil liberties
just as certainly as a prisoner who suffers at the hands of any mob," he wrote
Johnson.[21] Most Texans agreed. Half a million had moved from farms to cities
between 1941 and 1947. By 1950, 62 percent of Texans were urban dwellers. Inhibited by antiunion laws pushed through the legislature by O'Daniel and his
successors, by the prosperity that prevailed for most white Texans, and by the
ideology of rugged individualism, unions were never able to organize more than
15 percent of the state's 2.5 million nonagricultural workers.[22]

Johnson had been outspoken in denouncing wartime strikes. He shared
Truman's perception that union wage demands were excessive and threatened
the country with runaway inflation. In 1946, Johnson voted with the administration when the president asked Congress to establish fact-finding boards to
investigate labor disputes and compel laborers to return to work while the
boards deliberated. In May of that year, when a series of railroad strikes threatened to shut down the nation's transportation system and interrupt the flow of
life-saving goods to war-devastated Europe, Truman asked for permission to
draft strikers. Over the outraged protests of liberals, Johnson voted for the measure. He resisted efforts by the Communications Workers of America to unionize KTBC, pointing out that wages there were double the national minimum.[23]
He would have liked to believe that exercise of the franchise by manual laborers
was a more powerful means to self-advancement than unions and strikes, and

yet he knew better. Throughout the 1940s and 1950s, political expediency, paternalism, and a distaste for confrontation would place him on the side of those seeking to restrict the powers that labor had gained during the 1930s.

CIVIL RIGHTS WAS EVEN MORE OF A PROBLEM for Johnson than workers' rights. World War II had created a rising level of expectations among African Americans. During the war, labor shortages, coupled with pressure from civil rights activists and certain unions, had increased blacks' share of defense jobs from 3 to 8 percent. A million African American soldiers had fought to preserve democracy in Europe and the Pacific, and now they were determined to fight for full citizenship under the law and equality of opportunity at home. "I spent four years in the Army to free a bunch of Frenchmen and Dutchmen, and I'm hanged if I'm going to let the Alabama version of the Germans kick me around when I'm back home," declared one black veteran.[24]

The particular targets of civil rights organizations such as the NAACP and the Committee on Racial Equality (CORE), formed in 1942 (the name changed to Congress of Racial Equality in 1944), were discrimination in employment, disfranchisement through the poll tax and white primary, and terrorism through beatings, burnings, and lynchings.

Nonviolent black activists attacked racial barriers in both North and South. In Washington, D.C., Patricia Harris led the first sit-in to protest segregation and exclusion in public facilities. CORE staged a "freedom ride" to contest discrimination in interstate transport. CORE members also mounted lunch counter sit-ins in New York, New Jersey, and other northern states. The demonstrators were frequently beaten and arrested, but a growing number of public restaurants stopped segregating blacks and whites. In the South, African American veterans headed straight for their local voter registration offices. Most were threatened; many were beaten; some were murdered. In Atlanta, eighteen thousand blacks registered to vote, and in Winston-Salem, North Carolina, three thousand signed up. In these two cities and in Greensboro, North Carolina, embryonic black political machines began to emerge. Altogether, the number of blacks registered to vote in the South increased from 2 percent in 1940 to 12 percent in 1947, yet white segregationists continued to control much of the South, and race riots erupted in cities throughout the country.

LBJ was intensely aware of the difficulties black Americans faced in the first half of the twentieth century. Lady Bird's claim that "Lyndon, as a boy, did not see a Black person in the town where he grew up" is somewhat misleading.[25] The Peyton Colony, a community of several hundred black farmers, descendents of freed slaves, was located outside of Blanco. Austin boasted a sizable black population. One of Lyndon's Austin playmates remembers the two of them engaging in a popular pastime: chasing "nigger" kids away from Barton Springs, a popular swimming hole. Washington County, situated on the eastern end of the Tenth District, boasted a large black population.

Throughout his early public career, Johnson rubbed shoulders with a number of southern white radicals who were extremely advanced in their views on racial justice: Aubrey Williams, Maury Maverick, Clifford and Virginia Durr, and Charles Marsh.[26] But for all their enlightenment, these people were part of the elite, as Johnson was; they were paternalists. Moreover, the progressive businessmen on whom Johnson, Texas, and the New South were dependent were still profoundly conservative. "It is my opinion," Alvin Wirtz said to Johnson, "that people who seek to eradicate racial and religious prejudice by legislation are profoundly unwise. Legislation on racial and religious subjects only adds fuel to the flames. Racial prejudice was never so violent in the South as when Thaddeus Stevens [Civil War and Reconstruction–era congressman from Pennsylvania] and his brand of radicals in Congress and the Carpetbaggers in the South sought to legislate out of existence all prejudice and discrimination."[27] The Fair Employment Practices Commission (a federal agency proposed by liberals to further the cause of equality of opportunity) was an unconstitutional attempt to interfere with the sanctity of contract: "I have as much right to prefer a white secretary as Clark Foreman has to [prefer] a Negro," exclaimed the senator. Wirtz had repeatedly denounced the KKK and filed suit against its members during the 1920s, and he found the poll tax indefensible. Yet he did not like federal interference in state matters, and he feared that the Texas regulars would couple the race issue with red baiting and ride a red-and-black scare into power in 1946 and 1948.[28]

At the core of LBJ's attitude toward African Americans, a floor beneath which he would not sink, was a belief that blacks must be part of the body politic. Lady Bird remembered him campaigning in Washington and Lee Counties during the 1937 congressional contest. "He was talking to a crowd," she said, "so when he finished speaking, he began to go around and shake hands with everybody who was about—the heavily armed men, a few women, and out on the outskirts of the crowd, some black people. And he went around and he was shaking hands with all the black people on the edge of the crowd and later on, quietly, his manager for that county came up to him and said, 'Lyndon, I don't think you better do that next time. I think you're gonna offend some of the strongest people in this section.' And Lyndon made him an unprovoking answer as well as he could and went right on doing it."[29]

Beyond enfranchisement and equal access to government programs, however, the Lyndon Johnson of the 1940s was unwilling to go. During 1945–1946 he consistently voted with southern opponents of antilynching, anti–poll tax, and fair employment practices legislation. He claimed that he was acting not against blacks but for states' rights. He argued in private that there was nothing more useless than a politically dead liberal, citing Maury Maverick.[30] Besides, he argued, by going along with the Dixie association in Congress, he could win their support for more important bread-and-butter issues which were of vast importance to blacks. It should be noted that such southern progressives as J. William Fulbright also voted consistently against antilynching and anti–poll tax legislation, even going so far as to oppose Aubrey Williams's confirmation as head of the Rural Electrification Administration.[31]

As far as Johnson's personal feelings toward race were concerned, the signals are mixed. Robert Parker, a black sharecropper's son who worked occasionally for the Johnsons when they were giving dinner parties in Washington, claimed that LBJ "niggered" him unmercifully whenever other white southern racists were present. He cited the notorious Senator Theodore G. Bilbo of Mississippi as an example. Yet, there is no evidence that Bilbo, a crude boor as well as a racist, was ever a guest in any of the Johnson homes. Not only would Rowe, Corcoran, Fortas, and other of LBJ's New Deal cronies have been appalled, so would people like Richard Russell. Homer Thornberry, then a young politico at the University of Texas, recalled visiting Johnson in Washington when he was a congressman. On a streetcar ride to the Capitol, Johnson got up and offered his seat to a Negro woman who would otherwise have had to stand.[32] Black Congressman Adam Clayton Powell thought enough of LBJ to come to Texas and campaign for him in his congressional races. "Johnson is not a hater," Powell told Austin's black community.[33]

Of one thing Johnson was sure: if some degree of justice and opportunity were not offered to blacks, democracy and even the republic itself might not survive. In March 1948, when Horace Busby went to Washington to work for Johnson, they had an interesting opening conversation. "He said, 'You ought to know how I feel about everything.' And he toured the world and talked a lot about the prospects of war [with the Soviet Union], which was on everybody's mind . . . and then finally he said . . . 'And then there are the Negroes . . . They fought the war; they filled up the war plants, they built the bombers . . . And now they're back and they're not going to take this shit that we give them much longer' . . . The point of it was that we were in a race against time, and he said 'I hope we can, but I'm not sure we can get this system to respond on this. If we don't do it, blood will run in the streets.' "[34]

LYNDON CONTINUED TO SEE ALICE GLASS during the two years following the end of the war. One Saturday morning in the fall of 1945, he stopped by the apartment of Waddie Bullion, his friend and the family accountant. Bullion was still on duty with the navy, but his wife, sister-in-law, and infant son were there. Johnson had just dropped off his car for John and Nellie Connally, who lived down the hall, to use for the day. As Lyndon played with baby John, he explained unabashedly to the women how he was going to spend the day. Alice Glass was going to pick him up and they were going to enjoy each other's company. Waddie's wife, who knew who Alice was and about the affair, was appalled, but recalled that Johnson was almost aglow with anticipation.[35]

He also continued to coddle Sam Houston, who had taken to drinking himself into unconsciousness and running up hotel bills again.[36] "We do not see how a man in your brother's position can possibly afford to allow a matter of this kind to stand against his record," one creditor wrote to LBJ.[37] He continued to send money not only to Sam Houston but also to the wife and child whom his brother had abandoned.[38]

As THE 1946 CAMPAIGN SEASON APPROACHED, Johnson seemed unusually subdued. Harold Ickes observed that "he is toning down a bit. He is not so young and exuberant, as he used to be." Johnson would not have disagreed. "I have found that age has probably mellowed me some," he wrote Wirtz, "because in my younger days I didn't hesitate to charge hell with a bucket of water or ask a man to move out of his own house if it would help me. Now I am a little more considerate and those things are a little more distasteful to me."[39]

In fact, a series of illnesses, rather than age, probably had more to do with LBJ's "mellowness." In February 1946 he was hospitalized with yet another bout of pneumonia. Within a month of his release he had developed kidney stones. "I am not sure the kidney stone has been born yet," he wrote Wirtz, "but I am expecting the X-rays to show two possible stones and now they can't find any but they think maybe it could have gone into the bladder."[40] Despite allusions to the contrary, however, Johnson had no intention of retiring from public life.

John Connally was of the opinion that his boss ought to run for governor of Texas, in part because he coveted Johnson's congressional seat. During the closing months of 1945, Connally secured agreement from Homer Rainey, Buford Jester, state Attorney General Grover Sellers, and other potential candidates for the Democratic nomination that they would not run if Lyndon decided to seek the office. "When he got all this worked out and presented it to the Congressman," Horace Busby said, "the Congressman said he had absolutely no interest in the ticky little things that governors did. He wasn't interested in pardons, he wasn't interested in highway contract-letting, he wasn't interested in textbook contracts . . . they were all primitive and too conservative for him around there . . . The future lay in what people did in Washington." Connally stomped out, and the two did not speak for several weeks.[41]

To challenge Johnson in 1946, the regulars put forward Hardy Hollers, a forty-five-year-old attorney and decorated army colonel. In addition to a distinguished war record, Hollers could boast of having assisted Supreme Court Justice Robert Jackson in his prosecutorial activities at the Nuremberg war crimes trials. Over the next ten weeks, he and his handlers charged Johnson with virtually every kind of political and ethical wrongdoing imaginable. Hollers continually compared his extended service in combat to LBJ's single mission. He accused Johnson of using his position to enrich himself and his friends. He charged that Brown and Root had grown rich and fat on government wartime contracts secured for them by their congressman and that they had allegedly not only financed Johnson's political career but also enriched him personally.

Hollers also declared in speeches and newspaper interviews that his opponent had used improper influence with the FCC to secure broadcast business for his wife and friends. He made much of the fact that Lyndon and Lady Bird had acquired a "luxurious" duplex on Dillman Street in Austin from W. S. Bellows, a Brown and Root partner, and he insisted that Johnson's henchmen had offered him "a fat government job" if he would drop out of the race.[42]

Johnson, Wirtz, and Connally, who, mollified, had agreed to be campaign manager, decided that they would have to answer Hollers charge by charge. Johnson called a mass meeting for Wooldridge Park in downtown Austin and invited the media to come and pay close attention. With Lady Bird sitting on the dais at a desk piled high with tax records and canceled checks, Johnson dared the opposition to show that he had bribed, been bribed, or profited personally from his office. Neither he nor his friends had offered Hollers a job in the government. As for the house on Dillman (built by Bellows for his mistress, who committed suicide in 1943), he and Lady Bird had paid $15,490 in cash for the duplex and he had the canceled check to prove it. From there, Johnson departed for an intensive automobile canvass of the Tenth District.

"I had been working at the Austin papers for three years in 1946," newspaperwoman Margaret Mayer recalled. "One morning Buck Hood [editor of the *Austin American*] told me to bring a notebook and come with him. We drove out to 1901 Dillman and we went upstairs . . . There in the living room, sitting around mostly in yard chairs, because I think they hadn't furnished the apartment yet . . . were some ten men, as I recall. Johnson was lying on a couch. He was dressed or undressed as the case may be in a pair of shorts . . . They were just plain old boxer shorts. He was unfazed by my walking in. I was the only woman there."[43] The meeting was to plan "this ten-day whirlwind campaign with which he was going to beat Hardy Hollers."

Mayer covered the campaign. Each morning at the crack of dawn, the un–air conditioned Ford would set out with her in the back seat and Lyndon in the front, beside the driver. She was expected not only to write the day's story but to act as the candidate's valet. "Your job was not just to follow him around and report for the paper," she recalled. "You also took care of his Stetson, because he had two. He would wear his good one in the car. When he got out at the courthouse square you were supposed to hand him the worn one, the dirty one . . . You also kind of looked after his fresh suits, because he would change during the day, en route, at least once, and his throat lozenges and hand cream . . . You know, his hand would get raw."[44]

Johnson promised the good life for the common man and lambasted big oil. A popular song of the day was "Did You Ever See a Dream Walking?" LBJ would have a musical group sing the song and then he would begin to talk about his dream of a world of full employment, adequate housing, educational opportunity for all, and an end to poverty.[45]

As a springboard for a future Senate race, or to ensure that he had no opposition in 1948, Johnson wanted to win big. "I would like to get a landslide vote this time and thereby obviate the necessity of having to put up with any more Hollers[es] two years from now," he wrote Jim Rowe.[46] Toward the end of the campaign, Connally and his lieutenants put together "Johnson's Hill Billy Boys," a four-piece band that warmed up the candidate's evening crowds and played background for movie star Gene Autry, who came from California to lend support; Johnson had helped the movie star get into the Air Transport Command at the beginning of the war and had facilitated his discharge at the end. Autry sang his signature "Back in the Saddle Again," ending with the exhortation, "Let's put my friend Lyndon back in the saddle again, because that's where he belongs."[47]

Another come-on used by the Johnson campaign was to offer ice-cold free watermelon. On one occasion, the tactic backfired; a group of boys got into a watermelon rind fight right in front of the platform while the candidate was speaking. Forgetting to cover his microphone he yelled, "John, Jake, Joe, somebody, get those godamned kids out from in front of here . . . Watch out, Gene, one of them is going to hit you!"[48] For Washington County's heavily German American population, the Johnson forces carried the day by persuading Anheuser-Busch to supply free beer for campaign rallies.[49]

When the final vote was in, Johnson had bested Hollers by better than two and a half to one: 42,672 to 17,628. He carried all ten counties, even Washington. Nevertheless, Johnson complained of feeling beat up by the campaign. The 1946 election made him aware of his strengths and caused him to think of the Senate once again, but it also alerted him to the implacable hostility toward him by the state's most powerful conservatives.[50]

LADY BIRD had become pregnant again in 1945, but it turned out to be a tubal pregnancy, a condition from which her mother had suffered. It almost killed Lady Bird, too. Sometime during the first trimester, she began hemorrhaging. Lyndon was not home. Desperate with pain, she called her doctor, who sent an ambulance. "I knew that I was in a life-threatening situation," she recalled. "When they were putting me in the ambulance, I remember that I was glad that Lyndon and I were well off, that we had enough money, and wondered what it would be like to be that sick without any money at all."[51] An aide finally located Lyndon and he rushed to the hospital. The doctor informed him that his wife was losing a lot of blood and the choice basically was between saving mother or saving child. Lyndon did not hesitate. Horace Busby, then a brand-new staffer, recalled, "The idea of losing her filled him with panic. He told them to do whatever was necessary to save Bird."[52]

Happily, on July 2, 1947, Lady Bird gave birth to their second daughter, Lucy Baines. This, too, had been a difficult pregnancy. When at long last the doctor had the baby in his arms, Lady Bird remembered him saying, "I never thought I'd see you."[53] Apparently, she and Lyndon never considered her side of the family in the selection of first names. Lucy was named for Lucia, Lyndon's youngest sister and Lady Bird's favorite among his siblings.[54]

All the while Lyndon and Lady Bird were heading up a second family, the staff of KTBC and their spouses. It was at the radio station in Austin that Johnsonian paternalism appeared in its purest form. There were advantages to being a member of the family, but there was also a price to pay. The first benefit was security; employees were rarely fired, there were health insurance and a profit and stock sharing plan, and the Johnsons extended aid and sympathy that was at times heroic. Joe Phipps, who had signed on as morning announcer in late 1945, recalled that when the daughter of an employee was diagnosed with throat cancer, the congressman sprang into action: " 'Get me Jim Cain at Mayo's,' he orders the operator. 'We've got this girl down here, maybe dying,' he tells his personal physician. 'A monster's in her throat. Eating her up. Cancer . . . thyroid cancer . . . That's what the little bastard's eating on, her thyroid. You've got to cure her.' He listens, finally breaking in, 'The family doesn't have that kind of money. Hell, you know that. No family has that kind of money. They'll pay all they can. I'll give a little. You'll give a little . . . Your job is the easy one. You just have to cure her. She has the hard job. She has to go on living.' " [55]

On the debit side, no one at KTBC was allowed any freedom of expression; the development of radio "personalities" was verboten. Operational manuals governed every aspect of the day's work. Employees, including station manager Jesse Kellam, cleaned toilets until finally LBJ was prevailed upon to hire part-time janitorial help. Johnson advised female employees on matters of dress, when to have babies, and whom to choose as mates.

At the same time, young men on the staff were pressured to produce as many children as quickly as possible. "If three months went by after the wedding and Johnson could not detect the beginnings of abdominal swelling," Phipps said, he would grow almost distraught. Sensing a romantic void, he would approach the new bridegroom, press a $20 bill into his hand, and tell him, "Take your wife out to dinner. Candlelight. Soft music. Take her dancing. Give her a night of real romance. Soften her up. Get her to feeling 'dreamy.' Be gentle. Show how much you love her. Prove you're a man. I want a baby out of this." If males were among the subsequent offspring, at least one was expected to be named Lyndon. He could be brutal to Kellam, a spare, neatly dressed, prematurely gray man. Phipps recalled that an obviously angry Johnson would periodically storm into the manager's office, located on the first floor of the Brown Building. "Let's go for a walk," he would tell Kellam. "An hour or so later," Phipps recalled, "Kellam would return, red-eyed, then slump down at his desk as if his world had collapsed. His eyes would be wet. He'd cover them . . . I came to fear that internally KTBC's general manager was a mess." [56] The highlight of the year was the station Christmas party, at which Lyndon and Lady Bird presided, handing out presents, Lyndon delivering an inspirational pep talk. His remarks were partly thankful, partly self-serving, punctuated with guilt trips and ending with an appeal to loyalty.

IT HAD BECOME CLEAR that if LBJ wanted to enter the U.S. Senate it would have to be by way of Pappy Lee O'Daniel's seat. The thought of running again for the upper house filled him with anxiety. He would have to relinquish his congressional position and risk sacrificing his entire political career. "I just could not bear the thought of losing everything," he later told an interviewer.[57] The political tea leaves were extraordinarily difficult to read in 1948.

Out of the White House since 1932, the Republicans looked forward to the election of 1948 with a great deal of anticipation. Harry Truman's modest physical appearance, his lack of formal education, his failure to get his program through Congress, and his occasional public profanity combined to reinforce the popular notion that he was not fit to govern. The conservative wing of the party preferred Senator Robert Taft of Ohio, but the feeling among the moderate majority was that he was too austere and would prove to be a poor campaigner. Party leaders approached the hero of Normandy, Dwight D. Eisenhower, but he played coy. Thus it was that the Republicans turned to the man who had led them to defeat in 1944, Governor Thomas E. Dewey of New York. Dewey had compiled a progressive record as governor and firmly supported the policy of containment.

The Democratic party, meanwhile, was torn apart by internal disputes. Leading the charge against Truman and the Democratic establishment was former Secretary of Agriculture and Vice President Henry A. Wallace. He was the self-appointed champion of the blue-collar worker and small farmer, both black and white. Wallace charged that the Democratic party had been taken over by big business and southern segregationists. The Iowan also vehemently attacked the Truman administration's decision to get tough with the Soviet Union. In 1947, he organized the Progressive Citizens of America and notified the world that he would run on a third-party ticket. Democratic liberals, newly organized into the Americans for Democratic Action, maneuvered desperately to avoid choosing between Wallace and Truman. The two approached General Eisenhower, but he rebuffed them.

To make matters worse, southern Democrats were up in arms over the president's civil rights program. Truman had been a staunch opponent of the Ku Klux Klan in Missouri, and in 1947, at his behest, a prestigious commission had produced a study of race relations in America entitled *To Secure These Rights*. It was a searing indictment of segregation and discrimination and a resounding call for federal action to ensure that African Americans were accorded their constitutional rights. Truman enthusiastically endorsed its findings and recommendations.

When the Democratic Convention assembled in Philadelphia in July, the long-anticipated fight between liberals, headed by Mayor Hubert Humphrey of Minneapolis and the conservative, southern wing of the party, erupted. After a bitter floor fight, the convention adopted a civil rights plank demanding a Fair Employment Practices Commission and federal antilynching and anti–poll tax legislation. Delegates from Dixie made good on their promise to bolt if the party made a commitment to civil rights and immediately walked out of the convention. A few days later, the exhausted rump nominated Truman, largely because, a number of journalists observed, they had no other choice.

Meanwhile, disgruntled southern Democrats gathered in Birmingham, Alabama, waved Confederate flags, paid homage to Jefferson Davis, and founded the States Rights Democratic party. The Dixiecrats, as the southern dissidents were subsequently labeled, nominated South Carolina Governor J. Strom Thurmond for president. The segregationists hoped that they could capture enough electoral votes to throw the election into the House of Representatives, where they might strike a sectional bargain that would preserve their beloved racial system. "The Dixiecrat defection marked the exit of the South from the New Deal coalition," historian Kerry Frederickson writes, "and the reorientation of the national party toward its more liberal wing . . . By breaking with the Democratic party, the Dixiecrat movement demonstrated to conservative Southerners that allegiance to one party was 'neither necessary nor beneficial' and thus served as the crossover point for many southern voters in their move from the Democratic to the Republican column." [58]

In other words, 1948 marked the beginning of a two-party system in the South and a way station in the gradual transformation of that region into a Republican stronghold. Ironically, no one would do more to accelerate that trend than Lyndon Johnson.

CHAPTER 10

COKE

B Y 1948, SENATOR PAPPY O'DANIEL'S TIME HAD passed. His attacks on labor unions as bastions of communism and his continuing isolationism had made him a pariah in the national Democratic party, and several shady business deals had compromised his reputation as a man of the people. Johnson's real competition would lie elsewhere, from "Calculatin" Coke Stevenson, who was then governor. "Taking on Coke Stevenson was a very tricky thing to do," Jake Pickle recalled. "He was very popular in Texas. One of those strong, silent cowboy types. A typical rancher." Stevenson was an outspoken champion of states' rights, local control, and a balanced budget. "He could be the taciturn, wise, careful, prudent . . . public servant. That was his approach, and that was his philosophy too."[1]

Wartime prosperity had enhanced his reputation as state revenues had risen without any new taxes. Stevenson entered office with a deficit and left with a surplus. He was antiunion, anti-Roosevelt, and anti–civil rights. He was also appealingly direct. In 1947 he was interviewed by Johns Gunther for *Inside U.S.A.* Asked to enumerate his most significant decisions, Coke, puffing on his pipe, replied, "Never had any." In announcing his candidacy for the Senate, Stevenson proclaimed that he would ensure "the complete destruction of the Communist movement in this country."[2] To the bankers, insurance executives, and oil barons of Dallas, Fort Worth, and Houston, he was entirely safe.

Shortly after Coke announced, George B. Peddy, a Houston attorney who had gained something of a statewide reputation fighting the Ku Klux Klan, joined the fray. One poll indicated that 53 percent of qualified voters favored Coke. But in the same survey, 45 percent said that they preferred experience in Congress, compared to 27 percent who preferred experience as governor as a qualification for the Senate. Moreover, 85 percent said that they wanted the successful candidate not to be over fifty. Stevenson was coming up on his sixtieth birthday and Johnson his fortieth.[3]

As LBJ pondered his decision, Stevenson, through an intermediary, contacted the Brown brothers and others who had funded Johnson's 1941 campaign. The message was that Coke liked Johnson but that he stood almost no chance of winning. If the businessman in question contributed once again to a Johnson campaign, he would be pouring his money down the drain. Moreover, the congressman, who had brought in so many government contracts, would lose his seat. Why not back Coke, who would also serve their interests, and convince Lyndon to stay in Congress?[4]

On May 11, 1948, Johnson met with a group of his advisers in the backyard of the house on Dillman Street. The group included John Connally, Willard Wirtz, Claude Wild (who had had an offer to manage the Peddy campaign), Joe Kilgore, Buck Hood, Gordon Fulcher, Tom Miller, and Jake Pickle. There were a number of compelling reasons for the congressman to challenge Coke. The Dixiecrat revolt was looming, and Texas and the South desperately needed a progressive voice, a Roosevelt heir in the Senate and in the top echelons of the party.[5] Coke was the man who had fired Homer Rainey, the liberal president of the University of Texas who had challenged the regents over an anticommunist loyalty oath, and his racist views were so deeply held that he made no effort to conceal them.[6] A number of those present represented the large group of young veterans who were tired of the political establishment. "The thirties were not—in Texas they were not desperately poor times," said Horace Busby, "but they were stagnant times. You couldn't start a business without basically the consent of the banking community . . . The New Deal was bad in the eyes of such people because it was letting people who should not do things, do things. And I don't mean poor people, but people who should not be Chevrolet dealers were becoming Chevrolet dealers . . . This was an insurrection."[7]

As a young man on the make and a veteran of sorts, Johnson could pose as leader of this movement. But at the gathering, all the congressman could think of was the negatives. Polls still showed Stevenson's lead to be three to one. Johnson was obsessed with the fact that he was about to turn forty; he saw his life flashing before his eyes. "He kept raising objections," Connally recalled, "then declared he wasn't going to run. We agreed. That was the only way to deal with him when he was in one of those moods. There was a chorus of voices: 'Congressman, that's really the right decision. We really think you ought to step aside and let us put forward a younger man who can carry on this great tradition.' " He asked who they had in mind. John Connally, one said. "Well, just a minute. Let me think about this a little bit."[8]

The next morning the group met again. A spokesman asked Johnson to help them elect Connally and began discussing campaign plans. His mood darkening, Johnson called the gathering to order. He should have an announcement late in the day, he said, and walked out. That afternoon, from the penthouse at the Driskill, LBJ declared his candidacy. He had actually won in 1941, he told the packed press conference, but, like a good sport, had chosen not to challenge the result. He would have run again in 1942, but the war had intervened. At fifty-nine, Coke Stevenson was too old, he said. "I believe our senator should be young enough to have energy for the work . . . You've been fed up with has-beens."[9]

In February 1942, Johnson had hired Horace Busby as his staff intellectual. Busby, a journalism graduate from UT, had gained some degree of notoriety when, as editor of the *Daily Texan,* he had defended Rainey in his struggle with the Board of Regents and Governor Stevenson. A small, intense young man, Busby was the classic Texas intellectual: brilliant, imaginative, informed, simultaneously cynical and naïve, urbane but with a streak of populism.

For the rest of LBJ's public life, Busby would move in and out of his inner circle, working furiously to help Johnson reconcile his drive for power with his lofty goals, and then retiring for a time, exhausted by his boss's demands and idiosyncrasies. The evening after he announced, Johnson called the Washington office and asked to talk to Busby. "He came on the phone laughing," the aide later recalled, "and said, 'Well, Judge Busby'—the 'Judge Busby' was something that he called me—'The monkey's climbed the pole' [from the saying, 'If a monkey climbs a pole, he's going to show his ass']. And it was a fatalistic sort of laugh and comment, because he was being fatalistic about the fact that he had probably ended his career. He said, 'Do you think we're going to make it?' and I said, 'No, sir. I don't think that's in the cards.' He said, 'Well, do you want to try?' And I said, 'Oh, yes, sure, I want to try real hard.' "[10] At Johnson's insistence, Busby got off the phone, packed his bags—he was staying, not surprisingly, in the Dodge Hotel—got in his car, and headed for Texas.

Busby arrived in Austin around noon, two days later. He went to campaign headquarters, but no one was around. Gradually Connally, Wild, and others began to drift back from lunch. Where was the congressman? Busby asked. They had no idea, they said, and retired to meet with other staffers. Puzzled, Busby began to wander around. Introducing himself to the switchboard operator, he learned that Johnson had left a message for him. He was to come to the house on Dillman Street as soon as he got in. Lyndon and Lady Bird occupied the main apartment, which included the entire second floor. The Connallys lived in a smaller apartment below. The upstairs included a spacious living room–dining room with a kitchen on one end and a bedroom on the other. A large picture window overlooked Westlake Hills.

Busby rang the doorbell, but no one answered. He entered anyway, and there in the half-light, reclining on a couch in his shirt sleeves was Lyndon. He was smoking, using the long ivory cigarette holder with which he could eject cigarette butts up to ten feet away. The ash tray was full. Johnson just nodded. Busby sat down. Minutes passed. Cigarette butts were periodically ejected. An hour passed. Finally, LBJ said in a very low voice, "Do you think we have a chance?" Busby began waffling, but Johnson cut him off. " 'I asked you, do you think I have a chance?' I knew it was a yes or no question, so I said, 'No.' That's

good; I'd passed . . . I had not been unrealistic . . . he liked that. And he continued to lie there." The two men sat in silence. The phones—there were several
on thirty-foot cords—began to ring. One rang a dozen times, quit, and then
began ringing again. "He whispered to me as though the phone could hear us,"
Busby remembered. "He said, 'that's them' . . . I mouthed back to him, 'Who?
Who is them?' And he said whispering, 'Headquarters.' And he was careful not
to speak while the phone was ringing, as though that was a microphone."

The phone rang again in the apartment; this time Johnson got up and jerked
the cord out of the wall. He suddenly became animated. "He was talking about
the people, serving the people, what the people wanted," Busby recalled. "And
he got off on Roosevelt, that Roosevelt was the man that had the vision, and
Roosevelt was the man that had the feeling for people and that we didn't have
that kind of leadership." The country must have someone who cared about the
people, who knew about them, Johnson declared. He then began reciting large
portions of FDR's most famous speeches. All the while he was smoking and
ejecting the butts, sometimes from amazing distances, into an ash tray on the
coffee table.[11] The next day, LBJ appeared at headquarters, and the campaign was
off and running.

HOW TO DEFINE THE JOHNSON CANDIDACY? It was true that Texas
seemed in a conservative mood, tired of reform, frustrated with the federal bureaucracy, anxious to be left alone to drink beer, pray, procreate, and make some
money. Stevenson seemed their ideal representative, an antigovernment advocate of states' rights and a neo-isolationist. Yet, LBJ was of the opinion then and
later that Texans were more like other Americans than not. They had benefited
enormously from government programs during the New Deal and World War
II. They certainly desired no rollback of Social Security or government-insured,
low-interest loans. They felt threatened by godless communism and nuclear
annihilation, although it would be two years before the Soviets exploded their
first nuclear device.

As he had in the past, LBJ would run as a national candidate, the would-be
representative of a people who were not afraid of modernity, who favored
equality of opportunity if not condition, who, in their own interest and that of
the rest of the world, were ready to shoulder the burdens of collective security.
"I believe that we can have peace, progress and prosperity through a central government while my opponent cannot see further than the county courthouse,"
he would tell an audience in Denton. "I do not believe the courthouse can handle a 70-group air force. I do not believe you can halt hoof and mouth disease by
applying to the Commissioners Court. I do not believe the Courthouse can
build more REA [Rural Electrification Administration] projects . . . It is less
costly to prepare and make our nation so strong that no other nation will dare
jump on us than it is to have another war."[12]

He would ensure that Texas would not be relegated to the political and economic backwater, like states such as Arkansas and New Mexico. Such a posture

would appeal to the burgeoning white-collar middle class in Texas and to the tens of thousands of veterans who wanted to become part of the establishment.[13]

Johnson told the staff to prepare a fourteen-point program. "Worst thing ever happened to this country was those sixty-year-old senators, smelling of rat piss, doing Number One on Woodrow Wilson's Fourteen points," he declared.[14] The second order of business at these initial planning sessions was to select a candidate to run for Johnson's congressional seat. LBJ used the situation to put John Connally in his place. Creekmore Fath, a young Austin attorney, was considered but rejected as too independent for Johnson's taste. He had Connally ask Ralph Yarborough, a former assistant state attorney general and district judge who had just returned from military service in Japan, but he was not interested. After a number of other possibilities were explored with no success, Connally said, "I guess there's just little old me to serve up as the sacrificial lamb." Johnson exploded. "Get it out of your head, John. You'd be dead meat when they start zeroing in on you as 'Lyndon's boy.' " The congressman finally settled on Jake Pickle, another member of his staff, who he thought would avoid the "Lyndon's boy" tag. Connally did not even win the consolation prize of campaign manager. He would do the actual work, but Claude Wild would receive the title.[15]

The nerve center of the '48 campaign was the Hancock House, a two-storey mansion, tending toward decay, situated at the corner of 8th and Lavaca across from the U.S. Courthouse. In its day it had been a symbol of wealth in Austin, with its colonnaded veranda and green-shuttered windows. It was still an imposing structure. For the next five months, through two primaries and various legal wranglings, the building would be throbbing with activity as secretaries staffed a switchboard, managers from each of Texas's twenty-three congressional districts came and went, journalists hovered, waiting for the latest story, speechwriters wrote, and graphic designers turned out pamphlets.[16] "That old house sheltered us for a time as we raced and lumbered and laughed and shouted through it," campaign worker Joe Phipps remembered, "making it our headquarters for a volunteer crusade we saw sweeping the state . . . The once-upon-a-time, long-ago-rich-man's home became the center of our existence." [17]

There was a second headquarters that functioned intermittently; the backyard of the Dillman Street house. The staff found a rural telephone box and nailed it to a tree. It would shelter a phone connected to a jack in the house by a long cord. "If [LBJ] needed the phone, he just reached up and opened the mail box," Willard Deason recalled. It was here that Johnson frequently met with his brain and money trust: Alvin Wirtz, Charles Marsh, the Brown brothers, Tom Miller, and Roy Hofheinz of Houston.[18]

The campaign was set to open Saturday night, May 22, in Wooldridge Park. Johnson and his lieutenants planned every move, every pause, every phrase. Even Rebekah was brought in to Hancock House to give her input. During a break in LBJ's almost constant stream of instructions, she said, "There's a grammar error here, Son." Johnson turned on her, "Goddamnit it, Mama, I pay people to correct the grammar. You just put in the Bible verses. That's your job." [19]

On the afternoon of the big event, Paul Bolton, a KTBC staffer and speechwriter, went with fellow campaign worker Warren Woodward to Dillman Street to deliver a final draft of the address. They met Dr. William Morgan, the Johnson family physician, coming down the stairs. "Who's sick?" Woodward asked. The congressman, Morgan replied. He had a kidney stone that would not pass, and he had developed an infection. There were chills, fever, and excruciating pain. Morgan, who had given Johnson several injections, said that he did not see how a human being could function under those circumstances. Bolton and Woodward found LBJ in the bedroom, doubled over with pain, and Lady Bird helping him try to dress. He was determined to go on, he said. "At the appointed time, the Johnson car pulled up on the south side of the block near the public library," Woodward recalled, "and Mr. Johnson got out and was all dressed up; he looked beautiful in his well-tailored clothes . . . He ran to the center stage after his introduction, made his speech without a single hitch, and got a huge ovation from the crowd." He advocated preparedness, hailed the Truman Doctrine and Marshall Plan, railed against the abuse of big business and big labor and—true to form at this stage in his career—denounced the civil rights movement as "a farce and a sham—an effort to set up a police state in the guise of liberty." [20] After the speech, LBJ somehow managed to shake hands with the vast majority of a crowd estimated at more than two thousand.

The next morning, accompanied by Woodward and Bolton, Johnson took a Pioneer Airlines flight for Amarillo, stopping at San Angelo, Abilene, and Lubbock to phone local journalists and politicians. The candidate was sweating and in obvious discomfort, but insisted that he would pass his stone as he had passed previous ones. In Amarillo, he checked into the old Herring Hotel, and Woodward continued to ply him with aspirin. It was already hot in Texas, but Johnson seemed to be perspiring continuously and excessively. Woodward made a note to tell Zephyr Wright, the Johnsons' maid, to send more shirts; at this rate, the candidate would go through six or seven a day.

Tuesday afternoon, the trio boarded the train for Dallas, where Johnson was to meet with Secretary of the Air Force Stuart Symington to discuss making Sheppard Air Force Base a permanent installation. The train did not leave for Dallas until ten at night. LBJ, suffering alternately from bone-rattling chills and feverish sweats, spent the evening in bed. He and Woodward had the two bottom berths in an open Pullman. As the night wore on, Johnson moved in and out of delirium. When fever struck, he would make Woodward and the porter open his window. He would doze until the chills came, when he would cry out for blankets. "Finally, one time he asked me to get in the berth with him," Woodward said, "and I actually got in the berth with him on two occasions that night to try to give some heat from my body over to his and try to keep him warm." [21] After the train pulled into Dallas, Woodward got Johnson dressed, hailed a taxi, and conveyed his boss to the Baker Hotel. Johnson refused to let anyone call a doctor. He was still convinced he would pass the stone.

That afternoon, Symington and General Robert J. Smith, president of Pioneer, came by the suite. Woodward took them aside and explained the situation. Meanwhile, Johnson had showered and dressed. The three held their meeting on Sheppard, but by then LBJ had become desperately ill again. After much effort, Symington persuaded his friend to go to the hospital. The speech scheduled for Wichita Falls that night was canceled, but that was as far as Johnson would go. With the congressman throwing up in the hall, Woodward checked him into Medical Arts Hospital. Grudgingly, Johnson allowed his aide to call Connally in Austin and tell him. Under no circumstances was the press to be informed, however. Connally argued that it was impossible to keep the media in the dark; inquiries were already being made. Back and forth they went on the phone, with Woodward acting as intermediary. Finally, Johnson told his assistant to order Connally to keep quiet. Too late, Woodward reported, the press had already been informed that the congressman was in the hospital with a kidney stone.

LBJ grew quiet. "Well, if I can't run my own campaign, I guess I might as well [withdraw]; now is the time to get out." He had Woodward get his notebook and take down a withdrawal statement. Fortunately, Lady Bird was flying in from Austin. Woodward persuaded Johnson to do nothing further until he picked her up from Love Field. On his way out, he left instructions that Lyndon was to have no contact personally or by phone with anyone outside the hospital. When Lady Bird arrived, she managed to soothe and calm Lyndon until he drifted off to sleep.[22]

The next morning, the doctors in Dallas told Johnson that they were going to have to remove the stone surgically. He was adamantly opposed. The abdominal procedure would require five to six weeks of convalescence and would effectively eliminate him from the Senate race. While this conference was going on, Woodward took a call from the famed aviatrix Jacqueline Cochran. She had been in Arizona setting some air speed records in a P-51 but had come to Dallas to hear Symington's speech. She learned of her friend LBJ's plight and had called with a possible solution. At the Mayo Clinic in Minneapolis there was a famed urologist, Dr. Gerst Thompson, who might be able to do something. She could collect Johnson and his party at the hospital and they could depart in her Lockheed Electra at 1 A.M., arriving in Minneapolis around 6. LBJ agreed.

Johnson made the trip in a makeshift bunk in the fuselage of the plane. At the clinic, the doctors initially managed to control his infection with drugs. Johnson refused even to discuss surgery. Woodward and Lady Bird took him for auto rides on bumpy back roads and walked him up and down the stairs of the hospital in hopes of shaking the stone loose, but nothing worked. Finally, Dr. Thompson convinced him to let him and his colleagues use a new technique whereby they would insert a tube in his urethra and crush the stone. If it was lodged too far up for them to reach, however, they would have to operate. With

LBJ's political career hanging in the balance, the procedure worked and his fever cleared up rather quickly. Connally called, and the two talked as if there had never been a rift.[23]

Johnson would not have to be confined to bed. But how could he be everywhere at once in the vastness of Texas? Connally proposed a new kind of whistle-stop technology: the helicopter. The machines were a novelty in 1948, sure to attract a great deal of media and public attention. The candidate could cover an incredible amount of territory in a short space of time. Marsh had argued that LBJ should not rely on "a synthetic set-up of fat cats, newspaper publishers, small business interests, and veterans, and labor. They talk big but don't represent twenty percent." The task would be to contact and convert the great silent majority. Coke led merely because he was familiar to these people.[24] Working through Symington and General Smith, Connally made arrangements to rent a Sikorsky S51, a three-seat aircraft that could fly a hundred miles an hour, hover when necessary, and operate for up to 250 miles without the need to refuel. To avoid having the $25-a-day rental charged against the $10,000 ceiling imposed on campaign spending by law, Connally arranged for a group of one hundred Dallas-area veterans to pay for the helicopter as their contribution.[25]

On June 15, LBJ launched a seventeen-day speaking tour of north-central Texas, from Lubbock in the west to Dallas in the north, Texarkana in the east to Austin in the south. The helicopter touched down fourteen to sixteen times a day after hovering over assorted farmers, picnickers, and railroad work gangs while the candidate appealed for their support. Reporters dubbed it the "Johnson City Windmill," and it allowed him to reach an estimated 175,000 people. LBJ quickly abandoned the Sikorsky in favor of a smaller Bell helicopter. The machine was cheaper and the pilot, Joe Mashman, was a much more willing and involved campaigner than the Sikorsky pilot.[26]

The logistics for the tour were incredible. An advance team would race ahead, driving as fast as their cars would allow, to reach a given community before the flying circus. They would pick a landing spot free of wires and poles—an athletic field was ideal—distribute campaign literature, hire a local operator to invite residents, organize a reception committee, and then work the crowd once the candidate landed. The Beau Jesters, a barbershop quartet from Dallas, frequently traveled as part of the advance team to help warm up the locals. Meanwhile, high-octane gasoline trucks would have to be driven to designated refueling stops ahead of the helicopter. Following the advance men was a car with three or four reporters. Occasionally, Johnson would allow one to fly with him, but he or she had to sit on the floor.

From the beginning there was a weight problem. The Bell was a small machine. Mashman weighed 185 and the congressman weighed 195 or so. Once, when the campaign literature Johnson insisted on dropping clogged the air intake, the aircraft nearly stalled and crashed.[27] The long-suffering Warren Woodward remembered on one occasion that Johnson insisted on landing in downtown Rosenberg—not on the outskirts in a field, but downtown. What was a helicopter for if not to reach the people? Dutifully, Woodward convinced a service station owner to allow the Johnson City Windmill to land on his roof. But Mashman refused to descend unless and until the roof was reinforced. Frantically, Woodward and an elderly black man with horses and wagon hauled two-by-fours from the lumberyard and shored up the roof of the service station. "We had a good crowd," Woodward recalled.[28]

ON A TYPICAL DAY, Johnson would get up at five in the morning to make radio broadcasts to area farmers. He then would set off on the day's flight. His approach to a town was generally the same. "He'd circle the crowd, and then he'd speak over the PA system [attached to the runners of the helicopter]," Jake Pickle said. " 'This is Lyndon Johnson, your next United States senator, and I'll land in just a minute. I want to shake hands with all of you' . . . the helicopter would make one last swoop, and he'd open the door . . . wave his [Stetson], and then throw his hat from the helicopter. And everybody whooped and hollered."[29] The advance team had to retrieve the Stetson. "Everybody thought he was giving his hat to the crowd, but we always had to retrieve it. Or pay a dollar to the kid who had caught it and thought it was his."[30]

Because of the heat, the doors were removed from the Bell, which allowed wind-blown sand and dust to fill the cockpit throughout the flight, especially on landings and takeoffs. Johnson made no concession to fashion. Even in the poorest towns he would appear attired in suit, monogrammed white shirt with French cuffs, and a Countess Mara tie. Every other stop or so, filthy, he would shower (with a special double showerhead that he carried with him) and at least change shirts. Dorothy Nichols, his longtime secretary, had to travel in a separate car to accommodate his travel wardrobe.[31] Once, Phipps quietly chided him about his three baths a day and a fresh change after each. "My people aren't sending me to Washington," he said, "to watch hayseeds sprout from my nostrils or onion shoots coming out of my ears. They want someone to represent them they can be proud of, not a country yokel in a dirty shirt with snuff juice dripping off his chin."[32]

Virtually every evening there would be a banquet or service club speech, after which the advance team and candidate would meet to recap and go over the next day's routine. He would finally get to bed between 2 and 3 A.M. and then was up again at 5. Nichols, Mary Rather, and Dorothy Plyler, the congressman's three secretaries, alternated weeks on the road. Anything beyond seven days would have been beyond endurance.

BY THE END OF THE SECOND WEEK, LBJ was anxious and dissatisfied. He had had several advance men accompany him to warm up the crowds before he spoke and occasionally to impersonate him in the air. None had proved satisfactory. He decided to summon young Joe Phipps, the morning announcer at KTBC. "Here's how it will work," the congressman said. "Give me a one-minute, not more than two-minute, evangelical introduction that convinces them we are on the move . . . We're rolling. We're flying . . . Across the state, everyone is turning to Lyndon Johnson as the one, true hope . . . Use 'Texas' a lot and 'Texans' a lot . . . Use 'One' a lot. And 'First.' Then, when the crowd gets whipped up, I'll pull the mike away from you." He would speak for no more than three minutes, then Phipps would do the windup. "The trick is this," he told the young announcer: "Never give your audience a chance to find out what a truly bad speaker I am. At the same time, never let them think of you as being there. We are part of the same person." [33] Indeed, the relationship became a bit closer than Phipps had anticipated—or wished. It was decided that the new man would assume responsibility for laying out the candidate's clothes, waking him, and seeing that he was properly dressed and shaved.

Sometime in his youth, Phipps observed of his boss, Johnson had gotten the idea that he was ugly. Therefore, he was absolutely meticulous about his personal hygiene and appearance. Phipps recalled that "a sense of something awesome—almost magisterial—attached itself to the responsibility [of dressing the candidate], as with a master of the royal bed chamber for some medieval procession through the countryside." [34] At the appointed time on his first day, he touched the sleeping LBJ on the shoulder and presented him with a glass of water, as he had been instructed. Lyndon sat up and sipped. He spat it out, sputtering. "Warm water! Warm water, you son of a bitch!" (Phipps had brought iced.) "What are you trying to do? Lose me the election? Didn't your mama teach you anything. Cold water, you won't be able to shit all day." (This advice had come from Charles Marsh.) [35]

As he prepared to shave, Johnson told Phipps to summon "the girls." Dorothy Nichols and Dorothy Plyler appeared, notebooks in hand. As the candidate stood before the mirror to shave, towel loosely draped around his middle, they took turns standing in the doorway taking down his instructions in shorthand. After several moments, Phipps looked; Johnson was still barking orders and Nichols was still scribbling. The only change was that the towel had slipped off. [36] "I was to discover that nudity—his own in particular—did not seem to concern Lyndon Johnson at all. It was a natural state." [37]

It seemed to Phipps that Johnson was constantly alternating between the refined and the crude. Obsessively clean, immaculately dressed by day, "but in the privacy of an overnight hotel room on the road, he almost seemed to take pleasure in shocking the more protected of our little cadre, presenting himself as a hunk of lumpen flesh born with low animal circulatory, nervous, respiratory and digestive systems; belching, breaking wind, stalking into an adjoining bathroom to urinate or defecate without even bothering to close the door." But then he would launch into a description of some future utopia, identifying his central place in bringing it into being. "Inside, Lyndon Johnson harbored a romantic vision of the man he was meant to become: that same cruddy piece of clay born and named Lyndon Johnson, to be turned into a living work of art." [38]

From this point on, Phipps would be the master of ceremonies for the grand helicopter tour. Like many others, he was both repelled and attracted by Johnson. He recalled vividly the first staff meeting he attended. Johnson sat on a chair in the midst of a dozen or so secretaries and advance men. He began by issuing an endless stream of instructions: when to take off, where to land, whom to contact in Bastrop and Plano, what the next brochure should look like. Dorothy Nichols, Paul Bolton, Horace Busby, and the rest would all be sitting on the edges of their chairs, notepads on knees, taking copious notes. Suddenly, Johnson would shift gears, his eyes seemingly fixed on some distant utopia. "Firemen. Teachers. Farmers. Working men and women left out. Unrepresented. Disfranchised . . . Even if they belong to the National Grange, to the CIO, the Elks, the Woodmen of the World, the Mugwump Wing of the Republican party . . . No one really feels he has a voice. We will be that voice for all those beset by aloneness and helplessness by themselves." [39]

Phipps would later observe that his boss "had the capacity to split himself in two. Not the way a classic schizophrenic might . . . He could go back and forth across that hair-thin line which separated the practical ministry of running a political campaign and creating an almost mythological illusion of himself that he knew must be conveyed to voters if he were to be elected . . . The dramatic shifts from pragmatist to romantic, director to actor, and back again, occurred without warning over and over. Rhetorical flights mixed with down-to-earth instructions." [40]

By the end of the third week, LBJ was near exhaustion. At a reception in Lubbock, Plyler recalled, he "was literally propped against the wall . . . with somebody on each side of him." He greeted the "folks" lined up to meet him by weakly extending his left hand. Only catnaps on the helicopter allowed him to go on. [41] By the time the campaign reached east Texas, the candidate was showing signs of depression. Following a desultory speech in Lufkin, he and Phipps headed for the Angelina Hotel, where accommodations had been booked by an old friend of the Johnsons', Ernest Kurth.

Kurth had arranged for a corner suite where the breezes could sweep through unobstructed. Out of the bedroom appeared Lady Bird, radiant in a yellow cotton dress. Phipps describes the scene: "Her husband's mouth did not so much pop as it sagged open, his whole face softening, melting, then suddenly he was stumbling toward her, both arms wide, and she was rushing to him, fleet as a dancing girl, being folded to his body. His shoulders slumped roundedly as he drew her close, trembling, voice half strangled. 'Bird, Bird,' he was saying. 'I have needed you. More than I can say.' " [42]

The 1948 Senate race was one of the most expensive in American history to that time. Texas campaign laws allowed candidates to spend $10,000 total, $8,000 in the primary and $2,000 if a runoff became necessary. The loophole that had proved so helpful in 1941 still existed, however. The $10,000 limit applied just to the candidate and the organization directly under his control. "Voluntary" campaign organizations that sprang up to support one candidate or another did not count. Stevenson claimed that all in all, the Johnson campaign raised and spent more than a million dollars. He was probably not exaggerating by much. One statewide radio speech cost $1,500; in July alone LBJ delivered twenty-three. According to one campaign worker, the Johnson campaign ran up $30,000 in phone bills.[43]

But Stevenson was not far behind. With a few exceptions, Texas oil, banking, and insurance money backed the safe candidate. "Who is paying for the $1100 [full-page] newspaper ads and the $330 billboard posters for Stevenson on the highways?" Johnson asked in one speech. "In a twenty-five-mile stretch from Sugarland to Houston, there are seven such Stevenson billboards . . . I'm thankful I don't have to have $1100 advertisements saying I can't be bought."[44]

Johnson's financial support came from the usual cast of characters: Brown and Root, Hughes Aircraft, industrialist Sid Richardson, publishing magnates Marsh, Houston Harte, and Amon Carter, and Jewish and Hollywood executives rounded up in Washington and New York by Abe Fortas, Paul Porter, and Ed Weisl, who brokered contributions from wealthy Jews and movie industry executives.[45]

For all this seeming largesse, the Johnson campaign seemed continually strapped for money. "One day I was going down the road between Jasper, Texas, and Beaumont," Warren Woodward said, "and I ran across another Johnson campaign car coming the other direction. I passed him and he passed me. We recognized one another and hit the brakes at the same time. We backed up and got out of our cars and walked over to each other and the first thing we said, almost in unison, was, 'Have you got any money?' "[46] At the Hancock Building, Charles Herring, a Johnson campaign financial manager and future state senator, was forced to climb out of his second-storey office window to escape a bill collector.[47]

IN HIS SET SPEECHES, generally delivered at an evening venue, LBJ was careful to identify himself with those whose specific interests would be aided by the government programs he supported: doctors and federally funded hospitals, the elderly and a federally funded $50-a-month pension, veterans and the G.I. Bill, teachers and federal aid to education, businessmen and federally financed bases and defense contracts. To his rural audiences he played the populist, attacking Standard Oil and private utility companies for gorging themselves at the public's expense.[48] Though he had publicly denounced Truman's civil rights programs, he courted blacks and Hispanics privately and indirectly, arguing that they would benefit from continued government programs and full employment and implying that equal opportunity would come if they were patient.

At times, LBJ could be quite confrontational with segregationists. One day, the Johnson City Windmill set down in the public square in Cleveland, a hamlet situated in the heart of east Texas, which, like northern Louisiana, was one of the darkest and bloodiest racial battlefields in the nation. Lyndon was scheduled to address the local citizenry from a flatbed truck parked next to the railroad station. As he stood on the back of the truck, the single track stretched before him, with woods on the right and the town on the left. The crowd that gathered to the left of the tracks was all white. On the right, further down the rails, were a few black men and women. He could see others, including children in the woods, looking at him. "I'm not going to start speaking until those Americans over there on the right [he gestured] side of the track come over here and stand on the same side of the track with the other Americans over here. This is America. We don't do this." Nobody moved. He did it again, this time obviously exasperated and a little angry. "All right, come on. This is America. You Americans over there [he pointed at the blacks] now come on get over on this track." Some began to run for the woods. Three or four elderly blacks, however, sidled over closer to the track and up toward the speaker's platform. He made his speech.[49]

Back at the hotel, Horace Busby, who was advancing the trip, came into Johnson's hotel room. Johnson was ecstatic, Busby recalled, boiling over with excitement. "How many votes do you think we are going to get out of this county?" he asked. Busby held up ten fingers. Johnson shook his head and held up four fingers. "And he was happy, he was so happy," Busby recalled. "You know, it was Johnson; he had stuck it to them."[50]

ON JUNE 22, the Texas Federation of Labor held its annual convention in Fort Worth. Traditionally, the state branch of the AFL had avoided endorsing any one candidate over another, preferring to stick instead to specific bread-and-butter issues. But this time, anger over Johnson's votes on Taft-Hartley could not be contained. Various speakers denounced the congressman's antilabor votes as the six hundred delegates cheered. In the end, the organization voted to support Stevenson. Though he sensed he was being offered a two-edged sword, Coke decided reluctantly to accept the endorsement.[51] The CIO chose to remain uncommitted and privately denounced the Texas chapter of the AFL for endorsing Stevenson. Lyndon's advisers were elated. At their behest, Johnson issued a series of press releases accusing Stevenson of making a secret deal with labor bosses. What other explanation could there be? No one had been more antiunion than "Calculatin' Coke." There was a difference between labor bosses and the rank-and-file working men. "Both of us know," LBJ declared, "that since the Taft-Hartley became a law, there has been less than 30% of the strike idleness than there was before. I submit that the workers themselves have had more take-home pay since Taft-Hartley than they ever had before."[52]

FORTUNATELY FOR JOHNSON, if not for the country and the world, the Berlin Blockade Crisis erupted in late June. On the 24th, Soviet occupation authorities cut off land access to east Berlin, an isolated island in the Soviet occupation zone, from the American and British zones in the west. It seemed that if the Western democracies were not to abandon the people of noncommunist Berlin, they would have to push straight through the Russian forces. As a stop-gap measure, Truman ordered a massive airlift of food, medicine, and coal. Many predicted that the crisis would touch off World War III.

As midcentury approached, anticommunism and Russophobia in America were building to a perfect storm. It had long been rumored among Democrats that Coke Stevenson was an out-and-out isolationist. Johnson had tantalizing proof. He had discovered through Horace Busby that just before Stevenson delivered his announcement address in January, he had asked the press corps to excise a section from their advance copies. In the paragraph he wanted deleted, Coke had denounced Europe as a corrupt civilization that no longer warranted the sacrifice of American blood and treasure. Programs like the Marshall Plan were a waste of money. "We must follow the counsel of the good book," he wound up, "and not cast our pearls before swine." [53]

The members of the press, including Busby himself, complied, but remembered. As the Berlin Crisis deepened, LBJ whaled away at his opponent's stance on foreign policy. Those who opposed a large army and navy and aid to our allies abroad, he declared in one speech, are "of the same stripe of isolationist who got us into two world wars." [54] He believed in collective security; he equated Stalin with Hitler, and he was convinced that opposition to Soviet imperialism, if not domestic anticommunism, was completely compatible with liberalism.

MEANWHILE, Stevenson was touring the state, conferring with county judges and sheriffs and shaking as many hands as possible. All he had to do to win, he believed, was be himself. Coke sprang from rural poverty in west-central Texas, growing up in a log cabin in Kimble County. While working in a bank as a janitor and cashier, he read law and was admitted to the bar. Elected first as county judge and then state representative, Stevenson went on to the speakership of the Texas House in 1933, the lieutenant governorship in 1938, and then became governor.

Stevenson was not the benign Jeffersonian populist he appeared to be. He was a reactionary who built a budget surplus by slashing public services, including education and the Old Age Assistance Special Fund, which supported the aged, the blind, and dependent children. His reaction to a wartime lynching in Texarkana was to do nothing other than tell the press that "certain members of the Negro race from time to time furnish the setting for mob violence by the outrageous crimes which they commit." [55] If he believed in do-nothing government, he also believed in doing anything necessary to win an election.

On Saturday night, July 24, the Texas Election Bureau began releasing unofficial returns. All three of the frontrunners were disappointed. Up until the very end, Stevenson believed that he would win more than 50 percent of the vote and thus avoid a runoff. Instead, he polled 477,077 votes, 40 percent of the total. Peddy received a surprising 237,195, or 20 percent, but was eliminated. Johnson finished second with 405,617, or 34 percent. So there would be a runoff.

The day following the election, Lyndon and Lady Bird met with their political intimates in the backyard of the Dillman Street house. Johnson was ex-

hausted and despondent. To win, he would have to make up a seventy thousand-vote deficit in five weeks. It seemed impossible and, momentarily at least,
not worth the time and money. Lady Bird was most adamant about going on. "I
must say that was one time that I was very determined and tough, even belligerent," she said. "I told Lyndon I'd rather put in our whole stack, borrow anything
we could, work 18 hours a day . . . maybe we could even conceivably win."[56]

Immediately after the election, both Johnson and Stevenson left for Washington, the former to attend the famous "do-nothing" congressional session
that Truman had called to embarrass the Republicans, and the latter to better
identify himself with national and international issues. In Washington, LBJ paid
highly touted visits to the Department of Defense, after which he was able to
announce government plans to expand the workforce at the Fort Worth Con-
solidated-Vultee aircraft plant and the continued operation of wartime synthetic
rubber plants in Texas as part of the ongoing preparedness program.

Meanwhile, Coke made mistake after mistake. Texas newspapers carried a
picture of him standing in the Senate gallery pointing to a seat in the chamber as
if it were already his. Johnson enjoyed the unspoken support of both the Capitol Hill press corps and the White House, who saw him clearly as the more progressive of the two candidates. When Stevenson appeared before reporters, they
were ready for him. Where do you stand on Taft-Hartley? asked Jack Anderson,
Drew Pearson's assistant. Stevenson stammered, hemmed, and hawed. Anderson asked the question again. "What is your position on Taft-Hartley?" Coke finally responded, "You get me off up here away from my notes." Five times the
question was asked, but Stevenson never did answer.[57]

Pearson pounced. In a column widely reprinted in the Texas press, he wrote,
"Ex-Governor Coke Stevenson of Texas . . . on a recent trip to Washington
evaded more issues and dodged more questions than any recent performer in a
city noted for question dodging."[58] In subsequent speeches, Johnson would
parody his opponent, lowering his head to make a double chin and saying, "You
caught me away from my notes. I don't know quite what to think about that."
His audiences whooped and hollered.[59]

To eat into Coke's advantage in east Texas, LBJ first courted and then won
the support of former Governor Miriam "Ma" Ferguson, who agreed to write
her supporters asking them to vote for LBJ. Mindful of Peddy's attacks on him
for being soft on communism, LBJ red-baited and labor-baited with a
vengeance. The *Johnson Journal,* a campaign publication sent to rural voters, declared, "The big Northern labor unions, with their leadership which included
admitted Communists . . . have aligned their forces against Lyndon Johnson
and in favor of Coke Stevenson." These were the same people who "favor the
election of isolationist candidates . . . Wake up Texans! Don't let the Reds slip
up on you by any such cunning plot!"[60]

"Never easy with prepared remarks, on the stump—unburdened by notes
and pieces of paper—Lyndon Johnson became thunder and lightning," Joe
Phipps observed. "Even would-be scoffers remained to cheer as he lashed out at

undefeated and detested faceless enemies: organized labor (something different from the lone, unallied, horny-handed sons of toil); the rich, metropolitan 'kept' (as opposed to the struggling, small city, family-owned) press; 'big oil' (which fenced out the 'little independents' . . .); heartless mortgage bankers . . . ; out-of-state insurance companies (that wax rosy on the widow's mite)." [61]

In these diatribes, Johnson was not merely acting, however; he genuinely identified with the downtrodden, the working man and woman's fears, prejudices, limited horizons, hopes, and dreams. "Naked and alone," he paraphrased the Bible, "we come into a hostile world; Naked and alone, we shall depart it." [62] An old friend of Johnson's once remarked that if he had permitted himself a fantasy dream as a young politician when he drifted off to sleep, it probably would have been that he was the heir of Franklin D. Roosevelt—but he would awake in the morning to the realization that he was really the reincarnation of Huey Long. [63]

As LBJ's crowds swelled, Stevenson, to the anguish of his handlers, retired to his ranch to chop wood and dip stock. "Did you ever see a stump-tailed bull in fly time?" he asked reporters who wanted to know why he was not campaigning. [64] By the second week of August, however, Calculatin' Coke was once more scouring the state in his old Plymouth, chauffeured by his one-armed nephew. Not above red-baiting himself, Stevenson castigated his opponent for his votes against funding for the House Un-American Activities Committee. Johnson was nothing but a blowhard who had never introduced a meaningful piece of legislation in his eleven-plus years in Congress, he added. [65]

WITH TWO DAYS TO GO in the campaign, Johnson was, as usual, a physical wreck. Observers noted the dark circles around his eyes, his rail-thin appearance, and his speech, now reduced to a painful croak. On the last evening of the runoff, Lady Bird was scheduled to meet Lyndon in San Antonio, where she would make her first and only radio address of the campaign. That morning, she and Marietta Brooks, chair of the women's division of the Johnson operation, set off for a noontime reception in San Marcos. On the way, a truck ran them off the road. With Lady Bird at the wheel, the vehicle rolled over twice before landing upright. Bruised and battered, her dress and stockings torn, Lady Bird got out, flagged down a passerby, sent Marietta to the hospital, and hitched a ride into San Marcos. There she borrowed a dress from a friend and showed up in San Antonio in time to make her broadcast. She said nothing to Lyndon, who did not realize his wife had been in an accident until he saw her bruises later that night, while she was undressing. [66]

On the day of the election, Lady Bird reported for duty at the Austin campaign headquarters. She, Rebekah, and Lyndon's three sisters divided up the city phone book and began calling to solicit votes. Lyndon spent the day campaigning in San Antonio, where Stevenson had bested him by more than twelve thousand votes. Somehow, someway, Johnson had managed to get bitter political enemies Maury Maverick and Paul Kilday, the congressman who had defeated Maverick, to ride with him, one on one side and one on the other, in an open car through the barrio. He and James Knight, the pro-Johnson county clerk, made the rounds distributing cash to the ward and precinct bosses. "Don't misunderstand me," Knight said. "It's not a payoff or anything, because they've been standing here all day, drumming up votes, putting up posters. Five dollars for expenses . . . It was costing 'em that much money." [67]

As reports began coming in from the Texas Election Bureau, the unofficial vote-counting agency run by a consortium of state newspapers, prospects looked grim for LBJ. At midnight, Stevenson led by 2,119 out of 939,468 votes counted. Lady Bird was ready to concede. But a staffer reminded her that the Bureau was unofficial and had to rely on county officials, most of them campaign workers for the candidates themselves, to send in the vote totals.

By 9 P.M. Sunday, the next day, Lyndon held a 693-vote edge. "I was with Stevenson the night of the count . . . (Sunday)," recalled Charles Boatner, a Stevenson aide who would subsequently join LBJ's entourage. "[He] was doing one of his river barbeques . . . There was quite a bit of barbeque and quite a few beans and a lot more bourbon down there on the river and every vote count that would come in Stevenson was ahead . . . And finally . . . Stevenson's lead just dissipated, there was dead silence, and a few more drinks gulped . . . That night after they'd all left I drove back down the road from the ranch to the motel where we were staying and the next morning I got up pretty early and was putting my bag in my car when Coke came by just hell-bent for Austin. You could see the dust behind that car for five miles!" [68]

By Monday evening, Stevenson had regained the lead, with four hundred ballots still unaccounted for. When the Bureau reported its final totals on September 2, Stevenson was 362 votes ahead. [69] The Bureau reminded newspaper readers that its own tally was unofficial and that the State Executive Committee would meet in Fort Worth on September 13 for the official count, with the results to be presented to the state Democratic Convention the next day for confirmation. [70] Connally and his staff had not forgotten 1941. "We had been bitten once," he later recalled. "It would not happen again." [71] They knew that the Stevenson camp would instruct county officials loyal to their candidate to withhold or underreport some vote counts until it was apparent how many tallies would be needed to win. It was relatively easy to switch votes but hard to create new ones. "In 1948 we didn't urge anyone to get their votes in early because we knew the kind of shenanigans that might happen," Walter Jenkins said. "One of the first indications was when we got a call from a woman in Eastland County who was a supporter of Mr. Johnson and a telephone operator there. She called and said, 'I shouldn't listen in on conversations, but I just heard two men talking and they're going to take two hundred votes away from you in Eastland County tonight in a revision of the votes.' " [72] Johnson's managers complained but were never able to recover the two hundred votes.

Both sides arranged to have ballot watchers monitor the other camp's activities.[73] It was here that Johnson's energy and superior organization paid off. "Mr. Stevenson's more or less loose organization took a beating," said Bob Murphy, Stevenson's nephew and driver. "At this critical point of the campaign during this battle for ballots, after the election was over, Mr. Johnson's refined organization and the lieutenants that he had who were experienced in this type of activity shot us out of the water, just to be perfectly frank."[74]

The Johnson camp was able to monitor calls coming into and out of the Stevenson headquarters. When Coke would ask one of his managers to up the total in his county, Connally would have one of his people on the spot intervene or, failing that, call in some unreported votes for Johnson. Alvin Wirtz persuaded Ma Ferguson to contact some of her county judges in east Texas. Governor Stevenson will be calling, asking you to shift a certain number of votes, she said. Tell him you will, but do not. Sam Houston Johnson estimated that because of this ploy, Coke counted some twenty-four hundred votes that he did not really have.[75]

By September 3, the corrected returns turned into the Democratic State Executive Committee gave Lyndon a seventeen-vote lead. Twenty-four hours later, his margin had increased to 162. The previous Sunday evening, Stevenson had predicted that Johnson would try to win the election by calling in votes from the boss-dominated counties in south Texas.[76] In fact, the biggest increase—not a switch of votes from one column to another, but the discovery of additional ballots—came from Jim Wells County. Officers there had discovered an additional 203 ballots, 202 of which went to LBJ.[77]

Of the dozens of machine-controlled counties in south and east Texas, Jim Wells had been for Johnson from the beginning. Not for ideological or financial reasons, but because of a dispute with Coke over patronage. Calling the shots in Jim Wells and neighboring Duval County was forty-six-year-old George Parr, the so-called Duke of Duval. Parr's bases of operation were tiny San Diego in Duval and the much larger town of Alice in Jim Wells. Parr ruled his fiefdom by controlling the votes of thousands of Mexican immigrant laborers. As in the cities of the East and Midwest, the Parr machine located jobs, paid for medical care for children, and delivered groceries on Christmas.[78] It also paid the poll taxes of residents of Mexican descent, requiring them in return only to vote as they were told. "Most Latin Americans couldn't care less who was president of the United States or who was U.S. senator or governor," Jim Rowe observed. "The only one they were interested in was the sheriff because he was the law."[79]

Parr lived on a large estate complete with race track and swimming pool, while his fellow citizens wallowed in poverty and illiteracy. The Duke was a frequent partier with Dick Kleberg, until the latter failed to secure a pardon for him for income tax evasion. In previous elections, the Parr machine had delivered large majorities for Coke Stevenson: 3,643 to 141; 2,936 to 77, and 3,310 to 17. But when the governor refused to appoint Jimmy Kazen, a Parr protégé, as district attorney in Laredo, the Duke abandoned Coke.[80]

"Parr would have supported whoever was on the other side," said Callan Graham, an Alice attorney and Stevenson friend. "The fact that it was Lyndon in 1948 was incidental."[81]

Stevenson knew all of this. At a 1947 meeting with Manuel Ramon, Parr's ally in Laredo, he had been told, "We like you. We're not against you personally, but we've got to do this."[82] Nevertheless, Stevenson and his lieutenants decided to confront Parr and Johnson and contest the election. Returns from Duval on election day had Johnson ahead 4,197 to 40. At the end of the next day, when LBJ's overall 2,119-vote deficit turned into a 692-vote lead, Duval had added 425 more to his total. Six days after the election, officials in Alice, where Parr had a bank and a close working relationship with Ed Lloyd, the local boss, submitted corrected returns, giving Lyndon his additional 202 votes.

There is little doubt that fraud was involved. The Johnson man responsible for poll watching and vote totals in south Texas was Jim Rowe, who recalled, "I went to the meeting of the Jim Wells County Democratic Executive Committee where they canvassed the returns, and they announced this total for Box 13, and mouths fell open. I suddenly realized that here had been 200 votes added . . . One of the things that happened after the primary election was that the ballot boxes were taken to the jail . . . including Box 13, and they were kept by the Sheriff and not turned over to the County Clerk for several days. It's my belief that in that period is when the votes were added."[83] Thirty years later, Luis Salas, the election judge for Jim Wells County, told reporters that votes had been added illegally to the totals in Box 13. According to his account, Johnson came down to Parr's office in Alice and met with Parr, Lloyd, and himself. Johnson told them that Stevenson was ahead, and he needed an additional two hundred votes. Later that evening, in the sheriff's office, clerks added 203 names to the voter list from Box 13, copying directly from the poll tax list, not even bothering to change the alphabetical order.[84]

After Stevenson issued a public statement charging fraud, Lyndon went on a statewide radio hookup the night of September 6. He "did not buy anybody's vote," he declared and warned that a conspiracy was afoot to "thwart the will of the people." His opponent had received lopsided votes in Jim Wells and Duval Counties when he ran for governor. Why did he not protest then?[85] At the same time, his staff began collecting information on voting irregularities in counties that had gone for Stevenson, which was not hard to do. When Price Daniel, the state attorney general, refused to launch an investigation, Stevenson decided to take matters into his own hands.

On September 7, he dispatched aide Callan Graham and Kellis Dibrell, a former FBI agent and attorney practicing in San Antonio, to Alice to find out what had actually happened. They went to Parr's Alice National Bank to see Tom Donald, the manager who was also the Democratic county chairman. The contents of Box 13 were locked in the bank's vault, and he had no authority to release them, Donald said. At this point, Stevenson decided to intervene personally. He arrived in Alice with James Gardner, another ex-FBI agent, and

Frank Hamer, the ex–Texas Ranger famous for his role in helping track down Bonnie and Clyde.

As Stevenson and his colleagues approached the bank once again, they encountered two knots of armed men. Hamer stared them down, however, and the party was allowed to enter the bank.[86] They were joined by Harry Lee Adams, the incoming Democratic county chairman. Donald agreed to let only Adams into the vault and then for only five minutes. In that space of time he was able to copy twelve names off the list. Of those, several subsequently interviewed by Hamer and Dibrell claimed that they had paid their poll tax but never voted. Before Stevenson and his men left town, Hap Holmgren, the county clerk, fearful of being charged with fraud, allowed Dibrell and Graham to see the Precinct 13 ballots. The last 203 names were in alphabetical order and copied in a different handwriting from the rest.[87]

After two judges refused to allow election officials to reconsider the vote totals, all eyes turned to the meeting of the State Democratic Executive Committee scheduled for September 13 in Fort Worth's Blackstone Hotel, where the final vote tally would take place. The vote had been so close and contentious that committee chair Robert Calvert appointed a subcommittee of two Johnson delegates, two Stevenson delegates, and three chosen by him to do a preliminary count. The subcommittee meeting in the afternoon found that Johnson had won by eighty-seven votes, but they adopted by a four to three vote a resolution recommending the elimination of the Box 13 returns from Alice.

The full Executive Committee met that night in the jam-packed ballroom of the Blackstone. "The tension in that room was so sharp that anything could have exploded it," Jake Pickle recalled. "I was leaning up against a pillar in the back listening and trying to make tabulation on my sheet—and keeping tabs on my own heart!"[88] Lady Bird and Lyndon arrived, followed shortly by Stevenson. After greeting friends and supporters, they took seats in the front row, sitting about ten feet apart, Coke puffing on his pipe. Lawyers for both sides presented their respective cases. "I am here to prevent the stuffing of the ballot box," proclaimed one Stevenson representative.

LBJ's spokesmen insisted that they could give two examples of fraud for every one Stevenson presented, and accused Coke of dispatching a "goon squad" to Alice to intimidate the poor Mexican voters there.[89] And in fact, Wirtz had in hand evidence that the Stevenson people had switched or added votes in Dallas, Jack, Brown, Eastland, and several other counties.[90] Horace Busby later observed that "if you had recounted the election after throwing out ballots that were found to be fraudulent . . . Johnson would have won by four or five thousand votes."[91]

As the Executive Committee began its vote, Stevenson got off to an early lead, and it looked as if all was lost. But then Johnson began to gain. When the final tally was in, LBJ led twenty-nine to twenty-eight. That morning Jerome Sneed, a Johnson committee member from Austin, had collapsed in the lobby of a hotel with a heart attack. With his permission, Johnson had named Alvin

Wirtz to replace him. It looked for a moment as if the Sneed proxy would be the difference. But then a female delegate from Conroe County rose to declare that she was reversing herself. The vote count stood at twenty-nine to twenty-nine. Pandemonium erupted. Under the rules, Robert Calvert had the power to cast a tie-breaking vote. He was convinced, he later recalled, that the votes in Box 13 had been fraudulent, but he was aware that a state supreme court decision in 1932 had prohibited the Committee from doing anything but accepting the reported return. He decided that if necessary, he would vote for Johnson.

There were, however, still six Committee members unaccounted for. The clerk called the name of each; none of the first five answered. The sixth name, that of Charlie Gibson of Amarillo, was announced. Sam Houston would later claim that he fetched Gibson from the men's room, where he was being sick with a hangover. Gibson stood on a chair in the back of the room, demanding to be recognized. When he was, he cast his vote for LBJ. The tie was broken. The room broke into cheers and boos, and someone knocked Charlie Gibson's chair over.[92]

THE NEXT MOVE in the 1948 election was up to the general convention, whose two thousand delegates had gathered in Will Rogers Auditorium. Traditionally, the state convention accepted the recommendation of the Executive Committee without question, but 1948 was an unusual year. An unofficial head count taken by the Johnson people showed their candidate with a mere twelve-vote margin of victory. Illness, bribery, infidelity, and a host of other happenstances could easily change the outcome.

Fortunately, LBJ was saved by larger issues that pervaded the meeting. Wirtz and other loyalists were determined that the Texas delegation to the national convention support the party's regular nominee, Harry Truman, and not the Dixiecrat ticket of Strom Thurmond and Fielding Wright. They controlled the credentials committee and, after several fistfights on the floor of the convention, succeeded in barring a number of regulars who were real or suspected Dixiecrats. These delegates, of course, happened also to be supporters of Coke Stevenson. One of those ejected hailed from Fort Worth, and as such was part of the convention's host delegation. As he and his colleagues left the hall, they took with them chairs, desks, sound system, and typewriters. Standing in the bare hall, the Democratic loyalists overwhelmingly voted to accept the Executive Committee's decision and certify LBJ as the party's candidate for the U.S. Senate.[93]

THERE REMAINED ONLY COURT CHALLENGES, which initially went Stevenson's way, until Abe Fortas and other New Dealers convinced Supreme Court Justice Hugo Black to rule on the case. His stay of a state court decision in favor of Stevenson resulted in an order requiring that Johnson's name be listed as the candidate. In essence, he ruled that the federal courts, through which Stevenson had sought redress, had no jurisdiction. Human history is replete with irony. In 1948, a group of New Dealers, which certainly included Hugo Black, Virginia Durr's brother-in-law, used states' rights doctrine and counter-reconstruction litigation to confirm the election of one of their own, a liberal nationalist, to the U.S. Senate.

Several weeks after the election, when the tensions and stress had had a chance to ebb, LBJ told Vernon Whiteside a Box 13 joke that he would repeat periodically throughout his public career. "Well, this little boy was sitting on the curb Sunday morning at Alice," he said, "close to Box 13, crying, a little Mexican boy. And this fellow walked up and said, 'Son, are you hurt?' He said, 'No, I no hurt.' He said, 'Are you sick?' He said, 'No, I no sick.' He said, 'Are you hungry?' He said, 'No, I no hungry.' He said, 'What's the matter? What are you crying for?' He said, 'Well, yesterday, my papa, he been dead four years yesterday, he come back and voted for Lyndon Johnson, didn't come by to say hello to me.' "[94]

MUCH WOULD BE MADE of the election by LBJ's critics, from the reactionary J. Evetts Hailey to the liberal Texas journalist Ronnie Dugger, in an effort to portray him as a corrupt, feckless politician. "Landslide Lyndon," his own self-deprecating term, would be used derisively by segregationists opposed to his civil rights policies and antiwar protestors opposed to the war in Vietnam. Yet from the evidence, it appears that if all fraudulent ballots and counts had been thrown out, Johnson would have beaten Stevenson by 506 votes.[95]

Indeed, there is evidence of Stevenson fraud in Dallas County, where the Democratic party chair was the candidate's cousin, and in Navarro County, where all ballots were burned before they could be inspected by election judges.[96] Throughout the legal proceedings, Johnson's lawyers could not present specific facts refuting Stevenson's charges or submit charges of their own because they were contesting the authority of the federal court to hear the case in the first place.[97]

Indeed, there are other, more important questions to ask about the 1948 senatorial race. How, incredibly, had LBJ made up seventy thousand votes in a matter of a few weeks? The reason Calculatin' Coke lost was because he ran a truly abysmal campaign the second time around. An estimated 113,523 voters who opted for Stevenson in the first primary did not vote in the second, compared to only 4,054 Johnson supporters.[98] A number of conservatives were turned off by Stevenson's equivocation on Taft-Hartley and his acceptance of the Texas AFL endorsement. Veterans and their families were alarmed by his incipient isolationism. Most inportant, Johnson just flat outworked his opponent.

The campaign had showed Johnson at his best and his worst. He had been dogged, relentless, and at times inspiring. He had done a bit of demagoguing, but appealed mainly on the issues. With staff and supporters he had frequently been insensitive, gross, and even abusive. He thought nothing of chewing out campaign workers and volunteers in public. "You have to realize that a politician—a good one—is a strange duck," he told Joe Phipps at the height of the campaign. "Anyone who periodically has to get down on hands and knees to beg voters to prove they love him by giving him their vote is really sick. Depending on how obsessed he is, he could be very, very sick . . . Try to think of me as a seriously ill, a dear relative or friend who needs all the care, compassion, comfort and love he can get in order to get well, knowing that in time he will get well. The illness . . . won't come back till the next election rolls around."[99]

CHAPTER 11

A POPULIST GENTLEMEN'S CLUB

LYNDON JOHNSON'S PERSONALITY, LIKE THE NATURE OF Congress and, indeed, the human condition, was rife with opposites and the tension between them. Ambition versus public interest. One versus many. Faith versus doubt. The Declaration of Independence spoke not of community in its opening lines but of individual rights and dissolution of unjust governments. The Preamble to the Constitution, by contrast, focused on community, wholeness, oneness. As rhetorician Wayne Fields has noted, the Great Seal of the Republic symbolizes the tension: the eagle clutches in its beak a banner with *pluribus* emblazoned to the right and *unum* to the left. In a sense, Congress, rooted in particularism, regionalism, and parochial interest, represents the many, and the presidency, with its fictional persona speaking with the "national voice," the one.[1]

The dichotomy is certainly not absolute. Long before Johnson, nationalists in Congress such as Daniel Webster and John C. Calhoun in the nineteenth century and Sam Rayburn and Arthur Vandenburg in the twentieth had stepped forward to advance the cause of unity. Many of the great reform movements of the late nineteenth and early twentieth centuries—Populism, Progressivism, the New Deal–Fair Deal—were driven by legislators who had a vision of community rooted not just in liberty but in government as well. Although frequently used to buttress an unjust status quo and to protect vested interests, the conservative image of a Jeffersonian America in which the federal government served principally to preside over a nation of independent property-owning individuals was certainly a form of nationalism. Even the most parochial of legislators have held an image of the ideal community in their collective mind. The difference between liberals and conservatives, to oversimplify, has been that the left has argued that social justice is the primary glue of the American comity, as well as the core of true patriotism, and the right has insisted that maximum liberty is the cement of the republic and the defining element in patriotism. More-over, virtually all legislation passed by Congress is a result of compromise among contending interests, personalities, and regions in which representatives and senators are compelled to act in behalf of the larger good.

Nevertheless, the prospect of realizing the dream of one out of many through the mechanism of the bicameral legislature has often daunted Ameri-can nationalists. Observing the workings of Congress in 1869, Henry Adams was appalled:

> Within the walls of two rooms are forced together in close contact the jealousies of thirty-five million people,—between individuals, between cliques, between industries, between parties, between branches of the Government, between sections of the country, between the nation and its neighbors. As years pass on, the noise and the confusion, the vehemence of this scramble for power or for plunder, the shouting of reckless adven-turers, of wearied partisans, and of red-hot zealots in new issues,—the boiling and bubbling of this witches' cauldron, into which we have thrown eye of newt and toe of frog and all the venomous ingredients of corruption, and from which is expected to issue the future and more per-fect republic,—in short, the conflict and riot of interests, grow more and more overwhelming."[2]

HARRY TRUMAN'S 1948 CAMPAIGN had succeeded against all expecta-tion in part because he had chosen to run against Congress. He claimed to represent "the people," while castigating the people's representatives as "do-nothings." Now, in his annual message to Congress in January 1949, President Truman gave legislators a chance to redeem themselves by approving the vari-ous components of his domestic program, the Fair Deal. Over the next year, the now Democratic-controlled House and Senate handed him a number of victo-ries. They increased the minimum wage from forty to seventy-five cents an hour and extended the Social Security Act, bringing 10 million new workers under its provisions. Truman's greatest victory for the disadvantaged was the Housing Act of 1949, which appropriated large sums to clear slums and build 810,000 units of low-cost housing over the next six years.

There were defeats. In the wake of a gigantic lobbying effort by the American Medical Association, Congress rejected the president's plan for national health insurance. Led by the conservative coalition, the House and Senate also turned back the so-called Brannan Plan, which would have established a guaranteed in-come for farm families. Most disappointing for Truman was Congress's ob-structionism in the area of civil rights. During the 1948 campaign the president had placed himself squarely behind a broad program of civil rights legislation. Truman advocated federal protection against lynching, anti–poll tax legislation, the establishment of a permanent Fair Employment Practices Commission (FEPC), and the prohibition of segregation in interstate transportation. For the first time since Reconstruction, the status of African Americans had become a national issue.

Strom Thurmond and Fielding Wright had managed to carry only a handful of states in the Deep South in 1948, but because of the seniority system, the Dixiecrats maintained their strong position in Congress. Mississippi senator and outspoken segregationist James Eastland took over as chairman of the Judiciary Subcommittee. From this deceptively innocuous position, he wreaked havoc on the administration's civil rights program. John Stennis, Mississippi's other senator, headed a Rules Subcommittee that oversaw anti–poll tax legislation. In the House, William Colmer, congressman from Mississippi, used his position on the Rules Committee to preserve Jim Crow.[3] From these power niches southern states' righters continued not only to block civil rights legislation but also to present a compelling critique of the welfare state. The New Deal–Fair Deal's advocacy of collective bargaining for labor unions, welfare programs for the disadvantaged, and civil rights for blacks, especially the FEPC, gave rise to an uneasy alliance between the old planting aristocracy and New South industrialists. Their alliance was cemented with a virulent anticommunism. Presidential candidate Thurmond warned of a "federal police state, directed from Washington, [that] would force life in each hamlet in America to conform to a Washington pattern."[4]

IN DECEMBER 1948, preparing to assume his seat, LBJ summoned Bobby Baker, the chief page of the Senate. Though holding one of Washington's humbler positions, this twenty-year-old prodigy had become something of a power broker by virtue of his encyclopedic knowledge of the workings of the Senate and its personalities. "Mr. Baker," Johnson said (Bobby, a diminutive hustler who craved respect, was pleased by the formality), "I understand you know where the bodies are buried in the Senate. I'd appreciate it if you'd come to my office and talk to me."[5] For two hours Johnson and Baker discussed the power structure, the committee system, and the social roadmap of the Senate. "Lyndon and I became close very quickly because we both knew how to count, and he was very quick to learn all there was to know about each and every senator," said Baker.[6]

He was going to have to do some things that Truman and the liberal wing of the Democratic party would find offensive, Johnson told the young man. He would have to continue to support Taft-Hartley and he would have to support the oil and gas industry. "Frankly, Mr. Baker," he said, "I'm for nearly anything the big oil boys want because they hold the whip hand and I represent 'em. Yeah, I represent farmers and working men," he said, but "the New Deal spirit's gone from Texas and I'm limited in what I can do." And he would have to oppose the administration's civil rights program, especially the FEPC. "My state is much more conservative than the national Democratic party," he said. "I got elected by just 87 votes and I ran against a caveman."[7]

Johnson was forced to cram his sixteen-member staff—twice the Senate average—into the three rooms of Suite 321 of the Senate Office Building. LBJ pressed the leadership for one of the four-room suites reserved for senior members, but had to settle for a separate office on the next floor down and a fourth telephone line.[8] "When LBJ was first elected to the senate," recalled Leslie Carpenter, a Texas journalist, "he wanted his office open 24 hours a day. He did not want anybody calling Sen. Lyndon Johnson and his office didn't answer."[9]

LBJ announced in the Texas press that he would see every Texan requesting an audience, a potential queue of 7.5 million. He organized the staff into eight-hour shifts and expected them to handle up to 650 letters, 500 phone calls, and 70 visitors a day. Johnson continued to obsess on the mail. He actively solicited letters and laid down strict rules as to how they should be answered. "To Texans, Senator Lyndon B. Johnson is their Senator," a memo to his staff declared. "He is not an aloof, unapproachable figure about whom they read in the newspapers . . . They want the letter they receive in reply to be personal—almost like a father writing his son . . . It must never be forgotten that the voter is sovereign."[10]

To oversee his team, which included Walter Jenkins, Dorothy Nichols, Mary Rather, Warren Woodward, Glynn Stegall, and Horace Busby, Johnson persuaded John Connally to come up, at least for a shakedown period. Even then Connally was a lion to some, a jackal to others. Busby recalled with admiration his "lavish personality," great good looks, and obvious intelligence. "Rayburn had an extravagant, very high opinion of John Connally," Rayburn aide D. B. Hardeman recalled. "He said he thought he had more natural ability than any man of his age that he'd ever known."[11] "I thought he was a cold-blooded opportunist," said Virginia Durr. "I think John was essentially a servile character . . . He was a man who was always on the make, and he was always sucking up and buttering up people he thought could help him."[12]

Connally, who worked on and off for oil man Sid Richardson, represented basically the viewpoint of Richardson, Clint Murchison, and the Brown brothers. Texas and America were ideally the homes of swashbuckling capitalists, aided by subservient state and federal governments, who looked after the common people out of a sense of noblesse oblige and a desire to maintain social order. Civil rights definitely did not resonate. "My private opinion," Connally wrote Johnson concerning the Roosevelt administration's efforts to facilitate voting for military personnel stationed overseas, "is that this is but a cover up for these damn social workers who are trying to destroy the poll tax in the southern States to try to help the Negroes."[13]

When Connally returned to Texas in September to continue his quest to become a millionaire, Johnson named Walter Jenkins to replace him. Jenkins, a bespectacled, intense man, a Catholic who would eventually sire nine children, would remain an essential part of the LBJ team until he left under a cloud in 1964. Observers were unanimous in praising Jenkins for his loyalty, selflessness, intelligence, work ethic, and tact. He became familiar with every detail of the Johnsons' business enterprises as well as LBJ's political affairs. He never leaked to the press unless his boss told him to. According to Washington lawyer and

New Dealer Tommy Corcoran, no one other than Lady Bird was more central to Lyndon's success. "When they come to canonize political aides, he [Jenkins] will be the first summoned, for no man ever negotiated the shark-infested waters of the Potomac with more decency or charity or came out on the other side with his integrity less shaken," said future aide Bill Moyers.[14] But there was something unnatural about Jenkins's attachment to his boss. Moyers himself was secretly contemptuous of Jenkins's psychological dependence on LBJ.

TRUE TO FORM, Johnson was hard on himself and hard on his staff. He worked nonstop, frequently arriving at the office at 6:30 in the morning and working into the night, "arguing, listening, 'needling,' explaining, compromising, chain-smoking and chain-telephoning."[15] He expected the same intensity from his staff, whom he tended to absorb until they became mere extensions of himself. "He consumes people almost without knowing it," observed Senate aide Harry McPherson. "He wants everything once the deal is made, once the friendship is established . . . There's a period in which it's almost suffocating."[16] Early each day he would stop and pick up Mary Rather on his way to work, "and by the time I sat down he was giving me instructions," she recalled. "I learned to keep my notebook outside my purse. By the time we reached the office, he had outlined a whole day's work for me."[17]

The senator thought nothing of chewing out an aide in public for a mistake, real or perceived. George Reedy, who would become Johnson's lieutenant for political strategy and public relations, was a notorious butt of the senator's ridicule. The pipe-smoking, rotund Reedy was regularly blistered in front of reporters and staff for failing to come up with the right information at the right time. Johnson considered goading staff over work issues to be a perfectly legitimate method of management. But he was also capable of gratuitous cruelty. On one occasion, at a party where staff were present, guests were putting in drink orders. Rather requested a martini. Johnson, who was standing nearby, turned to her and said, "Um-huh, um-huh, there you are, there you are. We were out the other night and you had a little too many martinis and you made a complete ass out of yourself. I guess that's what you're fixing to do tonight." Ervin "Red" James, who witnessed the scene, recalled that the humiliated young woman just stood there, tears rolling down her cheeks. The next day, Johnson presented her with a new handbag.[18]

Norman Heine, who once worked for Johnson when he was a congressman, described the sometimes terrible vortex that he created around himself. "I felt even before I left that I was treated, not as an adult and an intelligent person," he told John Connally, "but as a child and inferior . . . When I was in the Navy, I often wondered whether I could get along on my own or not . . . It's been quite a mental relief for me to find that I actually can make the grade, and the only way I'd ever work for Lyndon again is to feel beyond a shadow of a doubt that I was actually needed by him, and be sure within my own mind, that it was not I who needed him."[19]

Strong personalities like Connally, Busby, and McPherson were able to stand up to their boss and accept the consequences. They appreciated his underlying idealism, his drive to succeed, and his unparalleled skills as a political tactician. To be associated with Johnson was to be always near the center of action and to be involved with causes that were worthwhile. He and those around him resided at the very heart of the American political enterprise, and that enabled him to continue to attract able and talented subordinates.

JOHNSON LEARNED THE WAYS of the Senate quickly. His meeting with Bobby Baker was only the beginning of a massive effort to gather intelligence on the upper house and to insinuate himself into its power structure. He proved spectacularly successful. Sometime later, LBJ granted an audience to historian Arthur Schlesinger Jr. "Most informative morning I ever spent," Schlesinger subsequently told John Kenneth Galbraith. "Never got a word in edgewise . . . Johnson went over every member of the Senate—his drinking habits, his sex habits, his intellectual capacity, reliability, how you manage him."[20]

Hubert Humphrey, the liberal from Minnesota who entered the Senate with Johnson, recalled, "He knew all the little things that people did. I used to say he had his own private FBI. If you ever knew anybody, if you'd been out on a date, or if you had a drink, or if you'd attended a meeting, or you danced with a gal at a night club, he knew it! It was just incredible!"[21] Johnson used personal information to prevent his colleagues from using his own peccadilloes against him and to ensure that they honored the bargains they had made with him. Though even when they did not, there is no evidence of his ever leaking personal information about a colleague to the press. And he rarely if ever asked a fellow senator to do something that would cause his electoral defeat.

Johnson was not a man to tolerate fools easily, however. Those in the upper house who were lazy, stupid, or unwilling to compromise were subjects of his scorn.[22] Infrequently, his contempt would burst forth in a public display. After one of his colleagues failed on the floor of the Senate to carry out his assigned duties, Johnson "just reamed him out like he was a bad boy in the family," Reedy recalled. When one of his staffers advised him that such outbursts could be counterproductive, LBJ replied, "But he's a stupid bastard."[23]

The power structure in the Senate, then as now, was more tightly controlled than that of the House. Clout resided primarily with the chairs of the permanent committees. Because seniority ruled, most of the committees were controlled by southerners, beginning with Richard Russell of Georgia. At the time, it was generally deemed impossible for a southerner to be elected president, so the best and the brightest political personalities south of the Mason-Dixon line aspired to the Senate.

Russell was generally considered the best of the best. Born in 1897 in Winder, Georgia, he had practiced law and then been elected speaker of the Georgia House, governor, and in 1933 U.S. senator. By 1949 Russell was a towering if lonely figure. A confirmed bachelor who resided in a suite at the

Mayflower Hotel, he spent most of his weekends reading or attending an occasional baseball game. His only love was the Senate. He knew its history and workings intimately and was devoted to its role as a stately brake on innovation, a preserver of American traditions. Russell knew as much about the constituencies of his fellow senators as they did themselves.[24]

Russell was a southerner, a segregationist, and a nationalist. His lifelong struggle was to devise a strategy that would defeat or slow the civil rights movement and at the same time keep his native region in the Democratic party and not far from the mainstream of American life. Like LBJ, he saw economic development as a key to progress in the South. He was a devoted servant of the military-industrial complex. His position as second in command to the ineffective Carl Hayden on the Armed Services Committee ensured the proliferation of bases and defense plants in Georgia and the rest of the South. He became self-appointed leader of the southern caucus or "Dixie Association," the senators from the eleven states of the former Confederacy who gathered regularly to plan the defeat of anti–poll tax legislation or forestall the creation of new FEPCs.[25]

Johnson immediately anointed himself a Russell protégé. He sought the Georgian's advice at every turn and began inviting him to the Johnson home most Sundays to dine and while away the hours. Lynda and Lucy were encouraged to call their guest "Uncle Dick." LBJ flattered the Georgian, listened to his stories, and encouraged him to run for the Democratic presidential nomination in 1952.[26] He made sure that his desk on the floor of the Senate was next to the Georgian's and he wrangled a seat on the Armed Services Committee.[27]

Johnson cultivated Russell because he resided at the seat of power in the Senate and shared some of LBJ's goals for the South and the nation. He was a master of the art of compromise and persuasion, an art the Texan greatly admired. He was, even when it came to the divisive issue of civil rights, a "patriot," able in the end to put the nation's interest ahead of the prejudices of white southerners. Russell in turn saw Johnson as the political figure that he could never be, a southerner with western ties, a nationalist who could hold the sprawling, diverse republic together, and perhaps even be the first man from a former Confederate state since Woodrow Wilson to sit in the White House.[28] Eventually, LBJ would gain the upper hand with the "Wizard of Winder," making him a handmaid, however reluctantly, to Johnson's vision of the future. "That goddamned Johnson!" Russell once remarked to Bobby Baker. "The son of a bitch, you can't say no to him!"[29]

THE SESSION OF CONGRESS that convened on January 3, 1948, featured eighteen freshmen senators, fourteen of whom were Democrats. Of these, eight had defeated Republican incumbents. The Class of '48, of which Johnson was a part, would be remarkable. It included Robert Kerr of Oklahoma, Hubert Humphrey of Minnesota, Joe Clark of Pennsylvania, Estes Kefauver of Tennessee, Mike Mansfield of Montana, Paul Douglas of Illinois, Frank Graham of

North Carolina, Clinton Anderson of New Mexico, and Russell Long of Louisiana. Kerr quickly rose to prominence as a debater and deal maker. The owner of $100 million in natural gas property, the Oklahoman made no apologies about acting as the chief spokesman for the oil and gas lobby. After LBJ acquired the family homestead in Stonewall, Texas, he, Kerr, and Wayne Morse of Oregon would lounge around the Senate cloak room and talk the talk of gentlemen ranchers.[30] Paul Douglas, former economics professor and marine hero, would become one of the Senate's most relentless liberals. But none of the newcomers would become better known for a commitment to social justice than Hubert Humphrey, the former mayor of Minneapolis who had gained national notoriety by delivering a fiery pro–civil rights speech on the floor of the 1948 Democratic National Convention.

Shortly after he took the office, Humphrey made the mistake of attacking Harry Byrd, a reactionary machine politician from Virginia who held senior positions on the Armed Services and Finance Committees. Unaccustomed to the mores of the Senate, Humphrey leveled his charges while Byrd was off the Senate floor and out of town for family reasons. The following day, senators from both parties stood to defend Byrd.[31] As a result, Humphrey was completely ostracized by his fellow Democrats. One day, while walking past a knot of southern senators, Humphrey overheard a remark by Russell obviously meant for his ears: "Can you imagine the people of Minnesota sending that damn fool down here to represent them?"[32] The naturally gregarious Humphrey was deeply hurt. Gradually, however, Humphrey, Douglas, and a number of other liberals were accepted into the club.[33]

Indeed, despite their profound differences over civil rights, unionization, the regulatory functions of the federal government, and other issues, a strain of populism united the senators from the South, West, and Midwest. Once, Harry McPherson recalled, Humphrey took the floor to speak against Republican Secretary of Agriculture Ezra Taft Benson's latest proposal on farm subsidies, based on a sliding scale. "He was bone-tired and in a passionate, hoarse-voiced, and angry ten minute harangue, he declared 'Hubert Humphrey did not come to the United States Senate to vote for sixty percent of living wage!' " Russell, who, during the early New Deal, had sponsored legislation creating the Rural Electrification Administration and the Farmers Home Administration, was heading out of the chamber. When Humphrey began to speak, he turned around, came back and sat down in front of him. Russell called to Olin Johnston, the son of a tenant farmer, now representing the Piedmont of South Carolina, and some others. "They all began to listen and to pound the table . . . It was a damned revival." "I used to notice the hands of men like Kerr and Johnson and Bill Fulbright and some others of that . . . class," McPherson later observed. "Their hands are generally big and scaly, freckled and hairy . . . There's a very common look about them—a worker's look—even though some of them, like Fulbright, had been an academic all their lives."[34] "I'm a reactionary when times are good," Russell once said. "In a depression, I'm a liberal."[35]

On the Republican side, the dominating figure was Senator Robert Taft of Ohio, son of the former president and perennial presidential aspirant. A states' rights conservative, he was a trenchant foe of the welfare state and the preeminent champion of business interests. He spoke for those Republicans who held a pseudo-religious view of America as a largely stateless society of self-regulating individuals. For them, the Great Depression had been a cataclysmic event that had paved the way for the greatest threats to democracy, free enterprise, and individual liberty that the republic had yet encountered: Franklin D. Roosevelt and the New Deal. With the defeat of Thomas Dewey in 1948, Taft assumed the role of "Mister Republican" and took the point in criticizing Truman and all he stood for. In the wake of the president's upset victory, Taft told reporters, "It defies all common sense to send that roughneck ward politician back to the White House." His philosophy as majority leader was summed up in a statement attributed to him: "The business of the opposition is to oppose."

Determined to get the most for his constituents, Johnson attempted to go straight to the top of the committee system. He wanted appropriations but in the end had to settle for Armed Services and Interstate and Foreign Commerce. From the one he was able to facilitate the growth of the military-industrial complex in Texas, and from the other, to protect the oil and gas industry. Using these power centers, he quickly racked up credits with constituents large and small: Reconstruction Finance Corporation (RFC) home loans to veterans, the bargain basement sale of government assets to the University of Texas, a huge RFC credit to the Lone Star State Steel Plant in northeast Texas, and government subsidies to a tin smelting operation in Texas City. Gradually, many businessmen, industrialists, and planters who had opposed Johnson began to come around. In the spring of 1950, former governor Jimmy Allred reported that virtually no one in south Texas had a negative thing to say about him.[36]

According to the program LBJ had in mind, there were two objectives that were in potential conflict: not to take positions that would be perceived as controversial in Texas and to cultivate close ties with the White House and the national Democratic party. The contradiction between these two was quickly highlighted by two issues: civil rights and regulation of the oil and gas industry. Legislative remedies for racial injustice had proved virtually impossible. Under existing Senate rules, the membership could end filibusters by a two-thirds vote, but cloture, as such action was called, was not applicable to debate on motions to consider a bill—thus the possibility for an interminable talkathon.

In March 1949, the administration launched a campaign to have cloture apply to all debate in hopes of paving the way for passage of its civil rights legislation. When Dick Russell called a meeting of the twenty-two members of the Dixie Association to plot strategy for preventing any modification of Rule 22, the cloture rule, Estes Kefauver and Johnson were conspicuously absent. The *Washington Post* took note. "I think the next morning must have been one of the most disillusioning mornings of Lyndon Johnson's life, ever," Horace Busby said. Telephone messages from old New Dealers such as Tommy Corcoran, Jim

Rowe, and Ben Cohen were stacked up. "Oh, no," Rowe said to Busby. "What does wonder boy think he's doing? That's not the way you play the game. He can't be a senator from Texas and amount to anything if he's going to start behaving like this. What is he, a goddamned idealist or something?"[37] LBJ's lieutenant recalled that he had never seen his boss more disgusted.

A day or two later, Russell made a formal appointment and came by to see Johnson. "Senator Russell just took him up on the mountaintop and gave him a picture of what lay ahead if he didn't keep faith with his southern colleagues," Busby recalled. "He'd never get recognized on the floor when he needed it, and he'd never get bills passed for Texas."[38] But Russell also expressed sympathy when Johnson stated his position: his opposition to the poll tax and lynching and his vision of an America with a progressive South as one of its essential components.

A few days later, LBJ summoned Busby and told him he intended to deliver his maiden speech in the Senate on Rule 22, but that he wanted to focus on cloture, not civil rights. In the meantime, Alvin Wirtz and Jimmy Allred had arrived in Washington. Together with John Connally, they convinced a reluctant Johnson that he could not placate white sensibilities unless he condemned Truman's civil rights program, especially the FEPC. The Senate was packed on the appointed day. "The galleries were filled with all these conspicuous figures from Washington's past; everybody came up there to see Johnson make his maiden speech," Busby recalled. "So they got there and he started out speaking and before long—he could get himself more wrought up making a speech, internally, than anybody I've ever seen. And he wasn't very long into the speech until the perspiration started showing on the back of his coat and on his forehead."[39]

Johnson began by staunchly defending the Senate's right to unlimited debate and attacked the administration's civil rights program, especially the FEPC. To Russell's delight, he took the high ground on cloture. The Senate had been established in part to protect the rights of the few against the passion of the many. The rights of all minorities were at stake. "When I say minority," the freshman from Texas declared, "I do not limit the term to mean only the South . . . It belongs to all the Nation, and to all the minorities—racial, religious, political, economic, or otherwise—which make up this nation." He went on to denounce racism. "No prejudice is so contagious or so dangerous," LBJ proclaimed, "as the unreasoning prejudice against men because of their birth, the color of their skin, or their ancestral background." The current debate had nothing to do with "the Negro race," with the South's desire to perpetuate bigotry and hatred. He was as opposed as any American to the poll tax and lynching, the junior senator from Texas declared, but federal laws, federal control had not been the answer in 1869 and were not the answer in 1949.[40] Subsequently, in May and July 1950, Johnson joined with Tom Connally to vote nay on a cloture motion during southern filibusters against the FEPC bill.[41]

Blacks in Texas and liberals in Washington were not pleased. The executive secretary of the Houston branch of the NAACP cabled, "The Negroes who sent you to Congress are ashamed to know that you have stood on the floor against them today. Do not forget that you went to Washington by a small majority vote and that was because of the Negro vote." The organization even sent a delegation to Washington to plead with Johnson directly, but to no avail. "Your old friends who remember the high stepping, idealistic, intelligent young man who came here as a bright young Congressman in 1938 expect more of you than that," Rowe complained.[42]

Johnson was infuriated by the mixed signals his New Dealer friend was sending. In response, he donned the mask worn by Booker T. Washington a half-century earlier. "I think all men are created equal," he wrote Rowe. "I want all men to have equal opportunity. Yes, I even think your civil rights slogans are eloquent and moving. But when you and Humphrey . . . reach the point of translating your humanitarian spirit into law you seem always to lose any sense of charity, faith in your fellow man, or reasonableness." What the nation was witnessing was "two blind unreasoning minorities" colliding.[43] What the country needed, he told Rowe, was a "frontal assault on the 'ill-housed, ill-clad, ill-fed' problem facing part of our nation. Until this problem is met, all your other legislation is built upon sand."[44]

Nevertheless, Johnson was stung by the criticism. With an eye to appeasing his liberal friends and to solidifying his position with Texas's largest minority, the junior senator in 1949 ostentatiously came to the aid of a Mexican American family victimized by white racism. In January of that year, Dr. Hector Garcia, a prominent south Texas physician, called LBJ asking for his help. It seemed that the white-owned funeral home in the small Texas community of Three Rivers was refusing the use of its facilities for the reburial of a Mexican American soldier, Felix Longoria, killed in the Philippines during World War II. Johnson told Garcia to try again, but if the Rice Funeral Home still insisted on discriminating, he and President Truman would see that Private Longoria was buried with full military honors at Arlington National Cemetery. Soon the Texas papers and then the national press had gotten wind of the story; both lauded Johnson's humanitarianism. The local mortician continued to refuse to see his chapel desecrated with the bones of a brown American, and the remains were duly buried at Arlington, with the Johnsons and Truman's military aide, General Harry Vaughn, in attendance.

In the aftermath of the civil rights battle in the Senate, LBJ proceeded to align himself with the White House on other measures. He voted for extended rent control, federal aid to education, additional low-rent public housing, a higher minimum wage, and expanded Social Security benefits. When a Fort Worth industrialist wrote to complain about wasteful government spending, Johnson lost his temper. "Would you have the government repudiate the national debt so that five billion dollars could be saved?" he asked rhetorically. "Would you scrap all our programs of Veterans' benefits and throw the Veterans recklessly on to the labor market, compounding the chaos of unemployment?" Should the nation dispense with food inspection, the Public Health Service, national defense and the court system as well?[45]

With the oil and gas lobby, Johnson faced a lose-lose situation. He had to oppose his president, who wanted to cut back the excessive subsidies enjoyed by these industries; yet he could never please industry bosses who were suspicious of him and always on the lookout for another Coke Stevenson. For example, throughout his second term, Harry Truman lobbied Congress to reduce the 27.5 percent oil depletion allowance, a huge tax break based on the gradual consumption of proven resources. But producers in Texas, Louisiana, Oklahoma, and California would have none of it. "We could have taken a 5 or 10 percent figure," Tom Connally later confided, "but we grabbed 27.5 because we were not only hogs but the odd figure made it appear as though it was scientifically arrived at."[46]

Arguing that the allowance was necessary to finance expensive exploration operations and to guarantee national self-sufficiency in petroleum, Johnson joined with the majority in defeating various amendments to reduce the depletion allowance. "One could simply not oppose the 27.5 depletion allowance and stay alive as a political figure in Texas," Harry McPherson said. Nevertheless, "his speeches on the floor in behalf of it were perfunctory and half-hearted."[47]

Much more controversial than the depletion allowance was the tidelands, or offshore oil deposits, issue. Truman favored federal control of tidelands oil deposits off the Texas coast. Almost to a person, Texans were adamantly opposed. "I've known of no other issue that aroused—even including civil rights—such a tremendous statewide emotion in Texas," George Reedy remembered.[48] Not only were the giant oil concerns and the independents up in arms, but middle- and working-class Texans were as well. The entire public school system plus the University of Texas were funded by proceeds from oil lands. Citizens of the Lone Star State were convinced that their livelihoods and the future of their children depended on oil. "A lot of Texans had an uneasy conscience about civil rights," Reedy said. "But there was no such thing as an anti-tidelands constituency."[49]

The issue was almost as emotional in the Northeast. Herblock ran a famous cartoon that was nationally syndicated entitled "Down by Smuggler's Cove," which depicted the nation's oilmen in the light of the moon gathering on the shore to steal the public's domain.[50] Johnson worked out a compromise in which the states would receive one-third of the proceeds from oil extracted from submerged lands and the federal government two-thirds, but the oil industry rejected it. Privately LBJ told friends that he favored federal control, but in public he staunchly defended states' rights. During the 1951–1952 session of Congress, he helped pass bills granting all affected states except Texas control over submerged lands three miles offshore. The Lone Star State would control out to ten and a half miles. Truman vetoed the bills, denouncing them as "robbery in broad daylight."[51]

Those who profited from fossil fuel in the Lone Star State were generally a greedy lot, conservative to the point of being crackpots. "I think they regarded Bob Taft with a bit of suspicion as being too liberal," George Reedy declared.[52] Thus it was that when Leland Olds, a member of the Federal Power Commission (FPC) since 1939 and an outspoken advocate of regulation of the gas industry, came up for reconfirmation, LBJ led the charge in opposing him. Olds was a fifty-nine-year-old New Yorker educated at Amherst College, where his father had been president. Following graduation, he became a Congregationalist minister, then from 1922 through 1929 worked as labor editor of the *Federated Press* until Governor Franklin Roosevelt selected him to head the New York State Power Authority. Then in 1939 Olds was tapped for the FPC. As a radical journalist in the 1920s, he had written a number of articles concerning the evils of capitalism and the inevitability of its collapse. He had subsequently moderated his views, but was still something of an icon to unions, consumers, and those favoring federal regulation of private enterprise.[53] As the nation's leading advocate for public power, he was anathema to the oil and gas interests.

It fell to LBJ to head the subcommittee of the Interstate and Foreign Commerce Committee that held hearings on Olds's nomination. Johnson realized that in the overheated atmosphere of the early cold war, the nominee's earlier writings praising Russia and communism would do him in. He met with Olds privately in an effort to persuade him to disavow the fifty-four articles published in "Labor Letter," his column for the *Federated Press*. When Olds brushed him off, Johnson decided to lead a no-holds-barred attack. South Texas Congressman John Lyle set the tone when he denounced Olds for sneering at the Fourth of July, referring to the church as "a handmaiden of the capitalist system," advocating nationalization of the coal, rail, and power industries, and preaching the communist doctrine of class struggle. Olds testified that he was not and had never been a communist and had changed his mind about Russia, but he also refused to disavow his earlier writings. Johnson's subcommittee voted seven to zero against confirmation, and the full committee concurred by a tally of ten to two.

LBJ should have let the matter rest there, but did not. He took to the floor of the Senate to denounce Olds for his "lifelong prejudice and hostility against the industries he now regulates."[54] "I do not charge that Mr. Olds is a communist," he said. "I realize that the line he followed, the phrases he used, the causes he espoused, resemble the party line today," but that did not make him a communist. Still, Johnson proclaimed, the issue before the Senate was: "Shall we have a Commissioner or a commissar?"[55] By a vote of fifty-three to fifteen the Senate overwhelmingly defeated the Olds nomination. "It was a pre–Joe McCarthy campaign," Joe Rauh later observed. "It was really vicious."[56] Drew Pearson, who was close to Olds, would never forgive Johnson. But the mail from Texas was overwhelmingly laudatory. Johnson noted that not only the consistently reactionary *Dallas Morning News* and *Houston Post* editorialized against Olds, but the vast majority of small dailies and weeklies did as well.[57]

Johnson's red-baiting was inexcusable, perhaps, but understandable. As historian Michael Gillette has observed, "The political atmosphere in October 1949 was one of suspicion against leftist government officials. The [Alger] Hiss trial was in the headlines; two days after the Senate vote [on Olds], eleven leaders of the American Communist party were convicted of conspiring to advocate the overthrow of the government . . . At that time most senators were far less interested in determining the accuracy of every accusation against Olds than they were in letting the public know and having the record show that they themselves did not vote for a man who was accused of being a Communist."[58]

Despite his wrecking job on the Olds nomination, Johnson continued to be a strong advocate of public power. He worked assiduously for the confirmation of Mon Walgren, a liberal from a public power state, to the FPC.[59] Indeed, according to George Reedy, Horace Busby, and D. B. Hardeman, Johnson was never close to his state's oil and gas industry. With a few individual exceptions, such as Wesley West, J. R. Parten, and the Brown brothers, big oil and gas continued to oppose him. H. L. Hunt, Sid Richardson, Clint Murchison, and others shared the view of E. B. Germany, CEO of Lone Star Steel, that LBJ was "the very essence of New Dealism and a stalwart of the philosophy of government which had brought this nation to the brink of disaster . . . He helped sow the seed for the harvest we are now reaping . . . [of] communists, fellow travelers, pinkos, and traitors to the American way of life firmly entrenched in . . . power."[60]

Personally, Johnson found the whole lot disgustingly self-centered and antidemocratic. Booth Mooney, an LBJ aide, recalled a meeting of oil and gas executives in which LBJ castigated them for opposing every piece of social legislation that came down the pike. " 'You make it goddamn hard for us to fight your battles up here,' he said. 'And it doesn't help any when stories come out in the papers about your private airplanes and your clubrooms with walls lined with the skins of unborn lambs and the fifty-grand parties you throw. You guys have about as much public relations sense as a tomcat on the prowl on Saturday night.' Some of his listeners snickered uncomfortably, but none undertook to answer his criticism."[61]

Neither was Johnson a soulmate of Dick Russell and the Dixie Association. LBJ, Hubert Humphrey observed, "was a close friend of Dick Russell's; a close associate of Walter George [the other Democratic senator from Georgia] . . . he was on good working relationships with every southerner, but he wasn't quite southern. He was a different cut. He worked with them on all the issues they were interested in, the depletion allowances, and in the early days on civil rights . . . But the relationship was never what I considered an emotional one, it was pragmatic."[62]

Soon after he entered the Senate, Johnson attended a meeting of the House-Senate Armed Services Committee conference. Harry Byrd Sr. of Virginia had been openly critical of those advocating a 70 group air force. Indignantly, Johnson demanded an apology from "as patrician a patrician as ever served in the Senate," for impugning the character, motives, and intelligence of 70-group supporters, of which he was one. A "flustered" Byrd apologized, directed that his remarks be stricken from the record, and asked that the committee move on with its business.[63] Although it was under different circumstances, when Hubert Humphrey, another freshman, had dared criticize Byrd, it had nearly ruined his career.

LBJ recognized early on that if he were going to be a power in the Democratic party and the U.S. Senate, he would have to build a working relationship with his liberal colleagues. His bridge to the twenty-five or so "bomb-throwers," as he called them, would be Hubert Humphrey. A year into their first term, Johnson began inviting the Minnesotan to his office for a drink and chats about the Senate and public affairs. It seemed an odd choice. Not only had Humphrey angered southerners and the Senate establishment—*Time* ran his picture on its cover with a tornado in the background, symbolizing the turmoil he would bring to Congress—but he was chair of the Americans for Democratic Action, the same organization that had led a campaign to dump Truman in favor of Dwight Eisenhower or William O. Douglas in 1948. But there was something about Humphrey, an echo of Maury Maverick, perhaps. He was smart, courageous, idealistic, and he wanted to make a difference. Johnson frequently invited Russell to join him and Humphrey for their chats.[64]

Humphrey and Johnson had both been schoolteachers, all three were from small towns, and each had an abiding sympathy for the rural poor. Johnson and Russell begin to think of Humphrey as "a more pragmatic fellow," who "wanted to learn how to live with people." To Paul Douglas and his other liberal friends, Humphrey began to argue that at his core Johnson was a New Dealer, but like all who hoped to remain in Congress, he had to adjust his ideas to the political realities of his home state. The liberals came to see Johnson as a man with whom they could do business, his way an avenue to social change, a means to both progress and union. "Johnson was an intensely ambitious man, anxious to get power and hold on to it," Douglas would say. "He had a progressive background, and I think this had entered into his spirit and was a fundamental feature of his character . . . But Texas after Roosevelt was a very different place than it had been. Gas and Oil came to the fore . . . They had become intensely anti-Roosevelt and anti-progressive, and yet they were the dominant characters in the state and in the Democratic party . . . Johnson, therefore, had this struggle within himself of his native tendencies, his Roosevelt idealism, faced with the hard facts of power politics and economic power."[65]

The key to Johnson's success as a senator was his skill in empathizing with his colleagues, but more than that, with his colleagues' constituents. His ability to get at the essence of other people was unparalleled, Harry McPherson observed. He perceived their fears, their hopes, their strengths, their weaknesses, their idealism, their pragmatism. June White, long-time family friend and wife of journalist William S. White, remembered that "he could read people almost on meeting them . . . It's almost as though he knew their assets, their plusses and their negative points, so that he could go . . . to their plus points and use them, even helping them to use themselves to their best advantage."[66] "He was like a novelist, a psychiatrist," Hubert Humphrey said.[67] He could identify with Jewish garment workers, Mexican American farm laborers, African Americans, both rural and urban, and white southerners jealous of their status and fearful of the future.

LBJ's relationship with the White House and Harry Truman was mixed. Truman had been unerring in his support of LBJ over Coke Stevenson in the 1948 campaign,[68] but the Texan's votes in favor of Taft-Hartley and his opposition to both the FEPC and the Olds nomination had rankled. Richard Russell had little respect for Truman, and he let Johnson know it. The junior senator from Texas was sometimes included in the group that the president and Clark Clifford, a principal adviser to the president, assembled to cruise the Potomac aboard the presidential yacht. There LBJ had a chance to rub shoulders with Chief Justice Carl Vinson, Clifford, Truman pal George Allen, and other luminaries. For an entire weekend Truman would preside over an eight-handed poker game lubricated with bourbon and branch water. "Everybody would come and show up in the dining room for breakfast," Clark Clifford recounted, "and they'd talk about conventions, and they'd talk about past experiences and the past political giants of the Democratic party."[69]

But there was always a distance. At the end of Johnson's first year in the Senate, Horace Busby asked why he did not spend more time at the White House. "It's this curly-headed fellow, Clifford." What has he got against you, Busby asked? "Clifford's one of those St. Louis aristocrats. He doesn't want the President to be around southerners and political types."[70] The two men would grow closer.

Eventually the relationship warmed. Johnson and Truman had too much in common for it not to. Both were genuine in their sympathy for the common man. Both were pragmatic politicians who detested pretension and thought racial prejudice absurd and a waste of time. LBJ played to Truman's "exaggerated masculinity," as George Reedy put it. "You know, his conversation was loaded with words that were so damn blue that even Johnson would blush occasionally . . . Johnson would always play this old game of contrasting Harry Truman to . . . some of the more effete liberals and intellectuals in the party. And Harry Truman wound up being a very strong Johnson supporter."[71]

IF LBJ SOMETIMES DIFFERED with the White House over aspects of domestic policy, he marched pretty much in lockstep with it in foreign affairs. By 1949 the notion prevailed among most Americans that they and their allies faced an international communist threat directed from the Kremlin and bent on world domination. They made little or no distinction between Marxist-Leninist ideology and Soviet imperialism. When China, the most populous nation in the world, fell to the communists in 1949, both government officials and the general public in the United States assumed that the Kremlin was responsible.

The triumph of the Chinese communists under Mao Zedong greatly intensified public and official anxiety in the United States and led directly to the Korean War. After the Soviet Union exploded an atomic device in 1949, Truman ordered the military to go ahead with development of a hydrogen bomb. At the same time, Secretary of State Dean Acheson ordered the policy planning staff, now headed by Paul Nitze, to come up with a new defense policy. The result was the National Security Council's policy statement NSC 68.

The premise underlying NSC 68 was that Marxism-Leninism was inherently totalitarian and expansionist and that the Soviet Union was determined to impose its will on the entire world. Nitze advocated a massive expansion of American military power to enable the United States to meet the threat posed by Soviet communism whenever and wherever it appeared. NSC 68 insisted that the U.S. economy could support a military budget that absorbed up to 50 percent of the GNP, and it recommended that defense spending be increased from $13 billion to $45 billion.

Before the globalist policies inherent in NSC 68 could be carried out, however, the cold war spread to the Korean peninsula and heated up. On June 25, 1950, the army of the communist republic of North Korea crossed the thirty-eighth parallel in an effort to reunify the country by force. South Korean (ROK) forces fled in confusion. Two days later, Truman ordered General Douglas MacArthur, who then headed the Allied occupation government in Japan, to use troops under his command to ensure that the South Korean army was not driven entirely off the peninsula. Subsequently, with American help, ROK forces were able to establish and protect an enclave around Pusan.

LBJ immediately declared his support for the Truman administration's decision to make a stand in Korea. Johnson hailed the president's action as one that "gives a new and noble meaning to freedom, gives purpose to our national resolve and determination, convincingly affirms America's capacity for world leadership."[72] Johnson was only being consistent. Throughout 1949 he had supported the administration's efforts to beef up the armed forces. "He was thoroughly convinced that we lived in a world where the United States would have no real voice or real prestige in international affairs unless it had the necessary defense strength to back it up," George Reedy observed. It was also clear that he believed in the concept of a monolithic communist threat. "Russia needs . . . and wants war," he told the Senate in a speech delivered some two weeks after the North Korean invasion, and placed the outbreak of hostilities in the context of the Soviet drive for world domination.[73]

As had been true during World War II, LBJ had no intention of sitting on the sidelines during the Korean conflict. Because of his experience in defense and military matters and his seat on the Armed Services Committee, Johnson's mind turned naturally to the idea of a special Senate watchdog committee that would oversee the relationship between the defense industry and the federal government, simultaneously ensuring efficiency in the war effort and protection of the reputation of the Democratic administration. Working through Russell and Millard Tydings of Maryland, the committee chairman, Johnson had little trouble bringing the special committee into being, with him as its chair.[74]

Between August and September, the committee produced its first wave of reports. They criticized the federal government for "paperwork preparedness," a "siesta psychology," and a "business as usual" attitude. They singled out the government Munitions Board for continuing to sell "surplus" property to the private sector at bargain-basement prices when there was a war on. One Texas operator had managed to buy $1.2 million worth of surplus airplane parts for $6.89 and then sell them back to the government for $63,000. For these and other transgressions, especially the failure to stockpile enough synthetic rubber, Truman summarily fired the chairman of the Munitions Board. The air force suddenly canceled a $1,650,000 order for white dress gloves for officers when it was rumored that Johnson was merely thinking about launching an investigation.[75]

Allied forces, made up primarily of South Korean and U.S. troops, were initially restricted to their toehold around Pusan on the southeastern tip of the peninsula. In the fall, however, MacArthur staged a daring amphibious landing at the port of Inchon on the west coast halfway between the thirty-eighth parallel and the southern tip of Korea. The assault was a success, with MacArthur's troops quickly establishing a beachhead. In the weeks that followed, U.S. marines and army personnel in cooperation with ROK troops pushed out from Pusan and Inchon. Confronted with this two-pronged offensive and Allied firepower, the North Korean army began to retreat, a retreat that quickly turned into a rout.

As MacArthur's soldiers neared the prewar boundary between North and South Korea, the Truman administration faced a dilemma. Should the UN command stop at the thirty-eighth parallel, or should it continue northward and reunify the country? MacArthur strenuously recommended the latter course, and Truman's advisers in Washington soon concurred, arguing to the president that it would be impossible to maintain an independent and secure South Korea as long as the communists were in control of the North. And, of course, the temptation to roll back the frontiers of communism in East Asia was hard to resist.

By the second week in November, MacArthur was within sight of the Yalu River, the boundary separating North Korea from China. With the bitter Korean winter setting in, three hundred thousand Chinese troops crossed the border and smashed the two Allied columns that had penetrated deep into North Korean territory. In his haste and overconfidence, MacArthur had had these two spearheads advance so quickly that they outran their logistical and reserve support. The communists killed or captured a large number of American soldiers, some twenty-three thousand in the vicinity of the Chosin reservoir alone. A remnant of MacArthur's force fought its way to the coast and escaped, while what remained of the shattered columns retreated before the advancing Chinese. Massing its reserves and utilizing its superior firepower, the UN command halted the communist offensive, but only after the Red Chinese and North Koreans had advanced well below the thirty-eighth parallel. Slowly, painfully, the Allies advanced up the peninsula once again until they reached a line corresponding roughly to the prewar boundary.

Following the Chinese intervention, Truman declared a state of national emergency, quadrupled his budget request for defense, and increased the size of the army by 50 percent.[76] Johnson's response was to criticize the administration for not having prepared earlier, declaring that "we have thrown up a chicken-wire fence, not a wall of armed might."[77] From late 1950 through 1952, he would urge the fullest possible mobilization of the nation's material and human resources. Meanwhile, the preparedness subcommittee launched one investigation after another into the defense effort. LBJ and the committee staff carefully avoided stepping on the White House's toes while at the same time satisfying the Republicans that they were not participating in a whitewash.[78]

Yet, by the fall of 1950, many Americans had become thoroughly frustrated with Harry Truman. Southerners were up in arms over his civil rights policies, liberals were disgusted with his inability to defeat the conservative coalition in Congress and with what they considered his personal vulgarity—he was then spending long hours writing wrathful and profane letters to columnists and reviewers who dared criticize him or his singing daughter, Margaret—and everyone was fed up with the Korean War. Public opinion polls taken in late 1950 indicated that 66 percent of the American people favored pulling out of the war, with 49 percent convinced that entering had been a mistake in the first place.[79]

NOT SURPRISINGLY, the Democrats took a beating in the midterm congressional elections, losing twenty-eight seats in the House and five in the Senate, among them the whip, Francis Myers of Pennsylvania.[80] There was not exactly a stampede to fill the now vacant leadership posts. Many considered them to be pathways to political oblivion because those who held them were diverted from the needs of their home states and their constituents. When Bobby Baker first mentioned the possibility of running for whip to Johnson, he laughingly replied, "You'll destroy me, because I can't afford to be identified with the Democratic party right now."[81]

But when Russell and Bob Kerr told Johnson that they would support him for whip, he decided to go for it. The chief obstacle was Senator Ernest W. McFarland of Arizona, who wanted to be majority leader and who did not want to have LBJ as his chief lieutenant. "Senator McFarland was not a strong leader," Bobby Baker recalled. "He in many ways was envious and jealous of Lyndon Johnson."[82] For Russell, however, the very fact of McFarland's weakness was reason enough to see Lyndon fill the number two position. Thus it unfolded that at the party caucus held on January 2, 1951, Lyndon Baines Johnson was selected by acclamation as the youngest whip in Senate history.[83]

The position hardly seemed worth the effort. It brought LBJ a small private office in the Senate and a desk in the middle of the front row on the chamber floor, but seemingly little else. Traditionally, the whip was nothing more than a vote counter for the majority leader, a job that secretary to the majority Felton "Skeeter" Johnson was more than capable of performing. The whip acted as leader when that person was absent, but McFarland was rarely gone. Nonetheless, LBJ was a master at exploiting whatever office he held. His influence grew as he helped one senator after another bring their pet legislative schemes to first committee and then full Senate vote. He had Russell's and Kerr's ear, and he continued to consult ostentatiously with Speaker Rayburn.

THE 82ND CONGRESS would become notorious for its investigative committees. More than 130 shined a legislative searchlight on everything from labor racketeering, to organized crime, to the national defense effort. They were considered effective mechanisms for members of the Senate and House to gain national and local headlines as guardians of the public welfare. Johnson's ongoing probe of the defense effort continued to be among the most conspicuous. With Reedy and Baker's help, LBJ successfully cultivated reporters from *Time, Newsweek,* and the *New York Times. Collier's* and the *Saturday Evening Post* both ran feature articles on the man and the politician. Indeed, virtually every national publication that covered Congress praised the work of the subcommittee, culminating with *Newsweek* featuring LBJ, the country's "watch-dog in chief," on the cover of its November 1950 issue.

As the media would learn, when evaluating the public career of Lyndon Johnson it was always prudent to distinguish between rhetoric and reality, although in politics, it should be noted, rhetoric sometimes creates reality. For example, it seemed in the waning months of 1951 that the majority whip, caught up in the passions of the cold war, had become an advocate of nuclear war with the Soviet Union. To audiences in west Texas and Dallas, he proclaimed that conflicts like Korea were part of a global plot hatched by the Soviet Union to dominate the world. Proxy wars in which the Kremlin escaped punishment for shedding the blood of others could not be allowed to continue. "Someday, somewhere, some way," he declared, "there must be a clear-cut settlement between the forces of freedom and the forces of communism. It is foolish to talk of avoiding war." Several weeks later: "We should announce, I believe, that any act of aggression, anywhere, by any communist forces, will be regarded as an act of aggression by the Soviet Union . . . If anywhere in the world—by any means, open or concealed—communism trespasses upon the soil of the free world, we should unleash all the power at our command upon the vitals of the Soviet Union." Challenged by a member of the audience, Johnson declared, "I realize full well the awesome potentialities of this proclamation."[84]

One of his biographers would dub Johnson "Senator Strangelove" for these Armageddon-like statements, but it should be noted that they were the stuff of brinksmanship and massive retaliation, the foreign policy doctrines that would sweep Dwight D. Eisenhower and John Foster Dulles into power in 1952 and keep them there for eight years. Moreover, when it came down to substantive acts, it seemed that Johnson preferred restraint and sought limited, not total, war.

By March 1951, the war had reached a stalemate, with both sides dug in in the vicinity of the thirty-eighth parallel. The "American Caesar," as one of his biographers would subsequently dub MacArthur, was not happy; he advocated not only retaking the North, but attacking China. In April, he addressed a public letter to Representative Joseph Martin, Republican minority leader in the House, in which he called for an all-out war effort in Asia to defeat the communists and criticized "diplomats" for being willing to fight with words only. "It seems strangely difficult for some to realize that here in Asia is where the Communist conspirators have elected to make their play for global conquest—if we lose the war to communism in Asia the fall of Europe is inevitable," MacArthur observed to Martin and through him to the American people. Truman was understandably furious. "The son of a bitch isn't going to resign on me," the president heatedly told General Omar Bradley. "I want him fired."[85] With the concurrence of the Joint Chiefs, Truman on April 11 relieved MacArthur of his command.

Acutely aware of the general's popularity, especially among conservatives, the Republicans prepared to blast the Democrats once more for being soft on communism and to charge the administration with not supporting its military commanders in the field. MacArthur's firing was a clear indication of the degree of communist infiltration of the federal government, Senator Joseph McCarthy of Wisconsin declared. "How can we account for our present situation," he asked rhetorically, "unless we believe that men high in this government are concerting to deliver us to disaster?"[86] He began referring to Dean Acheson, the nattily attired secretary of state, as "the Red Dean of Fashion."

The conqueror of Manila and Inchon was welcomed as a returning hero when he arrived in the United States on April 17. He made his way in a triumphal procession from San Francisco to New York, where a ticker-tape parade dumped an unprecedented sixteen tons of confetti on his motorcade. From there he traveled to Washington, where he addressed a joint session of Congress. It was from this lofty platform that MacArthur delivered his "old soldiers never die, they just fade away" speech. Unfortunately for the Truman administration, the general refused to do either. Former President Herbert Hoover declared MacArthur to be the "reincarnation of St. Paul into a great General of the Army who came out of the East." "I'll never forget watching him go up Pennsylvania Avenue," George Reedy recalled. "I had a very strong feeling that if he had said, 'Come on, let's take it,' and had started to charge toward the White House, that whole crowd would have gone with him."[87]

Johnson found MacArthur's performance disgusting and, increasingly, alarming. Since his days in the South Pacific he had never had much respect for the man. To LBJ, MacArthur's fault was not that he was a grandstander, but that he was lazy and inefficient.[88] Moreover, Johnson was then and would continue to be an ardent supporter of civilian control of the military. There was no doubt in his mind that the general was violating his constitutional oath and acting insubordinately against both Truman and the Joint Chiefs. "The basic issue is whether American policy shall be made by the elected officials of the government who are responsible to the people," he declared in a public statement, "or by military leaders who are responsible only to their immediate superiors."[89]

Johnson's was not a popular position in Texas. As he made his way across the nation, MacArthur had taken care to stop in Texas. In Houston, oil and banking magnates Jesse Jones, H. L. Hunt, and Hugh Roy Cullen, who had helped sponsor the visit, presented the hero of Inchon with the keys to a new Cadillac automobile.[90] Walter Jenkins recalled that the MacArthur controversy produced "the largest single mail that we ever had on one issue," the overwhelming majority favorable to MacArthur and calling for Truman's impeachment.[91]

IRONICALLY, it was the Republicans who provided the administration and its supporters with a strategy for extricating themselves from their dilemma. Shortly after the general's dismissal, congressional Republicans had begun calling for a full investigation into Truman's foreign and defense policies. Convinced that if given enough rope, the liberator of the Philippines would hang himself, Senate Democratic leaders, including Johnson, enthusiastically supported the idea of letting him testify. The person in charge of the hearings would have to be above reproach, all agreed. Immediately, the Senate gravitated to Richard Russell, a man clearly independent of the Truman administration but at the same time a proven Democratic loyalist. The MacArthur hearings, to be conducted jointly by the Senate Armed Services and Foreign Relations Committees, would require "a subtle mind," as George Reedy put it.[92]

From the beginning, LBJ played a leading role in the proceedings. Russell and Tom Connally, chair of Foreign Relations, would preside, but Lyndon Johnson would sit second chair. To help Russell prepare, Johnson lent him staffers George Reedy and Jerry Siegel. "There were almost daily morning sessions with Russell, Johnson, and myself," Reedy recalled. "I'd stay up most of the night analyzing the testimony . . . Then I'd wait until Russell came in, and he and Johnson and I would spend about an hour, sometimes a couple of hours, discussing what was going to happen during the day and thinking of all the various eventualities."[93]

The three decided that the worst thing that could happen was for the proceedings to become adversarial. MacArthur must be made to feel secure so that he would spin out his scenario and "the ridiculousness of it would eventually become apparent." Russell was convinced, and convinced Johnson, that the nation had arrived at a very dangerous point. The American people would not long continue to be willing to shed blood and treasure to preserve the status quo ante bellum—in Korea or anywhere else. The options to containment, however, were isolationism or Armageddon.[94]

Soon Johnson began to take charge of the questioning. He was exceedingly solicitous and patient. "Lister Hill [Democratic senator from Florida] had a favorite word that when you gave somebody honey, he called it a honey fucking," Bobby Baker said, "and Lyndon Johnson gave Douglas MacArthur the biggest honey fucking I have ever seen in my life."[95] Gradually, LBJ began to ask questions for which the general did not have good answers. The administration's chief witness was JCS Chairman General Omar Bradley. MacArthur had been out of the country too long, he said, and had lost sight of global strategy. "Taking on Red China," he declared at the hearings, would have led only "to a larger deadlock at greater expense." So long as the United States regarded the Soviet Union as the principal adversary and Europe as the chief prize in the cold war, the all-out conflict in Asia advocated by MacArthur "would involve us in the wrong war at the wrong place at the wrong time and with the wrong enemy."[96] Eventually, the logic of the administration's argument began to take hold, and the furor over MacArthur's firing died away.

When, in June 1951, the Soviet representative to the UN suggested an armistice in Korea with both sides withdrawing beyond their respective sides of the thirty-eighth parallel, Washington leaped at the offer. Tense negotiations began at Panmunjom and dragged on through 1952. The stalemated talks became an issue in the 1952 election, when the Republican candidate, General Dwight D. Eisenhower, promised to go directly to Korea to end the war. He did indeed make the trip, but it was probably his secret threats of nuclear strikes against North Korea and China if they did not agree to a permanent truce that ended the fighting.

THE KOREAN WAR was a "limited war," a unique and frustrating byproduct of the Soviet-American nuclear stalemate as well as a civil war with deep roots in Korean history. Though the United States possessed atomic weapons that could have been used to devastate North Korea and communist China, it dared not use them for fear of nuclear retaliation by the Soviet Union in East Asia and even Europe. Thus began a generation of limited, conventional conflicts; total mobilization and a complete commitment to victory were unthinkable as long as the world was under the threat of atomic annihilation. In a sense, however, Korea marked a clear-cut victory for the policy of containment. The United States and its allies had succeeded in "holding the line" against communist aggression. Just as the Berlin Blockade had reassured the noncommunist population of Europe that the Americans would walk the last mile with them, so, too, did the Korean war demonstrate to the people of East Asia that the United States would expend blood and treasure to defend them from the scourge of communism.

The question that the war did not answer was whether the policy of containment was capable of distinguishing between Marxism-Leninism as an economic theory and means to social justice on the one hand and Sino-Soviet imperialism on the other. And it reinforced the fear among the people of developing nations that in its obsessive anticommunism, Washington was willing to ally itself with autocratic regimes—that of Syngman Rhee in South Korea, for example—dedicated to maintaining an unjust status quo.

WHILE LYNDON BATTLED to stay afloat on the stormy seas of national politics, Lady Bird was busy raising two daughters and building the family fortune. In 1947, the year before LBJ ran for the Senate, KTBC listed assets of $213,140, including $82,191 in "undistributed profits." [97] Up to this point Lady Bird had been sole proprietor, but with the station on firm ground, she decided to incorporate. The five hundred shares originally issued by the Texas Broadcasting Corporation were mostly owned by Lady Bird and her daughters, with a small number sold to Jesse Kellam, station manager, Paul Bolton, news editor, nephew and employee O. P. Bobbitt, and Walter Jenkins. [98] LBJ was not a shareholder, but under Texas community property laws he was co-owner of his wife's shares. Occasionally, the company would issue debentures to him which he converted to cash and used to buy municipal bonds. [99]

At the same time, Lady Bird developed her holdings in Alabama. The properties in Autauga and Chilton Counties that she had inherited were seeded with pine trees, which were subsequently harvested and sold. By the late 1950s, Lady Bird was one of the largest tree farmers in Alabama. [100] What really turned LBJ Inc. into an imposing economic entity, however, was a new medium: television. In 1946, there were only eight thousand primitive black-and-white televisions nationwide; by 1960, 45.8 million high-quality sets adorned 90 percent of America's living rooms. The average television owner spent more time viewing than working. *TV Guide* became the fastest growing periodical of the 1950s, and the "electronic hearth" transformed the way Americans lived. Instead of reading, exercising, or conversing, the nuclear family gathered faithfully before "the tube" to watch their weekly mystery or variety show.

Lady Bird Johnson was one of a very few entrepreneurs in America who saw television's vast economic promise. When the FCC opened up television channels, broadcasting companies who received permits found the going rough. Both the Columbia Broadcasting System and Westinghouse Broadcasting actually turned back some of the permits they had purchased. [101] "I don't know how many stations were broadcasting in Texas in 1949," staffer Don Cook said. "I know that by the time we went on the air, there were only maybe six, and maybe five of them were losing big money." [102]

Yet, Lady Bird sensed that television was the wave of the future, and she had the capital to invest. The FCC issued Texas Broadcasting a license to operate KTBC television on July 11. The station went on the air on Thanksgiving Day 1952 to broadcast the annual University of Texas–Texas A&M football game. In the months that followed, Lyndon personally solicited contracts from the three major program producers: NBC, ABC, and CBS. [103]

KTBC television prospered, in part because it was well run and in part because it was the only VHF station in the state's booming capital city. As a monopoly, KTBC was able to charge comparatively higher rates for advertising. For example, the station's base hourly rate for ads was $575 in the early 1960s. Rochester, Minnesota, a roughly comparable city and market but with competition from stations in nearby Minneapolis–St. Paul, charged only $325.[104] Writing in the *Wall Street Journal* in 1964, journalist Louis Kohlmeier argued that there were other prospective competitors at the time KTBC was chartered, but they knew that with Johnson's political clout, the FCC would always favor Texas Broadcasting. He quoted Tom Potter, founding owner of WFAA-TV in Dallas: "Lyndon was in a favorable position to get that station even if somebody had contested it. Politics is politics." Perhaps so, but there was no law against public officeholders or their relatives engaging in legitimate business activities, and virtually everyone did. Moreover, there was no evidence that the Johnsons used improper influence to gain their license for KTBC.

The same cannot be said for their entry into the Waco television market. After issuing several hundred licenses in 1948, the FCC imposed a moratorium. In February 1952, LBJ contacted the commission in behalf of a constituent, the owner of KWTX Broadcasting Company in Waco, who wanted to apply for a VHF license. Writing on the stationary of the "Office of the Democratic Leader" (LBJ was then majority leader), he pressed federal regulators to give "serious consideration to this problem, based on its merits." [105]

Finally, on December 2, 1954, the FCC granted KWTX its television permit. The previous day, however, it had issued a license to Lady Bird to buy a debt-ridden UHF television station in Waco for $134,000. Lyndon's constituent complained that his license was almost worthless, because under the Johnson ownership, his UHF rival would command both CBS and ABC programming. Lady Bird quickly found a solution. In return for 29 percent of the stock in KWTX Broadcasting, she let the UHF station go under and persuaded CBS and ABC to commit to the new VHF station.[106]

Then in 1956, the Texas Broadcasting Company took over a debt-burdened station in Weslaco, a town situated in south Texas just above the Rio Grande. In return for 50 percent of the stock, Lady Bird paid the owner, O. L. Taylor, $5,000 and loaned him another $140,000. With major network affiliation, KRGT-TV prospered. In 1957, Texas Broadcasting bought the remaining 50 percent of the stock from Taylor for $100,000. In 1961, Bird sold KRGT for $1.6 million.[107] At the same time the FCC approved the Weslaco deal, it granted KTBC-TV another increase in power to 316 kilowatts and approved a request from Texas Broadcasting to change its name to LBJ Company. In April 1956, LBJ Company listed assets of $1,534,381. Three years later, the corporation's total value had climbed to $2,569,503.[108]

Throughout his political life, LBJ was terrified that he would be charged with using his political office to further his and his friends' financial interests. In Congress, he never voted on a single piece of legislation affecting radio or television, and he never went near the FCC. Both Paul Bolton and Leonard Marks insisted that their boss never threatened, cajoled, or coerced the federal bureaucracy to obtain a favorable decision. Yet, the FCC seemingly granted Texas Broadcasting's and LBJ Company's every request. KTBC's broadcasting boundaries were drawn so as to ensure its continuing monopoly in the Austin area.

The fact that Lyndon and Lady Bird Johnson were the proprietors was well-known to the staff and commissioners. The Johnsons were close friends with Clifford Durr, a commissioner from 1941 to 1948; Paul Porter, the chair of the Commission for fourteen months between 1944 and 1946; Rosel H. Hyde, who served for over twenty-three years beginning in 1946; and Robert T. Bartley, a Sam Rayburn nephew who held a seat from March 1952 through March 1972.[109] These individuals had every reason to pave the way for a Johnson broadcasting empire, not the least of which were ideological and political. All but Hyde were New Deal–Fair Dealers who wanted to see a moderate-to-liberal journalistic voice in Texas established to compete with the likes of the *Dallas Morning News* and *Houston Post* networks.

More important than this connection, perhaps, was LBJ's friendship with Frank Stanton and other media executives. In 1952, after the FCC had granted the license to operate KTBC, George Reedy reported to Johnson that a mutual friend, Theodore Granik, had called from New York. He had lunched with several NBC vice presidents, one of whom (Stanton) had recently met with the senator. "The reaction was extremely favorable," Granik reported. "[Stanton] . . . thinks your affiliation with the network would be a wonderful thing since 'everybody admires' you as a man who is doing a marvelous job for the country and who always stands behind his word."[110]

BY AMERICAN MIDDLE-CLASS STANDARDS at midcentury, Lyndon and Lady Bird Johnson were a successful couple. He was a U.S. senator and the youngest minority whip in the nation's history, and she had parlayed a modest inheritance into a small business empire. They began to search for a material badge of their success. For a variety of reasons, the couple turned to the Hill Country and the possibility of a ranch along the Pedernales. Lady Bird had come to love the limestone escarpments, the clear streams, the live oaks, and the bluebonnets of Blanco and Gillespie Counties almost as much as her husband. Ownership of a large farm or ranch would confirm Johnson's membership in the Senate, a body that one observer termed the most exclusive gentlemen's club in the world. Russell owned a country place near his home in Winder, Georgia; Kerr, Anderson, Everett Dirksen (GOP minority leader), and Morse all owned large ranches or farms. The time LBJ had spent at Huntland, George and Herman Brown's estate, and at Charles Marsh's Longlea had made a deep impression on him. Here the rich and powerful gathered to pay a kind of homage to the country squires who presided. Life could not have been more stimulating. Moreover, ownership of a substantial Hill Country spread would enable Lyndon to recoup psychologically for the humiliation of his father's failure. It would be an announcement to all of central Texas that he had fulfilled the dreams and atoned for the sins of his ancestors.[111]

In the fall of 1950, Lyndon took Lady Bird to visit his aged Aunt Frank Martin, who still lived in the two-story timber and fieldstone house on the banks of the Pedernales. The dog-trot cabin of his birth lay less than three-quarters of a mile away. Aunt Frank, then seventy-eight and increasingly unable to care for the house and the 243 acres on which it was situated, talked to Lyndon about how wonderful it would be if he and Lady Bird could buy the place and refurbish it as a retreat and site for family reunions. Lady Bird was appalled. The house was falling down and had a colony of bats living in its chimney.[112] It seemed to her to resemble nothing more than "a Charles Addams cartoon of a haunted house."[113] Yet, Lyndon had made up his mind, and privately he worked out the arrangements.[114]

Lady Bird, the woman who had had no home to call her own at the beginning of the 1940s, now had three. "I was really, thoroughly mad," she recalled, "but it was so obvious that Lyndon was ecstatic that to express my full anger would be like slapping the baby who had not moaned, it wasn't doing anything wrong . . . This was his heart's home. It was really where he wanted to get to."[115] She hired a local architect, and from February until July 1952 she would live with Lyndon's mother in Austin one week each month to oversee the renovations.[116]

That September the refurbishment had progressed sufficiently for Lady Bird and the girls to live in the Martin house while Lyndon campaigned for Adlai Stevenson around the state. It was raining on Tuesday morning, September 16, 1952, when Bird drove Lynda, then eight, across the wooden bridge to catch her school bus. The rain increased steadily throughout the day. Bird phoned a relative in Johnson City to pick Lynda up after school and keep her overnight. During the next thirty-six hours, twenty inches of rain fell in the Hill Country. Power failed, and every creek and stream in Blanco and Gillespie Counties became raging torrents. Lady Bird and Lucy, who dined in the dark on tomato soup and peanut butter sandwiches, could do nothing but watch the Pedernales rise, sweeping away topsoil, trees, and livestock. As the river approached the front porch, Bird read her daughter stories by the light of a coal-oil lamp. It finally stopped raining shortly after midnight on Wednesday. By midmorning the bright blue Texas sky was filled with rescue planes and helicopters searching for the injured and marooned. Lady Bird had survived the largest and most destructive flood in the Hill Country's recorded history.[117]

The ranch recovered and prospered. It became a vital part not only of Lyndon Johnson's private life but of his public persona as well. As historian Hal Rothman has noted, Johnson's acquisition and development of "the Ranch" coincided with the rise of the West in the popular imagination. The 1950s marked the heyday of the western in the movies and on television, from *Red River* in 1945 to *How the West Was Won* in 1962. In this mythic place, Americans, stressed by the tensions of the cold war and dulled by the monotonous conformity of suburbia, could find escape. "The American West became a parable for American society, the challenge that Americans faced in the past that offered ways to face, address, and solve new tensions in the present."[118] As a Texan, a rancher, a westerner, Johnson could pose as the new man, free of the taint of urban decay and southern racism.

But in addition, there was a different West, a new frontier that LBJ sought to lay claim to. It was the West of George and Herman Brown, of Sid Richardson, a frontier in which the ten-gallon hat and cowboy boots were but accoutrements to modernization and urbanization. Thus could LBJ pose as a problem solver, a herald of the new age of technology and skyscrapers but a man who was at the same time steeped in the traditions of the Turnerian frontier. The North and Midwest viewed the Southeast as the most backward part of the nation, the most resistant to change, and the most out of step with postwar realities. Southerners viewed the Northeast as economic exploiters and racist hypocrites. For many, the future and its answers were to be found in the West.

LBJ immediately adopted the guise of a rancher: Stetson, khakis, expensive boots, and horse (he was an excellent rider). As with most things in Lyndon Johnson's life, there were two ranches. There was the natural retreat whose vast blue dome, live oaks, wildflowers, and clear waters nourished his soul. He would rise early and spend an hour just walking and in the evening sit atop a ridge to witness the magnificent sunsets. "This country has always been a place where I could come and fill my cup, so to speak and recharge myself for the more difficult days ahead. Here's where we come to rest our bones and to collect our thoughts and to lay our plans."[119] And there was the public ranch, the endless pictures of LBJ hosting a barbeque for national and then international luminaries, the celebrity deer hunting, the inevitable inspection tours of cattle herds and fence mending.

PARENTING DID NOT COME NATURALLY either to Lyndon or to Lady Bird. Joe Phipps recounts a tale of Lyndon, the father of a three-year-old and a toddler, interacting with his offspring. One Sunday morning he and LBJ, still in his pajamas in bed, were going over campaign strategy. In pops Lady Bird declaring that Lynda and Lucy needed a kiss from their father. Delighted, LBJ straightened the covers and welcomed the giggling girls. For several minutes, father and daughters kissed, tickled, and laughed. As they continued to crawl all over him, their father's tone changed. "That's enough," he said, patting at them, trying to bring gleeful thrashings under control. "You've said 'good morning' to Daddy. That's enough. Take it easy." But neither of the children showed the slightest inclination toward being calmed. "At last, a tremendous roar unloosed, his face grew livid. He was shouting, 'Bird! Bird! Come get these little sons of bitches off my bed. They're crawling over me like baby dragons!' "[120]

For her part, Lady Bird had never had a mother and had no real model for the job. She loved both her daughters, but she made no bones about who came first:

Lyndon. Lucy even came to believe that she and her sister rated third after the family business. When the girls were in grade school, they lived half the year in Washington and the other half in Austin, sometimes with Lady Bird and sometimes with Willie Day Taylor, a former member of Johnson's staff who became their surrogate mother.

The other powerful figure in their life was the family's full-time cook, Zephyr Wright, a black college student from Marshall whom Bird hired in 1942.[121] Typically, the fall school term was spent in Johnson City and the spring term in a Washington, D.C., school. In Washington, most of the girls' classmates were Jewish because LBJ refused to live in a section of town with closed housing covenants. Lynda recalled that her classmates were nice and friendly, but she was rarely invited to parties or to sleep over. Her friends were to be found among the gentile offspring of staff members or among neighborhood children.[122]

Their father loved Lynda and Lucy and followed their upbringing, but he did so from afar. He left the house first thing in the morning and returned in the early evening or later. His contact with his daughters was limited to Sundays or to cocktail hour, when they would politely introduce themselves to the inevitable guests, do a bit of serving, and retire.[123] Father and daughters dealt with each other as 1950s stereotypes; only later, during his presidency, when they were increasingly self-aware young women and he was burdened with the trials of Vietnam did parent and children break in on each other emotionally and psychologically.

Johnson continued to look beyond his marriage for romance. By the time he entered the Senate, he had taken another lover. Madeline Brown was a twenty-three-year-old account executive working for Glenn Advertising, a firm that produced radio ads for KTBC. Lyndon spotted the five-foot, eight-inch, 118-pound beauty at a party in Dallas in the summer of 1948. He picked her out of the crowd and ordered Jesse Kellam to bring her to Austin at the first opportunity. On October 29, Brown flew to Austin on a Trans Texas airline ticket Kellam sent her. After attending a party at the Driskill sponsored by KTBC, she allowed herself to be seduced by Johnson. According to her account of the affair, his nickname for her was "Pussy Galore," and hers for him was "Sandow" (for Eugene Sandow, a famous nineteenth-century bodybuilder). "I threw away all my morals for him," Brown said.

He regarded Lady Bird as his "official wife," Lyndon reputedly told her. In fact, his wife's education, breeding, and business acumen benefited him in many ways, but emotionally and physically he felt the need to become involved with other women. In December 1951, Brown bore a son, Stephen, whom she claimed was Lyndon's. Using Kellam and Bolton as emissaries, he sent regular monthly payments to mother and child until his death in 1973. Privately, Lady Bird scoffed at Brown's claims, telling staff that she did not believe the affair had ever happened.[124]

CHAPTER 12

LEADER

LVIN WIRTZ, LBJ'S MENTOR AND GUARDIAN OF NEW
Deal Democrats in Texas, celebrated his sixty-third birthday in
1950. Political troubles were once again brewing in the Lone Star
State, but the power broker was confident that he would come out
on top. On October 27, he took time out from his busy schedule to attend a
football game between Texas, his alma mater, and Rice. In the midst of the excitement and hubbub, Wirtz suffered a heart attack and died. His death "was
kind of the end of an era . . . one of the final blows that ushered us into having to
stand on our own," Lady Bird later recalled. He was an "advisor and mentor and
friend and sort of court of last resort."[1] Lyndon found Wirtz's passing deeply depressing. It reminded him of his family's history of heart disease and his own
mortality. Johnson would soon sorely miss Wirtz's advice, as the ongoing intra-
party feud in Texas would turn ugly, smearing him as a murderer and, worse, a
disloyal Democrat.

As ever, LBJ's opponents were the Texas regulars, Democrats-cum-
Republicans. They had found a new, formidable champion in the person of
Allan Shivers. The lieutenant governor had become governor when Beauford
Jester had been found dead aboard his train on July 11, 1949. The forty-two-
year-old native of Port Arthur was tall, handsome, smart, ambitious, and Machiavellian. His father, a district court judge, had suffered one financial failure after
another, creating a deep-seated sense of financial insecurity in Allan. Shivers
was torn between a desire to be the ultimate political power broker in his native
state and its richest citizen.[2] If he could have both, so much the better.

On race, he had no real convictions. "Oh, I don't think Allan cared a thing in
the world about race," D. B. Hardeman said, "he could teach it flat or teach it
round."[3] The Brown brothers, Amon Carter, and Clint Murchison were a bit
too liberal for Shivers. He gravitated toward reactionaries like E. B. Germany of

Lone Star Steel and the oil crazies like H. L. Hunt. "Niggers in their place" and "The only good commie is a dead commie" were the slogans favored by his intimates. While Jester's body was still warm in his grave, Shivers began moving protégés of Coke Stevenson into high appointive positions in the state government.

In the runup to the state convention scheduled for September 1950, Shivers maneuvered to bring the Democratic party under his personal control, and he lured Jake Pickle away from the Johnson camp to help him. Having purged party workers at the precinct level who were not tried-and-true Shivercrats, the governor was in complete control of the state convention when it met. The delegates were so cowed that you could almost hear them moo, Sam Rayburn said.[4]

Shivers next set his sights on controlling the 1952 Democratic State Convention that would choose delegates to the national gathering. It became increasingly clear that the governor and, if he could help it, the state's delegation would support only a candidate who came out four-square for state ownership of offshore oil lands.

Initially, LBJ went out of his way to maintain a good relationship with Shivers. The two men "respected each other quite a lot as leaders," Walter Jenkins recalled, but there was never any warmth or intimacy between the two, as there was between Johnson and Connally.[5] Maury Maverick pled with LBJ to intervene and do battle with the Shivercrats in behalf of the loyalists, but Johnson was reluctant. Meddling in state politics had usually proven damaging to the careers of U.S. senators from Texas. Only three senators had represented the state for more than one term; Charles Culberson, Morris Sheppard, and Tom Connally. All three had scrupulously avoided entanglement in state politics.[6]

Nevertheless, if Shivers decided to challenge Johnson for his Senate seat in 1954, LBJ would need all the support from the loyalists that he could garner. For his part, Rayburn was convinced that if the Republicans nominated a candidate who was strong on the tidelands issue, and the Democrats did not, Shivers would lead Texas into the Eisenhower column. Rayburn and Johnson agreed that the speaker would find and persuade a solid, liberal Democrat to run against Shivers in 1952 while Johnson would work behind the scenes to persuade Shivers that it was in his best interests to support the national party.

IN FEBRUARY 1952, Rayburn and R. T. Craig, a leader of the loyalist Democrats, approached Ralph Yarborough. He was hesitant. "I didn't want to because I intended to run for attorney general, an office I believed I could win," he recalled. "They persisted and persisted, and finally I agreed when they assured me of all the financial help I might need."[7] In the meantime, Shivers told reporters that in his opinion, the delegates Texas sent to the Democratic presidential nominating convention should not commit to support any individual until his position on the tidelands and civil rights issues became clear. Shivers wanted Texas to control drilling rights up to twenty-seven miles offshore, and the Shivercrats and Dixiecrats wanted a nominee who would "get rid of the '48 civil rights stuff." Nevertheless, through intermediaries and then directly, Shivers promised Johnson and Rayburn that he would not bolt the party.[8]

Meanwhile, the governor had decided to flex his political muscles by running one of his protégés, Price Daniel, against the senior senator from Texas, Tom Connally. As Texas attorney general, Daniel had been outspoken in his support for state ownership of the tidelands. Statewide polls showed pervasive disenchantment with Connally, whom his enemies portrayed as far more interested in the Senate Foreign Relations Committee than the welfare of his fellow Texans. He announced his retirement in early 1952, virtually ensuring Daniel's election. Connally would later charge that Johnson had privately promised Shivers that he would support Daniel. Sweet revenge, perhaps, for the elder statesman's snubbing of him when, as a freshman, Johnson came around looking for support for a choice committee assignment. Connally, however, believed that the governor had thoroughly cowed LBJ. And, in fact, the junior senator had every reason to believe that Shivers was willing to play hardball.

In 1948, a deputy sheriff in Alice named Sam Smithwick had become involved in a dispute with a local radio commentator who was then denouncing him for operating a string of beer joints. Hearing that the clean government crusader was going to mention one of his children in a disparaging way, Smithwick sought out his nemesis, pulled his .45, and shot him dead, a deed for which he was sentenced to life in prison. In 1952, Smithwick wrote Coke Stevenson from prison, insisting that five days before the shooting, two Mexican Americans had delivered into his hands the contents of Box 13 from the famous 1948 senatorial campaign. In return for leniency from the state, he was willing to produce them. Stevenson set out immediately for Huntsville and the state prison. "I had left the ranch and got as far as Junction," Calculatin' Coke recounted, "when I got the information that he was dead."[9]

Indeed, the former deputy sheriff was found hanging from the bars in his cell. Shivers's friends began spreading the word that Johnson together with South Texas political boss Archie Parr had had Smithwick murdered to cover up their theft of the 1948 senatorial election. LBJ went so far as to confront Shivers over the matter, but he, of course, denied it: "I think it was a psychopathic case—an old, ignorant man about to die trying to get himself out of the pen, and getting no answer, he committed suicide."[10]

From Washington LBJ sought to put the matter in perspective. "I don't know what a convicted murderer might have done prior to committing suicide in an attempt to get release from prison," but Stevenson's (and Shivers's) release of the letter was "a continuation of a fight by a group of disgruntled, disappointed people."[11] Nevertheless, Johnson was shocked. "Shivers charged me with murder," he later told Ronnie Dugger with incredulity. "Shivers said I was a *murderer!*"[12]

WHEN THE DEMOCRATS GATHERED in their state convention on May 27, 1952, in San Antonio, the Shivercrats were firmly in control; thirty-five hundred of the four thousand delegates were loyal to the governor. Asked if he would support Sam Rayburn as a favorite son candidate, Shivers archly replied, "I would kill to know what his views [on civil rights and the tidelands issue] are." Upon hearing of Shivers's impudence, congressman Wright Patman, a loyalist, muttered, "Sam Rayburn's views were well known long before the governor was born."[13] Despite being overwhelmingly outnumbered, loyalists represented by Maury Maverick, fiery as ever, and Austin attorney John Cofer attempted to ram a loyalty oath through the convention. Shouted down, they marched their band of followers out of the convention hall, stopping for an occasional fistfight along the way.[14]

The Mavericks then held their own rump convention to select loyalist delegates to the national meeting. A firsthand observer described the crowd: "While most of the leaders were evidently of the professional and middle classes—lawyers, some businessmen, a few members of the academic profession . . . — without doubt, the majority of the rank-and-file were obviously working class people, many of them Negroes, and some Latin-Americans. Indeed, the general atmosphere was a unique mixture of western religious camp meeting (considering the fervor of most of the speakers), a labor union picnic, and a Tammany Hall clambake without the clams."[15]

Worried that he had gone too far and that the Democratic Convention in Chicago, where Rayburn would preside as permanent chairman, might not seat the Texas delegation, Shivers flew to Washington to confer with party leaders. Met at the airport by Johnson, the governor made the rounds, assuring any and all that he would support the Democratic ticket in the fall. Rayburn did not believe him. Neither did Maury Maverick, who showed up in Chicago with a rival delegation of loyalists. "Every night the rich Shivers gang parked in the best hotels in big private suites," journalist Alfred Steinberg recalled, "while the Maverick crowd jammed into small rooms at cheaper hotels, but during the day both armies were at the convention hall, where the credentials committee listened to their arguments."[16]

Finally, after LBJ arranged a face-to-face meeting between Shivers and Rayburn in Rayburn's hotel suite in which the governor once again pledged his loyalty to the Democratic ticket, the credentials committee consented to seating his delegation. Maverick and his followers were ordered up to the galleries. Defiant to the last, the fire-brand from San Antonio denounced national chairman Frank McKinney for "bootlicking the Dixiecrats."[17]

On the first ballot, Senator Estes Kefauver led with 340 votes, Illinois Governor Adlai Stevenson came in second with 273, and Richard Russell was third with 268. President Truman arrived in Chicago and made it clear in no uncertain terms that Stevenson was his choice. He captured the nomination on the third ballot, but the Texas delegation refused to make it unanimous, voting for Russell to the end.[18] It was another sign of the tension between southern Democrats and the rest of the party. Johnson hoped to be Stevenson's running mate—he even claimed Stevenson had "promised" the vice presidential spot in exchange for his peacemaking with Shivers and Russell—but the choice went to Senator John Sparkman of Alabama, a tried-and-true southerner whose loyalty to the national party was unquestioned. Johnson's name was never mentioned.[19]

As the election of 1952 approached and America's frustration with the Korean War drove Harry Truman's popularity ever downward, leading Republicans approached General Dwight D. Eisenhower, president of Columbia University (on leave), and supreme commander of NATO. The intensely ambitious Eisenhower was a novice at conventional politics. His military background and orthodox midwestern views convinced him, however, that the Republican party was a natural fit.

After some delay, he accepted the offer of support from GOP moderates, who were anxious to withhold the nomination from Senator Taft. He confided to friends that his overriding objective was to save the country from the perils of isolationism. Although the Taft people dominated the Republican National Committee, they were outmaneuvered at the national convention, and the wildly popular war hero was nominated on the first ballot. Among other things, he came out four-square for state ownership of the tidelands, thereby ensuring the support of many Texans.

During the ensuing campaign, Governor Shivers goaded Stevenson into stating publicly and aggressively his support for federal ownership of the mineral-rich offshore lands. Then, despite his pledge to the contrary, Shivers bolted the national party and threw the weight of his machine behind the Republican ticket.

At the Democratic party State Convention in early September, the governor won approval for resolutions backing Eisenhower and Richard Nixon, Ike's red-baiting running mate, and denouncing "the Federal larceny of our tidelands" and federal exploitation of minority groups through "class legislation" labeled "civil rights."[20] Rayburn was furious. "He felt that Shivers had lied to him and betrayed him," Booth Mooney said, "and it was the kind of thing that he didn't forget."[21]

AS THE FALL ELECTIONS APPROACHED, the speaker of the House and the minority leader of the Senate found themselves in a precarious position. Adlai Stevenson may have been the most unpopular man in Texas. With Eleanor Roosevelt, Jim Rowe, and other New Deal–Fair Dealers calling almost daily, Sam Houston Johnson told his brother that he had no choice if he aspired to high national office but to vigorously support the Democratic nominee. LBJ was hardly enthusiastic. "Well, Sam Houston," Lyndon exclaimed to his brother, "why should I be for him? Goddamnit, he promised Rayburn and Russell he'd put me on the ticket and then he didn't do it. And he couldn't have gotten it without Rayburn and Russell and me. And then—goddamn fool—he let Allan Shivers go up there and trip him on tidelands. What do you want to do, crucify me?"[22]

But support Stevenson he did. Johnson made speeches throughout the state and boarded the Stevenson campaign train when it came through Texas. In Fort Worth, Amon Carter let LBJ know that if he dared to introduce the Democratic candidate, he could forget about any future support from the *Star-Telegram*. Johnson introduced Stevenson, and it was years before Carter would even take a call from LBJ.[23]

Eisenhower won easily, including Texas, where he garnered 53 percent of the 2,075,946 votes cast. A statewide Belden poll indicated that Johnson's stand for Stevenson had caused his approval rating with voters to drop from 60 percent to 50 percent.[24] The *Dallas Morning News* observed hopefully that the campaign had left Lyndon vulnerable to Allan Shivers, who was "leaving all political doors open—including that of running for the U.S. Senate in 1954."[25]

Johnson continued to believe that he could finesse Texas while advancing his career on the national scene by staying on good terms with the national Democratic party. In fact, LBJ's support for Stevenson and Alben Barkley paid immediate dividends. Eisenhower's political coattails were not long, but they were long enough to give the Republicans a majority in the Senate, albeit a bare one. When former GOP Senator Wayne Morse of Oregon declared that he was an independent, the Republicans found themselves prevailing by a mere one vote. One of the Democrats defeated was Majority Leader Ernest McFarland, beaten by Arizona department store magnate and reserve air force general Barry Goldwater. The Democratic leadership was up for grabs.

AT FIRST GLANCE, becoming leader of Senate Democrats seemed an act of political suicide. Scott Lucas had assumed the post in 1949 and been defeated in 1950; McFarland suffered the same fate in 1952, after taking over the post the previous year. But LBJ had great confidence in his ability to get the most out of whatever office he held. Moreover, he reasoned that if he could not bring Texas to New Deal–Fair Deal America, he would bring the nation to Texas—states' rights, tidelands, military-industrial complex, and all. As minority leader he could unify a badly broken party. He could ingratiate himself with his constituents by cooperating with Eisenhower and the moderate wing of the Republican party.[26]

The leadership post was Richard Russell's for the asking. There wasn't a Democrat in the upper house who would vote against him. But Johnson knew the Georgian well enough to believe that he would not take it. LBJ was one of the first to get on the phone and urge Russell to become leader: "I'll do the work and you be the boss."[27] As Johnson had suspected, Russell wanted none of it. In the first place, the post was a minority position; the job was to merely react rather than lead. Second, the Georgian would have to give up his position as leader of the Dixie Association and moderate his public statements on race if he were to have any ties at all to Humphrey, Clark, Herbert Lehman, and the other liberals. Third, though he did not say it, he was simply not up to the stress and abuse that came with the job. When Russell declined his friend's offer, Johnson then asked Russell to support him for the post. As a southwesterner he could unify the caucus, and besides, he told Russell, he needed the prestige of the office to gain reelection in Texas. His friend readily agreed to support him.

Although Russell's backing made him a virtual lock for the job, LBJ left nothing to chance. The day after the election, Johnson, then at the ranch, phoned Bobby Baker and several senators. He solicited their support and had Baker persuade Senator Burnet Maybank of South Carolina to wire Russell urging him to take the leadership job but expressing his support for Johnson if this proved impossible. Baker then let it be known among other members of the Democratic caucus that LBJ was Maybank's second choice.[28]

Among the senators he contacted that day was Kentucky's liberal Earle Clements. Johnson promised the first-term Democrat the minority whip's position; within hours, Clements was on the phone with other liberals trying to convince them that LBJ was not the reactionary the Americans for Democratic Action (ADA) made him out to be. He contacted newly elected John F. Kennedy, who had defeated Henry Cabot Lodge in Massachusetts, and secured his vote. Johnson then phoned Allan Shivers to try to ensure that the governor would not take advantage of the distractions posed by the leadership position and run against him in 1954. He told Shivers he was considering running and asked his reaction. "I think it's great. You ought to do it," he responded. "The only thing that bothers me," LBJ said, "this position is open because [McFarland] has just been defeated . . . I don't want to take this position and get defeated in the next election." The governor got the message. "Well, "I don't think you run that risk," he said. "I think you ought to take it because you know how to do the job, and you'll do a great job and be a great service to the country and to Texas to have its own senator in that position."[29]

News that LBJ was lining up votes for the leadership did not sit well with liberals and several others like Bill Fulbright, who was mad at Johnson at what he believed was his lukewarm support of Stevenson. "The night that Eisenhower swept Stevenson off the boards," Joe Rauh, then head of the ADA, recalled with disgust, "most everybody did what I did—they got drunk! I had a hangover for a couple of days. But Johnson was too smart for that . . . The ADA did try in December [November] of '52 to see if there wasn't some way to get a rival candidate and defeat Johnson."[30] As usual, LBJ knew of the move almost before it got under way. "Jim Rowe called and said he just wanted to tell you that some of the Liberals are getting ready to try to knife you," Walter Jenkins told his boss. "The play is to try to put the heat on Lister Hill to run."[31]

Johnson's reaction to the machinations of this cabal was first to call Adlai Stevenson and see that he did not interfere. Paul Douglas's staff was going around spreading dirt about him, Johnson told him over the phone. Humphrey was trying to paint him as the Dixiecrat candidate. "If there is something I should do I would like to do it," Stevenson said. "I don't think there is anything you should do," Lyndon said. "The first thing the press says is that the Governor is telling the Senate what to do." Stevenson readily agreed to stay out of the matter.[32]

Johnson then called Humphrey and innocently asked for his support. He couldn't do it, Hubert replied. He was already committed to Senator James Murray of Montana, a senior member of the upper chamber and a staunch liberal. "There was no chance of defeating him," Humphrey later wrote in his memoirs, "but, after some discussion, we decided that we ought to nominate our own candidate, at least as symbolic resistance. At that state in American liberalism, it seemed important to have a symbol even if you lost with it." [33]

The Democratic caucus was scheduled to meet on January 2, 1953. Shortly before it convened, Humphrey and the liberals tried to trade their block of votes for some substantive concessions. Senator Lester Hunt of Wyoming and Humphrey called on Johnson and told him they would throw their support to him if he would put Paul Douglas and Herbert Lehman on the Senate Democratic Policy Committee. LBJ told them he didn't need their votes and curtly dismissed them. Shortly after returning to his office from that "awful meeting," Humphrey got a call from Johnson. "Come on down here alone. I want to talk to you." Humphrey complied and recalled finding him "in a take-charge, no-nonsense mood I would see often after that." Johnson asked him how many votes he had. Fourteen to seventeen, Humphrey replied. "First of all, you ought to be sure of your count. That's too much of a spread. But you don't have them anyway." He asked Humphrey to list those who were going to vote for Murray. "You don't have those senators," LBJ said. "I have personal commitments that they're going to vote for me. As a matter of fact, Senator Hunt, who was just in here with you, is going to vote for me. You ought to quit fooling around with people you can't depend on." His tone softening, Johnson said, "When this election's over and I'm leader, I want you to come back to me and we'll talk about what we're going to do. I want to work with you and only you from the bomb throwers." [34]

The caucus convened, and Richard Russell delivered a warm nominating speech. He hailed the Texan's record of party loyalty, his commitment to "human values," and his skills as a conciliator. Russell expressed "complete confidence" in Johnson's ability to serve the "party to which we adhere & [the] country & people we seek to serve." [35] Theodore Francis Green, representing the East, and Dennis Chavez of New Mexico, representing the West, delivered seconding speeches. On the first ballot, Murray received Humphrey's vote, plus those of Douglas, Hunt, and Lehman, as well as his own. Murray withdrew, and LBJ was elected unanimously. At forty-four, he was the youngest majority leader in history.

A HUMBLED HUMPHREY duly called on the leader as he had been ordered. "Now, what do you liberals really want?" he asked Humphrey. Jim Murray on the Policy Committee, Humphrey replied. All right, Johnson said, but it was a poor choice. "He's too loud," Johnson said. "He's going to go along with me on everything I want. You know that." He then agreed to liberal representation on the Steering Committee and the Finance, Judiciary, Commerce, and Appropriations committees. Once again, he told Humphrey to go back and tell his fellow "bomb throwers" that he was their designated representative to the leadership.[36]

Thus began an intimate political and personal relationship, frequently savage on Johnson's part. Nadine Eckhardt, a young Texan who went to work for Johnson a year or so later, recalled attending a small party for Eleanor Roosevelt at the Capitol. "I had been standing with Hubert having a drink and talking to him," she recalled. "Then I think I walked away and I heard LBJ say, 'Hubert!' and he snapped his fingers . . . Hubert jumped just like he had a little spring in him, you know, just right over like 'yes, Lyndon' [panting], and that really bothered me about Hubert Humphrey."[37]

George Reedy believed that LBJ genuinely liked Humphrey, and more than that, was a bit jealous of him. "He envied his ability to get up and talk about anything any time he felt like it," Reedy said. "and also Johnson would have dearly loved to have represented a state where he could be a free-wheeling [liberal] politician like Humphrey."[38] But to Johnson, Humphrey lacked toughness. "When I picture Hubert in my mind," he later said, "I picture him with tears in his eyes; he was always able to cry at the sight of something sad, whether it be a widow with her child or an old crippled-up man. And that part, it's just fine; it shows he can be touched . . . The trouble is that he's never learned to put feelings and strength together; all too often he sways in the wind like a big old reed, pushed around by the pressures of staff and friends and colleagues."[39]

WHEN LYNDON JOHNSON ASSUMED the leadership of the Democratic caucus in early 1953, the party was in shambles. Contemporary observers were fond of quoting Will Rogers's famous line: "I am not a member of any organized party. I am a Democrat."[40] According to George Reedy, there were at least four factions among Senate Democrats. "You had some of the far right, or some of the far segregationists," he recalled, "and you had some of the way-out liberals who were even to the left of Humphrey, people like Kefauver [and Mike Monroney of Oklahoma]. And you had the westerners. Then you had . . . some of the northern moderates."[41] There were only two men who thought that LBJ could bring order out of this chaos: Richard Russell and Johnson himself. "All of them were very, very skeptical of the Johnson leadership," Reedy said. "But there was just nobody else."[42]

The Republican party was triumphant but deeply divided as well. Reedy, who had become chief political analyst not only for Lyndon Johnson but also for the Democratic caucus in the Senate, again surveyed the scene. The GOP contingent in the upper house comprised three identifiable factions: the "Old Guard" Republicans who longed for the halcyon days of Hoover and Coolidge but who stood for a distinct program and were responsible politicians; a progressive wing that supported basic New Deal reforms but believed they should be circumscribed; and a group of "wild men," the product of twenty years of opposition psychology, who stood for nothing but were determined to seize political power through exploiting the people's fear of communism.

The glue that held these uneasy factions together was Robert Taft. Unquestioned leader of the Old Guard, he could constrain the wild men while playing to the progressives. The latter, strong in the East and West but isolated in Congress, were willing to help Taft in order to have some share of power.[43] Eisenhower's views on foreign affairs were clearly progressive. On economic and social issues, the new president was obsessed with balancing the budget, but he made it clear that he had no intention of dismantling the New Deal–Fair Deal programs put in place by his Democratic predecessors.

To conservatives like Bob Taft, Eisenhower was weak, naïve, and ripe for manipulation by the liberal wing of the party. He and his followers could not forget that Ike had been nominated at the Republican convention with the help of such eastern liberal Republicans as Henry Cabot Lodge, Nelson Rockefeller, and John Foster Dulles. Although Taft himself was intelligent and perceptive, his contingent of senators included Reedy's wild men, reactionary in domestic matters and isolationist in foreign affairs, who were determined to roll back the New Deal and resurrect Fortress America—Albert Jenner of Indiana and John Bricker of Ohio being prime examples. When he learned at a meeting at the White House in April 1953 that the administration's first budget would be $5.5 million in the red, Taft himself turned crimson, pounded the table, and told the president, "With a program like this, we'll never elect a Republican Congress in 1954. You're taking us down the same road Truman traveled. It's a repudiation of everything we promised in the campaign."[44] From that point on, the congressional wing of the GOP and the White House were frequently at loggerheads.

No one was better at the calculus of high politics than Lyndon Johnson. The number of factors and variables to be taken into account by one who would make sense of and manage American national politics at midcentury was mind-boggling. Each senator and representative had his or her own unique constituency. Powerful vested interests with deep pockets angled for influence. As always, the two major parties refused to display any ideological consistency. Over it all hung the shadow of the cold war and domestic anticommunism.

LBJ's goals in the aftermath of the 1952 election were, first, to convince the majority of voters in Texas, who had helped elect the Republican ticket, that despite his support of Stevenson, he was not too liberal to represent them in the U.S. Senate; second, as minority leader, Johnson was determined to unify the Democratic party insofar as possible, demonstrating to the American people that it was a fit instrument to rule.[45]

Just days after the election, George Reedy presented a concise recommendation to LBJ on the future of the Democratic party. Eisenhower may have won, but "it is practically a rebuke to the Republican party that they were unable to secure control (that is, firm control) of the House and Senate behind a candidate who rolled up one of the most astounding votes in history." The Democrats should disregard Robert Taft's admonition, delivered when he was minority leader during the Truman administration, that "the business of the opposition is to oppose."

If Eisenhower was going to succeed, he was going to do it on his own; Democrats must not be cast in the role of obstructionists. "The only real hope is to sit back and capitalize on Republican mistakes." By cooperating with the president on issues of foreign policy, especially foreign aid, in fending off attacks on the New Deal–Fair Deal status quo, and doing combat with the Taft-Jenner-McCarthy wing of the Republican party, the Democrats could assume the mantle of responsibility and plant in the public's mind the suspicion that Eisenhower was more of a Democrat than a Republican.[46]

Whatever the case, the politics of the 1930s and 1940s were gone; the New Deal coalition was moribund. "Eisenhower's great appeal is probably due to the fact that this is an era in which class and economic lines are becoming blurred," Reedy observed. "Roosevelt was a genius in putting together the blocs. But Eisenhower is the genius who makes those people think that the old blocs are just selfish interest groups and all 100 percent Americans will follow him . . . A political party which bases itself on bloc appeal will be sadly disillusioned."[47] Johnson was so pleased with the Reedy memo that he had it widely circulated among leading Democrats.

FROM 1953 THROUGH 1958, first as minority and then as majority leader, Johnson ostentatiously posed as leader of the loyal opposition, helping the president when he did battle with the forces of isolation and reaction. "Anyone who decides to enter into direct opposition to the President, must take into account the danger of leaving the country without any policy at all for the balance of the President's term," Johnson once observed to liberals who were criticizing his conciliatory approach to the administration. "Any responsible political leader will exhaust all possibilities of persuading the president to take the 'right' course before he seeks to block him from taking the 'wrong' course. He must always remember that a blockade of the 'wrong course' means 'no course at all.' There are times when such a drastic measure is justified but those times are rare, and it is a heavy responsibility to determine if they have arrived."[48]

A Johnson-Eisenhower alliance offered the opportunity to split the Dixiecrats off from the most reactionary elements of the Republican party, thus undermining the conservative coalition that had blocked reform and retarded the drive for social justice since the late 1930s. It would also help protect the party from charges that it was "soft on communism." McCarthyism was reaching its crescendo in 1952, and the political future of anyone other than a touch anticommunist was unsustainable.

Still, cooperation with the White House stuck in Johnson's craw. The president had surrounded himself with hard-faced businessmen: George Humphrey as secretary of the treasury, Charles Wilson ("What's good for General Motors is good for America") as secretary of defense, and Ezra Taft Benson as secretary of agriculture. Benson, an elder in the Mormon Church, was an avowed opponent of 90 percent parity, and both Humphrey and Wilson were devotees of a balanced budget, whatever the social cost. Eisenhower's priorities were clear; national defense, a balanced budget, a sound dollar, and then a social safety net with whatever was left over.

This philosophy ran exactly counter to LBJ's conviction that the only way to avoid class antagonisms and even race war was for the federal government to provide whatever resources were necessary to care for the ill-housed, ill-fed, and undereducated. His support of the administration made him feel like a hypocrite. Once, when he and an aide were thumbing through a portfolio of photographs, LBJ came across one of himself and said, "Have you ever seen a phonier smile in your life? . . . That's the way I always look when . . . I don't feel sincere. I try all the harder to look sincere and it looks all the worse every time."[49] Gnawing at Johnson was the belief that what he was doing might be in his best political interests and in the interests of the Democratic party, but that it was a betrayal of his populist roots, of his mother's Christian idealism, of what made politics worthwhile: the adulation of the masses in response to the authentic prophet of political democracy and economic justice.

As far as Johnson's thoughts on the new president himself, "I think he regarded Eisenhower as a man who was almost sublimely ignorant of many important things that politicians and people in a supremely political job like the presidency ought to know," said future staffer Harry McPherson. "He didn't exactly have contempt for Eisenhower, but he didn't have much respect for his judgment in some important fields."[50] George Reedy, who was rapidly becoming Johnson's alter ego when it came to political intelligence, summed matters up: "First, he is a General, with an American General's inordinate respect for economic nonsense when uttered by very rich men . . . Second, he is a General, and, like every American General, he regards politics as a dangerous labyrinth in which it is all too easy to go astray."[51]

Ironically, this created something of a bond between LBJ and Bob Taft. According to Sam Houston, shortly after leaving a meeting with the new president, Taft turned to LBJ and said with disgust, "You see what kind of pickle we're in. He doesn't know a damn thing, really, about what goes on. Lyndon, it's going to be up to you. I'm dying of cancer."[52]

IN 1949, the year Johnson arrived in the Senate, seventeen of the twenty most senior Democrats hailed from states below the Mason-Dixon line, the Southwest, or the small mountain states. Seven southern senators and four each from the Rocky Mountain and southwestern states chaired the fifteen standing committees. No Democratic senator from the East, the Midwest, or the Pacific coast presided over any permanent committee.[53]

LBJ had to change the balance of power, which meant converting the Steering Committee into a real instrument of power and modifying the seniority rule. The task before him was as daunting as changing the course of the Mississippi. "It was absolutely illogical to take a bunch of old men, which we had an abundance of," said Bobby Baker, "and give them all the plums in the Senate . . . I had seen these old men with their greed, not wanting to share their committee assignments."[54]

Johnson's first step was to fill three of the six vacant seats on the Steering Committee with liberals. Next he paid court to Richard Russell and persuaded him that it was in the interest of the party and sectional harmony for the corridors of power to be open to all factions.[55] With Russell's support, Johnson convened the Steering Committee and made a pitch for making aptitude and regional balance as well as seniority criteria for committee appointments. He used the oft-repeated and corny story of the Crider boys to make his point. "When I was a boy in Texas," he told the assembled committee, "I was a good friend of the Crider boys, Ben and Otto. Now Ben was older, and he was kind of sturdy and outgoing and popular among the boys, and Otto, well he was more shy and retiring." One day, said Lyndon, he asked if Otto could come and spend the night, but Otto's mother refused. The disappointed youngster protested, "But, mama, why can't I go? Ben, he's already been twowheres, and I ain't never been nowheres!"[56]

What sold the committee, in addition to Russell and Johnson's lobbying, was that the leadership could have its cake and eat it, too. The Republican majority had increased membership on each of the fifteen standing committees by one seat, with nine of the ten most desirable, including Appropriations, being increased by two.[57] Senior Democrats could keep their places while new spots went to deserving newcomers. In addition, the committee adopted the Johnson rule, which held that no senator could serve on more than one of the five most desirable committees until all other Democrats had had their first choice filled. Thus was LBJ able to appoint Hubert Humphrey and Mike Mansfield to Foreign Relations, Stuart Symington to Armed Services, John F. Kennedy, Price Daniel, and Russell Long to Finance, Albert Gore to Public Works, and George Smathers to Interstate and Foreign Commerce.[58] Johnson had not only built bridges to the young and hitherto marginalized among Senate Democrats, but created flexibility for the committees' future appointments. Dispensation of committee assignments would bond dozens of senators more closely to him.

To mute differences that could split the party, LBJ placed men on important committees, but ones that could not be used as soapboxes for their favorite cause. For example, he persuaded Humphrey to resign from Agriculture and Labor and Public Welfare, from whence he had launched tirade after tirade against agribusiness and the giant corporations, to take a seat on Foreign Relations. He kept Albert Gore away from the Judiciary Committee, where he might agitate for civil rights legislation.

A special problem was Wayne Morse, a maverick Republican from Oregon who had supported Stevenson in 1952. Liberal Democrats wanted to take in Morse, who had proclaimed himself the sole representative of the Independent Party of America, but LBJ refused, arguing that to do so would require displacing deserving Democrats from Armed Services and Labor, the committees on which Morse had previously sat. Reduced to Public Works and District of Columbia, Morse swore undying enmity toward the leader.[59]

The other instrument of power available to Johnson was the Policy Committee. In an infrequent fit of reform zeal, Congress in 1947 had passed the LaFollette-Monroney Act, sections of which established policy committees for the two major parties. These new bodies were to formulate positions on the major questions of the day so that debate would be clearer and more meaningful. The whole concept was absurd, "the product of some academic political thinking," said George Reedy. "Under our political system, you are never going to have clear-cut political positions that you can call Democratic or Republican in either the House or the Senate."[60]

So the Democratic Policy Committee became moribund—until Lyndon Johnson came along. The committee did have the power to schedule legislation, to decide when and in what order measures were to be submitted to committee for consideration. Johnson quickly recognized the latent power of this function and learned to maximize it: "Timing can make or break a bill," he said. "The first weeks provide the best opportunity to fight off a filibuster, the last weeks to avoid a conference committee, and the middle weeks to explore the issue. Sometimes the best tactic is delay—allowing time for support to build up and plunge—moving immediately to take advantage of momentum. Still other times the best timing inside the Senate depends on what's going on outside the Senate, such as primaries or elections or marches or something."[61]

Southern dominance of the Democratic caucus had ensured that the Policy Committee remained a conservative bastion. Johnson changed that, appointing four conservatives, two moderates, and three liberals. He also won agreement to a "unanimous consent rule," requiring that at least 90 percent of the committee approve the introduction of legislation before action was taken.

George Reedy was named chief of staff; he and Johnson subsequently assembled a group of experts to write position papers on issues and help draft legislation. Baker, as secretary to the leader, circulated among the members of the Democratic caucus, uncovering priorities and discovering what trade-offs were necessary to get a bill passed. In return for candid information on where a senator stood on a particular issue or his plans for a forthcoming investigation, Baker provided invaluable information on the forthcoming legislative calendar. "Baker's information was essential in planning your schedule," one senator observed. "As soon as he told you it would be safe for you to go home this Wednesday, you could pack up and go, knowing full well that your bill on wildlife would not be brought to the floor that day. Or he might say, 'You are interested in labor matters, aren't you. Well, you'd better stick around.' "[62]

In Reedy's words, the Policy Committee became "a gathering point for the leadership of the Senate to discuss legislation; to come to some conclusions; to help with scheduling; and to work out some of the necessary compromises that you have to have if you are going to get a bill enacted."[63] Belying charges of dictatorship from the liberals, LBJ was content to let the Policy Committee and the

Steering Committee decide appointment and scheduling matters on their own. "The truth is," said Harry McPherson, "that it was sort of a general leadership decision that Johnson was quite content with . . . It wasn't something that he forced down anybody's throat." [64]

LYNDON JOHNSON may have been the greatest intelligence gatherer Washington has ever known, and that in a city of information seekers and manipulators. LBJ wanted to know everything, attitudes, prejudices, philosophies, history, strategies, as well as just raw data. A chance encounter in the cloakroom was more than likely a planned interview. The leader might begin by offering advice that would benefit a colleague politically, or he might initiate the conversation by soliciting advice. He had Lady Bird and Zephyr Wright prepare intimate dinners for groups of legislators, journalists, and federal bureaucrats; hours of conversation preceded and followed. Lyndon missed nothing.

Over time, he assembled a gallery of mental portraits of each of his colleagues: his constituency, his aspirations, his work habits, his play habits, his religious beliefs or lack thereof, and, as Doris Kearns Goodwin noted, his image of himself, what kind of senator he wanted to be. He understood that in the complex world of the mid-twentieth century, senators had some leeway in the constituents they chose to represent and appeal to. It was in this gray area where there existed the most opportunity for persuasion, for Johnson to shape a colleague's political actions to his own purposes.

Much has been written about Johnson's persuasiveness, about the dynamics of his face-to-face private meetings with colleagues, about "the Johnson treatment." The stereotypical version was best rendered by Rowland Evans and Robert Novak—no friends of LBJ—in their 1966 book, *The Exercise of Power:*

> The Treatment could last ten minutes or four hours. It came, enveloping its target, at the LBJ Ranch swimming pool, in one of LBJ's offices, in the Senate cloakroom, on the floor of the Senate itself—wherever Johnson might find a fellow Senator within his reach. Its tone could be supplication, accusation, cajolery, exuberance, scorn, tears, complaint, the hint of threat . . . Its velocity was breathtaking . . . Interjections from the target were rare. Johnson anticipated them before they could be spoken. He moved in close, his face a scant millimeter from his target, his eyes widening and narrowing, his eyebrows rising and falling. From his pockets poured clippings, memos, statistics. Mimicry, humor, and the genius of analogy made The Treatment an almost hypnotic experience and rendered the target stunned and helpless." [65]

One "target" complained, "I came out of that session covered with blood, sweat, tears, spit, and . . . SPERM." [66]

LBJ thought the characterization was absurd. "I'd have to be some sort of acrobatic genius to carry it off," he told an interviewer, "and the Senator in question, well, he'd have to be pretty weak and pretty meek to be simply standing there like a paralyzed idiot."[67] The depiction was a function of the intelligentsia's contempt for him, he believed. "Most of the writing is done by the intellectuals who can never imagine me, a graduate from poor little San Marcos, engaged in an actual debate with words and with arguments, yet debating is what those sessions were all about." Never having had to persuade anyone of anything, columnists and political writers were like "a pack of nuns who have convinced themselves that sex is dirty and ugly and low-down and forced because they can never have it. And because they can never have it, they see it all as rape instead of seduction and they miss the elaborate preparation that goes on before the act is finally done."[68] Indeed, Hubert Humphrey would describe the Johnson technique as "making cowboy love."

Of course, the Johnson treatment was both debate and seduction. Only the significant were bullied or, more often, ignored. Each encounter was carefully planned and scripted. LBJ, Baker, Reedy, and other staffers would put their heads together as a pending piece of legislation headed for a vote. Baker provided a tentative head count. Those senators who were undecided or who were not fixed in place by conviction or political necessity were identified. Especially important were "umbrella" votes, votes that would provide cover for others. For example, if Richard Russell went along on a civil rights or defense issue, other southerners could safely follow suit. The group would analyze the individual's voting record and his constituency. Johnson would add his wealth of knowledge about the senator's personal characteristics and predilections. He would then prepare a list of points and questions. A chance meeting would be arranged and the treatment would begin.

The Texan was one of those men who was not afraid of physical intimacy with other males. If he was alone in a room with another man, he would sit next to him with their knees touching. Pats of affection, elbow squeezes, and other gestures were used to punctuate points. Actually, Johnson *had* to stand or sit close to other people in order to touch them. For a man of six feet, three inches, he had exceedingly short arms, so much so that Lady Bird had to special-order his shirts.[69] Nor was he afraid to tell other men that he loved them. The one-sidedness of the conversation depended on the stature and intelligence of the individual. Invariably, Johnson made his colleague feel that his was the crucial vote. His ultimate appeal was to the national welfare. "You are a patriot," LBJ would declare.

But the exchange was also substantive. No one knew the ins and outs of a legislative proposal better than Johnson. And he did not apply the treatment in behalf of causes in which he did not believe. A particular piece of legislation might be onerous on its face, but it was usually crucial to preserving a coalition that served larger purposes. "What convinces is conviction," he would often say. "You simply have to believe in the argument you are advancing. If you don't, you are as good as dead. The other person will sense that something isn't there, and no chain of reasoning, no matter how logical or elegant or brilliant, will win your case for you."[70]

For those who failed to succumb to the treatment, there was no retribution. That was reserved for those who did not keep their word. "When someone really cries out 'I can't do that,' there's something that snaps him back up," Harry McPherson said. "And I've seen him become almost tender with people who just said they couldn't do it, and he'd let them alone . . . And he hasn't gone out to try to ruin them later . . . He had considerable respect for such men."[71] Nor did he pressure his colleagues by threatening to obstruct legislation vital to their political survival. "This nonsense that he blackmails everybody," said Gerry Siegel, one of the Preparedness Subcommittee staffers, "is just sheer falsehood . . . This logrolling business, that was not his."[72]

Time-Life reporter John Steele, a not uncritical admirer of LBJ, has commented on the oft-leveled charge of deceit: "Those who know Lyndon least— the unknowledgeable journalist and observer—are those who describe Lyndon as 'crafty,' 'clever,' 'maneuvering,' 'conniving,' 'subtle.' This is bunk, as any well informed congressional observer knows. There is nothing indirect or crafty about the Johnson approach. More often than not, Johnson performs his feats out in the open—on the Senate floor in front of everyone who knows what's going on. Furthermore, he's quite open-handed and completely above board on what he's done—once his opposition won't profit from advance information."[73]

Johnson's power was enhanced by his continuing close relationship with Sam Rayburn, now relegated to the position of House minority leader. They continued to confer in the Board of Education or in the Senate leader's office. The two men saw eye-to-eye on Eisenhower and how to deal with him. "He's not better qualified to do that job [as President] than I was to do his [as supreme commander of Allied forces in Europe]," Rayburn said, "but you know how folks feel about fellows who come back from war with medals and ribbons."[74] But he agreed with Lyndon on a policy of constructive cooperation with the White House. "Any jackass can kick a barn down," Mister Sam told reporters, "but it takes a carpenter to build it."[75] Rayburn and Johnson benefited from having two Texans highly placed in the new administration. One was Secretary of the Navy (ultimately Secretary of the Treasury) Robert Anderson, a co-owner of KTBC before the Johnsons purchased it, and the other was Oveta Culp Hobby, former head of the Women's Army Corps and wife of Houston millionaire William Hobby, who headed the newly formed Department of Health, Education and Welfare.[76]

By all accounts, LBJ enjoyed a good working relationship with Majority Leader Robert Taft, less so with William Knowland of California, who succeeded to the leadership when Taft died in 1953. "He was a man of principle," Gerry Siegel recalled, but "a strange man, a bull in a china shop . . . He had no real political antennae that were reliable."[77] According to George Reedy, "He thought the leader of the party should raise a banner and that the party should rally around it. I remember he carried it so far that on occasions he would phys-ically leave the leader's seat and go to the back of the Senate and take a seat be-fore making a speech opposing Eisenhower."[78]

Knowland was such a relentless isolationist and Asia Firster that he became known as the senator from Formosa. No sooner had the Californian become leader than there was a test of wills with Lyndon. When the annual Jefferson-Jackson Day dinner drew Democrats out of town, Knowland agreed not to bring anything controversial to the floor of the Senate. He then proceeded to raise the issue of revising Taft-Hartley and several other touchy matters. When Johnson returned, he exploded. After castigating Knowland on the floor of the Senate, he moved to adjourn until all of his colleagues could return. To Know-land's embarrassment, virtually all of the Republicans, including Taft, who was then in a wheelchair, voted in the affirmative. "Johnson had to whip him a few times before he really began to realize what the situation was," Walter Jenkins recalled.[79] Soon, however, Knowland had become something of a Johnson dis-ciple. George Reedy recalled that on one of the fairly frequent occasions when LBJ threatened to resign the leadership, Knowland was in the forefront urging him not to do so.[80]

Actually, Knowland was the perfect foil for Johnson because he so often op-posed the administration on foreign policy matters. "It is a pity that his wisdom, his judgment, his tact, and his sense of humor lag so far behind his ambition," Ike said of the majority leader in his diary. Later, he went further: "There seems to be no final answer to the question, 'How stupid can you get?' "[81] The upshot was to make Eisenhower increasingly dependent on LBJ for action that he de-sired from Congress and to pave the way for a Democratic–progressive Repub-lican alliance that would help protect the New Deal–Fair Deal reform structure and advance the cause of internationalism.

THE 1950s WAS THE DECADE of the war generation. The typical service-man and -woman, over 12 million of them, had spent an average of three years in the military. That experience made domestic life doubly appealing and con-tributed to a huge bulge in the birth rate (the making of the baby boom genera-tion). The country suffered from an intense housing shortage that it attempted to meet in part with outlying housing developments financed by government-backed, long-term mortgages. In 1947 William Levitt, an aggressive New York developer, purchased twelve hundred acres of cheap Long island farmland and built 10,600 houses. The inexpensive three-bedroom homes were sold almost at once. Other Levittowns followed in Pennsylvania and New Jersey.

Thus was suburbia born. Long-held savings, continuing government spend-ing for both defense and entitlement programs, and technological innovations drove production, profits, wages, and real income ever upward. Installment buying, easy credit, and the shopping mall created a rampant consumerism that social critics lamented but that the average American thoroughly enjoyed. A burgeoning youth culture simultaneously consumed, conformed, and rebelled.

The popular culture icon of the 1950s was Elvis Presley, a working-class, southern kid who blended white country and western and black rhythm and blues. That amalgamation served as an interesting and important counterpart to racial conflict and the civil rights movement.

Two ominous clouds loomed on the American horizon at midcentury: racism, de jure and de facto, and anticommunism. Although Eisenhower made substantial gains among black voters in 1956, African Americans actually lost ground in their battle against discrimination during the first Eisenhower administration. For the first time since the Depression, black income began to decline in relation to white. Between 1937 and 1952, black earnings had climbed to 57 percent of that of whites, but during the next five years it dropped back to 53 percent.

The caste system continued to be most pervasive and most firmly institutionalized in the South. In 1944 in *Smith v. Allwright,* the Supreme Court had invalidated the white primary, a device that in the largely one-party South had meant disfranchisement for blacks. But neither Roosevelt nor Truman had followed up, and discriminatory application of existing statutes, together with the poll tax, violence, threats of economic reprisals, and other forms of intimidation, kept the voting rolls overwhelmingly white. In eleven southern states in 1957 only 25 percent of African Americans were registered, and far fewer than that were actually permitted to vote. Although the degree varied from moderate in the upper South to extreme in the lower, African Americans faced segregation or exclusion at lunch counters, on public transportation, in schools, in unions, and in the workplace. Violence continued to mar the region's social life. As late as 1955 a black youth from Chicago, Emmett Till, was killed in Mississippi for "admiring" a white woman. Class combined with caste to make the black southerner a virtual pariah in his native land.

Blocked in Congress and faced with an indifferent executive, African Americans turned increasingly to the courts. By the spring of 1954, the NAACP Legal Defense Fund was pushing five cases, all of which challenged the principle of educational segregation on its face. The five were combined and docketed under the name of Oliver Brown, who was suing in behalf of his daughter Linda, a Topeka, Kansas, schoolgirl who was forced to walk past her neighborhood white school to attend an all-black facility much farther from home.

Central to NAACP lead counsel Thurgood Marshall's argument, made to the U.S. Supreme Court on December 9, 1952, was that segregation conferred a cumulative stigma on black children. Separation implied inferiority, Marshall argued, and the denial of access to any and all educational institutions purely on the basis of race violated the Fourteenth Amendment to the Constitution, which guaranteed to every citizen equal protection of the laws and stipulated that no one could be denied life, liberty, or property without due process. His opponent stood on legal precedent. *Plessy v. Ferguson,* the 1898 decision condoning separate but equal, was the law, and sociological and psychological arguments were irrelevant.

On May 17, 1954, the U.S. Supreme Court ruled unanimously in the case of *Brown v. The Board of Education of Topeka* that racial segregation in the nation's public schools violated the Constitution. Education, Chief Justice Earl Warren declared in his opinion, constituted a central experience in life and was in fact the key to opportunity and advancement in American society. Those things that children learned in school remained with them for the rest of their lives. "Does segregation of children in public schools solely on the basis of race . . . deprive the children of the minority group of equal educational opportunities?" he asked rhetorically. "We believe that it does." The isolation of black children "from others of similar age and qualifications solely because of their race generates a feeling of inferiority as to their status in the community that may affect their hearts and minds in a way unlikely ever to be undone." The decision concluded: "Separate educational facilities are inherently unequal . . . Any language in *Plessy v. Ferguson* contrary to these findings is rejected."[82]

The *Brown* decision struck down a historic system of segregation, a symbol of the American caste system legally mandated in seventeen states, optional in four others. A major shift in the pattern of daily life had been mandated by Washington against the prejudices of millions. Initial reaction from the South was deceptively encouraging. Governor Francis Cherry of Arkansas declared, "Arkansas will obey the law. It always has."[83] Alabama chief executive "Big" Jim Folsom responded to reporters' questions by observing, "When the Supreme Court speaks, that's the law."

Several hundred school districts in the border states (Arkansas, Delaware, Kentucky, Maryland, Missouri, Oklahoma, and West Virginia) moved to integrate their schools. Many blacks were jubilant. Yet to be effective the *Brown* decision had to be enforced. In many parts of the South there simply were not enough supporters of the decision to move the mountains required. Demonstrations against Warren and the Court mushroomed. By some estimates, integration trends that had quietly begun without the Court's intervention actually slowed down or stopped for several years.

One of the cornerstones of white "massive resistance" was an effort to link the civil rights movement with the international communist conspiracy. Before 1945, communism did not inspire the hysterical fear that it did afterward, in large part because it was not linked to Soviet imperialism. With the onset of the cold war, however, antipathy toward communism mounted in the United States until it reached a fever pitch. In response to the House Un-American Activities Committee and charges from conservatives that the Democratic administration was soft on communism, President Truman on March 21, 1947, had issued Executive Order 9835, which mandated a loyalty investigation of each applicant for a federal job and made agency heads "personally responsible" for the loyalty of their employees. Still, the second Red Scare might have died aborning if it had not been for the communization of China, the detonation by the Soviet Union of its first atomic device years ahead of the date predicted, and a series of spectacular spy cases, the most celebrated of which was that of Alger Hiss.

The Hiss trial and the fears and prejudices it raised set the stage for the rise of Senator Joseph McCarthy and full-scale anticommunist hysteria in the United States. Born on a farm in central Wisconsin, McCarthy entered politics as much out of a lack of vocational alternative as anything else. Early in 1950, McCarthy decided that he could use the issue of communist infiltration of American institutions to revive his waning political fortunes. During the next four years he terrorized thousands of Americans through his brutal and indiscriminate charges.

When the Republicans gained control of Congress in 1952, McCarthy became head of the Committee on Government Operations and subsequently placed himself in charge of its permanent subcommittee on investigations. Within a year, his ongoing investigation had reached into the media, the entertainment industry, and colleges and universities. Anticommunist directors, producers, and actors vied with each other to come to Washington and denounce peers they suspected of communist sympathies. State legislatures swept up by the fervor of the witch hunt imposed loyalty oaths on the faculties of their state universities. Blacklists, usually the products of gossip and innuendo, ruined the careers of dozens of journalists, particularly in the broadcast field, as well as those of actors, writers, and directors. Indeed, by 1953, if not before, the search for communists and fellow travelers had become so widespread that McCarthy the man had been transformed into McCarthyism the movement.

Like other senators, Johnson originally underestimated the Wisconsin demagogue. "There were some things about McCarthy Johnson couldn't understand," George Reedy said. "He recognized him as a menace, but I think he thought that McCarthy was just a northern version of a southern demagogue. Now with the southern demagogue, once he had established his position, you could make a deal with him." Moreover, "at that time there was a feeling in the Senate that if the people of a state wanted to send a sonofabitch to the Senate, that was their business."[84] But LBJ and his staff quickly began to perceive that McCarthy was different. He did not have any set goals. He did not care a whit about the Republican party or the Senate. The latter was merely a stage upon which he could perform. McCarthy had managed to bring together "a large number of small fringe groups who were small in number but who had money, newspapers, radio commentators, enthusiastic followers," Reedy reported to his boss.[85] Gradually, LBJ realized that he was dealing with not only a dangerous individual—"a lethal rattlesnake," Bobby Baker termed him—but a movement that threatened the very foundations of the republic.

Liberals like Paul Douglas, Joe Rauh, and Drew Pearson argued that the Democratic party should make McCarthyism the centerpiece of its attack on the Republican party. "As leader of the Senate Democrats," Maury Maverick wrote Lyndon in 1954, "I hope you will do your part to stem the tide. Everybody in the Government is scared to death . . . There is nobody in Washington to take up for any part of the Constitution for anybody."[86]

LBJ sympathized, but he and his staff were convinced that to confront Mc-

Carthyism head-on would have been suicidal, for him personally, for the Democratic party, and for the nation. A 1954 *Fortune* poll indicated that McCarthy's popularity among businessmen was higher in Texas than any place other than Chicago.[87] As he put it to William S. White: "At this juncture I'm not about to commit the Democratic party to a high school debate on the subject, 'Resolved, that communism is good for the United States,' with my party taking the affirmative."[88]

Johnson warned Humphrey to keep away from McCarthy. "He just eats fellows like you," he said. "You're nourishment for him."[89] McCarthy is "the sorriest senator up here," he told Bobby Baker. "Can't tie his goddamn shoes. But he's riding high now, he's got people scared to death some Communist will strangle 'em in their sleep, and anybody who takes him on before the fevers cool—well, you don't get in a pissin' contest with a polecat."

What, then, was to be done? LBJ sensed that McCarthy lacked respect for the two-party system, the Senate, the entire American political process. He was subject to no discipline, and his thirst for attention knew no bounds. Eventually, he would turn on conservatives, southern senators who, though anticommunist, revered the rules of the Senate and adhered to a strict code of personal conduct, and institutions such as the army, which served as a touchstone for superpatriot and average American alike. Then McCarthy's opponents would have him.[90]

Reinforcing LBJ's determination to proceed cautiously was the attitude of the administration. Though he personally detested McCarthy and genuinely opposed extremism and witch hunts, Eisenhower contributed to the atmosphere of hysteria that both fed and was fed by McCarthy. In April 1953, the president signed an executive order authorizing the heads of federal departments to dismiss any employee about whom there was reasonable doubt concerning not only his or her loyalty, but his or her "good conduct and character" as well. After the Wisconsin demagogue libeled George Marshall, Eisenhower's mentor, pressure from friends in the military to take a public position in opposition to McCarthy mounted. Ike still refused, repeatedly telling friends and staff that he did not intend to dignify McCarthy's antics with public notice. "I don't intend to advertise this guy," he told General Lucius Clay.[91]

As Johnson had anticipated, McCarthy was soon putting the noose around his own neck. In the spring of 1952, he attacked Darrell St. Claire, the chief of staff of the Rules Committee, for actions he had taken while serving on the State Department's loyalty board. What McCarthy seemed not to realize was that the Rules Committee was chaired by Carl Hayden of Arizona, and St. Claire was a favorite of his. When Hayden objected on the Senate floor, McCarthy struck back at him, privately referring to the aged Arizonian "as an old, blind, deaf fuddy-duddy." "God," George Reedy later observed, "that was a stupid thing for him to do."[92]

Shortly thereafter, J. B. Matthews, one of McCarthy's staff members, published an article in the *American Mercury* entitled "Reds in the Churches," in which he accused one hundred leading members of the American Protestant clergy of being fellow travelers. One of these, Methodist Bishop G. Bromley Oxnam, was a close friend of Harry Byrd's. The conservative Virginian took to the floor of the Senate to demand that Matthews provide evidence to support his charges or "stand convicted as a cheap demagogue, willing to blacken the character of his fellow Americans for his own notoriety and personal gain." The day following, Lyndon encountered Hubert Humphrey in the cloakroom and pulled him aside. "I've told you," he said, "when you let one of these demagogues go long enough, he gets in trouble. This is the beginning of the end for Joe McCarthy." [93]

Humphrey was willing to give LBJ the benefit of the doubt, but others were not. Almost from the beginning of his career as a red-baiter, McCarthy had been embroiled in a running feud with syndicated newspaper columnist Drew Pearson. With the journalist denouncing McCarthy as nothing more than a demagogue, and the senator calling Pearson a communist, the conflict reached a climax at a cocktail party at Washington's exclusive Sulgrave Club. McCarthy kneed Pearson in the groin and slapped him repeatedly. "When are they going to put you in the booby hatch?" the journalist yelled. With McCarthy berating him almost weekly as a tool of the Kremlin, the columnist appealed to Johnson to come to his defense. Pearson recalled that he had supported the Texan in his 1948 bid for the Senate, but LBJ could not forget the Lyin' Down Lyndon crack. "Drew, you've not been kind to me lately," he said, and refused to lift a hand.

Pearson responded by tearing into LBJ. For six weeks in his columns and in a series of radio broadcasts, he attacked the leader's ethics. He accused him of playing footsie with the administration by suppressing Preparedness Subcommittee reports to the effect that General Motors, Secretary of Defense Charles Wilson's former company, was reaping unwarranted profits from defense contracts. In addition, he charged Johnson and Russell with blocking an investigation into waterfront racketeering in longshoremen's unions. "Drew is blackmailing me," LBJ complained to Al Friendly of the *Washington Post,* but he refused to budge on McCarthy. [94]

Meanwhile, Joe McCarthy's antics were threatening to plunge the nation into political chaos. By the close of 1953, he had turned from terrorizing the Democratic party to attacking his fellow Republicans and the army. During the course of his investigation into an alleged spy ring in the Signal Corps at Fort Monmouth, New Jersey, the junior senator from Wisconsin came across the case of Dr. Irving Peress, a New York dentist drafted during the Korean War.

McCarthy charged that the army had promoted Peress to the rank of major and given him an honorable discharge despite the fact that he had taken the Fifth Amendment when questioned about his allegedly communist activities. He demanded that the names of all persons connected with the Peress case be turned over to him. When Secretary of the Army Robert Stevens refused, McCarthy vented his spleen on General Ralph Zwicker, commandant of Camp Kilmer, where Peress had been inducted. Zwicker refused to criticize his superiors or to discuss security procedures in the army. McCarthy denounced him as a disgrace to the uniform and observed that he did not have the brains of a five-year-old child.

Stevens and the army counterattacked, filing twenty-nine charges against McCarthy, the committee counsel, Roy Cohn, and others. Among other things, the army claimed that the committee had sought a commission and special treatment for G. David Schine, Cohn's assistant, who had been drafted. McCarthy responded with forty-six charges of his own. Hearings were held from April 22 through June 17, 1954, by the Senate Committee on Government Operations, with Karl Mundt (R–South Dakota) in the chair.

As usual, McCarthy managed to dominate the proceedings, though it was he who was on trial. For thirteen days he browbeat Stevens as a rapt national audience watched over the new medium of television. McCarthy constantly interrupted witnesses, making insinuating comments or shouting "Point of order." When the Wisconsin senator implied that a young associate of army counsel Joseph Welch's was a communist sympathizer, Welch expressed the disgust felt by much of the committee and most of the onlookers: "Have you no sense of decency, sir, at long last?" Technically, neither the army nor McCarthy emerged victorious from the hearings, but the grand inquisitor had clearly lost. A Gallup poll revealed at the close of the hearings that McCarthy's approval rating had dropped to 35 percent. He had at last become a liability to the Republican party.

The moment of truth had finally arrived for the GOP. "It is a Republican problem . . . because they built Senator McCarthy to his present position of power," Reedy told Johnson. "They accepted his help gladly when he was attacking Democrats. They must now decide whether they will suffer the consequences."[95]

On June 17, 1954, two days after the army-McCarthy hearings ended, Senator Ralph Flanders, an elderly Republican from Vermont, introduced a resolution calling for McCarthy's removal from the Committee on Government Operations. The Wisconsin senator was as defiant as ever. Acknowledging that he sometimes played hardball, McCarthy declared that "as long as I am in the United States Senate . . . I don't intend to treat traitors like gentlemen." But the aura of fear and impregnability began to crumble. Flanders openly ridiculed him: "He dons his war paint . . . goes into his war dance . . . emits war whoops. He goes forth to battle and proudly returns with the scalp of a pink dentist."[96]

The distinguished television journalist Edward R. Murrow ran a series of film clips on his show, *See It Now,* showing McCarthy at his worst. As the opposition to McCarthy began to coalesce around Flanders, he and his supporters changed their proposal to a resolution of censure. Democratic liberals were ready to lead the public charge, but again Johnson restrained them.[97]

Finally, after the midterm elections in November, LBJ spoke out. The red-baiter from Wisconsin had publicly characterized Utah Senator Arthur Watkins as "stupid" and "cowardly" and alleged that his select committee then exploring censorship was doing the work of the Communist party. Such charges belonged more properly on the wall of a men's room rather than in the pages of the *Congressional Record,* LBJ declared.[98]

Behind the scenes, the leader lined up Democratic votes. All but one, Senator John F. Kennedy, who was then in the hospital recovering from back surgery, agreed to vote yea. Subsequently, by a tally of sixty-seven to twenty-two the Senate approved a resolution of condemnation. Though McCarthy would remain on the scene until his death in 1957, he was finished as a force in American life. "He never recovered," Harry McPherson recalled. "I would just see him lurch down the halls in the mornings, and he had a kind of bloated face with heavy jowls, he really looked terrible. And he would make those long, awful, incomprehensible speeches, seconded by other Republican drunks."[99]

Some liberals, such as Joe Rauh, would never forgive LBJ for what they considered his timidity during the McCarthy era. "Johnson was awful on Joe McCarthy, he was absolutely dreadful," he later observed. "Never said a word on McCarthy until the censure came through . . . Bullies are always scared of other bullies."[100] Those concerned with the welfare of the Democratic party were more complementary. "It took the genius of a Lyndon Johnson to completely castrate Joe McCarthy," Bobby Baker later claimed. "There was nobody else in there that had the mentality to destroy a Hitler-type person like . . . McCarthy."[101] An overstatement perhaps, but no one else had the power to restrain liberal Democrats from going after the junior senator from Wisconsin and in the process destroying themselves and the party. Both Humphrey and Douglas would give the Texan high marks for his leadership.

WITH JOE MCCARTHY'S DEMISE, the search for communists within the federal bureaucracy and military abated somewhat, but others had found a use for McCarthyism. In the years immediately following *Brown,* red-baiting the civil rights movement became an important part of the segregationist South's campaign against integration.

Conservative white southerners found anticommunist legislation and litigation particularly useful in harassing the civil rights movement. By spotlighting the backgrounds of those few activists who were communists and the more numerous who had participated in popular front activities during the 1930s, segregationists hoped to paint the entire civil rights movement red. By 1953 virtually all southern states had loyalty oaths on their books. By coupling these statutes with a drive to have attorneys general declare the NAACP and other civil rights organizations subversive, segregationists hoped to torpedo the mounting drive for racial justice. Southern racists joined with conservative Republicans in an effort to equate communism with socialism and socialism with liberalism. Thus could they invoke traditional states' rights doctrine to object to and obstruct federal efforts to regulate voting, education, hiring, housing, and public accommodations.

Unlike their Civil War forefathers, post–World War II southern conservatives were dedicated nationalists. Their goal was to link Americanism to states' rights. They defended decentralized, state-based government as a patriotic cause, often quoting Thomas Jefferson and John C. Calhoun in the same sentence. "Southerners devoted to 'Jeffersonian principles' are in control of Congress," George Reedy informed LBJ in February 1953. "They will launch a campaign to put the Democratic party back on 'the main road' . . . and destroy the control of 'Northern pressure groups' which are ruining the party."[102] Completing the circle, they linked state loyalty and security programs to their massive resistance to civil rights. By this arrangement, integration constituted a giant collectivist step toward federal control of economic, social, and political institutions. In this strategy, then, it was not just unsouthern to support federal over state control of important issues like education, race, and internal security. It was un-American.

Such was the world of Lyndon Johnson.

CHAPTER 13

PASSING THE LORD'S PRAYER

I T WAS HOT AS HELL IN TEXAS IN 1953 AND 1954—HOT and dry as an old boot. Summertime temperatures reached 114 in Austin, and Christmas Day 1953 saw the thermometer hit 90. Mothers armed their children with washrags to open car doors so they would not blister their palms. Normal rainfall in Amarillo was 20.8 inches a year; in 1953, only 13.05 inches fell. This came on top of three years of drought. At Laredo, the Rio Grande River bed dried up for the first time in recorded history.[1]

Residents of the Hill Country drilled deep into the limestone seeking to tap into an ever receding aquifer. The only animal that seemed to thrive was the buzzard. Everything was brown—the grass, the riverbeds, the dust-covered trees. Texans were reminded again that, despite all their oil, life was tenuous and prosperity uncertain. It was in this heat-blasted and stressed environment that Lyndon Johnson was compelled to run for reelection to the U.S. Senate.

By 1953, the individual who had emerged to become LBJ's chief political adviser and consultant was George Reedy, chief of staff of the Democratic Policy Committee. He was a most unlikely choice. Short, heavy-set, with short-cropped, prematurely gray hair, Reedy was a slow-moving, slow-talking, first-rate political analyst. A native of Illinois, he came from a long line of liberals. His grandfather had been a conductor on the Underground Railway. While a student at the University of Chicago, George had taken a number of classes under Paul Douglas.[2]

LBJ became acquainted with Reedy when the latter was working as a political correspondent for UPI. From 1953 until 1963, when be became President Johnson's first press secretary, Reedy poured out a steady stream of memos on virtually every subject under the sun, from Texas politics to Taft-Hartley to U.S.

policy in Indochina. He was a close reader of the national political scene and a master of the art of the possible. Reedy was, of course, skilled at protecting Johnson's political flanks, but he shared his boss's ideals. Jim Rowe recalled, "In many ways George was a mirror of the Senator's thinking. I had trouble deciding which was which."[3]

"George lived a life that only a political junkie could live," Harry McPherson recalled. "He would get to work very late in the day, late morning, and he . . . would . . . turn out these memos . . . He would leave the office about . . . six-thirty, something like that, and he would go over to northeast Washington to Gusti's, an Italian restaurant that used to be over on the Florida Avenue market. And he would drink an enormous number of martinis and he would hold court either with a secretary or whatever, a labor leader . . . And sometimes he would come back at eleven o'clock at night and dictate . . . Reedy would keep Geraldine [Williams, now Geraldine Novak] waiting unmercifully there until eleven-thirty or twelve o'clock at night and then come back and dictate to her."[4]

The Texas senatorial election was never far from Johnson's and Reedy's minds; in April 1953, Jim Rowe reported the views of John Lane, former aide to Congressman George Mahon, who had just returned from a six-week tour of the Lone Star State. "Lane saw a lot of people all over Texas," Rowe reported, "and he thinks [you] had better get home and do some work . . . He found a unanimity of feeling against you . . . The Eisenhower people didn't like you because you weren't one of them, and the Stevenson people didn't like you because you weren't one of them."[5] The first objective, Johnson and Reedy agreed, should be to torpedo or cripple potential challengers. "You had more people getting set to run against Lyndon Johnson for the Senate than you had voters in the average Texas precinct," Reedy later recalled.[6]

By tradition, Texas governors were limited to two terms, and there was widespread speculation that Allan Shivers would challenge LBJ. Another name batted about by the pundits was that of Attorney General John Ben Sheppard. Word was that Coke Stevenson was still bitter and was hosting Beat Johnson strategy sessions at his ranch. The red-baiting Martin Dies was always available. By far the most dangerous, of course, was Shivers, who, at the close of the 1952 campaign season, had gained complete control of the Democratic party machinery in Texas.

Early in 1953 Sam Houston Johnson arranged for a congressional banquet in Washington to honor his brother. Governor Shivers was, of course, invited. Traditionally, "these luncheons were strictly off the record affairs with no official press," Sam Houston recalled, but this time, quietly, he invited selected members of the fourth estate, especially correspondents from Texas papers. At the gala, both Sam Rayburn and Price Daniel delivered oral tributes. Not to be outdone, Shivers rose to declare, "I am proud to call Lyndon my personal friend . . . The state of Texas has never had a finer senator, and I personally hope he'll stay here a long time."[7]

"Shivers Endorses Johnson" ran the headlines across Texas the next day. The state's leading neo-Republican was furious, but there was little he could do. After Lyndon officially declared for reelection in October, newspapers quoted Shivers as saying that his wife did not want to raise their four children in Washington and hinted that he would make a run at a third term as governor.[8]

Nevertheless, the Johnson team concluded that the leader should conduct a two-and-a-half-week whirlwind preemptive campaign in Texas in the fall of 1953 to beef up his numbers in the polls, line up the big money, and drive out other potential contenders. In Houston, the senator spoke to the Mid-Continental Oil and Gas Association. His message was that the only thing standing between the petroleum industry and unfavorable rulings on the tidelands and depletion allowance was the senior Democratic leadership in Congress. They might not like it, but Johnson and Rayburn were all they had.[9] Amarillo, Lufkin, Tyler, and all points in between were recipients of the Johnson treatment. Reedy later estimated that the candidate made two to three speeches a day and shook a quarter of a million hands.[10] By the time the tour ended, LBJ's approval rating with voters had climbed from the 50 percent level in late 1952 to 63 percent.[11]

If anything, liberals both in Texas and nationally were more upset with Johnson than with conservatives. Creekmore Fath, a liberal lawyer from Austin, had written Drew Pearson contending that during the 1952 presidential campaign, LBJ had sat on his butt "while Texas went to pot."[12] Frustrated over having to choose between the interests of their state and the national party, the defeat of Ralph Yarborough in the governor's campaign, and their virtual exclusion from the state Democratic party apparatus, liberals vowed to get Johnson. In 1954, with the financial backing of Mrs. R. D. "Frankie" Randolph, a lumber and banking heiress from Houston whom one contemporary described as "a traitor to her class," a group of liberals merged two existing weeklies to create a statewide voice for the enlightened: The *Texas Observer*.

Meeting in a conference room in the Driskill Hotel, Randolph and other founders selected Ronnie Dugger, former muckraking editor of the *Daily Texan,* to be the first editor. For the next six years Dugger and the *Observer* would lead the attack against the oil and gas interests, the Shivercrats, and "the ledge" (Texas state legislature), which, according to Dugger, comprised the largest collection of self-seeking, special interest–dominated provincials ever assembled in one place. Convinced that Johnson was at best a reactionary and at worst an appeaser, the *Texas Observer* and Dugger in particular would be thorns in Lyndon Johnson's side from 1954 on.[13] At the same time, on the national level, Drew Pearson was joined by Democratic mainstays like the Louisville (Kentucky) *Courier-Journal* in complaining that Senate Democrats were being "led into the bondage of timid, calculating and narrow politics . . . to save the skin of a single colleague [LBJ]."[14]

JOHNSON'S RUN for a second term took place against the backdrop of the ongoing, bitter struggle between Shivercrats and liberal loyalists within the

Texas Democratic party. The conflict was far more than a factional dispute; it was ideological and both class- and race-based. Not only were Shivers and his followers advocates of small government and low tax regimes, they were for the most part out-and-out racists. Later, as chairman of the Board of Regents at the University of Texas, Shivers would declare that blacks would be admitted to the institution over his dead body. An admirer of Joe McCarthy, the governor was attracting national press coverage by advocating the death penalty for "convicted Communists."[15]

The working-class liberal loyalists in the Lone Star State supported unionization, government aid to the disadvantaged, and regulation of corporations and agribusiness. White-collar liberals were appalled by McCarthyism and generally supported the *Brown* decision. In 1952, shut out of the Democrat power structure, Maury Maverick and the liberals had bolted the state convention. "Who will go with me to La Villita?" the diminutive firebrand had asked and then led the liberal rump on a march in the rain to San Antonio's restored Hispanic district.[16] It seemed that the fortunes of former New Dealers and loyalists had reached rock bottom.

In the months that followed, however, Maverick and his followers, like Alvin Wirtz before them, took a page from the neo-Republican book. For the first time, they began organizing at the precinct level, and leaders like D. B. Hardeman worked to unify the faction: "We started in 1953 and 1954, you see, to work out a peace, a modus vivendi, between the loyal, moderate Democrats and the liberal Democrats, to get them to live together. There were a lot of people who were not for organized labor, we'll say, who still were loyal Democrats."[17]

Out of this came the Texas Democratic Advisory Council, an umbrella organization that oversaw the effort to mobilize voters at the grassroots level.[18] "There was the illusion that a lot of people had," said Hardeman, "that you could build a coalition of the Negro, the Latin American, the labor man, the loyal Democrats, and the liberal intellectuals, and you'd have 51 percent."[19]

The liberal loyalists settled on Ralph Yarborough to challenge whomever the neo-Republicans might put forward for governor in 1954, but try as they might, they were unable to recapture control of the party machinery. When liberal loyalists arrived in Mineral Wells for the state convention in 1954 they found that the state committee had not reserved any hotel rooms for them. Blacks were already barred from the city's hotels by custom. Some delegates had to stay as far away as one hundred miles. When a contingent attempted to hold a preconvention caucus in a city park, the sheriff's posse showed up and threatened them with billy clubs. Inside the convention hall, the liberal loyalists found that they had been relegated to the back of the room and allocated one seat for every two delegates. The chair refused to recognize liberal loyalist delegates who wished to speak or make a motion, and the keynote speaker referred to liberals as communists. The final indignity came at the close of the proceedings, when those out of favor discovered that their cars had been hauled off to the city pound, where they were forced to pay $13 each to liberate them.[20]

Unfortunately for LBJ, the election of 1948 would not go away. By February 1954, George Parr was in the headlines again, first when he became involved in "a bloody court house corridor brawl at Alice" with two Texas Rangers and second when state Attorney General Sheppard and U.S. Attorney General Herbert Brownell announced a state-federal investigation into the Duke of Duval's tax returns. All the old stories about Box13 began appearing in the state press. "This Parr business has been resurrected to the point where it is now the hottest it has ever been," Everett Looney, an Austin lawyer and Democratic activist, wrote Johnson. "Shivers and John Ben Sheppard seem to have an undeclared friendly war on between them to see who is to get the credit for slaying the dragon." [21]

Dudley T. Dougherty, a thirty-year-old, first-term state representative from Beeville, threw his hat in the ring in mid-February. He was both a naïf and an eccentric. A millionaire businessman and landowner, Dougherty had been Texas's single largest contributor to the Stevenson campaign in 1952. Amazingly, during his campaign run against Johnson he would accept financial help and advice from the Committee on Constitutional Government, a notorious anti-Semitic, pro-Nazi outfit. [22]

But Dougherty and his handlers had decided that the only chance an unknown had against an incumbent like LBJ was to run an extreme, McCarthyite campaign. Thus, at the time of his announcement, the Beeville tycoon declared himself an isolationist, called for a U.S. pullout from the UN, and denounced FDR, Truman, and Eisenhower as mentally incompetent pro-communists. [23] "It's the sort of thing you dream and pray and hope will happen," George Reedy later recalled with a smile. [24] During a campaign "talkathon" on television, Dougherty called Eleanor Roosevelt "an old witch." "Lyndon Johnson's the luckiest sonofabitch in the world," Maury Maverick observed to Creekmore Fath. [25] The contest, as everyone had predicted, was a charade; Johnson polled 883,000 to Dougherty's 354,000. [26]

Dougherty's token opposition to Johnson in 1954 hardly signaled an end to the internecine wars that plagued the Texas Democratic party. The national GOP had hoped to convince neo-Republicans—Shivercrats—to desert their nominal but traditional affiliation with the Democrats. Ike duly signed a quitclaim bill that gave Texas control of its tidelands, and he openly courted Shivers. Of course, the Shivercrats—as the self-proclaimed heirs of Thomas Jefferson, small government, and states' rights—claimed to be the true Democrats. They differed from Dixiecrats like Richard Russell in two important ways: there was none of the populism in them that appeared in so many southern legislators at midcentury, and they tended to be true believers in McCarthyism rather than mere political opportunists.

Once again, Texas liberals sent Ralph Yarborough forth to do battle with Shivers and the regulars. Yarborough, who had acquired his social conscience working as a harvester in the wheat fields of Oklahoma and as a roustabout in the oil fields around Bolger, Texas, boasted an enviable war record. He had ended his service in World War II with the rank of colonel. [27] Flowery in speech, temperamental, idealistic, and dogged, Yarborough would become synonymous with Texas liberalism for the next twenty years.

Shivers immediately took the low road by charging that his opponent's campaign was dominated by "Communist labor racketeers." Auspiciously for him, CIO-led retail workers in Corpus Christi walked out on strike in the midst of the campaign. The governor empanelled a special commission to investigate the extent of communist subversion in the Gulf Coast labor movement, and a subsequent special session of the legislature passed a measure punishing membership in the Communist party with a $20,000 fine and twenty years in prison. Shivers had wanted the death penalty.

Meanwhile, the governor's people retained an ad firm to put together a TV spot depicting the dire situation in Corpus Christi. The piece was shot at 5 A.M. and, not surprisingly, showed deserted streets, while the narrator warned that this was what all of Texas would look like if Yarborough won. Yarborough, who had stayed abreast of Shivers in the first primary, lost by eighty thousand votes in the second round. He blamed the Port Arthur story, and liberals looked toward the 1956 elections more embittered than ever.[28]

Of course, LBJ attempted to steer clear of the Yarborough-Shivers showdown. He worked to appease liberals by supporting New Deal–Fair Deal legislation in Congress during 1954, while quietly massaging and manipulating Shivers. "I am always going to know that whatever you do or say is not in any way calculated to do anything but help me," he told the governor over the phone in November. "I appreciate that," Shivers replied. "I think it would hurt you for me to endorse you."[29] But the split in the Democratic party was too deep, too emotional, too ideological for it to be finessed, and in the future, both sides would look constantly to Johnson for any signs of loyalty or apostasy.

JOHNSON'S RELATIVELY EASY RACE for reelection freed him up to focus on the 1954 midterm congressional elections. Typically, the party out of power gained seats in a nonpresidential election year, and both Sam Rayburn and Lyndon Johnson anticipated making the move from minority to majority leaders. In the campaign, LBJ was determined to portray the Democrats as the more unified of the two parties and, ironically, the most helpful to a still overwhelmingly popular president. All the Republicans seemed to have going for them was Ike's bland charisma and the soft-on-communism issue. One reason Johnson had played the McCarthy issue so carefully, waiting for the Republicans to take the lead, was so that the GOP could not use Democratic opposition to the Wisconsin demagogue in the midterm elections.

If LBJ thought that such a stratagem would spike the guns of such inveterate red-baiters as Vice President Nixon, he was wrong. In a forty-eight-day, thirty-one-state speaking tour, Nixon blamed previous Democratic administrations for the fall of China, the "defeat" in Korea, and the mess in Indochina. Any and all Democrats running for national office were both soft on communism and crypto-socialists.

Rayburn and Johnson, who privately referred to Nixon as a "fascist," struck back. The Senate minority leader declared to one campaign crowd, "They're trying to tell you there are nothing but a bunch of Communists among the Democrats in Washington. I suppose they mean that good old red Communist Harry Flood Byrd . . . Do you think that Walter George of Georgia is a Communist? . . . Do you think that Dick Russell is a Communist or Big Ed Johnson?"[30] LBJ's principal contribution to the 1954 midterm elections was a ten-day swing through the West, where liberals Jim Murray of Montana and Joseph O'Mahoney of Wyoming were in fights for their lives.

The results of the 1954 congressional elections did not meet LBJ's expectations, but they were sufficient. The Democrats gained seventeen seats in the House, returning Rayburn to the speakership. Both Murray and O'Mahoney won, as did Johnson and Humphrey, in landslides, but when the dust had settled, the Democrats controlled forty-eight seats in the Senate, the same number they had before the elections.

The difference was a quick and open rapprochement between Johnson and Wayne Morse. The Oregonian, a Republican who had declared himself an Independent in 1953, informed Johnson that he would vote openly and consistently with the Democrats in return for a seat on the Senate Foreign Relations Committee. "I don't know what he may want, but whatever he wants he's going to get it, if I've got it to give," LBJ said.[31] Fortunately, the Foreign Relations seat was his to give. With that deal concluded, LBJ was set to become the youngest Senate majority leader in American history.

Within two years of LBJ's accession to the position, the press would refer to him as the most powerful majority leader in American history, although that was not saying much. The only truly influential majority leader of the twentieth century had been Joseph T. Robinson of Arkansas, and his effectiveness had come during the New Deal years of 1934–1937, when FDR could exploit large Democratic majorities in both houses and reform was all the rage. In essence, the position of Senate majority leader, like that of minority leader, had no formal powers associated with it. But LBJ's influence with the Policy, Steering, and Campaign Committees meant that he would continue to dole out committee appointments to both the entrenched and the up-and-coming, control the scheduling of legislation, and have input into the expenditure of campaign funds.[32]

Under Johnson's rule, all Democratic newcomers were the beneficiaries of at least one desirable appointment; for example, Joe O'Mahoney and Alben Barkley, former senators who had just regained their positions, could have been treated like freshmen, but instead, Lyndon awarded them their first choices.[33] By 1955, LBJ had banked an impressive number of political debts, which he could collect when needed. He had helped pass numerous pieces of local and national legislation vital to the reelection prospects of various senators. He had protected others from having to take embarrassing positions on controversial issues. And his stumping during election time had proved undeniably effective.

With the Democrats in the majority, the Steering Committee became even more important.

LBJ understood just how important an ally or enemy the Capitol Hill press corps could be. As with his Senate colleagues, he quickly analyzed and categorized members of the fourth estate. William S. White, a friend from the National Youth Administration days, was then covering the Senate for the *New York Times.* "I knew that White admired subtlety," Johnson recalled, and he realized that with a little work he could be perceived as subtle rather than merely devious. "You learn," Johnson said, "that Stewart Alsop cares a lot about appearing to be an intellectual and a historian—he strives to match his brother's intellectual attainments—so whenever you talk to him . . . emphasize your relationship with FDR, and your roots in Texas . . . You learn that Evans and Novak love to traffic in backroom politics and political intrigue . . . Mary McGrory likes dominant personalities and Doris Fleeson cares only about issues, so that when you're with McGrory you come on strong and with Fleeson you make yourself sound like some impractical red-hot liberal." [34]

It was at this time that LBJ began the troubling habit of trying to manufacture images of himself for the press, to paint a portrait that he thought the public ought to see. It began innocuously enough, with exaggeration. One story on his life reported that his father spent twenty-four years in the Texas House of Representatives instead of the eleven he had actually served. The burgeoning communications empire in central Texas was Lady Bird's work alone; he had had nothing to do with it, he told reporters. [35]

Capitol Hill journalists however, were willing to cut the majority leader some slack in part because they viewed the man in the White House as a lightweight and an incompetent. Angered and frustrated by the obfuscation and nonsequiturs that characterized Ike's press conferences, Jack Steele of the *New York Herald-Tribune* quipped to Reedy that he was going to stop going to the president's press conferences "because they are too confusing. Aside from *Reader's Digest* and western stories, he did not appear to read—even newspapers. [36]

AFTER LBJ BECAME MAJORITY LEADER IN 1955, the physical seat of power in the upper house shifted to the quarters of the secretary of the Senate, in this case, Felton "Skeeter" Johnson of Mississippi, situated just off the floor. Senators gathered there to eat, drink, relax, talk, and gamble. "This is where Joe McCarthy lost thousands and thousands of dollars in there playing with Senator Kerr and Clinton Anderson," Bobby Baker recalled. [37] The Democratic Policy and Steering Committees gathered there. There were actually two chambers, a lounge, and a dining room. "We had a serious problem of people drinking too much," recalled Baker, who had become secretary to the majority. "John McClellan at one time was a notorious drunk and very belligerent, very difficult to get along with . . . But alcoholism is a horrible problem for politicians, because every place you go they've got a drink for lunch."

Nevertheless, Johnson's quarters were private, intimate, a place where the majority could get its work done. According to Baker, LBJ drank more liquid and consumed less liquor than anyone he had met. From the time he entered Skeeter Johnson's office until he left, he had a drink in his hand, Cutty Sark and soda. But the staff was under strict orders to use extra tall glasses when serving him and to pour no more than one ounce per drink. This could hardly be said of his colleagues, and, of course, the disparity in drink gave LBJ an edge, except with teetotalers like Kerr.[38]

As hyperactive as he was, LBJ could not be all places at all times. During his years as majority leader, Bobby Baker as secretary to the Democratic caucus was Johnson's principal factotum. Although only twenty-six, Baker was a veteran of the Senate. No one knew its personalities, procedures, and traditions better. He could count votes, deliver campaign funds, and arrange for legislation to be brought to a vote—or not. He was not well liked—many referred to him as "Little Lyndon"—but as an extension of the majority leader, he was respected. "He knew who was drunk," recalled one senator, "who was out of town, and who was out sleeping with whom. He knew who was against the bill and why, and he probably knew how to approach him to get him to swing around."[39]

Baker was short, dark, intense, a figure out of a Damon Runyon play, ever on the lookout not only for the interest of the Democratic party and his boss, but for his personal financial well-being as well. Lyndon trusted him implicitly. If LBJ was the Grand Calculator, Bobby Baker was his abacus.

LBJ LOOKED at a legislative session as a whole. Early on, he decided which measures would be desirable and necessary to pass. "He could see the combinations of support that had to be put together for each and how they would interrelate," staffer Gerry Siegel said.[40] If senators from agricultural states were assured that their northern colleagues would vote for 90 percent parity, they were likely to go along with legislation funding systems of mass transit. There were ways to vote for measures of racial justice other than laws guaranteeing equality under the law or advancing the cause of school integration—public housing, minimum wage, and extension of unemployment benefits, for example. Johnson was extremely flexible about blending interests and arranging compromises, but once the calculus of a session had been worked out, he was rigid, even ruthless, about enforcing it. His tone with his colleagues and members of the administration was economical, austere, and at times imperious. He used the logic of the equation he had produced with devastating effect. And he did not lie or misrepresent. "From my experience with him, in all those ballots we had when I was on the same side with him or against him," Alabama Senator John Stennis recalled, "he never did tell me anything false about the bill or what was in it. Or what he would or wouldn't do. He just didn't do it. And therefore he could always come back to you."[41] He had no use for those who would not play by his rules. Shortly after the opening of the 84th session, Estes Kefauver, who had repeatedly refused to toe the leader's line, called LBJ and asked to be placed on the Policy Committee. Johnson flatly refused. The Policy Committee was his "cabinet" and he was entitled to pick whom he wished.[42]

Johnson did not view the Senate as a debating society.[43] The body that he sought to master should not be a forum for the Websters and Calhouns of the world to persuade their colleagues and the public through grand rhetorical flourishes and paeans to patriotism. In fact, debate and unambiguous rhetoric could be quite damaging. For the legislative calculus to work, deals had to be negotiated directly among individuals and interest groups. The leader had to put on different faces for different audiences, and it was frequently unwise to provide information or argument that was not pertinent to the task. "The process itself," Johnson told an interviewer, "required a certain amount of deception. There's no getting around it. If the full implications of any bill were known before its enactment, it would never get passed."[44] Unrehearsed debates could only hamper, even cripple the process.

This approach put LBJ exactly in the center of the action. Only he had the full picture; only he was privy to all intelligence gathered, whether political or personal. All would have to turn to him and were in some respect dependent on him, the Senate's version of the Wizard of Oz. Horace Busby observed that Johnson was trying to make a virtue of the American political system which blurred distinctions and clouded issues. "His philosophy was the antithesis of parliamentary democracy," Busby wrote; it could be called "non-partisan nationalism." "We are a nation of financial conservatives" LBJ said in 1959. "At the same time, we are a nation of liberals in regard to our fellow human beings. In no other nation on earth is concern for human want and need and opportunity so nearly universal . . . Conservatism and liberalism always have—and I believe always will—go hand in hand . . . Our system of partisan politics—which had come to mean so much to us today—is not a system ordained and established by the Constitution."[45] In this sense, LBJ's political philosophy was much more akin to James Monroe's, Herbert Hoover's, and Dwight Eisenhower's than FDR's (pre-1938) or Woodrow Wilson's.

JOHNSON'S PHILOSOPHY of legislative leadership placed him once again on a collision course with the left wing of his own party. For liberals like Joe Rauh, conflict constituted the path to progress, whereas to liberals like LBJ, conciliation and cooperation were the best means to achieve the desired end. Rauh came to believe that Johnson was nothing more or less than an Eisenhower Republican seeking to patch together a coalition of moderate conservatives in the South that would marginalize northern and eastern liberals. "Some people would say, well he's got as good a voting record as [New York liberal Republican Senator Jacob] Javits," Rauh later observed. "But in the context of the Democratic party that was saying nothing." When Rauh was elected president of the Americans for Democratic Action (ADA) in the spring of 1955 his acceptance speech was an attack on the Johnson leadership.[46]

To LBJ's dismay, Adlai Stevenson used his influence—over LBJ's and Sam

Rayburn's objections—to have Paul Butler named chair of the Democratic National Committee. A slender, idealistic young lawyer from South Bend, Indiana, Butler was a fiery partisan who had nothing but contempt for Eisenhower
and his minions and for the policy of conciliation.[47]

WHEN LBJ ASSUMED the minority leadership in 1953, nearly everyone
doubted his ability to do the job. When he became majority leader two years
later, most Democrats were confident that he could unify and lead the Senate
contingent; the question was where he would lead it. But the differences between Douglas, Humphrey, and other Senate liberals and the leader had to do
much more with means than ends. LBJ always emphasized that it was the president's and not Congress's responsibility to develop and initiate a legislative
program. Congress could only react to what it received, and he publicly resisted
liberal demands that the Democrats in Congress formulate a program of their
own. But LBJ let the president know that this attitude depended on various department and bureau heads consulting closely with the Democratic chairs of appropriate Senate committees before drafting and introducing legislation. If the
Democrats were going to be in on any crash landings, they would have to be in
on the takeoff as well. Eisenhower proved amenable to a deal. "If there are any
roadblocks thrown in the way of cooperation, I am not going to be responsible,"
the president stated for the record.[48] Johnson sensed that Ike cared more about
foreign affairs, specifically foreign aid and military alliances, than he did about
blocking domestic reform, and he used this fact to broaden and deepen the New
Deal–Fair Deal reform structure during the 1950s.

THE 84TH SESSION, which LBJ would come to dominate, did not get off to
an auspicious start. For weeks, the leader had been bothered by pains in his
lower back. When Ike delivered his State of the Union message on January 5,
1955, Johnson was gasping with pain. Two weeks later, he took the train to
Rochester, Minnesota, where at the Mayo Clinic he was diagnosed once again
with kidney stones. His doctor, James C. Cain, a fellow Texan who was married
to Alvin Wirtz's daughter, advised him to rest to see if he could pass the stone. If
that tactic proved unsuccessful, surgery would be necessary. He rested as best he
could, but, as in the past, the stones refused to dislodge. Lyndon spent eleven
days at the clinic, was operated on, and recuperated at the ranch for another
twelve days.

Meanwhile, Sam Rayburn had become embroiled in a public feud with the
administration, just the sort of situation Johnson was determined to avoid. Populist to the core, Rayburn opened the session with an assault on the administration's Robin Hood–in-reverse tax policy. He introduced an across-the-board
tax cut of $20 for every man, woman, and child in the country. (The previous
year, the administration had pushed through a tax reduction measure, but it had
favored only the wealthy and corporations.) Conservatives—Taftites, progressive Republicans, and southern Democrats—rose as one to denounce the Ray-

burn proposal. The measure would cost the Treasury $2.3 billion a year and lead to runaway inflation. Rayburn's initiative, clearly rooted in the social justice movement, was bound to resurrect the conservative coalition that Johnson had been working so hard to break up.

Though still in pain, LBJ returned to Washington on February 12 to try to restore peace. The House had passed Rayburn's measure by a slim five-vote margin, but his measure died aborning in the Senate Finance Committee, with southern Democrats Harry Byrd and Walter George joining with seven Republicans to vote against it. As he struggled to work out a compromise, Lyndon was stricken again and had to return to the Mayo Clinic. Two weeks later, he was back, this time with the expelled stone in a jar and a steel-ribbed corset supporting his torso.[49] The best the leader could manage was a tax measure that accorded heads of households a mere $20 credit. Dependents would receive $10 and spouses nothing. The compromise satisfied neither liberals nor conservatives, and it went down to defeat.[50]

Despite this early disappointment, the 84th Congress would pass two hundred bills more than its predecessor. Though it considered some of the more controversial issues of the day, the first session produced nary a filibuster. Among LBJ's triumphs was a three-year extension of the Reciprocal Trade Extension Act, a measure traditionally anathema to Taftites and some southern Democrats. At Democratic urging, the Senate considered the first increase in the minimum wage in six years. The leader let the bill, which provided for a raise from seventy-five cents to a dollar an hour, languish until one day in June. With its principal opponents off the floor, he had it brought up and passed almost without debate. Spessard Holland of Florida, a leading opponent of the measure who was in the Senate dining room at the time, returned to the floor and began hollering and pounding the leader's desk. "Well, Spessard," Johnson replied calmly, "I had a little quorum call. If you fellows aren't on the job around here, I've got legislation to pass."[51] Johnson's support of the minimum wage bill initiated what was to be a lifelong friendship with David Dubinsky, the diminutive, dynamic Jew who headed the International Ladies Garment Workers Union.[52]

Perhaps LBJ's most satisfying legislative victory during the first 1955 session was passage of a public housing bill. The Republican-controlled 83rd Congress had virtually obliterated federally financed public housing. With the administration lukewarm, observers predicted that there was little chance of a new housing bill in 1955. Publicly, LBJ agreed, and the ADA blasted him for "affably acquiescing to the Republican assault on liberalism."[53]

Meanwhile, Johnson had helped guide through the Senate Banking Committee a bill sponsored by Alabama's John Sparkman that would build 135,000 units of housing over three years. Unwilling to completely expose itself on the issue, the administration, whose congressional spokesman on housing was Senator Homer Capehart of Indiana, proposed an amendment that would build 70,000 units over two years. Initial head counts indicated that southern Democrats would vote for the Capehart version. "Lyndon," said the corpulent conservative, "this is one time I've really got you. I'm going to rub your nose in it!"[54] But behind the scenes, the leader persuaded four northern liberals to support the Sparkman measure even though it did not go as far as they wished. He then appealed to the basic conservatism of his southern colleagues and convinced them to vote against both the Sparkman bill and the Capehart substitute. The leader gambled that the Sparkman bill would garner enough Republican votes to pass and he would not need the southerners. And that is what happened. As the final vote was announced—forty-four for and thirty-eight against—Capehart "was a slumped down hulk . . . And Bill Knowland, his face a fiery red, stared stunned at the . . . tally sheet in front of him."[55] Reedy remembers that "the press gallery nearly collapsed out of sheer shock, because they'd all written stories that morning predicting that this would be a major defeat for Lyndon Johnson as Democratic leader."[56]

QUIETLY, Johnson did what he could to contain the forces of extreme anti-communism. McCarthy the man might be discredited, but McCarthyism the movement was alive and well. As soon as the midterm elections were over, he and Rayburn began to plot the undoing of the House Un-American Activities Committee. Its functions could be transferred to "the much more responsible House Judiciary Committee, which has an excellent and deserved reputation for fairness and integrity," suggested George Reedy. Failing that, all communist-investigating bodies could be consolidated under a joint congressional committee under Senators Russell and McClellan.[57]

Meanwhile, Johnson had to come to the rescue of two southern liberals who were old friends of his and Lady Bird's, Aubrey Williams and Virginia Durr. Mississippi Senator James Eastland and William Jenner, an archconservative from Indiana, had decided to convene a session of the Internal Security Subcommittee of the Senate Judiciary Committee in New Orleans to investigate the doings of the Southern Conference for Human Welfare, a multiracial organization founded in the 1940s by the Durrs and other racial progressives. In a panic, Virginia called the majority leader. "What do you mean letting Jim Eastland come down here to crucify us?" she cried. He had heard nothing of it, Johnson said. He wasn't sure what he could do. "Make sure no other Democrat comes with Eastland," she replied. "Well, sweetie-pie, I love you; I'll do what I can," Durr remembered him saying.[58] There were no other Democrats with Eastland when he arrived in New Orleans. He did everything possible to paint his intended victims as Negro-loving communists, but to no avail. The only real drama came when Clifford Durr, Virginia's husband, attempted to leap over the courtroom rail to throttle Eastland and in the process suffered a mild heart attack.

Protecting Aubrey Williams and the Durrs from the Jenner-Eastland Committee was one of the actions of which Johnson was most proud during his years in the Senate. He recognized Eastland as a powerful force who was sometimes helpful on matters affecting the rural poor, but he had nothing but contempt for his politics. "Jim Eastland could be standing right in the middle of the worst Mississippi flood ever known," he quipped on one occasion, "and he'd say the niggers caused it, helped out some by the Communists."[59]

IN THE SPRING OF 1955, Lyndon Johnson was forty-six years old and at the height of his powers. As he bluntly put it, "Eisenhower couldn't pass the Lord's Prayer without my help." In June and July, *Newsweek,* the *New Republic,* and the *Washington Post* speculated on the possibility of his being nominated for the presidency in 1956 or 1960. He was "the first party leader in modern times to tame the independent Senate," the *Post* raved.[60] People respected the majority leader, found him exciting, even fascinating, but few genuinely liked him.

Johnson continued to drive his staff unmercifully and to attempt to control their individual lives, especially the women. His first private secretary was Mary Rather, who went to work for him in 1934. She became the prototype of the slavishly devoted secretary Johnson expected to have around him. A plump brunette whom LBJ snatched from Alvin Wirtz's office, Rather was soon receiving directions on losing weight and the proper clothes to wear. In 1951, she was succeeded by a vivacious twenty-one-year-old, another brunette, Mary Margaret Wiley. She was soon joined by a twenty-seven-year-old divorced mother of two, Ashton Gonella. Johnson was quick to establish his alpha male position. In his first encounter with Wiley he stuck his head in her office door, barked a few orders, and then vanished. "Blown away," she later recalled of the meeting, "and a little scared."[61]

LBJ made it clear from the beginning that he regarded his "girls" appearance as a direct reflection on him. "The first day I went to work for him, I wore my hair long and up in a chignon," Gonella recalled. "He told me if I wanted the job, I needed to get two pounds of hair cut off . . . He didn't want to look at me unless I looked the way he wanted. I cut my hair."[62] "He liked high heels and he liked lipstick, and he didn't want your slip showing," Wiley recalled.[63]

At the close of business, Johnson would sometimes hold court, with the secretaries sitting around and listening with rapt attention. He would rattle the ice in his glass until Gonella or Wiley or one of the other female staffers fetched him some more Cutty Sark. Serving coffee, drinks, and snacks was part of the secretaries' job description.[64] The year was 1955, and the cult of female domesticity (if not servility) was a prominent feature of American culture.

Feeling the need for a "liberal couple" in the office, in late 1955 LBJ hired Bill Lee Brammer, who had been working for Ronnie Dugger on the *Texas Observer,* and his wife, Nadine. "We were Ralph Yarborough liberals," she recalled. "I was from the [Rio Grande] River Valley, and I just was convinced that all those people were so ugly and nasty to those poor Mexicans. I joined the NAACP when I was a sophomore."[65]

"He was absolutely terrifying" at first, remembered Nadine. "He was so large and his eyes seemed magnified behind those glasses. It was as though he was a great Tasmanian devil, darting in and out of the office, pouncing on you before you knew it." One day, as LBJ was helping her out of the back seat of his car, "he took the opportunity to feel me up," she recalled. "It happened so fast I didn't even have a chance to complain."[66]

Johnson seemed incapable of separating women and sex. He wanted pretty, well-dressed, intelligent young women around the office because he assumed everyone would think he was having sex with them. They were part of his mid-century, male politician's harem, and he wanted nothing but the best and the brightest. "Sex to Johnson was part of the spoils of victory," said George Reedy. "He once told me that women, booze, and sitting outside in the sun were the only three things in life worth living for."[67]

The urge in him to seduce was almost irresistible. But he also craved the emotional support that women offered. Reedy believed that Johnson basically accepted his mother's Victorian view of gender: women were innately more cultured than men and invariably their moral superior; their approval was much to be desired. Thus did LBJ become luminous when women, especially strong women like Virginia Durr and Helen Gahagan Douglas, applauded his sacrifice for the common good.[68]

LBJ's relationships with his female staffers were not all one-way streets. They acquiesced in his behavior because it was the 1950s, and good-paying jobs for women were hard to come by. Sexual harassment, within limits, was a fact of life. But Johnson treated the women around him as more than just sex objects. His mother had embodied learning, especially in literature and the arts. LBJ gave the female of the species credit for having a brain and for having influence. Knowing Nadine Brammer's political predilections, he made sure to introduce her to and arrange an audience with Eleanor Roosevelt. When Nancy Dickerson was named national congressional correspondent for a major network, he and Lady Bird threw a party for her on Capitol Hill.[69]

And, of course, some were flattered by his attentions. Power and its display was no less an aphrodisiac in the 1950s than at other times.

To all appearances, Johnson's mental and physical fornications with other women did not weaken his relationship with his wife. Sam Rayburn once warned his protégé that his infidelity and gossip about it would limit him politically and expressed concern about Lady Bird. "Bird knows everything about me, and all my lady friends are hers too," LBJ replied.[70]

In fact, her response to a burgeoning relationship, with nonstaffers at least, was to attempt to ingratiate herself with the seduced. When her husband began sidling up to Nancy Dickerson, a former Badger Beauty at the University of Wisconsin and future NBC reporter, Lady Bird began calling to find out where she purchased her clothes. (After Dickerson made it professionally, they were Dior.) She, too, bowed before his propensity to "play Pygmalion," as she put it. Frequently, when LBJ was riding in the front seat of his chauffeured limousine and his wife, daughters, and/or female staff members were in the back seat, he would tell the driver to stop. He would then ask his female passengers to comb their hair and apply fresh lipstick, and they would comply.[71]

Lady Bird continued to revel in the role of political helpmate. She would come into the office several times a week, offering tours of the Capitol to constituents and making sure the Senate dining room served Texas-shaped hamburgers to the senator's luncheon guests. She would later say that these years were the most stimulating of her life. She went often to the Senate gallery and listened to debates, and she spent hours in the evening with her husband, Sam Rayburn, and others talking politics. "Lady Bird was the perfect politician's wife," Hope Riddings Miller, society editor for the *Washington Post,* observed, "because she always insisted on making the other person feel more important than herself. Her whole goal in life seemed to be to make other people feel big and herself small." [72]

Occasionally. Bird found it necessary to defend herself. One time, when Zephyr Wright served turkey hash during a post-Thanksgiving dinner for Sam Rayburn, Lyndon upbraided her in front of her guest. "Can't you have something better for dinner when we've got the Speaker here?" Lyndon fussed. Rayburn spoke up to say that turkey hash was one of his favorites. After he and the guests had departed, Bird turned to her husband and said calmly, "Dear, when we have guests, please do not complain about the food that's being served." He endured the rebuke in silence.[73]

Still, Bird seemed not only to accept her husband but to embrace him. At sunset on the ranch, while Lyndon was recovering from his gall bladder surgery, George Reedy caught sight of him and Lady Bird walking arm-in-arm, she with the most blissful look on her face.[74]

THOSE WHO WERE PART of LBJ's political calculus found him tough, aggressive, honest—and generally humorless. But this was not so for those with whom he felt comfortable. June White, wife of the journalist, remembered "a fascinating, charming evening" with the majority leader: "Impressions weaving in and out, humor weaving in and out. He was in a very, very good mood. There was no greater experience in life than spending time like this with Lyndon Johnson . . . You could see people, particularly when they were meeting him for the first time, just be charmed out of their wits." [75] Harry McPherson recalled a number of very distinguished, powerful individuals exclaiming after leaving a small meeting with him: "My God, if people could only see him that way." [76]

Johnson was a practiced mimic, hilariously cruel in depicting those of whom he disapproved, and warmly sympathetic to those of whom he approved. Horace Busby recalled an astonishing piece of one-man theater performed at one of their first meetings. Johnson reenacted the scene that had unfolded in Sam Rayburn's office the day FDR died. He played all the parts, Harry Truman, himself, and Rayburn in their respective voices, and was so caught up that he had tears in his eyes when he finished.[77] Johnson was frequently at his worst in large gatherings—big dinners or cocktail parties. "There was a streak—and people will think, anybody that ever reads or hears this will think I'm out of my mind—there was an enormous streak of shyness in him," Busby would claim. "He was always so afraid that in a graceful social setting that he wouldn't be mannered properly. Now he took over any party he went to . . . because if he didn't take it over it might bite him, in manners." [78]

Johnson's ego, though large, was extremely fragile. His antennae were constantly up for slights, for signs he was not being accorded his proper place in the pecking order. His behavior always depended on who he was with and his perception of that person. With the intelligent and sophisticated, especially those who he believed shared his values, he was intelligent and sophisticated. Over the years, his friends and intimates included some of the best minds in Washington: Richard Russell, Abe Fortas, Jim Rowe, Tommy Corcoran, Virginia and Cliff Durr. His mind was supple, quick, penetrating. Fortas claimed that Johnson possessed "one of the brightest, ablest minds I have ever encountered . . . He had a great power to retain information," which he could dredge up "accurately and effortlessly." [79]

Yet, these qualities existed in tension with LBJ's coarser self, which tended to emerge when he was bored or challenged. His belching, farting, public urinating, sexual boastfulness—in his office once he unzipped his pants, pulled out his penis, and asked rhetorically, "Have you ever seen anything as big as this?" in front of a friend visiting from Texas—frequently stemmed from indifference to the situation or an impulse to live up to a male stereotype that he had probably inherited from his father. [80] If the personal really is political, Johnson should have succeeded in politics only when he was in junior high school.

CHAPTER 14

BACK FROM THE EDGE

LYNDON EVALUATED HIMSELF—HE WAS ALWAYS GRADING himself and everyone around him—by the level of activity he was able to sustain. His day began at 6:30 A.M., when he awoke to skim the previous day's *Congressional Record*. Breakfast frequently consisted of black coffee and several cigarettes.[1] He rose and dressed in expensive silk double-breasted suits, and with cufflinks and tie in place, he departed for the Capitol at 7:30 in his chauffeur-driven limousine while perusing the *Post, New York Times,* and *Baltimore Sun* on the way. Arriving at the office, he would go over the day's schedule with Bobby Baker and Walter Jenkins.

The morning was spent in committee meetings and on the phone with committee chairs. Lunch, if there was time to eat, consisted of heavy southern fare: chicken-fried steak or meatloaf, for example, accompanied by some form of potato, preferably fried. The food was downed in huge, wolfing mouthfuls as rapidly as possible. During the afternoon, the leader was on the floor, managing the day's activities. Between five and six he would retire to the Board of Education or the Senate secretary's lounge to have a drink and rehash the day's events.

He frequently returned to his office to plan for the next day, not leaving for home until around ten. There, after consuming several drinks (not watered down at home) to relax, he would have dinner, invariably in the presence of politicians, journalists, or staffers he had invited on the spur of the moment. LBJ would then read himself to sleep, skimming memos, mail, and messages brought to the house around midnight by a Senate messenger. Frequently, he would awake in the middle of the night to phone a staffer or another senator with an item that needed immediate attention—at least in his opinion. At 6:30 the routine began again.

Bobby Baker estimated that the leader was consuming at least a fifth of Cutty

Sark a day, although he was never drunk, and he smoked incessantly. Johnson's weight soared to 225.

LYNDON AND LADY BIRD were scheduled to go to George Brown's posh estate in Middleburg, Virginia, on July 2, 1955, for the Independence Day weekend. Brown's country retreat was Huntland Farms, a historic 413-acre property complete with gorgeous five-bedroom home, two gatehouses, a gardener's cottage, stable, gardens, and a dairy, situated in the lush green, rolling hills of northern Virginia.[2] Lyndon would have to drive down for the July 4 celebration by himself. It was Lucy's eighth birthday, and she was suffering with a fever. Lady Bird would have to postpone until the next day, if she could come at all.

On the evening of July 1, Lyndon dined out with Sam Rayburn and Senator Stuart Symington. Rayburn noted that his friend was drinking more heavily than usual and had dark circles under his eyes. The speaker urged him to ease off, and Johnson promised that he would.

The next morning, LBJ went to his tailor's, where he was measured for two new suits, one brown and one navy blue. Before leaving town for Huntland Farms, he held an afternoon press conference with three wire service reporters. His plan was to tout the accomplishments of the first session of the 84th Congress and outline plans for the next session. One of the journalists, John Chadwick, a soft-spoken AP reporter, asked repeatedly why the Democrats were not pressing ahead with plans to amend the restrictive, anticommunist McCarran-Walter Immigration Bill. Herbert Lehman and other liberals were then advocating its outright repeal. Lyndon, who had been chain-smoking throughout the conference, blew up. He screamed at Chadwick, pounded the table, impugned his motives, completely lost control. The reporters and staff sat in stunned silence at this uncharacteristic outburst. Embarrassed, LBJ canceled the remainder of the session.[3]

Johnson and his chauffeur, Norman Edwards, were not able to leave Washington until nearly 5 P.M. No sooner had the limo crossed the Potomac than LBJ became uncomfortable. "I remember it suddenly began to seem terribly close," he later recalled, "and I told Norman to turn on the air conditioner. He said it was already on, and I said to turn it on full steam, and he said it was already on full steam and was getting very cold." Lyndon began experiencing severe pain in his chest and midsection. He remembered thinking that it was indigestion, perhaps the cantaloupe and hot dog he had wolfed down at lunch.[4]

When he arrived at Huntland Farms, he stayed downstairs in the trilevel house instead of going up to where the other guests were enjoying a drink before dinner. Hearing that the leader had arrived but was not well, George Brown went down to find his guest lying down in one of the bedrooms. He had had a bad day, Johnson told Brown: aggravating reporters and an unhealthy lunch. Did he have anything for indigestion? Brown gave him a bicarbonate of soda, but the pain continued. Johnson was sweating profusely. Suspecting heart trouble, Brown sent for one of the other guests, Senator Clinton Anderson, who had recently recovered from a major heart attack. Brown told Johnson of his fears. He had some digitalis prescribed for a heart murmur. Would LBJ like to try it? Anything, Johnson said.[5]

The pain was growing more intense. By this time Anderson had arrived. After Johnson described his symptoms, Anderson exclaimed, "My God, man, you're having a heart attack."[6] They should call a doctor immediately and have the leader rushed to the hospital. Johnson initially protested. The *Washington Post* was about to publish its article touting LBJ as a presidential possibility for 1956, and the Texan did not want the balloon popped before it even got off the ground.[7] But, overwhelmed by nausea and pain, Johnson quickly changed his mind, and the local doctor was sent for.

When Brown's physician arrived, he realized immediately that LBJ was suffering a major heart attack. He was surprised the digitalis had not exacerbated the situation and killed him. The patient would have to be rushed to Bethesda Naval Hospital, which had a major heart unit. Middleburg could boast but one ambulance, which doubled as a hearse. It was summoned and arrived some twenty minutes later.

With the mortician driving and the doctor in the front, the ambulance-hearse, with Johnson reclining in the back and Frank "Posh" Oltorf, Brown and Root's Washington lobbyist, at his side, set off for the hour-long trip north. Meanwhile, Brown had called Lady Bird and given her the news, which she took calmly. She set off to meet the party at the hospital. Fearing that he would die before they got to Bethesda, Johnson pulled Oltorf down close to his face and whispered the location of his will. It was in a drawer in his office at KTBC. "I've left everything to Lady Bird," he confided. "She's been the most wonderful wife in the world."[8]

Would he be able to smoke again? LBJ asked the doctor. "Well, Senator, frankly, no," the doctor replied. Johnson, who was thoroughly addicted, heaved a great sigh and said, "I'd rather have my pecker cut off."[9]

WHEN JOHNSON REACHED BETHESDA, Lady Bird, George Reedy, Walter Jenkins, and other staffers were there to meet him at the emergency entrance. He pulled Bird down to him and told her how much he loved her. While they were waiting for the elevator to take him up to the cardiac unit on the seventeenth floor, Lyndon asked for a cigarette. You can't smoke anymore, Senator Johnson, said Dr. Willis Hurst, the young navy doctor who would take charge of his care. Just one last one, he begged, and Hurst nodded his assent. "So, he had this—you never saw such a look of just savoring every second of that cigarette before he handed it back," Lady Bird said, "and it wasn't but a few moments before he turned gray, and I had never seen a person go into shock, and it really was scary. And at that moment, they gathered up speed, picked him up, took him away."[10] Lady Bird followed. What should she do about the two suits he had just been fitted for? she asked. Keep the dark blue one, Lyndon said. It would be suitable no matter how things turned out. As the doctors put him in the oxygen tent, Johnson almost died. His blood pressure dropped to zero over forty. For the next two days, it was nip and tuck, but with every passing hour, the leader's chances of surviving the coronary occlusion improved.[11]

Before being wheeled up to the seventeenth floor, Johnson had also spoken to Reedy. Call Earle Clements, he said, and tell him he was to assume the responsibilities of majority leader. Issue a statement to the press that he had had a heart attack, "a real belly buster," that Clements was going to take over the Senate, and that he was going to resign. Reedy called Clements and LBJ's friends in the press, but he made no mention of resignation. "I took it upon myself to let him think that one over, because I had a feeling that he would change his mind on it," Reedy said. He was right; Johnson did not castigate him for failing to mention resignation, and the subject was never raised again.[12]

ON THE MORNING OF JULY 5, Clements interrupted the proceedings of the Senate to read an announcement to his colleagues: "Senator Lyndon B. Johnson has had a myocardial infarction of a moderately severe character. He was quite critically ill immediately following the attack, but his recovery has been satisfactory. He should be able to return to the Senate in January."[13]

The statement touched off a chain reaction of sympathetic expressions from members of both parties. Herbert Lehman of New York, the liberal who had so often crossed swords with the leader, rose with a proposed resolution. It called on the Senate to "stand in silent prayer to the Almighty for the early and complete recovery of the majority leader, the beloved senior senator from Texas." For a full minute, senators, staff, and visitors stood in silence.[14]

"STAY WITH ME BIRD," Johnson had said to his wife before he went under. "I'd rather fight with you beside me." Realizing that Lyndon's recuperation would take weeks, Lady Bird moved into the room next to his and prepared for the long haul. She called the office and gave orders that important pieces of mail be brought directly to her so that she could sign them.[15]

The patient did not adjust to his post–heart attack regimen easily. As he recovered, he sank into the deep depression that is typical among heart patients as they realize that their lives will be forever altered and constrained. "When Johnson was in great despair," George Reedy recalled, "he'd just sort of lie there and sulk. Quite often you'd be with Johnson and all of a sudden, you'd feel that he wasn't there at all, that there was some representation of Johnson alongside of you, something mechanical, something—that he was a doppelganger."[16] Johnson had reason for despair: he could not eat, drink, smoke, fornicate, or politic. What would he do?

Soon the depression was punctuated by periods of mania. "Then one day he got up and he hollered to have somebody come up and give him a shave, and just in a matter of minutes that whole damned hospital started to click," Reedy said. "He took over the corridor, installed a couple of typewriters there, he was dictating letters, he was just going full speed."[17]

LBJ wheedled permission to listen to the radio from Dr. James Cain, friend and long-time family physician, who said okay, on the condition that his patient not listen to newscasts or any other programming that would upset him. Of course, as soon as he had the radio, Johnson did nothing else but listen to the news, and he ordered a separate transistor with an earplug so that he could tune in more than one program at a time.[18] When Lady Bird refused him cigarettes, he would have a screaming fit. Reedy remembered his keeping a pack in the table beside his bed so that he could obtain some small comfort from rolling one around in his mouth.

Gradually, Johnson began comforting himself by reading the hundreds of letters of condolences that came pouring in. "He'd read them over and over and over again," Reedy recalled. "It finally got to a point where we couldn't let them all in his room: there wouldn't have been enough room for him . . . There was sort of an unspoken yearning of his."[19] It was as if the letters were validations of his continued existence. Vice President Nixon came by to visit, as did President Eisenhower on his way out of town for a Big Four meeting in Europe. Hubert Humphrey wrote, "I miss having you get after me, I miss your good humor. Yes, we are just lonesome for you . . . Once you have recovered, God only knows what will happen around this town! Lyndon Johnson tired was a ball of fire; Lyndon Johnson rested will make the atom bomb obsolete!" Former President Truman wrote, and newspapers of all persuasions paid tribute to his leadership and political skills.

The patient's mood became more upbeat. During these weeks of convalescence, Lady Bird conferred with Dr. Cain, asking him if Lyndon's return to the Senate would mean a significantly shorter life. "We thought about this some," Cain later recalled. "I remember telling her that I didn't think he should retire from politics, that I thought if he were sitting on the porch at the LBJ Ranch whittling toothpicks, he'd have to whittle more toothpicks than anybody else in the country. Politics had been his life. It was what he knew, what he liked; and I told her that we had no evidence that continuing on working with a degree of moderation would shorten his life a bit."[20]

On July 22, the majority leader gave an interview to *Newsweek* and then a few days later granted an audience to a group of old reporter friends. When they commented on his weight loss, he had Sarah McClendon, the only female in the group, turn around and he then dropped his bed gown to show them just how thin he was. On August 7, he left the hospital and spent the following two weeks receiving colleagues, reporters, and well-wishers at home.

ON AUGUST 25, Lyndon and Lady Bird flew from Washington to Fredericksburg on millionaire Wesley West's private airplane. "He was the thinnest thing you have ever, ever seen, and his clothes were just hanging on him," Mary Rather remembered. "And of course, Mrs. Johnson looked bad, too."[21]

Dr. Hurst told Rather, who had agreed to stay through the fall recuperation, that the patient would be moody, one day demanding calls, mail, messages, and action and the next barely bothering to speak. He was right, but, of course, everything with LBJ tended to be exaggerated. He became obsessed with his exercise regimen and his diet. His doctors told him that he must walk at least a mile a day. So he got in his automobile and measured off a half mile, which took him from the ranch house to the gatepost in the fence surrounding the property. It was just a couple of hundred yards farther to Cousin Oriole's, so every evening he would walk to Oriole's house and back.

For the first time in his life, Johnson began to count calories. Bird and Mary Rather set up shop in the living room with books on nutrition and various devices to measure and weigh. Once, when he was being served some watermelon, he asked how many calories and Lady Bird told him sixty-five. When he subsequently learned that the caloric value of a slice was eighty-five, he blew up. "You would have thought the world had come to an end or he'd been betrayed," Reedy said.[22]

To facilitate his rehabilitation, Lady Bird had a swimming pool installed in the front yard. In addition to his daily walk, LBJ began paddling about in the water.

Johnson later wrote an article for *The American Magazine* entitled "My Heart Attack Taught Me How to Live." It was a maudlin if generally accurate account of his pre-attack excesses, the Middleburg episode, and his recovery. He claimed that his near-death experience had changed his life:

> My hours of reflection had made me painfully aware that my old life had not been a well-rounded one. In fact, it was so lopsided as to be ludicrous. After all, there was something in the world besides my job. I began consciously looking for some of the good things I had been missing . . . High on the list of those good things was getting acquainted with my two daughters. They had come to be 11 and 8 years of age, and I hardly knew them at all. Oh, I saw that they were fine, healthy, growing girls who got along well enough in school and seemed to enjoy themselves with their little friends. I was proud of them and loved them. I just didn't know them . . . Well, there was time now. I found myself falling easily into a happy relationship with Lynda Bird and Lucy Baines. We played games together—they could give me stiff competition at dominoes—and took turns reading aloud from their books. We watched our favorite television programs together. I was pleased beyond words by their ready acceptance of me. Why, they liked me![23]

LBJ's days were in fact more leisurely, and he did pay attention to Lucy and Lynda Bird. He would play with the girls, swim a bit, read some history and biography in the afternoons, and play dominoes with A. W. Moursund or Everett Looney, who would drive out from Austin. John Connally dropped by, as did Jake Pickle.[24] The pace was slower, and there was a prevailing mood of melancholy. "The awareness of his very bad heart attack made it such a long, sad time," Mary Rather recalled. "He had slowed down so much and the days were so long because we took very few phone calls. We had hardly any visitors and you knew that this worry about his health was on his mind and Lady Bird's mind every day, plus the big decision about what to do about being a member of Congress and what to do with his life if he didn't return to Congress."[25]

Rebekah arrived to help with her son's care. According to George Reedy, the staff awaited her coming with dread. By every word, body movement, and voice inflection, she conveyed to her son the message that he was shirking, that he was letting her and the country down, that he needed to get back on the job and prove himself. There were important things to accomplish, and her expectations to be met. "She was so damn mean to him," said Reedy. "She just had all these impossible standards. I would rather face ten of Al Capone's gangsters in a back alley than have to spend one hour alone with that woman."[26]

Instead of standing up to his mother, Lyndon took out his feelings of frustration and inadequacy on Lady Bird. In front of a large group, he accused his wife of "trying to kill me" when she served him food that he believed exceeded his caloric allowance. Soon Bird was emotionally exhausted. "When Lyndon is out of danger," she confided to a friend, "I want to go off alone somewhere and cry."[27]

ON AUGUST 24, news broke that President Eisenhower had suffered a major heart attack. Johnson was energized. He spoke to James Hagerty, Ike's press secretary, two or three times a day at first. Then Jerry Persons, the White House staff man for congressional relations called Lyndon daily to give him an update. Suddenly, 1956 seemed fraught with possibilities. "Our Republican friends are in a state of panic as of today," Bobby Baker reported from Washington. "The Dixiecrats have been so vicious that they cannot retreat to support either Stevenson, Harriman, or any one of the like stripe. They cannot afford to endorse Nixon or Warren since they know neither can carry a single southern State."[28]

On September 28 and 29, Sam Rayburn and Adlai Stevenson paid an official and much publicized visit to the ranch. Newton Minnow, then an adviser to Stevenson, recalled that he, Rayburn, and Grace Tully drove out from Austin and arrived late in the evening. The next morning, with LBJ in the middle, the three addressed a throng of reporters from chairs set up in the front yard. Johnson, looking surprisingly fit, dominated the proceedings. In response to a question, the majority leader declared that the three politicians had not discussed politics. There was one thing he wanted understood, though; "I like Ike." Sam quickly agreed: "We're not haters, we never hated Mister Eisenhower and we never will."[29] Stevenson opened his mouth as if to talk, but Johnson cut him off. He had supported Stevenson in '52 and would again if he were nominated. A reporter asked Stevenson if he thought Texas would return to the Democratic column in 1956. Before he could answer, LBJ interjected—"I think Sam and I are in a better position to answer that question"—and took over.

"All of the headlines carried such phrases as 'Big Three,' 'At the Summit.' 'Three most powerful men in the Democratic party,' " George Reedy subsequently reported. In the South, he said, "Republicans and Democrats alike are universal in their opinion that you alone, as far as our party is concerned, possess the character and integrity necessary to be President."[30] He followed up with a series of memos advising his boss on how to convince the electorate that he was indeed the hope of the nation. Reedy had arranged for the addition of Grace Tully to the Johnson staff. The presence of FDR's former secretary would reassure blacks, Jews, labor, northern liberals, and other members of the old New Deal coalition. After recovering his strength, LBJ should hit the ground running at the opening of the second session of the 84th in January 1956, showing that he had lost none of his energy or skill. Appear to be more a westerner than a southerner, Reedy advised. Most important, present a blueprint for action that will stand in stark contrast to the insipidness of Eisenhower Republicanism.[31]

Other prominent political figures followed Stevenson in paying tribute, even Estes Kefauver. The most interesting contact of that fateful fall, however, came from Joseph P. Kennedy. Using Tommy Corcoran as an intermediary, Joe urged Lyndon to run for president in 1956. If he would privately pledge to take on his son Jack as his running mate, Joe would arrange financing for the ticket. Johnson refused. He was not a candidate, he said. "Young Bobby . . . was infuriated," Corcoran recalled. "He believed it was unforgivably discourteous to turn down his father's generous offer." Jack himself wasn't upset, just curious. "Listen Tommy," Jack subsequently said, "we made an honest offer to Lyndon through you. He turned us down. Can you tell us this: 'Is Lyndon running without us?' " Corcoran replied, "Does a fish swim? Of course he is. He may not think he is and certainly he's saying he isn't. But I know God damned well he is. I'm sorry that he doesn't know it."[32]

LBJ realized that the elder Kennedy was attempting to use him as a stalking horse for Jack. It was likely that Ike would recover and that he would run for a second term. The Republicans had no one else; indeed, with the president out of commission the Taftites, progressives, and wild men were at each other's throats. Joe wanted to position his son for 1960 by having him named vice presidential candidate on the Democratic ticket in 1956. Ike was likely to win in 1956, but his margin of victory would be much smaller if Johnson rather than Stevenson ran. If Ike swamped Adlai again and Jack occupied second place on the ticket, the defeat could be blamed in part on Kennedy's Catholicism.

AT HIS DOCTOR'S INSISTENCE, LBJ had canceled all his speaking engagements for the remainder of 1955—except two: an innocuous tribute to Sam Rayburn to be delivered at the Texas State Fair in Dallas and a speech dedicating the new dam at Lake Whitney. With his health improving and his ambition pulsating, Johnson decided Whitney would be the place to announce his version of a domestic Fourteen Points. The staff was immediately thrown into a panic. Whitney, situated between Hillsboro and Waco, was tiny. The only possible venue was the National Guard Armory. The place would have to be packed, but how to attract a throng to the middle of nowhere?

But then word got out. Tommy Corcoran and Robert L. Clark, a Dallas lawyer, each sent $1,000 to buy tickets and distribute them for free admission. Democrats in Dallas and Fort Worth as well as Waco began making plans to attend. "The National Guard Armory was absolutely packed and jammed" when the leader arrived, Mary Rather recalled.[33]

The speech that LBJ delivered that evening had been prepared by George Reedy and Bob Oliver, the chief lobbyist for the United Automobile Workers. Titled "Program with a Heart," it was a New Deal–Fair Deal call to arms, including expanded Social Security coverage, federal subsidies for housing, school, and hospital construction, a guarantee of 90 percent parity to farmers, elimination of the poll tax, tax cuts for the disadvantaged, regional and national water conservation measures, amendments liberalizing the immigration and naturalization laws, and an agency similar to the Federal Power Commission to regulate interstate gas prices. When Johnson had finished reading his prepared text, he moved closer to the crowd and kept talking extemporaneously. George Reedy: "I had never before seen him take such complete command of an audience. It was virtually a mass orgasm."[34]

"I wish you could have been at Whitney," LBJ wrote Bobby Baker "I have never had a better audience, and it was composed of liberal, moderate and conservative Democrats, Shivercrats, Eisenhower-Democrats, and even Republicans."[35] Old New Dealers sensed a liberal Renaissance. "I have come reluctantly to the conclusion that your policy in the last two years had been correct," Tommy Corcoran wrote LBJ. "As you know, I thought it was wrong and told you so, since I believed in a frontal attack on Eisenhower. I think events, and I do not mean only his heart attack, have proved you right. You sensed the mood of the country far better than anyone else. I do not give Adlai too much credit on this because I think he is essentially a conservative at heart, while I have always believed you are a New Dealer at heart, despite the fulminations of our ADA [Americans for Democratic Action] friends."[36] Both Clark Clifford and Abe Fortas endorsed the goals LBJ had articulated and subsequently helped to flesh them out.[37]

In the context of the mid-1950s, the Whitney speech was remarkable—more liberal than anything Adlai Stevenson had ever uttered. The man who had supposedly caved in to the conservative mood sweeping Texas and the nation, the man who, according to the *Texas Observer,* was a tool of big oil, the corporations, and agribusiness, had staked his political future on a program that had essentially been written by UAW head Walter Reuther.

Indeed, many around Johnson saw the heart attack and the Whitney speech as a turning point in LBJ's life and career: George Reedy said, "1955 and 1956 were the two years in which he began to lay down some sort of a coherent program, largely a populist program, really, which gave a positive expression to his leadership."[38]

As Johnson saw matters, liberalism had lost its way. The focus increasingly was on remedies affecting the legal status of the disadvantaged and action to protect the civil liberties of Americans under siege by McCarthyism. Johnson was for these things, but the Whitney speech was a call to Democrats and the nation not to forget the ill-housed, ill-fed, and undereducated.

The event was cathartic for Johnson not only because it marked a return from his illness and the longest period of enforced idleness in his life, but also because it signified a return to the values he had been forced to move away from ever since his election to the U.S. Senate. Carl Albert later remarked that the Whitney speech was the beginning of the making of a president.[39]

IN THE AFTERMATH of the heart attack and the Whitney speech, LBJ's New Deal friends once again began to think of him as FDR's heir apparent. In November 1955, Tommy Corcoran wrote the Johnsons, "Lyndon can't keep out of politics because, as Holmes said, 'To live is to function: there is no other point in living,' and Lyndon's functioning is politics. But . . . the greater political function of Lyndon now is to find a broadening out of his interests in life that relieved his concentration on the infighting of politics and gives his subconscious time to function. His energy had successfully broken him through the gravitational pull that yanks down ordinary politicians."[40]

That same week. Jim Rowe sent Bird the latest one-volume biography of Abraham Lincoln for her to read to her convalescing husband. He had just returned to Washington from his first visit to the ranch. "Lyndon has a lot to learn from Lincoln," Rowe observed. "For one thing, when it comes to straight politicking, old Abe makes Lyndon look like an amateur . . . And it might interest him to know that Lincoln too had his waiting period, while he practiced law after he left Congress."[41]

AS THE SECOND SESSION of the 84th Congress prepared to open, the task ahead, as LBJ and his strategists defined it, was to continue to use the disjuncture between Eisenhower and the Republican party to further the interests of the majority leader and the Democrats. They continued to insist that the president, personally, was untouchable. In the minds of the American people, George Reedy observed, "he has become a myth—a myth which they themselves have created. They want a wise President so in their minds he is a wise President. They want a prudent President so in their minds he is a prudent President. They want a strong leader so in their minds he is a strong leader. It does not matter whether these descriptions are fitting or unfitting. They want the description to fit and they are determined that it will." Constant efforts to discredit Eisenhower would challenge the nation's judgment. "No man will admit—if he can help it—that he was a fool!"[42]

If the Democrats were to retain control of Congress and capture the White House in 1956, they were going to have to wean some 3.5 million voters away from the GOP. "While it is probably true that the old New Deal issues such as public power are dead, there is fortunately, a new kind of 'liberalism,'" Jim Rowe advised Johnson. "The American people want a variety of things which come under the heading 'general security.' The American economy is giving the people most of these without any help from the legislators. But there are certain things which can come only from the legislators . . . expanded Social Security, schools for their children, better roads, better health protection. The demands for all these things together can be the 'New Liberalism.' The politician who adequately articulates all these demands will become the successful leader."[43]

LBJ was on hand for the opening of the new Congress on January 5, 1956. He appeared a changed man, complete with a new routine. He did not arrive at his office until 10 A.M. and he stopped to take a nap every afternoon. The cigarettes were gone, alcohol consumption much diminished, and weight down to 187 pounds.

But life still had its pleasures. With the help of Joseph Duke, the Senate sergeant at arms, the leader lay claim to a small suite of rooms in the Page School on the west side of the Capitol. "He spent a fortune fixing it up down there," Bobby Baker recalled, "because it was hard to get the heating and air conditioning, because it was sort of what I call the bowels of the Capitol down there. It was on the inside, sort of facing the architect's office." Such hideaways were at a premium among the legislators, Baker recalled. "If they met a pretty constituent, they could take them there. If those rooms could talk, it would make a good gossip book . . . including Johnson."[44]

By the time LBJ arrived back in Washington, he had also beefed up his staff. Walter Jenkins was still there to run the day-to-day operations and take care of the minutiae. Arthur Perry continued to handle the Texas mail, still a crucial job; there were the Brammers and Booth Mooney.[45] Billy Brammer, a blossoming novelist, spent his days and early evenings serving Johnson and his nights holed up in his apartment, living on Kool-Aid and Butterfingers, writing a sweeping satire of Texas politics, later published as *The Gay Place*. To head up the Policy Committee, Jim Rowe was persuaded to leave his lucrative Washington law partnership with Tommy Corcoran. Rowe's recruitment was classic LBJ. "Lyndon Johnson went after me to come down there and run the Policy Committee, and I said, 'I'm not going to do it,'" as Rowe related the story. "He caused all kinds of people to get in touch with me and say that 'I think you have an obligation to our nation and to our party and to the Congress to go to help Lyndon Johnson.' It was embarrassing. I had to sound like someone who didn't care about any of those things to a lot of very nice people, very well-meaning people, but I could stand it until one night at dinner my wife wasn't speaking to me—Libby—and I said, 'What is wrong?' and she said, 'I just can't imagine why you're doing this to Lyndon.'"[46]

Perhaps the most important addition to the staff was a young lawyer from East Texas who came onboard as assistant to Gerry Siegel, the Policy Committee's legal counsel. A graduate of the University of the South, Columbia, and the University of Texas, Harry McPherson was a southern liberal of the Ralph McGill–Hodding Carter stripe. A devout Episcopalian, he viewed racial injustice as immoral, anticommunism as overblown and a threat to civil liberties, and the emergence of a labor-farmer-consumer-minority political coalition as a balance to big business as crucial to the future of the republic. McPherson was idealistic, self-deprecating, well-read, and tactful enough to stand up to LBJ without destroying himself. The young Texas attorney who had originally planned on becoming an English teacher would become a personal and political bridge from the New Deal–Fair Deal to the Great Society. "I came to admire his [Johnson's] politics and his principles . . . how the country works and how you get things done" McPherson later said.[47]

THE THORNIEST PROBLEM confronting Lyndon Johnson the would-be presidential candidate, LBJ the majority leader, and the Democratic party in general during the mid-1950s was civil rights. The *Brown* decision mandating desegregation of public schools marked the beginning, not the end, of the Second Reconstruction. On December 1, 1955, in Montgomery, Alabama, "the cradle of the Confederacy," a black seamstress and former NAACP official, Rosa Parks, refused to give up her seat to a white and move to the back of the bus. She was duly arrested. Three nights later, black community leaders gathered at the Dexter Avenue Baptist Church, formed the Montgomery Improvement Association, chose as its head the young, charismatic minister Martin Luther King Jr., and launched a bus boycott among local blacks.

Meanwhile, throughout 1954 and 1955, white supremacists in the South had been organizing to fight the *Brown* decision. By the end of 1955, no fewer than 568 separate segregationist organizations, including a revived Ku Klux Klan with a membership estimated at two hundred thousand, were operating in the United States. Senator Harry Flood Byrd (D-Virginia) called for a policy of "massive resistance."

Invoking the memory of John C. Calhoun, Georgia, Mississippi, and Virginia passed resolutions of interposition. "The Deep South Says Never" read the title of a series of articles by John Bartlow Martin on the segregationist movement.[48] "If we submit to this unconstitutional, judge-made integration law," declared a White Citizens' Council leader, "the malignant powers of atheism, Communism and mongrelization will surely follow."[49]

Throughout late 1955 and early 1956, state legislatures passed laws designed to frustrate *Brown*. Hundreds of different measures were enacted, some revoking the licenses of school employees teaching mixed-race classes, others appropriating state funds to subsidize tuition to all-white private academies, and still others completely shutting down school systems that had been ordered to desegregate.

Early in 1956, southern senators began meeting once again in Richard Russell's office. The gatherings were stormy. The radical racists—James Eastland (D-Mississippi), Allen Ellender (D-Louisiana), Strom Thurmond (D–South Carolina), and John Stennis (D-Mississippi)—were out for blood. Mob violence had accompanied the University of Alabama's rejection of Autherine Lucy, and passions were running high. Aside from their own personal feelings, the southerners were being pushed by extremists at home to stand up for Dixie, to show the North that white southerners would not be intimidated.

The heart and soul of the Dixie faction in the Senate continued to be Richard Russell, LBJ's friend and mentor. The party's and nation's rejection of him as a legitimate presidential candidate had shocked and embittered him. "Dick Russell had been a great leader, a great influence for good," Jim Rowe said, "but after he ran for the presidency and got knocked off as a southerner in 1952, I always thought that Dick became a much narrower southerner and was parochial."[50]

Beginning with the *Brown* decision, the senior senator from Georgia would become increasingly obsessed with civil rights. He was ably assisted by the mild-mannered but thoroughly reactionary Harry Byrd of Virginia. Praising the faithful and icing the wavering, Russell and Byrd continually emphasized that unanimity was the key to the bloc's success, and they made certain there were few defectors. Those who refused to conform risked ostracism and eventual political death. The Dixie Association quickly came to the conclusion that a statement of principles—the "Southern Manifesto"—was the proper response for sympathetic senators and representatives to make to the looming assault on hallowed southern institutions.[51]

Despite their general opposition to the *Brown* decision, southerners in the Senate were deeply split. Thurmond harangued the group with an uncompromising diatribe that called for resistance inside or outside the law, whatever the price. That was too much even for the other fire-breathers, and they turned to North Carolina's Sam Ervin, an unkempt, deceptively shrewd young lawyer who very much wanted to be reelected to the Senate. The *Brown* decision was based on neither law nor precedent, Ervin argued, but solely on "psychology and sociology." Given the fact that the Warren Court had usurped and exercised a power denied it by "the very instrument it was professing to interpret"—the Constitution—its decision was inoperative.[52]

Moderates like Fulbright, Sparkman, Lister Hill (D-Alabama), and Price Daniel (D-Texas) drafted their own version, which termed the *Brown* decision "unwarranted" and pledged that the signers would use all lawful means to bring about its reversal.[53] The upshot was a compromise. On Monday, March 12, 1956, nineteen senators and seventy-seven representatives issued their defiance. The Court, the "Southern Manifesto" declared, had substituted "naked power for established law," planted racial hatred and suspicion where there had been friendship and understanding. The signatories pledged to resist integration. Although they added the qualifying phrase "by any lawful means," the manifesto was taken by white supremacists as a call to arms.[54]

• • •

CONSPICUOUS BY THEIR ABSENCE on the list of manifesto signers were Albert Gore of Tennessee and Lyndon Johnson of Texas. Withholding his name from this paean to apartheid would be a source of pride for years to come for Lyndon. Senator Richard Neuberger, liberal Democrat from Oregon, described the leader's decision as "one of the most courageous acts of political valor I have ever seen . . . in my adult life."[55]

The leader's motives were several. First, of course, was his ambition for higher office. "Even though the time may have come when a Southerner could run for President and be elected, he certainly could not do so if he were known as 'the Southern candidate,' " George Reedy advised his boss. "The Nation as a whole might well accept a Southerner as a national leader but not as a sectional leader."[56] Johnson also believed that civil rights was an issue whose time was coming. In a sense, by presenting the white South with a fait accompli, the Supreme Court had done the region a favor. Nevertheless, it was absolutely necessary to mute his views and proceed very carefully. He managed to convince his colleagues in the Dixie Association and voters in Texas that, as he put it, "I am not a civil rights advocate."[57] His hands had been tied by his leadership position and by the need to act as a unifying force within the Democratic party.

Personal convictions aside, LBJ dreaded the possibility that Congress would have to consider a civil rights bill in 1956. Much like the Kansas-Nebraska Act a century earlier, a comprehensive civil rights measure had the potential to split the Democratic party right down the middle. According to the staff of the Policy Committee, there were four groups in the party supporting congressional action on civil rights: the "liberals," who were acting on both principle and emotion; labor, whose northern branches were seeking an accommodation with black workers and who saw the civil rights issue as a means to gain greater say in Democratic party councils; urban bosses, who viewed the black vote as increasingly important to their survival; and black organizations such as the NAACP.[58] But then, of course, the party included those most opposed to civil rights. A preelection tussle in Congress over the issue would fracture Democrats, resulting, perhaps, in another Dixiecrat bolt. The GOP could read the political tea leaves as well as Johnson and his staff, and they were determined not to pass up such an opportunity.

In 1955, the nation had been swept by a wave of revulsion in the wake of Emmett Till's lynching. Then there were the protests and police beatings that accompanied Autherine Lucy's attempt to attend the University of Alabama. As the Montgomery bus boycott dragged on into 1956, acts of terrorism by white thugs and local law enforcement officers increased, further offending moderates, liberals, and conservatives in the North and Midwest.

With a view to recapturing the black vote—the GOP was, after all, the party of Lincoln—and driving a stake into the heart of the Democratic party, Eisenhower and his attorney general, Herbert Brownell, decided to introduce a bill calling for a bipartisan commission to investigate civil rights abuses, a new division in the Justice Department whose sole duty it would be to prosecute civil rights violators, additional powers to enable the federal government to enforce voting rights, and amendments to existing civil rights statutes to protect those seeking their rights.[59] A watered-down version passed the House in July.

As the Senate prepared to receive the bill, LBJ surveyed the scene. Congress was scheduled to adjourn in just four days so that senators and representatives could attend their respective presidential nominating conventions. So far, the Democrats had managed to remain united. The leader consulted with Adlai Stevenson, Eleanor Roosevelt, Hubert Humphrey, and Wayne Morse. All agreed that a divisive debate over civil rights in the Senate would achieve nothing but the election of a Republican president and Congress. Hard-liners such as Paul Douglas and Herbert Lehman, urged on by the ADA and NAACP, however, were determined to force the issue.

Under normal Senate procedure, a bill coming from the House was read on the floor and then referred to the appropriate committee, in this case, most certainly Jim Eastland's Judiciary Committee. To prevent this from happening, Douglas planned to pick up the bill personally from the House, take it to the floor of the Senate, and ask for a direct and immediate debate by the whole body. Getting wind of the scheme, Johnson had the civil rights bill passed through a side door of the House chamber to a member of his staff. While Lehman, who had been tricked into leaving the floor, was absent, LBJ had the bill read and sent to Eastland's committee, where it was buried. Douglas, Lehman, and Rauh were furious, but Johnson had ensured that 1956 would not be a repeat of 1948.[60]

SAM RAYBURN approached the 1956 campaign season with grim determination. He was going to make an example of Allan Shivers. The governor, weakened by a series of insurance scandals and rumors of influence peddling within his administration, had decided not to stand for reelection, arranging for his protégé, Price Daniel, to quit the Senate and take his place in the governor's mansion. But Shivers was determined to head the Texas delegation to the Democratic National Convention scheduled for Chicago in August. Rayburn knew that Shivers would never agree to support Stevenson if he were nominated and suspected that the governor's plan was to once again deliver the Lone Star State to Eisenhower. He was right, of course. "I'll have to take that boy's pants before I'm through," the speaker exclaimed to a friend.[61]

Rayburn was concerned not so much about an Eisenhower victory in Texas, though he was thoroughly committed to Stevenson, as about the integrity and discipline of the state Democratic party. Ike threw his hat in the ring for a second term on March 1, and from that point on, political leaders in Texas conceded that Eisenhower was unbeatable. "This is the worst possible State in the country for personal attacks upon President Eisenhower," George Reedy advised LBJ. "When Texans voted for Eisenhower in 1952 they had to make a violent emotional break with their past traditions as in many parts of the State, voting Democratic is in the same category as going to Church on Sunday. When a man or a woman makes such a violent emotional break with the past, he or she bitterly resents any criticism of the move." [62]

But Eisenhower's victory, if he won, would be a personal and not a party victory. The GOP in Texas remained weak and marginalized. Its only hope was for Shivers to lead the neo-Republicans out of the Democratic party and formally merge them with the GOP. But how were the Democrats to stop Shivers without overtly attacking Eisenhower?

Shortly before his Whitney speech, LBJ had confided to Rayburn that he was considering running for the presidency as Texas's favorite son candidate. This would allow him to claim leadership of the Texas delegation and thus deal the coup de grâce to the Shivercrats. Rayburn was initially enthusiastic and agreed to support such a plan, but began to have second thoughts when it seemed that LBJ actually intended to make a serious run at the presidency. Using Jim Rowe as an intermediary, he told LBJ to back off. Rayburn wanted a smooth convention and a quick Stevenson nomination. A South-West coalition headed by LBJ would be sure to alienate labor, the urban machines, and northern liberals in general. "He said that you knew you could not have the first spot this time but he thought that what you wanted was the second spot," Rowe reported. [63] When LBJ assured the speaker that his candidacy was purely tactical, Rayburn released a telegram to the press on March 7 urging Lyndon to become the chair of the Texas delegation to the national convention as well as the state's favorite son candidate for the presidency. In a speech on April 10, Johnson accepted. [64]

The Texas that Shivers and Johnson struggled to control in the mid-1950s seemed more than ever a land of contrasts, a state in which new and old, modern and traditional, rich and poor, white and black seemed to live in juxtaposition with each other, side by side, without ever seeming to touch. Willie Morris painted a vivid picture of the Lone Star State in his *North Toward Home:* "Rigid fundamentalism flourished in modern, skyscraper cities, old Negro women carried laundry on their heads past the low-cut houses of the new suburbia, oil derricks rose high above swamps and cotton fields, television aerials decorated the roofs of sharecroppers' shacks. Republicans organized clubs in lazy courthouse-square towns that had never heard of two-party politics . . . I traveled all over Texas, from one end to another, and my memory of it as a physical place is like a montage, with brilliant lights and furious machinery in the background, and in the foreground a country café with old men in front, watching big cars speed by." [65]

It was clear from the beginning that if the Rayburn-Johnson forces were going to triumph at the state convention scheduled for May, they needed the support of the liberal loyalists, who had spent the past two years establishing a formidable organization at the precinct level. "There were 5,000 of these things—5,000 conventions," George Reedy said. "I think that a small group of dedicated Communists could very easily get into that thing one day and take over the whole party structure in Texas . . . You had to find these precinct conventions to begin with . . . They might be in somebody's back kitchen; they might be in a basement; they might be in a loft . . . The labor-liberal coalition . . . didn't have much of a popular [numerically large, voting] following in Texas, but machinery they did have." [66]

Before Johnson announced on April 10, he and John Connally, who had been picked to run the favorite son campaign if it materialized, asked Kathleen Voight, wealthy San Antonio liberal and leading light in the Democratic Advisory Council, to come to the ranch. Would the liberal loyalists support him in stopping Shivers, he asked. Voight had already consulted with labor leaders and her colleagues on the DAC. They would back Lyndon for chair of the delegation to the national convention in return for a substantial share of seats and would support him as Texas's favorite son—but only on the first ballot. Johnson was not pleased, but he agreed to her proposal. Voight then got on the phone with the editors of twelve of the state's largest newspapers. The deal was done. "Behold," said Johnson in his announcement on the 10th, quoting Psalm 133, "how good and pleasant it is when brothers dwell in unity! It is like the precious oil upon the head." [67]

A WEEK BEFORE the Democratic conclave opened in Dallas, Johnson had Connally bring Kathleen Voight to the ranch once again. Apprehensive as to what was in store, she had Jerry Holleman of the Texas AFL and Fred Schmidt of the CIO accompany her. After dinner, the leader let it be known what he wanted: support from the liberals on the delegation to Chicago to back him not only on the first ballot but on every succeeding ballot until he released them. The three protested that they had no authority from their constituents to make such a pledge. It did not matter, Johnson said; the convention would give him what he wanted. [68]

Connally arrived in Dallas early and began caucusing on the eighteenth floor of the Adolphus Hotel with various precinct chairmen. His lieutenants dispersed to distribute placards emblazoned with the slogan "Love That Lyndon," as triumphant liberal loyalists demonstrated in the halls demanding a purge of the Shivercrats. LBJ arrived on the opening day of the convention at the State Fair Grounds clad in white suit and white bow tie. He was presented with a white burro and a placard reading "Headed for the White House," while liberals paraded a black sheep across the auditorium stage with the sign "Shivers—Stray of '52." [69]

There were only two issues to be formally taken up by the gathering: selection of delegates to the national convention and the naming of Texas's national committeeman and committeewoman. Johnson appealed to the liberals to avoid a purge, to keep the door open to former Shivercrats who pledged loyalty to the Democratic party. His effort at reconciliation was greeted with catcalls and cries of "Throw 'Lyin-Down Lyndon' Out," but there was no purge, and a mixed slate of delegates was voted without serious debate. The group was bound to vote for LBJ for as many ballots as he required of them.

There was little conflict over the selection of a national committeeman, the progressive Byron Skelton of Temple, but the committeewoman was an entirely different matter. The liberals were determined to have the red duchess of Houston, Frankie Randolph, that traitor to her class, chosen. Connally hated her, and Johnson feared her. They threw all their weight behind the candidacy of Mrs. Lloyd (Beryl) Bentsen, wife of former congressman and wealthy south Texas businessman Lloyd Bentsen. When liberals began attacking her husband's ties to oil, gas, and agribusiness, however, she withdrew.[70]

The Connally-Johnson forces then made a last-minute effort to persuade Kathleen Voight, whom they viewed as more of an opportunist than an ideologue, into challenging the cofounder of the *Texas Observer.* Connally protégé John Singleton recalled the scene: "He [Johnson] was in the bathroom naked, shaving, and I was in the room when the knock came on the door. It was Kathleen Voight to come in to talk to John. Johnson said, 'Bring her on in,' so I brought her on in to the bathroom. They sat there and talked while Johnson shaved in the nude."[71]

Voight was not impressed. She had no intention of betraying Randolph and let Connally know in no uncertain terms. The next day, the convention selected Randolph to be the state's national committeewoman. Lyndon complained that "we got double-crossed, out-maneuvered and out-stayed when it counted."[72]

THROUGHOUT JUNE AND JULY, LBJ refused even to acknowledge that he was a true candidate for the presidency, much less make a run in the primaries. Meanwhile, Stevenson was being his usual coy self. "If the party wants me, I'll run again," he confided to a friend in late 1955, "but I'm not going to run around like I did before and run to all those shopping centers like I'm running for sheriff."[73] But after Estes Kefauver beat him in New Hampshire and Minnesota, Stevenson rolled up his sleeves and won in Florida, New Jersey, Oregon, Washington, D.C., and California.[74] When Kefauver withdrew, it appeared that Adlai was in the driver's seat. Perversely, the more Stevenson seemed to have the nomination sewn up, the more Johnson led reporters to believe that he would campaign in earnest. Connally opened a campaign headquarters and began organizing an LBJ floor demonstration. When a journalist asked him, "Are you just a favorite son, or are you a serious candidate?" Lyndon answered, "I'm always serious about everything I do."[75]

In the background, writing his biweekly memos, George Reedy kept his spur to the Johnson ambition. "Even though the primaries left Stevenson 'the front runner,' they still do not establish him as the man who can win in November," he advised his boss.[76]

On August 11, two days before the opening of the Democratic Convention, Harry Truman called a press conference at the Blackstone Hotel in Chicago and announced that he was supporting Governor Averell Harriman of New York for the nomination. Truman had lost all respect for Stevenson, having come to the conclusion that he was weak, ineffective, and, at heart, a conservative. Suddenly

Johnson seemed to be the man in control, the political kingmaker of 1956.[77] On August 12, he summoned reporters and formally announced his candidacy for the Democratic nomination for president. Rayburn and Rowe were appalled. The speaker, always a bit jealous of his protégé, remarked to reporters, "That damn fool Lyndon thinks he's going to be nominated president."[78]

The day Truman announced for Harriman, Rowe tried to rein Johnson in. The South was attempting to use Johnson as a stalking horse, and he should not let it happen. There was no way the Democratic party was going to nominate LBJ in 1956. Labor would not take a southerner: "Your personal friend, Walter Reuther, will lead the fight against you"; the northern bosses, who were increasingly sensitive to the Negro problem, would not take him; and the heart attack would be used by all against him. What Johnson should do was continue to hold himself aloof from the Dixie Association and position himself for 1960. "There is now a danger that Lyndon Johnson will become the Dick Russell of 1956," he concluded.[79]

Johnson's vanity had come to the fore, but there was another, more compelling reason for him to press his candidacy. Rumor had it that Harriman's mission at the Chicago convention was to push the South out of the party. He would use his candidacy as leverage with Stevenson, promising him that he and the labor-boss-Negro-liberal coalition that he represented would carry Adlai over the top when the vote began.[80] But Stevenson would have to stop temporizing on civil rights, Taft-Hartley, and regulation of big business.

Here again was the nightmare specter of the South falling into the arms of the GOP. Johnson regarded Harriman as nothing more than a cynical opportunist. During the preballoting jockeying, the New Yorker came to see Johnson. Jim Rowe was there. "Now, Lyndon, you don't have to worry about me on this civil rights business," Harriman said. "All I have to do to keep my people happy is to make a few speeches. I will make the speech, but I'm not going to do anything about it." After he departed, Johnson turned to Rowe and said, "You liberals, you're great!"[81] LBJ might have had one foot in the West, but he had to speak for the South. He could not stand by and see it driven out of the Democratic party.

Despite Stevenson's almost certain first-ballot victory, LBJ had John Connally go ahead with his nominating speech. It was faux Shakespeare: Johnson was a man who "knows people and they love him, and from that love burns an unquenchable flame of trust."[82] Allen Fear of Delaware made the seconding speech for Lyndon; when he began "Ladies and gentlemen, fellow delegates, President Truman, Lady Bird," a number of delegates could be heard murmuring loudly, "Who's Lady Bird?"[83] "They [the leadership of the Texas delegation] were after John Connally," Jerry Holleman recalled. "And John was on the phone talking to Lyndon, desperately trying to get Lyndon's permission to let them ask for the floor to switch their vote over to Adlai Stevenson. Remember, Mr. Rayburn was the chairman of the convention; he was the man with the gavel. He wanted Texas to switch its vote, and he waited and he waited and he waited for Texas to change its vote before he finally dropped that gavel, and Texas wouldn't change its vote because it couldn't get a release from Lyndon."[84] The first ballot saw Stevenson winning with 905.5 votes to Harriman's 210, Johnson's 80, and Stuart Symington's 45.5.

With the presidential nomination decided, all eyes turned to the second spot on the ticket. "Go and talk to Adlai," Johnson told Rowe. "Tell him I want it." Stevenson greeted the news with a flowery set speech praising the leader. After an hour passed with no word from the candidate, LBJ issued new instructions to Rowe: "Go back and tell Stevenson . . . that no Texan wants to be vice president. Not only Johnson but Rayburn, no Texan wants to be vice president. The only other thing is I want to be in the meeting where the vice president is selected. I don't want to be humiliated by not being called into the meeting."[85]

To everyone's consternation, Stevenson then announced that he was not going to pick a running mate; he would let the convention decide. The gathering avoided anarchy, but there was a mad scramble for the vice presidential nomination featuring Albert Gore of Tennessee, John Kennedy of Massachusetts, Hubert Humphrey, and Estes Kefauver. Johnson was determined that the Texas delegation not go to Kefauver. Southerners regarded him as a traitor to his region, and the party leadership still believed that he had used the mechanism of the Senate Investigating Committee to further his interests at the expense of the party's.

Johnson had the Lone Star State go for Gore on the first ballot. With no clear winner, he then favored Humphrey, but a quick canvass of the convention delegates showed little enthusiasm for the Minnesotan.[86] Johnson then settled on Jack Kennedy: "Texas proudly casts its fifty-six votes for the fighting sailor who wears the scars of battle," LBJ exclaimed over the microphone. Kefauver was selected on the third ballot.[87]

WHEN THE PRESIDENTIAL CAMPAIGN GOT UNDER WAY, Texas liberals assumed that LBJ would do nothing to help the Stevenson-Kefauver ticket. Some even spread the rumor that Johnson was, like his protégé John Connally, a closet Republican. They were mistaken. The majority leader wanted the Democratic ticket to carry the state, but he wanted it to happen without any overt attacks on Eisenhower. He flew to Santa Fe for a strategy meeting with Stevenson and Kefauver, spoke at fund-raisers in Norfolk, Virginia, and Baltimore, Maryland, and accompanied Kefauver on a tour of Texas. At the same time, with few illusions about Adlai's chances of defeating Ike, Johnson concentrated instead on seeing that the Democrats retained control of the Senate. He took a special interest in Alan Bible in Nevada, whom he had talked into running for reelection, Wayne Morse in Oregon, Warren Magnuson in Washington, and Frank Church in Idaho.[88]

The presidential contests produced some surprises. Adam Clayton Powell, the black congressman from New York, came out for Eisenhower, for example.

Reedy wanted to send the Powell speech to Shivers and have someone ask him publicly if he and Powell were now political bedfellows, but nothing came of it.[89] One Democratic political strategist wanted to attack the Eisenhower administration for being soft on communism, but the party decided to let that sleeping dog lie as well.[90] Nothing mattered. Eisenhower crushed Stevenson by a margin of 10 million popular votes and 457 to 73 in the electoral college. Stevenson, ironically, carried seven southern states, but Texas was not one of them.

There were hopeful signs, however. The Democrats retained control of both Houses, the first time a successful president had not carried at least one house for his party since Zachary Taylor in 1848. The Democrats would prevail in the Senate by a vote of forty-nine to forty-seven. To LBJ's dismay, however, the outcome was not decided until the 85th Congress had actually convened.

There were two potential obstacles to Johnson's retaining the majority leader's position. Price Daniel had captured the governorship of Texas, but there had been two years left on his senatorial term. Under law, it was the prerogative of the sitting governor. Allan Shivers, to name the individual who would fill the unexpired term. Shivers had worked hard to see that Eisenhower carried the Lone Star State, and many assumed that he would appoint a Republican. But the governor named William A. "Dollar Bill" Blakeley, a reactionary Democratic businessman, to fill Daniel's unexpired term.[91]

In Ohio, conservatives had elected Frank Lausche, nominally a Democrat but as conservative as any Republican. When he arrived in Washington for the opening of Congress, no one knew how he was going to vote. To LBJ's chagrin, Lausche did not attend the opening Democratic caucus. So confident were the Republicans that they actually offered William Knowland's name as majority leader. But when the decisive vote came, the Ohioan voted Democratic. Lyndon would be majority leader for another two years.[92]

No sooner had LBJ overcome these obstacles than he faced a challenge from another quarter, the Democratic National Committee and liberals inside and outside the Senate. Eleanor Roosevelt, Joe Rauh, and Adlai Stevenson himself were convinced that Johnson and Rayburn had not gone all out for the national ticket in 1956 and, more important, that their "me-tooism" was a strategy calculated to fail. They wanted Democrats in Congress to enact a legislative program that would clearly distinguish the party from Eisenhower and the GOP and give the 1960 Democratic candidate a platform on which to run.

At the opening of the 85th Congress, Hubert Humphrey and five other Democratic senators issued a sixteen-point manifesto that was intended to constitute such a legislative program. At the same time, Democratic National Committee chair Paul Butler announced the formation of a seventeen-member Democratic Advisory Council "to coordinate and advance efforts in behalf of Democratic programs and principles." The goal of this group was nothing less than enactment by Congress of each and every plank in the platform drafted at the Democratic National Convention in Chicago. "The DAC . . . was set up as a place where the then very substantial number of Democrats who weren't in office could express themselves . . . [and] take . . . some of the Texas image off the party," John Kenneth Galbraith, first cochair, recalled.[93]

A number of DAC activists were concerned, moreover, that Johnson was not using his position and the Senate to educate the American people. "The great leaders of the Senate did more than operate with other Senators in the lobbies and backrooms," Marietta Tree, a close friend of ADA luminary Arthur Schlesinger, wrote Jim Rowe. Didn't they see the Senate as a great forum for educating the public in the issues of the day? "The Johnson policy of doing good by stealth must only promote the Eisenhower policy of encouraging people not to think about politics."[94]

Johnson and Rayburn were appalled. This was a clear challenge to their power and a tactic guaranteed to drive southern Democrats into the arms of the Republicans. Johnson and Rayburn politely declined to become members of the DAC. Of the twenty congressional invitees, only Humphrey and Kefauver joined. What presumption, Johnson told Humphrey. "The American people will bitterly resent the idea that a group of appointive, professional politicians are supervising the work of the men they have elected to Congress."[95] The DAC duly constituted itself but was treated with cold civility by the two Texans, who now were arguably the most influential Democrats in the nation.[96]

CONTAINING THE RED-HOTS: FROM DULLES TO THE DIXIE ASSOCIATION

PRIOR TO HIS HEART ATTACK, JOHNSON HAD LIKED nothing better than to career over the hills of his beloved ranch in his Lincoln Continental convertible, shooting bucks from the front seat. The heart attack called for a less strenuous approach. The leader had had constructed a forty-foot-high tower topped by a glass-enclosed structure complete with a carpeted, air-conditioned dining room. The deer tower was situated where a large wooded area met an open field that had been liberally sewed with oats.

The routine called for Johnson and his guests, who invariably included his new business partner, Judge A. W. Moursund of Blanco, to have drinks and dinner, generally served by a coterie of black waiters, and then take their rifles to the deck. Johnson would throw the switch on a bank of spotlights, illuminating the oat field and freezing a number of deer in their tracks, where they were easy marks for the hunters. Roy and Jack Howard of the Scripps-Howard newspaper chain described their evening on the tower as one that "equaled hunting with the Maharaja of Mysore, who invited his guests to shoot tigers from a royally equipped and danger-proof structure in the jungles of India."[1]

IF LBJ WERE GOING TO BECOME A serious contender for the presidency, he would have to be seen to possess ongoing interest and expertise in matters international. In the course of World War II, defense and foreign policy issues had become inextricably intertwined; Johnson's long association with preparedness in both the House and Senate had familiarized him with the diplomatic problems of the day.

As in domestic affairs, the leader believed that the Democratic party ought to cooperate with the Eisenhower administration whenever possible. So-called bipartisanship in diplomatic and defense matters was easier than in social and economic, because the Republican administration that took office in 1953 did not differ fundamentally from its predecessor as to how the cold war should be conducted. Rhetoric notwithstanding, Dwight Eisenhower was not unhappy with the course of American policy since 1945. As NATO's first commander in chief, he had been a loyal advocate of Truman's containment policy. Like Acheson, Taft, and McCarthy, he believed in the existence of a monolithic communist threat directed from the Kremlin that, if the United States and its allies were not ever-vigilant, would spread communism across the globe through a combination of intimidation, subversion, and, if circumstances were right, armed aggression.

Eisenhower disagreed with both Taft and McCarthy in other areas, however. The principal threat was not communist burrowing from within. Rather, the chief menace was from abroad, and the battlefronts were economic and political as well as strategic. The problem posed by international communism was best dealt with by U.S.-led alliance systems and American-financed programs of overseas economic and military aid.

John Foster Dulles, the man whom Eisenhower chose as his secretary of state, was an articulate, bright, and intense man; he had written a number of treatises and pamphlets on international affairs. During the 1952 campaign he had taken the lead in criticizing Truman, Acheson, and the Democrats for opening up Eastern Europe to communist domination, allowing China to fall, and becoming involved in an indecisive quagmire in Korea. A prominent Presbyterian layman, Dulles appeared in public to be a dogmatic and uncompromising anticommunist. His rhetoric was laced with value-laden epithets such as "immoral," "enslavement," and "banditry." His critics would charge that he insisted on seeing every international crisis through the prism of the cold war, forcing nations to choose between the "free world" and international communism, and that he relied too heavily on military alliances and arms aid to achieve his foreign policy objectives. In reality, Dulles was generally patient and flexible in the behind-the-scenes negotiations that constituted the bulk of modern diplomacy. At times, however, he would find himself a prisoner of his own rhetoric.

JOHNSON AND REEDY gave careful consideration to the nature of the cooperation they were to offer the Eisenhower administration. Because they were responsible to the electorate, the president and his secretary of state were forced to take into account public opinion when they shaped foreign policy. Under the Constitution, the legislative branch was a partner, albeit a junior one, with the executive branch in the conduct of foreign affairs. The arrangement seemed to call for policymaking to be a two-party affair. Bipartisanship is especially critical to a president when he is confronted with domination of both houses of Congress by the opposite party.[2]

George Reedy was of the opinion that bipartisanship under the American system of government was not really possible. Under a presidential system, as opposed to a parliamentary system, only the chief executive could speak for the nation. The term he preferred was nonpartisanship.[3] The danger of course, was that the Eisenhower administration would commit the Democratic party to policies that it had no role in forming and then force it to share the blame when and if those policies failed. LBJ was determined that if he and his party were going to be in on the landing, share blame for the administration's failures, they should be aboard on the takeoff, share credit for its successes.

In his State of the Union address of February 2, 1953, Ike called openly for bipartisanship. He then institutionalized regular defense and foreign policy briefings for Democratic and Republican congressional leaders. The majority leader replied in kind. "We are facing a period in which it becomes increasingly important for the United States to speak with a single voice," he told the press. "The alternative is to be divided in the face of a threat from an aggressor nation that is united in its determination to spread communism throughout the world. The Democrats are ready at any time to enter into bipartisan consultation with the Republican administration." The Democratic party would oppose when they thought it in the national interest to do so. "But they will reject the course of opposition merely for the sake of some partisan gain."[4]

Bipartisanship did not get off to an auspicious start. For years, Taft, McCarthy, and other hard-line anticommunists in the Republican party had been blasting the Roosevelt-Truman administration for "selling out" the nations of Eastern Europe to the Soviet Union via the Yalta Accords. Eisenhower and Dulles would have preferred to let the matter rest, but following the election, both Taft and the wild men were out for blood. Thus, in the same State of the Union speech in which he called for bipartisanship, Ike criticized the Democrats for having concluded secret agreements that led to the "enslavement" of Eastern Europe.

What conservatives in his party wanted was a resolution that specifically repudiated the Yalta Accords. Instead, on February 20, the administration sent to the Hill a proposal that simply criticized the Soviet Union for using Yalta "to bring about the subjugation of free peoples."[5] Eisenhower and Dulles feared, of course, that if Congress declared the Yalta Accords invalid, the Soviet Union might feel justified in occupying all of Berlin and perhaps West Germany and Austria as well.[6]

The wild men were not to be placated, and McCarthy openly attacked the administration's proposal on the floor of the Senate. At this point, LBJ and the Policy Committee mounted up and came to the rescue, speaking unanimously in favor of the resolution as it had been received from the White House. Taft proposed a compromise in which an amendment would be added to the "captive nations" resolution, stating that it did "not constitute a determination by the

Congress as to the validity or invalidity" of the Yalta Accords. Johnson would have none of it. "How can we criticize the Russians for perverting understandings if we refuse to admit their validity?" he asked.[7] With relief, the administration allowed the captive nations resolution to be tabled.[8]

In September 1951, Senator John W. Bricker (R-Ohio) had introduced a constitutional amendment designed, he claimed, to protect the American people from executive tyranny and, more important, from the nefarious influence of foreign ideologies and cultures. A staunch conservative on domestic matters and an authentic isolationist in foreign affairs, Bricker was a favorite butt of liberal jokes. "Intellectually he is like interstellar space," declared John Gunther in *Inside U.S.A.,* "a vast vacuum occasionally crossed by homeless, wandering clichés." The Bricker amendment stipulated that executive agreements would become effective only after congressional action; no treaty of any kind, moreover, would become law until accepted by both houses of Congress. Any treaty provision that contravened the Constitution was to be automatically null and void.

The Ohioan's proposal to restrict the executive branch's freedom of action in foreign affairs was in part portrayed as an antidote to the "Yalta sellout." Never again would a treacherous president and secretary of state be able to appease the forces of evil. An important constituency for the Bricker amendment was the so-called China lobby, a group of conservative, influential Americans, including *Time-Life* publisher Henry Luce, who were MacArthur admirers and who agreed with him that the future course of civilization would be determined by events in Asia. They were close to both Chinese Nationalist leader Jiang Jieshi and Syngman Rhee.

Eisenhower, Dulles, and progressives such as Senator Alexander Wiley, chair and then ranking minority member of the Senate Foreign Relations Committee, were appalled by the Bricker amendment. If adopted, it would hamstring the executive in its ability to conduct the foreign relations of the country. Congress and conceivably every state would have to endorse a treaty or executive agreement before it could go into effect. The president and secretary of state would have no standing or credibility with foreign leaders. Privately, Eisenhower told GOP leaders that "he was duty bound to defend the Constitution" and "that acceptance of the Bricker Amendment would be a sellout of the Constitution."[9]

But Bricker, supported by Knowland and House Minority Leader Leverett Saltonstall, would not budge, and polls indicated widespread public support for the measure. "The Bricker amendment was probably the most divisive political proposal of the mid-fifties," Reedy recalled. "It got to the Senate, and it became apparent from the start that it could not be defeated on a straight-out vote. No one could vote against the Bricker amendment with impunity, and very few could vote against it and survive at all—at least, so they thought."[10]

It was tempting for the Democratic leadership to sit back and let the Republicans suffer the consequences of their own internal contradictions, but Johnson and his staff believed that such a course would be the height of irresponsibility. "If the split were merely over how foreign relations should be conducted, a reconciliation would be possible," Reedy observed. "But the split actually involves the differences between men who believe there should be foreign relations and men who basically believe there should be no foreign relations at all."

The country was going through a dangerous period. It had repudiated a Democratic administration and was growing visibly frustrated with the deeply divided GOP. There was a real possibility that the people would retreat completely from democratic politics and embrace political extremism, "something new that promised dramatic action," as Reedy put it. "This may well be the premise upon which Senator McCarthy's followers are operating."[11]

Most members of the Dixie Association were in favor of the Bricker amendment. In fact, following his humiliation in 1952, Richard Russell had become not only more of a segregationist, but more of a narrow nationalist in foreign affairs. In meetings with the Eisenhower administration, he repeatedly referred to the Baruch Plan, which envisioned UN control of atomic materials and weapons, as a mistake and opposed both the sharing of atomic information with America's NATO allies and the placing of U.S. troops under "foreign" command.[12] Once again the specter of an American fascism rooted in anticommunism and racism appeared to be raising its head.

Eisenhower needed help, but the leader could not come to his rescue if the president did not seek his aid. So overwhelming seemed sentiment in behalf of the Bricker amendment that Eisenhower felt he could not meet the issue head-on. For two years, between 1951 and 1953, the White House obstructed and delayed. When an exasperated Bricker finally introduced his measure, Secretary Dulles testified before Congress, lavishly praising the Ohio conservative while informing members of the Senate Judiciary Committee that his proposal went too far in restricting executive action in the field of foreign affairs.[13]

At this point, Lyndon sprang into action. He personally persuaded Walter George, originally a strong supporter of the Bricker amendment, to change his position and introduce an innocuous substitute. Knowland put forward his own compromise while Bricker stuck by the original. The Senate at the end of February rejected Bricker's draft by fifty to forty-two and then voted sixty-one to thirty to substitute the George version. When the vote was taken on it, however, it failed to win a two-thirds majority by a sixty to thirty-one count. Throughout, Johnson prowled the cloakrooms and Senate floor, arguing, cajoling, and promising.[14] "Had Lyndon Johnson not been the leader of the Senate, the Bricker Amendment would be part of your Constitution today," Bobby Baker said. "He was solely responsible, because of his parliamentary genius."[15]

THE PRINCIPAL FOREIGN and defense problem confronting Eisenhower, Dulles, Humphrey, and Wilson was how to reconcile a reduced defense budget with a militantly anticommunist posture around the globe. Humphrey and Wilson were afraid that the globalist responsibilities inherent in NSC 68 would cause the United States to spend itself into bankruptcy.

The answer they came up with was the policy of strategic deterrence, or what Dulles referred to as massive retaliation. According to this scenario, the administration would concentrate its funds on the air force, specifically the Strategic Air Command and its fleet of nuclear-armed bombers. Pursuing a diplomatic strategy of brinksmanship, the United States would have to convince the communists that it was willing to use nuclear weapons in virtually any situation, even anticolonial "wars of liberation" that the communists might attempt to co-opt. The defensive line NATO was committed to defend was too long, and the Russian Army was too large, Eisenhower told congressional leaders in 1954. An extended conflict would "exhaust our national economy," he insisted. As a result the United States must be "prepared to utilize atomic weapons in their many new forms." [16]

Johnson and the staff of the Senate Preparedness Subcommittee had grave reservations about the New Look, as the press dubbed the administration's defense policy. Most obvious was the fact that such an approach would rob defense strategists of any flexibility. "Does this mean that we turn every Korea-type war into an atomic raid on Moscow?" George Reedy asked rhetorically. "If it does not mean that, what does it mean in situations like Indo-China? Are not 'our vital interests' affected in Indo-China? Does 'massive retaliation' mean that we abandon our allies if they refuse to go along?" [17]

More important, the leader and his lieutenants were convinced that the nation was totally unprepared to fight and win the kind of war Eisenhower and Dulles projected. A May 1953 memo prepared by the committee's staff declared the existing American air defense system "almost wholly useless." It consisted primarily of some eighteen hundred Korean War–vintage fighter interceptors, the army's NIKE guided missile system, and a string of World War II–era radar stations strung along northern Canada. Intelligence estimates were that fighter interceptors would be successful in knocking down only about 30 percent of attacking aircraft; the NIKE missiles had a range of only ten miles and were subject to being thrown off course by chaff, the cloud of aluminum strips expelled by invading bombers; and the warning system left the country's two oceanic flanks unprotected. The Russians possessed a fleet of one thousand TU-4s, comparable to SAC's B-50s and B-29s. They were capable of piggybacking light IL-28 jet bombers. The Soviets were projected to have within two years a stockpile of four hundred 50-kiloton bombs, enough, according to intelligence estimates, "to knock out this country and force it to surrender to an enemy." [18] "The only real question is when the Soviets will assume they have enough bombs to launch a successful attack, and they unquestionably will have enough at some point in the future," Reedy advised Johnson. [19] The United States possessed a superior striking force and a larger arsenal of bombs, but the victory would go to the power that was willing to strike first.

What to do? The Democrats could attack the New Look frontally, which, given the conservative mood of the country and Eisenhower's popularity, would do no good. Moreover, massive retaliation was based on a kind of clear internal logic. If, in fact, all communist roads led to Moscow and every Marxist revolution threatened to expand the area of Soviet influence, it was absurd to battle the symptoms of the disease. The most efficient response was to destroy the source. Whatever their doubts, Johnson and his staff were convinced that the only alternative open to them was to aggressively but privately support the president in his efforts to secure funds from Congress to build adequate systems of air defense and to defend the president from budget cutters in his own administration.[20]

FOR THE MOST PART during the 1950s, the Soviets sought to project their power not by means of military aggression but through forging ideological links with anticolonial revolutionary movements in developing areas and providing non-Western governments with economic and military aid. Washington seemed oblivious to the fact that indigenous nationalism and local rivalries were far more important in most third world crises than the East-West confrontation. In its obsession with the cold war, the Eisenhower administration tended always to align the United States with entrenched, pro-Western oligarchies and to see revolutionary nationalism as part of the international communist conspiracy. As a result, U.S. policy frequently drove local nationalist movements into the arms of communist China and the Soviet Union.

The administration's conservative approach to combating the spread of communism was perhaps best revealed in its response to the crisis in Indochina. From 1882 until 1941, Laos, Cambodia, and Vietnam composed French Indochina, France's richest and most important colony. Forced to relinquish control to the Japanese following its surrender to Germany in 1941, the French returned to Southeast Asia in 1946 determined to regain their lost provinces. The war in the Pacific stimulated anticolonial movements throughout the area, and Indochina was no exception. Shortly after Japan's surrender, Ho Chi Minh, leader of the Vietminh, a broad-based, communist-led resistance movement, proclaimed from Hanoi the existence of a new nation, the Democratic Republic of Vietnam. His ultimate goal was unification and independence for all of Vietnam. The French, however, were determined to reclaim their colonial empire and, with the help of British and Chinese Nationalist occupation forces, reinfiltrated the country.

In 1946 war erupted between the French and the Vietminh. Despite massive economic aid by the Truman administration, the French were staring defeat in the face by 1954. Led by General Vo Nguyen Giap, Vietminh troops had surrounded a French garrison near Dienbienphu on the Chinese-Laotian border. In an ill-advised gamble, the French commander had positioned several thousand troops in an effort to cut off supplies coming from communist China to the Vietminh and to draw Giap's troops into a pitched battle in which supposedly superior French firepower would prevail.

In the midst of a horrific siege, the French chief of staff arrived in Washington and informed the Eisenhower administration that only direct U.S. military intervention could save the day. Admiral Arthur Radford, chair of the Joint Chiefs of Staff, supported him and urged that sixty B-29s pound the communist positions around Dienbienphu. General Matthew Ridgway, army chief of staff and a seasoned infantryman, argued against U.S. intervention. Once American lives were lost, he insisted. Congress and the public would demand total victory. That would require seven divisions—twelve if the Chinese intervened. A Pentagon study concluded ominously that three tactical nuclear weapons "properly employed" could lift the siege. Dulles and Nixon favored intervention, but Eisenhower made it clear that both Congress and Great Britain would have to go along before he would agree.

Johnson and the staff of the Preparedness Subcommittee believed that a line must be established and held in East Asia, but they were not sure Indochina was the best place to make a stand.[21] LBJ suspected that the French wanted to use the United States as "a junior partner," accepting matériel and manpower while remaining the primary power in the region.[22] If anything, liberals were more adamant than conservatives about holding the line there and about the efficacy of the domino theory: that if one major noncommunist stronghold fell to the communists, other free world nations in the area would follow like so many dominos in a chain reaction. "I personally am inclined to prefer this [war] to the first possibility [surrender of vital areas in Southeast Asia] only because I remember the road from Munich too well," Jim Rowe wrote Johnson.[23]

"A realistic appraisal of the military situation [might be] to find a line that can be held," Reedy argued. "This line might be in Indo-China; it might be Thailand or Burma; it might be Malaysia; or it might be in the islands that ring Southeast Asia. Wherever it is, it is essential to find the line because otherwise no realistic commitments can be made."[24] However, because of neglect of conventional forces under the New Look, the United States lacked the means to fight a land war in Southeast Asia, even if it had wanted to.

On April 2, the president had Dulles ask congressional leaders of both parties for discretionary authority to use American air and sea power against communist aggression in Southeast Asia. LBJ had already convened a meeting of the Democratic Policy Committee on the matter. Without much enthusiasm, Walter George made the case for going to the rescue of the French at Dienbienphu. Surprisingly, given his nationalism and anticommunism, Bob Kerr led the opposition. When George invoked loss of credibility if the United States did not act, Kerr smashed the table with his fist and declared, "Senator, if you'll forgive me, I'm not worried about losing my face, I'm worried about losing my ass."[25] Thus, in the meeting with Dulles, Johnson and Russell made it clear that at least forty Senate Democrats would not go along with a grant of authority. Eisenhower subsequently turned down the French, and Dienbienphu fell to the Vietminh on May 7, 1954.

The day following, the leaders of nine nations held the opening meeting of a conference designed to bring peace to Southeast Asia. By the time the Geneva Conference opened, the Vietminh controlled most of northern Vietnam, the communist-led Pathet Lao was struggling against French colonial rule in Laos, and the war-weary French people were ready to abandon Southeast Asia.

Though the United States was not an official participant in the Geneva deliberations, Dulles worked behind the scenes to ensure that at least part of Vietnam remained noncommunist. Because both the Soviet Union and communist China preferred to see Indochina "balkanized" rather than united in a confederation headed by Ho Chi Minh, American diplomacy was successful. Under the terms of the Geneva Accords signed in June, Cambodia and Laos obtained their independence. Vietnam was to be divided at the seventeenth parallel, the north to be ruled by Ho and the Vietminh, and the south by former emperor Bao Dai. All foreign troops were to be withdrawn from Vietnam within a year, and an international commission was to supervise nationwide elections to be held no later than July 1956.[26]

As Senate Democratic majority leader, LBJ was quick to realize that the president was trying to use bipartisanship for political purposes. He had frequently blasted the Democrats for being soft on communism in permitting Soviet domination of Eastern Europe and implying that his administration would move beyond containment and "roll back" the Iron Curtain. Now, here he was participating in a deal, tacitly at least, that allowed the northern half of Vietnam to go communist. When anticommunists protested, he could blame the Democratic-controlled Congress for not supporting him.

On May 6, 1954, the day before Dienbienphu fell, LBJ took the administration to task. "What is American policy in Indo-China?" he asked at a Democratic party dinner. "It is apparent only that American foreign policy has never in all its history suffered such a stunning reversal . . . Our friends and allies are frightened and wondering, as we do, where are we headed. We stand in clear danger of being left naked and alone in a hostile world."[27]

BEGINNING IN LATE 1955 and extending through early 1957, Chester Bowles, Truman's ambassador to India; Senators J. William Fulbright of Arkansas and John Sparkman of Alabama; and journalist Walter Lippmann began meeting and trading observations on the state of America's foreign policy. They quickly came to the conclusion that U.S. diplomacy was in shambles and that Democrats were allowing themselves and the nation to be duped by the Republicans. Polls indicated that 46 percent of the American people regarded foreign affairs as the number one problem facing the nation (farm policy was second at 8 percent), and 66 percent were of the opinion that the GOP was better qualified to conduct the nation's affairs than Democrats. And yet, Bowles argued in a far-reaching memo, the country's defense and foreign policy were in disarray.

Since 1916, the GOP had been split between internationalists and isolationists. The latter had now divided into two factions, one headed by Secretary of

Defense Humphrey that was classically isolationist, insisting that the country turn away from the rest of the world and concentrate on realizing the Jeffersonian dream. Others, like Knowland and Luce, were flirting with the concept of preemptive war as a cheap solution to the East-West confrontation. Dulles was a lawyer in diplomat's clothing, with all the rigidities of his profession, and Eisenhower was a simple-minded weakling, committed to flexible internationalism but unable to implement it. In reality, Bowles argued, his foreign policy was a reflection of his domestic policy. He dubbed himself a modern Republican: conservative when it came to finances, liberal when it came to human beings. The same was true in foreign policy, Bowles argued. The GOP loudly proclaimed that it was going to battle communism on every front and then had proceeded to reduce the defense budget from $50 billion to $35 billion. There was less and less strength to back up American diplomacy, and the results were becoming increasingly and painfully obvious.

Since the time of Peter the Great, Russia had been seeking gateways to the Mediterranean via the Middle East and India. Due to the administration's ineptness, the Soviet Union was making great headway with that goal. North Vietnam stood ready to overrun the South, and the only response available to the United States was nuclear war or withdrawal. The concept of massive retaliation was scaring the wits out of America's allies; it seemed that the only response they could expect if the Red Army attacked them in Europe was a rain of American nuclear bombs that would blow up the United States as well as the enemy.[28]

For the first time, the Democrats' demand for an alternative foreign policy fell on receptive ears.[29] LBJ had begun to suspect that the president was guilty of bad faith. In 1956, Eisenhower appointed Under Secretary of Labor Arthur Larson head of the United States Information Agency (USIA). A former Rhodes Scholar and dean of the University of Pittsburgh Law School, Larson had written a number of articles and a book praising Eisenhower's "modern Republicanism" and making the case for being liberal in human affairs and conservative on fiscal matters. Then, in April 1957, in a speech in Hawaii, Larson attacked Democrats as un-American. "Throughout the New and Fair Deals," he declared, "this country was in the grip of a somewhat alien philosophy imported from Europe."[30]

The next day, the House cut USIA appropriations from $144 million to $106 million. But this was only the beginning. For four days in May, Johnson presided over Senate hearings on Larson's operation. It was not only unethical but unwise to use taxpayer dollars to launch partisan attacks on one of the two major political parties, he declared. The Appropriations Subcommittee proceeded to take another $15 million from Larson's budget. The president complained bitterly to Johnson, but the majority leader would not relent.[31] More substantively, when in 1956 the administration committed a series of blunders in its Middle East policy, Johnson made it clear that he and the Democrats were not going to be made the fall guys.

In July 1952, the Egyptian government's inability to gain control of the Suez Canal from Britain together with domestic problems led to a bloodless revolution. Out of the group of junior officers who overthrew the corrupt regime of King Farouk emerged Colonel Gamal Abdel Nasser. The charismatic officer-politician transformed Egypt into a republic, launched a program of economic and land reform, and adopted an ultranationalist stance in foreign policy.

The centerpiece of Nasser's economic development plan was the High Aswan Dam, which, when completed, would increase Egypt's arable land by one-third and protect the thousands of farmers who lived in the Nile valley from floods. In December 1955, the United States offered an initial grant of $56 million, with Britain adding another $14 million. Nasser then delayed acceptance, dickering with the Soviets for better terms. By the following fall he had mortgaged Egypt's entire 1956 cotton crop in a huge arms deal with the government of Czechoslovakia.[32]

In May 1956, Nasser defiantly severed diplomatic ties with Nationalist China and recognized the government in Beijing. Infuriated, Dulles in July withdrew the American offer of aid in the construction of the High Dam. The secretary of state put the matter simply: "Do nations which play both sides get better treatment than nations which are stalwart and work with us?"[33] Humiliated and angry, Nasser announced a week later the nationalization of the Universal Suez Canal Company, which was owned mainly by British and French stockholders. Egyptians would run the canal, and the revenues earned would be used to finance the Aswan project.

Dulles's rash action threatened the interests of America's two principal allies, Britain and France. Not only did their citizens own the canal company, but the two Western European nations received massive amounts of petroleum and other raw materials through the waterway. Israel also felt threatened by the takeover and even more by an ongoing military buildup in Egypt. For more than a year, Palestinian fedayeen (guerrillas) operating out of the Sinai Peninsula had been carrying out hit-and-run attacks deep into Israel.

On October 29, the Israelis invaded the Sinai and drove toward the Suez Canal. Ignoring Dulles's pleas for calm, Britain and France issued an ultimatum to both combatants to keep their troops ten miles from either side of the Suez.[34] When Nasser refused, British and French troops parachuted into the zone and seized the canal. It became clear in retrospect that Tel Aviv, London, and Paris had acted in collusion.

On October 30, the United States placed a resolution before the UN Security Council calling on Israel and Egypt to stop fighting and for Israel to withdraw its troops. Britain and France vetoed this and a similar Russian resolution. Making the most of the situation, Moscow threatened to send volunteers into the area and rain missiles on London and Paris. Eisenhower responded by announcing that the United States would use force to prevent Soviet intervention. The UN subsequently negotiated a cease-fire, British and French troops withdrew, and the Egyptians began administering the canal fairly and efficiently.

On August 12, just as the Democratic National Convention was getting under way in Chicago, the president summoned LBJ and other congressional leaders to Washington for a quick consultation on the Middle East crisis.[35] The quandary facing the majority leader and his staff during the Suez episode was a familiar one. The administration had proceeded to make its own decisions regarding Nasser, the Aswan Dam, and its Western European allies without consulting the Democratic leadership. But now that the fat was in the fire, the White House invoked bipartisanship.[36]

Dean Acheson, the ultimate Atlanticist and advocate of great power politics, advised Johnson to back Britain and France unconditionally. "The facts of life, in the world in which we live, are that Big Peoples just cannot allow Little Peoples to interfere with their vital interests in this way."[37]

But Johnson realized that such a simple-minded course was fraught with danger at a time when the cold war was being fought in developing nations of the former colonial empire. LBJ met with Eisenhower and laid out two options: the United States could back Britain and France unconditionally, as Acheson had recommended, or it could do everything possible to prevent the European allies from using force, pointing out to them that "our real interest, and that of the British and the French, is to keep the ships moving through the Canal." As long as Nasser did not significantly interfere with this traffic, "we can take the view the Western World is all right . . . I personally tend a little bit to the second course."[38] And that was the line the administration would take.

Overall, American interests suffered as a result of the Suez crisis. Dulles's diplomacy had driven Nasser into the hands of the Russians, split NATO, and heightened Arab nationalism. To keep the warring parties apart, to ensure that armistice lines would hold for the foreseeable future, and to put the Russians on notice that Washington considered the Middle East vital to the national interest, Eisenhower and Dulles felt that they must give some sort of public guarantee to maintain the status quo.[39]

On January 5, 1957, the president stood before a joint session of Congress and asked the assembled legislators to approve a joint resolution authorizing him to devote up to $200 million in economic and military assistance to preserve "the independence and integrity of the nations of the Middle East," and also to use the U.S. armed forces in support of any Middle Eastern state facing "overt armed aggression from any country controlled by international communism."[40]

A number of Senate Democrats attacked the proposal as just another attempt by the administration to make them partners in a failed policy; the president didn't need such congressional approval under the Constitution. Rayburn and Russell introduced substitute resolutions backing "the preservation of the independence and integrity of the states of the Middle East," but eliminating any specific promises of economic and military aid.

Behind the scenes, LBJ worked furiously to achieve a compromise. The authority the administration was asking for was too sweeping, he believed, but it was "unthinkable" for a Democratic-led Congress to refuse the president the power to employ the armed forces of the United States.[41]

The first week in March, the leader defeated the Russell amendment. Dulles reported that LBJ told him "it was the hardest thing he had ever done, because Russell had ... consistently supported him ... for the Democratic leadership."[42] At the same time, LBJ forced the White House to accept his language: the United States "is prepared" to use force if the president "determines the necessity thereof, thus placing the ball back in the executive's court."[43] On March 5, Congress approved the so-called Eisenhower Doctrine by a vote of seventy-two to nineteen.

BY THE MID-1950S, racial tensions also were coming to a head. In January 1957, a month after the end of the successful Montgomery boycott, the charismatic Martin Luther King Jr. founded the Southern Christian Leadership Conference (SCLC) in an effort to bring black churches to the forefront of the struggle for racial justice and equal rights. In February 1957, *Time* magazine put King on its cover and praised his nonviolent philosophy as the solution to the nation's racial problems.

Eisenhower, who had served forty years in the segregated armed forces, had been lukewarm to the movement and had repeatedly maintained that one could not "legislate morals." But, following his victory in the 1956 presidential election, he agreed with Attorney General Herbert Brownell and Vice President Nixon that the time was ripe to move on civil rights. Embracing the issue would solidify the Republican party's hold on the black vote and drive a wedge into the heart of the Democratic party.

Indeed, Ike and his advisers had reason to believe that they could destroy the Democrats as a national political entity once and for all by giving limited backing to the Second Reconstruction. They recognized what George Reedy knew to be true: "The strength of the Democratic party at the present time is its ability to bridge the deeply emotional split in the United States over the civil rights issue. Should it be deprived of that ability, [it] would split into two confused halves, neither able to command a majority in the United States and both probably unable to outvote the Republicans ... the Republican party machinery had been captured completely by the Nixon-Brownell axis. This group has come to the cold-blooded decision that the South should be written off completely and that the way to win the 1960 election is to sell itself completely to the key minority vote of such states as New York, Pennsylvania, Illinois, New Jersey and California."[44] Eisenhower told GOP legislative leaders, "When someone tries to hit me over the head with a brickbat, I start looking around for something to hit him with."[45]

The measure the administration decided to support was identical to the 1956 bill. Parts I and II of HR 6127 proposed to create a bipartisan commission to investigate civil rights violations and establish a separate Civil Rights Division within the Department of Justice. In addition, Part I authorized the attorney general to seek a court injunction against anyone obstructing or depriving an individual of his or her right to vote. Part III empowered the Justice Department to file civil suits seeking injunctive relief for those whose civil rights had been violated in the areas of education, housing, public transportation, or voting. Finally, Part IV provided for trials by federal judges in cases involving civil rights contempt charges.[46]

"I personally think this is Armageddon for Lyndon Johnson," Jim Rowe wrote. If LBJ did not support some form of the civil rights law that would come before Congress, he could forget the presidential nomination; indeed, his position as majority leader would be irreparably compromised. He would thenceforward be perceived, as was Richard Russell after 1952, as purely a sectional figure. Without a leader, a bridge between southerners, northern liberals, and westerners, the Democratic party would disintegrate.[47] Johnson agreed. By 1957, he later observed, "I knew that if I failed to produce on this one, my leadership would be broken into a hundred pieces; everything I had built up over the years would be completely undone."[48]

There was really little question of where Johnson stood personally. "With LBJ I think that his basic attitude toward human beings has always been one characterized by an almost total lack of bias," George Reedy said.[49] Johnson was not above acquiescing in others' prejudices by playing to the galleries. "I heard him come into the Cloakroom of the Senate and tell Senator Douglas . . . : 'Paul, we're bringing up the civil rights bill again this afternoon,'" Harry McPherson remembered. "And about five minutes later I heard him say to some southerner . . . , 'I'm going to have to bring up the nigger bill again.'"[50] LBJ sympathized with those southern liberals whom historian Dewey Grantham identified as being caught in a bind: "Most of them, after all, were moderates and gradualists. They wanted an orderly, locally controlled process of racial change that would take account of community conditions and regional economic growth."[51] But with segregationists seemingly more implacable than ever, black Americans were out of patience. The country had reached a crossroads, LBJ sensed. Congress had not enacted a piece of civil rights legislation for eighty-two years. The legislative process in general and the U.S. Senate in particular must become responsive to this surging, disenfranchised minority or it would seek justice and equality of opportunity through other means.

The Brown decision had deeply divided the country; polls taken in February 1956 indicated that over 70 percent of northern whites who were interviewed supported the Supreme Court's rulings of 1954 and 1955; 80 percent of southern whites opposed them.[52] During the 1956 national convention, northern liberals and moderates, led by Averell Harriman and Arthur Schlesinger Jr., had seriously considered flushing the Dixiecrats out into the open and isolating them, even if that meant the Democratic party would lose the South. "The Southerners must understand that there is as much emotion on the subject of Civil Rights in the North as there is in the South," Jim Rowe had reported to LBJ at the time. Warned that forcing through a liberal civil rights program might break up the party, some of Harriman's lieutenants observed that that might be for the best. The only way the Democrats could win in 1956 or in the future was to be more "liberal" than they then were.[53]

Neither LBJ nor anyone on his staff believed, however, that the Democratic party or the nation could do without the states of the former Confederacy. He was fond of pointing out to the liberals that the only area Adlai Stevenson had carried in 1956 was the South. If the region was able to solve its racial problems and achieve the economic prosperity that had historically eluded it, the nation would survive. If it did not, the prospects for the Union were dim.

For the sake of his political future, as well as the future of the Democratic party and the nation as a whole, the majority leader would have to take charge. Originally pessimistic, Jim Rowe now saw a silver lining. "There was a man named Henry Clay who became known as the Great Compromiser," he observed to LBJ. "Lyndon Johnson could adopt this role."[54]

In December 1956, LBJ and his advisers huddled to devise a strategy. It was clear, they quickly concluded, that the South would never accept Part III of the civil rights bill, which gave the Justice Department power to enforce integration in housing, public transportation, and schools—nothing less than a reincarnation of the infamous Force Acts of the Reconstruction era. It would rub salt in the South's wounds, still raw over the *Brown* decision. The key, the leader and his staff believed, was to focus on voting rights. "One of the characteristics of southerners is that they really do believe in the Constitution as written," George Reedy observed. "When they have to take some stand that is clearly unconstitutional it worries them. Well, all you have to do is read the 14th, 15th, and 16th Amendments to see that they [blacks] were entitled to vote . . . And if they gave on that, then down the road it would be possible to branch out into other fields."[55] In addition, Johnson believed that when push came to shove, Richard Russell would prove to be more nationalist than racist.

At the opening of the 85th Congress, LBJ moved to demonstrate his loyalty to (and his power over) Russell and the South. In their quest to change Rule 22 to allow cloture by a majority vote, Senate liberals had gained the support of a valuable new ally, Vice President Nixon, who ruled in favor of the measure. But when Congress convened, the Senate still had to approve a rule change by a majority vote. At this point, LBJ called in all his markers with Democratic senators and then crossed the aisle. He let Republican leaders and the administration know that they could forget favorable action on the Middle East Resolution if the GOP voted to change Rule 22. The administration would get the kind of civil rights bill it wanted, but not if it stood by and watched the demise of the filibuster. In the ensuing vote, the majority leader prevailed by fifty-five to thirty-eight.[56]

From January through June, while the House debated the civil rights bill, Johnson huddled with Russell. He reminded his friend that Nixon was ready to rule at the beginning of the next congressional session that each new Senate could adopt its own rules. If such an eventuality came to pass, the solons could by a simple majority do away with Rule 22. The filibuster would be dead. He had held off the antifilibuster forces this session, Johnson told the Wizard of Winder, but he was likely to lose next time around.[57]

Russell agreed, grudgingly, to work to avoid a filibuster and to keep the South in the Democratic party, but his terms were hard. Any compromise measure must eliminate Section III, which would have empowered the federal government to press integration on the South. Russell described it as "a cunning device" to use "the whole might of the federal government, including the armed forces if necessary, to force a co-mingling of white and Negro children." And he insisted that anyone cited for contempt in federal civil rights cases would receive a jury trial. In the South, where voter rolls were lily white, this would ensure that no one would ever be convicted. What was left was a voting rights provision that would at best be difficult to enforce.[58]

When the House sent the civil rights bill to the Senate on June 18, proponents of the bill wanted to keep it from being referred to Eastland's Judiciary Committee, where it would surely be buried. In a vivid example of the truism that politics makes for strange bedfellows, William Knowland and Paul Douglas joined forces to sponsor a motion to have the bill brought up for debate on the Senate floor immediately, without referral to committee. Their proposal carried by a vote of forty-five to thirty-nine.

To show his solidarity with Russell and the South, LBJ voted nay. He also persuaded four liberal western senators—Wayne Morse, Warren Magnuson, Jim Murray, and Mike Mansfield—to vote to refer the measure to Eastland's committee. Their willingness to comply was part of a deal Johnson put together, whereby, in return for their votes on civil rights, the quartet could count on southern votes for federal subsidies for construction of the massive Hell's Canyon Dam on the Snake River in Idaho. The Hell's Canyon project, defeated fifty-one to forty-one the previous year, was subsequently approved.[59]

But Johnson and Russell had not enlisted the help of western liberals to block passage of the 1957 Civil Rights Act, only to have it modified to the point that it would meet with southern approval. On July 2, Richard Russell rose on the Senate floor to speak out against the pending legislation. He assaulted only sections of the bill, chiefly Section III, not the entire measure. The issue now became, as George Reedy put it, "the kind of bill that should be passed rather than whether a bill should be passed."[60]

What Johnson had in mind—what he and Reedy had had in mind all along—was passage of a voting rights act. Gradually the pieces began to fall into place. First, Eisenhower began to back away from Section III. At a press conference on July 3, he admitted that there were parts of the civil rights bill that he did not understand and that he wished only to protect and extend the right to vote.[61]

On July 11, Johnson inserted into the *Congressional Record* a Walter Lippmann column calling for a voting rights bill only.[62] To further soften up Senate liberals for compromise, Johnson solicited opinions from such Washington luminaries as former Secretary of State Dean Acheson and attorneys Abe Fortas and Ben Cohen that Section III was unconstitutional.[63]

At this point, Johnson arranged for Clint Anderson, a Democratic civil rights supporter, to join with Republican senators George Aiken of Vermont and Clifford Case of South Dakota to cosponsor an amendment to the civil rights bill eliminating Part III in its entirety. "It seemed to me," Anderson later said, "that a weakened bill was better than no bill at all, especially if the voting guarantees remained intact."[64]

On July 24, with the support of western liberals, the Senate voted fifty-two to thirty-eight to cut Section III from the bill.[65] Passage would now depend on reaching agreement on the jury trial provisions of Part IV. Southern senators were adamant that defendants accused of civil rights would have the right to a jury trial. They denounced Part IV as a clear violation of the rights of the individual by an overweening federal power. In this case, Russell and his colleagues had a strong argument. As freshman senator Frank Church put it. "The tradition of allowing men so accused to be judged by their peers was a very strong one."[66] But liberals countered that because in all but the rarest cases, blacks were barred from serving on juries in the South, no white man would ever be convicted of violating a Negro's civil rights. Again, compromise was the order of the day, but where, Johnson and his staff wondered, were there grounds here for half a loaf? Reedy found the answer in the pages of *The New Leader.* Carl Auerbach, a prominent Wisconsin law professor, suggested that the solution to the impasse lay with an ancient tradition that had its roots in English common law. Historically, the law had mandated jury trials in criminal cases but not in civil cases (such as contempt of court).[67]

Immediately, Johnson went to Joe O'Mahoney of Wyoming, Estes Kefauver of Tennessee, and Frank Church of Idaho and persuaded them to amend Section IV to require jury trials in criminal but not civil cases.[68] He then had Church add a provision guaranteeing "the right of all Americans to serve on [federal] juries, regardless of race, creed or color."[69]

Meanwhile, Brownell and Nixon had rebelled. The jury trial provision was too much. It would completely hamstring the attorney general in his efforts to enforce voting rights, much less the *Brown* decision, in the South. Roy Wilkins, president of the NAACP, had informed the vice president that blacks were totally opposed to the civil-criminal contempt compromise.[70]

As the vote on the O'Mahoney-Kefauver-Church amendment approached, Johnson and Minority Leader Knowland went head to head. Among other things, Lyndon promised Republican senators from Kansas and Maryland the right to fill newly created federal district judgeships in return for their votes. Knowland was convinced up until the last that he had thirty-nine Republicans when in reality he could command only thirty-three.

At the same time, Democratic liberals were grudgingly falling into line. "After the Senate, under Johnson's leadership, had knocked Part III out of the

House bill and had added the jury trial amendment to the voting rights section," Joe Rauh recalled, "the bitterness of the civil rights organizations against both him and what he had done knew no bounds." But "after a long day's argument, Roy Wilkins took . . . [Johnson's] view—that it was better to have a poor bill than no bill at all . . . and the whole group agreed to come out for the bill in a statement drafted on the spot." [71]

On August 2, at the close of a fourteen-hour session, the Senate voted fifty-one to forty-two for inclusion of the jury trial amendment. On August 7, the Senate voted seventy-two to eighteen to approve the entire bill.

Predictably, the Civil Rights Act of 1957 and Johnson's role in it pleased neither liberals nor conservatives. "Johnson did his party a great favor by his engineering of the Civil Rights Bill of 1957," a columnist for the *Dallas Morning News* wrote, "but he did himself no good at all in Texas"—or the South, he might have added. Liberals were even more dissatisfied. Rauh, who had been so instrumental in the measure's passage, later claimed, "Johnson's triumph was so tarnished that it proved his unfitness for national leadership." [72] Black leaders Ralph Bunche and A. Phillip Randolph declared that the measure as passed was worse than no bill at all. On its face, the Civil Rights Act of 1957 was, as Senator Paul Douglas put it, "like soup made from the shadow of a crow which had starved to death." [73]

But it was nonetheless historic. Johnson had maneuvered Russell and his Dixie colleagues into having to choose between the survival of the filibuster and passage of a civil rights bill, the first since the late 1860s. Like it or not, southern senators had, by abjuring a filibuster, acquiesced in the notion that the federal government, and specifically Congress, had the right to regulate civil rights in the states. The logjam was broken. No longer would the legislative branch of the federal government be denied to black Americans as a source of redress of grievance. "A man without a vote," Johnson observed to the press, "is a man without protection . . . He is virtually helpless." [74] Out of such feelings of helplessness were revolutions born.

In addition, the Civil Rights Act had arguably saved the Democratic party. "The real story of the Civil Rights Act is that five states left the Confederacy voluntarily—the healthiest thing that could have happened to this country in years," Johnson told party liberals. "The ultra-liberal position would have left eleven states solid—cut off from the rest of the country, dividing the Nation in an hour of peril. But now—by opening a division between those Southerners who have always been uncomfortable at the denial of so basic a right as the right to vote, and those who are determined from unshakable habit and prejudice to stand against everything for a Negro, we have passed a bill and have bought for ourselves needed time—time to reconcile the North and the South so we can present a united front in 1960." [75]

Thinking back on the making of the 1957 Civil Rights Act, Harry McPherson was moved to speculate whether "an intense political commitment and moral sensitivity were irreconcilable . . . If they were, then one could choose one or the other, though one led toward a brutal pragmatism, and the other toward ineffectiveness. Unless—one could choose a third way, and remain, as the modern theologians say, 'in the ambiguity'—acting forcefully, but conscious always that one's knowledge was insufficient and one's heart slightly corrupt; the best political men I knew seemed to have chosen this way . . . Ingenious and practical as he was, [Johnson] was also ethically sentient; he wished to be thought a good man as well as a clever one." [76]

IT MIGHT ALSO BE SAID of Lyndon Johnson that he was a fanatical gradualist. He was committed to social justice, and he recognized that that meant change. But in change, he believed, were the seeds of disunion. Throughout his years of public service, LBJ assumed that the average American, black, white, brown, or yellow, southerner or northerner, rural or urban dweller, wanted the same things. "What the man in the street wants," he insisted, "is not a big debate on fundamental issues; he wants a little medical care, a rug on the floor, a picture on the wall, a little music in the house, and a place to take Molly and the grandchildren when he retires." [77] Henry Wallace and Charles Marsh could not have said it better.

Harry McPherson remembered one extraordinary Johnsonian jaunt to west Texas. At a breakfast meeting in Abilene with several dozen farmers, ranchers, and Rural Electrification Administration executives, Johnson delivered

> one of the best extemporaneous political talks I've ever heard in my life . . . He talked about the commonality of state, of interest between you men and the automobile worker and the small farmer in Iowa and the little woman that sews dresses up there on Seventh Avenue in New York. He talked about high interest rates and he talked about the stake that the average American had in driving them down. He talked about the Republicans' just irresistible drive, their endemic love of high interest. The average hard working American was going to have to overcome his and her racial, regional, and religious prejudices. "When they say, 'We've got to have a little civil rights bill,' . . . you've got to go along with that a little bit. And when they say, 'I got to have a little minimum wage increase for these women that sit in these hot shops' . . . you got to be sympathetic, you've got to think, 'Well there's my friend and there's somebody that I'm on the same side with when it really counts.' " [78]

Given these truths, LBJ believed, with time, patience, and negotiation, a consensus could emerge and prevail: "So long as men try conscientiously to resolve their differences by negotiation, so long as they follow the prophet Isaiah to 'come now let us reason together,' there is always a chance." [79] As Tommy Corcoran said of Johnson following passage of the 1957 Civil Rights Act, "He is no 'mighty cannon loaded to the lips,' as Emerson said of Webster, but the fact is that Webster and his fellow giants, Calhoun and Clay, were conspicuous failures in trying to deal with the Negro problem, a problem which both Jefferson and Lincoln feared would split the country beyond healing." [80]

CHAPTER 16

LOST IN SPACE

O N OCTOBER 4, 1957, THE SOVIET UNION SHOCKED the West by sending the world's first man-made satellite, *Sputnik* ("traveling companion"), into orbit. That accomplishment, realized before the United States had perfected its own missile system, upset the scientific and, potentially, military balance between the two countries. Then, on November 2, the Russians launched *Sputnik II*, with a payload six times heavier than that carried by the first space vehicle, again proving their apparent superiority in missile technology. At that point, the Soviet Union also possessed the largest army in the world and was developing a navy second only to that of the United States. Secretary Dulles warned that Russia had overcome the "preponderance of power" that the United States had enjoyed since 1945.

In the wake of *Sputnik*, Americans became well-nigh obsessed with Soviet science and technology. Ignoring the fact that Russia had concentrated its resources on the military sector and in so doing doomed the rest of the economy to obsolescence and inefficiency, Americans were overcome by a sense of inferiority. Conservative Senator Styles Bridges of New Hampshire sounded the tocsin, declaring that the "time has clearly come to be less concerned with the depth of pile of the new broadloom rug or the height of the tail fin of the new car and to be more prepared to shed blood, sweat and tears."[1] *Sputnik* seemed to confirm Democratic charges that the GOP was the party of hedonism and materialism and that Eisenhower was more interested in playing golf than in defending the free world.

The Johnsons were at the ranch in Texas when news of *Sputnik* flashed across the nation's television screens. The majority leader understood the implications. The Russians had now achieved parity with the United States in delivery systems; the threat that gave massive retaliation and brinkmanship their credibility was gone. If the Soviets and Chinese communists decided to unleash their vast armies on the free world, what could the United States do?[2]

Not surprisingly, the White House tried to minimize the importance of the *Sputnik* launch. Eisenhower had left that Friday for a week of golf at his farm outside Gettysburg. Informed on Saturday morning of the successful orbit, he left the administration's response to Press Secretary James C. Hagerty and Secretary of State John Foster Dulles. They assured the media and the nation that *Sputnik* came as no surprise to Washington and that there was no cause whatever for alarm.

Press and public were not reassured. The editors of *Life* compared the launching of *Sputnik* to the shots fired at Lexington and Concord and called on Americans to respond as the Minutemen had.[3]

THE "MISSILE GAP" was an issue on which Democrats of all stripes could agree. For years, cold warriors like Senators Henry Jackson of Washington and Stuart Symington of Missouri had been raising a hue and cry about the deplorable state of the nation's defense under the penurious Eisenhower administration. Symington had been particularly vocal. Aside from the principles involved, the Missouri senator saw the *Sputnik* controversy as the perfect stepping stone to the Democratic presidential nomination in 1960. He urged Richard Russell to convene the Armed Services Committee and hold hearings.

On October 5, Russell himself told a Georgia audience, "We now know beyond a doubt that the Russians have the ultimate weapon—a long range missile capable of delivering atomic and hydrogen explosives across continents and oceans."[4] Two weeks later, the Democratic Advisory Council, which included former President Truman and Adlai Stevenson, accused the Eisenhower administration of "unilateral disarmament at the expense of our national security."[5]

No less than Symington, LBJ was mindful of the political moment, and he intended to take advantage of it for his and his party's benefits. "The integration issue is not going to go away," George Reedy observed. "The only possibility is to find another issue which is even more potent. Otherwise the Democratic future is bleak . . . Sputnik fulfills the requirements."[6]

But, as in the past, Johnson believed that the wisest posture for senatorial Democrats was one of constructive criticism. Early in his career he had sensed how powerful was the average American's loyalty to their commander in chief and the armed forces in times of crisis. Woe to those who were perceived to be undermining General President Eisenhower and the Joint Chiefs at a time when the nation faced a mortal threat from the forces of international communism. The leader believed that an investigation was in order, but it should be impartial and bipartisan—and he should be in charge.

Johnson beefed up his Preparedness Subcommittee staff with the addition of New York attorney Ed Weisl and Don Cook, plus three prominent scientists from Harvard, Rice, and Cal Tech. As the missile gap hearings prepared to get under way, LBJ emphasized the importance of fairness to the subcommittee's other members, Democrats Symington, Kefauver, and Stennis and Republicans Bridges, Flanders, and Saltonstall. The only guilty parties in the inquiry, he said, were Joseph Stalin and Nikita Khrushchev.[7]

BY THE TIME the Soviet Union launched its first *Sputnik,* an American missile program was well under way. Until the spring of 1954, the concept of an intercontinental ballistic missile (ICBM) capable of delivering atomic warheads to targets thousands of miles away had been impractical because existing atomic bombs had been too heavy and guidance systems too primitive. But then the United States successfully tested a hydrogen bomb in the Marshall Islands. A thousand times more powerful than the devices that destroyed Hiroshima and Nagasaki, a thermonuclear warhead was also much lighter. Moreover, one would have to land only roughly adjacent to a target to destroy it.

By October 1957, six major missile programs were under way in the United States at an annual cost of more than $1 billion.[8] Symington and members of the Joint Chiefs of Staff believed that this was far too little and warned that the United States was lagging behind the Soviet Union in the development of ICBMs. In November, several days after the launch of the first *Sputnik,* the Gaither Commission, impaneled to make recommendations on the nation's system of fallout shelters, delivered its report. It went far beyond civil defense and warned that the United States would soon be vulnerable to a Russian nuclear attack. The commission report recommended an increase in defense spending of $40 billion over the next five to eight years. But Eisenhower was as budgetary-minded as ever, and resisted pressure for increased spending. *Sputnik* or no *Sputnik,* the president declared, he was not going to bankrupt the nation.[9]

The president had another reason for not overreacting. Since 1956, high-flying U-2 reconnaissance planes had been taking photographs of the Soviet Union, pictures of a strip of Russian territory 125 miles wide by some 3,000 miles long, with images clear enough to make a newspaper headline legible. Eisenhower had known of the first two Soviet ICBM tests that occurred in 1957, and the CIA had warned him about *Sputnik.* U-2 observations showed that the Russians were only a couple of months ahead of the United States in missile technology and nowhere near ready to deploy ICBMs. The problem was that the existence of the U-2s was top-secret information. Ike had not shared it with the Gaither Committee, and he refused to reveal it either to the Preparedness Subcommittee or the American people.[10] He was certain that the existing missile program was more than adequate, but he could not prove it.[11]

LBJ WOULD DOMINATE the Preparedness Subcommittee hearings that opened in November. He introduced witnesses, led cross-examinations, and acted as principal spokesman to the press. His motives were several. Despite protestations to the contrary, there were partisan considerations. Here was what the American people should take away from the proceedings, Reedy declared: "It took the Russians four years to catch up with our atom bomb; it took the

Russians nine months to catch up with our hydrogen bomb; now we do not even have a timetable for catching up with their satellite."[12] There were political considerations. Johnson intended to contain Symington, so that he, rather than the Missourian, would become the recognized congressional expert on space and the missile gap. And there were economic factors. Johnson wanted American activities beyond the stratosphere to be dominated by a civilian agency rather than the military. He perceived the political benefits to himself but also the potential economic boon to the nation, and particularly Texas, of an accelerated space program. Finally, the *Sputnik* crisis might actually be the issue that got America moving again.[13] It could be the spark that led to the "realization of America's full potential," observed Abe Fortas, Johnson's friend and confidant.[14]

THE INDIVIDUALS WHO DOMINATED the first week of hearings were Edward Teller, "the father of the hydrogen bomb;" Vannevar Bush, who had mobilized the U.S. scientific community during World War II; and General James Doolittle, who had led the daring 1942 bombing raid on Tokyo. Bush, who enraged the Eisenhower administration by terming *Sputnik* America's greatest defeat since Pearl Harbor, observed that although the United States had fallen dangerously behind the Russians, it was not too late. With effort and commitment of resources, America could catch up. Rather than crash weapon development programs, Bush emphasized long-term investment in scientific research. Doolittle painted with an even broader brush, arguing for an "overhaul [of] our own educational program," with a view to producing more scientists and engineers.[15]

LBJ and his advisers took the argument one step further. *Sputnik* should be used to advance the cause of social justice and social security for all Americans. "The Romans dominated the world because they could build roads," George Reedy observed. "They did not learn to build roads because they were planning a military weapon but because they needed them for their whole economy . . . The British dominated the world because they could build the best ships. But these ships were not designed to be naval weapons. They were built because the British needed ships to carry their commerce and to explore the new world."[16]

On October 9, Eisenhower had rashly promised the American people that the United States would have a satellite in orbit by December, this despite the fact that the *Vanguard* missile that was to carry the payload had never been fully tested. Fearing a possible public relations disaster, the Defense Department closed the launch area, but more than a hundred reporters and TV cameramen gathered along the road to Cape Canaveral in Florida, the launch site. On December 6, *Vanguard*'s first-stage engine ignited. Amid a huge burst of flame and cloud of smoke the rocket lifted off the launch pad for a few feet, hovered, and then fell back and exploded. The national sense of humiliation and betrayal was almost palpable. "Flopnik," "Dudnik," "Kaputnik" were some of the names the press invented for the failure.[17] "How long, how long, O God," LBJ exclaimed to reporters, "how long will it take us to catch up with the Russians?"[18]

On January 7, 1958, the day before Eisenhower's State of the Union address, the majority leader addressed the Democratic caucus. "Control of space means control of the world," he declared. Republican budget constraints were endangering present and future generations of Americans. He subsequently submitted to Congress seventeen recommendations on space and the missile program, which, as intended, clearly identified the Democratic party with a topic that was at once fearsome and exhilarating: challenging and beating the Russians in missile technology and taking the lead in exploring outer space.[19] Johnson's handling of the *Sputnik* crisis was "a minor masterpiece," declared columnists Evans and Novak.[20]

On February 6, LBJ spearheaded a Senate resolution establishing a Special Committee on Space and Astronautics whose mission was to draft legislation for a national space program. To no one's surprise, he was chosen chair, and on April 14, he and Styles Bridges cosponsored an administration-backed bill creating the National Aeronautics and Space Agency (NASA).[21] Dry and dull as it seemed, organization would be everything, Jim Rowe told LBJ; it "may well determine whether life or death will be the fate of this planet."[22] Although Eisenhower originally favored placing the space program within the Defense Department, Vice President Nixon and presidential space adviser James R. Killian sided with Johnson.[23] Following a White House conference with LBJ in attendance, the way was cleared for the space measure to become law on July 29, 1958.[24]

The *Sputnik* crisis would set the stage for a period of national soul-searching. New Deal–Fair Deal liberals within the Democratic party would turn the missile gap into an education, health care, Social Security, social justice gap. With a vengeance, they would join the cold war to the cause of domestic reform. Without some degree of social and economic security for blacks, Reedy reminded Johnson, the civil rights issue would never go away. LBJ's lieutenant was thinking defensively as well. "It is vitally important that the defense emergency not be used as an excuse for cutting back on the social gains our country has made," he told his boss.[25]

But increasingly, Johnson would think offensively. The gap, real or perceived, could be used to fulfill the promise of the New Deal–Fair Deal and enable the Democrats to recapture the White House.

THE MISSILE GAP, coupled with a severe recession that began in December 1957, moved the Democratic Congress to action. John Sparkman called for more public housing, Robert Kerr more extensive and longer unemployment relief, Albert Gore a new Public Works Administration, Paul Douglas lower trade barriers, and Jack Kennedy higher levels of unemployment compensation. LBJ took these and combined them into a ten-point program, which he outlined at a dinner honoring Harry Truman. With Eisenhower fighting him every step of the way, the majority leader guided measures through the Senate that appropriated $1.8 billion for housing and $1.8 billion for highway construction and extended the Hill-Burton Hospital Construction Act for three more years. Congress also barred Ezra Taft Benson from reducing parity payments to farmers below 1957 levels. In addition, the House and Senate renewed the Reciprocal Trade Act, authorized the largest expenditure in U.S. history for medical research—$300 million—and increased Social Security benefits.[26]

In Johnson's opinion, however, Congress's most important achievement in 1958 was passage of the National Defense Education Act, which provided $1 billion over seven years for loans and fellowships to college students. Ed Weisl and Glen Wilson of the Preparedness Subcommittee staff had worked up a comprehensive study comparing the American and Soviet educational systems. "The Soviets are now producing scientists and engineers at more than twice the rate of the United States," they reported. "The magnitude of the need is difficult to comprehend. What is needed is money, in large amounts."[27] Wilson and committee staffer Gerry Siegel envisioned a "Johnson Plan," the heart of which would be a college scholarship program "based on the philosophy that in our country we must eventually extend the privilege of higher education to all who are able to receive it." Higher incomes earned by college graduates would swell the tax base and more than cover the cost of federally funded scholarships.[28]

BY THE SPRING OF 1958, Johnson had whipsawed the administration into accepting a full-blown partnership between Eisenhower and Dulles on the one hand and on the other, Johnson, Russell, and Fulbright, who would become chair of the Senate Foreign Relations Committee in 1959. Dulles and the majority leader talked frequently on the phone, so frequently that the Republican leadership began to complain.

By the midpoint of Eisenhower's second term, he and Dulles would not meet with Knowland and his colleagues on foreign policy issues without the Democratic leadership present, for fear of alienating Johnson.[29] The majority leader wanted to earn a reputation as a creative contributor to U.S. diplomatic and defense policy, while gaining leverage with the administration over other issues. He also wanted to embarrass the GOP for having openly attacked both the Roosevelt and Truman administrations during times of grave national peril. Accusing the political opposition of being unpatriotic was, for LBJ, beyond the pale.

"Lyndon Johnson has never ridden higher," John Steele wrote in the cover story that appeared in the March 17, 1958, issue of *Time,* "and he should be a happy man. But he is not and he may never be."[30]

Steele was right; one of the sources of LBJ's discontent was his portrayal by the national press. The *Time* piece he found particularly galling. The article took Johnson seriously as a political figure but not as an individual. No man had ever had more control over Congress, Steele wrote. LBJ had single-handedly held the Democratic party together during the difficult Eisenhower era. The journalist noted the quote by Edmund Burke prominently displayed on the leader's wall: "Those who would carry on great public schemes must be proof against the worst fatiguing delays, the most mortifying disappointments, the most shocking insults, and worst of all, the presumptuous judgment of the ignorant upon their designs."

But as an individual, Johnson was painfully imperfect: vain, simultaneously oversensitive and insensitive, undereducated, unsophisticated, complicated, maudlin, humorless, and self-pitying. "He sits at his command-post desk in Office G-14, Senate wing, U.S. Capitol, restless with energy, tumbling with talk," Steele wrote. "He flashes gold cuff links, fiddles with the gold band of a gold wristwatch, toys with a tiny gold pill box, tinkers with a gold desk ornament . . . His LBJ brand appears everywhere, on his shirts, his handkerchiefs, his personal jewelry, in his wife's initials, in his daughters' initials . . . Lyndon Johnson would rather be caught dead than in a suit costing less than $200." The LBJ portrayed in *Time* was gauche. "When host at his LBJ Ranch near Johnson City, Texas," Steele wrote, "he often serves hamburgers cut to the shape of Texas. But an unavoidable symmetrical flaw seems to bother him. 'Eat the Panhandle first,' he urges his guests." The final picture in the piece was of the ranch house with the caption "Eat the Panhandle First."[31]

LBJ ordered George Reedy to bar John Steele from the leader's offices. With difficulty, Reedy dissuaded him, pointing out that such discriminatory action would give the magazine an excuse for continued attacks.[32] Lady Bird and his staff labored to convince him that the article might have been "flippant" and "snide" but that on the whole it was positive, and the cover was a plus. "You are entirely too sensitive to press criticism," Jim Rowe told Johnson. "It has now become a subject of active and amused comment among the Washington press."[33]

Rebekah, who was delighted to have been quoted, was also reassuring: "The article in *Time* is basically good. It tells of your strength, accomplishments, consecration to service, high abilities, and outstanding qualities, but in the effort to picture you as one who has frailties and faults as well as virtues, the writer descends to exaggeration and superficiality." But as was always the case with his mother, in the midst of lavish praise there was the rebuke. "Clothes are merely incidental and not a matter of vital importance in the life of a great statesman," she scolded. "You want to stay near the people, to never lose 'the common touch,' to understand their interests, hopes and hardships, and most of them are poor people."[34]

Johnson may have been so upset by the Steele article because it depicted the Texan as a leading contender for the 1960 Democratic presidential nomination. Such talk, which had abounded in the national press for months, flattered Lyndon's ego but aroused intense anxieties as well. Would he be up to the job? Did he really have a chance to win? Could he stand rejection if he lost? What would a run for the presidency do to his health, mental as well as physical? Indeed, so overwrought did LBJ become at talk of him as presidential timber that he half believed that such stories were part of a plot by those out to get him. "I regret that all too frequently these past weeks my name and picture have been much in the news," he wrote his mother. "This fact creates many problems in assuaging the hurt pride of others. Then, too, I can envision the inevitable downfall that must and will come. I know the reaction of men to fame and I am fearful that there are some who seek by the means of a great and enormous publicity—an inordinate one—to bring about my destruction." [35]

So persistent was his boss in complaining about the damage presidential stories were doing to him, that, exasperated, Reedy observed that there was only one way to stop such talk: "Step down from any position of influence and prestige." [36] LBJ replied that he had already been considering giving up the leadership. Throughout his political career, Johnson had threatened to resign whatever position he held when he was feeling sorry for himself. But this time, apparently, was different. Ironically, although abdication would quiet the presidential speculation in the press, it would actually put him in a better position to compete for the highest office in the land. The leadership was a notoriously bad springboard to the White House. Indications were that the Democrats were going to win big in the upcoming midterm elections. A large majority would make it more difficult for the leader to control affairs. It would be Democrat against Democrat rather than Democrat against Republican. [37]

Johnson continued to consider resignation into May, but then decided against it. Without his power base, he would become fair game for those who hated him. "There will be people who will turn on you unexpectedly just because the wolf pack always turns on the fallen leader," Reedy told him. Drew Pearson would jump on his personal life with a vengeance. There would be much speculation that the Johnson heart was about to give out, literally and figuratively. And who, after all, would keep the South in the Democratic party? [38]

DURING THE TUMULTUOUS DEBATES over the 1957 civil rights bill, the Eisenhower Doctrine, and his leadership of the Democratic party, LBJ was periodically distracted by problems with his family's health. During the 1956 presidential nominating convention in Chicago, Rebekah informed Lyndon and Lady Bird that she had discovered "nodules" under her arm. A subsequent doctor's prognosis was chilling: lymph sarcoma. [39]

In 1957, Sam Houston, drunk more often than sober, had fallen in his own dining room, severely fracturing his leg. He subsequently developed osteomylitis, and after being operated on, was in a body cast from armpit to heel for a year. Lyndon hired him to join his staff as "political adviser." [40]

In July, Lyndon wrote his ailing mother: "I believe it is true that the adversity we suffer makes bigger persons of us all. I read a quote from Longfellow the other day that left a great impression on me. 'It has done me good to be somewhat parched by the heat and drenched by the rain of life.' The fullest, most complete lives are those that have known suffering and experienced setbacks. All my life I have marveled at the way you have borne with grace, discipline, and immense dignity the abundant difficulties and hardships that have filled your life. That's the reason you are who you are and when the balance sheet is totaled up it will be said of you that you are a great woman and the most wonderful mother a man ever had." [41]

On September 12, Rebekah Johnson died; she was seventy-eight. Her passing, together with the coming of his fiftieth birthday on August 27, sent Lyndon into a tailspin. He wallowed in memories of his childhood and talked frequently of going home to Texas. "He intermingled almost daily childish tantrums," George Reedy recalled, "threats of resignation . . . wild drinking bouts; a remarkably non-paternal yen for young girls; and an almost frantic desire to be in the company of young people." [42]

THE MORE POWERFUL Lyndon Johnson became, the more unpopular he seemed to be. In 1958 George Reedy noted a general revulsion against Texas and Texans, especially among northern liberals. In the first place, the Lone Star State was increasingly identified with Big Oil. According to a popular myth circulating among intellectuals and journalists, "The oil industry is evil and greedy and has been pampered by special privileges granted by the Federal government. Texas is the home of the oil industry and therefore is the home of evil and greed. Texas is populated by millionaires, indifferent to the welfare of the people, who ride around in gold-plated Cadillacs lighting dollar coronas with thousand-dollar bills." [43] An article in the March 1957 issue of *Harper's* by Ronnie Dugger claimed, "The very forms of government (in Texas) have been corrupted. Instead of the 'conflict of interest' of an occasional adviser in Washington, the government in Austin harbors entire agencies which act from an identity of interest with the industries they are charged to regulate . . . The rich think they can buy stock in the Legislature or an executive agency as they can in a corporation, and they can." [44] Jim Rowe advised Johnson, "The constant propaganda centering in New York that you and Rayburn run the Congress for the sake of Texas and will pay no attention whatsoever to the rest of the Democratic party outside of the Congress, is steadily growing." [45]

Typically, Johnson clung to the belief that there was a conspiracy in the press to "get him." Reedy dismissed the notion, but in such a way as to heighten Johnson's sense of isolation and persecution. "It is difficult—if not impossible—to conceive of Mark Childs, David Lawrence, *Time* Magazine, Doris Fleeson, the *New Republic* and the *Chicago Tribune* being bought or buying a bill of goods by the same person," he told his boss. [46]

Reedy was only partially correct. Not a conspiracy, perhaps, but there was a connection between the Democratic Advisory Council, the Americans for Democratic Action, the DOT, and its organ, the *Texas Observer*. "I'm a long-time contributor to the *Texas Observer* and very devoted to that paper," Joe Rauh declared in a 1969 interview. "You see, that was really my only source about Texas politics because I don't read the Texas papers." [47]

The image of LBJ that these organizations and the *Observer* projected throughout 1958 and 1959 was that of a venal hypocrite attempting to act the moderate liberal while serving the interests of Big Oil.[48] He was portrayed as a man obsessed with the 1960 Democratic presidential nomination but without the courage to say so, much less make an open run for it. A self-proclaimed heir of FDR, LBJ was a staunch supporter of Taft-Hartley. He was a stealer of elections and an exploiter of his office for private gain.[49] How could liberals trust a man who in December 1957 addressed the liberal Farmers Union convention in Abilene and then ventured to Houston to hobnob with "the plumed plutocrats . . . the Dixiecrats, Shivercrats, and Republicans"?[50]

The more enlightened perceived LBJ as weak rather than wicked. In May 1958, the respected political columnist and editor of the *New York Post* James A. Wechsler wrote a widely read piece on the Johnson leadership and the future of the Democratic party. LBJ was no reactionary wolf in liberal sheep's clothing. He was a "notably enlightened Texas senator." Wechsler's beef with him was that as majority leader, Johnson had conceived it his role to fashion a historic compromise between the state of Texas—essentially a small government, low-tax, individualistic, special interest–dominated entity—and the liberal forces of the Democratic party. He was being asked to support that compromise, Wechsler said, and he could not. He could not because there was no appreciable difference between the LBJ compromise and "so-called modern Republicanism."[51]

Then there was civil rights. "I do not regard the 1957 Civil Rights Bill as anything approaching the Magna Carta," Wechsler wrote Jim Rowe, who initiated an extended dialogue with the journalist following his editorial. "I am unwilling to proclaim to the Negroes of New York or of South Africa that we must all be indebted to Johnson for giving them so little so late. Again I must concede that if I lived in Texas I . . . might well be campaigning for him for Senator." But he did not live in Texas, and LBJ was Democratic majority leader, not just another legislator from the Lone Star State. "I thought Johnson was at his best when he talked about the essential spiritlessness of the country," Wechsler said. "But I think the lack of fire which he deplores is in large part a product of the essential conditions of compromise under which he operates."[52]

At one level, LBJ empathized with the *Post* editorial. He would have loved to have stood forthrightly with the forces of liberalism, railed against institutionalized racism and corporate exploitation of the working class, and touted the federal government as an instrument of social and economic justice. But the world was not that simple. He was the senior senator from Texas, not New York; his constituency was more conservative than those of senators from the urban Northeast or industrial Midwest.

But, Johnson was convinced, any fool could see that he was not kowtowing to the Shivercrats; he had first crushed them and now was opening the door for them to come onboard the political ark on his terms. He had humbled the Democrats of Texas and was battling the Democratic Advisory Council because if the former had their way, Texas would go Republican, and if the latter prevailed, the entire South would fall to the GOP. The Democratic party was and would continue to be the party of reform and social justice. "It has been many decades since the Republican party offered labor anything but a court injunction and a group of strikebreakers," as George Reedy put it.[53] And if the Democratic party was relegated to permanent minority status, as it would be if the South defected, what would happen to the cause of reform and social justice?[54]

There was the cold war to think about as well. "The United States simply cannot fight Jefferson Davis and Nikita Khrushchev at the same time," George Reedy noted.[55]

In effect, Johnson was trapped by his ideals and by geographic and historical circumstance, and he realized it. If he followed the course he knew to be in the interests of the masses and the party that served them, he was bound to be unpopular with the self-appointed spokesmen of his Texas constituents. And he craved the people's love and approval above almost all else. His angst was terrific, and its corrosive effect on the Johnson personality became increasingly marked.

THROUGHOUT HIS YEARS as majority leader, LBJ was able to gain some respite from his schedule and his obsessions by retiring with his family to the ranch. The big, comfortable house on the banks of the Pedernales was balm "to his spirit and heart," Lady Bird recalled. "This country," he remarked in 1957, "has always been a place where I could come and fill my cup . . . and recharge myself for the more difficult days ahead."

After Congress adjourned in August 1953, the Johnsons spent five months at the ranch. Following the 1954 recess, Lyndon, Bird, and the girls stayed in the Hill Country until Congress reconvened in January 1955. The heart attack kept LBJ at the ranch from summer through fall. In 1956 and 1957, he spent the greater part of the months of August, September, and October and half of November and December there. The fall and early winter were LBJ's favorite times. There was respite from the blistering summertime heat and drought, and there were doves and deer to hunt.[56]

During the 1958 campaigning season, a host of important politicos made the pilgrimage to the Pedernales. Visitors drove the sixty miles from Austin to the stone-pillared entrance to the ranch. LBJ could be found outside relaxing by the pool, sipping a diet Fresca, or inside taking phone calls.

Guests were ushered into the large living room, which was decorated with overstuffed sofas and chairs, a stone fireplace, and, in the corner, a domino table ready for action. LBJ rose at daybreak and found some way to let his guests know that they were to follow suit. There was the inevitable tour of the ranch house grounds, beautifully covered with bright green coastal Bermuda grass framed by fields of bluebonnets lovingly planted by Lady Bird. After dinner, LBJ usually insisted on leading his guest by flashlight to Cousin Oriole's cottage, about a half mile from the ranch house. He would call out to Oriole—Mrs. J. W. Bailey, whose mother was a Bunton—and the elderly lady would appear in bathrobe and slippers. Cousin Oriole was tall, rough-hewn, but gracious. She would invite one of the guests to sit in the horsehair love seat on the porch. Visitors could see that the house was simple but well cared for, with a white metal bed in the only bedroom. She would discuss religion and inquire after her uninvited guests' welfare. Often, Lyndon would bring her an autographed picture of himself.[57] One can only wonder what the old lady thought of this charade, of being a living relic of the poor boy past that Lyndon sought to create for his guests.

Deer hunts were usually by safari rather than from the hunting tower. Lyndon and his party loaded into late-model Lincoln Continentals or Cadillacs. At a preselected spot, where ranch hands had been driving deer toward the convoy, Lyndon would stop. Windows were rolled down and host and guests blasted away without ever getting out of the cars. On the way back to the ranch house, LBJ would drive among his swelling herd of cattle, blowing on his car horn, which roughly imitated the bellow of a bull in rut. Guests were treated to a harangue on the lineage and value of the animals. From the pastures he alerted the kitchen staff by car phone to have meals ready at a certain time.[58] The routine was repeated over and over as the roster of visiting politicians, journalists, and friends changed.

BY THE TIME the congressional campaigning season got under way in 1958, it was clear that Eisenhower could no longer carry the GOP. During the winter of 1957–1958, a severe recession gripped the country. Many of America's leading industries were operating at less than 70 percent, and unemployment mounted rapidly. *Sputnik* seemed to confirm Democratic charges that Eisenhower was a modern-day Nero who golfed while America burned. In contrast, the Democrats had demonstrated that they could stick together and were fit to rule. By July, pundits were predicting sweeping Democratic gains in both houses of Congress when voters went to the polls in November. Together with George Smathers and Earle Clements, LBJ ran the Senate Democratic Campaign Committee with skill and energy and made campaign appearances in eight states.[59] The results of the midterm elections were astounding, far surpassing the predictions of the most optimistic party strategists. In the House, the Democrats gained a nearly two-to-one advantage, 282 to 153, and in the Senate they increased their majority from two to twenty: sixty-four to thirty-four.[60] Never in American history had one party made such gains in that body.

Ironically, LBJ and Sam Rayburn were ambivalent about the severe thumping the GOP had taken. Both the speaker and the majority leader had predicted that with large majorities, Democrats would be much harder to control. Internecine warfare was likely to break out, with possible dire consequences for 1960 and for LBJ's leadership. And they were right. Jim Rowe warned LBJ that he would have to sever his tacit alliance with the Eisenhower White House and make substantial concessions to northern liberals. Much would be expected from the 87th Congress from voters looking for an excuse to vote Democratic in 1960.

To appease the fifteen new Democratic senators, five liberals and ten moderates, the leader announced on November 7 a twelve-point legislative program that would further extend the New Deal–Fair Deal, protect farmers, workers, consumers, and small businessmen from Republican reactionaries, and differentiate the Democratic party from the Eisenhower administration. Both Frank Church and Hubert Humphrey renewed their pledges of loyalty to both Johnson and his political strategy. But others were not so compliant. Joe Clark, a liberal blueblood from mainline Philadelphia, disliked the leader from the day he took his seat in the Senate in 1957. "He was a hypocritical s.o.b," Clark later said. "He was a typical Texas wheeler-dealer with no ethical sense whatever, but a great pragmatic ability to get things done." [61]

Clark was not Johnson's only liberal critic in the new Senate. As he had in 1958, LBJ delivered his own state of the union address to the Democratic caucus the day before Eisenhower gave his to the joint session on January 8, 1959. After outlining his legislative agenda, the leader adjourned the meeting, declaring that there would be no need for another caucus until the following January. Offended, first-term Wisconsin Senator William Proxmire dared to openly criticize the leadership. "There has never been a time when power has been as sharply concentrated as it is in the Senate today," he declared in a speech on February 23. In subsequent harangues he blasted the leader not only for "one-man rule," but for formulating Democratic policy in the Senate "on an ad-lib, off-the-cuff basis." Wayne Morse, Paul Douglas, and Joe Clark stood in the wings and applauded. [62]

So irritating did LBJ find Proxmire that he did him the honor of attacking him by name on the floor of the Senate. Proxmire needed a "fairy god-mother" or a "wet-nurse," Johnson told his colleagues. Frustrated, Clark and Proxmire gradually desisted, but Democratic liberals remained restive and their numbers were imposingly large. [63]

Resentment against Johnson was as much over form as substance. He was perceived by Washington insiders as both arrogant and grasping. On the eve of Ike's 1958 and 1959 State of the Union messages, Capitol wits declared that the majority leader "will resent Ike's interference in governmental affairs" and reported that "Senator Lyndon Johnson entered the House chambers to a sustained rising ovation. He was accompanied by the President." [64] Jack Kennedy, who had been returned to the Senate from Massachusetts by an astounding eight hundred thousand-vote margin, amused his campaign audiences with this story: God had told him in a dream that he not only would be reelected, but would be the next president. When he told Stu Symington about the dream, Symington had responded that oddly enough, he had had the same dream. When they both told Lyndon of their visions, he observed, "That's funny. For the life of me I can't remember tapping either of you two boys for the job." [65]

The leader's hoarding of office space while others, especially freshmen, suffered in cramped quarters was notorious. The *Chicago Tribune* dubbed him the "Maharajah of Texas." His domain consisted of twenty cathedral-size rooms, ornately decorated and thickly carpeted. "On the ceiling Constantino Brumidi's famous frescoes of Madonna-like women and cherubim look down on the majority leader as he talks to the unending flow of visitors to his office,"[66] a reporter for the *Dallas Morning News* wrote after visiting the leader in the historic chambers of the District of Columbia Committee. There were in addition, the offices occupied by his Preparedness and Space Committees, a private room off the gallery just over the Senate floor, the majority conference room on the second floor of the Capitol, and a seven-room suite across the hall from the Senate chamber. The new digs were decorated in green and gold with plush furniture. Visitors who managed to penetrate to the leader's inner office were greeted by the sight of a lighted, full-length portrait of LBJ himself.[67]

BY THE FALL OF 1958, Lyndon Johnson was considering the possibility that he might become president, although he continually denied his candidacy. "There is no vestige of a Johnson-for-President organization," John Steele wrote his editors. "But Lyndon has strong sinews of strength running through the South, the Southwest, the West up to the California line, and now in Indiana, Missouri, touching here and there in Illinois, south of Chicago. If such a line was to be consolidated with a Southwestern alliance at its heart, if there was a convention deadlock . . . Lyndon Johnson could find himself the nominee."[68]

Johnson would wake up in the morning desperately wanting to be president, George Reedy recalled, and then by afternoon be completely repelled by the idea. If he were not going to be a formal candidate, Johnson decided, at least he could make himself an attractive option.

The majority leader bullied the administration into allowing him to make a speech before the UN on the exploration of outer space. The national press gave the address positive reviews; so did international journalists, although they were somewhat nonplussed by the press conference that followed. He was "a country boy from Texas come to howdy and shake," LBJ told the assembled reporters. He quoted his daddy, Lady Bird, and Isaiah. Pulling a telegram from his pocket, he announced that his daughters, Lucy and Lynda, had congratulated him and Lady Bird on their twenty-fourth wedding anniversary. "We're so happy you married each other," he read. What had all this to do with international politics, the men and women from Reuters, *Le Monde,* and the *Manchester Guardian* wondered, but ascribed Johnson's performance to the eccentricities of American politics.[69]

Cornpone aside, Johnson boasted a sophisticated political philosophy that resonated with many Americans at mid-century. In a further effort to burnish his image as a statesman and political thinker as well as doer, LBJ published an article in the winter 1958 edition of the *Texas Quarterly*. Echoing FDR, he declared, "I am a free man, a U.S. Senator, and a Democrat, in that order. I am also a liberal, a conservative, a Texan, a taxpayer, a rancher, a businessman, a consumer, a parent, a voter . . . At the heart of my own beliefs is a rebellion against this very process of classifying, labeling and filing Americans under headings."[70]

In a sense, Johnson was a Madisonian. Like the Constitution that he helped write, James Madison did not envision the need for institutionalized political parties. Coalitions would form, but they would be temporary, and this was for the best. LBJ agreed. "Our system of partisan politics—which has come to mean so much to us today—is not a system ordained and established by the Constitution," he declared in 1959. "The spirit of the Constitution is hostile to the concept of competitive partisanship."[71]

As the nation came to grips with questions of wealth distribution, resource allocation, war and peace, civil rights, and political representation, positions were more likely to be determined by the content of particular disputes than by party labels or slogans. In a contest where today's enemies might be tomorrow's allies, conflicts were sure to be less severe, less damaging. Fuzziness, Johnson argued, was not simply a political expedient, but an authentic reflection of the "American people's own ambiguities of conviction and purpose."[72]

"With few rare exceptions," Johnson insisted, "the great political leaders of our country have been men of reconciliation—men who could hold their parties together. Lincoln never permitted the radical Republicans to drive more moderate elements out of the party. Woodrow Wilson appealed to elements throughout the nation and only went down to failure when he became too doctrinaire and too arbitrary. FDR successfully maintained a coalition that ranged all the way from [South Carolina senator and power broker] Jimmy Byrnes to [wealthy industrialist] Leon Henderson. Theodore Roosevelt was a great political figure up to the point that he split his own party."[73]

Johnson's "non-partisan nationalism," as Horace Busby termed it, was very much in tune with the pluralistic and consensus-oriented 1950s.[74] It was no accident that 1959 saw the publication of Daniel Bell's *The End of Ideology*.

The problem with Johnsonian-Madisonian pluralistic, consensus politics, critics argued, was that many groups and interests—minorities, the poor, uneducated isolated rural dwellers, migrant workers, and inner-city slum dwellers—were not granted access to the playing field. To critics of the Johnson philosophy, the American political landscape was like a high plateau with steep sides, with "legitimate" interests battling for position on the high ground and the disfranchised and voiceless struggling futilely to climb up the steep sides.[75]

LBJ would not have disagreed with such an analogy. He would have argued that all needed to be admitted to the playing field, and he would work to gain them access. He was also struggling to see that a significant group—white southerners—were not thrown off the plateau and into the pit of political oblivion. Unfortunately, the very aggregation he was trying to save was battling to keep another significant group—black Americans—off the plateau.

LBJ understood that, ironically, the fate of these two peoples were tied inextricably together. He believed that if southern whites were cast into darkness, southern blacks would find it that much more difficult, if not impossible, to ascend. Insofar as it was necessary to keep the South in the Democratic party, Lyndon Johnson and Richard Russell were in general agreement.[76] The difference between Russell and Johnson was that the Georgian wanted to make southern nationalism the cornerstone of mainstream politics, whereas the majority leader wanted to bring the South into the political mainstream.

WHEN CONGRESS CONVENED in January 1959, the national press was abuzz about the 1960 Democratic presidential nomination. Despite his Catholicism, the glamorous John F. Kennedy led the pack. Close behind were Hubert Humphrey, the darling of labor and civil rights groups, Stuart Symington, who hoped to capitalize on his reputation as an expert on questions of national defense, and Adlai Stevenson, the sentimental favorite of old New Dealers. And there was Lyndon Johnson.

In January, the *Saturday Evening Post* ran a generally laudatory piece by Stewart Alsop entitled "Lyndon Johnson: How Does He Do It?" Alsop predicted that LBJ would run for the presidency, but quietly, indirectly: "Johnson, with his hatred of failure, will not become an active candidate and thus risk the humiliation suffered by his friend Richard Russell as the Southern candidate in 1952."[77] Alsop proved to be right on the money.

Throughout the fall and winter of 1958, Jim Rowe had urged LBJ to declare and make an open run at the presidency. Johnson steadily refused, although he did nothing to discourage those who wanted to tout his candidacy. In January 1959, a frustrated Rowe cast his lot with Hubert Humphrey. Arthur Schlesinger later speculated that this "defection" fit in perfectly with the majority leader's plan. A vigorous run by the Minnesotan would help hold the Kennedy forces in check, and then, when a deadlock emerged at the convention, LBJ would have his old friend Rowe in a strategic position in the Humphrey camp.[78]

Johnson's strategy, then, continued to be to pose as the most effective majority leader the country had ever produced, a figure with a balanced view toward the civil rights issue, and a politician-statesman whose knowledge of the world was increasing daily. Johnson's Madisonian political philosophy was a reflection of the Texan's deeply held beliefs and his experiences but also a product of what he believed the American people really desired. Pragmatists to the core, Americans wanted a flexible, able person to lead them who could reach out to groups all along the political spectrum. They instinctively feared division and so could support a man and an approach that would contain the extremes that continually threatened to tear the country apart. "Someone must at all costs keep this broad and diverse country together," Jim Rowe wrote LBJ. "Slowly the problem is getting worse and slowly the men of good will in both sections of the country are beginning to wonder about, and therefore to accept, the possibility of defeat."[79]

ON RARE OCCASIONS, an issue came up in the Senate on which liberals and the Eisenhower administration could agree, and LBJ shone. Such an issue was statehood for Alaska and Hawaii. Statehood bills had come before a number of previous Congresses and had gotten nowhere. Southerners were opposed to

Hawaii's admission because of its racially mixed population. Senator Daniel K. Inouye later recalled that Hawaiian statehood was a pure civil rights issue: "The argument against the statehood bill, although not articulated publicly, was that if Hawaii became a state you would have representation by a strange looking people. As one senator said, 'How would you like to be sitting next to a fellow named Yamamoto?' "[80]

The Eisenhower administration favored statehood for Hawaii, convinced that it would enter the Union as a Republican state, but opposed Alaska out of the same political considerations. By 1958, pressure within and without Congress had built up for admission of Alaska. Opponents and supporters once again tried to link the two territories, but Johnson convinced John Burns, the delegate from Hawaii, not to go along. Backers of Hawaiian statehood should take the gamble that Alaska's admission would start a landslide for Hawaii. Burns, at great risk to his political career, agreed.

Alaska was duly admitted in 1958, and in March 1959 the Hawaiian statehood bill came up before the Senate. An observer recalled the scene:

At 3:34 P.M. on March 11, the day Governor William E. Quinn of Hawaii was to arrive, Johnson brought the bill up on the floor of the Senate and the speechmaking began. For the first three hours of the debate, Johnson wasn't even on the floor, having turned over the majority leader's duties temporarily to thirty-five-year-old Senator Frank Church of Idaho, one of his favorites . . . At 6:58 P.M. Johnson returned. He was impeccably dressed in an expensive gray suit, white shirt and conservative gray tie. He wore horn-rimmed glasses, as he always does except when being photographed . . . I was seated in the gallery with one of Johnson's assistants, who explained his every move. The assistant said, "He's talking to Willis Robertson of Virginia and now to Olin Johnston of South Carolina and now to Harry Byrd of Virginia, all opponents of the bill. He's keeping them soothed down. Now he's talking to Wayne Morse of Oregon. Lyndon wants him to limit his speech to a few minutes. Morse nodded, so I guess he'll keep it short . . ." While they spoke Johnson wandered from desk to desk, talking to about a dozen senators, both Democrats and Republicans, concentrating on the southerners . . . At 7:19 P.M., the speeches were still going on, but little attention was being paid to them. Johnson was moving all over the floor. Suddenly, he stopped and twirled his fingers. His assistant said, "That means he wants a fast roll call. All the pages are out rounding up the senators for a vote." Senators began to pour through the doors of the chamber, and in a matter of seconds, the room was filled for the first time since the debate began . . . At 7:36 P.M., Johnson himself got up to make the closing remarks. He said simply, "This is an important thing for the people of Hawaii and the United States, and I request a vote." The roll call began, and by 7:52 it was all over. Hawaii statehood had won by a vote of seventy-six to fifteen. In just over four hours Johnson had accomplished what no one had been able to do in forty years.[81]

BY THE FALL OF 1958, LBJ's patience with the Eisenhower administration and with bipartisanship was wearing thin. The president's numerous vetoes had embarrassed Congress generally and him specifically. When an opportunity presented itself to poke a stick in the administration's eye, Johnson, although somewhat reluctantly, took it.

In October 1958, Eisenhower nominated retired Admiral Lewis Strauss to be secretary of commerce. For a variety of reasons, Strauss's nomination did not reach the Senate until March 1959, when he had already been serving four months unofficially in the cabinet. Before being tapped to head Commerce, Strauss had served a five-year term as head of the Atomic Energy Commission. Aggressively conservative and arrogant, the former naval officer had managed to make a bitter enemy of Senator Clinton P. Anderson, chair of the Senate Committee on Atomic Energy. Moreover, Strauss had proven himself a determined foe of public power and an opponent of greater congressional oversight of the atomic energy industry. Finally, he, along with his pal, scientist Edward Teller, had angered liberals by arbitrarily singling out Robert Oppenheimer, chief scientist on the Manhattan Project, as a security risk.[82]

Strauss and Anderson had butted heads repeatedly, the admiral winning the undying enmity of the New Mexico senator, who did not possess a college education, by implying that he was not capable of understanding many of the complex issues associated with atomic energy. In fact, Eisenhower had moved Strauss from the AEC to Commerce because he was convinced that he could not win reappointment to the post he held.[83]

Anderson pressed the majority leader to mobilize the Senate to block Strauss from having a cabinet post. Johnson initially declined. Only seven times in the nation's history had the Senate denied a president his choice for a cabinet position, and not once since 1925. A quick head count indicated that despite his conservatism and uncooperativeness, Strauss would win approval from the Commerce Committee by a count of fourteen to three. Following a week of condescending and noncommittal replies, however, his margin had slipped to nine to eight. Both Gale McGhee, an outspoken opponent of confirmation, and Anderson pled with Johnson to intercede. He was still reluctant. "The vote is not even going to be close," the leader, uncharacteristically out of touch, told Earle Clements. Yes it will, Clements replied: "There are four votes that are going to vote just like you vote."[84]

Clements was right. Quietly, behind the scenes, the leader began to mobilize his colleagues against the Strauss nomination. LBJ did not publicly take a stand until June 19, the day of the vote. Kennedy, Symington, and Richard Neuberger followed Johnson's lead in voting no, and Fulbright absented himself from the

Senate floor. Minority Leader Everett Dirksen had counted on all four. The final tally was forty-nine against to forty-six for. In addition to the four Democrats, two other votes had been decisive, that of populist William Langer of North Dakota and Margaret Chase Smith of Maine, both Republicans. "Johnson had a lot of sway with Mrs. Smith," Harry McPherson recalled. "She thought he was pretty terrific, and he could usually get her vote . . . No one knew how it was going to come out except Johnson; he knew every vote. And the clerk said, 'Mrs. Smith.' 'No.' And there was 'Ahhh'—you could hear the breath exhale. And Barry Goldwater said, 'Goddamn!' And you could hear it all over the chamber."[85]

WITH THE END of the congressional session in September 1959, all political eyes turned to the forthcoming presidential race. Journalist Carroll Kilpatrick remembered accompanying Richard Nixon on a western speaking tour in the fall of 1959: "Late one night there weren't but four or five reporters with him and he invited us into one of the airport rooms while we waited for the plane to be refueled. We sat there for an hour or so and we talked about Johnson . . . He said, 'He is the ablest one . . . he would be a successful president, would be an able president . . . But he has two strikes against him: one that he is from Texas, and one that he has had a heart attack.' "[86]

Later, Kilpatrick and several colleagues had dinner at the National Press Club with John F. Kennedy. "Lyndon would make the ablest president of any of us running," JFK observed, "but he can't be elected."[87] Kennedy was of the opinion that the majority leader was too thoroughly identified with the South and thus unacceptable to the liberal-labor group. These observations were, of course, somewhat self-serving, but George Reedy thought it to his boss's advantage if this image of LBJ as qualified but unelectable be spread. "This leaves the public with the impression that a bunch of 'scheming politicians' are plotting to keep the nation from having its best leader because they are seeking to placate 'pressure groups,' " Reedy advised Johnson.[88]

Despite the urgings of Connally and some of his other advisers LBJ refused to declare his candidacy and made no preparations to enter the spring primaries. He believed that if he declared, he would immediately become the frontrunner and wind up as the target of a Stop Johnson movement that would probably be successful. But there was another reason. Johnson was profoundly distrustful of his ability to compete with the likes of Kennedy and Humphrey in a beauty contest. Charisma, charm, rhetorical flair that could be so apparent in one-on-one or small group encounters completely deserted LBJ in front of large crowds, especially when such appearances were being televised. And the more his presidential ambitions grew, the more tepid and noncommittal his speeches became.[89] His only chance, Johnson perceived, was to let the other Democratic hopefuls kill each other off and then have the party turn to him at the convention.

Being an unannounced candidate for president also would help LBJ's bid for reelection to the Senate in 1960, he and his staff believed. In the spring of 1959, the Johnson forces in Texas had succeeded in having state election laws altered to move the primaries up from July and August to May and June and to allow a candidate to compete for two national offices at the same time. Thus could LBJ run for reelection to the Senate in the spring and then stand for the presidency if the Democratic National Convention tapped him in July.

There seemed little to worry about as far as Texas was concerned. A Belden poll taken in May showed that LBJ had slipped alarmingly among minorities, low-income groups, and women; approval among Latinos was 40 percent, blacks 39 percent, and "lower socio-economic levels" 44 percent. But it also showed that in any contest matching him against either Price Daniel or Jim Wright, the popular young congressman from Dallas, Johnson would win in a landslide.[90]

But politics are fickle, especially in Texas. Conservatives could always choose to remember Johnson as an avid New Dealer, and even moderate liberals were barely reconciled.[91] In the end, however, Texas chauvinism could always be counted on. As long as Johnson was considered a legitimate contender for the presidency, voters in the Lone Star State would support him through thick and thin. "An awful lot of people want to play Presidential politics," George Reedy observed to his boss. "This is understandable because for many Texans this is the only chance they have ever had—or may ever have again—to be in on a serious Presidential show."[92]

CHAPTER 17

1960

IN OCTOBER 1959, LBJ HOSTED A VISIT BY MEXICAN
president Adolfo Lopez Mateos at the ranch. Here was an opportunity
for the majority leader to showcase himself as a major figure on the international stage and the ranch as a symbol of the growing power of the
West with LBJ as its spokesman. A Dallas newspaper called the gala put on by
the Johnsons in Lopez Mateos's honor "one of the most dramatic outdoor
shows since they produced Aida with live elephants."[1]

Lyndon and Lady Bird, together with Governor and Mrs. Price Daniel, were
on hand at Bergstrom Air Force Base to greet the Mexican president and his
party. Six helicopters then ferried the entourage to the ranch. En route, LBJ was
able to point with pride to the system of dams and lakes that made up the Lower
Colorado River Authority. On landing, the party was met by several hundred
guests that included Speaker Rayburn and former President Truman. While
those in attendance feasted on barbeque and beer under tents erected in the
pecan groves along the Pedernales, Rayburn and Truman discussed Lyndon's
presidential chances. Both had noted the numerous banners adorning the
grounds that read "Lyndon Johnson Sera Presidente." Truman told the speaker
that although he was nominally committed to fellow Missourian Stuart
Symington, his heart was with Johnson.[2]

Both Johnson and Lopez Mateos made speeches; the latter's was pro forma,
but LBJ proposed the creation of a new and better-funded Latin American development bank. The next day, Lopez Mateos and his party were helicoptered
back to Bergstrom for the return flight to Mexico City.

In the weeks that followed, pictures of Johnson, the western statesman at
home on his Ponderosa, were splashed across the front pages of the national
press.[3] During September and October, LBJ made several trips to Texas in behalf of his phantom presidential campaign. At the Palomas Ranch at Falfurrias,

he met with a group of deep pockets led by Herman Brown. "I'm thinking about running for president," Johnson told the group, "and if I do, it's going to cost all of you a lot of money. So, I want you to think about it." He had one of the men present list all the states on a pad of paper and he then went down the list, putting each one in either the Johnson or Kennedy camp. He, of course, won.[4]

From Falfurrias LBJ proceeded to Galveston, where he addressed a "Gulf Coast Hamburger Party" hosted by the Democracy Club of Galveston County. "His effectiveness is recognized by his colleagues and indeed by the nation," Walter G. Hall said in introducing him, "and it is the hope and prayer of many that the role he has played foretells greater things to come."[5] Leaving the Lone Star State, Johnson made a quick speaking trip through Missouri, Kansas, Nebraska, Iowa, and Arizona, states where he believed he had natural appeal.

It seemed that not a campaign season passed for LBJ but the ghost of 1948 reared its head. As 1959 came to a close, George Parr was fighting a mail fraud conviction. Fearful that the Duke of Duvall would spread incriminating rumors about him if he did not help, Johnson arranged to have Abe Fortas and Paul Porter represent Parr in his appeal, which he subsequently won.[6]

In February 1960, Jack Kennedy formally announced his candidacy for the Democratic nomination for president. He had already been running for over a year. "In the past forty months," he told reporters at his coming out, "I have toured every state in the Union. Any Democratic aspirant should be willing to submit to the voters his views, record, and competence in a series of primary contests." He already suspected that LBJ would not be willing to so expose himself. Kennedy later observed, "Johnson had to prove that a Southerner could win in the North, just as I had to prove a Catholic could win in heavily Protestant states."[7] By the time of Kennedy's announcement, his staff had built a central file of seventy thousand local Democratic leaders who were showered with autographed copies of *Profiles in Courage,* Christmas cards, and surprise drop-in visits by the candidate. "Everywhere he goes he leaves behind an organization," Sam Rayburn observed admiringly.[8]

By March, the usually sanguine George Reedy had become so alarmed that he was urging his boss to authorize a series of attacks on Joe Kennedy. "His [JFK's] real Achilles heel is that the American people are not going to stand for a wealthy man buying the Presidency for his son."[9] Before LBJ and his staff could react, Eleanor Roosevelt, an avid Stevenson backer, did their work for them. In a television interview, the former first lady lambasted the Kennedys for trying to spend their way into the White House. JFK asked for a retraction, but to no avail.[10]

As Stewart Alsop had predicted, Johnson anticipated using Hubert Humphrey as a stalking horse to stop the Kennedy juggernaut. If the Minnesotan could win some primaries and keep Jack Kennedy from accumulating a majority of delegates before the nominating convention opened in Los Angeles, LBJ would have a chance. "There were two Humphrey camps rolled into one," Joe Rauh recalled. "One Humphrey camp was for Johnson and was 'Stop Kennedy,' and the other Humphrey camp was for Humphrey and against Johnson. The ADA people in the Humphrey camp . . . were all for Humphrey 100% . . . The others in there were really for Johnson with Humphrey taking the Vice Presidency or whatever crumbs he could get." [11]

In April, Kennedy beat Humphrey in the Wisconsin primary, but did so by a small margin and only after a great deal of effort. All eyes turned to the West Virginia contest, where the voters were 97 percent Protestant. Aside from the religion issue, there were other reasons for optimism. Robert C. Byrd, the state's junior senator, was a Johnson supporter and promised to do all he could to help Humphrey. Humphrey announced that if he lost, he would withdraw from the race. But the combined efforts of LBJ and HHH were no match for the Kennedy money. In a state whose politics one journalist described as among the "most squalid, corrupt and despicable in the United States," Kennedy's people were able to outbid Humphrey's lieutenants for the allegiance of local bosses. Humphrey recalled that one of his operatives visited a county judge with a $2,500 payment in hand. He was told "we were not even close." [12]

Later, Judith Campbell, who at the time was the mistress simultaneously of Jack Kennedy and Mafia boss Sam Giancana, claimed to have carried messages and money between the two men regarding the buying of votes in West Virginia. Supposedly, Giancana dispatched Paul "Skinny" D' Amato to the impoverished state with a "suitcase full of money" ($50,000). [13]

Humphrey lost. Even without the Mafia, the Kennedy people had sufficient resources to accomplish their goal. Their money probably had the greatest impact in buying television time for the glamorous JFK.

After their loss in West Virginia, HHH and his advisers huddled. Rowe and company wanted Humphrey to stay in until the convention, but Rauh and the ADAers urged their candidate to withdraw and hope for a vice presidential bid. Humphrey elected to withdraw, but those who anticipated a Kennedy-Humphrey ticket were deceiving themselves. Joe Rauh recalled the scene when Bobby Kennedy came down to offer condolences and congratulations on a good race: "He walked over to Hubert and Muriel and he leaned down and kissed Muriel on the cheek. I swear to God I thought she was going to hit him. Humphrey's family and many of his supporters literally hated the Kennedys, and they urged Hubert not to run for Vice President with Jack Kennedy." [14]

Shortly after Humphrey dropped out, LBJ called Jim Rowe. Were there any options left? Could a Kennedy bandwagon be stopped? Perhaps they could persuade Stevenson to declare, Rowe suggested. "If you two get together, you might stop him," he said. "I don't think you can, but nobody else can." [15] LBJ met with Stevenson several times in the weeks that followed, but the most Adlai would agree to do was not commit to a Kennedy candidacy. "I think LBJ was using Governor Stevenson," said Newton Minnow, a Stevenson adviser. "I think he was attempting to keep the situation fluid in the hope that he, LBJ, might get nominated . . . But Governor Stevenson and I had a specific argument about whether or not he was being used by Johnson, and he did not think so. He thought Johnson was playing it straight." [16] Whatever the case, to the great irritation of Jack and Bobby, Stevenson continued to encourage his supporters to plan a draft at Los Angeles.

Following the West Virginia victory, the Kennedy machine viewed LBJ as the only real obstacle left in the way of nomination. Behind the scenes and in the press, the two men began to slug it out. Johnson got on the phone to Democratic leaders in the West and in farm states, arguing that Kennedy and they had nothing in common and that the American people would never elect a Catholic president. The Kennedys worked assiduously to portray LBJ as a stalking horse for Richard Russell and the Dixiecrats and insisted to labor leaders that as the ambassador to the United States from Brown and Root, LBJ had been and would continue to be antiunion.

By THE END OF MAY, LBJ's supporters were beside themselves at their man's coyness, or indecisiveness, or naïveté, or whatever it was that they believed was holding him back. He seemed to alternate between desperately wanting the nomination and feverishly planning how to capture it, with resignation at the probability that he could not obtain it. A number of the western states held their primaries very late. Gerry Siegel urged Johnson to enter the Oregon contest. He was popular in the West and sure to make a good showing. "You can't get out of that one," he told LBJ. "Go out there and try to either win it or make a hell of a strong showing." He just could not do it, Johnson told Siegel. [17]

But in late May, Johnson, appearing on a nationally televised political talk show, insisted that Kennedy's primary victories represented only a small fraction of the electorate. In the weeks that followed, he continued to telephone local leaders trying to undermine Kennedy's candidacy. Mr. Sam had hoped that Johnson would announce after he won the Democratic senatorial primary in Texas on May 7, but his protégé remained mum. Finally, the frustrated seventy-eight-year-old, who saw his dream of a Texan in the White House slipping away, took it upon himself to ask John Connally to open a Johnson for President campaign headquarters in Washington. "I thought that this had all been cleared with LBJ," Leonard Marks, the Johnson family attorney, later said. "Well, he was just furious. He called John Connally and he called Walter Jenkins and he called everybody involved, and he said, 'You get that sign down! I am not a candidate.' " [18] Then three days later, Connally received permission to open the headquarters.

By June, though Johnson had still not officially declared, his campaign began to look like it was in earnest. The Scripps-Howard newspaper chain announced its support. The Connally team divided the nation into six districts and began establishing contacts with state delegations. Eisenhower confided to Arthur Krock that "Lyndon Johnson . . . would be the best Democrat of them all as President from the viewpoint of responsible management of the national interest." Kennedy was nothing more than an "inexperienced boy." [19]

The last week in June, the majority leader persuaded Congress to recess rather than adjourn. The promise of a rump session following the conventions gave him added leverage, Johnson believed. Finally, on July 5, LBJ announced that he was a candidate for president of the United States. He predicted that he would win on the third ballot and told reporters that only his sense of duty as majority leader had kept him out of the campaign thus far: "But after July the bandwagons will be silent; the dark horses will be out to pasture; and we will stand face to face with whatever destiny this century holds for us." [20]

On June 11, the Johnson campaign had circulated a memo to reporters showing that LBJ would poll 526.5 ballots on the first vote at the convention. This was only 150 shy of the 761 needed to win. But Johnson's support was soft. "The Arizona delegation, where we thought we had it sewed up," recalled John Singleton, a campaign worker from Houston, "and at the last minute we learned that . . . one of the leaders . . . had a ten thousand dollar note at the bank that was suddenly paid. When it came down to the nut-cutting, Arizona voted for Kennedy." [21] Bill Moyers, another campaign aide, felt that these last-minute defections—"The Kennedy people came in and took delegates away, western delegates, there in his own backyard"—were decisive. He remembered Johnson remarking, "There I was, looking for the burglar coming in the front door, and little did I know that the fox was coming through the fence in back. When I woke up, the chickens were gone." [22]

The majority leader and Mrs. Johnson arrived in Los Angeles on Friday, July 8. Jack Kennedy did not come in until Saturday. He had no doubt been distracted by his father, who, having promised to keep a low profile, stopped in Las Vegas and bet heavily on his son, not to make money but to ensure that the odds favored Jack and hopefully contributed to a bandwagon mentality at Los Angeles. [23] The Johnsons occupied a suite on the seventh floor of the Biltmore. Kennedy and his entourage were two floors above, although he would take up residence at several different locations during the convention. Stuart Symington also stayed at the Biltmore, while Adlai Stevenson, in a fittingly symbolic move, booked rooms at the Beverly Hills, forty minutes away from the convention hall. Humphrey selected the Statler Hilton.

From the beginning, the convention was a melancholy affair for Lyndon and Lady Bird. "I was staying at a small hotel across from the Biltmore," remembered John Kenneth Galbraith, the Harvard economist who had signed on as a member of Kennedy's brain trust, "and fairly early on in the convention I was coming out from a meeting in the Kennedy headquarters late one night and there was a big crowd assembled at each side of the sidewalk, watching the notables coming in and out, including Kennedy . . . And as I came out, Johnson was coming in, and he was bowing to the crowd, and nobody recognized him." Jim Rowe recalled that he and Johnson had dinner together on opening night. As they watched Frank Church deliver the keynote address on television, Johnson said, " 'There's no way we can stop this fellow, is there?' Said it just as quietly as that. I don't think he had any illusions at all." [24]

Johnson rather liked Jack Kennedy but, like Bill Fulbright, did not initially think there was much to him. He had referred to him as a "playboy" and a "lightweight" who was good-looking and intelligent but certainly lacking in the drive required to become and be president of the United States.[25] He felt contempt for Bobby. When Jack had sent his brother and campaign manager to the LBJ Ranch in the spring to ask the majority leader directly what his intentions were, LBJ had a chance to play the alpha male. After telling Bobby that he was not a candidate but would not endorse Jack, Lyndon insisted on a deer hunt. Instead of arming the younger Kennedy with a deer rifle, the leader gave him a ten-gauge shotgun. When Bobby fired it, the recoil knocked him down, cutting his eye. Helping the thirty-four-year-old Bobby to his feet, LBJ remarked, "Son, you've got to learn to handle a gun like a man."[26]

But, as would become increasingly apparent, there was a world of difference between Lyndon's attitude toward JFK and his feelings about Bobby. He regarded the latter as incredibly arrogant—a sort of "liberal fascist," he would later term him—but he found Jack unassuming and appealing.[27] A mutual friend recalled a compelling scene from the 1956 presidential campaign: "Johnson and [John] Kennedy were at a motel on the edge of San Antonio. Kennedy was the main speaker at our rally there . . . I was in there talking to them, and the picture that stands out in my mind is John Kennedy sitting in a bathtub filled with hot water to ease the pain in his back, and LBJ sitting on the side of the tub pouring water on his back."[28]

Perhaps Johnson had no illusions about Kennedy being stopped, but his staff and supporters apparently had not gotten the word, and the days prior to the presidential balloting witnessed some nasty infighting. Two weeks before the convention opened, John Connally and his minions had decided to take off the gloves. In telephone calls, interviews with journalists, and press releases, they attacked the Kennedys for their intimacy with Joe McCarthy, Jack's poor voting record in the Senate, and Joe's fondness for fascism. They also hinted that the "boy" was hiding some grievous health defects. On the McCarthy issue, they received some much needed help from the Stevenson camp. Neither Senator Eugene McCarthy nor former first lady Eleanor Roosevelt, two of Adlai's biggest supporters, had much use for the Kennedy clan. McCarthy fancied himself Jack's intellectual superior and believed that if there were to be a Catholic in the White House, it ought to be he. Eleanor's husband had fired Joe Kennedy as ambassador to Great Britain. Referring to JFK's Pulitzer Prize–winning book, *Profiles in Courage,* she remarked to reporters, "A man cannot be President who understands what courage is, and admires it but has not quite the independence to have it."[29]

On July 4, Connally and India Edwards, former head of the DNC's Women's Division, held a news conference in Los Angeles. She had irrefutable proof that John F. Kennedy had Addison's disease, Edwards declared, a potentially fatal malady of the adrenal glands. Connally called for a full and frank evaluation of the Massachusetts senator's physical fitness to be president. Edwards for one had anticipated a firestorm: "John, let me do it," she had told Connally.

"I have no career ahead of me, and you're a young man. It will cause a terrible stink."[30]

She could not have been more prescient. "It was as though a bomb went off" in the Kennedy headquarters, Clark Clifford recalled. Jack's aides quickly arranged for a manufactured medical report giving him a clean bill of health. Whatever "adrenal insufficiency" Senator Kennedy suffered from was a minor holdover from "wartime shock and continued malaria."[31] Clifford also remembered that "Ambassador Kennedy, Senator Kennedy's father, was outraged by the charge. The entire family—Senator Kennedy, Bobby Kennedy, all the sisters and all the rest of them—was embittered as far as Senator Johnson was concerned. They felt it was grossly unfair."[32] Actually, according to Edwards, LBJ rebuked her for the Addison's story and announced that health should not be a consideration in the race at all.

But, of course, the charges were entirely true. Not only did JFK have a chronically bad back, he had been suffering from Addison's disease since 1950. The only thing that kept him alive was daily doses of cortisone, by mouth, by injection, and by pellets implanted in his thighs. Rumor had it that Kennedy senior had stashed supplies of the drug in safety deposit boxes all across the country. The Catholic Church had administered last rights to John F. Kennedy at least four times. But investigative reporting was still in its infancy in 1950, and the charges, unsubstantiated, ultimately generated sympathy for JFK rather than mistrust of him.[33]

DETERMINED NOT TO BE BEATEN by that "forty-two-year-old kid," LBJ made a last-ditch effort to block Kennedy's nomination. Making the rounds of state delegations he believed were still wavering, Johnson delivered another blow. "I wasn't any Chamberlain-umbrella policy man," he told the Washington state delegation. "I never thought Hitler was right."[34] The Kennedys cried dirty pool, but again, LBJ was but speaking the truth. As ambassador to Great Britain in the 1930s, Joseph Kennedy and his wife, Rose, had been close to Lady Astor and the Clivenden set, a high-society salon with reputed pro-Nazi sympathies. Ambassador Kennedy had lauded Prime Minister Neville Chamberlain's 1938 deal with Adolf Hitler at Munich. Kennedy's proposal to resettle the Jews of Germany as a solution to the dilemma posed in *Mein Kampf* revealed strong anti-Semitic tendencies.[35] Ironically, LBJ had been present in President Roosevelt's office the day he fired Joe Kennedy as ambassador.

If the shooting humiliation at the ranch were not enough, the Edwards-Connally press release coupled with LBJ's reference to Chamberlain converted Bobby Kennedy into an implacable foe of the Texan. Bobby Baker saw him at breakfast in the Biltmore on the morning of July 12. "Lyndon Johnson has compared my father to the Nazis and John Connally and India Edwards lied in saying my brother is dying of Addison's disease," he snarled to Baker. "You Johnson people are running a stinking damned campaign and you're gonna get yours when the time comes!"[36]

In a last-minute gambit, LBJ and his staff hit on the idea of having Johnson and Kennedy stage a televised debate before the combined Texas-Massachusetts delegations on Tuesday the twelfth. Phillip Graham, publisher of the *Washington Post* and by then one of LBJ's staunchest supporters, recalled that Johnson was exhilarated by the notion of debating Kennedy but also dog-tired from the long congressional session and last-minute campaigning. Graham convinced him to nap and subsequently described the scene: "A Negro couple from the Ranch were in the room throughout our lunch, and the three of us converged upon him, disrobed him, pajamaed him and got him to bed." He awakened after a thirty-minute nap completely refreshed.[37]

The debate was scheduled to begin at three, but no one was certain that Kennedy would participate. He and Bobby arrived five minutes late. LBJ eschewed issues of health and patriotism and concentrated on his opponent's terrible attendance record in the Senate. JFK disarmed him with humor. After telling the assemblage that there was little difference between his and Johnson's views on the great issues of the day, he expressed admiration for the Texan's attendance and voting record. He was the best majority leader the country had ever had and should continue in the position.[38]

By this time, the pressure on Hubert Humphrey to jump on the Kennedy bandwagon had become intense, but still he resisted. Jim Rowe recalled that one of the times he and Johnson were closeted with Humphrey and his aides discussing strategies for blocking Kennedy, there was a loud knocking on the hotel suite door. It was Joe Rauh who continued to bang and yelled, "HUBERT! HUBERT, I KNOW YOU'RE IN THERE!" Finally an aide to Humphrey, Pat O'Connor, opened the door and punched Rauh. Daunted, the leader of the ADA departed, and the meeting continued.[39]

On Tuesday the twelfth, the day before the presidential balloting, Bobby Kennedy rushed up to Humprey and, poking his finger in the older man's chest, said, "Hubert, we want your announcement and the pledge of the Minnesota delegation today—or else!" According to Humphrey, he jabbed a finger back at Bobby's chest and told him to "go to hell."[40]

IN THE LATE AFTERNOON of Wednesday, July 13, thousands of people began pouring into the Los Angeles Convention Center, including the 1,520 delegates who would select the Democratic party's nominee for the presidency. With Eleanor Roosevelt and Herbert Lehman looking on from the VIP box, Minnesota Governor Orville Freeman nominated John F. Kennedy. Sam Rayburn did the honors for LBJ. The speaker was not in good health, but he was still capable of a vigorous speech. With a noticeable quaver in his voice, he declared, "I have been a member of the Congress of the United States for nearly half a century. I have worked beside more than three thousand members of Congress from every nook and cranny of America. Every giant of the past half century in this country I have known personally. I think I know a great leader when I see him . . . This is a man for all Americans."[41] It was all for naught.

The quickness and decisiveness of the Kennedy victory stunned the Johnson camp. JFK won on the first ballot, polling 806 votes to Johnson's 409. Texas's favorite son had chosen not to attend, preferring to view the proceedings on television. "After Kennedy was nominated," campaign manager Booth Mooney recalled, "Johnson snapped off the television and said, 'Well, that's that. Tomorrow we can do something we really want to do—go to Disneyland, maybe.' " For the next few hours he lounged in his pajamas, receiving close friends, apparently relaxed and free of regret.[42]

JACK KENNEDY had won the nomination, but he could not triumph in November without Lyndon Johnson on the ticket. He was Irish Catholic, recently liberal, the darling of organized labor and civil rights organizations—in short, a reincarnation of Al Smith. The South and Southwest would have to have some reason, a good reason, to go to the polls and vote Democratic. Richard Nixon, the Republican nominee, might be a ruthless opportunist, but then again, Kennedy was a ruthless opportunist, and Nixon would be formidable. Jack Kennedy not Bobby or Joe or anyone else made the decision concerning his running mate. Lyndon Johnson, not Phil Graham, Jim Rowe, or anyone else, with the acquiescence of Sam Rayburn, made the choice to accept.[43]

In the runup to the nomination, Bobby had repeatedly promised Walter Reuther, Joe Rauh, and Roy Wilkins that LBJ would not be the vice presidential nominee, but Jack knew that in the end they would rather have the presidency than their choice of the second person on a failed ticket. And, in fact, if he mistrusted and disliked Lyndon Johnson, it would be better to have him in the innocuous position of vice president than as majority leader. "The son of a bitch will do us a lot less harm as Vice President than he will as Majority Leader," Kennedy said to Orville Freeman.[44]

What touched off twelve hours of confusion and turmoil the night of July 13 and morning of the 14th was the determination by Kennedy that his offer be accepted, and the determination by Johnson and Rayburn that they appear to be dragooned into accepting and not perceived as supplicants. Perhaps most important, Jack and Bobby wanted to humiliate Lyndon, to make him feel their spurs.

For their part, Lyndon Johnson, George Reedy, Jim Rowe, and Sam Rayburn had viewed the Senate leadership as a nonoption for nearly two years. With the sweeping Democratic victories in the midterm election of 1958, the majority had become virtually ungovernable. "He knew that no matter what was going to happen at the convention," Bill Moyers said, "the glory days of the majority leadership, in which he reveled, were over. That is, if a Democrat got the nomination and won the election, then that Democrat was going to be Mr. Democrat in the nation. Not Lyndon Johnson . . . Second, if Nixon got the nomination for the Republican party and was elected, Nixon was not going to be Eisenhower. Eisenhower was benevolent, passive, cooperative, collaborative, as

much a Democrat as a Republican . . . On the other hand, if Nixon were president—partisan, narrow, an in-fighter, a vehement man, not given to collabora-
tion, a loner, not trusting of the legislative process—Johnson knew that his
relationship with the White House was over."[45]

If the vice presidency were offered, LBJ would have to take it. If he hoped
ever to be president, he could not lay himself open to charges that he had
opened the door to a Republican victory in 1960 by turning down the second
spot on the ticket.[46] For political and personal reasons, Sam Rayburn would
never allow that to happen. "That man called me a traitor," the speaker said of
Nixon, "and I don't want a man who calls me a traitor to be President of the
United States."[47]

Moreover, there was the South to think about. No less a Kennedy loyalist
than Arthur Schlesinger Jr. recognized this as a prime motive. Johnson "had a
deep sense of responsibility about the future of the South in the American political system," Schlesinger later wrote. "If the Democratic party did not give a
Southerner a place on the ticket in 1960, it would drive the South even further
back on itself and into self-pity, bitterness and futility."[48]

In addition, George Reedy believed that the vice presidency would be of help
in the never-ending struggle to portray Lyndon Johnson as a national rather
than just a regional figure. "From your own standpoint," he had advised the
leader in June, "the Vice Presidency would give you an opportunity to grow in
depth that you do not have as majority leader . . . The Majority Leadership is an
action post which gives few people a real opportunity to find out about your
philosophy and your convictions. The Vice Presidency is not an action post and
strangely enough, this is somewhat of an advantage because it does give a man
an opportunity to think and to express his thoughts without fear of destroying a
legislative program."[49]

Finally, if India Edwards's information concerning JFK's Addison's disease
was correct, who knew what the future might hold? Clare Booth Luce, admit-
tedly no friend of LBJ, rode on the bus to the inaugural ball with him after the
election. She pressed him to tell her why, after a year and a half of denials, he had
agreed to accept second place on the ticket. "And he leaned close and said," Luce
recalled, " 'Clare, I looked it up; one out of every four presidents has died in office. I'm a gamblin' man, darling', and this is the only chance I got."[50]

THE DRAMA THAT PLAYED OUT the night of July 13 and the morning of
July 14 was, in fact, a charade, but a most interesting one, and one that has become part of American political folklore. Johnson and Rayburn knew very well
that Jack Kennedy would have to offer the vice presidency to the Texan.

On Monday, July 11, Phil Graham and Joe Alsop visited Kennedy and urged
him to pick Johnson for second place on the ticket. "He immediately agreed,"
Graham recalled, "so immediately as to leave me doubting the easy triumph and
I therefore restated the matter, urging him not to count on Johnson's turning it

down but to offer the Vpship so persuasively as to win Johnson over." The next morning the *Post* published a story reporting that "the word in Los Angeles is that Kennedy will offer the Vpship to Lyndon Johnson."[51]

For his part, Kennedy was reasonably sure that LBJ would accept. On the evening of July 13, the day of the presidential balloting, Massachusetts congressman Tip O'Neill waited outside a restaurant for forty-five minutes to tell the nominee that he had talked with Sam Rayburn, and after initial reservations, had agreed that LBJ should be vice president. Jack said that that was what he wanted but reiterated his desire not to be turned down. O'Neill arranged for a clandestine meeting in the stairwell of the Biltmore between Kennedy and Rayburn, during which the speaker assured JFK that Johnson would not say no.[52]

Johnson and Rayburn talked around midnight and then again at 2 A.M. They reaffirmed their decision that LBJ ought to accept the vice presidential nomination if offered, but only if Jack Kennedy was unequivocal in offering it and promised to make the office more than just a figurehead. At eight o'clock on the morning of the 13th the phone rang in the Johnsons' bedroom. Lady Bird answered. "Just a minute," she said. She shook her husband awake. "Lyndon, it's Senator Kennedy, and he wants to talk to you." LBJ sat up in bed and took the phone. "Yes, yes, yes, yes sure," he said, "come on down." Lady Bird said, "I wonder what he wants."[53]

Russ Brown, LBJ's old friend from law school, recounted what followed: "The next morning, Thursday, the LBJ group congregated in the Johnson suite . . . Sam Rayburn was there, Tommy Corcoran, [famed Washington hostess and Johnson friend] Perle Mesta, and ten or fifteen others . . . A little after 9 o'clock Bob Kennedy came by and went out to the bedroom to have a private talk with LBJ. He stayed about ten minutes and we learned he had said John Kennedy wanted LBJ to be the candidate for vice-president."[54]

Johnson did not immediately accept but told Bobby and his brother that they should make sure of organized labor, the big city bosses, and blacks. Around ten, Jack Kennedy telephoned. Johnson took the call in his bedroom, sitting on one bed with Jim Rowe on the other. Kennedy read Johnson the press release he was preparing. LBJ asked, "Do you really want me?" When JFK said he did, the Texan accepted. "That was the end of that," Rowe recalled.[55] At 10:58 Jack Kennedy came down to confirm the deal in person.[56]

According to Bobby Kennedy and Kenny O'Donnell, that was not the end of it. RFK later recounted to Arthur Schlesinger that his brother was in a panic following his conversation with LBJ. "You just won't believe it. He wants it," Jack told his brother. "Oh, my God!" Bobby declared. "Now what do we do?"[57]

What followed was a tumultuous several hours in which many of Kennedy's principal constituencies threatened to revolt. "I was vehemently against the Johnson selection," O'Donnell later wrote, "because it represented precisely the kind of cynical, old-style politics we were trying to get away from. I also knew our liberal friends would be appalled by it."[58]

He was certainly correct about the liberals' reaction. Labor leaders Walter Reuther, Arthur Goldberg, and Jack Conway of the UAW met with Jack and Bobby to protest the choice. Conway told Bobby, "If you do this, you're going to fuck everything up." "All hell broke loose!" Hubert Humphrey recalled. "They were just up in arms," he said of the delegates who had voted for Kennedy after news of his choice reached the floor of the convention. Black leaders accused the Kennedys of selling them out.[59] Joe Rauh and Governor G. Mennen "Soapy" Williams of Michigan declared that they could not vote for the ticket if Johnson was on it.[60] Mayor Richard Daley told JFK that having Johnson on the ticket would make it harder to carry Illinois.[61] Leonard Woodcock of the UAW remembered running into Joe Rauh, "who had tears literally rolling down his cheeks."[62]

Many of LBJ's supporters were just as vehemently against his accepting the second spot on the ticket as the liberals were. When Bob Kerr heard the news he went directly to the Johnson suite to try to talk his friend out of it. As a conservative oilman and an ardent Baptist, he was intensely anti-Kennedy. Price Daniel, who had spent the summer trying to convince Texans that Kennedy as president was an unthinkable idea, was opposed. So was Ed Weisl Jr., the wealthy New York Jew who had been a Preparedness Subcommittee staffer and was now a major Johnson supporter. "Joe Kennedy was a vitriolic anti-Semite," Harry McPherson recalled, "and had been on the board of Paramount with Ed Weisl, Sr. At one point, in one crucial meeting involving the future of Paramount, I think, Ed Weisl took a position opposed to that of Joe Kennedy, Sr. and Kennedy said, 'I don't have to sit here and listen to some kike lawyer.' "[63]

ON THE AFTERNOON OF THE 13TH Bobby made several trips to the Johnson suite to see if LBJ would be satisfied with something less than the vice presidency. In his account, written after his brother was dead and the hated Lyndon was president, RFK recalled again that he and Jack had had no idea that LBJ would accept and that JFK was genuinely trying to get out of the commitment. That explanation is surely incorrect. Labor leader Albert Zack remembered that early in the morning of the 13th, Reuther, Goldberg, and Alex Rose, head of the hatters union and of the Liberal Party in New York, visited Kennedy. JFK pulled Goldberg into the bathroom and told him it was LBJ. Later, Bobby paid the labor leaders a visit at the Statler and overruled their objections. "There's nothing more to talk about," he said, "the candidate's made up his mind."[64]

It may have been, as some have speculated, that Bobby and Jack were not communicating, but more likely Bobby's visits were for the purpose of appeasing distraught liberals. The Kennedys could argue that they had never dreamed that the proud majority leader would "trade a vote for a gavel," as LBJ once put it, referring to the vice president's role as president pro tem of the Senate, but then had had no choice when the Texan refused to back out.

Around 1:30 Bobby called the Johnson suite to say he was coming down. "Whatever it is, I don't want to see him," LBJ said. Bobby arrived—"He had that hair hanging down in his face," Rayburn remembered—and huddled with the speaker and John Connally. Things were in a terrible uproar, Bobby said. Labor and black leaders were threatening a revolt. Would LBJ accept the chairmanship of the Democratic National Committee? "Aw, shit!" Rayburn exclaimed and walked out of the room.[65] If Jack wanted Johnson to pull out, Jack was going to have to call personally and ask him to decline.

Bobby left but was back in ten minutes with the same story about impending revolt. In between RFK visits, Phil Graham had frantically called Jack Kennedy, asking him to do something. "Oh," JFK told him, "that's all right; Bobby's been out of touch and doesn't know what's happening." He then got Johnson on the phone and asked him to make a statement at once.[66] The Democratic ticket for 1960 was going to be John F. Kennedy and Lyndon B. Johnson.[67]

In fact, outside the Rauh-Reuther circle, the selection of Lyndon Johnson was a popular one with Democratic party leaders. Governors David Lawrence of Pennsylvania and Pat Brown of California had urged JFK to name the Texan. David Dubinsky, the influential head of the International Ladies' Garment Workers Union (ILGWU), was enthusiastic. Richard Daley quickly came around. Congressman Carmine deSapio of New York had told JFK that he would certainly lose without Johnson on the ticket, as had southern leaders like Buford Ellington and Luther Hodges, governors of Tennessee and North Carolina, respectively.[68]

Lyndon's name was placed before the convention on the evening of the 14th. With some difficulty, party leaders had managed to head off a floor revolt led by the Michigan delegation. Black delegates had been somewhat appeased when Johnson, at a meeting held at the Biltmore that afternoon, had assured them that he would support with enthusiasm the party's civil rights plank, which was more advanced than either the 1952 or 1956 versions.[69]

Phil Graham persuaded the irreconcilable Joe Rauh not to place Orville Freeman's name in nomination. LBJ could hear the proceedings as he waited in the tunnel leading up to the platform. Fearful of counterdemonstrations, the Kennedy people had arranged for Congressman John McCormack of Massachusetts to call for a voice vote and convention chairman LeRoy Collins to suspend the rules so that such a vote could be taken. When Collins called the question, the shouted "ayes" and "nays" seemed about evenly divided, but the chair declared the motion carried and Lyndon Johnson was nominated by acclamation. LBJ was joined on the podium by Lady Bird and Lucy. Somehow Lynda had not gotten the word and, to her father's intense displeasure, had gone off to Disneyland.[70]

THE RACE for the Republican nomination was a comparatively closed affair. The only serious rival to Vice President Richard M. Nixon was Nelson Rockefeller, who had defeated Averell Harriman for the governorship of New York in 1958. The GOP was still the minority party, and its leaders knew it. They had enjoyed control of the White House for the past eight years because of Dwight Eisenhower's popularity and not because of any major organizational or ideological victories. Consequently, the president's endorsement of the GOP nominee was crucial.

Ike did not like Richard Nixon, preferring the secretary of the treasury, John Anderson, a quiet Texan who had no chance at the nomination. The vice president seemed to Ike to be a tin man, incapable of conviction and even genuine feelings. Rockefeller was handsome and hard-driving, the epitome of an eastern, liberal Republican, but Eisenhower regarded him as a wealthy spendthrift who would permanently unbalance the budget. Reluctantly, the president endorsed the author of the "Checkers" speech.

Shortly after the Eisenhower announcement, Rockefeller withdrew from a race he had never really entered and focused his efforts instead on liberalizing the GOP platform for 1960. It just so happened that his campaign coincided with and complemented Nixon's attempts to moderate his own image as a red-baiting, partisan political opportunist.

In an effort to unify the party and stake out a claim to America's all-important political center, Nixon flew to New York for a secret meeting with Rockefeller. In the "Compact of Fifth Avenue," Nixon agreed to support a platform that called for preservation of New Deal–Fair Deal reforms and an ongoing effort to secure equal rights for African Americans and other minorities. Although the old Taft wing of the party denounced the compact as a betrayal of the hallowed principles of Republicanism, Nixon was easily nominated on the first ballot. He subsequently named Henry Cabot Lodge Jr., a prominent member of the eastern, liberal wing of the party, as his running mate.

THE KENNEDY'S MADE IT CLEAR that they expected LBJ to carry Texas and as much of the South as possible. The Lone Star State had gone Republican in every election since 1948, and the Democratic candidate had picked up only sixty electoral votes in the South in 1956 compared to Eisenhower's sixty-seven.[71] In this scenario, LBJ would be a purely regional candidate whose mission it was to "solidify the party" in the South and West, areas where Kennedy's Catholicism would hurt him most. In this way, Johnson could avoid speaking out on civil rights and remain firm on such issues as the oil depletion allowance. Jim Rowe, Booth Mooney, and George Reedy were adamantly opposed to such a role for their boss.

For a number of reasons, they insisted that LBJ run as a national candidate. He should campaign in the industrial Northeast and Midwest as well as the South and West. LBJ, they pointed out, was at last free to be himself. He could adopt reasonable, progressive positions on civil rights, labor issues, and matters of social security and justice. If he were to limit himself to the South and West and cater to Texas-style conservatism, Johnson would simply confirm the belief by his detractors that he was but a provincial phenomenon, placed on the ticket to appease Dixiecrats and Shivercrats. If LBJ accepted the role of regional candidate, he would be identifying himself with the old Democratic party, not the new.[72]

In fact, at the outset of the campaign, both Johnson and Kennedy resisted the notion that they must present themselves to the entire nation, not just those areas in which they felt most comfortable. Kennedy initially argued that he should stick to the Northeast and Midwest, where blacks, union members, city bosses, and Catholics, offended by the religious bigotry that was sure to play a part in the campaign, would carry the day. Indeed, if he could just get the Catholics in the suburbs who had defected to the Republicans in 1952 and 1956, he could win. But Jim Rowe, whom the Kennedys pressed into service as scheduler for both the presidential and vice presidential efforts, challenged him. He must appear in the South and West to demonstrate to voters there that at least he "did not have horns."[73]

Rowe made the same plea to LBJ, but it was not an easy sell. "There are three places that I will not go," LBJ told advance man James Blundell, "so don't even schedule me . . . New York, Chicago, and California." The three contained a huge number of electoral votes, Blundell pointed out. "Yes, but I'm not going in there and have those liberals beat my brains out and embarrass Kennedy and embarrass me."[74] But he did campaign in New York, Illinois, and California and did very well. Likewise, Kennedy ventured into Texas and delivered what some believed was the decisive speech of the election.

THE LAST WEEK IN JULY, Lyndon, Lady Bird, and selected staff members, accompanied by a bevy of reporters, flew to Hyannis Port for a strategy meeting with the Kennedys. For two days LBJ and JFK ostentatiously conferred. All the while, Lady Bird and Jacqueline Kennedy warily circled each other. Following the convention in Los Angeles, Jack had phoned Lady Bird at the ranch and asked her to head up the women's campaign. Jackie was pregnant and feared a miscarriage, he said. In truth, at Hyannis Port what struck Lady Bird most about the candidate's wife was her vulnerability. "She had a doll-like expression on her face and she spoke in a soft, airy voice," she recalled. While they toured the house, Jackie blurted out that she felt "so totally inadequate, so totally at a loss" to help with the campaign. To others in the Johnson entourage, Jackie seemed not helpless and vulnerable, but rude. "Jack Kennedy could not have been more gracious," Betty Hickman, an aide to Lady Bird, recalled. "He came over three or four times. 'Betty can I get you more coffee? What can I do?' But Jacqueline didn't even speak to Lady Bird. She hardly acknowledged that we were in the room."[75]

To reporters and fashion magazine editors, the two women seemed a study in contrasts. Jackie was the thirty-one-year-old debutante who had graduated from the Sorbonne, wore the latest designer fashions with style and grace, lived lavishly, and disdained the rough-and-tumble of everyday politics. Lady Bird was attractive but certainly not glamorous, the working politician's wife who could press the flesh with the best of them. She dressed very conservatively, deferring to her husband's preference for straight skirts and bright colors. And compared to LBJ, she was frugal. Lyndon, who had grown up in very modest means in the Hill Country, bought $200 suits six at a time, while Lady Bird, who grew up rich during the Depression, kept herself and the girls on a tight budget. The staff at Nieman-Marcus, where she shopped in Dallas, recalled that she would not go one cent over the amount she had allotted herself.[76]

One of the things Lady Bird and Jackie had in common was unfaithful husbands. JFK's staff lived in constant fear that his numerous affairs would become public knowledge. Jack's affair with Marilyn Monroe had begun in 1959, and it was she rather than Jackie who accompanied JFK to the Democratic Convention in Los Angeles. Meanwhile, Lyndon was in the midst of a long-running affair with Helen Gahagan Douglas, the movie star wife of actor Melvyn Douglas and one-time congresswoman from California. A tall, sophisticated, handsome brunette, Helen Douglas was in many ways comparable to Alice Glass. According to Horace Busby, the liaison began in LBJ's office in 1944, when both were in Congress, and continued off and on for the next twenty years.

During the Hyannis Port visit, LBJ seemed to observers to be more hyperactive than usual. He seemed never to sit still, never to stop talking. He dominated the closing press conference. Jack Kennedy later expressed satisfaction at this because, he said, it demonstrated how completely reconciled LBJ was to being his running mate. Behind their backs, the Kennedy staff made fun of "Mr. and Mrs. Cornpone."[77]

In fact, many in the Kennedy entourage were convinced that LBJ was as much a burden as an asset to the ticket. Arthur Schlesinger Jr., Harvard historian and ADA activist, reminded JFK how hard it had been to wean liberal intellectuals away from Adlai Stevenson. These were the "kinetic people" who had "traditionally provided the spark" in Democratic campaigns. "Putting Lyndon on the ticket . . . interrupted the emotional momentum of your drive," he wrote Kennedy. "The kinetic people . . . are not at the moment committed heart and soul to the Kennedy-Johnson campaign."[78]

From Hyannis Port, LBJ flew to Nashville to confer with a group of southern governors and Democratic party leaders who had congregated at Buford Ellington's mansion. The gathering ran the gamut from Luther Hodges and LeRoy Collins to Herman Talmadge. LBJ told the assemblage that he was a national candidate and, like JFK, committed to representing all the people, including blacks. But at the same time, he assured everyone that the new administration would be sensitive to the South's need for gradual change with the least possible amount of turmoil. Later, when LBJ was campaigning in that same city, he spied some racist graffiti. "I'll tell you what's at the bottom of it," he remarked to Bill Moyers. "If you can convince the lowest white man that he's better than the best colored man, he won't notice you picking his pocket. Hell, give him somebody to look down on, and he'll empty his pockets for you."[79]

At the gathering at the governor's mansion, Lyndon asked Robert Troutman, the prominent Georgia Democrat who had helped arrange the conference, to persuade Richard Russell to support the ticket. Troutman and others tried, but the Wizard of Winder insisted on sitting out the election. "I have turned them down in my own state and in South Carolina," he later told Walter Jenkins. "The Democratic ticket is going to win and I have bet $2,000 to that effect. I am not sure it will be a good thing for Lyndon if it does."[80]

THE PREVIOUS JUNE, LBJ had arranged for Congress to recess rather than adjourn. He believed that whoever the Democrats selected as their presidential and vice presidential candidates could use the session effectively in the campaign. If the Democratic majority was able to enact the progressive agenda LBJ had formulated at the beginning of the session, the ticket could claim credit. If conservatives in league with the Eisenhower White House managed to stymie such legislation, Democrats could, as Harry Truman had done in 1948, campaign against a "do-nothing" Republican party.

Jack Kennedy was still a senator, and he quickly embraced the strategy. He and Johnson pinned their hopes on four pieces of legislation: an increase in the minimum wage, Medicare for the aged, a housing bill, and a federal aid to education measure. Kennedy and Johnson's Senate colleagues immediately noticed some tension between the two. LBJ was the majority leader, but Kennedy was leader of the party. Suddenly the master of the Senate had to make way for a junior colleague noted for his indifference to the workings of the upper house. "This fellow who had just been one of the senators hanging around," as Kennedy aide Kenny O'Donnell put it, "was suddenly the boss calling the shots on what they do with the bills, and that irritated quite obviously."[81]

Nothing came of the rump session. Liberal Republicans were not going to cross the aisle in an election year, and they joined with conservative Democrats and the administration to block the Kennedy-Johnson program.[82]

NO CATHOLIC had ever been elected president of the United States, and there were large numbers of Protestants who were determined that one never would. Anti-Catholic sentiment was particularly strong in the South, including Texas. Even a person as liberal as Virginia Durr confessed that she opposed a Kennedy candidacy on religious grounds. On September 9, 150 Protestant clerics under the leadership of the Reverend Dr. Norman Vincent Peale, an Eisenhower disciple, congregated in Washington and issued a press release stating that in their opinion a Catholic president would have to subsume his will to that of the pope. At the same time, LBJ's contacts in Texas were telling him that the Democratic ticket was in deep trouble. "There are many responsible citizens," state senator Charles Herring wrote Walter Jenkins, "who believe the party is dominated primarily by Eastern liberals who take from the industrious and frugal and the financially successful for the benefit of the lazy and 'withouts.' " But above all there was the religious issue.[83] LBJ and Jim Rowe convinced Kennedy that he would have to confront the matter of his faith, and what better place to challenge southern white Protestants than in Texas.

At Johnson's urging, JFK accepted an invitation to speak before the Greater Houston Ministerial Alliance on September 12. LBJ and JFK rendezvoused that morning and proceeded to San Antonio for a noontime rally. When they arrived at the Alamo, the venue that had been selected, the two Democratic standard-bearers were greeted by protesters carrying signs reading "We don't want the Kremlin or the Vatican" and "We Want the Bible and the Constitution." Johnson immediately seized the podium. How dare anyone question the patriotism of Catholics or the religious beliefs of any American? At the Alamo 125 years earlier, "side by side with Bowie and Crockett died McCafferty, Bailey and Carey, but no one knows whether they were Catholics or not. For there was no religious test at the Alamo."[84] The crowd responded with a sustained ovation, and all but a few of the picketers put down their signs.

When the Kennedy-Johnson party arrived at the Houston Convention Center that evening, the tension was as thick and stifling as the humidity outside. One could feel all the old prejudices of 1928. Sam Rayburn had been totally opposed to Kennedy's visit to Houston. "These are not ministers," Mr. Sam told JFK. "These are politicians who are going around in robes and saying they're ministers, but they're nothing but politicians. They hate your guts and they're going to tear you to pieces."[85]

Rayburn was wrong. In his speech before three hundred mostly Protestant clergymen, Kennedy shone. "I believe in an America where the separation of Church and State is absolute," he proclaimed, "where no Catholic prelate would tell the president, should he be a Catholic, how to act and no Protestant minister would tell his parishioners for whom to vote . . . I believe in an America that is officially neither Catholic, Protestant nor Jewish . . . for while this year it may be a Catholic against whom the finger of suspicion is pointed, in other years it has been, and may someday be again, a Jew—or a Quaker—or a Unitarian—or a Baptist."[86] Gradually the tension ebbed, and the gathering concluded with a round of polite applause.

LADY BIRD, together with Ethel and Eunice Kennedy, JFK's sisters, was already in Houston campaigning. That afternoon, the trio had entertained some five thousand Texas women at a massive "tea party." While Bird was briefing her husband on the day's events, the telephone rang in their suite. It was her father's doctor calling from Marshall. Her eighty-six-year-old father, T. J., had developed blood poisoning, and one leg would have to be amputated. "I watched her on the phone," an aide remembered, "and saw her whole body flinch when she got the call."[87]

Lady Bird recognized that this was probably her father's last illness and told her husband that she would have to leave the campaign for a few days. He nodded. Early the next morning, she and Liz Carpenter, the tough-talking Texas newspaperwoman Lady Bird had hired as her assistant, left for East Texas. When they arrived, they found not only Mr. Taylor in the hospital but also his third wife, Ruth, who was being treated for prescription drug dependency. Ruth and Lady Bird had never gotten along, and T. J. Taylor's impending demise only made matters worse.

The patriarch of the Taylor clan died on October 22. LBJ helicoptered in for the service attended by several hundred people at the tiny Methodist church in Karnack. Taylor left the bulk of his estate, valued at more than $1 million, to Ruth. Included was the Brick House, from which Ruth subsequently barred Lady Bird until the former's death. Her father was gone, but his place in Lady Bird's life was more than taken by Lyndon. "I feel sure my ideas of what a man was were formed by my father," she later observed. "I adored him." She even admitted that she had married Lyndon in part because "subconsciously I suppose I was looking for my father."[88] "The key to understanding Lady Bird," Horace Busby observed, "is to understand that in her mind her father was the role model for how all men are and should be. It explains why she put up with LBJ's womanizing, and why she idealized him for being a public servant. She grew up with her father and assumed all men had a wife but also had girlfriends."[89]

ON OCTOBER 5, LBJ, Lady Bird, and their daughters departed on a five-day train trip through the South. It was time to make good on the implicit deal to deliver Dixie for the Democratic ticket. Lindy Boggs, wife of the Louisiana congressman, remembered that the Johnson staff dispatched an all-woman advance team, dressed in blue blazers, white pleated skirts, and blouses. The plan was to use the South's reputation for chivalry against its seething racial hatred. "What southern gentleman is not going to receive southern ladies when they are coming to his state and his city?" as Boggs put it.[90]

The idea of a whistle-stop campaign, reminiscent of Harry Truman's famous 1948 tour, appealed to LBJ. But it was a calculated gamble that could easily backfire. Much of the white South was up in arms over the lunch counter sit-in demonstrations and over Martin Luther King's campaign to end discrimination in the "cradle of the Confederacy," Birmingham, Alabama. They were convinced that the new leadership in the Democratic party would make matters worse. Not only had the Kennedys pressed successfully for an advanced civil rights plank in the 1960 platform, they had named a group of strident liberals, including Hubert Humphrey of Minnesota, Philip Hart of Michigan, and Joseph Clark of Pennsylvania, to their inner circle. "The only name missing is Thaddeus Stevens," George Reedy reported to LBJ with disgust.[91] JFK had stated publicly that he was opposed to Rule 22 requiring a two-thirds vote of the Senate to close debate. Thus did Richard Russell decide to sit out the election and thus was LBJ left with little maneuvering room in dealing with the South.

The tour, which began in Virginia and wound up in New Orleans, took the vice presidential candidate's party through the more conservative Piedmont.

Bobby Baker, who helped organize the event, described the daily routine: "We had a fantastic speaker system set up on the train that as we would come into the station you could hear, 'The Yellow Rose of Texas,' and as we would leave you could hear it. It was about a forty-minute production per stop by the time you introduced the locals and had your picture made with Lady Bird, and Lucy and Lynda and Lyndon and the local politicians." He and Kennedy would continue to support the South on its journey toward modernity and prosperity, Johnson told his audiences. In the twentieth century in America, religion should not, could not be an issue in politics. "He would always tell the story of Jack Kennedy's brother, Joe Junior, going down in that airplane with a copilot from New Braunfels, Texas," Jim Blundell recalled, "and he said, 'I'm sure that they didn't ask each other what church they went to. They both died for their country.' "[92]

The LBJ Special never knew what kind of reception to expect. In one of the first stops, at Culpepper, Virginia, the crowd was thin and generally hostile. Irritated, LBJ yelled, "What has Nixon ever done for Culpepper, Virginia!" as the train pulled out of the station. At Clemson University in South Carolina, a stronghold of southern conservatism, the band began to play "Hold That Tiger" every time Johnson started to speak. By contrast, the reception in New Orleans was a thundering success. A crowd of two hundred thousand led by Senator Russell Long, Congressman Hale Boggs, and Mayor DeLesseps Morrison met the train and gave the Johnson party ovation after ovation.[93]

IRONICALLY, given his reputation as a political wheeler-dealer committed to the notion that ends justified means, LBJ was obsessed with the ethics of campaign financing. A savings and loan executive had given LBJ $50,000 and then used the contribution as leverage to get a spot on the LBJ Special. When Lyndon heard about it, he had James Blundell physically eject the man from the train at Greenville, South Carolina, and return the donation.[94] The "Irish Mafia," the coterie of largely Irish staffers and family members close to JFK, had no such scruples; it would take money anywhere, anytime, and do whatever favors were called for in return. "Steve Smith, who was his treasurer in 1960, said that once a week he left his office, went out to Kennedy's house, and went through every suit, just collecting money," Jim Rowe recalled. "He collected cash, checks, etc., in all of Kennedy's suits, all contributions, and took them back and used them."[95] "Johnson was petrified of campaign contributions," Baker said.[96]

AS THE CAMPAIGN WORE ON, the press, noting that Kennedy and Johnson had not made a joint appearance after Houston, began speculating that a rift had developed. LBJ himself wondered if the Kennedys were holding him at arm's length. "Why don't they ever ask me to appear with Jack?" he asked an aide. "Nixon has Lodge with him quite often, but the Democratic candidates haven't appeared together."[97] Actually, both Kennedy's and Johnson's handlers had agreed early on that joint appearances were not a good idea. "The contrast between you and Kennedy, in my opinion, is always poor," Jim Rowe had told LBJ in August. "When you are together, Kennedy looks like your son. The Kennedy people also feel very strongly about this. Confidentially, they think the contrast hurts Kennedy."[98]

But the press continued to gossip and LBJ to gripe, so Leonard Marks and Ted Sorenson, LBJ and JFK aides respectively, arranged for a joint appearance in New York on the Thursday evening before the election on the following Tuesday. Johnson flew in from Los Angeles especially for the occasion. The schedule called for the candidates to meet at the Biltmore in the late afternoon to strategize before going on television that night. LBJ and his entourage ensconced themselves in the Biltmore and waited. Finally, word came from the Kennedy camp, which had been campaigning in Harlem, that JFK would be staying in the family apartment in the Carlyle. Marks loaded LBJ and his staff into waiting cars and proceeded to that hotel in a driving rain. No sooner had they settled in than they learned that Kennedy had just checked into the Biltmore. Johnson finally rendezvoused with his running mate, but he felt humiliated. Despite the confusion, the joint appearance received nationwide coverage and was seen by both camps as a definite plus.[99]

BY THE CLOSING DAYS of the campaign, LBJ and his staff had come to view Bobby Kennedy more as an enemy than a friend. In truth, JFK's younger brother and campaign manager would never forgive Johnson for the humiliation at the ranch and the slurs against his family at the Los Angeles convention. Bobby was more like his father, Joe, who reveled in his younger son's hardness. "You can trample all over him [Jack]," Joe told Tip O'Neill, "and the next day he's there for you with loving arms. But Bobby's my boy. When Bobby hates you, you stay hated."[100]

Prior to Jack's trip to Texas in September, Bobby had come down to discuss arrangements with LBJ's staff. Among other things, the Johnson advisers were concerned that Jack would say something inappropriate regarding the oil depletion allowance, still sacred to Texans. Campaign worker John Singleton met Bobby—"the most arrogant person I had ever met in my life"—at the airport. Singleton gave him a copy of a prepared, noncommittal statement about the depletion allowance. "He read it, tore it up and threw it on the ground and said, 'We're not going to say anything like that. We put that son of a bitch on the ticket to carry Texas, and if you can't carry Texas, that's y'all's problem.' "[101]

LBJ was not a natural politician. He was frequently uncomfortable in crowds, and he tried too hard with people.[102] Quite simply, he did not like to campaign. Insecure, compulsive, he quickly worked himself into a state of exhaustion and, usually, illness. Campaigning in 1960 was no exception. He blew up at his staff if his suits were not properly ironed, if his showers were not hot enough, if there was a glitch in the campaign schedule, which there inevitably was. He would rage particularly at Lady Bird, who stoically took it.[103] "I was so exhausted after one week of scheduling Johnson that I quit," Jim Rowe recalled.

" 'Get somebody else. I've scheduled Adlai, Kefauver, and Kennedy, but all three of them gave me less trouble in the whole business than you've given me in one week,' I said." [104]

Before he departed, Rowe wrote his fellow New Dealer a letter that would break their relationship until Johnson ascended to the presidency. "Somebody ought to tell you the truth occasionally—and there is no one around who does," it began. "I would tell you to your face but I have learned I can't get one word in edgewise with you . . . Don't you ever pause for a moment and wonder why such old and devoted friends—at least a quarter of a century apiece—like John Connally and Jim Rowe find it impossible to work for you? . . . I have not seen you pay one compliment, thank one person, be the sweet and kind and attractive Lyndon I used to know in all the time I have traveled with you. I have seen you do nothing but yell at them, every single one of them . . . And most of the time, you, LBJ, are wrong and they are right . . . They bend their heads and wait for the blows to fall—like obdurate mules who know the blow is coming. It makes me so goddamn mad I'd like to sock you in the jaw!" [105]

So frantic did LBJ become at one point during the campaign that Jack Kennedy told him, "I believe you're cracking up." [106] Among other things, LBJ was sick with worry over the prospect of losing Texas. "I need you as I have never needed you before," he cabled wealthy Fort Worth publisher Amon Carter. [107]

In a last-minute effort to generate support, LBJ decided to travel into that heartland of radical conservatism, Dallas. Aides in Texas scheduled a luncheon address at the Adolphus Hotel on November 4. Lyndon and Lady Bird flew into Fort Worth that morning and were picked up by Carl Phinney, a retired military officer and Democratic activist. Approaching the outskirts of Dallas, the Johnson party was stopped by city police and told that there was a "disturbance" at the Baker Hotel, where Lyndon and Lady Bird were booked. The officer in charge insisted on taking the Johnsons in through the back entrance of the hotel. There was no avoiding the lobby, however, and what Lyndon and Lady Bird found there was a throng of well-heeled Republicans led by the reactionary congressman from Dallas, Bruce Alger, and Lyndon's opponent in the Senate race, John Tower. The crowd, bearing banners reading "LBJ Sold Out to Yankee Socialists" and "Beat Judas," booed and hissed when they saw the vice presidential candidate. The party shouldered its way to the elevators.

While LBJ was dressing for his speech at the Adolphus, located just across Commerce Street from the Baker, his advance men urged him to allow them to take him and Lady Bird through the restaurant exit and then by auto to the back door of the Adolphus. LBJ flatly rejected the suggestion. "If the time has come when I can't walk through the lobby of a hotel in Dallas with my lady without a police escort," he said, "I want to know it." [108]

Commerce Street between the two hotels was a mob scene. In the forefront of the crowd were young, well-to-do Junior Leaguers Alger had whipped into a frenzy. "The Mink Coat Mob," one newspaper dubbed them. As LBJ clutched Bird to him, the crowd closed, shouting "Traitor," "Socialist," "Judas," and less polite epithets. A woman snatched Lady Bird's white gloves from her and threw them into the gutter. "It came upon me as a tremendous surprise and sort of an assault on my spirit," Lady Bird said, "because we had felt that we were working for them all these years." [109] Bird, her gorge rising, started to answer one young woman who was screaming at her, but Lyndon put his hand over her mouth. Suddenly, she noticed that her husband was moving very slowly, more slowly than he needed to. She also recalled that he had told Phinney and other staffers there to escort them to disappear. Finally, the vice presidential couple reached the friendly confines of the Adolphus, and Lyndon went on to speak. As he knew would be the case, the "Adolphus riot" received nationwide attention in both the print and broadcast media. A groundswell of sympathy for the Johnsons swept the Lone Star State. The next day in Houston, home to both conservative and liberal Johnson-haters, the couple was treated to a uniformly warm reception. [110]

IN AN EFFORT to cut into the Republican lead, the Kennedy camp challenged Nixon to a series of four debates. Only in this way, Democratic strategists believed, could their candidate answer the charges of inexperience and force Nixon into the position of defending a passive administration. The Republican candidate's advisers warned him to refuse, but he was proud of his forensic skill and psychologically incapable of dodging a challenge. Both candidates understood that the impressions they made in their first confrontation would be hard to alter. Kennedy prepared like a skilled trial lawyer, mastering position papers until the points were second nature to him.

On September 26 the curtain rose on one of contemporary history's most memorable dramas. Speaking first, Kennedy invoked the image of a revived, activist, successful America. He was handsome, suntanned, and well-groomed, radiating self-assurance and competence. Whether because of studio lighting or an inept makeup person, Nixon appeared unshaven and drawn. Worse, he perspired, causing his makeup to run.

A poll of radio listeners showed the debaters had tied. A postelection survey indicated, however, that of the 4 million Americans who indicated that they had been decisively influenced by the debate, 3 million had voted for Kennedy. Most rated the three remaining debates a draw, but the damage had been done.

CHAPTER 18

CAMELOT MEETS MR. CORNPONE

THE 1960 ELECTION WAS ONE OF THE TIGHTEST IN history, the closest since the disputed Hayes-Tilden contest of 1876. On election night, Lyndon and Lady Bird settled in at the Driskill Hotel in Austin, the stage on which their marriage drama had begun twenty-five years earlier, to await returns. Johnson conferred over the phone with JFK several times. "I see you are losing Ohio," he said to Jack during one of the calls. "I am carrying Texas and we are doing pretty well in Pennsylvania." [1]

Finally, at 7 A.M. on November 9, television anchors called the election for Kennedy-Johnson. The margin of victory in the popular vote had been razor thin: 112,881 out of nearly 67 million cast. In the electoral college the Democratic lead was more comfortable, at 303 to 219. In the South, Alabama, Arkansas, Georgia, Louisiana, North and South Carolina, and Texas had gone Democratic. Florida, Tennessee, and Virginia voted GOP, with Mississippi casting its electoral votes for an independent segregationist.

In the Texas Senate race, Johnson bested John Tower by 46,233 votes, a surprisingly small margin. That was almost precisely the number of votes by which Kennedy beat Nixon in the Lone Star State. Republicans would subsequently claim that the contest there and in Illinois was rife with fraud, but nothing came of it. Bobby Kennedy telephoned Johnson at the Driskill shortly after the election was called. "Well," he said, "Lady Bird carried Texas for the President." [2]

Lyndon was not amused. Moreover, the victory seemed to fill him with foreboding rather than anticipation. "The night he was elected vice-president," journalist Margaret Mayer recalled, "I don't think I ever saw a more unhappy man . . . There was no jubilation. Lyndon looked as if he'd lost his last friend on earth." [3]

• • •

THE DAY OF THE ELECTION, Tommy Corcoran, the New Dealer who had brought LBJ into Roosevelt's inner circle in 1937, wrote Lyndon and Lady Bird urging them to look on the bright side. "I know you didn't like what I said to you [several months earlier] about escaping from the cage of Texas," he began, "but your subconscious knew even then it was true . . . No matter how the votes fall today, you are a free force in the world, free to be right, free to be a national statesman, free to be a world statesman, free to free the greatness that FDR saw in you."[4]

At Lyndon's insistence, Jack Kennedy paid a visit to the ranch on November 16, just eight days after the election. Before a crowd of reporters and local residents, the mayor of Stonewall welcomed the president-elect and presented him with a Stetson. Despite the urging of photographers, Kennedy steadfastly refused to don the hat.

The next morning, LBJ awakened his guest for the customary deer hunt. Jack later told Jackie how much he "loathed" the prospect of shooting what amounted to an animal in a zoo. Jack and Lyndon departed the ranch house in a white Cadillac convertible. In a nearby pasture bordered by woods, ranch hands drove two deer into the hunter's path. Johnson subsequently told the *New York Times* that the president-elect had brought down his animal with a superb shot at four hundred yards. Actually it was 250 yards, and rumor had it that LBJ had played his old trick of firing simultaneously with his guest to ensure a kill. According to William Manchester's *The Death of a President*, Kennedy "looked into the face of the life he was about to take . . . He fired and quickly turned back to the car," but "he could not rid himself of the recollection. The memory of the creature's death had been haunting, and afterward he had relived it with his wife, vider l'abces, to heal the inner scar."[5]

Inner scar indeed, LBJ told his staff after the book was published. Jack Kennedy had jumped up and down and shouted like a schoolboy after the kill and insisted that the carcass be draped across the hood for all to see.[6] When LBJ subsequently shipped the president-elect his deer's head handsomely mounted, JFK remarked to Jackie, "The three most overrated things in the world are the State of Texas, the F.B.I., and mounted deer heads."[7]

JOHNSON'S ELECTION-NIGHT DEPRESSION did not let up. At the inauguration, in icy cold temperatures following a snowstorm, LBJ appeared glum and distracted. He sat somberly through Marian Anderson's rendition of the "Star-Spangled Banner." Johnson's closest friend in Congress and perpetual supporter, Sam Rayburn, administered the oath of office. Despite its simplicity, Lyndon stumbled over the words. He was in fact almost completely overshadowed by JFK's rousing call to arms in his inaugural speech. The oath-taking proceedings were a portent of things to come.[8]

The Texan had won election to a powerless job. In late December, prior to the inauguration, Lyndon had summoned Bobby Baker with a strange proposal:

"Bobby, I've been thinking about where I can do Jack Kennedy the most good. And it's right here on this Hill, the place I know best . . . All those Bostons and Harvards don't know any more about Capitol Hill than an old maid does about fuckin.' " He would help Mike Mansfield, the quiet, enigmatic Montanan whom JFK had selected to be majority leader, pass the Kennedy program, and Baker could continue to serve as his righthand man.[9]

Baker tried to warn his former boss that he could not continue to act as majority leader. But Johnson would not listen. Inexplicably, Mansfield agreed to support the idea before the Democratic caucus. The sixty-four Democratic senators gathered on January 3 and, after glowing tributes to LBJ's past leadership, unanimously elected Mansfield majority leader. The pipe-smoking Montanan rose, accepted the call to leadership, and then proposed that Lyndon preside at future meetings. The suggestion was greeted with stunned silence; then five senators rose to voice their opposition. "We might as well ask Jack Kennedy to come back to the Senate and take his turn at presiding," said Albert Gore.[10]

By threatening to resign, Mansfield managed to secure a forty-five to seventeen vote in favor of his proposal, but it was clear that the majority of those present thought the whole thing was a bad idea. LBJ attended the next caucus, when he turned over the gavel to Mansfield, but none thereafter. He took the affair hard. His colleagues had humiliated him in public, he later told Baker over drinks. "Now I know the difference between a caucus and a cactus," he said. "In a cactus all the pricks are on the outside."[11]

LBJ and his advisers could only try to wring power out of the notoriously powerless office of the vice presidency. Jokes alluding to the impotency of the office were legion. "There is the old story about the mother who had two sons," Hubert Humphrey told aides shortly after he himself came to occupy the second-highest office in the land. "One went to sea, and the other became vice-president, and neither was heard of again."[12]

Thomas Marshall, Warren Harding's vice president, compared the holder of the office to a cataleptic: "He cannot speak; he cannot move; he suffers no pain; yet he is perfectly conscious of everything that is going on about him."[13] In an interview with Judith Martin in 1968, LBJ summed up the vice presidential dilemma: "Everyone wants to talk to the President, get his quotes . . . and you sit there like a bump on a log, trying not to get in the way. You have no authority, no power, no decisions to make, but you have to abide by the decisions another man makes. If you're independent, you're disloyal, and if not, you're a stooge and a puppet."[14]

"BUILT NOT ON IDEOLOGY or a clear-cut sense of where they wanted to lead the country," historian James Hilty has written, "the Kennedys' ambition for office was personal."[15] That isn't completely fair; Kennedy was a strong anti-communist and he did have a moderately liberal vision of domestic affairs. Arthur Schlesinger and John Kenneth Galbraith, two of JFK's most influential house intellectuals, had been arguing since the 1950s that liberals must move

beyond the language and politics of class conflict that had sometimes characterized the New Deal era. By concentrating on ensuring increased production and
reducing barriers to international trade, the Kennedy administration could lift
all boats, avoid polarizing the country, and prolong their political reign.

Still, the great contest, John and Robert Kennedy believed, was between
communism on the one hand and capitalism on the other. JFK had ordered
speechwriters working on his inaugural address to drop the "domestic stuff."
"Who gives a shit about the minimum wage?" he asked rhetorically.[16] "Kennedy
liberalism," Hilty writes, "was more a political strategy than a set of beliefs, less
a scheme for social and economic change than an approach to resolve conflict
and to maintain economic and social stability."[17]

More than the Kennedys' lack of fervor and commitment to the cause of social justice, their inexperience and ineptitude would hamstring their legislative
program. Nowhere was their lack of insight more vividly demonstrated than in
the choice of Mike Mansfield to be majority leader. "Mike Mansfield is a
monk," Harry McPherson observed in 1972. "He has no desire to impress his
imprint on legislation, no desire, really, to be the Leader of the Senate . . . He is
a passive man except on a few things almost entirely in forging policy . . . I used
to get absolutely enraged because he would not do things which cried out for
doing."[18] Depending on Mansfield to whip Congress into shape was like wielding a noodle to lash an ox.

In the domestic arena, Kennedy began his presidency by focusing on what he
termed five "must" bills: an increase in the minimum wage, health insurance
for senior citizens, federal aid to education, housing legislation, and aid to depressed areas. Only the last, the area redevelopment bill, ever made it through
Congress.

The fight over medical insurance for the aged was typical. The American
Medical Association declared that Kennedy's proposal would introduce "compulsion, regulation and control into a system of freely practiced medicine." The
bill, introduced in February, would have levied a 25 percent increase in Social
Security payroll taxes to pay hospital and nursing costs incurred by individuals
eligible for Social Security old-age benefits. The White House mounted a public relations campaign which featured a televised address by Kennedy to a
throng of senior citizens in Madison Square Garden.

Despite opinion polls that showed a majority of Americans favoring the concept of Medicare, the Senate defeated the administration's proposal by a vote of
fifty-two to forty-eight. The result revealed an emerging pattern that would
characterize congressional action throughout the New Frontier period: only
five Republicans voted for the measure, and twenty-seven Democrats, mostly
from the South, cast their ballots in opposition. "By mid-1963 the deadlock between Congress and the White House was so unyielding that a real constitutional crisis existed," one observer has written. "Congress was not merely
balking at the President's proposals for new action; it was refusing to pass the
appropriations bills to pay for running the executive departments."[19]

Johnson was unable to break the logjam over Medicare in 1961; he had lost all of his leverage. First, whatever power he would have would come from the president. George Reedy observed to his boss that he was first and foremost understudy to JFK. "The Vice President must be a man who can step into the President's shoes tomorrow prepared immediately to make such decisions as dropping the atomic bomb," he memoed LBJ.[20] Second, he presided over the Senate, but was not of the Senate. The vice president was a national officer with no vote and no constituency. He had nothing to trade with members of the upper house and could only hope to influence them as a member of the executive. Third, the vice president represented the president on various foreign policy missions. The key word was "represent." He could make no commitment that was not specifically authorized. Fourth, the second man on the ticket accepted special assignments from the president, and here was the area of opportunity. In his backstairs meeting with Sam Rayburn the night before asking Johnson to be his running mate, Kennedy had allegedly promised the speaker that there would be significant tasks assigned, that his vice president would not be a political eunuch. If this turned out to be the case, the vice presidency held out the possibility of enabling LBJ to overcome his chief image problem, that of a skilled political manipulator with no philosophy and no substance.[21] The key then, would be to take what the president gave his second in command and make the most of it.

Unfortunately, the vice presidency bound LBJ to a body of men and women whose attitude toward him ranged from venomous hatred to mild, amused contempt. Bobby, of course, occupied the far end of the continuum; figures like John Kenneth Galbraith were situated at the near. Secretary of Defense Robert McNamara, who as president of Ford Motor Company had proven himself a genius at running large corporations, believed Johnson to be a second-rate man. Though LBJ would keep him on in his cabinet and tout him as his vice presidential running mate in 1964, McNamara observed that "Johnson lacked the education in history, philosophy, and political science which would have better prepared him to deal with extraordinarily complicated relationships among nations, and, as a matter of fact, with complicated relationships between the executive branch and the legislative branch, and between the government and the people of the United States."[22] Moreover, Johnson was perceived by the men and women of Camelot as socially unacceptable. McPherson observed that his boss wasn't someone whom one "would invite to get thrown in the Hickory Hill swimming pool or go to a fashionable party in New York."[23]

Of all the people in the new White House, JFK was most favorably disposed toward him, Johnson believed. He was wrong. The president thought his second in command was a boor. Jim Rowe was present when both JFK and LBJ attended the opening game of the Major League season in 1961. "I was watching Johnson talk incessantly to Kennedy," Rowe remembered. "[He] never bothered to look at the ball field all the time, and Kennedy was trying to watch the game. A year later they had Dave Powers sitting in between them."[24] Jack Kennedy supposedly had great respect for Johnson's political skills and regarded him as the most effective majority leader in the nation's history. Perhaps so, but he never saw fit to consult LBJ on legislative matters, much less use his vaunted skills to ram key measures through the House and Senate. Kennedy considered his vice president fundamentally dishonest. "Always remember," he told Jackie in 1963, "Lyndon is a liar." For the president, LBJ was a problem to be managed. "I can't afford to have my Vice President who knows every reporter in Washington going around saying we're all screwed up," he told his chief of staff, "so we're going to keep him happy. You're going to keep him happy."[25] "You're dealing with a very insecure, sensitive man with a huge ego," JFK told O'Donnell. "I want you literally to kiss his ass from one end of Washington to the other."[26]

JFK had duties in mind for LBJ, but before he could assign them, the vice president seized the initiative. His staff drafted an executive order for the president's signature. It would give the vice president direct control over a host of important government agencies, including NASA. The order would have agency heads report directly to LBJ. The president would simply rubber-stamp the vice president's recommendations in these designated fields. Half amused and half angry, JFK chose to ignore Johnson's proposal. But his staff leaked its contents to the press, and a number of columnists compared LBJ's move to a similar power grab initiated by William H. Seward, Abraham Lincoln's notoriously ambitious secretary of state.[27]

Nevertheless, Kennedy perceived that if he were to keep the frenetic Texan from dreaming Macbeth-like dreams, he would have to keep him busy. Jack and Bobby realized that, like it or not, civil rights was going to dominate the domestic scene for the next four years and play a role in Jack's plans for reelection. Martin Luther King and the Southern Christian Leadership Conference were then pulling in uneasy harness with the student protesters and sit-in demonstrators of the Congress of Racial Equality (CORE) and the Student Nonviolent Coordinating Committee (SNCC) to arouse the indignation of the black masses and the conscience of middle-class, white America. The White House believed that executive rather than legislative action would be the order of the day.

Jack, Bobby, and their congressional strategist, Lawrence O'Brien, were not anxious to take on the southern Democrats, who were still exceedingly powerful, especially in the Senate. On March 6, 1961, the president signed an executive order creating the Committee on Equal Employment Opportunities (CEEO), with the stated goal of removing "every trace of discrimination" from government employment and from work performed by the federal government by private contractors. Vice President Johnson was to chair the committee, which included Bobby.[28]

JFK also named Johnson to head the president's Space Council, the body that would oversee America's evolving space program and make recommendations for its sustenance and enhancement. The space issue was similar in kind if not degree to civil rights. Kennedy had made the cold war Project Number

One, and in lieu of Armageddon, the focus would be on peaceful competition. Both Johnson and Kennedy had worked hard during the dying days of the Eisenhower administration to convince the public that the measure of competition between the capitalist and communist systems was the space race. The diversion of billions of dollars into missiles and satellites was bound to be controversial: there would be a struggle between the military and civilian agencies for control of the program, and failures would not sit well with either Congress or the voters. If the drive for equal employment opportunity on the one hand, and dominance of outer space on the other, went well, Kennedy could take the credit; if not, LBJ could take the blame.

LIVING ACCOMMODATIONS were not a problem during Johnson's tenure as vice president. Senate Majority Leader Mansfield allowed Lyndon to continue to occupy the "Taj Mahal," the green-and-gold-decorated, seven-room suite opposite the Senate chamber. There was also the six-room suite on the second floor of the Executive Office Building next to the White House.

It was obvious to Lyndon and Lady Bird that the white brick house on Thirtieth Street was not a suitable abode for a vice president. While they looked for something grander, they lived in a four-bedroom apartment in the Sheraton Park Hotel. Then, in April 1961, they bought The Elms, a large French-style house situated atop a hill in Washington's fashionable Spring Valley. The home, complete with parquet floors in the library and Viennese paintings in the dining room, had belonged to Perle Mesta, a Johnson intimate and one of the city's most famous hostesses.[29] A restrictive covenant limiting ownership to whites was attached to the deed, but LBJ made the purchase with the explicit written understanding that he not be bound by it.[30]

THE WEEKS FOLLOWING THE INAUGURATION were ones of despair for Johnson. He felt trapped, useless, ridiculed. The vice president was by law a member of the National Security Council, and Kennedy invited Lyndon to attend cabinet meetings, meetings with House and Senate leaders, and pre–press conference briefings, but it soon became obvious that the president expected LBJ to be seen and not heard. Sometimes he wasn't even seen. JFK supposedly gave Kenny O'Donnell explicit instructions that the vice president was to be included in all important White House meetings, but the head of the Irish mafia "forgot" with increasing frequency, a strange omission for a man so scrupulously doglike in his devotion to JFK.

The Johnsons were rarely invited to the Kennedys' small, informal parties, which featured the McGeorge Bundys, the Schlesingers, and Ken Galbraith and his wife; worse, Lyndon and Lady Bird were frequently the butt of jokes at such gatherings. "Really, it was brutal, the stories that they were passing," said Kennedy friend Elizabeth Gatov, "and the jokes, and the inside nasty stuff about Lyndon. I didn't protest. It was a pretty heady period and they were young people mostly, and they were going to run the country for the next decade."[31]

George Reedy recalled that Johnson started drinking more heavily, and he would spend entire days in bed at home staring at the ceiling. His sense of humiliation was "like a demon in him," Reedy said.[32]

"I cannot stand Johnson's damn long face," JFK told Georgia Senator George Smathers. "He comes in, sits at the cabinet meetings, with his face all screwed up, never says anything. He looks so sad."[33] Why not make him a kind of ambassador-at-large? Smathers suggested. He could be received as a visiting head of state; all of the pomp and circumstance would provide more than enough nourishment for the Johnson ego. "A damn good idea," Kennedy responded and dispatched LBJ on trips to Africa and Asia in the spring of 1961. These would be the first of eleven sojourns to thirty-three foreign lands for the vice president.

The trips would show Lyndon at his best and his worst. In Africa, India, and Scandinavia he was almost buffoonlike, taking every occasion to outrage conventional manners, farting, belching, wolfing food and drink, making outrageous demands on the staffs of American embassies. On other occasions, he was an effective ambassador for the American values he held dear, particularly a commitment to social justice. In Vietnam and Berlin he was serious, businesslike, primarily because he had been given a real mission with consequences.

LBJ WAS FULLY IN TUNE with the activist foreign policies of the Kennedy administration. Unfortunately, Camelot's approach to international affairs suffered from a basic contradiction. The president and his advisers insisted that they were out to make the world safe for diversity, that under their leadership the United States would abandon the status quo policies of the past and support revolutionary movements for social justice and democratic self-determination, especially in the developing world. The Kennedy people did not object to Eisenhower's intervention into the internal affairs of other nations—only to the ineptness with which it was done. In a special address to Congress in May 1961, the president declared that "the great battleground for the defense and expansion of freedom today is . . . Asia, Latin America, Africa and the Middle East, the lands of the rising peoples."[34]

According to Arthur Schlesinger Jr., Kennedy fully understood that in Latin America "the militantly anti-revolutionary line" of the past was the policy most likely to strengthen the communists and lose the hemisphere. He and his advisers planned openings to the left to facilitate "democratic development." Specifically, the administration projected an ambitious foreign aid program that would promote social justice and economic progress in the developing nations and in the process funnel nationalist energy into pro-democracy, anticommunist channels. Modernization through American aid would ensure that the newly emerging nations would achieve change through evolution rather than revolution.

At the same time, the administration saw any significant alteration in the world balance of power as a threat to American security. Kennedy, McGeorge Bundy, Secretary of State Dean Rusk, and McNamara took very seriously

Khrushchev's January 1961 speech offering support for "wars of national liberation"; it was, they believed, evidence of a new communist campaign to seize control of anticolonial and other revolutionary movements in economically underdeveloped regions.

In Cuba, John F. Kennedy had had to confront the classic dilemma that faced all cold war presidents: What was to be done when anticolonial, nationalist revolutions embraced Marxism-Leninism? Despite his oft-repeated sympathy for anticolonial movements and socioeconomic justice in the developing world, Kennedy placed anticommunism at the top of his priorities and waged undeclared, mostly secret war on the Cuban Revolution. He made similar choices in regard to two other third world, cold war hot spots: the Congo and Vietnam. "Our first great obstacle," Kennedy said, "is still our relations with the Soviet Union and China. We must never be lulled into believing that either power has yielded its ambitions for world domination." [35] When confronted with a choice between communist-influenced revolutions and autocratic prowestern government, JFK would invariably choose the latter.

Determined to deal with the Kremlin from a position of strength, Kennedy and McNamara announced that America's nuclear arsenal would increase until it contained one thousand intercontinental ballistic missiles. "We dare not tempt [the Soviets] with weakness," the president declared. [36]

The nuclear buildup frightened Soviet Premier Nikita Khrushchev; as he well knew, the Soviet Union already lagged far behind the United States in delivery vehicles. Instead of stability, the Kennedy-McNamara buildup touched off an arms race that brought the world to the brink of nuclear war in 1962, during the Cuban Missile Crisis, and saddled the United States with a massive $50 billion annual military budget by 1963. But for Kennedy, McNamara, and Rusk, the nuclear arms race was just one aspect of the multifaceted contest with the communist powers.

Kennedy instructed the Special Warfare Center at Fort Bragg, North Carolina, to train a new type of soldier capable of fighting communist guerrillas on their own terms. In the 1950s, anticommunist forces in Malaya, the Philippines, and Greece had successfully employed guerrilla tactics to defeat insurgents, and the administration was convinced that these techniques were suitable for dealing with Khrushchev's wars of national liberation. The special forces at Fort Bragg, the Green Berets, increased from fewer than one-thousand to twelve-thousand during the Kennedy administration.

In January 1962, the White House created a Special Group (Counterinsurgency) chaired by General Maxwell Taylor and including Attorney General Robert Kennedy. Along with civil rights, poverty, and labor racketeering, counterinsurgency had captured the younger Kennedy's imagination. The Taylor group saw the special forces not only as a paramilitary unit capable of sabotage and counterterrorism but as a progressive political and social force that would assist local governments in winning the hearts and minds of indigenous peoples.

In the area of soft power, Kennedy proposed the Peace Corps. During a campaign rally at the University of Michigan in October 1960, the president asked ten thousand students if any of them would be willing to give two years of their lives working in Asia, Africa, or Latin America. Their enthusiastic response impressed him. Under its first director, Kennedy brother-in-law Sargent Shriver, the Peace Corps sent seven-thousand youthful volunteers to forty-four countries to teach English, train native peoples in the techniques of scientific farming and modern home economics, build hospitals, and combat disease. The stated objectives of the program were to provide a skill to an interested country, to teach other cultures about America, and to increase young Americans' understanding of other peoples. "The whole idea," declared one teenage volunteer, "was that you can make a difference . . . I really believed that I was going to be able to change the world." But for Kennedy, the Peace Corps was more than an exercise in altruism. He spoke of halting communist expansion by helping to develop the resources of the third world.

IN THE LATE 1950S, LBJ had made common cause with JFK and other Democratic aspirants for the presidency in attacking the Eisenhower administration's overreliance on atomic weaponry and its neglect of conventional forces. He respected hard-line balance-of-power proponents like Dean Acheson and Paul Nitze (Truman's secretary of state and chief policy planner, respectively, who were urging Kennedy to confront the communist superpowers directly) and Arthur Schlesinger and Walt Rostow who were urging the White House to emphasize democracy and social justice in third world areas as well as bases and alliances.[37]

Military preparedness and realistic diplomacy, LBJ believed, would contain communism within its existing bounds. To keep up morale among America's allies and satisfy hard-line anticommunists at home, the United States must hold fast in Berlin, oppose the admission of communist China to the United Nations, and continue to confront and blockade Cuba. He was aware of the growing split between the Soviet Union and communist China, and the possibilities inherent in it for dividing the communist world. The United States must continue its "flexible response" of military aid, economic assistance, and technical/political advice in response to the threat of communism in the developing world while nurturing its military alliances and maintaining its nuclear arsenal, but there was nothing wrong with negotiating with the Soviets at the same time in an effort to reduce tensions.

Insofar as Latin America was concerned, Johnson was an enthusiastic supporter of the Alliance for Progress; as a progressive Democrat he was drawn to the Schlesinger-Goodwin [presidential adviser Richard] philosophy of seeking openings to the democratic left. He did not buy into the concept of a monolithic communist threat. "Our real problem is not that governments go communist," as George Reedy put it, "but that they become part of the Soviet bloc. If Rumania, Hungary, Czechoslovakia and Bulgaria were genuine independent nations, we would regret the fact that they were communist but it would not be such great cause for concern." [38] Johnson was a cold warrior, but a flexible, pragmatic one.

The great difference between Kennedy and Johnson was that the Texan believed that idealism ought to be the driving force behind U.S. foreign policy, whereas the Kennedys saw social justice and democracy as tools with which to defeat Sino-Soviet imperialism. "To a considerable extent, our foreign policy has failed because it has been based on the assumption that we must do things simply to counter the Soviets," as George Reedy put it. "We have advertised to the whole world that we are willing to help India because we don't want India to go Communist. We have advertised to the world that we will help in the Middle East because we don't want Western Europe to lose the oil resources of Iraq, Iran and Saudi Arabia. This has, naturally, led to a great deal of skepticism among the uncommitted people." Instead, U.S. foreign policy ought to be based on the concept that "we do things because they are right." [39] America helps India because its people are starving, and it is incumbent upon the rich to help the poor. The United States offered aid to the nations of the Middle East because for generations they had labored under the yoke of foreign oppression and deserved help in their bid for economic and political independence.

As a number of historians have pointed out, the Kennedys were comfortable with elite politics, uncomfortable with mass politics. Jack and Bobby were of the elite and most adept at manipulating traditional elites, not unlike the tradition-bound U.S. foreign service. Johnson could manipulate legislative elites, but he was a firm believer in mass politics. The key to winning hearts and minds in the third world was to build personal, individual ties. Though a rural aristocrat of sorts, he was convinced, like that other great rural aristocrat, Franklin D. Roosevelt, that American leaders could and should articulate the needs and shoulder the burdens of the disadvantaged abroad as well as at home. "About all the average fellow wants is a chance to work from daylight to dark . . . to provide some food for the stomachs of his children, some clothes for their backs and a roof over their heads and a place for them to worship in, maybe a little recreation, and to maintain the freedom and dignity of the individual," LBJ declared in a speech to the Advertising Council in June 1961. "I believe all those people that I saw in Africa and Asia want the same thing and I think the average father and the average mother wants it, and I think they're going to get it." [40]

No sooner had LBJ returned from Africa than the president dispatched him on a goodwill tour of Asia to include stops in Laos, South Vietnam, Thailand, India, Pakistan, and the Philippines. By 1961 American policymakers, if not yet the American people, had become deeply concerned about the fate of Southeast Asia.

Throughout the 1950s, the Eisenhower administration had poured economic and military aid into Vietnam. Head of state Ngo Dinh Diem, a principled, patriotic man, briefly attempted land and constitutional reforms, but he proved unsuited to the task of building a social democracy. A devout Catholic and traditional mandarin by temperament and philosophy, he distrusted the masses and had contempt for the give-and-take of democratic politics. Increasingly, he relied on his family and loyal Catholics in the military and civil service to rule a country in which 90 percent of the population was Buddhist. His brother, Ngo Dinh Nhu, used the government-sponsored Can Lao Party, a thoroughly intimidated press, and the state police to persecute and suppress opponents of the regime.

As corruption increased and democracy all but disappeared, a rebellion broke out in the South against the Diem government. In 1960 Ho Chi Minh and the Democratic Republic of Vietnam decided to give formal aid to the newly formed National Liberation Front, the name assumed by the anti-Diemist revolutionaries.

A variety of factors prompted President Kennedy to view South Vietnam as the place where the leader of the free world would make his stand. He classified the conflict in South Vietnam as one of Khrushchev's wars of national liberation, a test of his administration's resolve just as much as Berlin or Cuba. Kennedy and his advisers fully accepted the domino theory. Following the administration's agreement in 1961 to the neutralization of Laos, a landlocked nation wracked by communist insurgency, Kennedy and his advisers believed that they had to hold the line in South Vietnam.

Experts in the State and Defense Departments and in the intelligence agencies were aware of the burgeoning Sino-Soviet split, but they believed that the communist superpowers would present a common front in any international crisis and that they were committed to promoting Marxism-Leninism in the developing world. In the fall of 1961, as the guerrilla war intensified, Assistant Secretary of State Walt Rostow and the president's military aide, General Maxwell Taylor, returned from a fact-finding trip to South Vietnam to recommend the dispatch of eight thousand combat troops. Kennedy decided against direct military intervention, but he ordered an increase in aid to Diem and the introduction of additional military advisers. The number of American uniformed personnel grew from several hundred when Kennedy assumed office to some sixteen thousand by 1963.

Johnson's 1961 Asia sojourn took him to several countries, including India. The focus, however, was Saigon and Diem's regime. Bribes and intimidation by civil servants and military officials had alienated peasant and urban dweller alike. Law 10/59, which the government pushed through the rubber-stamp national assembly, gave Ngo Dinh Nhu's police and special forces the power to arrest and execute South Vietnamese citizens for a wide variety of crimes, including black marketeering and spreading seditious rumors about the government. Nhu, Diem's brother and his minister of the interior, was a brilliant, erratic mandarin who catered to Diem's paranoia and elitism.

When JFK first suggested the Asian trip, LBJ was reluctant. He sensed the contempt in which he was held by State Department careerists, particularly foreign service officers serving abroad. "These State Department people think I'm going to go out there, and pat a little guy on the head and say, 'Little man, do this,' " he complained to a staffer. "They don't give me any credit for having any sense about how to treat people."[41] His fears were allayed somewhat when he learned that the president's sister, Jean, and her husband, Stephen Smith, were to go along. He rather liked the Kennedy women, and the presence of presidential kin would insulate him from the embassies' obsession with protocol. Nevertheless, when the party departed on May 5, aides noted that he seemed apprehensive and on edge. Over the Pacific he blew up at aide Horace Busby over some transgression and ordered him off the plane. "But we're over the Pacific," Busby protested. "I don't give a fucking damn!" Johnson replied.[42]

Upon landing in Saigon, the party made its way by motorcade from the airport to the presidential palace downtown. The vice president ordered the procession halted frequently so he could shake hands with some of the thousands who lined the route. He passed out pens, cigarette lighters, and gold and white passes to the U.S. Senate gallery. At the palace he made an arm-waving stump speech, calling Diem the "Winston Churchill of Asia."[43]

The next evening, following a dinner given by Diem for the vice president, the two men met privately for several hours. "Johnson decided to talk," journalist Sarah McClendon remembered. "[He] had one of those long line talks with Diem . . . Nobody could leave . . . and then they went into a room and decided that they would draft something . . . These diplomats still couldn't leave, and they didn't get away until one-thirty."[44]

As he had been instructed, Johnson praised Diem for his valiant struggle against the communist insurgency, but pressed him to undertake social, political, and fiscal reforms, especially to give his countrymen a greater say in the running of their country. Diem was friendly but remote when it came to specifics.[45] The South Vietnamese leader made it clear that he did not want American combat troops at that time, but did not rule out the possibility if the security situation deteriorated further.[46] "I don't know about this fellow, Diem," LBJ remarked to an aide at the time. "He was tickled as hell when I promised him forty million dollars and talked about military aid, but he turned deaf and dumb every time I talked about him speeding up and beefing up some health and welfare projects. I spent two hours and forty-five minutes with him; tried to get knee-to-knee and belly-to-belly so he wouldn't misunderstand me, but I don't know if I got to him."[47]

In Bangkok, where LBJ violated protocol by plunging into crowds and impolitely pressing the flesh, an early shot was fired in what would become Johnson's ongoing war against the press. He became irritated with the journalists accompanying him, so he called a press conference at 2:30 in the morning to "correct a misperception." Johnson then had George Reedy announce that there would be a tour of the Klongs, the famous water market in Bangkok. Journalist Carroll Kilpatrick remembered being awakened in the middle of the night and told that the event had been canceled. Then, at six in the morning, he was awakened again and informed, "You missed the trip because you didn't get there in time."[48]

Later, in Iran, when the corps skipped an afternoon village tour to file their stories, LBJ berated them: "What kind of bunch of goddamn pansies have I brought sixteen thousand miles only to have them sit around in air-conditioned rooms drinking whiskey while I am out meeting the people? No wonder we are not getting anything in the newspapers back home."[49]

Then, in Ankara, after visiting a bazaar, he flew into a rage because reporters and photographers were allegedly crowding him so much that he could not touch the people.[50] During his first press conference, he attempted to embarrass Carl Rowan, the black State Department information officer who was acting as his press secretary. Following the first probing questions, LBJ turned to Rowan and said loud enough for all to hear, "And you're the dummy who told me to submit myself to this?" As Rowan later put it, "Johnson wanted badly to be respected, even loved, by the press and couldn't understand that his personality was suited perfectly to rubbing the press the wrong way."[51]

Ambassador to India John Kenneth Galbraith and his wife, Catherine, flew to Bangkok to escort the Johnson party to New Delhi, the next stop on the trip. Before leaving to meet the vice president, Galbraith had written JFK, "Lyndon . . . arrives next week with two airplanes, a party of fifty, a communications unit, and other minor accoutrements of modern democracy. I . . . will try to make him feel good that he was on the ticket. His trip may not be decisive for the peace of Asia. The East, as you know, is inscrutable."[52]

After stopping in New Delhi, Johnson and company flew to Karachi, the capital of Pakistan. This stop echoed previous venues, with a few twists. On the trip into the heart of the city, LBJ jumped out of the car and jogged along shaking hands and distributing trinkets. When the motorcade approached an intersection, the vice president spied a shirtless camel driver with a particularly appealing face waiting to cross. Johnson halted the procession and jumped a muddy ditch to shake the man's hand and invite him to visit the United States. A cameraman and reporter for a Karachi daily captured the scene, and the next day Johnson and the camel driver, whose name was Ahmad Bashir, were featured on the front page. The vice president had invited the humble man to visit him in the United States and to stay at the Waldorf Astoria, the accompanying story declared. Johnson proceeded to hold his ceremonial conversation with President Ayub Khan, whom he took an immediate liking to, and then prepared to depart. By then, the invitation to Bashir had become front-page news across the globe.

State Department staff advised the vice president that his and his country's credibility was on the line. On his return, LBJ arranged for the Conference of Mayors to pay for a Bashir visit, but plans hit a snag when it was discovered that the Pakistani government had picked up Bashir and secluded him, fearing that this illiterate peasant would prove an embarrassment. LBJ appealed personally to Ayub Khan, and Bashir was released to make the trip.

Before proceeding to the ranch, the camel driver stopped in New York. Accompanied by a skilled interpreter, Bashir came off as a charming innocent. LBJ sent him back to India with a pickup truck donated by Ford Motor Company. All in all, the Bashir episode had proved something of a public relations coup for LBJ and America's crusade in the third world.[53]

PRESIDENT KENNEDY no doubt laughed with Ken Galbraith at LBJ's antics abroad. As his exclusion of Johnson from most diplomatic decision making indicated, he did not take the Texan seriously as a foreign policy analyst. But as his sponsorship of the Alliance for Progress, foreign aid in general, and the Peace Corps indicated, JFK did not believe that treaties, alliances, and power politics alone were going to win the cold war. Though he was no New Deal missionary like LBJ, Kennedy understood that America's demonstrated commitment to social justice was fundamental to winning hearts and minds in the third world. Hokily expressed though it might be, Johnson's sincerity was sure to make its mark.

Moreover, despite the skepticism of State Department officials and foreign service officers, LBJ had the confidence of Secretary of State Dean Rusk. "I want you to make sure that he sees the heads of state personally and alone," Rusk instructed one of the officers assigned to accompany the vice president. "There is no person in America that can equal Johnson in knee-to-knee conversation with another man."

LBJ's report to the president, submitted immediately after his return, argued that the free nations of Asia regarded the neutralization of Laos as nothing less than a sellout. American participation in this scheme had shaken confidence in the United States. There was no doubt, Johnson observed, that America must hold the line in Southeast Asia "or the United States, inevitably, must surrender the Pacific and take up our defenses on our own shores." Because getting troops and supplies into them would prove so very difficult, Laos and Cambodia were not the places to make a stand. The government of Thailand was so rigidly authoritarian that U.S. prestige would suffer by too close an association. The government of South Vietnam was problematical: "Diem is a complex figure beset by many problems. He has admirable qualities, but he is remote from the people, is surrounded by persons less admirable and capable than he." A decision to support Diem "must be made with the knowledge that at some point we may be faced with the further decision of whether we commit major United States forces . . . I recommend we proceed with a clear-cut and strong program of action."[54]

On Sunday, May 28, five days after delivering his report to President Kennedy, LBJ mounted the auditorium stage at Southwest Texas State to make the commencement address. He discarded his prepared text and for the next twenty minutes delivered a stem-winding, impassioned appeal to the assembled graduates to share the fruits of democracy, "to love freedom and liberty so much that you want everybody to have a little bit of it." All Americans had a "very special responsibility to your system—the system that produced you, the system that made it possible for you to have a trained mind and sound body . . . The three greatest friends that communism has are illiteracy, poverty and disease," Johnson declared. "And they're the three greatest enemies that our democratic system has."[55]

"Johnson was drinking a lot of Cutty Sark in those days, and the more he drank the meaner he got," remembered Carl Rowan. "He abused his staff verbally in ways that I could not believe. Yet, when sober or in one of his better moods, he spoke with greater eloquence and understanding about the economic and social needs of the poor nations, and about injustice in the United States, than any individual I ever knew in my life."[56]

JFK's determination to use Johnson as an instrument, if not a maker, of American foreign policy was demonstrated again in August 1961, when the president sent his understudy to Berlin in the midst of another of that beleaguered city's cold war crises. By the time JFK entered office, four thousand East Germans, most of them students, technocrats, and professionals drawn by the freedom and prosperity of West Berlin, had been crossing into the noncommunist sector of the city each week. The outflow not only gravely weakened East Germany but was a propaganda disaster for international communism. On Sunday, August 13, 1961, Soviet occupation authorities began construction on a barbed-wired and concrete wall that would eventually divide the city in two and serve as a symbol not only of the separation of East Germany from West but of a polarized world.

Three nights later, Lyndon was visiting Sam Rayburn in the speaker's apartment. Rayburn had been complaining of back pain for months and had steadily lost weight. His friends suspected he had cancer, but he insisted it was just a spell of "lumbago" and refused to see a specialist. While Lyndon was fussing at the speaker for not caring for himself properly, the phone rang. It was President Kennedy. "Lyndon," JFK said, "are you available to go to Berlin?" Kennedy asked him to come to a meeting the next day at the White House. The gathering included General Lucius D. Clay, commander in chief of U.S. forces in Europe and military governor of the American zone in Germany from 1947 to 1948, and former ambassador to the Soviet Union Charles "Chip" Bohlen. There was no discussion of an attempt to dismantle the wall by force, but all agreed that the West Berliners needed reassuring. That free city had become a symbol, *the* symbol, of America's commitment to Western Europe.

In addition to sending Lyndon to Berlin to reassure its anxious inhabitants, JFK and Clay decided to dispatch some fifteen hundred U.S. troops from West Germany to West Berlin. Privately, Johnson had some misgivings about the trip. There was a chance that the West Berliners would be angry, that the visit would be filled with recrimination, and that the affair would demonstrate cleavage rather than unity in the ranks of noncommunist Europe. He was also aware that JFK himself did not go because neither the West German government nor U.S. military authorities could guarantee his safety. Nevertheless, Johnson accepted the assignment, and threw himself into the task with his usual gusto.

On the transatlantic flight, Johnson stayed up all night reading briefing memos and preparing his speech. He was intensely aware of the importance of the occasion, and the possibility that if anything went wrong, full-scale war would result.

LBJ flew from Bonn to Templehoff Airport in West Berlin. He then rode to the city center in an open car, stopping frequently to shake hands with some of the one-hundred-thousand cheering Berliners who lined his route. At the Rats-haus, or City Hall, Johnson first addressed municipal officials and then emerged to make an open-air speech to the three hundred thousand who had gathered to hear him.

It was an inspiring effort—of the prepared speeches Johnson delivered in his life, one of the best. "I have come to Berlin by direction of President Kennedy," he declared. "To the survival and to the creative future of this city we Americans have pledged, in effect, what our ancestors pledged in forming the United States: 'our lives, our fortunes, and our sacred honor.' This island does not stand alone."[57] Wave after wave of thunderous applause and cheers swept over the vice president, who was visibly moved.

The next morning, LBJ and General Clay were at the Helmstedt entrance to the city to greet the fifteen hundred troops who had made the 105-mile over-land trip from West Germany. Papers across Europe and America headlined LBJ's mission and declared it to be one of the Kennedy administration's greatest successes. It was perhaps the closest LBJ would come to being identified with his charismatic boss, whose earlier trip to Berlin and "Ich bin ein Berliner" speech had already become part of diplomatic folklore.[58]

AMONG THOSE GREETING LBJ at the airport upon his return was Sam Rayburn. "I hadn't seen the Speaker in several weeks," Lady Bird remembered, "and my heart was in my throat at the way he looked."[59] Rayburn had been in and out of Bethesda Naval Hospital, but nothing seemed to work. Days later, he departed for Texas, never to return.

Shortly before Rayburn died in November 1961, LBJ visited him at the tiny hospital in Bonham. He helicoptered in, landing in the schoolyard across the street from the medical facility. "There were a number of people in Rayburn's room at that particular time," D. B. Hardeman remembered. "Vice President Johnson went over to the bed, and he took Rayburn's hand in his two hands, and he said, 'Hello, pardner.' A scene from his days as Dick Kleberg's secretary flashed across Johnson's mind. LBJ was in his room at the Dodge Hotel deliri-ous with pneumonia when he had awakened to find Rayburn asleep in the chair beside his bed, cigarette ashes spilled down the front of his suit coat."[60] Now, Lyndon leaned close and said again into his ear, "Hello, pardner." Rayburn showed no sign of recognition. "LBJ straightened up," Hardeman said, "and he had the most grief-stricken look on his face . . . I never saw [it] at any other time in his life. But he was a shattered man. He sort of turned on his heel and walked out, got on the helicopter, and went away." [61] That was the last time he saw the man from Flag Springs alive.

IN APRIL 1961, the Soviets put a man into orbit around the earth. It was years after *Sputnik,* yet America still lagged behind. Three weeks after Russian cosmonaut Yuri Gagarin's dramatic flight, U.S. astronaut Alan Shepard survived a suborbital flight, but the shortness of his trip—fifteen minutes—and a "sloppy splashdown" seemed to make the American effort a pale imitation of Gagarin's much longer flight.

On April 19, President Kennedy summoned LBJ to the White House and gave him his marching orders. "I would like for you as Chairman of the Space Council," the presidential directive read, "to be in charge of making an overall survey on where we stand in space . . . Do we have a chance of beating the Soviets by putting a laboratory into space, or by a trip around the moon, or by a rocket to land on the moon, or by a rocket to go to the moon and back with a man?" [62]

LBJ was ready. Before he left the Senate, he had arranged for his long-time intimate Senator Robert Kerr to be named to replace him as head of the Senate Space Committee. In the House, Texas Congressmen Overton Brooks and Olin Teague controlled the corresponding committee and Houstonian Albert Brooks headed Appropriation. Then, in February, LBJ succeeded in having Kerr's business partner and protégé, James Webb, chosen to direct NASA.

A North Carolinian by birth, Webb had served in the marine corps reserve and on the board of directors of Sperry Gyroscope before acting as Harry Truman's budget director. During the 1950s he had made his fortune with Kerr-McGee and landed a spot on the board of McDonnell Aviation. But Webb was more than just an engineer-businessman determined to make as much money out of technology as possible. Like LBJ, he was a visionary committed to public service. They embraced space as the new frontier where aeronautical technology would simultaneously advance the limits of knowledge, nourish the human spirit, and stimulate the national and global economies. "A Johnson or a Webb," historian Walter McDougall writes, "did not see a conflict between technocracy and freedom, between the expansionist state and the striving individual." [63] In the vastness of space, government and the individual could coexist as partners just as they had on the vastness of the American continent.

LBJ huddled with Webb and his congressional space team. He consulted with Secretary of Defense Robert McNamara and his staff as well as the country's leading rocket scientist, Werner Von Braun. All concluded, with some reservations, that the focus of the American space program should be a lunar landing. They were fully aware that such an effort would cost $30 to $40 billion over the next ten years. "If America was to win control over . . . men's minds through space accomplishments," Johnson advised Kennedy, the United States should embrace "manned exploration of the moon." His concluding sentence left Kennedy little wiggle room: "In the eyes of the world, first in space means first, period; second in space is second in everything." [64] Congress doubled NASA's budget in 1962 and again in 1963.

Talk of a missile gap began to subside when, on February 20, 1962, Lieutenant Colonel John H. Glenn flew around the earth three times in his Mercury space capsule, *Friendship 7,* and splashed down safely in the Caribbean. Suddenly, for the American people, all things seemed once again possible.

Perhaps more significant in the long run than the manned space flights was the launching on June 10 of Telstar, the experimental communications satellite developed by AT&T and Bell Laboratories. Soon it was relaying live television pictures from Andover, Maine, to France and Great Britain. A year later a secret military satellite released some 400 million tiny copper hairs into polar orbit, providing a cloud of reflective material for relaying radio signals from coast to coast within the United States.

To the surprise of no one, the site for the nation's new Manned Spacecraft Center was Houston. By the mid-1960s the Apollo moon shot complex looked like a giant crescent moon running around the littoral of the Gulf of Mexico from Texas to Florida. [65] As had happened so often in the past, a massive, federally funded project had been harnessed to the Johnson political wagon. Apollo was the newest and brightest jewel in the New South's diadem.

The U.S. space program benefitted immensely from LBJ's political sensitivity. The billions needed to explore and control the heavens was justified on military grounds alone, but advocates for the program should not leave it at that. Like others before him, Johnson compared the race for space with the competition among Britain, France, Spain, and Portugal to control the oceans of the globe in the fifteenth and sixteenth centuries. "The point is that the ability of people to move in outer space and the ability to deny outer space to others will determine which system of society and government dominates the future," he confided in a memo to JFK.

But military dominance as a rationale would not go over well with world opinion. Why not emphasize the many promising, enriching, constructive phases of space exploration: medicine, weather forecasting and control, communications? The United States should not only highlight these peaceful uses but offer to cooperate with the Soviets in advancing them. Thus could the United States have its cold war cake and eat it, too. [66]

PERHAPS JUST AS IMPORTANT as his role in the space program was Johnson's chairmanship of the President's Committee on Equal Employment Opportunity (CEEO). Its significance lay not in the concrete achievements of the committee, which were substantial, but in the dramatic rapprochement between LBJ and the black community that occurred as a result of it. John and Robert Kennedy, at least while he was acting as his brother's protector, could not really identify with the Second Reconstruction as a mass movement continually confronting the conscience of the nation. They were certainly not bigots themselves, but they were elitists. There was a certain amount of noblesse oblige in their commitment to civil rights, but they saw it primarily as historical inevitability.

Moreover, just as LBJ had when he was majority leader, the Kennedy brothers perceived it to be a problem to be managed. The Subcabinet Group on Civil Rights, chaired by Harris Wofford, was well aware that public opinion was running strongly against the civil rights movement in 1961. It was not a good time to challenge the Dixie Association in Congress.[67] President Kennedy chose instead to address the issue of employment opportunity through executive action. "I have dedicated my Administration to the cause of equal opportunity in employment by the government or its contractors," he announced in March. "I have no doubt that the vigorous enforcement of this order [creating the CEEO] will mean the end of such discrimination."[68]

LBJ was at first dubious about the assignment. "I don't have any budget, and I don't have any power, I don't have anything," he told JFK. The knowledge that Bobby, who had been named point man for the administration's civil rights effort, would be on the committee also gave Johnson pause. He suspected that he was being set up.[69] Whatever he and the committee did, they were bound to antagonize either northern liberals who felt he was not doing enough or southern segregationists who believed he was doing too much—or, more probably, both. He was aware that of all the Democratic party's civil rights initiatives since World War II, the Fair Employment Practices Commission had been most offensive to white southerners (and a number of white northerners as well), and the CEEO looked very much like a resurrected Fair Employment Practices Commission. But JFK insisted that Vice President Nixon had headed a similar body, and it would look very suspicious if Lyndon, a southerner, did not follow suit.[70]

There was no doubt that LBJ was committed to the goals of the CEEO: the elimination of racial discrimination in federal hiring and by contractors working for the federal government. Although blacks constituted 13 percent of federal employees, few held management positions. The Justice Department employed 955 lawyers, ten of whom were black.[71]

In one of its first actions, the CEEO surveyed companies under contract to the federal government and discovered that not a single African American was employed by twenty-five thousand of the thirty-five thousand contractors.[72] LBJ, who helped draft the executive order creating the committee, insisted that it require all firms doing business with the government to sign pledges that they did not and would not discriminate. He also wanted to empower the committee to cancel contracts with those that violated their pledges. At the same time, Johnson and George Reedy, the vice president's principal staffer on the committee, did not want the CEEO to turn into an enforcement agency, but a body seeking the voluntary cooperation of industry, labor, and civic leaders. The objective was nondiscrimination, not affirmative action.[73]

Unfortunately, the power to appoint staff was not solely in Johnson's hands. He shared that with the vice chair, Secretary of Labor Arthur Goldberg. The executive vice chair, the post that actually managed the mechanisms put in place by the committee, was Jerry Holleman, and his assistant was John G. Field, early Kennedy supporters with ties to the Texas and Michigan labor movements, respectively. They tended to be fairly hard-line, favoring a policy of mandatory rather than voluntary compliance.

No sooner was the committee organized and the staff up and going than Reedy was warning Johnson that Holleman and, to a lesser extent, Field were going to make an enforcer and thus a lightning rod of LBJ. As assistant secretary of labor, Holleman was Arthur Goldberg's man, not Johnson's. "He is not disloyal and is not an enemy," Reedy observed, but "even with the best of intentions, [he] will never comprehend your problems and your approach to them." If his philosophy prevailed, LBJ would "personally . . . have to become embroiled in every dispute concerning a Negro who felt that he had been discriminated against . . . You, personally, would have to become a cop with a nightstick running after hundreds of thousands of persons in arguments that you could never win."

Shortly after LBJ called a meeting of the hundred largest government contractors to outline the CEEO's plans and objectives, the committee received from the Georgia NAACP a list of complaints against the Lockheed Aircraft Company, headquartered at Marietta. Atlanta lawyer Robert Troutman was asked to investigate.[74] An energetic, charismatic self-promoter, Bobby Troutman had been a college chum of Joseph Kennedy Jr. and was a political intimate of Georgia Senator Herman Talmadge. He believed that voluntary desegregation was the key to prosperity and progress for the South.

Before Troutman met with Lockheed officials, he consulted Martin Luther King, George Meany, and Walter Reuther. Determined to avoid sanctions by the Department of Defense, Lockheed readily agreed to practice nondiscrimination in hiring and to promote existing Negro employees to higher-paying positions. With this feather in his cap, Troutman persuaded the CEEO to authorize him to undertake similar initiatives with other government contractors. The initiative was given the Soviet-style name Plans for Progress.[75] During 1962 Troutman persuaded some eighty-five corporations to sign voluntary pledges to end discrimination in hiring and to develop schemes for promoting black employees.[76]

Johnson was enthusiastic about the concept that underlay Plans for Progress but not about Bobby Troutman himself.

Through the NAACP and newspapers like the *Washington African-American,* the black community quickly began to express discontent with Plans for Progress. It was all happy talk, wrote Charles "Chuck" Stone, the aggressive editor of the *African American.* There were numerous plans but little or no real progress in hiring. "Under Robert Troutman," Stone wrote LBJ, "the emphasis had been on voluntary compliance with a total absence of compulsion. Perhaps Mr. Troutman's Georgia background has been the basic factor in deciding the pace of this program."[77] An investigator for the NAACP denounced Plans for Progress as nothing more than a "publicity stunt" and complained that Troutman was wasting money that should have gone into the compliance effort.[78] Privately, Johnson and Goldberg learned that the Georgian was promising companies who signed up that they would have "an easy out" and would not have to comply with the requirements of the president's executive order.[79]

A minor controversy soon ratcheted up to a potential scandal. John Wheeler, a black member of the CEEO, confided that the Sibley Law Firm of Atlanta, of which Troutman's father was a member, "is famous for infiltrating Negro causes and rendering them impotent by working from within." Noting the huge amounts of his own money Troutman was spending on Plans for Progress, Wheeler voiced the suspicion that the corporations involved had created a secret slush fund to finance his operation.[80]

Johnson would have forced Troutman out at once if it had not been for the objections of Bobby Kennedy.[81] Realizing that he was falling out of favor with the vice president, the secretary of labor, and the black community, Troutman attempted to insulate himself by splitting off the Plans for Progress program from the CEEO and giving it its own staff and budget. The new entity would report directly to the president. In Troutman's scheme, LBJ would have been stuck with an even less happy mandate. "It is not only somewhat of an insult to you but would leave you with a Committee doing absolutely nothing but chasing down a bunch of nit-picking cases," Reedy told his boss.[82]

Both sides resorted to attempted blackmail. "Abe [Fortas, whom LBJ had inserted into the dispute to draft a satisfactory restructuring document] says that Troutman is carrying around with him figures on negroes employed by the government and negroes employed in private industry and they show that private industry is doing better than the government," Reedy reported to Johnson. "Abe says the figures are 'pure dynamite' and Troutman implies that if he does not get pretty much what he wants the figures will be released. Troutman has the habit of flourishing them like a street peddler selling dirty pictures in Paris," Reedy added.[83]

But Troutman just as quickly lost the initiative when, after LBJ tried to force him to accept a black as chief of staff for Plans for Progress, the Georgian incautiously remarked to George Reedy that he could never get corporation presidents to talk to him in front of an African American. "If the word should circulate among negroes that a personal friend of the President has such an attitude," Reedy told Johnson, "the effects upon the 1962 and 1964 elections would be most interesting."[84]

In the end, Johnson was not able to get rid of Troutman, but succeeded in having Plans for Progress reorganized so that its director reported directly to him. It also became subject to an advisory board created by the president. The members of that body, as it turned out, were mostly black.[85] Finally, in late 1962, LBJ managed to secure the resignations of both Robert Troutman and Jerry Holleman. To head up the CEEO, including Plans for Progress, he selected a Texas-born black lawyer from Detroit, Hobart Taylor Jr.[86]

DESPITE ALL THE TURMOIL, by mid-1962 the CEEO had made some progress. Johnson personally badgered department and agency heads, and as a result, blacks in top government jobs increased 35 percent. In midlevel government positions the increase was 20 percent. Of the 1,610 complaints of discrimination from those seeking federal jobs, 72 percent had been resolved in favor of the complainants. Of the 2,156 in the private sector, the rate was 40 percent.[87]

Just as important were steps the CEEO took to end discrimination in labor unions. In most trades, workers could gain the necessary skills only by going through the union's apprenticeship training program. Because skilled crafts were generally handed down from father to son, and unions looked for ways to limit the number of skilled workers to keep wages up, blacks were almost never to be found in apprenticeship programs. "In this whole field of civil rights, the really crying scandal and shame is one that is mentioned the least," Reedy told Johnson, "the tremendous difficulties placed in the way of a Negro becoming a carpenter, an electrician, a plumber, or a railroad fireman." It was almost easier for blacks to become doctors or lawyers.[88] LBJ used Walter Reuther, an authentic liberal on civil rights, to apply pressure to the more conservative George Meany.[89] As a result, 118 international and 338 directly affiliated local unions of the AFL-CIO signed "Plans for Fair Practices," which committed them to abolishing segregated locals and segregated apprenticeship programs.[90]

The more progress the CEEO made, the more critical of it and its chair Bobby Kennedy became. All the while he had been pressuring LBJ not to fire Troutman, the attorney general was denouncing Plans for Progress in meetings with his staff and the president. "There was an awful lot of propaganda put out," he later recalled, "but when we started making an analysis, we found it really hadn't accomplished a great deal." The problem was Lyndon Johnson. "The CEEO," Bobby declared, "could have been an effective organization . . . if the vice president gave it some direction." When told of the CEEO's lack of progress, the president allegedly "almost had a fit." "That man can't run this committee," Bobby quoted him as saying. "Can you think of anything more deplorable than him trying to run the United States? That's why he can't ever be President of the United States."[91]

In committee meetings, RFK began openly confronting Johnson, criticizing and ridiculing him in front of the other members. He delivered a brutal dressing down to Johnson protégé James Webb for NASA's lack of progress in employing blacks.[92] One administration official remembered Bobby treating Lyndon "in a most vicious manner. He'd ridicule him, imply he was insincere."[93] Lyndon reported one of these encounters to a friend: "Bobby came in the other day to our Equal Employment Committee and I was humiliated. He took on Hobart and said about Birmingham, said the federal employees weren't employing them down there, and he just gave him hell." [94]

The real story of Lyndon Johnson and the CEEO, however, was the changed relationship between the vice president and the black community. When LBJ took the oath of office as vice president, he was regarded by most black leaders and opinion makers as, at best, a simple opportunist and, at worst, a power broker for white segregationists. Of Kennedy's choice for second place on the ticket, James Farmer, bloodied veteran of the 1961 freedom rides, had said, "Frankly, I considered it most unfortunate, probably a disaster, because of his Southern background and his voting record on civil rights." [95] Farmer was not alone. "If my sampling of opinion in my rather extensive travels about the country has any validity at all," Roy Wilkins, executive director of the NAACP, wrote an acquaintance in 1960, "most Negro citizens feel that . . . his background and identification with the most backward regions of the South bar him from consideration." [96]

By 1963, however, the opinion of many members of the black elite had changed dramatically. "One of the reasons I think I was sold on him," said black journalist-politician Louis Martin, "[was that] he talked so much like Roosevelt about the problems of poverty and the problems that faced us . . . The question of whether he was a liberal or conservative faded into the background in the light of his seemingly real passion of [sic] these things that I was obsessed with." [97] In the same letter in which he wrote LBJ denouncing Robert Troutman and Plans for Progress, Chuck Stone had exclaimed, "Liberals we don't need any more of. What we need are people of your intellectual and political ilk, of your almost psychogenetic restlessness for concrete achievement, of your concern for the real economic breakthroughs for Negroes." [98] Late in 1962, Whitney Young, head of the Urban League, confided to George Reedy that he had met "an increasing number of Negroes who wish that the Vice President were the President." [99] "I learned from the Los Angeles Director of CORE," Hobart Taylor reported to LBJ in the summer of 1963, "that Jim Farmer, in a private meeting made a statement that you understood the problem better than any white man in America, and that he was ready to support you for anything that you might want." [100]

For their part, Johnson and Reedy, pragmatists though they were, came to understand the civil rights movement as a moral and even a spiritual phenomenon. "It is obvious that this country is undergoing one of its most serious internal clashes since the Civil War itself," Reedy observed to Johnson in 1963. "The basic difference between the present situation and those in the past is that the Negroes are NOT fighting for limited objectives. In the past, the demonstrations involved swimming pools, or schools, or libraries, or city employment, or public parks. Today, they involve all of those things and something more—what the Negroes call 'freedom' but what actually means full status, full privileges, full dignity as an American citizen." [101]

In previous years, LBJ had insisted that state poll taxes could be done away with only through constitutional amendments. In 1962, he crusaded in behalf of repeal in Texas through a simple majority vote. "I appeal to you in the name of Texas, America and in fairness, decency and equality to go to the polls Nov. 9 and repeal this shame of Texas, this poll tax," he declared to a cheering audience in Beaumont.[102] In January 1963, in a speech at Wayne State University in Detroit, he exclaimed, "To strike the chains of a slave is noble. To leave him the captive of the color of his skin is hypocrisy."[103] Later, in a commencement address at Tufts University, he insisted that the United States could not long remain divided. "If we cannot permit each man and woman to find the rightful place in a free society to which they are entitled by merit, we cannot preserve a free society itself."[104]

But typically, LBJ refused to abandon the white people of the South, to see America's racial problems in the mid-twentieth century as merely an unresolved issue left over from the Civil War: "The settlement will be one that will try the souls and hearts of all men of all races and religions—North, South, East, and West. This is not a sectional problem because our society is unequal in every section. No part of our country is so without sin that it can cast the first stone . . . And somehow we must maintain our compassion . . . If we lose our compassion, we will merely substitute one injustice for another—and our agony will be in vain."[105]

"I do not think," Reedy told Johnson, "that you are regarded any more, even among extreme Liberals, as a tobacco-chewing Southerner roasting Negroes for breakfast. In fact, I think you may well turn out to be the dominant person in holding the minority vote."[106]

CHAPTER 19

HANGING ON

THROUGHOUT LATE 1961 AND 1962, THE LOVE AFFAIR between Jack Kennedy and the media flourished; out of the liaison came the myth of Camelot. JFK was the young, idealistic king, self-deprecating, brave, inspiring. He was surrounded by the best and the brightest, charismatic intellectuals and dedicated public servants committed to their leader and his cause, all the while sharing his zeal for the good life. Following a state dinner at the White House in October 1961, actors performed scenes from several Shakespearean plays. Not since Lincoln, Jefferson, and Adams had a president publicly embraced the Bard, applauded the *New York Times*. For the first time since 1904, when he appeared before Theodore Roosevelt, Pablo Casals performed for an American president and his guests. Ballets, poetry readings, string quartets followed in profusion, and the press swooned.[1]

Meanwhile, "Whatever happened to Lyndon Johnson?" stories began to pop up in papers from coast to coast.[2] When the popular television program *Candid Camera* asked unsuspecting interviewees who Lyndon Johnson was, they guessed a baseball player, an astronaut, anything but vice president of the United States.[3]

The White House staff fairly dripped with contempt for LBJ. Despite JFK's directive to kiss the vice presidential behind from one end of Pennsylvania Avenue to the other, Kenny O'Donnell "wouldn't give him the time of day," recalled another presidential aide. He deliberately failed to notify the vice president's office of cabinet and National Security Council meetings until the last minute, if at all.[4]

In mid-1962, at LBJ's direction, George Reedy took stock of the Johnson vice presidency. Things were not going well, the rotund house intellectual reported. The reasons were clear: "We lack goals; We haven't set our sights sufficiently high; We haven't organized ourselves properly to take advantage of the opportunities that are open to us."[5] The achievements of the CEEO were significant but obviously not sufficient. The space program was flourishing, but no one seemed to be willing to give LBJ credit for the vital role he was playing in it. Indeed, Johnson later recalled an incident that occurred just after Alan Shepard's successful sojourn in suborbital space. He, JFK, Shepard, and FCC head Newton Minnow were riding together to a meeting of the National Convention of Broadcasters. "You know, Lyndon," said Kennedy, poking him in the ribs, "nobody knows that the Vice President is the Chairman of the Space Council. But if that flight had been a flop, I guarantee you that everybody would have known that you were the Chairman."[6] Writing from Austin, Horace Busby argued that a conspiracy was afoot: "Today your activities are largely lost on the public because, in my judgment, both the Palace Guard and the jealous wing of the Senate are as fearful now as a year ago of your potential."[7]

Johnson was convinced that all could be made right if only he could establish a good relationship with Bobby. One night in 1962, after a social event at the White House, LBJ approached his nemesis. "Bobby," he said, "you do not like me. Your brother likes me. Your sister-in-law likes me. Your daddy likes me but you don't like me. Now, why?" The younger Kennedy would not answer directly, of course, but he had no intention of being reconciled. When LBJ denied that he had attacked Joe Sr. and cast aspersions on Jack's health at the 1960 convention, Bobby refused to believe him. Later he complained that Johnson "lies all the time . . . In every conversation I have with him, he lies . . . He lies even when he doesn't have to."[8]

LBJ would reach out again during the course of his public life, but the result would always be the same. Arthur Schlesinger Jr. argued that the barrier between the two men was cultural. Bobby was a reserved New Englander; LBJ was an expansive Texan who could not converse with another human being without touching him or her in some fashion. Bobby was cold-blooded, ironic; LBJ impulsive and overly earnest.[9]

But there was far more to it than that. Bobby was a unique combination of Irish clan chieftain, Catholic social worker, and prosecuting attorney. For him, things were black and white. He was intensely loyal to those he trusted and relentlessly antagonistic toward those he did not. "You have to admit, you have to face the fact that with all his generous heartedness and largeness, Bobby was just an awful hater," Joe Alsop later observed during an interview.[10] RFK refused to observe the dictum that in democratic politics one has no permanent enemies, that a person who opposes you one day may be your ally the next. Incredibly, during a 1962 trip to Indonesia, Bobby apologized for the Mexican War of 1848, implying that it was nothing more or less than an imperial escapade fomented by Texans and their American sympathizers.[11]

At a luncheon in New York a month before JFK was assassinated, LBJ shocked his listeners by making a striking comparison. Asked his views on the situation in South Vietnam, LBJ replied that actually Saigon and Washington were quite similar. Both places had chief executives in trouble because of the activities of "very strong" brothers, Bobby Kennedy and Ngo Dinh Nhu.[12]

For the most part, however, Johnson tried hard to get along. An inveterate leaker to the press as majority leader and subsequently as president, Johnson steadfastly refused to undercut either JFK or his policies. His feud was with Bobby, and it was competitive. "The Washington press corps is convinced that there is a well organized move afoot to groom Bobby Kennedy for the Presidency in 1968 and to shove you aside," George Reedy reported to him in January 1963.[13]

The stress of suppressing his combative instincts and remaining loyal to those who showed him nothing but contempt began to take its toll on Johnson. Periods of frenetic activity were punctuated with long spells of depression. "I was out at his house, The Elms . . . swimming one afternoon with him and with Abe Fortas," Harry McPherson recalled. "And he looked absolutely gross. His belly was enormous and his face looked bad, flushed, maybe he had been drinking a good deal. But he looked like a man who was not trimmed down for anything. His life was not causing him to come together physically, morally, intellectually, any way."[14] "I detested every minute of it," Johnson later told an interviewer.[15]

AT LEAST LYNDON AND LADY BIRD had plenty of time to expand their business empire. Lady Bird employed real estate agents to add to the thirty-eight hundred acres in Alabama she had inherited from her Aunt Effie and Uncle Claude. With the help of his business partner, A. W. Moursund, LBJ acquired three additional ranches adjacent to the original 438-acre spread purchased from Aunt Frank Martin. First was the eighteen-hundred acre Scharnhorst place, which included some of the best deer hunting land in Texas. Indeed, the inside of the red-painted frame ranch house that went with the property was festooned with the heads of deer killed by Lady Bird and Lynda. The vice president next paid $65 an acre for the Lewis farm. It comprised eight hundred acres and featured a fieldstone house that Lady Bird remodeled. The jewel in the Johnson empire, however, was the Haywood Ranch, a forty-eight-hundred acre spread acquired from Texas Christian University for $500,000. LBJ and Judge Moursund subsequently sold 242 acres of the Haywood place to the Comanche Cattle Corporation for $326,660. The owners of the Comanche Cattle Company were none other than Johnson and Moursund. Most of the land fronted Lake Granite Shoals, subsequently renamed Lake LBJ, and was divided up into some one hundred "ranchettes," which the partners sold.

Johnson, suddenly taken with water sports, built a boathouse on Granite Shoals near Lake LBJ to house his recently purchased speedboat and ninety-foot cabin cruiser. These acquisitions were made possible by profits from the Johnson broadcasting empire, which by 1961 amounted to more than half a million dollars annually.[16]

• • •

WHILE LBJ and the New Frontier languished, communist revolution and Soviet aggression were threatening America on its very doorstep. In Cuba, Fidel Castro's revolution had turned sharply leftward, and the Kennedy administration became involved in various schemes to overthrow it. LBJ had no influence on the Bay of Pigs fiasco, and only a modest consulting role in the Cuban Missile Crisis. Yet his views on the latter were revealing.

The Soviets began a massive arms buildup in Cuba during the summer of 1962, triggered by not only the Bay of Pigs invasion but also Operation Mongoose, a CIA covert operation designed to either oust Castro or assassinate him. The twenty-four medium-range (one thousand miles) and eighteen intermediate-range (two thousand miles) missiles gave the Soviet Union and its ally more than a defensive capability in the Western Hemisphere. Most likely, Khrushchev's gamble was the result of pressure from his generals, who were alarmed at the massive expansion of America's nuclear arsenal. The communists tried to keep construction of the missile sites secret, repeatedly lying to JFK.

Tipped off either by the CIA or Cuban exiles as to the existence of the missile sites, GOP congressional leaders demanded an investigation. U-2 spy plane photos taken on October 14 revealed the alarming truth. American intelligence indicated that if the sites were completed and armed, the Soviets and/or Cubans would be able to rain nuclear destruction down on as many as eighty U.S. cities.

Huddling with his advisers on an almost continuous basis throughout the next two weeks, Kennedy considered a variety of options, ranging from an immediate air strike and invasion to acquiescence in the buildup. Gradually, the White House settled on a naval blockade, or quarantine, of Cuba to prevent the arrival of additional missiles and warheads. U.S. diplomats would then demand the removal of existing weapons; if the communists refused, the military would invade and dismantle the sites forcibly.

On the evening of October 22, the president revealed the existence of the bases to the American people, denouncing their construction as "a clandestine, reckless, and provocative threat to world peace."[17] He announced the blockade, demanded the removal of the missile bases, and made it clear that if warheads were launched from Cuba, the United States would retaliate against the Soviet Union.

For the next six days, the world teetered on the brink of Armageddon. Castro mobilized his armed forces, the United States began assembling an invasion force of a quarter of a million men, and Soviet missile transports headed toward the gauntlet of ships set up by the U.S. Navy around Cuba. On Wednesday, October 24, the Soviet ships cut their engines and waited. Over the next seventy-two hours, the White House and the Kremlin exchanged a flurry of communications.

LBJ was an ex officio member of the National Security Council and participated in the meetings of "ExComm," its executive committee. He was with the president on October 16, when knowledge of the Soviet deployment first circulated among top officials. From October 17 through October 20, he was out of Washington campaigning in the West, but he returned for all of the crucial meetings during the week of October 21 to 28.[18]

Johnson sided with the hawks: "I would like to hear what the responsible commanders have to say. I think the question with the base is whether we take it out or whether we talk about it, and both alternatives are very distressing. But of the two, I would take it out."[19] On the crucial question of consulting Congress, LBJ was negative. "I realize it's a breach of faith," he said with regret, "but we're not going to get much help out of them."[20] For a brief period, ExComm considered offering to get out of Berlin if the Soviets would evacuate Cuba. Johnson was dead set against it. "I guess what he [Khrushchev] is really saying: 'I'm going to dismantle the foreign policy of the United States for the last 15 years in order to let you get these missiles out of Cuba.' Then we say: 'We're glad, and we appreciate it and we want to discuss it with you.' "[21]

On October 26, the Kremlin made two separate and distinct proposals to Kennedy. The first offered to remove Soviet missiles from Cuba in return for an American pledge never to invade the Ever Faithful Isle. The second, seemingly drafted by hard-liners in the defense and foreign ministries, suggested a trade-off. Russian missiles in Cuba for U.S. Jupiter missiles stationed in Turkey. Johnson argued strongly for accepting the second proposal. Although it was not generally known, the United States was already planning to replace the land-based Jupiters with submarine-based Polaris missiles.[22]

JFK agreed with the vice president. "We can't very well invade Cuba," he observed, "when we could have gotten them out by making a deal on the same missiles in Turkey. If that's part of the record, I don't see how we'll have a good war."[23]

But Kennedy refused to make an explicit deal, missiles for missiles. The crisis was resolved when JFK accepted the Kremlin's first offer and simply ignored the second—publicly at least. Privately, Robert Kennedy assured Soviet Ambassador Anatoly Dobrynin that after the Soviets pulled their missiles out of Cuba, the Jupiters would simply disappear; the president could not, however, link the two explicitly as a quid pro quo.[24]

The Kennedy administration, including LBJ, saw the Cuban Missile Crisis as a major cold war victory for the United States. The communist initiative in the Western Hemisphere had been blunted, Johnson told Joe Alsop. It should be clear to the American republics flirting with Marxism-Leninism that the Soviet Union would use little more than rhetoric in defending them.[25]

DURING HIS TENURE as vice president, LBJ added two more attractive young women to his staff, Vicky McCammon and Marie Fehmer. They continued a tradition. According to Juanita Roberts, the former WAC colonel who would hold the title of personal secretary to the president after Johnson succeeded to the presidency, there were always two secretarial staffs: the group that stayed on the ground and staffed the phones and the coterie that flew with LBJ when he was on his travels.[26]

First among the flight crew was Mary Margaret Wiley, the vivacious, attractive blonde who had gone to work for the Johnsons in 1951. She was widely rumored to have had an affair with LBJ and continued to enjoy a close relationship with him even after she married Houston advertising executive Jack Valenti in 1962.[27] Vicky McCammon, a striking coed from San Angelo, made friends with Susan Taylor, Lady Bird's niece, while both were attending George Washington University in Washington. McCammon caught Johnson's eye when Susan began inviting her to parties at The Elms. A political science major, she intrigued Johnson with her knowledge and self-confidence during an informal discussion of the dynamics of the Bay of Pigs fiasco. "And when I would be in Austin and he would come down to the ranch," she recalled, "he would call and he would talk and talk and talk. [He would] want to know how my courses were going and what I was studying and this and that . . . I think I was so young that it was almost like a teacher-student kind of thing."[28]

In the summer of 1962, LBJ hired Marie Fehmer, a slender brunette from Dallas, to replace Wiley, who would marry in June. She had just graduated from Texas with a degree in journalism and was planning to go to graduate school. The Johnsons had learned of Fehmer from the brother of journalist William S. White, for whom the young woman had done some work. In typical fashion, Lyndon summoned her to the offices of KTBC for an extended interview, including a hamburger lunch and a wide-ranging discussion that covered everything from typing speed to religion to politics. She went to work that afternoon and remained on the job until Lyndon Johnson's last day in the White House.

The vice president, fifty-four years old and unhappy, quickly fell in love with Fehmer. She went everywhere with Johnson and soon became accustomed to summonses at any and all hours. "I protested one time at the ranch," she recalled, "where a speaker phone went through the house and he would wake up about 8:00 in the morning and he would yell over the speaker phone, Marie do you want to go swimming? Well, no, I am in bed but I go, and we go swimming."[29]

One of the reasons Johnson found Marie so fascinating was that though she was obviously taken with him and his attentions, she refused to sleep with him. It provoked his curiosity. He believed that any meaningful relationship between a man and woman ought to end in sex. One day, when they were floating in the pool, he asked why she resisted him. I'm a Catholic, it's against my religion, she replied. Charmed, he had her explain at length. Lady Bird sensed the growing depth of the relationship and kept a close eye on the newcomer. In November 1962, Johnson made an astounding proposal to Marie. If she would agree to have his son, he would set her up in an apartment in New York. Fehmer refused, but their relationship only seemed to deepen.[30]

Some on LBJ's staff believed that Lady Bird not only knew about her husband's affairs, but condoned them. Fehmer remembered a trip to California with Mrs. Johnson shortly after she was hired. LBJ and Mary Margaret Wiley were already there, and when Lady Bird and Marie arrived, a woman's underwear was strewn all over the hotel room. Instead of being angry, Lady Bird seemed to go out of her way to be nice to Mary Margaret.[31]

Horace Busby recalled one weekend while LBJ was vice president. Johnson invited former congresswoman Helen Douglas to spend the weekend with him. Lady Bird conveniently arranged to leave on a shopping trip to New York shortly before Helen arrived. Busby recalled that Johnson and Douglas lounged around the pool holding hands and showing obvious affection for each other.[32]

VIETNAM WAS ONE of the issues that would define Johnson's presidency, but as vice president, he could do little but observe the White House's and State Department's maneuverings. One, in particular, was fateful. In August 1963, a group of South Vietnamese generals headed by Major General Tran Van Don, commander of the Army of the Republic of Vietnam, and Major General Nguyen Khanh opened secret talks with CIA and U.S. Embassy personnel concerning a possible coup against Diem and Nhu. What ensued was a deep split within the Kennedy foreign policy establishment. Roger Hilsman, the State Department's director of intelligence, Michael Forrestal, an aide to NSC Director McGeorge Bundy, and Undersecretary of State Averell Harriman were committed to a coup; Secretary of State Dean Rusk, Secretary of Defense Robert McNamara, CIA Director John McCone, and chair of the Joint Chiefs Maxwell Taylor were opposed to a forced regime change. From August 28 to September 2, the NSC met on almost a daily basis.

On August 26, Kennedy reluctantly approved a cable authorizing the agents in contact with the South Vietnamese generals to give them the go-ahead. Although Johnson had hitherto not been consulted, he was suddenly brought into the loop on August 28. McGeorge Bundy told Samuel Gammons, the State Department officer detailed to brief the vice president during the crisis, that there were some things JFK did not want Johnson to see but others were all right. Johnson was furious at having been excluded. "They don't pay any attention to my opinion (i.e. JFK)," he told Gammons "I went to SVN [South Vietnam] two years ago and they ignored my ideas; General Taylor a year later brought the same ones back and they carried them out!"[33]

When asked at an NSC meeting how he felt about the United States encouraging a coup, Johnson expressed his opposition. "Quit playing cops and robbers . . . put down your cap pistols," he said. On Sunday, September 1, 1963, Mike Forrestal came out to The Elms and briefed LBJ further on the coup plottings. Forrestal, who was up to his ears in the coup machinations, attempted to place all of the blame on Hilsman and Harriman.[34] Johnson seemed resigned. Two months later, the generals pulled off their coup. After being captured hiding in a Catholic church, Diem and Nhu were shot to death. LBJ would continue to believe that getting rid of Diem was a crucial mistake.

• • •

IT WAS THE OTHER MAJOR ISSUE of the Kennedy administration, civil rights, that drew Johnson into his most active role as vice president. By the end of 1962, Martin Luther King of the SCLC, James Forman of SNCC, and James Farmer of CORE had come to the conclusion that the Kennedy administration needed to be pressured. The president had expressed concern while avoiding action in deference to southern Democrats. Eight years after the *Brown* decision, in 1962, two thousand southern school districts remained strictly segregated; only 8 percent of black children in the South attended school with whites. At that rate, it would take fifty years for blacks to gain access to public facilities and a hundred years to achieve equality in job training and employment.

Adding to King's sense of urgency was his vulnerability to attack by Malcom X, leader of the Nation of Islam, and other black nationalists who charged that the SCLC's approach was too soft and gradualist. Malcolm ridiculed nonviolence and rejected the virtues of integration. Confrontation in all of its forms, militant self-defense, and black chauvinism were necessary to preserve both the physical and psychological well-being of African Americans, he argued. If King and his colleagues did not compel white America, including Jack and Bobby Kennedy, to act instead of talk, they would lose control of the movement to the radicals.

The staging ground that King and his advisers selected for the next act in the civil rights drama was Birmingham, Alabama, the most pervasively and rigidly segregated big city in America. Municipal authorities had closed down parks and other public facilities rather than integrate them. Fewer than ten thousand of the city's eighty thousand registered voters were black, although African Americans constituted 40 percent of the population. Between 1957 and 1967 Birmingham—local blacks nicknamed it "Bombingham" and their neighborhood "Dynamite Hill"—would be the scene of eighteen racial bombings and fifty cross burnings, all of which had been tacitly or expressly condoned by city authorities, including Police Commissioner Eugene T. "Bull" Connor. Stout, jowly, bigoted, Connor had devoted himself to "keeping the niggers in their place."[35] King believed that an assault on segregation in Birmingham would reveal southern "brutality openly—in the light of day—with the rest of the world looking on."[36]

King and his staff arrived in Birmingham in early April and immediately put into operation their secret Plan C—"C" for confrontation. They issued a public call for an immediate end to discriminatory employment practices and segregation of public facilities. In the days that followed, small groups of mainly black protesters staged lunch counter sit-ins and marched on city hall. During one of these protests, King was arrested and imprisoned. While incarcerated, he penned his famous "Letter from the Birmingham Jail." Written on a newspaper smuggled in to him, the nineteen-page missive was subsequently reprinted in scores of newspapers across the nation. The letter was an eloquent defense of civil disobedience; it argued persuasively that the protesters rather than the forces of law and order in Birmingham represented the Judeo-Christian ethic and the spirit as well as the letter of the Constitution. Hitler's laws were legal but manifestly unjust. It was profoundly immoral to continue to acquiesce in the oppression of black Americans.

Out of jail, King embarked on the greatest gamble of his career. On May 2, one thousand black children, some as young as six, set out from the Sixteenth Street Baptist Church in Birmingham headed for City Hall. Connor arrested them. When another thousand gathered in the church for a second march, he attempted to seal the building exits. As some escaped, he loosed police dogs and turned fire hoses on the children. Panicked black parents hurled rocks and bricks at the police, who in turn assaulted everyone in their path. A national television audience was horrified by the water hoses, which spewed streams strong enough to take bark off trees, by the snarling German shepherds, and by the truncheon-wielding police.

Time magazine painted a vivid picture: "There was the Negro youth, sprawled on his back and spinning across the pavement, while firemen battered him with streams of water . . . There was the Negro woman, pinned to the ground by cops, one of them with his knee dug into her throat . . . The blaze of bombs, the flash of blades, the eerie glow of fire, the keening cries of hatred, the wild dance of terror in the night—all this was Birmingham, Ala." [37]

The demonstrations continued throughout the first week in May, peaking on the seventh. With their city portrayed daily as a hotbed of racial violence, fearing even wider bloodshed, and under pressure from federal authorities, the Senior Citizens' Committee, a group of whites secretly selected by the Chamber of Commerce to negotiate with the black protesters, came to terms with King and his cohorts. The SCLC won its demand for desegregation of lunch counters and other public facilities and for "the upgrading and hiring of Negroes on a non-discriminatory basis," albeit in planned stages.

Birmingham galvanized even the poorest and most disorganized southern blacks, swelling the ranks of the SCLC, CORE, SNCC, and the NAACP. If Birmingham could be forced to accept integration, so could every other community in America. The descendents of those freed by the Civil War agreed with King, who, in his Birmingham Jail manifesto, had equated "wait" with "never." The major civil rights organizations became more militant, competing with each other in sponsoring protests, demonstrations, sit-ins, and law suits.

The Kennedys sympathized with the cause. The Civil Rights Division in the Justice Department under John Doar and John Siegenthaler filed forty-two lawsuits in behalf of black voting rights and helped push through Congress the Twenty-fourth Amendment to the Constitution outlawing the poll tax. The administration appointed a number of blacks to high-level government positions, including NAACP lawyer Thurgood Marshall to the New York Circuit Court of Appeals. Following the bloody freedom rides of 1961, the White House pressured the Interstate Commerce Commission to outlaw segregation in interstate bus terminals. [38]

Yet civil rights leaders criticized the White House for not introducing legislation outlawing discrimination in hiring, public accommodations, and all modes of interstate transportation. For all of the attorney general's bullying of the CEEO and his hard-nosed rhetoric, it all seemed for him a matter of political expediency. He saw civil rights as a problem to be managed in a manner that would ensure his brother's reelection in 1964.[39]

But then, in the wake of Birmingham, Jack and Bobby decided that justice and expediency had at last coincided, and the attorney general's office drafted an omnibus civil rights bill. But how could the administration get it through Congress? The Dixie Association seemed stronger than ever, and Republicans were more than willing to play both sides of the street to keep the Democrats divided. The administration had not even been able to get through Congress a literacy bill guaranteeing voter registration for anyone with a sixth-grade education. As RFK biographer James Hilty observed, "Throughout their careers, the Kennedys, and Robert in particular, had lacked a feel for coalitional politics and a willingness to bargain and compromise. It was highly improbable, then, at such a late date in their development (the summer of 1963), that either Kennedy would suddenly gain an appreciation for such skills."[40] Reluctantly Jack ordered Bobby and White House speech writer Theodore Sorensen to consult the vice president.

As THE CONGRESSIONAL DEADLOCK CONTINUED through 1962 and 1963, Johnson had looked on helplessly from his seat as presiding officer in the Senate. Larry O'Brien, Kennedy's congressional liaison, was "out of his element," Bobby Baker observed. Not once in two years had O'Brien ever stopped by his office, LBJ complained to Harry McPherson.[41]

Consequently, when RFK and Sorenson called, Johnson was both gratified and contemptuous. He peppered the attorney general with suggestions and concluded, "Well, Bob, I think you've still got a lot of homework to do." Juanita Roberts, who listened in on the conversation, recalled that the attorney general's resentment was almost palpable. With Sorenson, Johnson was even more pointed. "Now, I want to make it clear," he told Jack's chief speechwriter and adviser, "I'm as strong for this program as you are, my friend. But you want my judgment now, and I don't want to debate these things around fifteen men and then have them all go out and talk about the vice president and [what he thinks]." If he were going to be of any use to the president, moreover, he would have to be privy to the deliberations of his inner circle. "I don't know who drafted it; I've never seen it," he said of the bill. "Hell . . . I got it from the *New York Times*."[42] He then proceeded with a torrent of practical advice: whom to consult, in what order they should be consulted, legislative chits that could be given out and called in.

In reality, LBJ and his brain trust of George Reedy, Harry McPherson, Horace Busby, and Abe Fortas were not sure that introducing a comprehensive bill was the right move. All were dubious that the Kennedy team could get it through Congress. Black Americans were out of patience, Reedy observed: "From here on out, they will regard any measure which does not pass as a cynical gesture . . . The country will be likely to come to no conclusion—thus disillusioning the Negroes and strengthening the bigots in their conclusion that the country is 'really with' them. The Republicans will have a field day. And in addition to the civil rights cause, the President's whole program will go down the drain."[43] After reading the bill, which included a long list of "findings of fact"— specific instances of discrimination—Fortas observed, "It must have been written by children . . . This is embarrassing. It makes me cringe to think that my government could produce a document like this."[44] In the end, of course, Johnson and his staff decided to do all in their power to help.

Johnson's brain trust wrote an analysis of the state of race relations that showed more idealism and more political sense than was reflected in the bill. The longer the nation delayed guaranteeing full rights and nondiscrimination, they noted, the more radical the civil rights movement would become. "A number of stereotypes have gone by the boards. The NAACP is now the moderate, right-wing of the Negro protest movement. CORE is actually in the center. The various student groups are really to the left. And the role of the Black Muslims has been enhanced immeasurably." The only real choices facing the nation were integration or apartheid, and "the concept of apartheid is so repugnant and ridiculous that it would not require comment except for the fact that one branch of the Negro movement—the Black Muslims—has proposed it seriously."

Nevertheless, if the Union were to survive, the federal government could not compel equal rights and nondiscrimination through force of arms. The only means with any chance of success, as Martin Luther King had recognized, was moral compulsion.[45] "Strangely enough," LBJ's advisers told him, "both the Southern whites and the Negroes share one point of view in common—they are not certain that the government is on the side of the Negroes. The Southern whites feel that the civil rights issue is a matter of ward politics and the Negroes have an uneasy suspicion that they are receiving only token gestures of good will."[46]

Meanwhile, Johnson delivered stirring speeches in Detroit and Gettysburg. "Until justice is blind to color, until education is unaware of race, until opportunity is unaware of the color of men's skins, emancipation will be a proclamation but not a fact," he had declared to the crowd gathered at the nation's most famous Civil War battlefield.[47] Nor was the vice president bashful about carrying the message to the Kennedys. "Very serious consideration should be given to the President going into the South," he told the White House "not in a belligerent, bellicose mood but representing the conscience of the nation . . . The risks of such a course are great and could well amount to losing a number of Southern states in 1964. But those states will probably be lost anyway because of the action the President must take to enforce court decrees . . . If he states the moral issue face-to-face as their President—Southerners will at least respect his courage and will feel that they were on the losing side of an issue of conscience." [48]

JFK did not go to the South, but in June, after announcing that he was sending his historic civil rights bill to Congress, he went on television and delivered a stirring call to the nation to do the right thing by its black citizens. In the days that followed, the White House scheduled scores of meetings with journalists, union and business leaders, southerners and northerners to generate support for the measure. Arthur Schlesinger, who was present at these gatherings, termed the vice president's tone "evangelical." "Johnson was extremely effective," he later wrote, "I thought more effective than the President or the Attorney General." [49]

In the drama that followed, LBJ typically angered segregationists by ardently advocating the merits of the civil rights bill itself while refusing to alienate the South by backing yet another move to modify Rule 22. That provision required a two-thirds vote of the Senate to shut off discussion of a bill. It guaranteed virtually unlimited debate, and southern Senators continued to use it as a weapon to obstruct the passage of civil rights legislation. "Anxious as I am to choke off debate at times, this vice president is not going to choke off rules for a few people who ask the chair to do something they can't do themselves." [50]

There could be no question about Johnson's position on the issues addressed in the bill. It had several sections, but one in particular struck southern businessmen as an intolerable intrusion into their property rights. "Title II which prohibited discrimination in places of public accommodation was just as obnoxious as hell to the Southerners," Harry McPherson recalled.

> It was telling people what they could do with their private property and who they could associate with. The South was up in arms about the sitins. I was sitting up with Johnson at the chair of the vice president in the Senate. [Mississippi Senator John] Stennis walked by and LBJ motions him to come up. "How do you like that Title II of the Civil Rights Bill, John?" Stennis said, "Oh Lyndon, well you know, our people just can't take that kind of thing. It's just impossible. I mean I believe that a man ought to have the right to—if he owns a store or runs a café, he ought to have the right to serve who he wants to serve" . . . LBJ said, "Well, you know, John, the other day a sad thing happened. My cook, Zephyr Wright, who had been working for me for many years—she's a college graduate— and her husband drove my official car from Washington down to Texas . . . They drove through your state and when they got hungry, they stopped at grocery stores on the edge of town in colored areas and bought Vienna sausage and beans and ate them with a plastic spoon. And when they had to go to the bathroom they would stop, pull off on a side road, and Zephyr Wright, the cook of the vice president of the United States, would squat in the road to pee. And you know, John, that's just bad.

That's wrong. And there ought to be something to change that. And it seems to me that if people in Mississippi don't change it voluntarily, that it's just going to be necessary to change it by law." Stennis said, "Well, Lyndon, I'm sure that there are nice places where your cook and—." Then the vice president just said. "Uh-huh, Uh-huh," and just sort of looked away vacantly and said, "Well, thank you, John."[51]

DESPITE JOHNSON'S LABORS in the vineyard of civil rights, by 1963 rumors were circulating that the Kennedys were going to drop him from the ticket in 1964. When the vice president's name was linked with two highly publicized fraud cases, the speculation intensified. The leading citizen of Pecos, Texas, was a short, portly, bespectacled young man named Billie Sol Estes. A Jaycee Outstanding Young Man of 1953, Estes managed to make a fortune from the federal farm program. He collected millions in acreage allotments on land he bought on the slimmest of margins and then quickly sold. He collected additional monies on empty grain storage facilities. He sold nonexistent fertilizer tanks to farmers and then sold their mortgages to banks and lending institutions. So tangled was the Estes web of double-dealing that when he was arrested in 1962, no fewer than seventy-five FBI agents were working on his case.

News accounts reported that the Johnsons were sometime business partners of the West Texas tycoon, that LBJ had lobbied the Agriculture Department in behalf of Estes, and that Estes had given Lyndon and Lady Bird an airplane. Only the second was true; LBJ had lobbied for Estes. Yet, when Henry Marshall, an Agriculture Department official investigating the case, was found dead in Texas, public interest crested. Despite the fact that Marshall had bruises on his face and had been shot five times with a single-shot, bolt-action rifle, his death was ruled a suicide.

Twenty-two years later, during a grand jury investigation into Marshall's death, Billie Sol claimed that he, Lyndon, and Cliff Carter, an aide and old friend of the vice president, had hired a convicted murderer to kill the agent.[52] Although the grand jury ruled Marshall's death a murder, they uncovered no evidence linking LBJ to the incident. Moreover, although Bobby Kennedy and the Justice Department took an active interest in the case at the time, the FBI found nothing to substantiate charges that Lyndon and Lady Bird were part of the Estes scandal.[53]

Far more politically damaging to LBJ was the fall of his Senate protégé, Bobby Baker. By 1963, Baker had been working in the Senate twenty-one years, although he was then only thirty-four years old. Known as the "the 101st Senator," his stature was almost legendary. But Baker was thinly educated and narrowly focused. "To him the Senate was a mechanism that cranked out good things for Bobby Baker if he played it right," George Reedy said. "He had two major ambitions. He wanted to be a millionaire and he wanted to be the governor of South Carolina."[54] "Strangely enough," recalled journalist Leslie Carpenter, "there are some people who like to look crooked when they aren't. And

Bobby was one of those characters. He would always do the simplest thing in such a way to make it look like a deep dark plot that had been hatched in a back room with thousands of dollars laid on the table."[55]

During the 1950s, Baker's name had become inextricably intertwined with that of LBJ, so much so that he was known to some as "Little Lyndon." In 1962, the FBI launched an investigation into the funding and operation of a luxury motel in Ocean City, Maryland, of which Bobby was part owner. The other partners were apparently organized crime figures. Then, in October 1963, a vending machine company under contract to the federal government filed suit against Baker for having forced it out of a defense plant in a dispute over a kickback scheme. Baker resigned his post in the Senate.[56]

As Baker's shady past came to light, LBJ's name was increasingly mentioned in connection with his. News reporters dug up every favorable thing Lyndon had said about Baker and noted that the latter's two children were named Lynda and Lyndon Baines.[57]

On November 22, the day of the Kennedy assassination, Don B. Reynolds, an insurance executive in Silver Spring, Maryland, testified before the Senate Rules Committee, which had been assigned the task of investigating Baker, that after arranging for him to sell $200,000 in life insurance to the Johnsons, Bobby Baker and Walter Jenkins had advised Reynolds to buy $1,200 worth of advertising on KTBC. He also admitted giving the Johnsons a Magnavox stereo set worth $585.[58]

There was, however, no concrete evidence of wrongdoing. Nearly every crime Baker was accused of committing had occured after Johnson left the Senate.[59] Bob Kerr, Bobby's real patron, told Harry McPherson, "Johnson literally did not know a damned thing about the operations that Bobby got himself tied up in and I know that to be the case."[60] As vice president, Johnson continued to value Baker highly, but primarily as a devoted supporter and an unending and reliable source of information. During his troubles, LBJ expressed sympathy for the young man and persuaded Abe Fortas to look after his legal affairs.[61]

Of one thing LBJ was certain: the Baker scandal was Bobby Kennedy's doing. His informants told him that leaks concerning his connections with Baker were coming out of the Justice Department, not the Senate Rules Committee. Johnson believed that the attorney general had had his phones tapped. Hubert Humphrey later told the FBI that the "Kennedy crowd" at the Justice Department had plotted to use the Baker scandal to get LBJ off the ticket.[62]

THROUGHOUT THE SPRING AND SUMMER, both Kennedys vehemently and repeatedly denied that Jack was giving any thought to dumping LBJ.[63] When George Smathers repeated the rumors he had heard to the effect that Bobby was maneuvering to get rid of Lyndon, Jack Kennedy exploded: "George, you have some intelligence, I presume. Now who's Bobby going to put on the ticket, himself? . . . Lyndon's going to be my vice president because he helps me."[64]

Perhaps. But denying any intent to dump Johnson was good politics. There is no doubt that if scandal sank the vice president, not a tear would have been shed in the White House. More important, Johnson believed that the Kennedys wanted him off the ticket. Shortly after the Baker scandal broke, Johnson had dinner with friends, including Liz and Leslie Carpenter. Johnson's car took the couple home and Johnson rode with them. "Park in the driveway and let's talk a few minutes," Johnson said. "I think I'm going to announce that I'm not going to run again for vice president so that I can get off that ticket before they try to knock me off. What I would like to do is go back to Texas and be president of Southwest Texas State Teachers College." [65]

CHAPTER 20

INTERREGNUM:
DEATH AND RESURRECTION

L ITTLE DID JOHNSON KNOW THAT FATE, AND TEXAS, would change his plans. For some time, Jack Kennedy had been pressing Governor John Connally and LBJ to arrange a Texas speaking tour for him. The Kennedy-Johnson ticket had carried Texas in 1960, but only by forty-five thousand votes. John Tower had captured one of the state's two Senate seats, and Connally had barely won the governorship.[1]

Officials of the Democratic National Committee advised the White House that little or no money had come into party coffers during 1961–1962. Yet, neither Connally nor Johnson was enthusiastic about a Kennedy visit. "Many of the people who were Mr. Kennedy's most active supporters in Texas also tended to support my opponents [Ralph and Don Yarborough]," Connally said. "Many of my most active supporters did not lean toward JFK. To rally new support for him and to raise funds, therefore, I would have to appeal to my supporters— literally, to spend my political capital—while knowing that in the election of 1964, in which I too had to run again [for governor], many of Kennedy's backers would be fighting me."[2]

At the time, Johnson was feuding with both John Connally and Senator Ralph Yarborough. As a condition for accepting the vice presidency, LBJ had insisted that all federal patronage appointments for Texas be cleared through him, an arrangement that caused no end of friction between him and Yarborough. More fundamentally, LBJ's explicit speeches in behalf of civil rights had alienated many of Connally's conservative supporters.

JFK refused to take no for an answer. In June 1963, the president delivered the commencement address at the Air Force Academy, while Johnson did the same at Annapolis. Afterward, Kennedy had LBJ and Connally meet him in El

Paso. All three stayed at the Cortez Hotel, where they gathered in Connally's suite. He was going to tour Texas whether they liked it or not, Kennedy said. If we carry only two states in 1964, he exclaimed, they are going to be Massachusetts and Texas. And so it was that a presidential swing through the Lone Star State was arranged for late November 1963. The trip would include visits to Fort Worth, Dallas, and Houston.[3]

As the date for the Texas trip approached, apprehension increased among some of those close to President Kennedy, especially concerning the stopover in Dallas. "And then there was Dallas," Willie Morris had written, "always a cavernous city for me, claustrophobic, full of thundering certitudes and obsessed with its image . . . There was no other city remotely its size in America, except in the Deep South on the one issue of race, where . . . intolerance and the closed mind were so inclusive, and where violence could be so manifestly political."[4]

In late October, Adlai Stevenson had gone to Dallas to attend a meeting on United Nations Day. The radical right decided to counter this visit by holding a "United States Day," with General Edwin A. Walker as the speaker, just prior to Stevenson's arrival. A decorated veteran of World War II, Walker had been forced to retire from the army for distributing John Birch material among his troops. In his yard in Dallas he flew the American flag upside down to indicate where he thought the country was headed.

The day following Walker's appearance, handbills with photographs of the president of the United States, full-face and profile, appeared on the streets of the city captioned "Wanted for Treason." That evening many of Walker's partisans had appeared at the UN meeting to curse and spit on Stevenson. Talking with Arthur Schlesinger shortly thereafter, Stevenson remarked, "There was something very ugly and frightening about the atmosphere. Later I talked with some of the leading people out there. They wondered whether the President should go to Dallas and so do I."[5] But Kennedy was not to be deterred. He and the Democratic party needed the Lone Star State.

With plans for the trip set, Lyndon and Lady Bird decided to show President and Mrs. Kennedy real Texas hospitality. The schedule called for the first couple to spend the night of Friday, November 23, at the ranch. Lady Bird went down a week early to prepare. Lyndon arrived on the 19th. Lady Bird had to walk a fine line: she did not want to appear the rube, but she intended to be true to the mores of her beloved Hill Country—there would be a traditional barbeque. A special bed was shipped in to accommodate JFK's ailing back. The Johnsons knew that Jackie (who had just recently buried her third child, Patrick Bouvier, born prematurely) liked horses and champagne. They arranged to have a thoroughly trained walking horse on hand and plenty of France's finest.[6]

Johnson was at the head of a large crowd at the San Antonio airport when Air Force One set down on November 21. Though public opinion polls at the time indicated that only 35 percent of Texans approved of the way JFK was handling national affairs, the welcome was warm and enthusiastic. To facilitate his reception, JFK had brought along Congressman Henry Gonzalez and Senator Ralph Yarborough, whose popularity far exceeded his.

Yarborough was boiling mad. He had learned that at a fund-raising dinner scheduled for Austin Friday night, Connally intended to slight him by keeping him from the head table. He was not even invited to a reception following at the governor's mansion.[7] Yarborough retaliated by refusing to ride in LBJ's car into the city. He repeated the performance that afternoon in Houston.[8]

Late that afternoon, JFK summoned the vice president to his hotel suite. The two had a heated exchange that could be heard several doors down. Lyndon had better get hold of the situation. Open feuding between two Democrats was playing right into the hands of the GOP. Heal the breach or be responsible for losing the state. LBJ became defensive and left in a huff. What was that all about? Jackie asked, coming into the room. Texas politics, the president replied.[9] Yarborough got his head table seat and invitation to the reception.

The president and his entourage arrived in Fort Worth in a steady drizzle and settled into their hotel. A reporter noted that LBJ seemed dour and disconsolate. What the journalist did not know was that Johnson had decided to tell Kennedy that very evening that he would not run for the vice presidency in 1964.[10] Donald Reynolds was scheduled to testify before the Senate Rules Committee in the Bobby Baker case the next day, and Johnson feared the worst.

The next morning, Lyndon and Lady Bird flew on to Dallas ahead of Air Force One to head the delegation that would greet the first couple. Remembering their experience at the Adolphus Hotel, Lady Bird was a bit apprehensive. And in fact, H. L. Hunt and a number of other wealthy reactionaries had taken out a full-page, black-bordered ad in the *Dallas Morning News,* accusing JFK and virtually everyone in his administration of being a communist. But her and her husband's mood brightened as the sun came out and the motorcade set off in the midst of a glorious fall day. The route selected was circuitous, taking the president and his party through several residential areas and then downtown to the Trade Mart, where he was scheduled to give a luncheon address. To ensure a large turnout, the advance team had had the route published in the previous day's edition of the *News.* In the first car were the Kennedys in back, the Connallys seated in the jump seat, and the driver and Secret Service personnel in front. The Johnsons rode with Yarborough in the back seat of an open convertible, the fourth car behind the president's and two Secret Service vehicles. Originally, the president's car was to be covered with a bulletproof Plexiglas bubble, but at his insistence it was removed.[11]

The crowds lining the motorcade route were large and welcoming. At Houston Street, on the east edge of Dealy Plaza, the president's vehicle slowed nearly to a stop to make a right turn in front of the courthouse. Nellie Connally turned in her seat, full of pride, and said to JFK, "Well, Mr. President, you can't say that Dallas doesn't love you." "No, you certainly can't," he replied with a smile.[12]

On the edge of the plaza, on the sixth floor of the Texas Book Depository, a lone employee positioned himself with rifle and scope at a window. Lee Harvey Oswald, raised in a dysfunctional family, was a deeply disturbed child and adolescent who wound up in the marines. While stationed in Japan, he read Karl Marx's *Das Kapital* and became a self-proclaimed communist. He lived in the Soviet Union for a time and married a Russian woman. He subsequently returned to the United States, where he joined an organization called the Fair Play for Cuba Committee. He attempted to contact the Cubans directly, but they would have nothing to do with him, fearing he was a CIA agent. To further complicate matters, Oswald had family ties to a member of the Mafia who had spoken of his wish to kill Kennedy to stop the ongoing investigation of organized crime.[13] These bare facts have fueled an endless line of conspiracy theories, despite a consensus view that Oswald acted alone on November 22.

As the motorcade turned onto Elm Street, a shot rang out. Connally remembered being covered with a fine mist of blood and tissue. The president's head had been partially blown off. The second shot hit Connally in the back, passed through his body, through his hand, and into his thigh. A third shot rang out, but by that time pandemonium had broken loose. Jackie Kennedy, her pink suit splattered with her husband's brains and blood, cried, "Oh, my God, they have killed my husband—Jack, Jack."[14] She tried to crawl out of the car over the trunk but was pushed back in by Secret Service officers. They pulled the presidential vehicle out of line, and it sped off. It was 12:30 P.M.

WHEN RUFUS YOUNGBLOOD, the Secret Service agent assigned to the vice president, heard three explosive sounds and saw the president's car swerve, he immediately recognized that an assassination attempt was under way. He turned in his seat and grabbed LBJ. "Get down! Get down!" he yelled. Lyndon, Yarborough, and Lady Bird fell to the floorboard. Youngblood vaulted over the seat to cover Johnson's body with his own. LBJ remembered it vividly: "He got on top of me and he put his body between me and the crowd. He had his knees in my back and his elbows in my back and a good two hundred pounds all over me. And the car was speeded up. He had a microphone from the front seat that he'd pulled over with him, a two-way radio and there was a lot of traffic on the radio and you could hear them talking back and forth, and one of them said: 'Let's get out of here quick.' "[15]

On the floor, Lady Bird remembered the automobile accelerating faster and faster. Finally it slowed, wheeled around a corner, and braked. At last she and LBJ were allowed to raise their heads. A neon sign read "Parkland Hospital."[16]

Secret Service agents led Lyndon and Lady Bird into a small trauma room lined with sheets to block the windows. If there was a general conspiracy to wipe out the top echelon of the federal government, the vice president had to be kept secluded. Both Lady Bird and Lyndon sat quietly, erect. In one corner, Ralph Yarborough was hunched over, weeping. Men entered and exited—Congressman Homer Thornberry, Kenney McDonnell, Cliff Carter, various hospital personnel. Lyndon began conferring in whispers with Secret Service agents

Rufus Youngblood, Lem Johns, and Emory Roberts. Lady Bird remembered their being concerned about the whereabouts of the "black bag," the briefcase containing the secret codes the president could use to authorize a nuclear strike.

Lady Bird went off to try to find Jackie Kennedy and Nellie Connally to console them. The first lady was standing outside Trauma Room No. 1, where doctors were working feverishly over JFK. Jackie seemed in shock and did not respond when Lady Bird hugged her. Lady Bird and Nellie embraced and cried. Back in the waiting room Secret Service agent Emory Roberts came in around 1:20 and informed LBJ that Kennedy was dead.

Lyndon Baines Johnson was president of the United States.

The situation was extremely confused. No one knew if there was a lone shooter, if Dallas was the sole seat of violence, if the attack was communist-inspired or the product of a right-wing conspiracy. The immediate object was to protect the life of the new president, who now embodied the hopes and fears, the very identity of the nation. Continuity was everything.

The Secret Service agents advised LBJ that he should get back to Washington as quickly as possible. Not only was it the seat of power, but it would be much easier for the Secret Service, police, and military to protect him there. LBJ agreed. He reminded Youngblood, Johns, and Roberts that Lucy, then sixteen and a student at the National Cathedral School for girls in Washington, and Lynda, nineteen, then a sophomore at the University of Texas, would need Secret Service protection.

Throughout, LBJ was decisive, undemonstrative, self-contained. The agents rounded up Lady Bird and loaded her and Lyndon into unmarked police cars. The vice president's entourage and several journalists, including Charles Roberts, followed in similarly unmarked cars. "The Secret Service had ordered the sirens off on all cars going to Dallas Love Field," Roberts remembered, "because they didn't want to attract attention to the airport. So we went out there at about seventy miles an hour, with no police escort, in an unmarked car and actually, when traffic would get too heavy, we crossed the median strip and went down against the traffic, we went through red lights." [17]

For symbolic reasons and because of its communication equipment, Air Force One rather than Air Force Two was selected to transport LBJ and his party back to Washington. Before leaving Parkland, LBJ had conferred with Kenny O'Donnell. He would not return to Washington without the president's body and the first lady, LBJ said. [18] That would pose some difficulty, O'Donnell replied, because the Dallas coroner would insist on an autopsy before releasing the body. A homicide had been committed. The two agreed to do whatever was necessary to get the body aboard, however. [19]

At Love Field LBJ boarded Air Force One and began making phone calls from the stateroom. In his party were Lady Bird, of course; Jack Valenti, the Houston advertising executive who had been advancing the trip; Cliff Carter; Liz Carpenter; Marie Fehmer; and Congressmen Thomas, Thornberry, and Brooks. Bill Moyers, then an officer in the Peace Corps, arrived from Austin later and boarded the plane. While LBJ was talking on the phone, Kenny O'Donnell, Larry O'Brien, and Dave Powers, another Kennedy aide, arrived with the casket containing the dead president's body. Members of LBJ's staff could hear workers knocking out seats in the rear cabin to make room for the coffin.[20]

Jackie was startled to find Lyndon sprawled across the bed in the living compartment. Sensing her discomfort, he moved back into the stateroom, leaving the bedroom and rear compartment to the Kennedy entourage. As soon as the president's body was secured, O'Donnell sent Kennedy's air force aide General Godfrey McHugh forward to order the plane to take off. LBJ had him intercepted and reminded him that there was a new president, and he would decide when the plane should depart.[21]

Johnson instructed his staff to summon Federal Judge Sarah T. Hughes, an old Dallas friend, to the plane to administer the oath of office.[22] While he wolfed down a bowl of vegetable soup and saltines, Johnson conferred with O'Donnell and Powers. "It's been a week since I got up," LBJ remarked.[23]

Shortly after two o'clock, Judge Hughes arrived. By this time, the plane, which had been sitting on the ground without air conditioning for half an hour, was sweltering. The Johnson and Kennedy people convened in the stateroom. Four journalists from the press pool were summoned to witness the occasion. LBJ had O'Donnell go into the bedroom and ask Jackie if she would please come out and stand by as he was sworn in. He found her brushing her hair at the dresser. "Yes, I think I ought to," she said. "At least I owe that much to the country. . . . I should do it for the country."[24]

With Lady Bird on his right and Jackie, still wearing her blood-spattered suit, on his left, LBJ repeated the oath of office for president of the United States. Hughes's voice cracked several times; Jackie's face was "a mask of passive grief," as one onlooker described it. LBJ was somber, composed. After the swearing in, he turned and kissed Lady Bird, and then Jackie, whom he had repeatedly referred to as "Honey," on the cheek. The former first lady retired to the bedroom, and Air Force One took off for the two-hour-and-twenty-minute flight to Washington.[25]

The atmosphere aboard the presidential jet during the trip back was tense. Jackie, still in shock, brooded in the bedroom. Increasingly, she blamed Johnson and Connally for drawing her and her husband into a totally unnecessary and now disastrous trip to Texas. She had never liked Connally. "I can't stand being around him all day," she had told Jack in Fort Worth. "I just can't bear him sitting there saying all those great things about himself."[26]

O'Donnell, O'Brien, and Powers sat in the forward compartment and drank. "I thought they were just wine heads," LBJ later said in a closed oral history. "They were just drinkers, just one drink after another coming to them trying to drown out their sorrow and we weren't drinking, of course."[27]

The Irish Mafia began dredging up LBJ stories and contemplating with horror the future with Johnson as president. They became increasingly belligerent. When Marie Fehmer tried to wait on them, they angrily refused and made fun of her Texas accent. By the time the plane arrived in Washington, the Kennedy people were already casting LBJ in the role of crude usurper. Lyndon decided to put in a call to Rose Kennedy at Hyannis Port. "I wish to God there was something that I could do and I wanted to tell you that we were grieving with you," the new president said. Between sobs, the matriarch of the Kennedy clan thanked him: "I know you loved Jack and he loved you."[28]

As soon as the plane landed, Bobby Kennedy boarded through the forward door. He rushed straight down the aisle past the Johnsons without saying a word until he reached the back of the plane. "He didn't look to the left or the right," Liz Carpenter said, "and his face looked streaked with tears and absolutely stricken. He said, 'Where's Jackie? I want to be with Jackie.' "[29]

Johnson was prevented from coming aft, and another group of staffers blocked his departure by the forward gangway. In essence, he and Lady Bird were trapped in the stateroom until the Kennedys could make their getaway. One of the dead president's aides later confided to a reporter that "they felt Johnson wanted to use Kennedy's body for his own purposes."[30] "It was almost as if they were angry at Johnson," journalist Charles Roberts later recalled. There was absolutely no "appreciation of how important continuity was."[31]

Finally, LBJ was able to deplane. As he made his way to the microphones that had been set up for him, he conferred with several White House personnel, most notably National Security Adviser McGeorge Bundy, who reassured him that there were no major military movements around the world, and the assassination did not appear to be a prelude to an attack on the United States.[32] "We have suffered a loss that cannot be weighed," he told the assembled and those listening on radio and television. "For me it is a deep personal tragedy. I know that the world shares the sorrow that Mrs. Kennedy and her family bear. I will do my best. That is all I can do. I ask for your help—and God's."[33]

At 6:41 P.M. Lyndon, Lady Bird, McGeorge Bundy, Secretary of Defense Robert McNamara, Undersecretary of State George Ball, staffers Reedy and Jenkins, and Kennedy speechwriter Theodore Sorenson boarded an army helicopter for the ride to the White House. LBJ spent most of the time conferring with the three cabinet officers; the other department heads were aboard a jet over the Pacific returning from a trip to Japan. As he had with O'Donnell and O'Brien aboard Air Force One, the president asked them not to resign, telling each that he needed him more than Kennedy ever would. All assured Johnson that they would serve at his pleasure.[34]

The huge machine roared onto the White House lawn, blowing foam from the fountain over the group of officials, reporters, and photographers who waited near the swings and the seesaw that had been set up for Caroline Kennedy and her brother, John Jr. Johnson did not stop to address those who had gathered, but strode across the lawn.[35] He paused briefly in the Oval Office, surveying the seat of power, and then moved on to the cabinet room. There, conferring with Bundy, Ball, and others, the new president decided on meetings of the cabinet and National Security Council for the next day. He then proceeded to his suite on the second floor of the Executive Office Building and immersed himself in telephone calls.

After conferring briefly with Bill Fulbright and Averell Harriman, LBJ received a stream of congressional leaders who, like mafiosi to a godfather, pledged him their fealty. Just prior to his meetings with the leadership, LBJ had taken time to compose brief notes to each of the two Kennedy children. "Dearest Caroline," he wrote, "Your father's death has been a great tragedy for the nation, as well as for you, and I wanted you to know how much my thoughts are with you at this time . . . He was a wise and devoted man. You can always be proud of what he did for his country."[36] Finally, the new president retired to The Elms, where his family and a handful of friends awaited him.

LADY BIRD AND LIZ CARPENTER had arrived at the house earlier in the evening to find Lucy and Willie Day Taylor, who had picked Lucy up from school, waiting for them. The assassination meant that her father was now president, Lady Bird told her daughter. "Don't tell me that," she screamed. Lady Bird reassured her that though their lives would change, relationships would not; Lucy's and Lynda's would change the least. They called Lynda in Austin and Lady Bird asked her to fly up. "If there was something of a gulf between me and him [LBJ]," Lady Bird noted in her diary, "there never was anything of a gulf between Lynda Bird and him, and so I wanted her to be here."[37] Johnson and his entourage arrived. While he sipped an orange soda, he looked wistfully at a portrait of Sam Rayburn and said, "Mr. Speaker, I wish you were here tonight."[38]

The troubled souls gathered at The Elms ate a light supper at eleven o'clock, but Johnson still could not sleep. He insisted on watching televised reports of the day's events, but then the pictures, especially those of JFK moving about Fort Worth and Dallas just prior to his murder, began to bother him. "Turn it off," he told Horace Busby, his old friend and speechwriter. Then Busby and his wife, Mary, sat by LBJ and held his hand until he was calm enough to go to bed.

But he did not sleep. He had Cliff Carter, Bill Moyers, and Jack Valenti come into the bedroom to plan for the funeral, discuss staffing, and rough out a schedule. He asked Valenti to take two years off from his business to assist him in the Oval Office.[39] Bill Moyers recalled, as he mounted the stairs to one of the guest bedrooms, that he could see shadowy figures on the lawn: "The Secret Service had on a heavy guard."[40]

Then, around 3 A.M., Johnson summoned Busby, to talk long-range planning. When they began discussing an LBJ run for the presidency not only in 1964 but 1968, Lady Bird put in her earplugs, put on her eyeshades, and pulled the covers over her head.[41] Before he drifted off, Johnson recalled a conversation he had had with *Washington Post* publisher Phil Graham a year earlier. LBJ and Bobby were feuding, and communication had broken down entirely between the White House and the vice president. "No, just face it," Graham had said to Johnson, "you've got to face it: you're never going to be President."[42]

As he was dressing the next morning, LBJ summoned Busby again. "Buzz," he said, "do you realize that when I came back to Washington tonight as President there were on my desk the same things that were on my desk when I came to Congress in 1937?" It would be his duty and pleasure, he said, to remove the roadblocks that had been preventing the enactment of federal aid to education, Medicare, and a comprehensive civil rights bill.[43] "That whole [time]," Moyers recalled, "he seemed to have several chambers of his mind operating simultaneously. It was formidable, very formidable."[44]

Lyndon Johnson's first days as president were dense with activity, apprehension, tragedy, and hope. The new president knew that everything he did would be subjected to intense public scrutiny. "I took the oath," Johnson later said, a bit melodramatically, "I became President. But for millions of Americans I was still illegitimate, a naked man with no presidential covering, a pretender to the throne, an illegal usurper . . . The whole thing was almost unbearable."[45]

Unbearable or not, LBJ managed quite nicely. "Visiting with the new president in his office a few days ago," journalist John Steele wrote a week after the assassination, "provided a striking contrast with the fidgety, irascible, short-tempered, vain man we sat with only a few weeks ago in his capitol hill vice presidential office. . . . His voice in conversation these days is low and moderate; his demeanor almost a studied calm. His deliberation over every step he is about to take is apparent."[46]

For a variety of reasons, LBJ was determined to ingratiate himself with the Kennedys, Jackie in particular. He was aware that until the 1964 election at least, he would be viewed as the caretaker of the dead president's legacy, and he decided to embrace that role. He would mobilize the emotion and the tendency of Congress and the people to rally to a fallen martyr, to push the stalled New Frontier through the House and Senate. In international relations, he would hold fast to the commitments that he had inherited. And, in fact, a part of Johnson relished the role of caretaker, comforter of the afflicted, as well as guardian of the disadvantaged. That this strategy would enable him to push through Congress measures of social and economic justice that he had long dreamed of made the stratagem of dutiful heir even more appealing. The symbol of this approach would be his courtship of the bereaved widow.

During his first five weeks in office, Johnson called Jackie numerous times. Instinctively, awkwardly, he attempted to make what Hubert Humphrey referred to as "cowboy love" to her. A conversation the first week in December was typical: "Your picture was gorgeous. Now you had that chin up and that chest out and you looked so pretty marching in the front page of the *New York Daily News* . . . well," LBJ said, "I just came, sat in my desk and started signing a log of long things, and I decided I wanted to flirt with you a little bit . . . Darling, you know what I said to the Congress—I'd give anything in the world if I wasn't here today . . . Tell Caroline and John-John I'd like to be their daddy!"[47]

Rather than being offended, Jackie played the coquette and seemed to enjoy it. She giggled at his intimacy. " 'She ran around with two Presidents,' that's what they'll say about me," the former first lady told Johnson, who quietly chortled. She advised LBJ to make an afternoon nap part of his daily routine and not to sleep alone in the White House, at least at first.[48]

Nonetheless, Jackie would increasingly consider Johnson a graceless lout and a usurper. Robert had told her to put on her "widow's weeds," go down to the White House, and get all she could while the getting was good. The family wanted, for example, Cape Canaveral renamed Cape Kennedy. The widow found LBJ more than accommodating. Following this initial burst of intimacy, however, Jacqueline Kennedy ignored Lyndon and Lady Bird as well as the Johnson presidency.[49]

Some of the transition issues were utterly predictable, but no less delicate for that. The first was when and how LBJ and his staff would occupy the Oval Office and its environs. Johnson was worried about the appearance of rushing the Kennedy family and the dead president's staff, but McNamara, Bundy, and Ball emphasized the need to assure the world that there had not been and would not be a break in leadership.

Early on the morning of November 24, Bundy conferred with Robert Kennedy and Evelyn Lincoln, JFK's personal secretary, who asked for more time. Bundy left a note for LBJ to this effect, but he never got it. When Johnson arrived, he indicated politely but firmly to Lincoln that he would expect his secretaries and staff to settle themselves in the West Wing later that day. Lincoln rushed to RFK in tears. Learning of her distress, LBJ told Lincoln and her assistants to take all the time they needed to collect their boss's papers and belongings. But the damage had been done. Bobby recalled in a 1964 oral history that Johnson had been rude, preemptive, and totally insensitive during those first days.[50]

Lyndon, with Lady Bird in tow, took time off from a steady stream of briefings and visitors to pay tribute to President Kennedy, whose body lay in state in the East Room of the White House. "Lyndon walked slowly past the President's body," Lady Bird noted in her diary. "The catafalque was in the center and on it the casket, draped with the American flag. At each corner there was a large candle and a very rigid military man, representing each of the four services."[51]

From there, the president and first lady crossed Lafayette Square to attend a memorial service at St. Mark's Episcopal Church. Harry McPherson, who was a vestryman, was in attendance and remembered that the rector, William Baxter, delivered a brief but powerful sermon on the triumph and tragedy of the American experiment. In that moment of crisis, the country, in all its diversity, had come together and felt with one heart, breathed with one breath, he declared. That sense of unity should be treasured, preserved, because it was the key to the nation's future. "I remember Lyndon Johnson was weeping," McPherson said. "It was overwhelming."[52]

Following the service, Johnson asked McPherson to walk with him to his car. As they emerged from the church, a Secret Service agent stomped on McPherson's foot and elbowed him in the stomach. As he and another agent, presumably Rufus Youngblood, hustled Johnson to his waiting limousine,

McPherson lay on the ground, gasping for air. He managed to get to his feet and return to the parish hall. Just then somebody rushed in and exclaimed, "Jesus Christ, they've shot Oswald."[53]

It was true; Dallas nightclub owner Jack Ruby, a shadowy figure with close ties to both the Dallas police force and the Mafia, had fatally shot Oswald in front of television cameras as he was being transported. He did it, Ruby said, to spare Jacqueline Kennedy and her children the excruciating experience of an assassination trial.

AT 2:30 IN THE AFTERNOON, LBJ convened his first cabinet meeting. McGeorge Bundy had presumed to prepare some remarks for him to deliver. "A number of them . . . are quite numb with personal grief," he advised, "and in keeping with your own instinct of last night you will wish to avoid any suggestion of over-assertiveness." After opening the meeting with a prayer, Johnson paid tribute to his fallen predecessor and appealed to those present to help him and help the nation to realize a sense of continuity and then to implement the program that had meant so much to President Kennedy. "I want you all to stay on," he concluded. "I need you."[54]

Claiming his role as senior official present, Adlai Stevenson, U.S. ambassador to the UN, rose to praise LBJ's character and competence and to pledge the allegiance of all those present. Dean Rusk followed and gave a brief seconding statement. Toward the end of the meeting, Robert Kennedy entered. He would claim that he had not intended to come but that McGeorge Bundy had collared him in the Oval Office while he was looking after his brother's effects. Most of the cabinet rose and rushed to the still obviously grief-stricken attorney general. Johnson did not rise, and Bobby never acknowledged the new president. The meeting broke up awkwardly, the room suddenly filled with tension.

Shortly thereafter, Agriculture Secretary Orville Freeman, a liberal and great friend of Jack if not Robert Kennedy, went in to see his new boss. He was going to have great problems with the family, Johnson observed. Jackie was all right, but Bobby and his group of loyalists were going out of their way to humiliate him. Witness the events at Andrews and the just concluded cabinet meeting. "There was bitterness in Lyndon's voice on this one," Freeman noted in his diary, "and he said, what can I do, I do not want to get into a fight with the family and the aura of Kennedy is important to all of us."[55]

Later, intimates of Johnson and some historians would argue that it had been a huge mistake to keep the Kennedy people on. At the time, however, a number of influential individuals, including former President Eisenhower and Clark Clifford, had urged LBJ to keep Kennedy's cabinet in place. For the sake of continuity such a move was necessary, argued Clifford, who had been Truman's secretary of defense. "I outlined the key elements of the transfer of power in 1945 from Roosevelt to Truman—the rapid departure of the FDR loyalists, the condescending attitude of some of the Roosevelt holdovers, the unfortunate decision to make James Byrnes secretary of state, and the Henry Wallace fiasco."[56] Then there was the already burgeoning Kennedy legend. "It was very clear that after the assassination, President Kennedy's popularity grew all the time," Clifford observed. "He was revered in a manner after his death that perhaps didn't exist before his death. He had become a martyr president."[57]

Unlike a duly elected president, Johnson did not have the benefit of an interregnum during which to conduct a talent search. The justification that LBJ gave for retaining Kennedy's entourage was the obvious one: "I needed that White House staff. Without them I would have lost my link to John Kennedy, and without that I would have had absolutely no chance of gaining the support of the media or the Easterners or the intellectuals. And without that support I would have had absolutely no chance of governing the country."[58]

Kennedy's cabinet was distinguished, but not uniformly so. Not surprisingly, the stars were to be found mostly in the field of foreign affairs. The most impressive was Robert McNamara, the General Motors executive and sometime Republican whom Kennedy had convinced to take over the Department of Defense. A graduate of Berkeley and Harvard Business School, McNamara was the epitome of cool rationality. Repelled by the very thought of using nuclear weapons, he had presided over an immense strategic arms buildup so that nuclear war would never appear to be feasible.

If McNamara had an equal in the cabinet, it was McGeorge Bundy. The national security adviser was the product of an environment very similar to that in which the Kennedys has been raised: intellectual stimulation, physical competition, and so much confidence in family and status that snobbishness seemed absurd. Bundy was a Republican of the Theodore Roosevelt–Henry Stimson type. In fact, while a junior fellow at Harvard, Mac had helped Stimson, an old Bull Mooser and FDR's secretary of war, write his memoirs, *On Active Service in Peace and War.*

The third member of the Kennedy foreign policy triumvirate was Dean Rusk, a self-made intellectual with a deep, spiritually based sense of right and wrong. The son of a Scots Irish Presbyterian minister, Rusk was raised in the red clay hills of Georgia. One of twelve children, he worked his way through Davidson College and then attended Oxford as a Rhodes scholar. He served in the China-India-Burma theater during World War II and then worked for George Marshall, whom he worshipped, in the State Department. During the Eisenhower years, Rusk taught political science for a time and then went on to become head of the Ford Foundation. An intensely private, dignified, yet unpretentious man, Rusk abhorred public displays of emotion and tended to avoid controversy. Whereas McNamara and Bundy were bureaucratic aggressors, Rusk was a survivor.[59]

Treasury Secretary C. Douglas Dillon bridged the gap between international and domestic affairs. Like Kennedy, Dillon was a strong supporter of measures to facilitate the growth of international trade, but he was also determined to hold down wages, prices, and inflation. A member of the Wall Street banking firm of Dillon Reade, the secretary of the treasury, was a card-carrying Republican. To succeed Arthur Goldberg as secretary of labor, JFK had picked Northwestern University Law School professor Willard Wirtz. A veteran of the War Labor Board and National Wage Stabilization Board, Wirtz was an expert at solving labor-management problems. Heading up Interior was Stewart Udall. The son of a prominent Arizona family, Udall, a Mormon, had graduated from the University of Arizona School of Law, served in the air force during World War II, and been elected to Congress as a Democrat from one of the state's two congressional districts. He quickly associated himself with the liberal wing of the party, and as a member of the Committee on Interior and Insular Affairs became an expert on land, water, and conservation matters. Udall transformed the Interior Department into a national force for conservation in all its forms: preservation of natural resources, creation and protection of wilderness areas, construction of recreational facilities, and pollution control.[60]

Secretary of agriculture was former Minnesota governor Orville Freeman. A sometime protégé of Hubert Humphrey, Freeman was bright, liberal, and socially adept. He was able to champion the cause of the small farmer and still maintain a relationship with agribusiness and its mouthpiece, the Farm Bureau. To head Commerce, Kennedy had selected Luther Hodges, former governor of North Carolina. During the 1950s, Hodges had been a champion of the New South; he posed as a racial moderate but had provided more drag than sail to the civil rights movement within his state.

The Kennedy team entertained varying perceptions of the new president. At the instant of John F. Kennedy's death, Rusk, Freeman, Hodges, Wirtz, Udall, and Dillon were on a plane high above the Pacific returning from a trip to Japan. The party learned, to their horror, first that the president and John Connally had been shot, and then that JFK had died. Rusk came over the intercom: "Ladies and gentlemen this is the Secretary of State. I deeply regret to inform you that the president is dead. May God help our country." Cabinet members, wives, and staff sat in stunned silence. There were tears, memories—all agreed that the nation and the world had suffered a great loss, that had he lived, JFK would have been successful in combating poverty at home and tyranny abroad.[61]

Then the topic turned to LBJ. Somewhat surprisingly, his strongest supporter was Stewart Udall. Like Clinton Anderson, Udall was a western liberal who considered Johnson a member of the club. Freeman and his wife, Jane, recalled their conversation with JFK when, at Los Angeles, he had decided on Johnson as vice president; that it was better to have the son of a bitch in that innocuous office than as majority leader. But both paid tribute to Lyndon and Lady Bird's fundamental humanitarianism. "I do like him," Freeman said, but noted that he had often said of LBJ, "I wouldn't like to work too closely to him because he'd suck your guts out." Wirtz, who was close to Walter Reuther and Soapy Williams, the liberal governor of Michigan, had opposed LBJ's selection as Kennedy's running mate, but admitted he really did not know him. Dillon was dismissive, observing that Johnson was bound to be ignorant of balance-of-payment matters and other issues of international finance. Hodges, who spent most of his time with southern businessmen, observed with some feeling that the people of the South regarded Johnson as a traitor for his recent strong stand in behalf of civil rights.[62]

By far and away the most difficult of the cabinet members Johnson had inherited was his attorney general, Robert Francis Kennedy. Bobby was the third of nine children, behind Joseph Jr. and John Fitzgerald. Small, socially and physically clumsy, he lived for the approval of his brothers, who generally ignored him. Jack, funny, ironic, handsome, and easygoing, spent much of his time fighting with Joe, a muscular, overbearing bully of a boy. To please his mother, Bobby became a devout Catholic. To please his father, that ruthless, generally absent patriarch, he tried football at Milton Academy.[63] At Harvard, the younger brother continued to concentrate on football, at 155 pounds virtually willing himself onto the varsity. At age twenty-one, Bobby struck even his brothers and sisters as humorless and moralistic. After graduation, he married Ethel, and the couple moved to Washington to be near Jack. Bobby made the rounds as a staffer first for Joe McCarthy's Government Operations Subcommittee and then for Arkansas Senator John McClellan's Senate Committee on Labor Racketeering. Joe Sr. was adamantly opposed to the latter undertaking, thinking that it was both dangerous and impolitic.[64]

After 1948, Robert gave himself, his affection, his attention, his ambition, and his formidable will to Jack and his career. It was his role in the family, and it gained him, finally, the acceptance and approval of his father. The younger brother melded with the elder. Both Bobby and Jack fell in love with and had affairs with Marilyn Monroe.

The assassination did more than take away a beloved brother; it destroyed Bobby's purpose in life. "You couldn't get to him," Ethel Kennedy recalled. "His whole life was wrapped up in the President . . . He was just another part of his brother—sort of an added arm." He wandered around in a daze, turning the Justice Department over to Undersecretary Nicholas B. Katzenbach. "It was as though someone had turned off his switch," said college chum David Hackett.[65]

Bobby began to display all the signs of clinical depression: sleeplessness, moodiness, detachment, despair, and melancholy. He would take long nighttime rides in freezing weather in his convertible with the top down. What made his slough of despond particularly deep was that he feared that he might have been indirectly responsible for his brother's death. As counsel to the McClellan Committee, he had pursued the Mafia with relentless energy and had continued that crusade as attorney general. Could the mob have hired Oswald? And then there was the possibility that Castro had had Jack killed in retaliation for Operation Mongoose.[66] Lyndon Johnson believed that that was in fact the case. He commented to a staffer that the CIA and FBI, under Bobby Kennedy's overall supervision, was running a kind of "Murder Inc. in the Caribbean."

Several days after the president's death, Johnson related a story to Pierre Salinger, JFK's press secretary and a Kennedy family friend. It got back to Bobby, who was convinced that the story was intended for him. As he later told it, Johnson had said to Salinger, "When I was young in Texas, I used to know a cross-eyed boy. His eyes were crossed, and so was his character . . . That was God's retribution for people who were bad and so you should be careful of cross-eyed people because God put his mark on them . . . Sometimes I think that, when you remember the assassination of Trujillo [Dominican dictator Rafael, killed in 1961 supposedly with CIA complicity] and the assassination of Diem, what happened to Kennedy may have been divine retribution." [67]

The presidency would have been infinitely more comfortable with Robert Kennedy out of the administration, but LBJ did not believe it was in his or the nation's interest for the dead president's brother to leave. On December 4, LBJ asked Clark Clifford to meet with Bobby and persuade him to stay on. "We really had it out," Clifford reported, "and we covered it all. I think there are some arguments that he found unanswerable and I'm just authorized to say now that he's going to stay." [68]

Over the next few months, Johnson worked hard at a reconciliation. Through journalist Jimmy Weschler and labor leader Alex Rose, Johnson sent a message to the attorney general in early 1964: "President Johnson loves you, wants to be friends with you . . . The door at the White House is always open to you, and . . . there is nothing more important to him than to have a close working partnership with you." [69] "I know how hard the past six weeks have been for you," Lyndon wrote Bobby on New Year's Day 1964. "Under the most trying circumstances your first thoughts have been for your country. Your brother would have been very proud of the strength you have shown. As the new year begins, I resolve to do my best to fulfill his trust in me. I will need your counsel and support." [70] RFK would have none of it. What finally righted Bobby emotionally was his sense of duty to the Kennedy clan and to the legacy of his dead brother. And his hatred of his brother's usurper.

LBJ MAY HAVE KEPT Kennedy's cabinet on, but he had his own brain trust, a group he had assembled over the years, a collection of men whose pragmatic liberalism, tinged with the theological realism of Reinhold Niebuhr, he had both evoked and absorbed. There was George Reedy, who would become LBJ's first press secretary. Since 1952 Reedy had been Johnson's policy intellectual. He was the only member of the inner circle who was not a Texan. The son of a *Chicago Tribune* crime reporter, Reedy was blessed with a phenomenal mind. As a student at the University of Chicago, he had consumed books by day and lived the Bohemian life by night, drinking, arguing, and fornicating. Following a stint in the air force as an intelligence officer during World War II, Reedy went to work for UPI covering Capitol Hill, where LBJ discovered him. No one had done more to shape and reflect LBJ's pragmatic liberalism than Reedy, though Johnson at times found the portly, shaggy-haired Reedy too ponderous, too philosophical. "You ask him what time it is," LBJ complained, "and he discusses the significance of time before he tells you it's eleven-thirty." [71]

More important than Reedy, especially during these early months, was

Horace Busby. Buzz had grown up in Fort Worth, the son of a Church of Christ minister. As a student at the University of Texas, Busby had fallen in love with the written word, and he, like Reedy, decided to focus on journalism. During his editorship of the *Daily Texan,* Busby's commitment to reform, to the social gospel, to freedom of inquiry and expression, to public figures committed to the welfare of the common man rather than special interests, became evident. Running as a New Dealer against Coke Stevenson in 1948, LBJ had hired the twenty-five-year-old as his speechwriter. Thus began an on-again, off-again relationship that would last the rest of their lives.

Like LBJ, Busby was not antibusiness; indeed, he established and directed the American International Business Research Corporation. But he believed that government existed mainly to be an agent of social justice. He had a sharp political eye, especially when it came to LBJ's future. But he was a sensitive, dignified man, and unlike Reedy, Jenkins, and Valenti, would not put up with Johnson's tongue-lashings. Moreover, Johnson's occasional coarseness repelled him.

LBJ needed men like Reedy and Busby; he exploited them, and frequently did not give them the respect they felt they were due. "Buzz is a very sound, solid, able, good boy," Johnson once remarked. The condescension was infuriating. As a result, he moved in and out of the Johnson orbit, but he was a crucial figure during the early days of the presidency. The author of Johnson's powerful 1963 civil rights address at Gettysburg, Busby focused on domestic affairs and he wrote most of LBJ's Rose Garden speeches.[72]

The individual who held things together throughout the transition was Walter Jenkins, LBJ's friend, confidante, and loyal factotum. Jenkins was far from the simple, one-dimensional man that he seemed. Born on a hardscrabble farm near Wichita Falls, Texas, he managed two years at the University of Texas before he ran out of money and went to work for Lyndon. From 1952 to 1964, Jenkins left the extended Johnson family only twice, to serve in the army in North Africa and Italy during World War II and to run unsuccessfully for Congress in 1951.

Jenkins knew everything there was to know about Lyndon Johnson and his family—their dalliances, their business dealings, their friends, and their increasingly complicated social and political network. Jenkins was a quietly intense, mild-mannered man, but would harden instantly when anyone threatened his boss's reputation or interests. Like Bobby Baker, he was a great gatherer of information, and like George Reedy, he was a liberal, but that is where the resemblance ended. Jenkins was not ideological, was not well-read, and did not have a philosophical bent of mind. He was, as Eric Goldman, the Princeton historian who served for a time as White House intellectual, put it, "an enormously decent human being . . . who sought fair play and kindliness in the dealings between men."[73] A devout Catholic, he believed that to whom much was given, much was expected. It was incumbent upon America, a land blessed with genius and abundance, to help those who could not help themselves and to provide for average hard-working people a degree of physical comfort and security and the means to provide food, shelter, health care, and education to their children. Moreover, for a "provincial," Jenkins was remarkably broad-minded, an important characteristic for the person who would determine who should have access to the president of the United States. Jenkins made sure that LBJ was exposed to persons and points of view that ranged across the political spectrum, even those Jenkins found personally abhorrent.[74]

Observers expected Jenkins, Reedy, and Busby to assume the prominent roles they did in Johnson's White House, but Jack Valenti was a total surprise. Valenti's father was the son of a Sicilian immigrant who had earned $150 a month as a court clerk in Houston. Jack, a short, handsome, energetic youth with well-developed social skills, worked his way through the University of Houston as an office boy for Humble Oil. During World War II he became a decorated bomber pilot who flew fifty-one missions over Germany and Italy. Following V-E Day, Valenti realized a life-long dream by graduating from Harvard Business School. Back in Houston, he and a friend established a successful public relations business. Like Busby, Valenti became a devoted wordsmith. He was an avid reader, but his education was uneven. He liked popular nonfiction and the nineteenth-century English historian Thomas Macaulay. He was also given to perusing anthologies of famous quotes. Valenti caught Johnson's eye when he penned a worshipful portrait of him for the *Houston Post*. He worked in the 1960 election for the Kennedy-Johnson ticket and advanced the 1963 Texas trip. After the assassination, LBJ asked the sharp-dressing, ever accommodating Valenti to accompany him on Air Force One to Washington. He subsequently lived at The Elms and then at the White House until he could move his wife, the former Mary Margaret Wiley of LBJ's vice presidential staff, to Washington.

Until he departed the White House in April 1966, Valenti was LBJ's chief of staff and constant companion. He arrived at the White House at 6:30 every morning, and the two would begin discussing the day's schedule. Unless dispatched as ambassador to some discontented legislator, or as emissary to an interest group that was being courted by the White House, Valenti was at the president's elbow, frequently staying up with him until the wee hours of the morning as LBJ unwound. Intelligent, sensitive, and diplomatic, he proved skilled at assuaging hurt feelings and communicating the president's wishes. He was an uncritical admirer of LBJ. That and his belief in the efficacy of public relations sometimes worked to the detriment of his boss. During the early years, LBJ seemed an overly exposed headline seeker rather than a thoughtful statesman.[75]

Then there was Billy Don Moyers, the man who more than any other, until his departure in 1966, was perceived as the lieutenant who could truly speak for the president. He had grown up during the Depression in Hugo, Oklahoma. In search of a better life, the elder Moyers had moved the family to Marshall, an oil and gas town in East Texas that was heavily Baptist, featuring no fewer than four faith-based colleges. Bill was a star student at Marshall High and then earned degrees from North Texas State and UT. During the years that followed, he worked part time for the Johnsons at KTBC and attended Southwestern Baptist Theological Seminary. At Southwestern he studied under the liberal theologian Thomas Buford Matson, an outspoken advocate of racial justice and a champion of labor unions. He and young Moyers talked politics as much as they did theology. After working in the 1960 presidential campaign for the Kennedy-Johnson ticket, Moyers was selected to assist Sargent Shriver in directing the Peace Corps. He was the youngest person ever to be confirmed by the Senate.

Moyers proved to be the perfect New Frontiersman: a hard-nosed idealist. He would point with pride to the Jeffersonian quotation hanging on his office wall: "The care of human life and happiness . . . is the first and only legitimate object of good government."[76] At the same time, he appreciated power and aspired to it. He was an instinctive bureaucratic politician. Johnson named him appointments secretary, but he quickly became much more than that. Exuding confidence and the promise of influence, Moyers was able to attract other young men to him, and by 1965 could command a network of supporters that spread throughout the top echelons of the federal government. The constituency Moyers selected to represent was American youth. He addressed conventions of young people as if they were labor gatherings, posing to them and to the outside world as the representative of the 1960s generation.

Moyers proved to be loyal, but he could also be diplomatically critical. He was an independent voice in White House counsels. There was reputedly a father-son relationship between LBJ and Moyers, but that was an overstatement. Johnson trusted Moyers to carry out his instructions and, increasingly, to make decisions, but the two held each other at emotional arm's length. Moyers had received a Rotary scholarship and studied at Edinburgh University in Scotland. He fell in love with Europe, with literature, with social sophistication. The crew from Camelot fascinated him, and he managed to worm his way into its good graces. LBJ knew this and counted on Moyers to act as liaison with the Kennedys and the Georgetown cocktail circuit, but although Johnson found this role useful, he increasingly resented his aide for playing it.

To the extent that LBJ accepted Moyers as representative of America's youth, he erred. He was representative of the youth Johnson wanted America to produce: educated and idealistic but conventional and committed to existing institutions and processes. When the New Left and counterculture burst on the scene, Moyers was caught as unawares as LBJ.[77]

THE DAY FOLLOWING John F. Kennedy's assassination in November 1963, the new president told an aide, "I am a Roosevelt New Dealer. As a matter of fact . . . Kennedy was a little too conservative to suit my taste."[78]

In response to a genuine commitment to help the poor of all colors and ages, as well as with an eye to the 1964 election, Johnson declared "unconditional war on poverty" and embraced a program that was rooted in the New Frontier but that vastly transcended it. Instead of sleeping, Johnson spent most of his first few nights as president sitting up with Valenti, Reedy, Busby, McPherson, Moyers, and others filling yellow legal tablets with legislative proposals that would make a kindergarten through college education available to all; eradicate poverty in the nation's urban and rural slums; cleanse the environment of pollutants; enhance government benefits for the aged; guarantee equality under the law and equal opportunity for all Americans regardless of race, color, or national origin; change the nation's discriminatory immigration policy; provide federal support to enhance the arts and humanities; and launch a hundred other initiatives.[79]

On November 25, the day of JFK's funeral, Johnson delivered off-the-record remarks to the governors of several states: "We have to do something to stop . . . hate and the way we have to do it is to meet the problem of injustice that exists in this land, meet the problem of inequality that exists in this land, meet the problem of poverty that exists in this land, and the unemployment that exists in this land . . . I am going to be at it from daylight to midnight, and with your help and God's help we are going to make not only ourselves proud that we are Americans but we are going to make the rest of the world proud that there is an America in it."[80]

Anyone familiar with the mind-set and track record of those LBJ gathered around him during the closing days of 1963 could have predicted the administration's ensuing commitment to social justice, but he and his closest associates were largely a mystery, and LBJ knew it. He wanted there to be no mistake, in Congress's or the public's mind, that he intended to take up not where JFK but where FDR had left off.

A week after the assassination, LBJ met with Jim Rowe and Tommy Corcoran. He and Rowe had barely spoken since 1960, when the New Dealer had taken him to task for his rudeness and irascibility. "I've been thinking back over 1960 and thinking of where I am now," LBJ said, "and I need friends. I need help and you have been a friend to me and one of the wisest advisors I know. And I let you and I drift apart and it was my fault and I was foolish and short-sighted and I'm sorry and I hope that you'll forgive me and be my friend and supporter." With tears in his eyes, Rowe said, "My God, Mr. President, it wasn't your fault." Johnson said, "Yes, it was. Don't argue with me. Just be content to be the first man to whom the 36th President of the United States has offered his apologies."[81]

Abe Fortas and Clark Clifford, New Dealer and Fair Dealer, respectively, were a part of LBJ's inner circle from the very beginning.[82] Both were prominent attorneys and Washington insiders, but there was no comparison between LBJ's relationship with the two. Clifford was loyal to no one but himself. He would keep his star hitched to the LBJ wagon only so long as it suited his interests to do so. But for Johnson, he was a valuable tie to the Truman crowd. Fortas was Johnson's lawyer, but also a person whom Johnson trusted to advise him on any and every issue.

The son of middle-class Jewish parents from Memphis, Abe had attended

Yale Law School, where he found himself in the midst of the great debate between "conceptualists," whose home base was Harvard, and "functionalists," increasingly centered at Yale. The famous dialogue among legal scholars grew out of the Progressive Era and the dissent of jurists such as Louis Brandeis and Oliver Wendell Holmes. They had rebelled against the notion that the practice of constitutional law lay in discovering and abiding by a set of unchanging principles that had sprung from the minds of the Founding Fathers and were embedded in the Constitution. Brandeis, one of the fathers of functionalism, argued that America had changed dramatically since the eighteenth century and that practitioners of jurisprudence ought to factor in current social and economic conditions in handing down their decisions. The law was something organic and changing, to be interpreted always with an eye to the common good.

As editor of the *Yale Law Journal,* Fortas had embraced functionalism, and after graduation had moved on to take advantage of the opportunities New Deal Washington offered young Catholic and Jewish lawyers. He spent his New Deal years justifying government regulation of big business and promoting the cause of economic justice. He was the ultimate pragmatist, who agreed with the New Deal official who told his aides, "I want to assure you that we are not afraid of exploring anything within the law and we have a lawyer who will declare anything you want to do legal." [83]

Following the war, Fortas made a fortune representing the very corporations that he had once attacked.[84] In short, Abe Fortas was the perfect counselor to a pragmatic liberal like Lyndon Johnson.

ALL OF JOHNSON'S ADVISERS agreed that it was imperative that the new president address Congress and, through it, the nation and the world. For two days Johnson met with individuals in and out of government to gather ideas and to gauge the impact that his words would have on the immediate future.

LBJ ordered Valenti, Busby, and Theodore Sorenson (Kennedy's intense house intellectual, speechwriter, and political adviser) to work on the speech drafts. Meanwhile, he consulted with John Kenneth Galbraith, who had already been lobbying Democratic liberals to forget the past and work to ensure Johnson's election in 1964. Galbraith emphasized civil rights and the need not to become overextended in Indochina. Later in the day, Walter Heller, chairman of the Council of Economic Advisers, lobbied for a massive $11 million tax cut that the Kennedy administration had been considering.[85]

On Tuesday evening, before the Wednesday speech, Johnson met at The Elms for more than six hours with Abe Fortas, Hubert Humphrey, and others to go over drafts of the speech. Fortas remembered that one of those present urged Johnson not to give civil rights a high priority. Passage of the omnibus bill then before Congress looked pretty hopeless; the issue was as divisive as any faced by the nation; it would be suicide to wage and lose such a battle. LBJ looked at the man and then said, "Well, what the hell is the presidency for?"[86]

As Johnson stepped to the podium, Congress, the nation, and the world held its breath. Who was this man who was now president of the most powerful nation in history? Would he be a frontman for southern segregationists, as many northern liberals believed, or a turncoat integrationist, as many white southerners suspected? Where would he stand on foreign policy? Many at home and abroad feared that he would turn out to be a simple Texas jingo, crying "Remember the Alamo," willing to bring the world to the brink of nuclear destruction at the drop of a hat. Most important, was LBJ a simple political fixer, or was he a man of principle, with a value system that would advance the interests of peace, freedom, and social justice?

LBJ began quietly, so quietly that senators and congressmen in the back rows had to strain to hear. To no one's surprise, he paid tribute to John F. Kennedy—"The greatest leader of our time"—and emphasized continuity. JFK had had a dream "of conquering the vastness of space . . . the dream of a Peace Corps in less developed nations . . . the dream of education for all of our children—the dream of jobs for all who seek them and need them—the dream of care for our elderly—the dream of an all out attack on mental illness." President Kennedy had called to the nation, "Let us begin . . . I would say to all my fellow Americans, let us continue." [87]

After each dream was enunciated, Congress, the Supreme Court, the Joint Chiefs, foreign dignitaries, and the packed gallery broke into thunderous applause. Sensing that Johnson was about to address the issue of civil rights, southerners sat forward in their seats. "No memorial oration or eulogy could more eloquently honor President Kennedy's memory than the earliest possible passage of the civil rights bill for which he fought so long. We have talked long enough in this country about equal rights. We have talked for one hundred years or more. It is time now to write the next chapter, and to write it in the books of law." [88]

But civil rights was not only John F. Kennedy's cause, it was Lyndon Johnson's as well. "I urge you again, as I did in 1957 and again in 1960, to enact a civil rights law so that we can move forward to eliminate from this Nation every trace of discrimination and oppression that is based upon race or color." Again applause, although Russell and his followers were conspicuous by their silence. There was in their posture a mood more of resignation than defiance, however. Among black Americans there rose a collective sigh of relief. "You could hear 20,000 people unpacking their bags," comedian and civil rights activist Dick Gregory later joked. [89]

As to foreign affairs, there was to be peace through strength. "The Nation will keep its commitments from South Viet-Nam to Berlin," Johnson said, making a most significant linkage. And finally to the nation and the world's most immediate concern: "Let us turn away from the fanatics of the far left and the far right, from the apostles of bitterness and bigotry, from those defiant of law, and those who pour venom into our Nation's bloodstream." The speech ended with the first stanza of "America the Beautiful"—maudlin for most, under most circumstances, but somehow fitting coming from Lyndon Johnson's lips on November 27, 1963.[90]

The speech to the joint session of Congress was meant to evoke memories of JFK, but it was pure LBJ: military preparedness, peace through strength, holding the line against international communism, and social justice at home. The phrase to which Johnson's auditors should have paid most attention was "We will carry on the fight against poverty and misery, and disease and ignorance, in other lands and in our own."[91]

Johnson's ascendancy to the presidency made demands and presented opportunities that enabled him to transcend mere pragmatism. It was at this point that LBJ's value system and larger ambition came into play. "I do not accept Government as just the 'art of the practicable.' It is the business of deciding what is right and then finding the way to do it," he would declare in 1964.[92]

And there was a value system. Consider Johnson's self-acknowledged mentors: Huey Long; Maury Maverick; Charles Marsh, the Texas newspaper publisher who wrote speeches for Henry Wallace in 1948; Samuel Ealy Johnson, Lyndon's ardently populist father, and Rebekah Baines Johnson, his mother and a Christian social activist. "I am not a theologian. I am not a philosopher. I am just a public servant that is doing the very best I know how," LBJ would say to a group of southern Baptists in 1964.

> But in more than three decades of public life, I have seen firsthand how basic spiritual beliefs and deeds can shatter barriers of politics and bigotry. I have seen those barriers crumble in the presence of faith and hope, and from this experience I have drawn new hope that the seemingly insurmountable moral issues that we face at home and abroad today can be resolved by men of strong faith and men of brave deeds . . . Great questions of war and peace, of civil rights and education, the elimination of poverty at home and abroad, are the concern of millions who see no difference in this regard between their beliefs and their social obligations. This principle, the identity of private morality and public conscience, is as deeply rooted in our tradition and Constitution as the principle of legal separation. Washington in his first inaugural said that the roots of national policy lay in private morality.[93]

"You are using the 'moral imperatives of the times,' " John Roche, president of the Americans for Democratic Action, would write LBJ admiringly later that same year, "on the consciousness of the American people."[94]

BEFORE HE COULD GET ON with the job of improving the lot of humanity and containing communism, the new president had to lay to rest some burning issues left over from the assassination: Who had in fact killed John F. Kennedy? Was his death the product of a right-wing conspiracy, or an international plot hatched by the KGB, or perhaps Castro's intelligence service? If, God forbid, the communists had killed Kennedy, what should be America's response? That question would have to be thoroughly explored before the details of the plot were revealed.

To further complicate matters, there were those in the United States who wanted the communists to be found responsible, and even if they were not, to make it appear so in order to provoke a confrontation. Moreover, who should investigate and who should decide these issues? The FBI, which hungered for control, was suspect in the minds of many. The homicide had been committed in Texas, and Attorney General Waggoner Carr would claim jurisdiction. For many Americans, however, that would smack of trusting the investigation to a culture and political system that had been responsible for the deed itself. But if the inquiry into Kennedy's death were removed from the hands of Texas authorities, the Lone Star State, along with other former members of the Confederacy, would scream states' rights.

Contributing to the stress of the situation was Johnson's understandable fears for his own safety. "The President, after the Kennedy assassination, was very fearful of his own life," said Cartha "Deke" DeLoach of the FBI. "He was a man of courage, but also he didn't want to take any chances." Though he knew that he risked violating jurisdictional lines, LBJ had the FBI put an armed agent aboard Air Force One on almost every trip.[95] "There were times [during the 1964 presidential campaign] when he did not want to step off the plane in front of that crowd. It took a lot of guts. And once he did, he was exuberant; he felt liberated." Following one plunge into a Denver throng, Johnson, safely back aboard the plane, exclaimed, "No one shot at me."[96]

ON THE MORNING OF NOVEMBER 23, FBI Director J. Edgar Hoover had called Johnson to report on what the Bureau knew of the assassination. By that time, Oswald had been taken into custody, and his rifle and three spent shells had been recovered. It was also known that Oswald or a person fitting his description had visited the Soviet Embassy in Mexico City the previous September.[97]

The Soviets went out of their way to dissociate themselves from Oswald and the assassination. Horace Busby recalled that shortly after the return flight from Dallas, the State Department delivered a thick folder from the Russian Embassy. It was a day-by-day, hour-by-hour log of Oswald's movements. According to Busby, LBJ grinned and said, That's the Russian 'me no Alamo.' The soldiers in Santa Anna's army when they were captured at San Jacinto would raise the hands and say, 'me no Alamo.' "[98]

LBJ's initial reaction was to leave the investigation to Texas Attorney General Carr, who would convene a board of inquiry and rely on evidence collected by the FBI. Immediately, however, he came under pressure from a variety of sources to impanel a blue ribbon national commission to investigate. On November 26, the *Washington Post* ran an editorial to this effect. Figures from Yale

Law School Dean Eugene Rostow to columnist Joe Alsop lobbied the White House. Johnson continued to resist. "We don't want to be in the position of saying that we have come into a state, other than the FBI [and] told them that their integrity is no good and that we're going to have some carpetbag trials," he told Alsop. Showing the stress he was under, Johnson deluged Alsop with a flood of rhetoric, his voice shrill, verging at times on hysteria.[99]

Within hours, however, Johnson began to come around to the idea of a national commission. He received word that the assistant district attorney in Dallas intended to file a complaint against Oswald, charging that he had murdered Kennedy as part of an international communist conspiracy.[100] Senator James Eastland of Mississippi, a rabid anticommunist, was lobbying the congressional leadership to allow him to conduct his own investigation.[101] At the same time, Johnson received information from the CIA, FBI, and USIA that the Soviet military had gone on full alert. "According to our source," read the FBI report, "officials of the Communist party of the Soviet Union believed there was some well-organized conspiracy on the part of the 'ultra right' in the United States to effect a 'coup.' They seemed convinced that the assassination was not the deed of one man, but that it arose out of a carefully planned campaign in which several people played a part. They felt that those elements interested in utilizing the assassination and playing on anticommunist sentiment in the United States would then utilize this act to stop negotiations with the Soviet Union, attack Cuba and thereafter spread the war . . . Our source added that . . . it was indicated that 'now' the KGB was in possession of data purporting to indicate President Johnson was responsible for the assassination of the late President."[102]

This intelligence came at the very time Hoover was breaking the news to Johnson that Oswald was tied in with the Cuban Fair Play Committee, "which is pro-Castro, and dominated by Communism and financed, to some extent, by the Castro government."[103] It seemed as if the anticommunists and communists were determined to have a war out of the assassination. "Speculation about Oswald's motivation ought to be cut off," Deputy Attorney General Nicholas Katzenbach told Moyers, "and we should have some basis for rebutting the thought that this was a Communist conspiracy or (as the Iron Curtain press is saying) a right-wing conspiracy to blame it on the Communists . . . We can scarcely let the world see us totally in the image of the Dallas police when our President is murdered."[104]

LBJ agreed. "Some fellow will be testifying . . . comin' up from Dallas," he told Speaker John McCormack. "[He will say] I think Khrushchev planned this whole thing and he got our President assassinated . . . You can see what that'll lead us to right quick."[105]

On November 29, LBJ appointed a bipartisan panel headed by Chief Justice Earl Warren to investigate the circumstances surrounding President Kennedy's death. It included Democratic Senator Richard Russell of Georgia, Republican Senator John Sherman Cooper of Kentucky, Democratic Congressman Hale Boggs of Louisiana, Republican Congressman Gerald Ford of Michigan, former CIA Director Allen Dulles, and former U.S. High Commissioner of Germany John J. McCloy. Neither Warren nor Russell wanted to serve, the former because he did not think that such a role was appropriate for the chief justice, and the latter because he would have to serve with the author of *Brown v. Board of Education.* That Johnson was able to get these two men together was a testament to his persuasive power and relentless will. Russell required several conversations. "You've never turned your country down," he yelled at Russell. "This is not me . . . this is your country . . . and don't tell me what you can do and what you can't . . . because I can't arrest you and I'm not going to put the FBI on you but you're goddamned sure going to serve." Russell protested again, but in the end he caved in: "If it is for the good [of the] country, you know damned well I'll do it . . . and I'll do it for you, for that matter . . . I can serve with a Communist . . . and I can serve with a Negro . . . I can serve with a Chinaman."[106]

For the next ten months, the Warren Commission dug, sifted, and deliberated. "The White House never gave us any instruction," Warren later said, "never even looked at our work until I took it to the president. The president never once in any way, shape or form, made any suggestions; no limitations of any kind were put on us."[107]

In the end, the Warren Commission reported findings that LBJ and virtually everyone else with the national interest at heart hoped it would: President Kennedy had been killed by shots fired from a single gun at the hands of Lee Harvey Oswald, who was acting entirely alone. His murderer, Jack Rubenstein (Ruby), also acted alone, responding to motives that were entirely personal. The president "rambled about somewhat as to who may have caused it," Deke DeLoach later observed. " 'Could it have been the CIA?' And I said, 'No, sir.' And he didn't think so himself, he was just rambling in his conversation. 'Could it have been Castro? Could it have been the Soviet Union?' And I told him no, that the investigation had been very thorough . . . that there was no conspiracy involved and that Lee Harvey Oswald—and Oswald alone did it . . . He never really felt that the CIA did it; he never felt that anything was wrong with the FBI report, but he just wanted to make sure there was further confirming evidence and that's why he established the Warren Commission."[108]

It was time to move on.

CHAPTER 21

"KENNEDY WAS TOO
CONSERVATIVE FOR ME"

L YNDON JOHNSON PROVED TO BE THE MOST ARDENT
presidential lawmaker of the twentieth century. Presidents Theodore
Roosevelt and Woodrow Wilson had been the first to depart from
the Gilded Age maxim that Congress should legislate and the executive administrate. Wilson, in particular, the author of *Congressional Government*
and an admirer of the British parliamentary system, argued that the president,
while chief executive, was also leader of his party and the only official elected
by the body politic as a whole. As such, he should develop a legislative program
and, through persuasion or coercion, compel Congress to adopt it. In response
to the crisis of the Depression, Franklin Roosevelt set a new standard for activist
presidents during his first one hundred days. Yet LBJ's efforts eclipsed even
his, especially in view of the prosperity that prevailed during the 1960s.

From late 1963 through 1966, Lyndon Johnson interacted with senators and
representatives on a daily and even hourly basis. He became personally familiar
with the details of the more than one thousand major bills Congress considered
during this period. His memory banks were still full of information concerning
the political characteristics of the various congressional and senatorial districts
and the personal peccadilloes of those men and women who served them.
"There is but one way for a President to deal with the Congress," Johnson
would observe, "and that is continuously, incessantly, and without interruption.
If it's really going to work, the relationship between the President and the Congress has got to be almost incestuous. He's got to know them even better than
they know themselves. And then, on the basis of this knowledge, he's got to
build a system that stretches from the cradle to the grave, from the moment a
bill is introduced to the moment it is officially enrolled as the law of the land."[1]

As Congress passed one revolutionary piece of domestic legislation after another, the pressure on those involved became almost unbearable. "Don't assume anything," LBJ told himself and his aides, "make sure every possible weapon is brought to bear . . . keep everybody involved; don't let them slacken."[2]

LBJ's initial dealings with Congress were complicated, as he had to work around the Kennedy White House staff, all of whom he asked to stay on. There was Kenneth O'Donnell, JFK's chief of staff; Larry O'Brien, his congressional liaison; speechwriters Ted Sorenson and Richard Goodwin; house intellectual Arthur Schlesinger Jr.; Pierre Salinger, Kennedy's press secretary; and Lee C. White, deputy special counsel. "I knew how they felt," he later observed. "The impact of Kennedy's death was evident everywhere—in the looks on their faces and the sound of their voices. He was gone and with his going they must have felt that everything had changed. Suddenly, they were outsiders just as I had been for almost three years, outsiders on the inside."[3] O'Donnell initially could not even bring himself to come into the office. "Kenny O'Donnell sort of left the day that Johnson walked in," Vicky McCammon recalled. "Well, he didn't leave, he was there and still serving as appointments secretary supposedly, but spending all of his afternoons drunk over at Duke Ziebert's, crying, drunk at the bar."[4]

Salinger, the portly, fun-loving "Plucky" of Camelot fame, was overtly cooperative with the new president, but behind his back he oozed contempt. He decided to leave the first time LBJ, his voice low and seductive, tried to lure his press secretary to a naked swim in the White House pool.[5] The Kennedy staffers did make an effort to get along with Moyers, Valenti, Jenkins, and the rest of the LBJ people, although there were some grating incidents.[6] O'Donnell and Salinger departed rather quickly; Sorenson did not dally long, nor did Schlesinger; Goodwin lasted a year and a half. Only O'Brien and White made the conversion.

Larry O'Brien was a delightful surprise. He was a public relations expert who had joined Kennedy's staff in 1952. A gravelly voiced, amiable man with a good sense of humor, O'Brien was a traditional New Deal Democrat. Though the Kennedy legislative program was caught in gridlock by the time JFK was gunned down, that was no fault of O'Brien and his very capable assistant, Henry Wilson.

O'Brien and Johnson seemed to hit it off immediately. The Irishman had fallen in love with congressional politics, and like his new boss, he took a can-do, art-of-the-possible approach to the House and Senate. Perhaps most important to LBJ, O'Brien was tenacious and tireless. In turn, O'Brien was impressed with Johnson's openness, his commitment to social justice, and his high political ethics. Johnson kept his word, he did not lie or misrepresent, and he never used information about legislators' private lives to gain advantage. As in the past, he did not ask a representative or senator to do something that was going to get him or her defeated, unless the public interest absolutely demanded it, and then LBJ was up front about the matter.

The true instrument of the Johnson legislative will, however, was the telephone. Given his other duties as president, LBJ could not possibly have the same amount of face time with legislators as he did when he headed the Senate. During his first two and a half years in office, LBJ had most of his conversations taped and then transcribed by his secretaries. The purpose was not, as the tapes have subsequently revealed, to gather dirt on his former colleagues or to trick them into saying things or making commitments that could be used against them with others, but rather to keep track of the incredibly complex political math that underlay the hundreds of pieces of legislation that were enacted during these intense early years. What happened on an urban transit bill would have an impact on civil rights; that year's farm bill might be used to buy southern silence on certain aspects of civil rights legislation; a conservative might not be able to support both Medicare and federal aid to education and survive the next election, but he or she might be able to withstand one if federal funds were forthcoming to help build a new hospital or vocational school. Individual legislators had only to keep up with the part of the web that affected them directly; LBJ had to keep up with it all.

ON DECEMBER 7, some two weeks after the assassination, the Johnsons officially moved from The Elms to the White House. In her bedroom, Lady Bird found a bouquet of flowers and a note from Jackie: "I wish you a happy arrival in your new house, Lady Bird—Remember—you will be happier here. Love, Jackie."[7]

Lady Bird was not so sure.

Jackie had left another note, one that had an edge to it. When it came time to choose sleeping quarters, LBJ selected the Lincoln bedroom, Lady Bird the room adjoining. Opposite the large canopied bed was a white marble mantel that bore the inscription "In this room Abraham Lincoln slept during his occupancy of the White House as President of the United States, March 4, 1861–April 13, 1865." Beneath the Lincoln inscription, a new one had been carved. "In this room," it read, "lived John Fitzgerald Kennedy with his wife Jacqueline—during the two years, ten months and two days he was President of the United States. January 20, 1961–November 22, 1963."[8]

A month later, James "Scotty" Reston, the *New York Times* columnist, was visiting the White House and the president showed him the inscription. "Johnson nodded to it," Reston wrote in his memoirs, "and raised his eyebrows but didn't say a word . . . The stone has since been removed. By whom, nobody seems to know."[9]

Lyndon and Lady Bird planned to spend Christmas at the ranch in Texas, but on the way they intended to take a detour to attend the funeral of Pennsylvania Congressman William Green. The day before they were to leave, Johnson put in a call to Eddie Senz, the famous New York hairdresser. "All right now," the president said to the dumbfounded Senz, "I'm a poor man, and I don't make much money, but I got a wife and a couple of daughters, and four or five people that run around with me, and I like the way you make them look . . . This is your country and I want to see what you want to do about it." Senz replied that the president should not concern himself with the cost. He was honored to be asked and would fly down as soon as he could. Okay, Johnson said. "I'm going to leave you a hundred-dollar bill, and I'll pay your transportation, but I can't pay you like we normally do." [10]

Later that afternoon, he called Lady Bird, who was under the dryer. "When he gets through with Marie [Fehmer]," he told his wife, "tell him I want him to do Yolanda [Boozer, one of his secretaries], because she's got to have about a bale cut off if I'm going to look at her through Christmas." [11]

MEANWHILE, LBJ continued to court the Kennedys. When Pierre Salinger advised the president that he thought it best that Kenny O'Donnell and Ethel Kennedy ride on the same plane with Lyndon and Lady Bird to Bill Green's funeral, he replied, "Damn sure is better to ride with me than a separate plane . . . Wherever I go, Kenny O'Donnell and Ethel Kennedy go and anybody else named Kennedy—or anybody that's ever smelled the Kennedys." [12] Later, at the ranch on the 27th, he called Kenny O'Donnell and told him he wanted to appoint Jackie U.S. ambassador to Mexico. O'Donnell said that he did not think she would accept. "Hell," Johnson said, "I'd make her pope if I could." [13]

BACK HOME for the first time since the assassination, LBJ relished the Hill Country and ranch life and let the tensions and anxieties of the previous five weeks drain away. Over the phone his voice was soft and modulated, not frantic and shrill as it had so often been during the days following the assassination. He conversed and laughed with Judge Moursund and other old friends. With former Tennessee governor Buford Ellington as his guest, he took boat rides, watched the deer, and treated himself to two naps a day. [14]

THE FIRST ITEM on LBJ's legislative agenda when he returned to Washington was an $11 billion tax cut proposal inherited from the Kennedy administration. The politics of tax cutting in the 1960s was the opposite of today's: liberals supported cuts; conservatives opposed. Understanding why requires a bit of perspective. Famed economist John Maynard Keynes, to whom many New Dealers looked for guidance, believed that laissez-faire economic theory would work only under conditions of full employment. He devoted a good part of his time to proving that governmental acceptance of more responsibility for the smooth working of the economy, including full employment (approximately 95 percent), could increase human freedom and choice. Keynes never questioned the fundamental principles of private property, competition, self-interest, the market mechanism, or profit making. To Keynes, the object of government activism was to enable capitalism to work more smoothly and humanely. [15] If the task sometimes required deficit spending and/or tax cuts, so be it. The advent of prosperity would restore fiscal balance.

Meanwhile, congressional conservatives opposed tax cuts because in those days, they believed deeply in balancing the budget whatever the circumstances. Thus, the lines were drawn between spend-and-cut liberals and tax-and-save conservatives. The leading antagonists were Walter Heller, the liberal Minnesota economist who was chair of the Council of Economic Advisers, and Senator Harry Byrd, the hoary-headed reactionary from Virginia who was chair of the Senate Finance Committee.[16]

On November 25, LBJ met with the "Troika," the economic team that Kennedy had relied on to develop policy—Heller, Secretary of the Treasury Douglas Dillon, and Budget Director Kermit Gordon—to discuss the tax bill and budgetary matters in general. The first thing Johnson did was tell Heller to call off his liberal dogs. "Tell them to lay off, Walter. Tell them to quit lobbying. I'm for them. I know they have good programs, and that the economy needs to have that money pumped in. I want an expanding economy. The budget should be $108 billion."[17] But that was not politically realistic. If liberals expected to get the tax cut, the budget could not be a cent above $100 billion. If it is, he said, "you won't pee one drop." Dillon observed that they would have to pay the price for the tax bill but "then when you have it, you can do what you want." Right, said Johnson, "Like Ike did—talked economy and then spent."[18] In the short run then, tax cuts trumped expenditures for public works. Money for entitlement programs could be wrenched from the military-industrial complex.

In the days that followed, LBJ met with leaders of organized labor and big business, lobbying for a tax cut. He lobbied with individuals and groups. He telephoned Wall Street bankers and agribusinessmen. And he met almost continuously with Harry Byrd. The Virginian remained adamantly opposed to a tax cut. It would unbalance the budget and lead to economic and financial chaos, he said.

In the midst of these talks LBJ consulted Budget Director Gordon. He recalled that Johnson's first instruction was to get the budget down to $100 billion, which would not be very difficult, but then he began to press for more cuts. And more cuts. Farm programs suffered; so did education and space. Gordon and Heller became worried, concerned that they were dealing with a Herbert Hoover masquerading in Roosevelt's clothing.[19]

The president's principal ally in his budget-cutting campaign was, surprisingly, Secretary of Defense Robert McNamara. In various meetings he insisted that the United States had two and a half to three times the number of missiles, submarines, and airplanes as the Soviets and that they would never catch up.[20] Johnson even went so far as to tell CIA Director John McCone that he was thinking of pulling U.S. troops out of Europe and reverting to the Eisenhower "New Look" approach to save money.[21] With McNamara's blessing, the president sent letters to seventy-five hundred defense contractors demanding economies and cost reductions. Indeed, despite the fears of liberals, most of the reductions came in defense ($1 billion), in space ($600 million), and in atomic energy ($300 million).[22] "I am not going to produce atomic bombs as a WPA project," Johnson declared.[23]

At the crucial moment, LBJ invited Byrd to a private luncheon at the White House. Jack Valenti remembers it as the only time LBJ ever ate in the small room off the Oval Office. Johnson "personally . . . supervised the setting and the menu."[24] If he could get the budget below $100 billion, would Bryd let the tax bill out of his committee? "We might be able to do some business," the Virginian replied. Johnson subsequently called Byrd and told him that the administration would come in with a $97.9 billion budget. Byrd congratulated the president on his frugality: "I'm going to have to vote against the bill, but I'll be working for you behind the scenes."[25]

As the decisive votes approached, Johnson personally called every congressional waverer. "It looks like to me that you are not being very wise in your southern strategy," LBJ told Richard Russell, a member of the Finance Committee. "It is not up to me to tell you how smart you are, for the son to tell the father. But looks like you and Harry Byrd and Albert Gore [D-Tennessee] ought to let that damn tax bill come on out . . . What you will do [if you don't] is you will have every businessman in the country messing with your civil rights."[26]

In part, Johnson's aggressive budget and tax cutting was an attempt to reach out to the business community. He spent his first six weeks in office trying to repair relations that had become frayed under JFK, primarily by cultivating members of the Business Advisory Council, the private body established in 1933 to help ensure that the policies of federal agencies were acceptable to Wall Street and large manufacturers. Johnson understood that many industrialists and retailers appreciated the boost a tax cut could give to the economy, Taft-style conservatism notwithstanding. In early January 1964, he had the entire BAC membership to the White House for dinner, including W. B. Murphy of Campbell Soup, Albert Nickerson of Mobil Oil, and Frederick Kappel of AT&T. "It's the first time in our history," one executive remarked as he exited the White House, "that we've been invited to dine at the White House—it didn't even happen under Ike."[27]

At that dinner, LBJ told his audience of executives that he was going to cut future federal spending far below the levels projected by the Kennedy administration. One by one, cabinet officers rose to tell the corporate leaders exactly where the cuts were going to be made.[28] He also hinted at the moves he was going to make in the areas of civil rights, education, medical insurance, poverty, and area redevelopment. "President Johnson really gave the business guys the treatment," Orville Freeman recalled approvingly in his diary. "He emphasized more than anything else Civil Rights and told the story of his Negro cook. Later on in the week Bob McNamara said to me it was an amazing performance—then he kinda grinned and said, can you imagine John F. Kennedy telling these businessmen that the Negro cook had to stop along the road to relieve herself because there was no place to go to the bathroom, and yet he said, and he knew many of these people, that they were much more enthusiastic and much more convinced by Lyndon Johnson than they would have been by John Kennedy."[29]

Addressing the five thousand delegates to the national Chamber of Commerce convention, LBJ declared, "If you don't remember anything else that I tell you here today, I want you to remember this: 'If peaceful change is impossible . . . then a violent change is inevitable.' " He accused them of having "a martyr complex." He told them that they had a bigger stake than any other group in fighting poverty and ignorance. His talk was punctuated with waves of applause.[30]

Economically, the tax cut of 1964 was a stroke of genius. Month after month, quarter after quarter, the major indices of growth moved upward. Gross national product rose from $569.7 billion in the first quarter of 1964 to $631.2 billion in the last quarter of 1965. Disposable personal income shot up from $423 billion in the first quarter of 1964 to $486.1 in the last three months of 1965. The number of poor families in America, defined as earning less than $3,000 per year in 1965 dollars, dropped from 8.5 million in 1963 to 8 million in 1965. The number of people out of work dropped sharply from 4.1 million in January 1964 to 3.1 million in December 1965. Moreover, in the first half of 1965, government revenues had actually increased $7.5 billion over the prior pre–tax cut year. It was a president's dream and a supply-sider's harbinger: lower taxes and new funds for existing and even new domestic programs. The primary goal of the Kennedy-Johnson tax program was not ingratiation of the well-to-do per se, but creation of the political and economic capital to fund measures of health, education, and welfare.

Prosperity created by the tax cut of 1964 would have a profound impact on Lyndon Johnson and his crusade to create an American Utopia. By 1964 John Kenneth Galbraith, who, like Walter Heller, was an interpreter and applicator of Keynesian thought, was hard at work on a new book, the title of which would be *The New Industrial State*. Taking up where he had left off in his *Affluent Society*, Galbraith discussed the evolution of the modern corporation, demonstrating how, in cooperation with government and labor, it had acted effectively to minimize risk, protect itself from the vagaries of the free market system, and ensure its survival. What resulted was not stagnation but greater efficiency and productivity so that it had become possible to use the energies of the economy for nonindustrial purposes: "the expansion of public services, the assertion of the aesthetic dimension of life, widened choice as between income and leisure, the emancipation of education." What Galbraith proposed was that the emerging scientific and educational elite be harnessed to this purpose by the will of the federal government.[31]

LBJ had known and respected Galbraith for years. Throughout his presidency, Johnson would advocate a kind of corporatism, that is, prosperity as a result of labor-management-government cooperation. As a last resort, the federal government should and would compel cooperation, and it would not hesitate to use public monies to finance programs to help those who could not help themselves. Nevertheless, the private enterprise system *was* the economy. Johnson was determined that he and the federal government would do everything possible to nourish it. It would be the goose that lay the golden eggs of social and economic justice, of a higher standard of living for all Americans. Shortly after he assumed office, LBJ instructed Bill Moyers and Eric Goldman to go out into the byways of academe and assemble task forces that would address the great social and economic problems of the day and suggest policies to remedy them.[32]

Johnson, then, fully embraced the "politics of productivity." Given the affluence and technical expertise existing in America, the federal government could care for those who could not care for themselves, provide education and opportunity to the disadvantaged, and ensure social justice for all without taking from one group of citizens and giving to another. All could be invited to the table and all could be served. For Johnson, the class-based politics of the 1930s had given way to the interest-based politics of the 1940s but was now about to give way to the consensus-based politics of the 1960s. A reformer's dream was about to come true: justice and equity without conflict.

UNFORTUNATELY, Johnson would encounter conflict every day, starting with the press, who turned against him almost immediately. It began with an incident on the plane returning Johnson and the press corps from Texas after the Christmas holidays. During the flight, Johnson wandered into the section where the reporters were sitting and began kibitzing. Suddenly he became serious. "I'm the only President you've got," he said, "and I intend to be President of all the people. I need your help. If I succeed you succeed. We all succeed or fail together." He then made a startling proposition. "There's no reason why members of the White House press corps shouldn't be the best-informed, most respected, highest-paid reporters in Washington. If you help me, I'll help you. I'll make you all big men in your profession." But "if you want to play it the other way, I know how to play it both ways, too, and I know how to cut off the flow of news except in handouts."[33] Later, in conversation with an interviewer, Johnson aired his views on the press in all their cynicism. "Reporters are puppets," he said. "They simply respond to the pull of the most powerful strings. Every reporter has a constituency in mind when he writes his stories. Sometimes it is simply his editor or his publisher, but often it is some political group he wants to please or some intellectual society he wants to court . . . There is no such thing as an objective news story."[34]

This monologue indicated a complete misunderstanding of how the press perceived its role. In their collective minds, the White House press corps saw its relationship with the executive as primarily an adversarial one. They were there to report impartially, to uncover lies and deception, to expose hypocrisy, to be the watchdog for the body politic. The notion that they should become willing partners with a particular president in his efforts to see his program enacted and thus enhance his chances of being reelected was appalling. Johnson was reacting to his experience with Texas newspaper and radio stations owned and/or operated by business people who saw themselves as political operatives as well. Deals for support were made all the time. He was also reacting to the relatively new phenomenon of the national news pundit—figures like Walter Lippmann, James Reston, and Joe Alsop, who had actually helped write some of JFK's speeches. They had felt free to give presidents and secretaries of state advice. Indeed, they saw themselves as public intellectuals who were part of the policy-making process. But Johnson's refusal to either understand or cater to the press's self-image was a major misstep for which he was to pay dearly.

At his December 18 press conference, the president was asked about his budget for the fiscal year 1965. He was working with President Kennedy's $99 billion budget, he said. As a result of agency requests and new legislation in the areas of mental retardation, poverty, and area redevelopment, the budget would come in around $100.7 or $100.8 billion.[35] Then, at a New Year's Eve party at the Driskill, Johnson dropped by the bar for a drink with the journalists who had been assigned to cover him. He was struggling to make each and every cut he could, he said, but the best he could probably do was $100 billion. A number of reporters subsequently wrote sympathetic stories about the anguished decisions LBJ and his aides were having to make. Then came word in January that the 1965 budget would be $97.9 billion, lower than Kennedy's 1964 budget. Those who had written on the matter were furious. They had been manipulated into making Lyndon Johnson look like a financial wizard. The press corps would never quite believe what came out of LBJ's mouth thereafter. Their questions at press conferences were frequently provocative and needling. Johnson reacted in kind, in turn contemptuous, rude, and even hostile. Many, including Johnson himself, date the credibility gap to the knock-up over the 1965 budget.

IF THE TAX CUT of 1964 was the first building block in the edifice of Johnson's American Utopia, the second was the War on Poverty. Intertwined as it was with issues of race, public morality, and the proper role of government in society, the poverty program would come to define the administration as much as civil rights and Vietnam in the minds of public and press.

For 150 years, industrializing societies had struggled to come to grips with the problem of the permanently disadvantaged. Britain in the mid-nineteenth century, in the midst of industrialization and the enclosure movement, had become home to a burgeoning population of chronically poor people made famous by journalist Henry Mayhew. In the United States, mass awareness of the existence of a more or less permanent underclass grew out of the Progressive movement. Jacob Riis produced a score of books and articles, including *How the Other Half Lives,* describing the plight of those New Yorkers who struggled to eke out an existence in the city's tenements and sweatshops. Meanwhile Jane Addams and other social activists were attempting to mobilize local governments and political parties as well as philanthropists in a movement to alleviate not only the material but the spiritual plight of the poor. Believers like Rebekah Johnson were reading C. M. Sheldon's *In His Steps,* which argued that if Christians would live the lives Christ had called them to, it would be impossible for millions to walk the streets in search of food and for thousands of children to die each year from lack of adequate health care. The coming of the Great Depression spawned a new wave of revelatory and reform literature. John Steinbeck, LBJ's favorite author, aroused the consciousness of millions with his *Grapes of Wrath.* The pictures of rural poverty produced by the Farm Security Administration during the Dust Bowl reinforced Steinbeck's images. Then, in the 1940s and 1950s, some 3 million blacks migrated from the rural South into northern, southern, midwestern, and West Coast cities, where they were segregated into rat-infested ghettos. From the day in 1944 when the first mechanical cotton pickers were tested in Mississippi, African American farm workers were doomed to move or starve. Birmingham, Atlanta, Houston in the South; New York, Philadelphia, and Newark in the North; Chicago in the Midwest; and Los Angeles and Oakland in the West became home to a new urban underclass. Jobs were scarce to nonexistent, city services such as water and sewage were substandard, education was strictly segregated, and escape was virtually impossible. In 1962, Michael Harrington, a Catholic idealist and socialist, introduced Americans to the "culture of poverty" in *The Other America.* That same year CBS ran Edward R. Murrow's *Harvest of Shame,* a powerful indictment of poverty among migrant farm workers, and Harry M. Caudill published *Night Comes to the Cumberlands,* depicting the abject poverty of the half-million whites who lived on the Cumberland Plateau in the Appalachian Mountains.[36]

Plans to eradicate poverty excited Johnson's imagination, but he knew that government programs to achieve the objective would be controversial. As Sargent Shriver, whom LBJ would select to command the antipoverty effort, later observed, LBJ was attempting something revolutionary: "the only national effort ever conducted by the majority for the benefit of the minority."[37] The Roosevelt Revolution had taken place during a time when a huge proportion of middle-class whites were in dire straits. The Johnson administration would be attempting to use the federal government and taxpayers' money to eradicate poverty during a period of rising prosperity and growing racial tension. Walter Heller understood this; at the ranch during the Christmas holidays he, the president, Kermit Gordon, Bill Moyers, and Jack Valenti discussed ways and means. The administration's commitment to the cause would have to be loud and clear. "One thing I did know," LBJ later told journalist Douglass Cater. "When I got through, no one in this country would be able to ignore the poverty in our midst."[38] Johnson and Heller also agreed that if white middle-class America was going to join the fight, they would have to be assured that the campaign would destroy, not subsidize and perpetuate, the culture of poverty.

Heller's argument that "poverty was not only wrong, it was something we could not afford" was music to Johnson's ears.[39] His goal, as the president subsequently told conservatives like Richard Russell, Harry Byrd, and Everett Dirksen, was to "make tax payers rather than tax eaters" out of the disadvantaged. "This administration today, here and now, declares unconditional war on poverty in America," LBJ proclaimed in his State of the Union address on January 8, 1964. He envisioned area redevelopment programs, youth employment legislation, a National Service Corps paralleling at home what the Peace Corps was doing abroad, a broader food stamp program, Medicare for the elderly, and special education for the most depressed areas.[40]

Like other crusaders against poverty before him, LBJ would be swimming against a strong tide of individualism in American society, which prized self-reliance and condemned government largesse to the poor as counterproductive. Well into the twentieth century, many Americans accepted the conservative truism that poverty was the fault of the poor themselves, the product of character flaws beyond the reach of legislative remedy. Even the most hardened disciples of laissez-faire, however, admitted that there were in society those who could not care for themselves. The sick, the lame, widows with dependent children could not work and must be supported—they were the "deserving poor"—but the undeserving, the lazy, the venal, the improvident could not claim support by right and must rely on private charity.[41] Politically, poverty was primarily a Democratic issue, one that Republicans were more than willing to let them have. It was of great benefit to the GOP in its never-ending struggle to paint the Democratic party and liberalism in general as soft, emotional, and even anti-American. Campaigning for president in West Virginia in 1960, Richard Nixon denounced his Democratic opponent's assertion that 17 million people went to bed hungry every night. Such assertions only provided "grist for the Communist propaganda mill," he said and repeated Eisenhower's reaction to Kennedy's claim: "Now look, I go to bed hungry every night, but that's because I'm on a diet."[42]

When LBJ addressed the nation, neither he nor his advisers had a clear picture of the strategy and specific programs that would be involved. He needed a point man. Robert Kennedy let it be known that he would like such an assignment, but Johnson had no intention of giving a sworn enemy such a platform, especially as Bobby was then trying to position himself to be the Democratic party's vice presidential candidate in 1964. Galbraith suggested Moyers, but he was too young and inexperienced. Besides, Johnson needed him to be available for a variety of assignments. But Moyers's former boss in the Peace Corps, Sargent Shriver, was perfect.[43] A Catholic, he had worked with the poor as part of the Catholic Worker Movement in New York. Shriver was a disciple of St. Francis of Assisi and an active member of the St. Vincent de Paul Society in Chicago. As president of the school board there, he had worked to improve ghetto schools.[44] In addition to being an idealist, Shriver was a shrewd politician. He and the Peace Corps were perhaps the only two aspects of the New Frontier that were genuinely popular on the Hill.

Johnson recruited Shriver in typical whirlwind fashion. On the morning of February 1, the phone rang at Sarge and Eunice's home in Washington. Shriver had just returned from a Peace Corps trip to Europe.

"Sarge?" the president said.

"Good morning, Mr. President. How are you?"

"I'm gonna announce your appointment at that press conference."

"What press conference?"

"This afternoon."

"Could you just say that you have asked me to study this?"

"Hell, no. They've studied and studied. They [the press] want to know who in the hell is going to do this."

Shriver asked for a week's delay so that he could put some plan together. It would serve neither his, the president's, nor the program's interest if it appeared that he did not know what he was talking about. No, said Johnson, we'll announce you as head and tell the news people that you are putting together a team that will devise a workable program in the immediate future. Breathless, resigned, Shriver gave in.[45]

In the weeks that followed, Johnson made it clear that the administration's antipoverty program would not encompass welfare in the form of direct relief or a government jobs program that would compete with the private sector. During a cabinet meeting in February, Secretary of Labor Willard Wirtz proposed a massive jobs program similar to the WPA, costing $3 billion to $5 billion and financed by an increased tax on tobacco. Johnson wanted none of it. "I have never seen a colder reception from the president," a staffer in attendance said. "He just—absolute blank stare—implied without even opening his mouth that Shriver should move on to the next proposal."[46] Nor was LBJ interested in direct relief. "[Conservative House Rules Committee Chairman Howard] Smith has got to understand that I want these people taken off relief and trained to do something," he told Congressman Carl Albert (D-Oklahoma). "We're spending $8 billion on relief now . . . But I'm gonna cut down that $8 billion, if he'll let me, and put 'em to work."[47] Indeed, Johnson's War on Poverty might have accurately been termed a war on welfare. "Our American answer to poverty is not to make the poor more secure in their poverty but to reach down and to help them lift themselves out of the ruts of poverty and move with the large majority along the high road of hope and prosperity . . . The days of the dole in our country are numbered."[48] It was not that LBJ was opposed to government job programs or direct relief; he had supported both vigorously during the Depression. But the economic and political climate was far different in the 1960s from what it had been in the 1930s. The vast white middle class was prosperous, not impoverished. The disadvantaged had to be educated and trained to take advantage of opportunity.

In addition to the political problems that relief and public sector jobs would create, Johnson sensed that they were not the answer to the culture of poverty that had grown up in Appalachia and the nation's urban centers. "Very often a lack of jobs and money is not the cause of poverty, but the symptom," he declared in his first State of the Union address.

The cause may lie deeper—in our failure to give our fellow citizens a fair chance to develop their own capacities, in a lack of education and training, in a lack of medical care and housing, in a lack of decent communities in which to live and bring up their children . . . But whatever the cause, our joint Federal-local effort must pursue poverty, pursue it wherever it exists—in city slums and small towns, in sharecropper shacks or in migrant worker camps, on Indian Reservations, among whites as well as Negroes, among the young as well as the aged, in the boom towns and in the depressed areas.[49]

Despite his protestations to the contrary, Johnson saw the poverty bill very much as a civil rights bill. Moyers recalled that shortly after he assumed the presidency, LBJ had one of his secretaries dig up a flyer that had been published widely in Mississippi, Alabama, east Texas, and northern Georgia in 1959 by the White Citizens Council. "We intend to see that no negro who believes in equality has a job, gets credit, or is able to exist in our communities," it read. He kept it in his desk in the small office adjoining the Oval Office throughout the first year of his presidency. During the spring of 1964, the White House was bombarded with statistics showing that poverty was concentrated disproportionately among blacks. There was discrimination in hiring and discrimination in pay for those who were hired. In December 1963, Johnson met with Roy Wilkins of the NAACP and convinced him that the poverty program was a civil rights bill and a necessary complement to the pending public accommodations and voting legislation.[50]

LBJ was a great believer in symbolism, and America needed to get used to seeing black faces in unaccustomed places. Although he had exulted in astronaut John Glenn's orbital flight, he was overheard to say at the time, "Too bad it's not a Negro." He was already plotting to have Carl Rowan, the black journalist who had been serving as ambassador to Finland, named to head the USIA. And he wanted a black face around the Oval Office, preferably a pretty one. Shortly before ten in the evening on the day after the assassination, Gerri Whittington's phone rang. Whittington, an attractive African American woman, had been working as secretary to one of Kennedy's aides.

"Gerri? . . . Where are you?"

"I'm at home. Who's this?"

"This is the President . . . What're you doing?"

"Oh, I think someone's playing with me."

"No, no you're not [being played with]. I want to talk to you about our work, honey . . . Can you come down here immediately?"

"Oh, I'd be glad to."

"Come on down. I've got Jack Valenti here and we want to talk to you about a little reassignment."[51]

THERE WAS HARDLY a department or agency in the federal government that did not have an interest in or program bearing on the struggle to eliminate poverty: Labor; Health, Education, and Welfare; Agriculture; the Council of

Economic Advisers; the Bureau of the Budget; even Defense, which worried about the tens of thousands of young men who could not qualify for military service; and Justice, which faced the task of combating juvenile delinquency. At first, "the walls dripped with blood as the empire-builders clashed with the empire-wreckers," as one participant put it.[52] To Shriver's credit, he was able to impart to the 137-person task force that he convened a sense of mission and purpose that transcended their simple bureaucratic objectives. There was chaos, but it was exhilarating, "a beautiful hysteria," as one task force member described it.

Shriver's chief comrade in arms was Adam Yarmolinsky, a special assistant to Secretary of Defense Robert McNamara. He was, as Eric Goldman observed, one of those activist intellectuals tailor-made to raise the hackles of conservatives, especially southern conservatives. He was brilliant and arrogant, short, dark, Jewish, and a native New Yorker. A Harvard academic, Yarmolinsky was one of those aggressively liberal Charles River intellectuals who had come to Washington as a member of the Kennedy entourage. As a high school student, he had attended several Young Communist League meetings, but the totalitarian aspects of Soviet-style communism repelled him. In Defense, he had organized a commission to investigate racial discrimination in the armed forces and then headed the effort to implement its recommendations.[53] According to the scenario that Shriver envisioned, Yarmolinsky would draft the poverty bill, and he, Shriver, would drive it through Congress. Yarmolinsky would then head whatever administrative agency Congress approved to administer the poverty program. LBJ was enthusiastic about the Harvard academic's participation, but he sounded a warning: "I think he's very able," he told Shriver, "and very fine . . . wonderful fellow . . . he's a good friend of mine . . . You want to watch that background on the Hill though . . . I'd be worried a little bit about that."[54]

The Economic Opportunity Act that the administration sent to Congress in March 1964 combined several different approaches and philosophies. It proposed to spend $962 million, less than 9 percent of the estimated cost of eliminating poverty for one year. But Shriver and his lieutenants saw the EOA as only a beginning. Title I appropriated $190 million to fund a jobs training program for youths. The Job Corps would establish rural residential camps where trainees would receive basic educational and vocational training. In the cities, a Neighborhood Youth Corps would hire eighteen- to twenty-one-year-olds to work on minimum-wage jobs for the city, the county, or a nonprofit agency. The budget was $150 million. For students there was a work-study program that would employ youths at an educational or other public institution for a maximum of fifteen hours a week.

Title II established a community action program, Yarmolinsky's favorite, and what would prove to be the most controversial of the administration's poverty programs. The idea was for those who were caught in the culture of poverty to meet and design programs in education, employment, vocational rehabilitation, welfare, housing, and other fields that were particularly suited to their community. They would then apply to a new federal agency, the Office of Economic Opportunity, for funding. OEO would receive $315 million. In calling for "maximum feasible participation," community action was supposed to benefit the disadvantaged materially but also psychologically, by giving them a sense of empowerment.

Johnson was okay with community action as long as it did not become uncoupled from local political establishments. After the poverty bill passed, Moyers and Shriver suggested using some of the money to subsidize non-governmental organizations. "I'm going to re-write your poverty program," Johnson exploded. "You boys got together and wrote these things and I thought we were just going to have the NYA [National Youth Administration] . . . Do you know what I think about the poverty program? What I thought we were going to do? I thought we were going to have CCC [Civilian Conservation Corps] camps and I thought we were going to have community action where a city or a county or a school district or some government agency could sponsor projects . . . I am against subsidizing any private organization . . . I would prefer Dick Daley do it than the Urban League . . . I just think it makes us wide open and I don't want anybody to get any grants." [55]

Because LBJ was from experience sympathetic to rural poverty and because a number of representatives and senators who would be voting on EOA represented farming areas, the administration's bill contained something for the country-dwelling poor. Orville Freeman and his principal assistant for the poverty program, James Sundquist, wanted a provision "where significant quantities of land could be bought up, broken into family size farms, and sold at low interest on long term sales to Negroes, former sharecroppers and others, to rebuild these rural communities, and thus try and reverse the very damaging trend of people buying up big chunks of land and then operating it partly for pleasure, only partly for agriculture with hired labor, making virtually peons out of the displaced sharecroppers who have been driven North to the city slums." [56] As a result, Title III provided low-interest loans of up to $2,500 to poor families to purchase or improve small farms. The Office of Economic Opportunity would administer all of these programs. In addition, the director was also authorized to recruit citizens to Volunteers in Service to America (VISTA), who would work with Native Americans, migratory workers, the mentally ill, and the developmentally disabled. [57]

As LBJ, Shriver, and O'Brien turned their attention to Congress and the struggle to see the EOA pass, prospects looked bleak. Republicans under Senate Minority Leader Everett Dirksen and House Minority Leader Charles Halleck were determined to depict the War on Poverty as a hare-brained idea, the off-spring of soft-headed liberals, sure to bankrupt the nation. Southerners viewed the program as a civil rights Trojan horse, a federal initiative to empower blacks and further the cause of integration. When an administration official presented Arkansas Congressman Wilbur Mills with materials in support of the EOA, the chair of the House Ways and Means Committee threw it back at him, "said a few choice words about how he was not going to be involved in any program to help a bunch of niggers and threw me out of the office." [58]

The White House did not want Congress to enter into extended debates on the merits or demerits of the components of the EOA. Rather, its strategy was to focus on the plight of the poor in general to arouse a wave of public sympathy that would overwhelm Congress. Most of the sixty witnesses who testified before the House committee that held hearings on the poverty bill focused on the moral depravity of a society as affluent as America permitting children to go hungry, bed down with rats, and suffer from diseases that could easily be prevented. To highlight the plight of America's poor and to demonstrate that the EOA was intended to help whites as well as blacks, LBJ made two conspicuous tours of Appalachia in April and May. [59] In speeches there and in other venues, he evangelized. "It is almost insulting to urge you to enlist in this war for just economic motivations," he told the Advertising Council. "This is a moral challenge that goes to the very root of our civilization, and asks if we are willing to make public, personal sacrifices for the public good." [60]

The Appalachian trips, or "Poverty Tour," as the press dubbed it, offered Secretary of Agriculture Orville Freeman his first opportunity to experience the new president up close and personal:

> We went into town [in North Carolina], and I must say that he [LBJ] performed magnificently . . . He made inside the Courthouse a rather impassioned and most effective plea which was repeated in substance out in the street to maybe 20,000 or 30,000 people. He did lay it on the line where agriculture, small farm, family farm was concerned, with a real feeling, and I must say honestly that during the day a feeling for the people and effort to improve the lot of people, a dedication to the principles of the New Deal and Franklin Roosevelt, a constant repetition of the fact that the one-third of the ill-fed, ill-housed, ill-clothed Roosevelt Era, although down to 20 percent now must go down to 10 and 5 and be eliminated. He came through with a strength and a sincerity and intentness of purpose that was really quite stimulating." [61]

White House strategists perceived that in votes on the EOA, northern liberals and Republicans would cancel each other out. The balance would be held by southern Democrats. The outlook was gloomy. When LBJ pressed NAACP leader Roy Wilkins to go up on the Hill and lobby for the poverty bill, he at first refused. "Mr. President," he said, "going up there is like going to a KKK rally." [62] That the chair of the House Committee on Education and Labor and the Subcommittee on the War on Poverty Program that would conduct hearings on the EOA was congressman Adam Clayton Powell, the handsome, dapper black cleric who represented Harlem, helped somewhat, but brought its own problems. He had made a series of demands in return for his support of the poverty bill. "Christ, Powell has got a laundry list a yard long," Larry O'Brien told LBJ. "All he wants is for the federal government to finance the Hotel 2400 [a Powell investment property], to wipe out the $47,000 indebtedness to internal revenue, to get that judge to drop those threats of arrests." But after his demands were more or less met, Powell became an ardent, indispensable supporter.[63]

In what Yarmolinsky considered "a great stroke," LBJ persuaded conservative Georgia Congressman Phillip Landrum, coauthor of the antiunion Landrum-Griffin Labor Bill, to sponsor the EOA in the House. The president convinced Landrum that poor whites as well as blacks in his district would benefit. (Actually, the idea to use Landrum was Powell's.) That argument, together with the contention that the poverty program was a noninflammatory way to help blacks, was widely used among southern legislators.

Republicans believed initially that the race issue could be depended on to sink the administration's antipoverty program. When that possibility began to fade, they turned to religion. The GOP encouraged an amendment to EOA assuring that a portion of the funds made available would go to parochial schools. Sponsored by Congressman Hugh Carey of New York, the addendum would provide for money to be given not only through local school boards but directly to private institutions to conduct remedial reading and arithmetic courses. The National Education Association let the administration know that if it accepted the Carey amendment, it would "scuttle the bill."[64] "Halleck has got it going," LBJ complained to Shriver. "He's outsmarted you . . . He tried the Negro thing and that didn't get off the ground and now he's got the religious thing."[65] Johnson went on to assure Catholics that Shriver, who would administer the program and was a Catholic, would not discriminate against parochial schools. To Protestants, he declared that as long as Bill Moyers, "a Baptist preacher," was on the White House staff, the Catholic Church would not take over the poverty program, or as he put it, "we've got Moyers in on this program and he's not going to turn it over to the Pope."[66] Clearly, the race was going down to the wire. Anxiously, LBJ asked Larry O'Brien if the bill were going to pass. "Yeah, I think so," O'Brien replied, "if we can just keep the boys that should be sober, sober, and the ones that should be drinking, drinking."[67]

On July 16, Shriver predicted to LBJ that the poverty bill would pass the Senate by a two-to-one margin, but the House would be more difficult. A group of southern red-baiters headed by Congressman Harold Cooley (D–North Carolina) had decided to compel the administration to sacrifice Adam Yarmolinsky as their price for voting for the bill.

By 1964, Yarmolinsky had become something of an antihero to true believing anticommunists and southern segregationists, who had decided to use each other's movements to further their own cause. General Edwin Walker had been lambasting Yarmolinsky as nothing less than a "communist mole" in the Defense Department. His mother had been a "communist poet," conservatives charged, and Adam himself had been active in the communist youth movement. This was music to the ears of southerners, who blamed Yarmolinsky for the drive by the Defense Department to desegregate off-base facilities that catered to the military.

On August 6, Speaker McCormack summoned Shriver to a meeting in his office. Cooley and several other southern congressmen were there. Cooley informed him that if Yarmolinsky was given any role in administering the poverty program, he and his seven Carolina colleagues would not vote for the EOA. Shriver said that Yarmolinsky was extremely competent and his friend to boot, and he would not abandon him, but the decision was the president's. After several painful phone calls to the White House, Johnson persuaded Shriver to relent. It was all a plot by the National Association of Manufacturers, LBJ observed: "It is all a lie" and you should not be expected to "denounce the man because somebody is starting to lie on him," but keeping Yarmolinsky in Defense was a small price to pay for passage of the poverty bill.[68]

Subsequently, when conservative Congressman W. H. Ayres (R-Ohio) rose on the floor of the House to declare that Yarmolinsky would be the real power in the poverty program, not Shriver, but Phil Landrum cut him off: "So far as I am concerned, this gentleman, Mr. Yarmolinsky, will have absolutely nothing to do with the program." Shriver later recalled: "That was the most unpleasant experience I ever had in the government of the United States . . . I felt . . . as if I ought to just go out and vomit."[69]

But opponents of the poverty bill were not through. The conservative coalition offered an amendment to the measure requiring recipients to sign a loyalty oath, a pledge of allegiance to the United States, and a promise that they had never belonged to a "subversive" organization. The Senate had not included such an amendment, and if the House adopted it, the measure would have to go to conference. But to be referred to conference, the poverty bill would have to have a rule (setting the terms of debate) from Senator ("Judge") Howard Smith's committee. LBJ did not want his pride and joy to fall into the hands of the House's number one reactionary. Moyers and Shriver were opposed to the loyalty oath, but Johnson wanted his advisers to squelch their liberal impulses, go to the Senate, and get a loyalty oath in that chamber. "We'll handle the communist thing," he told his lieutenants. "We don't give a damn about that, that's professional liberals . . . but we'll kill the whole bill if we have to rely on Smith for another rule." Gradually he worked himself up to near hysteria. Calling Moyers and Shriver "children" and "school kids," he told them, "Learn this for all time to come so nobody'll ever have to teach it to any of you again, you can never get a bill into conference without a rule or unanimous consent. Call Mansfield and say please, oh please, dear God, this man has taken all the misery in the world because he got in with a bunch of social workers that never heard of parliamentary procedure . . . These amendments don't amount to a tinker's damn . . . Everybody that goes on the payroll . . . says I'm not a communist."[70] In the end, the loyalty oath failed to pass the House. The administration won the vote on the EOA 226 to 185. Southerners voted sixty to forty against, but the forty together with twenty-two Republicans were enough to carry the day. In a signing ceremony at the White House, Johnson declared that "for the first time in all the history of the human race, a great nation . . . is willing to make a commitment to eradicate poverty among its people."[71]

LBJ understood that the poverty program was a beginning, that Shriver and his staff were not at all sure where it was going or what the consequences of the policies they implemented would be. Hopefully the poverty program would produce institutions similar to Social Security, the minimum wage, or the TVA. Once in place, programs and agencies tended to develop a life and constituency of their own. Johnson regretted the sacrifice of Adam Yarmolinsky, but he concluded reluctantly that he had to be martyred to the cause. As Shriver subsequently told Yarmolinsky, "It was a question of whether we have this bill and the benefits it will bring to the hundreds of thousands or maybe millions of poor people, or you."[72]

LYNDON JOHNSON was a man absorbed equally with substance and image. He was also a man who desperately wanted to be appreciated, even loved. All chief executives pay attention to what the media say about them and the matters with which they are involved, but none more so than Lyndon Johnson. The Oval Office featured wire service tickers that provided the president and his staff with up-to-the-minute news reports. From his friend Frank Stanton, president of NBC, LBJ secured a panel of three televisions and a remote that allowed him to tune in and tune out the sound on each as he desired. At news time, the president could invariably be found watching all three TVs simultaneously and providing a running commentary to whomever he happened to be talking on the phone. He continued the practice he had begun as Senate majority leader of scanning the *New York Times,* the *Washington Post,* and the *Baltimore Sun,* as well as a Midwest and a West Coast paper every morning. He also checked the stories in the principal news magazines. "Lyndon Johnson was what they now call a media freak," news anchor John Chancellor later observed.[73]

In terms of policy, LBJ took very seriously what individuals like Tad Szulc of the *Times,* Walter Lippmann of *Newsweek,* and Chet Huntley of NBC said. He would quote them to staff, cabinet members, and military advisers and demand that they respond. White House tape recordings made during the first months of Johnson's presidency show him reading the AP ticker almost hourly and exploding whenever a story critical of him or his administration appeared, no matter how partisan or unreasonable. He invariably took the position that if something appeared in print or over the air, it was a force to be reckoned with, and it needed to be refuted or counteracted. He would call an affected subordinate and demand a new policy, or a revision, or that somebody be fired. By mid-1964, anyone who wanted to affect LBJ's decisions knew enough to plant stories or slant reports in a certain way. As time passed and Johnson's animosity toward the media grew, the more sophisticated came to realize that he frequently acted contrary to media interpretation, so they responded accordingly. For better or worse, reporters, broadcasters, and columnists played a major role in the decision making of the Johnson presidency.[74]

The relationship between the press and the president himself was even more complex and less healthy. By the spring of 1964, reports of bizarre presidential behavior began to appear in national news magazines. The first week in April, *Time* ran a story entitled "Mr. President, You're Fun," describing a ninety-mile-an-hour joy ride across the ranch in LBJ's cream-colored Lincoln Continental:

> At one point, Johnson pulled up near a small gathering of cattle, pushed a button under the dashboard—and a cow horn bawled from underneath the gleaming hood . . . Johnson talked about his cattle, once plunged into what one startled newswoman called a "very graphic description of the sex life of a bull . . ." During the tour, Reporter Marianne Means, her baby-blue eyes fastened on Johnson, cooed: "Mr. President, you're fun." Through all the fun, the President sipped beer from his paper cup. Eventually he ran dry, refilled once from Marianne's supply, emptied his cup again and took off at speeds up to 90 m.p.h. to get more . . . Someone gasped at how fast Johnson was driving. Quickly Lyndon took one hand from the wheel, removed his five-gallon hat and flopped it on the dashboard to cover the speedometer.[75]

Johnson was appalled at the story. To his mind, the reporters were his guests whom he was entertaining, and they had betrayed his hospitality by filing stories. Several weeks later, newspapers all across the country ran a photo of LBJ holding one of the family beagles up by its ears while the dog stood on its hind legs and howled. "Dog Lovers Bark at LBJ," ran the headline.[76] Johnson insisted to reporters that it was not at all unusual to get a dog to rear up by holding its ears, and he was merely responding to a request from one of their own to get a better look at the animals. An extremely literal-minded man at times, LBJ could not believe the brouhaha over the incident. "Who was it [who wrote the story]?" he demanded of George Reedy. "I want to know what that son-of-a-bitch looks like, and I want to give him the silent treatment for awhile."[77] Neither could Johnson understand the way he was caricatured in political cartoons. He had never worn a string tie in his life, he remarked to an aide with great indignation. Yet, Johnson's reaction to being portrayed as a coarse, crude cowboy was to act the coarsest, crudest cowboy he could imagine. Angry with what he considered East Coast, New England snobs (ignoring the fact that the typical national reporter was raised in a small town somewhere in the Midwest), he decided that he would act out whatever behavior they seemed to consider offensive, to further offend them.[78]

TO THE FRUSTRATION and increasing anger of the White House press corps, LBJ refused to release his travel schedule in advance. It seemed to them that he was being deliberately rude and inconsiderate. Perhaps, but there was another, more practical reason for Johnson's wanting to keep his schedule from the press: concerns about his personal safety. In the aftermath of the assassination, J. Edgar Hoover emphasized how vulnerable LBJ was and would be. He should always ride in cars with bulletproof bubbles and metal plating underneath, the director advised Johnson, "to take care of a hand grenade or bomb that might be thrown out and rolled along the street."[79] But Johnson loved the adulation of crowds and fed off pressing the flesh. Traveling in an enclosed vehicle surrounded by armed guards was anathema to him. Johnson had Horace Busby investigate past assassinations to see if there was a pattern. John Wilkes Booth had overheard the manager of Ford Theater saying that Lincoln would be attending that night's performance. Charles Guiteau, who shot Garfield, and Leon Czolgosz, who killed McKinley, had both learned from the newspapers of their prey's plans and route of travel. Lee Harvey Oswald had read the newspapers, too. "The argument," Busby concluded, "is strong against advance publicity. All the assassins had premeditated their crimes for weeks or days but would never have had the chance for their attempts without knowledge from news media.[80] Therefore, LBJ had his press staff do everything in their power to keep reporters from learning his plans in advance.

Johnson even refused to give advance notice of his press conferences, but for a different reason. "He knew that the Washington press corps was full of specialists," an aide recalled, "some of whom had devoted most of their careers to the study of foreign affairs, or the federal judiciary, or science or military affairs, and therefore not only knew their subjects, but probably knew more about them than he did. If he announced his news conferences in advance, they would come running with their well-informed and awkward inquiries. So he simply did not announce his news conferences."[81]

Somewhat paradoxically, LBJ's relationship with the press suffered because he also tried to be too intimate with various members of the Fourth Estate, and he cared too much about what they said about him. Franklin Roosevelt regularly scorned and ridiculed his questioners. He once pinned a Nazi Iron Cross on John O'Donnell of the *New York Daily News* during the Second World War, and ordered Robert Post of the *New York Times* to put on a dunce cap and stand in the corner. But he knew when to take them seriously and when not to, and he held the press at arm's length. Eisenhower, too, considered it beneath his dignity to socialize with mere reporters.[82] Johnson, by contrast, attempted to woo them and negotiate with them. He gave special attention to those whose stories pleased him, and ostracized or berated those whose pieces offended him. And he attempted to trade favors. Frequently, his idea of a press conference was to summon selected reporters to his office for coffee and a chat. On occasion, the president, reading a news report on the AP ticker, would call the reporter in question to make a correction or tell him he had the wrong slant on the story.[83] George Reedy believed that LBJ may have been the worst manager of the press ever to sit in the Oval Office. "The first six months he was in the White House he had the press eating out of his hand. But he kicked that away himself. He'd get mad at them . . . He simply could not understand why it was he could buy a reporter a drink and take him out to the Ranch, show him a good time, and that reporter would write a story he didn't like."[84]

AT TIMES, during those first weeks as president, Johnson was overwhelmed with doubt and a sense of inadequacy. In December, Katharine Graham, who took over as publisher of the *Washington Post* after her husband's death and who was a family friend of the Johnsons, made an innocent call to ask the president to speak at a publishers' dinner. Worried about his image, obsessed with Bobby Kennedy, and particularly impatient with Congress, whose members seemed to be out on perpetual holiday or speaking tours, he unloaded. Speaking in rapid-fire fashion, his voice increasingly shrill, the president would not let the stunned Graham get a word in: "Russell was in Winder [Georgia]. Dirksen was in Illinois. Humphrey was on the beach. Mansfield was on the beach in Miami . . . Charlie Halleck was out hunting turkey. Now there wasn't a human here. And they're not here now. And they are not working now. And they are not passing anything! And they are not going to! Now somebody has got to [write stories about congressional absenteeism] instead of just writing the stories about how the pages live or about Bobby Baker's girl. Whether he had a girl or whether he didn't is not a matter that is going to settle this country. But whether we have justice and equality is pretty damned important. So I'd like for them to be asking these fellows, 'Where did you spend your . . . holidays? Tell me about it, was it warm and nice?' " Referring to the pending civil rights bill, Johnson continued: "And write a little story on it . . . because if you don't, they are going to start quitting here about the 18th of December and they'd come back about the 18th of January and then they'll have hearings in the Rules Committee till about the middle of March and then they'll pass the bill and it will get over and Dick Russell will say, 'It's Easter and Lincoln's Birthday.' . . . He will screw them to death, because he's so much smarter than they are."[85]

The stress LBJ felt in late 1963 and 1964 manifested itself particularly in his dealings with the Secret Service. Though he was personally grateful to Rufus Youngblood, Lem Johns, and the other men who had protected him in Dallas, he did have some doubts about the Service as a whole following the assassination. He asked Deke DeLoach to assign an FBI agent to fly with him and to act as part of the security detail at the ranch. He displayed an irrational resentment toward the men assigned to him. At the ranch he would scream at agents whom he believed were following him too closely.[86] During the Poverty Tour in Georgia, a car carrying the Secret Service detail covering the president accidentally ran over a bystander's foot. Back in Washington, Johnson summoned James Rowley, head of the Service, and chewed him out: "Your damn secret service car stays up right behind me every trip . . . and you're going to kill more people than you save . . . It doesn't do any good to be right close to me . . . and all you're doing is running over little children . . . You ran over a man's foot here." All Rowley could say was, "Yes, sir."[87] When stories subsequently appeared in the press reporting low morale in the Service, Johnson once again summoned Rowley and told him to ask for the resignations of the dissatisfied. "Tell them to quit their bellyaching," he ordered. "If they don't want to handle the president, I'll send up an amendment and get the FBI to do it." Rowley: "Yes, sir."[88] But the storms would pass, and Johnson would lavish gifts on the agents who were assigned to him, and on their families as well.

The key to LBJ's preference for the FBI over the Secret Service was the former's apparent willingness to allow him to mix with crowds of people in public places. Johnson convinced himself that all he had to do to avoid an assassin's bullet was to conceal his travel plans, and particularly to keep his route secret until the last moment. "Between us, the Secret Service that covers me are a fine and dedicated group," he told Mike Mansfield, "but my judgment is that they are more likely to get me killed as they are to protect me. They're just not heavy thinkers; they're like the average cop. Hoover's the one . . . He doesn't object to my shaking hands with high school kids or people along a fence in Billings, Montana but he does object to my riding down the street in a car that's not bulletproof because that's where people hide. It's not likely that an assassin's going to be in with a bunch of high school band but it is that he gets in an upstairs window."[89]

As a constellation of ideas, as a vision of America, the Great Society had been taking shape in Lyndon Johnson's mind since he first heard the Great Commoner, William Jennings Bryan, orating in behalf of the people on his parents' Victrola in Johnson City. From his father's fervent populism and his mother's liberal Baptist faith, from the experiences at the Welhausen Elementary School in Cotulla, from Sam Rayburn and Charles Marsh and Franklin Roosevelt, from his love for the American political process, from his own messianic aspirations for himself came a cornucopia of programs that were intended to make America that land of social, economic, and political excellence that Sir Thomas More had dreamed of in 1519. What is exceptional about the thousand pieces of legislation that Congress passed during the Johnson presidency was that they were enacted not during a period of great moral outrage by the middle class at wealthy malefactors, or fears that the country was about to be overwhelmed by alien, immigrant cultures, or in the midst of a crushing economic depression that threatened the very foundations of capitalism. There seemed to be no sweeping mandate for change. JFK had barely beaten Richard Nixon in 1960. Much of the country was conservative. The Great Society was conceived and implemented during a period of growing prosperity. The country was immersed in the cold war and conflicted by the civil rights movement, but these phenomena were frequently power sources LBJ tapped into in order to realize his vision of a more perfect society.

The Great Society was certainly not the product of one man, but the Johnsonian will had more than anything else to do with the Civil Rights Acts of 1964–1965, Medicare, the National Endowment for the Arts and Humanities, immigration reform, the wilderness acts, and a hundred other initiatives.[90] "Johnson did have a capacity to almost hypnotize people," said Arthur Goldschmidt, head of technical assistance for the UN and a friend from congressional days, "to carry them beyond what might have been their almost cautious judgment when he seized upon something as an idea . . . The very people who were his architects were carried by his enthusiasm, his drive and his ambition, not only in the design of the program but in the speed of its implementation."[91]

The man in the Oval Office believed that the nation's priorities had gone askew. In 1964–1965 the federal government would spend a mere 1.6 percent of the GNP on purely domestic purposes, the lowest level of the postwar years and close to the level of 1929, when it was 1.1 percent. Despite its vast and growing wealth, the United States was investing less in "the renewal of our society than at any time since the pre-depression era."

Throughout the spring of 1964, in speeches, conversations, and off-the-record remarks, LBJ began to flesh out those ideas he had furiously scribbled down on yellow legal pads with his aides during the nights immediately following the assassination. In February, he sent a special message to Congress on consumer protection, promising to identify and empower this group so that it would have the same impact on national policy as business, labor, and agriculture.[92] In meetings with Moyers, Valenti, Fortas, and especially Busby, Johnson began to focus on the various facets of the Great Society, to try to digest the information that was already coming from the task forces Bill Moyers and Eric Goldman had assembled. Underlying their recommendations and LBJ's conclusions was the assumption of a strong executive. Like FDR, he was determined to move beyond the "deadlock of democracy," to use James McGregor Burns's phrase. "The presidency had been since 1789 the focal point of national pressures for progress and the leading edge of our progressive gains," Busby wrote in May 1964. In Johnson's view, he was the instrument of all the people, the only nationally elected official. A modern president could not afford partisanship, especially to be perceived as partisan. Within each of the two major parties there was an ongoing struggle between the forces of reaction and the forces of progress. Johnson's presidency must appeal to the enlightened of both parties. Insofar as interest groups sought the good life for those they represented and were willing to compromise with other entities in pursuit of their interests, they must be accommodated. Labor unions, corporations, defense contractors, minorities, the elderly, and consumers, all made up the political landscape which presidents must traverse. But segregationists were not an interest group and economic exploitation was not a legitimate enterprise. "The national office concept requires that the President—and the executive agencies which are his responsibility— . . . dispel rather than foment not only racial and religious division and discrimination, but, also, to exercise a wholesome, healing influence on the tendency to class division, regions division, labor-business divisions," Busby observed.[93]

No less a personage than Walter Lippmann was captured by the Johnsonian vision. Slogans like the New Deal and the Fair Deal imply a pack to be dealt, a clearly defined and limited pie to be distributed, Lippmann observed in a 1965 column. The possibility of managed affluence eliminated the need to think in those terms. "If a modern society like ours," he wrote, "need no longer think of itself as irreconcilably divided over the distribution of wealth, then it has become humanly possible to govern by obtaining wide agreement among the voters." [94]

There was in this mix a final and most important element: religion. The forces of conformity that were so strong during the early postwar period, coupled with the anxieties of the cold war, had led to a religious revival that was simultaneously intense, pervasive, and amorphous. Overall church membership increased from 64.5 million (49 percent of the total population) in 1940 to 125 million (64 percent) in 1965. All religions and denominations gained, but leading the way were Roman Catholics, Baptists, and southern Pentecostalists. Led by Norman Vincent Peale, whose *Power of Positive Thinking* sold millions of copies, many contemporary religious figures, especially in the mainstream denominations, concentrated on quieting the American middle class's anxieties in the nuclear age. Confronted simultaneously with the omnipresent threat of "the bomb," the implacable competition with international communism, and the corrosive effects of an overwhelming materialism, the American people were in dire need of reassurance as they confronted the second half of the twentieth century. The Protestant Council of New York instructed its television and radio speakers to abjure condemnation, controversy, and guilt. Their task was to "sell" religion, and to that end, their message "should project love, joy, courage, hope, faith, trust in God, good will." [95]

There were, of course, serious alternatives to this syrupy, sin-free approach to religion. The 1950s witnessed a new interest in revivalism and fundamentalism. One of the most striking preachers of the period was a young, well-dressed Baptist evangelist named Billy Graham. In sermons that stressed the sovereignty of God and the absolute wisdom of the Bible, the charismatic Graham drew hundreds of thousands of Americans to huge amphitheaters such as Yankee Stadium and Madison Square Garden. Graham and other fundamentalists offered clear moral and spiritual guidelines for middle-class Americans who craved substance and focus in their religion and for working-class Americans threatened by alcoholism, unemployment, and family disorganization. Meanwhile, the intelligentsia was drawn to the preachments of Reinhold Niebuhr, a theologian who attacked the "feel-good" religion propounded by the dominant culture. Niebuhr, who taught and preached at Union Theological Seminary in New York, was the towering theological and philosophical figure in the movement known as Christian neo-orthodoxy. He attacked the materialism, complacency, and conformity that seemed to permeate postwar America. World War II and the atomic age had proved that sin and evil were real and permanent and that man could not perfect the universe through his own efforts. Human beings were called upon not to ensconce themselves in a cocoon but to love the world and assume some responsibility for its problems. True peace involved the endurance of pain; the root of sin, he reminded Christians, was self-love.

Theologically, Johnson and his advisers—Busby, Church of Christ; Moyers, Baptist; Valenti and Shriver, Catholic; and McPherson, Episcopalian—were Niebuhrians. But LBJ's sympathy for and empathy with Jews was also deeply rooted. Like other Americans, he had been profoundly affected by the Holocaust. He was very much aware of the pervasive influence of evil in the world: racial prejudice, economic exploitation, political oppression, hunger, and disease. Believers must do the best they could under the circumstances, but LBJ was of the opinion that they should do it with a vengeance. He was both motivated by feelings of Christian charity and compassion, and determined to use religion in his quest to realize an American Utopia. His performances on two trips to Appalachia during the Poverty Tour could only be described as evangelical. He had met with the pope as vice president and would meet frequently with Billy Graham.

"From the time of the ancient Hebrew prophets and the dispersal of the money changers," LBJ told a group of civil rights leaders in the spring of 1964, "men of God have taught us that social problems are moral problems on a huge scale. They have demonstrated that a religion which did not struggle to remove oppression from the world of men would not be able to create the world of spirit. They have preached that the church should be the first to awake to individual suffering and the church should be the bravest in opposing all social wrongs . . . It is your job as men of God, to reawaken the conscience of your beloved land, the United States of America."[96] A devoted civil libertarian, Johnson was committed to the principle of separation of church and state, but that did not mean that men of state should separate themselves from faith and prayer or that people of faith should not apply their principles to their political decisions.[97]

LBJ realized that he needed a slogan for the broad program that was then germinating in federal agencies and task forces under his command. In early 1964, he began badgering Richard Goodwin, the Kennedy aide who had decided to stay on and write speeches for Johnson, to come up with a catchy phrase like New Deal or New Frontier. Although only thirty-two years old, Goodwin was already a prominent prowler of the halls of power.[98] He would spend his nights ridiculing LBJ and his days working to shape the policies of the man who had usurped JFK.

In February, LBJ summoned Goodwin and Moyers to the White House pool. As was his custom, the president was swimming in the buff. Goodwin was struck by the scene, and with Bobby Kennedy, Arthur Schlesinger, Kenny O'Donnell, and Pierre Salinger in mind, subsequently described it: "We entered the pool area to see the massive presidential flesh, a sun bleached atoll breaching the placid sea, passing gently, sidestroke, the deep-cleft buttocks moving slowly past our unstartled gaze. Moby Dick, I thought . . . 'It's like going swimming with a polar bear,' Moyers whispered."[99] The president had the two young men strip and join him. Johnson suddenly stopped, and began talking as if to some invisible audience in the distance. He wanted to build on Kennedy's accomplishments and dreams but go beyond them. America could be a land of plenty, but also one with a social conscience and an eye to excellence in all things public: education, conservation, beautification, cultural activities, and technological innovation. Despite himself, Goodwin was inspired. LBJ assigned his two assistants to draft a speech that would outline his vision and, more important, inspire the nation to support that vision.

Throughout March and April, Goodwin worked on a major address on domestic policy and searched for a title for the Johnson program. Goldman suggested "the Good Society," the title of a book written by Walter Lippmann some years earlier. Eventually, after consulting with Moyers, Valenti, and the president, Goodwin came up with "the Great Society," the title of a 1919 book penned by social psychologist Graham Wallis, who, not coincidentally, had been one of Lippmann's mentors.[100] The venue selected for the Great Society's coming out was commencement exercises at the University of Michigan scheduled for May 22.

On the appointed day, LBJ rose to the appreciative applause of the eighty thousand who filled the Michigan football stadium at Ann Arbor. It was a sunny, mild afternoon, and those in attendance were in a festive mood. "For a century," Johnson began, "we labored to settle and to subdue a continent. For half a century we called upon unbounded invention and untiring industry to create an order of plenty for all of our people. The challenge of the next half-century is whether we have the wisdom to use that wealth to enrich and elevate our national life, and to advance the quality of our American civilization. Your imagination, your initiative, and your indignation will determine whether we build a society where progress is the servant of our needs, or a society where old values and new visions are buried under unbridled growth . . . For in your time we have the opportunity to move not only toward the rich society and the powerful society, but upward to the Great Society . . . There are those timid souls who say this battle cannot be won," the president concluded, "that we are condemned to a soulless wealth. I do not agree. We have the power to shape the civilization that we want. But we need your will, your labor, your hearts, if we are to build that kind of society." [101]

The most intense period of reform in U.S. history was about to begin.

CHAPTER 22

FREE AT LAST

S THE SECOND RECONSTRUCTION GAINED MOMEN-
tum in the early 1960s, southern conservatives decided to try a
nonconfrontational approach. They convinced themselves that
the vast majority of their black fellow citizens were satisfied with
their second-class status. After all, most Negroes they knew went about their
business as tenant farmers, day laborers, or domestic workers quietly and without complaint. If only this message could be gotten across to the rest of the nation. A group of Chamber of Commerce types found an aged black man,
obviously deeply rooted in southern traditions, and asked him if he would tell
his story on a national television broadcast. He agreed to. The director brought
in to film the testimony insisted that it had to be spontaneous. The old man was
duly positioned on the porch of his ramshackle cabin, seated in his rocking
chair, attired in his tattered work clothes. The producer said, "Now when we
get ready we're going to give you the signal to go, and just start talking and tell
the people in your own words just how you feel." The red light came on and the
signal was given. He said, "Is it time to talk now?" The producer whispered,
"Yes, yes, go on." He said, "Now can I say anything I want to?" The producer
said with urgency, "Yes, yes, go on." The aged black man turned to the camera,
raised his voice, and shouted, "Help!"[1]

As LBJ SAW MATTERS, if civil rights was not resolved as an issue, it could
prevent progress on all other fronts, from education to health care to poverty.
And vice versa. The civil rights bill the Kennedy administration had introduced
was sweeping—and stalled. It would make completion of the sixth grade prima
facie proof of literacy for the right to vote in federal elections; compel access to
hotels, motels, places of entertainment, stores, restaurants, and other public facilities without regard to race, religion, or national origin; empower the com-

missioner of education to establish programs to desegregate public schools and the attorney general to file suit against school boards that did not participate; establish a Community Relations Service to mediate disputes over segregation and discrimination; require federal agencies to withhold funds from state and local entities and programs that discriminated; and establish a permanent Commission on Equal Employment Opportunity.[2] Unlike the 1957 civil rights bill, this one had teeth and was bound to elicit the unrelenting opposition of the Dixie Association. The key to breaking the logjam lay in a tacit partnership between the Kennedy-Johnson administrations and civil rights forces in the field.

The wanton brutality of Bull Connor's Birmingham, Alabama, police had sickened much of white America in 1962, and created a groundswell of sympathy for Martin Luther King's SCLC and the hundreds of young SNCC workers who staged sit-ins, registered rural blacks to vote, and conducted protest demonstration. "The picket line" now extends from the dime store to the United States Supreme Court and beyond that to national and world opinion," observed a Greensboro, North Carolina, newspaper.[3]

Frustrated, angry, paranoid, southern segregationists struck back. Cross burnings, night ridings, and bombings multiplied at a frightening rate during 1963. In June, Medgar Evers, NAACP field representative in Mississippi, was shot dead by a sniper outside his home in Jackson. Three months later, after black youths attempted to desegregate several previously all-white schools, a huge dynamite bomb shattered the Sixteenth Street Baptist Church in Birmingham. In the rubble lay the lifeless bodies of four girls, ages eleven to fourteen, who had been changing for choir practice.

On August 28, 1963, two hundred thousand Americans, black and white, had descended on Washington to express their support for the civil rights measure then pending in Congress. The participants, who included hundreds of nationally prominent church and civic leaders, marched peacefully from the Washington Monument to the Lincoln Memorial. There they heard pledges of support from politicians, the folk music of Peter, Paul, and Mary, and the gospel songs of Mahalia Jackson. The culmination of the March on Washington was Martin Luther King Jr.'s incomparable "I Have a Dream" speech.

Lyndon Johnson's decision to push the 1964 civil rights bill through Congress, no matter the cost, was fraught with danger. His advisers told him that he could not afford to lose, and he could not afford to compromise. African Americans were sick of palliatives. "The Negroes have seen two significant bills on civil rights [1957 and 1960] become law," George Reedy told him. "From here on out, they will regard any measure which does not pass as a cynical gesture." And there was good reason to believe that the measure would not pass. "It must be realized that the proper groundwork has not been laid," Reedy said. "Negroes are not convinced that the Administration is really on their side. Southern whites still believe that the turmoil is a combination of 'ward politics' and 'outside agitators.' Republicans believe that the issue is a matter of partisanship."[4] When Johnson subsequently asked Hubert Humphrey to spearhead the civil rights bill in the Senate, LBJ told him, "This is your test. But I predict it will not go through."[5] And what if it did pass? Southerners would be so embittered that there was a real possibility that white voters south of the Mason-Dixon line would abandon the Democratic party, and LBJ would be ignominiously defeated in the forthcoming presidential election. Moreover, the defection might prove permanent. Thus, in attempting to serve the cause of social justice, there was a very real possibility that Lyndon Johnson would become its primary victim.

Despite these negatives, Johnson never hesitated. There was, first, the very nature of the man. His parents, his upbringing, his psyche made for a compelling social conscience. Second, LBJ believed that the continued existence of the Union depended on the guarantee of civil equality and equality of opportunity for all Americans. In taking the lead in compelling adherence to the Constitution, the president and the federal government might be risking turmoil and even bloodshed in the short run, but if they did not, there would be hell to pay in the long. In the face of the Birmingham bombings, the murder of Medgar Evers, continuing police brutality, and ongoing segregationist intransigence, one could not expect the Negro to be realistic about the difficulties of getting legislation through Congress.[6] And then there was the South. Jim Crow had been a burden that the South had carried since the Civil War, and it had barred the region from full participation in the life of the republic. The end of segregation and discrimination would bring Dixie finally and firmly into the national mainstream, with all of the economic prosperity and political influence that would mean. Racial justice, Johnson believed, was just as much in the interest of southern whites as southern blacks.

In fact, the president and his counselors were convinced that if racial harmony were to come to America, it would come first to the South. Once white southerners realized that by integration and equal opportunity, blacks did not mean miscegenation or even social mixing, but a right to travel freely, live and work where they wanted, compete for jobs on an equal basis, and enjoy the comforts of public accommodation and the benefits of truly equal education, animosity would quickly subside. "If the Southerners understand this, they will solve the problem much easier than the North because Southerners have lived with Negroes longer than Northerners and really like them better," Reedy observed to Johnson.[7] This came not only from LBJ's white advisers but his black aides as well. "There's something in the folklore of Negro life that a reconstructed southerner is really far more liberal than a liberal Yankee," Louis Martin, the black journalist-politician who handled the African American press for the White House, observed.[8] Finally, Johnson believed that passage of a sweeping civil rights bill had at last become politically possible. Because he was associated with the civil rights legislation Congress was then considering, because he had gone on national television to condemn the church bombing in Birmingham, JFK's name had become identified with the Second Reconstruction. In the wake of his assassination, activists forgot his and his brother's timidity, and the fallen president became a martyr to the cause. What John Kennedy failed to do in life—make civil rights a compelling moral issue—he could do, or be made to do, in death.

POLLS TAKEN from the fall of 1963 through the spring of 1964 were revealing. As of June 1963, 49 percent of those queried favored a public accommodations law; 42 percent opposed. In January 1964, the approval rating stood at 61 percent. There was even some movement in the South, where opposition shrank from 82 to 72 percent. Most important, perhaps, polls revealed that southerners were becoming fatalistic about civil rights. Although the vast majority remained opposed to integration, 83 percent of those questioned believed racial integration to be inevitable; 49 percent predicted that it could come about in the South within five years.[9]

It was his political genius that caused Johnson to realize that the time had come, and his particular achievement to act on that realization. LBJ's role in civil rights reminded Harry McPherson of a quote from Sir Robert Peel, the eminent nineteenth-century English statesman: "Public opinion, as it is said, rules, and public opinion is the opinion of the average man. [Charles James] Fox used to say of [Edmund] Burke, 'Burke is a wise man, but he is wise too soon.' The average man will not bear this. Politicians, as has been said, live in the repute of the commonality. They may appeal to posterity, but of what use is posterity?"[10]

Johnson and his chief political strategists on the civil rights bill—Larry O'Brien and Deputy Attorney General Nicholas Katzenbach—began huddling within days of the assassination. Key to passage, they recognized, would be the civil rights organizations, labor, business, the churches, and the Republican party. The first order of business, Johnson perceived, was to reassure black leaders that he was and would continue to be their unwavering ally. On November 24, two days after JFK's death, LBJ talked with Whitney Young of the Urban League, asking his advice on congressional strategy. He also secured invitations to the Kennedy funeral for Young and other civil rights leaders.[11] Five days later, the president met with Roy Wilkins, head of the NAACP, and assured him that passage of the civil rights bill would top the new administration's list of priorities.[12] During the next six months, the president would talk and meet regularly with Wilkins, urging him especially to remind Republicans in Congress that the GOP was the "party of Lincoln," and to persuade firebrands in the civil rights movement to show some restraint until the fate of the civil rights measure became clear. Before the end of November, Johnson also spoke with Martin Luther King, James Farmer, and A. Philip Randolph. He explained that the poverty bill was basically a civil rights bill and that he wanted to secure its passage before the great battle over the accommodations and employment measure began. Don't go off half-cocked, he pled. "I don't want to stir up the folks on the Hill until we get ready to see the whites of their eyes," he told Randolph.[13] All did or would issue public statements expressing confidence in the new president, but they still were somewhat wary, not of LBJ's visceral commitment to civil rights but of his fondness for pragmatism and compromise. Johnson might indeed become "another Hugo Black," black intellectual and King adviser Bayard Rustin observed; he might "be able to control the South better than Mr. Kennedy did . . . SNCC must help Mr. Johnson—but to help Mr. Johnson means to create an atmosphere in which he is pushed even further." [14]

On his way to the office on the morning of December 4—the Johnsons were still living at The Elms—LBJ had his driver swing by and pick up George Meany, who lived nearby. During the ride, Meany promised that he would do everything possible to secure support for the civil rights bill from leaders of the AFL-CIO, no small task because the measure covered apprenticeship programs. A day later, LBJ gathered up House Republican Minority Leader Charles Halleck for the trip downtown. Halleck was noncomittal; Johnson made it plain that he was going to hold the GOP's feet to the fire on civil rights: "I'm going to lay it on the line . . . now you're either for civil rights or you're not . . . you're either the party of Lincoln or you're not . . . By God, put up or shut up." [15]

In January, Johnson spoke to business and corporate leaders who had agreed to participate in Plans for Progress. Urging them to take "affirmative action" to eliminate discrimination in hiring, he declared, "I can just almost guarantee each of you men that when your retirement time comes and you sit on your front porch in that rocking chair with your white Panama pulled down over your eyes and in retrospect look back over your days as a leader in your company, I can almost guarantee that one of your proudest moments and one of your greatest achievements will be the day that you took the leadership to destroy bigotry and bias and prejudice from the atmosphere of your own company." [16] At the same time, the president was not above appealing to conservative fears. "There's all this stuff [bombings, beatings, killings] going on," he told Robert Anderson, wealthy Texas businessman and Eisenhower confidante, "and we've been talking about this for 100 years . . . and I just think that we're going to have them out in the streets again if we don't make some little progress." [17] Johnson did not have to rally the churches. In the wake of the killing of the four black girls in Birmingham, Catholic, mainline Protestant, and Jewish organizations instructed their representatives in Washington to lobby in behalf of the civil rights bill.

Johnson and O'Brien next turned their attention to the House, Judge Smith, and the Rules Committee. Of the fifteen members on Rules, ten were Democrats and five Republicans, but four of the Democrats were from the Deep South. To Smith's delight, the conservative majority had been blocking measures of social justice for years. The most attractive option for bypassing the Rules Committee was a petition of discharge. If a majority of the House—218 members—so voted, a measure could be removed from the purview of the committee and introduced directly on the floor. Because it would appear to the public to be democracy in action, the president favored this option. Ninety of those sitting in the lower house were from the South, so fifty-plus Republicans would be required to achieve the requisite majority. Halleck told the White House to forget a petition; it would open the door to direct consideration of other liberal measures that the GOP opposed. But his was not the last word.

Two Republican members, William McCulloch and Clarence Brown of Ohio, were conservative on every issue but civil rights. They treasured their party's link to the Great Emancipator. Moreover, Wilberforce and Central, two predominantly black colleges, were located in Brown's district.[18] They indicated to Smith that if he did not release the civil rights bill, they would lead a revolt. "I know something about the facts of life around here," Smith confided to a friend, "and I know that many members want this bill considered. They could take it away from me and they can do it any minute they want to."[19] Consequently, the chairman of the Rules Committee announced that hearings on the bill would begin January 9, 1964. They were quickly concluded, and the measure was reported out with a positive recommendation on January 30.

In a last-ditch effort to cripple or defeat the civil rights measure, Howard Smith proposed an amendment to add a word to Title VII, which prohibited discrimination on the basis of national origin, race, and religion. That word was "sex." As the judge well knew, many conservatives, men as well as women, were opposed to legislation mandating gender equality. He assumed that a majority of those whites favoring advances in civil rights would not be willing to extend the same rights to women, that is, that most liberals were sexist. Smith was wrong. The House added the gender amendment by a vote of 168 to 133, and then on February 10, passed the Civil Rights Act of 1964 by a vote of 290 to 110.[20]

Johnson was jubilant. No sooner had the civil rights bill passed than one of the phones in the telephone area of the House cloakroom rang. It was LBJ looking for Joe Rauh, then vice president of the Americans for Democratic Action, and Clarence Mitchell, director of the Washington, D.C., chapter of the NAACP. "I don't know how he ever managed to get us on that phone," Mitchell later recalled, "but he was calling to say, 'All right, you fellows, get on over there to the Senate and get busy because we got it through the House and now we've got the big job of getting it through the Senate.' " At two o'clock in the morning, Johnson telephoned Congressman Jake Pickle, one of only six southerners to have voted for the bill, to congratulate him.[21]

Bill Moyers recalled that during a press conference in the midst of the fight over the civil rights measure, Jim Deakin, a reporter for the *St. Louis Post-Dispatch,* asked LBJ, "Mr. President, I don't understand. You didn't have a very sterling progressive record on civil rights either in the House or in the Senate, and yet here you have thrown the full weight of your presidency behind the civil rights movement. Would you, please sir, explain the contradiction?" Johnson paused a full thirty seconds before answering. Resisting the temptation to rationalize or to defend his past actions, he said, "Well, Jim, some people get a chance late in life to correct the sins of their youth and very few get a chance as big as the White House."[22]

On New Year's Eve, some five weeks after he had succeeded to the presidency, LBJ attended a party in honor of Horace Busby at the Forty Acres Club on the campus of the University of Texas at Austin. The club had been strictly segregated since its inception. Johnson swept in at the head of a small entourage. On his arm was his new, attractive black secretary, Gerri Whittington. Before they went in, Whittington had asked, "Mr. President, do you know what you are doing?" LBJ replied, "I sure do. Half of them are going to think you're my wife, and that's just fine with me."[23] From that point on, the Forty Acres Club accepted black members.

As a former colleague, Johnson felt close enough to several southern senators to appeal to them to moderate their opposition to the civil rights bill. He called young Robert Byrd of West Virginia and pled with him to allow the accomodations and employment bill to come to the floor for a vote. "No . . . No . . . No sir, I wouldn't make them vote on it because I know if they vote on it, they're going to get it," Byrd replied. "And if a man starts to coming to my house if I can't beat him with my fist . . . I'm going to take a poker to him . . . The only way we can win here is to not let them vote."[24] LBJ gave up. It was clear that the Dixie Association was going to filibuster, to "fight to the last ditch," as Richard Russell subsequently declared. "You can't do anything with the Southern Democrats," LBJ told Joe Rauh. "There ain't nobody that can get Thurmond or Olin Johnston, Dick Russell, or Talmadge."[25] Thus, it seemed that civil rights advocates were back to square one, where they had been in 1957 and 1960. But Johnson was now president of the United States, not the senior senator from Texas.

As the civil rights bill was being transferred from the House to the Senate, LBJ let it be known that he would not compromise, not even if the filibuster lasted the rest of the year. Shortly after the fight over the measure began, LBJ asked his old friend Dick Russell to the White House to have a frank talk. "The President sat in a wing chair," Jack Valenti recalled. "The Senator sat at one end of a small couch. Their knees almost touched . . . 'Dick, you've got to get out of my way. I'm going to run over you. I don't intend to . . . compromise.' 'You may do that,' " Valenti remembered Russell replying. " 'But by God, it's going to cost you the South and cost you the election.' " So be it, Johnson responded.[26]

The administration understood that it had the votes to pass the civil rights bill if it were ever allowed to be considered by the Senate as a whole. But the Dixie Association would use the filibuster to see that that never happened. Two methods were available for defeating Russell and his troops. The first consisted of exhausting the talkers, a stratagem LBJ had employed in 1960 and one he still favored. The rules of the Senate limited members to two speeches per calendar day. Once debate on a measure began, the calendar day lasted as long as the debate lasted—a week, a month. LBJ wanted to keep the Senate in continuous, twenty-four-hour-a-day session. Majority Leader Mike Mansfield, however, was opposed. The tactic had not worked in the past. Opponents of the filibuster had become just as fatigued as its supporters, and the result had been no measure or one so weakened as to be almost meaningless.[27] Mansfield favored a petition of cloture, which required two-thirds of the Senate to end debate and force a floor vote. The problem was that of the eleven past cloture petitions dealing with civil rights, all had been defeated, including two in 1962 on a bill that Kennedy had submitted dealing with literacy tests. LBJ thus resisted the cloture approach throughout the February 11 meeting at the White House. At a diplomatic reception immediately afterward, Johnson and Nick Katzenbach pulled two chairs together and continued the argument. "I think we've got fifty-eight votes for cloture," Katzenbach said. "Well, where are you going to get the others?" Johnson asked. Katzenbach pulled out a copy of the Senate roster and identified fourteen possible. "We get nine of those we'll get out sixty-seven votes." Finally, Johnson acceded.[28]

The key to both cloture and passage was Republican support. Of the sixty-seven Democrats in the Senate, twenty-one of them came from states of the former Confederacy. Unless twenty-three to twenty-five Republicans withdrew from the conservative coalition, there would be no breakthrough in public accomodations and employment. That meant winning over Minority Leader Everett Dirksen. As Johnson told Humphrey, "This bill can't pass unless you get Ev Dirksen. You and I are going to get Ev; it is going to take time. You make up your mind now that you've got to spend time with Ev Dirksen. You've got to let him have a piece of the action. He's got to look good all the time. Now don't let those bomb throwers [Paul Douglas, Joe Clark, and other liberal Democrats] talk you out of seeing Dirksen. You get in there to see Dirksen; you drink with Dirksen, you talk with Dirksen, you listen to Dirksen."[29]

The sixty-eight-year-old minority leader shielded a shrewd, agile mind with a veneer of buffoonery. Heavy-set with wavy, silver hair, a mellifluous speaking voice, and a broad face folded in wrinkles, Dirksen was a man who delighted in his own oratory. He was given to unusual words, like "baleful" and "felicitous." His speeches were often studies in digression. An avid gardener, he rose on the floor of the Senate every spring to propose that the marigold be selected as "the national floral emblem of our country."[30] He could be partisan, but he was jealous of his place in history. As a result, there was little consistency in his voting patterns: for foreign aid one day, against it the next, for example. Like Johnson, Dirksen was a shrewd calculator of men and counter of votes. He liked to deal and he could be dealt with. He was, in short, Johnson's kind of politician.[31] Friends worried about his health. Although he suffered from a peptic ulcer, Dirksen drank moderately but almost continuously. "Champagne is Mrs. Dirksen's favorite vegetable . . . and I prefer a fellow by the name of Jonathan Daniels," he told a reporter.[32] After he was elected minority leader, Dirksen cordoned off part of his office and named it the "Twilight Lodge." All of the numerals on the clock that hung there were fives.

Humphrey commenced the courtship. "I would have kissed Dirksen's ass on the Capitol steps" to secure his support for cloture, Humphrey later said, and he virtually did.[33] Appearing on *Meet the Press*, Humphrey responded to a question concerning Dirksen's stated reservations about the civil rights bill: "Senator Dirksen is not only a great senator, he is a great American, and he is going to see the necessity of this legislation. I predict that before this bill is through Senator Dirksen will be its champion." [34]

On February 26 the Senate adopted a Mansfield motion to bypass the Judiciary Committee and consider the civil rights bill directly. On March 9, 1964, the longest filibuster in the history of the U.S. Senate began. The debate over whether to take up the bill continued through March 26, when the Senate finally voted to make it the next order of business. Formal debate began on March 30 and continued for nine straight weeks. [35]

During the filibuster, LBJ worked assiduously to wrap white America in a moral strait jacket. How could individuals who fervently, continuously, and overwhelmingly identified themselves with a merciful and just God continue to condone racial discrimination, police brutality, and segregation in education and public accommodations? Johnson's language was not that traditionally wielded by liberal intellectuals—cerebral Jeffersonian phrases rooted in a deep faith in progress and reason—but the words of the believer who has encountered profound evil, Lincolnesque words founded in the notions of suffering and sacrifice. [36] Where in the Judeo-Christian ethic was there justification for killing young girls, denying an equal education to black children, barring fathers and mothers from competing for jobs that would feed and clothe their families? Was Jim Crow to be America's response to "Godless Communism"? Addressing business executives who had committed to Plans for Progress, LBJ said, "I don't know why you can't say, 'Except for the grace of God, I might be in his place and he might be in mine.' " Capitalism did not guarantee social and economic justice; only the consciences of God-fearing men and women could do that. The only way America could lay claim to world leadership would be "because of our moral standards and not because of our economic power." [37] To the Inter-religious Convocation on Civil Rights, Johnson pointed out that the story that Christ chose to illustrate the meaning of love was that of the Good Samaritan: "The Samaritan's attitude was one of good will born of a recognition of the fatherhood of God and the brotherhood of men—an attitude that expressed itself in action on the behalf of another's needs." [38] Even so conservative a newspaper as the *Fort Worth Star-Telegram* was moved by Johnson's sacred logic. "Now I knew that as President I couldn't make people want to integrate their schools or open their doors to blacks," he later said, "but I could make them feel guilty for not doing it and I believed it was my moral responsibility to do precisely that—to use the moral persuasion of my office to make people feel that segregation was a curse they'd carry with them to their graves." [39]

Johnson's decision to define civil rights as a moral issue, and to wield the nation's self-professed Judeo-Christian ethic as a sword in its behalf, constituted something of a watershed in twentieth-century political history. All presidents were fond of invoking the deity, and some conservatives like Dwight Eisenhower had flirted with employing Judeo-Christian teachings to justify their actions, but modern-day liberals, both politicians and the intellectuals who challenged and nourished them, had stayed away from spiritual witness.

Most liberal intellectuals were secular humanists. Academics in particular had historically been deeply distrustful of organized religion, which they identified with small-mindedness, bigotry, and anti-intellectualism. Moreover, as historian David Burner has observed, liberals "are most at home with the worldly vocabulary of law and education and the compromise of government."[40] Johnson distrusted organized religion to an extent, but he embraced Judeo-Christian teachings, particularly those found in Isaiah and the New Testament. For him, they offered the Western world's most compelling call to social justice. He did seem to foresee that to employ Christian moral philosophy might open the door, à la John Brown and William Lloyd Garrison, to appeals to a higher law. He was convinced that the U.S. Constitution was the ultimate expression of the Judeo-Christian ethic. Others, of course, were not. Out of the admixture of religion and civil rights would come nonviolent civil disobedience, a tactic that would arouse a great deal of angst in the thirty-sixth president.

IN THE SECOND WEEK IN MAY, the president electrified the nation by stumping Georgia in behalf of the civil rights bill. On May 8, he addressed a breakfast attended by members of the Georgia legislature in Atlanta, the city that Sherman had burned to the ground a century earlier. Governor and Mrs. Carl Sanders appeared on the dais with him, as did Senator Herman Talmadge and his wife. LBJ declared that the motto of the state of Georgia—"Wisdom, Justice, Moderation"—should be the motto of the nation in its time of trouble. Johnson quoted Atticus Haygood, president of Emory College, who in 1880 declared, "We in the South have no divine call to stand eternal guard by the grave of dead issues." How Georgia went, so would go America, the president proclaimed. "Heed not those who would come waving the tattered and discredited banners of the past, who seek to stir old hostilities and kindle old hatreds, who preach battle between neighbors and bitterness between States."[41] At Franklin D. Roosevelt Square in Gainesville, he declared, "Full participation in our society can no longer be denied to men because of their race or their religion or the region in which they live."[42] As remarkable as his words was the reception that he and his message were accorded. The crowd that lined the streets in Atlanta to greet LBJ numbered at least a half million. "I've never seen anything like it in my 18 years in Atlanta, even for 'Gone With the Wind' and Franklin Roosevelt," the police chief remarked.[43] The presidential motorcade took almost two hours to cover the fifteen miles in from the airport. Johnson stopped twenty-five times to address the cheering throng. The crowd in Gainesville, a town of eighteen thousand, was estimated at over fifty thousand.[44]

The filibuster wore on. Rhetoric from the Dixie Association was as fiery as ever, but close observers begin to sense an air of resignation. Russell, already suffering from the emphysema that would eventually kill him, seemed deflated. In December 1963, before the battle, Russell had visited with Orville Freeman. "He said that Lyndon Johnson was the most amazingly resourceful fellow," Freeman recalled, "that he was a man who really understood power and how to use it . . . He said that man will twist your arm off at the shoulder and beat your head in with it, and then he said, you know we could have beaten John Kennedy on civil rights, but not Lyndon Johnson."[45] After the filibuster began, Russell ran into Bill Moyers. "Now you tell Lyndon," he said, "that I've been expecting the rod for a long time, and I'm sorry that it's from his hand the rod must be wielded, but I'd rather it be his hand than anybody else's I know. Tell him to cry a little when he uses it."[46]

By mid-April, Dirksen was ready to move. On the afternoon of the 21st, Humphrey sat down beside the minority leader. As the southerners droned on, Dirksen declared that the administration's bill was a good one and he was ready to support it. He wished, however, to avoid a cloture vote; in fact, he did not think he could muster a sufficient number of his colleagues to shut off debate. Humphrey said no. The White House had promised Rauh, Mitchell, and the liberals that they would not stand for a watered-down bill. Besides, if he lost a cloture vote, Russell could claim to his segregationist supporters that he had fought to the last, but in the end had been overwhelmed by sheer numbers. Dirksen conceded the point. "The jig is up," Russell remarked privately.[47]

Dirksen proceeded to play out his self-scripted drama as the latter-day Abraham Lincoln. The minority leader arranged a meeting with the president for April 29. The day before, he told Republican leaders at lunch that he intended to give the Dixie Association one week to end their filibuster; if by then they had not, he would file a cloture petition. Over the next two weeks, Humphrey, Mansfield, and Nick Katzenbach met almost daily with Dirksen and in essence let him write the bill. There was no change in substance, but the language was Dirksen's, and he could proudly claim to be the coauthor. Johnson called the minority leader to thank him. "You're worthy of the Land of Lincoln," he said. "And the Man from Illinois is going to pass the bill, and I'll see that you get proper attention and credit."[48]

As the climax neared, the president opened his pork barrel to ensure success. He arranged for Secretary of Interior Stewart Udall to meet with Carl Hayden of Arizona. Representing a small constituency that was jealous of minority rights, Hayden had never voted for cloture. But when Udall promised administration support for the Central Arizona Water Project, a massive scheme to divert waters from the Colorado River to Tucson and Phoenix, Hayden offered his vote. To soften the blow for southerners, Johnson arranged for northern urban votes in support of the cotton and wheat bill.[49] That measure passed on April 9 by a vote of 211 to 103. "We just whipped the living hell out of your friend Charlie Halleck," he chortled to Russell (Republicans had opposed the measure), "and we had to do it with Yankees."[50] LBJ pressured a reluctant Kermit Gordon to approve $263 million for the Tennessee River–Tom Bigby project, a federally funded enterprise to improve river navigation from Tennessee to the Gulf.[51]

On June 10, following seventy-five days of debate, the Senate voted on cloture. Dirksen had the last, dramatic word. Relishing the moment, he quoted

Victor Hugo: "Stronger than all the armies is an idea whose time has come. The time has come for equality . . . in education and in employment. It will not be stayed or denied. It is here."[52] Humphrey predicted sixty-nine yea votes. He and Johnson followed the proceedings intently. Upstaging Dirksen was Senator Clair Engle of California, who, dying of a brain tumor, appeared on the floor of the Senate in a wheelchair. Unable to speak, he pointed to his eye when it came his turn to vote.[53] The final tally was seventy-one for and twenty-nine against, four more than needed and two more than Humphrey had predicted. The cloture vote, of course, ensured passage of the civil rights bill. Richard Russell was the last to speak, until he was cut off, with tears in his eyes. His protégé had finally succeeded in launching the Second Reconstruction.

IN THE WAKE of the passage of the Civil Rights Act of 1964, the leader of the Dixie Association counseled his constituents to be calm and obey the law, rather than invoking massive resistance. Perhaps the Georgian was a conservative, not a reactionary after all—a man committed to slowing change rather than obstructing it. For better or worse, his beloved South was entering the twentieth century, joining the political mainstream. Ambivalence, an awareness and even an appreciation of paradox, is the fate of all introspective individuals, and Russell was certainly that.

A jubilant Johnson scheduled a televised signing ceremony for July 2. But before the president could count his coup, the murder of three young civil rights workers in Mississippi threatened to touch off a cycle of violence that would undermine all of his plans for peaceful change in American race relations.

ALTHOUGH AFRICAN AMERICANS constituted 42 percent of Mississippi's population, only 5 percent were registered to vote. The median income for black families was under $1,500 a year, less than one-third of that for white families. Like its economy, Mississippi's politics was dominated by a tiny white elite that for a century had manipulated white working-class prejudices to keep blacks "in their place."

Early in 1964, Bob Moses and David Dennis of CORE had come up with the concept of Freedom Summer. Black and white college students, carefully trained in the techniques of nonviolent resistance and political activism, would spread out across rural Mississippi encouraging African Americans to register to vote, teaching in "freedom schools," and organizing a "freedom party" to challenge the all-white Mississippi Democratic party.[54]

On June 21, reports reached Moses and Dennis that three young project workers—Andrew Goodman, Michael Schwerner, and James Chaney—had disappeared near Philadelphia, Mississippi. Goodman and Schwerner were white, Chaney black. Six weeks later, the three were discovered buried in an earthen dam. Goodman and Schwerner had been shot in the heart and Chaney beaten to death. "In my twenty-five years as a pathologist and medical examiner," declared the attending physician, "I have never seen bones so severely shattered." Before the summer was out, three more civil rights workers died violently. A volunteer from the Mississippi Summer Freedom Project wrote home in July 1964: "Yesterday while the Mississippi River was being dragged looking for the three missing civil rights workers, two bodies of Negroes were found. Mississippi is the only state where you can drag a river any time and find bodies you were not expecting.[55] In McComb there were seventeen bombings in three months, and white extremists burned thirty-seven black churches to the ground.

After Schwerner, Goodman, and Chaney were reported missing, LBJ conferred daily with J. Edgar Hoover, urging the FBI director to leave no stone unturned to find the culprits and to make a case against them, even after it became apparent that local law enforcement officials were involved. "I asked Hoover . . . to fill up Mississippi with FBI men and infiltrate everything [the KKK, White Citizens' Councils, etc.]," he told Lee White, his assistant for civil rights matters. "I've asked him to put more men after these three kids . . . I've asked him for another report today . . . I'm shoving in as much as I know how."[56] On June 23, Hoover reported in: "Mr. President, I wanted to let you know we've found the car . . . [It] was burned and we do not know yet whether any bodies are inside of the car because of the intense heat . . . Apparently what's happened—these men have been killed."[57] That afternoon Johnson met with Schwerner's and Goodman's parents to console them. He then consulted with Mississippi Senator Jim Eastland, who predicted that the whole thing would turn out to be a hoax. There were no "white organizations" in that part of the state. Everyone knew that most of the so-called bombings were staged by local Negroes stirred up by outside agitators. The whole thing was a "publicity stunt."[58] Shortly thereafter, the bodies were discovered.

To make matters worse, the NAACP began picketing the White House to protest the federal government's inability or unwillingness to protect civil rights workers in Mississippi. James Farmer called to add his voice to the indignant. Civil rights leaders were only slightly mollified when the Neshoba County sheriff and several local Klan members were arrested.[59]

In the wake of his civil rights triumph, LBJ was characteristically conflicted. He had worked his will on Congress in a historic manner and won a place of honor for himself in the American social justice movement. But he felt for the white people of the South, people he had grown up with and loved. He appealed to LeRoy Collins, Buford Ellington, Luther Hodges, and other southern moderates to tell the governors, legislators, and people of the South that he had not abandoned them. "I moved a bunch of FBI people into Mississippi last night," Johnson told Hodges during the Schwerner-Goodman-Chaney crisis, "but I'm not going to send troops on my people if I can avoid it, and they got to help me avoid it."[60] He still hoped that when the scales of prejudice dropped from the eyes of poor whites in the South they could make common political cause with poor blacks within the context of the Democratic party. "I can't make people integrate," he told Richard Goodwin, "but maybe we can make them feel guilty if they don't. And once that happens, and they find out the jaws of hell don't open, and fire and brimstone doesn't flood down on them, then maybe they'll see just how they have been taken advantage of." [61] At the same time, Johnson was aware that the accommodations, employment, and education bill just passed was not the end of the struggle for racial justice in America. "He used to tell me," Humphrey wrote in his memoirs, " 'Yes, yes, Hubert, I want all those other things—buses, restaurants, all of that—but the right to vote with no ifs, ands, or buts, that's the key. When the Negroes get that, they'll have every politician, north and south, east and west, kissing their ass, begging for their support.' " Within days of passage of the 1964 Act he was badgering Nicholas Katzenbach "to write me the goddamn best, toughest voting rights act that you can devise." [62]

Johnson was afraid that the more militant members of the civil rights movement would become intoxicated by their success in passing the civil rights bill and press too hard. Immediately after the signing ceremony, Johnson met with Wilkins, Whitney Young, A. Philip Randolph, and other civil rights leaders and asked them to hold off on further demonstrations, lest they provoke a white backlash and prevent enforcement of the measure just signed. Young promised to help: "I know you are working on the southern governors and southern businessmen and . . . I don't want to see King and Farmer and everyone else talking about how they're going to insist on immediate compliance . . . If you can keep the southeners as you are from issuing defiance orders then we ought not to be talking about how we're going to test 'em." [63] But Johnson sensed, correctly as it turned out, that the movement was metamorphosing into something Young and the conservatives could not control. And then there was the political situation. The evening of the signing, Bill Moyers visited the president in his bedroom and found him deflated. Why so down, Moyers asked. "Because, Bill," he replied, "I think we just delivered the South to the Republican party for a long time to come." [64]

Unlike the *Brown* decision, the Civil Rights Act did not bring in its wake a wave of violence, calls for massive resistance, or even major defections from the ranks of the Democratic party. Richard Russell believed that the contrast was due to the *Brown* decision's being an edict of the court and the Civil Rights Act's being a series of laws enacted by a duly elected majority. As Johnson's remarkable reception in Georgia revealed, the relative calm was also due to the president's southern roots and his determination to make integration and nondiscrimination a gift to the nation from the South, not something that was imposed on the region from the outside.

THROUGHOUT THE SPRING and summer of 1964, Lady Bird basked in the reflected glory of her husband, but reflected glory was mostly what she had to settle for. Lady Bird recorded in her diary that she felt a "gulf" opening up between her and Lyndon after they entered the White House. He was putting in eighteen-hour days, and she had become First Lady, an office in and of itself with staff, permanent duties, endless invitations to functions, and unending correspondence. On one particular day, she received forty-four thousand communications. And there was the ongoing reminder that there were other women in her husband's life. Despite his health problems and the unflattering image picked up by the television cameras, Lyndon Johnson remained a physically compelling man. "Lyndon Johnson was giant-sized," recalled John Bullion, a historian and family friend. "He had huge bones, and he was carrying too much weight even for his expansive frame. But the overall impression was one of size, power, and force, not soft flabby fatness. His gut, though pooched out, looked rock hard, the result of hearty eating after heavy work, not the souvenir of hours idled away drinking beer . . . Both the image and the reality he was consciously projecting . . . were ones of powerful maleness."[65]

In early January, Johnson called Helen Douglas to ask her to fly to Liberia and represent him at a celebration commemorating the one hundredth anniversary of the founding of that country. Lady Bird was in the Oval Office at the time and overheard her husband tell Douglas that he was giving her four days' notice, "four days more than I usually give you." Douglas laughed and said she would have to ask her husband, Melvyn Douglas, quipping that, of course, "he never knew you the way I did." Near the end of the conversation, Lyndon put Lady Bird on, who was at her honeyed best: "Ah, Hell-en, so nice to hear you . . . honey." She remarked that she had recently met some women friends of Douglas's from California who seemed quite taken with Lyndon. She said, "I guess I'm used to it 'cause I like for women to like him, and I like him to like them."[66]

Two months later, LBJ ran into Helen Douglas at a banquet honoring Eleanor Roosevelt. Unbeknown to Lady Bird, he invited Douglas to spend the night at the White House. If Lady Bird was surprised to see her husband's consort the next morning, she did not let on. "He had supplied her, apparently, with my nightgown and robe," she recorded in her diary, "and there she was on the third floor. So at breakfast I called her to come down in her robe (my robe) and have breakfast with me in my room while we watched Lyndon depart by helicopter from the South Lawn . . . She is indeed the same vivid person I knew back in 1949–50 . . . She's an extraordinarily handsome woman, with an enormous appetite for life . . . I spent a wonderful hour and a half with her . . . and had simply loved it."[67]

Lady Bird may have been accommodating, but her husband's flaunting of Douglas hurt; she quickly grew lonely. Following several weeks of spending her evenings alone, she called the Oval Office. "I'm lonesome over here and I wish you'd come home," she told Lyndon, sounding almost desperate. He invited her over to swim with him and his aides, but she refused.[68] On another occasion, she showed up at the Oval Office at 8:45 in the evening to find LBJ with Marianne Means, the pert blond reporter who was another of Lyndon's flirtations. Again she accommodated: "I had a drink with them, asked her to dinner. We picked up Gerri Whittington. We stopped off by the pool. We found suits for both of them . . . Called up Marianne's date and asked him to join us, which he did presently . . . Lyndon was astonished that Gerri Whittington couldn't swim and in his very forthright way, he said, 'What's the matter, couldn't you go in any public pools?' And she, I must say, with very creditable poise, said, 'That is right, so I never learned to swim' . . . Lyndon and I and Gerri and Marianne and her date . . . had dinner and Lyndon rushed off, very much against my wishes, to put in an appearance at the Mexican Inter-parliamentary dinner." [69]

The marriage did have strengths. LBJ trusted Lady Bird implicitly, discussing affairs of state and politics with her. He made it clear that he respected her expertise as a businesswoman, journalist, judge of people, and observer of affairs. He was harsh with her, but rarely if ever devious. Her famous evaluation of him that followed his March 7, 1964, press conference—a tough one that featured questions about his relationships with Charles de Gaulle and Bobby Kennedy—was revealing. She called the Oval office: "You want to listen for about one minute to my critique, or would you rather wait until tonight?"

"Yes, ma'am. I'm willing now."

"I thought you looked strong, firm, and like a reliable guy. Your looks were splendid. The close-ups were much better than the distance ones . . . You were a little breathless and there was too much looking down and I think it was a little too fast . . . Not enough change of pace. Dropping voice at the end of sentence." Johnson tried to make excuses, but she would have none of it. "In general," she said, "I'd say it was a good B-plus." [70]

CHAPTER 23

CONTAINMENT AT HOME
AND ABROAD

EW PRESIDENTS, UPON ENTERING OFFICE, CARE MORE about foreign than domestic policy; Richard Nixon is at the head of a short list. More than most, however, Lyndon Johnson would have preferred to concentrate on domestic affairs. He had no overriding desire to remake the world in America's image, and he quite naturally hoped that ongoing hot spots like Korea, Southeast Asia, Berlin, and Cuba would remain calm. But after thirty years in Washington observing and participating in matters relating to World War II and the cold war, he labored under no illusions. The United States had faced threats first from the fascist powers and then from the forces of international communism. The cold war was a fact of life.

Johnson was not a triumphalist, but a Niebuhrian. Evil exists in the world. With an eye to the evil within themselves, righteous men and women must confront the evil without, knowing that they can never triumph completely but taking comfort in their willingness to struggle. Johnson had no comprehensive strategy for winning the cold war; as with most presidents, his policies and philosophies emerged in response to the management of specific situations and crises. He began with some basic assumptions, however. First and foremost was the avoidance of nuclear war.[1] At the first National Security Council meeting following Kennedy's assassination, Johnson read and reread a statement that had been prepared by McGeorge Bundy: "The greatest single requirement is that we find a way to ensure the survival of civilization in the nuclear age. A nuclear war would be the death of all our hopes and it is our task to see that it does not happen."[2] Throughout the 1964 presidential campaign, he made it clear that he rejected all notions of "limited nuclear war" and did not intend to delegate the decision to use atomic weapons to other persons or nations. In one of his most powerful speeches, Johnson told a Detroit audience in September, "Modern weapons are not like any other. In the first nuclear exchange, 100 million Americans and more than 100 million Russians would all be dead. And when it was all over, our great cities would be in ashes, our fields would be barren, our industry would be destroyed, and our American dreams would have vanished. As long as I am president I will bend every effort to make sure that day never comes."[3]

Like George Kennan and other apostles of containment, LBJ believed that the object of the cold war was to restrain the forces of international communism until the system collapsed of its own internal contradictions. He was convinced that any leader who placed an abstract idea above the interests of the individual was bound to fail. No one better understood that freedom had to be limited to protect the common good—big business had to be regulated to prevent abuse of the public interest, for example—but denial of the right of individuals to exercise a voice in their own government and to strive to better their lives transgressed against human nature and would not long be tolerated. To Johnson, containment meant not just bases, alliances, and weapons systems, but people-to-people aid. How to assist peasants and workers living in third world nations directly, bypassing the dictatorial and often corrupt regimes that ruled them, was a problem that occupied an increasingly large part of the president's foreign policy thought.

By the time Lyndon Johnson took the oath of office, a broad anticommunist consensus had emerged in America. It was accepted by virtually the entire political spectrum except for the far left, always a tiny minority. Its cutting edge was a small, fanatical minority on the far right. The 1960s had begun not only with the political triumph of a young, activist, progressive president but also, and perhaps not coincidentally, with the emergence of a new American radical right whose members *Time* magazine labeled "the ultras." Early in 1959, Robert H. W. Welch Jr., a fudge and candy manufacturer from Massachusetts, had gathered eleven of his friends in an Indianapolis hotel where, in due course, they founded the John Birch Society. The organization, which spread like wildfire for two years, was a semisecret network of "Americanists" dedicated to fighting communists by deliberately adopting some of communism's own clandestine and ruthless tactics—including the deliberate destruction of democracy, which Welch contemptuously described as government by "mobocracy." Meanwhile, in Tulsa, Oklahoma, the Reverend Billy James Hargis had launched the Christian Crusade ("America's largest anti-Communist organization"). The pink-faced, jowly evangelist specialized in coast-to-coast revivalist meetings, during which he delivered fundamentalist and anticommunist sermons, and organized Christian youth to combat the "Red Menace." Similarly, Dallas oilman H. L. Hunt financed an anticommunist radio program broadcast over three hundred stations.

Racism was a sometimes implicit, sometimes explicit feature of the radical right of the 1960s. Whether in the speeches of South Carolina Senator Strom

Thurmond or in the pages of the *Citizen,* the national publication of the white supremacist Citizens' Councils of America, segregationists lambasted the civil rights movement as a communist conspiracy to undermine American society.[4] The leaders of the radical right promised to make communism a tangible problem with which the average American could come to grips. As had the McCarthyites of the previous decade, the ultras argued vehemently that the real threat to the nation's security resided not so much in Sino-Soviet imperialism overseas as in communist subversion at home. They urged citizens to fight this subversion by keeping a close eye on their fellow citizens, scrutinizing voting records, writing letters, and generally raising the alarm. Above all, the ultras were extremists—they brooked no compromise. "You're either for us or against us," insisted a California electronics company executive. "There's no room in the middle any more." Mainstream conservatives shunned the ultras because of their religious fundamentalism, often blatant racism, and their flirtation with fascism. But they shared their view of communism. The intellectuals who wrote for the *National Review* in the 1950s and 1960s—Frank Meyer, James Burnham, Russell Kirk, William F. Buckley, Freda Utley, and Max Eastman—all viewed foreign affairs "as a titanic conflict of ideologies, religions, and civilizations." As Robert Strausz-Huppe of the University of Pennsylvania put it, "The Communist system is a conflict system; its ideology is an ideology of conflict and war . . . In spite of the twists and turns of the internecine power struggle, the communist system will endure so long as external pressures do not compound internal strains and bring the system crashing down."[5]

America's mainstream cold warriors, however, melded the philosophies of conservative anticommunists, who defined national security in terms of bases and alliances, and liberal reformers who were determined to export democracy and facilitate overseas social and economic progress. Spearheading the first group were former isolationists like Henry Luce, who believed that if the United States could not hide from the world it must control it. Joining these realpolitikers were liberals such as Arthur Schlesinger, Dean Acheson, and Hubert Humphrey. Products of World War II, these internationalists saw America's interests as being tied up with those of other countries. They opposed communism because it constituted a totalitarian threat to cultural diversity, individual liberty, and self-determination. Conservatives and their liberal adversaries may have differed as to their notions of the ideal America but not over whether America was ideal or over whether it was duty-bound to lead the "free world" into a new era of prosperity and stability.

Whatever his thoughts concerning their political shrewdness, Johnson identified with Humphrey, Rauh, and Schlesinger when it came to foreign policy matters. He was a liberal internationalist committed to containing communism through both military strength and foreign aid. He was also determined to prevent conservatives from painting the Democratic party and the social justice goals for which it stood as socialist-communist. Domestic anticommunism threatened the Great Society in general and the civil rights movement in particular. How to control these passions, he was not at all sure. In early 1968, during the height of the Vietnam War, Johnson would observe to a group of China experts that it was difficult to wage a major war against one communist entity without having the public and Congress wanting to go to war with all of international communism. He was immensely proud that he had been able to do battle with North Vietnam and the Vietcong and at the same time pursue a policy of détente with the Soviet Union—but could he control anticommunism at home? It was up to the United States to carry on an endurance contest in Vietnam in such a way as not to lead to inflexibility on other issues.[6]

Like other liberal internationalists, Johnson was convinced that communism was able to make inroads only in areas where the existing political system had failed to provide basic economic and social security for its citizens. Where there was hunger, disease, homelessness, and ignorance, fascism or communism would flourish. Men and women would always be willing to sacrifice their liberty for food, shelter, and a future for their children. It was thus incumbent upon the democracies to create the social and economic conditions where freedom could exist. Johnson's was a kind of Christian internationalism. It was based on the Social Gospel, not institutional engineering; on compassion, not more perfect government. Christian internationalism was not a substitute for multilateralism, but it was meant to transcend it. Indeed, in conversations with Bill Fulbright and others in 1964, Johnson expressed grave reservations about the efficacy of the assumptions that had been responsible for the original containment policy: the Munich analogy, the domino theory, and the notion of a monolithic communist threat. They were deeply embedded in the culture and could not be ignored. Yet they all boiled down to balance-of-power concepts that were irrelevant to Khrushchev's wars of national liberation. They presumed that conflict would be international rather than intranational. Addressing a celebration of the bicentennial of American Methodism in early 1966, he declared:

> From John Wesley to your leaders of today, Methodists have always believed that works of compassion among men were part of God's will in action . . . The Social Creed of the Methodist Church—written in 1940—is a most eloquent statement of that belief . . . "We pant for equal rights and complete justice for all men in all stations of life . . . for adequate provision for the protection, the education, the spiritual nurture and the wholesome recreation for every child . . . for the abatement of poverty and the right of all men to live . . . We believe that it is our Christian duty to do our utmost to provide for all men the opportunity to earn an adequate livelihood . . . We oppose all forms of social, economic, and moral waste . . ." It would be very hard for me to write a more perfect description of the American ideal—or of the American commitments in the 1960s . . . And while we are doing that I am not going to confine our efforts just to my own children or just to my own town or my own State or

my own Nation. I am concerned with all the 3 billion human beings that live in this world. I was concerned with the people of Europe when a dictator was marching through, gobbling up selfless countries and helpless countries . . . But just as I was concerned then—the human beings that were in concentration camps—I am concerned now with the little brown men in Southeast Asia whose freedom they are trying to preserve.[7]

LBJ's moral rhetoric was a justification for foreign policies undertaken for strategic and economic reasons, but they were also a natural outgrowth of his background, his family, the milieu in which he grew up, his concepts of right and wrong. He understood that freedom did not always translate into social justice, and he believed that democracy would not necessarily eradicate hunger, ignorance, and injustice. Only in the context of a morally compelling ethic could freedom and democracy do these things. If they could not, then they would be discredited in the eyes of the world, and alternative political creeds might very well triumph.

THE FOREIGN POLICY ESTABLISHMENT that LBJ inherited was headed by an impressive triumvirate: Robert McNamara at Defense, Dean Rusk at State, and McGeorge Bundy as NSC adviser.

Robert Strange McNamara, his middle name taken from his mother's maiden name, had grown up in a middle-class family in San Francisco and Oakland. His father, sales manager for a shoe firm, was a Catholic, but Bob chose the Protestant faith of his mother. After graduating from high school with honors, he entered Berkeley when Robert Gordon Sproul was turning it into a great university. At Berkeley, he balanced academics, socializing, and sports—mountain climbing and skiing—with ease. High marks came to him easily, so easily that he was able to read broadly and take an astounding array of courses. Upon graduation he entered Harvard Business School, where his mathematical and analytical skills made him a standout. He married an old friend, Margaret Craig, and settled down to teach accounting at Harvard. During World War II he served in the army air corps. Almost single-handedly, young McNamara developed the planning and logistics for the Allied strategic bombing of occupied Europe. Following the war, he took a job with Ford Motor Company, whose antiquated business practices had caused it to fall far behind General Motors in the race to dominate the domestic and foreign auto markets. He and a group of equally talented young engineers and statisticians worked to convert Ford from its archaic one-man-rule ways to the GM corporate model, which featured planning, rationalization, decentralization, and accountability. McNamara quickly became first among equals at Ford, but he was more than that. He was one of a new breed of corporate executives who did not come from business, but were well-educated technicians who relied on statistics and computers to rationalize every phase of the business operation. At work McNamara was totally focused, single-minded, driven, but out of the office he proved social, gregarious, philosophical, and philanthropic. "Why is it," asked Bobby Kennedy, "that they all call him 'the computer' and yet he's the one all my sisters want to sit next to at dinner?"[8] He had been president of Ford barely a week when Robert Lovett, who had been McNamara's boss in the air force, recommended him to the Kennedys to be secretary of defense.[9]

McNamara was already something of a legend when Johnson succeeded to the presidency. He was superb with charts and statistics. Once, while sitting at a CINCPAC (Commander in Chief Pacific) meeting for hours, watching hundreds of slides on the logistics of the Vietnam War, McNamara stopped the show. Slide number 869 contradicted slide number 11, he said. He was right, of course. As intended, his audience was intimidated. With his characteristic steel-rimmed glasses and slicked-back black hair, McNamara came to Washington to rationalize the Defense Department's $85 billion operation, to squeeze every globule of fat out of it, to make it the most efficient machine known to man. As he promised LBJ a week following the assassination, the foundation stones of his defense policy would be military strength at the lowest possible cost.[10]

But McNamara also intended to change the culture in Defense. In his view, the department had degenerated into groups of military spoilsmen, focusing on expanding the mission and assets of their particular branch without any consideration for the whole, strategically or politically. And they tended to respond to any and all perceived threats with contingency plans that called for maximum use of force.[11] He insisted that the Joint Chiefs be aware of and take into consideration not only the total defense picture, but political and diplomatic considerations as well. There was but one national interest, and it was defined by the president of the United States. In 1964, he promoted General Earle "Bus" Wheeler over several more senior officers for the job of JCS chairman. Cool, intelligent, articulate, educated, Wheeler was McNamara's kind of general.[12]

When he entered office, McNamara discovered that the belief that the use of nuclear power could in some circumstances serve the national interest was pervasive in the military and in Congress. He dedicated himself to correcting that view. And he was determined that congressional committees not be the tails that wagged the defense dog. "I did not believe that it was my function to yield to the pressures of narrow constituencies," he observed.[13] To help reform defense policy, McNamara brought in a new group of whiz kids, Rhodes scholars and editors of the Harvard and Yale *Law Review*s: Cyrus Vance, Roswell Gilpatric, Harold Brown, Paul Nitze, Alain Enthoven, Joseph Califano, and John McNaughton. This group worked almost as a fifth column within the Defense Department, laboring to bring it to heel.[14]

McNamara was a man of first-rate intelligence, dedicated to using the power that he craved, and proved so adept at accumulating, to serve the common good. The fact that he had contempt for his own department and little or no appreciation of the military as a human institution boded ill for the future. So, too, did his lack of experience in and feel for electoral or congressional politics. "McNamara . . . certainly is a 'can do' guy," Orville Freeman, his squash partner, observed, "but [he] . . . also has about as little perceptiveness, understanding and sensitivity in politics as anyone I've ever talked to." [15]

Second in the foreign policy triumvirate LBJ had inherited from Jack Kennedy was Dean Rusk. Two themes appear to have dominated the secretary of state's upbringing: Calvinism and militarism. Dean was the son of Robert Hugh Rusk, one of twelve children from a poor Scots-Irish Georgia family. After working his way through Davidson College, Robert Rusk studied to become a Presbyterian minister, abandoned that for life on a hardscrabble dirt farm, and finally settled his family in Atlanta. Dean, one of three brothers, was fond of church and reading the Bible; like so many other southern boys he revered all things military, read military history, and played war games at every opportunity. By the time Dean graduated from high school, the traits that would characterize his adult life had emerged: self-control, diligence, a sense of fatalism concerning the vagaries of life, and an overwhelming commitment to duty. Like his father, young Rusk attended Davidson College, where, because of his intelligence and hard work, one of his teachers suggested that he interview for a Rhodes scholarship. Dean was a candidate that would have warmed the cockles of Cecil Rhodes's heart; while earning Phi Beta Kappa honors, he played basketball and tennis at Davidson and took a leading role in both the ROTC and YMCA. At Oxford, Rusk focused on international affairs and won a number of prestigious academic awards. He returned to the States and took a teaching job at Mills College in California. [16]

During World War II, Rusk served in army intelligence and then as a plans officer in the China-Burma-India theater. There he caught the eye of George Marshall. Rusk was one of the soldier-intellectuals—John McCloy, Charles Bonesteel, and Andrew Goodpaster were others—whom Marshall identified to map out strategy for victory and peace in East Asia. After the war, he brought Rusk back to Washington to work in the State Department under him. Marshall—civil, selfless, austere, self-controlled, hard-working, and loyal—became Rusk's hero and role model. Both men were intelligent, with strong analytical minds, but they did not force their ideas on others; they demanded structure, obedience, and discipline of themselves and those who worked for them. Marshall and Rusk believed in good and evil but appreciated the difficulty of identifying both. They understood that man is a fallen creature, with only a very limited ability to do good, but it was humankind's duty to try, and they gloried in the struggle. Capitalism had its faults, but it was virtuous compared to communism. Capitalism, at least, was compatible, even conducive to democracy, but communism could coexist only with totalitarianism.

Following Eisenhower's election, Rusk retired from public life to head the Rockefeller Foundation. It was there that Jack Kennedy found him and decided to make him secretary of state. Rusk, who loved the office he held, believed it was his duty to discern the president's will and adhere to it. "I never let any blue sky show between his point of view and my point of view," he said of the presidents he served. [17] Unlike McNamara and Bundy, Rusk was not a member of the

Hickory Hill gang. Bobby Kennedy, Arthur Schlesinger, Ted Sorensen, and Pierre Salinger found him dull, pedestrian. They viewed his habit of speaking his mind only privately directly to the president as quaint and unproductive. But he was clearly dutiful, loyal, diligent, and hard-working—a difficult individual to get rid of.[18]

McGeorge Bundy, the national security adviser, was a man much more like McNamara than Rusk. Bundy's credentials as a Boston Brahmin were impeccable. His mother was descended from the Lowells, who had long dominated the intellectual and cultural life of New England. McGeorge was one of those "Harvards," as Lyndon Johnson referred to them, who reveled in his milieu but recognized its provinciality. He took care to profit from the education and connections that upper-class life in New England offered, but he flattered himself that he had transcended them. McGeorge was born in 1919 and attended Groton, the finest preparatory school in the East. There he dazzled, winning every academic honor. He played football, debated, and earned a perfect score on his college entrance exams. It was here that he entered the world of rich and privileged intellectuals-to-be who would opt for a life of public service rather than academe or business. Indeed, Groton's motto was *Cui servire regnare,* "To serve is to rule."[19] To broaden him, Bundy's parents sent him to Yale rather than Harvard because the former was thought to be somewhat more plebian than the latter. He earned Phi Beta Kappa honors, starred again as a debater, and wrote for the *Yale Daily News.* In one piece he addressed himself to the fascist threat then confronting Europe: "Let me put my whole proposition in one sentence. I believe in the dignity of the individual, in government by law, in respect for the truth, and in a good god; these beliefs are worth my life and more; they are not shared by Adolf Hitler."[20] From Yale McGeorge went to Harvard, but not as a regular graduate student; he was a junior fellow, enrolled in a special program funded by his great uncle, A. Lawrence Lowell, designed to allow the truly gifted to bypass ordinary doctoral work. Despite his poor eyesight, Bundy managed to get into the navy during World War II, serving as an aide to Admiral Alan Kirk. Following V-J Day he returned to Harvard to teach government.[21]

Bundy came to Kennedy's attention when the candidate was courting the Charles River intellectuals during the 1960 campaign. The two men took an instant liking to each other. Both had a strong sense of public service and sharp, incisive minds, and they both hated to bore and be bored. With his insightful, lucid analyses and his self-effacing arrogance—Bundy was contemptuous of and abusive toward those in government he considered unequal to the task at hand—Bundy quickly became Kennedy's chief foreign affairs lieutenant. The national security adviser was "a super pragmatist," observed James Thomson, his assistant for East Asia. He recalled a typical Bundy observation: "The fact of the matter is: We're here and what do we do tomorrow?" He believed, Thompson said, that "if you begin to suggest reconsidering the whole, unraveling the entire ball of yarn, you're in danger of being viewed as a sorehead and a long-winded fool."[22]

Johnson was initially deferential to his foreign policy team. He perceived that, whether from ambition or principle, they were willing to put the past behind them and work to make the Johnson presidency successful. At one level, the president viewed those who worked for him as both trophies he had won and reflections on the magnetism of his personality and the glamour of his agenda. He was intensely proud to have a Rhodes scholar, a former president of Ford, and the dean of Harvard College as his foreign affairs advisers. An observer recalled Johnson's visible appreciation of Mac Bundy's style: "A small amused smile would come to his face, like a hitting coach watching a fine hitter or a connoisseur watching a great ballet dancer. Mac was dancing, and dancing for him."[23]

Personally, LBJ felt most comfortable with Rusk. As he remarked to Sam Houston, the Georgian was not like some of the "bastards in the Kennedy administration: He's a damned good man. Hard working, bright, and loyal as a beagle. You'll never catch him working at cross purposes with his President."[24] But he viewed the State Department as undisciplined, filled with egotistical individuals willing to go off on their own and to leak state secrets if it furthered their agenda. To Johnson, Rusk would be primarily a furnisher of information. He appreciated Bundy but also felt, wrongly, that the national security adviser condescended toward him. LBJ loved technology, the notion that science and rational thought could work outside the box, solve the insoluble, and thus produce a better world. Thus did he find Robert McNamara attractive. He knew he would have to win the defense secretary's respect; consequently, during several initial cabinet and NSC meetings, LBJ demonstrated that his grasp of detail and ability to multitask was equal or superior to McNamara's. He agreed with the Defense chief that the uniformed members of the Pentagon staff should be carefully controlled, and he went out of his way to broadcast his position. "Tell the admiral . . . and tell the generals . . . that if they think they can pressure their commander in chief about what his strategy ought to be in war or what his decision ought to be in peace," he instructed Roswell Gilpatric, McNamara's deputy, "they don't know their commander-in-chief."[25] He seemed to trust McNamara implicitly, until he began to turn against the war in Vietnam. Though McNamara and Bundy had voted Republican for most of their lives, they, along with Rusk, were committed to social justice. McNamara especially would play a leading role in helping to make the Great Society efficacious.

Strong as they were, none of the three could match LBJ's force of personality. "I'm not afraid of him," David Bruce, the respected American diplomat, said, "but I must say that when he entered a room, particularly if you were going to be the only person in it, somehow the room seemed to contract—this huge thing, it's almost like releasing a djinn from one of those Arabian Nights' bottles. The personality sort of fills the room. Extraordinary thing."[26]

Under Eisenhower, the CIA, run by John Foster Dulles's brother, Allen, had played a major role in formulating and implementing the nation's foreign policy. The agency not only gathered information but conducted covert political and paramilitary operations from Guatemala to Iran. Angered and embarassed by the botched Bay of Pigs affair, Kennedy had relegated the CIA to intelligence gathering, although he did permit it to continue its conspiracy to kill Castro. The man whom Kennedy had selected to replace Dulles as head of the CIA, John McCone, deplored the "cloak and dagger" reputation the agency had acquired. "Our real contribution was to take all intelligence, including clandestine and technical intelligence, and meld it into a proper and thoughtful analysis estimate of any given situation," he once observed.[27] Almost as soon as he returned from Dallas, LBJ called McCone and assured him of his faith both in the agency and in the director personally.[28] "He said that he felt my work in intelligence was of greatest importance," McCone recorded in his notes of the meeting, "but he did not wish me to confine myself to this role. He said that he had observed that I had rather carefully avoided expressing myself on policy or suggesting courses of action and he suggested that it might be for interdepartmental reasons that I would wish to continue to do this in meetings . . . but nevertheless he invited and would welcome my coming to him from time to time with suggestions of courses of action on policy matters which, in my opinion, were wise even though they were not consistent with advice he was receiving from responsible people."[29] And, in fact, unlike Kennedy, LBJ appeared to want policy advice from the agency. As he would demonstrate, he was perfectly willing to conduct covert operations.[30]

Kennedy had relied heavily on the national security adviser but not at all on the National Security Council, two very different entities. The adviser was a person, Bundy, who presided over a staff of forty-eight people operating its own situation room in the White House. Bundy organized foreign policy meetings for the president, providing the documents that would enable him to evaluate the recommendations he received and make his own independent decision if he deemed it necessary. The NSC, on the other hand, was a large, unwieldy body that included not only the foreign policy cabinet officers but the vice president, the secretary of the treasury, and a host of other officials.

Johnson met regularly with the NSC for show. Except for the bombing of North Vietnam and the Dominican crisis of 1965, he did not jump down the chain of command on military diplomatic matters, and he didn't make decisions at NSC meetings. He preferred to deal solely with the relevant cabinet and agency heads or their deputies. Indeed, Johnson proved to be a fairly competent, disciplined administrator.[31] Under LBJ, the "Tuesday Lunch" meeting became an institution. On Tuesday, February 4, he convened Rusk, McNamara, and Bundy for an informal discussion of foreign policy. The same group met two weeks later, and regularly thereafter with the chairman of the Joint Chiefs, Bus Wheeler, CIA Director McCone, and (after he became press secretary) Bill Moyers. Johnson, who feared and detested leaks, favored these meetings. "They were invaluable sessions," Rusk recalled, "because we all could be confident that everyone around the table would keep his mouth shut and wouldn't be running off to Georgetown cocktail parties and talking about it."[32]

Johnson also had informal advisers. He frequently discussed thorny diplomatic problems with Abe Fortas, Clark Clifford, and Richard Russell. All were nationalists, Russell conservative, Fortas and Clifford more liberal, and all had a sharp sense of political reality. All were practical, pragmatic men who recognized the need to work within the parameters of the cold war consensus, and all wanted the Johnson presidency to succeed.

When it came to foreign affairs, LBJ was excruciatingly sensitive to the media. In January 1964, the *New York Herald Tribune* ran an article arguing that the Johnson administration seemed to have no plan of action for the international arena, preferring simply to react to events as they developed, to limit its role to that of crisis manager. That same month, Douglas Kiker wrote a series of articles for *Time* implying that LBJ did not know anything about foreign affairs; when it came to international relations, the country was adrift. Writing in the *New York Times,* James Reston observed that the president seemed "insecure" when it came to dealing with matters of diplomacy.[33] Convinced that the stories had been planted by Bobby Kennedy and his entourage, Johnson took momentary comfort in the fact that his top three policy advisers were Kennedy holdovers. But he could not help taking the criticism personally, and it spurred him to a frenzy of activity, meeting with every ambassador and foreign dignitary he could round up and lashing his aides to develop new initiatives. On New Year's Day, Soviet Premier Nikita Khrushchev had sent a widely publicized proposal to Johnson and other world leaders calling for an East-West nonaggression pact. LBJ felt as if he were being shown up. "I wonder why you don't get Rusk and the five ablest men in the State Department and go up to Camp David," he told Bundy, "and lock the gate this weekend and try to find some imaginative proposal or some initiative that we can take besides just reaction to actions and just let Khrushchev wire everybody . . . and us just sit back and dodge . . . I am tired, by God, of having him be the man who wants peace and I am the guy who wants war. And I'm just a big, fat slob that they throw a dagger into and I bleed and squirm just like a Mexican bullfighter."[34]

Of necessity, Johnson and his foreign policy team turned their attention first to Latin America. The goal of U.S. foreign policy had been and would continue to be to promote democracy, prosperity, and social justice south of the Rio Grande, without opening the door to communist infiltration. This objective proved virtually impossible to attain. Despite the election of democratic, civilian governments in Venezuela and several other countries, most Latin American republics were ruled by coalitions consisting of landed aristocracy and the business elite, the military, and the Catholic Church. For centuries, this unholy alliance had exploited peasants and workers while the Church's teachings on birth control contributed to a population explosion. U.S. military aid did nothing to feed, educate, or enfranchise the masses; indeed, it was often used to oppress the very people it was intended to help. Nonmilitary aid, too, was generally diverted by ruling elites into their own pockets or manipulated to safeguard their political position. By the time LBJ entered the White House, there were already signs that the Alliance for Progress was proving unequal to the task of fostering a social and economic revolution in Latin America. First, unlike the Marshall Plan, the Alliance offered loans rather than grants. Second, between 1961 and 1969, only a fraction of the $10 billion promised had been delivered, and much of it went to pay Latin American debts owed to the United States. Though the region's GNP grew at an annual rate of 4.5 percent during the 1960s, the per capita increase was only 2 percent because of population growth.[35] Social discontent increased accordingly.

Marxism-Leninism had been a part of the Latin American left since the 1920s, and it remained on the cutting edge of many worker-peasant movements from Chile to Mexico. With the rise of Castro in Cuba, that nation's increasingly close ties with the Soviet Union and communist China, and Castro's periodic promise to spread his revolution to the rest of Latin America, communism appeared to North Americans to be a real threat to the hemisphere's security. No one had been more alarmed than Jack and Robert Kennedy. Bobby had been obsessed with the plot to kill Castro, the administration's support for the coup in Argentina by the anticommunist military that ousted Arturo Frondizi in 1963, and the political warfare it waged against left-leaning Brazilian president João Goulart.[36] Indeed, by the time of Kennedy's assassination, U.S. Latin American policy had left Arthur Schlesinger and Richard Goodwin and their "openings to the left" strategy far behind. According to historian Stephen Rabe, by 1963 the Kennedy administration had ruled out "financing expropriations of land and actually opposed agrarian reform laws."[37] Kenny O'Donnell and Larry O'Brien asked Ralph Dungan, another Kennedy aide with foreign policy experience, to keep an eye on that "Goddamned Goodwin and Schlesinger, crazy nuts on Latin America."[38]

LBJ had been an outspoken supporter of the Alliance for Progress, and he believed that Operation Mongoose was counterproductive, ordering its end almost as soon as he became president.[39] At the same time, he was aware of the public's Castrophobia, which was shared by Congress and fueled by expatriate Cubans. At a foreign policy meeting with LBJ, Bundy, and others in December 1963, McCone reported that Cuban agents were hiding large caches of arms in Venezuela and recommended "a series of steps ranging from economic denial through blockade and even to possible invasion."[40] Yet when he was vice president, LBJ and his advisers had come to the conclusion that the threat posed by Castro in Cuba had been "grossly exaggerated." As George Reedy put it, "The facts are that Castro is a two-bit dictator who took over from another two-bit dictator. He maintains his position only because of his lifeline to Moscow and Peiping [Beijing]."[41] Nonetheless, not only Republicans but also ambitious Democrats would be waiting to pounce if the administration showed any sign of weakness.[42]

From all accounts, JFK's assassination had badly shaken Castro. He feared that Oswald's links to the Free Cuba committee would be used as an excuse for an outright U.S. attack. There were no longer any Soviet offensive missiles in

Cuba to use as leverage. Consequently, although Cuba had received renewed assurances from the Soviet Union of continuing economic aid and, if there was an invasion, military intervention, Castro intimated that Cuba was prepared to take significant steps to normalize relations with the United States. Johnson and his advisers decided to participate in supersecret talks with Castro, all the while keeping the economic blockade in place, attempting to penetrate the Cuban army and government with anti-Castro personnel, and sponsoring acts of sabotage that would create chaos in Cuba. A hypothetical conversation with Castro conjured up by Gordon Chase of the NSC staff summed up America's position in early 1964: "Fidel . . . we intend to maintain, and whenever possible, to increase our pressure against you until you fall . . . However, we are reasonable men. We are not intent on having your head per se, neither do we relish the suffering of the Cuban people. You know our central concerns—the Soviet connection and the subversion. If you feel you are in a position to allay these concerns, we can probably work out a way to live amicably together."[43]

In January 1964, LBJ appointed Thomas Mann assistant secretary of state for inter-American affairs and special assistant to the president. A native of Laredo, Texas, Mann had earned bachelor's and law degrees from Baylor before entering the foreign service. He had worked in the Eisenhower State Department as assistant secretary of state for economic affairs under Douglas Dillon and was ambassador to Mexico when Johnson tapped him. Fluent in Spanish, Mann had grown up in a border town where Latin American history had real meaning. He remembered as a very young child in 1915 being sequestered in a back room of his parents' house while Venustiano Carranza and Pancho Villa fought for control of Nuevo Laredo.[44] A committed noninterventionist and supporter of FDR's Good Neighbor Policy, Mann considered himself a liberal. He was, nonetheless, staunchly anticommunist. Though he remained close to Dillon and considered himself a friend of Jack Kennedy, he immediately found himself on the outs with the Schlesinger-Goodwin group. "Some of the supporters of President Kennedy, none of them in senior positions," he noted in his diary, "began to speak of the need for 'structural change' in all American societies; about the need to cultivate the 'angry young men' in Latin America and to compete with them for popular support in the area by proposing 'bold' changes of our own; about the need to disassociate ourselves from the middle and upper classes in Latin America and to identify ourselves with young revolutionaries who represented 'the wave of the future'; about the need for the United States to enforce respect for 'human rights' in other American states."[45] But Mann believed that the very middle- and upper-class moderates whom Schlesinger and Goodwin would have the United States abandon were the hope of the future.[46] Mann's critics accused him of wanting to rely only on the free enterprise system and inter-American trade to bring about social and economic progress in Latin America. In fact, he consistently supported such initiatives as a Nicaraguan Rural Electric Cooperative, $2 million to Chile for school construction, malaria eradication in Brazil, and farmer cooperatives in Uruguay. He preferred that

Latin American governments control inflation and impose austerity programs if necessary, but not if it would lead to widespread suffering.[47]

Undersecretary of State for Political Affairs Averell Harriman, a bureaucratic empire builder par excellence, predicted that Mann would "reverse the whole direction of Latin American policy." Schlesinger, now in official exile, denounced the Texan as "a colonialist by mentality and a free enterprise zealot." He considered Mann's appointment "an act of aggression" against Camelot. "Johnson has won the first round," he wrote Bobby Kennedy. "He has shown his power to move in a field of special concern to the Kennedys without consulting the Kennedys. This will lead people all over the government to conclude that their future lies with Johnson."[48] Following Mann's appointment, stories appeared in the *Washington Post, New York Times,* and other national papers quoting unnamed sources in the State Department that the Alianza was now dead, that Mann was too conservative and rigid to make it work.[49]

In fact, LBJ picked his fellow Texan not because of his substance but because of his form. He was considered an excellent, tireless negotiator, a superb diplomatic technician who could be counted on to carry out orders and get things done. "He's a coordinator," Johnson told journalist Jerry Griffin. "He's a shy, quiet, progressive fellow . . . Schlesinger, and Goodwin and some of these other fellows are not too happy about this, but you can understand that, if someone were brought in over you, you wouldn't be too happy either. If there is any flack about him becoming undersecretary we'll just make him special asst. to the president and let him use the power of the commander in chief. This doesn't mean we're going to give up on any of our idealism. We still believe you've got to have land reform and increased taxes. We want to build houses and we want to build schools."[50] He pointed out that George Ball, then undersecretary of state, Senators Fulbright and Morse, the latter a congressional expert on Latin America and a harsh critic of the U.S. foreign aid program there, all thought very highly of Mann.

The first hemispheric test for the Johnson administration came in January 1964, when rioting erupted in and around the Canal Zone in Panama, and that country's national guard informed Washington that it could no longer maintain order. Trouble had erupted when American students raised the Stars and Stripes in front of Balboa High School in the Zone. Panamanian students protested, and fighting erupted. The commander of U.S. troops in Panama, General Andrew O'Meara, stationed soldiers around the perimeter of the Zone. Meanwhile, as the embassy's Wallace Street observed, many of the Panamanian students seemed to grow markedly bolder. Soon snipers began firing on U.S. troops, who responded in kind; when the smoke had cleared, twenty Panamanians and four Americans lay dead, with hundreds more wounded. Roberto Chiari, the Panamanian president who would soon be up for reelection, declared that "the blood of the martyrs who perished today will not have been shed in vain."[51]

LBJ's in-house advisers were virtually unanimous in their opinion that the

Panamanian demonstrations had been taken over by communists and were being manipulated in hopes of destabilizing the government. The U.S. Embassy identified Victor Avilo, a "known Communist," as leader of the rock- and Molotov cocktail–throwing mobs. Mann was convinced that the leaders of the demonstrations were Castroites. Intelligence reports coming from the Southern Command in Panama blamed much of the fighting on the Vanguardia Accion Nacional, "a pro-Castro, violently anti-U.S. revolutionary group" that was determined to bring off "a Castro-type revolution in Panama."[52] In fact, there were a handful of communist agents involved plus a larger group of genuine Panamanian nationalists sympathetic to Castro. He and his revolution had become models to those in Latin America who identified oppression and economic exploitation with ruling elites historically supported by Washington. On January 10, LBJ called Chiari and talked to him directly. The Panamanian leader did not dissemble. "I feel, Mr. President, that what we need is a complete revision of all treaties which affect Panama-U.S. relations because that which we have at the present time is nothing but a source of dissatisfaction which has recently or just now exploded into violence which we are witnessing," he said. Johnson replied that the immediate need was to stop the violence and he was sending Ambassador Mann immediately to work out a solution. But he offered hope; "We want to look forward and not backward."[53]

Johnson was not averse to granting concessions to Panama over the canal; he acknowledged the justice of Panamanian charges of Yankee imperialism and agreed privately with Dean Rusk, who was of the opinion that eventually, supervision of the canal should be turned over to the Organization of American States (OAS). But he also believed that Chiari was playing demagogue, that Castro was more than ready to fish in troubled waters, and that American nationalists, to whom the Panama Canal had become something of an icon, had to be placated.[54] In response, a formula began crystallizing in Johnson's mind: contain the communists abroad, stroke the nationalists at home, and work for peaceful change.

While Tom Mann was explaining the facts of life to Roberto Chiari in Panama City, Johnson began work on Richard Russell, the bellwether of old-fashioned nationalists. Russell argued that the Panama Canal lay at the heart of the nation's strategic empire and should be protected at all costs. "I think this is a pretty good time to take a strong stand," he told LBJ. "The Panama Canal Zone is a property of the United States, the Canal was built with American ingenuity and blood, sweat, and sacrifices . . . [You ought to tell Chiari] that it was of vital necessity for the economy and the defense of every nation of this hemisphere and that under no circumstances would you permit the threat or interruption by any subversive group that may be undertaking such steps . . . We can't risk having it sabotaged or taken over by any Communist group and there's no question in my mind but that that is Castro's chief aim there."[55] Johnson assured his old friend that he was not going to let himself be intimidated and he was not going to renegotiate the canal treaty under duress, but "we are hurting, Dick," he said. "We're hurting in the hemisphere and the world. That damn propaganda is all against us."[56] In a subsequent conversation the president made it clear that he was not going to give up the right to defend the canal, but when substantive talks with the Panamanians got under way, "we'll find ourselves able to agree to significant changes in our existing relations."[57]

"When we finally arrived at the Palace, we were met by the President of Panama who seated us near a large window which looked out over the square in front of the Palace," Mann recorded in his diary. "No sooner were we seated than a crowd of people gathered in the square where they began to shout and to throw stones against the window nearest us . . . The noise caused by the shouting and by the sound of stone striking the glass made it necessary for us to raise our voices to hear and be heard."[58] Mann ordered everyone out of the room so that he could talk to the president alone. The United States had information that "Castroite communists" had penetrated the very highest level of his government, that Cuba was on the verge of flooding Panama with arms, and that a coup was imminent. Make no mistake, he said, Washington would invoke the right to defend the canal and take whatever military action was necessary to restore order. Chiari and his foreign minister, Galileo Solis, quickly backpedaled. They agreed to the restoration of diplomatic relations, and they pledged to protect U.S. citizens from mob violence. Panama would not disavow the 1903 treaty and would be satisfied with revision talks that could take up to three years.[59]

When word of this softening stance reached the street, however, nationalists called for Chiari's head, and rumors of an impending communist-led coup flooded Washington. At the same time, LBJ and his advisers received word that there were right-wing elements in Panama's national guard who were ready and willing to use the threat of communist subversion to stage their own coup.[60]

While Chiari hung by a thread, caught between the military and left-wing nationalists, Johnson resisted the urge to impose a settlement. Whatever solution emerged would probably have to include some revision of the Panama Canal treaty, and that meant Senate approval. Republicans were having a field day. New York GOP Senators Jacob Javits and Kenneth Keating proclaimed that "Castro-Communist agents" were spearheading the turmoil in Panama and declared that the canal belonged to America, period. Democrats were divided. Richard Russell led a group of hard-liners who wanted to take a tough line and give nothing away, while Humphrey and Fulbright argued for negotiations and concessions. From the UN, Ambassador Adlai Stevenson, much to Johnson's annoyance, pressed the White House to agree "to discuss and review everything in U.S.-Panamanian relations, including the canal treaties."[61] White House mail ran fifteen to one for taking a hard line.

The White House let it be known, not entirely convincingly, that it was opening conversations with Nicaragua, looking toward the construction of a new canal. A new waterway would deal a crippling economic blow to Panama. At the same time, the U.S. Embassy informed Chiari that the dozens of loan applications Panama then had pending with the United States would be reviewed and would not be approved unless the president could assure that there would be no recurrence of violence. "I don't want to settle Panama," Johnson confided to one of his staff. "I just pull out a little every day and sweat 'em a little more."[62] After repeated conversations with Russell, Johnson reached a tacit understanding with him that in any agreement to end the crisis, the United States would never approve the word "negotiate' in connection with the Panama Canal treaties, but would insist on the term "discuss."[63] On March 21, LBJ surprised reporters and his new press secretary, George Reedy, by paying an unannounced visit to that day's briefing. He was, he confided to the assembled journalists, shortly going to deliver to the OAS a statement clarifying his position on the Panama situation. In conciliatory tones, he said that he knew that the vast majority of Panamanians bore no malice or hatred toward the United States. That country had been one of America's earliest and staunchest allies during World War II. "We are prepared to review every issue which now divides us," he declared, "and every problem which the Panama Government wishes to raise."[64] An exhausted Chiari made one last unsuccessful attempt to have the term "negotiate" included and then gave in. The crisis ebbed, and talks that would lead to major treaty revisions a decade later got under way.[65]

The Panamanian crisis pointed up a key characteristic of Johnson's presidential decision making: like his mentor FDR, LBJ wanted to keep his options open until the last possible moment. His goal in consulting with the Bundys, McNamaras, Manns, Russells, and Fortases was to gather information or to check out a particular viewpoint or constituency. "When he wanted to do something," James Rowe observed of Johnson, "he would call a fellow, and he had a picture of exactly what this fellow was going to say to him in reply on any particular idea. When he got the response that he expected, he didn't pay much attention. But if he hit one of these fellows that responded differently, he sort of stopped and wondered what the hell was going on, why did this fellow say this . . . I think he would pause and try to figure that out. It was a very, very careful political technique."[66] "As far as expertise was concerned," observed Robert Komer, who served as the State Department's expert on the Middle East and who would head up the pacification program in Vietnam, "he had access to all the expertise he needed. He had expertise coming out of the gazoo. Let me tell you, as a guy who jousted with most of the experts . . . a guy with good, sound, political instinct and a feel for the jugular—and nobody ever said that Lyndon Johnson didn't have that—and who's a good horse trader—and nobody ever said he wasn't—is in business . . . It seemed to me a consistent principle of Johnson's conduct of affairs, as I saw it, was he did not want to make decisions before they had to be made. Now the bureaucracy is always pressing the President to make decisions as far ahead as possible in directions they want and so are all the foreign countries."[67] Even more so were pundits in the press who aspired to become players in the policymaking process, Johnson believed. "I've looked over the Matthews, Raymonds, Szulcs . . . background," he remarked to McGeorge

Bundy during the Panamanian crisis, "and they . . . have more to do with the running of this country than [the Bundys and McNamaras] . . . or [than I do] . . . I really honestly believe that . . . I think that they predict the day before and they get you in a position where you almost got to take it . . . I think they're very dangerous characters . . . And I don't think that we can allow them to get us boxed in here." [68] In Latin American policy as elsewhere, it would not become apparent to press and public what LBJ intended to do until he had acted, a fact that may have sharpened the effectiveness of his policy but that increasingly damaged his credibility with public intellectuals and journalists.

Above left: Lyndon at eighteen months.

Above right: Ready for school.

Right: Family gathering, circa 1912. Lyndon (four years old) is standing in front of the automobile. Sam Ealy is the third adult from the left, Rebekah Baines is in front of him, and Eliza Bunton Johnson is seated in the wheelchair.

Below: Johnson City boyhood home, circa 1915. Lyndon is standing by the family car.

Left: Sam Ealy Johnson Jr., circa 1930.

Right: Rebekah Baines Johnson as she saw herself, 1917.

The siblings, 1921: Lucia Huffman, Josefa Hermine, Rebekah Luruth, Lyndon Baines, and Sam Houston.

Class of 1924, Johnson City High School. Lyndon is in the top row, fifth from the left.

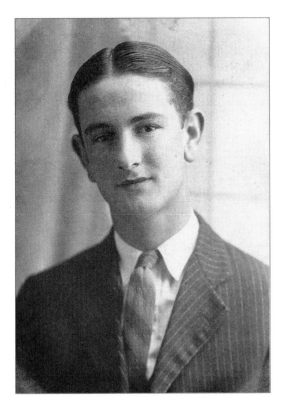

Lyndon, 1924.

Above left: Lyndon in California with Olga Martin, wife of Tom Martin.

Above right: College chums Alfred T. "Boody" Johnson and LBJ.

Left: The faculty at Welhausen School in Cotulla: Mrs. Elizabeth Johnson, Mrs. Jack Kerr, LBJ, and Mrs. Mary Wildenthal.

Below: Welhausen Athletic Club, Cotulla, 1928.

Above left: Lyndon and Lady Bird on their honeymoon in Mexico City, 1934.

Above right: The president and the protégé: FDR and LBJ in Galveston, May 11, 1937.

Right: Lt. Commander Lyndon B. Johnson, 1941.

Below: Hunting in comfort: LBJ, unidentified man, Tommy Corcoran, Herman Brown, and another unidentified man.

Above left: Wilbert Lee "Pappy" O'Daniel, 1941.

Above right: Governor Coke Stevenson, 1942.

Left: Lady Bird, 1941.

Below: On the hustings: U.S. Senate campaign, 1941.

Above: Momentary euphoria: LBJ and staff celebrating early returns in the 1941 Senate race.

Below: The "Johnson City Windmill," 1948 Senate race.

Above: Coke Stevenson and his supporters waiting for a verdict on the 1948 senatorial primary.

Below: Jim Wells and voting containers, 1948 senatorial primary.

Newsweek

SENATE REPORT ON REARMAMENT:
TOO MUCH BUTTER, NOT ENOUGH GUNS

DECEMBER 3, 1951 20¢

Lyndon Johnson: Watchdog-in-Chief

Above: Rising star in the Senate.

Below: Friends and adversaries: LBJ and Richard B. Russell.

Above: Texans in power: Lyndon Baines Johnson and Sam Rayburn, 1954.

Left: Eleanor Roosevelt and Rebekah Johnson, 1958.

Below: Nightclubbing in Acapulco: George Reedy, Mary Margaret Wiley, Lyndon, Lady Bird, Marjorie Jenkins, and Dr. and Mrs. Charles Bailey.

Who's having more fun? *Above*:
John F. Kennedy and Lady Bird; *right*:
Jacqueline Kennedy and Lyndon at a
Democratic fundraiser, Washington,
D.C., 1960.

Below right: Campaigning in Dixie,
1964.

Below left: The Democratic ticket,
1960.

Above: Men at war: Robert F. Kennedy and LBJ, 1964.

Below: LBJ and Martin Luther King Jr. at the White House, 1965.

Above: George Wallace and LBJ at the White House, 1965.

Below: LBJ appeals to civil rights leaders to restrain protesters and help curb urban rioting, 1966.

Above: Relaxing at the ranch, 1966.

Below: Recovering from abdominal surgery, 1966.

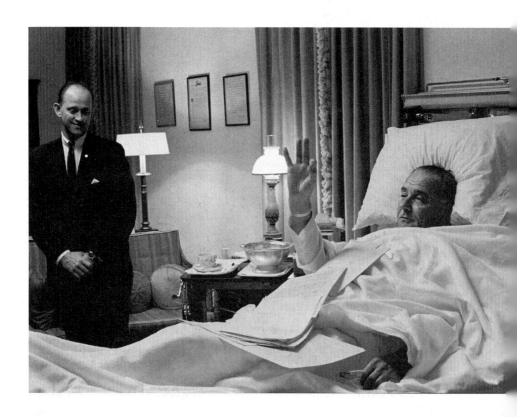

Above and right: The president visits Fort Campbell, Kentucky, 1966.

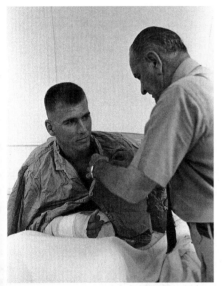

Left: LBJ visits with wounded soldier, Cam Ranh Bay, Vietnam, 1968.

Below: Foreign policy meeting at the ranch, 1967: Robert McNamara, LBJ, Dean Rusk, and Arthur Goldberg.

Above: Encounter at the Ranch, 1968: Spiro Agnew, Richard Nixon, Lady Bird, and LBJ.

Left: Togetherness: Luci Johnson Nugent, James Jones, Tom Johnson, Lynda Robb, Lyndon, and Lady Bird, 1968.

Below left: Gerri Whittington and President Johnson, 1968.

Below right: After the storm: LBJ in retirement.

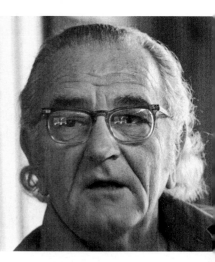

"THE COUNTRYSIDE
OF THE WORLD"

F OR MANY PEOPLE, LBJ BRINGS TO MIND TWO HISTORI-
cal phenomena: the Great Society and Vietnam. For almost everyone, Vietnam was the issue that brought him down and has forever
tarnished his reputation—whether in liberal eyes, for escalating the
war, or conservative ones, for badly mismanaging it. Yet both sides need to re-
think his fundamental commitment to the war. It touched on his deepest beliefs
and those of his fellow Americans.

Americans, Richard Hofstadter has written, are prone "to fits of crusading"
and "do not abide very quietly the evils of life." They are, Seymour Martin
Lipset observed, "particularly inclined to support movements for the elimination of evil."[1] Religion was a most significant dimension of anticommunism
during the cold war. Marxism-Leninism was repugnant in no small part because
it was "godless." Those in the 1950s, like Dwight D. Eisenhower, who had
sought to create an anticommunist monolith to compete with the Sino-Soviet
bloc had made the Judeo-Christian ethic its centerpiece. Christian realists like
Reinhold Niebuhr and Lyndon Johnson saw racism, imperialism, and totalitarianism as threats not only to America's strategic and economic well-being, but
to its spiritual and moral integrity as well. Among the most passionate supporters of the war in Vietnam were American Catholics, who were well aware that
the church constituted the backbone of resistance to the VC and NVA in South
Vietnam even after the demise of Diem and Nhu.[2] LBJ both participated in
these perceptions and inclinations and manipulated them to achieve his policy
objectives. "From our Jewish and Christian heritage, we draw the image of the
God of all mankind, who will judge his children not by their prayers and by
their pretensions, but by their mercy to the poor and their understanding of the

weak," he proclaimed to the Society of Newspaper Editors. "I tremble for our people if at the time of our greatest prosperity we turn our back on the moral obligations of our deepest faith."[3] Like freedom, democracy, and free enterprise, compassion was not divisible. "We made a basic national choice," Johnson told a group of clergymen visiting the White House. "We chose compassion. We put our faith in man—in the dignity and decency of individual man."[4]

BY THE MID-1960s, Khrushchev's calls for wars of national liberation had sent shock waves through chanceries and foreign offices throughout the non-communist world. Then, in 1965, Lin Piao, Mao Zedong's chief prophet, published a famous tract widely reproduced in the West. "On People's War" proclaimed that China's foreign policy was to encourage guerrilla wars in the "countryside of the world"—Asia, Africa, and Latin America—in order to encircle and destroy the imperialists in the "cities of the world," North America and Western Europe. No less a publication than *The Economist* declared Lin's article to be the beginning of the "Third World War" and insisted that Vietnam was the pass that must be held at all costs.[5] "It's now hard to realize how overwhelmingly and universally it was accepted that there was a great Chinese-sponsored tidal wave moving down through Indochina, across Thailand, into Burma, and right up to India," Harry McPherson noted some twenty years later. Two weeks before Johnson became president, the *New York Times* ran a feature story warning of just such an eventuality.[6] Throughout Johnson's presidency, public opinion polls would indicate support for a war to preserve a noncommunist entity in South Vietnam, if not for how that war was being conducted. Indeed, the citizens of the United States saw no moral alternative. At home, led by a southerner turned civil rights crusader, white middle-class Americans were undergoing a catharsis in which they were being forced to reconcile their Judeo-Christian principles with the evils of racial discrimination. Given the logic of the Second Reconstruction—that no believing person could deny equal opportunity and political freedom to another human being—how could the new America and its Texas prophet, trading in the angst of JFK, a fallen martyr, fail to come to the rescue of the nonwhite people of Vietnam in their struggle to resist communist totalitarianism?[7]

A majority of the American people did not want to repeat the Korean experience, did not want to get bogged down in a land war in Asia, and believed that Asians themselves ought to take primary responsibility for battling communism, but in the end they were not willing to stand idly by and see South Vietnam overrun by the North Vietnamese Army and the Vietcong, putative extensions of Maoist China.[8] Gallup polls taken in March 1965 indicated that 66 percent of those questioned believed that the United States should continue to do whatever was necessary to defend South Vietnam from the forces of international communism; 19 percent favored pulling out; and 15 percent offered no opinion. That consensus remained intact through the end of 1967.[9]

• • •

THERE ARE THOSE WHO ARGUE that shortly before his assassination, JFK had set in motion plans for an American withdrawal from Vietnam, thus making Johnson uniquely responsible for the war.[10] The best evidence for this is a meeting on October 2, 1963, when Kennedy gathered his top advisers to discuss Vietnam. After indicating that the Army of the Republic of Vietnam (ARVN) could complete the military campaign by the end of 1965, McNamara said, "If it extends beyond that period, we believe we can train the Vietnamese to take over the essential functions and withdraw the bulk of our forces. We need a way to get out of Vietnam. This is a way of doing it." General Maxwell Taylor, chair of the Joint Chiefs of Staff, agreed and insisted that this would "reduce this insurgency to little more than sporadic itching" by 1965. If we fail to meet this date, McNamara noted, "we nonetheless can withdraw the bulk of our U.S. forces according to the schedule we've laid out, worked out, because we can train the Vietnamese to do the job." Taylor interjected, "It ought to be very clear what we mean by victory is success. That doesn't mean that every Viet Cong comes in with a white flag, but what we do [is] suppress this insurgency to the point that the national security forces of Vietnam can contain [it]." McGeorge Bundy asked for clarification: "That doesn't quite mean that every American officer comes out of there, either." Taylor: "No, no." Bundy: "You're really talking about two different things. What you're saying is that the U.S. advice and stiffening function you may want to continue, but that the large use of US troops who can be replaced by properly trained Vietnamese can end." President Kennedy specified that the policy statement should say, "While there may continue to be a requirement for special training forces, we believe that the major United States part of the task can be completed by the end of '65."[11] But this was a plan for the Vietnamization of the war, not a scheme that would permit the fall of South Vietnam to the forces of communism, whether the Democratic Republic of Vietnam (DRV), the National Liberation Front (NLF), or a combination of the two.

Johnson's decision to commit to Vietnam stemmed from his Christian idealism; the way he fought the war was a function of his strategic perceptions. Like his predecessor, LBJ was determined to do everything in his power to see that the war in Southeast Asia was fought and won by those with the most at stake; noncommunist Vietnamese. But in the end, he decided that holding the line at the seventeenth parallel was worth both American treasure and American blood. He understood the dangers of such a course, that America, with little imperial history, would have no patience for fighting a protracted war whose outcome would remain inconclusive, that any government waging such a war would be caught between nationalists who would want to wage war to the fullest extent of existing technology and neutralists who believed that communism was preferable to war, at least for a powerless, nonwhite people halfway round the world. But Johnson and his advisers believed that given the imperatives of the cold war, particularly the strength of anticommunism in the United States, the alternative to limited war in Southeast Asia might well be a nuclear holocaust in which much of the settled world would be destroyed.

During the 1950s, the Eisenhower administration, wrapped in the assumptions of the New Look, neglected conventional forces while threatening either overtly or covertly to use nuclear weapons in confrontations with Sino-Soviet power. The president and his advisers made it clear repeatedly that though they dreaded a nuclear exchange, they would not shy away from it if it meant preventing the Free World from being overrun by communism. When Kennedy and McNamara came to power they were appalled by the idea that policymakers would even consider limited nuclear war as an option. Once the first bomb exploded, there would be no limits. JFK and his advisers set about taking the nuclear option off the table, by simultaneously rejecting it rhetorically as a possible course of action, embarking on a nuclear arms buildup that would assure America's enemies of total annihilation in case they were considering a first strike, and building up America's conventional forces to fight limited wars.[12]

LBJ was fully in accord with this strategic vision. If there was going to be a war on his watch, it would be a limited war. LBJ's old friend Bob Montgomery, the UT economist, recalled his saying that "if they [high-ranking military officers] were so hell-bent on having a war he'd let them have the war, but they would have to fight it on the ground so they would know what war was. In other words, they couldn't just fly over China and drop the bomb. Then of course, he was scared Russia would drop the bomb too."[13] To put it simply, the only alternative, short of submission, to unlimited war was limited war. But the threat of nuclear confrontation lurked even in this option.

If, to preserve a noncommunist South Vietnam, the United States and its allies invaded the North, China would intervene just as it had done in Korea. In addition to maintaining heavy troop concentrations along their border with North Vietnam, China had 170,000 uniformed personnel in North Vietnam helping with the war effort; they and their reinforcements would surely overwhelm any American expeditionary force. In such a scenario, there would be calls from virtually all quarters in the United States except pacifists and the extreme political left for the use of tactical nuclear weapons.[14] China would respond, touching off a chain reaction in which the United States would bomb Chinese nuclear facilities, the Soviet Union would be drawn by treaty into the war, and a full nuclear exchange between it and the United States would ensue. "I think it is important to note," Robert McNamara told congressional leaders in March 1965, "that Communist China signed the Sino-Soviet treaty in 1949, [by] the terms of which the Soviets agreed to come to the assistance of China in the event it was attacked. If we were to attack Communist China, the heartland itself, my personal view is that we can expect Soviet entry into the conflict."[15] Recently declassified documents in the former Soviet Union reveal that Beijing eventually made such a scenario explicit. In the summer of 1965, Premier Zhou Enlai communicated directly with LBJ through several neutral intermediaries. His message was clear: China would not provoke a war with the United States, but it would honor its international commitments to North Vietnam. If America bombed China, China would fight back on the ground; bombing would mean war, and it would have no bounds.[16]

The specter of a nuclear chain reaction that could get out of hand hung over the Vietnam decision-making process throughout the 1960s. Compared to a nuclear Armageddon, the possibility of another protracted brushfire war paled. Given the procrustean bed upon which they were stretched, Lyndon Johnson and his advisers would seem to have had little choice but to fight a limited war in Southeast Asia. Why the administration could not or would not make this iron logic apparent to the American people is another issue. This was the scenario, then, that emerged from the contingency planning of 1964: help the ARVN defeat the Vietcong on the ground in the South and hammer the North into halting infiltration across the 17th parallel and aid to the NLF. As students of military history are well aware, contingency plans have a way of becoming reality.

ON NOVEMBER 24, 1963, two days after the assassination, LBJ conferred with McNamara, Rusk, Ball, Bundy, McCone, and Ambassador Henry Cabot Lodge on the crisis in Vietnam. Lodge, who had supported the coup earlier that year against Diem and Nhu, painted a rosy picture. Political repression was ending and the people were rallying to the new man, General Nguyen Khanh. He "left the President with the impression that we are on the road to victory," minutes of the meeting recorded. McCone and the CIA disagreed, however, noting that far more of South Vietnam was under communist control than had previously been thought and that Khanh was totally unqualified to shape a political consensus out of the conflicted and conflicting parties that made up South Vietnamese society. There was no choice but to stay the course for the time being, McNamara observed. Johnson agreed.

LBJ was still angry over the decision to assassinate Diem. He placed much of the blame on Lodge, whom he regarded as a lazy, upper-class dilettente, whose paternalistic views had led the United States into the present state of affairs.[17] Nhu had been actively negotiating with the North Vietnamese, looking toward the creation of a unified Vietnam with Ho as president and Nhu as vice president, but he had been impossible to deal with. Diem had his faults, too, but at least he was not a military dictator and had a history as a noncommunist nationalist. Johnson understood that U.S. participation in the demise of both men had had the effect of deepening America's commitment to the conflict. Both the public and the foreign policy establishment were bound to feel more responsible for what had happened and therefore what was happening in Vietnam. At the November 24 meeting, LBJ also told his advisers that he had long been dissatisfied with the way the Vietnam situation was being handled; he wanted no more divisions, no more bickering in either Saigon or Washington.[18]

Two days later, LBJ initialed a National Security Action Memorandum that declared it to be the "central object of the United States in South Vietnam to assist the people and Government of that country to win their contest against the externally directed and supported Communist conspiracy." It promised to maintain programs of military and economic assistance at the level that had been obtained during Diem's rule, but also called for planning for possible "increased activity."[19] A month later, on New Year's Eve, Johnson addressed a public letter to Khanh: "The New Year provides a fitting opportunity for me to pledge on behalf of the American Government and people a renewed partnership with your government and people in your brave struggle for freedom. The United States will continue to furnish you and your people with the fullest measure of support in this bitter fight. We shall maintain in Viet-Nam American personnel and material as needed to assist you in achieving victory."[20] But how much aid, and what form should it take? When should aid be given, and what should the United States expect in return?

Over the next several months, Johnson was subjected to increasingly pessimistic reports on the situation in Vietnam, but could get no clear picture from his advisers as to what course to follow. Their lack of clarity was a product of their own indecision but also of domestic political considerations which, LBJ made clear, were of the utmost importance. The last week in December, McNamara returned from a fact-finding trip to Saigon. "The new government," he reported, "is indecisive and drifting. The Country Team [U.S. civilian and military leadership] . . . lacks leadership, has been poorly informed, and is not working to a common plan . . . Viet Cong progress had been great during the period since the coup, with my best guess being that the situation has in fact been deteriorating in the countryside since July to a far greater extent than we realized."[21] There were those outside the president's immediate policymaking circle who took the position that the situation was so bad that the United States should accept neutralization even if this led eventually to the communization of the Indochinese peninsula.

Early in February 1964, French President Charles de Gaulle announced that France intended to extend formal diplomatic recognition to communist China; military confrontation and diplomatic isolation had failed. He privately advised the Johnson administration to work toward neutralist status for both North and South Vietnam. China and Vietnam, he pointed out, were age-old enemies, and as neutrals, North and South Vietnam were more likely to act as barriers to Chinese communist expansion than as handmaidens of that expansion.[22] Senate Majority Leader Mike Mansfield agreed, warning LBJ in December and January of the "massive costs" of becoming bogged down in Vietnam. The strategic situation did not warrant it; there was no proof that the domino effect would apply. The United States and the Democratic party could not afford to fight and lose in Southeast Asia, he said. In his columns, Walter Lippmann took the position that Vietnam was simply not strategically important enough to warrant the kind of blood and treasure the United States had expended in Korea. In a conversation with LBJ and George Ball in May, he admitted that neutralization would in all probability be just a way station on the road to Chinese communist domination of all of Southeast Asia, but he argued that the United States could not stop this development under any circumstances. After a period, communist China would stabilize and mature like the Soviet Union; at that point, peaceful coexistence would be possible.[23]

At the opposite extreme was a coalition composed of Republican leaders, certain members of the military, and General Khanh. On January 22, the Joint Chiefs sent McNamara a memorandum recommending that the Untied States put aside many of the "self-imposed restrictions" barring bolder action in Southeast Asia and take the fight to North Vietnam. The government of Vietnam (GVN) should be induced to turn over the actual tactical direction of the war to Military Assistance Command–Vietnam, which would, in turn, "arm, advise, and support" the GVN in a bombing campaign and in covert operations directed against the North. More important, the United States should "conduct aerial bombing of key North Vietnam targets" to discourage the communists from infiltrating men and equipment into the South, and it should "commit additional US forces, as necessary, in support of the combat action within South Vietnam."[24] As Maxwell Taylor, chair of the JCS and soon to become ambassador to Vietnam, later observed, "We should never have been fighting the war in the South; we should have been fighting it in the North to begin with."[25] Khanh, who was growing increasingly frustrated with the unsettled political situation in South Vietnam, agreed. He and the country, Khanh told Lodge, were not prepared to endure "the long agony" that Washington and Hanoi apparently had in mind for them.[26]

Throughout the spring of 1964, as the presidential primaries unfolded, Republican leaders kept up a steady drumbeat of criticism for Johnson's allegedly weak and indecisive policy in Southeast Asia. In North Carolina, Richard Nixon complained about LBJ's lack of firmness in debunking de Gaulle's neutralization proposal. On February 3, Barry Goldwater told a Minneapolis audience that LBJ and his advisers were "napping" while the war in Vietnam "is drifting toward disaster."[27]

Finally, there were the Kennedys. Johnson did not know in which direction RFK, Schlesinger, Sorenson, and O'Donnell would turn. Publicly, Bobby, like Jack, had taken a consistently hard line on Vietnam, citing the domino theory and the Munich analogy, insisting that if the United States did not live up to its "commitments" to South Vietnam, all of Southeast Asia would fall to the communists and America's credibility as an ally would be destroyed. "We are going to win in Viet-Nam," Bobby had said during a trip to Saigon in 1962. "We will remain here until we do win."[28] As John Roche, head of the Americans for Democratic Action and a hardcore cold warrior put it, "Bob Kennedy made me look like a pacifist on the subject of Vietnam as of . . . 1965 and 1964 and 1963."[29] If Johnson did not play his cards right, the Kennedys could lead a charge against him within the Democratic party for losing Indochina through inexperience and indecisiveness. Following a dinner with the Clark Cliffords and Joseph Alsops in June 1964, Alsop and LBJ withdrew for a private conversation. The columnist told Johnson that if he did not commit combat troops to

Vietnam, he was going to preside over the first real defeat of the United States in history.[30]

There was no support among LBJ's advisers for de Gaulle's neutralization scheme. They were all staunch anticommunists and believers in the domino theory.[31] There were, McNamara told Johnson, four alternatives open to the administration.

> We can withdraw from South Vietnam. Without our support the government will be unable to counter the aid from the North for the Viet Cong. Vietnam will collapse, and the ripple effect will be felt throughout Southeast Asia, endangering the independent governments of Thailand and Malaysia, and extending as far as India on the west, Indonesia on the south, and the Philippines in the east . . . We can seek a formula that will "neutralize" South Vietnam. But any such formula will lead in the end to the same result as withdrawing support . . . We can send the Marines and other U.S. ground forces against the sources of the aggression. But if we do, our men may well be bogged down against numerically superior North Vietnamese and ChiCom [Chinese communist] forces . . . We can continue our present policy of providing training and logistical support for the South Vietnam forces. This policy has not failed. We propose to continue it.[32]

Bill Moyers remembered a conversation he had with the president shortly after his initial meeting with Lodge, McNamara, and company on the crisis in Southeast Asia. Clearly, Vietnam was a test, LBJ said: "The Chinese. The fellas in the Kremlin. They'll be taking the measure of us. They'll be wondering just how far they can go . . . I'm going to give those fellas out there the money they want . . . I told them I'm not going to let Vietnam go the way of China. I told them to go back and tell those generals in Saigon that Lyndon Johnson intends to stand by our word, but by God, I want something for my money. I want 'em to get off their butts and get out in those jungles and whip hell out of some Communists. And then I want 'em to leave me alone, because I've got some bigger things to do right here at home."[33] The first week in February, he wrote Khanh, "I am glad to know that we see eye to eye on the necessity of stepping up the pace of military operations against the Viet Cong."[34] By late February LBJ seemed ready to move north. "Again re North Vietnam," McCone recorded his saying in a meeting with his advisers, "he believed it essential to carry the fight to the enemy and that this be beyond pin-pricking, as the criticism of our passive position in the face of the deterioration of the situation is growing and can lead to a defeatist approach."[35]

Yet, after a story by Chalmers Roberts appeared in the *Washington Post* to the effect that the administration was planning to attack North Vietnam, LBJ drew back. He feared that Goldwater, Nixon, and Dirksen were attempting to entice him to reveal his hand on Vietnam. If he was shown to be weak and vacillating, he would become an easy mark for the GOP; if he took the war to the North, he could be labeled a "warmonger," as he put it, by liberals at home and abroad.[36] "I'm confronted," he told Richard Russell. "I don't believe the American people ever want me to run [abandon Vietnam]. If I lose it, I think that they'll say I've lost. I've pulled in. At the same time I don't want to commit us to a war. And I'm in a hell of a shape."[37] He also came to accept the argument that to act against the North, even to encourage Khanh to do so, would at this point be strategically premature. Finally, he felt the foreign policy establishment was spinning out of control. It was obvious from the Roberts article and others that one or more hawks in the administration had been talking to the press, perhaps, LBJ thought, to add to their sense of self-importance, perhaps to force his hand. He traced one of the leaks to Walt Rostow, the hard-line former MIT professor working the Asian desk in the State Department. "If you want to plan a war," Johnson told him, "you make it clear it's your war you're planning. And you go and fight it, because I don't want to fight it for you."[38]

Instead of going north, the president ordered a new plan for Vietnamization. "I want you to dictate to me a memorandum—a couple of pages . . . so I can read it and study it and commit it to memory," LBJ instructed McNamara on March 2. "We can say this is the Vietnamese's war and they've got two hundred thousand men, they're untrained, and we've got to bring their morale, and they have nothing really to fight for because of the type of government they've had. We can put in socially conscious people and try to get them to improve their own government . . . and we can train them how to fight . . . And that, after considering all of these, it seems that the latter [not withdrawing or escalating but continuing to do more of the same] offers the best alternative for America to follow. Now if the latter has failed, then, we have to make another decision. But at this point it has not failed."[39] The object of American policy henceforward, he remarked to a meeting of the National Security Council, was to achieve "a maximum effect with a minimum involvement."[40]

Critics of his dithering had a point: he was trying to have it both ways, at least until after the election. The maximum effect–minimum involvement plan contravened one of the fundamental tenets of warfare: never confront the enemy unless you are far superior in arms and men. To have maximum effect, there must be maximum effort. As Lincoln, Sherman, and North Vietnamese General Vo Nguyen Giap understood, victory required unlimited sacrifice of blood and treasure.

The situation in Vietnam continued to deteriorate throughout the late spring of 1964. Desertions from the ARVN outran enlistments. "The Government remains fragmented by dissension and distrust," McNamara reported after another trip in May. Indeed, at the time, Khanh's foreign minister was secretly telling the American Embassy that his chief had "possible Communist or neutralist connections."[41] None of the major figures in the American mission seemed to be talking to each other. When he was in Saigon, McNamara asked the commander of U.S. forces in Vietnam, General Paul Harkins, "Paul, how long do you think it will take to wind up this war?" Harkins replied, "Oh, I think we can change the tide in about six months."[42] Yet, Lodge was reporting to the White House that "a massive Communist success is possible which could end the war as a Communist victory" if the United States were not to react promptly.[43] Meanwhile, Khanh and the GVN initiated a public campaign in behalf of "marching North." While on the campaign trail, Reserve Air Force General, U.S. Senator, and GOP presidential candidate Barry Goldwater suggested the use of "low yield atomic weapons" to defoliate South Vietnam's borders and a U.S. conventional bombing campaign aginst the North.[44] Hard-liners within the JCS, notably Air Force Chief of Staff Curtis LeMay and Marine Corps Commandant Wallace Greene, continued to insist that "operations in Vietnam should be extended and expanded immediately."[45]

By May LBJ was frustrated, conflicted, anguished. "Let's get some more of something, my friend," he told McNamara, "because I'm going to have a heart attack if you don't get me something . . . Let's get somebody that wants to do something besides drop a bomb, that can go in and go after these damn fellows and run them back where they belong."[46] Later, in conversation with Dick Russell, he said, again, "I don't think the people of the country know much about Vietnam and I think they care a hell of a lot less." But if he were to lose Vietnam to the communists, Johnson said, there was not a doubt in his mind that Congress would impeach him. The JCS wanted to show the enemy an iron fist: "They don't believe that the Chinese Communists will come into this thing. But they don't know and nobody can really be sure."[47] Later that same day, he vented to McGeorge Bundy: "I don't think it's worth fighting for and I don't think that we can get out. It's just the biggest damned mess that I ever saw . . . I was looking at this sergeant of mine [his valet] this morning. Got six little old kids over there and he's getting out my things and bringing in my night reading . . . and I just thought about ordering his kids in there and what in the hell am I ordering him out there for? What the hell is Vietnam worth to me? What is Laos worth to me? What is it worth to this country? Of course, if you start running [from] the Communists, they may just chase you right into your own kitchen . . . But this is . . . a terrible thing that we're getting ready to do . . . No, we've got a treaty but, hell, everybody else's got a treaty out there and they're not doing anything about it."[48]

The solution that Johnson and his advisers came up with, one they hoped would contain hard-liners at home, pacify Khanh and others who were becoming increasingly doubtful concerning America's commitment to South Vietnam, and yet not enable liberals to label the president a warmonger, was to replace Lodge with a moderate military man and to authorize contingency planning for moves against the North, principally U.S. bombing of selected military and even industrial targets. Contingency planning did not constitute commitment, and yet if a crisis developed, as Lodge and Khanh were predicting, a mechanism would be in place for the United States to ride to the rescue.

In the late spring of 1964, to the great relief of the White House, Lodge announced that with the 1964 presidential campaign heating up, his party needed him and therefore he was resigning as ambassador to Vietnam and returning to the United States. Immediately, LBJ began casting around for a replacement. Both Rusk and McNamara volunteered, and Bobby Kennedy staged a minor campaign to be named to the position. LBJ decided that he needed all three in Washington for different reasons. Rusk and McNamara could be depended on to control State and Defense. As far as RFK was concerned, LBJ had no intention of sending his nemesis into harms' way, perhaps to return in triumph—another Caesar—to lay claim to the throne.[49] "I want him to stay right where he is," he told Bundy. Besides, the attorney general carried too much baggage. "Bobby is a very, very controversial character in the country," he confided. "I want this man to be above political matters of any kind and not to have been in any wars with Democrats or Republicans."[50]

Eventually, Johnson settled on Maxwell Taylor. His appointment had a number of advantages. The chairman of the Joint Chiefs was not of the Eisenhower, nuclear weapons persuasion. Indeed, he had resigned from the army in 1959 after making a public case for reemphasizing conventional warfare, especially counterinsurgency. After the Bay of Pigs, JFK called him back to service and jumped him over several senior officers to become chair. Taylor, multilingual, the author of several books, seemed the antithesis of single-minded war hawks like Curtis LeMay.[51] In many ways, Taylor was as hawkish as LeMay and Wallace Greene, commandant of the marine corps, but he was a gradualist. As could be expected from the author of *The Uncertain Trumpet,* Taylor was convinced that the United States and its allies could beat the communists at their own game in Vietnam.[52] From Johnson's perspective, Taylor was the perfect choice. He was a soldier and hence could "give us the cover we need with the country, with the Republicans and with the Congress," he observed to McNamara. But he was also an intellectual and a friend of the Kennedys, which would placate Lippmann and the liberals. "The only man I know," Johnson said, "who is not regarded as a war monger and who has a bunch of stars is Taylor."[53]

At the same time, Johnson named William Westmoreland to succeed Paul Harkins as commander of U.S. forces in Vietnam. Westmoreland seemed a military clone of Robert McNamara. A West Point graduate and veteran of both World War II and the Korean conflict, he was a thoroughly modern man, versed in systems analysis, a corporate executive in uniform who embraced his role as a team player. Westmoreland's diaries and papers reveal an Eisenhower-Bradley type of soldier; competent, committed to (and understanding of) democracy, comfortable with civilian control of the military, and essentially color-blind. There was nothing of the megalomania of MacArthur or the unbridled militarism of LeMay in him. Apparently, the principle of civilian control of the military was very much on the president's mind. "LBJ and I were both sharply conscious of the possibility of a parallel with MacArthur and Korea," Westmoreland recorded in his diary. "[Johnson] Made a blunt statement; have confidence you know what you are doing and hope to hell you don't kick over the traces like MacArthur . . . I submitted my plan, but even with the rejection, I deemed we had enough force to win in time. I thought it important that the military display a posture and image recognizing the military's subservience to civilian authority." [54]

Johnson believed that both Taylor and Westmoreland would have the patience and loyalty to do the job in Vietnam with the tools he chose to give them. "I will give you everything you want," Johnson told Westmoreland when he first met him in Hawaii, "because you want what I want in Vietnam. But I may have to give it to you a little slower than you want." The general replied, to LBJ's delight, "Mr. President, I may not want it as fast as you think I will. We cannot bring it in faster than Vietnam can absorb it." [55] Like Taylor, Westmoreland was fully aware of the political situation in the United States and was willing to accommodate himself and his mission to it. "With a presidential election coming up," the general noted, "LBJ did not want an image of being pushed around but he also wanted to appease the doves. Maxwell Taylor and Alexis Johnson [career diplomat who served as Taylor's assistant] came over with a plan to pressure Hanoi by bombing, but we were consciously holding down on making waves until after the election on orders from Washington." [56]

IN THE MANEUVERINGS and discussions of spring and summer of 1964, and especially in the contingency planning that Washington had decided to employ to appease Goldwater, LeMay, and Khanh, three themes stand out: the concept of limited war, military action as a form of communication, and credibility as a justification for U.S. participation in the conflict in Souteast Asia. Robert McNamara, among others, readily embraced the concept of limited war. From the first, the goal of U.S. policy was not to defeat North Vietnam per se but to crush the Vietcong in the South and to persuade Ho and his colleagues in the Lao Dong, the Vietnamese Communist Party, to withdraw support from the insurgency. [57]

Johnson, the ultimate persuader, did not believe that once committed in Vietnam, America could afford to fail. Credibility, the age-old notion that in international affairs, nations were only as good as their word, that if they reneged on an alliance, then in the future they would find it impossible to find new allies when danger threatened, carried a great deal of weight with LBJ, who remembered the great debate prior to American entry into World War II. If the peoples of the third world, particularly those in Asia who were contiguous to the communist superpowers, thought that Washington would abandon them at the drop of a hat, they were much more likely to make accommodations with Moscow and Beijing.

Following a conference of the East Asian chiefs of mission in the Philippines in 1967, the U.S. representative reported, "The Ambassadors were unanimous in the view that the determination which the U.S. has demonstrated in fulfilling its commitment to defend South Vietnam against aggression has had a major tonic effect on all the governments and people of the area. While all government leaders do not forthrightly speak out publicly to the degrees we wish, there is no free government in the East Asian area (except possibly Cambodia) which does not basically approve of what the U.S. is doing with respect to VietNam."[58] As the war dragged on, Japan, unarmed but a rising economic giant, continually expressed fear that the United States would lose its will and abandon Asia to the Chinese communists.[59]

In mid-1964 Hanoi launched a program to convert the Ho Chi Minh trail, which ran southward from North Vietnam through Laos and Cambodia, entering South Vietnam at various points, from a network of jungle trails to a modern transportation system. This, coupled with the decision taken earlier in the year to introduce regular North Vietnamese Army (NVA) units into the South, meant that by summer's end hundreds, soon to be thousands, of veteran North Vietnamese soldiers were taking up positions below the seventeenth parallel. The word "contingency" suddenly began to disappear from the memos of presidential advisers. Bundy urged Johnson to authorize the use of "selected and carefully graduated military force against North Vietnam . . . We should strike to hurt not to destroy and strike for the purpose of changing the North Vietnamese decision on intervention in the south."[60] Still Johnson refused. Then, at the Republican Convention in San Francisco in mid-July, a conservative insurgency swept Senator Barry Goldwater to the nomination. "Extremism in the defense of liberty is no vice!" Goldwater told the enraptured delegates in his acceptance speech, adding for good measure, "Moderation in the pursuit of justice is no virtue!" The Republican candidate had earlier urged that NATO commanders be given control of tactical nuclear weapons, and when asked about the situation in Southeast Asia had said, "I'd drop a low-yield atomic bomb on the Chinese supply lines in North Vietnam or maybe shell 'em with the Seventh Fleet."[61] Determined to protect his right flank in the forthcoming battle with Goldwater and fearful that North Vietnam's open commitment to the war in the South might lead to a collapse in the near future, LBJ decided to attack the North. But there would have to be a trigger.

As contingency planning for possible bombardment, blockade, or invasion of North Vietnam got under way in Washington, military intelligence began gathering information on a network of anti-aircraft missiles and radar stations installed by the Soviets on the bays and islands of the Tonkin Gulf. U-2 flights were able to photograph inland sites, but they were incapable of mapping the coastal installations. For this task, intelligence enlisted South Vietnamese commandos to harass the enemy radar transmitters, thereby activating them, so that American electronic intelligence vessels cruising in the Tonkin Gulf could chart their locations. In addition to these operations, code-named DeSoto missions, a State Department–CIA task force under McGeorge Bundy was coordinating OPLAN-34, a top-secret program of infiltration and harassment of North Vietnam by South Vietnamese covert operatives. As 1964 progressed, then, North

Vietnamese positions along the gulf coast were subjected to repeated attacks by the high-speed, heavily armed Norwegian speedboats used in the DeSoto program and to landings by OPLAN-34 operatives.

In July Admiral Ulysses Grant Sharp Jr., commander of U.S. forces in the Pacific, ordered the aircraft carrier *Ticonderoga* to the entrance to the Tonkin Gulf and instructed the destroyer *Maddox* to engage in DeSoto-type patrols off the North Vietnamese coast. On the night of July 30–31, South Vietnamese commandos in four patrol boats assaulted North Vietnamese positions on the islands of Hon Me and Hon Ngu, three and four miles, respectively, from the North Vietnamese mainland. Hon Ngu was only about three miles from Vinh, one of North Vietnam's busiest ports. The crackle of North Vietnamese radar signals and radio traffic triggered by the attacks was monitored aboard the *Maddox* and transmitted to a special American intelligence center in the Philippines.

At eleven o'clock on the morning of August 2, the *Maddox* was situated some ten miles out to sea, adjacent to the Red River Delta, the northernmost point of its circuit. Suddenly, from behind the island of Hon Me, three North Vietnamese patrol boats attacked. As the trio fired their torpedoes, missing, the *Maddox* opened fire and signaled for air support from the *Ticonderoga*. The skirmish, which lasted a bare twenty minutes, ended in a clear-cut American victory. A single bullet struck the *Maddox* harmlessly, while U.S. fire sank one hostile craft and crippled the other two.[62]

Reports of the incident reached Lyndon Johnson on the morning of the same day, Sunday, August 2. Because no American had been hurt, he told his staff, further action was unnecessary; he specifically rejected suggestions from the military for reprisals against North Vietnamese targets. The president instructed his spokesmen to play down the matter, and as a consequence, the initial Pentagon press release on the subject did not even identify the North Vietnamese as antagonists. At the same time, however, Johnson directed the *Maddox* and another destroyer, the *C. Turner Joy,* as well as protective aircraft, to return to the gulf. The commanders bore with them orders to "attack any force that attacks them."[63] The commander of the *Ticonderoga* task force radioed Captain John J. Herrick of the *Maddox* that the North Vietnamese had "thrown down the gauntlet" and should be "treated as belligerents from first detection."[64] Finally, on the 3rd, Dean Rusk, Robert McNamara, and Earle Wheeler, chairman of the Joint Chiefs, briefed a combined meeting of the Senate Foreign Relations and Armed Services Committees in executive session. They described the attack on the *Maddox* and the generally deteriorating situation in South Vietnam. In a conversation with Senator George Smathers of Florida, LBJ defended his decision not to retaliate: "You can't give them orders to chase the hell out and destroy a boat that they don't even know if they've seen."[65]

The night of August 3 was stormy and moonless. Around eight o'clock, intercepted radio messages seemed to indicate that communist patrol boats were bracing for an assault. Sonar began picking up bleeps on this night that one sailor later described as "darker than the hubs of hell."[66] An hour later the two destroyers started firing in all directions and taking evasive action to avoid North Vietnamese torpedoes. Their officers reported sinking two or perhaps three communist craft during the raid.

The battle report and traffic between the *Maddox* and Honolulu were monitored directly in the Situation Room in the basement of the White House. Duty officers summoned the president at once. McNamara asked permission to authorize the commanders of the *Maddox* and *Turner Joy* to "pursue any attacker and destroy the base of the attacker." Johnson not only concurred, but observed that "we not only ought to shoot at them, but almost simultaneously pull one of these things that you've been doing [aiding South Vietnamese commandos in attacking targets in North Vietnam]—on one of their bridges or something."[67] During the NSC meeting that followed, Douglas Dillon, whom Johnson knew to be very close to Robert Kennedy, observed, "There is a limit on the number of times we can be attacked by the North Vietnamese without hitting their naval bases." At 2:50, LBJ gave the order to retaliate.[68] Meanwhile, however, he had instructed McNamara to obtain verification of the second North Vietnamese strike. Unfortunately, Captain Herrick had begun to have second thoughts about whether or not an actual attack had occured. On the afternoon of the 4th, he cabled CINCPAC, Sharp's headquarters. The entire action had left many doubts, he reported, and he was conducting an immediate investigation. Several hours later, he cabled: "Review of action makes many reported contacts and torpedoes fired appear very doubtful . . . Freak weather effects and overeager sonarmen may have accounted for many reports. No actual sightings by *Maddox*. Suggest complete evaluation before any further action."[69] Late in the afternoon, McNamara sat down with the Joint Chiefs to evaluate the evidence to see if it could be safely concluded that a second attack had indeed occurred. The turning point was reached when he learned that someone in the administration had leaked to the press that a second attack had in fact taken place. There was no going back, then, he and Johnson concluded. If the administration were to take the position that evidence of the second attack was ambiguous, and not follow through with retaliation, it would open itself up to charges of deception and cowardice.

Though his information was still sketchy, Johnson called the congressional leadership, including Fulbright, to the White House on the evening of the 4th and announced that there had been a second, unprovoked, deliberate attack on the *Maddox* and *Turner Joy*. This time, he said, the United States had no choice but to retaliate, and he intended to ask for a resolution of support. After huddling briefly with Senators Fulbright, George Aiken, and Bourke Hickenlooper, Mansfield "read a paper expressing general opposition." Richard Russell supported retaliation in principle but voiced concern about whether the United States had enough manpower and equipment in the area to do the job. Should the United States continue to allow the North Vietnamese "to murder us from bases of safety?" McNamara asked incredulously. "I think I know what the reaction would be if we tucked our tails." At this point, Johnson chimed in: "Some of our boys are floating around in the water," he said. The Republican leadership—Saltonstall, Halleck, and Dirksen—all expressed support and promised to vote for a congressional resolution. Fulbright came away from the meeting convinced that both attacks had occurred, that they were part of a communist test of American resolve, as Rusk put it, and that the assaults would continue unless the United States responded.[70]

Johnson walked back to the Oval Office with Kenny O'Donnell. Speculating on the potential political effect of the crisis, they agreed that Johnson was "being tested" and would have to respond firmly to defend himself, not against the North Vietnamese but against Barry Goldwater and the Republican right wing. As O'Donnell later wrote, they felt that Johnson "must not allow them to accuse him of vacillating or being an indecisive leader."[71] Bundy subsequently observed to LBJ that separating Eisenhower from Goldwater was "the real object" of the exercise.[72]

Lyndon Johnson sensed that he was about to take a momentous step. Shortly before he was to go into another meeting of the NSC, South Carolina Senator Olin Johnston telephoned. "The newspapers called me today wanting to know if I was going to vote for you," he said. "I said yes. I'm for keeping us out of war and I'm for voting for Lyndon Johnson." "Well, I don't know whether I can do that," LBJ replied, clearly uneasy. "I'm going to do my best, Olin." Johnston pressed: "You are going to find in my state and in the South these mothers and people are afraid of war."[73] During the American military buildup in Vietnam a year later, LBJ would tell Robert McNamara, "We know ourselves, in our own conscience, that when we asked for this resolution, we had no intention of committing this many ground troops."[74] As LBJ prepared to announce to the press that the United States was going to attack patrol boat bases in North Vietnam in retaliation for the Gulf of Tonkin incident, Lady Bird called. "I just wanted to see you, beloved, whenever you're all alone, merely to tell you I loved you."[75]

Meanwhile, however, the White House believed that it had obtained independent verification that the second attack had occurred. Naval intelligence provided McNamara with a batch of intercepts of North Vietnamese radio flashes that seemed to be ordering their patrol boats into action. Although he was in Martha's Vineyard at the time and was not summoned back to Washington until the afternoon of the 4th, Assistant Secretary of State William Bundy recalled that the intercepts—"get ready, go, we are attacking"—were compelling. "These intercepts were certainly taken by all concerned to prove beyond a shadow of a doubt that there had been a second attack."[76]

As it turned out, evidence of the second attack was not even ambiguous; it was false. According to a recent article in the *New York Times,* midlevel officials in the National Security Administration, responsible for monitoring communications between North Vietnamese shore bases and their vessels at sea, had made numerous egregious translation errors. They subsequently falsified their intelligence reports, the reports that McNamara and the chiefs were relying on, to make it appear that a second attack had occurred on the night of the 3rd when it had not.[77]

As American jets lifted off the *Ticonderoga* and *Constellation,* Lyndon Johnson appeared on television to report to the nation that an unprovoked attack had taken place against American vessels on the high seas and that he had ordered retaliation. "Repeated acts of violence against the armed forces of the United States must be met not only with alert defense, but with positive reply. That reply is being given as I speak to you tonight . . . Aggression by terror against the peaceful villagers of South Vietnam has now been joined by open aggression on the high seas against the United States of America."[78] The strikes destroyed or damaged twenty-five patrol boats and 90 percent of the oil storage facilities at Vinh.

On August 5, LBJ summoned Fulbright to the White House to ask him to manage the resolution that Johnson would submit to Congress that day seeking approval for retaliation that had already occurred and for future military action to protect South Vietnam and American personnel in the area if it should become necessary. The chair of the Senate Foreign Relations Committee, who viewed Barry Goldwater and the ultras as the greatest threat to the liberty and safety of the country since Joe McCarthy, readily agreed. On the morning of August 6, George Ball met in the majority leader's offices with Mansfield, Fulbright, Russell, Saltonstall, and Aiken. There was no discussion of substance. "Our principal concern was one thing," Ball later recalled, "that there would be a kind of orgasm of outrage in the congress and that some of the right-wing hawk Republicans might take such action that would be in effect a declaration of war or would put the administration in a position where we had to do things which we thought would be very unwise, that might involve bringing the Chinese in or offending somebody else."[79] It was decided that Fulbright would introduce the resolution as soon as possible, with Russell, Hickenlooper, and Saltonstall cosponsoring. The Senate Foreign Relations and Armed Services Committees would hold perfunctory hearings on the morning of the 7th; passage, they anticipated, would come easily that afternoon.

The Gulf of Tonkin Resolution, introduced by Fulbright, authorized the president to take "all necessary measures to repel any armed attacks against the forces of the United States and to prevent further aggression."[80] On August 6, McNamara appeared before a joint session of the Senate Foreign Relations and Armed Services Committees to testify on the resolution. It was plain from the beginning that he would face little opposition. Opinion polls showed that 85 percent of the American people stood behind the administration; most newspaper editorials reflected this support. Nothing was said about the covert raids. Official reports indicated that the *Maddox* was engaged in routine patrols in international waters. The incidents were portrayed as "deliberate attacks" and "open aggression on the high seas."[81]

Congress responded to the administration's request with amazing alacrity.

Senator Ernest Gruening of Alaska attacked the resolution as "a predated declaration of war," and Senator Gaylord Nelson of Wisconsin pointed out that the
proposal amounted to a sweeping grant of authority to the executive. Wayne
Morse demanded to know why American war vessels were menacing the coast
of North Vietnam. George McGovern of South Dakota asked incredulously
why a tiny nation like North Vietnam would want to provoke a war with the
greatest superpower in the history of the world. One by one, Fulbright responded to the questions and criticisms. The *Maddox* had been attacked without
provocation, and the American reaction was entirely justified as an act of self-
defense under Article 45 of the UN Charter. "It would be a great mistake," he
declared, "to allow our optimism about promising developments in our relations with the Soviet Union and Eastern Europe to lead us to any illusions about
the aggressive designs of North Vietnam and its Chinese Communist sponsor."[82] The Senate debated the Gulf of Tonkin Resolution less than ten hours;
for much of the time the chamber was less than one-third full. Fulbright carefully guided the resolution through, choking off debate and amendments. Only
Morse and Gruening dissented; the final vote was eighty-eight to two.

For America, the war in Vietnam was about to begin in earnest.

CHAPTER 25

BOBBY

I T IS INCREASINGLY DIFFICULT TO WORK WITH THIS fellow Lyndon Johnson," Orville Freeman recorded in his diary in a mid-1964 evaluation of the new president. "Actually, I guess he is doing a great job. He's certainly enjoying every minute of it. But one never knows what to expect. There are about a half dozen people in the White House, any of them are apt to call at any time on any thing, and seldom does one know what the other is doing. [Johnson] lays out in all directions, you can't be sure when he really means it. He is quite a kidder but with a bite, and of course, a complete ham, grandstander, political par excellent [*sic*]. He reminds one very much of Humphrey without Humphrey's sensitivities really, but with all of Humphrey's ego drive and demand to grab and hold the limelight . . . He sure loves being President . . . On the other hand, in all fairness, a real human side comes out."[1] After witnessing LBJ's efforts to convince reporters that he was physically robust enough to be president by leading them on breakneck walks around the White House grounds, Freeman observed, "He is doing this kind of thing constantly. His whole life is involved in his job. His family, his recreation, his avocations—everything revolves around this and every person seems to be a target to be shot at, hit, and then consumed."[2]

It seemed a foregone conclusion that LBJ would be a candidate for president in his own right in 1964 and that he would win. And yet, as LBJ's friend Ed Weisl observed, "The real liberals never truly accepted Johnson. I don't know why, because he was more liberal than the most liberal of them . . . It's partly style, partly the fact that he's from Texas . . . They would tell you. 'He's good and he's wise and he's effective, but well, he just isn't our kind of a guy.' "[3] Commenting on the photo of LBJ in his 1964 campaign volume, *My Hope for America,* Murray Kempton wrote, "There is on this face both the effort to be-lieve everything and the experience to believe nothing. It is a low face of high aspiration . . . Being the king's face, it is innocent in a way in which General Eisenhower could not imagine being innocent; being also the minister's face, it is devious to a degree that Everett Dirksen would find serpentine. Of course, it lies to itself, and that is proper. Hervey said to Walpole: 'All princes must now and then be deceived by their ministers.' "[4] In short, in the view of most liberal intellectuals, LBJ was a man devoid of integrity. The hypersensitive Johnson sensed this disdain, of course, and it deeply embittered him. "What's the difference between a cannibal and a liberal?" he would ask. "A cannibal doesn't eat his friends."[5]

Johnson knew that he could do the job, and he was determined to prove his critics absolutely wrong. When a story by Rowland Evans and Robert Novak appeared in the *Washington Post* just a month after the assassination to the effect that Bobby would be a much stronger candidate than LBJ, the president called David Lawrence, former governor of Pennsylvania and a Democratic power broker. "Now I think you ought to talk to [Chicago Mayor] Dick Daley [a rumored Bobby supporter] and talk to three or four of them, and you ought to tell Mr. Evans and the rest of them that, by God, we're in better shape than we've ever been," Johnson said. "The Jews have been for me before they were for anybody else. I'm the leader in the civil rights thing with all the Negroes, and every one of them has said so when they come out of here. Labor unions were throwing their hats through the Cabinet Room the other day when I finished with them."[6] At another level, Johnson feared that his critics were right, that he was not equipped by education or temperament to be president, that he would be unable to unite the country. These doubts stemmed from Johnson's deep-seated feelings of insecurity, his vulnerability to sharp mood shifts, worries about his health, but also from a mind that was closely attuned to the political realities of the day. He later recounted what went through his mind as he considered the future in early 1964:

> I had decidedly mixed feelings about whether I wanted to seek a four-year term . . . in my own right . . . I knew enough, in those early months in the White House, that the Presidency of the U.S. was a prize with a heavy price. Scathing attacks had begun almost immediately, not only on me but on members of my family . . . There was, in addition the constant uncertainty whether my health would stand up through a full four-year term . . . I believed that the nation could successfully weather the ordeals it faced only if the people were united. I deeply feared that I would not be able to keep the country consolidated and bound together . . . And I did not believe, any more than I ever had, that the nation would unite indefinitely behind any Southerner . . . the metropolitan press of the Eastern seaboard would never permit it.[7]

Sometime after the New Year, Lyndon and Lady Bird sat down to list the pros and cons of running. She believed that if her husband did not offer himself for election to a full term, their remaining years would be a living hell. Enemies would speculate on unrevealed skeletons in the closet that had been responsible for driving Johnson out of a race that he surely could have won. Friends and supporters and the rank and file of the Democratic party would be embittered if the ticket lost in November, forever convinced that LBJ had let them down. True, he might live longer and could spend his remaining years at the ranch, but there would be the gnawing feeling that he could be doing better than whoever was sitting in the White House. "You may look around for a scapegoat," she said. "I do not want to be it. You may drink too much for lack of a higher calling." If he ran, she observed, he would probably win. There would be unfair criticism, personal attacks, some bad decisions, disappointment at the inadequacies of self and others, and perhaps an early death. But it would be worth it. "My conclusion," she said: "Stay in. If you win, let's do the best we can for 3 years and 3 or 4 months—and then the Lord letting us live that long, announce in Feb. or Mar. 1968 that you are not a candidate for reelection."[8]

Even more than Lady Bird's support, Johnson's hatred of Bobby Kennedy pushed him to run. Indeed, Pierre Salinger later opined that the only reason a reluctant LBJ had decided to throw his hat in the ring in 1964 was to keep Bobby out of the White House.[10] And so Lyndon decided to run, and having done so, he would devote every spare moment to the campaign, lashing his subordinates and supporters to redouble their efforts even when it was clear that he was going to win in a landslide, and stage-managing the 1964 Democratic Convention down to the last detail. Yet, he regularly considered dropping out. Ambition was a constant with Lyndon Johnson, but so was ambivalence.

LBJ CONSULTED with a wide variety of people concerning strategy—Rowe, Clifford, Fortas, Russell, Robert Anderson (Eisenhower's secretary of the treasury and a fellow Texan), Larry O'Brien, and many others—but his principal adviser was Horace Busby. The message that Busby continually conveyed during the spring and summer of 1964 was that the Democratic party was *not* the majority party in the United States (notwithstanding all evidence to the contrary) and that Johnson could lose the election. Busby claimed that Democrats were laboring under assumptions that were patently and dangerously false: that beginning in 1932, the political tide had set against the Republican party and was continuing to run against it; that the Democratic party was the majority party in 1964, not only in congressional and local politics but at the presidential level as well; that aside from its traditional base in the South, the Democratic party was the party with the broader national appeal; that the Republican incumbency during the 1950s was an aberration attributable to Eisenhower's war hero appeal; that the Kennedy-Johnson victory was a party victory that validated the previous assumptions. Wrong, wrong, wrong! Only when FDR ran for the presidency did the Democrats command a majority of voters, some 55 percent during his four elections. No Democrat since Roosevelt, including Harry Truman, had come close. The average for the four Democratic electoral victories in the twentieth century other than FDR's—Wilson in 1912 and 1916, Truman in 1948, and Kennedy in 1960—had been 46.6 percent.

Busby argued that polls taken in 1964 showing the party to be, by overwhelming margins, the majority party at the statehouse and courthouse levels did not translate to the national level. The cumulative plurality for the GOP in the four postwar presidential elections stood at 13,934,000 votes. If the South was removed from those totals, the figure rose to 15,725,750. The Democratic victory in 1960 was "the first victory in which the construction of the ticket and the positive electoral vote contribution of both Presidential and Vice Presidential candidates was responsible for the outcome, narrow though it was. A large number of voters were attracted to the ticket for reasons of religion, region, and factors other than loyalty to the Democratic party."[9]

Johnson's other advisers were similarly cautious. More and more, they worried, the Democratic party was coming to be seen as defender of the status quo, protector of those blocs and interests that composed the New Deal coalition. The one exception was in the area of civil rights, and that, as Henry Wilson, an aide to Larry O'Brien, observed, was an extremely dangerous exception. That issue alone, in the wake of *Brown,* Birmingham, and the Civil Rights Act of 1964, could cost the Democrats the presidency in 1964. "When race prejudice gets going," he warned, "organized labor can move right out from under its leadership en masse."[10] The Republicans, especially the Goldwater wing of the party, were posing as reformers. What they proposed to reform was bloated government that, acting in the name of special interests such as big labor, minorities, and the welfare community, was taxing the average American into penury and trampling on his and her liberties.[11]

Finally, Busby was blunt in assessing LBJ's liabilities as a campaigner: he was perceived as a mere tactician rather than a person of vision; he was given to exaggeration and excessive enthusiasm; everything seemed of pressing, immediate urgency, implying that Johnson had no sense of judgment or proportion; he was prone to sloganeering and building straw men to knock down; he pandered to the press; and he was vulgar.[12] This pessimism fed Johnson's insecurity but also served to motivate him. What Busby failed to stress—perhaps intentionally, to avoid complacency—was the fact that sympathy for the assassinated JFK washed over Johnson, and made it seem like an insult to the late president to reject his successor.

Philosophically, LBJ could not abandon the notion that the federal government was an instrument to be wielded for the good of the people. White House support for the poverty bill and the civil rights measure, as well as the Great Society speech delivered at the University of Michigan, had underlined the president's commitment to the notion of positive government action to end discrimination, guarantee equal opportunity, regulate the marketplace, and aid the disadvantaged. These goals would be obtained without revolution; indeed, they were an alternative to revolution. Eric Goldman urged LBJ to point out that positive action by the federal government actually enhanced individualism in America rather than detracted from it. The effect of antitrust legislation, worker safety laws, hours and wages legislation, a commitment to civil rights by the federal government, financial and occupational aid to the disadvantaged "has actually been to create much more opportunity for the American to be a genuine individual, with much more chance to express his individual self in both the practical and non-practical sense of living," he wrote LBJ.[13] Tactically, of course, Johnson had to reach out to traditional Republicans and whittle away at the GOP base. Given the likely defection of the South, such an effort was crucial. In an economic climate of a growing GNP, increasing wages and prices, and ever rising family incomes, Johnson could practice the "politics of productivity." "Until recently it had been assumed there was only so much pie," Walter Lippmann observed, and the social question was how to divide it. But in the current generation, a revolutionary idea had taken hold: you could make the pie bigger with fiscal policies, "and then a whole society, not just a part of it will grow richer."[14] Finally, LBJ should continue to pose as the "can-do" statesman, a prudent man of vision who could tease progressive legislation from the bureaucratic and political morass in Washington.[15]

April brought the perfect opportunity for LBJ to showcase his talents as political mediator and highlight the virtues of the corporate state. For five years the nation had been confronted with the possibility of a nationwide railway strike. By the spring of 1964, negotiations had completely stalemated, and the railroad brotherhoods made plans to walk out. Shortly before they announced their intentions, unknown agents dynamited a section of track, blowing up a locomotive and derailing twenty-seven cars.[16] Knowing that a prolonged work stoppage would threaten the health of the economy, Johnson summoned negotiators from both sides to the White House in a last-ditch effort to stop the walkout. Aware that the public had JFK's success in settling the 1962 steel strike on its mind and fearful of the political consequences for his prestige and the prestige of his office if he intervened and failed, LBJ was at his most intense. What Johnson wanted was for both sides to agree to give him time to work out a settlement before they inflicted a strike on the nation. He subsequently described the negotiations to his journalist friend from Texas, Marshall McNeil:

> I told them that this country couldn't stand this . . . It meant that everything we've done all year since I came in November would fall back. And that I wanted them to give me twenty days to see what I could do about it and for them to go off . . . and come back and tell me. They came back. And the carriers said, "We accept your proposal." The labor people said, "We do not accept your proposal . . . We've been at this four years and Presidents have asked us to postpone time and time again . . . and we just lost our ass every time . . ." I said . . . "I'm not going to take that kind of no. I'm supposed to be a great healer and a great pleader. You go in that President's private office by yourselves. Talk it over and see if you want to tell the people of this country that you said no to their President when he

hasn't had a chance . . ." Finally I went in there. I said . . . "There's a poll over on my desk—Gallup, says 77 percent approval Johnson for President . . . Now look at that, fellows. You wouldn't want me to say to the people of this country that you-all wouldn't give me two weeks to try to do my duty" . . . So . . . they came back and the old boy said . . . "We're going to go with you."[17]

LBJ brought the Illinois Central president and the head of the Brotherhood of Locomotive Engineers into the Fish Room, where he announced his achievement on national television. McNeil was impressed. "I thought you were just cuter than a pig on that television last night," he told Johnson.[18] Eric Goldman, who was present throughout, remembered the call to patriotism. "I want all of you to recognize," he remembered the president saying, "that we are in high focus throughout the world tonight. Please give me this opportunity to show that our system of free enterprise really works. As patriotic Americans, I tell you, you must delay."[19] Roy Davidson, head of the International Brotherhood of Locomotive Engineers, later said, "What else do you do if the President looks you straight in the face and tells you that it is your duty as an American?"[20]

During the next two weeks, Johnson oversaw negotiations in the Executive Office Building. Twice a day he would stick his head in, warning of the dire consequences of a strike and appealing to the participants' patriotism. "Every night Lyndon and I talk about what's happening to the railroad negotiators," Lady Bird recorded in her diary, "and I know how much is hanging in the balance for him."[21] In the end, management accepted most of the union's demands in return for concessions from the government. LBJ promised to press Congress to grant the railroads greater leeway in setting rates, and he intervened with Attorney General Kennedy, asking that Justice stretch the letter of antitrust laws and approve rail mergers whenever possible.[22] On April 22, over coffee, the two sides indicated to LBJ that they were ready to sign an agreement. Overjoyed, he swept up the four negotiators, stuffed them into the presidential limousine, and with police sirens screaming, drove directly to the local CBS affiliate, WTOP, where his friend, CBS president Frank Stanton, had arranged for a three-network broadcast. Jubilant, LBJ hailed the settlement as a triumph for American industrial democracy. The press reaction was more than LBJ's campaign staff could have hoped for. "The President scored a great coup—a 'miracle' some called it—in helping to settle the five-year-old railroad dispute that had defied all previous efforts at solution," declared a *New York Times* editorial. James Reston lauded "the tireless negotiating skill" of the president as "one of the vital natural resources of this country."[23]

THE END OF APRIL saw LBJ riding high in the polls. A political cartoon reflected the strength of the president's position. It showed him seated at a card table with a deck before him and "tax cut" cards tucked in the brim of his Stetson, "R.R. Settlement" and "Boom Times" cards coming out of his sleeves, and

"Common Touch" and "Poverty Fight" cards protruding from the cuffs of his pants. A smiling LBJ asked, "Now who'd like to play?"[24] Johnson was the only presidential candidate in history, complained the chairman of the Republican National Committee, to have both poverty and prosperity going for him. There even seemed some hope of capturing the South. In January, no less a Dixiecrat than Strom Thurmond declared in Houston that LBJ had a much greater chance of carrying the South than JFK would have had.[25] In July, southern moderates Luther Hodges, LeRoy Collins, and Buford Ellington embarked on a trip through the former Confederacy, meeting with every southern governor except Wallace of Alabama and Johnson of Mississippi to lobby for LBJ. You tell them "it's a hell of a lot easier to sit beside a Negro in a restaurant than to fight beside him with a gun overseas," LBJ instructed.[26]

Outside the Deep South, the only possible chink in the president's political armor was his home state of Texas, thanks to the continuing bitter feud between conservative and liberal Democrats and the love-hate relationship between Lyndon Johnson and John Connally. During the early months of 1964, it appeared unlikely that Connally would even support Johnson for president, much less nominate him. Johnson had called his protégé while he was still in the hospital recovering from Oswald's gunshot wounds. "I just wanted to tell you I loved you," LBJ said. "I didn't have a thing in the world—was just thinking about you, and I wanted to be damn sure you were doing all right." Connally thanked him, told him he was doing a whale of a job, but suggested, "For God's sake, meet with the businessmen. You been getting a little too much emphasis on meeting with the civil rights boys every day, and labor."[27] In the Texas senatorial primary, Johnson refused to support Connally protégé Joe Kilgore over Ralph Yarborough. The governor's hatred of Texas's second most successful liberal continued unabated.[28]

In February, during a presidential trip to Texas for the funeral of KTBC manager Jesse Kellam's wife, Johnson and Connally openly feuded. The governor turned down an invitation to the ranch, telling the president that he and Nellie were building a new ranch house at Floresville and he had "to pick out marble and brick and tile, fabrics, fixtures, and every other damn thing."[29] "I can be just as cold and hard as he is," LBJ subsequently remarked to Jack Valenti, "and let's just see who survives."[30] To make matters worse, liberal Democrat Don Yarborough, who had lost in the primary to Connally by only twenty-five thousand votes in 1962, announced that he was once again going to challenge for the governorship. Connally may not have believed that LBJ had put Don Yarborough up to running, but he did believe that he could have stopped it. When mutual friend Lloyd Hand suggested that the president call Connally and try to work things out, LBJ exploded: "I talked more with that son-of-bitch than with any of the other Governors in the United States put together."[31]

Connally, however, was unbeatable. He continued to be the darling of the Texas political establishment, and his November wounds had made him something of a folk hero. Liberals began to snicker about the "silver bullet" Oswald had offered up to Connally. "He ain't never done nothing but get himself shot in Dallas," Texas comptroller and liberal Bob Bullock quipped.[32] When he beat Don Yarborough two to one in the Democratic primary, however, Connally began to mellow, and he and Johnson reconciled.

Indeed, it was Big John who put Johnson's name up for nomination at the Atlantic City convention and subsequently acted as his emissary to the white power structure in the South. The Texas governor was the perfect intermediary. In 1963 Connally had come out publicly in opposition to the Kennedy administration's civil rights bill. He had made a survey of the Lone Star State's hotels, motels, swimming pools, and theaters, he said, and concluded that Texas was doing splendidly in the area of voluntary desegregation. At the same time, he refused to denounce integration per se, and at various southern governors' conferences was careful to distance himself from the likes of George Wallace, Ross Barnett, and Orval Faubus.[33]

As the nominating conventions approached and GOP aspirants fought it out in various state primaries, all the Republicans could do, it seemed, was keep the Bobby Baker scandal alive. Though the brouhaha was a tempest in a teapot, Johnson characteristically overreacted, and his paranoia and lack of candor created more problems for him than the charges themselves. It will be remembered that at the prodding of Republican Senator John Williams of Delaware, the Senate Rules Committee had opened hearings on the Baker case. Clearly, the secretary to the majority had been associating with underworld figures in his business dealings and was involved in a kickback scheme involving a vending company and a defense plant. But what was of particular interest to Williams and the GOP was the charge that Baker had compelled one Don Reynolds to buy several thousand dollars' worth of advertising from KTBC and to give a high-priced Magnavox stereo set to the Johnsons in return for a $200,000 life insurance policy that LBJ had purchased following his heart attack.[34] Johnson had gotten off on the wrong foot when he was vice president, when the scandal first broke, by telling reporters, "I hardly knew Bobby Baker!" George Reedy remembered being dumbfounded at the time: "My God! Bobby was one of his messiahs . . . He had just fantastic confidence in Bobby Baker," and everyone knew it. Johnson's claim, indeed, pointed to something of a character flaw. "You know, one of the things about Lyndon Johnson you always have to be careful of," Reedy observed. "Whatever Johnson tells you at any given moment, he thinks is the truth. The first victim of the Johnson whopper is always Lyndon Baines Johnson. In his own mind I don't think the man has ever told a whopper in his life."[35] The first week in February, acting on a tip from the White House, Drew Pearson and Jack Anderson wrote a column in the *Washington Post* charging that Reynolds had been dismissed from West Point and subsequently lied about it.[36] The Baker scandal quickly died down.

One of the problems facing LBJ and his campaign strategists as spring gave way to summer was that they were not at all sure who the GOP nominee would be. Former vice president Richard Nixon had thrown his hat in the ring, as had Governors Scranton and Rockefeller. Henry Cabot Lodge had returned from Vietnam hoping to be embraced as a heroic proconsul. Of these, Rockefeller seemed the strongest. JFK had always believed that if the GOP had run Rockefeller instead of Nixon in 1960, it would have won. Bright, attractive, Rockefeller was possessor of one of the most famous names in American history. But in a scandal that seems absurdly mild by today's standards, he had left his wife of thirty-one years to marry another woman who had also abandoned her marriage. Scranton of Pennsylvania was a feared contender among Democratic strategists. He was moderate, reasonable, intelligent, and seemingly trustworthy. He was also tough. "They say he's a real character assassin," LBJ observed, "but he does it in a Brooks Brothers style." Finally, Scranton would be able to rely on the support of internationalist Republicans with their money and press connections.[37] Fortunately for LBJ and the Democratic party, the Republicans were in no mood for moderation and reason in 1964. Contorted by internal bickering and frustrated by the Democratic resurgence of the late 1950s and early 1960s, the GOP abandoned the middle course it had been following since 1940.

THE DARLING OF THE NEW RIGHT was Senator Barry M. Goldwater of Arizona, the heir to a department store fortune and a reserve air force general who had first been elected to Congress in 1952. There seemed to be two Goldwaters, columnist Richard Rovere noted; one was the easygoing, affable southwesterner whom most senators knew personally. The other was the humorless, ideologically rigid author of *The Conscience of a Conservative*. That book, ghostwritten by Goldwater's handlers as a campaign tract, called for reduced government expenditures, elimination of government bureaucracies, an end to "forced" integration, reassertion of states' rights, an end to farm subsidies and welfare payments, and additional curbs on labor unions. Above all, Goldwater called for "total victory" over communism both at home and abroad. Laissez-faire in domestic policy and aggressive in foreign, Goldwater, who had never authored a bill, declared, "My aim is not to pass laws but to repeal them." On the other hand, containment was too defensive, "like a boxer who refuses to throw a punch."[38]

Early in the 1960s, conservative party operatives such as Peter O'Donnell of Texas, Clifton White of New York, and John Grenier of Alabama had set about capturing the party for Goldwater. They were the intellectual and political heirs of Robert Taft, convinced that the "me-tooism" of Thomas Dewey and the eastern, liberal wing of the party, which had controlled the presidential nominating process since the Roosevelt era, had bankrupted the GOP politically and failed to offer the voters a clear choice. As these true believers gained control of grass-roots organizations within the party and Goldwater assumed an ever-higher profile, the moderate wing of the party wallowed in disarray. Conservative activists held a rally at Madison Square Garden and thousands applauded as Brent Bozell, editor of the *National Review,* called on the United States to tear down the Berlin Wall and immediately invade Cuba.

Meanwhile, the moderate candidates were battering each other. Rockefeller managed to eliminate Lodge in the Oregon presidential primary but then lost to Goldwater in the crucial California contest. At the Republican Convention in San Francisco, held during the second week in July, the delegates chose Goldwater and, as his running mate, William E. Miller, New York congressman, chairman of the GOP National Committee, and an accomplished political polemicist. It was a raucous affair. Goldwater's supporters openly ridiculed Rockefeller and the moderate wing of the party. When the New Yorker derided the extremists and "kooks" he saw arrayed against him, the Goldwaterites jeered, rang cowbells, and blew horns to drown him out. One irate blonde in the galleries stood, shaking her fists, and screamed, "You're a lousy lover! You're a lousy lover!"[39]

Goldwater's nomination was stunning. Johnson and other observers believed it signaled the demise of the Republican party. The new right was "a pretty intense, fanatical group," the president told newspaper publisher Houston Harte, "a bunch of screwballs . . . the Birch Societies . . . I think it [will] probably mean the death of the Republican party . . . He [Goldwater] wants to drop atomic bombs on everybody. I don't believe the people will stand for that."[40] But the demise of the GOP did not necessarily translate into a victory for LBJ in November. The country seemed in a mood for extremism. An article in the *New York Times* by James Reston warned that America better take the Republican candidate seriously. Orville Freeman observed in his diary that "Goldwater has capitalized on a general frustrated feeling of people in a complex society, that he has picked up the backlash on the racial question, that he is capitalizing on the general fear of bigness and anti–big government attitudes, that he is emphasizing the individual in his efforts to maintain his identity in an increasingly large and collectivized society both publicly and privately."[41]

But Barry Goldwater was not the only figure in American politics in 1964 seeking to gnaw away the edges of the vital center. On May 19, George Corley Wallace won 43 percent of the vote in the Maryland Democratic primary against Senator Daniel Brewster, a stand-in for LBJ. In June 1963, the Alabama governor had become segregation's newest hero by standing in the door of the University of Alabama admissions building in an attempt to bar the registration of two black students, James Hood and Vivian Malone. Though he was forced to stand down, Wallace used the incident to whip white voters into a fury and to become a factor in presidential politics. When, on August 28, Martin Luther King led the famous March on Washington, Wallace made a point of declaring to reporters that he had better things to do than "waste my time" watching a march led by "communists and sex perverts."[42] When he subsequently announced that he was going to be a candidate for president on the Democratic ticket, pundits scoffed; many thought that the Dixiecrat card had been played and discarded in 1948. Others were not so sure. "Wallaceism is bigger than Wallace," King had warned CBS television reporter Dan Rather following the schoolhouse door incident.[43] The Alabama governor, one of his contemporaries observed, was "emotional, energetic, single-minded, rough-hewn, strong and appealing to the masses," a kind of redneck Ivanhoe "astride a great white charger," doing battle for the white people of Alabama and the South.[44]

Millions of working-class whites, not just in the South, but in the North and Midwest, felt socially and economically threatened by the civil rights movement and sided with Wallace. In July, rioting erupted in Harlem after an off-duty police officer shot a black teenager. Amid arson, looting, and violent clashes between the police and black youths, one died and more than one hundred were injured.[45] Reporting from his heavily Polish district in Illinois, Democratic Congressman Dan Rostenkowski told Jack Valenti that there was a definite white backlash among voters. A recent poll showed that 78 percent opposed the civil rights bill. Fear of job competition and declining real estate values had overridden the Catholic Church's strong stand in behalf of the Second Reconstruction.[46] Wallace subsequently dropped out of the race, but he had mobilized a potent constituency that would presumably switch their support to Goldwater. "It is time someone said to the President what apparently no one has yet said to him," a White House staffer memoed Bill Moyers, "that he could lose this election and that he could lose it despite having lined up all the press and the television networks, all the top labor leaders, most of the top business leaders, all of the negro vote, and perhaps even Lodge and Rockefeller." A Goldwater campaign based on "three potent commodities: Race prejudice . . . chauvinism . . . [and] simple answers to complicated questions" could produce an upset.[47]

The president's advisers need not have worried about their man. Johnson fought every campaign as if it were in doubt, as if every vote against him would be taken as a personal affront. He would leave no stone unturned in his search for support, no effort unexpended in campaigning. From his first run for Congress through the 1964 presidential campaign, he always ran scared. Even when the polls showed him far ahead and a sure winner, he worked tirelessly. Johnson coveted a landslide for his own personal gratification, but also as a mandate for the Great Society.

Johnson's biggest decision during the campaign was selection of a running mate. Early in the spring of 1964, Schlesinger, O'Donnell, and their allies in the press started a Kennedy for vice president boom. It worked. National polls indicated that the people preferred Bobby to his nearest rival, Hubert Humphrey, by a four-to-one margin. Syndicated columnist Stewart Alsop observed that it would be virtually impossible for LBJ to reject the attorney general as his running mate. To do so would risk losing Catholics, blacks, and the labor vote in the large industrial states of the East and Midwest.[48]

Three weeks after JFK's death, Johnson had told Kenny O'Donnell, "I don't want history to say I was elected to this office because I had Bobby on the ticket with me. But I'll take him if I need him." But he also said, "If I don't need him, I'm not going to take him."[49] LBJ later recalled the situation in a conversation with Doris Kearns Goodwin:

> Every day, as soon as I opened the papers or turned on the television, there was something about Bobby Kennedy; there was some person or group talking about what a great Vice President he'd make. Somehow it just didn't seem fair. I'd given three years of loyal service to Jack Kennedy. During all that time I'd willingly stayed in the background; I knew that it was his Presidency, not mine. If I disagreed with him, I did it in private, not in public. And then Kennedy was killed and I became the custodian of his will. I became President. But none of this seemed to register with Bobby Kennedy, who acted like he was the custodian of the Kennedy dream, some kind of rightful heir to the throne. I'd waited for my turn. Bobby should've waited for his . . . I simply couldn't let it happen. With Bobby on the ticket, I'd never know if I could be elected on my own.[50]

But how to get Bobby out of the unofficial race for the vice presidency without appearing to be mean and vindictive? To soften the blow, LBJ paid court to other Kennedys. His solicitous calls to Jackie continued, as they did to Joe Sr., bedridden with a stroke. When Ted suffered a broken back in a plane crash, LBJ telephoned him at the hospital. "Well, you're a great guy and you got lots of guts and stay in there and pitch and anything we can do, we're ready," Johnson told the youngest Kennedy, who would soon be campaigning for the Massachusetts Senate seat from the hospital. "And we'll elect you by a bigger vote than you got before."[51] May gave way to June and Bobby still refused to withdraw. Yet he told his friends that he was not sure he wanted the job. He had heard that LBJ had said that whoever became vice president, "I want his pecker . . . in my pocket."[52] And, of course, he hated Johnson. "He's mean, bitter, vicious—an animal in many ways."[53] In fact, Bobby wanted the second spot—and he wanted it desperately. "Well, he wants that job," McGeorge Bundy told the president in late July, having just conferred with RFK. "I don't think he finds fault with your right to have a view. I think he just plain wants it."[54]

On July 9, Johnson again met with Bobby in the Oval Office. This time, the conversation was dignified and to the point. LBJ told him that he had decided not to consider any sitting cabinet member for a running mate. Kennedy flushed slightly and then asked if he had settled on anyone. LBJ said no, but that he was faced with the same issues of geographic and philosophical balance that had confronted JFK in 1960. He told Bobby that he had a very bright future in the party and that he would do whatever he could to advance his career. He asked Bobby to stay on as attorney general. Not surprisingly, Kennedy refused and recommended Nick Katzenbach as his replacement. "He seemed to have expected what happened," LBJ subsequently told Clark Clifford, "but cherished the kind of hope. He kind of swallowed deeply a time or two. He wasn't combative in any way. I leaned over backwards not to be in the slightest arrogant." As he was departing, Bobby looked up at LBJ, smiled, and said, "Well, you didn't ask me. But I think I could have done a hell of a job for us." LBJ responded, "Well, I think you will do a hell of a job for us . . . And for yourself too."[55] Leaving the White House, Bobby met with O'Donnell and O'Brien at Sans Souci for lunch. "He told me he wouldn't take me under any circumstances and that's it," O'Donnell recalled his saying. "He [Bobby] was kind of laughing. He was mad but laughing."[56]

Obviously, Bobby felt humiliated, and it would have served Johnson well to have let the matter blow over as quickly as possible. But once again, he let stories in the media that he considered to have been planted by the Kennedys goad him into an error of judgment. Typical of the pieces was that by David Wise appearing in the *New York Herald Tribune.* He described the decision to keep RFK off the ticket as a "swift and final dumping" that constituted a "bitter blow" and "brought an end to a gay and glittering era that became known as 'The New Frontier.' "[57] Infuriated, LBJ invited reporters from the *Washington Post, New York Times,* and *New York Herald Tribune* for a four-hour lunch at the White House on July 31. He went into his meeting with RFK in great detail, exaggerating the attorney general's discomfort and implying that he begged for the vice presidency. LBJ mimicked a high squeaky voice and a man gulping. Bobby's Adam's apple had bobbed up and down like a cork in the water, he chortled.[58] Tipped off to the interview, an enraged RFK confronted the president and chastised him for breaching a confidence. When LBJ denied that he had met with the reporters, Bobby accused him of lying. He would check his calendar to see if he had made an error, Johnson replied. (Kennedy was convinced that Johnson had secretly taped their conversation. He had not.)[59] The feud was on again, full force.

If not Kennedy, then who? The Johnsons returned to the ranch to celebrate July 4th. In her diary, Lady Bird recalled breakfast with John and Nellie Connally, the Frank Ikards, and the Homer Thornberrys. "We discussed the vice presidency. Two of us there were for [Senator Eugene] McCarthy—the Thornberrys. Six were for McNamara [John Connally, who had served for a time as JFK's secretary of the navy, and Robert McNamara had become close friends].[60] They pretty much all agreed that Humphrey would be their third choice, although they've not forgotten the South's antipathy for him . . . No voice was raised for Shriver."[61] Johnson had earlier considered McNamara and rejected the idea. "I believe that the liberals, and I believe that the Negroes, and I believe that the labor folks, and I believe that the bosses . . . would revolt if I tried to cram Bob down their throats," he subsequently observed to McGeorge Bundy.[62] He had also considered Shriver, perhaps, as some said, to bait the Kennedys. But the brother-in-law had no real constituency.

In January, Johnson had encouraged Humphrey by telling him that he "could take confidential soundings and scout for support for the vice presidency."[63] Despite the fact that his advisers warned him that LBJ would "cut his balls off" if he took the job, Hubert Humphrey coveted the second spot.[64] It was probably his last, best chance to be president, a heartbeat away from a man whose heart had come perilously close to never beating again in 1955. LBJ kept Humphrey's appetite whetted. In the early spring, Jim Rowe, friend to both men, asked the ebullient Minnesotan to come to his house in fashionable Cleveland Park. There he told Humphrey that he was being considered seriously for the vice presidency. He then began to ask him personal questions: How much money do you owe and to whom do you owe it? Are there other women in your life? Above all, will you be loyal? Humphrey reassured Rowe on every count, but received no commitment in return.[65] "Two weeks before the convention," Eric Goldman recalled, "I watched him [Humphrey] eating lunch in the White House Mess. Despite his ebullience, his face was that of a man who was being drained. These days he was telling friends the sad little story of the girl whose hero was the handsome captain of the football team. He would keep phoning her—always to ask her opinion of some other girl and never for a date."[66]

Johnson wanted to keep the vice presidential issue open until the last possible moment, to focus press attention on him, the Democratic ticket, and the forthcoming convention at Atlantic City. He also took puerile satisfaction in torturing Humphrey. Moreover, though he genuinely liked Humphrey and knew that their political values were essentially the same, he also perceived that the Minnesotan was ambitious, had a strong ego, and would have difficulty standing in LBJ's shadow for four years. And there was Hubert's penchant for "bouncing verbosity," as Orville Freeman termed it.[67] Two days after the Gulf of Tonkin incident, Humphrey had given a wide-ranging interview to reporters during which he speculated about the origins and ramifications of the encounter. In the process, he revealed much of the information that had been imparted at the legislative leadership meetings. Johnson was angry and discouraged. "Our friend Hubert is just destroying himself with his big mouth," he told Jim Rowe. "He just has hydrophobia . . . and every responsible person . . . gets frightened when they see him . . . because he just blabbed everything that he had heard."[68]

On the second day of the convention, Rowe asked Humphrey to dinner and told him that he would be the nominee but that he could say not a word to anyone. The next day, Rowe phoned and told Humphrey that they would be taking a plane to Washington to meet with the president and that Connecticut Senator Thomas Dodd would be joining them. "What? Is Tom Dodd being considered too?" Humphrey inquired. No, no, Rowe assured him. The president simply wanted to maintain the suspense for as long as possible and give Dodd a boost in his bid for reelection. When the three men landed at Washington National, Jack Valenti picked them up and drove them around the city aimlessly while Reedy assembled the White House press corps. In due time, the limousine carrying the three men pulled up outside the executive mansion. Dodd was ushered in first while the exhausted Humphrey napped in the backseat.[69] "A knock on the car door awakened me," Humphrey wrote in his memoirs, "and someone said, 'Senator Humphrey, the President wants to see you.' I was led to the Fish Room, outside the President's office, and shortly Johnson himself appeared, saying, 'Hubert, let's go into the Cabinet Room.'" LBJ asked the Minnesotan if he wanted to be vice president, and Humphrey replied in the affirmative. Johnson warned him that the new relationship between the two men would probably ruin their friendship. "There is something about the jobs and the responsibilities that seem to get in the way of those friendships and understanding . . . You have to understand," he said, "that this is like a marriage with no chance of divorce. I need complete and unswerving loyalty."[70] Again Humphrey assured him, and the deal was done. LBJ proposed that they call Muriel Humphrey and give her the news. "Muriel," LBJ asked melodramatically, "how would you like to have your husband be the vice presidential nominee?" And then, "We're going to nominate your boy."[71]

THE APPROACH of the Democratic Convention in Atlantic City saw LBJ's paranoia and obsessiveness in full bloom. He asked J. Edgar Hoover to dispatch a secret team of agents to the site under the direction of Deke DeLoach to gather intelligence on potentially disruptive elements, including political enemies. Fearing a stampede to draft Bobby for the vice presidency, Johnson was asking the FBI director to spy on his immediate superior, the attorney general of the United States.[72] The director was happy to do so. Their rivalry dated back to the 1950s, when, as special counsel to the McClellan Committee, young Kennedy stole Hoover's thunder as the nation's top crusader against organized crime. At the 1960 Democratic Convention, Hoover had made no secret of his preference for LBJ as the nominee, and subsequently Jack had named Bobby attorney general, in no small part to keep a tight rein on Hoover. The Kennedys knew that the FBI had compiled a thick dossier on Jack's sexual exploits. Any possibility of reconciliation went by the boards when Bobby let it be known that the administration would not lift a finger to exempt the director when he reached mandatory retirement age in January 1965.[73]

No sooner had JFK's body been interred than Hoover began reporting directly to LBJ, bypassing Bobby.[74] The Hoover-Johnson relationship stretched back twenty years. The two men's homes in Washington were both on 30th Street, directly across from each other. The Johnsons would occasionally ask Hoover over for a drink, and they encouraged Lucy and Lynda to call him "Uncle Edgar." Privately, Johnson considered Hoover, who never married and lived alone in the same house with his deputy, Clyde Tolson, to be a hypocritical "queer."[75] But as Deke DeLoach recalled, the two men found each other useful. "President Johnson," he said, "knew of Mr. Hoover's image in the United States, particularly among the middle-of-the-road to conservative elements, and he knew it was vast. He knew of the potential strength of the FBI—insofar as being of assistance to the government and the White House is concerned."[76] There was an irony, also. By having Hoover and the FBI head investigations of abuse of civil rights activists by white supremacists, by involving the Bureau as deeply as possible in the movement, the president could give it some cover from segregationist charges that it was communist-inspired and -dominated. To seal their alliance, Johnson assured Hoover that he would be able to stay on as director well beyond the mandatory federal retirement age.[77] But, typically, LBJ never let the director forget who was boss. During one of their early conversations after Johnson had become president, he said, "Edgar, I can't hear you well. What's the matter, you got this phone tapped?" Hoover laughed nervously.[78]

Johnson had a reason other than subverting a possible Kennedy coup for dispatching a team of FBI agents to Atlantic City. The all-white Mississippi delegation was being challenged for its spot on the floor by the mixed-race Mississippi Freedom Democratic party (MFDP). The looming conflict, if allowed to get out of hand, might very well split the Democratic party and lead to a Dixiecrat walkout or to the disaffection of the party's increasingly important black constituency.

By the summer of 1964, Mississippi had once again become the principal battleground in the struggle over civil rights. The black population there was the most disfranchised in the nation. "Only 5 percent of black Mississippians [who made up 45 percent of the state's population] were registered to vote, the lowest rate in the United States," Juan Williams of the *Washington Post* reported. "With majorities in many counties, blacks might well have controlled local politics through the ballot box. But segregationists were not about to let blacks vote; many would sooner kill them."[79] In April delegates assembled in Jackson and voted to establish the MFDP.[80] During the ensuing Freedom Summer of 1964, local activists joined with volunteers from CORE and SNCC to try to register the disenfranchised. Rebuffed at every turn, they announced a "freedom registration" campaign. On August 6, twenty-five hundred people jammed into the Masonic Temple for the MFDP State Convention. There they selected sixty-four blacks and four whites to be the MFDP delegation to the Democratic Convention in Atlantic City. The plan was to challenge the regular all-white Mississippi delegation on two grounds: that it had racially discriminated and that its members would refuse to sign a loyalty oath and thus might bolt the party for Barry Goldwater and the GOP.[81]

The revolt among Mississippi's black voters frightened Johnson. As John Connally indelicately put it to LBJ, "If you seat those black jigaboos, the whole South will walk out."[82] Mississippi and Alabama were probably going to withdraw anyway if a loyalty oath was required, but this was not likely to precipitate a bolt by the entire South. "I think what they ought to do is to put Mississippi and Alabama near the nearest exit," Johnson told Speaker McCormack, "so that if they want to walk out, let them walk out . . . but [do] not let us throw them out."[83] In a telephone conversation with Roy Wilkins on August 15, LBJ declared, "If I were the Negro . . . I'd just let Mississippi [the all-white delegation] sit up on the platform, if they wanted to, and I'd stand at attention and salute the son of a bitch. Then I'd nominate Johnson for president . . . and I'd go out and elect my Congressman . . . And the next four years, I'd see the promised land."[84] "If I know anything, I know this," LBJ told Humphrey. "If we mess with the group of Negroes . . . who said we want you to recognize us and throw out the governor and the elected officials of the state . . . we will lose 15 states without campaigning . . . I don't want to do anything in Mississippi to lose Oklahoma for me and I don't want to do anything in Mississippi to lose Kentucky for me . . . and most of all I damn sure don't want to lose Texas."[85]

But the principal civil rights organizations, CORE, SNCC, the SCLC, and even the NAACP, were mobilizing in behalf of the MFDP. On July 17, Bishop Stephen Gill Spottswood, chair of the NAACP Board of Directors, sent a telegram to LBJ demanding that he take over administration of the state of Mississippi under Article IV, Section 4 of the U.S. Constitution.[86] On August 19, LBJ met with a delegation from the MFDP as well as CORE and SNCC. He pled with them to listen to reason. If the MFDP tried and failed, there were liable to be massive and probably violent demonstrations across the country. The ensuing white backlash could well undermine what he was trying to do in the area of civil rights. Law and order would be the bedrock of the fall campaign; it would be the base on which the administration would build its case in the South for obedience to the Civil Rights Act. His pleas fell on deaf ears.[87]

The MFDP delegation arrived by bus in Atlantic City on August 21. The group included a handful of experienced local politicos, but most were farmers, sharecroppers, and domestic workers. After settling in the tiny, rundown Gem Hotel, they began fanning out to lobby members of the Credentials Committee. On the 22nd, David Lawrence gaveled that body to order, and spokespersons for the MFDP and the regular, all-white delegation proceeded to make their cases in front of a bank of television cameras. Heading the regular contingent was Governor Paul Johnson, who had once joked that NAACP stood for "niggers, alligators, apes, coons, and possums."[88] The regulars cited the long history of Mississippi as an integral part of the Democratic party and denied that blacks had been barred from voting in their state. Speaking for the MFDP was Mrs. Fannie Lou Hamer, a black sharecropper from Ruleville who had been driven off her farm, jailed, and finally beaten for trying to vote. Before the Credentials Committee and a rapt television audience, she described her travails, and asked, "Is this America, the land of the free and the home of the brave, where we have to sleep with our telephones off the hooks because our lives be threatened daily, because we want to live as decent human beings, in America?"[89] Privately, Paul Johnson dismissed Hamer as "a bootlegger and a whore."[90]

To prevent a donnybrook on the floor of the convention, Lawrence appointed Minnesota Attorney General Walter Mondale as head of a subcommittee to investigate and recommend a solution to the Credentials Committee. Pressure for compromise was exerted by African American lieutenants of Chicago Mayor Richard Daley and white heavyweights like Abe Fortas and Governor Pat Brown of California. On Tuesday, the White House proposed a solution. Two MFDP delegates, Aaron Henry and Ed King, would be seated as delegates-at-large; only those members of the regular Mississippi delegation who signed a loyalty oath would be seated; and the Democratic party would prohibit discrimination in the selection of delegates to all future conventions.[91] The Credentials Committee was deeply divided, but in the end announced at a televised press conference that it had voted to accept the two-seat compromise. Despite the pleadings of Bayard Rustin, Martin Luther King, and others, the MFDP would have none of it. "We didn't come all this way for no two seats," Fannie Lou Hamer exclaimed.[92] The all-white Mississippi delegation, most of whose members immediately departed Atlantic City, were just as disgruntled. On Tuesday evening, twenty-one MFDP delegates, furnished credentials by friendly delegates, pushed their way into the seats vacated by the regular delegation. After an unsuccessful effort to evict Hamer and her colleagues, the sergeant at arms and his men simply ignored them, and the convention proceeded with its business.[93]

The MFDP brouhaha was a watershed in the history of the civil rights movement. It helped radicalize SNCC and CORE, and in the minds of some activists, it painted King, Whitney Young, Rustin, and Randolph as Uncle Toms. Civil rights activists in general became dubious about working within the Democratic party. For many people, observed SNCC's Joyce Ladner, "Atlantic City was the end of innocence." [94]

The fight over the seating of the MFDP traumatized Johnson. At 7:50 on the morning of August 25, he called his Texas friend and business partner, A W. Moursund. He was profoundly discouraged and depressed. He informed Moursund that he was leaning toward announcing later in the day that he was withdrawing as a candidate for the Democratic presidential nomination and retiring to Texas.[95] At eleven o'clock he broke the news to George Reedy by reading from a handwritten statement he had prepared: "On that fateful November day last year, I accepted the responsibility of the President, asking God's guidance and the help of all of our people . . . Our country faces grave dangers. These dangers must be faced and met by a united people under a leader they do not doubt . . . The times require leadership about which there is no doubt and a voice that men of all parties and sections and color can follow. I've learned, after trying very hard, that I am not that voice or that leader . . . I am absolutely unavailable." [96]

Racial politics aside, Johnson had been hurt by recent columns and news articles concerning him, his candidacy, and his presidency. "I look at the *Herald Tribune.* There's nothing but the things that we've done terrible," he complained to Reedy. "I read the *New York Times.* We had a 'pallid platform.' That was outrageous." He complained about a Henry Brandon piece in the *Philadelphia Inquirer* that described him as "a textbook caricature of a fast-dealing politician [who] has not aroused any excitement as a person or any emotion or enthusiasm as a human being." The previous week *Time* had run a long article on the Johnson family fortune, entitled "The Multimillionaire," that included a graceless swipe at Lady Bird's looks, clothes, manners, accent, and taste in music.[97] He was worried about his health, and the grave responsibilities of the office. "I don't want this power of the Bomb," he exclaimed. "I just don't want these decisions I'm being required to make. I don't want the conniving that's required. I don't want the disloyalty that's around. I don't want the bungling and the inefficiencies of our people."[98] In a subsequent conversation, he told Walter Jenkins, "I don't want to be in this place like Wilson" (who spent his last seventeen months in office incapacitated by a stroke).[99] He was disgusted by the ongoing political infighting in Texas and was not sure that he would even be able to carry his home state. But in the end, it was the knockup over the MFDP that had been decisive.

"I am absolutely positive that I cannot lead the South and the North," Johnson told Reedy. "And I don't want to lead the nation without my own state and without my own section. I am very convinced that the Negroes will not listen to me. They're not going to follow a white Southerner. And I think the stakes are too big to try to compromise." At the same time, he told Jenkins, "I don't feel good about throwing Alabama out and Mississippi and making them take an oath." Both Reedy and Jenkins, who had dealt with the Johnson doubts before, tried to talk him out of withdrawing. "I think this just gives the country to Goldwater," Reedy told his boss. "He's just a child. And look at our side. We don't have anybody. The only man around I'd trust to be President would be McNamara, and he wouldn't stand a chance." Johnson replied, "I don't care . . . I'm not seeking happiness. I'm just seeking a little comfort once in a while."[100] To Jenkins later: "People I think have mistaken judgment. They think I want great power. And what I want is great solace—and a little love. That's all I want."[101]

His aides began discussing whether to announce the decision from the Oval Office or at the convention in Atlantic City. After lunch, Johnson spent several intense hours with Lady Bird. She helped him work on his abdication statement, while struggling desperately to buoy his spirits and confidence and to talk him into staying in. "I do not remember hours I ever found harder," she later recalled in her diary. Following a long walk with Lynda around the South Grounds, Lady Bird wrote her husband, "Beloved, You are as brave a man as Harry Truman—or FDR—or Lincoln. You can go on to find some peace, some achievement amidst all the pain. You have been strong, determined, patient . . . I honor you for it. So does most of the Country. To step out now would be wrong for your country, and I can see nothing but a lonely wasteland for your future. Your friends would be frozen in embarrassed silence, and your enemies jeering."[102] At 2:30 Humphrey and Reuther phoned and informed LBJ of the two-delegate MFDP compromise. Neither Mississippi delegation was likely to be satisfied, but there would be no open floor fight, and if the southern delegations bolted, it would be over the loyalty oath and not race explicitly. Talk of withdrawal ended at once.[103]

The rest of the proceedings at Atlantic City were anticlimactic. On the evening of Wednesday, August 26, Lyndon's name was put in nomination by

John Connally and California governor Pat Brown. He was quickly and unanimously elected. The candidate stood in the wings and listened to the cheering and demonstrations for what seemed to many to be an interminable period. Finally, with Carol Channing singing "Hello Lyndon" to the tune of "Hello Dolly," her Broadway showstopper, the party's standard-bearer made his way to the podium and took the gavel from Speaker McCormack. He announced that his choice for running mate was Hubert Humphrey.

The following evening, the last of the convention, Johnson's and Humphrey's acceptance speeches were sandwiched between gala celebrations of Lyndon's fifth-sixth birthday. "The end of the Convention Hall is decked with five pictures," Orville Freeman noted in his diary. "Three small pictures across the top—Roosevelt, Kennedy, Truman—and on the side enormous Johnson pictures dominate the hall. This has been a Johnson show beginning to end with the complete dominance of the man evident at every hand." [104]

As the final night's proceedings unfolded, Bobby Kennedy waited patiently in a small room under the podium. When finally he was welcomed to the platform, the delegates went wild. For the next twenty-two minutes the assembled Democrats cheered, applauded, stomped, and whistled. Bobby then delivered a moving, graceful tribute to his brother, ending with a quote from *Romeo and Juliet* that Jackie had given him:

> *When he shall die*
> *Take him and cut him out in little stars*
> *And he will make the face of heaven so fine*
> *That all the world will be in love with night,*
> *And pay no worship to the garish Sun.* [105]

Garish sun my ass, thought Lyndon, as five thousand wept and applauded. Johnson's acceptance speech was tepid and uninspired, and paled in comparison with Humphrey's litany: "Most Democrats and many Republicans in the United States Senate . . . are for the nuclear test ban treaty. But not Senator Goldwater. Most Democrats and most Republicans in the United States Senate voted for the $11.5 billion tax cut for the American people. But not Senator Goldwater." As Humphrey continued, the delegates joined in each refrain, "But not Senator Goldwater." [106] The evening's festivities concluded with a huge fireworks display that featured a red, white, and blue portrait of Lyndon spread across the New Jersey skies. [107]

CHAPTER 26

BARRY

THE 1964 PRESIDENTIAL CAMPAIGN WOULD HAVE BEEN easier for Lyndon Johnson if Barry Goldwater had been a more conventional candidate. Goldwater and his advisers either had no feel whatever for the "vital center," or they were determined not to have anything to do with it. As journalist Richard Rovere observed after the GOP Convention in San Francisco, the Goldwaterites "are as hard as nails. The spirit of compromise and accommodation was wholly alien to them."[1] In a White House meeting with Johnson on urban unrest in late July, Goldwater seemed to imply that he was a prisoner of forces beyond his control. Johnson recalled his saying that he was not going to get personal in the campaign, but that there were a lot of conservatives out there, and he would not be able to dictate to them.[2]

Goldwater never had a chance. As Theodore White put it, "No man ever began a Presidential effort more deeply wounded by his own nomination, suffering more insurmountable handicaps. And then . . . he made the worst of them." In Florida, home to the nation's largest elderly population, he "warned against the outright hoax of this administration's Medicare scheme."[3] Instead of trying to shed or modify his image as a trigger-happy, heartless extremist, Goldwater embraced it. Some of Johnson's advisers came to the conclusion that the purpose of the Goldwater crusade was not to win but simply to damage LBJ as much as it could in hopes of crippling him and his agenda during the next four years. "Although Goldwater will almost certainly be beaten overwhelmingly," political strategist Fred Dutton observed to Bill Moyers, "our opposition will likely use October to try to blemish the President's long-term public standing as much as possible—the wheeler-dealer charge will almost surely be the main underlying theme to which they will keep returning."[4] "The aim is not your defeat in November," Horace Busby advised LBJ, "but your compromise after

January. Your Texas enemies and others failed to deny you the Presidency—a goal they long feared you would reach. But, having failed that, they now are driving for a final goal—to deny you a place either in the hearts of your countrymen or in history."[5]

What was important was how the campaign was waged. The rhetoric that Johnson employed, the interest he attracted to his political coalition, the hopes and expectations that he aroused would have a profound impact on the remainder of his presidency and on the country as a whole. LBJ fought the campaign as if the outcome were in doubt because that is what good politicians do, but also because he fantasized about exceeding Warren Harding's 60.3 percent of the vote garnered in 1920 and even FDR's total of 60.8 percent in 1936. He would be able to shed the JFK albatross once and for all, be president in his own right, and use his popular mandate to push through a revolutionary legislative program.

Johnson and his strategists operated initially on the assumption that Goldwater and the John Birch Society were their best assets.[6] To the extent that the Democratic campaign took Goldwater seriously, it should try to scare the hell of the American people. Such a stratagem would help offset possible voter complacency growing out of LBJ's continuing large lead in the polls. When the Goldwater campaign printed bumper stickers reading "In Your Heart You Know He's Right!" the Johnson machine responded "In Your Heart You Know He Might" and "In Your Gut You Know He's Nuts."[7] "The one thing we ought to get at," George Reedy told LBJ, "is mothers that are worried about having radioactive poisoning in their kid's milk . . . men that are worried about becoming sterile . . . kids that are being born with two heads."[8] To this end, Jenkins, Valenti, and Richard Goodwin contacted the ad agency Doyle Dane Bernbach (DDB) and arranged a series of television ads and radio spots contrasting the dangerously irresponsible Goldwater with an experienced, judicious Johnson. The most famous of these was the "daisy ad," a piece that depicted a young girl in the middle of a field plucking petals from a daisy. A voice in the background counted down from ten as she plucked. When the countdown reached zero, the camera zoomed in on the pupil of her eye, in which was reflected a mushrooming atomic cloud. As the scene faded, Johnson's voice came on: "These are the stakes—to make a world in which all of God's children can live, or go into the dark. We must love each other, or we must die." Then the narrator's voice: "Vote for President Johnson on November 3. The stakes are too high for you to stay home."[9] It became the most famous and least-watched ad in campaign history. The Republicans cried foul, and the ad ran only once. But it had the desired effect. Johnson acted out the charade of being shocked. After complaining about the spot to Moyers in front of several people, LBJ called him aside and asked, "You sure we ought to run it just once?"[10] Other DDB ads focused on Goldwater's extreme conservatism in domestic affairs. One quoted his wish to "saw off the Eastern seaboard"; another depicted a group of Alabama Klansmen burning a cross and quoted one: "I like Barry Goldwater. He needs our help."[11]

Despite Johnson's poor relationship with the press, most editors and columnists bought into the image of Goldwater as a dangerous radical. Drew Pearson and Jack Anderson repeated damaging material that the White House, via the FBI, provided on vice presidential candidate William Miller.[12] LBJ and his aides made it a point to have long conversations regarding the dangers posed by the Goldwaterites with Katherine Graham, James Reston, Walter Lippmann, and a host of others. Virtually all of the major dailies from coast to coast either condemned Goldwater, endorsed Johnson, or both.

In his crusade to win by the biggest landslide in the history of presidential elections, LBJ planned to leave no constituency behind: Catholics, Jews, Mormons, blacks, Hispanic Americans, women, the elderly, the poor, and the rich. All he wanted to leave the opposition to talk about was "beagles and speedometers," he laughingly told Henry Luce.[13] He set McGeorge Bundy to work persuading the Vatican to issue a statement absolving Jews of responsibility for the death of Christ. LBJ had the president of the Latter-Day Saints and the Mormon Tabernacle Choir to the White House.[14] The prize, Johnson believed, his ace in the whole, would be the business community and moderate Republicans.

If LBJ were going to capture the mainstream right, he would have to keep Eisenhower and Goldwater separated. His point man on this project continued to be Robert Anderson, the Texas financier whom Ike had favored for the GOP nomination in 1960. "I talk to him once a week . . . and you absolutely won the guy," Anderson told him.[15] In July, Walter S. Mack, former CEO of Pepsi-Cola and a prominent fund-raiser for the GOP, announced that he was forming the Independent Republicans and Citizens for Johnson. Mack had started the swing for Wendell Willkie at the 1940 Republican National Convention, supported Thomas Dewey over Robert Taft in 1948, and served as a fund-raiser for Eisenhower in 1952 and 1956.[16] Meanwhile, Henry Cabot Lodge volunteered to travel the country defending administration policies in Southeast Asia to prominent Republicans.[17] In the end, LBJ would succeed in seducing almost the entire liberal wing of the Republican party. He even nibbled at its far-right edges. Eddie Dicker, a Dallas oilman, announced that he was forming a Republicans for Johnson Committee in the Lone Star State. "We feel safer with LBJ," he told reporters.[18] "I've seen people that have never voted the Democratic ticket in their life—strong Republicans—and for the first time in their life, they're going to vote for you," Anderson confided to the delighted Johnson.[19] As LBJ put it to the Democratic National Committee, "You will find this: that for every backlash that the Democrats lose, we pick up 3 frontlash . . . And when you can get 3 to 1, it is always satisfying."[20]

Backlash or no, LBJ had no intention of conceding the South to the Goldwaterites. On trips to Georgia, Virginia, and Tennessee, he was encouraged by his reception. The Georgia delegation to the Atlantic City convention had included four blacks. "We've had a tremendous registration last year in our Negro vote," Governor Carl Sanders, a rising spokesman for the New South, reported to LBJ, "and we [are] still registering those every day."[21] Nevertheless, the situation looked bleak. Opinion polls taken in July indicated that the Democrats would not carry a single state from the former Confederacy. At the same time polls were indicating a total Democratic washout, southern governors and political movers and shakers had been telling the president through Connally that they would not support the national ticket if RFK were the vice presidential nominee; they liked HHH only a little less. You tell them, LBJ instructed Connally, that there were only three possible nominees available to Democrats: Johnson, Humphrey, and Kennedy. If they did not straighten up and get behind him, he would withdraw. In which case, Bobby would get the nomination, would most certainly become president, and then the South would really be screwed.[22] There was more than politics behind LBJ's southern strategy, however. He wanted to be president to all the people. He sympathized with those whites in the South who were being asked to leave their hallowed traditions behind them and enter unknown territory. "I think it is a mistake not to help them and leave them out in the cold," he told Alabama Senator John Sparkman. "I don't expect to carry them. I owe more obligation to those that I'm not going to carry than I do the ones I will."[23]

IF CONNALLY was LBJ's private ambassador to the South, his public emissary was Lady Bird. In early October, the first lady embarked on a four-day, 1,628-mile train trip through eight southern states. Her message would be clear: the Civil War was over; blacks and whites were fellow human beings and fellow countrymen; segregation and discrimination were unpatriotic and un-Christian. Once again, Johnson would be placing the South in a bind. Arguably, as of 1964 Lady Bird was the nation's most visible southern belle. Long known for its chivalry toward women, the region would either treat Bird with kindness and respect, or it would betray one of its most hallowed traditions.

On the matter of race, the first lady herself had had to make something of a journey. Her father had epitomized the tough southern boss, exploiting poor blacks and whites. In east Texas and Alabama, she had grown up in a strictly segregated, racist milieu. A photo of Bird and her brother, Tony, taken around 1913, when she was a toddler, showed them surrounded by six black servants, all clad in long aprons and floppy hats.[24] But she felt a natural affinity for the downtrodden, and it was emotionally and psychologically impossible for her to think of blacks as less human and less deserving than whites. Long association with the liberals on her husband's staff and among his friends had enlightened her. By the time she became first lady, Lady Bird had become a full if realistic supporter of the Second Reconstruction. Emerging from the signing ceremony for the Civil Rights Act of 1964, she predicted that the measure would produce "untold good and much pain and trouble."[25]

Lady Bird's chief assistant, Liz Carpenter, put together an eight-state whistle-stop tour in which Lady Bird would make dozens of appearances at southern towns and cities. Each would be covered by the national press, would highlight the administration's commitment to the New South, and hopefully would appeal to the hearts and minds of white southerners. LBJ and Kenny O'Donnell were at first reluctant because Democrats were begging the Johnsons to stay away. The project, now known as the "Lady Bird Special," also worried the Secret Service. The assassination was not yet a year old, and the South was in an extremely volatile mood. "I don't think assassination is part of my destiny," Lady Bird told reporters as she worked to reassure her husband. In the end, the temptation to use the white South's vaunted reputation for hospitality and chivalry as a lever to pry open its mind was too great. "Let's do it," Lyndon told O'Donnell.[26]

As preparations for the trip got under way, Lady Bird contacted southern senators, representatives, and governors asking if they and/or their wives would appear with her at one or more stops in their respective states. Initially, Richard Russell, Herman Talmadge, John Stennis, James Eastland, Allen Ellender, and Willis Robertson of Virginia all refused to appear, but then reluctantly came around.[27] The only enthusiasts were Louisiana Congressman Hale Boggs and his wife, Lindy, who was one of the chief organizers of the campaign and who accompanied the first lady from day one.

After the FBI received word that hate groups might blow up the train, the Secret Service arranged for a separate locomotive to travel fifteen minutes ahead of the first lady in order to detonate a bomb if there turned out to be one. Accompanied by a coterie of female campaign workers decked out in red-white-and-blue outfits and her twenty-year-old daughter, Lynda, Lady Bird set out on the morning of October 6. Lyndon rode with her during the first fifteen-minute leg of the trip to Alexandria, Virginia, the first of forty scheduled stops, and then got off. "The Constitution means the same for all the people," she told the crowd. "Lyndon has offered to unify this country, to put behind us things of the past."[28]

Lady Bird was particularly drawn to small towns and added them to the itinerary whenever possible. The citizens of Ahoskie, North Carolina, population five thousand, cabled her, "Nobody important has been through here since Buffalo Bill came through in 1916. Please have your train stop here."[29] She did, and ten thousand North Carolinians came out to welcome her. Not surprisingly, in rural areas crowds were composed mostly of poor whites, with knots of blacks on the periphery. One woman told her, "I got up this morning at three o'clock and milked twenty cows so I could be here."[30]

The Lady Bird Special first encountered real opposition on October 7 at Columbia, South Carolina. As the train pulled into the station, a large crowd began to chant, "We Want Barry!" When Lady Bird began to speak, the crowd drowned her out with boos. South Carolina Governor Donald Russell appealed to the "good manners and hospitality" of the crowd. The tight-lipped first lady pressed ahead as the heckling continued. Finally, she stopped in midsentence, held up a white-gloved hand, and said, "This is a country of many viewpoints. I respect your right to express your own. Now it is my turn to express mine. Thank you." The crowd quieted.[31] Four hours later, she confronted ten thousand mostly hostile South Carolinians at Charleston. One sign read: "Black

Bird, Go Home." Others declared "Johnson is a Communist" and "Johnson is a Nigger-Lover." This time the boos and catcalls did not stop. "I got thousands of loving friends and dozens of jeering enemies and I'll settle for that," she later told her brother, Tony.[32] That night, as every night of the tour, LBJ called. The conversations reveal an affectionate, concerned husband and father. "When he would call," Liz Carpenter recalled, "it was just like someone had waved a magic wand over Lady Bird."

Despite the hostility shown in South Carolina, the region was clearly conflicted. As the train crossed into Georgia, the *Atlanta Constitution* asked a key question: "Can Georgia turn away . . . from the first Southern President in a century?"[33]

The tour ended in New Orleans, and Lyndon flew down from Louisville to meet the train. When the Lady Bird Special pulled in at 8:16 the president bounded up the steps of the last car and embraced his wife and daughter. Exhausted, Bird momentarily broke down in tears. She then turned to address the huge throng—mostly black in the depot itself, mostly white in the plaza beyond. "I was on the station platform when they arrived," Kathrine Graham recalled. "It was a tremendously dramatic moment."[34] Later that evening, at a Democratic fund-raiser attended by Senators Allan Ellender and Russell Long and Louisiana Governor John McKeithen, LBJ delivered one of the most memorable speeches of his career. "If we are to heal our history and make this Nation whole," he declared, "prosperity must know no Mason-Dixon line and opportunity must know no color line . . . Robert E. Lee counseled us well when he told us to cast off our animosities, and raise our sons to be Americans . . . Whatever your views are, we have a Constitution and we have a Bill of Rights, and we have the law of the land, and two-thirds of the Democrats in the Senate voted for it [the Civil Rights Act] and three-fourths of the Republicans. I signed it, and I am going to enforce it." He then quoted Sam Rayburn: "I would like to go back down there [to an unnamed state of the Deep South] and make them one more Democratic speech . . . The poor old State, they haven't heard a Democratic speech in 30 years. All they ever hear at election time is 'Nigger, Nigger, Nigger!' " (The official transcript of the speech reads "Negro, Negro, Negro!" but numerous firsthand witnesses testify that he used the pejorative term.)[35] After a stunned silence, the racially mixed audience rose and gave the president a thunderous ovation.

What Johnson was doing during the 1964 campaign, of course, was attempting to cover the Confederate flag with the Stars and Stripes. "I say when you divide your country, that is wrong," he proclaimed to another Georgia audience. "The new South is here in America. What Americans want today is a new politics, a politics of national unity, a politics concerned with progress and peace for the Nation, a politics of honor, and a politics of decency for all . . . It is the sons of Georgia that have carried that flag to every corner of this globe, and they have brought her back without a tarnish on it. They know there is only one Nation, one people, one flag, one Constitution, united and indivisible under God."[36]

LBJ was not at all sure that his stratagem would work. Talking with Dean Rusk after the New Orleans speech, he recalled the story about the brilliant young defense attorney who defended a Negro against a rape charge. How did it go, asked his friend? It was the greatest speech of his life, the lawyer said; the jury was in tears when he finished. What about the verdict? "He said, well, they hung the son of a bitch. That's the way I feel."[37] Even if he lost the South, however, the trip had been worth it, Johnson believed. He was going to win, and he wanted to be president of all. "We didn't want those people to think we didn't care," he told a Texas friend. "We didn't want them to think they were left out. When a child gets to feel like he's hurt and mistreated he goes on home and don't come back and we don't want that to happen. We love those people and we thought the only thing to do was go tell 'em we loved 'em."[38]

Buoyed by the New Orleans experience, Johnson decided to beard the lion in his den. On Sunday, October 11, on his way to a swing through the West Coast, he stopped off in Phoenix. Speaking through a bullhorn from the back seat of his convertible, LBJ halted a dozen times on the drive from the airport into town to harangue spectators. "You really can't understand that campaign," Bill Moyers said, "unless you've seen Johnson rise out of the back seat of a car at dusk on a wide boulevard in Phoenix and bring the caravan to a screeching halt."[39] He would not be able to beat Goldwater in his home state, but he would come close, losing by fewer than five thousand votes.

Though he knew he would have to, LBJ initially resisted campaigning in the Northeast. He was convinced he would be eaten alive in this, the home turf of the Kennedys, liberals, Harvards, and national media. Moreover, Vermont, New Hampshire, and Maine had all gone for Nixon in 1960. To Johnson's utter delight, however, his fifteen-hour swing through Connecticut, Rhode Island, and the three Republican strongholds drew the largest and most enthusiastic crowds of the campaign. At Hartford and Providence, onlookers literally blocked the highway. After the first two stops, LBJ's hands were already swollen and bleeding. The cheers and ovations of New England intoxicated LBJ. "But he would really just go into complete metamorphosis," said Vicky McCammon, "almost, not a trance, but it was just 'the crowds, the crowds, the crowds, the applause.' "[40] This, Johnson mused, was why he had gotten into politics.

THE 1964 CAMPAIGN was characterized by ongoing tension between LBJ and the Secret Service. "He scared the Secret Service to death," recalled Vicky McCammon, "because here they had already had one horrible thing [the Kennedy assassination]. [They] would just raise hell with him all the time, telling him, 'Mr. President please now, you really shouldn't be getting out of the car. You really shouldn't stand up on the back of the convertible.' They didn't even want him in a convertible, period."[41] Johnson felt that he was being suffocated and, in fact, that his guardians' overzealousness was actually putting him at risk. He vented his spleen to his military aide: "They never do anything but endanger you. They notify everybody in town what time you're coming, how you're coming, where you're coming, and how to kill you, if you want to . . . And if they'll just let us go and get in the car and keep their damn mouth shut, we'll go down a back road and nobody ever knows we're there. But hey, get the si-renes going, forty cops leading you, and all that kind of stuff." [42]

THOUGH A PRAGMATIST and a political realist of the first order, LBJ set forth a vision during the 1964 campaign that was purely utopian. "I want all the ages of man to yield him [God] their promise," he proclaimed to an overflow crowd at Cadillac Square in Detroit. "The child will find all knowledge open to him; the growing boy will shape his spirit in a house of God and his ways in the house of his family . . . The man will find leisure and occasion for the closeness of family, and an opportunity for the enrichment of life. The citizen will enrich the Nation, sharing its rule, walking its streets, adding his views to its counsel, secure always from the unjust and the arbitrary power of his fellows . . . The least among us will find contentment, and the best among us will find greatness, and all of us will respect the dignity of the one and admire the achievements of the other." [43] The capitalist, the manager, the worker, the farmer, the banker, the clerk would all lie down together in green pastures.

The Johnsonian utopia was fine and good, members of LBJ's campaign team observed to each other, but it was somewhat unfettered from political reality. There seemed to be, Eric Goldman told Johnson, an underlying malaise in America. To many, the history of the United States during the past fifty years "can easily seem like an almost unending series of assaults" on American individualism. "This is true," he observed, "whether you listen to the corporation executive growling against unions which impede his 'freedom of action'; the factory worker complaining about distant union leadership; the executive or the worker irritated at taxes which 'spend his money for him'; the Italian backlasher protesting against the loss of his individual 'right' to pick his neighbor; the novelist railing against general 'conformity'; or the nice club lady, uneasily wondering whether the 'breakdown of individual responsibility resulting from the welfare state' has not led to crime in the streets." [44] In fact, the New Deal–Fair Deal–New Frontier–Great Society had made Americans more rather than less free, he reminded LBJ, had enhanced individualism rather than diminished it. State intervention had freed workers from wage slavery, provided the elderly an opportunity to retire, freed black Americans from the shackles of discrimination, protected business from unfair competition. Given the power and characteristics of the modern industrial state, government activism meant more not less choice, more control over one's life, not less. At the root of the Johnsonian philosophy, he and Horace Busby insisted, was "modern individualism." [45]

The modern individualism of which Johnson, Goldman, and Busby spoke was a combination of positive and negative freedoms. The traditional, libertarian notion of freedom emphasized liberty of speech, worship, and assembly, implying protection from avaricious power-hungry individuals, groups, or governments. [46] But for Johnson, Goldman, Moyers, McPherson, and other liberals, there was such a thing as positive freedom, that put forward a definition of liberty as not just the absence of external constraint but the enhancement of potential. LBJ and his lieutenants would devise a socioeconomic "bill of rights," which included, in addition to those listed in the Constitution, "the right to good education . . . the right to the best medical care . . . the right to a decent home, the right to live with dignity in old age . . . the right to a steady and secure job . . . the right to eat at a lunch counter or get a good night's lodging . . . the right to raise a family in a decent neighborhood . . . and the right to breathe clean air." [47]

If ever there was a person in American public life who believed that the individual ought to be willing to sacrifice private interests for the good of the community, it was Lyndon Johnson. But he came from a land that valued independence and self-reliance. He did not, like Samuel Adams, want to eliminate private enterprise and convert the United States into a "Christian Sparta." [48] The key lay in restraint by government. Citizens of the virtuous republic must be willing to sacrifice, but that willingness could not be abused. It was the duty of the Congress, the president, and the federal bureaucracy not to ask individuals and corporations to sacrifice their interests unless and until it was absolutely necessary. Fundamental to modern individualism, then, was the willingness of the individual to sacrifice and the restraint of government in calling upon that willingness. The events of the next four years would put both to a severe test.

THE PRESIDENTIAL ELECTION OF 1964 was fought against mounting concern about the war in Southeast Asia. The White House was understandably anxious to mute the issue until after the election, but the Goldwater campaign, the Joint Chiefs of Staff, Maxwell Taylor, and events would not permit.[49] In his speeches, Goldwater constantly implied that the Johnson administration was soft on communism and that the United States must carry the war into North Vietnam. If the move north provoked a war with communist China, so be it. Even moderate Republicans like Rockefeller and Scranton were calling for the United States to strike at the source of aggression, the Democratic Republic of Vietnam. So, too, were Ambassador Taylor and the Joint Chiefs. Khanh was exhausted, politically inept, and militarily impotent, Taylor reported. But there was no Churchill on the horizon. The alternatives available to the United States seemed to be either to stand by passively and watch the formation of a Popular Front coalition that would ultimately be dominated by the communists or to actively assume increased responsibility for the outcome of the war. "If we leave Vietnam with our tail between our legs," Taylor declared, "the consequences of this defeat in the rest of Asia, Africa and Latin America would be disastrous. We therefore would seem to have little choice left except to accept course (b)." [50] The Joint Chiefs wholeheartedly concurred. "Unless we move now to alter the present evolution of events," they wrote the president in October, "there is great likelihood of a VC [Vietcong] victory." [51]

But LBJ was having no part of wider war and would tolerate no new Gulf of

Tonkin incidents. On September 20, word came to the Pentagon of another possible communist torpedo boat attack on American vessels patrolling the gulf. "They think they destroyed three out of five [North Vietnamese torpedo boats]," McNamara told his boss.[52] Johnson immediately convened a meeting of his top foreign policy advisers. He "proved very skeptical abut the evidence to date," McBundy recorded, "and he was deeply annoyed that leaks apparently from the Pentagon were producing pressure . . . He made it clear that he was not interested in rapid escalation on so frail evidence and with a very fragile government in South Vietnam."[53] "I don't know why in the hell, some time or other, they can't be sure that they are being attacked," he complained to Bob McNamara in a subsequent conversation. "I don't want them just being some change-o'-life woman running up and saying that, by God, she was being raped just because a man walks in the room! And that looks like to me that's what happens in the thirty years that I've been watching them. A man gets enough braid on him, and he walks in a room, and he just immediately concludes that he's being attacked. And that's the basic argument between you and Goldwater."[54] Johnson's instincts were correct. By the next day, the Pentagon had concluded that no attack had occurred. Relieved, LBJ called Richard Russell: "They've decided to close up shop and let Peiping [Beijing] live another night."[55]

All the while, Johnson's advisers were warning him not to fall into the trap that had ensnared Woodrow Wilson in 1916 and Franklin D. Roosevelt in 1940, that is, in the heat of campaigning, promise that he would not send American boys into any foreign war when conditions indicated that he would probably have to do just that. Bundy was particularly adamant on the matter. "On Vietnam, I think you may wish to give a hint of firmness," he advised Johnson in preparation for a session on foreign policy with the bureau chiefs of AP, UPI, and Reuters. "It is a better than even chance that we will be undertaking some air and land action in the Laotian corridor and even in North Vietnam within the next two months, and we do not want the record to suggest even remotely that we campaigned on peace in order to start a war in November."[56]

As a result of these conflicting pressures, Lyndon Johnson decided to make the election a referendum on containment. "I didn't get you into Viet Nam," he told the American people. "You have been in Viet Nam 10 years." In his speeches, he emphasized his predecessors' efforts to contain communism. "In Greece and Turkey, and in Korea, President Truman halted Communist aggression," he told a group of New Hampshire newspaper editors. "In the Formosa straits President Eisenhower halted Communist aggression. In Cuba—and that was the last country that has gone Communist—remember, not a single country in the world has gone Communist since 1959—in Cuba, President Kennedy halted the Communist aggression which threatened the mainland of the United States itself. And in the Gulf of Tonkin, the Johnson administration acted, and will continue to act to halt Communist aggression."[57] The last week in September, LBJ created a new Panel of Consultants on Peace and National Security. Its members read like a cold war Who's Who. All of the architects and implementers were there: Dean Acheson, John J. McCloy, Allen Dulles, and Paul Hoffman, first administrator of the Marshall Plan.[58] Containment called for the United States to be strong, but it also called for it to be patient, they declared. What would be the point if America forced a showdown with Sino-Soviet imperialism and Armageddon resulted?[59] After the Scripps-Howard newspaper chain endorsed LBJ's candidacy, Harland Cleveland, one of Moyers's assistants, observed that the media conglomerate was probably speaking for a sizable majority of mainstream America "when it says—almost reluctantly but with evident relief—that post-war American foreign policy is beginning to pay off and that we better stick with it because it is the sounder and safer thing to do."[60]

In the late afternoon of October 14, LBJ was in a New York hotel, resting in preparation for a speech before two thousand wealthy Democrats. Exhausted from days of nonstop campaigning, the president was so hoarse that he could barely speak. Suddenly the phone rang. Abe Fortas and Clark Clifford were calling from Washington with shocking news. Walter Jenkins, a married Catholic, the father of six children, and Johnson's friend and chief lieutenant since 1952, had been arrested in the men's room in the basement of the Sixteenth Street YMCA, a favorite cruising ground for Washington, D.C., homosexuals, on a morals charge. Johnson listened in stunned silence and then said, "Tell me, can this be true?"[61] Fortas assured him that it could be and was. "He went over to the YMCA where there are dozens of them around there," Fortas said quietly. "The place is just full of that kind of fella and also of undercover cops . . . It was a pure pickup. There's something latent there," he told Johnson. "A psychiatric problem that Walter has mostly handled all these years. But exhausted and drunk . . . this thing just happened." The next morning, in conversation with Deputy Attorney General Nicholas Katzenbach, a still incredulous Johnson said, "It shocks me as much as though my daughter committed treason."[62]

For the better part of twenty years, Walter Jenkins had been LBJ's alter ego. All of the details and secrets of the Johnson life were either in his head or in the voluminous files of Jenkins's long-time assistant, Mildred Stegall. "Jenkins was one of the men you had to know in Washington," said Ben Bradlee, then managing editor of *Newsweek. "The* guy in the White House then."[63] But Jenkins had allowed himself to become LBJ's creature. Johnson not only trusted him but abused him. Following a rally in Detroit of UAW workers, Johnson had noticed a dearth of campaign paraphernalia. He called Jenkins immediately afterward: "Didn't I tell you I wanted every worker to have a button or an LBJ hat or sticker? Are you trying to make me lose the labor vote? I ask for things, and I expect to see them done."[64] Jenkins's close friend and fellow Catholic, Deke De-Loach, recalled seeing him so exhausted that he would fall asleep in midconservation.[65] Eighteen-hour days and seven-day work weeks were the lot of those who chose to follow the Johnson star. Most could take it for only brief periods, but not Jenkins. "Walter had no personal ambition," Jack Valenti observed. "It was all for the prince, following him into battle."[66]

Walter Jenkins's nightmare began on the evening of October 7, 1964. Uncharacteristically, he had agreed to take off work and meet his wife, Marjorie, at a reception being held by *Newsweek* to celebrate the opening of its new offices. The forty-six-year-old aide of aides arrived, had a martini, and socialized. He planned to go back to the White House to finish some work, and so, after an hour or so, he escorted Marjorie, who had a separate dinner engagement, to her car. Instead of returning to his office, Jenkins went back to the party and had several more drinks. He then left and proceeded to the Sixteenth Street Y, where he had previously been arrested in 1959 for making "indecent gestures." He went to the men's room, made eye contact with a sixty-two-year-old retired veteran who was hanging about, and entered one of the pay toilets with him. Shortly thereafter, two vice squad officers, who had been watching through a peephole, burst in, catching the two in a sexual act. They arrested them both, took them to police headquarters, and booked them on charges of public indecency. Both paid a $50 fine and departed.

Jenkins went to work the next morning as if nothing had happened. A week later, Liz Carpenter got a call from Charles Steib, an editor at the *Washington Star.* One of his reporters had been perusing the police blotter downtown and seen that Walter Jenkins had been arrested on a morals charge. He was calling to verify the story before he allowed it to run. Carpenter thanked him and called Jenkins. Rather than denying or affirming the truth of the story, he told Carpenter that he would take care of the matter.[67] Jenkins phoned Abe Fortas and subsequently rendezvoused with him and Clark Clifford at Fortas's house. As Jenkins told the two lawyers of his predicament, he became increasingly agitated and confused. Fortas called a physician, who came and sedated the distraught man. It would be better for Jenkins and for the president if he were incognito, the two lawyers decided, so Fortas and Clifford arranged for him to be admitted to Bethesda Naval Hospital for observation. It was then that they called LBJ in New York.[68]

In the 1960s, the gay rights movement was in its infancy. Only a tiny percentage of the American public entertained the thought that same-sex relationships could for some individuals be natural. At best, homosexuality was considered a moral weakness and at worst, moral depravity, a sin against nature. In the overheated atmosphere of the cold war, homosexuals in government were considered easy prey for blackmail by Soviet agents. As one government report issued at the time concluded, "The sexual pervert's . . . lack of emotional stability . . . and weakness of moral fiber make him susceptible to the blandishments of foreign agents."[69]

Johnson's first reaction was denial. How did the police know that Jenkins was going to be at that place at that time? It must be a frame-up by the Republican National Committee. "No, Mr. President," DeLoach subsequently told him. "It actually occurred and there is no indication it was a setup by the Republicans." How do you know? Johnson asked. DeLoach replied, "The arresting officers have been interviewed and I have the fingerprint card; I know it's true."

Besides, after initial denials, Jenkins had admitted that it was true, that he had been fighting the "instinct," but there had been, on rare occasions, previous incidents.[70] Johnson, who was given to conspiracy theories, was still skeptical, but the damage had been done.

LBJ's immediate instinct was to fire Jenkins at once. "If a President knows something like this and doesn't take prompt action," he told Abe Fortas, "what the goddamn hell confidence are they going to have in the Presidency? Pussyfooting and procrastinating."[71] Reedy was absolutely opposed. So were De-Loach and Lady Bird. "It's the worst thing you could do," the FBI executive told him, "because the man is sick; he has been sick. He's been working almost to the point of death for you, and for you to take an abrupt act like that would make it look like you're a cold, selfish, heartless individual."[72] It was agreed that LBJ would issue a statement expressing sympathy for Jenkins and his family and placing his aide on extended leave. In the meantime, Fortas, Clifford, and De-Loach would work to secure Jenkins's resignation.

Goldwater supporters began showing up at Democratic rallies bearing signs reading "Either Way with LBJ."[73] There were the inevitable comparisons of Jenkins with British Defense Minister John Profumo, who had recently been forced to resign his post after it was revealed that he was sharing the affections of a call girl with an attaché at the Soviet embassy.[74] Before Goldwater himself could react, the White House quietly reminded the GOP candidate that as a reserve air force general who was Jenkins's commanding officer in Washington, he had given him glowing evaluations. Moreover, there was the matter of Goldwater's own two documented nervous breakdowns. The Republican standard-bearer chose to steer clear of the matter in his public statements; in private, however, he quipped, "What a way to win an election: communists and cocksuckers!"[75]

By the third week of the scandal, Jenkins was in full denial, and both he and Marjorie were furious with LBJ for forcing him out of the White House. Shaken by an early morning call, full of reproach, from Marjorie, Lady Bird called her husband, who was at the airport about to board Air Force One. She intended to issue her own statement of sympathy and support and wanted to announce that the Johnsons were offering Walter a job at KTBC in Austin. LBJ paused, then said quietly, "I wouldn't do anything along that line now . . . I don't want you to hurt him more than he's hurt, and when we move into it . . . we blow it up." She persisted. They had to express public support for the Jenkins family. If not, she warned, "we will lose the entire love and devotion of all the people who have been with us . . . A gesture of support to Walter on our part is best." Still speaking quietly, if a bit desperately, Johnson said, "Don't create any more problems than I've got [by becoming] part of it . . . You just can't do that to the presidency, honey . . . The average farmer just can't understand [this], and your approving or condoning it . . . I am not opposed to giving him anything and everything we have, all of it . . . and letting him know it . . . But I don't want it blown up in headlines that I gave him advancement because he did this." But she was determined. "You're a brave, good guy, and if you read where I've said some things in Walter's support, they will be along the line that I have just said to you." He softened and then tacitly agreed. "You think I ought to call her [Marjorie]?" he asked.[76] Lady Bird said yes and subsequently declared the family's support for the Jenkinses. The Johnsons were as good as their word, allocating, among other things, a percentage of the family's ranching operations to Walter and his family.

On October 23, the FBI, after reviewing thousands of pages of documents and interviewing over five hundred people, issued a report certifying that Walter Jenkins had never been involved in a breach of security. LBJ called Hoover, who had not only given Jenkins a clean bill of health but also sent him a huge flower arrangement to the hospital with a card reading "J. Edgar Hoover and Associates." "I'm very grateful for your thoroughness and your patriotism and the way you have handled it," the president said.[77] But Johnson, who believed that Hoover was gay, could not help teasing him in a conversation a week later. "I never know who is and who isn't," LBJ said to the director. "You're going to have to teach me about this stuff. I swear I can't recognize them." Hoover replied stiffly, "You can't tell. There are some people who walk kind of funny. You might think they're queer."[78]

If there was any political steam left in the Jenkins story, it was drained off by two earth-shaking events the third week in October. First, the Chinese exploded their first nuclear device; second, Nikita Khrushchev was forced out of power in the Soviet Union, ostensibly for pursuing détente too vigorously with the United States and not vigorously enough with communist China.[79]

IN MID-AUGUST Johnson learned that Bobby Kennedy, who had lived in New York from 1925 to 1942, was thinking of challenging Republican Senator Kenneth Keating. It would be good to have the Kennedys diverted from seeking national office for a time, and the Great Society would benefit from having at least one Democratic senator from New York (the other being Republican Jacob Javits), Johnson admitted. But LBJ would prefer not have Bobby squatting on one of his prime pieces of political real estate. As Lyle Wilson of UPI put it, "The consensus on Robert F. Kennedy is that he is a young man of ruthless determination and of infinitely aggressive ambition. He is accustomed by reason of money, family position and brains to having his own way. It is reasonable, at least, to assume that Kennedy seeks to establish himself with a New York State political base which might be useful in another Kennedy thrust for the White House."[80] Johnson had little choice but to give the Kennedy campaign his blessing, but he was determined not to do any more than was necessary.[81]

The first week in September, Bobby found himself sitting in the Oval Office begging for money. The campaign was going to cost $1 million, he said. He did not mind going into debt $500,000 or $600,000, but there was no way he was going to raise an additional $300,000 in New York. LBJ bristled. "Well, I don't know where you're gonna get any of it out of the national fund. We need fifteen million . . . You've just got to go in there and make those folks and everybody you can in New York contribute." In an irritated and plaintive voice, Bobby replied, "I just can't do that Mr. President." His voice growing shrill, LBJ said, "I don't have the money. I haven't got it."[82] Rebuffed, Kennedy went back to New York and began raising money. Still, it looked like a race that would go down to the wire. Eight days before the election, RFK called LBJ and persuaded him to make a last-minute tour of Long Island.[83] Bobby wound up carrying New York by six hundred thousand votes against LBJ's margin of over 2 million.

The outcome of the general election exceeded LBJ's expectations, if not his dreams. Goldwater won only six states, five in the South, plus Arizona. "It was the picture of Negroes lining up to vote at the polling places early in the morning that turned the whites out," Olin Johnston subsequently reported to LBJ.[84] The president won 486 electoral votes to his opponent's 52. Only Roosevelt's 523 to 8 vote margin in 1936 was larger. Most important, however, Johnson's 43,129,484 popular votes against Goldwater's 27,178,188 represented the largest vote ever cast for a winning candidate, and his 61 percent majority was the largest in American history. The Republicans lost more than five hundred seats in state legislatures, thirty-seven in the House, and two in the Senate.[85] Johnson at last had the validation that he had so long craved. As one Republican senator put it, "That damn Lyndon Johnson hasn't just grabbed the middle of the road. He's a bit to the Right of center, as well as a bit to the Left of center. And with Johnson hogging the whole road, Right, Left and center, where the devil can we go except the ditch?"[86] Or, as Jim Rowe put it, "How are you going to beat Franklin Delano Hoover?"[87]

For Lyndon Johnson, whose life was politics, election to the presidency of the United States by a landslide was the ultimate triumph. And yet, characteristically, he could find bitterness in even the sweetest of sweets. At 11:28 the next day, Goldwater formally conceded. The Arizonan was not at his most gracious; reading from his telegram to LBJ, he told reporters that Republicans would assume "the part [role] of opposition when opposition is called for." Watching on television, LBJ exclaimed, "That damn son of a bitch!"[88] After reading a news story to the effect that the election was a repudiation of Goldwater rather than an endorsement of Johnson, he called his old friend Ed Weisl in New York. He believed that Weisl, whose client list read like a Who's Who of the publishing and broadcasting world, could help him mold the media. "Now Red Mueller [Merrill Mueller of NBC] started this story that they're just voting against Goldwater and they didn't like either one of us," he whined. "And that Johnson didn't have any rapport, and he didn't have any style, and he was a buffoon. And he was full of corn. The fact that he had drawn the biggest crowds in campaign history and had received the support of virtually every region and interest group seemed not to matter . . . They say, 'Aw-w-w, that doesn't amount to anything.' So the Bobby Kennedy group, they put out this stuff . . . that nobody loves Johnson. They are going to have it built up by January that I didn't get any mandate at all. That I was just the lesser of two evils, and that people didn't care."[89]

Lyndon and Lady Bird spent from election eve until November 15 at the ranch, returned to Washington for four days, and then flew back to Texas to spend the Christmas holidays. In anticipation of this extended stay, LBJ had decided to upgrade his informal wardrobe. He called Joe Haggar of Haggar Slacks. "I want a couple . . . of maybe three of the light brown," he told the startled executive, "kind of almost powder color . . . kind of like a powder on a lady's face . . . Then there was some green, and maybe some other light pair . . . I want them a half-inch larger in the waist than they were before." "Yes, sir," Haggar answered. But the president was not through: "Now another thing . . . the crotch, down where your nuts hang, is always a little too tight . . . so when you make them up, give me an inch where I can let it out there . . . They're just like riding a wire fence." [90]

During the six weeks the Johnsons were at the ranch in November and December, the president received a steady stream of reporters, dignitaries, cabinet officers, and advisers. First on the list were Hubert and Muriel Humphrey. There was something about Humphrey that brought out the bully in Johnson. No sooner had the vice president arrived than LBJ decided that he and his running mate should go for a horseback ride. "He called me into his bedroom and pulled out an outfit that dwarfed me," Humphrey recalled. "The pants were huge, so big that I thought I could put both my legs in one pant leg and still dance a polka. The jacket draped like a tent over a shirt whose neck was several sizes too large. I looked ridiculous and I felt ridiculous as I smiled wanly from under a cowboy hat that was made for his head and clearly not for mine." Instead of assigning Humphrey to a well-broken-in mount, Johnson had him hoisted up on a large, spirited horse. When it reared, Humphrey had to cling to it like a frightened child, with flashbulbs popping and reporters scribbling. [91]

Johnson decided to ask the Orville Freemans to come to Texas for a few days. Freeman noted the beauty of the ranch, particularly at sunset. He and Jane enjoyed the meals and Lady Bird's hospitality, but could not help but note Johnson's rudeness and churlishness. "Again the same shortness, the same crudeness and thoughtlessness this man has for the people around him came out," Freeman wrote in his diary. "He bellered several times into the communications system to one of the Secret Service guys . . . Then we stopped on top of the hill to get a drink and he was quite irked because the drink wasn't forthcoming rapidly enough. By the same token when he was backing a little cart out from their breezeway . . . and Lady Bird spoke up that he was going to bump the house, why he just told her to sit quiet and keep her mouth shut, and she did just that." [92] Sylvia Porter, a Washington reporter invited along, recalled with distaste Johnson's penchant for using a seduction analogy to describe any and every effort to accomplish a task: "He knew how it was that after all when you wanted to get a girl you didn't grab hold of her and say let's jump in bed that you at least started out at her knee and moved your hand up her leg slowly." "She thought that he was a crude, cruel man," Freeman recalled her saying, "but that he would be a great President . . . because he had his eye on the ball and that nothing was going to get in his way, and because people really didn't matter, it was really only reaching his objective—but she also said she felt he really was quite sincere about poverty and the Great Society and to make his place in history and that he would." [93]

Back in Washington, LBJ continued to torment his vice president. On December 10, after his first postelection cabinet meeting, LBJ called Orville Freeman into his office to talk farm policy. Humphrey showed up as well, and the president began on him. He accused the vice president of developing a publicity machine extraordinaire and of always wanting to get his name in the papers. He then showed Humphrey a memo from George Reedy repeating a rumor (untrue) that the president had a fatal liver disease and would be dead in six months. "You'd like that, wouldn't you Hubert," he said. " . . . But if it happens sooner than January 20, it won't do you any good will it?' " [94] And yet, when the Humphreys' son was diagnosed with throat cancer, LBJ immediately phoned the Minnesotan. "We are grieving with you," he said with obvious feeling. "All our thoughts and love are with you." [95]

As inaugural day approached, Lyndon became increasingly energized and excited. All week, he went from party to party coatless and hatless into overheated rooms and out into the frigid Washington air, sowing the seeds of pneumonia that would land him in the hospital two days after his swearing in. On Monday evening some ten thousand guests attended the Inaugural Ball at the cavernous Washington, D.C., Armory. The gala was hosted by Johnny Carson, Ann-Margret, and Alfred Hitchcock. LBJ became the first president to dance at his own inauguration, twirling nine different partners gracefully across the floor in thirteen minutes. The only incident that marred the occasion came when a photographer snapped a picture of the president dancing with the blond, extremely attractive wife of movie magnate Arthur Krim. At the sound of the flashbulb, Johnson stopped dancing and, visibly angry, took the photographer by the elbow and forcefully escorted him from the room. "You boys are vulgar," he said. [96]

The next morning, inauguration day, the Johnsons attended services at National City Christian Church. The Reverend Billy Graham delivered the sermon. He quoted Solomon ascending the throne of Israel: "Give me now wisdom and knowledge, that I may go out and come in before this people: for who can judge this thy people, that is so great?" [97] As the presidential motorcade made its way down Massachusetts Avenue, fifty-four hundred security officers watched from buildings along the route, and two military helicopters hovered overhead. Lyndon rejected the tuxedoes of tradition and took the oath in a dark business suit and four-in-hand tie. [98] As he quietly recited the oath, his hand rested on the tattered family Bible held by Lady Bird.

There was much on the Great Society and little on foreign affairs in the address that followed. Orville Freeman remembered the delivery more than the text: "It was a strange speech, an emotional speech, almost a prayer." [99] Nearly three thousand Texans had come to the capital for the crowning of their native son. Appointments Secretary Marvin Watson had felt it necessary to issue a warning to the Lone Star invitees: "All the world will be watching." He wrote them. "Let the others come in their boots and 10-gallon hats, but let us . . . present to the world the moderate and warm temperament of the true Texas." [100] Nevertheless, the national press portrayed the denizens of Lyndon's home state in full caricature. "True, there was one matron from Fort Worth who showed up in a tiara that lighted up and spelled T-E-X-A-S," *Newsweek* reported. "And there was a Texas State Society reception at the Statler-Hilton, where the assembled Texans raucously sang 'The Eyes of Texas,' with rebel yells. But a check after two-and-one-half hours of free-flowing booze revealed only two drunks, no fights, and no six-guns." [101] During the day Robert Kennedy made two ostentatious visits to his brother's grave in Arlington National Cemetery.

Ed Weisl reported a conversation he had with political humorist Art Buchwald at an election-night party after Johnson had defeated Goldwater. "Boy, now we're going to get this son-of-a-bitch." Weisl asked, "What do you mean, Art?" And he said, "Well, we were nice to this fellow while he was running against Goldwater because we were scared of Goldwater, but now we're going to get him because he's just a Texas clown." [102]

CHAPTER 27

A NEW BILL OF RIGHTS

T HE INAUGURATION OF LYNDON JOHNSON IN JAN-
uary 1965 was most important perhaps as a precipitate for the
Great Society, the details of which the president and his advisers
had been mulling over since that sunny afternoon in Ann Arbor
when the term was first articulated. Two weeks after his Michigan commencement address, Johnson had dispatched Bill Moyers and Richard Goodwin to
Cambridge where they lunched at John Kenneth Galbraith's house; there they
met with about thirty academics from Harvard, MIT, and other area institutions. Out of this and subsequent meetings came some fourteen task forces
composed of academics, government officials, and prominent citizens with instructions to devise recommendations for policy initiatives in the following
fields: transportation, natural resources, education, health, urban problems,
pollution of the environment, preservation of natural beauty, intergovernmen-
tal fiscal cooperation, efficiency and economy, antirecession policy, agriculture,
civil rights, foreign economic policy, and income maintenance policy. Johnson
insisted that the task forces operate in secret so that debate on the issues would
not start prematurely in the media and in Congress. He wanted the members to
be free, he said, to make recommendations without political considerations and
without regard to cost. When the reports were duly received at the White House
on November 10, 1965, they were sifted through by Goodwin, Moyers, and the
rest of the White House staff, to see which were workable from a political and
fiscal point of view. "If we had adopted all their ideas," said one bemused assistant, "we would have had to have come up with a budget of over $300 billion."[1]
There was, for example, $3 billion for a 200-mph, tube-encased, rocket-
powered railroad line linking Boston to Washington.

Moyers and his team delivered a twelve-hundred-page, condensed list of
programs to Johnson, who read them over during his stay at the ranch in No-

vember and December. He then summoned his advisers. As he lay in his hammock soaking up the Texas sun, the aides made their presentation. "I thought I
was being especially articulate," Moyers recalled, "but when I looked over at the
hammock, the President appeared to be asleep. So I stopped speaking, and for
five minutes we sat in silence. Then bang, bang, bang, the President spoke—he
had obviously heard everything that had been said—and he told us precisely
why the recommendation would not work and how it should be repackaged."[2]
Some of the programs envisioned in the Great Society were going to have a
price tag—potentially an enormous one—such as federal aid to education and
Medicare, but others, such as a voting rights bill and immigration reform,
would not, although their impact on American society promised to be just as
great. And as time would reveal, LBJ had his priorities.

The State of the Union address delivered at night, for the first time since
1936, to a joint session was an inspirational rally in behalf of the Great Society
rather than a detailed outline of program. Not surprisingly, the speech emphasized both change and continuity. The Great Society would mean a new day for
the 8 million American children who had never finished the fifth grade and the
54 million who had not finished high school. It would mean a new day for the
millions of elderly Americans who had no health insurance. It would mean a
new day for those black Americans so long denied the right to vote.[3] The Great
Society was not a dramatic departure but the fulfillment of dreams first
dreamed when Columbus came to the Americas. "A President does not shape a
new and personal vision of America," LBJ told the senators and representatives.
"He collects it from the scattered hopes of the American past. It existed when
the first settlers saw the coast of a new world, and when the first pioneers moved
westward . . . It shall lead us as we enter the third century of the search for 'a
more perfect union.' " His early years, he said, had been ones of witness to men
and women turning a howling wilderness into a land of milk and honey. "It [the
Hill Country] was once barren land. The angular hills were covered with scrub
cedar and a few large live oaks. Little would grow in that harsh caliche soil of my
country. And each spring the Pedernales River would flood our valley. But men
came and they worked and they endured and they built. And tonight that country is abundant with fruit and cattle and goats and sheep, and there are pleasant
homes and lakes and the floods are gone."[4]

The Great Society would be an attempt—halting, limited, constrained, but
groundbreaking—to change the status quo, a status quo that had embedded
within it racial discrimination, insensitivity to social and economic injustice,
and a self-serving attachment to laissez-faire. At one level, by seeming to ram
through Congress the programs that constituted the Great Society, LBJ would
be flying in the face of the American creed, which, as Samuel Huntington has
observed, is pervaded by an "anti-power ethic." All of its basic tenets—equality,
liberty, individualism, constitutionalism, democracy—are "basically antigovernment and antiauthority in character calling for the placing of limits on the
institutions of government. Individualism stressed freedom from government

control and egalitarianism emphasized the right of one individual to be free from control by another."[5] Thus could all of those with a vested or emotional interest in the status quo invoke hallowed American principles: segregationists who saw the Great Society as a conspiracy to foist integration on the South, manufacturers who saw the poverty program as a plot to rob America of its cheap labor force, physicians who perceived Medicare as a government scheme to prevent them from charging all that traffic would bear, employers who feared having to pay for a national health care system, Catholic and other faith-based groups that viewed federal aid to education as a scheme to crush parochial schools.

In addition to invoking the concept of modern individualism, Johnson's stratagem for combating conservatives wielding the American creed was to clothe his mandate with the rhetoric of consensus, a profoundly conservative term. " 'Consensus' is a word designed to conceal," a British political commentator noted in *The New Republic*. "What it tries to imply is that nothing exceptional is happening: that what has been achieved by precise (possibly new; possibly revolutionary) political methods, has, instead, 'just growed'—out of the goodness of heart, one is left to suppose, of big business and labor, of the cities and the countryside, of rich and poor."[6] Using the language of consensus as cover, LBJ, the newly, overwhelmingly elected, popular sovereign, intended to move the nation down the road of reform and social justice more quickly and more dramatically than it had ever been moved before.

Before he presented to Congress the sweeping program he had in mind, LBJ realized that he would have to identify the funds that would be needed to pay for them. First, he anticipated steady increases in tax revenue through natural growth in the economy. "Since the economy began its current expansion in the first quarter of 1961," the Council of Economic Advisers reported to him, "GNP has increased nearly \$150 billion or 30% . . . the growth in our 'real output' has been 22%, or an annual rate of 5.1%. This represents a substantial step up from the long-term historical performance . . . which has run about 3%. If we continue to advance at a rate of 4.1% for the remainder of this decade, our real output in 1970 will be 51% above 1960."[7] In addition, Johnson intended to squeeze every dollar he could out of the budgets of existing agencies and programs. "The Great Society will require a substantial investment," he told the cabinet two weeks after the election. "This means that as a nation we cannot afford to waste a single dollar of our resources on outmoded programs, which once may have been essential, but which time and events have overtaken."[8]

First and foremost among governmental entities to be squeezed was the Department of Defense. In this endeavor, Robert McNamara proved to be a willing ally. In the spring of 1964, he had made a formal, chart-laden presentation to his new boss "to show the President how I anticipated the percent of GNP devoted to defense should drop between 1964 and 1965 and subsequent years. I pointed out this should permit, by the saving in percent of GNP going to defense, a financing of both additional public and private goods."[9] "The point I want to make," LBJ told reporters at the ranch in January 1965, "is that every congressional district in this country that has a defense installation must understand that they are going to be reviewed from time to time. We want to save every penny we can every place we can so that we may have some much needed funds to fill unfilled needs—educational needs, health needs, poverty needs, needs generally." During 1964–1965, the Johnson administration closed more than four hundred military bases, naval yards, and air stations, creating an annual saving of $250 million.[10] Defense was not alone. Agriculture, Labor, and NASA, to name a few, experienced significant budget cuts.[11]

The effects of the Kennedy tax cut would eventually wear off, and to avoid a recession, the economy would require further stimulation either through another tax cut or through increased government spending.[12] What course would LBJ follow? Financial journals debated throughout early 1964 whether the president was a Keynesian, that is, whether he valued a balanced budget over all else or would be willing to use a variety of devices—tax cuts, increased government expenditures on public works, or manipulation of the interest rates—to keep profits and wages up and unemployment down.[13] Keynes had long been the punching bag of conservatives, portrayed as a rigid ideologue committed to permanent systems of public works, redistributive tax policies, public competition with the private sector, and expensive welfare programs. In reality, the economist advocated only temporary state intervention and manipulation to deal with unusual downturns in the economy. At different times in his life he had advocated protection and controls and free trade. As one jokester put it, "Where five economists are gathered together there will be six conflicting opinions and two of them will be held by Keynes."[14] Johnson denied that he was "a doctrinaire follower of any particular economic theory," meaning he was not necessarily a Keynesian, and in so doing ironically identified himself with the British economist, the ultimate pragmatist.[15] Clearly, LBJ was a Keynesian. He would not stand by and watch a recession overwhelm the economy in order to maintain a balanced budget and high interest rates.[16] He had cut his teeth on the New Deal, which was willing to create public works projects like the Works Progress Administration and National Youth Administration as temporary palliatives to shore up employment, which looked to plentiful energy provided by regional development programs like the Tennessee Valley Authority, and which sponsored government guarantees of loans and credit to create the conditions for prolonged prosperity. The wisdom of such an approach had been obscured by the impact of massive government spending during World War II, which had given the economy a huge shot in the arm and provided conservatives an out.[17]

Reasonably sure that the money necessary to launch the Great Society would be available, LBJ next turned his attention to Congress. He believed that he had a window of opportunity similar to that FDR had enjoyed in the wake of his sweeping victory in 1936. "He called me into the Yellow Room of the White House one late February or early March evening [in 1964]," remembered Bill Moyers.

Mrs. Johnson was sitting there . . . He was working with a white paper pad . . . He had written "November 22, 1963," and then a column of months that went to January 19, 1965, and then another from January 20, 1965 to January 19, 1969, and from January 20, 1969, to January 19, 1973 . . . Out to the side there was a scrawl which said "1964, win," "1965, P&P"—that means propose and pass . . . and then for 1967 it said "hold gains." He said, "Bill, I've just been figuring out how much time we would have to do what we want to do. I really intend to finish Franklin Roosevelt's revolution . . . In an ideal world . . . we would have about 110 months to his 144 months . . . I'll never make it that far, of course, so let's assume that we have to do it all in 1965 and 1966, and probably in 1966 we'll lose our big margin in the Congress. That means in 1967 and 1968 there will be a hell of a fight." [18]

Johnson believed that he had approximately twenty months to pass Medicare, reform the immigration laws, pass a voting rights bill, dramatically expand the federal nature conservancy, and do approximately nine hundred other things that had or would come to mind. For this to happen, Congress would have to be a lean, mean, bill-passing machine, not the stifling logjam it had so often been since those halcyon days of the Second New Deal.

At first glance, the national legislature would seem to have posed little or no problem. The Democrats enjoyed two-to-one majorities in both Houses. Despite this Democratic dominance and his 16 million vote mandate, however, LBJ insisted that the Great Society was in for rough sledding. "I've watched the Congress from either the inside or the outside, man and boy, for more than forty years," he remarked shortly after the election, "and I've never seen a Congress that didn't eventually take the measure of the President it was dealing with." [19] And he was right. During the first session of the 89th Congress, as more than one hundred administration-backed bills passed, the average margin of victory in the House was only 235 to 200. The bulk of the support was provided by 213 Democrats who supported the president at least 70 percent of the time and 22 Republicans who supported him at least 55 percent of the time. "A shift of a mere 18 votes—just half of the Democrats' net gain in 1964—would have meant the failure of much of the program," White House staffer Douglass Cater later noted. [20] LBJ realized that if he approached Congress with a mandate on his hip, threatening, talking tough, showing up representatives and senators, he would get exactly nowhere. In his State of the Union address, consequently, the president was almost obsequious. "I am proud to be among my colleagues of the Congress whose legacy to their trust is their loyalty to their Nation," he intoned. [21] After one proposal, he ad-libbed, "And I welcome the recommendations and constructive efforts of the Congress." Democratic Senator Vance Hartke noted the passage approvingly and observed, "He told us in effect that there was room for difference without difference of principle." [22] "The most important people you will talk to are senators and congressmen," Johnson told

Jack Valenti. "You treat them as if they were president. Answer their calls immediately. Give them respect. They deserve it."[23]

Every cabinet department, every agency was to have its own liaison team to
work with Congress, the overall effort to be coordinated by Larry O'Brien and
his staff. Johnson insisted that the liaison personnel get to know members as he
had during his congressional heyday. And they did. "It's not something that you
can put in a computer and get out an answer," said Wilbur Cohen, who headed
the Social Security Administration and who was one of the administration's
most effective lobbyists.

> Every man is different and every woman is different . . . Again, a man is
> very different if he's the bottom man of a committee or he's the chairman
> . . . [If] he wants to run for the United States Senate in five years—he's
> obviously going to do different things than if he isn't . . . Russell Long has,
> for instance, a certain heritage from his father Huey Long; and while there
> are many things that Russell Long is in favor of that would make his father
> turn over in his grave—he stands with the oil interests in preventing an
> amendment of the depletion allowance—Long still has a strong, strong,
> populist, radical, share-the-wealth attitude . . . And you've got to under-
> stand that Wilbur D. Mills comes from a little town of 2,500, which is a
> small, rural town but he nevertheless is a Harvard Law School graduate.[24]

LBJ would court members of Congress, flatter them, drink with them, above
all, pay attention to them; it was not unusual, for example, during crucial periods in the battle over a major component of the Great Society for LBJ to talk to
twenty members in a single day. At the same time, there was a subtle warning to
the House and Senate in his State of the Union message: "You will soon learn
that you are among men whose first love is their country, men who try each day
to do as best they can what they believe is right."[25]

Late in February, LBJ presided over a meeting of key members of the House
and Senate in the State Dining Room. He singled out the effective for praise and
chided the recalcitrant. "There was this great range of emotions displayed,"
D. B. Hardeman recalled, "from near anger to ribald humor, to history—appeals to history; it was a very fascinating intellectual and dramatic display . . . It
was an evening that held you on the edge of your seat."[26] "In some ways," Johnson confided to a friend, "Congress is like a dangerous animal that you're trying
to make work for you. You push him a little bit and he may go just as you want
but you push him too much and he may balk and turn on you. You've got to
sense just how much he'll take and what kind of mood he's in every day. For if
you don't have a feel for him, he's liable to turn around and go wild."[27]

The order in which the components of the Great Society were presented to
Congress would be extremely important. Federal aid to education, the antipoverty program, voting rights, Medicare, welfare reform, area redevelopment, and aid to urban areas would all be voted on by the same representatives

and senators who were politically, emotionally, and/or ideologically attracted to or repelled by a particular proposal. The task, as Johnson viewed it, was to prevent the coalescing of Republicans and southern Democrats into an antireform bloc.

Labor constituted an absolutely crucial element of the Great Society coalition. Since the passage of Taft-Hartley, unions and their lobbyists had been obsessed with securing repeal of Section 14b, the provision authorizing states to pass right-to-work laws, which in turn undermined the unions' prerogative to organize and bargain collectively. LBJ told UAW head Walter Reuther that if labor insisted on forcing an early congressional showdown on 14b, "that will wreck everything. We oughta do it but the first thing we ought to try to put through, if we can, is medical care. The second thing is the excise taxes to put a little soup in this economy. The third thing is unemployment insurance. The fourth thing and simultaneously if we can ought to be Appalachia and maybe some ARA [area redevelopment] to end these distressed areas . . . If we bring that other other thing up first that'll drive the South and the Republicans together in an old bloc again."[28] Reuther was persuaded, and during the first year of the Great Society, organized labor worked strenuously for Medicare, voting rights, and area redevelopment while waiting patiently for revision of Taft-Hartley.

THE ANGLO-TEXANS with whom Lyndon Johnson grew up worshipped at the shrine of education. None more so than his own family. The Germans who settled the Hill Country emanated from a culture known for its accomplishments in science, philosophy, and music. For Rebekah Baines, education was one of the joys she shared with her beloved father and the key to her elevated social status, real and imagined, in Johnson City. One of the reasons Lyndon was so rebellious in school, a notorious truant at times, was that his home was a school. Lessons, recitations, and discussions of public affairs were never-ending. Central and south-central Texas produced more teachers than any other area of the state; San Marcos was a teachers college. "I came from a family that is interested in public life and in education," LBJ told the National Conference on Educational Legislation in 1965. "My mother was a teacher and my father was a teacher. My great grandfather, my mother's grand-father, was the second president of Baylor University when it was located down at Washington on the Brazos."[29] And LBJ was a teacher, the only profession he had ever known besides politics.

But there was more to Johnson's commitment than the Anglo-Texans' respect for education, and more than the American pragmatist's belief that education was the gateway to a better material life for oneself and humankind in general. LBJ was a man who was acutely aware of the vastness of the American republic and the centripetal forces—race, religion, region, class, ideology, and national origin—that continually threatened to tear it apart. In an extensive republic like the United States, which had no established religion and which was flooded periodically with immigrants, an integrating educational system was not important—it was crucial. It was not surprising that the "common school" envisioned and championed by Horace Mann originated during the 1830s and 1840s in the midst of one of these tides of influx. Systems of public education could not eliminate prejudices, eradicate differences; indeed, racial and ethnic minorities traditionally received unfair, even brutal treatment at the hands of textbook authors, who not so subtly held up white Christianity as the ideal. But the teaching of mathematics, science, logic, rhetoric, which were universal, together with respect for the Constitution, democracy, republicanism, and the other tenets of American political culture, would unify and integrate.[30] Johnson, the democratic nationalist, the prophet of pluralism, shared Horace Mann's faith, stripped of its New England prejudices.

By 1964, elementary and secondary education for both public and parochial students was in a woeful state. There was a shortage of teachers, who were grossly underpaid, classrooms were overcrowded, many school buildings were rundown and dilapidated, and textbooks were worn and outmoded. The postwar baby boom had flooded public and private institutions with students that they simply did not have the resources to handle. It was worse in some areas than others—much worse. Mississippi spent $241 per student per year compared to New York's $705.[31] Nearly all monies for public education came from local property taxes and state subsidies; the federal government provided only 3.5 percent of the funds spent on elementary and secondary education. "Millions of students," social historian Irving Bernstein writes, "were denied a proper education because they lived in states too poor to provide one, or in central cities in which the schools were beggared, or suffered from physical or emotional handicaps in localities which offered no or, at best, inadequate special education."[32]

Federal aid to education, championed by both Robert Taft and Harry Truman, had foundered on a number of rocks. Segregationists had fought it, seeing it as a weapon wielded by on overweaning federal authority to force integration on the South. Conservatives like Howard Smith continued to denounce the concept as an unwarranted interference with states' rights that would lead to federal dictation of everything from dress to curricula. But the real sticking point for federal aid to schools was religion. Protestants and Jews were enthusiastic supporters of federal aid to education, but only to public school systems. If Catholics, and for that matter fundamentalist Christians and orthodox Jews, wanted to send their children to private schools, let them and their churches pay the bill. Over the years, the National Education Association, the powerful teachers union, the National Council of Churches, which included the major Protestant denominations, and the principal Jewish organizations had adamantly opposed federal aid if any was to go to parochial schools.[33] Conversely, Catholics, who operated 85 percent of the nation's parochial schools for some 5 million pupils, insisted that the "free exercise" of religion guaranteed by the Constitution included the right to religious education and that it was unfair for Catholic parents to pay taxes to support schools that their children would not attend.[34]

The Kennedy administration had submitted to Congress a federal aid to education bill that provided funding to public but not private schools under a formula weighted to give disproportionate help to systems in the poorest states and in inner-city ghettoes. As a Catholic, JFK felt he could not afford to champion aid to private institutions. Yet, led by James Delaney, a Catholic congressman from New York, parochial school forces in the House managed to block passage.[35] Thus did it fall to LBJ's task force on education to find a way around the impasse. LBJ and his advisers knew that there would be no federal aid to education bill if parochial students were not somehow included. The key, the task force realized, was to focus on the child and not the institution. In 1947, in *Everson v. Ewing Township,* the Supreme Court had approved the use of state funds to provide bus transportation to parochial schoolchildren; the benefit was going to the individual pupil, not the institution, the Court ruled. The Elementary and Secondary Education Act (ESEA) that was introduced into Congress in January 1965 was based on a rather simple formula. The federal government would provide each state funds in the amount of the number of children in the state from low-income families (less than $2,000 a year), multiplied by 50 percent of the state's average expenditure per pupil.[36] Title I provided funds to public institutions to help the children of low-income families, but services in these institutions would be available to public and parochial students alike. Title II funded textbooks and library materials that state agencies could distribute to both private and public institutions. Title III would create supplementary educational centers to provide physical education, music, languages, advanced science, remedial reading, television equipment, and teaching innovations for both public and private schools.[37] It was estimated that private school children would receive between 10.1 and 13.5 percent of the dollars appropriated under ESEA, slightly less than their per capita ratio.

It was time for Johnson the evangelist. "Nothing matters more to the future of our country," he declared of the education bill. If Congress did not act for the 30 million boys and girls slated to enter the job force during the forthcoming decade, 2.5 million would never see the inside of a high school; 8 million would never earn a high school diploma; and more than 1 million qualified to attend college would never go.[38] He envisioned, he said, a doubling of federal spending on education from $4 billion to $8 billion, with $1 billion going to elementary and secondary students. Eric Goldman and Horace Busby were assigned to draft the president's special message to Congress on education. When they ended with a quote from Lincoln, LBJ suggested that he use the famous "Lamar" quote instead. After some digging, Goldman discovered that Lamar was Mirabeau B. Lamar, the Republic of Texas's second president, famous for his hard-line approach to Indians and Mexicans and for his expansionist vision. In an effort to persuade the Texas legislature to fund a public school system in

1838, he had exclaimed to its members, "The cultivated mind is the guardian genius of democracy. It is the only dictator that free man acknowledges. It is the only security that free man desires." [39]

In his quest to pass a landmark education bill, LBJ was able to count on a number of assets. As noted previously, passage of the 1964 Civil Rights Act had drawn some of the venom from the segregationists. The energy mobilized in behalf of the poverty bill would spill over into the fight for ESEA. It was framed in part as an antipoverty measure, and who could be in favor of poverty? Moreover, some of the anti-Catholic prejudice that at one time had been as strong as anti-Semitism in the United States was waning. There were signs that both public and private school advocates were coming to the conclusion that if they did not compromise, the very thing they professed to be serving would continue to deteriorate. That is, by demanding equal treatment for parochial schools, Catholics were getting no help at all; by insisting on nothing for religious schools, non-Catholics were getting nothing for themselves.

The bill was introduced in the House on January 12, 1965, by Carl Perkins of Kentucky, chair of the General Education Subcommittee, and in the Senate by Wayne Morse, chair of the Education Subcommittee. The Senate had always been more favorably inclined toward federal aid to education, and so O'Brien, Cater, and their troops concentrated on the lower house. All seemed well when the measure was referred to the House Labor and Education Committee, chaired by Adam Clayton Powell of New York. A cleric and a fiery crusader for civil rights, Powell had previously insisted that any federal aid to education measure include a compulsory school desegregation proviso. With passage of the equal accommodations provision of the 1964 Civil Rights Act, there was no longer any need to single out education. Powell was certainly a supporter of public funding for schools, but he had personal needs that had to be met. A strikingly handsome and charismatic man, Powell was a notorious playboy, making frequent trips to the Caribbean with one beauty or another. "The Abyssinian Baptist Church was the biggest organization and the largest black church in the country," Louis Martin, Johnson's liaison with the black press, remembered. "Adam was absolutely as handsome as a man could be. He was also almost white . . . He was olive . . . he was also amiable. You know, smiling, and when he walked into a room, the lights go on . . . Mrs. Kennedy even talked about how good-looking the son of a bitch was." [40] The Powell lifestyle required money. When the House refused to increase his committee's expense account from $225,000 to $440,000, Powell retired to Puerto Rico and refused to take phone calls. Holding his nose, LBJ lobbied key congressmen to give the reverend his money. [41] Pointing out that Powell had been key to passage of the poverty bill, Johnson observed that the chair of Labor and Education was like Bob Kerr; "He always took something out of every pot but he by God put more into it than he took out." [42] His coffers now overflowing, Powell returned from self-imposed exile to lead the charge. He announced that the committee would meet all day, every day, including Saturday, until the bill was passed.

In the Senate, Morse drove the measure through in a matter of days. He saw to it that there were no amendments, thus obviating the need for a potentially contentious conference committee. There were cries of "railroad" and paeans to the Force Acts of Reconstruction days. Senator Winston Prouty of Vermont declared, "The principal issue facing the nation today is not education. It is the future of the Senate as a co-equal partner in the legislative process." The final count was seventy-three to eighteen.[43] In a mere eighty-seven days, Eric Goldman noted, Congress had acted on legislation that had been pending for twenty years and had established a federal-state partnership in one of society's fundamental activities.

LBJ decided to hold the signing ceremony in Texas in front of the one-room schoolhouse at Junction, a mile and a half down the road from the ranch. He picked the spot because it was a reminder of his own origins and journey, and he hoped it would become to LBJ what the log cabin was to Abraham Lincoln. The structure had been bought by an Oklahoma couple for a vacation home, but they readily agreed to let the president use it. The White House arranged for former students from Houston and Cotulla to be bused in. Gene Latimer and Luther Jones, LBJ's former star debaters, both came. So did Mrs. Katie Deadrich Looney, Johnson's first-grade teacher. Liz Carpenter found some old desks of World War I vintage and had them arrayed in the front yard. There were picnic tables for a barbeque. "It was an accurate, warm, corny setting," Lady Bird wrote.[44] The president's remarks were as much a reminiscence as a speech. "In this one-room schoolhouse Miss Katie Deadrich taught eight grades at one and the same time," he told the more than three hundred that had gathered. "Come over here, Miss Katie, and sit by me, will you? Let them see you. I started school when I was 4 years old, and they tell me, Miss Katie, that I recited my first lessons while sitting on your lap."[45]

Back in Washington, he presided over a more formal ceremony attended by all the big names in education and politics. "I will never do anything in my entire life," LBJ said, "now or in the future, that excites me more, or benefits the nation I serve more, or makes the land and all of its people better and wiser and stronger, or anything that I think means more to freedom and justice in the world than what we have done with this education bill."[46] He quoted Thomas Jefferson: "Preach, my dear sir, a crusade against ignorance; establish and improve the law for educating the common people."[47]

ESEA was only the first of a two-pronged attack on the nation's educational problems. The second was the Higher Education Act of 1965. The nation's twenty-three hundred institutions of higher education were straining to accommodate the children of the World War II generation. Libraries at 50 percent of the four-year and 82 percent of the two-year institutions failed to meet minimum standards of books per student. Qualified children from poor families could not afford to go to college, or if they did, they could not afford to stay. As of 1960, 78 percent of high school graduates from families with incomes over $12,000 attended college; only 33 percent from families with incomes under

$3,000 did so. Twenty-two percent of college students dropped out during their first year; the overriding reason was financial distress. There would be no public-parochial debate during deliberations on the higher education bill. Most of the nation's colleges and universities had begun as private, faith-based entities, and in 1960, 41 percent still were. It would make no sense at all to starve one and feed the other when all were bulging at the seams and the United States was involved in a cold war with the forces of international communism.

The Higher Education Act of 1965 provided funds to colleges and universities to develop programs focusing on housing, poverty, health, and other public interest areas. It proposed to pump millions of dollars into long-neglected libraries. The heart of the bill, however, comprised scholarships, low-interest loans, and work-study programs for lower-income students. In addition, any student enrolled full time in an accredited postsecondary institution would be eligible to borrow without regard to need up to $1,500 per academic year to a limit of $7,500. President Johnson signed the Higher Education Act in the Strahan Gymnasium at Southwest Texas State College in San Marcos on November 8, 1965. "I shall never forget the faces of the boys and girls . . . [at that] little Welhausen Mexican school . . . and the pain of knowing then that college was closed to practically every one of those children because they were too poor." [48]

ESEA and the Higher Education Act were universal in design, but Johnson had one group chiefly in mind. "It's the Negroes," he had exclaimed to Hubert Humphrey. "Now, by God, they can't work in a filling station and put water in a radiator unless they can read and write. Because they've got to go and punch their cash register, and they don't know which one to punch. They've got to take a check, and they don't know which one to cash. They've got to take a credit card, and they can't pull the numbers." [49] But of course, federal aid to education did not end poverty, and it did not prove to be the escape route for children born in inner-city ghettoes. The culture of poverty was too complex. The ESEA did not wind up helping poor students exclusively or even overwhelmingly. Historian Allen Matusow quotes a 1977 study showing that "nearly two-thirds of the students in programs funded by Title I were not poor; more than half were not even low achievers; and 40 percent were neither poor nor low achieving." [50]

Nevertheless, ESEA was a historic piece of legislation and of monumental importance to the nation. Education took its place alongside national defense as an overriding concern of the federal government. The measure facilitated desegregation and helped make America's colleges and universities the envy of the world and its population the most educated in history. By 1970, one out of every four college students in the United States was receiving some form of financial assistance provided by the Higher Education Act. [51] In 1993, 36 percent of Americans between the ages of twenty-five and sixty-four held college degrees.

AGAIN, Johnson chose a general program to help build broad support for the Great Society as a whole. The next jewel in the diadem would be Medicare, a system of health insurance for elderly Americans. Of all the advanced industrial democracies in the 1960s, only the United States did not have in place a government program to protect the elderly from the often catastrophic costs of health care. Britain, France, Sweden, and Denmark all boasted either a nationalized health system or national health insurance. There were no federally or state-supported nursing homes, no help for aged Americans afflicted with cancer, diabetes, heart disease, and stroke who did not have private means. In 1934, FDR had suggested including a program of national health insurance in the Social Security Act but had backed off in the face of opposition from the American Medical Association. In 1939, liberal Democrats had sponsored legislation to create a system of national health insurance, but it had gotten nowhere. Harry Truman included plans for a national health insurance program in the Fair Deal, but Robert Taft and the conservative coalition sided with the AMA and private insurance companies, and the man from Missouri was stymied.[52]

In 1959, George Reedy had warned his boss that the absence of government-supported health care for the aged was a national disgrace and would only get worse. "In 1900," he noted, "there were three million people in this country over sixty-five. Today, the number is close to fifteen million, and in ten years there will be about twenty-one million . . . Somehow, the problem must be dramatized in some way so that Americans will know that the problem of the aging amounts to a collective responsibility. America is no longer a nation of simple pioneer folk in which grandmother and grandfather can spend their declining years in a log cabin doing odd jobs and taking care of the grandchildren."[53] LBJ was innately empathetic with the afflicted, particular those who were dependent. Memories of his paralyzed and wheelchair-ridden grandmother who had had to live with him and his family still haunted him. More than this, however, LBJ wanted to define health care—like education, a healthy diet, and adequate shelter—as a basic right. He remembered discussing education and the Constitution in a college theme; he received an F, he recalled. The Constitution said nothing about education—or health care. But they were implied, Johnson would insist. Like trial by jury and freedom of speech, he told aide Harry Middleton, adequate health care ought to be a federal guarantee: "A person who comes into birth in this country ought to have those rights, whatever the price is."[54] In November 1964, on the eve of the election, when a reporter asked if a health insurance bill for the aged would be a priority if he were elected, LBJ replied, "Just top of the list."[55]

In 1961, JFK had asked Wilbur Cohen, long-time administrator of the original Social Security System, who was then teaching at the University of Michigan, to head his task force on health and Social Security. What Cohen and his colleagues came up with was a scheme of contributory medical insurance for the nearly 14.8 million Americans receiving Old-Age Survivors and Disability Insurance—Social Security. The AMA responded by launching the biggest and costliest lobbying campaign in American history. Seventy publicists toiled away at the organization's Chicago office, and no fewer then twenty-three lobbyists patroled Capitol Hill. The AMA spent more than $50 million on the effort. In their campaign, doctors were ably and liberally assisted by the private insurance industry. While they eyed their incomes and profit statements nervously, physicians and insurance executives cried that Medicare would undermine individual initiative and open the door to socialized medicine, another fateful step in the liberal drive to convert America into a welfare state. The third roadblock in Medicare's path was Congressman Wilbur Mills (D-Arkansas), chair of the powerful House Ways and Means Committee, who opposed the legislation for his own reasons. Thus was Medicare still languishing when LBJ came to the presidency that day in late November 1963.

Mills was a stocky man of average height, noted, like Robert McNamara, for his slicked-back hair and steel-rimmed glasses. He was the son of a small-town merchant and had attended Hendrix College, where he so excelled in his studies that he was able to gain entry to Harvard Law School. In 1934 he was admitted to the Arkansas Bar and four years later was elected to Congress to represent the Second District, which included the Ozark Mountain region in the northwest, an area of small farms in the north-central part of the state, and the Mississippi Delta to the east. His district was poor and thinly populated. Labor unions were virtually nonexistent.[56] Sam Rayburn took young Mills under his wing, taught him the traditions and procedures of the House, and helped him land a seat on Ways and Means. The Arkansan was not a reactionary, but a conservative New Dealer. Despite representing a region that clung tenaciously to the nineteenth century, Mills believed that in a modern society, order and justice required that the federal government play an active role, protecting the defenseless, regulating the economy, and guarding the nation's security. "Do not be misled," he said in 1948, "economic policies of Government both at home and in international relations determine to a great extent these periods of prosperity and depression."[57] Yet Mills was obsessed with maintaining the fiscal integrity of existing government programs, especially Social Security. "In the Social Security field," Wilbur Cohen observed, "Mr. Mills is probably the only man out of the five hundred and thirty five people in Congress who . . . is completely conversant with the basis for making the actuarial estimates and all of the factors that enter into it."[58] Mills was not opposed to the notion of health care for the aged, but he believed that the proposal under consideration would discredit and/or bankrupt Social Security. Existing benefits under Social Security were cash payments based on payroll deductions and employer contributions. These payments could be predicted and controlled. Under the existing Medicare proposal, Social Security was to pay for medical services the cost of which could neither be predicted nor controlled. Experts told him that the most workers would agree to have withheld from their paychecks without rebelling was 10 percent. Mills could see Medicare producing costs that would spin out of control.

Throughout 1964, Wilbur Cohen barely left Mills's side. He read the transcripts of the chairman's speeches, quipped Cohen's biographer, "the way that Sinologists studied statements from Mao."[59] On the surface, the two men seemed not at all compatible. Cohen, the son of Jewish immigrants, had attended the University of Wisconsin and its Experimental College. There he had read Lincoln Steffens and Henry Adams and flirted with socialism. "I come from a tradition of social reform in Wisconsin under the La Follettes and under Professor John R. Commons, which brought me into the New Deal," he later said of himself."[60] Yet, both men had great respect for each other. "He is a man of great capacity and a man of great ability, and the most important part of that is that he has the respect of his colleagues in Congress," Cohen said of Mills.[61] Despite their excellent working relationship, the two Wilburs were not able to put together a satisfactory Medicare compromise before the election. "Now they've [Republicans and the AMA] got us screwed on Medicare," Johnson told House Majority Leader Carl Albert. "We're screwed good."[62]

Then came the election of 1964, with LBJ's sweeping mandate and the additions to the already large Democratic majority in the House. Public opinion polls were showing a two-to-one margin in favor of some type of national medical insurance for the aged. For many middle-class families, matters had reached the point where they had to choose between proper medical care for aged parents and college for their children. Johnson appealed to Mills. "If you can get something you can possibly live with and defend," he told the chairman of Ways and Means, "that these people will not kick over the bucket with, it'll mean more than all the bills we've passed put together and it'll mean more to posterity and to you and to me."[63] The morning following the election, Mills informed reporters that he "would be receptive to a Medicare proposal in the upcoming session."[64] Desperate, the AMA backed a bill that it dubbed Eldercare. Persons over sixty-five could purchase Blue Cross/Blue Shield or commercial insurance by paying all or none of the cost depending on their income. The expense would be borne by the states and the federal government. Then on February 4, 1965, Republican John Byrnes introduced "Bettercare," a plan that would cover hospital and doctor bills as well as selected patient services. The government would pay two-thirds of the cost from the general fund and the remainder would be defrayed by premium payments scaled to income. To Wilbur Cohen's horror, Mills told Byrnes that he liked the idea behind Bettercare.[65] He then proposed what he called a "three-layer cake." The bottom layer would be a plan to take comprehensive care of those without means. Medicare would be the middle layer, providing hospital care for those covered by Social Security. Topping off the confection would be Bettercare, a voluntary system to defray the cost of doctor bills. Cohen was stunned—and delighted. No sooner had Mills made his proposal than everyone in the committee room knew "that it was all over," said one committee member. "The rest would be details. In thirty seconds, a $2 billion bill was launched, and the greatest departure in the social security laws in thirty years was brought about."[66] The subsequent "debate" in the House lasted one day. When Mills stepped to the podium to present his plan, he received a standing ovation from both sides of the aisle. The House passed the three-layer cake by a vote of 313 to 115.

On the morning of March 26, after Mills's committee had voted out the Social Security Amendments Act of 1965 (Medicare), LBJ summoned the congressional leadership of both houses to the White House for a discussion of the measure. Unbeknown to his guests, Johnson had arranged for television coverage. Before the cameras LBJ praised Mills and his three-tiered plan and then turned to the venerable Harry Byrd, chairman of the Senate Finance Committee and an archenemy of Medicare. "Senator Byrd, would you care to make an observation?" Startled, the conservative Virginian said he had not studied the measure but was prepared to hold hearings on it. "And you have nothing that you know of that would prevent that coming about in reasonable time?" "No," said Byrd quietly. "So when the House acts and it is referred to the Senate Finance Committee, you will arrange for prompt hearings." "Yes," Byrd replied, even more quietly.[67] As he was leaving, the congressman observed wryly to reporters that if he had known he was going to be on television, he would have dressed more formally. Byrd was as good as his word. Hearings proceeded without a hitch, and on July 9 the Senate approved the amendments to the Social Security Act of 1965 creating Medicare and Medicaid by a vote of sixty-eight to twenty-one.[68] "Biggest Change Since the New Deal," trumpeted *Newsweek's* headline.[69] Johnson was ecstatic. "[This] gives your boys [in Congress] something to run on if you'll just put out that propaganda," he chortled to Larry O'Brien. "That they've done more than they did in Roosevelt's Hundred Days."[70]

There was one final hurdle to be cleared. Some people feared that the AMA might refuse to participate in Medicare and Medicaid. The Ohio Medical Association, representing ten thousand physicians, had already adopted a resolution to boycott the new programs. When, subsequently, some twenty-five thousand doctors gathered in New York on June 20 for the annual AMA convention, the House of Delegates directed its officers to meet with the president to discuss implementation of the legislation. Shortly before the gathering was to take place, AFL-CIO president George Meany called to express his concern. Johnson asked him, "George, have you ever fed chickens?" "No," Meany answered. "Well," the president said, "chickens are real dumb. They eat and eat and eat and never stop. Why they start shitting at the same time they're eating, and before you know it, they're knee-deep in their own shit. Well, the AMA's the same. They've been eating and eating nonstop and now they're knee-deep in their own shit and everybody knows it. They won't be able to stop anything."[71]

On June 29, the AMA leadership assembled in the West Wing and were promptly given a large dose of the Johnson treatment. LBJ began by saying what wonderful people doctors were, recalling how the local physician in Johnson City had made numerous house calls to treat his ailing father. He stood and stretched; they stood. He sat. They sat. LBJ then delivered a moving statement about "this great nation and its obligation to those who had helped make it great and who were now old and sick and helpless through no fault of their own." He stood again. They stood. He sat, and they followed suit, now perfectly clear as to who was in control.[72] Suddenly Johnson brought up Vietnam. Would the AMA help in arranging for physician volunteers to serve for short periods in that country to help the civilian population gain a modicum of health? "Your country needs your help. Your President needs your help." In unison, the AMA officials said that they would be glad to participate. "Get the press in here," Johnson shouted to a lieutenant. To the journalists, the president announced the AMA's commitment to help in Vietnam and praised their patriotism. One of the reporters asked if the AMA was going to boycott Medicare. Johnson piped up with mock indignity: "These men are going to get doctors to go to Vietnam where they might be killed. Medicare is the law of the land. Of course, they'll support the law of the land. Tell him," LBJ said, turning to the head of the delegation. That worthy nodded and said, "We are, after all, law-abiding citizens, and we have every intention of obeying the new law." A few weeks later, the AMA announced its intention to support Medicare.[73]

"The application of Medicare to twenty million people on July 1 was perhaps the biggest single governmental operation since D-Day in Europe during World War II," Wilbur Cohen subsequently observed.[74] By early May 1966, 16.8 million elderly, 88 percent of those eligible, had voluntarily enrolled for medical insurance. By that date, over 90 percent of the nation's accredited hospitals and more than 80 percent of nonaccredited facilities had applied for participation. Over the years, Medicare and Medicaid transformed the lives of millions of American families. The impoverished, elderly, and dependent no longer had to go without health care; middle-class families no longer had to choose between college for their children and proper medical care for their grandparents. But Wilbur Mills had been right to be worried. There were no effective controls on costs. Hospitals and physicians were entitled to be reimbursed for reasonable costs, which were whatever hospitals and physicians said they were. Total Medicare expenditures amounted to $3.5 billion in the first year of the program; by 1993 total costs had risen to $144 billion, and Americans were spending approximately 15 percent of the gross national income on health care.[75]

As was true of many of the Great Society measures, Medicare was a civil rights as well as a health care bill. In those hospitals and doctors' offices that participated, "colored" and "white" signs disappeared from waiting rooms, restrooms, and water fountains. Harry McPherson remembered that in the days following passage of the Act, the White House was deluged with letters and telegrams from outraged southerners. Noting that federal law required hospitals and clinics not to discriminate and to desegregate to receive federal funds, one correspondent told the president, "And they won't Lyndon. You know that. Do you want to be responsible for closing the St. Francis Hospital in Biloxi, Mississippi? That's what will happen if you put this thing into effect . . . Doctors won't treat the coloreds, and the nurses won't treat them."[76] It was a great gamble, McPherson recalled. "Whatever he decided," he said of the president, "thousands of people, either the elderly or the blacks, might have been deprived of hospitalization. It was an excruciating decision to make, but he made it. Comply. And they did."[77]

CHAPTER 28

THE CRUX OF THE MATTER

T HE CAMPAIGN FOR REFORM IN EDUCATION AND
health care unfolded in the midst of the ongoing struggle by black
Americans to achieve political power in the South. The 1954
Brown decision had opened the door to school integration, and the
Civil Rights Act of 1964 had outlawed Jim Crow policies in parks, theaters, hotels, and public transportation. But in six southern states—Alabama, Georgia,
Louisiana, Mississippi, South Carolina, and Virginia,—the vast majority of
blacks still could not vote.[1] As part of the Freedom Summer Project of 1964, the
Council of Federated Organizations and SNCC had established freedom
schools in Mississippi to build support for the Mississippi Freedom Democratic
party. More than eighty thousand black Mississippians had voted for the MFDP
delegation that traveled to Atlantic City. But that political process had taken
place outside the regular voting mechanism, still dominated by the white power
structure and still closed to African Americans. Only 6 and 19 percent, respectively, of voting-age blacks were on the rolls in Mississippi and Alabama.[2] In
some counties in those two states in which the majority of residents were black,
not a single one was registered to vote. White registrars in league with local
sheriffs used the poll tax and literacy tests to discourage black voting, but if these
did not suffice, those seeking to exercise the franchise could be fired from their
jobs, arrested on trumped up charges, or simply beaten up.

Given his philosophy and experience, LBJ believed that the vote was everything. In a remarkable conversation with Roy Wilkins of the NAACP, Johnson
spelled out his faith in democracy. His only hope for really empowering his people, LBJ told the civil rights leader, was to get behind the movement for mass
enfranchisement and registration for poor whites as well as blacks. "I know you
get disheartened," he told Wilkins,

and I do, and you think that there is no use trying to get an illiterate [white] truck driver and tell him what is best for him because he has been mistreated—and how he will not cooperate and so forth. I feel that way every day. But when the chips are down and you hurt a man and you whip him, chain him and handcuff him and make the vox populi go to the polls, he has a better smell and better sense of values and knows better what is better for the country than [banker-turned-diplomat] John Mc-Cloy . . . This old farmer that rides looking at the back end of the mule on the cultivator all day long—he just sits there and thinks. It is his boy that is in Viet Nam, his sister that is out of a job, his brother-in-law that got his car repossessed—and somehow or other, they just add up and they will do what is right . . . I will resign my office twelve months from now if I am not right, you will see the people [blacks] come into power in every Southern state if you will let them vote . . . Everyone of these states that you consider the worst ones in the Union will wind up being the best.[3]

"Now let's just go register," Johnson told Wilkins, "and anybody that is not registered is not patriotic."[4] In his January 1965 State of the Union address, the president informed lawmakers that he was going to press for the elimination of "every remaining obstacle to the right and the opportunity to vote." Privately he asked Nicholas Katzenbach, the acting attorney general, to draft legislation that would enforce the constitutional guarantee of the right of every adult American to cast a ballot.[5]

Working closely with LBJ to secure the franchise for black Americans was Martin Luther King. From the beginning, the alliance was an uneasy one. Throughout his political career, LBJ had preferred to deal with black leaders such as A. Philip Randolph, Roy Wilkins, Whitney Young, and even Adam Clayton Powell.[6] They were people from the world of politics, or they were associated with interest groups who sought protection and power in the political arena. He had leverage with them; they were subject to deal making and compromise. They seemed willing to trust his superb sense of political timing and his prioritizing. Not so Martin King. The head of the SCLC was both an intellectual and a spiritual leader. His and Johnson's values were similar, but they relied on dramatically different means for putting those values into action. Like William Lloyd Garrison, Martin Luther King lived in the tension between conscience and law. "Civil disobedience presupposes that conscience must obey not statutory or constitutional law but a higher moral law," historian David Burner has observed.[7] In the South, King and his associates realized that the law was the bulwark of injustice and thus morally invalid in many cases. Consequently, King deliberately flouted the law and went to jail, and he encouraged others, including children, to do the same. During the debate over the 1964 Civil Rights Act, he had told his lieutenants that he was going on a hunger strike. He would tell the nation, "Either you stop the filibuster and pass the Civil Rights Bill . . . Or let me die."[8] Johnson valued the parliamentary process, the orderly working of democracy, as much as the social justice that the system was supposed to produce. He believed in this sense that means and ends were inseparable. Demonstrations, deliberate violation of the law, the politics of confrontation, all of which King and the SCLC practiced, made LBJ extremely uncomfortable. Confrontation could easily spiral out of control into violence, black rage, white backlash, and even, ultimately, racial war. At the same time, LBJ understood the political value of demonstrations and sit-ins; he realized that they created the energy necessary for reform. Moreover, he recognized that the laws that the white power structure in the South were trying to enforce were unconstitutional.

There was also the religious dimension. Martin King was first and foremost a Christian minister, a preacher, a spiritual leader. As a mass movement, the Second Reconstruction was in no small part an evangelical religious crusade.[9] Johnson acknowledged the validity of prophets and preachers, but the world in which they lived was alien to him. Out of faith and an experience of the divine came social values, and it was proper at times to invoke religion in behalf of social justice in the rhetoric of politics, but Johnson feared a world in which religion transcended law and politics. In this he was not unlike other liberals of his day. The Schlesingers, Galbraiths, and Lippmanns were ambivalent about civil disobedience and social action based on faith and testimony. Liberals felt most at home in the ordered world of courts and laws, of science and universities; the nonviolence practiced by King and his followers was rooted in the southern black evangelical church, with all its fervent spirituality and emotion.[10] Unlike many liberals, LBJ was not a secular humanist, but he believed that morality and religion must be harnessed to and not pitted against the existing order. For his part, King understood and appreciated Johnson, but unlike Wilkins and Young, insisted on holding him at arms' length. In his recorded conversations with the president, King is cordial but formal and restrained. If the civil rights game had been played solely by Lyndon Johnson's rules, King believed, the Second Reconstruction would have died aborning.

The relationship between King and Johnson was further complicated by the machinations of J. Edgar Hoover. The FBI director was obsessively protective of the Bureau's reputation. Martin Luther King's name first came across his desk on a letter to the incoming Kennedy administration that called for a more integrated FBI; the agency had virtually no black employees other than janitors and maids. Hoover, who thought blacks unworthy of the Bureau, was indignant. Then, in 1962 King, when asked why he thought the FBI had not arrested whites who had openly assaulted nonviolent protesters in Albany, Georgia, speculated that the local FBI agents were white southerners who were culturally and emotionally linked to local racists.[11] In August 1963, the FBI marked King internally as "the most dangerous Negro to the future in this nation," and Hoover persuaded Bobby Kennedy to authorize wiretaps of King's home and his SCLC offices in Atlanta and New York.[12]

In December 1963, the FBI began delivering massive amounts of raw data to the White House on a variety of subjects; J. Edgar Hoover thought the information might be "of interest" to the new president. These were the famous "raw files" consisting of uncorroborated secondhand information, but also excerpts from wiretaps that, though spun by the Bureau, still provided valuable political intelligence. These reports were for LBJ's eyes only and were kept in a safe by Mildred Stegall, Walter Jenkins's secretary. Among the communications were special memos signed by Hoover himself designed to portray Martin Luther King as dangerously unstable and a tool of communists who had thoroughly infiltrated the civil rights movement. Every communication ended with a paragraph listing the "communist credentials" of King's top aides. A March 9, 1964, letter was typical: "As of July, 1963, [Stanley] Levinson [adviser and fund-raiser for King] was a secret member of the Communist Party, USA. [Clarence] Jones [another King aide] has been identified as a person in a position of leadership in the Labor Youth League . . . designated as subversive pursuant to Executive Order 10450 . . . [Bayard] Rustin has admitted joining the Young Communist League in 1936." [13]

As he turned to confront civil rights, the most compelling and potentially divisive issue facing America, Johnson was chilled by the knowledge that Hoover and the FBI were waiting in the wings, ready to provide the Dixie Association with intelligence, real or manufactured, that the Second Reconstruction was nothing more than a Trojan horse for the Communist International and Martin Luther King nothing less than a stooge of the Kremlin. Matters were further complicated by the fact that the Justice Department had to rely almost entirely on the Bureau to investigate civil rights crimes and gather the evidence necessary to bring the guilty to justice. In its criticism of the Bureau, an increasingly enraged black leadership might push Hoover into open alliance with Russell and Eastland. Conversely, if the federal government did not legislate equality and protection for black Americans and then protect them in the exercise of those rights, it would deliver the movement into the hands of extremists. The line he would have to walk, LBJ perceived, would have to be fine indeed.

Then, in early 1964, the FBI's campaign against King reached a new low. On the night of January 6, agents, with the cooperation of the management of the Willard Hotel in Washington, installed bugs in King's suite. Following a day of business, the civil rights leader and several of his assistants returned to the hotel room. At least two women were already there. The FBI recording machines picked up the sounds of clinking glasses and cocktail party conversation. As the hours passed the gathering became more lively, eventually resulting in group sex. At one point, King's voice could be heard above the others: "I'm not a Negro tonight!" [14] Upon hearing the tapes, Hoover was both appalled and ecstatic. "King is a 'tom cat' with obsessive, degenerate sexual urges," the director wrote in a memo on the incident. If being a "communist dupe" was not enough to discredit the civil rights leader and undermine his position as America's preeminent civil rights leader, perhaps evidence of sexual "perversion" was. In February, Deke DeLoach delivered the FBI's voluminous file on King and his associates to the White House.

To Hoover's consternation, LBJ observed that he knew he could trust the agency to ensure that the dirt on the civil rights leader did not become public, and he proceeded to meet with King, Wilkins, and Young to plot strategy to get the public accommodations bill through Congress. LBJ was hardly one to hold nonmonogamous activity against another man.[15] When Whitney Young heard a rumor of the existence of the King sex tapes and pictures, he went directly to Johnson to ask if they were true. The president said, "Yes, it's true." Young asked to see some of the evidence, and LBJ obliged. Appalled, the civil rights leader said to Johnson, "This is terrible. You've got to do something. What are you going to do about it?" Meaning, what was the president going to do about reining in the FBI? Johnson replied, "Well, what are you going to do about it? You're the civil rights leader!" Meaning, what was Young going to do to force King to be more discreet?[16]

On December 18, 1964, the Johnsons had welcomed Martin and Coretta King to the White House following their return from the Noble prize festivities in Oslo. In his acceptance speech, King had declared, "All that I have said boils down to the point of affirming that mankind's survival is dependent upon man's ability to solve the problems of racial injustice, poverty and war." LBJ could not have put it more succinctly.[17] The two men were in total agreement concerning the next great goal of the civil rights movement: voting rights. Where they differed was on timing and tactics. In January 1965 in Selma, Alabama, King addressed a cheering crowd of several hundred. "Today marks the beginning of a determined, organized, mobilized campaign to get the right to vote everywhere in Alabama," he declared. "If we are refused, we will appeal to Governor George Wallace. If he refuses to listen, we will appeal to the legislature. If they don't listen, we will appeal to the conscience of the Congress . . . We must be ready to march. We must be ready to go to jail by the thousands . . . Our cry to the state of Alabama is a simple one. Give us the ballot!"[18] What King wanted was an ironclad national voting rights bill. So did LBJ, but he was not sure it could or should be done in 1965. The political and racial waters were still roiled from the fight over the Civil Rights Act of 1964. Johnson was in the process of placing the main components of the Great Society program before Congress, and he was afraid another major debate over civil rights would polarize the House and Senate and bring his beloved reform program to a halt.

LBJ also continued to see himself as the hope of the white South, segregationists as well as liberals. "We've got to have some understanding," he told Ed Clark, an old Austin friend. "We've got to have some leadership; we've got to have some sympathy; we've got to have some kindness. I called them in South Carolina yesterday and Georgia and told them that as long as I was in the White House the door would be open to them and they would be treated with respect . . . I love Alabama and I love Mississippi and I'm going to tell 'em so and they can tell me to hell with you if they want to," but in the end they would come around, he said. "We've got to educate 'em [white southerners] and you can't be putting 'em off by themselves," he declared following his victory in the 1964 election. "That creates a juvenile problem right off the bat. The first thing that happens the sociologists say is that . . . you develop an inferiority complex and the rest of your life you're hitting at people when you think they're going to strike you even when they're not."[19] Indeed, it may have been that domestically, LBJ's greatest impact was on white southerners. "I ran for governor in 1958," Buford Ellington recalled, "and was elected on an anti–civil rights stand here in Tennessee, because I just couldn't bring it to my mind that anybody had any business telling us what we had to do in our state. Yet in less than two years I was traveling the country for this man, trying to help him in his fight to bring it about."[20]

Martin Luther King, too, was interested in redeeming the white South, but he was determined to do it sooner rather than later and even if the recipients of his beneficence had to be dragged to grace kicking and screaming. Montgomery civil rights leader Reverend James Bevel was named to head a statewide voting rights campaign that would begin in Selma. Large numbers of blacks would appear at the courthouse on registration days, and there would be marches and demonstrations until all were registered. Selma, a city of some twenty-nine thousand, was still entirely segregated in 1965. The *Brown* decision and the 1964 Civil Rights Act seemed to have made no impression at all. Parks, restaurants, schools, water fountains, public restrooms—all were segregated. In Dallas County, of which Selma was the county seat, there were 14,400 whites and 15,115 blacks of voting age. Exactly 156 African Americans, or 1 percent, were registered. Chief enforcer of Jim Crow in Dallas County was Sheriff Jim Clark, the stereotypical southern law officer, complete with paunch, jowls, campaign hat, pistol, and cattle prod. He had at his command not only his deputies and the Selma police but also white "posses," whose members salivated at the thought of forcibly disbanding marches and breaking up demonstrations. The mayor, Joe T. Smitherman, was somewhat more progressive. He felt the sight of police dogs and water hoses being used against black women and children was not conducive to economic development, but he was a segregationist, and his hold over Clark was quite tenuous. In league with Clark was Circuit Judge James Hare, an amateur anthropologist who believed that Alabama blacks were particularly retrograde because they were descended from the Ibo tribesmen of Nigeria and had no Berber (Arab) blood.[21] Presiding over this motley crew was Governor George Corley Wallace, who was just as determined to stand in the schoolhouse door as always.

Though Bevel was the principal organizer for the Selma voting rights effort, King planned to be its chief symbol. Judge Hare had issued a decree forbidding some fifty named individuals and fifteen organizations from holding meetings of more than three persons. Among other things, King intended to convene gatherings in defiance of the order and get himself arrested. Beginning Monday,

January 18, he led waves of local blacks to the courthouse to register, where they were confronted by Clark and ordered to disperse. They did, but subsequently returned. The demonstrators were duly arrested, made bail, and then returned again. As the organizers had anticipated, Clark's temper quickly frayed. He and his officers began to rough up the marchers. In the second week of the demonstrations, Clark shoved Mrs. Annie Lee Cooper, a dignified, sturdy woman, who hit him in the face. As he staggered back, she delivered two more punches, kicking him in the groin. Enraged, Clark got up and knocked the woman down and jumped on top of her, his baton in hand. The next morning that picture appeared on the front page of the *New York Times.* On February 1, the next regular registration day, King was arrested and thrown in jail.[22]

LBJ and Nick Katzenbach, meanwhile, were monitoring events closely in Washington. Justice had dispatched trouble-shooter John Doar to the scene to try to keep a lid on things. The first week in February, he persuaded U.S. District Judge Daniel Thomas to issue an order suspending Alabama's literacy test and demanding that Selma speed up registration. King was still not satisfied. From jail, using his aide Andrew Young as a messenger, he asked LBJ to send a personal representative to Selma, declare his support for voting rights in Alabama, and use his office and his influence with Congress to see that those rights were realized.[23] The day after King's release from jail, the White House announced that it was going to send a voting rights bill to Congress before the end of 1965.[24] On February 9, King traveled to Washington to meet with Katzenbach, Humphrey, and a somewhat reluctant LBJ.[25] Emerging from the chat, King assured reporters of the president's commitment to voting rights, but he returned to Alabama in a fairly pessimistic mood. The state, the nation, and the president would need additional prodding, he had concluded.

King found tempers were on the rise in Selma. Police had shot and killed a young demonstrator, Jimmie Lee Jackson, who was planning a march to protest the arrest of a local SCLC leader in the nearby town of Marion. King delivered a moving, fiery eulogy at the interment, and James Bevel announced that there would be a march from Selma to Montgomery, the state capital, situated some fifty-four miles to the east on Highway 80. The Reverend King would lead the way and present petitions to Governor Wallace and the state legislature demanding that all voting-age Alabamans be allowed to cast their ballot. The march would get under way on Sunday, March 7. On the evening before the demonstration, word came that Governor Wallace had declared the event to be an unauthorized assembly and dangerous to the public order. He ordered Albert J. Lingo, head of the Alabama State Troopers, to assemble just off the Edmund Pettus Bridge, which arched Highway 80 over the Alabama River east of Selma, and use whatever means necessary to stop the march. Wallace had personally recruited Lingo, who was known as "hell on niggers."[26]

As the five hundred or so marchers crossed the Pettus Bridge, they came face to face with Major John Cloud and his contingent of state troopers. Lurking behind them were Sheriff Clark and his deputies. Whites lined the south side of the road. Major Cloud ordered the marchers to disperse. When they did not, his troopers, many on horseback, charged. Several fired teargas canisters into the crowd. As the knot of demonstrators broke and ran for town, state police rode them to the ground, where dismounted officers and Clark's men beat them with billyclubs, kicked, and stomped them. The next day a vivid, blow-by-blow account of what came to be known as "Bloody Sunday" appeared on the front page of the *New York Times*.[27] ABC interrupted its regularly scheduled programming that night to present a long televised report on the brutality.[28] King immediately announced that the marchers would try again on Tuesday. He called for sympathetic volunteers from around the country to come and join the column. Stirred by images of violence on television and in the newspapers, hundreds responded.

As he had feared, LBJ was caught between King and the civil rights activists on the one hand and Wallace and the segregationist power structure in Alabama on the other. On the scene, John Doar, LeRoy Collins, head of the Federal Mediation Service, and Buford Ellington tried to work out a compromise. Somewhat ironically, Wallace wanted federal intervention. If LBJ was forced to nationalize the Alabama National Guard and send the troops in, Wallace could claim to bitter-end segregationists that he had been overwhelmed by a greater force. "This damned little Wallace!" Lister Hill, the other senator from Alabama and a friend of Johnson's, told the president. "That's a hell of a decision to have to make, because when you move in there, the people down home are going to think, My God, he [LBJ] just moved in there and took over for this King!"[29] And LBJ most certainly did not want to send an occupying force to Alabama. Neither did his advisers. At the same time, he and Katzenbach seriously considered arresting both Clark and Lingo for violating the civil rights of the marchers. "Hell, we've got three cases against Sheriff Clark now," Katzenbach said.[30]

Meanwhile, in Selma, the Reverend James Reeb, a Unitarian minister working for the American Friends Service Committee in Boston who had flown to Selma to march with King, was assaulted along with two other white ministers by four thugs. One of them shattered Reeb's skull with a three-foot-long bludgeon. He died in a Birmingham hospital on Thursday evening. King, who confided to Doar and Katzenbach that he was in fear for his life, more so than usual, led some two thousand marchers across the Pettus Bridge the next day. The procession halted before Lingo, Clark, and their massed forces. King led the group in singing "We Shall Overcome," the group knelt in silent prayer for several moments, and then got up and walked back into town. King put everyone on notice, however, that he was still determined to march to Montgomery.

In an effort to retake the initiative from King and Johnson, Wallace asked for a summit meeting with the president. He should have been alarmed by the alacrity with which LBJ accepted. In fact, the president had already decided to invite the governor to the White House when he received Wallace's request.[31] Just before noon on February 13, a smiling Johnson welcomed Wallace and his attorney general, Seymore Trammel, to the Oval Office. The president had the

diminutive Wallace sit in the large overstuffed sofa while he occupied the rocking chair opposite, pulled so close that when he leaned forward his nose nearly
touched the top of the governor's head. It seemed to him, Johnson offered in a
friendly voice, that all the demonstrators wanted was the right to vote. "You cannot deal with street revolutionaries," Wallace replied sternly, "you can never satisfy them . . . First, it is a front seat on a bus; next, it's a takeover of parks; then
it's public schools; then it's voting rights; then it's jobs; then it's distribution of
wealth without work."[32] Johnson pulled closer, reached over, and gripped
Wallace's knee and launched into an hour-long monologue on his vision of a
just and prosperous America. "You can be a part of that," he kept saying. Stop
"looking back to 1865 and start planning for 2065." As Wallace seem to shrink,
Trammel tried to interrupt, invoking "the growing menace of the Communist
demonstrators in Alabama." Johnson turned slowly. "He looked at me like I was
some kind of dog mess," remembered Trammel. Johnson thrust a pencil and
tablet in his hands and told him to take notes. Why, oh, why was Wallace abandoning his liberal roots? "Why are you off on this black thing? You ought to be
down there calling for help for Aunt Susie in the nursing home." Then he went
to the crux of the matter. "Why don't you let the niggers vote?" Wallace
protested that he had no power over county registrars. Johnson suddenly stiff-
ened. "Don't you shit me, George Wallace," he said.[33] Rising, Johnson put both
hands on the back of the sofa, leaned over Wallace, and said, "George, you're
fucking over your president. Why are you fucking over your president?"[34]

   After three hours, Wallace emerged looking like a wilted plant. In the subsequent press conference in the Rose Garden, Johnson continued to dominate.
"The Governor expressed his concern that the demonstrations which have
taken place are a threat to the peace and security of the people of Alabama," LBJ
told the more than one hundred reporters who had assembled for the occasion.
"I said that those Negro citizens of Alabama who have systematically been denied the right to register and to participate in the choice of those who govern
them should be provided the opportunity of directing national attention to their
plight . . . I am firmly convinced, as I said to the Governor a few moments ago,
that when all of the eligible Negroes of Alabama have been registered, the economic and the social injustices they have experienced throughout will be
righted, and the demonstrations, I believe, will stop."[35]

LYNDON JOHNSON WAS NOT A MAN to ignore the power of circum-
stance. His advisers and his instincts told him that the time had come for the administration to exploit the momentum created by Martin Luther King and his
followers, to lead rather than follow in the struggle for dignity and equality for
African Americans. "What the public felt on Monday [the day following Bloody
Sunday], in my opinion, was the deepest sense of outrage it has ever felt on the
civil rights question," Harry McPherson told the president. "I had dinner with
Abe Fortas Monday night. That reasonable man was for sending troops at
once."[36] On the evening of March 14, LBJ met with congressional leaders of

both parties, and the group decided on a televised presidential address to a joint session to denounce the Selma outrages and introduce his voting rights bill. With only twenty-four hours to prepare, Johnson summoned McPherson, Goodwin, Busby, Valenti, and company. "I sat with my staff for several hours," Johnson later recalled. "I described the general outline of what I wanted to say. I wanted to use every ounce of moral persuasion the Presidency held. I wanted no hedging, no equivocation. And I wanted to talk from my own heart, from my own experience."[37] According to Goodwin, he drafted the speech, but the substance and, in the end, the wording were entirely Johnson. "It was by me," he said, "but it was for and of the Lyndon Johnson I had carefully studied and come to know."[38]

As the time for LBJ's evening address approached, the Capitol and the nation sensed that something extraordinary was about to happen. The House chamber was packed. In addition to the legislators, all of the Supreme Court justices, the entire ambassadorial corps, and the cabinet were present. Even the aisles were filled, an unprecedented occurrence. The galleries were jammed with whites and blacks, some in street clothes fresh from demonstrations and others in business attire. Lady Bird and Lynda sat among them, as did J. Edgar Hoover. The entire Mississippi congressional delegation boycotted the event. Virtually all Americans were aware of the historic moment, and most had their television sets on in anticipation. At 9 P.M. Johnson entered the hall, tall, erect, smiling, making the customary handshakes as he proceeded to the podium. He wasted no time. "I speak tonight for the dignity of man and the destiny of democracy," he began in a slow melodious tone. "At times history and fate meet at a single time in a single place to shape a turning point in man's unending search for freedom," he intoned. "So it was at Lexington and Concord. So it was a century ago at Appomattox. So it was last week in Selma, Alabama."[39] Those who were there remembered almost total silence, a collective holding of breaths.

The nation had reached a moral juncture brought there by "the cries of pain and the hymns and protests of oppressed people [who] have summoned into convocation all the majesty of this great government . . . Rarely in any time does an issue lay bare the secret heart of America itself," Johnson declared, his voice rising, his pace quickening. "The issue of equal rights for American Negroes is such an issue. And should we defeat every enemy, should we double our wealth and conquer the stars, and still be unequal to this issue, then we will have failed as a people and as a nation . . . For with a country as with a person, 'What is a man profited, if he shall gain the whole world and lose his own soul.' "[40] He was interrupted by the first burst of applause, hesitant, solid, then thunderous. No president, not even Abraham Lincoln, had so forthrightly identified himself, the Constitution, and the values of the country with the cause of equal rights for African Americans. One shrewd heartland politician was finishing what another had started.

The next great step in the march to equality was a national voting rights law. He was, he said, sending to Congress immediately following his speech a special message that would put in place machinery to register black voters in areas where local officials were unwilling to do so and to provide protection to them in their exercise of the franchise. What president who took his oath of office seriously could do less? By now, LBJ's voice was inspired, rolling, ringing, a Texas version of the southern Baptist rhythm and tenor that Martin Luther King had mastered. "There is no constitutional issue here," LBJ declared. "The command of the Constitution is plain. There is no moral issue. It is wrong—deadly wrong—to deny any of your fellow Americans the right to vote in this country. There is no issue of States rights or national rights. There is only the struggle for human rights." The real heroes of the hour were the civil rights activists who were demonstrating, going to jail, and dying. "Their cause must be our cause too. Because it is not just Negroes, but really it is all of us, who must overcome the crippling legacy of bigotry and injustice."[41] And then, the president of the United States, remarkably, raised his arms over his head and proclaimed slowly, deliberately, "We—shall—overcome!" The assembled throng rose almost as one and delivered a roaring, prolonged ovation. In the galleries and on the floor, long-time laborers in the vineyard of civil rights wept openly. Watching from their homes, stunned, black Americans dared to hope that at last their dream of full citizenship might actually come true. As Lady Bird and Lynda departed the chamber, a reporter asked the president's elder daughter how she felt about the speech. "It was just like that old hymn," she said. " 'Once to every man and nation comes a moment to decide.' "[42]

Johnsonian rhetoric notwithstanding, Martin Luther King intended to keep the pressure on. Alabama was still a long way from Washington, and he sensed no softening in the attitudes of the George Wallaces, Al Lingos, and Jim Clarks of the world. On March 17, Federal District Court Judge Frank Johnson, sitting in Montgomery, issued an order sanctioning the SCLC's planned march from Selma to the capital and declaring that participants were entitled to state protection. Wallace was at last trapped. On March 18, he called the president. "These people are pouring in from all over the country," he whined. "Two days ago . . . James Forman suggested in front of all the nuns and priests that if anybody went in a café and they wouldn't serve 'em, they'd 'kick the fuckin' legs of the tables off' . . . It inflames people . . . I don't want anybody to get hurt. But . . . I don't want to be in the position of intimating that I'm asking for federal troops . . . A Negro priest yesterday asked all the patrolmen what their wives were doing, whether some of their friends could have dates with their wives. You know, trying to provoke them . . . These fifty thousand people . . . They're going to bankrupt the state." LBJ listened patiently, but remained firm. It would be much better, much less divisive if the national guard acted as state rather than federal troops. But Wallace would not give.[43]

That night, Wallace told the Alabama legislature in a televised speech that the state could not afford to activate the guard. He demanded that the president send federal authorities to Alabama. LBJ was furious. "You're dealing with a very treacherous guy," he told Buford Ellington. "He's a no good son of a bitch

... Son of a bitch! He's absolutely treacherous."[44] Later, Wallace wired the White House that he did not have the assets available to protect a march from Selma to Montgomery. Absurd, Johnson told reporters. The governor had available to him ten thousand Alabama national guardsmen, but if Wallace could not or would not call them up, he would dispatch federal troops to protect King and his fellow demonstrators.[45] The president issued orders federalizing the Alabama National Guard and dispatched a sizable contingent of regular army troops to Maxwell Air Force Base to stand by if needed. "Be sure what ever we do is measured, fitting, and adequate—like in Viet Nam," he told Katzenbach, Ellington, and Justice Department official Burke Marshall.[46]

On March 21, 392 marchers with King at their head set out on foot from Selma to Montgomery. Federalized guardsmen lined the route, and there were only minor incidents along the way. The entire march was covered by television cameras and print journalists. The trek, some fifty-four miles, took several days. It was bitterly cold at night, and King slept in a trailer that accompanied the marchers. By the time the demonstrators reached the outskirts of Montgomery, their numbers had swelled to twelve hundred, including show business celebrities Peter, Paul, and Mary; Joan Baez; Dick Gregory; Frank Sinatra; and Marlon Brando.[47] The morning after the marchers arrived, King addressed a throng of some twenty-five thousand that had gathered on the plaza in front of the state capitol. The redoubtable Wallace peeked at the proceedings from behind Venetian blinds in his office.

That night a white civil rights activist from Detroit, Viola Liuzzo, was shot in the head and killed as she drove Le Roy Moton, a young black man, back to Selma from Montgomery.[48] In his subsequent report on the incident, Hoover informed LBJ, "We found numerous needle marks indicating she had been taking dope although we can't say that definitely because she is dead." To Katzenbach he reported that Mrs. Liuzzo "was sitting very, very close to the Negro in the car . . . It had the appearance of a necking party."[49] The White House ignored Hoover's innuendoes and ordered the FBI to apprehend the perpetrators at once. In response to questions from reporters concerning the Liuzzo murder, the president described the Klan as a "hooded society of bigots."[50] The thing to do, Johnson subsequently told Katzenbach, was to turn the House Un-American Activities Committee loose on them.[51] That would spike Hoover and the segregationists' red-baiting guns.

Focus now shifted to Congress and the voting rights bill. "We needed something where you didn't have to litigate for fifteen years before you finally get . . . some relief," Deputy Attorney General Ramsey Clark said.[52] The legislation that the White House presented to the Hill on March 17 began by echoing the Fifteenth Amendment. It prohibited the denial of the right to vote on the basis of race or color. The measure invalidated "any test or device" that was used to discriminate in any federal, state, or local election in areas in which, as of November 1, 1964, fewer than 50 percent of the persons of voting age were not registered and did not vote in the presidential election. Twenty or more residents of a jurisdiction were empowered to petition the attorney general, charging that they had been denied the right to vote on the basis of race. If the complaint was validated, the Justice Department would appoint examiners to check the qualifications of voter applicants and certify them to vote if they were twenty-one or over and legal residents. Finally, no person could be denied the right to vote for failure to pay a poll tax.[53]

Even legislators of the Deep South were not willing to argue publicly that qualified individuals did not have the right to vote. Russell Long let the White House know that he was going to vote for the measure, and he predicted that he would be able to carry eleven other southern senators with him. Everett Dirksen and the Republican leadership never gave serious thought to holding hands with southern conservatives on the issue. The black vote was coming to the South, and the GOP did not want to be left out. Led by Robert Kennedy, liberals in the Senate made a brief but unsuccessful attempt to toughen the administration's measure by outlawing the poll tax altogether.[54] Johnson, of course, believed that the move was just one more attempt by his archrival and the liberals to upstage and embarrass him.[55] The Voting Rights Act of 1965 passed the Senate by a vote of seventy-seven to nineteen. The majority included five southern and border state Democrats. The House followed suit on July 9 by a vote of 333 to 85. Among the majority were thirty-three Democrats and three Republicans from the South. On August 6, 1965, LBJ proudly presided over a televised signing ceremony in the rotunda of the Capitol.[56]

Throughout the fall and indeed for the remainder of his administration, LBJ badgered Justice, local officials, and civil rights leaders to pursue voter registration relentlessly. "I will go to any meeting," he told Roy Wilkins. "I will issue any proclamations. I will go to Cleveland. I will go to Huntsville. I will go to Birmingham or Little Rock. And let's just say 'let every person in this State vote' . . . I don't care if you are Mexican, American, Negro, Baptist, Catholic, Jew—just vote. Questions of race and religion would then disappear; with every person voting his best interests, social justice would inevitably follow and it would be based on democracy, on 'home rule' rather than federal edict."[57]

By July 14, 1965, federal agencies had identified eight counties each in Alabama, Mississippi, and Louisiana along with four in Georgia that did not meet the 50 percent rule. Operating from Civil Service offices in Atlanta and Dallas, supervisors opened local offices in the affected areas. By the end of January 1966, the campaign would claim 93,778 new voters, 91,212 black and 2,566 white. Of the 310,641 potential black voters, 30 percent had been registered. Progress was slow but steady. In March 1966, the Supreme Court would hold the basic components of the Voting Rights Act constitutional.[58] Southern conservatives quickly recognized the handwriting on the wall. "[Virginia Democratic Congressman A. Willis] Robertson is in a great mood these days," White House aide Mike Manatos reported to LBJ in February 1966. "He is looking at those Negro votes. He told me point blank one day, he said you know they have registered about 200,000 Negroes down there and he said I just want to be on the good side of 'em." [59] By the 1968 presidential election, Mississippi had reached 59 percent, and black registration in the eleven former Confederate states averaged 62 percent. In 1980 only 7 percent fewer blacks proportionately than whites were on the nation's voting rolls. [60]

DURING THE DEBATE over the poverty bill, LBJ had come to understand that the story of the disadvantaged in America was a complicated one, and that even if white attitudes changed overnight, the culture of poverty would still persist. The White House began to get an inkling by the summer of 1965 that the number one racial battleground of the future would be the large urban areas of the Northeast and Midwest, where millions of blacks had migrated between 1940 and 1970. In August 1965, *Newsweek* ran a piece entitled "New Crisis: The Negro Family." The article, citing a Department of Labor report, painted a dismal picture of overpopulated urban ghettoes teeming with unemployed youths, fatherless children, drug addicts, gang members, rats, and predatory white shopkeepers. "The evidence—not final, but powerfully persuasive—is that the Negro family in the urban ghettoes is crumbling . . . This is the time bomb ticking at the very heart of America's 'most dangerous social problem.' " [61]

In his conversation with black leaders and the architects of the Great Society, LBJ had made it clear that he considered the Office of Economic Opportunity and other facets of the War on Poverty to be civil rights programs. Implicit in this strategy was the assumption that equality under the law, equal access, and voting rights were not enough. The history of the African American was quite different from that of other ethnic, immigrant groups. Slavery had deliberately fractured families, prohibited literacy, and denigrated notions of self-worth. The sharecrop, crop-lien system, and Jim Crow were steps up from slavery but miles short of equality. Even with *Brown* and the Civil Rights Acts of 1964 and 1965 in place, blacks were not simply working-class whites ready to move up to the next rung on the socioeconomic ladder. By virtue of education, income, IQ, and other accepted measures of achievement, African Americans did not measure up.

The War on Poverty had spawned a number of government studies that sought to uncover the historical and social roots of the culture of poverty. One of those, a report on the black family by Assistant Secretary of Labor Daniel Patrick Moynihan, had been circulating in the West Wing and throughout the federal bureaucracy for four months. The Moynihan report ticked off the statistics and then focused on that most widely accepted criterion of social stability and progress: the family. One-quarter of city-dwelling black women who had ever been married were now divorced, separated, or deserted—22.9 percent compared to 7.9 percent for whites. As a result, one black family in four was fatherless. More than half of all Negro children would have lived in broken homes by their eighteenth birthday. Twenty-five percent of all black babies born in America were illegitimate, compared to 3.07 percent of whites. As a result, recipients of Aid to Families with Dependent Children had become primarily unmarried black females and their dependent children. More than half of all Negro children subsisted on AFDC checks at some time during their childhood. At the same time, the birthrate for ghetto-dwelling blacks was 40 percent higher than for whites.[62]

The intention of the report, Moynihan later recalled, was not to indict the black family but to use it as "the best point . . . at which to measure the net, cumulative plus or minus impact of outside forces on the Negro community. All the abstractions of employment, housing, income, discrimination, education, et al. come together here."[63] With its focus on the African American nuclear family, the Moynihan report proved to be a bombshell, however. Harry McPherson recalled that when Moynihan, a close friend and intellectual soul mate, finished his study, he, McPherson, was in the hospital recovering from a hernia operation. Moynihan showed up with the document and a full bottle of Johnny Walker Black scotch. As McPherson read, he grew drunker and increasingly alarmed. It would be fodder for every racist who was trying to discredit the values and morality of African Americans.[64] He was right. Black activists, especially the more radical in SNCC, CORE, and the Black Power movement, insisted that the government was trying to blame the victim for the crime. It seemed to be saying that if only blacks would take control of their lives, embrace monogamy, and nurture their children, all would be well. But where would the jobs come from, where the schools, where the rat-control programs, where the health care? How could inner-city blacks reach the suburbs, where the jobs were, without transportation?

Initially, George Reedy recalled, Johnson and his staff were not willing to accept preference for blacks, with the notion of hiring quotas that it implied.[65] By the summer of 1965, however, LBJ began to shift gears. The first week in June, the president delivered the commencement address at Howard University, in which he justified and defined affirmative action. "You do not take a person who, for years, has been hobbled by chains and liberate him, bring him up to the starting line of a race and then say, 'you are free to compete with all the others,' and still justly believe that you have been completely fair," he declared. It was not sufficient simply to open the gates of opportunity; all must be able to enter those gates. Equipping black Americans to take advantage of the opportunities available to them would be "the next and more profound stage for the battle for civil rights. We seek not just freedom but opportunity. We seek not just legal equity but human ability, not just equality as a right and a theory but equality as a fact and equality as a result." Summarizing the Moynihan report, LBJ emphasized the historical role that racial prejudice and exploitation had played in blighting black youth and their families. "Ability is stretched or stunted by the family that you live with," Johnson told his all-black audience, "and the neighborhood you live in—by the school you go to and the poverty or the richness of your surroundings." It was the responsibility of all Americans to see that this blight was lifted from those who suffered from it. Typically, LBJ quoted Scripture: "I shall light a candle of understanding in thine heart, which shall not be put out."[66]

"The strategy of the speech," Moynihan later observed, "was that by couching the issue in terms of family . . . white America could be brought to see the tired old issues of employment, housing, discrimination and such in terms of much greater urgency than they ever evoked on their own." Moreover, family as an issue raised the possibility of enlisting the support of conservative groups for quite radical social programs. The architects of the Howard speech recognized that "the intense moralisms of conservative Catholic and Protestant religion" were "simply a clumsy effort to maintain standards of family stability that most of us regard as eminently sane."[67]

In fact, the administration got the worst of both worlds. Conservatives for the most part chose to view the disintegration of the black family as proof of the innate depravity of inner-city blacks, and many blacks elected to treat the Moynihan report and references to the family in the Howard speech as attempts by the white power structure to blame the victim. And then there was the reaction to affirmative action, especially to Johnson's new, more radical definition of it. The president did not develop the notion of affirmative action with any specificity, but his allusion to equality of condition as well as equality of opportunity pointed to the righting of historic wrongs through hiring quotas and preferences. Traditional civil rights leaders like King, Young, Randolph, and Wilkins hailed the Howard speech as historic. Some white liberals were not so sure, however. Quotas and preferences violated the "American philosophical creed," libertarian Daniel Bell wrote. Special subsidies for the poor were acceptable, but a plan that would end up discriminating "against others" was not.[68] The managing editor of *Christian Century,* Kyle Haselden, agreed. "Compensation for Negroes is a subtle but pernicious form of racism," he editorialized. "It requires that men be dealt with by society on the basis of race and color rather than on the basis of their humanity."[69]

In part, the Howard speech was an attempt to dissipate the storm that was gathering in America's ghettoes before it burst upon the nation and created a white backlash that would undo all that LBJ and his colleagues had accomplished. But, despite its promise, it was too little too late. Just days after LBJ signed the Voting Rights Act in August 1965, riots erupted in Watts, Los Angeles's teeming black ghetto.[70] The violence began when a white policeman attempted to arrest a black youth for driving under the influence. As the officer tried to push the young man into his patrol car, he began to struggle. By this time, the youth's mother had arrived, accompanied by a crowd from nearby street corners. Suddenly, she and the onlookers began pelting the police with rocks and bottles. Reinforcements arrived, and a major confrontation ensued. Fueled by chronic unemployment, poor schools or no schools at all, rat-infested tenements, police brutality, and the general hopelessness and frustration of ghetto living, Watts boiled over. A mob estimated at five thousand roamed the streets, looted stores, attacked whites, and fire-bombed white- and Korean-owned businesses. When police and firemen responded, isolated sniper fire from surrounding rooftops greeted them.[71] At this point, the governor of California called in the national guard. Still the looting and violence continued. Crowds of young blacks chanted "Burn, baby, burn" and prevented firefighters from dousing flames. After a curfew was imposed, soldiers and policemen began shooting indiscriminately. For six days Watts was turned into a combat zone. When the rioting was finally quelled, thirty-four lay dead, one thousand were injured, four thousand had been arrested, and large sections of the ghetto had been reduced to a smoldering ruin.[72]

"If a single event can be picked to mark the dividing line of the sixties," *Life* editorialized, "it was Watts." The outburst of violence "ripped the fabric of democratic society and set the tone of confrontation and open revolt."[73] Martin Luther King flew to the scene to appeal for calm only to be heckled by young militants. A feud had long been brewing between the older generation of civil rights leaders like King and Randolph and the younger, more radical elements in CORE and SNCC who had grown disillusioned with the American political process and nonviolent civil disobedience. Revolutionary activists such as Stokely Carmichael, H. Rap Brown, and Bobby Seale took over existing organizations or formed new ones that called for whatever means necessary, including violence, to achieve equality and opportunity for African Americans. They were aided and abetted by black writers and intellectuals such as Eldridge Cleaver (*Soul on Ice,* 1967) and James Baldwin (*The Fire Next Time,* 1963), who moved beyond Richard Wright and Ralph Ellison in their anger and their vision of an apocalyptic end to the struggle of African Americans against oppression and exploitation. The new militants even questioned the value of integration. "Integration," Stokely Carmichael wrote, "is a subterfuge for the maintenance of white supremacy."[74]

The ultimate prophet of the new militancy, which the press dubbed "the Black Power movement," was Malcolm X, who had risen to the leadership of the Black Muslims, or Nation of Islam. The organization was a puritanical association of African Americans that practiced a variation of the Islamic creed and that drew its converts primarily from the pimps, drug pushers, and generally down-and-out of the big-city ghettos. Malcolm X argued that blacks had been abused and reviled for so long that the only way they could liberate themselves spiritually as well as politically and economically was through violent struggle. "If someone puts a hand on you," he told his followers, "send him to the cemetery." *Newsweek* called him a "spiritual desperado . . . a demagogue who titillated slum Negroes and frightened whites."[75]

For Johnson, the rioting in Watts was the ultimate nightmare. Up to this point, he had been relatively successful in denying conservatives use of the "law and order" issue. During the 1964 campaign, Goldwater and the ultras had tried to raise the specter of lawlessness, subtly attempting to link civil rights demonstrations with communist subversion and inner-city crime.[76] They had gotten nowhere. Johnson had turned the law-and-order table on conservatives by comparing the Klan to the Communist Party and pointing to the lawlessness of anti–civil rights forces in the South. Indeed, his final, unanswerable appeal to southern whites faced with the Second Reconstruction was the demand and the expectation that they "obey the law." Now the nation was faced with the reality of black violence and, worse, black leaders who were hailing the therapeutic value of violence and denouncing white society and white political processes as impotent and irrelevant. Johnson's first reaction to Watts was incredulity and then denial. "How is it possible," he asked "after all we've accomplished? How could it be?" When he first received word that mass violence had erupted in South Los Angeles, LBJ was at the ranch, celebrating the signing of the Voting Rights Act. Stunned, he drove around his pastures alone for hours refusing to return calls from White House domestic adviser Joseph Califano, who was quickly besieged by California Governor Pat Brown, Los Angeles Mayor Sam Yorty, and other state officials pleading for federal aid.[77]

On the second day of the rioting, LBJ began to emerge from his shell and grapple with the situation. He and his advisers at once realized how symbolically important would be the manner in which the federal government reacted to Watts. There was obviously an overriding need to get at the roots of the rioting, lest other American cities go up in flames. The White House dispatched Ramsey Clark and a team of troubleshooters to Los Angeles to confer with Mayor Yorty and black leaders.[78] The president agreed to meet with King.

"What should we do?" LBJ asked. "Get the Poverty Program going in L.A.," King replied.[79] Johnson ordered Katzenbach to put together an emergency task force to develop summer job programs and funnel government funds into the "rehabilitation of recreation centers and playgrounds." The government had initiated such programs in Washington, D.C., where violence had been predicted during the summers of 1963 and 1964. At the very least, Katzenbach observed, such moves would "show the children and juveniles that their government cared about their problems."[80] But such aid would have to be discreet lest the federal government appear to frightened whites to be rewarding violence and lawlessness. "The riot had, you know, just stunned and polarized the community there particularly, but also the nation," Ramsey Clark noted. Gun sales to white suburbanites skyrocketed, and so did the popularity of law-and-order candidates like actor-turned-politician Ronald Reagan. "And there was great concern that what we would do might appear to reward rioters," Clark observed.[81] Joe Califano, who had moved over from Defense to the White House to handle domestic affairs after Moyers became press secretary, recalled how worried the president was that out of frustration, hopelessness, and ignorance, poor blacks would lash out and undermine the very programs he was initiating to help them.[82]

Despite his frustration, disappointment, and occasional anger, however, Johnson had no intention of abandoning inner-city blacks to their fate. "We are on a powder keg in a dozen places," he told John McCone, whom he was trying to persuade to head up an inquiry into urban unrest. "You just have no idea of the depth of the feeling of these people. I see some of the boys that have worked for me, have 2,000 years of persecution, now they suffer from it. They [ghetto dwellers] have absolutely nothing to live for, 40% of them are unemployed, these youngsters live with rats and have no place to sleep, and they all start from broken homes and illegitimate families and all that narcotics circulating around . . . We have just got to find some way to wipe out these ghettos and find some housing and put them to work."[83] At the same time that he appealed to the compassion of liberals, he tweaked the fears of conservatives. "I got 38 percent of these young Negro boys out on the streets," he told Arkansas Senator John McClellan. "They've got no school to go to and no job. And by God, I'm just scared to death what's going to happen . . . You take an old hard-peckered boy that sits around and got no school and got no job and got no work and got no discipline. His daddy's probably on relief, and his mama's probably taking morphine. Why, he ain't got nothing hurt if he gets shot. I mean, he's better off dead than he is where he is."[84] By the end of August, the administration had allocated more than $29 million to help rehabilitate Watts alone.

In the months ahead, LBJ would turn his attention once again to the War on Poverty, now perceived as both an exercise in idealism and an emergency fire station to keep the American house from burning down. At the same time, the president increasingly employed the language of law and order. A few days before announcing the new federal programs for Watts, he addressed a White House Conference on Equal Employment Opportunities. "A rioter with a Molotov cocktail in his hands is not fighting for civil rights any more than a Klansman with a sheet on his back and a mask on his face," he declared. "They are both more or less what the law declares them: lawbreakers, destroyers of constitutional rights and liberties, and ultimately destroyers of a free America. They must be exposed and they must be dealt with."[85]

CHAPTER 29

DAUNTED COURAGE

W HILE TRYING TO UNRAVEL THE COMPLEXITIES of the civil rights movement and urban unrest in the United States, LBJ was also confronting an increasingly chaotic situation in Vietnam. Following American reprisal raids against the North in the wake of the Gulf of Tonkin incident, General Nguyen Khanh, prime minister of South Vietnam, was suddenly imbued with a new and unfamiliar sense of confidence. Opting for authoritarianism rather than conciliation, he declared a state of emergency, reimposed censorship on the press, and hastily drafted a new constitution that, among other things, elevated him to the post of president. These sudden moves shattered the tenuous calm in Saigon. Beginning on August 21, 1964, students took to the streets demonstrating against Khanh and calling for democracy and civilian rule. Soon they were joined by militant Buddhists, who claimed Khanh was controlled by the Catholic-dominated Dai Viet Party and former Diemists who were plotting once again to suppress their religion.

Intimidated, Khanh sought out the two most prominent monks, Thich Tri Quang and Tam Chau, and asked them what they required of him to halt the demonstrations. They demanded that he scrap the new constitution, guarantee freedom of religion, and commit to free elections no later than November 1965. Revealing his political naïveté, he told them that he would have to confer with the Americans. Immediately, the street protests took on an anti-American tone. Khanh promised a return to civilian rule in the near future, but the Buddhists and students were not satisfied.

In his search for a viable political base, ironically, Khanh proved willing to recognize the legitimacy of the National Liberation Front and forge a political agreement that would cut out the Americans and preserve Vietnamese sovereignty. In December 1964, the general began talking with the NLF directly.[1]

Meanwhile, his fellow officers in the Military Revolutionary Council (MRC) recoiled at Khanh's weakness and, smelling blood, began to intrigue against him. Especially prominent among the new aspirants to power were Nguyen Van Thieu, army chief of staff, and Nguyen Cao Ky, the youthful, flamboyant head of the South Vietnamese Air Force. Thieu was a convert to Catholicism and Ky a nominal Buddhist.

McGeorge Bundy described the new crisis in Vietnam to LBJ, telling him that it "could hardly be more serious." There was a very real possibility that the president would have to order "substantial armed forces" to secure the area. "I myself believe that before we let this country go, we should have a hard look at this grim alternative, and I do not at all think that it is a repetition of Korea."[2] September witnessed Catholic activists confronting Buddhists in the streets, four days of mass mayhem by roving street gangs armed with sticks and bottles, a civilian prime minister who lasted two weeks, and an abortive coup attempt by two generals who had been relieved of their commands. In October, Khanh allowed himself to be replaced as prime minister by the sixty-year-old schoolteacher and former mayor of Saigon, Tran Van Huong. To be chief of state, Khanh and the MRC chose Pham Khac Suu, an octogenarian who had once worked for Bao Dai and who insisted on advertising his obsolescence by wearing the traditional black mandarin gown.

The pressure in the administration for mounting a greater and more direct U.S. military effort in Southeast Asia, momentarily deflated by the November election, began to mount once again. State, Defense, the CIA, the Joint Chiefs, and the American mission in Saigon, diplomats and soldiers (some for very different reasons), came to the conclusion that the United States would have to make one last effort to get the South Vietnamese to pull their socks up, but if they could not, rather than abandoning the area, Washington should assume direct responsibility for winning the war.

Increasingly in State, the driving force for escalation was Walt Whitman Rostow, head of the Policy Planning Staff, the post that the venerable George Kennan had occupied. For all his brilliance, enthusiasm, and sincerity, Rostow was an individual whose reach frequently exceeded his grasp. He was one of three sons of a Russian Jewish immigrant, the other two sons bearing the authentic American appellations of Eugene Victor (Debs) and Ralph Waldo. Walt Whitman Rostow was the archetypal child prodigy, first in everything in school, a young graduate of Yale, an infant Rhodes scholar. He had spent World War II picking targets for the strategic bombing effort in Europe. He returned to the States to earn a Ph.D. in economics and then a tenured position at Yale. When he came to Jack Kennedy's attention in 1959 as the candidate was scouring the banks of the Charles River for liberal intellectuals with which to temper his Irish mafia, Rostow was a well-published scholar. His most recent work was entitled *The States of Economic Growth: A Non-Communist Manifesto*. Rostow was an amiable, seemingly open-minded man, with well-honed social skills, a person whom enemies found hard to dislike. But as David Halberstam pointed out in

The Best and the Brightest, Rostow could be agreeable and forthcoming because he was absolutely secure in his beliefs. His ideal was capitalism with a conscience. The American model could be successfully exported to the third world and, where applied with care, it would bring about social justice and general prosperity, thus sparing emerging societies the evils of revolution and communist totalitarianism. Rostow was a committed cold warrior. The Truman Doctrine and Marshall Plan had saved the Near East and Western Europe. Strategically, he lived in a world that began in 1942 and ended in 1949 with the Berlin airlift, a world replete with Munich analogies and falling dominoes. In Greece, for example, the United States had weathered chronic political instability, noncommunist dictatorships, and guerrilla warfare and had succeeded in stopping Stalinism at the gates of Europe. So, too, could it halt the forces of international communism in Southeast Asia. Finally, Rostow was a firm believer in the efficacy of strategic bombing, the findings of the U.S. Strategic Bombing Survey notwithstanding.[3]

Rostow considered himself a quick study. When it appeared that Kennedy had a chance to win, he had taken a three-month sabbatical to educate himself on the intricacies of Asian economics and politics. Thus was he able to sell himself to the new administration as an expert on East Asian affairs.[4] "Having examined the problem of Vietnam, I early concluded that it was the most dangerous case of guerrilla warfare I had ever seen," Rostow later wrote. "The reason was that there was not only a deeply embedded Viet Cong infrastructure in the South, but—much more serious—there was a long open frontier across which men and supplies were already moving at a dangerous rate in 1961. It is difficult if not impossible to win a guerrilla war with an open frontier. Looking at that frontier and the problem of monitoring it from inside the borders, I concluded quite early that we might be driven, at some time, to force an end to infiltration by striking at its source."[5]

Meanwhile, the continuing reports from South Vietnam describing a revolving door government, less rather than more consensus, continuing Vietcong gains in the countryside, and intelligence that the Democratic Republic of Vietnam was in fact assuming a much more direct role in the war in the South had Robert McNamara, the can-do activist, searching for answers.[6] He did not want to become involved in a conflict that would draw in communist Chinese land forces, an eventuality that would likely compel him to authorize the use of tactical nuclear weapons. By mid-November, the defense chief and his colleagues had fully embraced the logic and tactic of limited war. Force would be employed in Southeast Asia to communicate with the enemy. "I am convinced that we should not go forward into the next state without a US ground force commitment of some kind," Rostow advised McNamara. "The withdrawal of those ground forces could be a critically important part of our diplomatic bargaining position." The United States must decide to bomb the North, not to obliterate its war-making power but to "instill the principle that they will, from the present forward, be vulnerable to retaliatory attack in the north."[7] For these men, war did not mark the cessation of diplomacy but its continuation in a different form.

The American mission in Saigon was in agreement on the need to strike directly at the North, if not on the strategy of limited war. "After a year of changing and ineffective government, the counterinsurgency program country-wide is bogged down and will require heroic treatment to assure revival," Ambassador Maxwell Taylor wrote from Saigon. "The northern provinces of South Viet-Nam which a year ago were considered almost free of Viet-Cong are now in deep trouble . . . Once more we are threatened with a partition of the country by a Viet-Cong salient driven to the sea." He continued even more bleakly: "It is impossible to foresee a stable and effective government under any name in anything like the near future . . . We sense the mounting feeling of war weariness and hopelessness which pervade South Viet-Nam, particularly in the urban areas." Taylor observed that it was nearly impossible for the United States to provide economic aid and military support through a government apparatus that did not really exist; moreover, "it seems highly unlikely that we will see such a government of South Viet-Nam in the time frame available to us to reverse the downward trend of events." The only way to save the situation was for the United States to bomb the North, beginning with supply depots between the seventeenth and twentieth parallels and infiltration routes from Laos and moving up to military-industrial targets around Hanoi and Haiphong if the insurgency in the South continued.[8]

LBJ had said repeatedly throughout the summer and early fall that he did not want to initiate an air campaign against the North with the South in such a weakened condition. He did not, he said famously, "wish to enter the patient in a 10-round bout when he was in no shape to hold out for one round. We should get him ready to face 3 or 4 rounds at least."[9] When, on the night of October 31, 1964, Bien Hoa airfield came under a mortar attack that killed four U.S. servicemen, wounded thirty, and destroyed or damaged twenty-seven aircraft, Johnson had refused to approve retaliatory air raids against the North. But the message that Taylor and others were sending to the president was that the patient was dying, not getting better. If the United States did not step in and take a direct role, there would be no South Vietnam to defend.[10]

By the late fall of 1964, the issue within policymaking circles seemed to be viability versus credibility: the viability of the South Vietnamese government as opposed to the credibility of the United States with its cold war allies. Inexorably, the latter was overshadowing the former. CIA Director John McCone continued to express the opinion that social cohesion and political stability in South Vietnam would be almost impossible to achieve, but that the United States ought to at once initiate a graduated bombing campaign against the North.[11] Secretary of State Dean Rusk was a firm believer that security was the dog and political stability the tail. "Korea, so far as he was concerned, had been a great success," Undersecretary of State George Ball recalled. So I would say, 'Look, you've got no government. It's impossible to win in a situation where you've got this totally fragile political base. These people are clowns.' Where-upon, he'd say, 'Don't give me that stuff. You don't understand that at the time of Korea that we had to go out and dig Syngman Rhee out of the bush where he was hiding; there was no government in Korea either, and we were able to come though.' "[12] "It is essential—however badly Southeast Asia may go over the next 2–4 years—that US emerge as a 'good doctor,' " Assistant Secretary of Defense John McNaughton told his boss. "We must have kept promises, been tough, taken risks, gotten bloodied, and hurt the enemy very badly."[13] The Joint Chiefs never wavered. They continued to consider "Southeast Asia to be an area of major strategic importance to the United States, the loss of which would lead to grave political and military consequences in the entire Western Pacific, and to serious political consequences world-wide."[14]

Still, LBJ resisted. Bombing, especially a graduated program to force the North Vietnamese Army to cease and desist in its support of the insurgency in the South, as opposed to tit-for-tat retaliatory bombings such as that which fol-lowed the Gulf of Tonkin incident, would intensify the war and probably result in the introduction of U.S. ground combat units. How in God's name could he keep a lid on things? In conversations with those outside his policymaking cir-cle, LBJ was doom and gloom. He and Richard Russell agreed that the operative figure from Texas history was not the hero of San Jacinto, Sam Houston, but the martyr of San Antonio, Ben Milam.[15] In the early stages of the Texas Revolution, Colonel Ben Milam, an elderly impresario, had led a force of Texan volunteers against a superior Mexican force holding the town of San Antonio de Bexar. The Texans finally managed to prevail, but Old Ben Milam was shot dead.[16] "I wish we could figure some way to get out of that, Mr. President," Russell ob-served to his friend in November. "I think if we get in there and get messing around with those Chinese, we could be in there for the next ten years. But I don't know how we can get out. I told John McCone he ought to get somebody to run that country [who] didn't want us in there . . . then . . . we could get out with good grace."[17]

Then there was Johnson's beloved Great Society to consider. "If we get into this war, I know what's going to happen," he confided to a group of visitors to the White House in late 1964. "Those damn conservatives are going to sit in Congress and they're going to use this war as a way of opposing my Great Soci-ety legislation. People like [John] Stennis [senator from Alabama]. They hate this stuff, they don't want to help the poor and the Negroes but they're afraid to be against it at a time like this when there's been all this prosperity. But the war, oh, they'll like the war. They'll take the war as their weapon. They'll be against my programs because of the war . . . They'll say they're not against it, not against the poor, but we have this job to do, beating Communists. We beat the Communists first, then we can look around and maybe give something to the poor." One of his auditors later observed that the monologue was like listening to a man who had had a premonition of his own death.[18]

As his advisers pressed a bombing campaign on him, LBJ defiantly tried to force them to focus on the venality, selfishness, and uncooperativeness of the military-political figures who were jockeying for control in South Vietnam. Why and how did the deteriorating political situation in the South add up to a greater American commitment? "Why not say, 'This is it!' " he argued to his advisers. "Not send Johnson City boys out to die if they are acting as they are." Had the United States overemphasized the strategic importance of the region to itself and to the South Vietnamese? "Are they drunk on Alsop?" he asked rhetorically. He did not want to "send a widow woman to slap Jack Dempsey." [19] In response, the president's advisers, in conjunction with Taylor, developed a plan whereby bombing and the introduction of U.S. combat forces could be used as bargaining chips to force Khanh, his generals, Tri Quang, and the other actors in the South Vietnamese drama to get their house in order. But once the United States had decided the issue of credibility versus viability, it really had very little leverage with the government of Vietnam and the Army of the Republic of Vietnam (ARVN). [20] As a GVN official confided to journalist Stanley Karnow at the time, "Our big advantage over the Americans is that they want to win the war more than we do." [21]

It was at this point that George Ball, at the president's invitation, presented the case for a de-escalation leading to eventual withdrawal. Working nights and weekends, the undersecretary of state prepared a seventy-five-page memorandum that challenged every assumption that underlay the recommendations for escalating the war in Vietnam. Southeast Asia was not comparable in strategic or economic importance to the Near East and certainly not to Western Europe. To equate Berlin with Saigon was absurd. Moreover, there were limits on American military and political power. If the United States threw in its stack, to use an LBJ term, in Vietnam, it would not have the resources to defend its interests elsewhere. Moreover, there was really, in political and sociological terms, no such thing as South Vietnam. Vietnamese nationalism, the drive to unify and not be dominated by an outside force, was stronger than either communism or anticommunism. Given the long history of Vietnamese-Chinese antagonism, a unified Vietnam under Ho Chi Minh was likely to become a barrier to Chinese communist expansion rather than a conduit for it. The notion that by the use of limited bombing of the North the United States could affect the outcome of the struggle in the South was absurd, Ball, insisted. And this from a man who had participated in the bombing survey that had called into question the efficacy of the Allied bombing campaign in Europe during World War II. The United States had made every effort to help the South Vietnamese help themselves. If, as was proving the case, they were unable to get the job done, the United States should arrange for negotiations and make a graceful exit. [22]

Only five copies of the summarized memorandum existed; circulation was limited to LBJ, Rusk, Mac Bundy, Ball, and Bill Bundy. In various conversations with his colleagues, the NSC adviser referred to Ball's evaluation as "the 'devil's advocate' exercise," but Ball would insist that although he was a team player, his recommendations represented his true views together with those of Clark Clifford, Averell Harriman, and others.[23] In a 1967 interview with journalist Robert Manning, LBJ observed, "When Ball was here, he was good about arguing the opposite viewpoint even when he, Rusk and McNamara were actually together on something."[24] McNamara "was absolutely horrified" when he first saw the memo, Ball recalled. "He treated it like a poisonous snake."[25] The secretary of defense believed that the mere knowledge that U.S. policymakers were seriously considering withdrawing would have disastrous results in Hanoi and Saigon.[26] Nevertheless, LBJ thoroughly familiarized himself with Ball's points, confronted the escalators with them, and forced Rusk, McNamara, and MacBundy to respond in detail to each argument.

To say that the president stage-managed his administration's meetings on foreign affairs would be going too far. He did not know in advance what the outcome of these gatherings would be, what consensus would emerge, but he was determined not to be surprised by positions taken or information offered in support of those positions. He read the most important memos almost as soon as his subordinates did. He had individuals in the various departments and agencies—Joe Califano in Defense, for example—who reported to him directly on the arguments and probable recommendations that he would hear in a more formal setting. He treasured such foreknowledge and went to great lengths to keep his network secret. "The president's connection with such matters as U-2 flights, and the fact that he knows about the views of the Chiefs before they are formally presented," McGeorge Bundy told Califano, "are both sensitive, and the written record should either omit such matters or be handled very tightly indeed."[27]

MEANWHILE, in Saigon, the South Vietnamese political situation proceeded with all of the decorum and idealism of a Chinese fire drill. Although a nominally civilian government under Prime Minister Huong had been installed, the Buddhists were not satisfied. Thich Tri Quang in particular was convinced that the Catholic Dai Viet generals were still in charge and that the U.S. mission was backing them. By late January, Saigon and Hue, a Buddhist stronghold, were witnesses to almost daily demonstrations by students and Buddhist activists. Subsequently, rumors circulated in Saigon and Washington that Khanh and Tri Quang had made a deal to negotiate a cease-fire with the Vietcong and work toward the creation of a neutralist government in South Vietnam.[28] Sensing that Khanh had fallen out of favor with the Americans—which indeed was the case with the embassy in Saigon, if not with Washington—Air Marshal Ky and Chief of Staff Thieu began to plot a coup. After further maneuverings, on the morning of February 20, 1965, the MRC voted to strip Khanh of his authority and to name him ambassador-at-large. Three days later, the general flew out of Saigon—never to return.[29]

The veneer of a civilian government remained for four more months, but then in June the generals moved once again to take direct charge of the government. Phan Huy Quat, who had replaced Huong, was ousted as prime minister and the venerable Pham Khac Suu was forced out as premier. Ky became prime minister, with Thieu stepping in as chief of state.[30] William Bundy observed of the new leadership in Saigon: "The bottom of the barrel, absolutely the bottom of the barrel."[31]

BY LATE JANUARY 1965, the logic of credibility over viability began to constrict Lyndon Johnson the decision maker. Not that doubts and misgivings did not remain. "In January of 1965," Douglass Cater recalled, "some of us were gathered working on a domestic message around nine-thirty in the evening, and the President came in . . . He sat down, and either Bill [Moyers] or Joe [Califano] attempted to brief him swiftly on what we were doing here. He didn't hear a word of it. He said, 'I don't know what to do. If I send in more men, there will be killin'; if I take out men, there will be killin'. Anything I do, there will be killin'.' "[32] "Every time I get a military recommendation," LBJ observed to Ambassador Taylor, "it seems to me that it calls for large-scale bombing. I have never felt this war will be won from the air."[33] He continually badgered the State Department to line up "third country support," indicating that his decisions on escalation would rely heavily on proof that America's allies in the cold war were willing to step forward in Southeast Asia. And there was still no evidence that South Vietnam was moving toward a stable political system capable of withstanding the pressures of escalation and taking the fight to the enemy. "The Deadly and Perplexing War," read the headline in a major *Newsweek* story on the conflict in Southeast Asia.[34]

Then, in conversations with the president on January 26 and 27, Mac Bundy and McNamara convinced LBJ that the United States could no longer risk holding Saigon's hand, no matter what the situation there. Bundy insisted that "what we are doing now, essentially, is to wait and hope for a stable government." The only alternative, he continued, was "to use our military power in the Far East and to force a change of Communist policy."[35] After receiving assurances once again from McCone and the CIA that a graduated, restrained program of bombing against targets just north of the seventeenth parallel would not result in direct Chinese intervention, LBJ gave the word to initiate new DeSoto patrols in the Gulf of Tonkin and to be ready to use the next direct attack on American forces as an excuse to begin the bombing of North Vietnam.[36]

At two o'clock on Sunday morning, February 6, 1965, a Viet Cong suicide squad exploded thirteen satchel charges against the concrete perimeter wall guarding Camp Holloway, a U.S. base near the central South Vietnamese city of Pleiku. Shortly thereafter, mortar shells began raining down on the encampment while guerrillas, entrenched some three hundred yards away, peppered U.S. personnel with small arms and recoilless rifle fire. Nearly all of the shells and bullets were U.S.-made, fired by American weapons taken from the ARVN. Famed military cartoonist Bill Mauldin happened to be at Holloway visiting his son, a helicopter pilot. Within minutes after the attack began, he recalled, "there was a big streak of wounded moving toward the infirmary. The infirmary itself was a real charnel house. Dead and dying were everywhere and everything was covered with blood." When the smoke cleared, seven U.S. servicemen lay dead with another 109 wounded.[37]

That afternoon, LBJ assembled his principal advisers on Vietnam together with the speaker of the House and the Senate majority leader. It just so happened that McGeorge Bundy was then in South Vietnam on a fact-finding trip. He had rushed to Pleiku just hours after the attack, and in an emotional conversation with the president had relayed the U.S. mission's request for permission to strike four targets just across the border in North Vietnam. General William Westmoreland recalled that "Bundy was very intense, abrupt and arrogant. I saw that as with many civilians, when they had smelled a little gunpowder and had some troops under their control, they developed a sort of Field Marshal psychosis."[38] But Bundy was no more bellicose than his hosts. Indeed, the impulse to strike back had been building within the American mission in Saigon for months.[39]

In the post-Pleiku meeting with his advisers, LBJ relayed the request to attack and went around the room asking each person if he concurred. George Ball was particularly emphatic on the need for retaliation. Only Senator Mansfield dissented. John McCone recorded Johnson's response to the majority leader: "The President took the opposite opinion, emphasizing that he had kept the shotgun over the mantel and the bullets in the basement for a long time now, but that the enemy was killing his personnel and he could not expect them to continue their work if he did not authorize them to take steps to defend themselves. He commented that 'cowardice has gotten us into more wars than response has.' He particularly recalled the fact that we would not have gotten into World War I if we had been courageous in the early stages, nor World War II. He then said he realized that there was a risk of involving the Soviets and Chinese but that neither of these are friendly with us and the problem is to face up to them both."[40] At two in the afternoon, only twelve hours after the Pleiku attack, American land- and carrier-based aircraft began taking off to bomb the North Vietnamese Army (NVA) military barracks at Dong Hoi, just north of the seventeenth parallel. Bad weather obscured the targets, and additional raids had to be launched throughout the evening and during the next several days. "In the night," Lady Bird recorded in her diary, "we were waiting to hear how the attack had gone. It came at one o'clock, and two o'clock, and three, and again at five— the ring of the phone, the quick reach for it, and tense, quiet talk . . . It was a tense and shadowed day, but we'll probably have to learn to live in the middle of it—for not hours or days, but years."[41]

There is no doubt that Pleiku, the killing of American servicemen, was the spark in Johnson's mind that triggered the decision to launch Rolling Thunder. But this was not simply a knee-jerk reaction to the shedding of American blood. The last week in January the president had approved a graduated bombing campaign of the North in principle; that is, he had agreed that it was preferable to continued deterioration and defeat, but he had not approved putting that option into action. For LBJ, Pleiku was the last falling domino, to use a famous analogy, pushing him toward a decision he did not want to make. For Bundy and McNamara, Pleiku was a long-anticipated event that would lead to implementation of a decision they had favored since the summer of 1964. For example, Chester Cooper of the NSC staff observed that the policymakers, including Defense and the JCS, were just waiting for a Pleiku. Cooper later expressed the opinion "that if the Viet Cong had chosen an entirely different approach . . . had decided to lay off the Americans and concentrate their energies on the South Vietnamese military, concentrate on subversion in Saigon . . . it's conceivable that Johnson might have been ready to back off rather than move ahead on the escalatory track." [42]

During the days immediately following Pleiku, military leaders and Johnson's advisers were unclear on exactly what the president had approved. Was he committed to tit-for-tat retaliation or to a gradually escalating campaign of bombing against the North in an effort to force the Democratic Republic of Vietnam (DRV) to abandon the insurgency in the South? "The President said we face a choice of going forward or running," McCone recorded in his meeting notes. "All of us agree on this but there remains some difference as to how fast we should go forward." [43]

On February 10, the Vietcong struck again, tossing grenades and pouring small arms fire into a U.S. enlisted men's barracks at Qui Nhon. Two days later, without extended debate, the Johnson administration initiated Rolling Thunder, a campaign of gradually intensified air attacks against North Vietnam. These strikes would be launched not in response to Vietcong or NVA provocation but according to a prearranged plan and time schedule. [44] "We were attacking those targets for three reasons," Taylor later recalled. "One, to give the feeling in South Viet Nam that for the first time they were being allowed to strike the homeland of the enemy, the enemy that had been making their lives miserable . . . Second, to restrict and make more difficult the infiltration of men and supplies from North Vietnam to South Viet Nam. The third reason was both psychological and political. It was to remind Ho Chi Minh and his council that were sitting up in Hanoi running a war at no expense that they were going to start to pay a price, and an increasing price as long as they continued." [45]

Johnson would call the Situation Room in the basement of the White House at all hours of the night asking for updates when he was aware that American aviators were in the air over hostile territory: how many planes had been lost, the status of rescue operations. As the bombing campaign got under way, Lady Bird made a notation in her diary: "While Lyndon and Hubert [Humphrey] were talking, I was rather startled to hear [Lyndon] say something that I had heard so often, but did not really expect to come out of his mouth in front of anyone else. 'I'm not temperamentally equipped to be Commander-in-Chief,' he said. They were talking about the crisis in Vietnam, the long nights with phone calls about planes going out . . . the necessity of giving orders that would produce God knows what cataclysmic results. He said, 'I'm too sentimental to give the orders.' "[46]

Public opinion polls taken in February both reassured and frightened LBJ—reassured him because they indicated approval of the course he was following, frightened him because they pointed to a consensus that viewed the conflict in South Vietnam as a direct challenge by communist China, a challenge that had to be met whatever the costs, although respondents seemed to indicate a preference for bombing over direct participation in the war by U.S. ground troops. Of those queried, 26 percent believed that North Vietnam alone was behind the insurgency in the South; 53 percent pointed to communist China. The polls indicated that 83 percent approved of the bombing of the North. In the view of 79 percent the United States was fighting to prevent the communists from taking over all of Southeast Asia, and 69 percent were convinced that the security of the United States was involved. Some 48 percent favored sending "a large number of American troops to help save South Vietnam," while 40 percent were opposed.[47]

Despite Rolling Thunder, the security situation in the South continued to deteriorate. Intelligence reports warned ominously that at the current rate, within six months government control might be reduced to a series of islands surrounding the provincial capitals. From the outset, LBJ had insisted on maintaining tight personal control over the air war: "They can't even bomb an outhouse without my approval," he was quoted as saying.[48] But that resolve quickly melted away. He allowed the JCS to authorize the use of napalm to ensure greater destructiveness and to permit pilots to strike alternative targets without obtaining prior permission. In April 1965, American and South Vietnamese pilots flew a total of thirty-six hundred sorties (one sortie equals one flight by one combat aircraft) against North Vietnamese targets. What the White House did retain control of was the geography of the bombing. Everything above the twentieth parallel was off-limits. Attacking the power stations, oil storage depots, rail and ship yards around Hanoi and Haiphong might kill Soviet and Chinese advisers and provoke a strong military response from the two communist superpowers.[49]

Anticipating Vietcong attacks against U.S. air bases in retaliation for Rolling Thunder, Westmoreland in late February urgently requested two marine assault battalions to protect the mushrooming air base at Da Nang. Ironically, Taylor, the father of counterinsurgency, did not support the request. He questioned whether American troops were adequately trained to fight a guerrilla war in the jungles of Southeast Asia. Moreover, he warned that by taking a direct combat role in the war, Washington would be providing a disincentive to the South Vietnamese to row their own military boat. Finally, once Americans troops began fighting and dying on a daily basis, it would be virtually impossible for the United States to reduce its role and certainly to withdraw.[50] Nevertheless, LBJ approved Westmoreland's request, and on March 8 two battalions of marines, fitted out in full battle dress, with tanks and eight-inch howitzers in tow, splashed ashore near Da Nang. They were welcomed by South Vietnamese officials, television cameras, and pretty girls who adorned them with leis. "I'm scared to death of putting ground forces in," LBJ had confided to McNamara, "but I'm more frightened about losing a bunch of planes from lack of security."[51] "I guess we've got no choice," he told Dick Russell, "but it scared the death out of me. I think everybody's going to think, 'We're landing the marines. We're off to battle' . . . Of course, if they [the Vietcong] come up there, they're going to get them in a fight. Just sure as hell. They're not going to run. Then you're tied down."[52]

Westmoreland was still not satisfied. He feared a major Vietcong–NVA offensive in the Central Highlands and was convinced that the induction and training of South Vietnamese soldiers would not be sufficient to meet the threat. As a result, in mid-March, he concluded that there was no option but for the United States to step in and take the offensive. He requested two U.S. Army divisions, one to be assigned to the highlands and the other to the Saigon area. The JCS urged him to request three divisions, but Taylor continued to drag his feet. "The increasing presence of more Americans will give Peiking [sic] grounds to press military reinforcements on Hanoi," he cabled Washington. "Frictions will grow between the [South] Vietnamese and their white allies; it will become increasingly difficult to steer US and GVN policy on parallel lines. The net effect may be not an expediting of victory but its retardation."[53] At this point, it should be noted, the Johnson administration was planning for defeat in Vietnam. "Two of the three of us think that the chances of a turn-around in South Vietnam remain less than even," Bundy reported to LBJ the first week in March. "The brutal fact is that we have been losing ground at an increasing rate in the countryside in January and February." Pacification was making absolutely no headway, he reported, and Ambassador Taylor was cordially detested by all parties in the South.[54]

Frustrated, LBJ ordered the principals to gather in Honolulu in late April and settle on a plan. There, Taylor and the JCS put aside their differences and hastily improvised a strategy whose objective was to "break the will of the DRV/VC by depriving them of victory." They agreed to maintain bombing at its current level for six months to a year and to introduce forty thousand additional U.S. grounds troops into Vietnam. These personnel were not to be used in the highlands or given an unrestricted mission, as Westmoreland and the JCS wanted. Rather, they would be used in the more cautious "enclave strategy" suggested by Taylor. Deployed in pockets around the major U.S. bases with their backs to the sea, they would be authorized to undertake operations within fifty miles of their base areas only. In this, Taylor was supported by Dean Rusk, who had opposed escalation all along.[55] LBJ and his advisers hoped that this limited commitment of forces would be adequate to deny the enemy a knockout blow, thus allowing time for a South Vietnamese military buildup and for the bombing to take its toll on Hanoi. He was not sanguine. "Airplanes ain't worth a damn,

Dick!" he declaimed to Russell, "They just scare the countries, they just scare their prime ministers . . . They did it in the Ruhr. And I guess they can do it in an industrial city . . . But they can't do it in the barracks. Hell, I had 160 of them over at a barracks, and twenty-seven buildings, and they set two on fire . . . That's the damndest thing I ever saw. The biggest fraud. Don't you get your hopes up that the Air Force is going to defend this." [56]

THE BOMBING OF THE NORTH stimulated the infant antiwar movement in the United States. Faculty at Michigan, Syracuse, and Harvard held "teach-ins" against the war, and students staged small protest meetings. Meanwhile, in the Senate, a small but growing clique opposed to escalation decided to speak out. Mansfield had been hammering away in behalf of a neutralist settlement within the halls of power for months—with no result. In January, the young, first-term senator from South Dakota, George McGovern, screwed up his courage and made an appointment with the president. McGovern, a veteran of thirty-nine World War II bombing missions over occupied Europe, attacked the notion of a monolithic communist threat and the domino theory. He dared to point out that the Chinese and Vietnamese had been fighting each other for a thousand years. Finally, the president exploded: "Goddamn it, George, you and Fulbright and all you history teachers [McGovern had earned a Ph.D. in history from Northwestern]. I haven't got time to fuck around with history. I've got boys on the line out there. I can't be worried about history when there are boys out there who might die before morning." [57]

On the afternoon of March 1, Idaho Democrat Frank Church formally opened the Senate debate on Vietnam. It would continue for the next eight years. "He began by reminding his colleagues that he is a confirmed internationalist and a consistent supporter of U.S. foreign-aid programs," *Newsweek* reported. " 'But,' he had declared, 'the pendulum of our foreign policy can swing from one extreme to the other. Once we thought that anything which happened abroad was none of our business; now we evidently think that everything which happens abroad has become our business . . . We have plunged into these former colonial regions as though we had been designated on high to act as trustee in bankruptcy . . . There are limits to what we can do in helping any government surmount a Communist uprising . . . If the people themselves will not support the government in power, we cannot save it.' " [58] In April, twenty thousand assembled in Washington to demonstrate against the escalation. They sang along with folksingers Joan Baez and Judy Collins and listened to Paul Potter, president of Students for a Democratic Society (SDS), call for a massive social movement to change America. Members of the crowd waved placards that read "Get out of Saigon and into Selma," "Freedom Now in Vietnam," and "War on Poverty Not on People." Public intellectuals like Walter Lippmann openly questioned the rationale for the war. In his columns, he insisted that it was absurd for the United States to think that mainland China would not be the dominant force in East Asia, and he repeatedly called for negotiations leading to a unified, neutralized Vietnam. UN Secretary General U Thant echoed his appeal. In what was perhaps the cruelest blow of all, Martin Luther King told a Virginia rally in the early summer, "I'm not going to sit by and see the war escalated without saying anything about it." The Vietnam War "must be stopped . . . We must even negotiate with the Vietcong."[59]

Johnson responded to this criticism by sending the best and the brightest in his administration across the nation to explain his policies and whip up support for the war. "I would ask [McGovern and Church] to your office," he suggested to McGeorge Bundy, "and . . . say . . . 'I have just returned [from Saigon] . . . and one of the biggest problems we have is stability in government. We've had nine of them, and the thing that causes them to just pee in their pants is to read a speech by [Senator Wayne] Morse saying . . . we ought to run out—or Mansfield . . . Let them know that there is no greater disservice that they can render. Then if they want to do it, then they are on their own."[60]

Always thin-skinned, overly sensitive to criticism, LBJ was hurt and frustrated by criticism of his policies in Vietnam. He was also taken off guard. "The notion that people would get tired of it if nothing happened in three years I think was never far from his mind," McGeorge Bundy remembered. "But the antiwar movement as such I think was a surprise." The president "underestimated and I think we all did, the virulence and the earliness of the opposition to the war."[61] As usual, LBJ took matters personally; he began to see communist sympathizers or Bobby lovers under every bed and behind every tree. "Every facility that the Communist world has at its disposal is being used to divide us," he told Senator Gale McGee (D-Wyoming), a supporter of the war. "Edgar Hoover was very upset about it. Brought [the files] over last night. They're going into the colleges and the faculties and the student bodies, and trying to get them to send . . . wires . . . that come right out of Communist headquarters."[62]

Not only did Johnson organize and direct a public relations counteroffensive, but he began vilifying and confronting his tormentors in person. Canadian Prime Minister Lester B. Pearson delivered an address in Philadelphia in the first week in April criticizing the escalation of the war in Vietnam. Afterward, at Camp David, LBJ remonstrated with his guest. When subsequently asked by a cabinet member what had really transpired at the presidential retreat, Pearson recounted the story of a British policeman giving evidence at a murder trial. " 'My Lord,' the policeman told the judge, 'acting on information received, I proceeded to a certain address and there found the body of a woman. She had been strangled, stabbed and shot, decapitated and dismembered. But, My Lord, she had not been interfered with.' " At Camp David, Pearson explained in conclusion, he had at least not been "interfered with."[63]

By March Vietnam was taking a toll on LBJ's emotional and psychological health. The depression that had plagued him earlier in his life returned in full force. Bill Moyers recalled that even in the best of times LBJ was given to fits of paranoia and periods of deep depression, but at no time was this more pronounced than during the decision to escalate the war in Vietnam. "He would just go within himself, just disappear—morose, self-pitying, angry," Moyers recalled. "He was a tormented man." One day the press secretary found his boss lying in bed with the covers pulled almost over his head. Vietnam was a Louisiana swamp "that's pulling me down," he said.[64] He rarely got to sleep before two in the morning and continued to insist on being awakened to receive action reports. "I want to be called every time somebody dies," he instructed the Situation Room.[65] During a March 23 conversation with Drew Pearson, Johnson verged on hysteria: "I don't believe I can walk out . . . If I did, they'd take Thailand . . . They'd take Cambodia . . . They'd take Burma . . . They'd take Indonesia . . . They'd take India . . . They'd come right back and take the Philippines . . . I'd be another Chamberlain and . . . we'd have another Munich." The aggressors feed on blood, he exclaimed, his voice rising to a scream. "I'm not coming home! They may get another President, but I'm not going to pull out. Now the second thing is negotiation . . . I'll go anywhere, I'll do anything . . . So the third thing is the [Curtis] LeMay viewpoint. I can take my bombs, and I can take my nuclear weapons, as Barry [Goldwater] says. I can defoliate, and I can clear out that brush where I can see anybody coming down that line, and I can wipe out Hanoi, and I can wipe out Peiping . . . But I think that would start World War III."[66]

Lady Bird fretted over the "erosion" noticeable in her husband's personality. In mid-March, she had LBJ's longtime private doctors and friends, Dr. Willis Hurst of Emory University and Dr. James Cain of the Mayo Clinic, to the White House to evaluate the president's health. "All the basic organs and functioning thereof . . . were fine," she recorded them as saying, "but there is this heavy load of tension and fog of depression."[67] Unable to stand the alternating abuse and self-pity, she left Washington for a six-week stay at the ranch in the spring of 1965. Lady Bird later recalled LBJ's agony over the war: "It was just a hell of a thorn stuck in his throat," she told historian Robert Dallek. "It wouldn't come up; it wouldn't go down . . . It was just pure hell and he did not have that reassuring, strong feeling that this is right, that he had when he was in a crunch with civil rights or poverty or education. It didn't have that: we'll make it through this one: Win or lose, it's the right thing to do. So, uncertainty . . . we had a rich dose of that . . . True, you can 'bear any burden, pay any price' if you're sure you're doing right. But if you do not know you're doing right . . ."[68]

For weeks, Horace Busby, among others, had been badgering LBJ to take the lead in justifying the war to the nation. Suddenly, impulsively, the president decided to accept a long-standing invitation to deliver a foreign policy address at Johns Hopkins University and named April 7 as the date he would justify the war to the nation. He wanted to define the conflict once again in cold war, Munich analogy terms, but also to throw some crumbs to the antiwar movement by indicating a willingness to negotiate. More important, LBJ felt the need to justify the war to himself. In the end, the only way he was able to do that was to cast the conflict in Southeast Asia in Great Society terms. As he contemplated ways the United States could compel North Vietnam to cut off aid to the insurgency in the South, Johnson's mind turned naturally from sticks to carrots. Just before he had departed on his trip to Vietnam when he was vice president, LBJ had received a letter from Arthur Goldschmidt, an old New Deal friend and the director of technical assistance for the United Nations. Goldschmidt drew Johnson's attention to a plan then in embryo to develop the Lower Mekong River Basin through an Asian version of the TVA. If realized, the scheme could bring Cambodia, Laos, and both Vietnams economically into the twentieth century.[69] Perhaps, LBJ began to think in the spring of 1965, North Vietnam could be seduced by peace if peace was gilded with prosperity. He recalled the Mekong development plan. Notes of a meeting he had with his foreign policy advisers on April 1 record him saying, "If we can first get our feet on their neck. Rural electrification—Brotherhood Operation."[70] A TVA for Southeast Asia—who could resist that?

LBJ began his talk at Johns Hopkins by describing the horrors of guerrilla war and justifying American participation in the Vietnam conflict in classic World War II–cold war terms. He then humanized the enemy. "For what do the people of North Viet-Nam want?" he asked rhetorically, spreading his arms for effect. "They want what their neighbors also desire: food for their hunger; health for their bodies; a chance to learn; progress for their country; and an end to the bondage of material misery. And they would find all these things far more readily in peaceful association with others than in the endless course of battle." He called for "a much more massive effort to improve the life of man in that conflict-torn corner of our world." Johnson then announced that he was going to request a $1 billion appropriation from Congress to help fund a giant Mekong River development project that would bring electricity with all of its benefits to the people of the region. Overseeing a task force to plan the project would be Eugene Black, the former head of the World Bank, a man respected in both financial and diplomatic circles. "The ordinary men and women of North Viet-Nam and South Viet-Nam—of China and India—of Russia and America—are brave people," he said. "They are filled with the same proportion of hate and fear, of love and hope. Most of them want the same things for themselves and their families." As icing on the cake, the president declared that the United States was ready for "unconditional discussions" with North Vietnam and other concerned governments looking to a negotiated settlement to the conflict.[71]

Now at last, Johnson could take some psychic comfort in the war. The United States was fighting not merely for geopolitical reasons, but to feed, clothe, and educate the underprivileged. Vietnam now could be seen as a piece of the Great Society, along with the civil rights movement, the poverty program, Medicare and Medicaid.[72] South Korea then had one of the highest economic growth rates in the world and one of the highest living standards in Asia. LBJ hoped for the same for South Vietnam and its neighbors. Regional economic development was the idea that made all the terrible things about the war endurable—and necessary.

To Johnson's consternation, the press paid virtually no attention to the Mekong development announcement but focused instead on the offer to negotiate. For this, LBJ was roundly praised from the editorial rooms of the *New York Times* to the *Times of India,* which declared the speech "a triumph for sanity, realism, and good sense." In France the Gaullist *Paris-Press* termed the Johns Hopkins address "the first ray of hope."[73]

On April 12 and 13, the DRV responded to the Baltimore speech by articulating its "Terms for Settlement": immediate cessation of air attacks; the withdrawal of all foreign bases and forces from Vietnam; settlement of South Vietnamese affairs by the people of the south "in accordance with the program of the Front [NLF]; and the peaceful unification of Vietnam without outside interference." The Mekong River development project was a "trap," Mai Van Bo, DRV ambassador to France, declared.[74]

In truth, the administration had no negotiating strategy because it was not committed to making concessions on basic questions. Johnson had offered to talk but at the same time had stated categorically that the United States would not settle for anything less than an "independent South Vietnam—securely guaranteed and able to shape its own relationships to all others—free from outside interference—tied to no alliance."[75] The speech was designed to mollify critics of the war and soothe the presidential psyche rather than produce a negotiated settlement. At McGeorge Bundy's urging, LBJ met with Walter Lippmann in the Oval Office the day before the Baltimore speech. While the columnist was flipping though the pages, LBJ blurted out, "I'm not just going to pull up my pants and run out on Vietnam. Don't you know the church is on fire over there . . . You say to negotiate, but there's nobody over there to negotiate with. So the only thing there is to do is to hang on. And that's what I'm going to do."[76] As long as the United States was committed to maintaining an independent, anticommunist state south of the seventeenth parallel, there would be no basis for negotiation. Ho Chi Minh, according to statements coming out of Hanoi and to American intelligence reports, was determined to reunify the country, expel foreign troops, and establish his version of a socialist system. The communist-led NLF viewed the military government in Saigon as a foreign-controlled, puppet regime dominated by northern Catholics intent on exploiting and oppressing the predominantly Buddhist south.

Unbeknown to Washington, however, the communist camp in Vietnam in 1965 was in many ways as conflicted as the leadership in the United States. There is no doubt, historian Robert Brigham writes, that the NLF was an extension of the DRV. The Lao Dong, the Vietnamese Communist Party, encompassed both, but there were certainly differences. The initiation of Rolling Thunder divided the communist leadership in Hanoi. A majority wanted to escalate, but a vocal minority on the Lao Dong Politburo called for a reexamination of the party's priorities. The bombing might destroy the North's economic base, thus threatening the socialist entity that already existed above the seventeenth parallel. Some questioned whether continued support for the insurgency in the South was worth it. "We feared that northerners who had friends in the Political Bureau, were so blinded by socialism," a southern communist observed, "that they would sacrifice the South to save the North." Thus did some southerners believe that Hanoi was willing to put the long-term interests of the North before liberation of the South.[77]

In one of the most important decisions of the war, the leadership of the Lao Dong decided to pursue a two-pronged strategy. Hanoi would increase its military commitment to the southern battlefield and at the same time pursue negotiations to limit the war. "Decisive victory" would come in the South through waging a protracted war. Le Duan, secretary general of the Lao Dong, outlined the DRV-NLF strategy for the years 1965–67. Hanoi would dangle peace feelers before Washington's eyes, compelling it to initiate periodic bombing pauses. Revolutionary forces would then take advantage of the lulls to destroy the bulk of ARVN troops while inflicting sufficient damage on American forces to compel the United States to withdraw.[78]

The struggle against Saigon and its American sponsors enjoyed the support of both Moscow and Beijing, although the Chinese were much more enthusiastic than the Russians. Indeed, the bombing of the North and the introduction of U.S. ground forces triggered a competition between the Soviet Union and communist China as to which could provide the most aid and thus gain maximum influence in North Vietnam and among the emerging peoples of the third world. Moscow dispatched surface-to-air missiles, IL-28 bombers, and MIG fighters.

Nevertheless, at the very time the United States was choosing to escalate the war in Vietnam and Russia was stepping up its aid, the Johnson administration was pursuing a policy of détente with the Soviet Union. Policymakers regarded Khrushchev's ouster as a setback, but they continued to view Russia as an increasingly conservative, status quo power that perceived armed revolution to be counterproductive to its interests. Repeatedly Washington appealed to Moscow to use its good offices to persuade Hanoi to see reason, even to mediate the dispute between South and North. But the Kremlin steadfastly refused. The United States, it insisted, must negotiate directly with the DRV and NLF.[79]

There were those in the Politburo who saw the war as a dangerous nuisance that could only benefit the Chinese, but Russia could not afford to appear less revolutionary than their community rivals. And what of communist China? In essence, Beijing had committed to mirroring the U.S. effort in behalf of South Vietnam. If the United States used its navy and air force to support a South Vietnamese attack on the North, China would provide naval and air support to the DRV; if the Johnson administration committed land forces to a drive across the seventeenth parallel, the Chinese communist army would enter the fray. Beginning in June 1965, China sent ground-to-air missiles, antiaircraft and artillery batteries, and engineering units into North Vietnam. By 1967 there were 170,000 Red Army personnel in the north.[80] The Chinese went out of their way to let American intelligence know their troops were there. Soldiers wore their regular uniforms and operated in the open. "The presence of troops," historian

Qiang Zhai has written, "along with the large base complex that China built at Yen Bai in northwest Vietnam, provided credible and successful deterrence against an American invasion of North Vietnam." It was at this point, on June 5, 1965, that Chinese Foreign Minister Chen Yi drew a line in the dirt for the United States. If Washington limited its air assaults to North Vietnam, and did not attempt to invade the North, Beijing would not enter the war. But if America attempted to invade the North or to bomb China, Beijing would commit and "would go all the way if it did come in."[81]

Ironically, the strategy developed by the DRV in 1965 was essentially the same one that the Johnson administration attempted to follow. During the period from late April to July 1965, LBJ decided on a two-pronged approach; at the same time the military was escalating the war on the ground in the South and continuing to bomb infiltration routes, arms depots, and enemy barracks between the seventeenth and twentieth parallels, diplomats would launch a peace initiative holding out the possibility of a negotiated settlement to the DRV and NLF. Such a strategy would help defuse the antiwar movement at home, win the propaganda battle abroad, and provide the communists with a channel if they did in fact decide to cry uncle.[82] Johnson berated Rusk and McNamara for not doing enough to build public and congressional support for escalation, and he directed Ball to prepare a memorandum outlining the justifications for a peace initiative. Meanwhile, reports from South Vietnam seemed to indicate that the war was going a bit better, at least in terms of enemy body count, increasingly the criterion for progress in the war.

Johnson's advisers assured him that he had adequate legal authority under the Constitution as commander in chief and under the terms of the Tonkin Gulf Resolution to put ground troops into Vietnam, but LBJ continued to fret about congressional opposition.[83] Indeed, in conversations with Mansfield and other congressional doves, the president seemed to share their misgivings. "I cannot see staying out there with the forces that I can see building up against it [the American presence]," he told the majority leader. "On the other hand, I do not see exactly the medium for pulling out . . . I want to talk to you and probably to McCormack . . . Rusk . . . McNamara . . . Bundy does not know I am thinking this. I have not talked to a human." He was convinced, he said, that the current request for more troops was just the beginning: "If they get 150, they will have to get another 150, and they they will have to get anther 150." He noted that opinion polls indicated the public approved escalation, "but I am not sure that they want to do that six months from now." To Senator Birch Bayh (D–Indiana) he confided, "I really believe they will last longer than we do. One of their boys gets down in a rut and stays there for two days without water, food, or anything and never moves, waiting to ambush somebody. Now an American stays there about 20 minutes and he got to get him a cigarette."[84] He did not want to go any further without congressional approval, Johnson told Mansfield. "I think you've might near gotta have a debate," he said. Mansfield warned him against such a move: "Well if you make another approach to the Congress, I think really the roof will blow off this time because people who have remained quiet will no longer remain silent." [85]

The first week in May, LBJ submitted a $700 million military appropriation bill to Congress to help defray the mounting costs of the war in Vietnam. This was no ordinary appropriations bill, he said in his accompanying message. "Each member of Congress who supports this request is also voting to persist in an effort to halt Communist aggression in South Vietnam." With public opinion polls running strongly in favor of continuing to hold the line in Southeast Asia and American soldiers fighting and dying in the field, the House and Senate voted the money by overwhelming margins. [86] RFK supported the measure but declared in a May 6 Senate speech that no one should consider his vote as a "blank check" to pursue a wider war. The course the administration was presently following risked sending "hundreds of thousands of American troops" to Southeast Asia, "a development that might easily lead to nuclear warfare." [87]

Then, in mid-June, just as Air Marshal Nguyen Cao Ky was seizing the reins of power, such as they were, in Saigon, the military situation took a sharp turn for the worse. [88] On June 5, McNamara reported to LBJ, "We've had a very unhappy week. The losses have been extremely high . . . In terms of killed, wounded, and missing in action, the total will be a thousand. We've had several serious setbacks, including an attack . . . by a Vietcong battalion-size force only ten miles from Saigon." [89] What do you think? LBJ asked. Westmoreland wanted forty-five thousand more men, the defense chief said, but he would recommend an increase of only about twenty-five thousand: "We have to slow down here and try to halt at some point the ground troop commitment." [90] "I don't believe they're ever going to quit," LBJ said. "And I don't see . . . that we have any . . . plan for a victory—militarily or diplomatically." [91]

Johnson trusted McNamara only up to a point—and Bundy even less so. He never forgot that the two men had been part of the Kennedy team and continued to socialize with Bobby and Jackie. At times, he thought he was being sucker-punched, with McNamara and Bundy pushing him toward greater involvement and RFK gearing up to reap the political harvest when he became bogged down in Vietnam. When Bundy disobeyed Johnson's orders not to publicly debate critics of the war, he directed Bill Moyers to ask for the national security adviser's resignation. As Moyers sat speechless, LBJ declared, "That's the trouble with all you fellows; you're in bed with the Kennedys." [92]

By this point, Westmoreland was pressing not only for an increase of fifty thousand troops but permission to abandon the enclave strategy for "search and destroy." If the tide were to be stemmed, American combat units would have to be able to roam freely throughout the country conducting spoiling operations and waging a war of attrition against the enemy. Neither Westmoreland nor his superiors, who eventually approved his request, envisioned escalation as anything more than a tactical response to an immediate situation; it was not a strategic decision to Americanize the war. The forty-four battalion request was intended to first blunt the enemy's conventional attack, then mop up Vietcong base and staging areas, and finally to force communist fighters out to South Vietnam's borders with Laos and Cambodia.[93]

Still LBJ refused to commit. He, Lady Bird, and the girls were scheduled to go to the ranch for the Fourth of July weekend. Two days before they departed, eighteen-year-old Luci (she had changed the spelling of her name) converted to Catholicism in a ceremony at St. Matthew's Cathedral in Washington. Lady Bird recalled that her younger daughter had seemed to be searching for something all her life. The structure of Catholic theology and the beauty of the liturgy appealed to her. She had taken instruction for nine months and deliberately scheduled the ceremony to coincide with her birthday. Her parents and Lynda accompanied her, but Lynda was in tears as they left the cathedral. Both Lyndon and Lady Bird had been opposed to the decision but had deferred to their daughter's will.[94]

Once he was esconced at the ranch, LBJ, and thus his guests, began to relax. While Luci showed off to her friends the Corvette she had gotten for her birthday, Lyndon roared around the lake in his speedboat. "Took all of the pretty girls he could gather . . . for a ride," Lady Bird recorded in her diary. "I think I do not remember three successive days at the ranch with such a minimum of calls from McNamara and McGeorge Bundy and Dean Rusk. Briefly the world has stopped to take a breath." Then it was time to return to Washington. "[I] said goodbye to Lyndon in his city clothes," Lady Bird recalled. "I almost look upon them as fighting uniforms these days. And it is a little sad to say goodbye to him heading back to the city of troubles."[95]

ON JULY 15, while on business in London, Adlai Stevenson dropped dead of a heart attack. Johnson had never been close to the dapper, articulate former Democratic standard-bearer. He had always thought Stevenson was a conservative masquerading as a silk-stocking liberal. Philosophically and temperamentally, the two men were as different as night and day. Stevenson had clashed with LBJ over Panama and most recently over Vietnam. Indeed, some of his friends in the Americans for Democratic Action had been pushing him to resign in protest over the decision to bomb the North. Still, Stevenson was valuable to Johnson because he was who he was. As he became more deeply involved in the Vietnam conflict and subsequently in the unrest in the Dominican Republic, LBJ needed a liberal internationalist in his diplomatic entourage. The UN ambassador would be perfect for the peace campaign the president was planning. "That Stevenson!" Johnson remarked shortly after the ambassador's demise. "Who am I going to get to take his place?"[96] He first considered Frank Church and then George Ball, but settled on Arthur Goldberg, the long-time labor lawyer whom Kennedy had chosen to be his secretary of labor and then named to the Supreme Court. Goldberg's appointment would serve two purposes. He was known to be in favor of a negotiated settlement in Vietnam, even if that meant neutralization, and his spot on the Court could be filled by long-time Johnson intimate Abe Fortas. The only possible drawback was reaction to the appointment in the Arab world. Goldberg was a Jew and an ardent Zionist. "What would it do to the Arabs, Dick?" he asked Richard Russell rhetorically. But those attributes could also be a plus. "I think this Jew thing would take the *New York Times*—all this crowd that gives me hell all the time—and disarm them. And [I'd] still have a Johnson man." [97]

LBJ called Goldberg to the Oval Office and offered him the UN post with "a key role in the Vietnam situation." [98] Goldberg put him off, and then on the plane to Stevenson's funeral, LBJ applied the pressure. After helping to make peace in Vietnam, Johnson told his mark, he might just be in line to become the first Jewish vice president. Goldberg said he wanted to think about it. On the plane ride back, LBJ told his guest that he was going to announce his resignation from the Court and his appointment to the UN post and that was that.

In early July, LBJ sent Robert McNamara and Henry Cabot Lodge, whom he had just named to succeed Max Taylor as ambassador to Vietnam, for one more firsthand appraisal of the situation. The new regime in Saigon headed by Air Marshal Ky had let Washington know that it considered the former ambassador much more sensitive to Vietnamese sensibilities and politics than Taylor, who had tended to treat the generals like a group of fledgling "cadets." [99] General Earle Wheeler was also part of the American contingent that landed in Saigon on July 16. That evening they dined with Prime Minister Ky and Premier Thieu. Ky appeared dressed in a tight white jacket, tapered trousers, patent leather shoes, and red socks, "looking like a saxophone player in a second-rate nightclub," as Stanley Karnow put it. "At least no one could confuse him with Uncle Ho," commented one member of the U.S. party. [100]

The American team returned to Washington for an almost continuous round of meetings beginning on July 21. McNamara seemed to have abandoned his reservations concerning an open-ended troop buildup. Westmoreland was not only asking for the first increase to eighty thousand men but an additional seventy-five thousand to be inserted between August and December. Both the defense chief and Bus Wheeler supported the request. Seventy-five thousand now would be "just enough to protect bases—it will let us lose slowly instead of rapidly," the JCS chair argued. To bolster Ball's position against escalation and for negotiation looking to withdrawal, Clark Clifford had been invited to sit in. The doves were logical and persuasive, but so were McNamara and Wheeler. This was the first war of national liberation, they argued; if the United States failed to respond, there would be another and another and another. Wheeler promised that the U.S. command would be able to reverse the downward trend in one year and be well on the way to victory in three years. [101] LBJ expressed doubt and indicated his belief that the conflict would eventually require the presence of half a million American soldiers.

During these crucial days of decision, LBJ's natural ebullience muted. "Normally," recalled John Connally, "he dominated any conversation, and all his listeners. He was restless, confident, persuasive. But when faced with a great decision, he changed. He fell silent, almost brooding. He questioned without revealing his thoughts. All his energy appeared to be focused on the decision." [102]

By the end of the week, Johnson seemed ready to commit. But then on Friday afternoon, April 23, he told the group gathered in the Cabinet Room, "I've got just a little weak spot in my stomach; the answer is 'no'; I'm going up to Camp David." [103] Lady Bird later recalled waking up the night before just before dawn and hearing her husband saying aloud to himself, "I don't want to get in a war and I don't see any way out of it. I've got to call up 600,000 boys, make them leave their homes and families." [104] As Johnson pondered his options, *Newsweek* was reporting that "physically and psychologically, South Vietnam [was giving] unmistakable signs of crumbling in the clutches of the Communist guerrillas . . . A fresh bomb plot against the life of retiring U.S. Ambassador Maxwell D. Taylor was foiled with only minutes to spare . . . And outside Saigon, the Viet Cong tightened their stranglehold on the capital city with equal ease. In a matter of only 72 hours, the guerillas blew up seven bridges and set up three roadblocks . . . Of the five major highways connecting Saigon with the countryside, only one—Route 4 leading to the rice-rich Mekong Delta—remained safe for travel and then only during daylight hours." [105]

The official guests at the presidential retreat that weekend were the John Connallys, but Rusk, McNamara, Goldberg, and Clifford traipsed in and out. The constant topic was Vietnam. "It was a short night," Lady Bird recalled in her diary. "I waked at five-thirty, with the birds chirping the dawn." The day was filled with individual and small group discussions on the situation in Southeast Asia in Aspen Lodge and other spots in the wooded compound. That evening the dinner conversation focused on the story of the 1960 convention, "LBJ versus RFK," as it was described in Arthur Schlesinger's recently released book. "In Aspen Lodge, late on Sunday afternoon, LBJ sat down, drinking a glass of Fresca with Goldberg, McNamara, and Clifford to talk about Vietnam. When the defense secretary suggested calling up the reserves and putting the nation on a war footing, Goldberg told Johnson, 'You do that and you don't get my letter of resignation!' " When Goldberg described his wish to take Vietnam to the UN, Clifford objected, warning that the risks outweighed the potential gains. The "counselor to the presidents" said he doubted that America could win the war. "Until January 1966, they should 'underplay Vietnam' in public, with 'no talking about where and why we are there,' " Lady Bird recalled his saying. "Then, after the monsoon season, they should find a way 'to get out.' " McNamara briskly replied that without a rapid military buildup, Saigon would fall. LBJ abruptly said that no one wanted peace more than he did. Then the man who so craved having people around him spent two hours driving and walking the grounds of Camp David alone. [106]

The last week in July 1965, LBJ authorized the dispatch of fifty thousand additional combat forces immediately and an additional seventy-five thousand by the end of the year. The JCS approved Westmoreland's search-and-destroy strategy. At the same time, the White House rejected the Joint Chiefs' and CIA's request to expand the bombing to include military-industrial targets in the northern part of North Vietnam. "Russia doesn't want war," he told those with whom he had been deliberating during the previous six months. "China doesn't want to get into a war, and you damned well know that we don't want to get into the big war. We can do this thing without bluster, without throwing our weight around. And we can do it, still making clear that we have committed our honor and our power."[107] The Pentagon announced that there would be additional troop levees, hinting at an enlarged draft and a partial call-up of the reserves, but it was not specific.[108] At noon on July 30, when the television and radio audiences were sure to be small, LBJ addressed the nation: "I have asked the commanding general, General Westmoreland, what more he needs to meet this mounting aggression. He has told me. And we will meet his needs. We cannot be defeated by force of arms. We will stand in Vietnam."[109]

Stepped up military operations would be only the first part of the two-pronged strategy to achieve peace with honor in Southeast Asia. "I told McNamara that he's my right hand punch," as he described it to journalists John Steele and Hugh Sidey. "I told him to take the power of this country and with it keep our word and keep our honor and our treaty, and protect the lives of our boys to the maximum extent possible. I told Rusk and Goldberg [punching the air now with his left fist] that they're my left hand punch and for us to get out. I told them to keep us in there with power and strength and to work to get us out."[110] The peace offensive would mean pursuing every lead, responding to any and every opportunity, private and public, to communicate with the enemy.[111] LBJ put it succinctly to Birch Bayh: "We are in a war of nerves; [hoping that] over several months that they'll finally say, 'Well, let's talk.' "[112]

Thus did the United States embark upon its limited war in Southeast Asia, a conflict that had as its goal not total victory but a return to the status quo as it had existed in 1954. While American ground forces and their ARVN allies "found, fixed, and finished" the Vietcong in the South, Rolling Thunder would compel the DRV to stop providing military support for the insurgency in the South. "We went in there with limited objectives," General John P. O'Connell recalled, "and we fought a limited war . . . It never was the intent to destroy the government of North Vietnam or destroy the North Vietnam nation itself. If it had been that intentional, we could have done it. We could have done it with air power and naval power in six weeks."[113] The entire effort was in a sense an exercise in communication. But it was in the area of communication that the Johnson administration committed its greatest blunders, or at least was preordained to commit such blunders by the premises that underlay the war. On the one hand, Washington was trying to scare and bluff Hanoi, attempting to leave the impression that it would increase the level of violence in the North until the DRV was incapable or unwilling to continue its effort to unify the country under a communist regime. On the other hand, the Johnson administration was trying to reassure Moscow and Beijing that there were certain and definite limits to the lengths it would go to force the North to submit to its will.[114]

Just as significant was the way the Johnson administration chose to communicate with the American people and Congress concerning the objectives and strategy that underlay the war. As numerous historians have noted, LBJ chose to try to fight a hot war in cold blood. He chose not to mobilize the reserves or declare a state of national emergency lest he create a wave of anticommunist hysteria that would push the nation into a major conflict with the Soviet Union and/or communist China. LBJ had taken care to sound out former President Eisenhower, the architect of victory in Europe. In both public and private, Ike proved to be an ardent supporter of air strikes against the North and eventually the introduction of ground combat troops. But he also made it clear that if the Chinese communists entered in force, he would call for the use of tactical nuclear weapons.[115] In addition, LBJ did not want to give conservatives an excuse to block passage of the remaining components of the Great Society. He knew what happened to a democratic society fully mobilized for war. Patriotism and xenophobia would run rampant, respect for civil liberties would decline, the war machine would consume every available resource, and any chance of domestic reform would disappear.[116] To prevent conservatives from using the war to undermine the Great Society, he would simply refuse to declare war.

At times, LBJ was so deliberately cloudy on the steps he intended to take in Vietnam that his own government was overcome with doubt and anxiety, "I understand . . . that you do not want to give a loud public signal of a major change in policy right now," McGeorge Bundy wrote LBJ after Rolling Thunder had gotten under way. Nevertheless, he and the rest of the foreign policy advisers believed that the decision to bomb the North was a "major watershed decision," and he pled with the president to make it clear that he agreed. It was imperative that "this decision be known and understood by enough people to permit its orderly execution."[117] Determined to keep his options open until the last minute, LBJ refused to outline a long-term, fixed strategy for his advisers or to select among those that were presented to him. At first, at the urging of Bundy and others, LBJ tried to stay out of the public limelight where Vietnam was concerned, letting Rusk, McNamara, and Ball, who had declared his unwavering commitment to the cause now that the decision had been taken, explain the motives behind and objectives of administration policy. Very quickly, however, it became apparent that the media would accept no substitute for the commander in chief, "The big story in Washington—and the only story," Busby told him, "has become what you think. Anything less is laughable."[118]

Gradually, LBJ began to speak out, first through a series of detailed briefings to groups of representatives and senators, and then in press conferences and speeches. His and his subordinates' utterances on the war in 1965 were characterized by strategic certainty and tactical ambiguity. The context of the cold war—communism versus capitalism, freedom versus totalitarianism, good versus evil—was clear; the rhetoric of limited war with its emphasis on communication and contingency was not. On the one hand were the shibboleths of the monolithic communist threat, the domino theory, the Munich analogy, and the Social Gospel. "We have come to one very clear conclusion," George Ball, with LBJ at his side, told a gathering of congressional leaders. "And that is that any withdrawal . . . of American power . . . from South Vietnam . . . would be a very real catastrophe, not merely for the United States, but for the whole Free World . . . And what is really involved in the longer range in the effort in South Vietnam is whether the Free World will be able to limit the expansionist drive of Communist China, not merely in the Southeast Asian peninsula, but on down through those very soft islands . . . Indonesia . . . the Philippines . . . [and] ultimately threaten Australia."[119] Spanning the globe, McGeorge Bundy compared America's commitment to Berlin with the obligation it had to Saigon.[120] At his April 27 news conference, LBJ declared, "If the price of ending aggression is blood and men, we are ready to pay that price. We do this . . . because it is right in this world that the strong and the wealthy should help the poor and the weak."[121]

On the other hand were the complexities of fighting a limited war designed to persuade rather than destroy, of a guerrilla conflict in which it was difficult to tell friend from foe, of defending an autocratic military regime in South Vietnam in the name of freedom and democracy. "The United States still seeks no wider war," LBJ told reporters in late March. "We threaten no regime and covet no territory."[122] As he rallied the nation to a greater effort in Southeast Asia, LBJ seemed at times almost apologetic. "I regret the necessities of war have compelled us to bomb North Vietnam," he declared in a statement to the press at the ranch. "We have carefully limited those raids. They have been directed at radar stations, bridges, and ammunition dumps, not at population centers. They have been directed at concrete and steel, and not human life."[123] If North Vietnam was the site of all this evil and the seat of aggression, why not strike at it and strike hard? Why the regret? Then there was the question of his ally's resolve. The South Vietnam that the media described and that administration spokesmen admitted existed seemed not to care nearly as much about their freedom and independence as did the United States. "The country is politically new," Bundy told congressmen. "It is divided into four religions and many more internal tendencies within the religions. There is a delicate balance of force between the military and the politicos. In order to have a stable government . . . we've got to understand what the Buddhists are doing. Yet every time I asked the question, when I was there—What do the Buddhists want? I got nothing but blank stares."[124] "We have had nine changes in the government of South Vietnam," LBJ himself admitted. "The best people that we have had out there have been unable to mash a button and get the kind of government they want."[125] Again and again, LBJ and his lieutenants told the American people and the world that the United States was fighting solely to enable the denizens of South

Vietnam to determine their own destiny, to protect the hallowed principle of national self-determination. But to most American minds, national self-determination implied democracy; a nation could not act or speak authentically unless and until popular sovereignty prevailed.[126] But in South Vietnam, democracy was nowhere to be seen.

At times, the president seemed totally confused. "Now, we are not going to leave that area as long as they will let us stay and want us to stay," he told an assemblage of House and Senate leaders. "And as we get into these skirmishes and as we suffer these losses and as the aggressor comes on us, why we are going on him. And what evils that will lead to, God only knows . . . We are going to try to keep them [U.S actions] steady and adequate and measured . . . And we hope some way, some how, and some time they will see the light. And if they don't, we hope we can deter them, whether we can diminish them. And if we have to, we can destroy them." [127] According to top administration officials, the purpose of the bombing of the North was to compel Ho and his lieutenants to negotiate, but according to these same officials, the DRV was not willing to parley and probably never would be. When Robert Goralski, an NBC correspondent, reported that talks and a negotiated settlement were the objects of the air assault against the North, LBJ blew his top. If the hawks believed that, they would turn on the administration in full force. "This stuff [reports that the object of the bombing was to get the DRV and NLF to the bargaining table rather than defeating them] creates all kinds of problems when the Senators see it," LBJ complained to Bundy. "They think we are going under." [128] To Robert McNamara: "Well my reaction is, ain't a damn bit of use [in] going out and bombing all morning and telling them all afternoon you didn't mean it and you want to talk at a conference table." In fact, the administration sounded conflicted and ambivalent because it was conflicted and ambivalent. "We're drifting from day to day here," McNamara replied to his boss, "and we ought to have inside the government some thought as to what we're going to say tomorrow and the next day and next week." [129]

Following the introduction of U.S. combat troops, the war in Vietnam became a distinct entity with momentum of its own. The Johnson administration and the American people were increasingly subject to what columnist Emmet John Hughes referred to as "the tyranny of accomplished facts": the blood spilled, the billions spent, the rhetoric of justification uttered. Except in the face of abject defeat or complete exhaustion, retreat had become unthinkable. Nevertheless, to many in Congress, the press, and academia, the war would come to seem anachronistic and unreasonable. Why this wrenching, dangerous war halfway around the world during a period of détente with the Soviet Union, increasing isolation of communist China, and growing independence among lesser communist states? Then there was the goal of a democratic, self-sufficient, noncommunist South Vietnam. Even to those who paid the most superficial attention to the situation in Southeast Asia, this seemed an unattainable, even ludicrous objective. Opinion polls taken in the summer of 1965 showed public support for escalation, but 73 percent of Americans expressed absolutely no confidence in the government of South Vietnam. In March of that year the first major news report to use the term "credibility gap" appeared. As Hughes put it, "The laws of politics do not allow even the mightiest nation to win a victory it cannot define." [130]

CHAPTER 30

CASTRO'S AND
KENNEDY'S SHADOWS

A T 4:40 IN THE AFTERNOON OF APRIL 28, LYNDON Johnson sat down with Dean Rusk, Robert McNamara, George Ball, McGeorge Bundy, and presidential aide Bill Moyers to discuss the perilous situation in Vietnam. An hour into the meeting President Johnson was handed a cable marked "critic" (critical) from Ambassador W. Tapley Bennett in Santo Domingo. The Dominican military had spilt into at least two factions, and one was arming the populace in an effort to seize power. "Regret report situation deteriorating rapidly," it stated. "Country team unanimously of opinion that time has come to land the marines . . . American lives are in danger." After conferring with his advisers, all of whom approved intervention, President Johnson ordered four hundred marines to proceed to the Dominican capital at once. Rusk rushed off to inform all the Latin American embassies in Washington, and Moyers departed to set up a briefing session in the Cabinet Room for congressional leaders later that evening.[1]

When Johnson and his advisers closeted themselves with the House and Senate leaders, Rusk stressed that the administration's decision to intervene had been based on the need to protect American lives. Newly named head of the CIA Admiral William "Red" Raborn declared that there had been "positive identification of three ring-leaders of the Rebels as Castro-trained agents." Everett Dirksen and John McCormack immediately warned of the danger of allowing another Castroite regime to emerge in the hemisphere and declared their support for armed intervention. Bill Fulbright's only contribution to the council of war was to recommend that the Organization of American States be involved.[2]

But on April 29, Richard Goodwin warned that the Dominican crisis could be as costly "as the Bay of Pigs invasion itself." The marine landing, he reminded Johnson, was the first military intervention in Latin America since U.S. troops left Nicaragua in the 1920s. It contravened the charter of the OAS and violated the spirit of the Good Neighbor Policy. Goodwin, coarchitect with Arthur Schlesinger of the Kennedy administration's Latin American policy, insisted that President Johnson not put himself in the position of suppressing a popular revolution against military rule. Still, he concluded, "I agree that anything, including military intervention, should be done if essential to prevent another Castro-type takeover in the Caribbean."[3]

The following day, as Dean Rusk advised reporters to play down "the ideological aspects of this thing," Johnson met with McNamara and General Wheeler.[4] He asked them, John Bartlow Martin later wrote, "What they would need to take the republic." One or two divisions, they replied. Martin, a former ambassador to the Dominican Republic whom Johnson had decided to send down on a fact-finding mission, recalled LBJ's motives as he stated them: "The President said he foresaw two dangers—very soon we would witness a Castro/Communist-dominated government in the Dominican Republic, or we would find ourselves in the Republic alone without any support in the hemisphere. He didn't want either to happen." Anticipating the criticism that was to come, Johnson declared that he had every intention of working through the OAS, but that he did not intend "to sit here with my hands tied and let Castro take that island. What can we do in Vietnam if we can't clean up the Dominican Republic?"[5]

The causes of the Dominican Republic's many troubles were varied, but most were rooted in the thirty-year dictatorship of Rafael Leonidas Trujillo Molina. Trujillo had brutally suppressed all opposition, turned the army into his personal palace guard, and ravaged his country's fragile economy. Then, in the summer of 1961, assassins had shot him through the head. His family tried to perpetuate his tyranny, but failed and fled into exile. In December 1962, the Dominicans elected the liberal intellectual Juan Bosch president. Tall, handsome, and charismatic, Bosch was immensely popular with peasants, workers, students, and some members of the middle class. Much as FDR had with his countrymen, he was able to project a sense of empathy with the travails of everyday life for the mass of Dominicans.[6] At the same time, he alienated the army, landed elite, and Catholic Church by forging a live-and-let-live agreement with the communist-dominated 14th of June movement and by presiding over the writing of a constitution that guaranteed basic civil liberties and legalizing divorce. By the summer of 1963, the oligarchy had decided that Bosch had to go, and on September 24, 1963, he was ousted in a military coup that forced him into exile in Puerto Rico.[7]

Heading the triumvirate that subsequently presided in the Dominican Republic was Donald Reid Cabral, scion of one of the nation's wealthiest and most powerful families. The Caribbean nation was absolutely dependent on the sugar industry, and Reid Cabral had the misfortune to be in power when the world price for that commodity collapsed.[8] Dull and uninspiring, Reid Cabral also lacked his predecessor's sympathy for the common man. Indeed, under his rule, trade union leaders were jailed, left-wing newspapers were banned, and the death squads that had been such a prominent part of the Trujillo regime returned. Reid Cabral soon established a cordial relationship with the U.S. ambassador, W. Tapley Bennett Jr., a veteran diplomat and a Georgian who was very close to Richard Russell and his family.[9] The Dominican Revolutionary Party (PRD) which Bosch had helped found began to make a comeback among peasants, workers, and even a contingent of left-leaning military officers.

The spring of 1965 found the Dominican military deeply divided. A minority were committed to Bosch's return, but the majority regarded him as a dangerous revolutionary who would "open the door to the communists" and, not coincidentally, do away with the military's privileges. When, in the spring of 1965, officers loyal to Reid Cabral attempted to arrest some of their fellows for plotting against the government in behalf of Juan Bosch, the PRD declared a general uprising and seized the presidential palace. At this point, the anti-Bosch military, led by the pious and thoroughly reactionary General Elias Wessin y Wessin, issued an ultimatum to the PRD, demanding that it turn over the palace to the army. Wessin y Wessin had become convinced that Bosch and the PRD were encouraging the Castroite 14th of June movement. When the rebels ignored his demand, air force planes began bombing and strafing the palace, as well as the slums of Santo Domingo, which were Bosch strongholds and, in the minds of the military, seedbeds of communist agitation. The brutal attacks inflamed the population, which subsequently flooded into the streets in response to calls from the PRD.[10]

By April 24 armed civilians, including leaders of the PRD and 14th of June movement, and dissident troops led by Colonel Francisco Alberto Caamano Deno controlled the center of the capital, Santo Domingo, including the presidential palace and Radio Santo Domingo. In a poor third world country like the Dominican Republic, in which half the population was unable to read, control of the radio waves was very important. Even the poorest barrio contained dozens of transistor radios. Meanwhile, the anti-Bosch, or "loyalist," faction within the military under General Wessin y Wessin began to organize to storm insurgent positions. Their base of operations was the main military base at San Isidro on the outskirts of the city.[11] At this point, P-51 Mustangs from the San Isidro air base once again began bombing and strafing the palace and subsequently the inner-city barrios where the insurgents were dug in. Over the next three days, a handful of rebels and dozens of civilians were killed. On April 26, the violence mounted, with street gangs looting houses in the more affluent part of Santo Domingo, and rebel forces besieging police stations in the areas under their control.[12]

On April 27 the battle for Duarte Bridge, connecting the suburbs of Santo Domingo with the rebel-held inner city, began. By this point, more than a thousand Americans had taken shelter in the Ambassador Hotel, the largest luxury hotel in the city. At midmorning some thirty rebels entered the building looking for the editor of a small, far-right newspaper, *La Prensa Libre,* who had played a role in ousting Bosch. The armed band held several American tourists at gunpoint, conducted a fruitless search for the journalist, fired some rounds into the air, and departed. This intrusion convinced the American Embassy that its nationals had to be evacuated. Half were bused to two ships that had arrived at the port of Haina, while the other half were flown by helicopter to the USS *Boxer,* an aircraft carrier situated some five miles out to sea. There were no incidents.[13] It was in the midst of this evacuation that Tapley Bennett had sent his cable to the White House urgently requesting the dispatch of marines.

From late April through June 1965, Lyndon Johnson would spend more time on the situation in the Dominican Republic than he would on any other issue, including civil rights and Vietnam. By the time the crisis had ended, the United States had positioned twenty thousand troops in the island nation, one of the largest military interventions in the troubled history of U.S.–Latin American relations. As in so many other foreign policy crises during his administration, LBJ pursed a policy of double containment; containment of communism abroad and anticommunism at home. In the end, LBJ and his foreign policy team were able to quell the violence in Santo Domingo and bring forth a government that represented neither the far left nor the far right in Dominican politics. He believed that he could do the same thing in Vietnam.

THE PEACEFUL CONCLUSION of the Cuban Missile Crisis had not ended the blood feud between Castro and the United States. The Russians had supposedly dismantled their missiles and left, but many in the United States feared that they would return, or worse, that when the Soviets had departed, they had left secreted offensive weapons in the hands of the mercurial Cuban leader. What was certain was that the Russians had turned over their surface-to-air missiles to Castro, who had sworn to use them to halt Yankee overflights.[14] The huge anti-Castro Cuban exile community in Florida and the communist government in Havana were constantly at each other's throats. The U.S.-led economic boycott of the Ever Faithful Isle continued to take its toll. And there seemed to be a never-ending series of minicrises to plague relations between the two countries. In the spring of 1964, the U.S. Coast Guard had seized four Cuban fishing boats plying their trade in North American waters. Castro responded by cutting off the water supply to the American base at Guantanamo Bay. The incident was resolved peacefully, but as LBJ remarked to Richard Russell, "I think there's a latent feeling there one of these days, they [the American people] are going to say well we've just been a bunch of asses. [We cannot] continually just back down and give away and say excuse me every time we come in collision with one of these little countries just because they're small and particularly communist countries and nobody will know just when the boiler is ready to give on it."[15] Indeed, conservatives like Richard Nixon, Everett Dirksen, J. Edgar Hoover, and the editors of the *National Review* were convinced that the threat of Castroism spreading throughout the hemisphere was very real. The GOP stood as ready as ever to denounce the Democrats for being soft on communism.

Just as vociferous, if not as numerous, were liberals who believed that U.S. intervention into the affairs of its sister republics was immoral and counterproductive no matter what the circumstances. Heading critics of U.S.–Latin American policy was a group of U.S. senators—Ernest Gruening of Alaska, Wayne Morse of Oregon, George McGovern of South Dakota, Frank Church of Idaho, and Bill Fulbright of Arkansas.[16] McGovern's first speech was entitled "Our Castro Fixation versus the Alliance for Progress." Fidel's revolution, the South Dakotan suggested, "forced every government of the hemisphere to take a new and more searching look at the crying needs of the great masses of human beings."[17] Out of power, Arthur Schlesinger and Robert Kennedy increasingly gravitated toward this group and its arguments. "This damn Schlesinger is going all over the world denouncing us," LBJ complained to Assistant Secretary of State for Latin American Affair Tom Mann. He was saying "how our whole policy in Latin America has changed and we had abandoned the Alliance."[18]

The task confronting LBJ in the Dominican crisis, as he saw it, was to steer a middle course between the anti-imperialists and anticommunists at home and reactionaries and revolutionaries in Latin America. He regarded Castroism as an authentic threat to peaceful change and to democracy, but no more than the autocratic, privileged elites who would use the red menace for their own purposes. To a degree, these divisions were reflected within the foreign policy establishment as it pertained to Latin America. Dean Rusk, Tom Mann, Mann assistant Jack Hood Vaughn, and Tapley Bennett were anticommunists first, democrats and social reformers second. McNamara, Bundy, and particularly Abe Fortas, whom Johnson brought in to troubleshoot during the Dominican crisis, tended to err on the side of democracy and social reform. Not that they were willing to countenance the emergence of another Cuba in the Western Hemisphere, but they believed that the threat of communist infiltration and takeover must be evaluated realistically and every effort made to work with and co-opt indigenous revolutions.

With a thousand Americans trapped in the Ambassador Hotel and a showdown looming between the rebels holed up in the center of Santo Domingo and the loyalist military advancing on them from San Isidro, LBJ, at seven-thirty in the evening on April 28, had ordered the first contingent of five hundred marines into action. An hour later, he went on television to announce that the troops were being dispatched "to protect American lives."[19] That night, U.S. helicopters landed on the polo field next to the hotel and began the evacuation. The administration now had to decide whether to pull out and leave the Dominicans to themselves or to intervene massively to determine the outcome of the onrushing civil war.

By this point, Bosch in Puerto Rico had accepted the rebels' invitation to return as president and was broadcasting appeals to all freedom-loving Dominicans to support the insurgents. The issue for LBJ was the extent to which communists had taken control of the revolution. According to testimony subsequently given by Mann and others before an executive session of the Senate Foreign Relations Committee, there were three significant communist contingents in the Dominican Republic in the spring of 1965: the 14th of June movement, with an estimated membership of between three and four thousand that looked to Havana for leadership; the Popular Democratic Socialist Party, subsequently the Dominican Communist Party, with seven hundred to a thousand members that looked to Moscow for guidance; and a Beijing-oriented faction, the Popular Dominican Movement, with a following of some five hundred.[20] In Mann and Rusk's opinion, Bosch was an ivory-tower intellectual, weak and vulnerable to manipulation by the ruthless Marxists who had infiltrated the PRD and were assuming control of the insurgency. "Bosch writes books," Mann observed to the president. "He's the most impractical fellow in the world. Sort of an idealist. We don't think that he is a Communist [but we] don't think that [he] understands that the Communists are dangerous."[21]

On the afternoon of April 29, the U.S. Embassy and the marine detachment guarding it came under insurgent sniper fire. "I sure don't want to wake up and find out Castro is in charge," Johnson remarked gloomily to McGeorge Bundy.[22] The Latin Americanists within the State Department, Richard Goodwin, and various press pundits continued to urge Johnson to work through the OAS. On the 28th the president had appealed to that body to authorize a joint military operation to restore peace in the Dominican Republic. To his intense frustration, the head of the OAS informed the White House that it would take time to even get the delegates together much less agree on the wording of a statement.[23]

Suddenly, Johnson began to panic. When the revolution had gotten under way, he had arranged for his friend and confidante, Abe Fortas, to go to Puerto Rico and confer with Juan Bosch to attempt to persuade him to disown the communist influence within the insurgency and accept a compromise settlement with the loyalist military. Fortas had come to know Bosch through a mutual friend, Jaime Benitez, chancellor of the University of Puerto Rico, when Fortas had been undersecretary of the interior.[24] Late in the morning of the 30th LBJ called his friend, who was operating under the code name "Mr. Davidson," in San Juan. Suffering from a terrible cold, his voice harsh and shrill, he was barely comprehensible:

> They're killing our people. They've captured tanks now and they've taken over the police, and they're marching them down the street and they're saying they're going to shoot them if they don't take over. Now, our CIA says this is a completely led, operated, dominated—they've got men on the inside of it—Castro operation. That it started out as a Bosch operation, but he's been moved completely out of the picture. Since last Saturday Bosch lasted for a few hours. Then Castro started operating.

They got forty-five more in there last night—Castro-trained, Castro-operated. They are moving other places in the hemisphere. It may be a part of a whole Communist pattern tied in with Vietnam. I don't think that God Almighty is going to excuse me for sitting with adequate forces and letting them murder human beings.[25]

To Mike Mansfield later in the day LBJ said, "The Castro forces are really gaining control. We begged the OAS to send somebody in last night. They won't move. They're just the damndest fraud I ever saw, Mike, these international organizations ain't worth a damn, except window dressing."[26]

That afternoon, LBJ and his advisers hit on the idea of sending several battalions of regular army troops to establish an "international safety zone" extending from the U.S. Embassy out to the polo field where the marines had rallied. Nationals of all countries seeking safety from the fighting could congregate there, and it would give the United States cover with the international community for intervening militarily in what was clearly a civil war.[27]

With Johnson scheduled to go on a nationwide television hookup that night at 8:40 to inform the country of his decision, a nasty argument broke out among his advisers as to what justification should be used. Mann and the CIA wanted Castroism and the threat of another communist regime in the hemisphere to be front and center. LBJ wholeheartedly agreed with them. Both hard-liners like Russell and liberals like Mansfield and Morse were telling him that it was on these grounds and these grounds alone that Congress and the public would accept massive armed intervention in a civil conflict. McNamara was of the opinion that the Red card ought to be played, but that the president's advisers and not the president ought to do it: "I think you have got a pretty tough job to prove that [they] have got a handful of people there but you don't know that Castro is trying to do anything. You would have a hard time proving to any group that Castro has done more than train these people, and we have trained a lot of people. I think it puts your own status and prestige too much on the line." LBJ asked him if the CIA would be able to document the fact of communist domination of the insurgency. McNamara said he did not think so. The agency might be able to demonstrate that certain people had been trained in Cuba but not that Castro was directing the rebellion in Santo Domingo or even had any control over the people he had trained.[28] Moyers also wanted to keep the cold war out of the speech. "The CIA Cuban Man tells me Havana is still taken off balance by this," he observed. "Their hope is that we don't give some push to Cuba to try to get in there in a way they're not in there now."[29] Bundy agreed. He did not want the president to get "pinned to a civil war against Communists that aren't in charge."[30]

By six o'clock, Johnson was nearly beside himself. "While we were talking yesterday, we ought to have been acting," he told Bundy. "I think they're going to have that island in another twenty-four hours. We've run under the table and hid." When Bundy said that some in the State Department were afraid that the

OAS might take references to communist domination of the insurgency in the Dominican Republic as an effort to stampede the membership, LBJ blew his top. "All right," he screamed at Bundy. "Let's see if we can satisfy that bunch of damn sissies over there on that question! Let's cut it [reference to communist influence] and say they're 'great statesmen!' "[31]

Johnson's address to the nation delivered on the evening of April 30 was a disaster. He felt rotten. The klieg lights were too close, partially blinding and overheating him. In the midst of his speech, the teleprompter stopped; Johnson read the same paragraph twice. "I begged George Reedy to go [fix] it," he complained to Fortas after the speech, "[but] he is the laziest, no-good son of a bitch!"[32] He announced that he was sending marines and army personnel to the Dominican Republic to prevent further killing and restore order. "At stake are the lives of thousands, the liberty of a nation, and the principles and the values of all the American Republics." He reviewed events and indicated that forces outside the hemisphere were attempting to take advantage of the situation. The United States must intervene to stop the bloodshed and to see a freely elected, noncommunist government take power.[33]

Two nights later, Johnson gave a more extensive explanation. Some advised waiting, he asserted, but when the entire nine-member U.S. team in Santo Domingo indicated that without U.S. forces, " 'men and women—Americans and those of other lands—will die in the streets'—well, I knew there was no time to talk, to consult, or to delay." He then played the Red card. In the midst of the unrest, events "took a tragic turn," he said. "Communist leaders, many of them trained in Cuba, took increasing control. And what began as a popular democratic revolution was taken over and really seized and placed into the hands of a band of Communist conspirators. The American nations cannot, must not, and will not permit the establishment of another Communist government in the Western Hemisphere."[34]

Opinion polls taken shortly thereafter indicated popular approval for the president's actions, but dissidents in Congress, the press, and in other American republics began to question the extent of communist influence in the insurgency and the wisdom of U.S. intervention. As they did, LBJ became more shrill and exaggerated in defense of his actions. Had the United States not intervened, blood would have run in the streets, he repeatedly told the White House press corps. Warming to the subject, LBJ declared, "Some 1,500 innocent people were murdered and shot, and their heads cut off, and six Latin American embassies were violated and fired upon over a period of 4 days before we went in. As we talked to our Ambassador to confirm the horror and the tragedy and the unbelievable fact that they were firing on Americans and the American Embassy, he was talking to us from under a desk while bullets were going through his windows and he had a thousand American men, women, and children assembled in the hotel who were pleading with their President for help to preserve their lives."[35] Johnson's extravagant rhetoric, of course, betrayed a fundamental anxiety about the correctness of his course. "If I send in Marines, I can't live in the hemisphere," he told congressional leaders on May 2. "If I don't, I can't live at home."[36]

As to the wisdom of the Dominican intervention and the motives behind it, opinions vary. The question of communist influence aside, Assistant Secretary of Defense Cyrus Vance, who was part of the negotiating team, believed that the U.S. intervention had averted a bloodbath. "Indeed," he confided to an interviewer, "Caamano told me privately in one of my conversations with him that if the United States had not interposed itself between the contending forces that thousands and perhaps scores of thousands of Dominicans would have been killed."[37] "I think you have to read this in terms of American domestic politics at the time," said George Ball, who was in the Oval Office when LBJ made his decision. "The clamor that if we had permitted the Dominican Republic to become another Cuba, which was the thing that was on the President's mind, I think it would have been devastating; that, plus the fact that he was getting a lot of what I thought were highly dubious reports from J. Edgar Hoover about the number of communists."[38]

Once the decision to intervene had been made, the U.S. Caribbean Command moved quickly. By May 1, there were sixty-two hundred U.S. combat soldiers in the Dominican Republic. By May 17, the intervention force had reached its maximum of 22,200 soldiers. The first week in May, the OAS agreed to send a delegation representing five member states to oversee a cease-fire and mediate between the two sides. Fortas and Moyers persuaded LBJ to appoint former ambassador to the Dominican Republic John Bartlow Martin to go to the island and join the American negotiating team. As U.S. troops occupied a zone between the Ambassador Hotel and the Embassy, effectively inserting themselves between the loyalist forces and the insurgents, Martin and his team convinced the junta and the rebel forces to sign a cease-fire. The loyalists, suddenly grown braver, insisted that in any final settlement the rebels surrender unconditionally and accept the punishment they had coming to them. As Martin advised Washington, "The gutless Generals" were "waiting for the U.S. to do the job for them."[39]

As U.S. troops poured into Santo Domingo, Colonel Caamano, who had been approved by Bosch as temporary provisional president of the insurgent republic, reported to his exiled leader that the Americans were aiding loyalist troops, tightly constricting the rebel zone while allowing the junta to move its forces into position on his perimeter. And, in truth, the American press was full of reports of such prejudicial treatment. It seemed for the moment that Washington might side openly with the anti-Bosch forces. On May 2, reports came into the White House Situation Room that American troops at the Ambassador Hotel and the polo field were under fire, with two marines dead and twenty wounded.[40] "These attacks were during the night and they were carried out by very well organized, prepared, and armed men," Martin subsequently reported to the president. "So the rebels violated the cease fire line they had agreed to."[41] "Got raging disorder, concentrated mobs, Castro oratory reported. Real Holocaust. Castro Communist elements have taken over movement," LBJ scribbled on his notepad during a meeting held that day to discuss the Dominican crisis.[42]

LBJ followed closely and with increasing anguish the mounting critical and sometimes incredulous press reports on the intervention. "I just watched the television shows tonight," Johnson complained to McGeorge Bundy, "and the CBS reporter from down there said we ran wild through the rebel zone and just invited people to shoot us and try to stir up trouble. We are just mean sons o' bitches and outlaws and they are nice, virtuous maidens."[43] Characteristically, he could not leave well enough alone. Johnson called NBC correspondent John Chancellor, whom he regarded as one of his few allies in the press: "Now what happened is . . . Bosch people started it," he confided. "Then these fellows [the communists] move in just like they do in a Negro demonstration. 8 of them were identified by midnight. 58 are identified as of last night." Chancellor mumbled assent. "I have to be very careful," the president added, "because I don't want to say a guy who disagrees with me is a communist or I'm a McCarthy."[44] On May 5, Johnson called *New York Times* correspondent Charles Mohr. "This was not a fight between a great literary, fine, sweet poet and mean old Wessin," LBJ proclaimed. "It was a fight between two goddamn thugs!"[45] At the same time the White House stepped up pressure on Raborn and the CIA to come up with the names and credentials of more Castroites within the insurgent movement.[46]

While U.S. marines and army units labored to contain the insurgents and build up the morale of loyalist forces, Johnson's Dominican team, which by now included Mann, Deputy Secretary of Defense Cyrus Vance, Martin, General Bruce Palmer, commander of U.S. forces in Santo Domingo, and Fortas, labored to come up with an interim government that would be noncommunist without being fanatically anticommunist, one that would at least tolerate advocates of social reform. During the first ten days of May, Fortas and Bundy ferried back and forth between San Juan and Santo Domingo, trying to find an appropriate figurehead and negotiate a settlement under which peace and stability could be restored. Fortas, and to an extent Martin, sympathized with Bosch but believed him unfit to rule. If he were to return to assume the presidency, he would either become a tool of the communists or a victim of right-wing extremists. After meeting with Bosch, Martin reported him to be "a broken man." "Probably the most we can get out of him is silence but of course that is something," he told the president.[47] On the other hand, he observed, "there is not a goddamn thing in the Junta."[48]

If the situation were not volatile enough, the Kennedys now chose to enter the fray. On May 6, RFK rose on the floor of the Senate to deliver a speech criticizing the administration for not working through the OAS. The text had been drafted by the ubiquitous Arthur Schlesinger. Working on another front, Schlesinger took it upon himself to confer with Venezuelan President Romulo Betancourt, a democratically elected progressive whom Trujillo had attempted to assassinate, on the Dominican situation and report to the White House. Intensely annoyed, but cognizant of the need to not appear to be acting unilaterally, LBJ agreed to meet with Betancourt. To Johnson's delight, the Venezuelan seemed to be thoroughly in accord with his thinking. As for Bosch, he observed, "He is the best short story writer and the worst politician in Latin America, and he should spend the rest of his life writing short stories." But he agreed with Martin that Wessin y Wessin and the other extremists were unacceptable as well. Betancourt agreed to team up with former Costa Rican President Jose Figures and the former governor of Puerto Rico, Luis Muñoz Marin, and develop a plan for an eventual OAS trusteeship for the Dominican Republic. LBJ agreed to support the effort with a massive aid package to reconstruct the war-torn republic.[49]

In mid-May, Fortas came up with the name of Silvestre Antonio Guzman Fernandez as a possible compromise interim president. He was a leader of the moderate wing of the PRD, had remained loyal to Bosch, but was staunchly anticommunist. But when the junta got word of the Guzman option, it reacted violently. As a Bosch protégé he was totally unacceptable.[50] Wessin and his colleagues put forward the name of General Antonio Imbert Barreras, a man who had first served Trujillo and then joined with those who had assassinated him.[51] All through the night of May 14, LBJ spoke with one adviser, then another. "The political emotions here are just at this particular time absolutely indescribable," Tom Mann reported. "I've never seen anything like it."[52] In the end, LBJ was forced to choose between Imbert and Guzman, and thus between Mann and Fortas, between their respective approaches to the situation.

The dispute was over more than just personalities. Rusk and Mann insisted that any provisional regime give categorical assurances that there would be no communist participation in the new government and that communists or suspected communists found to be engaged in subversive activities would be either deported or imprisoned. Fortas, Bundy, and Vance believed that such assurances were not necessary; the new regime should have an opportunity to co-opt members of the 14th of June movement in particular.[53] LBJ felt a strong sense of loyalty toward Mann, whom the press and anti-imperialist senators had increasingly targeted as an uncritical supporter of the junta. "Well, now, really, honestly," he told Fortas, "I have more confidence in Mann's judgment than I do in Bundy's. I have never found Mann wrong." Fortas said that he did not think that Mann was a reactionary, merely unimaginative and inflexible. "I don't think he's quick to adjust his own fundamental notions to changing strategic situations," he told Johnson.[54] He could not see how backing Imbert and the junta could do anything but lead to a repeat of the present situation, and the United States would once again identify itself with the forces of reaction in Latin America. LBJ asked if stories were true to the effect that U.S. troops were actively aiding the loyalists. Fortas replied that they were not now but had been in the past.[55] Later that day, LBJ discussed the situation with Moyers. Imbert, he observed, "will never have mass support," but Guzman seemed to have support only from liberals and seemed not to have "much character, much guts." Nevertheless, "between Abe and Tom, as of the moment I would favor Abe."[56]

While these discussions were going on, Imbert and loyalist troops began cleaning insurgents out of the northern part of Santo Domingo, home to the city's major industrial plants. The rebel main force was prevented from coming to their aid by the cordon of American troops. In response, they vented their rage against the presidential palace, now in loyalist hands. Marines who were still guarding the structure responded to insurgent mortars and small arms fire in kind. In the cross-fire a young colonel, Rafael Fernandez Dominguez, was killed. A protégé of Bosch's, he had flown in just a few days before, ready to play a prominent role in any provisional government.[57] Caamano, furious, charged that Fernandez had been shot in the back by "Yankee assassins." He cabled the UN that the incident was just "one more proof of the assistance which the invaders have been giving to the reactionary military forces." "Sometime in the middle of the night," Lady Bird recorded in her diary, "Lyndon came and crawled into bed with me. This morning, haggard and worn, he looked at me and said, 'The most awful thing has happened!' He said Bosch's friends, five of them, were returning to Santo Domingo. The one who was the key to the situation was shot in street fighting and killed. Lyndon said he had only slept two hours Monday night and very little last night."[58] With great difficulty, Guzman was persuaded to keep his hat in the ring.

Johnson's solution to the Dominican problem was to draft Guzman to head a provisional government but to force him to agree to exclude known communists and to crack down on the 14th of June movement and any other groups linked to the forces of international communism at the first sign of trouble. "I can't sell [this proposal] to Russell and to Dirksen and to Ford and to the George Mahons [Texas congressman] for one dollar," he cried to Fortas. "I just can't! I can't stand the pressure if we have a government that's soft or sympathetic or even kind in dealing with the Communists. I'm not ever going to get Schlesinger's support or the liberals' support. It's really got to be anti-Communist and pro-liberal."[59] "First thing that's going to happen," he told his friend, "they're going to go tell Tom Dodd [Connecticut senator and staunch anticommunist]—Hoover is—that I didn't check it and I've got a notorious communist as secretary of the Army. That's what they'll do and I'll be destroyed."[60] "George," LBJ remarked to Ball in 1965, "the great beast is the reactionary elements in the country. Those are the people that we have to fear."[61]

During the hectic days in late April, when Johnson had been coming to the decision to intervene and subsequently to justify that intervention, he had made the mistake of asking the FBI to join the CIA in hunting for card-carrying reds in the Dominican Republic. Hoover had been more than happy to oblige. From the beginning he was convinced that "this so-called Bosch fellow and his stooge down there [Caamano] were either communists or fellow travelers." There was no doubt, he said over and over to LBJ, that "the communists are holding and directing the principal policy of the rebel forces down there." Now Johnson found himself hostage to the instrument he had hoped to wield to protect his right flank. As he struggled to find a satisfactory arrangement, LBJ repeatedly tried to appease the director by volunteering, in advance, the dossiers of individuals being considered for positions in the Guzman regime. From June until the end of the year, the State Department struggled to get the FBI and Hoover out of the Dominican picture, but to no avail.[62]

Gradually, Caamano and Imbert faded into the background. Privately, the U.S. negotiating team arranged for "overseas assignments" for Wessin y Wessin and other, more extreme members of the junta and for the three most prominent leaders of the insurgency.[63] In September 1965, moderate Hector Garcia Godoy was installed as president of a provisional government. A year later, Juan Balaguer peacefully, if fraudulently, defeated Juan Bosch for the presidency of the Dominican Republic.[64] With the advent of economic stability, if not social justice, a troubled calm settled over the island. The same could be said of Lyndon Johnson. "I have nothing in the world I want, except to do what I believe to be right," he cried out to Abe Fortas. "I don't always know what's right. Sometimes I take other people's judgments, and I get misled. Like sending troops in there to Santo Domingo. But the man that misled me was Lyndon Johnson. Nobody else! I did that! I can't blame a damn human . . . I know how it looks. It looks just the opposite of the way I want to look. I don't want to be an intervener."[65]

THE DOMINICAN CRISIS OF 1965 marked the beginning of an open breach between LBJ and the chair of the Senate Foreign Relations Committee, J. William Fulbright, a break that would have profound consequences for the Johnson presidency.

On September 14, McGeorge Bundy was tipped off by "friendly newspapermen" that Fulbright was going to deliver a major address the next day indicting the administration for mishandling the Dominican situation and then intervening to no good purpose.[66] Fulbright's Dominican address was indeed a devastating indictment. After laying out the chronology, the chair of Foreign Relations blasted Bennett for underreacting and then overreacting. The embassy was paranoid concerning the threat that Castro and communism posed to the hemisphere, he said. "If we are automatically to oppose any reform movement that Communists adhere to, we are likely to end up opposing every reform movement, making ourselves the prisoners of reactionaries who wish to preserve the status quo," Fulbright declared. Intervention had undermined the OAS and generated anti-Americanism in Latin America that had not been seen since the 1920s.[67]

Fulbright's dissent coincided with and reflected growing animosity toward LBJ by two of twentieth-century America's most important image makers: the press and intellectuals. By the 1960s the distinction between the two had blurred somewhat with the emergence of individuals like columnists Walter

Lippmann, James Reston, Joseph Kraft, Emmet Hughes, Stewart and Joe Alsop; reporters-turned historians such as David Halberstam, Malcolm Browne, and Neil Sheehan; and celebrity intellectuals such as Arthur Schlesinger, John Kenneth Galbraith, Hans Morgenthau, James McGregor Burns, Margaret Meade, and David Reisman. These "public intellectuals" were read and respected by both academics and educated laypeople. LBJ and his staff had always recognized the power of the press, but they were also mindful, like the Kennedys, of the growing power of the intelligentsia. "It is quite probable that within the next few years," George Reedy had observed to his boss in 1962, "university professors will become much more potent politically than Mayors, County Judges, Sheriffs or political chairmen." [68] He knew they were important, but to his everlasting detriment, LBJ proved either unwilling or unable to understand either the press or the intellectual community. In fact, beginning in early 1965, the president commenced a war with the national media that would escalate to grotesque dimensions.

As EVERY JOURNALIST in America knew, the public was fascinated with the presidency, "with the scope of its dramatic possibilities, the amazing range of interpretations the role can tolerate, and the considerable body of contradictions it indulges," to use linguist Wayne Fields's words. [69] Though it claimed absolute freedom of thought and independence of judgment, the national media was made to be used by the modern presidency. The White House press corps was absolutely dependent on the entity it covered for news. Presidential words and actions were immediate front-page material. Consensus historians like Schlesinger and political scientists like Richard Neustadt had made the presidency the center of the nation's civic life. Franklin Roosevelt, who ran successfully four times against the overwhelming opposition of the nation's editors and publishers, had dominated the press corps by bullying and manipulating them. His skill as a speaker, particularly a radio orator, allowed him to bypass, to a large degree, editorial opinion. After the bland and often deliberately inarticulate Dwight Eisenhower, the press had been swept off its collective feet by the eloquent, candid, self-effacing JFK.

LBJ initially thought he could co-opt and control the national media, singling out individuals whom he favored for privileged interviews and freezing with total silence those who had fallen into disfavor. Stories concerning the president's efforts to secure, intimidate, and control were legion. Joe Alsop remembered that as majority leader, LBJ always wanted to write a reporter's story for him or her. "It seemed an inconceivable waste of precious time for this immensely able, desperately busy man to spend 20 minutes of a half-hour talk compulsively and fruitlessly peddling a lemon, thus leaving only ten minutes for the practical discussion of practical affairs—which might just reveal a bona fide Johnsonian accomplishment that could be reported with bona fide enthusiasm and of course the problem is immeasurably worse now that he is President." [70] Johnson's drive to control was overwhelming. He read virtually every major newspaper and magazine story having to do with the administration, and of course, the three Oval Office television monitors were always on during the news. No story, particularly one he interpreted as critical, went unnoticed. He would call up Bundy or Moyers and direct him to contact the offending reporter and set him or her straight. Occasionally he would do the job himself, although most of the time he would use his personal touch to get a journalist that he considered favorably inclined toward him, like John Chancellor, to write a positive story he wanted to see in the press. Johnson nonplussed his press secretary when, during the 1964 campaign, he directed Reedy to get Peter Lisagor, Philip Potter, and other reporters whose papers had endorsed him to "send him a little note" outlining what they were going to do for him during the last three weeks of the campaign.[71] Leonard Marks, who replaced Carl Rowan as head of the USIA, recalled presenting the president with a survey of public opinion journals around the world on the activities of the Johnson administration. Many of the views expressed were negative. "You have ten thousand people working for you and you have a budget of two hundred million dollars," LBJ said. "Some of them are very good people. Why can't you tell the world what we are doing? Why don't they understand us?" To LBJ's consternation, Marks replied, "Mr. President, they understand us—they don't agree with us!"[72]

The desire to shape and control the presidential image has been characteristic of all administrations. "You tend to view everything in terms of whether it hurts your Administration, your President and that sort of thing," Harry McPherson explained. "Or helps. You look at almost nothing from the point of view of whether it's true or not."[73] George Reedy put it another way: "The most important, and least examined, problem of the presidency is that of maintaining contact with reality," he said.[74] But Johnson's attention and sensitivity to the press seemed grotesque.

LBJ would show his spurs to the members of the Fourth Estate in a variety of ways. He was fond of leading the White House press corps on extended, rapid walks around the White House grounds, especially during the stifling summer months, carrying on an extended monologue that might or might not contain newsworthy tidbits. Frank Cormier described one of these jaunts in his memoir of the Johnson years: "As we negotiated lap after lap, our ranks thinned considerably. A reporter for the *Chicago Sun Times* dragged himself into the pressroom and phoned a half-frantic, half-admiring message to his bureau chief in Atlantic City: 'He's going around again. Twelfth time. We're dropping like flies. It's a death march!' "[75]

The president could be particularly brutal with reporters who covered the Texas White House. He continued to believe that the press had no business following him around as he toured his pastures, sunned aboard one of his motorboats, or attended a nearby church on Sunday. To him it seemed proper that in his own domain, the press ought to appear only when summoned either to cover some stage-managed event or to be his guests. When they reported on events while enjoying his hospitality, it infuriated him. Journalist Lewis H.

Lapham recalled one mass humiliation by auto. Emerging from church one Sunday to find the entire press corps assembled in a line of cars to follow him wherever he might go, LBJ grinned mischievously and crooked his finger for the journalists to follow. "Picking his way along a series of back roads and trailing a high cloud of dust," as Lapham described the incident, "the President first returned to the town of Blanco. To continue to Johnson City he had only to make a simple right turn at the main intersection, but instead he turned left and drove slowly, in a full circle, around the town square. The resulting confusion was extensive. Some of the cars got halfway around the square before guessing the President's intention. Others stopped short. Some, at the end of the line, turned left and passed Mr. Johnson's car going in an opposite direction. All players again maneuvered for position, and their collective trickiness resulted in a stalemate: all cars stopped, the drivers beating helplessly on their dashboards in frustration and rage. The President meanwhile drove serenely back onto the highway, smiling and waving at those he recognized."[76] "If I can't go to an adjoining place, somewhere I'm working on a house, eleven miles without somebody having flack [complaining that they had not been notified]," he once complained to George Reedy, "well, they're little chickenshits." He instructed his press secretary to tell them that there was an area of forty or fifty miles that he felt he ought to be free to move in without calling a press conference.[77]

LBJ found press conferences to be excruciating. He was frequently brusque, rarely forthcoming, and sometimes rude. When a reporter asked him during a question-and-answer session at the ranch shortly before the inauguration if he would give the press a hint about his future travel plans, he replied, "No!" The journalist persisted: "Could you give us a clue?" LBJ interrupted, "I said no!" Later in the session, he observed that there was no point in giving out information, because he would only be misquoted, and he accused reporters of being patsies for leaks from overly ambitious administration officials who did not know "come here from sic em!"[78]

Increasingly, LBJ blamed his deteriorating relationship with the press on George Reedy. The president was acutely aware of the Georgetown cocktail circuit, where members of the cultural and political elite convened to network and gossip, frequently about LBJ and his personal and professional shortcomings. There the Schlesingers, Achesons, Fulbrights, Lippmans, Alsops, Galbraiths, Bundys, Kennedys, and Freemans participated in an open-ended salon in which all matters of import were discussed with verve and wit. LBJ could never hope to be part of the Georgetown scene, but he wanted an emissary—not Bundy or McNamara, who would always be suspect in his eyes—but one of his own. He expected his press secretary to be such a figure. Reedy, slow-talking, slow-moving, overweight, ungainly, simply lacked the sparkle to fit the bill. More and more often, LBJ would complain to McNamara and others about Reedy's dullness, his laziness, and his lack of imagination. Johnson upbraided Reedy personally about his weight and his rumpled appearance. "I'm going to try to build you up," he told Reedy when he named him press secretary. "You're entitled to prestige . . . you've worked for it harder than anybody else . . . but you've got to help me yourself. You don't help yourself, you come in those damned old wrinkled suits . . . and you come in with a dirty shirt . . . and you come in with your tie screwed up . . . I want you to look real nice . . . put on your corset if you have to . . . But look like a top-flight businessman. You look like a god-damned reporter."[79] And Johnson bullied him unmercifully. Finally, in July 1965, Reedy resigned, using impending foot surgery as an excuse. Liz Carpenter staged a "hospital send-off party" with guests bringing pajamas and reading materials as gifts and Luci dressing up in a nurse's uniform.[80] Though LBJ gave Reedy one of his old Lincoln Continentals and helped him find a lucrative job in the private sector, his long-time aide was not amused and with the passage of time would become increasingly bitter.

To replace Reedy as press secretary, LBJ named Bill Moyers. He knew that the Kennedys liked and trusted Moyers and that the Georgetown crowd found him marginally acceptable. And, in fact, the White House's relationship with the press improved markedly in the aftermath of the change. The press corps was flattered that LBJ would appoint one of his advisers of substance to be their liaison.[81] "George had reached the point where he was impossible," journalist Charles Roberts observed. "He was afraid to say anything, tell you anything. Bill came in: he was very articulate and would tell you not only what the President was doing, but what he was thinking and what he might do and his reasons for doing the things he did. He was interpreting the President to us and since he had so much access to him, his guidance was good."[82] But not even Moyers's wit, charm, or cultivation of Arthur Schlesinger Jr. could overcome LBJ's suspiciousness, his tendency to try to manipulate the press and abuse it if he could not, and the press's growing conviction that the president was either the biggest deceiver in American political history or a man with multiple personalities, each completely walled off from the other.[83] In this suspicion, journalists were not alone.

"It is always a sign of trouble when a leader loses the support of the intellectuals," former Tennessee Valley Authority head David Lilienthal observed in his diaries in 1965. "This seems to be happening with Johnson because of Vietnam, and it will probably also happen because of the Dominican affair."[84] In truth, the alienation of the intellectuals had to do with those foreign policy crises but also with other factors as well. There was first of all the burgeoning Kennedy mystique. "President Johnson is to most of us an ideological cipher," political scientist and Americans for Democratic Action president John Roche wrote Bill Moyers, "and as I told you, we suffer from a certain urban parochialism which tends, I suspect, to exaggerate the political virtues of the late President at the expense of his successor."[85] In the wake of the assassination, the *New York Review of Books* had run a special edition, with such luminaries as David Reisman, Richard Hofstadter, Norman Mailer, Irving Howe, Dwight Macdonald, and Hannah Arendt speculating on the reality and promise of the fallen president. "People in other countries, oppressed by the ham-handed or iron-fisted or flabby leadership of elderly non-intellectual men," Reisman wrote, "looked to President Kennedy with admiration and even a touch of envy." Hofstadter saw him as the ultimate democratic ruler: "He belongs to those men in all times for whom politics has been a distinguished and demanding craft." David Bazelon put it in more romantic terms: "He made love, to be succinct, to the American people. He concentrated on it, and he managed to get the people to love him. So he left a nation of unfulfilled lovers behind him." [86] In trying to pinpoint the hold that JFK came to have on the imagination of educated Americans and in-tellectuals in particular, Gary Wills quoted Walter Bagehot on Bolingbroke: "There lurks about the fancies of many men and women an imaginary concep-tion of an ideal statesman, resembling the character of which Alcibiades has been the recognized type for centuries. There is a sort of intellectual luxury in the idea which fascinates the human mind. We like to fancy a young man in the first vigor of body and first vigor of mind, who is full of bounding enjoyment, who excels all rivals at masculine feats, who gains the love of women by a magic attraction, but who is also a powerful statesman, who regulates great events, who settles great measures, who guides a great nation." [87] Such was much of ed-ucated America's view of John F. Kennedy. It was an image that never tarnished, but was only burnished, because JFK was not alive to disappoint. It was with such a mythic figure that Lyndon Johnson had to compete.

Of course, the entourage that gathered around the heir apparent did their best to keep the Kennedy mystique alive and be sure that it was transferred to RFK. At a speech delivered to the eighteenth annual convention of the Ameri-cans for Democratic Action in the spring of 1965, Arthur Schlesinger attributed the concept of the Great Society entirely to New Frontiersman Richard Good-win. All of LBJ's men—Valenti, Busby, Reedy—were against the idea, Schlesinger insisted, arguing that the "dreamy vague proposals would be inter-preted as a hangover from the Soviet Union's series of unsuccessful five-year plans." Warming to his audience, he hailed the triumph of Goodwin's proposals as "a clear victory of the liberal cause of American politics over the messianic conservative complex of the President's Texas mafia." [88]

The degree to which LBJ had become demonized in the collective mind of the Kennedys became clear during a 1969 interview that Kenny O'Donnell gave on his time at the White House. "All I can say is that in my opinion he [LBJ] was the worst politician I've ever seen in my life," O'Donnell insisted, "just unbe-lievably bad." [89] Clearly, Bobby and those around him reveled in stories that LBJ had someway, somehow been complicit in JFK's death. "He was regarded as a usurper and, no doubt by millions of people around the world, as probably re-sponsible for Kennedy's death. In Asia, Latin America and parts of Europe, it was inconceivable that a President assassinated in the Vice-President's home state had not been killed as part of a coup by the Vice President," Harry McPherson observed. "Other people also believed it in a milder way. As Hamlet says to his uncle, 'he was to you "as Hyperion to a Satyr." ' " [90]

It was often not the substance of the Johnson policies that offended journalists and intellectuals, but the ways they were presented, articulated, or justified. Reedy and Johnson had believed that JFK's staff and cabinet were too visible, that in their speeches, articles, and public appearances they had become minicelebrities that detracted from the president and the presidency.[91] After he succeeded to the White House, LBJ swore his staff to anonymity. In the first days of the Johnson administration, the media attempted to develop stories on the men around the president. He flatly refused to let Moyers, Valenti, and Busby be interviewed, much less profiled. They were to be neither seen nor heard outside the political apparatus that Johnson sought to manage.[92] Rumor had it that LBJ had sent McGeorge Bundy to Santo Domingo during the Dominican crisis to prevent him from debating Schlesinger, Morgenthau, and other critics of administration policy at a teach-in in Washington. "I don't think a White House staff member ought to be doing these things, except the press secretary," he told Moyers.[93] Horace Busby, among others, tried to convince LBJ that by keeping his staff in the background, his image was suffering. In large part, the JFK mystique had been created by Schlesinger, Sorenson, Goodwin, and O'Donnell. "The Kennedy 'image' was—for the president personally—the foam atop a heady brew of intellectual ferment, in Washington and out," he told his boss. "If the people around him had been hesitant, reluctant or simply ill-equipped to talk about plans for the future, the now-existing Kennedy image would never have risen to the top. President Kennedy was the beneficiary of the accessibility and self-confidence of his associates, intimate or peripheral. But, by contrast, the edginess, evasiveness and simple 'in the dark' ignorance of persons in this Administration works against any successful image program."[94] But Johnson would not listen. Busby left the White House staff, disgusted, within a year. Thus, reporters and columnists were left to talk among themselves or with LBJ's enemies about the very peculiar man who had succeeded JFK in the White House.

Those who would understand Lyndon Johnson were confounded by his habit of inventing versions of himself and putting them up for inspection and approval.[95] There was Johnson the Son of the Tenant Farmer, Johnson the Great Compromiser, Johnson the All-Knowing, Johnson the Humble, Johnson the Warrior, Johnson the Dove, Johnson the Romantic, Johnson the Hard-Headed Pragmatist, Johnson the Preserver of Traditions, Johnson the Crusader for Social Justice, Johnson the Magnanimous, Johnson the Vindictive. The only person really capable of writing a biography of LBJ, George Reedy observed, was the Italian playwright Luigi Pirandello, whose best-known plays *Six Characters in Search of an Author* (1921) and *Henry IV* (1922) exploited the notions of multiple personality and the relativity of reality.[96] Some of these LBJs were carefully calculated to appeal to a particular constituency or audience, some a reflection of the various roles presidents are expected to play. Indeed, Johnson's commitment to consensus led him at times to try to be all things to all people. "He sent out all kinds of wrong signals to the people," John Chancellor observed. "He would send out liberal-conservative signals at the same time. He would send out internationalist-isolationist signals at the same time. He could get up and make a speech at Howard University on the Negro family and what we would do about the Negroes, which was one of the most inspiring speeches I have ever heard in my life. And yet what did you see when the speech was being made? You saw somebody with that long face and the regional accent and that sort of high collar white shirt and that sort of luminescent suit he used to wear, that all added up to a visual impression of a man who couldn't possibly be saying anything good about blacks." [97]

Some of Johnson's role-playing was an involuntary response to the unbelievable stress he endured. In his anger and desire to strike back, LBJ adopted the ironic and self-defeating habit of acting out a caricature in front of those whom he believed caricatured him. Thus his exhibitionism and crudeness in the company of those, usually perceived to be part of the Eastern establishment, whom he believed were whispering about his credentials behind his back. In the presence of "the Ivy League types," Reedy said, "there would come bubbling to the surface a very intense crudity, an obviously deliberate effort to be disgusting in their sight." [98]

FROM THE VERY BEGINNING, journalists and public intellectuals had predicted that foreign affairs would be LBJ's Achilles' heel. In late January 1964, Douglas Kiker, writing in the *New York Herald Tribune,* cited "mounting evidence" that the new president "has yet to develop an effective technique for the day-to-day conduct of foreign affairs." [99] Johnson responded by constantly listing the numbers of meetings he had held with foreign heads of state and ambassadors. But it all seemed for naught. A year later, *Newsweek* ran a feature article on Johnsonian diplomacy entitled "Foreign Policy: Drift or Design?" [100]

LBJ's penchant for venting sometimes confused his friends in the press and played into the hands of his enemies. In early 1965, Stewart Alsop cited an interview with the president, who, after listening to questions concerning Vietnam, Panama, the Middle East, and Central Africa, spoke in exasperation of the United States pulling back from its commitments. "The President said in effect," Alsop wrote, "this country had been 'listening too much to our own propaganda about being leader of the free world.' Perhaps it had been too easy for tin-pot dictators to blackmail us by saying, 'Pay me or I'll go Communist.' Maybe it was time to 'let some people sweat a bit—let them go right up to the end of the street and see what happens.' Maybe it was time we let the other side have a try at running the world." What a contrast with Kennedy, Alsop wrote. [101] Four months later, following a flood of presidential rhetoric declaring that America would never abandon its righteous mission to defend the free peoples of the world from the scourge of communism, that it would never "tuck tail and run" in Vietnam, that it would never permit another Castro in the Western Hemisphere, luminaries such as Walter Lippmann and Hans Morgenthau were blasting LBJ as a simple-minded interventionist whose sole foreign policy reference was the Alamo. [102]

Throughout the spring and summer of 1965, voices inside and outside the White House criticized LBJ for not providing a compelling rationale for a U.S. presence in Vietnam and for not rallying the American people and Congress to support a war that clearly America had decided to take over. "By not talking about the enlarged operational mission for enlarged U.S. military forces," John Steele wrote his editors, "he [LBJ] appeared to me to be raising a crisis of confidence with the people. By generalizing, by down playing, by emphasizing the unlimited nature of his willingness to talk, by an unwillingness to sacrifice at least for the moment his lust for a Great Society, by postponing until a later day the rendering of the real bill, he seemed to me to bring into question the American purpose." [103] Johnson's rhetorical excesses and confusion during the early days of the Dominican crisis produced a spate of stories in the *New York Times* and scores of other journals blasting him for overreacting and then inventing a Castroite communist menace to cover his mistake, for claiming that he worked through the OAS when he clearly did not. "There is now a deep-seated distrust because of a feeling that we are not fully and frankly explaining what we are doing," James Reston advised McGeorge Bundy.[104] It was in the summer of 1965 that that famous term "credibility gap" began to appear in news stories.

Most upsetting to the press and public intellectuals was Johnson's tendency to question their right to dissent, to imply that they were being at best irresponsible and at worst disloyal. Increasingly, he complained that naysayers were uninformed armchair quarterbacks and unwitting dupes of the communists. Most annoying, he seemed to be equating those who dissented with those appeasers who had opened the door to the Nazis and Japanese imperialists in the 1930s and 1940s. "If the President's version of history is correct," Lippmann wrote indignantly, "it follows that when there is an issue of war and peace, the only safe and patriotic course is to suspend all debate and rally around the President." [105] The objects of his attacks responded by wondering aloud if the president had not crawled in bed with the very mindless hawks he had defeated in 1964. "The testiness of the President is not mysterious," Emmet John Hughes wrote in May 1965. "It is not pleasant to receive the most candid critiques from the Fulbrights or the Mansfields in his own party. It must be yet more disconcerting to be cheered on by Barry Goldwater and the *New York Daily News*. But it might be expected that this very discomfiture would force some twinge of doubt on whether he had not, perhaps, slipped into the wrong pew in a strange church." [106]

To Lyndon Johnson, an intellectual was, benignly, a wordsmith and idea machine, and, malignantly, an ideologue. It was not that LBJ could not think abstractly: he was a master at political calculus. He was given to utopian dreaming and at times a kind of Emersonian, transcendental mysticism. "I have heard him, when we were on his ranch going by and watching the animals," Wilbur Cohen recalled, "refer to all sorts of sexual characteristics of the animals and of people, and then five minutes later you could stand on the hillside there watching the sunset and you'd find a man who was a poet in describing the sunset and the relationship of the land to the people and his hopes and aspirations for people."[107] He seemed to respect Walter Lippmann initially and made repeated attempts during his first year and a half in office to cultivate him.[108] But Lippmann was different from Morgenthau and academic celebrities in general. He was himself a pragmatist, "a philosopher with an intense interest in how Government works—not the mechanics but the actual manipulation of power," as George Reedy put it.[109]

LBJ was enamored of expertise. As one architect of the Great Society points out, the number of task forces he established and the number of Ph.D.s (especially from Harvard and MIT) he recruited for cabinet and subcabinet positions exceeded those of any other president in the nation's history. But LBJ made a distinction between experts and intellectuals. Johnson identified the latter with liberals like Paul Douglas and Joe Rauh, individuals possessed by rigid ideologies and fixed agendas. Shortly after he left office, LBJ blurted out to an aide, "I didn't let them control my mind; I didn't let them control my mind." LBJ agreed with Sam Rayburn and John McCormack, who once exclaimed to a reporter who had called him a liberal, "Don't you call me that! Liberals are those people who want to own your mind. I'm a progressive."[110] To LBJ, most liberal intellectuals were ideological imperialists attempting to entrap those who exercised power within a preordained philosophical structure that placed the interests of the system before the interests of the individual.

Eric Goldman, among others on the White House staff, insisted to LBJ that, as a Democratic president with dreams of fulfilling and transcending the promises of the New Deal, Fair Deal, and New Frontier, he must maintain an amicable relationship with liberal intellectuals. Wandering in the political wilderness since the days of FDR, the Galbraiths, the Schlesingers, and the Balls had been overjoyed to be welcomed back to the halls of power by JFK. They were ripe, indeed anxious to be courted by LBJ, Goldman and Goodwin argued. To this end, in June 1965, the White House staged a gala Festival of Arts.[111] For thirteen hours, more than four hundred poets, novelists, actors and actresses, historians, playwrights, musicians, composers, and artists hobnobbed at the White House. Lunch was held in the National Gallery's East Garden Court. After dinner that evening at the White House, George Kennan addressed the group on the artist's place in contemporary society. Soprano Roberta Peters accompanied by the Louisville Orchestra entertained, and then excerpts from four American plays and several movies were shown.

The proceedings were marred by an undertone of discontent, however. The distinguished poet Robert Lowell, who had been a conscientious objector during World War I, had ostentatiously returned his invitation in protest over administration policies toward the Dominican Republic and Vietnam. During the festival, cultural critic Dwight Macdonald circulated an antiwar petition. Despite the fact that Macdonald garnered only nine signatures, LBJ was not pleased. Informed of Lowell's protest beforehand, he memoed Dick Goodwin,

"I've been very dubious about this from the beginning—when you get in a pen with pigs you get some of it on you."[112] Although Lady Bird was prominent throughout the proceedings, the president appeared only briefly, striding out onto the White House lawn to deliver a few remarks. "Your art is not a political weapon," he said tersely. "Yet much of what you do is profoundly political." He shook a few hands and then turned on his heel and marched back to the Oval Office.[113]

By fall, the intellectuals were in full revolt. Writing in the *New York Review of Books,* Hans Morgenthau observed that the principal motive for U.S. involvement in Vietnam seemed to be credibility; America's credibility and its prestige with its allies in the cold war. But, he insisted, to become bogged down in a guerrilla war that it could not win, a war fought for dubious purposes, would destroy, not enhance, America's prestige. The article was embellished with a David Levine cartoon depicting LBJ crying giant crocodile tears.[114] Perhaps most important, Reinhold Niebuhr, the man who had provided moral justification for the war against the Axis, the conflict in Korea, and containment in general, put his dissent on record. Interviewed by the *New Republic,* he declared, "The analogy between our defense against Nazism and our defense of South Vietnam against the Communist North is flagrantly misleading. Nazism's military nationalism threatened the moral substance of Western culture, the Jews with extinction, and non-German continental nations with slavery. None of these issues is involved in a civil war between two portions of a partitioned nation, one Communist and the other non-Communist."[115]

The White House remained defiant. Warned by James Reston that military intervention in the Caribbean and Southeast Asia was alienating much of the nation's cultural elite, McGeorge Bundy rebuked him. "I went on to tell Reston," he reported to LBJ, "that any President who was asked to choose between the understanding and support of the American people, and the understanding and support of the intellectuals, would choose the people."[116] It was all Bill Moyers could do to persuade an angry Johnson not to abolish the Medals of Freedom award program, which recognized individual excellence in the arts, humanities, sciences, and public service.[117]

The first week in July, Jack Valenti attempted to refurbish his boss's failing image. Unfortunately for him and the White House, his rhetoric got out of hand. "He is a sensitive man, a cultivated man, a warmhearted and extraordinary man," the effusive and somewhat sycophantic Valenti gushed. "The President, thank the Good Lord, has extra glands, I am persuaded, that give him energy that ordinary men simply don't have. I sleep each night a little better, a little more confidently because Lyndon Johnson is my President."[118] When the text of the Valenti speech was reprinted, "The whole town exploded in a hilarious howl of disbelief," the *Wall Street Journal* reported. Political cartoonists such as the *Washington Post*'s Herblock had a field day. He depicted three cringing White House staffers, bare to the waist with their backs deeply lacerated, striding away from the president, who was holding a bullwhip. The piece was captioned "Happy Days on the Old Plantation."[119] Significantly, LBJ could see nothing wrong with Valenti's remarks and was infuriated by the satire.

By the fall of 1965, the American people were being assailed with a number of conflicting images of the thirty-sixth president. There was still Lyndon the Compassionate. "At no time since the New Deal, and probably not even then, has this country had such a clear sense of purpose on the home front as it has today," James Reston wrote in the *Washington Post*. "President Johnson is working toward a just and compassionate society with remarkable vigor, skill and success."[120] Walter Lippmann could still speak of the president's "Inexhaustible Gift of Sympathy."[121] Then there was Lyndon the Competent. Jim Bishop hailed the president as "A 'Can Do' Man. Mr. Johnson has not only assumed the office of president, but he has taken complete charge."[122] Most pleasing of all to LBJ were Lyndon the Emancipator and Lyndon the Consensus Builder. Shortly after the assassination, British commentator Alistair Cooke had compared LBJ favorably to Abraham Lincoln. Both hailed from humble origins, Lincoln born in a simple log cabin on the nineteenth-century American frontier and Johnson "to a tenant farmer on the central plain of Texas, a 400-mile stretch of pulverized concrete planted with mesquite and cat's claw." Both men were possessed of a "deep conviction that good men ought to differ but can be decently made to collaborate" and "a solemn sense of the national good."[123] A political cartoon in the *Louisville Courier-Journal* posed LBJ as a grinning Statue of Liberty, clutching tablets labeled Voting Rights and Medicare, and captioned "Give Me Your Rich, Your Poor, Your Old, Your Young, Your Black, Your White, Your Huddled Masses Yearning to Breathe Free."[124]

But increasingly, as Vietnam and urban rioting came to overshadow the Great Society, negative images would come to overshadow positive. "The contrast of the home front with policy and direction on the foreign front is startling," Reston wrote in the spring of 1965. "The President's goals and priorities are clear at home. They have been defined and broadcast to the nation in a remarkable series of speeches and messages to the Congress, and this is precisely what has been lacking in the foreign field."[125] As unease metamorphosed into distrust, portraits of the thirty-sixth president grew more sinister. There had always been Lyndon the Westerner. "The man who is the 36th President of the United States is a big, breezy, rough-cut man of the plains and of the dust, 'the drought, the hail and the wind'—as Walter Prescott Webb put it," Tom Wicker wrote in early 1964.[126] The papers were still full of LBJ in khakis and Stetson, inspecting his cattle, instructing ranch foreman Dale Malechek in the art of fencing, presiding over vast barbeques for visiting dignitaries, riding, hunting. But that image began to take on a negative tone, that of a hip-shooting Texas Ranger with an Alamo mentality and a mind capable of thinking only in simple black and white.[127]

Then there was Johnson the Uncouth, an image that included several shadings. There was LBJ the Hick, a subset of Lyndon the Westerner. Russell Baker parodied the president's speech pattern with a piece entitled "Let's All Escalate Up to the Purdnalis." [128] Writing in the *Texas Monthly,* Nicholas Lemann captured the essence of the hick image, which seemed particularly evident on television. " 'Mah fell' Ummurrukuns'; 'Yew-nited States'; 'Futher' instead of 'further'; 'Tinnytive' instead of 'tentative'; 'Wahr' instead of 'telegram'; 'Prospairity'; 'Coontribyit.' And that's not to mention his whole demeanor: the hair slicked straight back; the upper teeth concealed by a flabby lip; the lower lip shooting out to the side when he talked; the nervous, false little smile; the blinking; the tidal rise and fall of his eyebrows; the dark, hooded eyes." [129] Describing LBJ's rush to the television studios to announce the end of the rail strike, T.R.B., writing in the *New Republic,* declared, "He introduced the rival spokesmen like a Head Scout producing two troop members who had just won the rope-tying contest . . . There he was, proud as a new father, his big ears fairly shaking with gratification." [130]

Then there was Lyndon the Satyr. Although 1965 was a time in which the press still eschewed stories concerning the sexual improprieties of public figures, at least heterosexual improprieties, tales concerning the president's longterm affairs and casual intercourse made the rounds of the Washington gossip circle with increasing frequency. Lyndon the Vulgar became a staple. By pulling up his shirt to show reporters his appendix scar, by continuing to skinny-dip in the White House pool, by burping and farting his way through innumerable conversations, Johnson seemed to feed this image with a vengeance. Johnson the Ogre had been around ever since the Texan had first assembled his staff. The Kennedys, particularly Bobby, never tired of recounting tales of LBJ's abusive outbursts to his underlings. Humiliated and increasingly embittered by his rude dismissal after years of faithful service, George Reedy began to vent his spleen. "As a human being, he was a miserable person," he wrote, "a bully, sadist, lout and egoist. He had no sense of loyalty (despite his protestations that it was the quality he valued above all others) and he enjoyed tormenting those who had done the most for him. It was customary for his staff to excuse his deplorable manners and his barnyard speech as 'the simple ways of a man who was born and lives close to the soil.' That was incredible nonsense. Most of his adult life was spent in Washington, D.C., which is not exactly the hookworm and pellagra belt. His lapses from civilized conduct were deliberate and usually intended to subordinate someone else to his will." [131] Even Valenti would later comment on this trait: "I never lost the fascination of simply being around him, because he was very exciting. But he was also one tough son of a bitch and he was a hard, cruel man at times. I remember once I was sitting in his bedroom and on an open car phone he lashed into Bill Moyers like I had never heard anybody lash into anybody. And when I tried to take Bill's side of the argument, he damn near blew me away." [132]

Finally, with the publication of *The Making of the President: 1964* by Theodore H. White, Johnson the Usurper made its reappearance. After paying lip service to all the LBJ positives, White portrayed him as an obsessively vain, ambitious man without values and without magnanimity. Most important, he came across as not only an accidental but a completely unworthy successor to his cultured, idealistic, and sophisticated predecessor, almost a cruel parody of him. "When he thought of America," White wrote of Johnson, "he thought of it either in primitive terms of Fourth-of-July patriotism or else as groups of people, forces, individuals, leaders, lobbies, pressures that he had spent his life in intermeshing. He was ill at ease with the broad phraseologies, purposes, and meanings of civilization."[133]

Hurtful images indeed, but what president, even Washington and especially Lincoln, had not been pilloried and vilified? Polls indicated that the people approved the way the president was handling Vietnam by 57 percent to 43 percent. There was no dearth of voices pointing out to LBJ that his obsessive sensitivity was counterproductive. After interviewing Johnson in May 1965, David Brinkley called Jack Valenti. "I think he pays too goddamn much attention to what the papers say about him," he exclaimed. "If I was president of the U.S., I'll be goddamn if I'd read the papers to find out anything about foreign policy. Who gives a goddamn what John Oakes [editorial page editor for the *New York Times*] writes? . . . For Christ's sake what does he care? He knows a hundred times more about what's going on than any of us. What the hell does he read 'em for? It's silly."[134] During a frank conversation in September 1965, Connecticut senator Abraham Ribicoff advised Johnson to stop pressing: "You are doing so well that I would just be Lyndon Johnson and figure if I had 70% I was doing so damn well that I am not entitled to 100%. No man is entitled to 100%. I think if you try to reach for love, nobody can make it because love is an ephemeral thing. Now you have got the greatest ingredient of any man that I know of in the presidency and you have got universal respect."[135] But LBJ did continue to read critical news stories and he continued to care—deeply. "The attitude of the *Post, Times,* and *Newsweek*," he complained to George Reedy before he left, "—not just the Baker thing, or the gold cufflinks, or the Texas hat, or the string bow tie—on things such as Panama, the editors are still critical. Even though things worked out well and were done the right way, 'the fella is still a son-of-a-bitch.' " The press was showing the same attitude toward him as "Mississippi shows toward Harlem."[136]

Increasingly, the president's interviews deteriorated into an ongoing effort to refute misperceptions and misjudgments he believed the press held about him, punctuated by occasional efforts at reconciliation. In a remarkable interview with *Newsweek*'s James Cannon and Charles Roberts, he said, "Liberals like to talk about a lot of things without doing them; we like to do them. We don't twist arms. Most of that comes from people who are not informed. Now they say that Bobby's against me, that he's my sworn enemy. But Bobby came in here and asked me to keep Katzenbach as Attorney General, and I did. Now some of you fellows criticized me on the Dominican Republic, but if you look at Gallup, Harris, Quayle and all the other polls, you'll see that we went up from 63 percent to 69 percent." Denying stories that he was planning to dump Dean Rusk as secretary of state, LBJ exclaimed, "They don't try you fellows for writing stories to the contrary. They don't shoot you for it. You've got that First Amendment. I can't be responsible for the veracity of your profession. Somebody ought to do an article on you, on your damn profession, your First Amendment." Then, "I never go to bed without thanking the Good Lord for the people who are helping me as President."[137] James Reston perhaps best summed up LBJ's impossible relationship with the Fourth Estate. "If you don't tell the precise truth about him, which is almost inevitable, he thinks you are dishonest, and if you do, he feels you are disloyal."[138]

What, then, were the sources of this grotesque relationship with the media? "The one thing that I'm positive about," George Reedy said, "is that whatever else may be said about him, he was a tormented man. I don't know what tormented him."[139] Nancy Dickerson recalled a bizarre conversation with LBJ at the 1960 Democratic Convention. "I am like an animal, a wild animal on a leash," he blurted out. "I always keep that leash in a very tight rein. My instinct is always to go for the jugular."[140] Most obvious, Johnson's goals for himself continued to be absurdly high. His mother was watching, his father was watching, FDR was watching, God was watching, grading, always grading. In 1968 Harold Lasswell, an expert on psychology and the political personality, made some observations about the Johnson psyche: "One thing of outstanding interest is the extent to which Johnson had to struggle to achieve independence from his mother. She was an ambitious, domineering woman who thought she had married beneath her. She was determined that this lad would be a great success and she pushed him very hard. It puts the son in a conflict. On the one side there is a tendency to accept domination and on the other hand a rebellious tendency to reassert one's independence and masculinity and sense of adequacy. It is a reasonable inference that Johnson was very much concerned about remaining independent of outside influence. His subsequent political career— with his demand to make his own decisions and his demand to control a situation—has these very deep roots."[141] Horace Busby observed that LBJ believed that a president must be knowledgeable about everything of real or potential national importance. He believed that those in power in the executive branch, in Congress, and in the press expected this of him.[142] That was an incredible burden to bear, one that made the presidency much more of a pressure cooker than it already was.

Most simply and most profoundly, however, LBJ was multifaceted, elusive, combative, and, at times, paranoid with the press because he literally internalized the incredible diversity and ambiguity of the American republic during the turbulent 1960s. He felt it was his duty, if not his destiny, to take on the burdens of the nation—throwing off two hundred years of racism, obliterating poverty, protecting the free world from communism without leading it into Armageddon—and it whipsawed his already conflicted personality. Like a moth circling the flame, Johnson was drawn irresistibly to the storms of American life, even though they would consume him. After reading an article in *Life* in 1958 about

General James Gavin, Lyndon had written his mother, "One quote from him struck me as particularly good: 'I went forth to seek the challenge, to "move toward the sound of the guns," to go where danger was the greatest, for there is where issues would be resolved and decisions made.' I think that is a wonderful thought . . . because I always seem to be right up to my neck in problems and decisions it appears to me to be more than an adequate justification for what I can't seem to help anyway." [143]

LBJ was committed to the common men and women of America, the tenant farmer, the factory worker, the ghetto dweller, the shoe salesman, the domestic worker, and the pharmacy owner. Outside of the white South, he was generally respected, and among black Americans, even revered. "I admire President Johnson because he stands on his own feet, and he's firm in his beliefs," Cosby Harrell, a black manual laborer from Lake Purdy, Alabama, told an interviewer. F. L. Pippne, black owner of a prosperous dry-cleaning establishment, commented to pollsters that he thought the president's "personality is wonderful" and that he admired him because he "has helped everybody, but especially the underprivileged people." William Nalomski, a welder from Chicago, responded when asked his opinion, "He's a thinker, not quick with his judgments. He's got a big load on his shoulders—you can see it in his face. He may turn out to be another Lincoln." Glen Lochem, a farmer from Plainfield, Illinois, said, "I like him, because he doesn't believe in letting those Communists push him around in Vietnam." Johnson's approval rating on the economy was 77 percent to 23 percent and on Vietnam 65 percent to 35 percent. Among modern presidents, respondents rated him better than Truman and Eisenhower but worse than FDR and Kennedy. [144]

But for LBJ, that was not enough. He may have dismissed the best and the brightest rhetorically, but their disapproval served as a constant goad to him. However, given his values, Johnson could see no other course in foreign and domestic affairs than the one he was following and he was who he was; thus was LBJ doomed to wander for the rest of his presidency among those whose respect he craved but could never obtain. Typically, LBJ's response was to try harder.

CHAPTER 31

A CITY ON THE HILL

THE WAR ON POVERTY REMAINED AT THE VERY CORE of the Great Society. It was perceived to be the key to social justice, vitiating class animosities, giving substance to the civil rights movement, quelling urban unrest, and demonstrating to the world that capitalism was superior to communism. By 1965, Sargent Shriver and the Office of Economic Opportunity were getting help to millions of poor Americans. Local antipoverty programs were already under way in forty-four states; fifty-three job corps centers, many of them at converted military bases, were processing sixty hundred applications a day. Some twenty-five thousand welfare families were receiving employment training, and ninety thousand adults were enrolled in adult education programs. Neighborhood Youth Corps were operating in forty-nine cities and eleven rural communities, and some 4 million Americans were receiving benefits under AFDC. In March, LBJ submitted a $1.5 billion request to Congress to continue and expand these programs. One of the most significant increases was for Operation Head Start, "pre-school programs primarily for inner city children designed to compensate for cultural disadvantages" and get them up to speed for the first grade.[1]

As the House and Senate took up the administration's 1965 poverty bill, the campaign against want was receiving mixed reviews. Complaints came pouring in from the poor that bureaucratic red tape was preventing mass access to OEO and other antipoverty offices. "The pipeline is getting clogged up," Connecticut Senator Abraham Ribicoff, a supporter of the poverty program, told LBJ. "And we are going to have indigestion in the country; you have oversold the program . . . This is going to start kicking back in everybody's teeth within the next year."[2] When a riot erupted at the Job Corps Center at Camp Breckenridge in Kentucky over discriminatory hiring practices at the facility, conservatives denounced the camps as no more than breeding grounds for urban revolutionaries.[3] Mayors and governors complained with increasing shrillness about Shriver's willingness to give control of poverty funds to private organizations that circumvented local political machines. Welfare had long constituted the base of political power for big-city organizations and they were loath to give it up. Leading the charge was the powerful mayor of Chicago, Richard Daley, and Adam Clayton Powell, whose HARY-YOU project in Harlem was one of the major relief projects in New York City. "What in the hell are you people doing?" Daley asked Bill Moyers. "Does the president know he's putting money in the hands of subversives . . . to poor people that aren't a part of the organization?"[4] Southern governors joined northern mayors in clamoring for control. Their motives, Shriver and his staff suspected, were not of the purest. Initially, OEO stuck to its guns, insisting that the poor constitute a majority on local Community Action Program boards and removing segregationists from positions of power in the poverty program in Louisiana and other southern states. The perennially tanned and energetic Shriver came under increasing attack as a result. In an effort to appease critics, he agreed to give up the Peace Corps to concentrate on poverty, but the criticism continued.

Not surprisingly, LBJ preferred to work through established political authority. Ribicoff, an increasingly influential voice in matters of poverty and urban unrest, argued to LBJ that for the War on Poverty to succeed, "you have to have the political establishment, you have to have labor, you have to have industry, you have to have civil rights and the poor. Now setting up what they [OEO] are doing now, setting up a new power base with the poor is absolutely dynamite because it has to lead to anarchy when the vicious men who have never been able to achieve power, seek power through the poor. Now you have to start with smart mayors and work all of them in together."[5] The problem was that "the poor" and many urban civil rights leaders sided with Shriver and the OEO radicals. Labor was split, with Meany supporting the establishment and Reuther and the UAW working to set up local nonprofits outside the existing power structure. Meanwhile, representatives of the National Governors Conference attached amendments to the Economic Opportunity Act of 1965 providing for a gubernatorial veto of all poverty program decisions in their respective states.[6]

Inevitably, the War on Poverty had to address the thorny issue of birth control. Economists and demographers estimated that over a generation, 1 million poor women practicing contraception meant five hundred thousand fewer poor children. Under existing guidelines, the Department of Health, Education, and Welfare could provide federal funds for family planning, but only if states requested and administered such aid. Anthony Celebrezze, the secretary, was a Catholic and insisted that federal activity in the area of birth control ought to go no further. Shriver, also a Catholic, violently disagreed. He, along with Harry McPherson and Bill Moyers, believed that the federal government through the OEO ought to undertake an aggressive campaign of education and provide free contraceptives not only to married poor women but to unmarried as well. Indeed, it was unmarried women and women not living with the father of their children who were responsible, biologically, for the population explosion. "If the purpose of our policy is to slow down the making of babies in conditions of squalor and intellectual degradation," McPherson observed to Moyers, "the choice seems clear."[7] Johnson was leery. The subject was a minefield. As McPherson pointed out, the great mass of Catholics would prove acquiescent, but if the Vatican chose to make an issue of the matter, there would be trouble, particularly if it allied with white religious fundamentalists who would see federal birth control programs as attempts to subsidize immorality. Finally, there would be those in the Black Power movement who would cry genocide. Nevertheless, the OEO proceeded to make grants to private nonprofits to distribute information and contraceptives among both inner-city and rural poor.[8] Early in 1966, John Gardner, the new HEW secretary, issued a directive to his army of agency heads, informing them that they had the authority to render family planning assistance to their clients immediately.[9] In May of that year, Congress passed legislation authorizing specific HEW grants to state and local agencies and private nonprofits for family planning, including the distribution of free contraceptives.[10]

IN LATE JULY, the president took time off from lobbying for the poverty bill to secure long-time friend and confidant Abe Fortas's nomination to the Supreme Court. Johnson knew how groundbreaking and controversial his Great Society programs were and, to ensure that they would be upheld on judicial review, he needed the liberal majority on the Warren Court to remain intact. Moreover, he knew he could depend on Fortas to keep him abreast of the changing mood of the Court as it responded to new personalities and changing circumstances. Fortas had always insisted that he did not want to leave his lucrative practice for the high court. Ever since LBJ had become president, Fortas, egged on by his wife and fellow attorney, Carol Agger, had deflected talk of an appointment. She wanted him to wait five or six years until the couple had ensured their financial security; then Abe could enjoy the ermine of the bench in his declining years. On July 28, LBJ summoned his friend to the White House and told him that in minutes he was going to address a press conference announcing that he was sending an additional fifty thousand troops to Vietnam, and that he was nominating Fortas for the vacant position on the Supreme Court.[11] Faced with a fait accompli, the lawyer dutifully—and gratefully—accepted. Carol Agger was furious, hanging up on LBJ when he called to explain why he had to have her husband on the bench. "She would not talk to Johnson for the next two months, and her relationship with her husband during that period was also tense," Fortas biographer Laura Kalman writes.[12] Eventually, she forgave both.

During Fortas's confirmation hearings in August, some senators expressed worry that his close relationship with the president might compromise his judicial independence. "There are two things that have been vastly exaggerated with respect to me," Fortas declared with some disingenuousness. "One is the extent to which I am a Presidential adviser and the other is the extent to which I am a proficient violinist. I am a very poor violinist but very enthusiastic, and my relationship with the President has been exaggerated out of all connection with reality." Despite the fact that members of the John Birch Society and other right-wing groups flooded Washington with telegrams urging rejection of the nomination on the grounds that Fortas was a Jew, a liberal, or even a communist, he was approved unanimously.[13]

As Congress debated the 1965 poverty bill during the summer and early fall, LBJ stepped up the pressure, calling members of congress, goading labor leaders and civil rights organizations to enter the fray, and subtly threatening conservatives with the specter of urban revolution.[14] On October 9 Congress passed the Economic Opportunity Act Amendments of 1965. The OEO was only 20 percent of what had become nearly a $20 billion War on Poverty that included Social Security, direct relief, food stamps, Department of Education aid to slum schools, federal expenditures for public housing, and area redevelopment.[15]

There was always a sense of fevered urgency surrounding any project LBJ chose to back, but in 1965 poverty had been a special case. In the wake of Watts, Martin Luther King had advised the president that the antidote to urban rioting as far as the federal government was concerned was the OEO and its attendant programs. While publicly mouthing the rhetoric of law and order, LBJ and his staff worked frantically behind the scenes to forestall Watts-like eruptions in other urban centers. Not only did the White House lobby intensively for passage of the 1965 EOA general amendments bill, but they focused poverty programs on south Los Angeles in an effort to convince potential rioters elsewhere that there was hope. On August 26, LBJ announced that the federal government was going to immediately spend between $200 million and $300 million in Watts for a special employment program, establishment of pilot child care centers, creation of a small business center to foster black-owned enterprises, a vigorous back-to-school program, construction of low-income housing, and an expanded surplus food distribution initiative.[16] But Abe Ribicoff, Walter Reuther, and others advised the president that special programs beyond OEO and AFDC were needed to address the complex problems facing the nation's cities, problems such as mass transit that would bring the poor to available jobs and slum clearance that would do more than simply replace tenements with middle-class housing that the poor could not afford.[17]

Independently, Walter Reuther attempted to sell the White House on a "pilot cities" program in which business, labor, and the federal government would cooperate "to carve out significant portions of decayed areas of center cities and rebuild them with rehabilitation, new housing, new commercial buildings, new workers, professional people, Negroes, Whites, etc."[18] LBJ was sympathetic, despite his dislike of Reuther; he confided to an aide that whenever he sat across from Reuther in the Oval Office, "I'm sitting in my rocker, smiling and thinking all the time, 'How can I get that hand out of his pocket [Reuther had been maimed by a would-be assassin's bullet] so I can cut his balls off!' " [19] It was no accident that Watts simultaneously demonstrated the highest population density, the highest disease rate, the highest unemployment rate, and the highest rate of narcotic use in the country, he commented to network executive Al Friendly. "If we don't face up to the problems [that we have now] ultimately [we will] not only have to face up to the ones we got now, but we [will have to] face up to a bunch we have created that flow from failure to face up to the ones we got." [20] Standing in the LBJ Ranch swimming pool at the beginning of August, Johnson proclaimed to his new domestic adviser, Joe Califano, "I want to rebuild American cities. I want a bill that makes it possible for anybody to buy a house anywhere they can afford to." [21] The upshot was that LBJ proposed a new cabinet-level department, Housing and Urban Development (HUD), to Congress. On September 9, 1965, both houses overwhelmingly approved legislation to create the new agency.

Although the president was required to name a director for HUD no later than November 1, he agonized for more than three months before announcing his choice. Ever since his accession to the presidency, LBJ had made noises about naming the first black Supreme Court justice and the first black cabinet officer. He was aware of the tremendously symbolic importance of appointing a black cabinet officer. He knew "how many little Negro boys in Podunk, Mississippi," would be uplifted by it, he told Roy Wilkins. "Now I am very anxious, in the limited time the Good Lord is going to give me, to just not talk but to do and to do by example and to put the coon skins on the wall and not just talk and promise and then make big speeches." Nearly everyone anticipated that the president would name Robert Weaver, the administrator of the Housing and Home Finance Agency and an African American, to head HUD. But as he confided to Wilkins, he had serious misgivings. He liked Weaver, but he feared that racism in Congress and within the urban power structures would prevent him from getting the job done. "I rather think that a white man can do a hell of a lot more for the Negro than the Negroes can for themselves in these cities," he observed to Wilkins. "I think having a Negro heading up housing is just every time they take any kind of step creates a problem." [22] "In my judgment you are liable to get yourself in the same shape you did after the Reconstruction and it will take you another hundred years to get back," the president confided to Katzenbach. "I doubt that this fella can make the grade and he will be a flop and he will be exhibit number one." [23]

LBJ had other reasons for delaying. He wanted to use Weaver's appointment with civil rights leaders to compel them to follow the moderate path he had chosen, and he wanted to impress upon Weaver the importance of his appointment and the debt he would owe to the president as a result of it. In his conversation with Wilkins, he indirectly chided the leadership of the traditional civil rights organizations for not anticipating urban unrest and acting to prevent it, for fostering demonstrations that contributed to the white backlash, and for not getting out to register black voters. Significantly, Wilkins told LBJ that he and the blacks that he knew would abide by whatever decision he made. "I can criticize you and will," he told LBJ, "but I still believe in your heart."[24]

As the weeks passed, Weaver became more and more anguished. He twice threatened to resign his existing position. "Yesterday I think he decided not to resign," LBJ said to Wilkins, "then last night he said he was going to put it off another day and I haven't heard what he has done this morning. My judgment is he is not going to resign. He is a damned fool if he does and if he doesn't have any more sense than that, he should not be in the Cabinet."[25] Of the incident, Joe Califano later wrote, "He [LBJ] gave me a glimpse of the trait that sometimes drove him to crush and reshape a man before placing him in a job of enormous importance, much the way a ranch hand tames a wild horse before mounting it. To Johnson, this technique helped assure that an appointee was his alone."[26] All the while LBJ kept Weaver and the black community in suspense, he had been running interference for him with Richard Russell, Russell Long, other southern senators, and, surprisingly enough, with Adam Clayton Powell. "I am a little worried about Powell," LBJ confided to Roy Wilkins. "He has told me that under no circumstances should I name Weaver." Wilkins advised him to ignore the reverend. "I feel, if I may say so," Wilkins said, "Powell's opposition goes back to the fact that Weaver is Harvard and high in an appointed position, out of the reach of Powell as an operating Congressman."[27] When LBJ finally sent Weaver's name up in January, the Senate took a mere four days to give it unanimous consent.

A month later, LBJ let it be known that he was going to nominate Andrew Brimmer, a black Harvard-educated economist, to fill a vacancy on the Federal Reserve Board. William McChesney Martin, the conservative head of the Fed, opposed Brimmer's appointment for ideological reasons. Martin was an advocate of tight money; fighting inflation came before everything—jobs, wage levels, politics—whereas Brimmer, like Johnson, believed in maintaining the lowest possible interest rates for as long as possible. When Martin put out the word that he would have to resign if he found himself in a minority on the board, LBJ exploded. "I don't think anybody is indispensable and goddamn these fellows that say I am going to be on a board of seven members and if you don't appoint anybody I want I am going to quit. I had a cabinet officer tell me one night I just feel like I will be called upon to resign if this policy that you announced is carried out and I said, 'Do you want to do it orally or in writing?' He is still working for me effectively."[28] Johnson appointed Brimmer, and Martin did not resign.

THE FIRST WEEK IN OCTOBER, the nation was reminded that racism was alive and well in the South. The previous August, in Lowndes County, Alabama, Thomas A. Coleman, a highway engineer and unpaid deputy sheriff, had emptied his shotgun into two civil rights workers, Jonathan M. Daniels, a twenty-six-year-old white Episcopal seminarian, and Richard Morrisroe, a black Catholic priest of the same age, killing the former and gravely wounding the latter. Coleman's trial took place in the slave-built, whitewashed courthouse in Haynesville. Circuit Judge T. Werth Thagard refused to allow Alabama Attorney General Richmond Flowers to direct the prosecution, and he refused to delay the trial until Morrisroe was well enough to testify. The clerk of the court was Coleman's cousin; the local football field had been named for his father. Lowndes County prosecutor Arthur E. "Bubba" Gamble dominated the proceedings. Joyce Bailey, a slight, nineteen-year-old black woman took the stand and described the scene at the Cash Store, which a mixed group, including Daniels and Morissroe, was trying to integrate. She repeated Coleman's order to Daniels: "Get off this property, or I'll blow your goddamn heads off, you sons of bitches." Gamble joined the jury and spectators in prolonged laughter. She described the blast at Daniels: "He caught his stomach and then he fell back." With Father Morrisroe, she started running. After the priest was shot down, she testified, "I was still running." More laughter; then from the gallery somebody yelled, "Run, you niggers." More laughter. Coleman was duly acquitted.[29]

The White House was as repelled as the rest of the nation. Reedy, who had rejoined the LBJ team as special adviser, and his cohorts mulled over various options, including reviving the Force Acts, federal legislation to reform the jury system, and a sub rosa campaign to convince southern officials that if they did not put a halt to these courtroom farces, the civil rights movement would be driven underground, "where it is likely to act like the Viet Cong." But there was little in the short run that the administration could do.[30] In November, the Justice Department did intervene in behalf of Charles Morgan Jr., a Birmingham lawyer who had filed suit in federal court charging discriminatory jury selection in Haynesville.[31]

In his Howard speech in June 1965, LBJ had called for the convening of a massive White House Conference, "To Ensure These Rights," to be held in the spring of 1966. In November, some two hundred civil rights leaders gathered at the Washington Hilton to plan for the spring meeting. By this point, the black backlash against the Moynihan report was in full swing. If Negroes had a family problem, declared black intellectual and civil rights activist Bayard Rustin, "it is not because they are Negro but because they are so disproportionately a part of the unemployed, the underemployed, and the ill-paid." Honorary chairman A. Philip Randolph, seventy-six, the courtly president of the Brotherhood of Sleeping Car Porters, called for a "100 billion dollar 'freedom budget' to be spent on eradicating ghettos."[32] Actually, Moynihan agreed. Harry McPherson recalled, "Pat's answer was rather simple—a family allowance plan. He was very disturbed from the very beginning about community action. He said, 'You realize what you've done, don't you? You've ruined the poverty program . . . effort with community action. It's wild; these people are out to destroy you.' He took the position that all the remedial programs in the world were for naught unless there was an income base in the family. You could build on that; they would stay home and you'd have an interacting family. This was a Catholic middle-class view."[33] Given LBJ's commitment to consensus, his determination to sell antipoverty and civil rights to conservatives as well as liberals, and the mounting costs of the war in Southeast Asia, such an approach, which could cost $11 billion to $12 billion a year, was impossible.[34]

THROUGHOUT HIS PRESIDENCY, LBJ was obsessed with avoiding scandal, not only obvious corruption, but even the hint of wrongdoing. His obsession with public virtuosity morphed into a fixation on cost cutting. He lived in constant terror that his enemies, especially his Republican enemies, would charge him with excessive spending. Thus did he order lights at the White House turned off if they were not in immediate use. At one point, he attempted to cut his aides' allowances for journals. The president complained constantly that the security measures taken by the military and Secret Service were too extensive and too expensive. Periodically, Lady Bird would have to put her foot down. One morning in August, she was summoned to the Oval Office to hear her husband's complaints about the cost of protecting the girls in their modest travels and of advancing a trip Lady Bird was planning to the Grand Teton. She blew up. "I took the position that my few speeches, my few trips for Head Start, beautification, and so forth had to be advanced and ought to be paid for. My own personal ticket I would buy. And then I walked out, angry and hurt." Shortly after returning from a beauty parlor appointment, she was told the president would like to see her in the Oval Office. "He put his arms around me and said, 'You don't have to worry about anything. You ought not to worry about money. I'll get you whatever you need.' I was speechless and closer to tears than I had been in four or five years. I hugged him and walked out, not trusting myself to talk. Poor man, trying to walk the tightrope between loving and wanting to please his family and make them comfortable, and wanting to live up to the ethics, a sort of thrift, for the private actions that could face public scrutiny."[35] Nevertheless, to the delight of political satirists, the lights stayed off. Harry McPherson later speculated on the source of this ostentatious frugality. "I think that he may have been spooked by impressions that I certainly know I heard in Texas in 1962," he said, "when I would go down to see my family, that this was all just a big swimming pool party up here and a lot of whoring around and boozing and a lot of dilettantes having a ball. And he may have felt that the country felt that."[36]

TO SIMULTANEOUSLY FINANCE THE WAR in Southeast Asia and the Great Society, it was imperative, LBJ believed, to hold prices and wages down lest runaway inflation ravage the economy. Beginning in August 1964, the Johnson administration had worked to persuade labor and management to adhere to an unofficial wage-price guideline of 3.2 percent. The first great challenge to this standard, which corresponded to the estimated annual growth rate in productivity, came from the steel industry.[37] The United Steel Workers, headed by newly elected I. W. Abel, and the steel industry, represented by R. Conrad

Cooper, had attempted to work out a new contract throughout the summer, but to no avail. The union demanded wage increases of approximately 5 percent, with steel offering half that amount. If it were forced to go above 2.5, industry spokesmen said, prices would increase well above the 3.2 percent guideline. Abel had been elected on a promise to achieve the same wage increase recently won by the can and aluminum workers, and he would not budge. Cooper, banking on White House intervention, also remained adamant. On August 17, LBJ summoned Abel to the White House to try a little persuasion. "I made commitments to the members who elected me," Abel told the president defensively. "You're starting to sound just like Dick Russell," Johnson observed, cunningly. "He sat on that very couch talking to me about my civil rights bill in 1964. I asked him not to filibuster. 'We've got to make a stand somewhere,' he said. He sounded just like you." Smiling, LBJ softened and repeated a favorite anecdote. "I told Dick Russell the story about the Negro boy in bed with the white gal, whose husband arrived home unexpectedly. 'Hide! hide,' she whispered. 'He'll kill you and then he'll kill me.' " The president described how the black youth hid in the closet. "At this point," recalled Joe Califano, who sat in on the conversation, "Johnson bolted from his rocker, stood upright, arms stiff at his side, legs straight, tight together, back and shoulders ramrod straight." He described the enraged husband charging through the bedroom shouting that he knew someone was there, banging doors open. Finally, he came to the closet where the culprit was hiding. " 'What the hell are you doin' here?' this little white gal's husband shouts, fire in his eyes. 'Everybody's gotta stand somewhere, boss,' this Negro boy answers." The group laughed. Johnson leaned into Abel and said softly, slowly, "Everybody's gotta stand somewhere," he repeated. "Just like that Negro boy he wanted to keep down, Russell stuck himself in a closet with nowhere to go on civil rights. Mr. Abel, I know you gotta stand somewhere. But you gotta stand where you can move around a little, not just pinned in the linen closet." [38]

In the days that followed LBJ met with both labor and management, appealing typically to both parties' patriotism. A strike would end the nation's fifty-five-month economic expansion. A price rise on steel would percolate throughout the economy, providing justification for price increases on thousands of consumer items. A recently conducted Harris poll indicated that 87 percent of America's housewives were worried about inflation. [39] Negotiators pushed LBJ to permit selective price increases that would allow a better wage offer to the union. "No price increase," he told Califano. "None. Zero," making a circle with his thumb and forefinger. [40]

In fact, observers remarked on the enthusiasm, confidence, almost joy with which LBJ intervened in the steel dispute. He continued to pop in on union and industry negotiators, at the same time sending Clark Clifford, counsel to Republic Steel, to tell company executives that there would be no guideline-busting settlement, and dispatching Goldberg to union leaders to tell them the same thing. [41] On September 3 a gleeful Johnson was flanked by Abel and

Cooper, neither of whom shared his mood, to announce that a settlement had been reached and that it was well within the administration's 3.25 guideline. Comments in the press and among economists were generally laudatory. " 'Masterful' is the word for the way you brought the steel crisis to a successful solution," former Council of Economic Advisers head Walter Heller wrote him. "You struck a key blow for continued cost-price stability and the country's economic health." [42]

In reality, LBJ's ostentatious intrusion into the steel dispute ended his honeymoon with the business community. In the midst of the White House–brokered negotiations, conservative economist Milton Friedman wrote an article for the *National Review* entitled "Social Responsibility: A Subversive Doctrine." A businessperson's first and overriding obligation must be to his or her stockholders. To introduce other factors into the decision-making process would be to subvert the free market system. It was his experience, Friedman wrote, that "the appeal to 'social' responsibility or 'voluntary' restraint has always occurred when the governmental agency which is responsible for the area of policy in question has been unable or unwilling to discharge its own responsibility." Here was an attack on the whole notion of Johnsonian corporatism, the idea of business-labor-government cooperation to bring stability and predictability to the marketplace. [43] Executives and business academics chastised LBJ for undermining the very system he was trying to save. George Shultz, dean of the Graduate School of Business at the University of Chicago and a prominent labor arbitrator, warned that "it undermines private collective bargaining to have the President and government come in so strongly." Lawrence Harvey, president of California's Harvey Aluminum, agreed: "Soon there will be no more unions, in effect, and no more collective bargaining. The government will control the terms of every contract." [44] What a classic dog in the manger, Johnson thought.

In the end, LBJ's attempts to limit price-wage increases short of mandatory controls proved futile. In January 1966, John V. Lindsay, the newly elected liberal Republican mayor of New York, agreed to give striking transit workers a 6.3 percent pay raise. During the walkout that had paralyzed Manhattan, LBJ had considered a number of options, including asking Congress for a resolution authorizing the executive to impose a settlement. He tried to pressure Lindsay, but given that the mayor was not a member of his party, that proved difficult. Johnson called George Meany and threatened to sit on his hands when 14b came up for debate in Congress. But it was all to no avail. Everybody was in bed together in the New York situation, Willard Wirtz reported. "We are dealing with the most corrupt system for settling labor disputes in the country. That New York situation is rotten all the way through." [45] Then, in the summer, steel defied LBJ by increasing prices. A subsequent settlement between the International Machinists and Aerospace Workers and the country's airlines gave the union a 4.9 percent raise, and in the words of the IMA president, "destroy[ed] all existing wage and price guidelines now in existence." [46]

· · ·

AS THE GLORIOUS 89th Congress neared its end, LBJ increasingly permitted himself the luxury of comparing the achievements of the Great Society with those of the New Deal and himself with FDR. As with his predecessor's program, there was something for everyone, even the venomous and ungrateful intellectuals and artists who were then criticizing him for everything from his Vietnam policy to his haircut. The previous March the president had submitted to Congress legislation creating a National Foundation on the Arts and Humanities. The legislation sped through the Senate and bogged down briefly in the House. A little presidential prodding, however, freed the bill from the conservatives' embrace. On September 29, LBJ signed the new measure and promised that a National Theater, a National Opera, and a National Ballet would follow. The legislation created two twenty-four-member bodies: a National Council on the Arts/Humanities to select projects worthy of funding and a National Endowment of the Arts/Humanities to administer the grants awarded. Thus was launched the first comprehensive effort by the federal government to materially support artists, historians, musicians, writers, critics, philosophers, sculptors, painters, and dancers. As chairman of the Arts Council, the White House chose Roger Stevens, playwright, art impresario, and, not coincidentally, chair of the Kennedy Center.[47]

Stevens's selection was part of LBJ's intermittent campaign to reconcile with the Kennedys. Indeed, LBJ had Bob McNamara on continuous duty with the family trying to convince them that the president was really their friend. He was very fond of Jackie, LBJ told the defense chief during a conversation in August. He had stopped calling her for fear she was becoming annoyed. He was pleased, he said, to see that Bobby had attended several bill-signing ceremonies. You have so much power and prestige that you can afford to bend over backward, McNamara told his boss. But he could not expect the still grief-stricken Jackie to come to the White House. She would not come, and she would not have anything publicly to do with President and Mrs. Johnson. Both he and Lady Bird understood, Johnson said.[48] But then, a week later, Jackie had her first coming-out party in New York. It began in her fifteen-room duplex apartment with a dinner honoring John Kenneth Galbraith. Kennedy in-laws held simultaneous dinners for other luminaries. Then the group, numbering about a hundred, took over the Sign of the Dove, a converted greenhouse-and-garden restaurant. Wearing a strapless, off-white evening dress, Jackie danced the night away with guests Truman Capote, Bob McNamara, and John Galbraith while Wendy Vanderbilt and Pierre Salinger looked on. New Frontiersmen Schlesinger, Goodwin, and Sorenson beamed at each other, while Bobby Kennedy and McGeorge Bundy were seen leaving the festivities arm-in-arm around 1 A.M.[49]

LBJ did not comment directly, but the coming out, the worshipful press coverage, and the obvious intimacy of some of his closest advisers with those who despised him, rankled. He again caved in to feelings of cultural and personal self-pity. Told that *Life* wanted to do a pictorial feature on the ranch, LBJ reacted negatively. All the magazine cared about was running derogatory articles on him. It had published nonrevelations concerning his personal finances and all but libeled Lady Bird and the girls. "I know the utter contempt they and these sophisticated alleged intellectuals have for the people of Johnson City and that little town and they think it is dirty and nasty and uncouth and illiterate." All *Life* and the other publications were doing was commercializing the presidency for their own profit. When, however, Liz Carpenter told him that the person heading the *Life* team was a Texas boy, LBJ relented.[50]

ON THE AFTERNOON OF OCTOBER 3, at the base of the Statue of Liberty, LBJ signed the Immigration Act of 1965, thus putting in place one of the least-noticed but most important components of the Great Society. In theory, according to historian Philip Gleason, to be an American, "a person did not have to be of any particular national, linguistic, religious, or ethnic background. All he had to do was to commit himself to the political ideology centered on the abstract ideals of liberty, equality, and republicanism."[51] This was allegedly what set America off from the rest of the world. Citizenship was not to be based on blood, national origin, kinship, heredity, or color, but on a commitment to certain governing political principles. But, in reality, as particular ethnic, religious, or racial groups within the United States struggled to gain or maintain political and cultural dominance, they sought to identify American nationality as peculiarly white or Protestant or Anglo-Saxon. In turn, Congress passed citizenship laws that institutionalized those myths.[52] Throughout most of the history of the United States, laws were on the books that declared the vast majority of the people in the world legally ineligible to become full citizens solely because of their race, original nationality, or gender. Even indigenous peoples were not immune from discrimination. Until the second half of the twentieth century, African Americans and Native Americans were considered beyond the pale. There was in the late nineteenth century a flurry of immigration from China and Japan, mostly manual laborers who were willing to work on the railroads, in the mines, and in the white households of the booming West. It was this influx that produced the first immigration law that discriminated on the basis of race or nationality, the Chinese Exclusion Act of 1882.

By the turn of the century, the pseudoscience of eugenics (from the Greek, meaning "noble in heredity") began to take root in the United States. Appealing alike to white southerners who were busily erecting Jim Crow statutes and to nativists who wanted to keep the impure from America's shores, eugenicists such as Dr. Harry H. Laughlin were writing popular articles positing the existence of a chain of being, setting up racial classifications in descending order, with the whitest and hence most civilized and most intelligent at the top and the darkest and hence least intelligent and least civilized at the bottom. Others equated race with nationality. Thus Poles, Italians, Russians, and Jews were biologically different from the English, Scots, Germans, and Norwegians. The former, it came to be believed, were "inferior" and the latter "superior." By the eve of the Great War a vast nativist movement had emerged, insisting that immigration to the United States had to be regulated on the basis of national origin.[53] The Immigration Act of 1917, passed over Woodrow Wilson's veto, assuming that Western Europeans were literate and southeastern Europeans were not, imposed a literacy test on would-be immigrants. When it turned out that most residents of southern and eastern Europe could indeed read and write, Congress passed the National Origins Act of 1924, which accorded nations immigration quotas based on their percentage of the U.S. population as of 1910. The annual British quota was sixty-five thousand, while those of Greece and China were one hundred, the minimum.[54] The McCarran-Walter Act, enacted during the height of second Red Scare, reaffirmed the old quota system and established a bureau within the State Department to screen all would-be immigrants for ties to communism.

The leading proponent of immigration reform was Representative Emmanuel Celler of New York. The entire concept of quotas based on national origin was racist, he argued. Shortly after he became president, LBJ met with Celler, Myer Feldman, the White House aide who had handled immigration issues for Kennedy, and Abba Schwarz, a Jewish activist and expert on displaced persons. LBJ, who had helped smuggle European Jewish refugees into the United States before and during World War II, needed little persuading that change was in order. On January 13, 1964, he met with sixty representatives of church, nationality, and labor groups that supported immigration reform as well as congressional leaders and asked for prompt and positive action on the bill the Kennedy administration had devised and introduced in the House. But nativists kept the measure bottled up in committee until after the 1964 election. Then the large Democratic majorities elected to both houses broke the logjam. On September 3, 1965, Congress passed the Immigration Act Amendments of 1965. Under the provisions of the law, the national origins system, the central feature of U.S. immigration policy for forty years, was to be phased out by July 1, 1968. Thereafter, immigrants would be admitted by preference categories—family relationships to U.S. citizens and resident aliens, and occupational qualifications—on a first-come, first-served basis without reference to country of birth.

At the signing ceremony, LBJ proclaimed that the new law repaired "a very deep and painful flaw in the fabric of American justice." The national origin system, he said, "violated the basic principle of American democracy—the principle that values and rewards each man on the basis of his merit as a man . . . It has been untrue to the faith that brought thousands to these shores even before we were a country."[55] The Immigration Act of 1965 did nothing less than ensure that America remained a land of diversity whose identity rested on a set of political principles rather than blood and soil nationalism. Since 1920 the percentage of foreign-born individuals residing in America had been declining. The census of 1980 showed the first reversal of that trend, and the percentages would grow gradually but steadily thereafter.[56]

• • •

THERE WAS in the Johnson program protection for the environment, consumers, and workers as well. "The water we drink, the food we eat, the very air we breathe are threatened with pollution," Johnson told Congress in February 1965. "We must act . . . For . . . once our natural splendor is destroyed, it can never be recaptured."[57] As was true of much of the Johnson program, environmental protection had its roots in the Kennedy administration. In 1961, JFK had named Arizona Senator Stewart Udall secretary of the interior. Udall and Kennedy had become friends in the 1950s, and the Arizonan had played a key role in delivering his state to the Democrats in the 1960 presidential election. Udall and the environmentalists of the 1960s went beyond the narrowly gauged conservation movement that had characterized environmentalism since the Progressive Era. In line with the liberal philosophy being espoused by Schlesinger and Galbraith, they insisted that the goal was not simply to conserve pockets of beauty, wildlife, and natural resources but to preserve and enhance the "quality of life" in cities and towns as well as mountains, forests, lakes, and deserts. Udall declared, "No longer is peripheral action—the 'saving' of a forest, a park, a refuge for wildlife isolated from the mainstream—sufficient. The total environment is now the concern, and the new conservation makes man, himself, its subject. The quality of life is now the perspective and repose of the new conservation."[58]

The Kennedy administration had sponsored a White House conference on the environment in 1962 and pushed through Congress legislation creating the Cape Cod National Seashore, but it was not until publication of Rachel Carson's *Silent Spring* (1962) that nationwide support began to build in behalf of the new environmentalism. A marine biologist with the U.S. Fish and Wildlife Service, Carson had written a celebrated series of nature essays collected and published in 1951 as *The Sea Around Us.* As the economy exploded in the years after World War II, she had become increasingly disturbed by the pollution of the nation's rivers, lakes, and underground aquifers by DDT and other pesticides. Because it was used to eliminate malaria-carrying mosquitoes and insects that destroyed food and fiber crops, DDT had been hailed as a wonder chemical and used indiscriminately. In *Silent Spring,* Carson demonstrated through massive research that widespread use of toxic chemicals was poisoning the nation's water supply and food sources, thus threatening the health of human beings and animals alike. Though pesticide manufacturers mounted a massive campaign to discredit Carson as a hysteric, *Silent Spring* became the text of the burgeoning environmental movement.

Environmentalists were initially pessimistic about LBJ and his commitment to their cause. They remembered him as the oil senator from Texas. But once again, reformers were pleasantly surprised. "You'll recall this Rachel Carson book, *Silent Spring,*" Orville Freeman prompted his boss in mid-1964. "I think it's very important politically that we be doing something about this because we've got to use pesticides in agriculture and in our forests . . . we've just got to go ahead and do the right thing."[59] Throughout his first year and a half in office, LBJ invoked the memory of Theodore Roosevelt and promised to take up where the Rough Rider had left off. "There is no excuse for a river flowing red with blood from slaughterhouses. There is no excuse for paper mills pouring tons of sulphuric acid into the lakes and the streams of the people of this country. There is no excuse—and we should call a spade a spade—for chemical companies and oil refineries using our major rivers and pipelines for toxic wastes."[60]

Under the Water Quality Act of 1965, all states were required to enforce water quality standards for interstate rivers, lakes, and streams within their borders. The following year, Maine Senator Edmund Muskie pushed through Congress the Clean Waters Restoration Act, authorizing more than $3.5 billion to finance a cleanup of the nation's waterways and to block further pollution through the dumping of sewage or toxic industrial waste. From that point on, LBJ tended to take violation of his environmental standards personally. White House aide Lee White recalled that when the president received a series of complaints that sewage waste was being allowed to contaminate drinking water in a particular locale, he called Udall up. "I don't know what the hell you guys are doing but that dirty-water program just ain't working. I've got all kinds of complaints." Udall replied, "Mr. President, that may be the case, but the truth of the matter is that that program is in the Health Service, in the Department of Health, Education and Welfare." Incredulous, the president exclaimed, "What's it doing there?" "That's where it's always been," Udall answered. Johnson said, "Well, I think that's outrageous. When I think of dirty water, I think of you." He then turned to White and Califano, who had also been present during the conversation, and ordered them to use the president's reorganization authority and get the clean water program transferred from HEW to Interior.[61]

It was a natural step for environmentalists to move from concern about water purity to a focus on clean air. President Johnson's Task Force on Environmental Pollution, established in 1964, documented the damage being done to the environment by toxic emissions from coal-burning factories and auto exhaust systems. The nation was shocked to learn that air pollutants created "acid rain," which fell back to earth, tainting food crops and further corrupting the water supply. On Thanksgiving Day 1965, New York City experienced an ecological catastrophe, an air inversion that concentrated almost two pounds of soot per person in the atmosphere. Eighty people died and hundreds were hospitalized. In the wake of the Third National Conference on Air Pollution in 1966, Congress passed the Air Quality Act of 1967, which set progressively stricter standards for industrial and automobile emissions. The polluting industries invested billions of dollars in lobbying for restrictive amendments, and in the end the legislation provided that standards were to be set jointly by industry and government. In 1969, Congress passed the National Environmental Policy Act, requiring, among other things, that federal agencies file environmental impact statements for all federally funded projects. The following year, the House and Senate established the Environmental Protection Agency. These were but the first shots fired in the ongoing battle to protect the public and nature from air- and waterborne pollutants.

On another environmental front, Udall joined Lady Bird to launch a preservation and beautification movement that would protect wilderness areas and make inhabited regions as visually attractive as possible. In 1889, John Muir had formed the Sierra Club in an effort to save the giant redwoods of California's Yosemite Valley. During the years that followed, the Sierra Club and other wilderness preservation groups made some headway, but they were no match for the lumber companies and mining interests, which insisted on the unrestricted right of private enterprise to exploit the public domain. From the time LBJ had been director of the National Youth Administration in Texas, Lady Bird had taken an intense interest in preserving portions of the environment in their natural state and cleaning up the American landscape. During the 1930s she had cofounded a movement to establish a system of roadside parks. Along with her husband and Stewart Udall, she helped persuade Congress to pass the Wilderness Act of 1964, a legislative initiative the Sierra Club and Wilderness Society had been touting for ten years. The measure set aside 9 million acres of national forest as wilderness areas, protecting them from timber cuttings and strictly regulating public access. The following year, the Wild and Scenic Rivers Act extended federal protection over portions of eight of America's most spectacular waterways. Mrs. Johnson was gratified by these successes, but she was determined to do something about populated areas as well.

At the first lady's behest, in 1964 the president convened the Task Force on the Preservation of Natural Beauty. The national beautification movement focused first on Washington, D.C. Hoping to convert the nation's capital into a model community, Mrs. Johnson worked through the National Park Service and private donors to beautify Pennsylvania Avenue and create a system of parks throughout the city. She and LBJ subsequently championed the Highway Beautification Act of 1965 in the face of stiff opposition from the Outdoor Advertising Association. Beautification was good business, the president insisted to the Chamber of Commerce. Tourism in Europe was booming, he observed, but it was declining in the United States. "Yet a few men are coming in and insisting that we keep these dirty little old signs up in these dirty little old towns," he proclaimed to an environmentalist group, "and that this is going to affect free enterprise.[62] The highway bill cleared the Senate but stalled in the House. LBJ sent word to the Hill that he considered a vote for highway beautification "a matter of personal honor" because his wife was involved. The day the measure came up for a vote, October 7, Lady Bird was to host a previously scheduled White House dinner. LBJ sent word that no member of Congress would be welcome at the executive mansion unless and until the highway bill was voted through.[63] As finally passed, the compromise law banned or restricted outdoor billboards outside commercial and industrial sectors and required the fencing of unsightly junkyards adjacent to highways.[64]

Critics of the administration dismissed leaders of the beautification movement as dilettante elitists, "the daffodil and dogwood" set. Rats, open sewage, and unsafe buildings were more of a problem than green space, advocates for inner-city dwellers argued. Mrs. Johnson responded by persuading Walter Johnson to head the Neighborhoods and Special Projects Committee, a body whose goal was to clean up and beautify the mostly black, poorer neighborhoods of Washington, D.C. Compared to racism, war, poverty, and social injustice, the beautification movement paled, but it was an authentic aspect of the larger environmental movement and important in part because it involved members of the American aristocracy.

That portion of the environmental movement that sought to protect human beings and the national habitat from polluting industries reinforced and was reinforced by the consumer protection movement. Congress's enactment of a bill imposing the first federal standards on automobile emissions marked a victory for both groups. In 1965 Ralph Nader, a muckraking young lawyer who would become the guru of consumer advocacy, published *Unsafe at Any Speed,* an attack on giant automobile companies like General Motors, which allegedly placed design and cost considerations above safety. He played a key role in securing passage of the Fair Packaging and Labeling Act and the Automobile Safety Act, both passed in 1966. Near the close of Johnson's term, Congress enacted the landmark Occupational Health and Safety Act, which imposed new federal safety standards on the American workplace.

Lady Bird's decision to embrace national beautification was natural for her. As a girl, she had reveled in the outdoors, in the simple beauties and spirituality to be found in flowers, forests, rivers, and mountains. It was also a function of her determination "to be a useful First Lady," to be identified with Eleanor Roosevelt rather than the high-fashion, decorative, uninvolved Jackie Kennedy. Indeed, Lady Bird dressed smartly and well but made no attempt to compete with her predecessor as a fashion icon. Whereas Jackie had been among the most photographed first ladies, Lady Bird was among the least. She moved to establish her own identity, setting up an office in the East Wing to accommodate her staff and the press that covered her. At state dinners, opera and classical music were replaced by Broadway stars and American music. Bird exchanged Jackie's pretentious and high-strung French chef, Rene Verdon, with Zephyr Wright. She chose china with a native wildflower pattern and shopped at Garfinckel's, Washington's traditional department store. She made herself accessible to the press and treated its members with respect. As a result, in contrast to her husband, she enjoyed an excellent relationship with journalists and was depicted generally as a genuine, caring, intelligent, long-suffering woman, and a person altogether to be admired.

But immersion in the movement to clean up the nation's highways and urban centers, to expand its national parklands, and to make aesthetic sensibility part of the national life was also an escape from her husband and the pressure of national affairs. As both LBJ and Lady Bird threw themselves into the roles into which they had been cast by JFK's assassination, they grew apart. There was obviously much less occasion for intimacy. The best time was in the wee hours of the morning, before the day's business began, but Vietnam, urban unrest, and the "vicious" media intruded even then. LBJ kept up a separate sexual life. There was not time for long-term affairs, but from 1965 on, the daily White House logs are full of notations of forty-five-minute and one-hour private sessions in the Oval Office between LBJ and a half-dozen women whom he bragged to others about having sex with. As usual, Lady Bird seemed to accommodate herself. In January 1964, she welcomed Alice Glass to the East Room of the White House to hear Robert Merrill of the Metropolitan Opera sing excerpts from Rossini's *Barber of Seville.* The arrangement whereby she acceded to her husband's affairs in return for being accorded a place of honor, influence, and respect by him remained intact.

There is no doubt that Lady Bird empathized with Lyndon in his trials and supported his policies. One wintry afternoon in February 1965, while greeting guests in the East Room, she spied a group of civil rights protesters kneeling in the snow outside singing "We Shall Overcome." Suddenly she sank into a chair and began weeping.[65] In June, just before the Festival of Arts was to get under way, she heard that writer John Hersey intended to read aloud portions from his book, *Hiroshima,* about the atomic bombing of Japan, as a protest against the war in Vietnam. She tried to get Eric Goldman to withdraw the invitation, but he convinced her that such a move would be a public relations disaster. Hersey did attend and did read. Throughout, Lady Bird sat in stony silence and refused to applaud at the finish. Vietnam—the deaths on the battlefield, her husband's angst, and the increasingly strident antiwar demonstrations—drove her to distraction. "I couldn't handle the war in Vietnam," she later commented to her staff. "I wasn't big enough."[66]

By the spring of 1965 her diary entries show increasing signs of depression. Nothing in her public or private life would be construed as a challenge to her husband; her existence was an exercise in subjugation. In this way, she was different from Eleanor Roosevelt. As Liz Carpenter put it, "Mrs. Roosevelt was an instigator, an innovator, willing to air a cause without her husband's endorsement. Mrs. Johnson was an implementer and translator of her husband and his purpose. She was, first and foremost, a wife."[67] Within six months of her husband's landslide election to the presidency, Lady Bird was fantasizing about retirement. Her diary entry from Sunday, March 7, read, "For some time I have been swimming upstream against a feeling of depression and relative inertia. I flinch from activity and involvement, and yet I rust without them. Lyndon lives in a cloud of troubles, with a few rays of light. I am counting the months until March 1968 when, like Truman, it will be possible to say, 'I don't want this office, this responsibility, any longer, even if you want me. Find the strongest and most able man and God bless you. Good-by.' "[68]

Bird lived in constant dread that Lyndon would die in office. His health was more fragile than anyone but she and his doctors knew. "We came home Tuesday morning," she recorded after a trip to the ranch, "and last night was not a good night. An old enemy returned. Lyndon sweated down two or three pair of pajamas. This has been a symptom of his illness for all the years I have known him, so I should have expected it." He was still carrying a stone in his left kidney.[69] By April 1965, Johnson had let his weight rise to 226, more than he had carried in 1955, when he had his heart attack. Lady Bird was disgusted. "I don't know whether to lash out in anger or sarcasm," she wrote. She did neither but instead issued strict instructions to those serving her husband his meals: one helping of oatmeal at breakfast, one helping of chili at lunch, and no more than one jigger of Cutty Sark before dinner. Late one night, after everyone else had retired, Lady Bird awoke to find herself alone in bed. She got up and went out into the hall, where she heard a strange metallic scraping sound. She followed it to the kitchen, where she found Lyndon wolfing down a bowl of tapioca pudding, his favorite desert. Silently she took the spoon and bowl from him. The next day Johnson ordered one of his Secret Service attendants to go out and purchase a wooden spoon.[70]

In the fall, LBJ was compelled to enter Bethesda Naval Hospital for a gall bladder operation. For once, he seemed determined to provide full, advance information to the press. On October 5, he called a press conference at the ranch to announce the event.[71] He was mindful of the impact that his going under the knife and being anesthetized for an extended period, especially with his record of heart disease, could have on international affairs and the domestic stock market. He reminded everyone that Vice President Humphrey would be in charge and that matters would proceed as usual. "Thus began three days of tension and concern that no amount of reassuring pronouncements from the doctors could quite dispel," *Newsweek* reported, "but which the President took in even larger stride than usual, combining the aplomb of a ringmaster with the bravado of a lion tamer, managing all the while to seem as pleased with himself as a small boy who has been promised a gallon of ice cream after he has had his tonsils out."[72] Three weeks later he was cleared to leave the hospital, but his physicians insisted that he spend most of the next two months recuperating at the ranch. Before leaving Bethesda, he lifted his sport shirt to show reporters the scar from his operation, a twelve-inch incision that appeared to be healing nicely.[73] For Lyndon and for Lady Bird, the gall bladder operation was something of a disguised blessing. It was back on the diet, with Fresca instead of scotch in the evening.

At the same time that LBJ left the hospital, the "Fabulous 89th," as the press labeled the sitting session of Congress, adjourned. Its record of achievement was unparalleled: Medicare, Medicaid, voting rights, federal aid to education, the NEH and NEA, a battery of antipoverty programs, highway beautification, a heart, cancer, and stroke bill that pumped new funds into the National Institutes of Health for research, area redevelopment, a new Department of Housing and Urban Development. LBJ was intensely proud of what he and Congress had done; he desperately wanted to be compared to his hero, FDR. It was not to be. "The President has been lucky," Senate Majority Leader Mike Mansfield told reporters. "Don't overlook that. If Clarence Cannon were still alive, he'd have plenty of headaches with his appropriation bills. But the House Appropriation Committee is headed by George Mahon of Texas who is a close friend of the President's."[74] Others pointed out that every measure that Congress had passed had had the support of a majority of Americans. The one item that did not pass—repeal of Section 14b of the Taft-Hartley Act, the so-called right to work proviso—was voted down in both houses. The Republican National Committee estimated that the cumulative cost of the top fifty Great Society bills would be $112 billion. "Think of it!—$112 billion!" exclaimed National Committee Chair Ray C. Bliss. "This spending program dwarfs into utter insignificance all past spending programs, by all nations, all over the world."[75] Columnists who were willing to give LBJ the credit he felt he deserved for the legislative achievements of 1965 were careful to couple their praise with a critique of his foreign policies as aimless and reactive.[76]

LBJ did not take these blows gracefully. He felt he should get credit for resolving some of the great issues of the twentieth century, resolving them in favor of the poor, oppressed, and disadvantaged without polarizing the nation and stoking the flames of class warfare. In the fall, he agreed to give an interview to political historian William Leuchtenburg. "Mr. President, this has been a remarkable Congress," Leuchtenburg said. "It is even arguable whether this isn't the most significant Congress ever." LBJ responded, "No, it isn't. It's not arguable." He then launched into a two-hour tirade against the press, liberals, and the inflated reputations of both JFK and FDR. Roosevelt, he declared, "was like the fellow who cut cordwood and sold it all at Christmas and then spent it all on firecrackers. Social Security and the Wagner Act were all that really amounted to much, and none of it compares to my education act." Johnson was aware that his guest was the author of a laudatory account of the New Deal and that he was an admirer of the Kennedys. "No man knew less about Congress than John Kennedy," LBJ followed up. Every press story he read was full of lies, the president added. "We treat those columnists as whores," he shouted to Leuchtenburg. "Anytime an editor wants to screw 'em, they'll get down on the floor and do it for three dollars."[77]

Johnson ordered his staff to put together a series of White House dinners that turned into tributes to LBJ and the Great Society. "A moment ago I left the White House at the conclusion of another of the President's great circuses," Orville Freeman recorded in his diary, "where the business community is beguiled, seduced, enraptured and then coaxed into thunderous applause about the great God, LBJ. At my table a Mexican-American who started as a shoeshine boy made his statement of dedication to America and of course LBJ. Then two Negroes also spoke. There wasn't a single critical note in the crowd. What does it mean? I really don't know. On the one hand I feel a sense of purpose and direction, consensus, mobilization, and it's good. The troublesome thing is, it is kind of enshrined in a kind of hero worship, exhibitionism."[78]

• • •

IN OCTOBER, WHILE LBJ was in the hospital recuperating from gall bladder surgery, John Kenneth Galbraith wrote urging him to take an extended vacation. "While no one who lives in the eye of the hurricane will ever think so," he observed to the president, "historians will describe these as rather tranquil times. There is no depression; no fighting except for a minor jungle conflict with a fourth-rate power; no major legislative battle impending here at home."[79] If only you knew, LBJ thought. His advisers were telling him that the war was going to require at least another one hundred thousand troops. He was going to have to go to Congress and the American people and ask for an additional $15 billion to $20 billion to fight the war, a step that would knock the notion of a balanced budget into a cocked hat, raise the hackles of conservatives, and threaten present and future Great Society programs. Meanwhile, moderate civil rights leaders like Martin Luther King, increasingly driven to take more radical positions on public issues by the burgeoning Black Power movement, were speaking out against the war. The antiwar movement among blacks coupled with ongoing urban rioting would alienate working-class whites, thus shattering any hope LBJ had of fashioning a rainbow coalition that would ensure ongoing peaceful change in the United States. Something had to be done.

Earlier, on July 8, LBJ had Moyers summon the heads of the various task forces he had put together to design components of the Great Society. In the White House mess, LBJ thanked Robert Wood, John Gardner, and the other action intellectuals who had devised everything from Head Start to Medicare. "In an extraordinary evening lasting until after one the next morning," Wood writes, "Johnson conveyed his appreciation, his determination to continue his domestic initiatives, and his conviction that guns for Vietnam and butter for the cities were possible simultaneously. Toward the end of the evening, several academics politely questioned that assumption."[80] But LBJ would have none of it. At that point, his economists were telling him that the American economy was more than robust enough to turn back the communists in Southeast Asia and feed the hungry, educate the ignorant, and train the unemployed in America.[81]

Then, on December 1, 1965, McNamara stunned his boss by informing him that in order to continue to fight the war in Vietnam at present levels, Defense was going to have to ask Congress for an $11 billion supplemental to the FY 1966 budget. And that was not the worst of it. If Phase II of the war was implemented—that is, more troops and more extensive bombing—the Defense request for FY 1967 would be $61 billion, putting the total budget over $115 billion.[82] Told of the news, Gardner Ackley, chair of the Council of Economic Advisers, advised the president that such a budget would require a huge tax increase. The GNP for 1966 would have to grow 7.5 percent to pay the bill, and that was not going to happen. Such a tax increase could touch off a recession; to prevent inflation, there would probably have to be mandatory wage-price controls.[83]

LBJ's first reaction to this unwelcome news was to attempt to split money for Vietnam out of the regular budget.[84] Told that such a tactic would not alter the impact that total federal spending would have on the economy, he turned to economies in existing programs. He summoned the cabinet heads to the ranch and ordered them to scour their departments for cuts. LBJ had no intention of abandoning his dream of a just and prosperous polity, but emphasis would have to be placed on quality of life programs that cost little or no money and on the problems of the inner cities.[85]

As part of his effort to have guns and butter simultaneously, LBJ converted the Defense Department itself into an antipoverty agency. In late 1965, planning began on Project 100,000, a scheme to use "advanced educational and medical techniques" to qualify one hundred thousand of the approximately six hundred thousand young men who failed the Armed Forces Qualification Test each year.[86] The scheme, which had its roots in the Kennedy administration, was designed simultaneously to increase the pool of individuals available for service in the military, to ensure that the number of nonwhites in the armed forces matched the number in the general population, to reinforce the poverty program by providing education, job training, discipline, and employment to impoverished young men, and to undercut discontent in inner-city ghettoes—40 percent of those who failed the AFQT were African Americans—by removing their most volatile populations.[87]

The task force report, written largely by Pat Moynihan, was duly submitted to LBJ in January 1964.[88] He was fascinated and excited by its recommendations. "I've seen these kids all my life," he remarked in a cabinet meeting. "I've been with these poor children everywhere. I know that you can do better by them than the NYA or the Job Corps can. The Defense Department can do the job best." Go to it, he told McNamara.[89] The defense chief needed no convincing. Here was a program if ever there was one that could demonstrate his and the Pentagon's commitment to the social justice goals of the Great Society, to the notion "that Defense Department operations can be shaped to support both military and social objectives without significant penalties to military readiness."[90]

LBJ believed that the black community would welcome a program to train disadvantaged young men through military service. Throughout the history of the republic, black leaders, aware that such service constituted the ultimate badge of citizenship, had fought for the right of their young men to wear the uniform of their country, and especially to serve in combat units. That seemed no less true during Vietnam. "The re-enlistment of Negroes is up 3% over whites," the president noted in 1967. "We would have an all-Negro Army if we took them all, if we accepted all who want to re-enlist."[91] Based on information that Moynihan supplied in 1965, Johnson and his advisers came to include the military among those American corporations who were doing a particularly poor job of ending job discrimination. "The single most important and dramatic instance of the exclusion of Negro Americans from employment opportunities in the United States is that of the Armed Forces," Moynihan reported to the White House. "If there was a proportionate racial balance in the Armed Forces, the unemployment rate for young Negro men would be lower than that for whites!"[92] Then came the skyrocketing budget projections of December. "I just hung up with Bill Moyers," LBJ reported to McNamara. "I'm trying to get him to sit with Shriver and tell him if you'll let Bob McNamara take 300,000 of your boys and take care of them in the service for their education and health . . . if you will just get along with what you had last year, we'll give you the first supplemental when the war ends."[93] When the OEO chief and black activists protested, Johnson had Moyers threaten Shriver: "I'm ready to kill it [the poverty program] quietly through George Mahon [chair of the House Appropriations Committee] . . . and get the damn thing out of the way if the niggers are just going to be that mean to me and Shriver's group is going to be disloyal."[94]

In August 1966, appearing before the Veterans of Foreign Wars, McNamara announced the launching of Project 100,000. He was, he said, going to uplift the "subterranean poor" by taking into the military each year one hundred thousand young men who would normally be rejected. As Clark Clifford put it, "Every man taken under this program reduces problems in the cities."[95] Unlike the Kennedy administration plan, which had called for an initial appropriation of $32.1 million, Project 100,000 could be accommodated within the existing Defense budget. Immediately, various branches of the service began accepting "New Standards" men, as they were called. Unfortunately for LBJ, Project 100,000 and other attempts to realize the goals of the Great Society on the cheap yielded only anemic dividends.

CHAPTER 32

BALANCING ACT

AS OF THE FALL OF 1965, THE BASIC OUTLINE OF American strategy for winning the war in Vietnam had not changed. It was clear that communist China was not capable of launching a nuclear strike at the American heartland, but because Washington continued to see Southeast Asia as "the first domino" and to assume the existence of a monolithic communist threat in East Asia, it felt compelled to fight to restore the status quo established by the Geneva Conference in 1954. "China, like Germany in 1917, like Germany in the West and Japan in the East in the late 30's, and like the USSR in 1947—looms as a major power threatening to undercut our importance and effectiveness in the world, and, more remotely but more menacingly, to organize all of Asia against us," McNamara observed to LBJ in November. Liberal democracy in one country was not possible. "Our ends cannot be achieved and our leadership role cannot be played if some powerful and virulent nation—whether Germany, Japan, Russia or China—is allowed to organize their part of the world according to a philosophy contrary to ours."[1] But there continued to be limits on what the United States could do and how far it could go in enforcing its will on Southeast Asia. Communist China had made it clear that if it were attacked directly or if North Vietnam were invaded, it would go all out. McNamara, Rusk, and Bundy continued to assume that the Sino-Soviet Treaty of 1949, in which the Soviets agreed to come to the assistance of China in the event it was attacked, was in force. There was still the likelihood that if confronted with the full force of the Chinese Communist Army, Washington would authorize the use of tactical nuclear weapons, thus risking a general nuclear exchange between the United States and the USSR.[2]

In the summer, the Johnson administration had authorized General William Westmoreland to abandon the restrictive enclave strategy and embark on a war of attrition the strategists named "search and destroy." In terms of body count, territory liberated, and population pacified, this more aggressive approach showed immediate results.[3] But there were negatives. American forces became involved in a two-front war: against regular North Vietnamese Army formations in the northern part of South Vietnam and against Vietcong guerrillas everywhere else. The last week in November 1965, U.S. troops fought a bloody battle with NVA regular units in the shell-scarred Ia Drang Valley near the Cambodian border. American forces claimed fifteen hundred communist dead, with 175 lost on their side. During the action, a battalion of the First Cavalry was ambushed and one entire company wiped out. Vietcong scoured the battlefield after dark, bayoneting and shooting wounded GIs while enraged Americans shot NVA prisoners in cold blood.[4]

U.S. forces found the Vietcong to be dedicated, tough, resourceful, flexible, elusive, and ruthless. The guerrillas refused to wear uniforms and hid among the civilian population, or rather, were indistinguishable from the civilian population. Plantation workers, landless peasants, students, refugees driven from their land by the war, veteran nationalists, the VC were experts at terror, indoctrination, and persuasion. They came into the villages of South Vietnam after dark, slitting the throats of government-appointed officials and collaborators. The Army of the Republic of Vietnam claimed to have killed more than seventy-five thousand since 1960, but their number was estimated at over one hundred thousand in 1965, and they controlled territory that included more than 50 percent of the country's inhabitants. When they targeted an outpost, the VC usually bribed or threatened a local worker or soldier to inform them of the layout. They approached silently in small groups and then attacked. In one assault, about one hundred VC dressed only in swimming trunks and sneakers, with hand grenades strapped across their chests, crept up to the high barbed-wire fence surrounding a government encampment. Catapulting each other over the fence by twos and threes, the sappers dashed into the defending foxholes and blew themselves up along with the defenders. On patrol, ARVN and U.S. troops were liable to crash through a light covering of twigs into a deep pit, impaling themselves on sharpened bamboo stakes, or trip over a vine bringing down a rotten log embedded with poisonous snakes.[5]

It was the willingness of the locals to support, tolerate, or acquiesce in the insurgency that caused the most difficulty. When government troops appeared ready to lay down fire on a village suspected of harboring VC, local mothers with babes in arms would come out and beg the soldiers not to attack. Sometimes they succeeded, earning them the sobriquet "the cannon spikers."[6] Frustrated, angry, ARVN and subsequently American soldiers began shooting and burning indiscriminately. In August, a CBS news correspondent narrated as a detachment of marines conducted a sweep through the village of Cam Ne looking for VC. "The marines," reported Morley Safer, "had orders to burn the hamlet to the ground if they received so much as one round." They did, and replied by laying down a rocket barrage that killed an infant and wounded three women. Then they moved into the village and proceeded, "first with cigarette lighters, then with flame throwers to burn down an estimated 150 dwellings. Old men and women who were pleading with the marines to spare their houses were ignored . . . The operations netted about four prisoners—old men." The filmed report was aired during the primetime news and shocked many Americans. "On the one hand," observed *Newsweek,* "the incident at Cam Ne raised a moral question as old as war itself: can the punishment of a whole population for the activity of only some of its members possibly be justified? On the other hand, what happened at Cam Ne was an inexorable result of the U.S. decision to change the nature of its commitment in Vietnam from an advisory role to that of a no-holds-barred combatant."[7]

For a week Cam Ne was the talk of the West Wing. "Multiply that a thousand times and we will lose whatever good will we have in Viet Nam and become instead the white terrorists whose presence is death in the countryside," Harry McPherson observed to Bill Moyers. "The effect on Americans is no less negative."[8] Johnson complained that once again he and his soldiers were being unjustly vilified by a biased media.[9] So distraught was the president over the incident that when a North Carolina clergyman returned from Vietnam to report that the CBS presentation was "badly distorted" and that GIs were regularly delivering babies, helping with surgery, and doing everything they could to aid the local populace, he invited the man and his wife to spend the night at the White House.[10]

By the fall of 1965, press reporting from Vietnam had become a major concern to the president and his advisers. David Halberstam and other journalists published widely read books that did not question the rationale for U.S. involvement in Vietnam, that is, anticommunism, but denounced the military-political regime in Saigon as unworthy of support and the tactics being employed against the VC as counterproductive of U.S. goals. "In my two weeks in Saigon," Edward P. Morgan, a sympathetic journalist, reported to White House aide Douglass Cater, "I found the relationships between the press corps and the U.S. government establishment shockingly tense and full of mutual distrust. The daily 5 o'clock press briefings . . . verged on farce. Briefers were contemptuous of reporters and refused to provide the most mundane information. Arthur Sylvester [press officer for the American Mission] held a backgrounder that was apparently beyond belief . . . This was not a backgrounder but an angry argument, insulting at times on both sides, that lasted for hours." Some of the correspondents heckled and baited in response to official stonewalling. "Most of this baiting seems to come from a flock of very junior reporters," Morgan observed, "quite young and edgy but monstrously ambitious." Despite the grief dealt the administration by reporters in Vietnam, LBJ and his advisers never considered censorship. "The official guidelines for newsmen in Vietnam are minimal and only concern the handling of information that could, if prematurely publicized, be detrimental to the safety of our forces there," Bill Moyers wrote NBC chief Frank Stanton.[11] Indeed, Vietnam was the most censorship-free war in American history. For better or worse, the American public was treated to daily reports of bloody combat and suffering refugees from the battlefronts in the print media and on nightly TV broadcast.[12]

Mounting cynicism in the Saigon press corps was accompanied by increasingly insistent dissent within Congress. There were those like Rivers, Eastland, Ford, and Dirksen who were arguing that the United States was not doing enough militarily and those such as Fulbright, McGovern, Morse, and Church who argued that it was doing too much. And then there was Russell, "a cross between Curtis LeMay and Fulbright," as LBJ put it. As the fall progressed, McGovern, Morse, and Fullbright challenged the administration publicly, the former two over Vietnam, the latter over the Dominican Republic, while behind the scenes Mansfield spoke for a score of other senators who had grave doubts about the course the United States was following in Vietnam. "I am afraid that eventually, Mr. President," the Montanan opined, "some government in Saigon is going to have to enter into negotiations with the Viet Cong."[13]

Congressional doves were echoed by a variety of groups in the general population. Traditional pacifists such as A. J. Muste and the organizations they headed, the Fellowship of Reconciliation and the War Resisters League, spoke out against the carnage in South Vietnam because they were against all wars. The taking of human life, no matter what the reason, was immoral. Antinuclear activists who had organized the Committee for a Sane Nuclear Policy (SANE) in the mid-1950s opposed the war in Vietnam because they feared it would lead to a nuclear confrontation between the United States and the communist superpowers. Student activists who, energized by the civil rights movement, formed the Students for a Democratic Society in 1960 enlisted in the antiwar movement as part of a larger campaign to fundamentally alter American society. SDS members and their academic mentors formed what came to be known in intellectual circles as the New Left. Building on the economic determinism of Charles Beard and Fred Harrington, New Leftists insisted that because it was a capitalist society, America was dominated by financiers and manufacturers who, having subdued the American proletariat and exploited the nation's resources in the nineteenth century, set out to establish their economic hegemony throughout the rest of the world in the twentieth. Because politics always follows economics, the government and military were permanently and primarily committed to Wall Street's cause. Liberals of a more moderate stripe, concentrated in one wing of the Americans for Democratic Action, had become convinced by the end of 1965 that the war in Southeast Asia was a perversion of the liberal internationalism that they had espoused since the end of World War II. In its quest to protect democracy and liberty from communist totalitarianism, the United States was allying itself with brutal military dictatorships and facilitating the murder of thousands of innocent people. Finally, the Quakers and elements within the other major religious denominations began denouncing the war in Vietnam, some because they thought the whole enterprise unjust, some because they deplored the indiscriminate and brutal taking of civilian life, and some because they were appalled at the spectacle of the richest, most powerful nation in the world attempting to bomb into submission a tiny, fourth-rate power situated halfway around the world. In October 1965, the Reverend Richard Neuhaus, Rabbi Abraham Heschel, and Father Daniel Berrigan formed Clergy Concerned about Vietnam.

On the evening of November 2, while attending a meeting at the Pentagon, Robert McNamara was drawn to the windows of the conference room by a commotion below in the parking lot. There an agitated crowd had gathered around something that was burning. An ambulance arrived and covered the object with blankets. Shortly thereafter, McNamara was shocked to learn that a thirty-one-year-old Quaker pacifist, a husband and father, had drenched himself in kerosene and burned himself to death to protest the war.[14] Later that month, Sanford Gottlieb of SANE persuaded a group of prominent liberals to call a march on Washington for the 27th to agitate for a cease-fire, a unilateral bombing halt, and negotiations among all warring parties. The organizers were careful to coordinate with the White House beforehand, and they rejected plans for civil disobedience, repudiated communist participation, and insisted that marchers carry only flags and banners that had been approved by the sponsors. The event was massive but peaceful and dignified.[15] The bitterest dissent was reserved for the president himself. Writing in 1965, Norman Mailer declared, "If the Lord of the Snopes [President Johnson] went to war in Vietnam because finally he didn't have the moral courage to try to solve an impossible mix of camp, red-neck, civil rights, street violence, play-boy pornography and all the glut which bugs our works . . . well, what he didn't realize was that the war in Vietnam was not going to serve as a cloaca for our worst emotions but instead was going to up the ante and give us more camp, more police society gone ape, more of everything else Lyndon was trying to ship overseas."[16]

A natural target for the antiwar movement was the draft, designed by Selective Service Director General Lewis B. Hershey as a system for effectively managing human resources, but in its administration seemingly discriminatory and unfair. College students received deferments; so did married men. The very poor and unskilled could not qualify, leaving the war to be fought by the sons of the American working class. If they could mobilize and convert this traditionally conventional and patriotic sector of society, opponents of the war realized, they would have struck a mighty blow at the Vietnam consensus. In Michigan in the fall of 1965, thirty-one students staged a sit-in at the Michigan Draft Board headquarters. A number of New York pacifists held a major draft card–burning ceremony in Manhattan's Foley Square on November 10.[17]

Infuriated, General Hershey authorized Michigan draft authorities to revoke the deferments of the students who had burned their cards and induct them immediately into the service. "Getting a deferment is a privilege," he told the *Washington Star.* The White House moved immediately to stifle the general. "[HEW Secretary John] Gardner believes that this kind of loose talk is bound to stir up tremendous reaction in the university community," Doug Cater advised the president.[18] What kind of signal was Hershey sending, George Reedy asked

LBJ: that military service was some kind of punishment? "The Government should think very carefully before it equates Pleiku with Alcatraz," he told the president. "Even a hard shell conservative will sense an uneasy suspicion that a weapon employed against pacifists today can be swung against Republicans tomorrow." [19]

The burgeoning antiwar movement was profoundly disturbing to the White House generally and the president specifically. He was angst-ridden under normal conditions; criticism, organized criticism, criticism from people whom he believed were his philosophical bedfellows, drove LBJ nearly to distraction. The first week in August, he and Lady Bird asked a group of friends to Camp David for the weekend. The invitees included columnist Marianne Means and her date, soon-to-be-named USIA chief John Chancellor, Cissy Morrissey of *Life,* and the Johnsons' new acquaintances, Arthur and Mathilde Krim. Krim was a wealthy New York attorney whose clients included the Motion Picture Association of America. His wife was beautiful, elegant, and discreet—just Lyndon's type. "After dinner we went into a meeting that I will never forget," Krim recalled. "It started with a rather casual discussion about a whole variety of things . . . Along about nine or ten o'clock Lady Bird went to bed . . . that left in the room Marianne Means, Cissy Morrissey, John Chancellor . . . Vicky McCammon . . . and me. The meeting lasted until six in the morning. It was an extraordinary window into much of the President's subliminal frustrations." What set Johnson off was Chancellor and Means making light of Jack Valenti's "I sleep better at night" tribute to him. LBJ launched into a lecture on the value of loyalty. "He did a lot of drinking that night, fixed the drinks himself, must have had ten or twelve Scotch and soda[s]." Means, Chancellor, and Morrissey persisted that such a gushy tribute was inappropriate and counterproductive. "The President was very strong in his characterizations of the press, spoke of the fact that the three networks were dominated by communists. He attacked one of his own cabinet members as a pinko. Bobby Kennedy was nothing more than a wire-tapping law breaker." He talked about Vietnam: "He did say that he was following the Kennedy program in Vietnam, and that he couldn't have come in after the assassination to be the president that would abort the operation there . . . He talked about his prediction that he would die at the age of sixty . . . At the time he was talking he was fifty-seven . . . I remember that I was absolutely and completely bewildered by the fact that he did that with three members of the working press in the room." [20]

LBJ's personal sensitivity aside, he and his advisers were worried that the demonstrations would convey to enemies and allies alike a lack of unity and commitment. [21] Johnson recognized that fighting a limited, prolonged war was absolutely foreign to a noncolonial power (at least in its own mind) like the United States. "I think that in time it is going to be like the Yale professor said," he confided to McNamara. "That it is going to be difficult for us to very long prosecute effectively a war that far away from home with the divisions we have here and particularly the potential divisions. That really has me concerned . . .

and I am very depressed about it."[22] Moreover, the movement would have consequences that reached beyond foreign policy. The participation of King and other civil rights leaders was adding to the white backlash initiated by urban rioting. The white middle class and, to a lesser extent, the white working class were key to the success of the Second Reconstruction, the former because of its overt support and the latter because of its acquiescence. To the degree that whites identified the civil rights movement with the antiwar movement, the campaign in behalf of civil rights could become stalled.[23]

To make matters worse, doubts about the war were growing within the administration itself. "The more I study and learn," Henry Cabot Lodge reported from Saigon in late October 1966, "the more impressed I am with the savage and thorough way in which the Viet Cong has destroyed the political structure of this country. Everything that I have read about successful counter-guerilla activity says that one must start in each hamlet by picking out a good man to be chairman of a committee of up and coming young men. In this country the 'good man' all too often has had his head cut off, the grade B people have been driven out and what is left are the old and the weak and the children . . . I thought the war veterans would be a likely nucleus but I now learn that 80 percent of the war veterans are afraid to live out in the country and have gathered in the cities."[24] McNamara kept repeating that the objectives of bombing the North were to cut off infiltration into the South, weaken the enemy's will to fight on, and force the DRV to the negotiating table. But at the same time, he was advising the president that the communists' will seemed to be increasing rather than decreasing, and the amount of men and matériel flowing into the South from the North was growing rather than shrinking. From the State Department LBJ was hearing that Hanoi was not likely to attend a general peace conference, or if it did, not negotiate in good faith. The lesson that Ho and his colleagues had learned from the 1954 Geneva Conference was that the great powers, even the communist ones, would willingly sacrifice North Vietnam's interests to their larger concerns.[25] "I don't see how we have any way of either a plan for a victory militarily or diplomatically," Johnson complained to McNamara. "And I think that is something you and Dean [Rusk] have to sit down and try to see if there are any people that we have in those departments that can find us any program or plan or hope."[26]

LBJ's intelligence sources on Vietnam were unbelievably bad. Neither the CIA, the National Security Administration, nor the intelligence divisions of the military branches were able to give him any reliable information about the dynamics of the decision-making process within the DRV, NLF, or Mao's regime. Frustrated, LBJ dispatched Clark Clifford on an intelligence-gathering mission in early November. "Mr. Clifford," reported Edward Rice, a consular official in Hong Kong who was present at a secret meeting of regional intelligence officers, "said that the President spends much of his time on Vietnam, and feels forced to make a great many decisions on the basis of inadequate information. What we lack and what he wants is . . . definite information about the Viet

Cong. What about their attitudes? Are they re-evaluating their position? Are their attitudes softening or hardening? . . . What is the thinking in Hanoi? Are the leaders there determined, or are they 'seeking a way out'?" The response of the gathering after much hemming and hawing was that they could not with any authority say.[27] At a meeting with his principal advisers at the ranch the first week in December, LBJ blurted out, "What makes it so tough: I've had little real sympathy with Fulbright, but I don't see any light down that barrel. We're getting deeper and deeper in . . . Where we were when I came in—I'd trade back to where we were."[28] At a subsequent meeting with the same individuals: "Then, no matter what we do in the military [field], there is no sure victory?" To everyone's shock, McNamara agreed: "That's right. We have been too optimistic. One [chance of victory] in three or two in three is my estimate."[29]

Confronted with mounting dissent in and outside of Congress, LBJ attempted to reach out to the Republican party, to use bipartisanship as a political backstop for the Vietnam consensus. He found the GOP a prickly partner, to say the least. Nixon, Dirksen, and Ford were not about to be outflanked on the right. While "supporting" the administration on the war in Vietnam, the GOP kept up a constant drumfire of criticism that the Defense Department was not getting weapons and ammunition to troops in the field in a timely manner, that "politicians" were intruding into decision making that properly belonged to the military, and that the war ought to be fought more aggressively, particularly against the North. Eisenhower agreed to be part of Johnson's Vietnam team— but only up to a point. In August, LBJ went to the well once too often, citing a 1954 agreement with the Diem regime as justification for U.S. involvement in the war. Pressured by Republican leaders, Eisenhower told reporters that his commitment to the government of South Vietnam had been economic and not military. "Military Pledge to Saigon Is Denied by Eisenhower," headlined the *New York Times*. He and Johnson subsequently made up, but Ike and the GOP had put the president on notice that the current decisions on Vietnam were his and his alone, and he would be held responsible.[30]

Beginning in October 1965, the Johnson foreign policy team began debating the wisdom of instituting an extended, unilateral bombing pause. There were a number of pros. The Russians had made it clear that Hanoi would never agree to talks while American aircraft were strafing and bombing its territory. The DRV would look upon discussions during the bombings as "a plea from a position of weakness," Soviet Ambassador Andrei Gromyko told Rusk.[31] In November, Barbara Ward, LBJ's favorite historian, reported on a trip to New York, where she surveyed opinion within "the 'Establishment'—Council on Foreign Relations, Commonwealth Fund trustees, Wall Street bankers and lawyers." She described a "general malaise" over the Vietnam War. "These were almost without exception moderate men supporting the President," she told Jack Valenti. "Yet they all in one way or another seemed to express the same fear— that mounting casualties coupled with some popular uncertainty about the purposes of the war could erode away the whole of the middle ground upon which the President stands." The solution: an offer to the North Vietnamese to nego-tiate without precondition.[32] Then there was the international arena. Johnson and Rusk believed that in the wake of a bombing halt, the Soviet Union might seize the initiative from communist China and pressure Hanoi to sit down at the negotiating table.[33]

The Joint Chiefs were adamantly opposed; indeed, they wanted to expand the bombing to include oil storage facilities and industrial targets in and around Hanoi and Haiphong. Lodge and the U.S. mission in Saigon were also against a halt, arguing that the conflict was not going to be resolved through a negotiated treaty: "The communists do not like to sign papers in which they admit that they were defeated," Lodge observed. The goal should be to control the coastal plains, eliminate the VC from the Saigon-Delta area, and continue to hold the forty-three provincial capitals. Then, as was the case with the Philippines and Malaysia, the communists would just melt away.[34] Johnson himself expressed serious doubts concerning the efficacy of a bombing halt. The chiefs were in-sisting that a unilateral halt without precondition would allow the NVA to pour men and supplies into the South without inhibition, and he believed that was true. Moreover, a halt would have a very negative impact on morale in Saigon and among the ARVN and U.S. troops. And what if a halt did not produce results? The pressure on the administration to resume, and resume with a vengeance, would be overwhelming. The doves would be in full retreat and the hawks in charge. "That is the most dangerous aspect," LBJ told his advisers. "Don't we know a pause will fail? If we are in worse shape then, won't we be bringing a deadly crisis on ourselves?"[35] By December, McNamara, both Bundys, Ball, and others had come down on the side of a unilateral pause to last roughly from Christmas Eve to the end of January 1966, coupled with an offer to Hanoi of direct negotiations.[36] But ultimately, it was not his advisers' input that convinced LBJ, but the results of various opinion polls taken in November and December.

"It is evident that the American public has supported the military increases made during the past year," White House staffer Hayes Redmon advised Bill Moyers. "Yet, if the public supports our military increases to date, they are even more overwhelmingly in favor of attempts at negotiated settlement . . . During the past year every negotiating proposal that has been put to the public has had overwhelming approval." Citing the Korean conflict, during which public sup-port for the war slipped from 65 percent in August 1950 to 38 percent in January 1951, Redmon warned of the threat of mounting frustration and war-weariness. "If we are to have public support for our policies—if we are to blunt mounting frustration," he told Moyers and through him LBJ, "it is absolutely essential that the public be constantly assured that we are doing all we can to get an honorable negotiated settlement. A majority does not now believe it."[37]

On Christmas Eve 1965, the constant pounding of NVA positions between the seventeenth and twentieth parallels that had been going on since May sud-denly stopped. Immediately, a small army of diplomats headed by Ambassador-at-large Averell Harriman departed for various European and Asian capitals with much-publicized instructions to leave no stone unturned in its quest for a nego-tiated settlement. Four days after the pause went into effect, Rusk cabled Lodge: "For your own personal guidance, a major factor in the decision [to halt the bombing] is the action which will have to be made public in January. The prospect of large scale reinforcement in men and defense budget increases of some twenty billion for next eighteen month period requires solid preparation of American public. A crucial element will be clear demonstration that we have explored fully every alternative but that aggressor has left us no choice . . . We do not, quite frankly, anticipate that Hanoi will respond in any significant way."[38]

It is ironic that LBJ would allow public opinion, or at least the White House's estimation of it, to largely determine his decision on a bombing pause. He was permitting strategy in Vietnam to be set by a political entity with which he had consistently refused to be candid. Johnson was much impressed with the way FDR had handled events leading up to American entry into World War II during the 1940–1941 era. Roosevelt had perceived that war was inevitable and be-lieved it to be in America's interests to join the struggle in Europe, but he did not seek a vote of Congress beforehand; rather, he let events take their course, trusting that Congress and the American people would approve after the fact. "Pleiku was a little Pearl Harbor," Moyers remembered Johnson saying.[39] But Pleiku was not Pearl Harbor. There was no catharsis. In a sense, administration policy never moved beyond the 1940–41 analogy.[40]

As THE THIRD YEAR of the Johnson presidency began, the White House staff had experienced some important changes, important because, in the world of LBJ, individuals were far more significant than organizations. Johnson was never able to find a replacement for Walter Jenkins. Several months after the 1964 election, the president had named Marvin Watson to be his appointments secretary, with the title of special assistant to the president. The Huntsville na-tive had worked his way through Baylor, served as a marine in the Pacific, and then returned to Texas, where he rose to become the righthand man of E. B. Germany, the reactionary president of Lone Star Steel Company. He was not a proto-fascist like his boss, but a parochial Texan with limited experience who still clung to the rural political values of a bygone era. He was loyal, hardwork-ing, and unimaginative. He was also literal-minded and tactless. When LBJ told him to do something, he did it no matter how outrageous or counterproductive. Where Jenkins had been solicitous and attentive to all with the slightest bit of in-fluence or importance to his boss, Watson was frequently brusque and dismis-sive.[41] Shortly after coming to the West Wing, Watson angered other staffers, the Washington press corps, and pundits in general by ordering White House switchboard operators to record the name, business affiliation, and office tele-phone number of all callers. McGeorge Bundy and others protested, and Joe Alsop denounced in print "the curious espionage system to which members of the White House staff are subjected."[42] More ominously, Watson served as a tacit ally of J. Edgar Hoover in his effort to instill in LBJ an anticommunist paranoia.[43]

The new year saw Jack Valenti still on board, but he was wearing out. Ever since that fateful day in November 1963, he had been constantly at LBJ's side. "Jack Valenti performed a function that has been described as 'valet,' " Harry McPherson observed, "but it was a hell of a lot more important than that. Because of his proximity to the President and because he is an almost hyper-active man, he was into all kinds of things, especially in the daily doings of the President, what the President said, who the President saw. Jack would be there early in the morning and late at night."[44] Valenti found Watson to be his exact opposite in personality and philosophy. Moreover, his stint at the White House, his constant intimacy with the president, was taking its toll on him psychologically.

Staffers talked of "the Valenti syndrome," the tendency to judge oneself by LBJ's prevailing appraisal. When you were in favor, you were on top of the world; when you were not, you were in absolute despair.[45] In May, Valenti departed to become president of the Motion Picture Association of America at $150,000 per year, four times his White House salary. "I feel like I'm tearing out my heart and leaving it here on the floor," he told Newsweek's Charles Roberts. "I love this man, and let me tell you, he has eaten me up with love."[46]

Following his foot surgery, George Reedy had returned to the White House as "a sort of resident, long-range idea-man," particularly on civil rights and labor. He, too, departed in May to take a lucrative job as vice president of a New York public relations firm. The man who had been with LBJ the longest, Horace Busby, had already withdrawn to Texas. He had resented particularly Bill Moyers's instant intimacy and influence with LBJ. Busby viewed Moyers as a bureaucratic imperialist and a secret ally of Bobby Kennedy.[47] There was much truth in the first perception and a bit in the second. John Roche, who had replaced Eric Goldman as the resident White House intellectual, observed that Moyers had more allies in more departments and agencies than the president himself. He frequently knew what was going on before a cabinet officer or agency head did. His critics murmured that in briefings with the White House press corps, Moyers frequently confused his views and persona with those of the president.[48] And as his ongoing relationship with Arthur Schlesinger and his habituation of the Georgetown cocktail circuit indicated, he found the heirs of Camelot extremely seductive. But Moyers worked tirelessly and loyally for LBJ. He was intelligent, principled, pragmatic, and shrewd. He was absolutely committed to what the president was trying to do at home and initially abroad. "Bill contributes a certain quality of brilliance, of wit, and a mixture of aloofness from us," Lady Bird wrote in her diary, "with yet enough devotion to us that Lyndon needs. I could not bear to lose him."[49]

The vacuum that was left by the departures of Valenti, Reedy, and Busby was partially filled by Joseph A. Califano Jr., who had come to the White House in the fall of 1965 to replace Moyers as chief domestic adviser. The thirty-three-year-old Brooklynite was the son of an Irish American mother and an Italian

American father. After graduating from Holy Cross and Harvard Law School, he landed a job with the New York law firm headed by Thomas E. Dewey. Califano, who, like Pat Moynihan, was a member of the Catholic social work movement and a liberal Democrat, and the former GOP presidential candidate were strange bedfellows. Thus, when the opportunity to become one of McNamara's Department of Defense whiz kids opened up, Califano jumped at the opportunity.[50] He took over the task forces from Moyers and began building relationships with those departments and agencies most concerned with domestic affairs. He proved to be devoted to the Great Society and to his boss, and was ruthless in defending both. Moynihan once asked Califano how one acquired power in the White House. "You take it," he replied. "There are vacuums everywhere, and if you do it, if you take it and seize it and run with it, it's yours, and you develop a certain right of adverse possession."[51]

A major shakeup among LBJ's foreign policy advisers also occurred in 1966. On February 28, McGeorge Bundy departed as national security adviser. Bundy had grown tired of LBJ's pettiness and his absurd insistence on staff anonymity. He realized that Vietnam was going to be a long, protracted conflict. He might have stayed the course for Jack Kennedy, but not for Lyndon Johnson. His wife had been against the conflict from the beginning. And there was the constant tension generated by the Bobby-Lyndon feud, with both the president and the Kennedys alluding to Bundy's disloyalty.[52] In April, Bundy was named to head the Ford Foundation. The man who succeeded him as national security adviser was Walt Rostow. Contemporaries remembered Rostow exhibiting a genial but stubborn certainty on the cold war and the conflict in Southeast Asia. Communists were "scavengers of the modernization process," and the communist attempt to overrun South Vietnam was as sure a test of American resolve and principles as the Japanese attack on Pearl Harbor and Hitler's drive to overrun Europe. In truth, LBJ did not expect startling new insights from his new national security adviser. "I think Rostow would probably give us a little more protection [than Robert Komer, whom Johnson was also considering] from the intellectual and the college crowd," he remarked to Dean Rusk. "I believe he would be loyal and he seems to be very friendly with you and me."[53] Tom Mann resigned as the State Department's chief Latin American expert, to be replaced by career diplomat Jack Hood Vaughn. It was Tweedle-dum and Tweedle-dee. As one critic of the changes observed, "This is a triumph of the curators . . . of past policies."[54] The only appointment out of the ordinary was LBJ's selection of Attorney General Nicholas Katzenbach to replace George Ball as undersecretary of state. Ball was a team player, but his misgivings concerning Vietnam were real. Some viewed Katzenbach's transfer as a demotion, but he had wearied of civil rights and particularly the frustrations associated with the growing urban unrest and the Black Power movement. Even before his move from Justice to State, he, along with Komer and Rostow, had with LBJ's approval constituted themselves as a "kitchen cabinet" on Vietnam.[55]

Almost unnoticed by the press—much to LBJ's gratification—was the growing influence of Harry McPherson, the literate, open-minded Texas liberal who became counsel and then special counsel to the president. From the summer of 1966 on, he was the chief architect of all of Johnson's speeches. McPherson's humanity, his Christian realism, his political experience and sensitivity, his independence of mind, and his loyalty would serve LBJ well as he descended into the paradoxes of America in the 1960s.

Conspicuously absent from Johnson's inner circle was Hubert Humphrey. When the president learned that Joe Califano had asked Humphrey to participate in the planning for Phase II of the Great Society, he exploded. "You are never, never to let the Vice President attend any meeting on the legislative program," he roared at Califano. "He has Minnesota running-water disease. I've never known anyone from Minnesota that could keep their mouth shut. It's just something in the water out there." It turned out that Humphrey had alluded in several speeches to Reuther's suggestions for the creation of demonstration cities and Whitney Young's ideas for a Marshall Plan for urban areas. Johnson told Califano to tell the vice president to shut up. "The President will talk about what he wants to do in the State of the Union message and he doesn't need the Vice President to try to commit him to some crazy, Goddamned expensive idea that Congress will never approve anyway."[56]

Obviously, Johnson approached the 1966 State of the Union address with a troubled mind. He would have to rally the country to stay the course in Vietnam. At this point, he still held out hope that if things went fairly well on the battlefield, at the negotiating table, and in the political arena in South Vietnam, the United States could begin withdrawing troops in 1967. But a number of his advisers warned him that the economy would not be able to produce enough largesse in 1966 for both guns and butter.[57] Budget Director Charles Schultze pointed out that budget requests and appropriations did not match the amounts authorized when various Great Society bills were passed. "States, cities, depressed areas and individuals have been led to expect immediate delivery of benefits from Great Society programs to a degree that is not realistic."[58] There was no question about funding existing programs, but, for a variety of reasons, LBJ also opposed a moratorium on new ones. He would still have liberal majorities in both houses of Congress in 1966, something he could not count on after the midterm elections. Many Great Society programs were also civil rights programs. To back away at that point would be to undercut moderate leaders like Whitney Young and Martin Luther King and open the way for a takeover of the movement by Stokely Carmichael, Floyd McKissick, and other advocates of Black Power. That would in turn exacerbate the white backlash, fueling racial tensions in the nation's cities and giving encouragement to segregationists everywhere.

During a nose-to-nose conversation with Joe Califano in the pool at the ranch in July 1965, LBJ had been emphatic about the two things he wanted, in addition to a Department of Transportation. "I want to rebuild American cities," he had told the frantically dog-paddling Califano. "I want a fair housing bill.

We've got to end this goddamn discrimination against Negroes. Until people whether they're purple, brown, black, yellow, red, green or whatever [he jabbed his besieged aide hard on the shoulder as he enumerated each color]—live together, they'll never know they have the same hopes for their children, the same fears troubles, woes, ambitions." [59] Most important, LBJ continued to believe that it was his moral and religious duty to bring a better life within reach of as many people as possible. During the early months of 1966, LBJ carried around two quotations from Scripture in his pocket. The first was from Acts: "Then Philip went down to the city of Samaria, and proclaimed unto them the Christ. And the multitude gave heed . . . when they heard and saw the signs which he did. For some of those that had unclean spirits that came out crying with a loud voice and many that were palsied and were lame were healed. And there was much joy in that city." The second was from Second Peter: "And besides this, giving all diligence, add to your faith virtue; and to virtue knowledge; and to knowledge temperance, and to temperance patience; and to patience godliness; and to godliness brotherly kindness; and to brotherly kindness love." [60] That April, the president delivered a speech on the bicentennial of American Methodism in which he proclaimed "The Social Creed of the Methodist Church," written in 1940, to be the "perfect description of the American ideal [and] the American commitments in the 1960s." [61]

During the summer and fall of 1965, Joe Califano had set up a series of new task forces to plan the second phase of the Great Society. Government officials and distinguished citizens (from Kingman Brewster, president of Yale, to Walter Reuther to John Kenneth Galbraith and Barbara Ward) focused on pollution control, transportation, urban renewal, population control, education, housing, foreign aid, and civil rights. On December 29 at the ranch, Califano walked LBJ through the proposed program. Johnson was particularly taken with a vast international health initiative, which, among other things, aimed at a complete eradication of smallpox by 1975. LBJ also wanted to expand a proposal to enrich kindergarten and summer programs for poor children by making free lunches available to those who could not afford them. The idea had come to the White House through aide Larry Levinson, whose friend, Father Charles Woodrich, a Denver priest, had experimented successfully with the notion as part of the local antipoverty program. The lower-priced meals had been served in one secondary and three elementary schools; immediately attendance improved, attention spans expanded, and dropout rates and disciplinary problems declined. [62]

LBJ knew what he wanted to ask Congress to support, but he seemed unusually tentative. Aides remembered that the 1966 State of the Union speech preparation process was the wildest, most hair-raising to date. Valenti (he would not depart until May) suggested bringing Richard Goodwin back onboard to draft the domestic portions. To Goodwin's intense irritation, LBJ insisted on editing every line, and he refused to meet in person with him. At 4 A.M. on January 12, the day of the speech, Goodwin, Califano, and Valenti sent what they anticipated would be the final draft to the president's bedroom for approval. Instead of giving them the go-ahead, he summoned six aides, excluding Goodwin, and told them to rewrite the whole thing, reducing it by a third. Work on the address continued until just an hour and a half before delivery.[63]

More than half of the final speech dealt with Vietnam. The president began well enough, with an uncompromising call to arms. "We will not permit those who fire upon us in Vietnam to win a victory over the desires and the intentions of all the American people," LBJ declared. "This Nation is mighty enough, its society is healthy enough, its people are strong enough, to pursue our goals in the rest of the world while still building a Great Society here at home." Then, uninspiringly, he simply ticked off the goals of his domestic policy: continuation of "the great health and education programs," including the antipoverty program enacted the previous year; more money for foreign aid "to make a maximum attack on hunger and disease and ignorance in those countries that are determined to help themselves"; "a program to rebuild completely, on a scale never before attempted, entire central and slum areas of several of our cities"; a clean water act; a measure prohibiting discrimination in jury selection; a new Department of Transportation; a fair housing measure; consumer protection laws; repeal of Section 14b of Taft-Hartley; and a constitutional amendment "extending the terms of congressmen to four years to match that of the President."[64] Johnson admitted that the war in Vietnam would create budget constraints, but by economizing in government, holding down inflation through restraining prices and wages, and maintaining the pace of growth, the nation could have both guns and butter.

In truth, the recommendation for LBJ's second hundred days differed from those of the first almost as much as FDR's did for the so-called first and second New Deals. The emphasis of Phase II of the Johnsonian program would be on regulation and reform rather than relief. Demonstration cities and, to a lesser extent, transportation were big-ticket items, but the rest were not. Consumer and environmental protection, fair housing, and nondiscriminatory jury selection were largely regulatory proposals designed to improve the quality of life for Americans by preventing encroachment on their rights as traditionally defined.

LBJ and his lieutenants spent an inordinate amount of time during 1966 in efforts to preserve the economic space that would make guns and butter possible. LBJ lashed NASA, Agriculture, Interior, and Defense (in non-combat-related areas) to trim their budgets. When conservatives began to threaten funding cuts for Great Society programs, he let them know that he might veto their favorite pork barrel projects and leaked to the press that it was Congress and not he nor the war in Vietnam that was unbalancing the budget.[65] "It came through," Orville Freeman recorded in his diary, "that he was rather enjoying the position he had Congress in which he could contend that he was being so frugal and careful and that Congress was not going along with these cuts . . . but insisting on increasing all of them . . . At the same time this protects some of the other programs such as rent subsidy, poverty program, [and] teachers corps that he is bound and determined to hold regardless . . . He could be dramatized himself as being frugal and could answer those who holler, which he knew they would with the Vietnam war on, to cut these new programs. He has never said this; he is too smart to let anyone know because it might leak."[66]

As spring turned into summer, the economy continued to grow at a healthy pace and unemployment remained low, but the rate of inflation crept steadily upward. A fight broke out between the White House and organized labor over the minimum wage. David Dubinsky of the ILGWU and Jacob Potofsky of the Amalgamated Clothing Workers were struggling with industries who were taking their union shops from the high-wage North to the low-wage South. Speaking for them, Meany insisted that the administration propose legislation that would establish a $1.60 minimum wage beginning immediately and moving to $1.75 or $1.80 by 1968. Califano and Gardner Ackley, who had replaced Walter Heller as Chair of the Council of Economic Advisers, advised the president that such legislation would be grossly inflationary. Johnson agreed. "I don't see how I can break [my own] guidelines," he remarked to Califano.[67] To Johnson's vast irritation, Labor Secretary Willard Wirtz seemed to have abandoned the administration for an open alliance with Meany. In 1966 the labor secretary had begun to press for an increase in the minimum wage from $1.25 to $1.40 by the end of 1966 and $1.60 by the fall of 1970.[68] LBJ let it be known that he agreed to $1.60, but it would have to be phased in over a four-year period. Dubinsky, Potofsky, and other labor leaders denounced the administration in the press, and a confrontation with Meany followed. "I don't mind telling you that I've got a very unhappy bunch of boys here," Meany said. "Well, I am unhappy too," LBJ replied. "I have worked and fought and bled and died for them, and am still ready to do it, but I don't want my motives questioned and I don't want my sincerity questioned."[69] The 1966 amendments to the Fair Labor Standards Act passed on September 23 raised the minimum wage to $1.60 an hour by 1971 and expanded coverage to include seven hundred thousand federal employees.

Public unrest over the steadily rising rate of inflation grew apace during 1966. "Rising Prices: How Long, How High?" a *Newsweek* headline asked.[70] In August pollster Lou Harris called the White House to report "a crisis of major proportions" for the president. An informal survey of corporation heads and investment bankers revealed a total lack of confidence in LBJ on the issue of inflation. The latest poll gave LBJ a 90 percent unfavorable rating on his handling of the economy.[71] LBJ understood that inflation had destroyed more governments in modern history than any other issue. Nevertheless, he persevered. No let-up on the domestic front or in Vietnam, and no tax increase. "I think it is as important to take care of our poor that are on social security or on relief as it is to meet our commitments under some treaty," he told congressional leaders in September. "Because I don't think we can do those things [enforce collective security agreements] if we neglect the health and the education and the economic well being of our people. I think that in an economy that is running 750 billion dollars a year, gross national product, I think that we can do what we are doing in

Vietnam and do these other things without taking it out of the hides of the poor, or the head start kids, or the education bill."[72] Johnson began carrying a new Bible verse in his pocket, one from the Seventy-second Psalm: "He shall deliver the needy when he crieth; the poor also, and him that hath no helper."[73]

With Vietnam, inflation, and the need for a surtax converging, and conservatives waiting in the wings to take an ax to the budget, LBJ perceived that he had a narrow time frame in which to realize Phase II of the Great Society. As his support of beautification indicated, Johnson was committed to improving the quality of life for all Americans, not just the poor and infirm. His vision of Utopia was solidly middle class. To the degree that the peoples of the earth were able to experience enough social and economic security to be able to raise their families, live independently, and look forward to a better future, to that extent would there be social stability and international peace. Moreover, there was the political angle. During the fifteen years following the end of World War II, the vast majority of Americans had joined the middle class. Without their support, Johnson realized, there could be no civil rights campaign, War on Poverty, or commitment to hold back the communist tide in Southeast Asia. This awareness had as much as anything to do with measures such as Medicare and the various education bills. And now, with transportation.

BY 1966 THE NATION'S TRANSPORTATION SYSTEM was in danger of being overwhelmed by a tangle of conflicting authority and bureaucratic red tape. For a century and a half Congress had provided funds to construct a system of roads and canals linking the East with the trans-Appalachian West, for subsidizing the construction of a national rail system, and finally for establishing a national network of highways. As of 1966, more than thirty agencies and bureaus attempted to regulate the trucking, airline, and railroad industries, to oversee the merchant marine, and to build and regulate airports, harbors, and inland waterways. Transportation, so vital to the domestic economy and to any foreign conflict in which the United States might find itself, cried out for a central authority to direct it.

In March LBJ sent a dramatic Special Message on Transportation to Congress, asking it to bring together under one cabinet-level Department of Transportation the almost one hundred thousand employees and almost $6 billion then allocated to transportation in the federal government. Pointing out that nearly fifty thousand Americans had died in traffic accidents the previous year, he also proposed creation of a National Transportation Safety Board under the new secretary of transportation as well as passage of the Traffic Safety Act of 1966 that would, among other things, set safety standards for motor vehicles operating in the United States.[74] LBJ and Joe Califano had spent endless hours with the constituencies involved—railroad executives and unions, truckers, auto manufacturers, shipbuilders, airline industry executives—getting them onboard. It was a gargantuan task that perhaps only a person of Johnson's energy and drive could have accomplished.

After the White House reluctantly agreed to exclude the Maritime Administration from the new department—labor and management had joined forces to lobby for its exclusion, fearing that LBJ would find it easier to reduce federal subsidies for shipping than would Congress—the transportation bill passed the House. In the Senate, the principal obstacle would be the hard-drinking, conservative senior senator from Arkansas, John McClellan, who headed the Commerce Subcommittee that would conduct hearings on the bill. McClellan's pet scheme was the Kerr-McClellan Navigation Project, which had transformed the Arkansas River into a major inland waterway. He objected to the transportation bill's demanding standards for the construction and operation of such navigation systems. During the early stages of the hearings, "Big John" refused to even meet with Califano. Upon hearing of the Arkansan's intransigence, LBJ proposed that his aide leak a story to the press to the effect that McClellan was holding up the bill because he wanted the Corps of Engineers to build a dam on property he owned, enabling him to realize a huge profit when the government condemned and bought the land. Califano asked if this was true, and LBJ responded by telling him a story from his earliest days in politics. "The first time Mr. Kleberg ran for Congress," LBJ said, "he was back home making a tub-thumper campaign speech against this opponent. I was sitting on the steps at the side of the platform, listening. Mr. Kleberg said: 'It isn't easy, but I guess I can understand why the good citizens of the hill country might let themselves be represented in Washington by a man who drinks too much. It isn't easy, but I guess I can even understand why the good citizens of the hill country might let themselves be represented by a man in Washington who carouses with city women while his wife and children are back here working the land. But, as God is my witness, I will never understand why the good people of the hill country would let themselves be represented by a man who takes female sheep up into the hills alone at night!' " Well, the president said, "I jumped up and shouted, 'Mr. Kleberg, Mr. Kleberg, that's not true.' He just looked down at me and said, 'Then let the son of a bitch deny it!' " According to Califano, they did not have to resort to the leak; the president instead talked directly to McClellan and convinced him to at least agree to a dialogue.[75]

Over the next two weeks, Califano and McClellan negotiated standards for the Corps of Engineers water projects. Upon reaching an agreement, the aide returned to the West Wing and proudly presented it to his boss. After scanning it, LBJ told his aide to stand up and unzip his pants. Califano smiled nervously, not because he took Johnson literally but because he suspected he had erred. "Unzip your fly," LBJ said again, standing up, "because there's nothing there. John McClellan just cut it off with a razor so sharp you didn't even notice it." LBJ had the White House operator get McClellan on the telephone. "John," he said, "I'm calling about Joe Califano. You cut his pecker off and put it in your desk drawer. Now I'm sending him back up there to get it from you. I can't agree to anything like that."[76] Eventually the Transportation Bill cleared a House-Senate conference committee almost as it had originally been received.

LBJ was so mad at the leaders of the maritime corporations and unions that he did not invite them to the signing ceremony.

JOHNSON HAD ESTABLISHED the Department of Housing and Urban Development to solve the problem of urban blight, to give ghetto dwellers from Los Angeles to Newark hope, and to build a backfire against the urban rioting that loomed in 1966 and 1967. But he and Califano believed that HUD would have to do more than expand the programs and practices of the past. Despite his dislike and distrust of Walter Reuther, Johnson was enthusiastic about the labor leader's demonstration cities plan. Up to this point, urban renewal had consisted almost exclusively of demolishing existing slums and replacing them with low-cost public housing, which inevitably turned into slums themselves. Demonstration cities proposed to create local action committees consisting of business, labor, government, and local residents, both blacks and whites, to improve not only housing but local education, health care, transportation, and recreation. "Instead of urban renewal programs that moved poor people out of their neighborhoods, and homes," Joe Califano remembered, "he envisioned a program that would allow them to stay there, in remodeled or new dwellings, with jobs, police protection, recreation, and community health centers."[77]

In the wake of Watts, LBJ had instructed Califano to put together a task force specifically for the purpose of fleshing out Reuther's ideas. Leading lights on that body were HUD Undersecretary for Metropolitan Development Charles Haar, Senator Abraham Ribicoff, and Ben Heineman of the Chicago & Northwestern Railroad. Haar wanted to focus on one city. Reuther had proposed six. LBJ settled on sixty-six—six with populations over 500,000, ten between 250,000 and 500,000, and fifty with fewer than 250,000. LBJ pointed out that to get demonstration cities through Congress, urban areas of all sizes and regions would have to be included. Estimated costs were $2.3 billion over five years, with the federal government providing 80 percent and local entities 20 percent. Federal funds would be concentrated in housing and in block grants to neighborhoods for specific projects.[78]

Members of Congress reacted to the demonstration cities bill as if a dead fish had been thrown among them. Conservatives insisted that the nation could not afford such a costly experiment in time of war. Liberals complained that the funding was woefully inadequate. Mayors who were convinced their cities would not be picked weighed in. Those caught up in the white backlash seized on the project's title, proclaiming that the measure was nothing more than a scheme to reward demonstrators and looters.[79] In May the *New York Times* declared the measure dead.

LBJ instructed Califano and Humphrey to line up the interest groups that would benefit from the bill and get them to mobilize their lobbyists on the Hill. Persuade the House subcommittee to bring their hearings to a close and report the measure out, he instructed his allies in Congress, but then have the House hold it up. In an election year, the House would not act unless the Senate was first committed. The Senate would be a problem. The chair of the Banking and Currency Subcommittee on Housing was John Sparkman of Alabama, a moderate segregationist who was up for reelection. Second in seniority was Paul Douglas of Illinois, who was an enthusiastic supporter of the bill but who was facing a tough reelection campaign against the popular Charles Percy. He would not have the time to give demonstration cities the attention that it required. That left Edmund Muskie of Maine, a rural state whose concern with urban decay was minimal at best. When Califano pointed out that Muskie did not have a single city in the state of Maine that would be eligible for the program, LBJ chuckled and replied, "Well, he has one now." [80]

Muskie labored mightily, but a head count showed that demonstration cities would fail in the subcommittee. The administration needed one more vote and settled on Senator Thomas McIntyre, a Democrat from New Hampshire who was up for reelection. Unfortunately, the Portsmouth Naval Base, which employed a large number of McIntyre's constituents, was scheduled for closure. Moreover, New Hampshirites were renowned for their frugality. Nevertheless, after the White House promised to delay the base closing until after the election and allowed McIntyre to amend the bill reducing the amounts requested from $2.3 billion to $12 million for planning grants and $900 million for the first two years, he switched his vote, and demonstration cities cleared committee on August 19. [81]

Having run the conservative gauntlet, the bill now faced the wrath of liberals. A subcommittee of the Government Operations Committee headed by Abe Ribicoff examined the White House proposal for demonstration cities; for the rest of August, he, Bobby Kennedy, and GOP Senator Jacob Javits of New York took turns blasting the administration for not doing enough for the cities and especially the black ghetto dwellers who lived in their decaying cores. LBJ saw the "City Hearings," as they were called, as a vehicle to promote Bobby's presidential candidacy. As for Ribicoff, "Abe wants to be America's first Jewish Vice President." [82] To divert public attention from the hearings, LBJ embarked on a three-day swing through the Northeast to gin up support for his urban renewal bill. Upon his return, he called Ribicoff. "Abe, if you want to eat from the cake, don't piss on it," he said. [83] The Senate passed the bill on August 16, and the House followed suit on September 1. At the signing ceremony in the East Room on November 3, LBJ referred to the measure as the Model Cities Act and instructed administration officials to refer to it as such from then on. Leaving the ceremonies with Califano, Johnson turned to his aide and said with mock hostility, "Don't ever give such a stupid Goddamn name to a bill again." [84]

Johnson and the framers of the Model Cities Act were determined that it not turn out to be just another pork barrel measure, but they were equally committed to seeing that it did not fall into the hands of irresponsible radicals. Guidelines were stringent: funded projects had to be integrated in terms of housing, education, health, jobs, and recreation; in terms of race; in terms of politics, bringing together local political establishments and marginalized neighborhood dwellers; and in terms of business-labor participation. For the first two years of Model Cities, all HUD did was process applications; by May 1967, the agency had received 193. Over the next year and a half, HEW Secretary Weaver and his lieutenants approved 108.

Model Cities was a noble dream. "Along with new buildings to replace the crumbling hovels where slum dwellers worried out their deprived existences," Johnson wrote in his memoirs, "we needed to offer those slum dwellers a genuine opportunity to change their lives—programs to train them to jobs, the means of giving their children a better chance to finish school, a method for putting medical clinics and legal services within their reach."[85] But there was no flood of new jobs, no new health and transportation infrastructures, few new housing projects and parks, little or no immediate relief. There was only the beginning of local political/administrative structures that would, over the years, hone their skills as grant writers and win the support and trust of local residents and city halls alike.[86] That a model cities bill passed Congress at all in 1966 was remarkable. In the summer of that year pollsters asked Americans whether they had a favorable or unfavorable opinion of the Great Society. Of all respondents, 32 percent answered favorable, 44 percent unfavorable, and 24 percent gave no opinion.[87]

CHAPTER 33

DIVISIONS

THE GREAT SOCIETY HAD MANY GOALS, BUT CER-
tainly among its most important was to facilitate the Second
Reconstruction, thus simultaneously preventing race war, an
American apartheid, and the permanent marginalization of the
white South. "I will sleep tonight in the house where Lincoln slept," LBJ told the
White House Conference on Civil Rights in June 1966. "It was 100 years ago that
a civil war was fought in this country to free the Negro from slavery. The Negro
won that war, but he lost the battle still to come. Emancipation was a proclamation," Johnson exclaimed to the twenty-two hundred delegates assembled at the
rambling Washington Sheraton Hotel, "but it was not a fact. I came here tonight
to tell you that in the time allotted me, with whatever energy and ability I have, I
do not intend for history to repeat itself."[1] But since the Watts riot and the white
backlash that surged in its wake, LBJ had felt the power to affect the course of
civil rights in America slipping from his hands. Watts was but a prelude. That uprising was followed by upheavals in the summer of 1966 in thirty-eight cities, including Minneapolis, Atlanta, Philadelphia, Chicago, and Cleveland. Images of
black youth yelling "Burn, baby, burn!" as they torched stores and stoned the fire
fighters who came to douse the flames sent waves of fear through white middle-
class America, scabbing over the very consciousness that the civil rights movement had depended on to succeed. Surveys taken at the end of the summer
indicated that 86 percent of whites believed that blacks were getting a better
break in finding jobs than they had five years previously. Of those polled, 54 percent were convinced that Negro children were receiving as good an education as
whites. But 70 percent were of the opinion that blacks "are trying to move too
fast." Virtually all who so responded blamed the federal government in general
and Lyndon Johnson in particular for opening Pandora's box. A July 1966 congressional survey of twelve thousand constituents showed that a large majority

favored cutting poverty programs, welfare, and urban renewal in order to finance the war in Vietnam. There was support for consumer protection and environmental measures, but an astounding 90 percent opposed additional civil rights measures.[2] "For the first time," Abe Fortas wrote Jack Valenti, "I am becoming concerned about the signs of resentment and reaction which I see, even in persons who have been sturdy advocates of the Civil Rights program."[3]

Of those African Americans surveyed in an August 1966 poll, between 50 percent and 60 percent testified that they felt more satisfaction with their jobs, found it easier to eat in restaurants, believed that their children were getting a better education, and found it easier to vote in 1966 than they had in 1963.[4] The problem was that, as Pat Moynihan put it, "things were going to hell at the bottom." From 1960 to 1965 family income in the nation went up 14 percent and nonwhite family income rose 24 percent. But a government survey of south Los Angeles following Watts found that in the Watts area, with a quarter of a million black residents, family income went down 8 percent. The number of female-headed households went up, the proportion of adult males in the population went down, and the proportion of persons living with both parents dropped from 56 percent to 44 percent. As much as anything else, it was ghetto dwellers' self-comparison with the rest of the country that bred frustration and anger. It was the alienated black lumpen proletariat that the rising Black Power movement appealed to and spoke for. The influence within the civil rights movement of SNCC and CORE, of opponents of nonviolent civil disobedience that was so noticeable after Watts, grew apace through the spring and summer of 1966.

In June 1966 James Meredith, who had desegregated the University of Mississippi in 1960, decided to return to his native state after three years of study in Nigeria and at the Columbia University School of Law. He had been haunted by continuing stories of repression and persecution of blacks in his native South. Meredith decided that if he could walk unarmed across Mississippi during the approaching primary season, it would encourage other blacks residing in the rural South to come out and register to vote. A mile south of Hernando, Mississippi, a white unemployed hardware clerk from Memphis rose up out of the underbrush and shot Meredith twice with birdshot from a 16-gauge shotgun. Meredith fell to the ground wounded, but not mortally. Within minutes he was on his way to a Memphis hospital. As news of the shooting flashed across the nation over television and radio, civil rights leaders—Martin Luther King of SCLC, Floyd McKissick of CORE, and Stokely Carmichael of SNCC—rushed to Meredith's bedside.[5] It was decided immediately to continue the march with all groups participating. At Greenwood Carmichael was arrested when the marchers violated a city ordinance by pitching tents on the grounds of a black school. Freed on bond, he told an agitated crowd of six hundred, "Every courthouse in Mississippi ought to be burned tomorrow to get rid of the dirt. Now, from now on when they ask you what you want, you know what to tell 'em?" Then he answered his own question: "Black Power!" As he repeated the slogan, the crowd thundered back time and again, "Black Power! Black Power!"[6]

Over the next two years, it was the Black Power movement, headed by Carmichael, McKissick, and, to a degree, Malcolm X, that captured national headlines and came to symbolize the movement for many white Americans. With the focus of the civil rights movement shifting from South to North and the outbreak of race riots in northern and western cities, the movement as a whole underwent a transformation, historian Dewey Grantham noted, "from a religious to a secular emphasis, from nonviolence and integration to greater militancy and black separatism, from attacking the immorality of segregation to a harsh critique of the economic and social order."[7]

Johnson's response to the Black Power movement alternated between outrage and empathy. In conversations with congressional friends and advisers, he would rail against the handful of "hoodlums" and "commie agitators" who were stirring up America's ghetto dwellers. But when he paused and reflected, he knew that this was a gross oversimplification. "God knows how little we've really moved on this issue," he said to a group of aides. "As I see it, I've moved the Negro from D+ to C-. He's still nowhere. He knows it. And that's why he's out in the streets. Hell, I'd be there too. It was bad enough in the South—especially from the standpoint of education—but at least there the Negro knew he was really loved and cared for, which he never was in the North, where children live with rats and have no place to sleep and come from broken homes and get rejected from the Army. And then they look on TV and see all the promises of a rich country." But he also understood and empathized with working-class whites who were repelled and angered by urban rioting and Black Power doctrine. "There are thousands of people . . . who've worked hard every day to save up for a week's vacation or a new store," he said, "and they look around and think they see their tax dollars going to finance a bunch of ungrateful rioters. Why, that's bound to make even a non-prejudiced person angry."[8]

Johnson understood that, tragically, the Black Power movement and urban rioting were costing black Americans the moral high ground in their struggle to achieve economic and social justice. Like Martin Luther King, LBJ recognized that religious and moral sensibilities were African Americans' greatest allies. Even more than during the crusade to abolish slavery, advocates of racial justice during the 1950s and early 1960s had been able to occupy the moral high ground, a crucial achievement given the evangelical Christian leanings of so many southern segregationists. Moreover, LBJ and his allies had been able to count on white America's affinity for law and order. George Wallace, Bull Connor, and Ross Barnett were violating the Constitution and, worst of all, employing violence to maintain a status quo that was not only unjust but illegal. The Black Power movement's rejection of "the system" and the violence and lawlessness associated with the urban riots forfeited the legal high ground as well. In September 1966, LBJ addressed the Bishops' Council of the African Methodist Episcopal Church. He noted the fundamental importance of the black church in the modern civil rights movement: "Headquarters for the battle in almost every community have always been a church and often an AME church

. . . The battle cry was not a shout, it was a song. The victory was not conquest, but was reason and reconciliation." But the movement was on the verge of taking an ominous turn. "What if the cry for freedom becomes a sound of a brick cracking through a store window, turning over an automobile in the street, or throwing of rocks, or the sound of the mob . . . If that sound should drown out the voices of reason, frustration will replace progress and all of our best work will be undone." Do not abdicate, he begged the bishops, but there was a tone of resignation, even hopelessness, in his plea.[9]

The only thing Johnson knew to do was to press ahead with existing and future programs, to appoint more blacks to the federal bench, to see that as many as possible were hired by the federal bureaucracy, to use the armed forces as a tool to integrate American society and to provide job training for blacks, to ask for new legislative initiatives, and to expand and refine the poverty program. He would not admit that the existing social and political order could not accommodate the stresses and strains of the Second Reconstruction.

Throughout the fall of 1965 and spring of 1966, LBJ pressed the case of school integration, ordering the Departments of Education and Justice to submit daily reports on the progress southern school districts were making. By 1966, 88 percent of school systems had filed compliance plans and the number of black children attending integrated facilities tripled. Still, integration of the southern educational system moved at a snail's pace, as the vast majority of the school districts dragged their feet, seeking to comply with court orders and HEW guidelines under Title VI with merely token integration. Up until 1966, HEW and the courts had used freedom of choice as the principal criterion for judging compliance. In 1966, that changed. Under new guidelines, compliance was based on the number of black students actually attending formerly all-white schools. Conservatives screamed that the federal government had embraced quotas and reverse discrimination, but the courts upheld the 1966 guidelines, and integration in the South began to move at a much brisker pace.[10] Progress there was, but much of it was painful. In September, when 150 black students showed up for the first day of class at formerly white schools in Granada, Mississippi, many of them had to run a gauntlet of spitting, cursing whites. A group of young white men beat a twelve-year-old black boy bloody. A seventy-year-old apostle of the segregation cause told fourteen-year-old Emerald Cunningham, "You are a fool to try to go to a white school. We'll kill all of you, black ass nigger." He then attacked her with an iron pipe.[11]

Compelling southern school districts to integrate was one thing, but forcing compliance on northern counties and districts was another. As the Johnson administration soon learned, it had built a political coalition to force equality of opportunity and access on the South with northern constituencies that were not themselves committed to those principles. In October Commissioner of Education Francis Keppel announced that HEW was withholding $30 million from the Chicago school system because of widespread complaints of discrimination. Both Dirksen and Democratic Congressman Roman C. Pucinski announced that their respective houses were going to open investigations into HEW's administration of Title VI. Richard Daley rushed off to New York to confront LBJ, who was there to sign the immigration bill and meet with the pope, who was on tour. After LBJ became president, both he and Daley had put the 1960 convention behind them and had become cordial political allies. Daley had helped deliver the Illinois congressional delegation on a number of important Great Society votes. "I am a Daley man," LBJ had proclaimed to the mayor shortly after the 1964 election. When the mayor reached Johnson in New York, he was incoherent with anger. Keppel was an idiot, he declared. If this was how the administration was going to treat its friends, then he wanted no part of it.

Upon his return to Washington, LBJ called Keppel and HEW Secretary John Gardner on the carpet and gave them "unstinted hell." Wilbur Cohen was immediately dispatched to Chicago to confer with Daley and school system superintendent Benjamin C. Willis. Willis insisted that no discrimination had taken place, and Cohen emerged from the meeting to announce that Chicago's Title VI money was being restored. Keppel was transferred from his post as commissioner and resigned from the administration later in the year.[12]

As LBJ contemplated his next move in the area of civil rights, the political intelligence he was receiving was not encouraging. Congress was in no mood to expand the Second Reconstruction, especially in the field of housing, which polls continued to show as a flashpoint in white attitudes toward the civil rights movement. The Republicans were not anxious to hand the president another series of victories, especially in an election year. Everett Dirksen had already gone on record as opposing a fair housing measure.[13] Besides, whites were hearing from the new generation of black leaders that Negroes did not want to integrate. But LBJ was not to be deterred, especially on the housing issue. He continued to assume that "racial isolation" was perpetuating racism and inequality, and he perceived that the problem went beyond segregation imposed by law to include "housing patterns, school districting, economic stratification and population movements."[14] Many of his friends and advisers were telling him to pull back, warning that the housing issue in particular was one on which he could only lose. But as Harry McPherson told him, "You are the principal civil rights leader in the country—in a time of turmoil, as in a time of unity and progress . . . In my judgment, you cannot shake off that leadership. You are stuck with it, in sickness as in health . . . If you do nothing to exercise your leadership, you will be damned by the Negroes, who will turn increasingly toward extremist leaders, and by the whites, who will still identify you as the Negroes' protector . . . The pressure will grow for you to silence the protests . . . But the Negro is not about to return to subservience now . . . He will not listen to—and will bitterly resent—those who tell him to stop where he is now and consolidate his gains."[15]

In April, LBJ sent a new message on civil rights to Congress. In it he asked the House and Senate to pass legislation forbidding racial discrimination in the sale and rental of housing. "The ghettos of our major cities—North and South, from coast to coast—represent fully as severe a denial of freedom and the fruits of American citizenship as more obvious injustices," he declared. "As long as the color of a man's skin determines his choice of housing, no investment in the physical rebuilding of our cities will free the men and women living there." [16] LBJ called civil rights leaders from Young to King to McKissick to the White House and assured them of his commitment to the program, but he warned them that "the situation in Congress is a good deal different with respect to civil rights than it was in 1964 or 1965." It would not just be a matter of lining up labor, the big-city machines, and northern liberals to compel Dixie to respect the Constitution. Housing represented a new frontier. As Nick Katzenbach put it, "The difficulty with housing legislation is that this is the first civil rights proposal which has a major impact outside a few states in the South." They were going to have to lobby as they never lobbied before. [17]

THOSE AROUND LBJ during the spring of 1966 noticed that he seemed physically uncomfortable, his moods alternating with unusual frequency and severity—even for him. "I'm afraid, just terribly afraid that I'm going to have to go back in the hospital and get this side taken care of," he at last confided to Bill Moyers. Bothering you, his aide asked? "Oh Hell," Johnson said, "it's just been unbearable, just excruciating all day long. Whenever you catch me waspish with people, irritable, real irritable you can just bet that it's two things: I can't get my breath or I'm just aching somewhere. I just can't control it . . . They've got the story out again that I've got cancer." [18]

POLLS CONTINUED TO SHOW that of all societal groups, African Americans were most opposed to the war in Vietnam. Conservatives in both parties were sure to use this fact to impugn the patriotism of blacks and stir up opposition to any new civil rights legislation. If blacks wanted full citizenship, Republicans and southern Democrats would argue, they would have to be prepared to bear the burdens of that citizenship. Conservatives would ignore that, anti-Vietnam sentiment aside, blacks were volunteering for the military and serving in Southeast Asia in disproportionate numbers. LBJ decided to seize on the posthumous bestowal of the Medal of Honor on Private First Class Milton Olive II, the first black medal winner from Vietnam, to spike this particular segregationist gun. "If Negroes can give their lives for their country," he declared at the award ceremony, "surely a grateful nation will accord them opportunity to live in any neighborhood they can afford, and to send their children to any school of their choice to be educated and developed to their fullest capacity." [19]

But when it came to housing, the northern white conscience proved impervious to Johnson's guilt trips. In August, Martin Luther King's lieutenants in Chicago sent racially mixed teams into two all-white residential sections, Gage Park–Chicago Lawn, a mostly Lithuanian, Polish, and German area on the southwest side, and Belmont-Cragin, a northwest side colony of Poles and Italians. In both "tests," real estate agents offered to sell to whites but not to blacks.

Despite numerous telephoned threats on his life, King personally led protest marches into the two neighborhoods.[20] In Belmont-Cragin a howling mob that eventually reached fifty-four thousand waved rebel flags, sported Nazi insignia, and pelted the marchers with rocks and beer bottles. In Gage Park a white mob taunted and assaulted marchers to the tune of a ditty entitled "Alabama Trooper":

> *I wish I were an Alabama trooper,*
> *That is what I would truly like to be;*
> *I wish I were an Alabama trooper*
> *'Cause then I could kill the niggers legally.*

Bruised and battered, King commented, "I think on the whole, I've never seen as much hate and hostility before, and I've been on a lot of marches."[21]

By October Congress had made it clear that it would not pass a civil rights bill with a fair housing section in it. LBJ and his advisers decided that it was better to have no bill at all than one without housing. The White House let it be known that it was giving up—but only for the moment. It would be back again after the midterm elections, however they might turn out. Meanwhile, Congress busied itself with the white backlash. The House Un-American Activities Committee announced plans to investigate "subversive elements" that were no doubt responsible for the riots. The Judiciary Committee began hearings on a stack of eighty separate antiriot bills.[22]

In the wake of its failure to get a civil rights measure through the 90th Congress, the White House stepped back to take stock. Everyone agreed that it was pointless to try to deal with the likes of Carmichael and other Black Power advocates. But Young, Wilkins, and Randolph were too old and too identified with the white establishment. McPherson wanted the president to build bridges to a new generation of moderate black leaders. The problem was that no such group could be found.[23] King was the new generation, but, as Pat Moynihan observed, he and white liberals such as Schlesinger, Bobby Kennedy, and Joe Rauh had abandoned the administration, kowtowing to Carmichael and the militants for political advantage. "The President was badly let down by the white liberal community which panicked at the thought that it might have to pursue for a moment a line of thought unpopular with the Negro militants, leaving the administration in a hopelessly exposed position from which it had to withdraw."[24] Typical of the new, radicalized liberal was Andrew Kopkind who, in the *New York Review of Books,* had attacked Martin Luther King, and implicitly LBJ, for being out of date and irrelevant. Racism and capitalism had joined hands in a "practically invulnerable" alliance. The efficacy of nonviolent civil disobedience was always an illusion. "Morality, like politics, starts at the barrel of a gun."[25] The distinguished black intellectual Ralph Ellison disagreed. The way envisioned by Johnson and the prerevolutionary King was the only way in a white-dominated, essentially conservative society. "He [LBJ] is far ahead of most of the intellectuals—especially those Northern liberals who have become, in the name of the highest motives, the new apologists for segregation," Ellison declared in a magazine interview in early 1967. "President Johnson's speech at Howard University spelled out the meaning of full integration for Negroes in a way that no one, no President, not Lincoln nor Roosevelt, no matter how much we love and respected them, has ever done before."[26] Intellectual though he might have been, Ellison actually spoke for the rank and file of black Americans.

More disturbingly, those around the president concerned with civil rights began to suspect that there were no answers to the problems of the urban ghettoes. Evidence began to mount that none of the administration's programs was having any impact at all on the denizens of America's inner cities. If the problem was the black family, as Moynihan had argued, no amount of integration, job training, park construction, or improved sewage could change attitudes ingrained by decades of oppression, economic deprivation, and social disorganization. The massive Coleman report on black education was submitted to Congress toward the close of the year. It found that spending money on special classrooms and equipment did not help black students much. Neither did a low pupil-teacher ratio, superior teachers, nor integration. What did make a difference was family and peer attitudes, a sense in the student that education mattered and that it was truly possible for a black, ghetto-dwelling youth to "control his own destiny."[27]

BLACK AMERICANS WERE NOT THE ONLY ONES struggling in 1966 to control their own future. In late February, French President Charles de Gaulle called a press conference to announce that France was withdrawing from NATO. He expected the removal of all American forces from his country forthwith. In a separate note to LBJ, he explained that his country was determined to "reassume on her territory the full exercise of her sovereignty, which is at present impaired by the permanent presence of allied military elements." France would no longer participate in the integrated military operations of the treaty organization. At the same time, de Gaulle assured the White House that it stood by the basic treaty, first signed in 1949, committing the fifteen Atlantic nations to regard an attack on one as an attack on all, and would sign it again when it came up for renewal in 1969.[28] France had been the political and strategic fulcrum of the alliance structure erected to protect Europe from communist aggression. A number of observers predicted that NATO could not survive. The European ball was now squarely in the court of the man from Johnson City.

Charles de Gaulle was one of the first foreign leaders LBJ met with during John F. Kennedy's funeral in November 1963. With the American press de Gaulle was full of praise for Johnson. In President Kennedy one could see America's mask, he remarked; in President Johnson, its real face. In conversations with French journalists, de Gaulle was less kind. "I rather like Johnson," he said. "He doesn't even take the trouble to pretend he's thinking."[29] Like most

Europeans, the French leader believed that LBJ was a shallow, uneducated, rural politician whom chance had thrust into the most powerful office in the world.[30] In the wake of U.S. intervention into Vietnam and the Dominican Republic, many on the left concluded that he was a right-wing, fanatical anticommunist and an imperialist.[31] German political leader Kurt Birrenbach paid a visit to Washington in the spring of 1964 and subsequently observed that LBJ was a product of "Innenpolitik," who, unlike Woodrow Wilson, FDR, and JFK, "did not speak the language of Europe."[32] He predicted that Johnson and the United States would be supplanted by France and de Gaulle as leaders of the Western alliance. He could not have been more wrong.

By the time LBJ became president, continental Europe had recovered from the famine and pestilence of World War II and was in the midst of a major economic boom. At the same time, the raison d'être for the alliance—fear of Soviet aggression—had lessened considerably. As a result, Europe wanted a greater say in American decisions regarding NATO, and Washington, especially Congress, looked forward to greater European "burden-sharing," especially in providing for the commonn defense. Of America's principal European allies, Britain was still the closest. It alone of the European powers was partnering with the United States in the global effort to contain communism. Despite the usual British carping about Yankee arrogance and naïveté, the "special relationship" was still very much intact. Yet Britain's ability to stay the course as a world power was very much in doubt. Since the late 1950s the United Kingdom had been running a chronic balance of payments deficit that continually threatened the value of its currency, the pound sterling. The British public was growing increasingly impatient with footing the bill for an empire on which the sun was rapidly setting. Throughout the Johnson presidency, the threat that Britain would withdraw its fleets and bases east of Suez, leaving the United States as the world's only policeman, hung over Anglo-American relations.

Since 1958 "le grande Charles" had presided over the French political scene like the proconsul he pictured himself to be. For many French men and women, even those who did not agree with his politics, de Gaulle—tall, austere, proud—was a living antidote to the humiliation French forces had suffered at the hands of the Germans in World Wars I and II. He had with some difficulty compelled the Americans to recognize him as head of Free French forces in North Africa in 1943–1944 and had persuaded Eisenhower to include him and his army in the liberation of Europe. Like most other French citizens, de Gaulle rankled at the invasion of American culture and Washington's domination of the North Atlantic alliance. When his calls for the creation of a Franco-American-British directorate to dictate defense policies fell on deaf ears, he aimed at making France independent of the alliance.

Under the fourteen-year reign of West German Chancellor Konrad Adenauer, the Federal Republic had embraced democracy and prospered. By the 1960s its economy was one of the fastest growing in the world, but Germany's continued division coupled with its Nazi past earned it the sobriquet later coined by Helmut Schmidt of "economic colossus, political pygmy." Adenauer had coupled close cooperation with the Federal Republic's NATO partners with an adamant refusal to recognize the legitimacy of a divided Germany. He worried continually that Washington would sacrifice Germany's interests in its new-found desire for détente with the Soviet Union. As a result, he cultivated de Gaulle, intimating that Germany might opt to make common cause with France in creating a European "Third Force" that would counterbalance the American and Soviet blocs.[33] In the fall of 1963, Adenauer was succeeded as chancellor by the genial, cigar-chomping Ludwig Erhard. Erhard favored a simpler, more straightforward, pro-American policy, but he was not strong politically; indeed, Adenauer remained chairman of their political party, the Christian Democratic Union, and kept Erhard on a tight rein. The latter was later criticized for having "no government." Adenauer disagreed. "That is quite wrong. There are at least three governments, and he's not in charge of any of them."[34]

The United States had led the way in creating NATO with two objectives in mind. The first was to deter and if necessary to defeat an assault on Western Europe by the Soviet Union and its allies in the Warsaw Pact. The second was to rehabilitate West Germany militarily within the context of NATO. Making the resuscitated German military part of an integrated European force would simultaneously strengthen NATO and quiet fears both in Western Europe and the Soviet Union about the revival of Nazi-style German militarism. Under no circumstances should West Germany be given access to nuclear weapons. But how to persuade the Germans to stand up to the Soviet Union, a nuclear superpower? The answer was to place the Federal Republic clearly within the American security perimeter. The United States promised to retaliate against a Soviet conventional attack with large numbers of combat troops stationed in Germany and to a nuclear attack with an American nuclear response directly against the Soviet Union.

At the same time it tried to reassure Europe concerning its commitment to the continent's security, the Johnson administration was working to ensure that the day of reckoning would never come. Following the Cuban Missile Crisis of 1962, Soviet-American relations had experienced a dramatic thaw; both JFK and subsequently LBJ actively pursued a policy of détente toward the Soviet Union. In July 1966, LBJ signed a national security directive that declared that "in consultation with our Allies—we actively develop areas of peaceful cooperation with the nations of Eastern Europe and the Soviet Union."[35] At the same time, economic considerations fueled a "bring-the-boys-home" movement in Congress that began in 1958 and crested in 1966. Led by Senate Majority Leader Mike Mansfield, American taxpayers increasingly took the position that with the return of prosperity to Europe, de Gaulle, Adenauer, and British Prime Minister Harold Wilson could afford to pay for their own defense. With the escalation of the war in Vietnam, Secretary of Defense McNamara became a bureaucratic ally of the force cutters. He had long been convinced that American superiority in nuclear weaponry and delivery systems made the possibility of a

Soviet first strike against Europe remote to impossible.[36] The Europeans could and should assume more of the burden of defending themselves, and an American build-down in Europe would free up funds for the conflict in Southeast Asia. There were, moreover, wider economic concerns; the massive American military presence in Europe was creating a rather dramatic balance of payments deficit. Funds expended by the U.S. government to station and supply American military personnel and their dependents caused a sizable net outflow of dollars to most of the European allies, but especially Germany. The problem was exacerbated by a massive influx of European consumer products into the United States and by increasing American tourism in Europe. By the end of 1964, the United States was showing an annual deficit of $5 billion, and matters only promised to get worse.[37]

Lyndon Johnson resolved that neither French nationalism, nor American neo-isolationism, nor British financial weakness, nor German domestic politics would destroy the Atlantic alliance. "I was determined to leave office with NATO stronger than when I entered the Presidency," he wrote in *Vantage Point,* "stronger not only as a military shield but as a forum for allied consultation and a tool for action in nonmilitary affairs. I was also determined to leave my successor a solid transatlantic foundation for a healthy world economy." Johnson was convinced that nothing could do more to advance détente with the Soviet Union than a strong NATO. Confronted with a stable, unified Atlantic community, Moscow would be more likely to make concessions than if NATO were weak and divided. He also recognized that whatever Soviet leaders might say about American imperialism, they tacitly supported the presence of U.S. troops in Germany as insurance against the revival of German revanchism. "This effort to strengthen security and economic health in the Atlantic community absorbed the time, energy, and talent of some of the best men in government and private life," LBJ observed, "[and] absorbed much more of my time and attention than most people realized."[38] His personal views on America's three principal allies mirrored those of the average American: he liked and felt kinship with the British; perceived the Germans to be strong, hard-working, but politically untrustworthy people; and regarded the French as culturally powerful but politically immature.[39]

Then, on February 21, 1966, de Gaulle announced that France was withdrawing from NATO. The move was hardly unanticipated in Washington. For two years de Gaulle had been criticizing the structure of NATO and the way it functioned. He had repeatedly called for reforms and in 1965 withdrew French naval officers from NATO's planning operation. During conversations with George Ball, de Gaulle wondered whether the United States would risk its own annihilation to protect interests that were purely European. What nation in a similar situation would? In the spring of that year, the French leader initiated what Bohlen referred to as a "rather indecent flirtation with the Soviet Union."[40] In June 1965 Bohlen flatly predicted a French withdrawal. Still, when it came, the announcement was shocking. As Ball had observed to de Gaulle during his 1965 visit, the United States saw NATO as an integrated whole. The American people had committed themselves under Article V to fighting and dying to defend Western Europe on the assumption that the Western European nations were willing to do the same for them and for each other. American officials feared that France's withdrawal would open the door for other members to go their own way, to join with France in constituting a third force, or even working out their own modus vivendi with the Soviet Union.[41] Moreover, the move could have grave domestic consequences, stimulating neo-isolationism and playing into the hands of both Republicans and Kennedy liberals who had long argued that LBJ was grossly mismanaging America's European policies.

In many ways, LBJ's handling of the NATO crisis of 1966 was his finest hour as a diplomat. The dangers of a misstep were enormous. NATO and the events surrounding its formation constituted the very basis for America's commitment to participate in world affairs following World War II. Traditionally an isolationist nation, America had been persuaded that in the modern world it could not stand alone, that with aircraft carriers and intercontinental ballistic missiles, the United States could no longer be safe within Fortress America. The public and Congress had been persuaded to view the nations of Western Europe as its gallant allies in the struggle against the forces of international communism, just as they had been in the struggle against the forces of international fascism. But unilateralism—the impulse to act independently in world affairs—if not outright isolationism was still a tempting course for many Americans. The collapse of NATO would provide tremendous impetus to those who wanted the United States to go it alone. That France, who had defaulted on its multibillion-dollar World War I debt and had collapsed in six weeks before the Nazi onslaught of 1941, was rejecting NATO was particularly galling for Americans.

In Europe, the feeling that the United States would not risk nuclear destruction to save NATO was not limited to France. Most Europeans saw U.S. involvement in the war in Vietnam as a mistake. America was frittering away its resources, attention, and prestige in a conflict that was peripheral to the interests of the Atlantic community, the seat of Western civilization and the heart of the noncommunist world. If America's commitment to internationalism and the Western alliance were to be saved, LBJ recognized instinctively, he would have to act strongly yet subtly.

To be sure, the French withdrawal from NATO, when it came, as well as other signs of independence from America's European allies, annoyed and frustrated Johnson. "I am not an isolationist and I don't want a fortress America but I am being driven to it more and more every day," he complained to Russell. "The trouble is . . . everybody just treats us like we all used to treat our mother. They impose on us. We just know that she's sweet and good and wonderful and she is going to be kind to us and she'll always know that we came out of her womb and we belong to her and every damned one of them talk to me that way . . . I just talk to 113 nations and they just screw us to death."[42] But this was just typical Johnson rant. LBJ refused to get into "a pissing match," as he put it to

George Ball, with le grande Charles. France was a second-rate power, Johnson observed. The United States was the dominant player and should act as such. "He was," Ball recalled, "inclined to give him very soft treatment."[43] He understood that the general was a "proud, egotistical man who closely identifies himself with France" and would have to appear and to an extent be independent of the world's superpowers. But Johnson believed that there was no fundamental difference of interests between the two countries and that when "the chips were down," as he told Richard Russell, "France and America would stand shoulder to shoulder." He knew this to be so because de Gaulle had privately but repeatedly told him so. The general was in fact playing to the crowd and let LBJ know it.[44] In March 1964, using former Treasury Secretary Robert Anderson as intermediary, the two leaders opened a private channel of communication.[45]

But many believed that de Gaulle's public posturing was more significant than his private reassurances. In the aftermath of France's declaration of independence, LBJ's advisers split, with Bohlen and the White House staff counseling patience and restraint, and the State Department, which viewed NATO as the cornerstone of American foreign policy, favoring a strong rhetorical denunciation of France followed by moves to isolate that country within the European community. Indeed, State wanted the White House to inform de Gaulle that "if he won't play his part in the organization, France will no longer enjoy the protection of the treaty."[46] Public anger at de Gaulle and France was palpable. A popular political cartoon depicted the general standing in the center of an Allied cemetery. Framed by row after row of white crosses, he asks, "Why do you Americans stay where you're not wanted?"[47]

In the months that followed, LBJ rejected the temptation to use de Gaulle as a foil, much to the annoyance of American nationalists and neo-isolationists, concentrating instead on reassuring the other allies of the U.S. commitment to them. By repeatedly pointing out that in his notice of withdrawal from NATO, de Gaulle had stated explicitly that France would come to the military aid of the other treaty signatories in case of "unprovoked attack," Johnson tacitly acknowledged that the organization and the treaty could be separated. In so doing he saved the Atlantic alliance from being done in by Gaullist nationalism.

While struggling to preserve NATO, LBJ also worked to fashion a coherent aid policy for developing nations that would prevent the forces of international communism from feeding on social and economic discontent among their people but at the same time help them to economic independence and compel them to stand up and be counted in the cold war. Johnson and Orville Freeman decided that food aid to famine-plagued India, as to other developing nations, would have to be put on some sort of rational, long-term basis, with congressional participation in the planning and approval of the final result. Such a scheme would have to take into account that as of 1966, the world was confronting a food crisis of frightening proportions. "We are in a sense playing a game of Russian roulette," Freeman recorded in his diary, "and I awaken often in the middle of the night in a cold sweat in connection with it. Since World War

II, famine has been avoided and wherever disaster has struck, American food has been there almost within hours. With heavy surpluses we could do this and the rest of the world has depended upon us to do it."[48] The countries of Western Europe and Japan had promised to contribute, but they were just paying lip service. During the time Freeman was secretary of agriculture, the world's population had grown by nearly 350 million, while U.S. farm surpluses had shrunk dramatically. To avert disaster, both Freeman and LBJ agreed, two things were going to have to happen: PL-480 legislation was going to have to be changed so that shipments of food to developing countries were built into the farm program, budgeted, as it were, and other developed nations were going to have to be persuaded to contribute:[49] The first idea would be a hard sell in Congress. Conservative farm state representatives such as the powerful Allen Ellender of Louisiana were adamantly opposed to making taxpayers fund food aid to third world countries through farm subsidies. He and his fellows argued vehemently that such aid should be limited to whatever surplus existed in any given year. Moreover, in its current anti–foreign aid frame of mind, Congress was not going to commit to open-ended support. There would have to be the promise of eventual self-sufficiency. There was also the expectation that recipient countries side openly with the West in the cold war. On February 10, the White House sent a special message to Congress asking that it implement a new Food for Freedom program, which would involve a budgeted food aid program but also self-help by recipient nations and burden sharing with other affluent societies.[50]

Shortly before the White House broached the Food for Freedom idea on the Hill, Indian Prime Minister Lal Bahadur Shastri suddenly died. He was replaced as leader of one-seventh of the world's population by Indira Gandhi, daughter of Jawaharlal Nehru. Feeling the need to impress on India's new leader his determination to link food aid to economic self-help and strategic cooperation, the president invited her to Washington for a state visit. Monsoon rains were not what they had been in past years, and despite New Delhi's commitment to the agricultural sector, the country once again faced famine. Freeman informed the president that thousands of Indians would starve if the United States did not ship at least a million tons of wheat a month.[51] The president was bombarded with memos from Indophiles like Chester Bowles, Ken Galbraith, and McGeorge Bundy and editorials from the *Times* and the *Post* urging him to make a generous, no-strings-attached, long-term aid commitment to Gandhi and her vast, fragile democracy. He vented to Freeman: "I get fourteen memos from everybody in the government—it starts with Bowles and then it goes to State and then it goes to every Indian lover in town and then it goes to all the do-good columnists . . . I feel kind've like they are getting ready to rob my bank, I have to put up the bars and close the doors . . . Now what I am going to tell [Indian Ambassador B. K.] Nehru is very simple. I am not going to make any big commitments and I am not going to underwrite anything. I am going to say to him today . . . I am waiting to see what kind of a foreign policy we can have with your people . . . I am not just going to underwrite the perpetuation of the government of India and the people of India to have them spend all their goddamn time dedicating themselves to the destruction of the people of the United States."[52] Nevertheless, the following day, Johnson announced that he was sending 2 million tons of wheat and 1 million tons of sorghum, more than any of his advisers had recommended.[53]

Four days before Gandhi arrived in Washington on March 27, Ambassador Bowles met with the president and urged him to go all out, to commit without conditions to the delivery of 6 million tons of grain as soon as it could be shipped. "This is an emergency situation growing from an unprecedented drought, the worst in 65 years," Bowles told Johnson.[54] From the other side, Robert Komer was pressing for the continuation of the "short-tether" policy. The Indians must be told that U.S. aid would actually be disbursed only in response to concrete Indian self-help measures. Moreover, Gandhi and Nehru must understand that "we count on India to play more of a wise great power role in Asia vis-à-vis both Pakistan and China."[55] The prospect of actually having to starve people to death to compel India to meet American foreign policy goals deeply disturbed LBJ. On the evening of the 27th, he dined at the Indian Embassy with Gandhi and Nehru. Orville Freeman, who was also there, recalled that the president was like a cat on a hot tin roof. "He sat directly across from me and next to Madame Gandhi. It was an interesting interchange . . . She is of course urban, highly sophisticated. The President, with this massive size and sometimes aggressive mannerisms, towered over her literally and figuratively . . . He seemed to be in one of his compulsive moods. During the meal he draped himself all over the table. He was eating with both hands and talking with his mouthful [*sic*]. He would lean over and talk to her with great concentration. One had the feeling that he repelled her and yet kind of fascinated her, too. I felt as I watched him that he was ill at ease, unhappy with her, and generally frustrated."[56]

The formal discussions between the president, Gandhi, and Nehru actually went quite well. The prime minister expressed understanding and support for the principles of self-help and burden sharing. She also readily agreed to expand her government's campaign to limit population growth through a vigorous birth control program. On April 19, Congress approved a measure specifically authorizing U.S. participation in an international food relief scheme for India.[57]

Still, the crisis did not abate. Monsoon rains in the summer and fall of 1966 were light to nonexistent. Canada, Australia, and other grain-producing nations had still not stepped forward. Meanwhile, the administration's Food for Freedom legislation languished in Congress. Aside from continuing conservative opposition to foreign aid food budgeting, there were other snags. Led by Congressman Clement Zablocki, pro-life forces in Congress objected to the population control components of the Food for Freedom program. On this, however, the administration was not about to budge. American overseas efforts in this regard were noncoercive and purely educational, McPherson told the president. Indian women, for example, were readily employing intrauterine devices; indeed, New Delhi could not keep up with the demand. It was absurd for the United States and other donor nations to keep subsidizing through its food shipments unrestrained population growth.[58] In addition, LBJ got into a spat with George McGovern and other congressional liberals over the title of the program. McGovern wanted Food for Peace. Proponents argued that Food for Freedom smacked of ideology and coercion. Johnson would have none of it. "We want freedom," he instructed his congressional liaison.[59] If McGovern insisted on "Peace," he could sign the bill.

To generate pressure on both India and Congress, LBJ suspended all grain shipments to India from August to December 1966. Indophiles screamed to the press. "I was pictured as a heartless man willing to let innocent people starve," LBJ recalled in his memoir. Both the *Post* and the *Times* ran editorials criticizing him. Still he would not budge. In September Congress passed the Food for Freedom bill. By December, Australia and Canada, after heavy lobbying by the Indians, committed to shipping a quarter of a million tons of wheat. That month an American congressional delegation returned from a trip to India to survey drought-stricken areas. They were appalled and recommended to their colleagues that they approve whatever shipments the president saw fit to propose. In early 1967 the grain began to flow again. Following record monsoon rains, the food crisis in India began to ease.[60]

LABOR HISTORIAN IRVING BERNSTEIN has penned the standard view of Lyndon Johnson and high culture: "The notion of Lyndon Johnson as a latter-day Lorenzo de Medici, patron of the arts, is ludicrous on its face. He was a Texas hill country philistine. There is no evidence that he ever read a poem or a novel of his own choice. His interest in painting seems to have been confined to the noted western artist Peter Hurd who painted the first official portrait of Johnson, which the President hated. Music, the theater, opera, ballet held no attraction. At the Kennedy White House parties for artists, writers, and musicians he stood about with his hands in his pockets and a sour expression on his face."[61] Johnson actually liked visual art but not the pretension that usually surrounded it. McPherson remembered that when abroad, he frequently purchased paintings, some abstract, most representational. During a trip to Italy, the president was offered a Renaissance painting featuring a Rubenesque nude. Riding back to the embassy with G. Frederick Reinhardt, who, according to McPherson, was something of a "nose-in-the-air fellow, a slightly effete Easterner," LBJ turned to him and said, "He [the art dealer] wants $3,000 for it. I told him I'd give him $1,500, but I also told him that I would give him the whole $3,000 if he'd take about twenty pounds off her ass."[62] And yet, no chief executive in American history did more for the arts and humanities.

As of 1960, public support for the arts in America was practically nonexistent. Among the elite of the Republican party were some of the most generous and enthusiastic patrons of music, painting, sculpture, and dance, but the official position of the GOP was that this support should remain private and philanthropic. The Democratic party in the twentieth century, dominated for the most part by representatives of farmers and laborers, did not give the fine arts a high priority. With the advent of Jack and Jackie Kennedy, that changed. They turned the White House into a stage for violinists, sopranos, ballerinas, and novelists and threw their support behind the establishment of a National Cultural Center. LBJ preferred Tony Orlando to Robert Merrill, but he recognized that the fine arts should be nurtured by any society that considered itself great. Under his leadership, the federal government matched the $15.5 million that had been raised by private subscription for the center. The legislation appropriating the funds, passed in January 1964, renamed the facility, completed in 1971 at a final cost of $71 million, the John F. Kennedy Center for the Performing Arts. Taking further advantage of the Kennedy legacy, the president had encouraged Congress to put public funding for cultural matters on a permanent footing by creating the National Endowments for the Arts and Humanities. In 1966 he and Lady Bird approached the multimillionaire art collector Joseph Hirshhorn about donating his magnificent collection of paintings and sculptures to the Smithsonian Institution. He agreed, but only on condition that the federal government build a separate building to house his treasures. Harry McPherson, who was acting as liaison, urged the president to comply. "Hirshhorn's collection is among the very best in private hands anywhere," he advised LBJ. "Washington has long lacked a significant connection with the world of 20th century art, and this will provide it. It is the sort of thing the art, magazine, and education worlds will remember about your Administration." Johnson needed little urging, "I agree with all this," he replied, "and get the message ready for me— the strongest one ever written—I want to see that our people go to see every member of that Committee and explain it to them."[63] Following a year of intense lobbying by the White House and various cultural entities, Congress appropriated the necessary funds. The Hirshhorn Museum, with its nearly six thousand works by Rodin, Degas, Renoir, Picasso, Calder, and Matisse, was one of the Johnsons' greatest gifts to the nation. Finally, LBJ induced Congress in 1967 to create the Corporation for Public Broadcasting, with a one-year appropriation of $10.5 million for construction and $9 million for operations. From this initiative grew National Public Radio and its television companion, the Public Broadcasting System.[64]

IF HIGH CULTURE did not resonate particularly with Lyndon Johnson, wilderness preservation did. "Everybody needs beauty as well as bread, places to play in and pray in," wrote John Muir, "where Nature may heal and cheer and give strength to body and soul alike."[65] LBJ had benefited immensely from his almost transcendental relationship with the Texas Hill Country; he believed that all Americans—"the mechanic that gets Saturday off, who wants to pack his six children, his wife, and mother-in-law into a station wagon to relax a little bit, to free himself from some of the 20th century frustrations"—ought to have that experience open to them. The Johnson administration identified three stages in the conservation-environmental movement. The first comprised federal and state legislation fencing off areas of natural beauty, protecting them from the ravages of modern civilization. The second involved soil conservation and water power development projects such as the TVA. The third put government in the business of building and maintaining a system of national parks and recreation areas.[66]

In September 1964, LBJ signed legislation creating the National Wilderness Preservation System. Starting with 9.1 million acres of Forest Service lands, classified as wilderness, the system grew to eventually include more than 100 million acres, or 5 percent of the nation's land mass. Then, in 1966, LBJ signed six separate bills designating new National Park and Recreation Areas, including the Fire Island Seashore in New York, Pictured Rocks National Lake Shore in Michigan, and the Big Horn Canyon National Recreation Area in Montana.[67]

"MAKE NO LITTLE PLANS," wrote Danish astronomer Tycho Brahe. "They have no magic to stir men's blood."[68] Lyndon Johnson was no maker of little plans, and his schemes most often stirred his countrymen's blood—often in unforeseen ways. One of the overriding goals of the Great Society was to achieve a basic redistribution of power in America. As Joe Califano observed in his commencement address to the students of Mercy College, the Johnson administration was concerned with economic redistribution, to finish what FDR had started. "We are now asking the many to give to the relatively few—the 15 percent of our society who comprise the remaining 'have nots' in the wealthiest nation in the world."[69] In that quest, the White House had achieved a remarkable degree of success in a very short period of time. From 1964 through 1967, federal expenditures on education tripled, from $4 billion to $12 billion. There was more than a tripling on health, from $5 billion to $16 billion. By then the federal government was spending $4,000 a year on each poor family of four, four times the amount spent in 1961.[70] In 1959 America defined 38 million of its citizens as poor; in 1967, 25.9 million. The 14 percent of whites and 47 percent of nonwhites in poverty had declined to 10 percent and 35 percent, respectively.

But, as the Moynihan and Coleman reports observed, jobs, education, and health care alone would not break the cycle of poverty, "This mood of our people is captured in large measure in Paul Goodman's phrase, 'the psychology of being powerless,' " Califano said. If the disinherited could become convinced that the good things in life were coming to them through the exercise of their own political muscle rather than the charity of philanthropists or government, they would be rid of the enervating feelings of dependency and powerlessness.[71] This, of course, was the rationale for the Community Action Programs. Those involved in the War on Poverty, especially LBJ, saw maximum feasible participation by the poor as a counter to the dole, as a gateway to opportunity, and thus resonant with the traditional American values of hard work and self-reliance. If ever there was a believer in the virtues of access to political power, it was Johnson, and he thought of the CAPs as powerful vehicles to achieve that end.[72] The problem was that by 1966, more than one thousand CAPs had sprung into existence, and they were being penetrated by opportunists, Black Power advocates, and representatives of the New Left, who saw maximum feasible participation as an antidote and not a complement to the existing political system.

Initially, Johnson and his advisers, who drew the community action concept in part from New Left literature, saw the movement as an ally rather than an adversary in their campaign for social justice. It was only later that they realized that the movement was out to destroy and not reform liberal capitalism. As an explicitly political protest movement, the New Left traced its origins to 1960, when Al Haber and Tom Hayden, two University of Michigan students who had been profoundly influenced by Jack Kerouac and other members of the beat generation, the civil rights movement—especially SNCC's voter registration campaign—and the working-class radicals of the 1930s, founded the Students for a Democratic Society. Two years later, Hayden penned the "Port Huron statement," which was a call to arms to university and college students to rise up against a political and social system that oppressed the poor and nonwhite and that swallowed up individual freedom in a sea of conformity.[73] For the authors of Port Huron, freedom was not the possession and exercise of the vote or the protection offered by the Bill of Rights, but individual action from moment to moment in accordance with intelligence and conscience, hopefully in concert with other like-minded people.[74] Hayden and his fellow activists soon adopted the name New Left to distinguish the movement from the more explicitly Marxist Old Left of the 1930s. The Free Speech movement (FSM), born on the University of California, Berkeley, campus in 1964, was distinct from the New Left, but in its demand for student rights and freedom of expression, it was complementary.

Over time, members of the SDS and sectors of the FSM became increasingly preoccupied with national politics and foreign affairs. Appalled by the ongoing war in Vietnam, by the persistence of racism, by the pervasiveness of the military-industrial complex, and by the perceived hypocrisy of middle-class morality, students and academics turned out first a comprehensive critique of American politics and society and then a devastating indictment of American foreign policy.

In his 1966 essay, "Power and the Myth of Progress," SDS president Todd Gitlin denounced free enterprise as nothing more than a fraud. But he did not stop with an attack on the inequities of capitalism. As a willing tool of monopoly capitalism, government itself was at fault.[75] Equality in America could be achieved only by building egalitarian "counter-institutions" that would be free of corruption from the larger society. These counterinstitutions included renters' unions, freedom schools, experimental universities, community-formed police review boards, and antipoverty organizations controlled by the poor, specifically the CAPs. SNCC, SDS, and other groups found ready converts in the squalor of the nation's inner cities. "The poor in our cities," Bill

Moyers observed, "have been the wards of the political machines. The machines needed them to exist, and they needed the machines to survive, and the benevolence of the politicians toward the poor kept the arrangement going . . . Suddenly we discovered that these people wanted more than merely the illusion of being in; they wanted political power, a sense of control. They were no longer contented with the meager paternalism by which the system had been held together."[76] Under the flag of maximum feasible participation, CAPs challenged local political leaders and established institutions such as schools, welfare agencies, and housing authorities to attract and control poverty funds. No less a liberal than Jim Rowe directed LBJ's attention to a *New York Times* feature on a Syracuse, New York, CAP whose $300,000 OEO grant was being used to finance protests by the poor against the city's Housing Authority. In Washington, D.C., "high minded . . . innocents" at the OEO's national headquarters were "giving instructions and grants to local private groups for the purpose of training the Negro poor on how to conduct sit-ins and protest meetings against government agencies—federal, state, and local."[77] Tired of being sued, demonstrated against, and having their offices occupied by sit-in protestors, the members of the U.S. Conference of Mayors, led by Richard Daley and Sam Yorty, passed a resolution condemning the CAPs for promoting "class struggle and insisting that local programs remain under the control of local officials."[78]

Eventually some of the more radical elements in the CAPs decided that maximum feasible participation was just a ruse by the political lackeys of capitalism to keep the poor impoverished. Beginning in Manhattan's Lower East Side in the winter of 1965–1966, the OEO financed the establishment of the Committee of Welfare Families. The object of the organization was to get as many mothers and children on the welfare rolls as possible. Struck by the fact that only about half of those eligible for public assistance under the existing terms of the Social Security Act received relief, Richard Cloward and George Wiley, who had just been defeated by Floyd McKissick in the contest to become national director of CORE, formed the National Welfare Rights Organization. The goal of the new group was "a massive drive to recruit the poor onto the welfare rolls," just the opposite of what LBJ had been promising middle-class America that the War on Poverty would achieve.[79] From 3.1 million people on AFDC in 1960, the number rose to 4.3 million in 1965 and 6.7 million in 1969. At the same time, the percentage of nonwhites on welfare grew steadily, from 32 percent in 1950 to 46 percent in 1967. OEO activists worked to bring legal services to the residents of America's inner cities, but they soon found that welfare recipients wanted to use those services in contravention of the rehabilitation goals that the poverty warriors brought with them. Planners wanted strong families; ghetto residents used legal services to obtain divorces. One of the primary rationales of the War on Poverty was to reduce the welfare rolls, but inner-city dwellers used legal services to challenge denials of welfare grants. "The actions and attitudes of legal aid lawyers," historian Edward Berkowitz writes, "tended to make the system more permissive not more oriented toward rehabilitation."[80]

What bothered LBJ more than the perversion of the War on Poverty from opportunity to entitlement and the challenge the CAPs were posing to local political machines was the perception that the OEO had become a Trojan horse within his administration to advance the fortunes of Robert F. Kennedy. The internecine warfare between the Kennedy and Johnson camps had, if anything, intensified since 1964. LBJ naturally gravitated toward those who had a low opinion of the Kennedys. John Roche, the political scientist who had replaced Eric Goldman as White House intellectual, was typical. "While I had immense admiration and respect for John Kennedy, I thought Bob Kennedy was a little shit," he later told an interviewer. "Ted Kennedy seemed to me to be a genial idiot. There's nothing wrong with Ted that, say, a hundred points in I.Q. wouldn't help, you know."[81] For his part, Bobby continued to view LBJ as something of a monster. "Our president," he told his Hickory Hill friends, "was a gentleman and a human being, and . . . this man is not. He's mean, bitter, vicious—an animal in many ways."[82] There was the sniping on Vietnam, but RFK's principal strategy seemed to be to build a liberal-Negro alliance to challenge LBJ for the presidency in 1968. "He is trying to put himself into a position of leadership among liberal Senators, newspapermen, foundation executives, and the like," McPherson advised his boss. "Most of these people mistrusted him in the past, believing him (rightly) to be a man of narrow sensibilities and totalitarian instincts. A number of brave votes for pure liberalism, and a number of internationalist . . . speeches such as the one on nuclear proliferation, and he will seem to them like St. George slaying the conservative dragons . . . As we know, the intellectuals are as easy a lay as can be found."[83] In October 1966, *Newsweek* ran an article on RFK under the banner headline "The Bobby Phenomenon."[84] Straw polls indicated that Democrats favored RFK over LBJ for the 1968 nomination.

The temptation for the president to turn his back on the poverty program, and especially community action, was great. It would throw a bone to conservatives and to big-city mayors who continued to swamp the White House with complaints. "It's [community action] the most dangerous problem we've got facing us today," Richard Daley complained to LBJ. "You've got a lot of people on poverty that are subversive . . . They're [members of inner-city gangs] going in and telling the people, you'll either pay us off or we will knock your windows out or give you a Molotov Cocktail . . . We've gotten in our city reports on RAM which is a pro-Castro outfit operating out of New York . . . What they do is move all around the country . . . I think it's going to happen in every major city."[85] In distancing himself from the poverty program, Johnson could outflank Bobby on the right. The junior senator from New York had joined with Jake Javits and Abe Ribicoff to conduct hearings on America's urban problems, hearings that generally laid the blame on the doorstep of the Johnson White House. If Kennedy wanted to take charge of the urban problem, why not let him have it?

By late 1965 Sargent Shriver was arousing presidential suspicions by pressing continually for more funds for OEO and by refusing to restrain the radicals in his organization who were giving grants to local CAPs to stage demonstrations and sit-in strikes. LBJ subsequently complained to Wilbur Cohen that everybody at OEO was "disloyal to him . . . always trying to undermine him." [86] On a couple of occasions, the White House did intervene to try to rein in OEO projects that its political allies in Congress or city hall found particularly objectionable, most notably a literacy program conceived by James Farmer that Daley and Yorty objected to and the Child Development Group of Mississippi, which had set up eight Head Start centers in forty communities staffed by poor blacks and objected to by Appropriations Committee Chair John Stennis.

Generally, however, LBJ was content to let matters take their course. He rejected suggestions that he break up OEO and transfer its components to other government agencies, and he refused to fire Shriver. Despite all the angst he experienced over the Kennedys, Johnson chose to follow Harry McPherson's advice. "It is possible, in my opinion, for people to work hard for you, maintain confidences, and still find the Kennedys attractive and adventurous," he had told his boss. "The test of our people should be whether they are smart, imaginative, and working to carry out your policies." [87] Nor did the White House declare war on the CAPs. In 1967 Congress modified the original OEO legislation, allowing mayors and governors to take over community action entities if they so desired. The White House opposed the legislation; ironically, of the 940 mayors with CAPs in their jurisdiction, only forty chose to take them over. [88]

CHAPTER 34

CIVIL WAR

THE ISSUE OF WHETHER OR NOT TO PROLONG THE Christmas bombing halt of 1965–1966 provoked an intense debate in the White House and beyond. The chief proponent of a continuation was Robert McNamara. When the Joint Chiefs were able to produce statistics showing a dramatic increase in infiltration during the halt, McNamara pointed out that it was the dry season and this was to be expected. But by early 1966, the defense chief was privately telling Schlesinger, Goodwin, and Galbraith that "he did not regard a military solution as possible. Infiltration from the North seemed to increase at a steady pace whether the United States bombed or did not bomb."[1] Moreover, he predicted that if the bombing were resumed and expanded—the two seemed inseparable—within the year U.S. aircraft would be engaging Chinese communist fighters directly.[2] The CIA agreed, continuing to insist that bombing had had no impact on the North's willingness or ability to infiltrate and that the assault from the air would continue to be ineffective. From Saigon, Henry Cabot Lodge, under intense pressure from General William Westmoreland, railed against the pause. On Christmas Day alone, he reported to Johnson, "1,000 North Vietnamese soldiers were reliably observed entering South Vietnam." "Every day increases their capability in the South," Earle Wheeler insisted to Johnson, and he called for a full-scale air assault on Hanoi.[3] Nguyen Van Thieu added that with every day of a bombing pause, the chances of a coup against the government of South Vietnam increased. "His point was that cessation of bombing suggested appeasement of the communists and eagerness to negotiate which was not consistent with the policy of his government," Westmoreland told his superiors.[4]

Increasingly, hawks rejected the notion of limited war, seeing negotiations not as a means to but as an alternative to victory. "We find that the vast majority of Americans are in full accord with your Vietnam policy," L. Eldon James, national commander of the American Legion, wrote LBJ. "There is increasingly expressed, however, a concern that emphasis has shifted from pursuit of the war effort to pursuit of negotiations with the enemy. Loyal Americans do not want another 'peace without victory' as in the case of the Korean war."[5] More ominously, Eisenhower, whose advice Johnson was soliciting on a weekly basis by early 1966, was expressing the view earlier offered by Richard Russell that the American people would not stand for a protracted war with an indefinite and unpredictable result. He urged LBJ to do as he had done during the Korean stalemate: threaten the communists with nuclear annihilation.

By January 20 Johnson had made the decision to resume the bombing of North Vietnam. In no small part, the pause had been initiated to appease domestic doves and prove to the world that the United States was reasonable, flexible, and pragmatic, whereas the DRV and Beijing were fanatical militarists unwilling to give an inch.[6] By the third week in January, LBJ had become convinced that that goal had been achieved. Hanoi had repeatedly rejected the pause and invitation to negotiate as a hoax. Talks could begin when and only when the last American soldier had left Vietnam.[7] Political and diplomatic considerations aside, LBJ could not bear the thought that he was letting America's fighting men down. On the evening of the 25th, Johnson met with the entire congressional leadership. He read from Bruce Catton's *Never Call Retreat* on Lincoln's anguish over decision making during the Civil War. "He [Lincoln] had told a friend," LBJ read, "that all of the responsibilities of the Administration 'belong to that unhappy wretch called Abraham Lincoln.' And as he tried to meet those responsibilities the last thing he needed or wanted was a contrived or enforced harmony."[8] Senators Dirksen, Russell, McCormack, Bourke Hickenlooper, Carl Albert, and others urged the president to resume and even expand the bombing; only Mansfield and Fulbright spoke out for a continuation of the pause.[9]

On January 28 Johnson assembled the "Wise Men," a bipartisan group of diplomats and soldiers—Dean Acheson, Robert Lovett, John McCloy, General Omar Bradley, Allen Dulles—to give him their views on Vietnam. All had been principal architects of the containment strategy and all were for holding the line in Southeast Asia.[10] Clark Clifford, the establishment's liaison with the Democratic party, argued that bombing was the best, probably the only way for the United States to exit Vietnam.[11] As the consensus for resumption mounted, McNamara's resolve melted away. At a meeting in the Cabinet Room on the 27th he was unequivocal. "Any further delay in the resumption of the bombing," he said, "can polarize opinion in this country. I feel that we should resume the bombing and I recommend that we send an execute order tonight."[12]

On January 31, 1966, American fighters and fighter-bombers took to the skies once again and struck bridges and staging areas north of the seventeenth parallel. Johnson hoped resumption would compel the North Vietnamese to "show their ass before we showed ours." His public justification was done with a bit more rhetorical flourish. "They persist in aggression," he announced in a broadcast from the White House theater. "They insist on the surrender of South Vietnam to communism. It is, therefore, very plain that there is no readiness or willingness to talk, no readiness for peace in that regime today." [13]

That evening, J. William Fulbright appeared on CBS to declare the war morally wrong and counterproductive to the interests of the country. The administration, the chairman of the Senate Foreign Relations Committee declared, was still a prisoner of the Munich analogy, a comparison that was totally inapplicable to Southeast Asia. To him, Vietnam did not represent Soviet aggression, but a genuinely indigenous revolt against colonialism. Fulbright and the staff of the Foreign Relations Committee, headed by Carl Marcy, proceeded immediately with plans to hold public hearings on the war in Southeast Asia. On February 3 the Committee met in executive session; Fulbright, Gore, Morse, and Aiken persuaded the others to authorize hearings not just on the pending $415 million supplemental aid bill for Vietnam but on the war as a whole. The hearings were to be public, and Marcy was directed to obtain the widest possible exposure. As soon as the meeting broke up, the chief of staff got on the phone with executives from the major television networks and persuaded them to carry the hearings.

On February 3, 1966, without telling any of his aides, Johnson decided to call an impromptu summit meeting with Nguyen Cao Ky to be held in Honolulu. That day, Chester Cooper, McGeorge Bundy's chief assistant on the National Security Council, had gone out for lunch. Upon his return, he discovered that his boss had been searching frantically for him. " 'For God's sake, where the hell you been? Don't you know we're going to be meeting in Honolulu on Saturday?' " "Westmoreland was then on R&R in Hawaii," Cooper recalled, "and the president had decided that it was a good time—in the midst of Fulbright's SFRC hearings—to go out and visit with his commander. Then, he hit upon the idea of making it a summit conference to include Ky and Thieu, whom he had never met, and to emphasize America and the South Vietnamese government's commitment to social justice and pacification." [14] By four o'clock Cooper had an agenda ready; twenty-four hours later, the White House informed the world that the president was going to Hawaii for a summit with his advisers and his South Vietnamese allies. "No international conference of modern times had begun amidst quite so much helter-skelter improvisation as the strategy talks staged in Honolulu," observed *Newsweek*. [15] Indeed, Lodge, Ky, and Thieu did not learn of the impending summit until the night of the 3rd.

The U.S. entourage arrived in Honolulu in moderate disorder, trailing journalists with their shirttails out and their toothbrushes in hand. Cooper recalled that on Friday, "they sent telegrams to the two big hotels in Honolulu and said, 'we're coming; we need'—God knows how many rooms, 'and we'll be there on Saturday.' And out went the Secret Service that night and the communications guys and so forth, and they just tore these hotels apart right in the height of the season." [16]

LBJ spent Sunday, February 6, closeted with Westmoreland. "LBJ was intense, disturbed," the general recorded in his diary. "I think he was torn by the magnitude of the problem and felt insecure about his bombing strategy." Much depended on his performance, Johnson told Westmoreland, and assured the general that Washington would give him what he asked for in terms of troops and matériel. And then, "I hope that you do not pull a MacArthur on me," that is, appeal to the hawks in Congress and through them to the American people to force the White House to wage all-out war against the North. "I felt it not appropriate for me to answer on this," the general recorded.[17]

The first plenary session was held in a large room at Camp Clark, with the Americans and Vietnamese seated across from each other on either side of a long table. With press and observers, there were perhaps a hundred people in the room. In addition to Rusk and McNamara, Agriculture Secretary Orville Freeman and HEW Secretary John Gardner were among the Americans, highlighting the priority to be given to pacification and reconstruction. In his opening statement, Prime Minister Ky outlined four goals: defeat the Vietcong, eradicate social injustice, establish a viable economy, and build true democracy.[18] He struck the Americans as candid, self-effacing, and sincere. "We must have a record of considerably more progress than we have been able to accomplish so far," the mustachioed, diminutive former air marshal said. "We must create a society where each individual in Vietnam can feel that he has a future . . . that he has some chance for himself and his children to live in an atmosphere where all is not disappointment, despair, and dejection."[19]

LBJ responded in kind. "The President opened with a typical Johnson approach leaning across the table talking intently to Chairman Thieu and Prime Minister Ky," Freeman recorded. "He spoke about being close to the people . . . He referred again to his own closeness to REAs [rural electrification] . . . We must take a new look at AID [Agency for International Development] which he had recommended to the Congress and go for not only steel, highway building, but emphasize education, children learning to read and write at ages of 6 and 7, concentrated health facilities . . . to eliminate the killer diseases."[20] LBJ and Ky then retired to the King Kalakaua Suite in the Royal Hawaiian Hotel. The president pulled his chair up close to the youthful Vietnamese leader, occasionally thumping him on the knee for emphasis. He pointed out that 85 percent of the South Vietnamese were peasants who had suffered terribly for ten years. That must stop and the regime must have the support of the people.[21] "The plans are fine," he said, "but what we needed is results, results." Then he added, "We want to see those coonskins nailed to the wall." He repeated the coonskins analogy at the second and final plenary session on Tuesday. "Vietnamese much perplexed," Westmoreland noted. "They have no coons and were unfamiliar with the frontier tradition behind the remark."[22]

At session's close, the two sides issued the Declaration of Honolulu, in which the United States and South Vietnam pledged to keep fighting until an honorable peace could be negotiated and to launch immediately an accelerated program of social, economic, and political reform. Freeman was enthused by the proceedings. "I came away with the feeling that the Vietnamese were absolutely sincere at least to the extent of knowing they had no alternative but to win the support of their people or lose the war."[23] LBJ himself was somewhat more restrained, more realistic. "I knew nothing about Ky and Thieu," he subsequently told India's ambassador to the United States, B. K. Nehru. "The impressions, the titles, the military backgrounds, the generals, the air marshals, the field marshals . . . They never have been very impressive to civilians in Johnson City, Texas, cause we didn't have many storm troopers out there . . . He [Ky] certainly knows how to talk. Whether he knows how to do as well as he knows how to talk is different."[24] At a press conference before departing for Saigon, Ky told reporters that under no circumstances would his government agree to allow the National Liberation Front to be a party to negotiations and that "destroying the military targets in North Veitnam is a necessity." Yet, LBJ had told him emphatically that there would be no escalation of the war and Ambassador-at-Large Averell Harriman had declared that the administration would be prepared to accept the NLF as a separate party to peace talks.[25]

Before they departed Honolulu, LBJ informed Ky that there would be another meeting somewhere in the Pacific in three to six months to evaluate the progress toward social justice and democracy that had been made in South Vietnam.[26] The president could not leave Honolulu without a blast at Fulbright, Morse, and other congressional detractors. He warned America that the war effort was being hampered by "special pleaders who counsel retreat in Vietnam."[27]

FULBRIGHT'S HEARINGS stretched across more than two weeks; the Honolulu Conference could be only a fleeting diversion. He and Marcy had intended to mix administration figures with prominent dissidents, but the White House had no intention of cooperating. McNamara and Rusk refused to appear in open hearing, so most of the testimony was from those with reservations about the war. General James Gavin presented the case for the enclave strategy that Fulbright and Walter Lippmann had earlier advocated and that the Johnson administration had already discarded. Fulbright was able to persuade Korean War hero Matthew Ridgway to submit a letter to the committee endorsing this approach. On February 11, Fulbright and Marcy pulled out their big gun: George Kennan. The author of the containment strategy agreed with Gavin that it was essential to avoid further escalation, and he also urged that the war be ended "as soon as this could be done without inordinate damage to our prestige or stability in the area." There could be no clear-cut military victory, given the threat of full-scale war with China.[28]

Like the Kefauver crime investigations of 1951 and the army-McCarthy encounters of 1954, the Vietnam hearings were watched and discussed by millions. Worried by the attention, Lyndon Johnson called Frank Stanton of CBS and demanded that he cease coverage. On February 10, the network abandoned the hearings and ran its normal daytime fare, including reruns of *I Love Lucy*. Only after respected news director Fred W. Friendly resigned over the incident did CBS resume coverage. NBC carried the entire proceeding, however, including Kennan's powerful testimony.[29]

With each day that the hearings continued, Johnson became more and more distraught. On February 19, he called J. Edgar Hoover and ordered the FBI to "cover the Senate Foreign Relations Committee television presentation with a view toward determining whether Senator Fulbright and the other Senators were receiving information from Communists." The Bureau obliged by drawing "parallels" between presentations made at the hearings and "documented Communist Party publications or statements of Communist leaders." Shortly after the hearings ended, Johnson had Fulbright and several other Senate doves placed under strict FBI surveillance.[30] "The criticism from the Executive is becoming bitter and mean," Fulbright complained to a constituent.[31]

In late February, Bill Moyers reported to the president that the approval rating for his handling of the war had dropped in one month from 63 percent to 49 percent. "Never have I known Washington to be so full of dissonant voices as it is today," Moyers wrote to Theodore H. White.[32] Most important, perhaps, Kennan's and Gavin's testimony and Fulbright's cross-examination made it respectable to question, if not oppose, the war. On February 26, Robert Komer, McGeorge Bundy's top aide, reported to Johnson that the New York business community was getting cold feet. If, as they suspected, the administration was going to spend $10 billion and then get out of Vietnam following the 1966 congressional elections, then it ought to get out at once.[33]

Johnson could not help but note that Robert Kennedy took pains to associate himself with the Foreign Relations Committee and the hearings. Appealing as he always did to the president's worst instincts, John Connally told him that Bobby was "the motivating force behind the Senate hearings."[34] Kennedy's dissent was especially galling. Had LBJ had his wish, Diem would never have been assassinated and America would never have become bogged down in a land war in Asia. Vietnam, a cancer that LBJ already suspected would destroy his presidency, was a gift bequeathed to him by Jack Kennedy. Johnson could understand how and why JFK became involved in Vietnam and bore him no grudge. In public or private he never uttered a word criticizing his predecessor's policies. Diem, LBJ was convinced, was not JFK's doing. But now here were the ex-president's brother and Fulbright joining forces to attack him for pursuing a policy that they had once fully supported.

LBJ's decision to resume the bombing of the North did not constitute a decision to do what was necessary to win the war militarily. The Joint Chiefs were unanimous in wanting to expand the bombing to include the oil storage facilities and power plants around Hanoi and Haiphong. But the president, McNamara, Bundy, and Rusk were determined to keep a tight leash on the aerial assault to control dissent at home and to keep Chinese communists out of the conflict.[35] American and Vietnamese soldiers might have to continue to die, but there would be no Armageddon. Johnson was convinced that he and his advisers had examined every option and that limited war was the only means to achieve double containment—of communism abroad and anticommunism at home. LBJ's 1966 State of the Union address, half of which had been devoted to Vietnam, was a Niebuhrian call to stay the course. "Scarred with the weakness of men," he had declared, "with whatever guidance God may offer us we must, nevertheless, and alone with our mortality strive to ennoble the life of man on earth."[36]

Johnson wanted the leadership of South Vietnam to build a viable nation, something that had never existed south of the seventeenth parallel. There was, as State Department analyst Philip Habib put it, "a strong sense of peoplehood but no sense of nationhood."[37] During the long years of French rule, the colonial authorities had done everything in their power to prevent the emergence of an authentic Vietnamese nationalism. They had pursued and jailed leaders not only of the Vietnamese Communist Party but also of the Vietnamese Nationalist and Constitutionalist Parties. They had pitted Catholic against Buddhist and encouraged the development of the Cao Dai, Hoa Hao, and other sects. Then came Diem and Nhu and their failed experiment in personalism. The revolving door of military governments had made little or no attempt to develop a viable political culture. The Americans had only made matters worse. They had gotten rid of Diem, Nhu, and the "Dragon Lady," Madame Nhu, but they had not been able to solve the riddle of which came first, military security or democratic, representative government. Now the United States was taking over the war directly. The conflict was no longer between Vietnamese communists and Vietnamese nationalists, wrote Ton That Thien in the *Far Eastern Review,* but between the United States and the forces of international communism. Vietnam was destined, it seemed, to become one vast military base either for America or communist China. He noted that Ky had recently stated that "so long as the Vietnamese people have no democratic spirit and habits, so long as they still do not know what democracy is, elections are useless." Given these circumstances, "what is there left for the Vietnamese nationalists to fight for?"[38]

And, in fact, the Americanization of the war was ripping the already delicate fabric of Vietnamese life. The fighting and bombing had driven an estimated 4 million South Vietnamese from their homes, some 25 percent of the population. These alienated, destitute villagers settled in squalid refugee camps or drifted into the cities looking for work. Rootless and hostile, they proved to be an excellent source of recruits for the Vietcong. The influx of hundreds of thousands of American troops and billions of dollars into South Vietnam had a devastating impact on urban life as well. Saigon and other large cities became boomtowns, crowded to the scuppers with human beings, automobiles, foot taxis, and garbage. To fight inflation, the Americans flooded the country with consumer goods, but among other things, this influx destroyed South Vietnam's few native industries and made the economy ever more dependent on outside forces. By 1967 much of the urban population was employed providing services to the Americans. The port of Saigon became permanently clogged with ships backed up out to sea as far as the eye could see, waiting to unload.

The port was the center of a network of corruption that spread throughout the country, with military officials extorting money from importers, and importers grossly overcharging the U.S. government. In addition, South Vietnamese officials rented land to the U.S. mission at inflated prices; required bribes for driver's licenses, passports, visas, and work permits; extorted kickbacks for contracts to build and service facilities; and participated enthusiastically in the thriving opium trade. By 1966 the nation was in the grip of runaway inflation. In Da Nang, for example, the price of chicken had risen 1,000 percent since the coming of the Americans.[39] Seedy bars with their innumerable prostitutes were everywhere, offending the normally permissive Vietnamese.

The government, such as it was, was purely a military regime. Ky, Thieu, and the directorate of officers that backed them were dependent almost entirely on the support of the commanders of the four military districts into which South Vietnam was divided. The government was relatively strong in II, III, and IV Corps, but I Corps (the northernmost sector, which bordered the seventeenth parallel and included some of the most densely populated and revolutionary-minded areas of the country) was a different matter.

In truth, South Vietnam in 1966 consisted of two separate regions and cultures, the center and the south. The center ran from the seventeenth parallel down to the outskirts of Saigon and included the Central Highlands populated by the ethnically distinct Montagnards and the coastal plain. Comprising tiny parcels of relatively poor land, the region could not support itself and was dependent on the south for much of its rice. The south, formerly the French province of Cochinchina, included Saigon and the Mekong Delta, one of the great rice-producing regions of the world. Historic differences tended to follow geographic lines. The center, part of the former French province of Annam, was the seat of the imperial court, a haven for Buddhist monks and scholars. It was also the historic seat of strong resistance to both Chinese pressure from the north and French pressure from the south. The south was a frontier province of the center, settled rather late and in large land holdings. When they came, the French found it much easier to co-opt the large landowners of the south, who became typical clients of the colonial power—rich, French-educated, and totally divorced from the uneducated peasant masses.[40]

The commander of I Corps, which comprised the northern half of the center, was the charismatic General Nguyen Chanh Thi. Unlike other warlords, Thi relied on more than clubs and bullets to maintain his position. He had established ties with local mayors and village chiefs, the intellectual community centered in Hue, Vietnam's ancient capital and a symbol of nationalist sentiment, and with the Buddhist leadership, particularly Thich Tri Quang, head of the United Buddhist Church. For many Buddhists in South Vietnam, Tri Quang epitomized Mahayana Buddhism. He had organized the immolations and street demonstrations that had played such a key role in Diem's and Nhu's ouster, and he and his followers had acted as the people's conscience to all the military regimes that followed. Lodge, Westmoreland, and the rest of the U.S.

mission misunderstood, misrepresented, and generally despised Tri Quang.[41] Whatever the case, the bonze's mission was clear and consistent: to organize resistance to any government that exploited peasants and workers and did nothing to relieve their suffering by refusing to seek a negotiated settlement to the war.

Upon his return from Honolulu, intoxicated by the attention and praise that had been paid him, Ky decided to move on his rival and reassert Saigon's control over I Corps. He called the members of the directorate together—minus Thi—and informed them that if they did not authorize him to dismiss Thi, he would resign and go back to running the air force.[42] Reluctantly, they agreed. Within days, antigovernment demonstrations flared up in Da Nang, the seaport headquarters of I Corps, and, with a population of some two hundred thousand, one of the country's larges cities. In Hue students and faculty members of the university ran amok in the streets of the normally placid city. In the days that followed, Tri Quang and his associates announced the creation of the "Buddhist Struggle movement" and listed four demands: the return to Vietnam of ousted generals such as Duong Van "Big" Minh and Tran Van Don; the return of general military officers to purely military duties; the establishment of institutions characteristic of independence and democracy; and the launching of a social revolution to better the life of the masses.[43] A leader of the movement pledged to reporters that he and his followers would work "to the last drop of blood, to the last breath" to achieve these goals.[44]

The first week in April, riots broke out in Saigon. Gathering by the thousands in the city's central market, demonstrators nailed pictures of Ky and Thieu to posts which the government had used in the past for the execution of Viet Cong agents and war profiteers. "Hue and Da Nang are now virtually out of control," Rusk reported to LBJ on April 2. "The themes of the so-called 'struggle' movement are spreading to other areas . . . In addition to the Buddhist-backed 'struggle' group, the important Cau [Cao] Dai sect has now said that the present government is 'illegal.' Catholic discontent is also evident and would probably become acute if the government made special concessions to the Buddhists."[45] Johnson closely monitored developments from the White House. "It looks like to me, Bob, that there's a very serious danger that there's been a complete infiltration of the power base by the communists," he observed to McNamara.[46]

The threat of secession by I Corps, a civil war within a civil war, brought the Johnson administration to the brink of withdrawal from Vietnam. As Westmoreland told a member of the directorate, if the American people found out that 228 U.S. soldiers had been killed and 850 wounded during the month of March while all this "foolishness" was going on, there would be hell to pay.[47] "I note that, for the third successive week, our casualties have exceeded those of Vietnamese forces," Earle Wheeler cabled Westmoreland. "Rightly or wrongly, this latter fact is taken by the American people as proof of the position that . . . the United States forces are fighting the war against VC/NVA forces while the South Vietnamese, whose freedom and country are at stake, squabble pettily among themselves to achieve political advantage . . . I think I can feel the first gusts of the whirlwind generated by the wind sown by the Vietnamese . . . My purpose in addressing you is to convey my own deep distress and concern that the lives, the resources, and the political capital we have expended in our effort to preserve South Vietnam as a part of the free world approach the point of having been in vain."[48] To make matters worse, the Buddhist Struggle movement began to take on a decidedly anti-American tone. After it was learned that U.S. planes had ferried Saigonese troops to Da Nang, the leadership cabled a protest to Lodge, and demonstrators paraded through Hue with banners reading "Down With the CIA" and "End Foreign Domination of Vietnam." Johnson expressed his frustration to his secretary of state: "Now Dean what are we going to do . . . how are we going to justify and explain throwing in the towel if these people just take over that government and tell us to get out or if it just looks like we're in the middle of a civil war? . . . Are we moving to the point where it would be difficult for us to ask people to continue to die out there with this going on every two or three months?"[49] On April 2, LBJ observed to Rusk, McNamara, Rostow, Moyers, and Valenti that the United States must be prepared to make a terrible choice: to leave Vietnam entirely and make a stand in Thailand. He subsequently ordered Defense to draft a scenario for a withdrawal, possibly to be achieved within weeks.[50]

In mid-April, the State Department asked Lodge and Ky to stop labeling opponents of the existing regime communist and insisted that there must be concessions to the Buddhist Struggle movement, principally a constitutional convention with elections to follow. From March 20 to 22, LBJ met once again with Westmoreland and Ky, this time on the island of Guam. He made it clear that he intended to stay the course in Vietnam, but he also let the South Vietnamese leader know that he expected democratic reform. "My birthday is in late August," he told Ky. "The greatest birthday present you could give me is a national election."[51] The prime minister returned to Saigon, seemingly chastened.

Then suddenly, on May 15, 1966, Ky dispatched two thousand soldiers to Da Nang and staged a surprise attack on antigovernment forces. In house-to-house fighting, more than one hundred antigovernment troops and civilians were killed. Several pagodas were damaged or destroyed.[52] Tri Quang, along with scores of other students and Buddhist leaders, was jailed indefinitely. LBJ, to put it mildly, was upset. "It seems to him that internally we cannot permit this thing to go on," Moyers told Rusk. "It will tear us to pieces and [LBJ] thinks time has come for us to try to push whatever buttons we have to push."[53]

On the same day that he ordered the attack on Da Nang, Ky appeared before the National Political Congress, just convened by the government of Vietnam, and signed a decree mandating free, universal elections for a constitutional convention to be held within three to five months. The delegates, who stood and cheered, subsequently adopted rules barring "communist and neutralist elements from participating in the convention but offering amnesty to those who had participated in the struggle movement."[54] Elections were scheduled to take place sometime between July 5 and September 5, preferably in August to meet LBJ's birthday deadline. "The problem," Maxwell Taylor observed, "is to instill order in South Viet-Nam under a cooperative government capable of an effective prosecution of the war, while progressing toward a constitutional, freely elected government."[55] That had always been the problem. Those around the president were not particularly sanguine. Rostow reported that the consensus was that "we face, say, a 10 to 15% chance of chaos and total paralysis; a lower percentage possibility that a government might emerge that would seek to end the war on almost any terms and that would ask us to leave; a 50% probability that the government continues somewhat weakened and in no position to prosecute with full vigor the non-military programs; and a modest, perhaps 25% possibility that . . . we will have an even better situation than in the past."[56] Discouraged, dismayed, LBJ nonetheless refused to fold. The war would continue.

With U.S. jets flying around-the-clock sorties against targets north of the seventeenth parallel, LBJ went on national television to reassure Americans and the world that the United States had no intention of escalating the war, but that it would keep on doing what it had been doing in order eventually to wear the enemy down. At the same time, UN Ambassador Arthur Goldberg told a specially called session of the Security Council that the Johnson administration would welcome its help in securing a negotiated peace and invited it to reopen the Geneva Peace Conference of 1954.[57]

Two weeks later, Robert Kennedy called a press conference and issued a statement declaring that the willingness of the administration and the Ky government to admit "discontented elements in South Vietnam," including the National Liberation Front, "to a share of power and responsibility is at the heart of the hope for a negotiated settlement."[58] Bobby took pains to warn Russia, China, and North Vietnam not to assume that if he were to become president of the United States, they could expect a policy of appeasement. "Coming from any other senator," *Newsweek* observed, "the suggestion might have stirred a ripple of controversy; coming from a Kennedy, it jolted the Administration with the force of a Claymore mine planted in Dean Rusk's in-basket."[59] LBJ was appalled both at the substance and the tone of RFK's statement. "I think it's tragic," he told Dean Rusk. "It's so presumptuous . . . He says that he doesn't want the Russians and the Communists to be over-gleeful and expect him to be elected President because if he were elected President it wouldn't mean that he'd have an easy surrender himself . . . Well hell, he don't have to become President to do that—that's what he's trying to do now." Johnson jumped to the conclusion that Kennedy and the liberals were getting ready to stab him in the back again and expressed the fear that the balance of power was tipping in their favor even within his own administration. Bundy had gone over to the dark side and now McNamara. "You know Bob McNamara has felt that while we ought to have limited objectives," he confided to Rusk, "that we ought to make it abundantly clear that we did not necessarily have to have everybody of our own choosing in this government, that it could be a Communist government . . . a very dangerous position to me . . . but he has said to me a number of times that he thought that we ought to give serious consideration to this. And then when he said the other day that we only have one chance out of three of winning, it just shocked me."[60]

During a subsequent conversation, Joe Alsop told Harry McPherson that the reason for RFK's coalition speech was that he was convinced that LBJ would not "stay the long course" in Vietnam and he, Bobby, did not want to get stuck out on the right wing when the administration worked out a negotiated solution.[61] "Bullshit," LBJ exclaimed. "You make it clear on the Hill," he told Larry O'Brien,

> that there is all the difference in the world between [my] position and Bobby's concerning the NLF . . . We don't believe in favoring the communists, we are trying to kill 'em and we don't favor them in the government before or after the election. We say that we are willing to let their voice be heard but we do not recognize them as a government and if they come to the peace table they would have to come through North Vietnam. He [RFK] favors permitting them to sit as an equal. We do not. He favors permitting them in the government. We do not.[62]

Actually, Johnson was telling Congress one thing and Saigon another. He and Rusk did not accept the Lodge-Ky position about prohibiting any participation by the Vietcong in the forthcoming elections specifically and the political life of South Vietnam generally. "We believe the GVN [government of Vietnam] . . . would be wise to exclude communists," Rusk, Komer, and Rostow advised the president, "not by name but by barring as candidates 'agents of any external power committed to the overthrow of the GVN by force or subversion' and they should even be prepared to give the vote to persons from VC-controlled areas if they can be properly identified."[63] Rostow in particular was and would continue to be an advocate of one man, one vote in South Vietnam, believing that the communists could be defeated legitimately at the polls. At the Honolulu meeting LBJ had urged Ky and Thieu to develop better contacts with the Vietcong to gain insight into the movement.[64]

Kennedy and Fulbright's perceived treachery continued to eat away at LBJ like a cancer. "Bobby is behind this revolt up there on Viet Nam," he complained to Nick Katzenbach. "He made this damn fool speech [on including the Vietcong in the political process in South Vietnam] . . . Four different people told [me] that Schlesinger had written this speech . . . He has an idea . . . that I am an evil man that is trying to trip him up. I am not . . . My daddy used to say 'some people are so damned crooked themselves, they think everybody else is,'—and some people are so evil themselves and are so manipulating themselves, they think everybody else is . . . I have no objections to Bobby becoming President of this country. I just, by God, want to be a President myself and I think it ill-behooves the Kennedys after all I have done for them to not reciprocate the treatment I have given them."[65]

On the evening of May 12, 1966, Johnson addressed a congressional dinner held in the National Guard Armory. "I am delighted to be here tonight with so many of my very old friends as well as some members of the Foreign Relations Committee," he declared. "You can say one thing about those hearings, although I don't think this is the place to say it." Following a call to stay the course on the Great Society, he said, "Our people have learned that aggression, I think, in any part of the world, carries the seeds of destruction to American freedom."[66]

The Armory speech appalled McPherson, and he let his boss know it the next day: "I felt it was harsh, uncompromising and over-militant . . . The speech does not read as bad as it sounded. The combination of tone, emphasis, and frequent glances down at Fulbright made it wrong . . . Mr. President, I am one who believes we are right to stand in Viet Nam. I abhor the kind of vapid, sophomoric fighting that Fulbright is producing nowadays, but there are questions about Viet Nam and about our appropriate role in the world that are extremely difficult for me to resolve . . . Churchill, rallying Britain in 1940, is not the only posture a wise and strong leader can assume today." LBJ's reaction to these observations was to call McPherson in and chew him out.[67] He was angry because he recognized the wisdom of McPherson's remarks. He would grow closer to, not more distant from, this particular adviser as time wore on, even as he and others in the executive branch began to drift apart. What drove him to distraction about Fulbright's dissent was its refusal to recognize the ongoing power of domestic anticommunism. Though one part of him ached, à la Richard Russell, for a leader to come to power in South Vietnam who would ask the United States to leave, another part perceived that neutralization and the communism of Vietnam would revive the conservative coalition and stall the Great Society and particularly the Second Reconstruction, thus exacerbating the urban rioting that was threatening to tear the nation apart. Fulbright, who had done battle with Strom Thurmond and the ultras throughout the Kennedy administration, should have known better.

Both Lyndon Johnson and Dean Rusk convinced themselves that the chairman of the Senate Foreign Relations Committee's opposition to the war in Vietnam stemmed from his racism; the yellows, blacks, and browns of the world were just not worth bothering about. Fulbright had signed the Southern Manifesto and voted against the 1964 and 1965 Civil Rights Acts. "The President said that on one occasion he was having a discussion with him," Orville Freeman remembered, "and had asked Fulbright why he was so against Vietnam. Fulbright just said to him, 'they're not our kind of people' and then with real vehemence the President said that means what Fulbright is really saying is 'nigger, nigger, nigger.' "[68] More ominously, in his never-ending conversations with sympathetic politicians and news people, LBJ began implying that Fulbright, Church, Morse, and Clark were tools of the Kremlin. "Now the Soviet Union has a hell of a campaign on," Johnson confided to Georgia Senator Herman Talmadge. "They are seeing I guess ten Senators per day on various phases of Viet Nam policy . . . This last pause originates with a fellow like Fulbright who eats dinner out there [at the Soviet embassy] and stays until 1 o'clock."[69] Johnson realized he was walking a fine line. He wanted to intimidate the dissenters, but he did not want to unleash a full-scale witch hunt. "Mr. President, I am basically a gut fighter," Russell Long blurted out during one conversation with the president. "Now if you have got that information that Bill Fulbright was at the Soviet embassy . . . won't you please let me put that on him on nationwide TV?" Not a good idea, LBJ responded immediately: "Well they would make a McCarthy out of you and they would just destroy you in the damn press and they would say that we were spying on them and they would give you hell."[70]

BIOGRAPHERS AND HISTORIANS have long painted Vietnam as a tragic mistake that undercut Johnson's reforms at home. In fact, by 1966 the two projects had become closely linked in the president's mind: Johnson wanted to build a strong, free society in both places. The concept of nation building lay at the very core of the Johnsonian vision; the Great Society itself, especially the Second Reconstruction, was nothing if not an experiment in nation building. In the midst of the I Corps crisis, LBJ had burst out during one meeting, "Dammit, we've got to see that the South Vietnamese government wins the battle . . . of crops and hearts and caring."[71]

It was inevitable, perhaps, that the president and his advisers would transfer their vision of Utopia from the American heartland to the jungles and paddies of Southeast Asia. There was first and foremost Johnson's idealism. "I am going to start this year or try as best I can," he told Roy Wilkins, "to commence it [Head Start] in the African countries and Latin American countries and Asian countries . . . I am going to take some of my AID money and start Headstart Programs in these countries and have the children come in and get examined physically then have a health program where they will all get inoculated for cholera and things of that kind. Then I am going to have them learn how to read and write instead of all these Ph.D.'s coming to exchange under the Fulbright program of $50 to $60 million."[72] Not far behind idealism, perhaps inextricably intertwined with it, was guilt. Just as Woodrow Wilson found it psychologically and emotionally necessary to justify the shedding of blood in the Great War in terms of making the world safe for democracy, so too did LBJ feel compelled to justify the carnage in Vietnam in terms of exporting the Great Society.

From a strategic and ideological perspective, there was still the perceived need to demonstrate to the third world that democracy and regulated free enterprise, "modern individualism," brought about higher living standards, a better quality of life, and greater psychological well-being than Marxism-Leninism. Much of Walt Rostow's meaningful intellectual life had been devoted to developing a noncommunist alternative for the peoples of the developing nations in their pursuit of social justice in the midst of decolonization. The United States had to be more than just a shining example to the rest of the world, he argued to Joe Califano. America must not only get money and land into the hands of

South Vietnamese villagers, must not only bring them literacy, hygiene, and electricity, but must impart to them a sense of empowerment. If community action programs were appropriate for Watts, why not for Bien Hoa province.[73] But, of course, it was not that simple. Outside of traditional village communalism, democracy was a foreign concept south of the seventeenth parallel. Nor did there exist the institutions—legislative bodies, quasi-independent federal agencies, and a federal court system—by which Americans had traditionally sought political empowerment and socioeconomic justice.

Actually, Johnson had been talking for more than six months with Robert Komer about how to win "the other war" in Vietnam.[74] Komer, whom LBJ would appoint special assistant to the president to oversee "U.S. non-military programs for peaceful construction relating to Vietnam" and who was almost as hyperactive as Johnson, defined the other war in the broadest possible terms. Working through the government in Saigon, the American mission must control inflation; enforce discipline on the port of Saigon to see that commodities were duly landed and distributed; increase the number of AID workers (then three-thousand compared to 3 million military personnel) and send agricultural, health, and educational specialists into every village; provide security for the Americans and their Vietnamese counterparts as they struggled to win the hearts and minds of the peasant population; and compel the government in Saigon to institute a program of land reform and follow through on its promises of free elections. The other war would also involve counterinsurgency efforts to demoralize, intimidate, and, if necessary, eradicate the Vietcong. At the heart of the new pacification effort would be the already established Revolutionary Development (RD) program, by which, in a conscious imitation of NLF tactics, the U.S. mission assembled fifty-nine-man teams of Vietnamese, trained them in propaganda and social service, and inserted them in the villages of South Vietnam, there to build popular support for the government and undermine the appeal of the communists.[75] Komer, Johnson, and the American mission wanted desperately to work through the South Vietnamese political and military power structure. "We cannot just take over from the Vietnamese—the growing US presence is already creating its own problems," Komer observed to the president.[76]

The commanders of the other war, Komer and his chief lieutenant, William Leonhart, reported immediate problems. Lodge, who was bored by social and economic issues, had to be forced to focus on pacification.[77] Many of those who were willing to acknowledge that something needed to be done on the nonmilitary side took a very simplistic, if not simple-minded, view of pacification. "We found that in our frontier days we couldn't plant the corn outside the stockade if the Indians were still around," Maxwell Taylor observed. "Well, that's what we've been trying to do in Viet Nam. We planted a lot of corn with the Indians still around, and we've sometimes lost the corn . . . [If] security becomes greater . . . pacification will move along much better."[78] Other than the marines, who lobbied constantly to be given control of pacification, the military, including Westmoreland, had little time for the other war. Ky was no more interested in economic and social questions than Lodge was. "The weakness of the GVN is the biggest bottleneck," Komer told LBJ.[79] RDs, militia, and police were under the command of the generals who headed the four corps areas, and they thought in purely military terms. Those who were assigned to protect the pacification cadre were loath to stay the night in the villages they were assigned to protect. As a result, many a dawn found the resident RDs with their throats slit. During a seven-month period in 1966, 3,015 RD personnel were murdered or kidnapped.[80] Frequently, ARVN soldiers would undo any good the cadre had done by forcibly conscripting young men from the villages and imposing arbitrary and exorbitant taxes. Much of the money earmarked for RD found its way into the pockets of local military commanders.[81]

In August, the White House turned to David Lilienthal, the legendary force behind TVA, and asked him to oversee the pacification effort in Vietnam. Reluctantly, he agreed, but his talents were, as the administration should have foreseen, far more suited to peacetime reconstruction.[82] By September, Komer had decided that for bureaucratic as well as substantive reasons, the other war had to be placed under military control, "I still favor (as does McNamara) giving the whole job to [Westmoreland]—and it will probably come to this if we want solid results," Komer told Johnson.[83] AID, State, and the CIA all strenuously objected, for obvious bureaucratic reasons, but also because they believed that the military could never get its priorities right, that it would focus primarily on physical security and let politics and reform fall by the wayside.[84] They were able to delay the transfer, but only until spring, when LBJ made Westmoreland commander of both wars.

BY 1966, ALTHOUGH OVERALL SUPPORT FOR THE WAR remained high, polls suggested plummeting support for Johnson's handling of it. "Many people are simply not satisfied with the official explanations," Harry McPherson observed to Bill Moyers. "They cannot believe we are there to 'defend the freedom of South Vietnam.' Why should we pick that place, to defend the freedom of those people? . . . Several people said . . . they wished the President would put the whole thing in the simplest terms of Realpolitik: we are there to fight China. She is trying to take Asia . . . So we are involved in an elemental, if dangerous, power struggle; that is acceptable, we are a power; to hell with 'fighting for freedom and self-determination.' "[85] In fact, Fulbright hearings and street demonstrations aside, the White House was feeling more pressure from the hawks than the doves in 1966. In surveys of states from West Virginia to Tennessee to Michigan, pollsters found that an average of 65 percent of those who gave LBJ an unfavorable rating on the war wanted "to go all out, short of nuclear attack." Of all people surveyed, 50 percent wanted to "bomb Hanoi" and 60 percent wanted to blockade North Vietnamese ports.[86]

As soon as it became apparent in January that the White House was going to resume bombing, the Joint Chiefs began to ask for the air raids to be extended to include petroleum storage facilities in and around Hanoi and Haiphong. Wheeler also pressed the president to allow his aircraft to bomb the two railways connecting communist China and North Vietnam and to mine all of the harbors through which the DRV was receiving supplies from both China and the Soviet Union. As usual, LBJ resisted. He wanted to exert the maximum possible pressure on the enemy without escalating the war. "I am convinced that if I carried out all the recommendations made to me," he told a group of representatives and senators gathered at the White House, "we'd be in World War III right now." [87] Yet he continued to believe that America could not afford to fail in Vietnam. In arguing that the United States could not fall back to Thailand, Rusk had opined that "even if sophisticated leaders understood the Vietnamese political weaknesses and our inability to control them—to the mass of the Thai people the failure would remain a US failure and a proof that Communism from the north was the decisive force in the area . . . Thailand simply could not be held in these circumstances and the rest of Southeast Asia would probably follow in due course." [88] Johnson did not argue the point.

Every military twist and turn was agonizingly debated. On June 22, LBJ called a meeting of his advisers to discuss extending the bombing to include the petroleum storage facilities. Rusk was for it; so were Humphrey, Rostow, William Bundy, Wheeler, and McNamara. [89] The defense chief had consistently opposed bombing the facilities in the past, but he had changed his mind. With no petroleum, the enemy's supplies would dwindle to a trickle and there would be no trucks available to carry regular NVA units into the South. [90] Of LBJ's advisers, only Arthur Goldberg and George Ball spoke up in opposition. The Chinese communists would eventually send MIG fighters in to protect key installations in North Vietnam, and U.S. planes would have to engage them they argued. Moreover, the president was going to lose liberal opinion once and for all if he escalated the war. [91] Johnson took their words to heart. "They [McNamara and the Joint Chiefs] think it's a tragic mistake not to destroy that petroleum that's supplying ten thousand trucks that are coming down now," the president told Mike Mansfield. "I seem to be the only one that's afraid that they'll hit . . . a hospital or hit a school or something." [92]

In truth, Johnson was continuing to have nightmares about unforeseen events that would cause him to lose control of the situation in Southeast Asia. "You're familiar with our battleship Maine," he remarked to McNamara. "Now what's going to happen if we hit their tanker there . . . We've got to analyze this very carefully . . . and we have . . . do we get enough out of this for the price we pay?" McNamara responded that it would indeed be serious if a Soviet tanker were hit, but that American pilots would exercise every caution. In his opinion, the defense chief told Johnson, the administration really had no choice. "This is a minor incident in the war. I don't see how you can keep fighting out there, frankly, Mr. President without doing this . . . I don't think you can keep the morale of the troops up and I don't think you can keep the morale of the people in the country that support you up . . . I believe it has military value, although I don't put the weight on it that the Chiefs do. But I don't put the cost on it that the people in State do, Ball, for example."[93] Then, on the 24th, a story appeared in the *New York Times* by Max Frankel that the Pentagon was planning to bomb targets in and around Hanoi and Haiphong. Johnson was furious and frightened. He had visions of the reinforced and forewarned enemy lying in wait for the American assault aircraft. "I wish I could put Frankel in the first plane," he told Cy Vance.[94] On June 28, LBJ gave McNamara the go-ahead to strike the two major petroleum storage facilities in the Hanoi-Haiphong area. What ensued was the most intense and sustained aerial offensive of the war to date.

From 1 A.M. to 3 A.M. during the initial assault, LBJ stayed on the phone with Rostow and Vance asking for minute-by-minute reports. From their vantage point in the Situation Room, they related that 60 percent of the targets had been hit, with no bombs falling outside the target areas, then 80 percent. Reports were coming in of mushroom clouds reaching twenty thousand feet. To Johnson's intense relief, not a single U.S. plane was lost.[95]

"WASHINGTON IS A CITY OBSESSED by Vietnam," Ronald Steel wrote in the *New York Review of Books* in 1966. "It eats, sleeps, and particularly drinks this war. There is virtually no other subject of conversation worthy of the name, and no social gathering or private discussion that does not inevitably gravitate toward the war. Never, one feels, has a war been so passionately discussed, so minutely examined, so feverishly followed—and so little understood—as the war in Vietnam . . . The administration . . . has not had the time, or the aptitude, or perhaps the understanding to explain this war in terms that could reconcile it with traditional American values. As a result, it has lost the support of much of the nation's intellectual community."[96] In a spate of essays and books LBJ began to appear as a power-mad Machiavellian figure who was establishing in America an "imperial presidency." When Johnson pointed out in a speech in Omaha that he was the only public official in America elected by all the people, Walter Lippmann's pen scratched defiance: "This is such an extraordinary conception of the American Presidency that if it is taken at face value . . . the President has unlimited and arbitrary power in the making of war and peace."[97]

"There's a great infiltration in the government and in the press particularly and in the networks of folks that have little faith in our system and who want to destroy it every way in the world they can," Johnson complained to George Brown.

> They are making an all out pitch against everything—getting out of Vietnam . . . I think we're going to have to start a drive to run 'em underground because they're getting to a point now where they're dangerous . . . No mother and no daughter and no married woman wants her husband or her son to go to Vietnam. The only thing that would . . . compel 'em to go would be love of country and their honor and their duty. But

they no longer think it's an honor or duty; they think it's a terrible thing to do. So pretty soon you'll get no one to do the fighting and all you'll do is just have a little reaching and then by god they are gonna come eat us . . . I don't think they do any good to the morale of our people . . . when they raise a doubt and a question based on misinformation about everything we do. Because a mother sits there and it's anguish enough for her to give up her boy anyway without some goddamn senator say[ing] that he's being manipulated and maneuvered and unfairly sent. It's just too cruel, too brutal. It's all right if they have an alternative and debate the alternative, but to say that you're maneuvering 'em and lacking candor and you're lying . . . it just goes a little bit further than it oughta go.[98]

In a series of articles, University of Chicago political scientist Hans Morgenthau took it upon himself to reveal the truth about the tyrant who was corrupting American life and institutions. Johnson was about power, he declared in one piece; intellectuals (read: dissenters) were about truth. The two could never meet.[99] In an essay entitled "The Colossus of Johnson City," Morgenthau wrote, "What is so ominous in our present situation is not that the President has reasserted his powers, but that in the process he has reduced all countervailing powers, political and social, to virtual and seemingly permanent impotence. What the Founding Fathers feared has indeed come to pass; the President of the United States has become an uncrowned king. Lyndon B. Johnson has become the Julius Caesar of the American Republic."[100] Suddenly, even conservatives like Emmet Hughes, who had been a speechwriter for Dwight Eisenhower, began to bemoan the threat posed to the Great Society by the war in Vietnam.[101] How much more so liberals? "Who could have foreseen it?" opined the *New Republic.* "The Great Society exponent, the practitioner of common sense, compromise, and consensus, has become The War President—sworn to prevent at any cost one set of Vietnamese (unfriendly, we have guaranteed that) from overcoming other Vietnamese (who could not hold power without us)."[102]

A number of books published in 1966 reinforced the negative stereotypes that intellectuals had been attempting to instill in the reading public's mind since 1965. The kindest was by Philip Geyelin, *Lyndon Johnson and the World,* which portrayed the thirty-sixth president as a simple-minded idealist who, when his attempt to substitute the Great Society for armed intervention failed, resorted to the outworn shibboleths of the 1930s and 1940s. Geyelin quoted a White House aide: "You will search without success for any evidence of deep commitment or firm philosophy."[103] In January, Theodore Sorenson *(Kennedy)* and Arthur Schlesinger *(A Thousand Days)* published books lauding JFK and Camelot. There again was the incomparable Jack: handsome, witty, urbane, self-effacing, cool under pressure, inspiring.[104] There was Johnson, the supernumerary who accidentally and quite undeservedly became president. Later in the year, Rowland Evans and Robert Novak published their *Lyndon B. Johnson: The Exercise of Power.* Larry King reviewed the book: "It is all there: the hoohawing, indiscriminate profanity and compulsive flesh-pressing; LBJ's crying need to be loved by all and yet retain a drill sergeant's iron-fisted control; the little miracles and helpful deceits which form the foundation stone of Lyndon Johnson's career . . . They understand Johnson's troubled Jekyll-Hyde existence: parochial nose-pick politician on the one hand and frustrated national figure on the other." [105]

Feebly, ineptly, the White House tried to fight back. When columnist Joseph Kraft wrote that President Johnson couldn't hold and attract the most competent men from the "knowledge community" because he "uses them only for cosmetic purposes," the White House pointed to John Roche, the Brandeis University political scientist, and to LBJ's long-time relationship with novelist John Steinbeck. [106] LBJ was particularly bitter about the charge that his administration was devoid of first-rate brains. "He concluded our visit," Orville Freeman recorded in his diary, "by saying that it's alright if they said he couldn't speak without dripping tobacco juice on his shirtfront, but it was grossly unfair to say that he did not have intellectuals in his Administration." [107] Roche heaped scorn on what he termed "Highbrow Illiterates." "Mainly the New York artsy-craftsy set," he told columnist Jimmy Breslin, "they're in the *Partisan Review* and the *New York Review of Books* and publications like that. The West Side Jacobins, I call them. They intend to launch a revolution from Riverside Drive." [108] Johnson suggested to Arthur Krim that he persuade Hollywood to produce a picture based on *The Mission,* a memoir by one of the men with whom the president had flown in the Pacific. [109] When John Wayne approached the White House and Defense Department about making a patriotic movie on the war in Vietnam—ultimately *The Green Berets*—Valenti and Moyers convinced LBJ to approve government cooperation. "My own judgment is that Wayne's politics are wrong," Valenti told his boss, "but insofar as Vietnam is concerned, his views are right. If he made the picture he would be saying the things we want said." [110]

Johnson himself pled with literate Americans to look at both sides. "So when you hear these voices in the days to come, the men who exercise the right to dissent," he beseeched an Indiana crowd, "I hope you will ask yourselves the question: 'I just wonder why we don't talk about all the war? I just wonder why they are so anxious to get us to stop bombing to protect our men and they never say a word about stopping them from infiltrating and killing our men? Why don't we talk about both sides sitting down?' Your President is ready." [111]

Meanwhile, the administration's press continued to worsen. When Marvin Watson insisted on monitoring incoming and outgoing calls between reporters and members of the executive, the media, led by the imperious Joe Alsop, responded with a slew of denunciatory articles. "You can tell the President from me," Alsop wrote Moyers, "that the rather considerable debt that he owes me has been very ill repaid, in my opinion, by this kind of response to the independence which no self-respecting newspaperman can ever sacrifice. He may not think so, but he would be very ill served if all the members of my business were transformed into the type of waffling sycophant that appears to be the current White House ideal."[112] June and July saw a series of stories on LBJ's personal unpopularity. "Many Americans Seem to Dislike, Distrust President," ran a Tom Wicker Story in the *New York Times*.[113] Johnson read every negative article, every column. "It is awfully goddamn hard to have a foreign policy if they [the *New York Times*] don't approve of it," he grumbled to Eugene McCarthy. The government had done everything the pundits recommended, but they were never satisfied. "They started with . . . Diem you remember," he said. "He was corrupt and he ought to be killed so we killed him. We all got together and got a goddamned bunch of thugs and we went in and assassinated him. We have really had no political stability since then."[114] "They wanted Khanh gone so he left. They wanted a bombing pause, so they got a bombing pause. They wanted negotiations, so we offered unconditional negotiations." The president spent hours on the phone with publishers Walker Stone and Henry Luce trying to explain the administration's position on Vietnam.[115]

Johnson could not give the press and the American people the answers they wanted, and he knew it. "I cannot say 'when' and 'how' about Vietnam," he remarked to McGeorge Bundy. "Can you?" "No," Bundy replied.[116] "We have by-and-large blunted the communist military initiative," McNamara reported to Johnson following a fact-finding trip to Vietnam in early October. "My concern continues, however, in other respects. This is because I see no reasonable way to bring the war to an end soon. Enemy morale has not broken—he apparently has adjusted to our stopping his drive for military victory and has adopted a strategy of keeping us busy and waiting us out (A strategy of attriting our national will)."[117] "I think that I have failed you and I've failed the American people in my inability and my incapacity to bring about the united front that I would like to see in this country in connection with our objectives there [Vietnam]," Johnson subsequently told a group of representatives and senators. "I have been ineffective in communicating our position there."[118]

Following the extension of the bombing to petroleum storage sites around Hanoi and Haiphong, LBJ's approval rating shot up six points, but it quickly fell back to the high forties. When a September poll asked who the Democrats would run for president in the next election, an astounding 46 percent responded that they did not know.[119] There was too much consensus and too little decision, Emmet Hughes opined in *Newsweek*. What Richard Russell feared was coming to pass. The American people were psychologically and historically unprepared to fight an extended war of uncertain outcome, and Johnson's attempt to conduct one was endangering the whole containment regime that had been so painstakingly constructed in the United States. "When I was that young girl," Nancy Harjan remarked in an oral history of World War II, "I saw on the news films the Parisian people, with tears streaming down their faces, welcoming our GIs. They were doing what I wanted them to do. When the Holocaust survivors came out, I felt we were liberating them. When the GIs and the Russian soldiers met, they were all knights in shining armor, saving humanity."[120] What these

same Americans saw in 1966 was burning villages, corrupt Saigonese, and an inconclusive war for indeterminate ends.

IN THE CONTINUING SEARCH for compelling justifications for America's
war in Southeast Asia, LBJ, Dean Rusk, William Bundy, and other administration spokesmen repeatedly resorted to the issue of credibility—that if the
United States abandoned its SEATO ally, none of the other of the forty-odd
agreements the United States had signed with foreign powers would be worth
the paper they were printed on. What about reciprocity, Fulbright and other dissenters had asked? Why didn't the British and Canadians have troops in Vietnam? What about those most directly threatened by communist expansion?
Besides Korea and Australia, no other Asian power could claim a significant
combat presence in Vietnam. To undercut this criticism, the White House announced that the president would embark on a ten-day Asian tour highlighted
by a gathering in Manila of representatives from the SEATO nations. White
House advance men fanned out across the Pacific, and dozens of destroyers,
cruisers, and other warships moved into position along Air Force One's planned
line of flight.[121] The tour would include South Korea, Thailand, Australia,
Malaysia, and New Zealand. First stop was New Zealand. Lyndon, Lady Bird,
and their formidable entourage were greeted by Prime Minister Holyoake and a
Maori delegation. The chief of the Maori, "very fierce looking in appearance,"
stuck out his tongue, rolled his eyes, and commenced a frantic dance. He interrupted his dervish three times to lay ceremonial gifts at the president's feet. The
prime minister picked up each and handed it to LBJ, informing him that accepting the gifts meant he had come in peace. Then the whole group, men and
women, clad in all their aboriginal finery, began dancing and singing. One of
LBJ's staff could not help but notice that one of the troupe was humming the
Beatle's hit "I Want to Hold Your Hand" under his breath.[122]

From Christchurch, the presidential party proceeded to Australia. Seven
hundred thousand Aussies turned out to cheer the Johnson motorcade and
shower it with confetti. The president stopped his automobile more than a
dozen times to get out and shake hands. There were also antiwar hecklers; two
of them threw red and green paint bombs at the bubble-top limousine carrying
the guests of honor, causing it to stop momentarily. Once the windshield and
Secret Service agents were cleaned up, however, the motorcade proceeded to
Government House without further incident.[123] "You have given me a very colorful welcome," Johnson joked in his opening remarks. Later in the evening,
the president invited the press corps, who were having to stand outside in the
dark and cold, in for a drink. "Remember this," he quipped, "all this is off the
record—both what I say and how much you drink."[124]

While in Melbourne, LBJ took a side trip to visit Dame Mabel Brooke, who
had entertained him more than twenty years earlier during his Pacific tour. Back
in Canberra, the capital, the Johnsons had dinner with Premier Harold Holt
and his family, and the president briefly addressed a cabinet meeting at Parlia-

ment House. In his comments, he referred to how "bigoted" he had been concerning Asia and the Pacific early in his life. He had originally opposed statehood for Hawaii because, like most Americans, he was an Atlanticist, and regarded the people of the Pacific as somehow different. Then, during the war, he had traveled the area and seen that there was no fundamental difference. He had been appalled at how the Pacific theater had been given such short shrift in the allocation of war matériel. After a swipe at Harold Wilson and the British— "God forgive them for they know not what they do"—(Wilson had refused to commit troops and repeatedly expressed doubts about the war) he went on to praise steadfast allies, the sanctity of treaties, and foreign policies that made room for both guns and butter.[125]

From Australia, the presidential party proceeded to the Philippines and the Manila Conference. Behind the scenes, LBJ met with Philippine President Marcos and South Korean President Park. His message was consistent: "We must remain united at this conference; secondly, we must demonstrate our determination that we shall not pull out and that Hanoi cannot win; third, [we must] focus the world's attention on the problems of Asia." There was also a warning: "You cannot impose freedom on people who don't want it," he said, "but if they love liberty and freedom, we will stay with them and support them. If they don't want freedom the U.S. can look after itself and meet the threat at Honolulu."[126] He met with Ky and Thieu, telling the former that his forthcoming speech at a conference plenary session would be very important. As usual he had some advice: "Lean as far away as you can from the 'imperialist' Johnson, from the hard-liner Rusk, and that fellow with stars on his shoulders, Westmoreland. You just hold the Bible in your hand tomorrow. You be a man of good will; love your neighbor; but indicate, of course, that you will not take steps which tie your hands behind your back when they are still shooting."[127]

Following the last session of the Manila Conference, LBJ called Rostow, Moyers, Lodge, Clifford, and Westmoreland together. He wanted to make a surprise visit to Vietnam the next day. Westmoreland eventually agreed to arrange for American forces to receive Johnson around five o'clock in the afternoon at Cam Ranh Bay. There began one of the more frantic twenty-four hours in Westmoreland's career. He cabled his lieutenants that he wanted a major awards ceremony at Cam Ranh the following day and ordered them to round up America's finest soldiers from units throughout the country. The huge military complex became a beehive of activity. The First Cavalry Band was flown in by Caribou. Preparations were completed a bare thirty minutes before the president and his party arrived.[128]

Meanwhile, aboard Air Force One, LBJ had slipped into his "cowboy" outfit, as White House reporters referred to it: tan gabardine slacks and a matching zipper jacket bearing the gold seal of the president of the United States on the right breast. To minimize exposure to possible enemy fire, the presidential aircraft made a steep and rapid descent. On the ground, LBJ and Westmoreland boarded a jeep and stood in the back as it drove past the seven thousand American service men and women who had assembled for the occasion. Johnson reviewed the nine-hundred-man honor guard and then pinned medals on heroes. "A grateful nation . . . ," he repeated over and over.

Then it was time to address the troops. Among them were some of the wounded from the nearby base hospital. The soldiers were quiet, attentive. "I came here today for one good reason," Johnson began strongly, "simply because I could not come to this part of the world and not come to see you. I came here today for one good purpose: to tell you, and through you, tell every soldier, sailor, airman and marine in Vietnam how proud we are of what you are doing and how proud we are of the way you are doing it . . . I give you my pledge: We shall never let you down, nor your fighting comrades, nor the 125 million people of South Vietnam, nor the hundreds of millions of Asians who are counting on us." Then, his voice breaking, "We believe in you. We know you are going to get the job done. And soon, when peace can come to the world, we will receive you back in your homeland with open arms, with great pride, and with great thanks." [129]

After brief stops at the hospital and mess hall, the president and his party departed. They had been in South Vietnam a little more than two and a half hours. "It was obvious that he was speaking as much with his heart as with his mind," Farris Bryant, who was a member of the entourage, later recalled. He was "as emotional as I have ever seen him." [130]

Hubert Humphrey would later make an insightful observation concerning LBJ's empathy for those fighting and dying in Vietnam: "When you send men into battle, you know some are going to lose their lives. That is an awful part of political power. I don't suppose it is easy for anyone, but military people are at least trained in war. Most politicians are not. Yet the compassion breeds an irony: once an early order causes the first person to die, leaders feel required to justify what has been done. Thus, the compassion helps to create an insidious condition that leads, I fear, not to less killing, but to more." [131]

CHAPTER 35

BATTLING DR. STRANGELOVE

I

T HAD BEEN DEEMED TOO DANGEROUS FOR LADY BIRD to accompany Lyndon to Vietnam, so she stayed behind on the island of Corregidor, where Air Force One had touched down briefly to pay tribute to the heroes of the Bataan Death March. She had relished the Asian tour, however, because it provided a rare opportunity for her to spend time with her husband. She had given up much to be Lyndon Johnson's wife. So had her daughters, Lynda and Luci. When their father had suddenly become president, Luci was sixteen, a junior at National Cathedral School for Girls in Washington, D.C., and Lynda nineteen, a sophomore at the University of Texas at Austin. Reluctantly, Lynda agreed to transfer to George Washington University and move into the White House with the rest of the family. Among other things, Lady Bird had hoped that Lynda could help manage and calm the high-strung, sometimes melodramatic Luci. But the two girls were as different as sisters could be and were as often thorns to each other as comforts. "I love her. I just don't like her very much," Luci once remarked indiscreetly to a White House reporter.[1] Both young women felt abandoned by their parents and resented it. "I never understood why my mother had to leave and travel with my father," said Luci. "I remember one time [when I was a little girl] I clung to her skirts and tried to keep her from leaving. I screamed at her, 'You're not a real mother! A mother stays home!' "[2] Lynda also felt orphaned, but she reacted differently. She remembered going into her mother's room when she was gone, feeling her bedcovers and clothes and smelling her perfume to take some of the sting out of her loneliness. She typically reacted with accommodation. As a teenager, Lynda became a student of politics, reading the *Congressional Record* in her room after school, trying to impress her father with her knowledge of public affairs.

Luci perceived that one of her primary roles was to be "the pretty one." She was periodically obsessed with her weight.[3] After the family moved into the White House, Luci's search for an independent life continued. There was the conversion to Catholicism and then, at midnight on Christmas Eve 1965, the family announced from the ranch that she had become engaged to Patrick Nugent of Waukegan, Illinois. Nugent, a twenty-two-year-old senior at Marquette, had been introduced to Luci a year earlier at a Washington party by Beth Jenkins, Walter's daughter.[4] Everybody in the family believed that at nineteen, Luci was too young to get married and had tried to talk her out of it. But as usual, she had not listened. Lynda responded by striking up an affair with George Hamilton, the tan, dark-haired, strikingly handsome movie actor. The two first appeared together when a more glamorous Lynda appeared on George's arm at the Sugar Bowl game in New Orleans on January 2, 1966.[5] Both Lyndon, who called Hamilton "Charlie" behind his back, and Lady Bird worried initially that Lynda was out of her league and that the actor was just trying to take advantage of the first family for publicity purposes, but eventually, Lady Bird at least warmed to the relationship. "He was extremely good for her—he really brought her out as a woman," she observed in a 1997 interview.[6]

There was an undertone of competition in the Luci-Pat, Lynda-George relationships. When a Women's Wear Daily story placed all three Johnson women in their worst-dressed in America category, Luci blamed Lynda for being deliberately plain and frumpy. The older daughter responded by losing more weight and had George introduce her to the Hollywood hairdresser George Masters. He persuaded her to abandon the UT coed, puffed bouffant for a more relaxed hairstyle. After one subsequent capital soiree, the Washington Post described her as "resplendent in a white dress with dark hair down over her shoulders."[7]

Luci and Lynda frequently complained about life in the White House. "If I'm drinking a glass of milk at a party," Lynda told Newsweek, "it gets reported as milk punch and some nice WCTU lady will write me saying 'the sins of the flesh move upon you.' " "When my grades weren't so good, complete strangers scolded me," says Luci, "and when they got better and we sort of leaked the news about my B average, people said I was bragging." Lynda quipped, "Caesar's daughter must be above reproach." But as Lady Bird said, "They wear their bonds rather lightly."[8]

All three Johnson women seemed to enjoy preparations for Luci and Pat's August nuptials. The wedding was preceded by a week of parties. Lyndon struggled not to overwhelm. "All I'm going to do is put on a cutaway and walk down the aisle and pay the bills," he told reporters. But one thing the Johnson family never lacked was sentiment and affection. The president did nothing to hide how much he was going to miss his younger daughter. At lunch at the White House, journalist John Steele recorded a prewedding moment between father and his elder daughter. "Quietly Lynda Bird slipped through the room in a dressing gown, then appeared again attractively attired to kiss her father on the top of his head, hold his hand for a long moment. The two looked somewhat soulfully at one another."[9] The wedding ceremony was an hour-long extravaganza in the cavernous National Shrine of the Immaculate Conception. Seven hundred guests sweltered in the oppressive Washington heat. Both bride and maid of honor, Lynda, nearly fainted, but with some assistance they remained upright. Wedding party and guests retired to a White House reception featuring a wedding cake that stood eight feet tall and weighed three hundred pounds.[10]

Luci's wedding was a highlight in the Lyndon–Lady Bird relationship, but their marriage continued to be plagued with the roughness and misunderstanding that seemed always to characterize it. Two weeks after the wedding, Lady Bird returned from a shopping trip to New York. She found her husband at work in the Oval Office. On his desk was a small package. At first she thought it was for him; he would be fifty-eight on the morrow. But he gestured for her to open it. Inside was a large, obviously expensive diamond ring. Lady Bird had pretended to be content with the $2.50 Sears and Roebuck ring Dan Quill had bought for her on Lyndon's behalf so many years ago. "All these years I've taken a rather condescending view of women who wanted or needed diamonds," she wrote in her diary. "Now I find myself, at 53, proud to have that shiny rock, delighted to be told that I am cherished."[11] For his birthday, Lyndon received from Lady Bird an antique wooden seaman's chest, circa 1840, that had been owned by a German immigrant family. He was insulted. It was like giving your wife a toaster oven for her birthday. "If I live long enough I guess Lady Bird will get enough of these chests," he announced to the thirty-two guests who had gathered at the ranch for a birthday feast of barbeque and peach ice cream.[12] She was humiliated.

ALTHOUGH OUTWARDLY BUOYANT, Democratic leaders approached the midterm elections of 1966 with apprehension. "The American people are concerned about Vietnam," Orville Freeman recorded in his diary. "There is a dark void there, and they don't know exactly where we're going as a Nation . . . The same thing seems to be true about the economy. The President's obsession with it, with inflation, with what should be done about it, and the failure to act . . . and certainly these civil rights disturbances and riots everywhere and the whole white backlash problem is another where there is such doubt and indecision."[13]

Further contributing to Democratic gloom was a growing awareness that the president had grossly neglected the party and its machinery. Indeed, Johnson was proving to be one of America's least partisan presidents. "I hear rumors you were a politician," John Roche told LBJ, "but have no evidence of it."[14] Part of his conflict with Richard Daley had stemmed from Johnson's contempt for the patronage system. The Johnson administration featured a running feud between John Macy, LBJ's chief talent scout who was also head of the Civil Service Commission, and Jim Rowe. Without success, Rowe continually hounded Macy to recommend some good party loyalists for appointment to government office. In answer to one of Macy's polite but noncommittal responses, Rowe replied, "I am delighted . . . you are grateful for my words of wisdom and encouragement . . . However that ain't what I want! What I want are some Democrats appointed to something." And again, "Perhaps you can train some of those career men to run the political campaign in 1968."[15]

LBJ was driven by his search for excellence and expertise, as well as by his determination to be above reproach. "You know," he told Rowe, "I can only feel safe if I pick civil servants or military men, because their whole life has been under such complete scrutiny, they won't surprise me . . . You lawyers, you are not trustworthy, you have always got a client some way or other that's embarrassing."[16] Johnson's neglect of the Democratic National Committee was common knowledge. He did not consult it, use it, or even acknowledge it. One sign of his indifference was that he did not bother to remove John Bailey, a man for whom he had utter contempt, as national chairman.[17]

As the campaign season got under way, the Johnson administration discovered that the two-party system was alive and well. By 1966, the GOP was well on its way back to the center of political life in America. Heading this resurgence was a new, sleeker, more relaxed Richard Nixon. Since his 1960 presidential defeat and his loss in the 1962 California gubernatorial contest, Nixon seemed to have shed the insecurity and humorlessness that had plagued him. "Remember when the Democrats tried to run with LBJ?" Nixon asked a whooping throng of Republican loyalists. "Now they're trying to run away from him."[18]

The Kennedys could have cared less about the midterm elections; they had their sights set on 1968. On the war in Vietnam (the administration was too inflexible), on the Great Society (the administration was quitting too early), and on the plight of the cities (the administration was not doing enough), RFK worked to stake out an alternative position. But the "exquisitely modulated battle," as *Newsweek* termed it, between RFK and LBJ was having an immediate and detrimental impact.[19] Polls by both Gallup and Quayle taken in the first week in September indicated that Democrats favored Bobby 40 to 38 percent for the 1968 presidential nomination and independents preferred him by 38 to 24 percent. If the election were held then, Kennedy would beat George Romney easily by 55 to 39 percent, and LBJ would squeak by with 48 to 44 percent.[20] To many voters, the Democrats seemed disorganized and demoralized.

To campaign or not to campaign, that was the question facing the president as Democratic and Republican hopefuls hit the campaign trail in August. He sensed some ambivalence among Democrats about the attitude they should take toward the administration, and it created more than a little ambivalence in him. Nevertheless, in the last week in August he made a campaign swing through New York and New England, remembering fondly the tumultuous welcome he had received there during the 1964 campaign. Momentarily dispelling doom and gloom among Democratic strategists, he was greeted by large, enthusiastic crowds and seemed to be at his press-fleshing best. A week later, he traveled through Michigan and Ohio, ending up at the Fairfield County Fair Grounds in Lancaster, Ohio, where twenty-five thousand, including some two thousand high school band members from around Ohio, turned out.[21] Two weeks thence, Air Force One made visits to Idaho, Wyoming, and Colorado.

At all of his campaign stops, Johnson hammered away on the achievements of the Great Society. Inflation there was, but relative purchasing power continued to increase. Crime on the streets was a growing problem, but it had not reached epidemic proportions, nor was it exclusively an African American problem. The president condemned rioting and looting, pointing out that 99 percent of black Americans did, too.[22] He was particularly energized by a sight he had seen in Denver. On his way to a speaking engagement, his motorcade had driven through a nice, lower-middle-class neighborhood. With growing excitement, Johnson noted that the residents were black. Repeatedly, he stopped and got out of his car to walk and chat with them.[23] At a subsequent news conference at the ranch, he described what he had seen: "You drove through the places where you would expect to see the ghettoes in Denver and you saw modest homes. I said to some of my people that it looked very much like my mother's home in Austin, Texas, a three-bedroom little home with one bath, with a beautiful lawn, small, attractive, with flowers growing in the windows, well kept with great pride, and happy people living in it . . . It would have been difficult to believe that those were Negro homes, if you hadn't seen them standing there."[24]

From every quarter, the White House was advised that Vietnam was on the nation's collective mind and that voters wanted to see some light at the end of the tunnel. This, of course, was one of the major reasons LBJ undertook his whirlwind Asian tour in October. But at the end, all the American people could see when they looked ahead was continued darkness.[25]

Election day proved to be humbling, if not disastrous, for the Democrats. The GOP gained forty-seven seats in Congress, three in the Senate, eight governorships, and, perhaps most significant, over five hundred seats in state legislatures. Critics of the administration were elated.[26] Liberals predicted a revival of the Dixiecrat-conservative coalition. Some Democrats saw a silver lining, however. "It is, I think, a brand-new ball game," political activist Frank Mankiewicz wrote Bobby Kennedy after the elections. "In every contested election the young, attractive, more non-political candidate won. And the oldest, least attractive, most political candidate is LBJ."[27] Vietnam was not as important in explaining GOP gains, Arthur Schlesinger told reporters, as "the picture—true or false—which people have about President Johnson's character."[28] LBJ tried to put the best face on the outcome. Democratic margins had been reduced from 249 to 187 in the House and sixty-four to thirty-six in the Senate—still workable majorities. And though he did not say it, LBJ believed that some of the newly elected Republicans might be easier to get along with than some of his liberal fellow Democrats.[29]

IN DECEMBER 1966, BILL MOYERS LEFT the White House to become publisher of *Newsday*. A break had been in the offing since he first took the job as press secretary. At the time, Moyers had remarked to his wife, "This is the beginning of the end, because no man can serve two masters," meaning LBJ and the press.[30] Particularly when those two masters were so continually and vexatiously at odds. Johnson was dissatisfied with his relationship with the media and, increasingly, he tended to blame his press secretary. The White House press corps began to view Moyers less as a witty, informed, sincere individual who was doing his best to accommodate them than as the defender of the paranoid, arbitrary, dishonest man in the White House. In the summer of 1966 Moyers had gone to the hospital with a bleeding ulcer.

There were many former and current members of the Johnson entourage who did not like or trust Moyers. George Reedy and his assistant, Joe Laitin, detested him as a Johnny-come-lately, a bureaucratic imperialist, a trafficker in the ideas and influence of others. Jake Jacobsen, who worked in the White House for a time, felt that Moyers talked too much, and too frequently presumed to speak for the president. Everybody outside his own circle, especially his boss, believed that Moyers was too close to the Kennedys and too active on the Georgetown cocktail circuit. Then there was the war. By the late summer of 1966, Johnson's press secretary was beginning to question, both in house and out, the efficacy of the bombing of North Vietnam.[31] Moreover, he had been extremely upset about the growing power of Appointments Secretary Marvin Watson and especially the decision to censor the staff's contacts with journalists.

Still, Johnson was fond of Moyers and continued to regard him as immensely capable. There was a sense of inevitability in the relationship between the two men, an understanding that no one of Moyers's intellect and independence of mind could continue indefinitely in the press secretary's job. During the pressure and confusion leading up to the 1966 State of the Union address, Johnson and his protégé had had a falling out. Moyers had been intensely irritated with the way LBJ was treating Richard Goodwin, with his perfectionism and hypercriticism. When LBJ implied that Moyers was behind all of the anti-Watson stories then circulating, his aide had stalked out of the room and during the rest of the day had given Johnson a taste of his own deep-freeze medicine. Finally, at 1:30 in the morning, LBJ called him. "I had the feeling that you got angry this morning and kinda sulked all day long . . . puffed up like a powder pigeon," Johnson remarked. Moyers didn't deny it. The press secretary's job was hellacious, the president observed: "I don't believe you are constitutionally and physically and temperamentally and emotionally fitted. I know I am not . . . All I am trying to do is struggle and preserve for myself until my last heart beats a complete succumbing to their [journalists'] domination." But he realized, he said, that as press secretary, Moyers was inevitably part of the Fourth Estate. Did he want out, LBJ asked? "I find it an exciting job," Moyers replied. "I find it an unsatisfying job for the way I am built," the president observed. "A man like you or a man like me are never going to be satisfied by the press secretary job." "Anytime you want out," Johnson said, "I'll understand and help you find another position as long as you come to me first." Again he asked, "Is there any job you would rather have that you want to go to?" Moyers sighed, "No sir. There is not another job that I believe that I should do right now." Both men clearly understood the phrase "right now."[32] The very day Moyers left the White House, he agreed to lunch with Bobby Kennedy at Sans Souci. The next day the *Washington Star* ran a front-page picture of the two in rapt conversation. "Of course," John Roche observed, "after that nothing would ever convince Johnson that Moyers really hadn't been on the Kennedy payroll for years and years."[33]

THE NEW YEAR BEGAN WITH a brouhaba over the official portrait of the thirty-sixth president. LBJ had long admired the work of portraitist and western landscape painter Peter Hurd. As a result, the White House Historical Association had commissioned him to render the official portrait. As Hurd later put it, the president had "no idea of the obligations of a sitter to the artist." In the spring of 1966, LBJ viewed the preliminary work at the ranch and pronounced it "the ugliest thing I ever saw." He then sent Hurd a flock of White House photos to work from. The first week in January, the artist announced that he had lost interest in the project and was going to put his original work on public display at the Gallery of Fine Arts in Columbus, Ohio. LBJ incurred further derision from habitués of high culture when he indicated his preference for a sketch of him done by Norman Rockwell.[34] But LBJ was right. The Hurd portrait was flat and lifeless, although Johnson had no one to blame but himself.

DESPITE VIETNAM, HIS TROUBLES WITH THE PRESS, and GOP gains, LBJ's appetite for reform had not abated. As he prepared for his fourth State of the Union address, he was as determined as ever to forge ahead on the domestic front. Any other man might have been satisfied with the enormous progress made to date: since 1963 unemployment was down from 5.7 percent to 3.7 percent; industrial production was up by 25 percent; GNP had increased more than $100 billion, or 17 percent; real income was up by 14 percent; profits had grown by 36 percent; 4 million Americans had moved above the poverty line; 8 million disadvantaged children in seventeen thousand school districts were receiving aid under the Elementary and Secondary Education Act; 8 million more workers were covered by minimum wage; and never-before-provided federal health care was available to millions of disabled and elderly Americans.[35]

Shortly after Christmas, Joe Califano arrived at the ranch to go over the next year's program. For months, Johnson had been thinking about upgrading nursing homes. At the president's direction, Califano had put together a task force to make recommendations. LBJ's charge to the members had been memorable. As he described some of the conditions he had witnessed, his voice rose and he became more agitated, "Fire traps, rat traps, a disgrace . . . no one of you would let your mother near one." He invoked the Bible and the commandment to honor thy father and mother. "I want nursing homes that will be livable, happy places for people to serve out their old age, places where there will be a little joy for the elderly, but most of all places that take care of their special needs." There needed to be "flat floors, and grades, so that the wheelchairs can easily be used . . . And when you design toilets . . ."—at this point he leaned sideways on his left but-tock, put his elbow on the arm of his chair, took his right arm and hand, and strained to twist them as far behind himself as he could, and, grunting and jab-bing his hand behind his back, he continued—"make sure that you don't put the toilet paper rack way behind them so they have to wrench their back out of place or dislocate a shoulder or get a stiff neck in order to get their hands on the toilet paper."[36]

Califano suggested legislation requiring tobacco companies to reveal the tar and nicotine content of cigarettes on their packaging. LBJ was sympathetic but did not want to do anything further to alienate the tobacco states. His civil rights initiatives were doing enough. LBJ was enthusiastic about lowering the voting age to eighteen, but wanted to wait a year (he proposed a constitutional amend-ment to that effect in June 1968). He wanted a truth-in-lending bill, the presi-dent told his advisers. Earlier that year, Califano's son, Joe, had swallowed the contents of an aspirin bottle and had had to have his stomach pumped. "There ought to be a law that makes druggists use safe containers," LBJ declared on hearing of the accident. "There ought to be safety caps on those bottles so kids like little Joe can't open them." Thus was born the Child Safety Act, which Congress eventually passed in 1970.[37]

Johnson continued to believe that the answer to urban unrest—both rioting and everyday murders, muggings, drug use, and theft—was better housing, more education, jobs, and health care, but he also recognized that the public felt unsafe and wanted government to reaffirm its commitment to law and order. In addition, he believed that, in the long run, such a commitment was just as much in black America's interest, if not more, than white America's. He instructed Califano, Harry McPherson, and Ramsey Clark, then in the Justice Depart-ment, to come up with a recommendation that would demonstrate the admin-istration's support for law and order. "When I sent Harry McPherson an early draft of the message," Califano recalled, "I wrote, 'Please get mean and nasty be-fore you start work on it, since the President wants a tough anticrime mes-sage.' " The president instructed his subordinates to pay close attention to the title of the proposed legislation. They should be "godamned careful what you call these bills. Don't name them at midnight when you're tired and should be doing something like answering mail or returning calls. Do it in the morning. And then count to ten."[38] Califano liked "Safe Streets Act." Clark objected that the streets could never be made completely safe, not in a free society, and sug-gested "Crime Control Act." LBJ settled on "the Safe Streets and Crime Con-trol Act." He understood that policing the nation was a function of local and state governments. He had envisioned federal grants to improve existing police and criminal justice systems, to encourage the development of innovative law enforcement programs, and to fund modern crime labs and police academies. He also intended to ask Congress for a gun control law and more money to fight drugs through prevention and rehabilitation.

To balance the Safe Streets Act and to put law-and-order zealots on notice that they could not flout civil liberties, Johnson planned to submit a Right of Privacy Act that would ban all wiretapping and electronic eavesdropping, except in national security cases, and even then to prohibit the use of evidence gathered in this manner in court. Writing in the *New York Times* near the end of the Johnson administration, journalist Sidney Zion observed that LBJ's record on civil liberties was perhaps the best of any twentieth-century president. He did not impose censorship in Vietnam. In the face of urban rioting and subversive activities by groups like the Black Panthers and the Weather Underground, he sought no exceptional authority for the federal government, no suspension of rights.[39] Indeed, he seemed at times fanatical about the subject. In May 1966, Missouri Democratic Senator Edward Long, chair of a subcommittee investigating electronic eavesdropping, had singled out the IRS and accused its director, Sheldon Cohen, of trampling on the rights of taxpayers. LBJ subsequently demanded an explanation. Cohen tried to defend electronic snooping to catch tax evaders and perpetrators of fraud. What the IRS was doing, he said, was not wrong "in the eyes of the law or of reasonable people." Johnson disagreed. "Sheldon—Stop it all at once," he scribbled on Cohen's memo, "and this is final—no microphones—taps or any other hidden devices, legal or illegal, if you are going to work for me."[40]

Charged with drafting a White House position paper on wiretapping, Joe Califano and Lee White suggested three alternatives: unlimited official wiretapping, a complete ban on all taps, and a middle ground permitting wiretapping under stringent controls. Next to the complete ban, LBJ scribbled, "I like this best."[41] At first glance, this Johnsonian commitment to civil liberties seemed to go against the grain. Here was a man who had based his political life and effectiveness on information gathering, knowing more about an issue and the men who would decide it than anyone else. He had a Dictabelt system installed on his phones so that at his signal his secretaries could record incoming and outgoing calls. He read voraciously the "raw files" J. Edgar Hoover sent over. He relied on the Bureau to run careful background checks on individuals he proposed to nominate to federal office. According to Jim Jones, the young White House aide who sat at LBJ's right hand from late 1967 thorough 1969, "Homosexuality, run-ins with the law, and habitual drunkenness were red flags for the president."[42] But at the same time, he thought Hoover "weird" for collecting the data. There is no evidence that LBJ ever used personal information to blackmail; he liked to know an individual's weaknesses so that he could predict his or her actions and to decide whether the person could be depended on, but he did not blackmail. "Johnson was an excessive man in many ways," Harry McPherson observed, "but he had a sense of proportion about the government and the governed and about the Congress and Executive; he was prudent."[43]

By late 1967, LBJ was under pressure from law-and-order advocates in Congress to have the Justice Department actively prosecute urban rioters and violent antiwar demonstrators, using various communist control statutes if necessary. In January 1968, the president began to badger Ramsey Clark to refer cases to the Subversive Activities Control Board, a congressionally created watchdog agency. But Johnson did so not out of a lack of respect for civil liberties, but because Everett Dirksen, whose support LBJ needed to pass the 1968 civil rights bill, had assumed control of the committee overseeing the board and needed some action for publicity purposes.[44] There was another reason for Johnson's high profile on civil liberties; it would show him in sharp and favorable contrast to Bobby Kennedy. In late 1966, following reports that the FBI had used electronic surveillance to arrest and charge defendants in criminal cases (including Bobby Baker), Ramsey Clark, also a lion on civil liberties, ordered an investigation that revealed that the FBI had indeed engaged in widespread eavesdropping. When news of the investigation leaked to the press, Hoover responded by declaring that his boss, then Attorney General Robert Kennedy, had ordered the wiretaps. Bobby denied that he had ever done anything other than authorize electronic eavesdropping in national security cases, but the fat was in the fire. It was in response to this brouhaha that Congressman Edward Long's committee began its work. Bill Moyers confided to Richard Goodwin of Long, "He is out to get Bobby. Johnson is egging him on."[45]

LBJ and his advisers picked the evening of January 10, 1967, for the State of the Union address. Johnson did not want to conflict with Ev Dirksen's birthday party scheduled for the 11th and he did not want to shoulder aside popular television programs. "I don't want millions of people looking at me for an hour and thinking, 'This is the big-eared son of a bitch that knocked my favorite program off the air,' " he told Califano.[46] Still, the 10th turned out to be an unfortunate choice. "On the Hill today there had been a death [the aged Congressman John E. Fogarty of Rhode Island] and an expulsion," Lady Bird recorded in her diary. "Adam Clayton Powell had been expelled from the House [for misuse of public funds and other offenses] in an atmosphere tense with violence and hatred."[47]

Observers noted a different LBJ who strode into the House chamber that January evening. There was a diffident, almost apologetic smile on his face. His tone was subdued, his rhetoric measured. He admitted that sundry "mistakes" and "errors" marred his leadership. He alluded to the need sometime in the future for a tax increase. He promised safer streets, maintenance rather than extension of most Great Society programs, and, as in 1966, emphasis on quality of life issues. Johnson mentioned civil rights only briefly. The theme was not what the federal government was going to do for America, but what could be achieved in partnership with state and local government.[48] James Reston hailed the speech as the beginning of a new and creative federalism. In a laudatory column entitled "Johnson and the Age of Reform," Reston wrote, "This is not a conservative but a radical program. He is not trying to follow but to transform the New Deal. He is not proposing to console the poor in their poverty but to give them the means of lifting themselves out of poverty. He is not using Federal funds to keep them where they are or to impose Federal control over the states and cities, but to finance the passage of the poor into useful, effective jobs, and create new partnerships between Washington and the state capitals and the cities and other political centers in the world."[49] Johnson was in fact saying to the South Vietnamese, to African Americans, to the white middle class, to labor, to management that he had carried forward and modernized the Roosveltian vision; he had put in place the tools with which to achieve the goal of a just, peaceful, diverse, and democratic society. Now it was up to the people to determine whether they had the will and wisdom to sustain that vision.

On the war itself, the president offered little solace. "I wish I could report to you that the conflict is almost over," he said. "This I cannot do. We face more cost, more loss, and more agony. For the end is not yet. I cannot promise you that it will come this year—or come next year." America and its allies would prove equal to the task, however. Significantly, Johnson did not cite the cold war as justification, did not pitch the battle in terms of a cataclysmic clash between the good of capitalism and democracy and the evil of communism and totalitarianism. "One result of our stand in Vietnam is already clear," he declared. "It is this: The peoples of Asia now know that the door to independence is not going to be slammed shut. They know that it is possible for them to choose their own national destinies—without coercion."[50] The subtle listener would notice the shift to national self-determination rather than simple anticommunism as a justification for the war and conclude that the president was laying the groundwork for public acceptance of a coalition government in South Vietnam, a government that would include the National Liberation Front, communists and noncommunists alike. Indeed, starting in 1966, LBJ had begun talking more in terms of moderation versus extremism than communism versus freedom. America's policy of "patience and daring, of commonsense and vision, of the wise use of power and its wise restraint when needs be," he told a Democratic gathering in Des Moines, "has made possible a rebirth of moderation and commonsense, not just in the United States but throughout all the continents of the world. In the last few years, in country after country, on continent after continent, extremist leaders have suffered one defeat after another. They have been replaced by men of moderation."[51]

Two weeks later, the United States endured its first manned space tragedy. Air Force Lieutenant Colonel Virgil I. Grissom, Navy Lieutenant Commander Roger B. Chaffee, and Air Force Colonel Edward H. White II were burned to death when a ball of flame engulfed their *Apollo I* spacecraft at Cape Kennedy as they rehearsed one of the steps designed to take man to the moon. Grissom, Chaffee, and White were buried on a clear wintry day in Arlington Cemetery. Both Lyndon and Lady Bird attended the service. One photograph showed the president bent almost double shaking the white-gloved hand of eight-year-old Shelly Chaffee.[52] When Lady Bird stopped to offer condolences to White's widow, the young mother pulled her down and said, "Please tell the President that Ed loved him. Now will you remember to tell him that?"[53]

• • •

By 1967, the war in Vietnam was Lyndon Johnson's principal preoccupation, not merely because American lives and treasure were bleeding out all over that land, but because the course of the war would have a major impact on the future of domestic reform and especially the Second Reconstruction. If the war could not be won, it would have to be managed in a way that kept the conservative coalition from joining hands with disgruntled liberals in gutting the administration's domestic programs and foreign aid. As 1967 began, some commentators suggested that the Johnson administration was having to fight two wars: one in Vietnam against the North Vietnamese Army and Vietcong and one at home against opponents of the war. Johnson continued to believe that he could not withdraw from Vietnam over the objections of the hawks, and he could not take the land war to North Vietnam and interdict Soviet and Chinese supply lines running into the enemy's heartland, both because that would risk a wider war and because it would completely alienate the doves. There was another possibility: that hawks and doves, both convinced that the war could not be won or that the administration was unwilling to do what was necessary to win it, would join forces and compel American withdrawal from Southeast Asia. They would in fact unite behind the neoconservative vision of Robert Taft and Herbert Hoover in which the United States would forswear a military presence on the Asian mainland and be content for its defense on a string of island bases stretching from Japan to the Philippines.

In truth, by 1967 LBJ was willing to accept the communization of Indochina by peaceful means. "He is prepared for a cease fire and phased withdrawal of all combatants in Vietnam," James Reston, a not uncritical observer of the president, noted in the *New York Times*. "He is willing to dismantle American bases in that peninsula; he is in favor of neutralization of all Southeast Asia, and he is prepared to let the peoples of South and North Vietnam decide their own political future even if this means a coalition with the Communists."[54] What Johnson could not permit, under any circumstances, was the overthrow of the Saigon regime by force of arms. To do so would threaten the entire containment regime so painstakingly built by Dean Acheson and the Wise Men in the post–World War II era. If America chose to abandon rather than modify containment, it would soon find itself alone in a dangerous world. But for a variety of reasons, Hanoi, if not the NLF, proved unwilling to renounce the military option and to consider participating in a political coalition with the Saigon regime. For fear of destroying South Vietnam's will to war and alienating the hawks forever, LBJ could not speak openly of neutralization. So Bill Fulbright, Walter Lippmann, and George McGovern did not believe that he truly did want to turn the war over to the Vietnamese and let matters take their course. To his mind, LBJ would have to continue to steer a middle course between appeasement and Armageddon until either the communists and Saigon agreed to a coalition government, or Hanoi's will to war evaporated, or a hawk-dove, neo-isolationist consensus materialized. In the meantime, thousands of young men, white and yellow, were fighting and dying, thousands of civilians were being incinerated,

maimed, and rendered homeless. "Now is indeed 'the Valley of the Black Pig,' "
Lady Bird recorded in her diary on January 5. "A miasma of trouble hangs over
everything . . . It is unbearably hard to fight a limited war."[55]

AS 1966 CAME TO A CLOSE, heavy fighting in Vietnam was increasingly
concentrated in I Corps, the northernmost part of South Vietnam that bordered
on the demilitarized zone (DMZ). North Vietnamese main force units had
massed just north of the border, periodically thrusting southward to isolate and
decimate ARVN positions. U.S. marines and Special Forces engaged the enemy,
inflicting heavy losses, but were frustrated by their inability to strike across the
border into North Vietnam and Laos. So frustrated, in fact, that General Westmoreland's command began to develop plans for an antivehicular, antiperson-
nel "barrier" to be built along the southern edge of the DMZ extending into
Laos. The barrier would consist of mine fields, concertina wire fences, sensing
devices, foot patrols, air-mobile troops, and constant air reconnaissance.[56]
Meanwhile, the fighting on the ground continued. The first week in October,
American casualties had soared to a record 142 killed and 825 wounded as
marines attempted to clear units of North Vietnam's crack 324B Divisions from
the "Rockpile," a rugged, seven-hundred-foot-high outcropping that dominated the main valley approaches to northern South Vietnam. A journalist embedded with the Americans reported, "As we thread our way along the ridgeline
between the two hills, I notice a few bone fragments on the trail. Then dried,
bloodstained Marine flak jackets and fatigues . . . we pass a skull on a stake at the
side of the trail. A few yards further a crudely penned note on a branch says in
English: 'We come back kill marines.' "[57]

On the other side of the country, the Vietcong headquartered in War Zone C,
a tangled jungle tract in South Vietnam's Tay Ninh province near the Cambodian border, continued to set up roadblocks, terrorize villagers, and operate a sophisticated system of tax collection. "We fight 'em, we pull back, we regroup,
and we go back and fight 'em again," observed Corporal Robert Lee Cotton of
the 101st Airborne. "We get soft, and then we go jump off again for five or six
days and kill 300, maybe 400 VC, and then we come back and sit on the hill for
another month. I can't say whether I'm for this war or not. I can't say whether
we should be here or not. But I will say this: since we are here, we can't leave."[58]
Lyndon Johnson could not have put it better.

SOME THREE WEEKS FOLLOWING the midterm elections, James Reston
observed to Bob Komer that if the president did not settle Vietnam by the end of
1967, "the ensuing ruckus will tear the country apart."[59] Similar feelings pervaded the foreign policy establishment. "The time is ripe" for negotiations, Bill
Bundy, assistant secretary of state for East Asian Affairs, advised Rusk just before
the New Year. The American people were not prepared to stay in South Vietnam indefinitely. At some point, the citizens of that putative nation were going
to have to pull their socks up and admit the NLF/VC to the electoral process. In

terms of both political survival and ideological consistency, it was in the Johnson administration's interests to see this happen. The task ahead, therefore, was to begin talks with the enemy—sure to be protracted—while South Vietnam grew stronger politically and militarily until at some point, hopefully before the end of 1967, it would be safe to involve the NLF/VC in the political life of the nation. The bombing of the North would continue but under close restraint. "If we are to pursue a serious negotiating track on a 'package deal' basis," Bundy concluded, "we simply must accept that we will not hit politically sensitive targets, and specifically the Hanoi and Haiphong areas." [60]

American officials later tallied as many as two thousand attempts to initiate peace talks between 1965 and 1967. Some, obviously, were taken far more seriously in Washington than others, and all were tied up with decisions concerning the bombing of the North. Lyndon Johnson rarely had a conversation with an individual—and he had thousands of them—without an ulterior motive. He was determined to convince those with reservations about the war that he was going the last mile to secure a negotiated settlement and those who were committed to the struggle that he would never submit to a "dishonorable" peace. He would continue to bomb, but he wanted to show the doves that he was the image of restraint, that he would do nothing to precipitate a "wider war."

At the same time, Johnson worked to prevent a revolt within his own military, which was having to fight a war knowing that it had the power to destroy the enemy but could not use it. In a November 1966 conversation with McNamara, LBJ outlined the position he would take on bombing: "I think if we're causing 'em damage and they're hurtin' but we haven't got their children's hospitals afire and so forth, I think Moscow can say to Hanoi, 'Goddamnit, this thing is getting awfully costly on you and on us and on everybody else. Let's try to find an answer here' . . . I think that this pressure must be as steady but—this looks like a contradiction but I don't want it to be—steady but as undramatic as we can make it." [61]

Johnson exhausted his advisers with endless conversations and meetings, demanding that both supporters of the bombing campaign and advocates for negotiations defend their positions. To those internal opponents of bombing, he played the hawk, and to the generals he played the dove. In so doing he hoped to squeeze every personal prejudice and bureaucratic interest out of them. He hoped that negotiations would succeed, that the enemy would weary of the war to the point of, if not surrendering, then agreeing to a mutual North Vietnamese—U.S. withdrawal from the South followed by free elections. Johnson believed that under the circumstances, given all of the factors that needed to be taken into consideration, he was doing the best he could. The casualties deeply distressed him, but increasingly he found the spiritual means to deal with the anguish and guilt. What infuriated him, at times unbalanced him, was the mounting criticism from liberals whose idealism had in no small part been responsible for the war and who now seemed to be determined to burn down the barn to get rid of the rats. Harry McPherson later recalled that this friend, Pat

Moynihan, often spoke of Vietnam as being " 'our war,' meaning the war of the liberal intellectuals really, because they were the ones who were most upset over the Eisenhower-Dulles massive retaliation policy. They were the ones who called for a capacity to meet limited wars and keep them limited. They were the ones who wanted the helicopters and the Green Berets, who thought that by a combination of this skillfully applied military power and economic resources and a commitment to political democracy, that we would settle just about any problem anywhere in the world." [62] Johnson truly believed that in Vietnam he was sustaining the legacy bequeathed him by his predecessor, the darling of his liberal critics. "I've tried my best to play fair with Jack Kennedy," he told Larry O'Brien in 1967. "I think I have; my conscience is very, very clear on that point and I think on Vietnam that he's right where I am and I'm carrying out his policy." [63]

The first week in January, Walt Rostow speculated that the North Vietnamese wanted "to get out of the war but don't know how." North Vietnamese Premier Pham Van Dong and his colleagues could not openly negotiate with Washington. To do so would risk a split within the communist Lao Dong Party and alienation of Beijing. The communists in Hanoi would have to have before them the minimum terms for a face-saving settlement before negotiations were acknowledged. He suggested direct communication between the president and Ho Chi Minh, either outlining the terms of such a minimum arrangement or setting up top-secret, face-to-face talks, or both. [64] Johnson agreed to a strategy whereby in a letter to Ho, he would propose that the United States agree to an immediate halt to the bombing and a freeze on the buildup of military personnel in the South, in return for a commitment from Hanoi to halt NVA infiltration into the South. At the same time, through a variety of channels, the administration tried to signal Hanoi what an acceptable final settlement would look like. "Thus far the greatest unanswered question," he told Mike Mansfield, "is whether they are prepared to see the third of their four points [unification of the country] settled by free, democratic elections in the South rather than by force." [65]

At the close of January, the beginning of the Vietnamese New Year, or Tet, Johnson authorized a four-day bombing halt and, through intermediaries in Moscow, sent a letter to Ho offering an indefinite suspension of the bombing and troop freeze in return for the closing of the Ho Chi Minh trail. After some delay, the North Vietnamese representative rejected the notion of placing conditions on a bombing halt. [66] At the same time, Washington took advantage of a meeting between British Prime Minister Harold Wilson and Alexey Kosygin in London to send a different message. If Hanoi would secretly agree to respond after a short period of time to an American bombing halt and troop freeze by de-escalating the war, the United States would agree to a "unilateral halt and freeze." As a sign of good faith, the Tet bombing suspension was extended. [67] In essence, the Johnson administration was pursuing the same tactic Kennedy had employed during the Cuban Missile Crisis, offering a hard and a soft choice to the enemy simultaneously. But then, LBJ and his advisers got cold feet. The White House communicated through Kosygin and Wilson that if Hanoi accepted its soft proposal, it would have to allow the U.S. mission to announce that the communists were winding down the war and there would have to be instantaneous proof that this was indeed happening. "We will take whatever actions we can to verify it and to observe it by land, sea, air, tunnel, and everything else," Johnson told McNamara, "that they just be sure they close down and do not one damn thing on infiltrating," and this "within a period of very minimum necessary hours."[68] Wilson, who did not know of the direct, harder offer Washington had made to Hanoi, pled with Johnson to relent, but he would not.[69] On January 12, without waiting for a reply from Hanoi, the president ordered a resumption of the bombing.

The degree to which Hanoi was seriously considering negotiations is a matter of speculation. "Pham Van Dong, chief figure in the so-called moderate clique, firmly believes that the war is going so badly for the North Vietnamese that if it is not ended in a matter of months, North Vietnam would need massive Chinese intervention," the CIA reported. However, he and his associates feared Chinese occupation almost as much as American.[70] Whatever the state of the DRV's mind, it was still not master of its own ship. From 1965 through 1968, Beijing opposed any and every attempt at a negotiated settlement. As one peace initiative after another popped up on the radar screen, China pressured its tiny neighbor not to compromise. If cajoling were not enough, Beijing would threaten a cutoff of aid and even military occupation. The war in Vietnam, Mao and Zhou Enlai perceived, could do nothing but improve China's international position. If successful, it would vindicate the concept of "wars of national liberation." The conflict was tying down American forces and sapping its will, thus giving a fillip to other liberation movements. The war could also prevent the Soviet Union from turning the international communist movement into some kind of revisionist compromise with the West. Finally, Beijing feared another Geneva Conference where it would once again be relegated to a secondary position behind the traditional great powers.[71]

The Russians continued to prefer a cessation of hostilities in Vietnam, but they had to be very careful lest the Chinese get wind of any effort they might make to mediate peace between Hanoi and Washington. Mao could blame anything less than total victory on the cowardly revisionists in Moscow, thus discrediting them with those parts of the world still struggling to throw off the bonds of colonialism.[72] In addition, if the Soviets were not careful, Kosygin and his colleagues believed, they would inadvertently turn North Vietnam into a communist Chinese colony. During their meeting, Kosygin had told Harold Wilson that 3 million Chinese soldiers were poised to invade North Vietnam if it showed any weakness in the struggle with the imperialists.[73] Neither Hanoi nor Moscow wanted another Geneva Conference because, especially after the Cultural Revolution got under way, neither nation wanted communist China involved in any peace negotiations.[74]

On the 15th Ho officially responded to LBJ's letter: "The government of the United States must stop the bombing, definitively and unconditionally, and all other acts of war against the Democratic Republic of Vietnam, withdraw from South Vietnam all its troops and those of its satellites, recognize the National Liberation Front of South Vietnam and allow the people of Vietnam to settle their problems by themselves."[75] There would be no negotiations.

Suddenly, Johnson was consumed with anxiety lest both doves and history view him as inflexible, uncompromising, and deceitful. "I think it is extremely important that you not be put in the position of torpedoing peace again," Mc-Namara advised his boss. "And this is just exactly what Wilson would try to do to bring glory to himself. He had it all made, and you screwed it up."[76] LBJ instructed McNamara to draft a cable to Wilson praising him for his efforts in behalf of peace and reiterating that the United States would negotiate anytime, anywhere. "I think we ought to try to write a wire, and when Fulbright thinks he's got you and getting ready to railroad you and sends you right to jail, you can read this wire and he'll say, 'I'll be damned, you did all a human could.' " To Wilson, they should say, " 'I think you ought to pursue this, because you've done a noble job here, and I'm going to say so to the world, and I think that every freedom-loving person will admire it.' And let's just play this one for the record. And you be thinking all these things that we stuff up his bottom good and let him dilate before we shoot in the second one."[77]

It was all to no avail. Wilson subsequently issued a statement saying in effect that peace had been at hand but Washington had spoiled things by prematurely resuming the bombing.

With the collapse of Sunflower, as the early 1967 peace initiative was code-named, the foreign policy team's attention switched to the bombing, surely the most controversial and most studied aspect of the entire Vietnam War. As Rostow had put it in early January, "If we do not get a diplomatic breakthrough in the next three weeks or so, it probably means that they plan to sweat us out down to the election of 1968."[78] Westmoreland, General Wheeler, and the JCS continued to argue that any and all bombing was good. "The air campaign directed against North Vietnam is an essential element of our strategy for achieving U.S. objectives in Southeast Asia," U. S. Grant Sharp cabled Wheeler. Indeed, he insisted the bombing had provided the "balance of power" that had kept the enemy from gobbling up large chunks of I and II Corps. U.S. and ARVN troops were outnumbered by NVA units operating just north of the DMZ. "A stand-down of air operations against enemy forces in or within supporting distance of the DMZ for even the shortest period of time would create the gravest of risks to the security of friendly force."[79] At his meeting with Johnson at the ranch in August, Westmoreland pled with the president at a minimum not to stop the bombing of supply lines and troop concentrations in the southern panhandle of North Vietnam from the DMZ to Vinh.[80]

In late 1966, LBJ confided to several of his cabinet members that Fritz Hollings, newly elected senator from South Carolina, had taken a trip to Vietnam and then come in to see him. "He had been out in Vietnam," Orville Free-man remembered LBJ saying, "had talked to some general who had told him the war would be won in a week if there was more bombing and that if Johnson would only give the go-ahead the whole matter would be taken care of." [81] From the other side, Averell Harriman and his team, supported by Arthur Goldberg at the UN, pressed continually for one more bombing halt to jump-start peace talks. Statistics and world opinion were on Harriman and Goldberg's side. Studies by both the CIA and Defense Intelligence Agency indicated that the bombing had destroyed much of the economic and industrial infrastructure of North Vietnam but that it was having little or no effect on the war. Moreover, "There is no concrete evidence that the air strikes have significantly weakened popular morale." [82] "There is no evidence that any significant portion of the pop-ulation blames the Hanoi regime for the bombing," Westmoreland's intelli-gence branch reported to him. "Instead, US 'imperialism' is the focus of hatred." [83]

On December 21, 1966, the *New York Times* began publishing the first of fif-teen dispatches from North Vietnam by Assistant Managing Editor Harrison E. Salisbury. His vivid reports detailed the suffering the bombing was causing in the North; in addition to those civilians killed and maimed by the air war, thou-sands were homeless and suffering from malnutrition. [84] Just before Christmas, LBJ declared the area in and around Hanoi-Haiphong off-limits to American attack aircraft. His decision probably had more to do with public opinion than a desire to get negotiations on track. "We were just starting to put some real pres-sure on Hanoi," Sharp complained to Wheeler. "Our air strikes on the rail yard and the vehicle depot were hitting the enemy where it was beginning to hurt. Then, Hanoi complains that we have killed a few civilians, hoping that they would get a favorable reaction. And they did, more than they could have hoped for . . . Let's roll up our sleeves and get on with this war." [85]

Beginning in the fall of 1966, McNamara argued that the conflict would be won or lost in the South. He pressed not only for a timely end to the bombing but a ceiling on U.S. troop levels and a shift of responsibility for the fighting to ARVN. McNamara was undoubtedly correct; if the United States did not want to turn South Vietnam into a colony or the fifty-first state, the South Viet-namese would have to assume responsibility for their own fate. But as of late 1966 and early 1967, they were both unable and unwilling to do so. Saigon and environs were just starting down the long road to democracy—elections would not be held until August 1967—and the American decision to assume control of the fighting was undercutting any move the South Vietnamese might make to-ward taking the war into their own hands. From 1965 through 1967, South Vietnamese and U.S. aircraft dropped more than a million tons of bombs on South Vietnam, more than twice the tonnage dumped on the North. American fighter bombers staged retaliatory raids against villages suspected of harboring Vietcong. Entire areas of Vietnam were designated Free Fire Zones that could be pulverized indiscriminately. The expansion of the war drove an estimated 4 million South Vietnamese, 25 percent of the population, from their native villages. Some drifted into the already teeming cities; others settled in squalid refugee camps. Washington provided $30 million a year to care for victims of the war, but corruption drained most of this away before it reached the intended recipients. Thus, a large portion of the population was left rootless and hostile, a fertile breeding ground for the Vietcong.

At the same time, what went on north of the DMZ in late 1966 and 1967 was crucial to the course of the war. North Vietnamese main force units were tying down large numbers of U.S. and ARVN troops in I Corps. The casualties they inflicted contributed to growing antiwar sentiment in the United States. Hanoi's ability to supply its troops and the Vietcong was crucial to the war effort. That ability in turn depended on a continuing flow of supplies from the two communist superpowers. Rostow's World War II analogy was absurdly wide of the mark. There were no Axis superpowers immune from Allied attack sitting on Germany's flanks ready and willing to resupply Hitler's forces, as there were in Southeast Asia. As Clark Clifford remarked in a meeting with the president and Maxwell Taylor, "As long as the supplies continue to reach the troops in the South coming in from Laos, over the Northeast railway, through Haiphong Harbor, and down from Cambodia we can't get the war over. As long as the faucets are on, we cannot reach our objective."[86]

There was another option. The United States could bomb the system of dikes the North Vietnamese had so laboriously built up over the years to control flooding in the Red River Delta. In 1967 the delta area and the surrounding plain where the dike system was concentrated contained 9 million people. Eighty percent of the rice grown in North Vietnam was artificially irrigated through the man-made system of waterways.[87] Bombing the dikes would destroy one of the enemy's principal sources of food. But the specter of thousands of drowned and starving civilians prevented the Johnson administration from ever seriously considering such a move.

Attacking Chinese supply lines and cutting the Soviets off by blockading Haiphong harbor also continued to be unattractive courses of action. The CIA advised the White House that "the Soviets would not enter the war directly unless American forces sought to physically occupy North Vietnam, but that Soviet convoy commanders had orders to shoot their way through any blockade."[88] Besides this, there was the whole issue of détente. NATO was still the bedrock of American foreign and defense policy, and prevention of an East-West confrontation in Europe was priority number one. Washington's perception was that Moscow would have liked to have a compromise settlement of the war in Vietnam. Johnson's advisers speculated that the Russians secretly hoped that a continued American military presence south of the seventeenth parallel would act as a counterweight to the expansionist Chinese.[89] Why risk a confrontation with a blockade?

Communist China continued to be a dangerous enigma. By the opening weeks of 1967, the Cultural Revolution showed signs of running out of control.

"From Mukden to Canton," *Newsweek* reported, "the Red Guards marched and countermarched; sound trucks rolled through the streets spitting charge and counter charge; the airwaves rang with threats, cajolery and baleful maledictions; and on every city wall the battle of the posters raged on." Trains all but ceased to run on schedule. Production at China's huge Taching oil field, in Manchuria, dropped sharply when ten thousand student workers left for Beijing.[90] Inevitably, the denunciations and humiliations, and ultimately the violence against intellectuals, bureaucrats, and even army officers, produced a backlash. Workers walked off their jobs in protest, and rural militias formed to fight the Red Guard. Mao, as one observer pointed out, despite his brilliance, was essentially a provincial. He had been out of China only twice, both times to the Soviet Union. What he seemed to want was perpetual revolution, which had as its principal goal his own glorification.[91]

What did the Cultural Revolution mean for the war in Vietnam? Why not take advantage of communist China's distraction to press the war more vigorously in the north, even to the point of bombing Chinese supply lines? Still too risky. China might be weakened by its internal upheaval, the Johnson administration concluded, but it remained a military giant with a huge land army and nuclear weapons. Its very vulnerability made it dangerous. As all autocratic regime leaders did when threatened internally, Mao and his colleagues blamed outside forces for their domestic problems. Indeed, in an interview with journalist Simon Malley, Zhou Enlai insisted that there existed a tacit but increasingly strong antirevolutionary alliance between the United States and the Soviet Union and that war between the People's Republic and those two powers was probably inevitable.[92] Even such an ardent advocate of bombing as Walt Rostow thought that it was far too risky to try to "close the funnel," that is, blockade the North Vietnamese coast and bomb Chinese supply lines.[93] Johnson continued to be haunted by the specter of a stray bomb that would escalate into a nuclear confrontation. Lynda would come in from a date and find him still up, he told senators and representatives at a congressional briefing. " 'Daddy, you look like you're twenty years older. What's the matter?' And I said: 'Well, we may wake up in World War III. Now, just sit down here and I'll give you a little lesson in American history. Our planes are going into Hanoi and Haiphong tonight. And when they get in that harbor, that port, why some old Texas boy will be in the lead bomber and drop one right down a Russian smokestack. And we know what happened to the battleship *Maine,* the *Lusitania,* and a few things. And we might very well be in war in the morning. So it's time to do some heavy thinking and deep praying.' "[94]

CHAPTER 36

THE HOLY LAND

A T THE BEGINNING OF THE NEW YEAR, WASHINGTON decided that it needed a new team representing the United States in Saigon. Henry Cabot Lodge was popular with the generals—too popular, Dean Rusk and Johnson decided. He continued to insist that the National Liberation Front was nothing but a gang of terrorists who deserved to be shot rather than negotiated with. The pacification effort was still stagnant, and the United States needed an ambassador who would act as a disinterested power broker during the runup to the fall presidential elections. The White House and State Department settled on seventy-two-year-old career diplomat Ellsworth Bunker. A tall, dignified New Englander known for a combination of toughness and tact, Bunker had come to the president's attention when he had presided over a political settlement that brought peace and security, if not democracy, to the Dominician Republic. Eugene Locke was to replace William Porter as deputy ambassador, and Bob Komer would head up the pacification effort. Being third in line was a disappointment for Komer, but he had developed a reputation for excessive happy talk, the administration's Guildenstern, as *Newsweek* termed him, always willing to tell the president what he thought Johnson wanted to hear.[1] Lodge and Porter stepped down officially the second week in April. General Westmoreland and his staff held a dinner for them, during which Westmoreland presented the two with 9 mm Browning pistols complete with shoulder holsters and a plaque reading "Honorary Field Marshal."[2]

In March, LBJ traveled to Guam, the westernmost outpost of American power in the Pacific, to introduce his new team to Ky and Thieu and to say good-bye to the old. At the Guam conference, Johnson told Ky that everything depended on a free and fair election. Only with a transparent democracy and the emergence of authentic noncommunist political parties could South Vietnam be assured of continued support from the United States. Moreover, the Military Revolutionary Council must reconcile itself to participation in the political life of the nation by members of the NLF and Vietcong, at least as individuals if not as an organized communist party.[3] Johnson also talked privately with Bunker. "My recollections are that the president emphasized the fact that he wanted to see the training of the Vietnamese accelerated and speeded up to enable us to more quickly turn the war over to them," Bunker later recalled of the conversation.[4]

Shortly before the Guam Conference convened, UN Secretary General U Thant attempted to jump-start negotiations by proposing an unconditional bombing halt, a cease-fire in South Vietnam, and internationally supervised elections.[5] But LBJ was through with peace feelers for the time being. "I proceed from one negotiation to the other constantly waiting for something that never comes and usually find myself in worse shape at the end of the proposal than I do at the beginning," he complained to Dean Rusk. Why couldn't U Thant, Bill Fulbright, Harold Wilson, and other would-be negotiators see that?[6] The army of peacemakers needed to be told,

> "You bring us something and you'll find a pleasant and favorable response, but you don't take anything from us until you get something from them." . . . Now we constantly do that, three years of it, and we're on borrowed time now and just a few months before the judgment day . . . I'm terribly afraid of these negotiations at this stage because I don't think they want them and I don't think they're ready for them and I don't think they're prepared to give a damned thing. And if they were prepared, I'd be more frightened than I am because I don't think they're prepared to give what we must have . . . We have a limited time to go ahead and get ourselves in condition [to hold free elections and pull out] and I don't want anybody interfering with it . . . We get their [the American people's] hopes up . . . and then they're nailed again each time we strike out . . . I think that with this Constitution, if it comes through out there and if we can get an election in 90 days and have that work out well, I think that we're going to be in a lot better condition than we are now.[7]

As the president and his party winged their way back home, Ho Chi Minh stole most of the Guam headlines by publishing the texts of his and Johnson's top-secret exchange of the previous month. The press speculated that he wanted to reassure China and other societies engaged in or contemplating wars of national liberation that North Vietnam would never relent. Immediately, Bobby Kennedy called a press conference to denounce the administration for having increased the price the United States was asking for peace. Previously, said Bobby, LBJ had demanded only a de-escalation of the war by Hanoi in return for a bombing halt; now, Kennedy maintained, Mr. Johnson had upped the ante by demanding "evidence that Hanoi has already ceased infiltration before we stop the bombing."[8] Arthur Schlesinger had been hammering away at his impressionable young friend. "Americans will never in a hundred years be able to bring democracy to the countryside of South Vietnam," he wrote Bobby. "It is, so far as we are concerned, an alien, mysterious and impenetrable culture . . . And it is not our sort of thing anyway. We wouldn't be able to do it in Latin America, despite the common moral and cultural heritage; we can't even do it in Mississippi and Alabama."[9]

IN THE MIDST OF URBAN RIOTING in the summer of 1966, Bobby had cosponsored Senate hearings to prove that LBJ was not doing enough to help the cities. Now the heir apparent had "declared his independence" from the administration on Vietnam. The first step had come in early February 1967 when, during a tour of Western Europe, Kennedy had met with two officials from the Quay d'Orsay, the French Foreign Ministry. The Frenchmen suggested that if the United States would stop the bombing of the North, negotiations and an agreement on mutual de-escalation would soon follow. Immediately afterward, a story appeared in *Newsweek* to the effect that Bobby had been in indirect touch with the North Vietnamese and the terms for negotiation had been agreed on.

Soon after his return, the president asked Kennedy to come to the White House to discuss his trip and the story in *Newsweek*. Rusk advised Johnson to have a "witness" present. Consequently, both Walt Rostow and Nick Katzenbach sat in during the hour-long discussion late on the afternoon of February 6.[10] From all accounts, it was a stormy interview. Bobby tried to downplay his discussion with the French. Johnson implied that RFK, an uninformed and unauthorized U.S. senator, was interfering with and threatening legitimate American efforts to work out a negotiated settlement of the war in Vietnam. He was particularly irate about the leak to *Newsweek*. It probably came from your State Department, Bobby remarked. "It isn't my State Department; it's your State Department," LBJ retorted. Johnson insisted that Kennedy inform the press that he had had no contact with the North Vietnamese, and he sullenly complied.[11]

Then, a month later, Bobby rose on the floor of the Senate to declare, "We are now at a critical turning point . . . between the rising prospects of peace and surely rising war, between the promise of negotiations and the perils of spreading conflict." He outlined a beguilingly simple peace plan. First, the United States should halt the bombing and announce its readiness "to negotiate within the week." Second, the negotiators would agree that neither side would "substantially increase" its war effort. Third, some "international presence" should gradually replace U.S. troops while the two sides worked out a settlement permitting all major political interests—including the communists—a voice in determining South Vietnam's political destiny.[12] Kennedy was being disingenuous, and everyone with any inside knowledge knew it. Joe Alsop later told an interviewer, "You have to bear in mind about Bobby, and I don't mind saying it and I know it'll hurt Ethel if she reads these damn things, but Johnson continued President Kennedy's policy, and Bobby . . . was, by implication, rather violently attacking his own brother's policy." [13]

Johnson was convinced that Kennedy's demarche was intended primarily for the 1968 presidential election campaign, but publicly he took a soft line. "We have help and suggestions from members of the Senate," he told a televised press conference. "I have no particular fault to find or criticism to make of others . . . I must grant to them the same sincerity that I reserve for myself." [14] He also believed he could invoke Jack to defeat Bobby. LBJ had Rostow research his predecessor's speeches. Citing JFK's commitment to SEATO, his acceptance of the domino theory, and his repeated comparison of South Vietnam to Berlin, Rostow observed, "I don't believe any objective person can read this record without knowing that President Kennedy would have seen this through whatever the cost." [15]

With the approach of the 1968 presidential election, Johnson feared, the American people, war-weary, increasingly uncertain about the wisdom of expending American blood and treasure to protect a tiny piece of real estate halfway around the world, would be unable to resist RFK's siren song. "As this process goes forward," LBJ confided to Orville Freeman, "there would be a real danger of a settlement on very bad terms which would subsequently blow up and which would, of course, destroy the president and the country in the process." [16]

The new confrontation with Bobby came in the midst of the publication of a another book on President Kennedy that further demonized LBJ and news reports that Lee Harvey Oswald had not acted alone in killing the president. Just before Christmas 1966, *Look* published excerpts from William Manchester's long-awaited *Death of a President*. It was an emotional, vivid account of the fateful trip to Dallas and the days that followed. It featured extensive interviews with all of the Kennedys and anybody remotely associated with them, but none with LBJ. In the text the narrator kills LBJ with kindness while allowing Ted Sorenson, Kenny O'Donnell, and others to engage in character assassination. [17]

At the same time, attacks on the Warren Commission as an LBJ-orchestrated cover-up moved from gossip column to courtroom. Beginning in late February, New Orlean's flamboyant district attorney Jim Garrison bragged that he had cracked the murder mystery of the century, the assassination of JFK. At a preliminary hearing before a three-judge federal panel, two witnesses testified that at a mid-September party in 1963, they had heard Clay L. Shaw, fifty-four, a retired businessman, and David W. Ferrie, an unemployed charter pilot, conspire with Lee Harvey Oswald to assassinate the president, including such details as the angulation of crossfire. [18] A week before the trial was to begin, Ferrie had apparently committed suicide. The judges ruled the witnesses credible enough to convene a grand jury. LBJ briefly considered reopening the investigation, but after talking with Joe Califano, Lee White, and John Roche, he decided that only Chief Justice Warren himself could do that. [19]

In late February, an off-Broadway neo-Shakespearean satire about the

Kennedys and Johnson, entitled *MacBird,* opened. Written by a precocious Berkeley coed, the mock-heroic parody and satire opened with a Lyndonish MacBird introducing himself with a "Howdy folks," and calling the Earl of Warren "Boy." His "Smooth Society" came off fairly well but not his foreign policy, "Pox Americana." The Stevensonian Egg of Head was made a Hamlet-like figure vacillating between action and acceptance. Most telling was the implication that Macbeth/Johnson was involved in the death of Duncan/Kennedy.[20]

If LBJ took note of *MacBird,* there is no record of it, but the Manchester book and its implications gnawed at Johnson. In mid-March he unburdened himself during an off-the-record talk with Drew Pearson. Chief Justice Warren was also present. "Bobby says he's gong to have twelve books written about me and twelve books written about him before the next election," LBJ griped. Every columnist in Washington from [Joseph] Kraft to Evans and Novak were writing for Bobby. How could O'Donnell and the others have such a vivid memory of what happened on the plane back from Washington? They were all drowning their sorrow. "This fellow Manchester wanted to talk to me, I told him I would answer written questions, which I did. But I could tell he was a screwball by the questions."[21]

LBJ HAD NO INTENTION OF ALLOWING Hanoi to escape the consequences of its refusal to begin talks. In early April, the White House authorized an expansion of the bombing in the North. American fighter-bombers and B-52s destroyed two power plants in Haiphong, plants that had previously been off-limits to U.S. aircraft. Then air force and navy jet fighter-bombers pounded industrial targets just miles from the heart of Hanoi.[22] Meanwhile, on the ground, Westmoreland's aggressive strategy was gobbling up more and more men. By the end of 1966, 431,000 American military personnel were involved in the war.

By late 1967, U.S. and allied forces had inflicted a quarter of a million casualties on their opponents. Unfortunately, two-hundred-thousand Vietnamese reached draft age each year, and in the spring of 1967 Westmoreland sent word that he still did not have enough men to do the job. The first week in March he confided to Earle Wheeler that the American mission had been grossly misrepresenting the level of enemy activity. From January 1966 to January 1967, Saigon had reported forty-five battalions and larger size enemy-initiated action. In reality, there had been 174 enemy actions. Instead of an average of four a month, there had been an average of eighteen. In January 1967 alone, the mission had reported one such engagement, when in reality there had been twenty-five. Wheeler was flabbergasted. "If these figures should reach the public domain," he cabled back, "they would, literally, blow the lid off of Washington. Please do whatever is necessary to insure these figures are not repeated, not released to news media or otherwise exposed to public knowledge."[23] It could very well sabotage the military's requests for more troops.

As the war escalated, the administration was reeling from repeated blows by the surging antiwar movement. As television displayed the horrors of Vietnam on a daily basis and deepening American involvement produced a dramatic expansion of the draft, the increasingly student-driven antiwar movement gained momentum. Opposition to the conflict in Southeast Asia took many forms. Students against the war burned their draft cards, fled to Canada, or even mutilated themselves as part of a dual effort to protest the conflict and avoid serving in Vietnam. By war's end the draft resistance movement had produced 570,000 draft offenders and 563,000 less-than-honorable discharges from the military. Folk singer Joan Baez refused to pay that part of her income tax that went to support the war. Muhammad Ali filed for conscientious objector status, a move that produced some derision given his career as a professional pugilist. Three enlisted men, the Fort Hood Three, challenged the constitutionality of the conflict from their encampment in Texas and refused to fight in what they termed an "unjust, immoral, and illegal war." [24] But it was the mass demonstrations broadcast by the major networks that had the greatest impact on the public and White House. In the spring of 1967, five hundred thousand marchers of all ages converged on New York's Central Park, some of them chanting "Hey, hey, LBJ, how many kids did you kill today?" [25]

At the same time, the reservations concerning the war within the Johnson foreign policy team that first appeared in 1966 grew apace. Alain Enthoven, assistant secretary of defense for systems analysis, submitted a pessimistic report to McNamara on the probable course of the war. "The "dangerously clever" North Vietnamese strategy was working. The enemy was absorbing the losses inflicted by Westmoreland's war of attrition and counting on American public opinion to grow frustrated and eventually withdraw its support for the war. Washington was in a race to build a viable nation in the South before the domestic consensus supporting the conflict evaporated, and it was losing. [26] In part, Robert McNamara's assistants were reflecting his thinking. Shortly after the Manila Conference he had confided to LBJ, "I don't think we ought to just look ahead to the future and say we're going to go higher and higher and higher and higher—600,000 [troops] 700,000, whatever it takes. It will break the economy of that country and it will substitute U.S. soldiers for South Vietnamese and will distort the whole pattern of conduct in South Vietnam if we do." [27] He continued to voice his misgivings to the Kennedys and to Averell Harriman. The United States could not win the war militarily, he told the ambassador-at-large. After the presidential election, the United States ought to come down full force on Saigon to negotiate a settlement with the NLF. Others in the cabinet were beginning to have their doubts, too, especially Willard Wirtz and Stewart Udall, both of whom had been members of JFK's cabinet. [28]

In April 1967, the White House summoned Westmoreland to Washington to justify his course of action in Vietnam. He met first with Mendell Rivers, John Stennis, and other congressional hawks and assured them that the Johnson administration was not overruling him and the military command in Vietnam and was in fact providing the men and matériel he needed to win the war. The general then proceeded to the White House for a face-to-face meeting with LBJ and his advisers. He reported that the war was going well. With the troops he had, he could survive and probably wear the enemy out, but it would take five years.[29] From the White House, the U.S. commander in Vietnam proceeded to the Hill to address a joint session of Congress. Resplendent in an immaculately pressed uniform, his chest adorned with six rows of ribbons, Westmoreland spoke with "calculated optimism" of the war in Southeast Asia. As he recounted the exploits of U.S. and allied forces he was interrupted four times by standing ovations. At the conclusion of his speech he turned to Vice President Humphrey and Speaker McCormack and saluted smartly, then wheeled and repeated the gesture to the assembled House and Senate. Once again his auditors rose as one, showering Westmoreland with wave after wave of applause.

Reluctantly, Johnson and McNamara agreed to give their field commander another fifty-five thousand troops.[30] At the same time, they made it clear that that was it; there would not be another significant increase; everyone in the American mission should focus on Vietnamization—empowering the Vietnamese to build a viable society capable of defending itself. All those concerned with the war effort should "emphasize consistently that the sole US objective in Vietnam has been and is to permit the people of South Vietnam to determine their own future." Wheeler cabled Sharp following a May policy review: "Suggest that you batten down for rough weather ahead."[31]

BEGINNING IN 1966 Allard Lowenstein, a former student activist at the University of North Carolina at Chapel Hill, a past head of the National Student Association, and a leader of the reform wing of the Americans for Democratic Action, launched a campaign to persuade the ADA to support someone other than Lyndon Johnson for president in 1968. Though Lowenstein did not succeed, the National Board at its annual meeting in Washington in the spring of 1967 denounced the war in Vietnam. At the same time, a group of antiwar enthusiasts in New York opened the "Citizens for Kennedy-Fulbright" headquarters in preparation for the 1968 presidential election. In July the group organized some fifty former delegates to the Democratic National Convention who sent a public letter to the president urging him not to run in 1968. Because of deep divisions over foreign affairs, they declared, "millions of Democrats will be unable to support Democratic candidates in local, state or national elections."[32] From that time on, Lyndon Johnson viewed the ADA as nothing less than a "Kennedy-in-exile" government.

Meanwhile, a series of events in the Congo had persuaded Richard Russell, the powerful chairman of Armed Services, that the administration had to be confronted lest America become involved in one Vietnam after another. Throughout the Congo's bloody struggle for independence from Belgium and the civil strife that followed, the United States had acted to shore up the pro-Western, anticommunist government of President Joseph Mobutu. In June

President Johnson dispatched three C-130 cargo planes and 150 military personnel to the central African republic. The American presence was necessary, Mobutu claimed, to help him suppress a major rebellion against his government. On July 8, shortly before the planes departed, Rusk called Russell and Fulbright to inform them of the enterprise. He gave the impression that the purpose of the expedition was to rescue Americans about to be butchered in the jungle. The following day, however, Rusk called again and said that the planes would be used to move Mobutu's troops "around the Congo to deal with revolutionary elements."[33] On July 10, Russell seized the floor in the Senate to sharply criticize the administration. The situation in the Congo, he said, was purely an internal conflict and one in which the United States should not become involved. Americans must not become bogged down in "local rebellions and local wars" where the nation had "no stake and where we have no legal or moral commitment to intervene."[34] He had protested privately to the administration, he said, but his objections had gone unheeded.

Fulbright moved quickly to take advantage of the opening. During a long lunch in the Senate dining room, the Arkansan broached the subject of a national commitments resolution to his old friend from Georgia and urged him to introduce a bill embodying it. The document that Carl Marcy and his staff produced was a masterpiece, the chairman observed, one that "seems to me to come pretty close to expressing what I would guess is a nearly universal Senate view." It provided that a national commitment by the United States to a foreign power "necessarily and exclusively results from affirmative action taken by the executive and legislative branches of the United States Government through means of a treaty, convention, or other legislative instrumentality specifically intended to give effect to such a commitment."[35] Thus was planted the seed that would flower into the Hatfield-McGovern and Cooper-Church resolutions as well as the War Powers Act. The long, bitter struggle against the imperial presidency had begun.

ON JULY 25 Lyndon Johnson convened what he expected to be a routine gathering of Senate committee chairs. The group included Henry Jackson of Washington, Allen Ellender, James Eastland, Mike Monroney, Warren Magnuson—all committed party-liners on the war—as well as Mansfield and Fulbright. The president thanked the group for their "experience, friendship and judgment," and invited comments. "Mr. President," Fulbright exclaimed, "what you really need to do is to stop the war. That will solve all your problems." Johnson's face reddened. He sensed a change in the attitude of his colleagues toward the conflict in Vietnam, Fulbright declared. Even such a hawk as Indiana Senator Frank Lausche had called for an end to the bombing of the North. Senator Russell was very upset about being lied to on the Congo situation. "Vietnam is ruining our domestic and our foreign policy. I will not support it any longer," he said. By now Johnson's steely gaze was fixed on the Arkansan. The group was absolutely still. "I expect that for the first time in 20 years I may vote against foreign assistance and may try to bottle the whole bill up in the Committee," Fulbright warned. Johnson exploded. If Congress wanted to tell the rest of the world to go to hell, that was its prerogative. "Maybe you don't want to help the children of India, but I can't hold back." He then dared the leaders to defeat foreign aid. Fulbright refused to be intimidated. "Vietnam is central to the whole problem," he declared. It was unbalancing the budget and undermining the nation's foreign policy. "Bill," Johnson responded, "everybody doesn't have a blind spot like you do. You say don't bomb North Vietnam on just about everything. I don't have the simple solution you have." Turning to the group, the president said bitterly, "If you want me to get out of Vietnam, then you have the prerogative of taking out the resolution under which we are out there now. You can repeal it tomorrow. You can tell the troops to come home. You can tell General Westmoreland that he doesn't know what he is doing."[36]

"Lyndon Johnson is a complicated human being," Walter Lippmann opined. "There are at least two spirits wrestling within him. One is that of the peacemaker and reformer and herald of a better world. The other is that of the primitive frontiersman who wants to be the biggest, the best, the first, a worshiper of what William James called the bitch-goddess, success."[37] Fool! LBJ thought. Could he and the others not see that the cause of domestic reform, especially the fate of the civil rights movement, was inextricably intertwined with the course of the war in Vietnam? If the administration failed to prevent a direct military confrontation with the communist superpowers on the one hand or secure an "honorable peace" in Vietnam on the other, there could only be reaction, not reform, on the home front.

By the spring of 1967, Lady Bird was pining for LBJ's retirement. "Many months ago I set March 1968 in my own mind as the time when Lyndon can make a statement that he will not be a candidate for reelection," she recorded in her diary. "I was following the pattern of President Truman . . . For the first time in my life I have felt lately that Lyndon would be a happy man retired. I feel that there is enough at the Ranch to hold him, keep him busy, and that he can pour himself into some sort of therapeutic work at the University of Texas—in the Johnson School of Public Service perhaps." She was convinced that her husband would not survive a second term. Indeed, in February 1965, she had bought a black funeral dress in case Lyndon should die suddenly.[38] In mid-May she talked with Abe Fortas about a 1968 retirement. The president must not, could not, make any such announcement until March 1968 at the earliest, he said. The consensus in behalf of the war and the Great Society would fall apart. Moreover, if things were not going better in the country than they were then, it would be his duty to run again.[39]

In late summer, LBJ summoned George Christian to his bedroom for an early morning confab. Lady Bird was there. He had decided not to seek another term, Johnson told his press secretary, and asked him to research exactly how Harry Truman had gone about withdrawing his name from consideration in 1952. LBJ explained that every time he looked at Woodrow Wilson's portrait in the White House, he became more determined to step down before he became physically or politically incapacitated, or both. "The feeling I had that morning was that he was living under a sword," Christian said. "He knew his days were numbered and he didn't have four more years in him." As Christian left the room, the president said, "Nobody knows this but you, me, and Bird."[40]

IN JUNE 1967, in the midst of LBJ's preoccupation with the war in Vietnam and eroding support for the Great Society, Israel staged a preemptive strike against Egyptian forces. The war later widened to include Jordan and Syria, thereby threatening to precipitate a military confrontation between Washington and Moscow. The roots of the Six Day War are well-known. Relations between pan-Arab nationalists, led by Egypt's Gamal Abdel Nasser, and Israel had grown increasingly tense in the years following the 1956 Suez crisis. In 1964 Nasser joined with other Arab leaders in sponsoring the Palestinian Liberation Organization (PLO), whose objective was to destroy the state of Israel and secure the return of the hundreds of thousands of Palestinians who had been driven from their homes in 1948.

The Kennedy administration had announced that it would pursue an even-handed policy in the Middle East. During the 1960 presidential campaign, JFK, prompted by a desire to counteract his father's reputation as an anti-Semite and by the knowledge that Jewish intellectuals were one of the mainstays of American liberalism, had courted and largely won over the Jewish vote in the United States. He had named two acknowledged Zionists, Abe Ribicoff and Arthur Goldberg, to his cabinet and set up a de facto Jewish affairs desk under special assistant Myer Feldman. In September 1962, acting on the advice of these friends of Israel, Kennedy had approved the sale of Hawk surface-to-air anti-aircraft missiles to Tel Aviv. In so doing, he broke with the long established, though unwritten, American policy of no arms sales to the Middle East. His pro-Israeli advisers observed that the Soviets had not taken such a self-denying pledge and were supplying Egypt with tanks, planes, and artillery pieces. Besides, they said, the Hawks could be used for defensive purposes only. At the same time, in accord with the Schlesinger-Goodwin-Galbraith doctrine of building bridges to anticolonial third world leaders, Kennedy attempted to cultivate Nasser. He spoke frequently and sympathetically of Arab nationalism. He increased American aid to Egypt, especially shipments of food under PL-480. In part, the president was responding to pressure from the State and Defense Departments, always cognizant of the strategic importance of the Arab states because of their large populations and the massive oil deposits in the region.[41] This, then, was the situation when Lyndon Baines Johnson became thirty-sixth president of the United States.

For those Jews who knew of his past, Lyndon Johnson's standing could not have been higher, but for the rank and file, who were aware only that he hailed from oil-rich Texas, the new president was an object of suspicion. In truth, LBJ counted Jews, along with other minorities, as one of his natural constituencies.

From his days as National Youth Administration director, when he had facilitated Jewish emigration from Nazi Germany, to the 1956 Suez crisis, when he had vociferously opposed a movement within Dulles's State Department to impose sanctions on Israel, LBJ had demonstrated his fealty to the Zionist cause. Orville Freeman quoted him on his ties with the American Jewish community: "He . . . said wryly that in all his political life when people had been against him, looking to Texas now, that always, the Mexicans, the Negroes, the Jews had been his friends and he didn't forget it." [42] Harry McPherson recalled reading an article by a Jewish writer at the time on the typical non-Jewish Jew and the typical Jewish non-Jew. "And the classic non-Jewish Jew was a Texan, just generally, the Texan being loud and wearing his heart on his sleeve, and being full of complaints, and fun, and being a little bit too much at all points . . . And Johnson was kind of a non-Jewish Jew in that sense; he was outrageous and he talked too much and demanded too much and was never satisfied and was a lot of fun." [43] He could have added that Johnson was sentimental, ardently attached to family and clan, generous, gregarious—and neurotic. Shortly after being sworn in as president, Johnson had remarked to an Israeli diplomat, "You have lost a very great friend, but you have found a better one." [44]

Johnson's close relationship with Abe Fortas and other Jewish New Dealers was well-known. He retained Myer Feldman until 1966 and embraced David Dubinsky and the heavily Jewish ILGWU. During the 1964 election Lyndon and Lady Bird struck up a friendship with Arthur and Mathilde Krim (Mathilde had served briefly with the Irgun, the Israeli counterterrorist organization, in her youth). Indeed, the Krims became such close friends that they purchased land and built a house near the ranch in order to be available to the president on his frequent Texas vacations. [45] As far as the Arab states were concerned, Johnson felt a natural antipathy for Nasser as a disturber of the status quo. While Johnson was still in the Senate, George Reedy had convinced his boss that Nasser's bread and butter was the poverty and ignorance of his own countrymen; the Egyptian leader would continue to blame the West for their lot while doing nothing substantively to improve it because he could continue to exploit their discontent to keep himself in power. [46]

At the same time, Johnson was determined to hew to the line that separated Israeli and American interests. As a congressional expert and advocate of preparedness, he was well aware of the importance of Arab oil to the strategic well-being of the United States. He also understood clearly that the Soviet Union was poised to take advantage of any and every tension in Arab-American relations. Typically, Johnson was careful in his diplomacy toward the Middle East, very careful. While showering Israel with rhetorical assurances concerning America's commitment to that state's well-being and cultivating American Zionists, the president did everything in his power to strengthen conservative, status quo powers in the Arab world and, when possible, to placate Nasser. For example, in early 1964, ardently supported by various Zionist organizations in the United States, Israel began pressuring Washington to sell it a hundred tanks, pointing out that the Soviets were rapidly arming the Egyptians and Syrians. Abe Feinberg, chief fund-raiser in the United States for Israeli causes, Feldman, and even Robert Komer, then the resident NSC Arabist, argued for the sale, warning Johnson that if it were not forthcoming, the GOP might well wean the Jewish vote away from the Democrats. Johnson chose to wait. The sale would be the first transfer of weapons that could be used for both offense and defense and was sure to anger Arab nationalists and strengthen Nasser's hand. He did not know how long he would be able to resist Tel Aviv and New York's blandishments, but he intended to get something for the tanks if and when the sale was made.

The White House was extremely worried about nuclear proliferation in the Middle East. Israel had constructed a top-secret nuclear reactor at Dimona.[47] During a visit by Prime Minister Levi Eshkol to the ranch in 1964, LBJ had secured a commitment to allow American inspectors to check Dimona at regular intervals to verify that no weapons were being developed. Still Johnson hesitated. He told Eshkol that Israel should attempt to purchase the tanks it needed from West Germany, France, or Britain. If that were not possible, the United States would deliver. In the end, the Europeans could not match quality or price, and the American marker was called in.[48]

As the Johnson presidency began, Israel found itself prospering amid insecurity. Its population had tripled to 2.9 million since the founding of the state, and the annual economic growth rate was among the highest in the world. Prejudice there was, against Sephardic (non-European) Jews, but Israel was an open, diverse, dynamic democracy. The Israeli Defense Force (IDF), with its élan and egalitarianism—saluting and marching were rare and authority continually questioned—was a formidable force, claiming twenty-five brigades, 175 jets, and nearly one thousand battle tanks. In terms of training, equipment, and spare parts, if not in numbers, the IDF was the most potent military force in the Middle East. At the same time, Israel was circumscribed by 639 miles of hostile borders manned by thirty Arab divisions. Egypt was in a position to strangle Israeli trade by blockading the Straits of Tiran. The Palestinian Liberation Organization, or Fatah, attacked and harassed from bases in Egypt, Jordan, and Syria. Finally, antipathy to Israel was the one unifying factor in the Arab world.[49]

At a Pan-Arab Summit Conference held in Cairo in January 1964, the Arabs approved a plan to divert the Jordan River at its source in hopes of turning all of Israel into a desert. They also approved creation of a United Arab Command with a $345 million, ten-year budget. The UAC would become operational in 1967.[50] Later that year, U.S.-Egyptian relations reached the breaking point. Rioters, egged on by Nasserian rhetoric, burned down the American Embassy library. Then Egyptian forces accidentally shot down a plane belonging to John Mecom, a prominent Texas oilman. When Lucius Battle, the U.S. ambassador, suggested to the Egyptian president that he moderate his tone, the latter replied, "The American Ambassador says that our behavior is not acceptable. Well, let us tell them that those who do not accept our behavior can go and drink from the sea . . . We will cut the tongues of anybody who talks badly about us. We are not going to accept gangsterism by cowboys."[51] This from a man who led 29.5 million residents who earned an average of $140 a year, lived to the age of thirty-five, and were 50 percent illiterate. Johnson had no intention of rewarding pseudo-revolutionaries who exploited rather than served their people. By 1965 Washington was working to block Egypt's efforts to refinance its massive international debt. American food aid—shipments from the United States accounted for 60 percent of all Egyptian bread—was suspended.[52]

Increasingly, Washington, Cairo, and, to an extent, Tel Aviv saw Jordan and its youthful monarch, Hussein, as a key to the solution of the Middle East riddle. Short, dapper, soft-spoken, Hussein's smiling demeanor and mild manner concealed a shrewd intelligence and inner tenacity. He had survived no fewer than thirteen coup and assassination plots since taking over the throne in 1953. Indeed, his father had been shot by a Palestinian extremist.[53] Jordan, devoid of natural resources, had long depended on foreign aid, first from the British and then from the United States, to feed and employ its people and to provide for its defense. With the rise of Nasser and pan-Arab nationalism, however, Hussein had had to wean his nation from the West, turning to Saudi Arabia and the Gulf emirates for the subsidies his state needed to survive. As far as the Arab-Israeli conflict was concerned, Hussein had to perform a dangerous balancing act to keep from being swallowed up by his powerful neighbors. Nasser's agents continually fomented unrest among Jordan's huge Palestinian population, while Israel issued threat after threat to annihilate Jordan if it did not put a stop to Fatah raids emanating from its territory into Israel.[54]

At the Pan-Arab Summit in Cairo, Soviet arms dealers had been much in evidence. Egypt and Syria wanted to let Russia be the sole armorer for the UAC. Hussein, supported by the Saudis, resisted. It would be unwise for the Arab brotherhood to become dependent on one source of supply. In desperation, the king turned to the United States. If Washington wanted to keep Soviet arms and United Arab Republic trainers out of Jordan, it would have to cut an arms deal. With the tacit approval of Israel, the United States had been "subsidizing nonviable Jordan": $56 million in FY 1964 and $46.5 million in FY 1965. But Johnson and his advisers knew that overt military aid would deeply offend the friends of Israel. Tel Aviv might eventually understand, but American Jewish organizations, always more strident than the Israelis themselves, would view an arms deal with a frontline Arab country as a betrayal. As Komer observed to Ed Weisl, "The real trouble is that Israel's US friends are much less knowledgeable about the real state of affairs than the Israeli Government—and thus more emotional."[55]

Komer and the State Department favored extending Jordan some $55 million in arms aid, ground weapons only. "So long as we can keep Hussein out of Nasser's camp," Komer observed, "Israel cannot be effectively hemmed in."[56] To make the case with the Israelis, LBJ chose Komer and Averell Harriman, Komer because of his hard nose and Harriman, as George Ball put it, because the former governor had "a lot of vested capital with the New York Jewish community."[57] Prime Minister Eshkol and Foreign Minister Golda Meir finally consented, but only in return for a public commitment to sell more and better arms to Israel. As Komer confided to LBJ, "Israeli aims are rather different from our own. They've consistently felt nervous about US support in a crunch, so have long favored tying us to them publicly (security guarantees, arms aid), regardless of whether this would throw the Arabs into Soviet hands or cost us our position in the Arab world."[58] There would be no public commitments, but Washington agreed to help Israel acquire some advanced supersonic aircraft from other suppliers. As had been the case with the tanks, Western European sources did not work out, and the United States ended up selling Israel several squadrons of A4 fighter-bombers. At the same time, the Johnson administration went ahead with its arms package to Jordan.[59] These arrangements satisfied Abe Feinberg and other American Zionists but, of course, infuriated Nasser. He had to stand idly by while the United States armed both the Israelis and his moderate/progressive enemies within the Arab bloc.

During 1966 LBJ's natural sympathy for Jews in general and Israel in particular was partially eclipsed by his anger over growing antiwar sentiment in the American Jewish community. Led by columnist Walter Lippmann, political activist Allard Lowenstein, and New York Senator Jacob Javits, Jewish political activists and intellectuals questioned the assumptions that underlay American involvement in Vietnam and participated in various end-the-war and dump Johnson movements. LBJ was dumbfounded. How could a people so educated and intelligent not see the connection between Southeast Asia and the Middle East? In the summer of 1966, Israeli President Zalman Shazar called at the White House. Johnson used the occasion to protest. "If because of the critics of our Vietnam policy," LBJ asked, "we did not fulfill our commitments to the sixteen million people in Vietnam, how could we be expected to fulfill our commitments to two million Israelis?"[60] Johnson pointed out to newly named Israeli Foreign Minister Abba Eban that Hanoi had issued several statements in support of the PLO. At one point, Johnson became so frustrated he told Tel Aviv that if they did not get their American friends off his back over Vietnam they could forget about further aid. Eban and Eppie Evron, Israel's minister in the United States, tried, calling on Fulbright and assuring him of their total support of the administration's position on Vietnam. But in fact they were able to make little headway. In Israel, the labor-dominated left was adamantly opposed to the war in Vietnam. Lippmann and Lowenstein felt far more strongly about Southeast Asia than they did the Middle East.[61]

Throughout the Middle East crisis a principal dilemma for the United States was whether or not to support Arab unity. In its effort to prevent Soviet penetration of the region—Moscow was continually trying to exploit Arab nationalism and play the radicals off against the moderates—Washington seemed called on to keep Nasser, Hussein, and King Faisal of Saudi Arabia talking and cooperating. The Johnson administration chose unity both out of cold war considerations and because it believed moderating Arab radicalism was the only long-term solution to the Arab-Israeli conflict. "We have succeeded in maintaining satisfactory working relationships on all sides of a series of local disputes that have threatened to drive us and the USSR into opposing camps," NSC Middle East expert Hal Saunders observed to Rostow. "We have long believed that splitting the Middle East is a major Soviet objective. Our interests in the area are wide and varied enough that we judge it essential to avoid that kind of split. Carrying water on both shoulders sometimes seems immoral and is always difficult. But for a power like the U.S. with its far flung conflicting interests there seems no other choice." [62]

During an interview with Rabbi Philip Bernstein and I. L. Kenen of the American-Israel Public Affairs Committee in March 1966, Bob Komer observed that the "Arab-Israeli standoff is . . . one of the most stable crises in the world." [63] He could not have been more wrong. The February 1966 coup in Syria that brought an ardently socialist and militantly anti-Israeli Ba'thist regime to power had further roiled the troubled waters of the Middle East. Damascus and Moscow embraced rhetorically and militarily. In 1966 alone the Soviets poured over $400 million into Syria. Russian became the nation's second language. From Syrian territory, Fatah guerrillas began raiding Israeli settlements on an almost weekly basis. Over the course of 1966 Israel recorded ninety-three border incidents—mine explosions, shootings, sabotage. [64] From positions on the Golan Heights, Syrian artillerymen shelled Israeli settlements. At the same time, PLO fighters continued to operate with almost a free hand along the Jordanian-Israeli border. On November 10, an Israeli police vehicle struck a mine that had been planted by Fatah guerrillas along the Israeli border. Three soldiers died. Three days later, an Israeli force of four-hundred men, under the cover of jet fighters, crossed into Syria and surrounded the small Jordanian town of Samu, suspected of harboring the guerrillas. As the force began to demolish more than one-hundred houses, a Jordanian infantry brigade arrived, and an intended surgical strike became a pitched battle. When the smoke and dust had cleared, the Israeli commander and fifteen Jordanian soldiers had been killed. [65] Then on April 7, 1967, the Israeli Air Force launched raids against the Syrian gunners on the Golan Heights. In the air battle that followed the Israeli fighters blasted the Syrian MIGs out of the air and buzzed Damascus for effect.

In mid-May 1967, Nasser began to give way to pressure from Syria and militant Arab nationalists in Egypt and elsewhere to redeem himself and all of Islam by standing up to Israel. Citing Eshkol's public pronouncements proclaiming his intention to wipe out Fatah camps in Syria, Damascus was deluging Cairo with dire warnings of an impending Israeli invasion. On May 16, he ordered the UN peacekeeping force out of the Sinai. Secretary General U Thant complied immediately without a murmur. Then on May 22, as Egyptian troops occupied Sharm el Sheikh on the Strait of Tiran at the entrance to the Gulf of Aqaba, Nasser announced that he was closing the waterway to Israeli shipping. At the same time, he began to mass troops along Israel's southwestern border.[66] These moves put an already nervous Israel into an "apocalyptic" frame of mind, as Eppie Evron put it. Abe Feinberg and his companions besieged the White House with requests for meetings with LBJ. "The Egyptian build-up of armour and infantry in Sinai, to the extent so far of approximately four divisions including 600 tanks, is greater than ever before, and has no objective justification," Eshkol cabled Johnson.[67] He insisted that the United States live up to its "commitment" to Israel.[68]

Meanwhile, Hussein told the American ambassador to Jordan that he was convinced that Israel had long planned to annex all or part of the West Bank to improve its security position. The current Egyptian buildup and Syrian posturing offered the Israelis the perfect justification for a preemptive attack. He wanted no part of a war with Israel, but if attacked, Jordan would have to defend itself. Would the United States live up to its commitment to ensure that his kingdom was not overrun?[69]

From the last week in May through the end of June, Johnson and his advisers met several times a day on the mounting crisis in the Middle East. Where did American obligations lie? "We have no specific written commitment to Israel's defense," Harry McPherson wrote Hubert Humphrey. "But as the President said in Ellenville, New York on August 19: 'What do you do when little Israel calls on you for assistance and help? I'll tell you what you do. You do what is right—you stand up for freedom, whatever the price.' "[70] But that was rhetoric. During the runup to war, LBJ made it clear to the Israelis that the United States did not have an "attack-on-you-is-an-attack-on-us agreement." He could not and would not give such assurance without the express consent of Congress. In fact, of course, the president did not want and did not seek such approval. His advisers told him that Israel would prevail in any war with the Arabs—in five days if they attacked, in ten if they were attacked. "The judgment of the intelligence community is that Israeli ground forces can maintain internal security, defend successfully against simultaneous Arab attacks on all fronts, launch limited attacks simultaneously on all fronts, or hold on any three fronts while mounting successfully a major offensive on the fourth. The key was the war in the air. If Israel's air force were not damaged beyond repair in an Egyptian preemptive strike, the Israelis would prevail."[71] But despite what the Arabs and Soviets would later say, the White House did not want war under any circumstances. U.S. emissaries rushed to assure the Egyptians that Israel was not preparing to attack Syria and the Israelis that Egypt was not readying a preemptive strike against them.

At 6:10 on May 23, 1967, LBJ went on a national radio and television hookup to address the rising tension in the Middle East. He expressed concern about the warlike activities being conducted by the states of the region against each other, and he regretted the hasty withdrawal of UN troops from the Sinai. Blockade of Israel through closing the Straits of Tiran was unacceptable. The United States would uphold the right of free, innocent passage of this and other international waterways, he declared, and was "firmly committed to the support of the political independence and territorial integrity of all the nations of the area." [72]

On May 25, Abba Eban arrived in Washington for talks with the president and his advisers. The historic split between the State and Defense Departments on the one hand and the friends of Israel on the other came into sharp relief. McNamara and Rusk insisted that if Israel chose to attack first, it should expect no help from the United States. Abe Fortas and Clark Clifford argued that the administration must give Eban something to take home. At the very least, the president must assure the foreign minister that America would use force if necessary to open the straits. At one point, Dean Acheson, looking directly at Clifford, observed that it would better for all concerned if Israel had never been created. Clifford, as he knew, had played a crucial role during the Truman administration in helping bring the Jewish nation into being. No assurances, Johnson ultimately said, but he would consider a plan to put together an armed flotilla comprising ships from the major maritime powers to force entry through the straits. The key, LBJ observed, was whether the UK had enough interest to "stand up with us like men." [73]

Meanwhile, the task at hand was to keep the Israelis from launching a preemptive strike. The atmosphere was tense as Johnson and Eban, with their advisers in tow, convened at the White House. Israeli intelligence was wrong, the president began. The Egyptians and Syrians had no intention of attacking; the mobilization was purely defensive in nature. Eban listened intently. Even if there were an attack, Johnson said, the IDF would "beat the hell out of them." The United States was not going to give public guarantees for Israel's security, and Israel must not, LBJ emphasized, make itself responsible for initiating hostilities. Slowly, solemnly he said, "Israel will not be alone unless it decides to go it alone." Eban sat in silence for a moment. He had to take something back to the cabinet, he finally said, as it attempted to deal with the "apocalyptic atmosphere" in his country. The United States was firmly committed to the right of free passage through the Straits of Tiran for all nations, LBJ replied. "I would not be wrong," Eban inquired, "if I told the Prime Minister that your disposition is to make every possible effort to assure that the Strait and the Gulf will remain open to free and innocent passage?" LBJ replied that he would not be wrong. [74] A day later the Israeli cabinet met and voted to take no action for the time being in response to the Arab buildup. [75]

The next seven days were a blur of diplomatic activity. American officials approached the British, French, and Canadians about putting together an armed maritime flotilla to force the issue in the Gulf of Aqaba. France flatly refused, Britain was supportive in principle, and the Canadians provisionally promised a couple of ships. After due deliberation, Johnson's advisers told him that any attempt to force open the Straits of Tiran by military means would require congressional approval. In turn, congressional leaders informed the president that although both houses were overwhelmingly sympathetic to the Israeli cause, they would not support unilateral action by the United States and urged Johnson to work through the UN.

Shortly after the Arabs began mobilizing, McNamara had the Sixth Fleet, stationed in the central Mediterranean, turn and steam slowly toward the eastern littoral, a move not lost on the Soviets. Soviet Premier Alexsey Kosygin wrote LBJ warning that the Israelis were preparing a first strike, urging him to restrain his "ally," and implying that Russia would not stand idly by if the United States intervened in an Arab-Israeli war.[76] Through an intermediary, Nasser attempted to explain his position to LBJ: "Now is the time when all Arab people are waiting to see an act of friendship on the part of the USA. His urgent request is that the U.S. undertake no direct military action in the form of landings, shifting of naval fleet, or otherwise."[77] At the end of May the U.S. ambassador to Egypt reported that "he [Nasser] would probably welcome, but not seek, military showdown with Israel."[78] Though no one on Johnson's foreign policy team said it, a Jewish victory that deflated Nasser and the militants and left Israel with more defensible borders would not be unwelcome. On the 31st Rostow had drinks with Eppie Evron. "Am I wrong in assessing the President's personal determination [to come to Israel's aid if it were threatened with extinction] as I did?" Evron asked. "You have known President Johnson for a long time and have a right to make your own assessment," the national security adviser replied. Rostow remembered his saying with tears in his eyes, "So much hinges on that man."[79]

LYNDON JOHNSON and his advisers did not want war in the Middle East. They had done everything in their power to prevent it. True, LBJ had shifted from a policy of no arms aid to potential combatants, to seeking a balance through arming both sides. But massive Russian arms shipments to the frontline states had made passivity impossible. On June 1, 1967, McNamara met for forty minutes with General Meir Amit. The Israeli later recounted their conversation. "I told him that I'm personally going to recommend that we take action, because there's no way out, and please don't react. He told me it was all right, the president knows that you are here and I have a direct line to the president." McNamara asked only two questions: How long would the war last— "seven days"—and how many casualties would Israel sustain?[80]

"Like a cocked pistol, like a bomb with a dozen detonators," ran a *Newsweek* story on the Arab-Israeli confrontation, "the Middle East last week exuded the ugly aura of imminent slaughter. In the souks of Damascus, reluctant shopkeepers were put through air-raid drills. In the mosques of Cairo, priests [sic] exhorted their congregations to holy war. And in the sacred city of Jerusalem, long divided between Arab and Jew, Israeli children were asked to supply two sandbags each to fortify their schools."[81] On June 5, 1967, the pistol went off. As the blistering summer sun rose over the Negev, wave after wave of Israeli Air Force fighters took off, flying straight out over the Mediterranean and then wheeling and coming in low from the northwest to attack Egyptian airfields and troop concentrations. At the same time, Israeli armored columns drove south into the sands of the Sinai to engage Nasser's forces, by then some eighty thousand strong. To the east, Israeli tanks and armored personnel carriers rolled toward Jordan and joined battle with Hussein's Arab Legion. On the third front in the north, Israeli artillery opened up a barrage on Syrian positions perched atop the heights overlooking the Sea of Galilee.

At 11 A.M. the Egyptians announced they had shot down forty-four enemy planes, nearly 10 percent of Israel's air force. Radio Amman and Radio Damascus told their listeners that the Zionists were on the run and would soon be defeated. By nightfall, however, the truth had become clear. The Israelis had caught Nasser's air force completely by surprise, destroying some 410 aircraft, most of them on the ground. In the Sinai, Israeli tank columns had captured three key road junctions and trapped more than ten thousand Arab troops in an indefensible pocket along the Gaza Strip. On the border with Jordan, Israeli forces pushed the Arab Legion back against the banks of the river and occupied all of the Old City of Jerusalem.[82]

As chance would have it, Harry McPherson, who had been acting as liaison with the American Jewish community after Myer Feldman left to join a Washington law firm, was in Israel the day the war started. He had flown in from Saigon via Hong Kong, where he had been on another fact-finding mission for the president. He arrived at three in the morning and was whisked away to the U.S. ambassador's home for some sleep. At eight o'clock McPherson was awakened by air raid sirens and was informed that the war had started. After huddling with the ambassador, Wally Barbour, in the air raid shelter at the embassy, the president's emissary met with Abba Eban and the Israeli chief of military intelligence General Aharon Yariv at army headquarters in Jerusalem. The Israelis indicated that the Egyptians had started the fighting and they had merely counterattacked—but they were vague: "Big artillery barrages . . . big movements down in the Sinai." McPherson insisted that they be more specific; President Johnson would want to know whether he was going to be speaking in behalf of a country that was being attacked or had itself delivered the first blow. At that point, the air raid sirens went off again. Should not everyone head for the air raid shelter? Barbour asked. Yariv paused a long moment and then replied, "No, that won't be necessary." Suddenly it dawned on McPherson: all of the Arab airplanes had been destroyed on the ground by the Israelis' first strike. Immediately, he and Barbour informed Washington that it would have to cope with a war started by the Israelis.[83]

The first of LBJ's advisers to learn of the onset of war was Walt Rostow. The Situation Room woke him at 2:50 A.M. with news of fighting in the Sinai. He dressed, arrived at the White House at 3:25, conferred with Rusk, and then called the president at 4:35. By then, Robert McNamara had arrived at the Pentagon. Shortly after seven, one of his staff officers informed him that Prime Minister Kosygin was on the "hot line"—actually a teletype rather than a telephone—and wanted to speak to the president.[84] Kosygin and Johnson hastened to reassure each other that they had done their best to restrain their respective clients in the Middle East, deplored the outbreak of hostilities, and promised to work together through the UN Security Council to secure a cease-fire as soon as possible. During their exchange, LBJ had addressed his counterpart as "Comrade Kosygin." At 10:01 A.M. Radio Cairo announced that it had information from King Hussein that American aircraft were participating in the attacks on Arab positions. Immediately LBJ got on the hot line again, denied the charge, and asked Kosygin to persuade Nasser to stop spreading lies lest every American legation in the Middle East be burned to the ground. It was already too late for that. In Arab cities with an American consulate, angry demonstrations besieged U.S. offices, breaking windows and setting fires. The frontline states broke relations with the United States and the United Kingdom, and Arab oil ministers announced that they were going to meet; oil shipments would be halted to any nation found guilty of aiding the Zionists.[85]

Just before noon on the 5th, LBJ gathered with his foreign policy advisers: Dean Rusk; McGeorge Bundy, who had been called in to troubleshoot, Dean Acheson; and Clark Clifford, who was still serving as chair of the president's Foreign Intelligence Advisory Board. Bundy later recalled that the meeting was "mainly concerned with the awful shape we would be in if the Israelis were losing. We didn't really know anything about the situation on the ground. When, in the course of that day, it became apparent that the Israeli Air Force had won, the entire atmosphere of the problem changed. It was in a way reassuring when it became clear that the fighting was the Israelis' idea and that the idea was working. That was a lot better than if it had been the other way around."[86] At the meeting's conclusion, LBJ asked Bundy to return to temporary duty and head the team dealing with the Middle East crisis. Rostow, like virtually everyone else, was absorbed with Vietnam. Bundy readily agreed.[87] Throughout the crisis, LBJ, who could become hysterical over trivia, demonstrated the coolness and deliberation that his staff had come to expect in times of great peril or uncertainty. That morning, Paul Glynn, LBJ's military valet, was on duty and later recorded, "Found President quiet—watching TV. Pres. gave no indications of it being anything but a normal day—showered, shaved and dressed and left for SitRU."[88]

By the second day of the war, the issue facing LBJ, Bundy, Rusk, and Rostow was whether to join the Soviets in pressing for an immediate cease-fire. Initially, the Israelis had assured Washington that they would not use the war to annex Arab territory. But the rapid and overwhelming success of their arms quickly changed their minds. The Israelis and their American supporters were convinced that in 1956 the Great Powers had forced them to disgorge lands they had conquered legitimately by force of arms, thus rendering the state indefensible. They were determined that this would not happen again.

State and Defense, understandably distraught over the prospect of a cutoff of Arab oil to the West, pressed Johnson to support an immediate cease-fire. Others, such as Walt Rostow, argued that the Israelis should be left alone for a while to expand and consolidate their gains. Only until Nasser and the militant nationalists were discredited and Israel acquired defensible borders would there be a chance for a permanent long-term settlement of the Arab-Israeli conflict. With the "moderates" in charge, a comprehensive agreement, including recognition of Israel's right to exist and justice for Palestinian refugees, just might be possible.[89] Johnson was drawn to the latter position. He remembered his conversations with George Reedy following the Suez crisis to the effect that Nasser was dedicated to permanent revolution and there would be no peace in the Holy Land until he was removed, or at least discredited. He knew that a majority of Americans agreed with Rostow. As Orville Freeman put it, "I hope they don't have to kill too many of them [soldiers of the frontline states], but I hope they destroy their military resources and complete[ly] discredit them and eradicate the power of Nasser and make it clear once and for all that Israel is around to stay for a long, long time."[90] Finally, the intelligence LBJ had available to him indicated that the Soviets would not intervene to save the Arabs. Privately, the men in the Kremlin were admitting gross "miscalculations" by both themselves and the Arabs. They had overestimated the military prowess of the Egyptians and underestimated the commitment and effectiveness of the Israelis. In the days that followed, Johnson had Arthur Goldberg cooperate with the Soviets, but Washington did nothing to restrain Israel when it maneuvered to delay Security Council action for as long as possible.[91]

The president had another reason for not moving strongly to bring the fighting to an immediate halt: the mounting anger among American friends of Israel at what they considered his unsympathetic stance toward their brethren in arms. On the morning of the 5th, the White House press officer had told assembled journalists, echoing Woodrow Wilson, that the United States intended to remain neutral in "thought, word, and deed." The Jewish community reacted as if the administration had just announced its intention to bomb the Wailing Wall. Larry Levinson and Ben Wattenberg, White House staffer and speechwriter, respectively, alerted Johnson that there would be a mass rally in behalf of Israel in Lafayette Park on the 8th. They and Mathilde Krim urged the president to make a mollifying statement, lest the gathering turn into a Hate LBJ session.[92]

The president, who believed that he had been bending over backward to help Israel, was infuriated. He called Levinson into Joe Califano's office to rebuke him. He told him how disappointed he was in some of his Jewish friends, their lack of trust in him, their lack of gratitude. A little later, LBJ spotted Levinson in the hall outside the Oval Office. He shook his fist at him and yelled, "You Zionist dupe! You Zionist dupe! You and Wattenberg are Zionist dupes in the White House! Why can't you see I'm doing all I can for Israel? That's what you should be telling people when they ask for a message from the President for their rally." Levinson later told Joe Califano that he felt "shaken to the marrow of my bones by the encounter."[93]

Having blown off steam, LBJ once again became the cautious diplomat. The

Israelis had made it clear from the beginning that they did not expect the United States to come to their rescue. "[Israeli intelligence chief Moshe] Bitan told us on the first day that they didn't want our troops or planes," McPherson reported to Johnson, "they would do the job themselves; they just wanted us to keep the Russians off their backs, and they wanted 'two or three days to finish the job.' "[94] Moreover, although pro-Israeli sentiment was running strong in Congress, leaders from both houses made it clear to the president that they did not want him to take unilateral action. Everything should be done through the UN.[95] Consequently, LBJ worked through Feinberg, the Krims, Ed Weisl, and other contacts in the Jewish community to spread the word that he remained as firm a friend of Israel as ever. "Neutrality does not imply indifference," Rusk told a news conference.[96]

At 8:10 A.M. on June 8, the American intelligence ship, USS Liberty, operating some thirteen miles off the Egyptian coast, reported that it was under attack—from Israeli aircraft. The Mirages made six strafing runs against the vessel. Twenty minutes later, three torpedo boats closed at high speed, and after first circling the Liberty, two of them launched torpedoes. One passed astern, and the other struck the starboard side in the area occupied by the ship's intelligence-gathering and communication equipment. The weather was clear, the Liberty was flying the Stars and Stripes, and its hull number was prominently displayed. The ship began listing, and the Israelis called off the attack, convinced, apparently, that the Liberty was sinking.[97] As a result of the assault, the ship suffered more than two hundred casualties, with thirty-four dead or dying.

As soon as the incident was reported, the U.S. aircraft carriers America and Saratoga scrambled jets with orders to defend the Liberty. "You are authorized to use force including destruction as necessary to control the situation," the commander of the Sixth Fleet ordered. "Do not use more force than required; do not pursue any unit towards land for reprisal purposes."[98] By the time the U.S. aircraft arrived, the Israelis had already departed the scene. Forty-four minutes after the attack, Tel Aviv "discovered" that they had nearly destroyed an American war vessel in international waters. Ambassador Avraham Harman called at the White House to apologize, and Abba Eban wrote LBJ, "I am deeply mortified and grieved by the tragic accident involving the lives and safety of Americans in Middle Eastern waters."[99]

LBJ was angry, of course, but he realized that he would have to tread carefully. He had cabled Kosygin that he was sending the America and Saratoga to the area to investigate. The initial CIA report indicated that it had all been a mistake. The information that the Liberty was a U.S. vessel had never made its way up the tactical chain of command in Israel.[100] But subsequent probes by Naval Intelligence and other sources rendered that scenario highly unlikely. As Clark Clifford, a long-time friend of Israel, told LBJ, "It is inconceivable that it was an accident."[101] According to a later theory, a high-ranking Israeli official—Defense Minister Moshe Dayan's name was mentioned—had ordered the attack in the belief that the Liberty was spying on Israel and was about to spill the beans concerning a forthcoming surprise attack on Syria. Whatever the case, Johnson did not subsequently press the matter with the Israelis. Rusk delivered a harsh protest to Ambassador Harman, but then let the matter go.[102] Among other things, LBJ believed, the attack on the *Liberty* would get Feinberg and the American friends of Israel off his back and give him some leverage with the Israelis as the terms of a peace settlement came to be worked out.

The Israeli decision to attack Syria drove the Soviet Union to the brink of war. Their chief proxy, Egypt, had been militarily annihilated. The USSR's massive investment in the region seemed for naught. The Chinese were crowing, and respect for Soviet power was changing to contempt in many quarters of the globe. On news of the Israeli invasion, the Kremlin had broken diplomatic relations with Tel Aviv. Kosygin got on the hot line and warned of a "grave catastrophe" and announced that unless the Israelis halted their incursion into Syria immediately, the Soviet Union would take "necessary actions, including military." LBJ immediately huddled with CIA Director Richard Helms, McNamara, Clifford, Bundy, Rostow, and Ambassador to the Soviet Union Llewellyn Thompson. The CIA chief later recalled that the meeting was one of the tensest he had ever attended. After due deliberation, LBJ ordered the Sixth Fleet to set sail for the eastern Mediterranean.[103] At the same time, he cabled Kosygin that he would do his utmost to persuade the Israelis to stand down. Fortunately, early in the afternoon of June 10, Israel signed a truce agreement with Syria, and by June 11 all was still in the Holy Land.

In the days following the end of the Six Day War, Rostow continued to push LBJ to use the occasion to convince all parties that the time had come for a comprehensive settlement. The problem was, as Harry McPherson pointed out to the president, the Israelis and their American supporters were in no frame of mind to make concessions. They were drunk with victory and mesmerized by the vision of permanently secure borders impervious to future Arab and Soviet attacks. Tel Aviv began stalling on U.S. inspection of the atomic facility at Dimona and flatly refused to follow International Atomic Energy Agency nonproliferation guidelines. To ask Israeli intellectuals and religious leaders to give up the Old City now would be like talking to deaf men.[104] Finally, it was highly unlikely that the Kremlin, despite its disgust with Nasser, would be willing to stop fishing in troubled waters. Both Nasser and Hussein had survived. In the wake of their devastating military defeat, both became temporarily more flexible, especially in dealing with the United States, but both continued to plead that their very existence depended on their ability to avoid direct negotiations with Israel, the only precondition Tel Aviv set for relinquishing the gains that it had achieved as a result of its blitzkrieg.[105]

On June 19, LBJ delivered an innocuous speech outlining an entirely predictable plan for peace: freedom of innocent passage through all international waterways in the region; a settlement (unspecified) of the refugee problem; respect for the political independence and territorial integrity of all parties; an arms control agreement; and the right of all countries to physical security. Peace,

Johnson emphasized, was up to the parties involved. The United States could not and would not pressure the Israelis to sacrifice if their neighbors were not even willing to talk with them. As he was well aware, American opinion continued to be decidedly pro-Israeli. "Harris told me last week that in all his years as a pollster, he had never seen a more sweeping . . . registration of overwhelming support for one side of a question," McGeorge Bundy reported to LBJ.[106] John Roche, who had prepared the president's speech, told him after one draft, "It is still a bit much for my taste, but I confess that I look on the Israelis as Texans and Nasser as Santa Anna."[107]

That November, the UN Security Council approved Resolution 242, which was designed to bring about a negotiated settlement to the ongoing Middle East crisis. It called for a multilateral guarantee of Israel's borders in exchange for a return of the territory seized in the Six Day War. In addition, Israel would enjoy free access to "regional waterways" (Nasser had ordered the Suez Canal blocked with sunken ships shortly after Israel attacked) in the area, while the Palestinians could look forward to "a just settlement of the refugee problem," a provision that they interpreted to mean the conversion of what used to be called Palestine (Israel and parts of the current state of Jordan) into a multinational state including both Jews and Palestinians.

The United States supported Resolution 242 but was sympathetic to Israel's fears concerning its security. Tel Aviv insisted that the Arab nations would have to extend formal recognition and give guarantees before the land seized in the Six Day War was returned. As the United States continued to replace Israeli military equipment and to subsidize the Israeli economy, an angry Nasser severed diplomatic ties with Washington. When Israel refused to evacuate the Sinai and return the Gaza Strip, the West Bank, and the Golan Heights, Moscow broke relations with Tel Aviv. Washington and various third parties attempted mediation but with no success. Fedayeen border raids and terrorist attacks mounted in number, while Israel ruled the territories under its control with an iron hand. The region remained ripe for another explosion.

LBJ thought, all things considered, that the United States had handled the Middle East crisis rather well: there had not been a general war involving the Soviet Union and the United States; the conflict had been of brief duration; and Israel was more secure than it had been before the fighting started, rendering the possibility of another war more remote. Others did not agree. "U.S. Ignored Crisis Signs in Mideast," ran a headline in the Baltimore Sun. "The result has been one of the worst failures of United States foreign policy since the miscalculations in the early days of the Vietnamese war."[108]

CHAPTER 37

BACKLASH

S HORTLY AFTER THE SIX DAY WAR, THE KREMLIN AN-
nounced that Premier Kosygin would travel to New York to address
the United Nations. Friends and foes alike urged the president to
meet with his Russian counterpart. Despite their vast differences over
Vietnam, Lippmann, Fulbright, and Johnson were in fundamental agreement
about the need for détente with the Soviet Union.[1] They felt it important to
stand up against the kind of mindless anticommunism that had produced Mc-
Carthyism and the ultra movement of the early 1960s.

At the time, the Johnson administration was actively pursuing a Soviet-
American agreement on the issues of nuclear nonproliferation and strategic
weapons limitations. At lunch at his house in April with Soviet Ambassador
Anatoly Dobrynin, McNamara assured the Russian that the administration had
no intention of proceeding with an antiballistic missile system. This would only
upset the balance of power, causing the Soviet Union to expand its offensive capability. Both nations would suffer financially and wind up being less secure.
America could be safe only "if it were assured of having a force so strong as to be
able to absorb a surprise attack and survive with sufficient power to inflict unacceptable damage on the nations of the [Warsaw] Pact. We believe the Soviets' requirement for a deterrent is the same as ours. We believe they have that
deterrent today." Why not agree to a freeze on the development of new systems
and focus on preventing the spread of nuclear weapons into the hands of third
parties?[2]

Then there was the conflict in Southeast Asia. From Moscow, Ambassador
Llewellyn Thompson advised that Kosygin spoke for the advocates of détente
within the Politburo and that there was still a good chance he would be willing to act as intermediary with the North Vietnamese to effect a mutual de-
escalation. LBJ could not be perceived to be less enthusiastic for peace than

Kosygin. A summit would perhaps take some of the air out of the anti-Vietnam war movement.

Some initial sparring occurred over location. LBJ could not be perceived to be coming to the Russians; besides, Manhattan was likely to be packed with antiwar demonstrators. If, on the other hand, Kosygin came to Washington, the world headquarters of the capitalists-imperialists, the Red Chinese would make a laughingstock of him. In the end, the State Department and Soviet Foreign Ministry settled on the campus of Glassboro State College in Glassboro, New Jersey, approximately halfway between Washington and New York and much less accessible to antiwar protestors.[3]

Johnson and Kosygin met on Saturday, June 23, and then again on Sunday morning. LBJ and his party arrived first by helicopter at the baseball field. An hour later, the Russians made their entry by motorcade. Hollybush, the home of Glassboro State President and Mrs. Thomas Robinson, had been selected to house the conference. When Kosygin arrived, Johnson came out on the porch to meet him. The two exchanged pleasantries and posed for photographs before shaking hands and entering. They met with interpreters only, LBJ seated in a padded rocker and Kosygin in an easy chair drawn up alongside. Each scribbled notes as they talked.[4] The conversations, civil but frank, roamed across the Middle East, Vietnam, and arms control. Johnson observed that the two powers should act the role of "older brothers" to the inhabitants of the Middle East. Kosygin noted that Moscow had been successful in restraining the Arabs, but the United States had failed with the Israelis. There could be no peace in the area unless and until Israel agreed to give up the lands it had conquered. If there were no compromise, there would surely be war, Kosygin asserted, or, as he put it, "They would be sure to resume the fight sooner or later. If they had weapons, they would use them. If they did not have them, they would fight with their bare hands or buy weapons and surely someone would be found to sell them these weapons." At this point, LBJ leaned forward and said very quietly, very slowly, "Let us understand one another. I hope there will be no war. If there is a war, I hope it will not be a big war. If they fight, I hope they fight with fists and not with guns. I hope you and we will keep out of this matter because if we do get into it, it will be a 'most serious' matter."[5]

In a gracious toast to Kosygin at lunch, LBJ declared, "We both have special responsibilities for the security of our families, and over and beyond all our families is the security of the entire human family inhabiting this earth. We must never forget that there are many peoples in this world, many different nations each with its own history and ambitions." Because of Russia's and America's strength and resources, "relations between our two countries [must] be as reasonable and as constructive as we know how to make them."[6] Following the meal, the two leaders discussed arms control but were not able to get beyond generalities.

On Vietnam, Johnson showed some interest when Kosygin remarked that if the United States halted the bombing of the North, peace talks could begin at once. Kosygin went on to say that Vietnam was spoiling relations between the two nations, allowing China "a chance to raise its head with consequent great danger for the peace of the entire world."[7] At the close of the summit, Kosygin and his party got in their cars and began to drive away, but stopped when a knot of onlookers began cheering. They set up a chant: "We want Kosygin!" The Soviet leader got out, stood atop a small embankment, and spoke briefly. "I want friendship with the American people," he said. "I can assure you we want nothing but peace with the American people."[8]

Later, in an interview with Bob Thompson of Hearst Newspapers, Johnson remarked, "He came over here to try to get some of the polecat smell off of him. His policies in the Middle East have been a flop and a failure." The Soviets seemed terribly worried about China, he remarked.[9] One thing was certain: the Soviet Union's failure in the Middle East would make it less willing to act the honest broker in Southeast Asia. Beijing was actually making a bid to wean Syria away from the Soviet orbit. The wars of national liberation desperately needed a winner, and North Vietnam looked like the best bet as the summer of 1967 gave way to fall. Johnson was right. "The Russians have given up any attempt to try to influence Hanoi," Rusk reported to the president the first week in October.[10]

SHORTLY BEFORE LBJ HAD DEPARTED for Glassboro on June 21, he had been awakened by a telephone call from Austin. Luci had given birth to her first child, a son, Patrick Lyndon. "A boy," said the president, pleased. "That's fine." Lynda was then in the last stages of her relationship with George Hamilton. Shortly thereafter, she went on a trip to London without him and then began dating Charles Robb, a marine corps captain who had commanded the White House Color Guard. Less than a month later, on August 10, she burst into her parents' bedroom and informed them that she and Charles intended to get married. The match, despite the suddenness of the courtship, seemed to please both Lyndon and Lady Bird. Robb, a 1961 graduate of Wisconsin and two years later of the University of Virginia Law School, seemed the all-American boy.[11]

THERE HAD ALWAYS BEEN A COMPLICATED but crucial connection between the civil rights movement in the United States and the war in Vietnam. The moral imperative that Lyndon Johnson, Martin Luther King, and others had invoked to persuade white, middle-class America to support the drive for racial equality had reinforced and been reinforced by the liberal internationalist notion that the United States had an obligation to help the nonwhite peoples of the third world resist communist domination. Johnson's talk of internationalizing the Great Society and of transforming the Mekong Delta into another TVA had woven the connecting fabric tighter and tighter. But as the Black Power advocates co-opted the civil rights movement and intimidated white liberals, and as a new wave of urban rioting swept the nation's cities, a white backlash had erupted that threatened not only the Great Society and the Second Reconstruction, but the war in Vietnam as well. Liberals who surrendered to the New Left and who joined with Tom Hayden and Stokely Carmichael in indicting American institutions and political processes played their part in eroding the Vietnam consensus, but it was the growing doubts among the average American that the Judeo-Christian ethic could or should be applied to social problems at home and abroad that did the real damage.

Harry McPherson persuaded LBJ to take advantage of Lincoln's birthday anniversary on February 12 to speak out on race, to affirm the administration's continuing commitment to equal opportunity and equality under the law both at home and abroad.[12] Standing before the majestic Lincoln Memorial, LBJ gestured to the statue designed by Daniel Chester French and called the crowd's attention to an aura "of brooding compassion, of love for humanity; a love which was, if anything, strengthened and deepened by the agony that drove lesser men to the protective shelter of callous indifference." Speaking for himself as well as the Great Emancipator, LBJ said, "Lincoln did not come to the Presidency with any set of full-blown theories, but rather with a mystical dedication to this Union—and an unyielding determination to always preserve the integrity of the Republic." Then the link between civil rights and internationalism: "Today, racial suspicions, racial hatreds and racial violence plague men in almost every part of the earth . . . The true liberators of mankind have always been those who showed men another way to live—than by hating their brothers."[13]

What Johnson and McPherson were trying to do, of course, was to persuade black Americans to acknowledge a positive connection between the Second Reconstruction and the war in Vietnam: both were struggles for self-determination, campaigns to spread the blessings of freedom and democracy to nonwhite peoples. Instead, the Black Power movement, the SDS, SNCC, and the leadership of the SCLC, including Martin Luther King, were joining hands to portray the war in Southeast Asia as just another attempt by the white power structure in the United States to exploit and oppress colored people everywhere. There was a link, but black soldiers ought to be fighting with the Vietcong against American imperialism rather than with the Armed Forces of the United States. Only the most radical went that far, of course, but increasingly black revolutionaries like Floyd McKissick and New Left leaders like Tom Hayden were joining with evangelical civil rights activists like King in calling for an immediate withdrawal from Vietnam in order to free up funds for the antipoverty program and other aspects of the Great Society.

The SDS and SNCC had begun collaborating as early as 1966, but King did not emerge as a prominent antiwar figure until February 26, 1967, when in Los Angeles he called on the country's "creative dissenters" to "combine the fervor for the civil rights movement with the peace movement . . . until the very foundations of our nation are shaken."[14] A month later, he and Dr. Benjamin Spock, a prominent pediatrician and anti-war leader, led a Holy Saturday procession of eighty-five hundred people down State Street to the Chicago Coliseum. But his most memorable antiwar statement came at New York's Riverside Church on April 4. The nation's soul was once again in peril, King proclaimed. The war in

Vietnam was "a symptom of a far deeper malady" that throughout history had prompted the United States to oppose revolutions in behalf of social justice and self-determination by the nonwhite peoples of the third world.[15] King's public prominence, his receipt of the 1964 Nobel Peace Prize, and his organizational connections made him an immediate focal point of the antiwar movement, but it was his stature as a spiritual leader that would be most telling. The Judeo-Christian ethic he had wielded so effectively to mobilize the black masses and shame the white middle class would now be enlisted in the aid of the anti–Vietnam War crusade.

Actually, King's position on the war was moderate: bombing halt, cease-fire, negotiations, and implementation of the 1954 Geneva Accords. But the White House, recognizing the significance of his rhetoric, came to see him as "the crown prince of the Vietniks," as Harry McPherson put it. LBJ and his advisers believed that by blaming the war in Vietnam for society's ills, King was undercutting their efforts to bring the Second Reconstruction to fruition. Conservatives were aching for a justification to starve the Great Society of funds. While the administration argued for guns and butter, leaders of the conservative coalition could cite the "dubious loyalty" of figures like King to block further appropriations.[16]

Not surprisingly, the administration did everything in its power to mobilize and highlight black supporters of the war. And there were supporters, although most were unenthusiastic. A. Philip Randolph, Whitney Young, Roy Wilkins, and even James Farmer had varying reservations about the conflict in Southeast Asia. They worried that it would divert attention and funding away from antipoverty and other programs vital to African Americans, but they kept these sentiments to themselves. "I felt that the civil rights movement should not get involved in this," Farmer later recalled. "I felt it would simply confuse the issue."[17] Wilkins and Young recognized the idealism, misguided though it may have been, that was responsible for America's decision to go to war. The White House encouraged Young to make a trip to Vietnam and applauded when he subsequently reported to the Saigon press corps that black soldiers seemed to be faring no better or worse than their white counterparts, that they generally supported the war, and that, for the most part, they saw service in the military as a way to get ahead in the world.[18] The Board of the NAACP voted on April 10, 1967, that any attempt to merge the civil rights and peace movements would be "a serious tactical mistake."[19] At the prompting of the White House, General Hershey and the Selective Service Board made a concerted effort to get blacks on local draft and appeal boards in the South. In response, between December 1966 and June 1967, the number of blacks on local boards increased from 267 to 413, including Florida with five and Louisiana with eight. The White House ordered a study to determine if African Americans were fighting and dying in Vietnam in a higher proportion than their percentage of the general service population. (The study found that blacks were serving in disproportionately high numbers in combat, but those in combat were dying at the same rate as whites.)[20]

Ironically, LBJ's staying the course in Vietnam won him scant credit with the ultranationalist white South. While most whites approved of the war, they continued to disapprove of him. A September 1966 poll in Louisiana showed the president's job rating at 31 percent favorable and 69 percent unfavorable. When divided by race, the numbers stood at 16 percent to 84 percent among whites and 94 percent to 6 percent among blacks.[21] As hawkish South Carolina Congressman Mendell Rivers told White House aide Henry Wilson, his constituents loved the bombing but hated the federal registrars.[22]

JOHNSON DID NOT BELIEVE IN TOKENS, but he believed in symbols. Early in his administration he had brought Clifford Alexander, a black Harvard graduate, into the White House to advise him on appointments. Alexander, who knew nearly everybody in the black elite and who would eventually head the Equal Opportunity Commission, was a fanatic on the appointment of African Americans to mid- and high-level federal positions. He tattled on recalcitrant agencies and put forward a steady stream of black talent for the president's perusal. He had been relentless in pushing Bob Weaver for HUD, and he badgered LBJ about appointing a black to the U.S. Supreme Court. The logical candidate was Thurgood Marshall, the pioneering NAACP lawyer whom Kennedy had appointed to the U.S. Court of Appeals.

In July 1965, LBJ had nominated Marshall to be solicitor general. When the first vacancy on the Court came up, Johnson felt duty-bound to offer it to Abe Fortas. But he was as enthusiastic as Alexander about having a black on the Supreme Court. He wanted "every little Negro boy in the country," he told a journalist, to wake up knowing that he had as much chance to occupy a cabinet position or sit on the Supreme Court as anyone else. There were other reasons. The threatened takeover of the civil rights movement by Black Power advocates and the promise of more urban rioting was cutting the moral ground out from beneath the Second Reconstruction. Its other pillar, the law, was also being threatened and needed affirmation. Marshall was perfect. The fifty-eight-year-old African American was a seasoned jurist with a stellar record as an attorney and a judge. Johnson found it gratifying that he had risen from humble origins, although, given the range of black experience, being the son of a Pullman car steward and kindergarten teacher could hardly be called humble. "This is a man who understands people, understands what they're about," he would tell Clifford Alexander. What he meant, Alexander later mused, was that "he's like me."[23]

Marshall had grown up in racially segregated Baltimore. He confronted segregation with dignity and determination. Denied admission to the University of Maryland Law School, he graduated first in his class from Howard in 1933. As a disciple of pioneering civil rights lawyer Charles H. Houston and later director of the NAACP's Legal Defense Fund, Marshall stood for a philosophy of activism within the system, for using constitutional guarantees and the legal process to redress grievances. Among segregationists, no laborer in the vineyard of civil rights other than King was more hated. During Marshall's confirmation hearings for the Court of Appeals, Jim Eastland had stalled for nearly a year, finally telling JFK that he would "give him the nigger" if Kennedy would nominate the racist Mississippi judge, Harold Costo, to a district court seat.[24]

First, however, there had to be an open seat. In February, LBJ had maneuvered to have Tom Clark retire from the high court to make way for his son, Ramsey's, appointment as attorney general. Joe Califano recalled that during one of the early morning staff meetings in the president's bedroom, LBJ mentioned that Clark would be officially stepping down on June 13 and asked for suggestions for a replacement. They bandied about some names, and then LBJ said he was thinking of appointing a woman. Lady Bird encouraged him. You have already done so much for blacks; why not choose a woman, she said. Several were mentioned, including Shirley Huffstedler, then a judge in California. But more than likely Johnson had long ago settled on Marshall. (He would later appoint Huffstedler to the Court of Appeals for the 9th Circuit.) A couple of weeks later, Johnson was talking with Connally aide Larry Temple, who would soon join the White House staff. He was thinking about the Supreme Court vacancy and was considering a Negro, the president said. Any suggestions? Temple mentioned Judge A. Leon Higginbotham, a Johnson appointee to the Federal District Court for Eastern Pennsylvania. Temple recalled that LBJ leaned forward, fixing him with his unforgettable gaze. "Larry," he said, "the only two people who ever heard of Judge Higginbotham are you and his momma. When I appoint a nigger to the bench, I want everyone to know he's a nigger."[25]

Typically, before announcing the appointment, the president tried to put doubt in everyone's mind. Marshall "wasn't worth a damn as an administrator," LBJ told Louis Martin, a prominent black newspaper publisher and Johnson's emissary to the black press.[26] But nominate Marshall he did. There was the predictable southern opposition from Ervin, Russell, and particularly John McClellan. Tellingly, however, they did not oppose him on racial grounds or even on qualification, but rather on philosophy. He was too much of an activist, too likely to be easy on the criminal element. Marshall was confirmed on August 30 by a vote of sixty-nine to eleven.[27]

JOHNSON, MCPHERSON, CALIFANO, and Ramsey Clark, who had been serving as acting attorney general, were anticipating another summer of unrest in the nation's inner cities. During late 1966 and early 1967, they had continued to struggle with causes and remedies. Moynihan's focus on the dysfunctional black family seemed logical, but what to do about it, especially in the long run? To make matters worse, the Moynihan report was being denounced daily by Black Power spokesmen as just another racial slur.[28] More parks, more summer camps, more job training, more subsidized housing, and better educational opportunities were needed.[29]

On February 15, LBJ delivered a special message to Congress on equal justice. He called on lawmakers to enact a fair housing law, provide specific punishments for those interfering with existing federal rights, approve a measure that outlawed discrimination in jury selection, and extend the lives of both the Committee on Equal Employment Opportunity Commission and the U.S. Civil Rights Commission.[30] LBJ was most specific about fair housing. Under his plan, a flat ban on discrimination would go into effect for large apartment houses and real estate developments in 1968 and for all housing in 1969. "I am proposing fair-housing legislation again this year," he said, "because it is decent and right." And there was an effort to mobilize sentiment, if not for the war in Vietnam, for the soldiers fighting there in behalf of civil rights. "The bullets of our enemies do not discriminate between Negro marines and white marines." And he recalled the promise of the Howard speech. "Freedom," he declared, "is not enough. You do not wipe away the scars of centuries by saying: Now you are free to go where you want, do as you desire."[31]

Marshall's nomination and Johnson's message to Congress may have swelled the hearts of the vast majority of African Americans, but it did not do a thing for urban ghetto dwellers confronted with a landscape of unremitting hopelessness. Moreover, unlike their rural brethren, they were in a position to vent their anger. The second week in July, violence erupted in Newark, New Jersey, when police arrested a black cab driver on traffic charges and scuffled with him outside a station house. A glowering crowd from an adjacent housing project gathered, shouted insults, then rocks and bricks from the knot of angry blacks and finally a Molotov cocktail were hurled at police. Ghetto dwellers by the hundreds poured out onto the street, setting fires and looting. Police and firefighters who responded to calls were stoned and eventually fired on by snipers. Rioters dragged passing whites out of their cars, mauled a Good Humor ice cream vendor, and overturned and set fire to his truck. "We're getting bombed out here," one cop radioed. "What should we do?" "Leave," said his dispatcher. Six days of rioting took twenty-six lives, injured fifteen hundred, and left much of the inner city a burned-out shell.[32] State and local police responded with a vengeance.

LBJ wanted to avoid a federal presence in Newark. Whatever the administration did, conservatives who would say it wasn't doing enough and liberals who were saying it was doing too much would whipsaw U.S. marshals and troops. As luck would have it, New Jersey Democratic Governor Richard Hughes was one of Johnson's strongest supporters. The president offered aid, but to his great relief, Hughes replied that state and local authorities could handle matters. On Saturday afternoon, July 15, UPI reported that Vice President Humphrey had called the governor and offered "federal aid." Johnson was furious. He ordered Califano to rein in the vice president: "He has no authority, spell it out, N-O-N-E, to provide any federal aid to Newark or any other city, town or county in America."[33] Humphrey subsequently denied to Califano that he had made any such promise, but LBJ remained unconvinced. In truth, Johnson was taking his anger at white liberals out on Humphrey. All the while, Congress was whittling away at his Great Society programs, Kennedy, Ribicoff, and Clark were blasting the administration for abandoning the nation's cities.

Congress found itself in the grip of a Newark backlash almost immediately. In a special message to the House and Senate earlier in the year on urban and rural poverty, LBJ had proposed the Rat Extermination Act to provide federal funding to control and exterminate the millions of rats that bred in collapsed buildings and bit terrified children. The measure had breezed through the Senate, and the administration expected quick passage in the House. But three days after Newark, a coalition of southern Democrats and Republicans by a vote of 207 to 176 blocked the measure. They derided it as a "civil rats" bill and suggested that the president allocate funds to hire an army of cats.[34] Johnson was appropriately appalled. He issued a scathing statement the afternoon of the defeat, calling the House action a "cruel blow to the poor children of America . . . We are spending Federal funds to protect our livestock from rodents and predatory animals. The least we can do is give our children the same protection we give our livestock."[35] Following a massive lobbying effort by the White House, the House reversed itself and added a rat extermination provision to the Partnership for Health Act, which the president signed on December 4, 1967.[36]

At 4 A.M. on Sunday, July 26, Detroit police staged a raid on a "blind pig," an after-hours drinking club on the city's west side in the heart of the ghetto. As the officers herded some eighty patrons down the stairs of the club, knots of angry blacks gathered in the muggy streets. Soon a crowd had surrounded the police and began hurling rocks and then bricks at them and their cruisers. The besieged officers defended themselves but did nothing to disperse the crowds. Mayor Jerome Cavanaugh had been elected by black votes and had implemented a walk softly approach to police-minority relations. Encouraged by the cops' passivity, the crowd emptied garbage into the streets and set it afire. Then the looting began. Bricks crashed through shop windows, and roaming gangs set fire to what they did not take. There would be more than fifteen hundred blazes in the days to come. Cavanaugh and Michigan Governor George Romney huddled and decided to call in seventy-three hundred national guardsmen to reinforce the city's four thousand police. The guardsmen turned out to be, in *Newsweek*'s words, "a ragged, jittery, hair-triggered lot, ill-trained in riot control." Said one young citizen-soldier, "I'm gonna shoot anything that moves and is black." By midmorning, Detroit was paralyzed. A pall of smoke hung over the entire city as intermittent sniper fire crackled in the air.[37]

Just before 3 A.M. on Monday morning, Romney made the first of a series of calls to Ramsey Clark. Romney, "a Republican with a conscience," was positioning himself for a run at the 1968 GOP presidential nomination. Attractive, articulate, moderate, he was to LBJ's mind a more formidable adversary than Richard Nixon. Under the 1795 law that governed the federal government's response to civil unrest, the president was authorized to send in troops at the "request" of a governor to put down an "insurrection." In his conversations with

Clark, Romney stated that he would probably have to "recommend" that troops be sent in. Each of these conversations was reported to LBJ. Abe Fortas warned that Romney was going to try to draw the administration into the peacekeeping effort in Detroit and then scream federal intervention. From then on, Johnson's antennae were up. Throughout the morning Clark and Romney sparred.[38] The governor would have to formally request the troops before they could be sent, Clark said. After Romney agreed, the attorney general insisted that his message to LBJ also use the word "insurrection." The governor angrily pointed out that insurance companies did not pay for damages caused by insurrections and slammed the phone down. He then told the press that he had requested troops, the president had agreed to send them, but that he had then withdrawn his request out of the conviction that federal forces would be needed to put down disturbances in other U.S. cities. The implication was that the government was losing control of the country. In fact, Congressman Gerald Ford, also of Michigan, had been touting this line, and that very day the Republican Coordinating Committee had issued a statement charging that "widespread rioting and violent civil righters have grown to a national crisis since the present Administration took office."[39]

At 10:46 Romney cabled a formal request for federal troops. Meanwhile, Cyrus Vance, whom LBJ had dispatched to the riot scene to represent him, reported that the situation was worsening: more fires, more sniper fire, more shootings by guardsmen. Johnson ordered McNamara to assemble a contingent of troops at Selfridge Air Force Base some thirty miles from Detroit. To no one in particular, LBJ remarked despondently, "Well, I guess it is just a matter of minutes before federal troops start shooting women and children."[40] He then told Vance to get on the radio, or loudspeakers, or whatever was available and issue a call for peace and quiet before troops were sent in. There wasn't time, Hoover interjected: "They have lost all control in Detroit. Harlem will break loose within thirty minutes. They plan to tear it to pieces."[41] Finally, at 11:22, an exhausted Johnson signed the executive order dispatching federal troops to Detroit. Fortas helped draft a statement for him to read over television. The address was a disaster. The seven-minute statement mentioned Romney fourteen times, spelled out to the minute when the president received the governor's wire and when he responded, and emphasized the "undisputed evidence that Governor Romney of Michigan and the local officials in Detroit have been unable to bring the situation under control."[42] CBS President Frank Stanton, a friend of LBJ's, later observed to Joe Califano that the statement was transparently political and beneath the president at such a time.[43]

The violence in Detroit continued for three more days. When peace was finally restored, forty people lay dead, another 2,250 were injured. Police had arrested more than four thousand citizens, and property damage was estimated in the hundreds of millions of dollars. *Newsweek* described the scene and summed up the national mood: "Whole streets lay ravaged by looters, while blocks were immolated in flames. Federal troops—the first sent into racial battle outside the

South in a quarter century—occupied American streets at bayonet point. Patton tanks—machine guns ablaze—and Huey helicopters patrolled a cityscape of blackened brick chimneys poking out of gutted basements. And suddenly Harlem 1964 and Watts 1965 and Newark only three weeks ago fell back into the shadows of memory. Detroit was the new benchmark, its rubble a monument to the most devastating race riot in U.S. history—and a symbol of a domestic crisis grown graver than any since the Civil War." [44]

Even before the ashes of Detroit had cooled, the conservative coalition had moved to portray the rioting as part of a well-orchestrated communist conspiracy to rip apart the fabric of American society. Figures on the right from Gerald Ford to Richard Russell, aided and abetted by J. Edgar Hoover, saw an opportunity to simultaneously generate support for the war in Vietnam and cut the ground out from under the Second Reconstruction and the Great Society. The ghetto uprising, Black Power rhetoric, and King's antiwar speeches were proof positive that the war in Vietnam and the drive for social justice in the United States were not part of the same struggle but antithetical to each other. What African Americans needed was law and order, discipline, not more costly programs. Head Start and the antipoverty program were indirectly subsiding anarchism and riots, and playing into the hands of Hanoi, Moscow, and Beijing.

To the delight of conservatives, in the wake of Newark and Detroit, Stokely Carmichael flew to Castro's Cuba to address the Organization for Latin American Solidarity. The gathering of Marxists-Leninists from throughout the Western Hemisphere was held in the Hotel Havana Libra, whose three-storey lobby featured an enormous derrick replete with machine guns, automatic rifles, Molotov cocktails, and banners proclaiming the OLAS motto: "The duty of every revolutionary is to make revolution!" Carmichael was appropriately radical. "Yankee imperialism has existed too long," he declared. "We are ready to destroy it from the inside. We hope you are ready to destroy it from the outside." [45] His remarks made front-page news in papers across the United States. At the same time, SNCC's new national chairman, H. Rap Brown, proclaimed that the organization would thereafter celebrate August 18, the anniversary of the 1965 Watts riot, as Independence Day instead of July 4. One GOP congressman declared that by preaching resistance to the draft and the use of violence to achieve the goals of the civil rights movement, Carmichael had violated the treason laws of the United States. He must be arrested and severely punished. If the president did not take action, the nation could and probably would descend into chaos. [46]

For months, Hoover had been deluging LBJ with "proof" that the riots were communist-inspired and probably communist-run. King's support for the antiwar movement was further evidence that he was nothing more or less than the dupe of his red handlers, Bayard Rustin and Stanley Levinson. LBJ was tempted to buy into the theory. The Black Power movement, with its apocalyptic anti-administration rhetoric and advocacy of violence in the nation's inner cities, continued to distress him. How could blacks, for whom he had done so much, be so ungrateful? But if the GOP's plans to derail domestic reform were to be thwarted, the riots and Black Power movement must be portrayed as an indigenous aberration, the acts of a misguided, but tiny, minority. Besides, the CIA, which was in a much better position than the FBI to judge what role if any was played by Sino-Soviet agents provocateurs, found that there was no connection between the riots and the forces of international communism.[47]

While Kennedy, Ribicoff, and King assailed the administration from the left, accusing it of doing too little, too late on behalf of the nation's cities and implying that the war in Vietnam was draining away funds from the Great Society programs, Ford, Dirksen, and the Republican Coordinating Committee attacked from the right. The GOP issued a statement, endorsed by former President Eisenhower, flailing LBJ for having "totally failed to recognize the problem" of the American city on the same day its authors appealed to the president to cut back federal spending for the antipoverty program and Model Cities. It insisted that the administration "must accept its national responsibility" for the rioting. It was unclear whether the Republicans regarded Johnson's $10 billion request for urban areas, a 250 percent increase over seven years, as a plus or a minus. There was no choice, LBJ told his aides and members of the cabinet, but to keep plugging away on behalf of housing, education, jobs, and health.[48]

At Harry McPherson's suggestion, LBJ met with his informal black cabinet, Randolph, Young, Wilkins, et al. "To the Black Power crowd, these people are Uncle Toms," McPherson admitted. "[But] I don't think we should let the Carmichael crowd deter us by their scorn of men like these."[49] LBJ and his staff found the group discouraged, even despondent, with nothing to offer but the same old remedies. Do not punish the 97 percent of the law-abiding citizens because of the 3 percent who riot. Get more housing; reconsider Young's Marshall Plan for the ghettoes.[50] They seemed to LBJ to be out of touch with the currents that were then shifting in both the ghettoes and Congress. Columnist Emmet Hughes observed that the "movement" had recently come "to suffer the baleful prominence of two men supremely skilled in the art of alienating—the smirking Adam Clayton Powell and the snarling Stokely Carmichael."[51]

On July 27, LBJ went on national television to appeal for peace and calm. He designated the following Sunday a national day of prayer and announced that he was establishing the National Advisory Commission on Civil Disorders. LBJ wanted a blue ribbon commission whose report would sensitize white America to the plight of ghetto dwellers, and he wanted to head off congressional investigations of the riots that would no doubt assail him from both the right and the left. To this end, he planned to stack it with white liberals and black conservatives. For chair he chose Illinois Governor Otto Kerner, a Democrat, and for vice chair John Lindsay, the Republican governor of New York. Both Roy Wilkins and Republican Senator Edward Brooke of Massachusetts, an African American, were included. In his speech, LBJ condemned the rioters and promised that they would be punished, but he warned, "It would compound the tragedy . . . if we should settle for order that is imposed by the muzzle of a gun . . . The only genuine, long-range solution for what has happened lies in an attack—mounted at every level—upon the conditions that breed despair and violence." [52]

The president dispatched his aides to St. Louis, New York, Boston, Washington, D.C., and other breeding grounds for urban rioting. Cliff Alexander, Louis Martin, and Harry McPherson went to Harlem and Bedford-Stuyvesant. McPherson's report was chilling: "It is awful in most parts of Harlem. In one block we saw four separate empty lots . . . that were piled high with rubbish and filth, and that were no doubt breeding rats by the thousands. Harlem looks like Calcutta: filthy streets, broken doorways (affording no security for those who live there), trash in the halls, condemned buildings where junkies sleep overnight and sometimes start fires that threaten the whole neighborhood." And Harlem was Shangri-la compared with Bed-Sty. In their effort to quell discontent before it erupted into violence, Mayor Lindsay and local black leaders sometimes found themselves forming unusual alliances. "We heard of a conversation between Rap Brown and a man named Bumpy Johnson— allegedly the top Negro in the Mafia rackets," McPherson told the president. "After Brown spoke, Johnson told him, 'I agree with a lot of what you said. Except I don't want any riots. I got to raise $60,000 to buy off some people downtown on a narcotics rap. I can't do that if there's a riot. You start a riot and I'll kill you.' Brown is said to have left town the next day." [53]

Predictably, Detroit and Newark hardened racial stereotyping among many whites. Blacks were lazy, immoral, less intelligent—people who wanted something for nothing. White America had extended its hand, and look what happened. Public opinion polls taken in the wake of the rioting showed that whites believed by 71 percent that the uprisings were organized and by 45 percent that the organizing was done by outside agitators. [54] White blacklash, red-baiters, demagogues, and political opportunists aside, there was a growing feeling among well-intentioned Americans that nothing really could be done about the residents of the third world, whether they lived in inner-city Philadelphia or the rice paddies of South Vietnam. "This kind of world outbreak, the failure to follow law and order and accepted procedures," Orville Freeman confided to his diary, "might very well lead us to what is the big problem in most of the less developed countries around the world that they simply can't get together, work together, and cooperate to get anything done." [55] In the wake of the rioting LBJ's approval rating fell to an all-time low of 39 percent. [56]

BY 1967 LBJ had become convinced, very reluctantly, that he could not continue to have guns and butter without a tax increase. He knew how Americans hated taxes; he knew that "higher taxes and federal spending" were the issues that conservatives could always make political hay with, but the budget had soared to $126.7 billion for FY 1967 and was projected to reach $135 billion for FY 1968. The administration had estimated that around $12 billion would be needed for Vietnam; the figure turned out instead to be $21.9 billion. The Johnson budget called for only $1.9 billion more for Great Society programs—just $280 million over FY 1967 for the War on Poverty—but the president refused to abandon other programs he regarded as essential. The Council of Economic Advisers predicted a budget deficit of $10 to $12 billion. Johnson declared that the country could afford—financially, politically, socially—no more than $2 billion. To pay for guns and butter, LBJ asked Congress to consider enacting a 6 percent surcharge (a tax on a tax) on corporate and individual incomes.[57]

For six months, the administration's surtax proposal lay dead in the water. Members of the conservative coalition did not want to give the administration additional funds because they opposed most aspects of the Great Society program; liberals did not want to give the administration more money because they opposed the war in Vietnam and wanted to make LBJ choose between domestic programs and the conflict in Southeast Asia. The first week in June, LBJ met with his economic advisers; they presented him with devastating news. The projected cost of the war was continuing to increase, as was the cost of Medicare, Social Security, and other domestic programs. The administration was looking at a projected deficit for FY 1968 of from $23 to $28 billion.[58] Several days later, he presided over a cabinet meeting. "The country could not tolerate a deficit of from $25 to $30 billion," Johnson said. Either there would be new taxes or programs would be cut. Each cabinet officer, each agency head must cultivate every representative and senator they could gain access to. While they were applying a thick coat of butter to the solons, he would be "tailing em up." He explained that in Texas, when there was a drought or bad weather and the cows became very weak and could not eat and refused to get up, the cowboys would go out and grasp the cow's tail, twisting it around and around until the animal became so uncomfortable that it got up on its feet and began to eat.[59]

On July 26, LBJ had Wilbur Mills to the White House. Why did the economy need a tax cut in 1964 but now need a tax increase? Mills inquired. Times and conditions were different, Johnson replied. Mills helped draft a new tax request message to Congress, but made it clear that he would not come onboard until there were dramatic cuts in domestic programs.[60] On August 3, the president sent his message to Congress, asking this time not for a 6 percent but for a 10 percent surcharge on personal and corporate income taxes. Congress's response was to threaten virtually every component of the Great Society program, from education to Medicare to Social Security to rent supplements to public broadcasting. All right, if they want cuts, LBJ responded, we'll give them cuts. He contemplated telling Congress that if it did not enact a tax increase, he would request the House and Senate to cut all appropriations by 10 percent. "Including defense," McNamara interjected. "I'd stick it to Mills," he said, implying that he was leading a congressional charge that would not only undermine existing domestic programs but threaten the war in Vietnam.[61] All the while, Johnson continued to lash his cabinet officers, telling them that if they did not lobby the hell out of Congress, he would sacrifice their budgets first. In a spate of interviews with journalists, LBJ laid out the situation and placed the blame at Congress's door. Wilbur Mills, he told columnist Joe Kraft, was the "chief Blackmailer."[62]

In mid-November LBJ held a spirited press conference on the economic situation. He abandoned his podium and teleprompter, instead walking among reporters with lavalier microphone pinned to his lapel, speaking extemporaneously: "One of the great mistakes that the Congress will make is that Mr. Ford and Mr. Mills have taken the position that they cannot have any tax bill now. They will live to rue the day when they made that decision . . . I know it doesn't add to your . . . popularity to say we have to have additional taxes to fight this war abroad and fight the problems in our cities at home. But we can do it with the gross national product we have. Who should do it [if we don't]?"[63]

The day following, the British devalued the pound for the first time since 1949 and raised interest rates. To protect the dollar, the Fed, followed by commercial banks, raised the prime lending rate. Johnson attempted to seize the crisis to push his tax bill and to eliminate congressional addons to his budget. But Mills was still not moved. To Johnson's consternation, the chairman added a freeze on welfare payments for dependent children to the administration's Social Security bill, an amendment that, if enacted, would keep another 1.3 million Americans from rising above the poverty line. In a last-ditch effort to get the Arkansan to back down, LBJ met with him in the Oval Office. The freeze was unfair, LBJ protested. "Mr. President," Mills said, "across town from my mother in Arkansas a Negro woman has a baby every year. Every time I go home, my mother complains. That Negro woman's now got eleven children. My proposal will stop this." Moreover, he declared, there would be no tax bill until there were more and deeper cuts in domestic programs.[64]

CHAPTER 38

OF HAWKS AND DOVES,
VULTURES AND CHICKENS

I N MANY WAYS, BY 1967 HARRY McPHERSON HAD BECOME
as important to Lyndon Johnson as George Reedy had been during the
1950s—even more, perhaps. McPherson was smart, an intellectual, an
idealist, but a practical one—and he was a Texan. LBJ might argue with
McPherson, might momentarily bridle at his bluntness, but he trusted McPherson's judgment, both moral and political. The English major turned lawyer
served as LBJ's eyes and ears in America's ghettoes, in the Middle East, and in
Vietnam. And McPherson was disinterested—a true patriot, as LBJ defined the
term. He could see Vietnam with clear eyes. It wasn't a pretty sight.

In early June, McPherson returned from his latest visit. What struck him
first, he told Johnson, was the massive U.S. presence in that tiny country. "At
1500 feet in a Huey on any given afternoon, you look out on two or three Eagle
flights of choppers going in to chase VC's; an air strike in progress; artillery
'prepping' another area; a division camp here, a battalion forward area there;
trucks moving on a dozen roads . . . Flying north along the road to Danang, you
see why the highway is secure: great areas have been scraped off the hilltops
every five miles or so, ringed by 105's [mobile howitzers] and covered with
troops and tents." The other thing one noticed was the lack of security. "You just
can't go down that country road, although it looks peaceful. You can't spend the
night in this area. You take off from a rice paddy with your .50 caliber gunners
aiming at an impassive crowd of peasants standing on a dike. This PF [Popular
Forces] outpost was overrun last week." He could see why the Vietcong continued to gain traction. Corruption was everywhere. The peasants hated the police
because they arbitrarily imposed and collected "taxes" on every bag of rice they
came upon. "It sounds romantic to say so, but if I were a young peasant living in

a hamlet, and had had none of my family hurt or killed by the VC; if I saw that the ridiculous Vietnamese educational system would almost certainly deny me the chance to go beyond the fifth grade; if I was frustrated by the lack of opportunity, and bored by the limited life of the hamlet; if I had no sense of commitment to today's South Vietnamese action, because the Saigon government had given me no reason to have it; and if I were offered the possibility of adventure, of striking at my Frenchified oppressors and their American allies . . . I would join up."[1]

LYNDON JOHNSON WAS SIMULTANEOUSLY a shrewd rationalist and a hopeless sentimentalist. His acute sense of empathy did not serve him well as commander in chief. By 1966 the Situation Room had grown used to late-night or early-morning calls from the president asking for casualty reports. LBJ forced himself to visit military hospitals in the Washington area, the burn center at Walter Reed Hospital in San Antonio, and wounded veterans during his trips to the Pacific. "I saw him cry a lot over Vietnam," Marie Fehmer, the secretary who was closest to him, recalled, "mostly at night while we were waiting for the bombing raids . . . for the boys to come home. Then the next morning he had to sign the letters that went out to the families of the boys who didn't make it."[2] "I am convinced that every casualty report stabbed him to the heart," George Reedy said. "Sometimes he would pass old friends without even an eye blink of recognition. He was not seeing them because his eyes were focused instead on rice paddies in Vietnam."[3] He and Lady Bird began attending two and sometimes three services at various churches on Sunday morning. He was particularly attracted during this period by his daughter Luci's and Marie Fehmer's Catholicism. He began dropping in at the tiny Catholic mission in Stonewall, Texas, and struck up a friendship with its assistant priest, Father Wunibald Schneider. In Washington he went to the chapel at Saint Dominic's Priory to sit and think and pray after the day's work was done.[4] In the midst of the incredible complexity and ambiguity of the world in which he lived, Johnson was particularly attracted by Catholicism's simplicity and certainty. He revived an old friendship with the archbishop of San Antonio, Robert E. Lucey.[5]

During his trips to church, LBJ did not always hear what he wanted to hear. On November 11, Lyndon and Lady Bird spent the night in Colonial Williamsburg and the next morning attended services at the Bruton Parish Episcopal Church. In his sermon, the Reverend Cotesworth Pinckney Lewis expressed support and admiration for the president but then launched into a critique of the war. Attacking from the right and the left, he declared first that he was "appalled" at the fact that "this is the only war in our history which has had three times as many civilian as military casualties" (a totally erroneous claim) and then he was "mystified" by news accounts that "our brave fighting units are being inhibited by directives and inadequate equipment from using their capacities to terminate the conflict successfully." Then, looking LBJ directly in the eye, he asked, "While pledging our loyalty—we ask respectfully, WHY?"[6] LBJ kept his cool, pumping the preacher's hand after the service, but he was humiliated. "I think our aims . . . have been very clear," he subsequently remarked to reporters, "and . . . I thought that even all the preachers in the country had heard about it."[7]

IN MAY, GENERAL WESTMORELAND and Admiral Sharp, alarmed by the antiwar movement and general war weariness, decided once again to ask for enough force to deliver a knockout blow. "The Vietnam war is unpopular in this country," they observed to McNamara. "It is becoming increasingly unpopular as it escalates—causing more American casualties, more fear of its growing into a wider war, more privation of the domestic sector, and more distress at the amount of suffering being visited on the non-combatants in Vietnam, South and North. Most Americans do not know how we got where we are, and most . . . are convinced that somehow we should not have gotten this deeply in. All want the war ended and expect their President to end it. Successfully or else . . . This state of mind in the U.S. generates impatience in the political structure of the United States. It unfortunately also generates patience in Hanoi." What Westmoreland and Sharp asked for were an additional two-hundred-thousand men—half immediately and half in the next fiscal year—and thirteen additional tactical air squadrons for South Vietnam. This would require calling up the reserves, the addition of five hundred thousand men to America's armed forces, and an increase of nearly $10 million in the defense budget. McNamara told LBJ that such a move would generate irresistible pressure to escalate the war: to move into Cambodia and Laos to eliminate communist sanctuaries; for unlimited bombing of the North; for a blockade of rail, road, and sea routes into North Vietnam; and ultimately, an invasion of the North to control infiltration routes.[8] McNamara, of course, was adamantly opposed to such an escalation. So, too, was his boss.[9] On August 3, LBJ announced that another fifty-five thousand men would be sent to Vietnam and set a new ceiling of 525,000 GIs by June 30, 1968. In light of their intent to turn the war over to the South Vietnamese, anything above this would be counterproductive, he had concluded.[10]

In truth, Westmoreland, Sharp, and Wheeler had long since accommodated themselves to fighting the war within the restraints that politics placed on them. However, other service chiefs and their allies in Congress had not and were growing restive by the summer of 1967. The second week in July, two marine companies operating in the jungle near Con Thien in the narrow neck of northern South Vietnam were ambushed and nearly annihilated by a force of more than one thousand North Vietnamese Army soldiers. The enemy, able to operate freely north of the DMZ and in Laos and Cambodia, had managed to infiltrate behind U.S. lines. In the initial onslaught, one entire American company was wiped out. "We were all wounded," recalled Corporal Mike Hughes, "and the men were just lying there firing. I shouted, 'get up and move back,' and somebody said, 'We can't.' I said: 'You want to live you got to move.' " By the time U.S. fighter bombers and a relief column arrived, nearly all of the marines had been killed or wounded. "Bodies of dead American marines lay everywhere, and there was evidence that the North Vietnamese had executed some of the wounded after overrunning the U.S. positions," the combat reporter accompanying the unit later wrote.[11] Westmoreland won permission to conduct secret sweeps north of the DMZ south of the Ben Hai River. He subsequently reported that these operations were successful, but American casualties were high because of enemy artillery fire north of the river. Washington refused to give him permission to go further north or to conduct sweeps into Cambodia and Laos.[12]

Bombing in the North remained limited. American aircraft were permitted to hit electrical stations and petroleum depots in and around Hanoi but not Haiphong. "The Haiphong Port is the single most vulnerable and important point in the lines of communications system of North Vietnam," General Wheeler complained. "In March, 142,700 metric tons of cargo passed through the port."[13] In June, U.S. aircraft attacking an anti-aircraft battery at Cam Pha, fifty miles north of Haiphong, struck the Soviet freighters *Turkestan* and *Mikhail Frunze*. Washington quickly apologized and promised Moscow that in the future no harm would come to their vessels.[14] "We have hit two ships," LBJ subsequently commented to a group of labor leaders. "You know how emotions run in this country when ships are hit. Remember the *Lusitania*. We do not want to get the Soviet Union and China into this war."[15]

The first week in September the military staged a minor revolt. As General W. E. Depuy of the JCS staff argued, "If U.S. disengagement has the flavor of a military defeat, or even military frustration, it will take years to repair the damage to morale, the traditions, and even the concept for employment of military forces in the national defense."[16] That week, Army Chief of Staff Harold Johnson and Marine Commandant Wallace Greene testified before Stennis's Senate Preparedness Subcommittee that McNamara and civilian authorities were preventing the military from taking the steps necessary to win the war. Both generals advocated attacking Haiphong, mining the harbor, and bombing five targets in the thirty-mile buffer zone near China. Greene and Stennis subsequently took their campaign for wider bombing to the American Legion convention in Boston. The commandant of the marines called the Vietnam War more important than urban unrest, and warned that if the United States didn't win, "We're not going to have any city problems . . . to worry about." In a blistering report, the Stennis committee charged that McNamara's "gradual" approach had allowed Hanoi to build up "the world's most formidable anti-aircraft defense" and in this way "almost certainly contributed" to heavy U.S. losses.[17]

LBJ worked to repair the damage, calling a news conference to inform reporters that the differences between McNamara and the chiefs had been blown all out of proportion. Privately, the president told Harold Johnson and his colleagues to come up with some imaginative ideas to bring the war to a conclusion. "He said he did not want them to just recommend more men or that we drop the Atom bomb," the notes of the meeting recorded LBJ as saying. "The

President said he could think of those ideas."[18] "Bus," he told Wheeler, "your generals almost destroyed us with their testimony before the Stennis Committee."[19] It should be noted that at this point Westmoreland and his colleagues were being less than candid with the White House, the press, and the public regarding the course of the war. Westmoreland had steadfastly maintained that the United States was winning the war, that it had turned the tide, and that the two-year buildup of American men and matériel was beginning to have its effect. The enemy was hurting, and if the pressure were increased he would, in the foreseeable future, collapse. This was particularly true of the war against NVA main force units. Yet, at a Military Assistance Command (Vietnam) Commander's Conference in Saigon in mid-May, he had noted, "The main force war is accelerating at a rapid, almost alarming rate . . . The NVA is taking over the main front war in I, II, and III Corps. This relieves the VC to move to the local level . . . Infiltration continues and at a greater rate than in the past. Individuals and units are better equipped and have some of the best weapons from the USSR; we now are seeing much anti-tank, rocket, and recoilless rifle capability."[20] Westmoreland told Johnson what he thought he wanted to hear, even when he knew the truth lay elsewhere.

Thanks to McPherson and others, however, Lyndon Johnson had a relatively accurate picture of the actual situation in South Vietnam. Following his trip to Southeast Asia in October 1966, McNamara reported, "By and large, the people in rural areas believe that the GVN [government of Vietnam] when it comes will not stay but that the VC will; that cooperation with the GVN will be punished by the VC; that the GVN is really indifferent to the people's welfare: that the low-level GVN are tools of the local rich; and that the GVN is ridden with corruption."[21] LBJ was much impressed with an unofficial evaluation of the situation by Michael Deutsch, a U.S. aid worker who had just returned from a year in Vietnam. "I have a visceral feeling that we underestimate the size, organization and potential threat of the VC terrorist machine in the south, which the GVN cannot eradicate . . . I doubt that the new . . . U.S. organization can achieve tangible results at this late date, or that the underpaid ARVN [Army of the Republic of Vietnam], lacking in ideology, can be trained fast enough to actually clear and hold the villages and swing the people away from the VC."[22]

Johnson wanted elections in South Vietnam and he wanted them to be as free as possible in order to have a viable entity capable of temporarily taking over the war and negotiating a political settlement with the National Liberation Front. "We do not want to conquer Vietnam," he told news anchor Harry Reasoner. "All we want to do is to prevent them from taking South Vietnam by force. If they take it by votes, that's a different matter, ok . . . When infiltration and violence ceases, we will get out. We may go to Thailand or to the Philippines, but we will get out. I told Kosygin that."[23] National Security Adviser Walt Rostow put it well. There was a direct corollary between the "Negro problem" in the United States and pacification in Vietnam. Whether one was talking about peasants and workers in South Vietnam, the disadvantaged of America's ghettoes, or the struggling masses of the third world in Latin America and Asia, the heart of the matter was self-determination.[24]

Central to Johnson's hopes was a new South Vietnamese constitution, written in April, calling for elections for the presidency and Senate on September 1 and the lower House on October 1. Following the constitutional convention, Dr. Phan Quang Dan, who had been imprisoned for two years under Diem, called on Henry Cabot Lodge to congratulate the Americans on their light hand. The constitution, most delegates felt, was an authentic Vietnamese document, rather than a tract dictated by occupiers. To a remarkable degree, U.S. authorities allowed matters to take their course, providing aid and advice to all candidates.[25] In the weeks that followed, the American mission turned its efforts to preventing the Military Revolutionary Council from intimidating the opposition and rigging the election. A task, as it turned out, that proved to be a full-time job.

"If the military establishment can agree on a single slate and a single presidential candidate to support," the CIA reported, "none of the potential civilian candidates appears likely to develop the organization and broad spectrum of support necessary to seriously contest the military's choice."[26] The two top contenders were Ky, a northerner and a Catholic, and Nguyen Van Thieu, a southerner and a Buddhist-turned-Catholic. During the previous year, the American mission had become increasingly impressed with Thieu. He seemed to Westmoreland and Ellsworth Bunker less impulsive, less ambitious, a shrewder judge of domestic and world opinion than Ky.[27]

On May 5, Ky announced to his fellow officers that he was going to be a candidate for president. Complaints began to trickle in from the civilian aspirants that the government would not allow opposition newspapers to operate and would not permit television time to be sold to nonmilitary politicians. A month later, on June 14, Thieu threw his hat in the ring. The American mission's nightmare had at last come true; the military was split. The Military Revolutionary Council held a climactic meeting over the weekend of June 28–30 to resolve the matter before the campaign went any further. "Sessions were long, emotional, and sometimes heated," Westmoreland confided to his diary. On the evening of the 29th it was decided that Thieu would be chief of the armed forces and Ky would continue to run for president. The following morning, Thieu announced that he would resign from the army and run as a civilian candidate. As pressure and dissension mounted, Ky suddenly announced that he would withdraw and return to the air force. To everyone's surprise, Thieu declared that this would be unacceptable. It was then that the two decided to campaign on the same ticket, with Thieu as the presidential candidate and Ky as the vice presidential.[28] The election outcome was now a foregone conclusion.

IF DISSENT WAS WITHERING on the vine in South Vietnam, it was blooming in America. The summer featured three new antiwar initiatives. On April 24 in New York, in an effort to mobilize politically moderate, socially conventional

Americans concerned about the war, King, Rauh, Galbraith, Schlesinger, and Victor Reuther of the UAW established a new organization, Negotiations Now! Projecting an image of reason and fairness, the organizers called for an unconditional bombing halt, a cease-fire in the South, and internationally supervised elections. At the same time, other antiwar activists announced in Cambridge the formation of Vietnam Summer. Modeled after the 1964 Mississippi Summer project, Vietnam Summer was intended to train students in the techniques of peaceful protest. Finally, on thirty college campuses, students and faculty established draft resistance movements. By the summer, they had begun to move beyond the walls of academia to recruit in working-class neighborhoods and even the ghettoes.[29] Then, on Tuesday, October 17, thirty-five hundred radicals tried to shut down the army induction center in Oakland, California. When the police broke up the picket lines, sending some twenty people to the hospital, ten thousand outraged Berkeley residents gathered to protest. Two thousand police confronted them. Fighting erupted, and the melee eventually encompassed more than twenty city blocks.

Johnson had no sympathy whatsoever with draft card burners, and he periodically needled Ramsey Clark about his reluctance to prosecute those who openly defied conscription. But it also came to his notice that a large number of young Americans were quietly and effectively using legal means to avoid serving in Vietnam. In mid-1966 *Newsweek* ran an article entitled "The Draft: The Unjust vs. the Unwilling." While some young men were publicly registering their dissent by fleeing to Canada and destroying their draft cards—and usually suffering for it—a far greater proportion of draft-age Americans were joining national guard units, flocking to graduate schools, making sudden decisions to join the Peace Corps, and doing everything in their power to fail their draft physicals. "For the first time in American history," *Newsweek* noted, "avoidance of service at a time when U.S. soldiers were at war and casualty lists were mounting had become socially acceptable."[30] Angered by the draft resistance movement, hawks in Congress were ready to consider legislation making it a criminal offense not only to refuse service but to advocate draft dodging. "Let's forget the First Amendment," proclaimed Louisiana Democrat F. Edward Hebert. Congress had to act, Mendell Rivers declared: "The Justice Department hasn't got the nerve to prosecute these riff-raff."[31]

LBJ and his aides worried that conservatives would come to view the poor and especially minorities as unpatriotic, or at least to portray them as such, as part of an effort to discredit the Great Society programs. "We must denounce those who are trying to divide the poor and the rest of the country," Harry McPherson told his boss. The administration must make the point that "every American, no matter what his economic condition, race or creed, has a vital stake in the defense of freedom in Viet Nam."[32] In July 1966, the president had named a National Advisory Commission on Selective Service headed by Burke Marshall, by then known for his prominent role in the federal government's struggle against racial violence and injustice in the South, to examine the draft and make recommendations for change. The original Selective Service Act had been passed in 1940—Johnson was fond of recalling his role in pushing that controversial measure through the House—but was allowed to lapse for a period after the end of World War II, only to be revived in 1948. It compelled all eighteen-year-olds to register, and provided for drafting the oldest first out of the prime eighteen-to-twenty-six-year-olds. Deferments were available for those enrolled in postsecondary institutions, for married fathers, and for those working in selected fields deemed important to the national interest. On March 6, 1967, Johnson forwarded his recommended changes, based on the findings of the Marshall Commission. Among the most important provisions were these: nineteen-year-olds were to be drafted first; no further postgraduate deferments would be allowed except for medical and dental school; and Selective Service would establish a fair and impartial random system of selection. He noted that a majority of the commission wanted to do away with college deferments altogether but that he and his advisers had decided that the disruption in a young man's life would be greater if service came at the end of high school rather than college.[33] In an attempt to satisfy hawks, Johnson and Clark announced that individuals who did something improper affecting their own status—burning their draft card, for example—would have their draft into the service accelerated as promptly as possible; all who violated federal law by doing something improper against the system generally—blocking a troop train, for example—would be promptly prosecuted by the Justice Department.[34]

CONGRESS, THE HOTHOUSE THAT HAD nurtured Johnson, the wellspring of both the New Deal and the Great Society, was now his enemy. Mills was blocking the much-needed surtax. Rivers and Stennis were attacking from the right, Fulbright and Bobby Kennedy from the left. Mike Mansfield, the taciturn Montanan, was proving increasingly ineffectual. So much for the Democrats. Dirksen and Ford, the Republicans, were acting as a chorus to Democratic hawks, denouncing the administration for doing nothing to save the cities, while moving to cut appropriations for programs that were designed to rehabilitate the nation's ghettoes. Periodically, Johnson would have Mansfield, Dirksen, and even Fulbright to the White House and ask them to hold off or at least tone down congressional hearings on the war. He would even give them the latest top-secret information on back-channel contacts with the North Vietnamese. The solons would express sympathy, and then return to their respective chambers to pound away again.[35]

Inevitably, Johnson would lose his temper. In a late February 1967 meeting with congressional leaders, he read a letter from John Steinbeck, who then had two sons serving in Vietnam: "In our anxiety about liberty, we've spawned anarchy. I have not the slightest doubt that the protest marchers, the full-page advertisements, the attacks on what is called our foreign policy, the shrill and fully reported cries that we get out of Vietnam and leave these people and the rest of Southeast Asia to mass murder—I believe that these activities and the political main-chancing have prolonged the war, have been responsible for the death and the crippling of our finest and our bravest young men . . . And I am angry at the bastards who find patriotism a dirty word, and gallantry in bad taste."[36] Johnson also played the race card. "Fulbright and Lippmann . . . will protect the whites and they do not care for the colored," he told Indian journalist Durga Das. "I stand for all alike, for the colored who are two-thirds of the people of the world."[37] These outbursts in turn produced a spate of essays by Walter Lippmann, Hans Morgenthau, and others to the effect that LBJ was a would-be dictator intent on crushing dissent and destroying the Bill of Rights.

Meanwhile, relations between the White House and the press went from bad to worse. The administration continued to be dismayed by what it considered biased and irresponsible reporting on the war in Vietnam in both the United States and South Vietnam. In conversation with William McAndrew, president of NBC News, LBJ said that in his opinion all the networks, with the possible exception of ABC, were slanted against him. They were "infiltrated," and he had "to be ready to move on them if they move on us."[38] American reporters were "immature, naïve and hostile," Bus Wheeler observed during a meeting with the president and his foreign policy advisers. "They are out there to win Pulitzer prizes for sensational articles rather than objective reporting," remarked another in attendance.[39] Every effort by Rostow, McPherson, and Robert Kintner, hired by the White House to improve media relations, to work out a rapprochment between LBJ and the press failed. "I thought you were pretty abrupt at the beginning of the CBS meeting tonight," McPherson commented after one presidential encounter with the media. "You kept challenging your questioner to tell you who said what about the bombing, indicating . . . that he was a boob to bring it up at all. I thought you bullied him pretty bad, and changed what felt like a pretty receptive occasion into a somber affair."[40] Some of the reporting was in truth harsh and negative, but LBJ was naïve and self-deluding to expect otherwise. Generally, the press reported what the administration knew to be true: South Vietnam was not a viable country, politically, economically, or militarily. Neil Sheehan and David Halberstam could see what McNamara and McPherson could see. Moreover, the White House's rhetorical efforts to steer a middle course between hawks and doves at home made it appear at times that it was doing one thing and saying another.[41]

In July 1967, *Newsweek* published a Louis Harris poll that was surprising, given the national hysteria that was allegedly gripping the country. On Vietnam, LBJ received a 46 percent approval rating, up from 41 percent two months earlier. His overall approval rating was an astonishing 62 percent. Indeed, as far as the conflict in Southeast Asia was concerned, Johnson seemed to be doing more or less what the vast majority wanted.[42] Americans continued to believe that it was in the nation's interests to make a stand against the forces of international communism somewhere in South Asia and that Ho and the NVA represented the forces of international communism. But those figures were an outgrowth of a "support our troops" mentality. By October polls indicated that although 58 percent of those questioned continued to support the war, 69 percent disapproved of the way the conflict was being handled.[43] Lack of clear and consistent justification continued to be an issue: "The problem is that people still can't get it deeply in their bones that we ought to be in Vietnam," McPherson advised Johnson. "What difference does it make to us? Even if he wins, Ho poses no threat to the United States. It is silly to talk about a rag tail revolutionary like Ho attacking Hawaii or California . . . Talk about defending freedom in the South also falls on deaf ears. South Vietnam is a semi-country run by a junta of generals who were raised in the North and imposed on the South. Why should we care if their own people knock them off?" [44]

In an effort to deflate antiwar critics on the left, reassure moderate opinion that he was indeed focused on negotiations, and pressure the Saigon government to get its house in order, LBJ broached a new peace formula during a speech at a National Legislative Conference in San Antonio. The plan was one that had been put to Hanoi by Harvard academic and sometime diplomat Henry Kissinger during a new peace initiative that had begun in late July. Through two French intermediaries, Kissinger, as authorized by the State Department, had suggested that the United States would be willing to stop the aerial and naval bombardment of North Vietnam if this would lead "promptly to productive discussions between representatives of the U.S. and DRV [Democratic Republic of Vietnam]." The discussions could proceed either publicly or secretly; it was up to Hanoi. In turn, "the DRV would not take advantage of the bombing cessation." [45]

Instead of rejecting the proposal out of hand, Pham Van Dong insisted on the unconditional and permanent cessation of bombing raids against the North, but then went on to make some conciliatory statements. The NLF would have to be "present" when South Vietnamese matters were discussed, but the United States would not have to commit to dealing exclusively with the NLF in matters of war and peace or recognize the NLF as the genuine voice of the South Vietnamese people. He also acknowledged that U.S. troops would have to remain in the South until a political settlement was worked out.[46] In early September, the United States had scaled back its bombing campaign in the North. Two weeks passed without anything meaningful coming out of Hanoi or Paris. LBJ's frustration began to show. During an interview with an Australian broadcaster on September 20, he complained that the media was ignoring the restraint he was showing. "But the television doesn't want that story," he declared. "I can prove that Ho is a son-of-a-bitch if you let me put it on the screen but they [the networks] want me to be the son-of-a-bitch . . . NBC and the *New York Times* are committed to an editorial policy of making us surrender." [47]

During a meeting with his advisers a week later, LBJ complained that the North Vietnamese "are playing us for suckers. They have no more intention of talking than we have of surrendering." [48] He now wanted to not only resume bombing but to escalate. Nick Katzenbach, as head of the informal interdepartmental committee on Vietnam, tried to dissuade him. "The significance of the

Paris-Kissinger exercise lies in the fact that it is the closest thing we have yet had to establishing a dialogue with North Vietnam," he observed to LBJ.[49] Johnson agreed to give peace one more chance.

In San Antonio the president unveiled his new formula. "The United States is willing to stop all aerial and naval bombardment of North Vietnam, when this will lead promptly to productive discussions," he proclaimed. "We, of course, assume that while discussions proceed, North Vietnam would not take advantage of the bombing cessation or limitation," meaning it would not accelerate the flow of men and supplies into the South nor launch new military initiatives. The press generally hailed the "San Antonio Formula," which in fact was a significant departure from previous offers that had required an end to infiltration, but nothing came of it.[50] There is some doubt that LBJ ever believed North Vietnam would agree to negotiate. During one meeting with Johnson and his foreign policy advisers, Dean Acheson observed, "We must understand that we are not going to have negotiations. The bombing has no effect on negotiations. When these fellows decide they can't defeat the South, then they will give up. This is the way it was in Korea. This is the way the Communists operate."[51] If the San Antonio Formula was not going to get negotiations started, John Roche observed to his boss, nothing would. "I doubt if Hanoi would negotiate now if you offered them California," he quipped. "Tell him I agree with that," LBJ scribbled on the memo.[52]

Meanwhile, the antiwar movement continued to fragment between moderates and radicals. On Labor Day weekend some three thousand delegates from 372 organizations gathered at the Palmer House in Chicago to attend the first convention of the National Conference for a New Politics. No one knew what the "new politics" was, exactly, and the proceedings quickly degenerated into a scene, as one observer put it, "worthy of Genet or Pirandello, with whites masquerading as either poor or black, blacks posing as revolutionaries or as arrogant whites, conservatives pretending to be communists, women feigning to be the oppressed, and liberals pretending not to be there at all."[53] A 150-member black delegation demanded that the gathering pass a resolution denouncing Zionism and calling for immediate reparations payments to all African Americans. Shortly thereafter, forty antiwar radicals met with North Vietnamese and NLF representatives in Czechoslovakia. SDS leader Tom Hayden attended and was quoted afterward: "Now we're all Viet Cong."[54]

The outrageous activities of the far left seemed to momentarily unhinge LBJ. Up to this point, aside from an occasional rhetorical outburst, the president had weathered the domestic storm over the war with relatively little stress.[55] But the antics of would-be revolutionaries, especially in Washington, D.C., a city he loved, threatened to push him over the edge. A week after fifty thousand protesters tried to shut down the Pentagon, he burst out, "I'm not going to let the Communists take this government and they're doing it right now." He told his advisers that he had been protecting civil liberties "since he was nine years old," but "I told the Attorney General that I am not going to let two-hundred-thousand of these people ruin everything for the 200 million Americans. I've got my belly full of seeing these people put on a Communist plane and shipped all over this country."[56] Johnson instructed the CIA to place leaders of the SDS, SANE, the Yippies (Youth International Party), Mothers Against the War, and other antiwar groups under surveillance and to do everything possible to gather evidence that they were communist-controlled, even operating on orders from foreign governments. This program, later institutionalized as Operation Chaos, violated the CIA's charter, which prohibited domestic operations.

The war against the peace movement soon shifted from surveillance to harassment and disruption. Dr. Spock, among others, was indicted for counseling draft resistance. Agents provocateur penetrated various organizations, encouraging division, sabotaging demonstrations, and gathering evidence of illegal activities. Not surprisingly, the FBI got into the act. Shortly after the Vietnam Veterans Against the War was formed, Hoover's men infiltrated the organization, encouraging activities that they hoped would discredit the movement.[57] Still, violations of civil liberties during the Vietnam conflict were insignificant compared to other wars. In this respect, LBJ compared favorably with Abraham Lincoln and, if anyone, resembled Jefferson Davis. Davis, fighting for slavery, tended to permit too much democracy and dissent within his country, whereas Lincoln, fighting for human freedom, succeeded in part because he was willing to crack down on domestic dissent.

As his hopes for peace foundered, LBJ decided to keep up the military pressure on the North Vietnamese and Vietcong through the 1968 presidential election. "If we cannot get negotiations," he asked McNamara and Wheeler during a meeting in the last week in October, "why don't we hit all the military targets short of provoking Russia and China? It astounds me that our boys in Vietnam have such good morale with all of this going on."[58] On November 17, Westmoreland outlined his plan of operation for 1968, which he codenamed York. It called for action against the enemy command center in the Vietcong's Military Region 5 in the Central Highlands, while the second phase would consist of destroying Vietcong munitions and supply stockpiles in the Ashau Valley. A third force composed of the 1st Air Cavalry would be assembled to be used either to launch an amphibious hook north of the DMZ or, if that proved politically impossible, to sweep clear of enemy troops the provinces from Quang Tri to Quang Ngai. Referring to the 525,000-troop level that had been authorized, Westmoreland told the chiefs, "For the first time I will have enough troops to really start grinding them down."[59]

IN THE MIDST OF THIS PLANNING, the White House announced that Robert McNamara was resigning as secretary of defense to take a job as head of the World Bank. The circumstances surrounding McNamara's departure were a matter of intense speculation in the media and on the Georgetown cocktail circuit. Rumor had it that the defense chief was near a nervous breakdown. He looked haggard, and despite his twice-a-week squash games with Orville Free-man, jowly. His wife, Marge, was suffering from an ulcer, and it was well-known that his children were adamantly opposed to the war. Stories circulated of his ranting incoherence and tearful breakdowns. LBJ reportedly expressed the fear that McNamara would "pull a Forrestal" on him, that is, commit sui-cide. In a subsequent interview with historian Bob Dallek, McNamara offered a qualified denial. Rumors of his "emotional and physical collapse" were greatly exaggerated, he said. "I was indeed feeling stress. I was at loggerheads with the President of the United States; I was not getting answers to my questions; and I was tense as hell. But, I was not under medical care, not taking drugs except for an occasional sleeping pill, and never contemplated suicide." [60] In truth, McNa-mara was tired of presiding over a stalemate, tired of getting kicked simultane-ously by Stennis and Fulbright, and desirous of campaigning openly for Bobby Kennedy in 1968. Larry O'Brien recalled that in 1967 the defense secretary had come around to his office to "make a strong pitch that Bobby should run for president." As an alternative, O'Brien suggested that they work internally to change Johnson's position on the war. No, McNamara had said, it was impera-tive that Kennedy run and be the party's nominee. [61] McNamara would, how-ever, continue in office for five months after the announcement of his departure.

The civilian whiz kids in the Pentagon were by this point almost to a person opposed to continuation of the war. It was time for a political solution in the South—now. "There is only one answer," McNamara confided to Averell Har-riman. "representatives of the VC must be admitted to the coalition govern-ment and the VC recognized as a legitimate party." [62] At lunch on November 1, McNamara told the president "that continuation of our present action in Southeast Asia would be dangerous, costly in lives, and unsatisfactory to the American people." He gave him a memorandum outlining an alternative course, namely, to announce "a policy of stabilization of our military effort, with no further increase in American force levels and no expansion of the war against the North . . . To further increase support for the war effort and to probe the possibilities of a negotiated settlement, I recommend we plan on a halt in the bombing of the North." He emphasized the pointlessness of further buildup. "The additional numbers of combat troops will not produce any significant change in the nature of our military operations," he wrote. "The increase in numbers is likely to lead to a proportionate increase in encounters with the enemy, and some increase in the number of casualties inflicted on both sides. But neither the addition of troops not scheduled nor augmentation of our forces by a much greater amount holds great promise of bringing the North Vietnamese and Viet Cong forces visibly closer to collapse during the next 15 months . . . I suggest we examine our military operations in the South with a view to taking steps which will reduce our casualties and increase the role of the Vietnamese." [63]

LBJ was reportedly angered by McNamara's initiative, complaining that his secretary of defense had gone "dovish" on him. On the memo, LBJ had written, "Chapter and verse—Why believe this?" In his memoirs, McNamara insisted that his critique of the war had done "one thing; it raised the tension between 2 men who loved and respected each other—Lyndon Johnson and me—to the breaking point."[64] In fact, there was little difference in the positions of the two men. McNamara was more ready to stop the bombing than his chief and more willing to recognize the NLF as an organization rather than a group of individuals, but on fundamentals the president and his defense chief were headed in the same direction: stabilization of the fighting at its present level, imposing a ceiling on the U.S. troop buildup, and doing everything possible to accelerate the Vietnamization of the war with the ultimate result of a negotiated settlement between the Ky-Thieu government and the NLF. McNamara's departure was for personal and political reasons.

In Truth, Johnson and Westmoreland had been working on a plan for getting out of Vietnam since 1965. American units were introduced into combat not to assume responsibility for a strategic offensive against Hanoi. Rather, they were there to conduct three phases of warfare: to blunt the enemy's conventional attack, clean out major communist bases and staging areas within South Vietnam, and finally push communist units out to South Vietnam's border with Laos and Cambodia. Once those tasks were accomplished, South Vietnamese forces would carry the brunt of any continued combat with the Vietcong and American combat units could disengage. Westmoreland originally envisioned the completion of Phase III in late 1967, but was forced to push that forward by a year.[65] Johnson's goal was to avoid being forced out of Vietnam before Vietnamization could be implemented. The NVA and Vietcong could not accomplish that task, but the antiwar movement, especially dissent within the halls of power, could.

Using McNamara's "alternative" as a foil, LBJ went through an elaborate procedure, calling the Wise Men together and consulting advisers past and present, including Fortas and Clifford, with the goal of shoring up his Vietnam consensus. All except Ball advised rejecting the McNamara approach. Acheson and company agreed that "there is great improvement and progress" evident in the conduct of the war. The United States should continue to bomb the north. Unilateral withdrawal from Vietnam was "unthinkable."[66] Fortas and Clifford were emphatic. "Our duty is to do what we consider right," Fortas advised LBJ. The administration should persevere, including continuing to bomb the North, "unless and until the people through Congress or the polls make it impossible for the administration to do what it considers to be right in the national interest."[67] "The President and every man around him wants to end the war," Clifford exclaimed. "But the future of our children and grandchildren require that it be ended by accomplishing our purpose, i.e., the thwarting of the aggression by North Vietnam, aided by China and Russia."[68]

In November 1967, LBJ once again recalled Westmoreland to buck up the home front. The commander of American troops in Vietnam made an appearance before the Armed Services Committees and then attended a Medal of Honor ceremony in the Rose Garden. That weekend, the Westmorelands and the Johnsons briefly escaped to Camp David. Richard Russell came down for dinner. He and the women present retired early, leaving the president and his field commander alone. LBJ broke the news that McNamara was leaving for the World Bank and that Clark Clifford was going to replace him. He then told Westmoreland that he did not plan to be a candidate in the 1968 presidential election and asked what the reaction of the troops would be. They would understand, the general replied. "President explained that his health was not good and that he and Lady Bird were tired," Westmoreland subsequently recorded in his diary. "[He] recalled the fact that the constitution did not provide for an invalid president—a reference to the illness of Pres. Wilson and Pres. Eisenhower. The President emphasized the sensitivity of our discussion." [69]

LBJ, of course, had long been considering not running, but he had not made up his mind. Even a political naïf could see that the road to reelection in 1968 was going to be a rocky one. Bobby Kennedy was giving every sign that he was not going to wait until 1972. Egging him on was Arthur Schlesinger, who argued that there was a better than fifty-fifty chance that LBJ was going to escalate the bombing. "Psychologically he is a bully who has made his way in life by leaning on people," Schlesinger wrote Kennedy, "and he recently has been extending the bully's approach to Hanoi . . . He would probably count on the invasion generating a great surge of chauvinism, which would silence his critics, unite the country and perhaps carry him though 1968. I imagine he thinks that, the larger the conflict, the more families involved and therefore the more support for the war." [70] Both Kenny O'Donnell and Richard Goodwin delivered a series of speeches attacking LBJ's record in the cities and Vietnam. Bobby made an emotional appearance on *Face the Nation* depicting the war in Vietnam as horrific and indefensible. [71] In Congress, figures like George McGovern in the Senate and Brock Adams in the House made no secret of their preference for RFK over LBJ. One of the White House's allies, Congresswoman Julia Hansen of Washington, reported that Adams "is like a great number of Kennedy people who 'deep down' have a feeling of vengeance because President Kennedy was assassinated in President Johnson's home state." [72] All the while, the Kennedys continued to glitter. "Saturday night we went to the big 17th Anniversary Bob Kennedy party," Orville Freeman recorded in his diary. "We started at the Averell Harrimans for dinner and then out to Hickory Hill. It was a lavish and expensive party. The women in extreme gowns of various kinds, some in mini skirts to the long ones, fast music, lots of liquor and food, and all the 'best' people there." [73]

By the fall an organization calling itself Citizens for Kennedy/Fulbright began soliciting pledges. Most outspoken of the dissidents was Allard Lowenstein, a thirty-eight-year-old New York attorney who seemed determined to merge the Democratic party with the New Left. In October he announced a conference for all those interested in dumping LBJ.[74] But taking on an incumbent president, especially if that incumbent was Lyndon Johnson, was a daunting prospect, and Bobby refused to throw his hat in the ring. Desperate for a rallying point for the Stop LBJ movement, dissident Democrats persuaded Senator Eugene McCarthy, a Minnesota Democrat, to make himself available. Best known for his eloquent speech nominating Adlai Stevenson in 1960, McCarthy was described by *Newsweek* as "a scholarly, witty, somewhat lazy man who writes books, reads poetry and laces his lectures with dollops of theology."[75] He was not the only challenger.

It was clear that George Wallace was going to make another run at the presidential nomination as a Democrat. But Johnson's advisers were divided as to whether the Wallace candidacy would hurt or help. If the Republicans nominated a neo-Goldwaterite like Governor Ronald Reagan of California, Wallace would drain away segregationist and superhawk votes in the South and the working-class neighborhoods of the North from the GOP, but if the Republicans nominated a moderate like Romney, the Wallace challenge would hurt.[76] Finally, the administration was faced in 1967 with a minor farm revolt. Although net farm income per person had doubled between 1960 and 1965, it had dropped sharply between 1966 and 1967. Most of the decline was caused by skyrocketing prices for beef, the one commodity for which there was not a federal price support program. "The projection is that if elections were held next month we would lose every non-southern state with farm voter population of 9% or more," one of Orville Freeman's analysts advised him. "This would mean the loss of about 86 electoral college votes out of the 270 required."[77]

More than ever, LBJ's personality had become an issue, "an issue, indeed, that seems increasingly to be producing almost as much criticism and contention as the war in Vietnam and the tumult in the ghettos," observed one news magazine. In Pocatello, Idaho, a sixtyish grandmother and a life-long Democrat told an interviewer, "I'm beginning to hate that man!"[78] Johnson's staff had been acutely aware of the problem at least since the fall of 1966. With trepidation they had approached the president about making some changes. "The problem is that the press considers us humorless," McPherson had observed to Moyers. "The press believes the President is unable to laugh at himself, and that his staff is too frightened to laugh at anything that goes on around the White House . . . We don't go out to lunch; we don't play touch football or softball; we just work."[79] Johnson was not going to be persuaded to take up touch football, but perhaps he could learn to modulate his mood swings, avoid absolutes, and stop indulging in public paroxysms of self-pity. As Journalist John Steele observed, "In this day of instantly seen television, his downs look like gravel pits, his ups like the stratosphere. He's never had any real personal, emotional balance . . . When he gets emotional, he gets emotional all over the place."[80]

Johnson tried, and the press tried to respond. "Is It Superman? No, It's LBJ," ran a *Newsweek* headline in March 1967 on the new, more modest, more restrained chief executive.[81] In interviews with selected columnists and reporters Johnson attempted to appear self-effacing, satisfied, philosophical. "During my four years, on balance, I have had a good press," he told Hugh Sidey. "I like the job. I am much more at ease and much less volatile," he said when asked how he had changed. "We have one of the finest staffs we have ever had." To Helen Thomas and Jack Horner: "When I was a little boy coming along, I thought I had been denied a lot of things other people had. But I can never cease to be grateful enough and thankful enough. I rarely ever have a pain . . . No man who ever lived had a better family . . . My job is excellent . . . I have a good cabinet . . . I have good care, good friends, good staff, good dogs, wonderful family. You have never heard me whine." [82] Things were tough in Vietnam but generally going well. "The common thing about them [American soldiers] is that all of them love the South Vietnamese," he told Sidey with a straight face. "They go out at night to teach them, to care for their wounds, and to help in any way they can." [83]

The correspondents did not miss the anger, abuse, and self-pity. But at the same time, they felt insulted. LBJ's new vanilla, I'm okay–you're okay persona reeked of insincerity. In an effort to present a different, more modest, mellow image, he came off as being either patronizing or manipulative—or both. It also could not last. LBJ was incapable of hiding his feelings, of not striking out when he felt he was being treated unfairly, of not defending himself and his policies, of not unmasking those he felt guilty of hypocrisy. Why, Max Frankel asked during an interview in September, was such a strong figure like the president having trouble inspiring and moving people to his causes? He wasn't the problem, Johnson replied defiantly. "The Republicans, factionalism of the Democratic party, the war in Vietnam, plus the *New York Times*" were the problems. Liberals were married to Bobby's ambition, "and they want to return to this house at the earliest possible hour." If he was such a bad speaker, had no charisma, and was not a good campaigner, how had he managed to win so many elections? "Why do people dislike you?" Frankel asked. He replied, "I am a dominating personality, and when I get things done I don't always please all the people . . . Remember people booed [baseball superstar] Ted Williams, too." And don't forget, "the protests are Communist led." [84]

Despite all this doubt and turmoil, LBJ still believed he could win. Liberals—doves, hawks, farmers, labor unionists, intellectuals, environmentalists, blacks—might be dissatisfied, but where were they going to turn? If they embraced Bobby or McCarthy, the Democratic party would lose the South and the election. He was still the only Democrat who could win, and he would capture the nomination if he decided to pursue it. A Quayle poll, taken the last week in November, showed that Democrats preferred LBJ to RFK by 47 percent to 36 percent, with 11 percent undecided. A Harris survey showed an LBJ-HHH ticket leading Romney-Reagan by 57 percent to 43 percent.[85] In November LBJ briefly hit the campaign trail, and delivered a series of speeches lauding the accomplishments of the Great Society and the bravery of America's fighting men.

At a White House press conference, he lambasted the Vietnam naysayers in Congress. To a pro-union crowd he called for passage of the tax surcharge. In a ceremony swearing in newly elected members of the Washington, D.C., City Council, he declared war on "crime in the streets." He lambasted the GOP for its social irresponsibility. "Some have called the passage of this act [an appropriations bill for HUD] a legislative victory," he remarked at the signing ceremony. "It might better be called a legislative miracle." "Ninety-three percent of the House Republicans voted to recommit and kill rent supplements. Eighty percent voted to . . . delete all funds for model cities."[86] In December he flew to Bar Harbor, Florida, to address the twelve hundred delegates to the AFL-CIO Convention, which had just voted to endorse him.

During this flurry, he gave what by all accounts was the best press conference of his presidency. Armed once again with a lavalier microphone clipped to his lapel, he stepped out from behind the podium and delivered a thirty-seven-minute, stem-winding defense of his policies. He was funny, inspiring, expressive, engaging. LBJ had at last "showed the nation the compelling, free-swinging form he usually reserves for private persuasion," *Newsweek* exulted.[87] "When I came away from the White House I felt good inside for the first time in too long," Hugh Sidey wrote Johnson after the conference. "I suddenly sensed just how much I want to you to succeed and just how much better I feel when things go well for the President of the United States." Johnson was warmed. "Thanks much for the time it took to write me and the heart that produced the understanding and encouragement," he wrote back.[88]

Part of Johnson's image problem was that in terms of popular culture, he hailed from the wrong side of the tracks. During the 1960s it seemed that half of middle-class white America listened to the Beatles, danced the frug, and went to James Bond movies, while the other half watched westerns, listened to Tony Orlando and Tony Bennett, and bowled. Lyndon Johnson definitely fell into the latter category.[89] "Lyndon Johnson roamed the country in a green suit . . . in the age of muted gray," Hugh Sidey wrote. "He was an avuncular figure who eschewed the seashore when the ads beckoned all America to seek the sand and surf. He had never skied in his life, and he hunted from the air-conditioned interior of a white Lincoln Continental. His golf was poor. Amid the great crush of culture, he knew neither Beatles nor Brahms. His artist was Norman Rockwell."[90] In planning for the 1968 campaign, George Reedy, back again at the White House on a temporary basis, suggested putting together "one of those electric guitar 'musical' groups to travel around to meetings. It is not too difficult to get some kids with long hair and fancy clothes and give them a title such as 'The Black Beards' or 'The White Beards' and turn them loose." Johnson was intrigued. "This may deserve attention," he scrawled on Reedy's memo.[91]

The counterculture, the youth movement, cultural change, and rebelliousness in general confused and upset Johnson. One staffer remembered his angrily denouncing the assumptions that underlay the movie *The Graduate,* after watching it in the converted hangar at the ranch. "When he was a young man, a college education was a tremendous prize," George Reedy observed. In the world of the 1960s it was viewed as more of an entitlement by many middle-class white Americans. "Second, their lifestyle was totally different from his lifestyle as a young man. When he was a young man, as soon as you graduated from college you were very careful to comb your hair right and tie your tie right, get a pressed shirt, pressed suit, and you'd start making the rounds looking for a job . . . The long hair bothered him, the careless, sloppy clothing, the blue jeans, and he'd look around the White House and he'd see a lot of young people that looked exactly like his ideal . . . And so to him that was the real American youth. I don't know where he thought those people outside came from, probably Mars or Neptune." [92]

Entertainment at White House social functions usually featured light-hearted song and dance: Victor Borge, the wisecracking pianist, for example. Lyndon and Lady Bird were particularly enamored of Carol Channing. On the fourth anniversary of her Broadway hit *Hello Dolly!* there was a celebration at the executive mansion. She and the cast performed thirty minutes from Act II that featured the line "Money is like manure. It doesn't do any good unless it is spread around." The presidential couple, the vice president and Muriel Humphrey, the chief justice, and other honored guests were delighted. Afterward, they danced. There was always dancing at any Johnson White House function. "Lyndon led Carol out on the floor," as Lady Bird described the scene. "Her feathered hat covered his face as they danced. Rather than join in, nearly everybody made a circle and watched." [93]

Johnson continued to take sustenance, spiritual and physical, from the adoring women who surrounded him. Juanita Roberts, his personal secretary, wrote him the morning after a Victor Borge concert at the White House: "I want to thank you for the lovely colored picture and for the very sweet inscription. You were so very, very generous on my birthday, my emotion tongue-tied me. The picture will keep those wondrous moments alive for me always." [94] Rumors of a romantic relationship with Jewell Malechek, wife of his ranch foreman, were already rampant around Johnson City. [95] In part, his relationships—which at this point in his life were almost certainly not sexual—were a function of the LBJ persona, and in part they were a result of feelings of loneliness and isolation. Lyndon and Lady Bird found themselves apart more and more as their rounds of official duties took them in separate directions. Yet he seemed, emotionally and psychologically, more dependent on her than ever. "Sometime during the evening Lyndon called, and I could sense the loneliness in his voice and the desire just to talk to me," Lady Bird wrote in her diary in mid-August. "I try to keep that loneliness at bay and I felt torn between doing what I was doing, which must be done, and being with him. The 'Mary' and the 'Martha' in my life have an eternal war." [96]

Both Lyndon and Lady Bird were feeling vulnerable about themselves and about each other. That same month, Lady Bird was scheduled to return to Washington from New York, where she had been on a shopping trip. The weather was bad and the pilot came on to announce that they would have to sit on the runway for a while until the storms let up. Suddenly Lady Bird's security men whisked her off the plane. The LaGuardia tower had received an anonymous telephone call threatening to blow up the five o'clock shuttle.[97] A month later, at the ranch, LBJ spent all one day talking with John Connally, who had announced that he was not going to run again for the governorship, and Jake Pickle, then a U.S. congressman. The subject was retirement. The three men started off the morning by riding horseback around the wooded ridges and pastures, analyzing the pros and cons. "He was blowing hot and cold on his decision," Pickle recalled. Connally could not see his patron-rival putting himself through another four years. Peace demonstrators around the White House were now so thick and constant that a presidential foray into the world outside had become a major ordeal. Pickle, on the other hand, could not see Johnson giving way to Bobby Kennedy. Around seven that evening Lyndon summoned Lady Bird to join the discussion. With her hair still in rollers she joined the three men for dinner on TV trays. She was unequivocal in her opposition to another term. She reminded her husband that his father had died at sixty. Like Lyndon, Lady Bird feared a debilitating illness while they still occupied the White House. She brought a laugh when she quipped, "If we ever get sick, I want to be sick on our time."[98] The following month, family physician Willis Hurst called the first lady and told her that he was worried about the president's health. She asked him straight up if he was fit enough for another term. Hurst did not answer, but he suggested that she do two things: limit her travel schedule in order to be close to Lyndon's side and have a physical to assure that the strain of her position was not ruining her own health. That night she had another long talk with her husband about retirement. "Our mood was bleak and dispirited and no answers came," she remembered.[99]

In mid-December, Lynda Bird and Chuck Robb were married in the East Room of the White House in an Episcopal ceremony. Five hundred guests, including eighty-three-year-old Alice Roosevelt Longworth, moved through the receiving line in the Blue Room. The president seemed in good spirits, if a bit fatigued. Carol Channing again created a stir in an outfit of yellow mini-bloomers and yellow stockings. The newlyweds would have only two months of married life together in their rented split-level house in Arlington before Chuck reported for a year of active duty in Vietnam. "I'm a professional military man," he reminded reporters.[100] Before he left, Robb turned over a written statement to Liz Carpenter to be released if he were captured or killed. "I believe in what we're doing in Vietnam," he told Lady Bird's chief of staff. "If the enemy should try to broadcast some phony statement or claim, you and the Pentagon know my views and can release them."[101]

CHAPTER 39

TET

W HEN LBJ LASHED HIS AIDES AND CONGRES-
sional allies mercilessly in 1965, saying, "We have so little
time, we have so little time," they wondered why.[1] He had
won in a landslide. Liberal majorities in both houses waited
to do his bidding; the country was then in the midst of an incredible economic
boom. But Johnson had been right. Reform is rare and difficult in the United
States, a deeply conservative country. And political unity is not its natural state.
Now, in 1968, time was almost up. Dissension was high. Urban riots, the white
backlash, and the Black Power movement were whipsawing the country. The
Vietnam conflict was corroding the public spirit.

Yet Johnson would not give up. He wanted to raise taxes and to spend more
money not just to fight crime, but to build affordable housing and to fund jobs.
As he prepared for the 1968 State of the Union address, he took John Roche and
Harry McPherson's advice to heart: "We have to utilize 'conservative' tactics to
protect the substance of liberalism—'liberalism,' as enacted over the past three
years, has to become *the* status quo."[2] Standing before Congress, the president
spoke quietly, conversationally. He renewed his request for a 10 percent income
tax surcharge and presented a $186 billion budget, an increase of $10 billion
over the previous fiscal year. Joe Califano had wanted the president to go at
Wilbur Mills head-on. The Arkansan, he told his boss, "wants either (or both)
(1) to force . . . you to your knees or (2) to dismantle great hunks of the Great
Society."[3] Johnson agreed. "I warn the Congress and the Nation tonight that
this failure to act on the tax bill will sweep us into an accelerating spiral of price
increases, a slump in homebuilding, and a continuing erosion of the American
dollar," he said. He asked Congress for $455 million in new job program funds,
most of it to initiate a public-private, three-year plan to train and employ five-
hundred thousand of the least qualified jobless. He proposed $1 billion for

Model Cities and $2.2 billion for the War on Poverty. To rousing applause, LBJ told the joint session that in his safe streets and crime control bill, he was doubling the money he had originally asked for, but he also renewed his call for gun control: "Those who preach disorder and those who preach violence must know that local authorities are able to resist them swiftly, to resist them sternly, and to resist them decisively."[4]

As 1968 opened Lyndon Johnson was more worried about the prospect of a race war in the United States than he was about losing the war in Vietnam. In the fall of 1967 novelist William Styron's *The Confessions of Nat Turner* had been published. The book, an immediate bestseller, was a fictionalized account of a black slave revolt that took place in the tidewater country of southern Virginia in 1831. An educated black slave and preacher with apocalyptic visions, Nat Turner led the uprising. For two days Turner's band of seventy-five runaways rampaged though the countryside, slaughtering fifty-five white men, women, and children before being overcome by a hastily formed white militia. Those who were not killed immediately were summarily executed. James Baldwin, who read the book in manuscript, declared it historically accurate and socially relevant. Throughout 1967 and 1968, as riots erupted in Detroit, Washington, Newark, and Memphis, a white backlash gained momentum north and south of the Mason-Dixon line. In primarily Catholic, blue-collar, white south Boston, segregationist Louise Day Hicks declared her candidacy for mayor.[5]

Propagandists in North Vietnam made the most of the unrest. "To display solidarity and support for the just struggle of the U.S. Negroes in the United States in claiming their basic national rights, a struggle which is completely consistent with the just struggle of the South Vietnamese people for independence, democracy, and peace," the National Liberation Front in November released three black servicemen it had held captive.[6] John McCone told LBJ and his cabinet, "The very stability and future of the United States was gravely threatened by the current racial problem with the Negroes."[7] Martin Luther King was getting into bed with Stokely Carmichael, and Congress was criticizing the commander of U.S. troops in the Detroit riot for not issuing a "shoot on sight" order. "In other words, as one looks at it," Orville Freeman recorded in his diary, "it might seem that the world was about to come to an end."[8]

As his and the nation's troubles mounted, the president spent what little spare time he had reading the speeches of Abraham Lincoln. He ran across an antislavery address that his predecessor had delivered at Edwardsville, Illinois, in 1858. "Now when by all these means," he had said to the South, "you have succeeded in dehumanizing the Negro; when you have put him down and made it forever impossible for him to be but as the beasts of the field; when you have extinguished his soul and placed him where the ray of hope is blown out in darkness like that which broods over the spirits of the damned; are you quite sure the demon which you have roused will not turn and rend you?"[9]

Johnson's strategy through early 1968 was to try to placate blacks by distancing the administration from the Moynihan report and by focusing on jobs and housing, while trying to appease whites with tough law-and-order rhetoric.[10] The White House reintroduced legislation outlawing discrimination in the sale, renting, and leasing of housing, the touchiest of all subjects among white urban dwellers. A similar bill had helped Ronald Reagan defeat California Governor Pat Brown in 1966. Yet Johnson was determined.

The second order of business was jobs. Sargent Shriver suggested public works, but Johnson felt they would take too long and were unaffordable. The key was the private sector. LBJ wanted to "get some ghetto grime under those highly polished executive fingernails."[11] He succeeded in persuading Henry Ford to chair the National Alliance of Businessmen, a voluntary organization committed to persuading the nation's corporations to hire and train the hardcore unemployed. The federal government would pay for most of the training, including health care and literacy instruction. On January 27, 1968, LBJ hosted the first executive committee meeting of the NAB. In addition to Ford, the CEOs of Mobil Oil, Safeway Stores, ITT, and ALCOA were in attendance. "We're faced with the hard core unemployed," Johnson told them. "You all are going to have to teach them how to wash and stay clean, how to read, how to write. All the things everyone around this table got from their mommies and daddies. Only these people don't have mommies and daddies who give a damn about them. Or if they do, those mommies and daddies can't read or don't know how to help them." One of the executives said, "This is a tough job, Mr. President." LBJ turned to him and said, "I didn't invite you here to tell me how tough a job this is. I invited you here to get the job done . . . This economy has been so good to you that you can afford to give a little back."[12] In late January 1968, LBJ sent a special message to Congress entitled "To Earn a Living: The Right of Every American." Among other things, he asked the House and Senate to fund a $2.1 billion manpower-training program.[13] By the end of 1968 the NAB had succeeded in seeing one hundred thousand of the poorest, most disadvantaged Americans trained and put to work. The subsequent retention rate was almost 75 percent.[14]

With the law-and-order forces demanding raw meat, Johnson saw no reason why Stokely Carmichael should not be offered up. Had he not, after all, preached violent resistance to authority, particularly to the draft, using Havana as his pulpit, no less? LBJ and the White House wanted the Black Power advocate prosecuted under the Logan Act, an eighteenth-century statute prohibiting private citizens from attempting to influence diplomatic relations between the United States and a foreign government. The problem was, Attorney General Ramsey Clark pointed out, most of the evidence against alleged subversives like Carmichael had been gathered by illegal wiretap.[15] The Justice Department had a better chance of making a case against George Romney than Stokely Carmichael, he told presidential aide Larry Temple. Clark was much more interested in going after the South Carolina State Police after they fired shotgun blasts into the ranks of peaceful protesters at the all-black State College at Orangeburg. Three were killed and thirty wounded.[16] Johnson made no secret of his irritation with his attorney general. He ranted to Russell and Dirksen, denouncing Clark in their private conversations, but in the end, typically, he listened to reason. As Clark pointed out, what the vast majority of urban-dwelling blacks wanted was law and order, protection from looting and violence, safety for their children. To stretch or even violate the law in order to satisfy vigilante groups was to start down a dangerous, slippery slope. Moreover, as Clark argued, "I think that the notion that you can control dissent by convicting a few of the most outspoken radicals is absurdly naïve. If there's nothing to it but the charisma of a few leaders fanning flames, why, it's not a very serious problem."[17]

In mid-March the Kerner Commission famously announced that the riots of 1967 had social and not conspiratorial roots. The commission's report emphasized the existence of a pervasive white racism and warned that more violence would ensue if cities, states, and the federal government did not move massively and rapidly to improve living conditions in urban ghettoes. Conservatives were predictably outraged. Presidential candidate Richard Nixon condemned the report because it "in effect blames everybody for the riots except the perpetrators."[18] LBJ withheld comment for six days. Eventually, however, he relented, telling a group of black newspaper editors that the Kerner report was "the most important report made to me since I have been President." He asked all cabinet officers to come up with plans to remedy the inequities identified.[19] Harry McPherson later explained why Johnson was so conflicted about the commission's findings:

> The only thing that held any hope for the Negro was the continuation of the coalition between labor, Negroes, intellectuals, . . . big city bosses and political machines, and some of the white urban poor . . . In other words it required keeping the Polacks who work on the line at River Rouge [Michigan auto plant] in the ball park and supporting Walter Reuther and the government as they try to spend a lot of money for the blacks. That's the only way they'll ever make it, because the people [in office buildings] don't give a damn about them. They're scared of them, always have been; they're middle-class whites . . . Then a presidential commission is formed and goes out and comes back and what does it say? Who's responsible for the riots? "The other members of the coalition. They did it. Those racists." And thereupon the coalition says, you know, a four-letter word, and "we'll go find ourselves a guy like George Wallace, or Richard Nixon."[20]

PARTLY OUT OF IDEALISM and partly out of a desire to placate white, middle-class America, Johnson announced the first Occupational Health and Safety Program. Then in early February, with Ralph Nader's image splashed across the front pages of America's newspapers and magazines, LBJ sent to Congress another special message entitled "To Protect the Consumer Interest." It called for sweeping new legislation to outlaw deceptive advertising, investigate the auto insurance industry, ensure quality control in fish and poultry processing, strengthen auto safety standards, and appoint a government ombudsman to represent the consuming public. Nader, a lanky, sallow-faced young lawyer, had converted a one-man crusade for consumer protection into a national movement. Working eighteen-hour days, he had directed his controlled outrage at the likes of Henry Ford II and Harvey Firestone over auto safety issues and then spread out to diseased fish, unnecessary dental X-rays, and deceptive labeling. Public opinion polls indicated that federal action in these areas had almost universal approval.[21] Finally, proclaiming education to be "the Fifth Freedom," Johnson asked Congress to increase annual appropriations for the Head Start program from $340 million to $380 million, for a new Stay in School program at $30 million, and for adult education at $50 million.[22]

JUST BEFORE MIDNIGHT on January 22, 1968, the telephone rang in Walt Rostow's bedroom. It was the Situation Room, reporting that an American intelligence-gathering ship, the USS *Pueblo,* cruising off North Korea, just outside the territorial limit, was under attack. The *Pueblo* was a small cargo vessel that the navy had recently converted into an electronic intelligence ship operating under the joint direction of the National Security Administration and Naval Intelligence. The ship and its eighty-three-man crew had departed Sasebo, Japan, on January 11 with orders to monitor and collect North Korean and Soviet radar, sonar, and radio signals and to analyze maritime activity along the North Korean coast. On the afternoon of January 23, North Korean trawlers supported by aircraft approached the *Pueblo* as it lay dead in the water. According to the ship's navigational equipment, it was outside the twelve-mile limit, and so its captain, Commander Lloyd "Pete" Bucher, anticipated simple harassment. However, when the *Pueblo* ignored the North Korean order to heave to and turned to escape, the communist vessels opened fire, killing one and wounding four. Bucher, with no real means to defend his ship, stopped and allowed the *Pueblo* to be boarded.[23]

Rostow reported to the president just before 3 A.M. Johnson asked a few questions and then went back to sleep. At the next day's meeting of the National Security Council, McNamara, who had agreed to stay on through February, observed that the incident was preplanned and was "a conscious effort to provoke a response or a lack of response"; the Soviets had known of the ambush beforehand, and the North Koreans had no intention of returning the men or the ship. CIA chief Richard Helms spoke for all: "This is a very serious matter. It appears the North Koreans are doing this in support of the North Vietnamese against us. It looks, at this time, like collusion between the North Koreans and the Soviets."[24]

With the GOP and conservative Democrats demanding retaliation, a story broke quoting a captured North Korean soldier who claimed that a thirty-one-man team was on its way to Seoul to blow up the presidential palace and kill South Korean President Park Chung Hee. Many predicted the onset of a second

Korean War. Senator Henry Jackson (D-Washington) told reporters, "If they really make an all-out effort in Korea, that is to reopen another Korean war, I'm afraid we'll be getting into the use of nuclear weapons." The president ordered the nuclear-powered USS *Enterprise,* the largest ship in the world with more than one hundred warplanes aboard, to set sail for North Korean waters, and he called up nearly fifteen thousand air force and naval reservists. "Clearly, this cannot be accepted," he told a television audience.[25]

In fact, Johnson was determined to do everything in his power to avoid having the *Pueblo* incident deteriorate into a general war. He told Orville Freeman and other cabinet members that "he was most thankful that the Admiral over there and the Skipper of the ship had not perpetrated a major incident." An attempt to rescue the crew and ship through military action was out of the question, he said. The air base at nearby Wonsan was the largest in North Korea and any attempt at armed rescue would have resulted in "overwhelming loss."[26] He appointed a *Pueblo* Advisory Group, including Rostow, Rusk, McNamara, Ball, and Helms, to develop an overall strategy for dealing with the crisis. As he anticipated, they recommended negotiations. Eleven months later, the much abused crew of the *Pueblo* would be released, but only after a coerced confession by Commander Bucher.[27]

EVEN AS THE PUEBLO CRISIS unfolded, LBJ was harboring hopes of a peace agreement in Vietnam. The North Vietnamese had offered to negotiate if America stopped bombing. But on January 31, it became painfully clear that this was a diversion. Throughout the previous month, the North Vietnamese Army had reinforced its positions around Khe Sanh, a U.S. marine outpost located in rough terrain near the DMZ. Soon two divisions, forty thousand men, had surrounded the firebase. With the press predicting another Dienbienphu, Westmoreland dispatched six thousand marines to defend the garrison, and wave after wave of B-52s dropped 1,200,000 tons of ordnance on a five-square-mile area. LBJ followed the action closely in the White House Situation Room, assuring anyone and everyone that he would not allow Khe Sanh to fall to the enemy. Then, the first day of the month, a force numbering initially fifty-eight thousand and quickly rising to approximately eighty-four thousand Vietcong and NVA regulars launched a surprise offensive of extraordinary intensity and astonishing scope. Violating a truce that they themselves had pledged to observe during the Tet season, the communist forces barged into more than a hundred cities and towns, including Saigon, and audaciously shifted the war for the first time from its rural setting to a new arena: South Vietnam's supposedly impregnable urban areas. Nothing was safe, not even the American Embassy. Nineteen heavily armed Vietcong blasted their way through the compound's reinforced concrete outer wall with a 3.5-inch bazooka. The heavily armed men, some dressed in black peasant pajamas with red armbands, others in green shirts and slacks, fanned out through the four-acre enclosure. For six hours the enemy pounded the embassy itself with rockets and machine gun fire. Finally, the attack was repelled by American MPs and soldiers of the Army of the Republic of Vietnam. The enemy had come within an inch of occupying, indeed obliterating the heart of the U.S. mission in Vietnam.[28]

American and ARVN forces quickly rallied. Within days, U.S. and South Vietnamese soldiers had cleared Saigon. In the weeks that followed, they drove the communists from virtually every other city and town they had occupied, forcing them deep into the countryside and inflicting huge casualties. In Hue, the occupying forces held out for three weeks. Allied forces pounded the ancient city into rubble and then cleared what remained of the enemy in house-to-house fighting. More than forty-thousand communist soldiers were killed or wounded. The infrastructure of the Vietcong lay shattered, never fully to recover.

If the communists suffered a military setback as a result of Tet, they gained a major psychological victory. American casualties were high—eleven hundred killed—the ARVN lost twenty-three hundred men. The fighting also took 12,500 civilian lives and created as many as 1 million new refugees. But the real casualty was morale on the home front. The images from the Tet Offensive that flashed across America's television screens were horrific and haunting: U.S. diplomats in shirtsleeves firing out of the windows of the American embassy; air force and navy planes dropping canisters of exploding napalm on South Vietnamese villages; house-to-house fighting amid the rubble of Hue, once one of Southeast Asia's cultural treasures; the haggard faces of the besieged marines at Khe Sanh; and the image of Saigon's police chief casually firing his revolver into the head of a captured Vietcong. "We had to destroy it in order to save it," declared an American officer standing on the outskirts of what once was a Mekong Delta village.[29]

As soon as Johnson learned of Tet, he remarked to his foreign policy advisers, "It appears to be the judgment of our enemies that we are sufficiently weak and uncertain at home, sufficiently stretched in our military dispositions abroad, and sufficiently anxious to end the war in Viet Nam so that we are likely to accept, if not defeat, at least a degree of humiliation."[30] On the morning of February 1, LBJ addressed a presidential prayer breakfast. "In the hours of this night just past," he intoned, "I found these lines of prayer that were repeated a quarter of a century ago by another President. It was in 1942—when we were challenged in both oceans—at a season when the winds of the world blew harsh and the dawn of a brighter day seemed very far away, Franklin Delano Roosevelt offered to this Nation these words and I repeat them in these times now: 'God of the free, we pledge our hearts and lives to the cause of all free mankind . . . Grant us a common faith that man shall know bread and peace, that he shall know justice and righteousness, freedom and security, and an equal chance to do his best, not only in our own lands, but throughout the world. And in that faith let us march toward the clean world our hands can make.'[31]

Americans had been led to believe by Westmoreland's optimistic accounts that victory was just around the corner. But how could that be, when the Vietcong could penetrate the very symbol of U.S. power in Southeast Asia, the American Embassy compound in Saigon? "What the hell is going on?" demanded the respected CBS television anchor Walter Cronkite. "I thought we were winning the war." In the weeks that followed, Cronkite and other former administration supporters advised the president to negotiate a withdrawal. The United States had acted honorably and done all in its power to ensure the survival of freedom and democracy in Southeast Asia. Now it was up to the Vietnamese. Further roiling the waters were reports that the administration was deploying tactical nuclear weapons to Vietnam.[32] All across the nation, the Tet Offensive caused Americans to verbalize doubts that had been lurking in their subconscious: Was there really a viable nation south of the seventeenth parallel? If so, why were the Vietnamese not willing to fight and die to defend it? How could the U.S. military command have been caught so off-guard? Did Tet indicate that American strategic thinking was either fatally flawed or totally unrealistic? As opinion analyst Samuel Lubell noted, Americans shared a "fervent drive to shake free of an unwanted burden."[33] Citizens were confused, frustrated, and impatient. One housewife commented, "I want to get out but I don't want to give in."[34]

Ten days into the Tet Offensive, Generals Wheeler and Westmoreland decided that "free world" forces in Vietnam were on the verge of a major victory. The ARVN, which had been the primary military target of the NVA–Vietcong attacks, had suffered heavy casualties, but in general had stood and fought, bravely and effectively. The popular uprising, one of the enemy's prime objectives in launching the Tet Offensive, had not materialized. But they also perceived that a number of battles had been "very close things." The enemy had come within a hair, for example, of overrunning Ton So Nuht Air Base, the giant U.S. facility near Saigon. The battle for Khe Sanh was still raging, and the U.S. commanders saw that as the centerpiece of a communist drive to overrun I Corps. Both men compared the Tet Offensive to the 1944 Battle of the Bulge, the last-ditch German offensive that stretched the Seventh Army to the breaking point. American forces managed to prevail, however, and their victory signaled the beginning of the end for the Axis forces in Europe.[35] The two battles were tactically comparable, of course, but strategically and politically quite different. The military was vaguely aware of the public discontent in the United States caused by Tet, but they saw that as all the more reason to treat the battle as a victory to be followed up on rather than a defeat to be absorbed. "Indeed," Westmoreland later wrote, "from a psychological viewpoint, it seemed to me imperative that we exploit the ultimate failure of the enemy's offensive, 'close ranks,' and prosecute the war to a successful conclusion."[36] A consensus existed then that the U.S. command in Vietnam should ask for more troops, for relief from the 525,000 ceiling (there were then five hundred thousand American soldiers in Vietnam) to keep on the offensive and deal the enemy a knockout blow.

During the next few days, with Wheeler's rather inept coaching, Westmoreland made an increasingly urgent and yet ambivalent appeal for the permanent stationing of more troops in Vietnam. "This has been a limited war with limited objectives," he cabled Washington, "fought with limited means and programmed for the utilization of limited resources. This was a feasible proposition on the assumption that the enemy was to fight a protracted war. We are now in a new ball game where we face a determined, highly disciplined enemy, fully mobilized to achieve a quick victory. He is in the process of throwing in all his 'military chips to go for broke.' "[37] Then later that day: "I am expressing a firm request for additional troops, not because I fear defeat if I am not reinforced, but because I do not feel that I can fully grasp the initiative from the recently reinforced enemy without them. On the other hand a set back is fully possible if I am not reinforced and it is likely that we will lose ground in other areas if I am required to make substantial reinforcement of I Corp."[38]

On the 12th, with unanimous support, LBJ authorized the immediate dispatch of 10,300 men, 3,800 from the 82nd and the 6,500 marines from the 27th Regimental Landing Team. "Does this give Westmoreland what he needs?" LBJ asked Wheeler. "Yes, sir," the chairman replied, meaning, of course, for the present.[39]

That week, Bobby Kennedy delivered a major foreign policy address. "The time has come to take a new look at the war," he declared. The nation must rid itself of the illusion that Tet was some kind of victory. "The Viet Cong . . . have demonstrated despite all our reports of progress . . . that half a million American soldiers with 700,000 Vietnamese allies, with total command of the air [and] sea, backed by huge resources and the most modern weapons, are unable to secure even a single city from the attacks of an enemy whose total strength is about 250,000 . . . We have misconceived the nature of the war."[40]

On February 20, Fulbright convened Senate Foreign Relations Committee hearings on the Gulf of Tonkin incident. Over the next two weeks, the committee staff leaked documents to the press proving that the *Turner Joy* and *Maddox* had been on a secret mission in support of the South Vietnamese and that the second attack had never happened.[41] If Johnson had misled Congress and the American people concerning the North Vietnamese attack on the two American destroyers in 1964, then the Gulf of Tonkin Resolution, the very justification for the presence of American troops in Vietnam, was invalid.

Johnson's own advisers continued to show signs of dissent. Harry McPherson sent the president a copy of a commentary by Eric Sevareid on CBS television. The broadcaster had criticized the U.S. command in Vietnam for trying to dress up a disaster. "I agree in every particular," McPherson told his boss. "I don't agree with any of it—thanks for your judgment," LBJ scribbled on his aide's memo.[42] Later that day, Johnson sent Clark Clifford the famous quote on war by John Stuart Mill: "War is an ugly thing, but not the ugliest thing: the decayed and degraded state of moral and patriotic feeling which thinks nothing worth a war is worse . . . A man who has nothing which he cares about more than his personal safety is a miserable creature who has no chance of being free, unless made and kept so by the exertions of better men than himself." [43]

As his advisers were conferring on what strategy to pursue in the wake of Tet, Johnson left Washington to visit some of the troops who were getting ready to ship out to Vietnam. He went first to Fort Bragg, North Carolina, to see those elements of the 82nd scheduled to go. Commenting on his trip later to his aides, Johnson said, "Those boys expressed no sentiment, but it was obvious to me that none of them was happy to be going . . . About 50% of the men down there were Negroes. I understand they volunteered because of the high morale in the Airborne and the extra pay." [44] From Fort Bragg, the president and his entourage flew cross-country to visit the 27th Marine Regiment stationed at El Toro, California. After his remarks, he walked across the tarmac to talk and shake hands with the soldiers as they boarded their transport plane. "I am at heart a sentimental guy at times like those—that I sure regret having to send those men," he said. "One soldier really melted me and brought me to my knees. I asked a boy from Ohio if he had been to Vietnam before. He said yes . . . I asked him if he had a family. He said yes, sir, he had a little baby boy born yesterday. There wasn't a tear in his eye. No bitterness showed in his face. But I can assure you I sure stopped asking any men questions for awhile." [45]

Before returning to Washington, LBJ spent the night aboard the aircraft carrier *Constellation,* scheduled to depart for Vietnam in June. At breakfast with some twenty sailors, LBJ asked one what he would change about the war if he could. "I would hit them more," he said. The remark unleashed a torrent of words from Johnson, a torrent that summed up his dilemma as he saw it. If the United States closed the ports of North Vietnam through blockade, it would only make the NVA more dependent on communist China. If the U.S. bombed indiscriminately in the North, there was a chance of hitting a Soviet or Chinese ship. "If you hit two or three ships in the harbor—it is like slapping me and I would slap back. We don't want a wider war. They have a signed agreement that if they get into a war the Russians and Chinese will come to their aid. They have two big brothers that have more weight and people than I have. They are very dangerous. If the whole family jumps upon me—I have all I can say grace over now . . . We are trying not to make this a wider war." [46] Inflamed though his patriotism was and as hurt as his ego might have been, LBJ could not see an escape from that strategic logic. [47]

Back in Washington, LBJ seemed oppressed and exhausted to those around him. Speaking to some visiting students at the White House, he said, "I don't know how to do anything better than we are doing it. If I did, I would do it. I would take the better way. We have considered everything." On Abraham Lincoln's birthday he spoke briefly from the steps of the monument to a meager crowd that shivered in the cold February wind. "We live in a time that Lincoln would have well understood," the president declared. "He heard the charges that the war was long, and wrong. He saw Americans die—600,000 of them— and he brooded; he saw dissent, riot and rebellion; he saw heavy taxes and inflation; he saw hunger and poverty. Sad, but steady, always convinced of his cause, Lincoln stuck it out." Then, speaking deliberately, drawing out his words, he finished, "Sad, but steady, so will we."[48]

On February 23 the chairman of the Joint Chiefs arrived in Saigon for a major policy review. "Wheeler was told to go out and talk things over with Westmoreland," Califano said. "LBJ wanted . . . some talk without all 'that cow-shit I am always hearing from over there.' "[49] Matters had reached a crucial stage in Washington, the JCS chief told his field commander. The fighting in Vietnam, tensions in Korea, and the depleted state of the nation's military reserves were forcing the administration to make some major decisions. Westmoreland wanted forty thousand additional men, but it seemed inconceivable that the administration would make such a commitment without a general call-up of the reserves. If that were the case, he and Westmoreland should think in larger terms: both men assumed that Tet was just the beginning of a major year-long offensive designed to gain as much ground in the South as possible before the enemy would "try to lock us into a negotiation at his peak position before we can counterattack."[50] The United States must not allow that to happen. Their goal, like the president's, was to turn the war over to the South Vietnamese. In the short run, the prospects were not good, the two soldiers concluded, but in the long run they were.

Westmoreland insisted that Tet was the best thing that could have happened as far as Vietnamization was concerned. He would not have "fortressed up" Saigon and the other cities and defended them even if he had wanted to. If Thieu, Ky, and the ARVN were not willing to fight for their cities, then there was no hope anyway. "The VC getting into Saigon was a blessing," he subsequently told an interviewer.[51] The South Vietnamese had fought for their cities, and, though severely bloodied, had won. That there was no popular uprising as the Vietcong had hoped was extremely heartening to the leadership. From 1964 through 1967, Westmoreland later observed, "the South Vietnamese government was afraid to arm the people. Really afraid. But Tet convinced them the concern was false. The people were crying for arms."[52] Wheeler and Westmoreland fleshed out a strategy that called for nationwide attacks on Vietcong and NVA units and supply bases in the South; accelerated bombing of the North, including the port of Haiphong; cutting the Ho Chi Minh trail in Cambodia and Laos; and launching an amphibious hook across the DMZ. Such a strategy would require many more troops and would lead to a general call-up of reserves. Either the administration would mobilize the nation for war or it would not.[53] What did Wheeler think of the prospects? Westmoreland asked. Wheeler said he did not know, but was encouraged by the fact that Clark Clifford, an outspoken hawk, was replacing McNamara as secretary of defense.[54]

On February 27, with the president in Texas to attend a birthday party for John Connally, Rusk, McNamara, Clifford, Katzenbach, Bill Bundy, Rostow, Califano, and McPherson met with Wheeler to consider the military's request for troops to deliver a knockout blow. The JCS chair outlined what they hoped to accomplish and then gave the figures: 105,000 additional troops by May 1 and 100,000 more in two increments, part by September 1 and the rest by December 31. "In many areas the pacification program has been brought to a halt," Wheeler wrote. "The VC are prowling the countryside, and it is a question of which side moves fastest to gain control. The outcome is not at all clear . . . If the enemy synchronizes his expected major attacks with increased pressure throughout the country, General Westmoreland's margin will be paper thin."[55] McNamara reckoned that, at a minimum, 150,000 reservists would have to be called up and draft numbers increased substantially, reaching a total of four hundred thousand new uniformed personnel at least. Rostow was enthusiastic, McPherson appalled. "This is unbelievable and futile," he blurted out. Was the U.S. military in Vietnam poised to take the offensive or teetering on the edge of defeat?

Johnson returned to Washington later that day and the next morning met with Wheeler and his foreign policy advisers. What were the alternatives to 205,000 additional men, LBJ asked? Loss of the northern two provinces of South Vietnam, Wheeler replied.[56] Joe Califano later described the mood of the meeting. "It was just about the most crepe hanging session I ever sat in on," he told an interviewer. "Everybody was way down because of all the hell being raised on the hill and out in the streets against the war. Harry was convinced that we had to do something pretty damned dramatic to keep from being politically lynched. McNamara looked like he wanted to cry and kept saying the bombing got us into this fix and we had better fight against any more escalation. Clifford played like a trial lawyer, asking snappy questions . . . and NEVER making a suggestion of what to do. He had all the questions and none of the answers. Bundy looked like he was holding class with a group of unbright students. He agreed that we had 'spit in the political soup' here at home and needed to 'pet the dove somehow.' By this time everybody was ready to declare peace and get the hell out except Rostow."[57] The gathering broke up without taking a firm position.

When McNamara bade his farewell to the Defense Department staff on February 29, he and the president were marooned on an elevator for thirteen minutes on their way to the ceremony. It was fate's commentary, some said. But the architects of war were rescued, and McNamara bade a tearful farewell to his coworkers.

With Clark Clifford sworn in as his successor, the "Clifford Task Force," essentially the entire foreign policy team, was directed to prepare an evaluation of the 205,000-troop request and to recommend alternatives. Clifford huddled with Wheeler and the JCS almost continuously through late February and early March. He found the results of those conversations most unsatisfactory, he subsequently reported to LBJ. The chiefs could not promise him that another two hundred thousand would suffice, that increased bombing would turn the tide or even reduce American casualties. American troops would have to continue to carry the military burden for the foreseeable future. There was, he later wrote in an account of the sessions, "no plan for victory in the historic American sense," and there was "no agreement on an answer" as to how long it would take to win the war of attrition.[58] On March 4 Clifford met privately with LBJ to present his findings and recommendations and then appeared before a larger meeting that included Rusk, Humphrey, Wheeler, Helms, Maxwell Taylor, Rostow, George Christian, and Marvin Watson. The hawk had now turned into a dove. The infusion of another 205,000 troops, Clifford said, would probably inhibit rather than promote the emergence of "our purpose—which is for a viable South Vietnam which can live in peace." There was every indication that the enemy would be able to match the U.S. buildup body for body, gun for gun. Consequently, the president should approve additional forces necessary to meet contingencies for only the next three to four months—perhaps thirty thousand men. "This is as far as we are willing to go."[59]

Some later accounts have suggested that LBJ was shocked, incredulous, angry at Clifford's recommendations and that he felt betrayed. In fact, Clark Clifford was speaking for Lyndon Johnson. LBJ did not permit "surprises" in his meetings. Clifford had talked repeatedly with the president about his impressions of where the war in Vietnam was headed. Indeed, in this particular situation, the counsel to the president was nothing more than a cipher. The position that he articulated at the meeting on March 4 represented Johnson's thinking precisely. "It just grabs my ass when everybody and his brother-in-law tries to win the damn peace prize by claiming to fight for the mind of the president," LBJ later told journalist Don Oberdorfer. "There was no fight. I listened to all their talk and made up my own mind."[60] It also reflected a consensus within the foreign policy establishment, excluding Walt Rostow and Max Taylor.

In the days following the March 4 meeting, LBJ "consulted" with Congress. At an evening meeting at the White House with Senators Mansfield, Sparkman, Aiken, and Hickenlooper, Fulbright told LBJ that the Gulf of Tonkin Resolution would be null and void if the president decided to dispatch another two hundred thousand troops to Vietnam. Johnson replied that he did not regard the resolution as binding on Congress. If the members were opposed to another escalation, they ought to speak out. "I know full well that all of you are my friends and all of you want to help the president," he said. "I also know that you do have differences. Your intentions and your good judgment and your experience are well known to me. I have never doubted them." Fulbright was sympathetic. He knew nothing about how to run a war, he said; the United States needed to get out, but there was no good way to do it. "I just think this war is a disaster," he said. "I think that we are going down the drain if we continue with it. This is their country . . . they are poor and don't have much tolerance. We have a lot to lose. In my opinion we are playing the Communist game. We just ought to get out of that country any way we can."[61]

Separately, LBJ turned to the hawks. During a conversation with Richard Russell, he claimed that the doves were all over him, threatening to revoke the Gulf of Tonkin Resolution, bullying Rusk, harnessing themselves to the political machinations of Bobby Kennedy. The Foreign Relations Committee was busy turning itself into another Civil War–era Committee of Congress to supervise the war. Russell was appropriately disgusted. "Fulbright doesn't know what he is talking about," he said. Nonetheless, the Georgian said, he was coming to the conclusion that if the United States could not go all out in Vietnam, it ought to get out.[62]

After March 4, the issue was not whether to escalate, but whether to take another bite of the peace apple. On February 21, after the American–South Vietnamese counteroffensive had taken its toll, UN Secretary General U Thant had reported to LBJ, "If the republic of North Vietnam were to be officially notified of a cessation of hostilities [bombing] from the United States, then the talks could start immediately." Johnson responded with this proposal: the United States would call a bombing halt for the area above the DMZ; discussions would start within two or three days; these talks would be "substantive and not vituperative and just harassment—he did not want another Panmunjom"; both sides would continue to supply their forces but there would not be "a crash program to try to overrun us at the DMZ."[63] Johnson's conversation with U Thant was more than just another attempt to appease world opinion and pour water on the antiwar fire at home, to "pet the dove," as Bill Bundy had put it. On February 28, Dean Rusk proposed to LBJ an unconditional bombing halt north of the twentieth parallel. "All this time [during the debate over the 205,000 figure]," notes journalist-historian Don Oberdorfer, "Johnson had in hand Rusk's bombing halt proposal—in writing—and he kept it all to himself."[64]

A plan was beginning to take shape in the president's mind. He had already decided he would not run for reelection. In early January, he had asked Horace Busby to draft a withdrawal statement. John Connally, who was privy to the decision, had suggested that the State of the Union address would be an excellent venue for the sure-to-be-dramatic announcement. "The longer he waited," Connally observed, the more it would help Bobby Kennedy, who "was free to operate while others were not."[65] But Johnson decided that the time was not right. It was too soon. He still had some blows to strike, and he did not want to become a lame duck yet. Before leaving for the Capitol to deliver the address, he handed Lady Bird his withdrawal statement to let her know of his decision.[66]

In January and February, the president had had several remarkable conversations with HEW Secretary John Gardner. As Gardner later recalled, "I had become increasingly concerned about the state of the country, about the war, about the riots, about the course of events as I saw them . . . We were discussing what could be done to insure the reelection of President Johnson . . . And I found to my consternation some time in early January that I did not think that the president should run for reelection . . . I wrote a letter of resignation [for Johnson], took it in and handed it to him, and he read it and laid it on the table and asked me why I did it . . . And I said, 'Well, I just don't believe that you can unite the country. I just think that we're in a terrible passage in our history and that you cannot do what needs to be done, with the best will in the world. I just think that is not in the cards for you . . . ' And he said, 'Well, I've had the same thought myself many times.' "[67]

March 1968 proved one of the most tumultuous months in American political history. As the spring primary season approached, LBJ's political advisers urged him to give some attention to the forthcoming campaign. Polls showed Eugene McCarthy lagging far behind the president, but Bobby was waiting in the wings. "I am sure that B K is sponsoring a 'War of Liberation' against you and your administration," John Roche observed to LBJ.[68] Orville Freeman and other party luminaries had pressed Johnson to give them the go-ahead to organize the reelection campaign. In early January, he had, but in an almost offhanded way, and with a few exceptions, he turned away requests to meet with party leaders. Jim Rowe agreed to head a volunteer effort to generate grassroots support, but LBJ took little notice.[69] Intimates and close observers murmured that electoral politics seemed to have lost its interest for the president.

Defections from the ranks of Johnson's Democratic supporters became a weekly and even daily affair. Jesse Unruh, the powerful speaker of the California Assembly, was reportedly ready to jump ship, as was Walter Reuther. From every corner of the country Democratic governors warned the president's men that if matters did not take a dramatic new course in Vietnam, they would all go down to defeat in November.[70]

By 1968 liberals had divided into a pro-war faction typified by Henry Jackson and Hubert Humphrey and an antiwar segment led by Bobby Kennedy, Frank Church, and George McGovern. To the delight of conservatives, antiwar liberals seemed to be willing to go to any lengths to stop the war and get rid of LBJ, even to the point of sacrificing Democratic rule. With another wave of rioting looming as summer approached, urban ethnic Democrats were attracted by the candidacy of George Wallace, a southerner, a populist, and a law-and-order segregationist. Southern Democrats were breaking away from the Great Society consensus and joining with the GOP to block further initiatives in the areas of health, civil rights, public works, and Social Security. This in turn would further embitter the disadvantaged, and the country would be plunged into an endless cycle of black rage and white reaction. Perhaps, LBJ believed, if he could remove himself from the picture, this disaster could be avoided. Perhaps the fanaticism of the anti-Johnson liberals would cool, and the New South could once again join hands with the northern liberal-labor coalition. Moreover, out of contention, the president could work for an "honorable peace" in Vietnam. It was a long shot, but worth a try. Thus, though he was at times ambivalent, reluctant to give up, hungering for more approval at the polls, desirous of revenge against his enemies, LBJ decided not to run for the very reasons John Gardner had laid out. He could do more for his country—and his reputation—politically dead than alive. Johnson ordered his speechwriters to prepare a major address on Vietnam to be delivered the evening of March 31.

On March 12 Eugene McCarthy and his "Children's Campaign" shocked the nation. Predicted to win no more than 11 or 12 percent of the vote in the New Hampshire primary, the Minnesotan captured 42.4 percent compared to LBJ's 49.5 percent. "Dove bites Hawk," a journalist quipped. Exit polls indicated that most of McCarthy's support came from those disenchanted with the war, both hawks and doves. With the exception of speechwriter Richard Goodwin, students directed the entire McCarthy effort. McCarthy's success, and Johnson's distress, were more than Bobby Kennedy could bear. On March 14, using Clark Clifford as an intermediary, Bobby proposed a deal to the White House. If LBJ would appoint a national commission to investigate the war effort in Vietnam, headed presumably by him or brother Ted, and make recommendations, presumably binding, he would not jump into the race. All he wanted, Bobby said, was peace in Vietnam.[71] LBJ told Clifford to tell RFK that he and his views on Vietnam were always welcome at the White House, but that the deal being proposed would alienate everyone if it became public knowledge, which it surely would.[72] Two days later, RFK threw his hat into the ring.

Writing in the *New York Review of Books,* Andrew Kopkind commented on RFK's persistent appeal. "By luck and pluck he has become the last, best hope of the Sixties and the first of the Seventies," Kopkind observed.

> The luck is his family, his fortune, and the assassin (or assassins) of Dallas. The pluck involves the development of a style and a rhetoric compounding some of the more attractive aspects of Bob Dylan and Fidel Castro: tousled hair, plaintive croon, underdoggedness, undefined revolutionism. His special charm is for those temporarily or permanently out of power; they sense that he is, either directly or metaphorically, their ticket to the top . . . Everybody knows that Robert Kennedy was soft on McCarthy and vicious to Hoffa, that he plays rough in touch football and tough in election campaigns, and that his father is a scoundrel and his social life a three-ring circus. But those who believe in him don't much care . . . They see his ruthlessness as pragmatism, his sentimentality as humanism, his single-mindedness as dedication.[73]

Johnson hardly seemed devastated by McCarthy's showing. Speaking to a VFW group the night of the New Hampshire primary, he observed that he had had an early report on the voting. Of the first twenty-five votes cast he had not received one. "I said to Mrs. Johnson, 'What do you think about that?' She answered, 'I think the day is bound to get better, Lyndon'."[74] A few days after Kennedy's announcement, Orville Freeman saw the president during a cabinet meeting. "As usual he was a half hour late . . . Finally about 8:00 he drifted in, in an exceptionally good humor. It was really quite impressive. Actually, I don't think he could have put it on."[75] But Freeman found the president's nonchalance unsettling. "Mr. President," he said, "what we really need now is someone that's calling the signals on this [campaign]." Johnson remarked that he thought Georgia Governor Terry Sanford was coming in to do that. "All in all," Freeman observed, "what comes through loud and clear is that at this point, this is almost like a big ship without a rudder."[76]

On March 22, LBJ formally rejected Westmoreland's two hundred thousand–plus troop request. He then summoned the Wise Men to a meeting at the White House on March 26. Prior to the gathering, the commander in chief had his briefers paint as bleak a picture of the military and fiscal situation as possible. The group—Acheson, Ball, McCloy, McGeorge Bundy, Cyrus Vance, General Matthew Ridgway, Maxwell Taylor, Robert Murphy, Lodge, Fortas, and Goldberg—were appropriately gloomy. A minority advocated holding the line and even escalating the war if necessary, but the majority favored immediate steps to de-escalate. Acheson spoke for all when he said that "the United States could no longer do the job we set out to do in the time we have left and we must begin to take steps to disengage." Johnson was reportedly furious. "The establishment bastards have bailed out," he is said to have remarked after the meeting.[77] He was playing to the galleries. The "establishment bastards" were doing just what he wanted them to do. Indeed, that same day, in a tense meeting with Wheeler and General Creighton Abrams, Westmoreland's successor, Johnson pled with the military to support his peace overtures. He lamented the deteriorating fiscal situation, divisions at home, and his own "overwhelming disapproval" in the press.[78]

The war continued to take its toll on the president's family. In mid-January the first lady had hosted a luncheon of some fifty "Woman Doers" on what women could do to prevent crime on the streets. During a question-and-answer period, black vocalist Eartha Kitt stood and pointed her finger at Lady Bird and said in a shrill voice, "You send the best of this country off to be shot and maimed. No wonder the kids rebel and take pot. They don't want to go to school because they're going to be snatched off from their mothers to be shot in Vietnam." With tears welling in her eyes, the first lady tried to defend herself. Just because there was a war on, the women of the nation should not stop working for better education, health care, and job opportunities for the nation's young people.[79] Adding to Lady Bird's stress was the fact that both of her recently married daughters had husbands that had gone or were going to Vietnam. She wanted Lyndon to announce that he was not going to run, but she was not at all sure what he was going to do. America had all the spiritual and material resources in the world but seemed determined, in a fit of self-flagellation, to destroy itself, she lamented to Orville Freeman.[80]

On March 28, LBJ met with Califano and McPherson over lunch to discuss his forthcoming speech on Vietnam. They mulled over the bombing pause and tax surcharge and then the president suddenly asked, "What do you think about my not running for reelection?" McPherson said that personally, he would not run if he were the president, but both he and Califano insisted that Johnson had to win another term. Otherwise, the country would become hopelessly deadlocked. It is already deadlocked, Johnson observed. "Others can get things done," he said. "The Congress and I are like an old married couple. We've lived together so long and we've been rubbing against each other night after night so often and we've asked so much of each other over the years we're tired of each other." [81] Later, alone with Califano, LBJ asked, "If I don't run, who do you think will get the nomination?" Bobby Kennedy, Califano said.

"What about Hubert?"

"I don't think he can beat Kennedy."

"What's wrong with Bobby? He's made some nasty speeches about me, but he's never had to sit here . . . Bobby would keep fighting for the Great Society programs. And when he sat in this chair he might have a different view on the war. His major problem would be with appropriations. He doesn't know how to deal with people on the Hill and a lot of them don't like him. But he'll try . . . Whether Kennedy or Nixon won, at least the leadership would support them in the first year or so . . . And that might provide the necessary time to heal the wounds now separating the country." [82]

Califano recalled that LBJ looked exhausted. During the week, Johnson read and reread Lincoln's second inaugural address: "With malice toward none; with charity for all; with firmness in the right, as God gives us to see the right, let us strive on to finish the work we are in; to bind up the nation's wounds; to care for him who shall have borne the battle, and for his widow and his orphan . . . to do all which may achieve and cherish a just and lasting peace among ourselves and with all nations." [83]

Meanwhile, Horace Busby had been working secretly on an addendum to the March 31 "peace with honor" speech on Vietnam. [84] Early Sunday morning, the 31st, found the president surrounded by his staff, working on his address scheduled for that night. Only Busby had the withdrawal paragraphs. Lady Bird was allowed to see the portions on Vietnam, of which she very much approved, but not the abdication material.

At seven o'clock Lynda returned from California, where she had said good-bye to her husband at Camp Pendleton. He would leave in a fortnight for his first thirteen-month tour of duty in Vietnam. She was pregnant with her first child. Lady Bird recalled being stunned by her appearance. Looking like a "wraith from another world," Lynda stared directly at her father and asked, "Why do we have to go to Vietnam?" Her father just stared at her, and Lady Bird later wrote that she had not seen such pain in his eyes since his mother had died. [85]

Around 10 A.M., LBJ gathered up aide Jim Jones and Luci and drove to St. Dominic's to attend mass. During the service, he instructed Jones to get the Secret Service to fetch the draft of the speech, including the Busby material, from his bedroom and to call Vice President Humphrey and tell him that they were coming over. When the speech and LBJ arrived at the Humphreys' apartment, the second couple was preparing to fly to Mexico City for a state visit. "At the Vice President's apartment in southwestern Washington," Jones later wrote, "Mrs. Humphrey and Luci visited while the President gave Mr. Humphrey the speech. When he got to the final paragraph, the Vice President's face flushed, his eyes watered and he protested that Mr. Johnson could not step down. 'Don't mention this to anyone until Jim calls you in Mexico tonight. But you'd better start now planning your campaign for President.' Humphrey's face went slack, his shoulders hunched. 'There's no way I can beat the Kennedys,' he said."[86]

Back at the White House, the president continued to fiddle with the wording of the Vietnam sections of the speech. He glanced at the newspapers, which included a just-released Gallup poll showing his approval ratings at an all-time low; only 36 percent endorsed his overall job performance and 26 percent his handling of the war in Vietnam.[87] Late in the afternoon, LBJ had George Christian call John Connally and ask him once again if he thought withdrawal was the right thing to do. Connally said yes. The president should have done it in the State of the Union, and if he was going to step down, he must wait no longer. He owed it to the party and to the country.[88]

Just after six o'clock Johnson met with Soviet Ambassador Anatoly Dobrynin and told him that he was going to send an additional 13,500 troops to Vietnam but that he would couple it with an announcement that the United States would cease bombing above the twentieth parallel for an indefinite period. The United States was prepared to go ninety percent of the way toward peace; now it was time for Moscow to get the North Vietnamese to go the remaining 10 percent of the way. It was up to the United States and the USSR to end the war soon and prevent hostilities from spreading.[89]

The address was scheduled for 9:15. At 8:15 Jim Jones took the last two pages over and had them put on the teleprompter. The president rattled off a series of names of people that Jones and Christian should call—cabinet members, party leaders, and lifelong friends—once the speech had started to tell them about its punch line. Both Lynda and Luci were in tears. Lynda was particularly distraught. How could her father think of not running? What would happen to Chuck and the other soldiers in Vietnam? "Now I'll be free to work for them full time," her father told her.[90]

A somber, somewhat haggard president went on national television to announce that henceforward the bombing of North Vietnam would be limited to the area just north of the DMZ below the twentieth parallel. The United States, he declared, was ready for comprehensive peace talks anywhere, anytime, and he announced that Averell Harriman would represent the administration should such talks materialize. The nation, he said, had done its very best to keep faith with the words spoken by John F. Kennedy, to "pay any price, bear any burden, meet any hardship, support any friend, oppose any foe to assure the survival and the success of liberty." But without "the unity of our people," the United States could do nothing. "There is division in the American house now. There is divisiveness among us all tonight. And holding the trust that is mine, as President of all the people, I cannot disregard the peril to the progress of the American people and the hope and the prospect of peace for all peoples."[91]

Lyndon Johnson and the republic to which he was committed had come to a crossroads. They had embarked on their nation-building enterprise believing that freedom was indivisible, that historically, intellectually, and morally the United States was bound to combat communist totalitarianism on every front. But they had discovered that there were limits to American power, that in its pursuit of liberty for the Vietnamese the nation was verging on forfeiting its own freedoms. The moral imperatives that Lyndon Johnson invoked to justify the Second Reconstruction and the conflict in Southeast Asia were not equivalent. The sins of racial injustice were America's own; the sins of communism, of Sino-Soviet imperialism belonged to others. For the first, the nation could and should risk self-immolation, but not for the second. The most America could do in a dangerous world was protect itself and protect only those others who were vital to the nation's survival. For a variety of reasons, Johnson could not simply withdraw from Vietnam. Historical errors are not that easily corrected. But he could sacrifice himself. The Texan then dropped his bombshell. "I shall not seek, and I will not accept, the nomination of my party for another term as president," he told a stunned nation.[92]

In the wake of the dramatic announcement, friends and cabinet members gathered in the West Wing. LBJ appeared relaxed, increasingly confident that he had done the right thing. Johnson loved surprises. And he had just pulled off one of the great surprises of twentieth-century political life. Given his personality, of course, the Texan found the notion of self-sacrifice deeply satisfying. "[He was] telling stories and jokes and laughing," Vicky McCammon remembered, while staff and guests huddled in knots, talking in hushed tones.[93] LBJ stayed up until well after midnight taking calls from well-wishers, telling his Texas friends to polish up on their dominoes, remarking several times that he was looking forward to spending more time with his grandson, Patrick Lyndon Nugent.[94]

The next morning Sam Houston sent his brother a congratulatory note. "Last night was the happiest moment of my life," he wrote. "I am proud to be your brother."[95] In the days that followed, LBJ basked in the public adulation that had once been his, but since 1966 had become nothing more than a fond memory. On April 4 he flew to New York for the installation of Terence Cooke as Catholic archbishop. The crowd that had assembled on the steps of St. Patrick's Cathedral cheered him. Striding down the center aisle, Johnson was momentarily taken aback when the congregation rose as one and treated him to a prolonged ovation. The next day, a Lou Harris poll revealed that the March 31 speech had completely reversed the president's fortunes. His 57 percent disapproval rating had transformed into a 57 percent approval rating.

CHAPTER 40

A MIDSUMMER NIGHTMARE

T HE PRESIDENT'S EUPHORIA WAS SHORT-LIVED. AT 7:30 P.M. on April 4, 1968, as LBJ was preparing to depart the White House to attend a Democratic fund-raiser for Vice President Humphrey, he was informed that Martin Luther King had been shot in Memphis. Earlier in the day, a white petty crook, James Earl Ray, had told his brother that he was going to "get the big nigger."[1] That evening, he did just that, shooting King while he stood on the balcony of the Lorraine Motel. At 8:20 George Christian informed LBJ that King was dead. "Everything we've gained in the last few days we're going to lose tonight," he remarked dejectedly to Joe Califano.[2]

As news of King's death went out over radio and television, new waves of rioting racked the nation. "When white America killed Dr. King," declared Stokely Carmichael, "she declared war on us." In Washington, D.C., over seven hundred fires turned night into day, and smoke from them completely obscured the Capitol. LBJ instructed his aides to convene a meeting of congressional leaders and prominent black activists the following morning. Among those invited were Whitney Young, A. Philip Randolph, Roy Wilkins, Bayard Rustin, Mayor Carl Stokes of Cleveland, and NAACP field director Charles Evers of Jackson, Mississippi. Johnson asked King's father to attend, but his doctors would not allow him to travel. Told that the president's prayers were with him, the elder King replied, "Oh no, my prayers are with the President."[3]

The meeting got under way at eleven the next morning. As the talks continued, Floyd McKissick, accompanied by two other men, suddenly showed up at the White House gates. He demanded that all three be admitted. When the guards told him that only his name was on the guest list, he and his companions turned on their heels and left.[4] Inside, Johnson paid tribute to King and promised to continue to work day and night to realize his dream. The real question was what his murder would mean to America. "Let us be frank about it," he said. "It can mean that those—of both races—who believe that violence is the best means of settling racial problems in America, will have had their belief confirmed" Black Americans must recommit to nonviolence and white Americans to "root out every trace of racism from their hearts."[5] The black leaders were generally receptive, but they warned that time was short. "The large majority of Negroes were not in favor of violence, but we need something to fight back with," declared Reverend Leon Sullivan. "Otherwise we will be caught with nothing."[6] From the White House the president and his guests motored to the National Cathedral to attend a memorial service for King. Back at the Rose Garden, LBJ, flanked by prominent blacks and congressional leaders, issued a proclamation declaring Sunday, April 7, a day of national mourning for the fallen civil rights leader. He dashed off a note to Coretta Scott King: "My thoughts have been with you and your children throughout this long and anguished day . . . Since early morning, I have devoted all my hours and energy to honoring your good husband in the manner he would most approve. I have sought—by word, deed and official act—to unite this sorrowing and troubled nation against further and wider violence."[7]

From the Situation Room the president received hourly reports: "As of 8:00 P.M., 6 deaths, 533 arrests and 209 injuries treated at hospitals [in Washington, D.C.]; 8:55 P.M., confirmed report of four men with rifles on top of the Hawk and Dove Restaurant in the 300 block of Pennsylvania Avenue, SE."[8] General Westmoreland, in town for a meeting with LBJ and Clark Clifford, recalled that the capital "looked worse than Saigon did at the height of the Tet offensive." He quipped that in 1814 the British had burned Washington, but this time we were doing it ourselves.[9] From Chicago, Mayor Daley advised that he was probably going to have to request federal troops to quell post-assassination disturbances. Burnings and shootings were reported from Detroit, Cleveland, and Houston.[10] Somehow, Johnson managed to keep a sense of humor. Upon hearing rumors that Stokely Carmichael was organizing a group at 14th and U Streets Northwest to march on Georgetown and burn it down, the president smiled, and said, "Goddamn! I've waited thirty-five years for this day!"[11]

By late Saturday night the White House had received reports of rioting and looting in more than a hundred American cities. The first contingents of nearly fourteen thousand regular army, marine, and national guard troops began to deploy in Washington. Roadblocks were set up around the White House, and soldiers took up positions at the southwest gate. Johnson was determined that the world would not be treated to scenes of Americans shooting Americans, as he put it, in the nation's capital. He ordered troop commanders and police to use the absolute minimum force necessary to maintain order. Senator Russell called Johnson to complain that marines guarding the Capitol grounds had not been issued live ammunition. Senator Robert Byrd of West Virginia phoned to ask why martial law had not been proclaimed and to insist that adult looters be shot on sight.[12] The president stuck to his unloaded guns.

The next day, April 6, was Palm Sunday. LBJ gathered up Luci, Marie Fehmer, Jim Jones, and Joe Califano and left to attend mass at St. Dominic's. By Monday reports of sporadic violence continued to trickle in, but black anger seemed to have crested. The president had every intention of attending the funeral scheduled for Monday in Atlanta, but by that morning, the Secret Service and FBI were reporting several threats on Johnson's life.[13] From New York, UN Ambassador Arthur Goldberg called: "The President should not . . . leave Washington and should stay right in the White House. This could be very explosive. His presence in the White House is a stabilizing influence."[14] LBJ dispatched Air Force One with Vice President Humphrey and top black administration officials, including Thurgood Marshall and Robert Weaver. One of Richard Nixon's aides called the White House to suggest that Nixon, McCarthy, and Kennedy be invited to fly with the official party to show national solidarity, but Johnson demurred, so they flew on their own. Bobby, who the day before had walked the streets of a burned-out neighborhood in northwest Washington, was cheered. Nixon was booed. McCarthy was ignored.[15]

As with the Civil Rights Act following JFK's assassination, Johnson used the tragedy of King's death to push through another major civil rights initiative: fair housing. Perhaps only a trauma of such magnitude could have generated sufficient energy to ram through such a controversial measure. "When Johnson had sent his fair-housing bill to Congress in 1966," Califano later recalled, "it had prompted some of the most vicious mail LBJ received on any subject and the only death threats I ever received as a White House assistant."[16] The Senate had passed the Civil Rights Act of 1968 in March, but the House, whose members were being besieged by white middle-class constituents determined to keep blacks out of their neighborhoods, balked. Though Johnson had not been simpatico with King and resented particularly his outspoken opposition to the war, he was more than ready to use his martyrdom to get the fair housing bill passed. In the days following the assassination, LBJ never missed an opportunity to invoke King's name and to brandish his "dream" before Congress and the public. On April 10 the House passed the fair housing bill and sent it to the president for his signature.[17]

UNBEKNOWN TO MOST, throughout 1967 and 1968, LBJ could count on a devoted constituency of his own in the black community. LBJ's true emissary to African Americans was Louis Martin, a black politician and journalist who during the 1960s served as deputy director of the Democratic National Committee. Shrewd, intelligent, politically savvy, Martin was a loyal Democrat and a devoted LBJ man, a person who kept Lyndon Johnson and the Negro community together longer than anyone else assumed they could be kept together. Martin cultivated three main constituencies: the black press, the Negro churches, and black politicians. "Every year," McPherson recalled "once or twice a year, the Rose Garden would be filled with three or four hundred black faces, all of them voted into office, in there to see the man whose sponsorship of voting rights legislation had made it possible for them to be elected. It was a love feast every time . . . almost an orgy."[18]

MORE IMPORTANT THAN EVEN HOUSING, to the president's mind, was the pending tax surcharge bill. Perhaps the time was right. "It seems to me," White House aide Harold "Barefoot" Sanders observed, "that the President's decision not to run and the assassination of King may have created a climate in Congress for a dramatic new approach to the financial crisis. That new approach should not emphasize appropriations cuts, but, rather, the need for new revenues."[19] Unfortunately, Wilbur Mills, from his chokehold position as chair of the House Ways and Means Committee, seemed totally unmoved by the events in Memphis and the March 31 abdication speech. Joe Califano argued that more was at stake than just the tax increase. "For the past month we have been moving with increased power and ability to get things done," he wrote LBJ, "as well as an increased sense of confidence because the American people believe you are doing whatever you do without any ax to grind and only because it is right. This has all resulted from your pulling out of the race. But this remarkable assertion of power in a lame duck status could deteriorate rapidly if Wilbur Mills rolls over us on the tax legislation."[20]

By the close of April, LBJ had persuaded liberals in his administration and organized labor that the best that could be gotten from Congress was a tax surcharge bill that would require $5 billion in spending reductions for FY 1969. In conversations at the White House, Johnson told Mills, "If I could appoint you president, I would take Ways and Means and [you could] do what you think about it . . . My God, I have given all I have got. I have given my life—my political life . . . I don't want to see this country go down the drain . . . And I think I know more about it than you do. I don't think you see what is happening . . . And I think that there has got to be a position somewhere in between what you want in the way of a tax bill and what we want."[21] Mills told Johnson that he believed the nation could "get by" with the $5 billion figure. Then, on May 2, the chair of the House Ways and Means Committee announced that the president would have to agree not only to a $6 billion cut in his budget but also have to give up an additional $14 billion in new obligational authority.[22] At his news conference on May 3, LBJ came out swinging. "I want to make it perfectly clear to the American people," he told the assembled reporters, "that I think we are courting danger by this continued procrastination, this continued delay . . . I proposed a budget. If they [members of Congress] don't like that budget, then stand up like men and answer the roll call and cut what they think ought to be cut. Then the president will exercise his responsibility of approving it or rejecting it and vetoing it."[23] That night he recalled to Joe Califano Senator Alvin Wirtz's statement to him some thirty years earlier that one could tell another man to go to hell, but making him go was another matter. "Well, I just told someone to go to hell," he chuckled to his domestic policy adviser.[24] Over the next six weeks the president called scores of members of Congress, warning liberals that if the tax cut were not enacted, runaway inflation would gobble up the monies available to finance programs of social justice, and conservatives that the soundness of the dollar and the stability of the international economy depended on passage.[25]

THE PACE OF LBJ's LIFE had quickened rather than slowed after the March 31 speech. The daily routine that he had followed since his first days in the White House had changed very little, but there seemed more to do. He described a typical twenty-four hours in a televised interview with Mel Stuart:

> I have two working days. I get awake in the morning, six-thirty—six, six-thirty—and I work straight through to about three o'clock . . . I have my lunch and then I break my day . . . I go and take a nap—thirty minutes, forty-five minutes, sometimes over an hour . . . Then I wash my teeth, have my shave, and take my shower and start my second day. And that keeps me here generally, unless I have a state dinner or something, 'til eleven in the evening. And I go home and I have my meal and then I start—my dinner, my evening meal—and then I start to work on night reading and I finish that about one or one-thirty. I have a masseur that comes in and gives me a rub. And as I'm reading that mail and he's rubbing me, I go to sleep two or three times . . . He leaves, I turn out the light and I'm asleep in five minutes. One of my roommates in college said when I was a young man, "We'll never have to worry about Lyndon committing suicide—he'll go to sleep thinking about it."[26]

Johnson may have been busier than ever, but fewer and fewer of his hours were spent in public. Antiwar demonstrations were so predictable and widespread that Johnson spent his time away from the White House at the ranch, at Camp David, and in Washington, sometimes on the presidential yacht, *Sequoia*. Johnson's reluctance to indulge his fondness for spontaneous encounters with the masses during 1967 and 1968 stemmed from fear of humiliation more than of assassination.[27]

While LBJ twisted congressional arms, minds, and consciences in an effort to pass his housing and tax bills, some three thousand "poor people" trekked to the nation's capital by rail, bus, mule train, and automobile. During the last two weeks in May they threw up a shantytown made of plywood and canvas huts on Anacostia Flats, the site of the settlement established by the Bonus Expeditionary marchers during the Hoover administration; they named their encampment "Resurrection City." The Poor People's Campaign was the brainchild of Martin Luther King. Indeed, his trip to Memphis had been designed both to highlight a sanitation strike and to launch the march on Washington. Following his assassination, King's successor as head of the SCLC, Ralph David Abernathy, took up the gauntlet. "It isn't going to be a Sunday-school picnic like the '63 march on Washington," said Andrew Young, now one of Abernathy's aides.

"Something is going to change or we'll all be in jail. This is do or die—not just for nonviolence but for the nation."[28] White House officials met with Abernathy and an advance party of some sixty people to try to establish ground rules for what promised to be a prolonged and perhaps inflammatory demonstration.[29] "I want you to listen very closely and sympathetically to their appeals," Johnson told his cabinet. "See if there is anything that your departments may have left undone that would help them."[30] Out of that dialogue came dozens of proposals, including a summer school program for the nation's one hundred largest cities and one hundred poorest counties.[31]

"I'm sitting here waiting for the delegation from the Poor People's March to appear," Orville Freemen wrote in his diary. "What a comedy of uncertainty and errors this performance is. They've got this town standing on its head. The problem of course is one of uncertainty. In the first place they can't control their own people, although they are doing much better than I would have dreamed possible. They already have sent home by bus some gangs from various cities and groups that make trouble. This morning an off-shoot group went to the hill and when Mills wouldn't see them began to picket and sing in a restricted area."[32] On the anniversary of Malcolm X's assassination, black nationalist groups marched, distributed leaflets, and forced black merchants to close for the day, but true to King's philosophy, the march remained peaceful.[33]

LBJ's immediate concern was to see that the inevitable friction between the capital police and the residents of Resurrection City did not get out of hand. He told journalist Ken Crawford that he had been in Washington during the Bonus March and did not want a repetition of that sorry episode.[34] Then, on May 21, CBS aired a heart-wrenching documentary entitled *Hunger in America* depicting black, female-headed, inner-city families and white Appalachian and southern families, all of them with malnourished infants and toddlers, some of them suffering from tuberculosis and influenza. Liberals in Congress simultaneously launched an investigation, which concluded that the administration was "permitting" 14 million Americans to go hungry every day.

On June 19, Abernathy addressed fifty thousand people at the Lincoln Memorial and blasted the administration and Congress, calling the Great Society's record on social justice and civil rights a series of "broken promises." For Johnson, this was the last straw. He complained to Orville Freeman that "the very people we are seeking to help in Medicare and education and welfare and Food Stamps are protesting louder and louder and giving no recognition or allowance for what's been done. Our efforts seem to have resulted only in anarchy . . . The women no longer bother to get married, they just keep breeding. The men go their way and the women get relief—why should they work?"[35]

Johnson claimed to see Bobby Kennedy's fine hand behind the Poor People's Campaign. And, in fact, in the wake of the King assassination, RFK had met publicly with Abernathy, who subsequently declared to reporters, "In it white America does have someone who cares." Indeed, as several of RFK's aides later admitted, the King assassination gave their man's candidacy new life. Bobby had jumped into the presidential race after McCarthy's strong showing in the New Hampshire primary. If the election were to be about LBJ, Bobby would be the perfect challenger, heir to the programs and vision that the Texan was allegedly betraying. But then Bobby's great foil had withdrawn. Now, with King's assassination, RFK could pose as champion of the Negro, the Hispanic, and the downtrodden in general.[36]

To make matters worse for the administration, the student movement turned increasingly violent in the spring of 1968. In late 1967 a faction of the Students for a Democratic Society led by Tom Hayden had rejected participatory democracy and nonviolent civil disobedience. He could "shoot to kill" if necessary, Hayden declared. The organization also became more authoritarian and dictatorial. V. I. Lenin replaced Jean-Jacques Rousseau as the SDS's philosophical guru and icon. In April 1968, Mark Rudd, head of the SDS chapter at Columbia University, led a demonstration to protest the university's decision to build a gymnasium in a long-established black neighborhood. A confrontation ensued between administration officials and student protesters as Rudd and his followers occupied university buildings, ransacked administrative offices, and forced the cancellation of classes. Columbia officials called in the police, who attacked the students with clubs and fists. After dozens of bleeding protesters were driven off to jail in waiting paddy wagons, the campus paper denounced the whole affair as a "brutal, bloody show." The violence created sympathy among previously neutral components of the student body, and a strike shut down the university for the remainder of the semester. Similar clashes, most of which centered around antiwar demonstrations, broke out at Harvard, Cornell, and San Francisco State University. Richard Nixon declared that Columbia was the "first major skirmish in a revolutionary struggle to seize the universities," and Congressman Robert H. Michel warned that the radicals' next target would be "City Hall, the State Capitol, or even the White House."[37]

LBJ and his aides were, of course, afraid that the Poor People's Campaign, *Hunger in America,* violence on college campuses, and RFK's machinations would create a white middle- and working-class reaction that would make passage of the fair housing bill and the tax surcharge impossible. "It's a real challenge as to how we handle this and keep them active and participating and making progress without permitting them to become destructive of the functioning of Government and our society and without creating the resentments and apprehensions that will result in a middle class white backlash," Freeman observed.[38] But things did hold together. Congress passed the housing bill and in the last week in June enacted a 10 percent tax surcharge; LBJ had to agree in principle to a $6 billion spending reduction for the coming fiscal year, but he intended not to take the initiative, suspecting that when it came down to it, Congress would not have the will to make specific program cuts. He was proved right. Congress was unable to cut even $4 billion in pending expenditures. Fiscal year 1969 ended with a $3.2 billion surplus and with most of the Great Society programs intact.[39]

• • •

FROM THE EVENING OF MARCH 31, when he announced he was not going to run, LBJ's overriding objective was to keep himself and the presidency above politics so that he could preserve as much of the Great Society as possible and secure what he believed would be an honorable peace in Vietnam, two goals, he believed, that were inextricably intertwined. During a congressional leadership breakfast on April 2, several of those present asked if they could talk politics briefly. Johnson refused. He said that he was "tired of begging anyone for anything. I had a partnership with Jack Kennedy and when he died I felt it was my duty to look after the family and stockholders and employees of my partner . . . [Now], the divisions are so deep within the party that I could not reconcile them." [40] Later, he promised both Bobby Kennedy and Hubert Humphrey that he would stay out of the campaign.

Through Joe Califano, LBJ let his cabinet officers and agency heads know that he did not want them participating in the race for the presidency either. If they felt the need, they should resign, like Postmaster General Larry O'Brien, who had departed to work for Bobby. Though he knew that Freeman, Willard Wirtz, Wilbur Cohen, and others wanted to attend Humphrey's announcement luncheon on April 27, he would not let them. Freeman especially was incensed. He was a fellow Minnesotan and would undoubtedly be asked to participate in and even manage the Humphrey campaign, he told the president. Johnson would not budge. [41]

Of course, Johnson did not want Richard Nixon to be president. Like Sam Rayburn, he detested the man, believing him to be devoid of principle, the ultimate political opportunist. But he also thought that Nixon would be hardest to beat. Johnson felt fairly confident that he could defeat Nixon, but he was not sure either Humphrey or Bobby Kennedy could. As a result, for six weeks in the spring of 1968 the president did everything in his power to persuade Nelson Rockefeller to run and touted him to Republicans who had voted for LBJ in 1964. The two men had long expressed mutual regard for each other. In 1962 Rockefeller had drawn the ire of Catholics and conservative Protestants when he divorced his first wife, Mary Todhunter Clark, and then a year later married Margaretta (Happy) Murphy. Johnson told friends that he felt "Nelson took a terrible beating in the press for marrying Happy," and repeatedly invited the couple to White House dinners to "put a stamp of approval on that marriage." [42] In April, LBJ and Lady Bird hosted a private dinner at the White House during which the first couple worked to persuade Rockefeller and his wife that the country needed them. So determined were both parties to keep the encounter secret that Jim Jones arranged for the Rockefellers to come to the west basement entrance and have Larry Temple escort them to the mansion. [43]

By May Bobby Kennedy's well-financed campaign was in high gear. That month he defeated a favorite son candidate who was running as a Humphrey stand-in in the Indiana primary. Instead of focusing on organizing and fundraising, the Humphrey campaign wallowed in self-pity. [44] When Eugene Mc-

Carthy triumphed in Oregon, he and Kennedy prepared for a showdown in California, a state whose large electoral vote made it crucial to any presidential campaign. McCarthy's young supporters stuck by him, but he was no match for the handsome, charismatic RFK. A bland speaker who seemed to lecture his audiences, the Minnesota senator sounded like "the dean of the finest English department in the land," as Norman Mailer put it.[45] The grinning Bobby, hair flopping, hand perpetually extended, blitzed the state and called in all of his family's political debts. Shrieking young women vied with large contingents of Mexican farm workers for a glimpse of the candidate. On June 4 Kennedy won with 46 percent of the vote to McCarthy's 42 percent. He was well on his way to the nomination.

At midnight Bobby collected Ethel and headed downstairs to address campaign workers in the ballroom of the Embassy Hotel in Los Angeles. Exhausted by the grueling primary campaign, he had spent the morning at Malibu body surfing with six of his ten children. He appeared fresh and exhilarated, and he addressed his worshipful audience with characteristic humor, self-effacement, and inspiration. At the last minute his aides had agreed to a press conference following the speech. Led by NFL football great Roosevelt Grier and Olympic decathlon champion Rafer Johnson, Kennedy took a shortcut through the hotel pantry. Waiting for him there was a short, dark Palestinian named Sirhan Sirhan. As Bobby approached, Sirhan pulled a .22 caliber pistol and shot him twice, once in the head and once in the armpit. As bodyguards struggled to subdue the assailant, the heir-apparent to the Kennedy dynasty lay motionless, his eyes open, staring blankly.[46] Finally, an ambulance arrived and whisked him off to the hospital, where he hovered between life and death.

At 3:31 A.M. on the morning of June 5, Walt Rostow wakened LBJ to give him the news. "Too horrible for words," Johnson responded. It was too horrible for words at many levels. If RFK should die, as his doctors privately predicted he would, the nation would be treated to yet another violent death and bound to sink once again into a slough of despondency and self-questioning. All the momentum toward peace and reconciliation that had begun with the March 31 speech would be lost. And LBJ's hopes of being remembered as one of the nation's most effective and dedicated presidents would evaporate. The bookends to his administration would be the two Kennedy assassinations, he reduced to a cipher and they elevated in the public imagination to the level of political demigods embodying the youth, vigor, and idealism of the nation.

This time LBJ kept his self-pity to himself and focused on the tasks at hand: comforting the Kennedy family and the nation and reassuring them that the attack on Bobby was the responsibility of the perpetrator only and not the American people as a whole. Shortly after the King assassination, the White House had set the wheels in motion to have Congress approve Secret Service protection for all candidates in a presidential election, but nothing had been done as of early June. Johnson on his own ordered protection extended to Humphrey, Wallace, McCarthy, and the surviving members of the Kennedy family. He then telephoned congressional leaders and asked them to act, which they did the following day. He called Ted Kennedy and issued a statement of condolence.[47] As the president awaited news of Bobby's condition, he lunched with Califano, McPherson, and Christian. Informed that Kennedy would almost certainly die, he said, "God help the mother of those boys. Thank God He's given her such faith that she can withstand the tragedies the Good Lord has seen fit to subject her to."[48] That evening he had Dirksen and Mansfield to the mansion for drinks. They briefly discussed the wisdom of constituting another Warren Commission. The president decided against it. Word from the FBI was that the shooter was acting alone, a deranged young man angered by Kennedy's wealth, privilege, and devotion to Israel.[49] Existing law enforcement would suffice for the investigation. He asked Dirksen and Mansfield not to launch a congressional investigation, which would only divide the country and further devastate the family. He told them that he intended to create a national commission on violence headed by Milton Eisenhower (the president's brother and a former president of Johns Hopkins). The panel would seek to uncover the root causes of violence in America, not the specifics of the RFK shooting. He continued to get minute-by-minute reports on Bobby's condition: "8:50 P.M.—Heart getting weaker . . . 8:55 P.M.—[Doctors] Asked all members of the family to gather at the hospital."[50]

The president had scheduled a ten o'clock broadcast to the nation, and he worked feverishly with his aides to come up with the proper words. "A young leader of uncommon energy and dedication, who has served his country tirelessly and well, and whose voice and example have touched millions throughout the entire world, has been senselessly and horribly stricken . . . We pray to God that He will spare Robert Kennedy . . . It would be wrong, it would be self-deceptive, to ignore the connection between . . . lawlessness and hatred and this act of violence. It would be just as wrong, and just as self-deceptive, to conclude from this act that our country itself is sick, that it has lost its balance, that it has lost its sense of direction, even its common decency. Two hundred million Americans did not strike down Robert Kennedy last night any more than they stuck down President John F. Kennedy in 1963 or Dr. Martin Luther King."[51] At 5:01 A.M. the next morning, LBJ was informed that Senator Kennedy had died. "It seems impossible," Orville Freeman wrote in his diary. "That strange, moody, intense, combative, competitive but really gentle and sensitive human being is gone like the brother before him."[52]

There was some apprehension among Johnson and his aides that the family would ask for a full state funeral with the body on display in the Capitol Rotunda. Only heads of state were eligible for this type of commemoration. They need not have worried. Ethel and Ted decided on a funeral mass at St. Patrick's Cathedral in New York, with a burial near JFK in the Arlington National Cemetery. There was to be no honor guard or military salute at the gravesite. LBJ ordered his staff to provide every assistance to the family. White House operators transmitted invitations to the funeral, and the president sent a government plane to California to pick up the children. Johnson was determined to attend the funeral in New York, but he did not want to intrude. He arranged with Archbishop Cooke, who would preside, to slip in after the family had been seated, just minutes before the service was to begin. As the appointed time neared, reports of death threats against the president kept coming in, and the Secret Service urged him not to go. He insisted. Joe Califano, who, along with Jim Jones and Lady Bird, were the only people to accompany LBJ, recalled that the tension was so thick after they entered the cathedral that one could cut it with the proverbial knife. The pews were filled with hundreds of people who had loved Bobby and shared his antipathy for LBJ. Many blamed the Texan for the division and violence that gripped the nation and that had played a part in Kennedy's demise. And many in attendance had been turned back when they seemed once again poised to prowl the corridors of power. To LBJ's everlasting gratitude, Archbishop Cooke in his homily thanked the president for pointing out that one man and not the whole nation had fired the shot that killed RFK.[53] As Lyndon and Lady Bird boarded the helicopter in Central Park that would take them to the airport, the president learned that James Earl Ray had been captured in London.

Once again Johnson moved to take advantage of a fallen hero's martyrdom. He had been pressing Congress for gun control legislation since John Kennedy's death, but to no avail. On the day of Bobby's funeral, the White House taped and aired a gun control message. Two days later, LBJ met with the members of the National Commission on the Causes and Prevention of Violence. He pointed out that one in every five presidents since 1865 had been assassinated and one in three had been the target of attempted assassinations. The crescendo of shootings associated with attempts to suppress the civil rights movement and with urban rioting had been made immeasurably worse by the ready availability of firearms. He asked the blue ribbon panel to draft a sweeping justification for gun control. Shortly thereafter, the president called on Congress to ban all mail order and out-of-state sales of handguns, rifles, and shotguns; halt the sale of firearms to minors; and require the national registration of all guns. After a brutal behind-the-scenes battle, the administration's bill was defeated. Congress did present the White House with a gun control measure, but it said nothing about registration and licensing. LBJ signed the measure but lashed out at the National Rifle Association. "The voices that blocked these safeguards," he declared, "were the voices of a powerful lobby, a gun lobby, that has prevailed for the moment in an election year . . . We have been through a great deal of anguish these last few months and these last few years—too much anguish to forget so quickly."[54]

Congress reacted to RFK's death not with effective gun control legislation, but with a revised Safe Streets Act that posed a clear threat to the Fourth Amendment. "It barely resembles the Safe Streets Bill we sent the Congress with such high hopes and ardent pleas," Ramsey Clark observed to his boss. "The bill is far more a reflection of the fears, frustration and politics of the times than an intelligent carefully tailored measure." It retained funds to support local police, which the administration supported, but authorized wiretapping and electronic surveillance, which it did not. "Thousands of local and state officials are authorized to tap for nearly any serious crime for 30 days with unlimited 30-day extensions possible," the attorney general warned. As a direct slap at Clark, whom many members of Congress considered soft on crime, the revised bill established a three-person Law Enforcement Administration, independent of the attorney general, to make grants to state governments. There was a gratuitous denunciation of the *Miranda* decision. LBJ was tempted to veto the bill, but even Clark advised against it. "From a practical standpoint," he told Johnson, "the result might be a worse bill . . . If the Congress acted again it might . . . limit the jurisdiction and habeas corpus powers of the federal courts. This would be disastrous."[55] The president clenched his teeth, held his tongue, and signed the bill into law. Five years later, Congress would be forced to investigate abusive wiretapping by the FBI, and state surveillance programs such as Mississippi's would become national scandals.

As Lyndon Johnson watched the conservative coalition once again assert itself, he moved to erect a judicial barrier around his Great Society programs. Like FDR in 1937, LBJ in 1968 was worried that a conservative court, sure to emerge if a Republican like Richard Nixon won the presidency, would issue decisions dismantling Medicare, the various civil rights measures passed during his administration, and federal aid to education. On June 13, Chief Justice Warren informed the president that he intended to retire "effective at your pleasure." Warren admired Johnson and hated Nixon. If he could give LBJ a chance to appoint a new chief justice, he believed, it would be worth an early retirement.[56] Johnson had long since decided that if Warren stepped down, he would nominate Associate Justice Abe Fortas, his long-time friend, confidant, and personal lawyer, to be chief justice. From the outset he knew that it would be a tough fight. Fortas's credentials as a liberal jurist had made him persona non grata among conservatives. As a teacher, practitioner, and justice, he had worked to perpetuate Justice Brandeis's philosophy that jurists must adjudicate not only according to precedent, but also according to social and economic conditions that changed over time. He was an activist who would not defer to Congress as often as most justices. In 1950 he had defended Owen Lattimore against the red-baiting assaults of Joe McCarthy. Nor was he inclined to defer to the states. Fortas was an original New Dealer who defended Roosevelt's decision to use the federal government to achieve a degree of economic justice. In *Gideon v. Wainwright,* which established the right of an indigent to publicly funded defense counsel, he had defended Clarence Gideon on appeal.[57] Fortas had proved a staunch advocate for laws furthering the Second Reconstruction, and he was a known intimate of Lyndon Johnson, either of which alone was sufficient to raise the hackles of conservatives.

To fill the seat that Fortas's elevation to chief justice would create, Johnson rather unwisely chose Homer Thornberry, a former congressman and LBJ protégé whom the president had elevated to the Fifth Circuit Court of Appeals. The Texan reflected Johnson's values. The Fifth Circuit included the Deep South, and Thornberry had proved himself a staunch defender of civil rights. It was not that he was unqualified, a number of jurists had been placed on the Court with lesser credentials. Nor was there a real question about his independence. He had ruled against the state in a case involving the arrest of some University of Texas students who had picketed an LBJ speech in Kileen.[58] Nevertheless, Thornberry was sure to be depicted by White House opponents as just another crony of the president. Larry Temple, the aide that Johnson had plucked from John Connally's staff the previous year, tried to object. Johnson lashed out at him: "What political office did you ever get elected to? . . . Don't come to me as any great knowledgeable political expert until you've run and gotten elected to a political office."[59] The very vehemence of the reaction indicated that he knew Temple was right. The Fortas-Thornberry nominations were a case of Johnson's heart trumping his brain.

Republicans were not about to stand idly by and see Johnson have his way with the high court. They resented the fact that the president had hedged his bets. In his response to Warren's letter of resignation, the president had said, "With your agreement, I will accept your decision to retire effective at such time as a successor is qualified."[60] If the Fortas nomination were to fail, LBJ wanted Warren still on the Court. Yet the presidential election was only five months away. Dirksen and other GOP stalwarts believed that Nixon had an excellent chance of winning, and the victor ought to have the right to nominate whom he wanted to the Court.[61] Law-and-order advocates despised Warren for his rulings in the *Gideon, Miranda,* and other landmark civil liberties cases. Southerners would forever remember the Californian as the author of the famous *Brown* decision, and they saw Fortas as a philosophical replica of the man he would replace.

Freshman Senator Robert Griffin of Michigan took it upon himself to lead the opposition. As a matter of principle, he would never support a Supreme Court nominee made by a lame-duck president, he announced. If necessary, he would lead a filibuster. Robert Byrd, Russell Long, and Sam Ervin let it be known that they would vote no. John McClellan of Arkansas told Jim Eastland that he was looking forward to having "that SOB formally submitted to the Senate," so that he could fight his nomination. Eastland, chair of the Senate Judiciary Committee, told Mike Manatos, White House congressional liaison, that he "had never seen so much feeling against a man as against Fortas."[62] Eastland himself was under tremendous pressure from his white constituents in Mississippi. The state's racist governor, John Bell Williams, was then blaming the chair of the Senate Judiciary Committee for permitting confirmation of those justices who had struck down various "freedom of choice" school plans. Indeed, Williams was threatening to run for the Senate himself in the next election.[63]

From the outset, Johnson took personal charge of the lobbying campaign to secure Fortas's nomination. He called Henry Ford and urged him to mobilize members of the National Alliance of Businessmen. He contacted Pennsylvania Federal Judge Leon Higginbotham and asked him to have every black lawyer in the state write or call their senator, Hugh Scott. And LBJ played the Jewish card at every possible turn. He told all who would listen that anti-Semitism had much to do with the opposition to Fortas's nomination. How would it look, he asked Albert Jenner, chair of the American Bar Association committee that reviewed federal judicial nominees, if the Senate turned away "the first Jew ever nominated for Chief Justice"?[64] Fortas was not at all religious, and LBJ appreciated the irony of his plea. When Harry McPherson uncovered a photo of Fortas and philanthropist David Lloyd Kreeger wearing yarmulkes as they played a violin duo, he offered to circulate the image among Jewish groups. Johnson turned to his aide and said, "This doesn't mean a damn thing. I've had on more of those than Abe has."[65]

Still, initially, prospects for the Fortas nomination were far from desperate. Johnson managed to get both Richard Russell and Everett Dirksen on record in favor. Russell had long known Fortas and respected both his mind and his judgment in crisis situations. Dirksen was loath to identify himself and his party with religious and racial bigotry. But then, inadvertently, LBJ gave grave offense to his friend from Georgia. Normally, presidents accepted the recommendations of senators from their own parties for federal judgeships. Several months earlier, the Wizard of Winder had nominated Alexander Lawrence Jr., a close personal friend from Savannah, to a federal judgeship. But then an article appeared in the *Atlanta Journal* intimating that Lawrence was a racist.[66] Ramsey Clark objected to the nomination. Johnson wavered. He did not want to commit the same error President Kennedy had by allowing southern senators to stop the drive to integration by seeing defenders of the Lost Cause appointed to the federal bench. Clark continued to drag his feet, and Lawrence's nomination was still pending when the Fortas matter came up.[67] Deeply offended, Russell informed the White House that he considered himself "released from any statements that I may have made to you with respect to your nominations."[68] Johnson bypassed Clark and sent Lawrence's nomination to the Senate Judiciary Committee, but it was too late. Russell informed Senator Griffin that he could count on his support in opposing Fortas. (Lawrence was subsequently confirmed and proved himself to be a champion of school integration in Georgia.)

From July 16 through 19, Fortas testified before the Senate Judiciary Committee, the first nominee for chief Justice and the first sitting justice to do so. He successfully turned aside questions concerning his liberal voting record, citing separation of powers and the need to respect the Court's independence. But he did agree to address himself to charges that he had had an inappropriately close relationship with President Johnson while he was on the Court. He denied that he had violated the separation of powers or given advice improperly to LBJ. Yet Fortas had been a regular at White House meetings on everything from Vietnam to labor disputes. He had helped draft Johnson's 1966 State of the Union address. All of this he denied. Asked whether he had written the president's statement on sending troops into Detroit during the 1967 riots, he said no. It was another lie. "Fortas' testimony was so misleading and deceptive," Joe Califano later wrote, "that those of us who were aware of his relationship with Johnson winced with each news report . . . Cronyism was now the least of the charges some of us feared."[69]

LBJ saw nothing at all wrong with his seeking Fortas's advice while he was on the high court. Vicky McCammon described the relationship as Fortas and Johnson saw it: "I don't think at all that President Johnson ever, or would ever, try to influence what Abe Fortas did on the Court. I don't think he would even mention it out loud, much less think it, because of the respect each of the men had for each other . . . By the same token, I don't see Fortas influencing a decision on a President for the benefit of something else that he was trying to do. It wasn't the two of them trying to buy each other or trying to influence each other. I think it was more the two of them trying to work out what they considered the best social policies for the country."[70] The White House pointed out to any journalist who would listen that since the beginning of the republic presidents had solicited and received advice on policy matters from members of the Supreme Court: Washington from Jay, Jackson from Taney, Wilson from Brandeis.[71] But it was all to no avail. The charge of cronyism stuck.

Still, LBJ was hopeful. With August approaching, Congress would have to adjourn for the presidential nominating conventions. Just as the Senate Judiciary Committee appeared to be winding down its hearings, Senator Strom Thurmond of South Carolina, now a Republican, raised a new issue. Both as private counsel and as a Supreme Court justice, Fortas had given aid and comfort to pornographers. Thurmond cited especially a case in which the New York courts had found that the film *Flaming Creatures* had violated that state's obscenity laws. Fortas had stood alone among his colleagues in voting to reverse the conviction.[72] Dirksen began to waver. Sam Ervin declared that he could not vote on Fortas's nomination because no vacancy had occured. Warren should either resign or not resign. Thurmond promised to show the Judiciary Committee every salacious film on which Fortas had ruled. Behind the scenes, Nixon pressured Dirksen to rise above his friendship with LBJ and help block the Fortas nomination.[73]

The White House fought back. Spokesmen pointed out that never in the history of Supreme Court nominations had one failed due to filibuster. Johnson, who by this time had come to regard the fight over Fortas as a personal battle between him and his reactionary enemies, lashed his subordinates to renewed effort. "We're a bunch of dupes down here," he told Califano and Temple. "They've got all the wisdom . . . they're smarter than we are. We're a bunch of ignorant, immature kids who don't know anything about this . . . We've got to do something."[74] He had one of his aides draft two papers, one depicting Fortas as a liberal activist and the other as a strict constructionist. When the aide suggested that the White House might be criticized for sending out contradictory signals, LBJ reminded him of the story of the young man who was interviewing for a teaching job in a rural Texas district. The climax of the interview came when the redneck chairman of the school board asked the extremely stressed candidate, "Do you teach that the world is flat or do you teach that the world is round?" The young man hesitated and then replied, "I can teach it either way."[75] The object of the exercise, LBJ reminded his staffer, was to have Fortas named chief justice. In the first week in September, LBJ called Orville Freeman and told him he was thinking of retaliating against southern opponents of the nomination by vetoing the farm bill. It had been brought to his attention that wealthy white agribusinessmen in the South were receiving huge subsidy payments while their black tenants were starving to death. Jim Eastland was getting an annual payment of $157,000 from the federal government not to plant on his thousands of acres while black and white tenants driven off the land had to live on $35 a month in relief. But Freeman convinced him that to veto the farm bill was to assure a Republican victory in November.[76]

After the August recess, shortly before the committee reconvened on September 13, the White House learned that Griffin had come into possession of more damning evidence. Paul Porter, Fortas's former law partner, had raised $30,000 from past and present clients to pay Fortas to teach a series of seminars at American University Law School. Some of the contributors could expect to have cases to which they were a party reach the high court. Fortas had already been paid $15,000. At the time, that was a significant sum of money, greatly increasing Fortas's income through an arrangement that risked creating conflicts of interest. Though no actual conflicts were claimed, it was a far more damaging scandal that any pornography decision or White House conversation. The Fortas nomination was dead.[77] Later that month, Abe and his wife, Carol, went to dinner at the White House. "When they came," Lady Bird later recorded in her diary, "Carol was bouncy and strong and expressed her observations in salty and, I thought, healthy language . . . Abe was very quiet, contained, and dignified . . . I wondered if they could stand to see us, the unwitting architects of all the agony they have been going through."[78] Thus did LBJ botch his effort to leave the Supreme Court in liberal hands. Richard Nixon would make three appointments.

WAS THERE ANY HOPE for a Democratic White House after Johnson's abdication and RFK's assassination, pundits asked. If the void were to be filled it would have to be by Hubert Humphrey. Prior to June 5, the Happy Warrior's chances of capturing the Democratic nomination seemed dim indeed. His beloved Americans for Democratic Action had voted to endorse Eugene McCarthy. But then, tragically, Bobby was removed from the scene. "Clean Gene" was clearly the peace candidate, but he was proving a disappointment as a campaigner. Jack Newfield, a liberal journalist who was an early activist in behalf of McCarthy, had changed his mind by early 1968. "Let the unhappy brutal truth come out. Eugene McCarthy's campaign is a disaster . . . McCarthy's speeches are dull, vague, and without either balls or poetry. He is lazy and vain."[79]

Humphrey had the support of organized labor and, irony of ironies, the still Democratic South. "The rumor is that the South and Southern delegates generally are moving in behind Humphrey," Orville Freeman noted. "Goodness how the wheel turns."[80] Black voters, who had supported Bobby, were up for grabs.[81] Whether working-class whites voted for Humphrey, Wallace, or Nixon, if he proved to be the GOP nominee, depended on where Humphrey stood on the war. To attract some of McCarthy's supporters, he was going to have to create some distance between himself and the president, but not too much distance lest he lose the hardhat vote. And not so much distance that he rouse the infamous LBJ ire. In this context, the ability of the administration to move peace negotiations with the North Vietnamese toward some type of resolution would prove crucial to the 1968 presidential contest.

Johnson wanted his vice president to win, but he doubted whether Humphrey could or even should be president. Above all, LBJ believed, his liberal protégé would have to sit tight on Vietnam. Meaningful negotiations were crucial to Humphrey's successful candidacy. In order to ensure negotiations that would give Vietnamization a chance, and a settlement that would not enrage conservatives, the North Vietnamese Army and Vietcong would have to first be beaten bloody and then convinced that the best deal they could get from their enemy would be sooner rather than later. If Humphrey in his quest to attract Kennedy-McCarthy supporters prematurely called for de-escalation, a bombing halt, and even unilateral withdrawal, all would be lost—on the political battlefield at home and the military battlefield in Vietnam. In the White House's view, Humphrey's best bet was for LBJ's plan to work: for there to be period of all-out war in Vietnam followed by meaningful negotiations that would give the nation a glimpse of peace with honor and thus vindicate the foreign policy with which he had so long been identified. But the vice president would have to hold his water.

For LBJ the elements of the Vietnam equation had not changed. He had to convince the North Vietnamese that they could not prevail in the South militarily, the South Vietnamese that he was not going to sell them out, the doves in the United States that he was sincere about peace, and the hawks that he was not going to appease the forces of international communism. On April 3, to the joy of the White House and the nation, Hanoi announced that continued American bombing of the North notwithstanding, the Democratic Republic of Vietnam was ready to meet with representatives of the United States to discuss peace. Indications were that LBJ's abdication announcement had caught Ho and his associates off-guard. To avoid relinquishing the propaganda initiative to the Americans, they had to respond to the president's act of selflessness.[82] Three weeks of wrangling ensued over an appropriate site for the peace talks. Finally, the two parties settled on Paris. During a conversation with Averell Harriman on April 1, Anatoly Dobrynin asked what kind of settlement the administration envisioned. Harriman reported that that could only be determined when the negotiations started. "You mean to say the United States hasn't got a policy?"

Harriman reported his asking. "I said there were some differences of views at present. We were not as disciplined as the Soviet Union. In any event, a great deal depended upon developments in South Vietnam and South Vietnamese attitude. I personally hoped that Saigon and the NLF [National Liberation Front] would be able to work out an acceptable settlement."[83] The peace Washington eventually offered would depend on events on the battlefield.

There were those then in the Johnson administration who believed that a cease-fire and political settlement in the South could not be fashioned in negotiations between Washington and Hanoi. The two combatants were too locked into their positions by ideological considerations, the dynamics of the cold war, and alliance politics within their respective spheres. The best that could be hoped for was ongoing discussions that would reduce the level of violence between U.S. and NVA forces while southerners worked out their own future. Indeed, in the last week in April, Rostow made this assumption explicit: "Why not encourage Thieu to take the initiative and actively seek private negotiations with 'a member' of the NLF, using a trusted man. There are three virtues, if he could see it that way: the [key to] peace is the southern political settlement anyway; the southern political settlement will, in my view, have to be negotiated secretly and, quite probably, separately from any formal conference generated by Washington-Hanoi . . . ; it would put Thieu and the GVN [government of Vietnam] in the center of things—taking the initiative to shape its own destiny—rather than awaiting anxiously the outcome of U.S.-Hanoi talks."[84] LBJ was certainly amenable to such negotiations; his focus was on preventing the North from overrunning the South militarily.

On May 6 the president met with his foreign policy team, including the principal negotiators who were about to leave for Paris. "I'm glad we're going to talk, but I'm not overly hopeful," he said. "Some of you think we want resolution of this in an election year. I want it resolved, but not because of the election. Don't yield anything on that impression."[85] Following that meeting, Clifford complained to his staff, "The gang around LBJ is turning against settlement— No settlement—just beat the hell out of them."[86] Yet Johnson did not remove Harriman. Nor did he seek to muzzle Clark Clifford, who would repeatedly plead for a softer line in the negotiations with Hanoi. As a signal to all, however, that he intended to accept nothing less than an "honorable peace," LBJ named General Andrew Goodpaster, Eisenhower's protégé and liaison with the administration, to be part of the U.S. negotiating team.[87]

In late April the president gave a remarkable off-the-record interview with a group of editors and columnists from the *Washington Star.* On the March 31 announcement and the war in Southeast Asia, he said, "I had the impression— rightly or wrongly—that as a candidate, being in the nose cone, so to speak, or the volcano, or the typhoon, that others in the world would misjudge our situation and feel like they had pressures on the President that would require him to take actions that he might not think were most desirable because of his own political problems." He felt great sympathy with the South Vietnamese on the eve of the opening of the Paris negotiations: "They're frightened to death . . . that if this ball bounces the wrong way that they—all of them—will be assassinated and they would be run over, they would be locked up and they would be in concentration camps and they'd be slaves—if the Communists take over." What he hoped was that the United States and North Vietnam would both agree to withdraw from the South and let matters take their course. Of course, the North Vietnamese would never give up a prize they were so close to winning, and Johnson knew it. "I think presently he [Ho] feels like he is entitled to South Vietnam and he's going to try to get it if he can and I don't think he can get it during my political lifetime . . . He had his eye on this country all these years." [88]

Johnson was certainly right about the mood in Saigon. His withdrawal statement had shaken Thieu and the other generals to their collective core. Despite his outward equanimity, Thieu was already deeply suspicious of the Americans. The CIA reported a March 18 conversation between him and Lieutenant General Khang, III Corps's commander. Thieu expressed concern that the American Embassy was plotting a coup that would lead to a coalition government that would include the NLF. He asked Khang if there was any evidence that the United States had assisted the Vietcong during the Tet Offensive. [89] A bit paranoid perhaps, but Thieu was far from being alone in his fear of a coalition government. Harry McPherson reported to Johnson a conversation he had had with a member of the South Vietnamese National Assembly, a veteran of the Vietminh, a liberal who believed that the GVN should include wider representation. "I said, 'What do you think about a coalition government?' He looked at me as if I had just defamed his mother. 'If you offer the NLF a part of the coalition government now,' he said, 'you'd better have your troops at the docks and airfields. The people and the ARVN [Army of the Republic of Vietnam] will turn on you. They will know—no matter what you say—that the war is over and that the communists have won it.' " [90]

Meanwhile, the level of violence in South Vietnam accelerated dramatically. The number of NVA troops detected moving south increased from six thousand in February to twenty-nine thousand in March and ten thousand for the first week alone in April. From May 4 to 15 the communists launched a series of attacks in and around Saigon. On one level, this "second offensive," like its predecessor Tet, was a disaster for the NVA. The enemy lost 11,633 killed compared to 907 for ARVN and American forces. But the attack created 125,000 new refugees in Saigon and Gia Dinh and destroyed or damaged sixteen thousand houses. Every sign pointed toward a third offensive to take place probably some time in late August. Johnson debated an expanded bombing campaign, but decided that it was unnecessary. [91]

On the Vietnamese political front, Thieu's efforts to broaden his military base, pave the way for greater participation of civilians in the government, and generally to prepare his country for one-man, one-vote rule, were encountering stiff resistance from Ky and the officers close to him. When in late May Thieu, without consulting his associates on the Military Revolutionary Council, named Tran Van Huong to be prime minister, he was barely able to avert an open revolt. In the weeks that followed, he began to move against Ky slowly and, at first, with some fear for his safety.[92] Then, on June 3, a U.S. helicopter gunship carrying out operations against suspected Vietcong positions in Saigon accidentally sent a rocket into the very ARVN command post from which it was receiving direction. The blast killed a number of high-ranking South Vietnamese officers close to Ky, including his brother-in-law and the administrator of the port of Saigon, who was Ky's confidant and the source of much of his family's income. To make matters worse for the Ky clique, General Nguyen Noc Loan, the ruthless commander of the national police, was then laid up in the hospital with a serious leg wound. Ky was convinced that the Americans, at the behest of Thieu, were responsible for the attacks on his supporters. On June 4, Ambassador Bunker and General Abrams called on the vice president to express their condolences. "Unlike his usual easy and friendly welcome," Bunker reported to Washington, "he greeted us grimly, and as he talked it was clear he was in a dark, depressed and despondent mood."[93] But the air marshal's wings had been clipped. "There is no chance that Ky will react violently to these developments, such as staging a coup. Ky lacks the strength, and the military most likely want no part in any such activity," U.S. intelligence sources reported to the White House.[94]

Three days after Bobby Kennedy's assassination and the rocketing of the ARVN command post, Premier Kosygin wrote LBJ suggesting a total cessation of bombing in the North as part of an effort to get the Paris talks jump-started. "I and my colleagues believe—and we have grounds for this—that a full cessation by the United States of bombardments . . . could promote a breakthrough in the situation that would open perspectives for peaceful settlement," he said. "Such a step cannot bring about any adverse consequences whatever for the United States neither in the sense of a loss for the interests of their safety nor even in the sense of a loss for their prestige."[95] Clifford was overjoyed, Wheeler aghast. "We have a great opportunity here," the secretary of defense told Johnson and his other advisers. "We should take serious advantage of it." The risk was too great, Wheeler replied. The enemy would be free to mass on the DMZ. "Some units might be overrun," he insisted.[96] Johnson was conflicted. In a conversation with Nelson Rockefeller on June 10, he observed that there were signs the North Vietnamese were moderating their position. Xuan Thuy, chief negotiator for the DRV, and his colleagues in Paris were no longer denying that there were NVA troops in the South, and the DRV delegation had begun pressing for substantive agreements.[97] Johnson had long hoped Moscow would use its good offices to end the violence in Vietnam. "We are prepared to end the bombardment of the Democratic Republic of Vietnam if we know it will lead to a deescalation of the war," Johnson subsequently wrote Kosygin.[98] But he took the position that he could not stop the bombing without assurances that the Vietcong would cease their rocket attacks on Saigon, an almost daily occurance, and that American soldiers south of the DMZ would not be exposed to greater danger. As he later remarked to Richard Nixon, all a bombing halt would mean at that point was "that my son-in-law down in the DMZ with the rifle company would have to take 30 percent more cuts [attacks] than they have ever faced there before because we are stopping 30 percent of them that are coming through there." [99]

Increasingly, LBJ was attracted by Rostow's notion that the conflict in Vietnam would not be settled by negotiations between the United States and North Vietnam, but rather by direct talks between the NLF and the Thieu government. The president was getting reports—from pacification official John Paul Vann, among others—that at last pacification was going reasonably well and that the Thieu government was in fact mobilizing Vietnam's youth for the fight ahead. [100] The last week in June, Bunker reported to Rusk that both Huong and Thieu "most confidentially" had agreed to talks with the NLF if the contact originated with that organization. [101] Whether or not the North Vietnamese would go along with a coalition government and one-man, one-vote in the South was a matter of conjecture, but there were signs that it would. The Russians, it appeared, were pressuring Hanoi to acquiesce in such an arrangement. Intelligence reported that the communist Chinese, disgusted at Hanoi's willingness to talk with the Americans and disappointed in their hopes for a war in Southeast Asia of indefinite duration, were beginning to sharply cut back on aid to the DRV. [102] Then in Paris in mid-June, NVA negotiator Le Duc Tho observed to Harriman and Cyrus Vance that "there can never be a settlement of military matters without prior agreement on a political solution." [103]

LBJ felt the need to talk to Thieu, whom he was beginning to trust, face-to-face, and he told his lieutenants to arrange a meeting for July 19–20 in Honolulu. Before sitting down with their counterparts, the members of the U.S. team held their own highly contentious meeting. Clifford insisted that they play hardball with Thieu and his colleagues. He argued that there was no way that the United States and its allies could terminate the war militarily, but the Saigonese wanted the conflict to go on forever. According to notes of the meeting, he said, "They're protected by 540,000 U.S. [troops] & golden flow of money . . . they think we're soft & good for anything they ask for. Corruption is through all this. All the U.S. candidates [were] moving away from the war. Therefore LBJ should tell Thieu every effort should be made to settle war in 6 mos." Rusk fought back. Clifford subsequently reported to his subordinates, "Rusk is rigid & frozen in the hard-line hawk attitude—Hit 'em again & again!" [104]

The direct talks between Thieu and LBJ ranged over a variety of topics: corruption, the Paris talks, Ky, the NLF, the state of American and South Vietnamese public opinion. Johnson assured Thieu that when substantive negotiations began in Paris, the GVN would have a voice in them. At the close of the meeting the two leaders issued a concise communiqué expressing their solidarity and promising to fight on until an honorable peace—presumably one that would allow electoral politics to proceed in the South without the threat of violence—should be won.[105]

One of the reasons Clifford was so frantic at Honolulu was that by that point, it had become clear that the GOP nominee for 1968 would be Richard Milhouse Nixon, red-baiter-turned-moderate and long-time bête noire of the Democratic party. The previous year the antihero of the "Checkers" speech had looked like a long shot for the nomination. The front-runner was the handsome, moderate governor of Michigan, George Romney. Governor Ronald Reagan of California had emerged as claimant to the Goldwater wing of the party, and the liberal Nelson Rockefeller, with LBJ's encouragement, had made himself available. But Nixon had ingratiated himself with party regulars by working tirelessly in the successful 1966 midterm elections and by speaking at innumerable fund-raisers in every corner of the country. A devout Mormon, Romney's explicit religious rhetoric raised the hackles of some in the party. Then in August 1967, he had openly denounced the war in Vietnam. In a taped interview with WKBD in Detroit, Romney said, "When I came back from Viet Nam [in November 1965], I'd just had the greatest brainwashing that anybody can get."[106] The vast majority of Republicans were hawkish and were appalled by the Michigan governor's charge. Moreover, how smart could a person be if he was susceptible to brainwashing? The only centrist candidate left was Nixon.

Throughout June and July, LBJ labored to persuade the leading presidential candidates not to take positions on the war and the negotiations in Paris that would tie his hands. As he told Nixon at the White House on June 26, in a favorite rhetorical technique, if he were the Democratic nominee and Nixon were president, he would issue a statement to the effect that he (Johnson) was not responsible for the country until he became president. He had similar conversations with Rockefeller, Humphrey, and Wallace. But not McCarthy; the other candidate from Minnesota was hopeless, Johnson believed. The contenders duly agreed to do everything possible not to interfere or narrow the president's options. But because he was vice president, Humphrey's silence would link him irrevocably to Johnson's polices. There were dangers for Nixon as well. Privately and publicly he had indicated support for the war in Vietnam, for the assumptions that lay behind it, and for the notion of military victory. His criticism had been that the administration had been too timid, had placed too many restraints on the military. If Nixon continued this hawkish support for LBJ and his policies, and nothing changed, all would be well; but what if sometime during the fall and before the election, the administration initiated a bombing halt, and the talks in Paris began to move toward a settlement? Nixon would be left hanging, twisting in the wind, to anticipate a phrase.

By late July, as Wheeler and the Joint Chiefs were reporting massive infiltration of NVA troops into the South and predicting the start of the third offensive sometime in mid to late July, probably timed to coincide with the Democratic National Convention, Harriman and Vance were urging the administration to consider a bombing halt.[107] At this point, members of the Democratic Platform Committee gathered in Chicago to draft a plank stating the party's position on the war and the talks in Paris. McGovern had already called for an immediate withdrawal of 250,000 American troops from Vietnam.[108] A bitter fight ensued between administration loyalists, led by Senator Gale McGhee, and a large minority of Kennedy-McCarthy peace advocates, led by Philip Hart of Michigan. "What they're [the peace Democrats] asking me to do is be the biggest boob of our time," LBJ complained to his friend, Governor Richard Hughes of New Jersey. "Just as the Communists get ready to hit us, they want me to do what I did at Tet—take a vacation . . . and call off our bombing, let them hit me full length, and I just—I just—I just don't see it . . . Although, God, I want to be a hero, and I want to get the war over." [109]

Johnson believed that Humphrey ought to firmly and repeatedly echo the administration's hard line in public, and he blamed the vice president for not quashing the peaceniks on the platform committee. During a conversation with Orville Freeman, Johnson launched into a tirade against the Happy Warrior. "He pointed out that Humphrey was all over the place, that he didn't need to try and go after the McCarthy delegates that he couldn't get hold of them any way, that he was gaining nothing, fostering a lot of uncertainty," Freeman wrote. "He claimed that Connally had told him he was about ready to walk out on the whole business . . . He, the President, had two son-in-laws in Viet Nam, that Chuck Robb had had more than half of his Company shot out from under him already." (What Johnson did not say was that military intelligence had learned of a Vietcong plot to kidnap Robb, and he had been secretly reassigned.) The North Vietnamese were refusing to promise to refrain from shelling cities in the South and not to accelerate the rate of infiltration. At that point, Luci came in with Lyn, LBJ's grandson, and the president softened. "Humphrey had been great on television last Sunday on 'Meet the Press,' " Freeman recorded his saying, "but . . . he should be careful not to always have the answer to everything so quick." He had heard how despondent Humphrey was and felt for him. "Don't tell him I'm cross because it will upset him." Freeman concluded, "He's for Humphrey all right, but he also is bleeding himself and it really showed through." [110]

There was another reason for LBJ's frustration. Unbeknown to all but a few of his closest advisers, the president was planning a trip to the Soviet Union for a summit meeting with Kosygin and Communist party Chairman Leonid Brezhnev. It would be the crowning achievement of his administration. He and the Soviet leaders would begin talks on an across-the-board arms control agreement, which when concluded would forever link Johnson's name with détente.[111] As a prelude, representatives from the United States, the Soviet Union, Great Britain, and more than fifty other nations had met in July at the White House to sign the Nuclear Nonproliferation Treaty. LBJ, Rusk, and their lieutenants had been working on the agreement since 1963. Nonnuclear powers who signed the pact agreed not to press for the right to bear nuclear arms in return for promises from members of the nuclear club to work toward disarmament.

But then on August 20, the Soviet Union invaded Czechoslovakia. Beginning in the spring under the leadership of Alexander Dubček, liberals within the Czech Communist Party had been lessening government controls over the press, freeing dissidents from jail, and paving the way for the participation of noncommunists in the political life of the nation. In July, the Soviets, fearing that these dangerous reforms might spread throughout Eastern Europe, undermining their authority, began massing tanks and troops on the Czech border. Encouraged by students, intellectuals, labor leaders, and others, Dubček pressed on. Then in August, hundreds of Soviet tanks and tens of thousands of Eastern Bloc troops poured into Czechoslovakia. There was some bloodshed in Prague, but Dubček quickly succumbed.[112] LBJ met with his cabinet on the 22nd. "We do not believe that any intervention is in our interest," he said. Rusk chimed in, "Let us be very clear about one thing. Military intervention means nuclear war . . . So world public opinion is our resort."[113] Yet the Moscow summit and further progress toward détente were no longer possible during what was left of the Johnson administration. The Czech crisis and the administration's passive reaction to it would provide ample grounds for Nixon, Wallace, and the American right in general to once again portray the Democrats as soft on communism without Johnson's adding to it by going to Moscow.

Two days after the Soviet invasion of Czechoslovakia, Ellsworth Bunker informed Washington that the communist third offensive was under way. "The pattern of enemy military activity changed abruptly during the past week," he reported. "The lull which had existed for some weeks past came to an end with a series of coordinated attacks on Tay Ninh Province and city; on Loc Ninh which had been the scene of heavy fighting last October; and Dak Seang in Kontum Province."[114]

IF 1968 HAD NOT ALREADY PROVEN ITSELF to be a disastrous year, through two assassinations, more urban rioting, and continued agony in Vietnam, events at the close of August were about to remove any doubt of it. The Democratic National Convention in Chicago would be one of the most memorable in American history. The meeting itself was an angry, bitter affair in which the delegates quickly polarized into antiwar and pro-war factions. The Platform Committee had been unable to reach a consensus on a Vietnam plank, and they came to the convention with a majority and a minority report. The hawks, led by Mayor Daley, who was speaking in effect for Lyndon Johnson, voted down the "peace" plank advocated by McCarthy and McGovern and adopted instead a statement endorsing the administration's quest for "an honorable and lasting peace" in Vietnam. The doves' plank, declared Ohio Congressman Wayne Hays, would play into the hands of radicals who want "pot instead of patriotism, sideburns instead of solutions. They would substitute riots for reason."[115] Yet more than a thousand delegates voted for it.

McCarthy managed to attract some of Kennedy's delegates, and he consistently led Humphrey in the polls. Nonetheless, the vice president easily captured the nomination on the first ballot. Most professional politicians distrusted McCarthy and had heaped ridicule on his "Children's Crusade." Without winning one state primary, Humphrey had worked behind the scenes to line up almost fifteen hundred delegates. He had also made it clear that he supported "Johnson's war." "Nothing would bring the real peaceniks back to our side," confided an aide to a reporter, "unless Hubert urinated on a portrait of Lyndon Johnson in Times Square before television—and then they'd say to him, why didn't you do it before."[116] As his running mate, the Happy Warrior chose the environmentalist and moderate liberal Edmund Muskie of Maine.

On the floor, black delegates from the Northeast sneered at white southerners, calling them racists, while antiwar delegates and administration supporters traded insults. Daley's beefy security men were everywhere. As the nation watched, CBS reporter Dan Rather was knocked to the floor while covering the ejection of a regular Georgia delegate. Watching from his anchor booth, Walter Cronkite was incensed. "I think we've got a bunch of thugs down there," he said, his voice quivering.[117]

Unbeknown to the media, the delegates, and the American public, the chief challenger to Hubert Humphrey's nomination at Chicago was Lyndon Johnson. From the outset, LBJ labored to ensure that nothing transpired at the 1968 Democratic National Convention in Chicago without his knowledge or approval. His chief lieutenant in this effort was John Criswell, the treasurer of the Democratic National Committee and chairman of the convention. Criswell, a long-time friend of the Johnsons, headed a team that included Marvin Watson, presidential aides Jim Jones and Larry Temple, and Arthur Krim, among others. For a variety of reasons, the president worked to keep his hand as hidden as possible, although in the fight over the Vietnam plank in the platform, that proved impossible. Among other things, the Jones-Criswell team made sure that a tribute to Bobby Kennedy was placed in the schedule after the nominating procedure, lest the convention be stampeded by its emotions and draft Ted Kennedy. LBJ also saw to it that the convention was set to coincide with his birthday, August 27, much to Humphrey's dismay. The late date would leave the Democratic nominee relatively little time to campaign.[118] According to a plan developed by the Criswell team, Daley, in behalf of the Arrangements Committee, would issue a secret, open-ended invitation to the president to attend. No mention would be made in the program of LBJ's visit. Johnson had expressed concern about being caught up in and embarrassed by antiwar demonstrations that were sure to occur. This would not be a problem, Criswell reported to the White House. "On Tuesday morning—we could make firm recommendations and we would not even need to know the decision until take-off from the ranch. We would be flexible enough with the program so that it could be broken at whatever point for the president."[119] Ideally, LBJ would fly to Chicago and address the convention after the showing of a film tribute to the Great Society narrated by Gregory Peck. He would then attend a gala birthday celebration, replete with fireworks, along Michigan Avenue.

As the date for the opening of the convention approached, LBJ began to fantasize about a draft. Initially, there were some encouraging signs. In late July, Criswell wrote Jones, "I feel certain he [Daley] doubts the Vice President's pulling power . . . In the several conversations and a long lunch with him last week he is consistently mentioning the president and favorably." [120] The second weekend in August, LBJ and Lady Bird had Jim Eastland to the ranch to lobby him on the Fortas nomination. During a tour of the ranch, he remarked to Bird, "You know your husband is going to be nominated, don't you?" Lady Bird denied that he would accept if drafted, but she really did not know what her husband was going to do. [121]

His ambition reawakened, Johnson began to show open displeasure with Humphrey. At a cabinet meeting on August 22, he challenged the vice president over Vietnam, lecturing him to the effect that the only way the communists would be persuaded to talk was if they were faced with a tough, hard position. "Humphrey looked terrible," Freeman recalled. "I've never seen such dark pouches under his eyes." [122] Two days later, the not-so-happy warrior flew to Chicago and immediately became immersed in negotiations over the Vietnam plank. LBJ had told him to clear any compromise with Dean Rusk. After hours of negotiations with the McCarthy and Daley forces, the vice president came up with wording that Rusk agreed to, but it was not enough for LBJ. The two had a tension-filled conversation. "This plank just undercuts our whole policy and, by god, the Democratic party ought not to be doing that to me and you ought not to be doing it; you've been a part of this policy." [123] Meanwhile, Humphrey had learned that Johnson was exploring the possibility of a draft.

Working through Jones, the president had John Connally survey southern governors to see how an LBJ candidacy would go down with them. [124] He also instructed Arthur Krim to have a quick poll run to see how he would stack up against Nixon. On Sunday, LBJ's lieutenants relayed bad news: "Nixon 42; LBJ 34; Wallace, 17; undecided 7." Connally reported that he found absolutely no support in the South at this stage for an LBJ candidacy. Finally, according to Krim, Daley was balking: "He said, 'the President has got to announce or do something to show that he wants it. Otherwise there's nothing I can do.' " At this point, Johnson told all concerned to go all out for Humphrey. [125]

As the Democratic delegates jousted Chicago's cavernous amphitheater, a wrenching spectacle was unfolding on the streets outside. An army of antiwar protestors, antiestablishment crusaders, and counterculture figures had descended on the city. Tom Hayden told reporters, "We are coming to Chicago to vomit on the 'politics of joy,' " a reference to Humphrey's campaign slogan. "We are coming . . . to expose the secret decisions, upset the night club orgies, and face the Democratic party with its illegitimacy and criminality." [126] From the earnest and well-scrubbed supporters of Eugene McCarthy, to the SDS, to the nihilistic Yippies, the crowds spanned the antiwar spectrum. Most were bent on peaceful demonstration, but a faction led by Abbie Hoffman—who told reporters that his "conception of revolution is that it's fun"—were determined to provoke violence.[127] And, in fact, it was counterculture extremists who managed to seize the spotlight. A former SNCC organizer and would-be standup comic, Hoffman represented all that respectable, middle-class America detested. Ridiculing the notion of "character" and conventional morality, he declared marijuana and LSD to be the only sure paths to higher consciousness and enlightenment. The Yippies spread rumors that they were going to put LSD in Chicago's water supply and use female members to seduce Humphrey delegates.

Mayor Daley ordered an army of twelve thousand policemen to cordon off and control the demonstrators. He persuaded the governor to station some six thousand Illinois National Guardsmen armed with rifles, flame throwers, grenade launchers, and bazookas outside the city as backup. He also ordered his plainclothes police to infiltrate protest organizations and prevailed on the federal government to dispatch a thousand agents to Chicago. For every six demonstrators during the convention there was one undercover agent. The *Chicago Tribune* published a series of revelations concerning "plans by Communists and left-wing agitators to disrupt the city." When some of the Yippies and SDS members began hurling bags of urine and screaming obscenities, the police went berserk. For three days, a national television audience watched as Daley's men beat not only the demonstrators, but some innocent bystanders as well. As journalist Nicholas Von Hoffman noted, the police had "taken off their badges, their name plates, even the unit patches on their shoulders to become a mob of identical, unidentifiable club swingers."[128] Watching from the ABC studios in Chicago, commentators William F. Buckley and Gore Vidal nearly came to blows when anchor Howard K. Smith compared the protestors hoisting the Vietcong battle flag in Lincoln Park with fascists running up the Nazi flag during World War II. Vidal reported, "Well, there are no Nazis here, except perhaps Bill Buckley, a crypto-Nazi." Buckley reddened and he said, "Listen, you queer, stop calling me a crypto-Nazi, or I'll sock you in the goddamn face and you'll stay plastered."[129]

At the ranch the Johnsons' staff members and some of their Texas friends had gathered to watch Humphrey's nomination. The group congregated in front of the three television sets in the living room. Lady Bird recalled that she could not tear them or herself away long enough for dinner. "It was a three-ring circus," Lady Bird said of the convention. "There was a Stop Humphrey Movement by McCarthy and McGovern and a Draft Teddy Kennedy movement, with the TV commentators running in a circle from one Kennedy supporter to another, trying to stoke the fires under it . . . Finally the forces of the south moved in and favorite son delegations began releasing their delegates for Humphrey . . . The convention moved on toward the bitterest fight of all, the crucial Vietnam plank in the platform. And so, in spite of all the hell raised on the floor and in the city, the work of the convention did go forward . . . The whole strange week was characterized by Luci as 'the longest wake I ever attended.' "[130]

CHAPTER 41

TOUCHING THE VOID

C HICAGO WAS INDEED A WAKE FOR THE DEMOCRATIC party, for the Great Society, and, for all practical purposes, for Lyndon Johnson. He would live for five more years, a tortured man, watching his legacy erode before his eyes.

Politically, the 1968 election was a turning point. The Nixon campaign had a number of things going for it, but the two most important were urban and student unrest—the so-called law-and-order issue—and Vietnam. Law and order was clear-cut. Nixon was for it and the administration, especially Ramsey Clark, was apparently against it. Initially it appeared that Nixon would have to share that issue with George Wallace, who told delighted crowds from Wisconsin to Georgia that if a demonstrator lay down in a street on which he was driving, he would run him over. But Wallace proceeded to outflank himself on the right by selecting Curtis LeMay as his running mate. LeMay announced that a Wallace-LeMay administration would not hesitate to employ nuclear weapons to defeat godless communism, thus ending whatever chance he and his running mate had of winning.

Vietnam was a much more difficult issue for Nixon. Since 1964 he had been "supporting" the administration's policies in Southeast Asia, while at the same time criticizing LBJ for being too weak and timid in pursuing them. Characteristically, he had never missed an opportunity to play the anticommunist card, keeping the specter of McCarthyism and the soft-on-communism charge always in the back of LBJ's mind. Following the March 31 speech, Nixon had announced that as far as he was concerned, Vietnam was off-limits politically. He would support his president. On September 15, after he received the nomination, Nixon sent word through the Reverend Billy Graham, who had now declared himself to be a Republican, that he would "never embarrass him [President Johnson] after the election. I respect him as a man and as the president." And he promised that he would "do everything to make [Johnson] . . . a place in history because you deserve it."[1] But Nixon was ambivalent about a bombing halt. If the administration announced one and negotiations stalled, or the North Vietnamese Army stepped up the war and Johnson had to resume bombing, the Democratic administration would appear once again to have been duped. But if the bomb halt led to productive negotiations and those negotiations dovetailed with a Humphrey campaign that was moving toward de-escalation, withdrawal, and peace, he would be dead. To Richard Nixon's great discomfort, the ball was in Lyndon Johnson's court—and in Hanoi's.

Even more than Nixon, Hubert Humphrey's political fate was in Johnson's hands. Opinion polls taken in early September showed the vice president running well behind Nixon nationwide and third in some southern and midwestern states behind both Nixon and Wallace. "On television tonight," Orville Freeman noted on September 11, "both Wallace and Nixon got more play than Humphrey and the TV made a big point of the fact that he was being snubbed by Jess Unruh in California, Connally in Texas, and by McKeithen in Louisiana."[2] Humphrey was a committed cold war liberal and had accepted the conflict in Southeast Asia for ideological, strategic, and political reasons.[3] But he was also deeply committed to the Great Society and civil rights in particular. Many of those like McGovern, McCarthy, and Michigan Senator Philip Hart who were opposing the war had long been his colleagues in the great liberal struggle. Emotionally, ideologically he was drawn to them. On how close or how far to position himself in regard to LBJ, Humphrey's advisers were split. Orville Freeman and Jim Rowe believed it was suicide for him to part ways with the administration. Adlai Stevenson had virtually disowned Harry Truman and look what had happened to him. The best bet was to tout Medicare, voting rights, clean air and water, and to keep silent on Vietnam.[4] "Make Nixon seem irresponsible," another adviser said, "a Wallace with shoes on."[5] But others insisted that LBJ was probably the most unpopular man in the country in 1968. America wanted peace and would vote only for a candidate who promised not more of the same in Vietnam, but a resolution to that agonizing conflict.[6] Caught between the two camps, Humphrey's anguish became palpable.[7]

Johnson recognized the value a bombing halt and substantive negotiations would have for the vice president's campaign, but neither in fact nor appearance did he want politics to govern his last decision on Vietnam. By the end of September, just over twenty-nine thousand Americans had died in the war, 14,073 in 1968 alone.[8] The president wanted to stop the carnage. An end to the fighting would allow the nation to focus its attention on domestic problems. And Johnson was thinking about his own place in history.[9] But he also believed he had to tough it out a little bit longer. He called Mansfield and Dirksen to the White House and told them, "Now I want you all to know one thing. If I don't have anybody here except me, I'm not going to give in . . . So there is no use of any pressure speeches or anything else that is going to do one damn bit of good . . . If the Congress does not agree to what I am doing, all you have to do is to repeal your Tonkin Gulf Resolution."[10] "Johnson feels this very strongly," Freeman noted in his diary, "and it isn't a matter of his own personal position or personal pique, in my judgment, it's more basic than that. I am convinced that the president believes that the only and best chance for peace during his Administration and to make any progress in Paris is now to be just as tough as can be and to make it clear that Hanoi will profit not at all by waiting . . . Charley [Murphy] said today that he was convinced that the President would rather see Nixon elected than to see any equivocation on this very key issue."[11]

Humphrey was whipsawed. "Now, the way I see the thing," LBJ told Everett Dirksen, "there are 43 percent of the people for Nixon, 28 percent for Hubert, 21 percent for Wallace. So when you take 43 and 21 on Wallace and Nixon that's 64 percent. Now these McCarthy people. That doesn't do him any good. If he puts 8 percent with his 28, he's just got 36. So he's got to do something to get at some of the Nixon [supporters] back or some of the Wallace people back."[12] In truth, on Vietnam, Humphrey could not resist the temptation to be all things to all people. He supported the president's tough line, but shortly after the convention he told reporters that he believed the United States could begin bringing home some troops after the first of the year. Several days later, at the end of a long day, obviously exhausted, Humphrey let it slip that he could live with the minority plank on Vietnam if it came to that.

All of this, of course, sent Johnson up the wall. "I saw the president yesterday," Freeman recorded, "he only had 10 minutes by the time I got in and he really went after Humphrey. He called him a coward . . . He's trying to back off from his own family and unidentify himself with this program . . . He was furious that he is, as he put it, ogling McCarthy who is just treating him with contempt . . . On and on he went. A lot of the language was four letter words." Then his face softened and he said, "Now don't tell Humphrey anything about this . . . After all he's the candidate, it's hard going, I know he's discouraged . . . so you don't tell him that I've been so harsh with him and let's see if we can't help him."[13] Later, Johnson put it to his vice president directly. McCarthy was not his friend and was not supporting him, LBJ said. "Hubert, somebody could knee you in the balls and you'd just come up giggling and saying 'Knee me again.' You're going to have to hang tough. Don't get off on a Vietnam issue. If you stay tough, Nixon has a way of blowing it. He'll blow it. But you've got to stay tough and on a single path, not go jump[ing] all over the lot."[14]

By mid-September, LBJ had decided on three preconditions for a bombing halt. The North Vietnamese would have to respect the DMZ, foreswear further rocket attacks on Saigon and other cities, and accept the government of South Vietnam as a negotiating partner in Paris.[15] Rumors of a peace deal swirled through Washington. On the 24th, Dirksen, who had become the go-between for LBJ and Nixon, paid a secret call at the White House. The GOP candidate, he said, had heard that the administration was leaning toward a settlement "that might be regarded as something of a sellout." Not without reciprocity, LBJ replied. "I am getting criticism [from members of my own party] on not hitting

Nixon," he told the minority leader. "Now I don't want to be a hypocrite at all. I want Humphrey to win just like you want Nixon to win. On the other hand, I want Communism defeated in Southeast Asia and this country more than I want anybody to win and that's why I took myself out of it March 31st." [16] Harriman and Vance subsequently broached the president's terms to Xuan Thuy, but he refused to budge. "The North Vietnamese have come back with no counter proposals," Rusk reported to the president and his other advisers. "They repeat merely that after we stop the bombing, they will discuss issues which either side wishes to raise. They refuse to agree to take any action which implies reciprocity for our present limitation on the bombing of North Vietnam." [17]

By this point Harriman, Vance, Ball, and Clifford were well-nigh beside themselves. The North Vietnamese were clearly in a mood to talk, they believed. They had not rejected the president's proposals out of hand but said that there would need to be a pause before they could discuss them. There had been signs from Oslo, where the Norwegians were in contact with representatives of the DRV, that Hanoi would accept a GVN presence in Paris. [18] The Soviets were reporting through several channels that their allies were ready to enter into meaningful talks. The election was just over a month away. On September 25 Ball, who had been appointed U.S. representative to the United Nations on May 14, resigned. "I cannot permit myself to remain quiet any longer about Nixon," Clifford reported Ball as saying. "He is a liar, dishonest, and a crook. This is my country. We would get poor leadership." He must be free to help Humphrey, he said. [19]

By the last week in September Humphrey was beginning to gain on Nixon in the polls but not quickly enough to catch up. At his public appearances, the vice president was being picketed and heckled both by followers of Wallace and by students who had supported McCarthy. In Salt Lake City on the evening of September 30, he delivered a major speech on Vietnam. It was taped, and excerpts were broadcast on all three networks. Humphrey declared that if he were elected president, he would immediately institute a total bombing halt. The only condition would be that the North Vietnamese respect the DMZ, that is, that the abatement would not further endanger U.S. soldiers in I Corps. He expected Hanoi to negotiate in "good faith"; if it did not, the bombing would resume. [20]

The speech seemed to win the McCarthy-McGovern wing of the party over completely. A few days after the Salt Lake City speech, the vice president made an appearance in Boston. Humphrey recalled in his memoirs, "As I approached the hotel . . . I found myself surrounded by hundreds of students carrying signs that read, 'We're for you, Hubert,' or simply, 'Humphrey for President.' This was the same Boston that only a few weeks earlier had been the scene of noisy demonstrators who heckled . . . me." [21] Fifteen minutes before the speech, Humphrey called LBJ to tell him what he was going to say. Both men were cordial but frank. Johnson did not seem unduly upset. He had already seen a draft that had been released to the press earlier in the day. Quoting from it, he said, "You do require evidence of direct or indirect, or deed or word on the restoration of the DMZ?"

Humphrey replied, "Absolutely."

Johnson: "I'll turn it on."

Humphrey: "God bless you. Thank you."[22]

Johnson understood intellectually that Humphrey had to try to carve out an independent position, and as he told George Ball, whom he phoned during Humphrey's speech, there was little substantive difference between Humphrey's position and his own. But the Salt Lake City speech was likely to have dangerous repercussions, Johnson believed, especially because Ball and other Humphrey advisers were telling reporters in background interviews that Humphrey was committed to a bombing halt no matter what.[23] Nixon had called Johnson in a huff on the 27th, complaining that rumor had it that Humphrey was going to come out for an immediate unconditional bombing halt. Were the White House and the vice president planning to pull the rug out from under him? No, Johnson replied, and repeated his three conditions.

Then there were the South Vietnamese, specifically Thieu and Ky. The two were more suspicious than ever of the Americans. On September 10, Ky had paid a visit to Thieu and told him that rumors of a coup were in the air. Was it possible that the Americans were planning to oust them before the election so that Humphrey might win? Thieu replied that the same thought had occurred to him. It was quite possible that the Americans would either stage a coup or make a sudden decision to stop the bombing, accept a cease-fire, and press for a coalition government. Both men agreed that they, who had the most to lose if the Americans suddenly caved, should be on constant guard.[24] Johnson recognized clearly that if the Thieu-Ky regime perceived that it was going to be cut out of the loop and sacrificed on the altar of American politics, they would do everything possible to stall any breakthrough in the peace talks and help Richard Nixon win in November.

As the election approached, the president alternately pulled Humphrey to him and pushed him away. In mid-October Humphrey went to the White House for an off-the-record visit with the president. But because a report of the meeting had leaked to the press, LBJ refused to see him. "It's the same old business of the President's petulance and pettiness," Freeman observed. "This is what has made it difficult for him and why he has lost his personal popularity. How and why he could be this narrow and petty, even making allowances for the fact that he resents and dislikes what he calls Humphrey's mouthiness . . . is just incredible."[25] A week or so later, the meeting took place. Jim Jones recalled the encounter: "Mr. Johnson would drink scotch and soda and he had a special jigger that just [held] almost a thimbleful of Scotch. He'd chug those down . . . and they would be equivalent to about four or five regular mixed drinks . . . Humphrey was trying to keep up with him, but the Filipino houseboy that was mixing the drinks didn't have the same small jigger for Humphrey . . . At eleven or midnight or so when they finally wound up their conversation, Humphrey came bounding out of the President's office into my office. He was about ten feet off the ground, just happy and smiling and running around, and he walked into two closet doors, thinking that was the door out into the hallway." [26]

IN THE MIDST OF THE MANEUVERING surrounding a possible bombing halt, the Johnsons accepted an invitation to dine with General and Mrs. Westmoreland on the evening of October 8. The president was temporarily detained, and Lady Bird and Luci went ahead. "We drove up to Quarters one at Fort Myer," Lady Bird subsequently recorded in her diary, "and looked down below, through the trees in the valley to the lights of Washington—a glorious view, with the Washington Monument as its chief jewel. At first there were only the four of us, and then General and Mrs. Earle Wheeler joined us." Lyndon came in very late, around nine. "Looking as tired as I have ever seen him, as worn—the fight temporarily gone out of him. He was warm to the company he was in, even sentimental." The conversation ranged over the older people's lifetimes: World War II, MacArthur, Vietnam. The three men discussed the Paris peace talks. LBJ slept all the way on the drive back to the White House. Lady Bird noticed that the little motorcade did not enter through the Southwest Gate as usual, but instead through a series of closed-off streets and through the front entrance on Pennsylvania Avenue. She asked the Secret Service why. "There has been a penetration," he replied. Someone had gone over the fence. The individual was apprehended without incident, but Lady Bird later learned that during his presidency there had been more than six thousand threats on LBJ's life. [27] The next day, it was Vietnam again.

EVEN BEFORE THE SALT LAKE CITY SPEECH, LBJ had begun leaning toward a halt. He sent General Andrew Goodpaster out to Saigon to survey the situation directly. The general reported back on October 8: "We do not wish to say this in public, but things are going very, very well. All we need here is some time and it will come out fine." [28] A week later, Rostow told LBJ that both Creighton Abrams and Ellsworth Bunker "were comfortable about facing negotiations now in view of the improved military situation in Vietnam." Westmoreland, who was in on the conversation, declared, "The enemy is militarily bankrupt." The DMZ and the shelling of the cities were now off the table. In this same meeting, Rostow reported that in private talks with Harriman and Vance during the previous weekend in Paris, the North Vietnamese had indicated that the GVN could sit at the negotiating table. [29] Peace was in the air. "We are going to be charged with moving now for political reasons," the president observed. "We will be asked why we did not move earlier . . . However, it would be on my conscience if our negotiators were put in a position to say that the president had held them back and kept them from reaching agreement." [30]

But Johnson and his advisers had underestimated Richard Nixon, Thieu, and Ky. The administration had to have South Vietnam's agreement to conclude a deal, and Saigon was determined to keep fighting, a fact the GOP candidate was determined to turn to his advantage. The president and his advisers settled on a bombing halt announcement at midnight on Wednesday, October 16. That afternoon, however, Thieu's foreign minister had called in the ambassadors of Korea, Thailand, Australia, New Zealand, and the Philippines (the troop-contributing countries) and told them that the United States was about to institute a bombing halt. "I just think we oughtn't send Thieu anymore stuff," LBJ exclaimed to Rusk. "To hell with him. I don't care. I am just tired of the son-of-a-bitch making up that kind of stuff. It is just awful that his Foreign Minister and all that stuff just causes us all this damn trouble. I feel about the same way about these little jerks that have got one battalion over there."[31] That same day, the North Vietnamese in Paris informed Harriman and Rusk that they would have to contact the NLF and arrange for it to send a delegation to Paris before substantive talks could begin. Johnson described the exchange to Mansfield. "We went all the way through it, and they said, 'this is all fine, but . . . you say here that you'll meet the next day with us with the Government of Vietnam. We have to have the NLF, and we don't know how long it will take to get them.' Now we said, 'well, that's all right. We'll be glad if you'll go get them.' They said, 'No, we think you better stop bombing and then we'll go look for them.' Now we said, 'No, you said in your talks that if we would stop bombing that you'd be willing to start discussions the next day.' "[32] Clifford reported to his staff: "I don't know whether it's a real hitch or not . . . LBJ was in good humor all yesterday, until last nite [*sic*], when he was in 'slough of despair' over the hitch . . . The man hangs over the ticker in his office until he's hump-backed. I wish somebody would blow the damn thing up."[33]

On October 19, with the election two and a half weeks away, Thieu went on television and announced that the DRV had done nothing to earn a bombing halt and to declare that he and his government were adamantly opposed to the NLF being present at the Paris negotiations.[34] Not a day passed that did not produce news stories from Saigon and Paris on the widening gap between the GVN and the Johnson administration and the impossibility of reaching terms suitable to both Saigon and Hanoi. All the while, Rusk was frantically negotiating through the Russians with Hanoi, trying to narrow the gap between the effective date of a bombing halt and the beginning of substantive negotiations. By October 22 it was two to three days versus ten days.

On October 24 Lynda and Chuck Robb's first child was born at Bethesda Naval Hospital. That evening as Luci, Lynda, and Lady Bird were departing for the hospital, Johnson wrote his son-in-law: "Dear Chuck, This has been a week of waiting, of rumors, and of hopes for a turn toward peace, which have not been fulfilled . . . While we ache to see this turn in the road, I must be absolutely sure that every step we take is consistent with our national interests and honor and consistent with the sacrifices made by our men in the field and with their security . . . We all send our love."[35]

The day before, Johnson had summoned General William W. Momyer, former commander, 7th Air Force, Vietnam, to the White House. He did not want to jump the lines of command, he said, but he had to know: Would a bombing halt put American soldiers in Vietnam at greater risk? The monsoon season was just beginning, Momyer replied. Bombing from the eleventh to the nineteenth parallel for the three months following would have to be done by radar. That would mean bombing only fixed points and not trucks moving south. Normally, the air force would concentrate instead on bombing supply routes running through Laos. If that could be continued there would be minimal risk. "If you were president, would you do it?" LBJ asked. Momyer paused briefly and then said, "Yes, sir." [36]

The last week in October, the White House finally learned that the Nixon camp was secretly parleying with Thieu and Ky, promising them better treatment under a Republican administration and encouraging them to obstruct matters until after the election. The campaign's go-between with the South Vietnamese government was Mrs. Anna Chan Chennault, the Chinese-born wife of General Claire Chennault. Mrs. Chennault was president of Flying Tiger Airlines, a frequent visitor to Asia, and a long-time intimate of Chinese Nationalist leader Jiang Jieshi and the members of the China lobby in the United States. In 1968 she was cochair of the Republican Women for Nixon. Once he became convinced in mid-October that LBJ was indeed working toward a bombing halt before the election, Nixon had his campaign manager, John Mitchell, telephone her. "Anna," Mitchell said, "I'm speaking on behalf of Mr. Nixon. It's very important that our Vietnamese friends understand our Republican position and I hope you have made that clear to them." If she could persuade Thieu not to go to the negotiating table, it would offset the effect of any preelection bombing halt announcement. LBJ would appear to be a cynical politician who was willing to abandon a valiant, long-time ally. [37]

When Johnson got wind of what was happening, he ordered the FBI to begin tailing Madame Chennault. He also instructed Deke DeLoach to send a team to install a listening device on the phone in her apartment in the Watergate building. Would it also be possible, he asked, to put a bug onboard Nixon's campaign plane? After all, this was treason. [38] DeLoach hedged. The Watergate was a huge building with a lot of traffic. The risk of discovery if his men tried to put a listening device there or on Nixon's plane was too great. If the operation were revealed, both the agency and the president would be disgraced. [39] "The thing that amazed me," Jim Jones later observed, "was the total inability of the FBI to turn up any kind of hard evidence when they had been able to do it on so many other cases," [40] But Johnson had other instruments at his disposal: the CIA and the National Security Administration. [41] From intercepts collected by these agencies, he learned the full story.

LBJ called Jim Rowe, who was on the campaign trail with Humphrey. "He had the Vietnam embassy tapped, and he called me out in, I think, Peoria," Rowe later recalled. "It was an open-air speech. I was in the crowd listening to Humphrey, and the Secret Service tapped me on the shoulder and said, 'the president wants to talk with you . . . Come over to the hotel.' Johnson got on the phone. He told me about Anna . . . He said, 'I just want Humphrey to know about it. Tell him about it, and tell him I don't think he ought to do anything about it, but that's his problem.' I told Humphrey, and Humphrey didn't ever say anything about it."[42] Rostow and Johnson had talked about how to proceed on the Chennault matter. "The materials are so explosive that they could gravely damage the country whether Mr. Nixon is elected or not," Rostow observed. "If they get out in their present form, they could be the subject of one of the most acrimonious debates we have ever witnessed . . . For the larger good of the country, you may wish to consider finding an occasion to talk with Mr. Nixon."[43] LBJ agreed.

On October 29, top-secret orders went out to the U.S. military command in South Vietnam to "stop all air, naval, and artillery bombardment and all other acts involving the use of force against the territory of the DRV as of 0001 GMT Wednesday [the 30th]."[44] Walt Rostow would later observe that October 29 through 31, 1968, would be the most hectic, intense, and dangerous days he had spent since the Cuban Missile Crisis.[45] The key would be the posture the government of South Vietnam chose to take. On the 29th a member of the American mission paid a visit to Ky at the presidential palace. There could not be an unconditional suspension, Ky declared. "Although the U.S. wants a bombing halt in the interest of the number of votes for Vice President Humphrey, it is impossible without the concurrence of the Vietnamese Government, and there cannot be the ruination of [a nation] for the sake of one person."[46] LBJ met in almost continuous session with his advisers. Even Clark Clifford was alarmed at Saigon's mood. It would be "extremely serious" if Thieu and Ky refused to go along. "Ky is a guy who is capable of committing suicide," Rusk observed. "We've invested 29,000 killed and $70 billion . . . The whole thing could blow up."[47]

Later, LBJ described the situation as he saw it: "The Nixon forces have been working on South Vietnam . . . We can't walk out, quit, split. We have got to hold together. We must tell them we won't stand for their vetoing this . . . If he [Thieu] keeps us from moving, God help South Vietnam—because I can't help him anymore, neither can anyone else who has my job."[48] On the morning of the 30th Washington instructed Bunker to see Ky and Thieu and make the administration's position crystal clear. Thieu remained adamant, however: the United States must secure assurances from the DRV that it would negotiate directly with the GVN and that the NLF would not be treated as a separate entity at Paris. "Thieu kept circling around the problem," Bunker reported. "I finally told him point blank that since we cannot get these assurances, if he insists on making his agreement conditional on such assurances, we shall have to go our separate ways. I warned him of the consequences if he forced us into this position."[49] Washington held its breath.

Meanwhile, the United States notified both the Russians and the North Vietnamese of the impending halt.[50] Bunker met again with Thieu. "Thieu reacted emotionally and disjointedly," he reported. " 'You are powerful, you can say to small nations what you want. We understand America's sacrifice for Vietnam. All Vietnamese know our life depends on US support, but you cannot force us to do anything against our interest. This negotiation is not a life or death matter for the US but it is for Vietnam.' I think they may take us right to the brink." [51] Meanwhile, from Paris, Vance reported that the DRV had agreed that your-side, our-side negotiations could begin in Paris on November 6, the day after the election. [52]

By noon on October 31 the announcement speech was ready. The president, who had a bad cold and spoke hoarsely, was scheduled to go on television at eight that evening. At 6:05 LBJ telephoned the three presidential candidates and told them what he was going to do. At seven he called Humphrey a second time. LBJ was frank about what he had made clear to both Hanoi and Saigon and what he expected to happen over the next few weeks. They talked about Nixon's efforts through Madame Chennault and the South Vietnamese ambassador to the United States, Bui Diem, to persuade Thieu to obstruct negotiations. He was all for him, the president told Humphrey, and went over plans he had to hit the campaign trail between then and November 5. "We've been talking about our programs, Mr. President," Humphrey said. "I want you to know one thing: if I can do half as good a job as you've done, if I am elected, I will be happy."

LBJ: "Well, you will do good."

Humphrey: "I have been wanting to call you all the time."

LBJ: "Don't you do it. Don't you do it. Don't worry about me. You don't have to . . . don't mess with me." [53]

After he hung up, LBJ watched his taped speech with family members and staff in the Oval Office. One of his aides took notes: "He said it was the most important decision he had ever made. He further said he was not sure it was the right decision but was what he felt had to be done. Said he couldn't guarantee Thieu, what Thieu wanted. 'I could only tell him I was taking them on faith— that the times demanded this action. This is a step toward peace." [54]

In the wake of Johnson's announcement, Humphrey drew virtually abreast of Nixon in the polls. Going on the attack, the Democratic nominee challenged his opponent to a debate. When the Republicans refused, Humphrey dubbed Nixon "Richard the Chickenhearted." A week before the election, McCarthy endorsed his party's selection in his typically cynical fashion: "I'm voting for Humphrey, and I think you should suffer with me." The tantalizing question remained: Should Johnson go public with Nixon's secret deal with Saigon? On the evening of November 2 LBJ called Dirksen. We know what you are doing, he said. Tell Nixon to cut it out. "We're skirting on dangerous ground," he warned. "Some of . . . your old China crowd, and here's the latest information we got . . . she's—they've just talked to the 'boss' in New Mexico [Spiro Agnew, Nixon's running mate, was then campaigning in New Mexico], and he says that 'you [Thieu] must hold out'—just hold on until after the election." Then Johnson put his cards on the table: "Now I can identify them because I know who's doing this. I don't want to identify it. I think it would shock America if a principal candidate was playing with a source like this on a matter this important . . . I know this—that they're contacting a foreign power in the middle of a war . . . And it's a damn bad mistake." Dirksen said he would pass along the information—and the warning.[55]

But Nixon refused to call off Madame Chennault. Instead, GOP spokesperson Robert Finch informed the press that LBJ had misled the presidential candidates into thinking that he would stand firm in Vietnam; the failure of the Thieu government to endorse the bombing halt showed how bankrupt and duplicitous the administration's Vietnam policy was. In Saigon, Ky leaked various cables and transcripts of conversations in which Bunker had tried to persuade him and Thieu to agree to a bombing halt. Bunker was livid. "We obviously will never again be able to repose any confidence in Ky," he told Rostow, "and indeed it is difficult to know how we can deal in future with this government, given this kind of irresponsibility at the top."[56]

On November 3, Nixon called LBJ to tell him that he had heard from Dirksen. Johnson repeated his accusations. Nixon just laughed. Everyone knew that Hanoi believed that it would get a better deal from a Democratic rather than a Republican administration. "That's one of the reasons you had to go forward with the pause," he said. "But . . . my God, I would never do anything to encourage Hanoi—I mean Saigon—not to come to the table."[57] But of course, he had, did, and would.[58]

On November 4, the day before the election, LBJ and his advisers discussed once again the wisdom of leaking the Chennault affair. Rusk was against it: "I do not believe that any President can make any use of interceptions or telephone taps in any way that would involve politics. The moment we cross over that divide we are in a different kind of society." Because of his desire to see Washington continue to take a strong line in Vietnam no matter who was in the White House, the secretary of state's views were somewhat suspect. Clifford, for once, supported him. "I think that some elements of the story are so shocking in their nature," he declared, "that I'm wondering whether it would be good for the country to disclose the story, and then possibly to have a certain individual elected. It could cast his whole administration under such doubts that I would think it would be inimical to our country's interests." So be it, Johnson declared.[59]

When the final tallies were counted on election Tuesday, Richard Nixon had won a narrow victory. The Republican ticket polled 31.7 million votes, 43.4 percent of the total, while Humphrey and Muskie rolled up 31.2 million, 42.7 percent of the whole. Wallace received 13.5 percent, which was strong for a third-party candidate, and had almost taken enough votes away from Nixon to have changed the outcome. Almost, but not quite. In a sense, the election was close, but in another sense, it amounted, as Theodore White observed, to a "negative landslide" of gigantic proportions. Since 1965 the Democrats had squandered a plurality of more than 16 million votes. The fragile consensus that

Johnson had stitched together had been ripped apart by Vietnam, inflation, urban rioting, and the white backlash against the Second Reconstruction. More important, perhaps, the Great Society was proving an ironic success, elevating the poor into the working class and the working class into the middle class, accelerating the trend that had begun after World War II and pushing the country relentlessly to the right. Economically, the vast majority of Americans were no longer aggrieved. The Democrats saw defections from nearly every component of the New Deal coalition: labor, the South, urban ethnics, and farmers. Humphrey won a mere 38 percent of the white vote. Massive majorities among blacks and Jews helped, but even the reliable black vote fell 11 percent from 1964. Nixon had spoken of a "silent majority," and he turned out to be right. "Nixon's forgotten men should not be confused with Roosevelt's," observed columnist Kenneth Crawford. "Nixon's are comfortable, housed, clad and fed, who constitute the middle stratum of society. But they aspire to more and feel menaced by those who have less." [60]

Johnson spent election day at the ranch. Arthur Krim recalled that he was relatively quiet as the returns came in showing Humphrey with an early lead but then shifting to Nixon. "When I got up around seven or eight o'clock, it was all over," Krim later recalled. "I went downstairs and there was LBJ and so many thoughts swept through my mind about is he going to blame himself, how is he going to handle the Nixon thing? . . . He was, I would say, obviously deep into himself about the impact of it." [61]

It would take Nixon five long years to reach a peace agreement in Vietnam, through alternate periods of brutal aggression, reluctant concession, and endless talks. Ultimately, nothing he and Henry Kissinger, his national security adviser, could do could stop the North from winning the war. Johnson's legacy would suffer with each twist.

TWO WEEKS AFTER THE ELECTION, the Nixons paid a visit to the White House. The president and Lady Bird were waiting beneath a South Portico canopy when Pat and Dick arrived. The Johnsons greeted the first couple–elect warmly, LBJ even throwing his arm around the shoulders of the man who had driven his lover, Helen Gahagan Douglas, out of office some twenty years earlier in an acrimonious campaign. The two couples chatted for a bit. Nixon asked Johnson why he had not swept out the Kennedy people in December 1964, after his election. LBJ paused and answered thoughtfully: "Well, there are several reasons. One, respect for President Kennedy. He had trusted me and I tried to put myself in his shoes. How would I have felt if, as soon as I was gone, he had disposed of all my people? I wanted to be loyal to him. Two, I didn't know for a good while whether I had an excellent man or an incompetent. And Three, I didn't always have all the troops I needed . . . Maybe I made a mistake." [62]

After lunch, Lady Bird gave Pat a tour of the mansion while Lyndon and Dick went out into the Rose Garden to meet the press. President Johnson, Nixon announced, would speak "not just for this Administration, but for the nation and . . . for the next Administration as well," until January 20.[63] Of course, nothing could have been further from the truth. In person, the president-elect would continue to be defferential. "Every time during that whole transition or the briefings prior to the election," Jim Jones recalled, "Nixon was like a boy scout around Johnson. It was like Johnson was a big, hulking professional football player and Nixon was the autograph seeker."[64] But everyone knew who held real power, and it wasn't Johnson.

The press tried to be kind. Stewart Alsop paid tribute in a column entitled "Well, Good-Bye, Lyndon." In it, he praised the president for his selflessness in not running and his dogged pursuit of an arms control agreement with the Soviet Union.[65] The *Washington Post* ran an editorial recalling the calm LBJ had brought to the nation in the wake of the assassination, the huge advances he had made in the area of civil rights and poverty alleviation, and his commitment to civil liberty. Johnson was pathetically grateful. "Kay dear," he wrote Katharine Graham, the publisher of the *Post,* "I thank you and any others who contributed to the [editorial] . . . Through the years you and yours have given me courage and strength when I needed it most. Love, LBJ."[66] But for the most part, Johnson left office unreconciled to the media. "There are people who write with great authority about the president and the presidency who have never been in this room," he complained in his taped interview with journalist Mel Stuart. "And a great deal of their stuff is imagination. There's a great press credibility in this country. One man can write an article that someone has planted with him and they're planted every day by certain people, serving their own ambition . . . So many people read what one man writes and then they clip it and then they re-write it and then the folks of the country start repeating it and repeating it and pretty soon it becomes an accepted fact and then they have two polls to come along and confirm it. And then you've had it."[67]

On January 14, LBJ delivered his last message to Congress. It turned out to be a warm, sentimental occasion. The president entered to a five-minute standing ovation. In a measured, almost understated voice, he reviewed the achievements of the past five years. They were monumental: voting rights, fair housing, Medicare, the poverty program, environmental protection, federal aid to education, the wilderness program. He expressed disappointment at not obtaining a gun control bill and voiced his hope for a just and speedy peace in Southeast Asia. He paid tribute to Congresses past and present, and singled out the Wizard of Winder, Richard Russell. His closing was eloquent and moving. "Now," he said, "it is time to leave. I hope it may be said, a hundred years from now, that by working together we helped to make our country more just, more just for all of its people . . . That is what I hope. But I believe that at least it will be said that we tried." He took his time leaving, shaking as many hands as he could reach as his colleagues sang "Auld Lang Syne."[68]

The day before the inauguration was a blur of friendly faces and fond farewells for the Johnsons. Humphrey called with a warm good-bye. The Marine Corps Band came by to serenade with the "Pedernales River March" as the president watched from the Truman balcony. Dean Rusk and Averell Harriman dropped in to pay their respects. Early in the evening, Lyndon and Lady Bird stopped by the staid, exclusive F Street Club to attend a party being thrown by the Henry Fords.[69] From there, it was back to the White House to host a cocktail buffet for family and staff. Johnson mingled easily, telling stories and expressing a few regrets. "Perhaps it would have been different with Fulbright," he told Joe Califano, "if we had only talked to him more, had him over here more, found some things to agree with him on." Later, he warned Califano about Nixon. Recalling what he had done to Helen Douglas, he said, "It's not enough for Nixon to win. He's going to have to put some people in jail."[70] He warned his aide to pay $500 extra in federal taxes each year to keep the IRS off his back. The group sang "For He's a Jolly Good Fellow." LBJ paid warm tribute to his staff, and Harry McPherson spoke eloquently about the privilege it had been to work for a man with such lofty goals. Lady Bird and Lyndon left the party and went to bed around eleven.

Shortly after the inauguration the next day, the four Johnsons flew back to Texas, landing at Bergstrom Air Force Base outside Austin. An enthusiastic crowd of some five hundred friends and well-wishers were on hand to greet them. The University of Texas Band played "The Eyes of Texas" and "Ruffles and Flourishes." The former first couple arrived at the ranch around dusk. "The weather was mild and warm," Lyndon later recalled. "After we changed into comfortable clothes, Lady Bird and I walked around the yard together." In the carport behind the house the luggage was piled in a giant mound. For the first time in five years there were no aides to carry the bags inside. Lady Bird looked at the scene and began to laugh. "The coach had turned back into a pumpkin," she said, "and the mice have all run away."[71]

THE LIFE THAT LYNDON JOHNSON envisioned for himself after the presidency was that of rancher-businessman and teacher. In fact, it would be an abbreviated life of spiraling sickness and isolation from public affairs. His presidential library would be built in Austin. Longhorn football games would be attended. Annual wedding-anniversary parties would provide carefree relief. He would draw closer to his family. But overall, it was a time of reflection and decline.

LBJ was consumed by a fit of depression during his first few months back on the ranch. Visitors found him irritable, self-pitying, uncharacteristically withdrawn. He had begun smoking on the plane back to Texas on inauguration day and he never stopped again. His drinking and eating habits became completely undisciplined. In the spring, Elizabeth Goldschmidt received an emergency call from Lady Bird begging her and her husband, Arthur, to come down and spend Easter with them. "She was trying desperately to find a way to pull Johnson out of what was clearly a depression," Goldschmidt recalled. "And he refused to discuss anything that was less than twenty-five years old."[72]

Then suddenly LBJ snapped out of it. "I was very, very worried," Luci said. "I thought thirty-five years in public service and this is going to be like putting him in a tomb. But he discovered play . . . And he discovered his grandchildren and it was a delightful time." [73] His health improved somewhat and he began sleeping uninterruptedly from ten in the evening until six or seven in the morning. The house filled with people again as LBJ had Lady Bird and her staff on the phone constantly, inviting people to lunch and dinner. He began taking short trips, initially in state and then further afield. [74] And his sense of malicious fun returned, at least for a time. In December 1969, National Security Adviser Henry Kissinger began giving LBJ periodic foreign affairs briefings. After he returned from his first trip to the ranch, he told a Cambridge friend that the president was crazy. What do you mean? he asked. "When I first got down there, he called me 'Dr. Kee-sing-er' . . . Like I was the prime minister of Germany." His colleague told Kissinger that LBJ was putting him on. No, said Kissinger; he is crazy. "And then he got me all mixed up and called me Dr. Schles-ing-er." [75] Johnson knew perfectly well who the new national security adviser was and that he had been up to his neck in the Chennault affair. This was his way of having some fun and keeping yet another "Harvard" off balance.

By the end of 1969 Lyndon and Lady Bird's social life was booming and their horizons broadening. They began hosting each year on December 21 a rollicking party at the Argyle Hotel in San Antonio to celebrate their wedding anniversary. [76] Lyndon and Lady Bird had become fast friends of former Mexican president Miguel Aleman. Every February, and spontaneously at other times of the year, the Johnsons would fly to Acapulco and stay in Aleman's villa there. Typically, LBJ would invite guests at a moment's notice; the former president's plane would land and disgorge passengers—some dressed in business attire, others in tropical shirts—and mounds of baggage. LBJ always insisted on bringing his own food and water, a memorial to a bout with dysentery on an earlier trip. As was true at the ranch, LBJ played lord of the manor. If he wanted to golf, everyone golfed. If he wanted to go to the beach, everyone went to the beach. If he decided to watch the famous cliff divers, everyone went to view the cliff divers. Arthur Krim, who had bought a spread an hour's drive from the LBJ Ranch, and his wife, Mathilde, usually came, bringing with them the latest movie releases. [77] Sometimes Aleman would take the Johnsons to his ranch, Las Pampas, in the interior. The stark beauty and remoteness of the location made a lasting impression on LBJ. On these trips he would invariably bring containers of contraceptives, food, and over-the-counter medicines for distribution to the local peasantry.

When the Johnsons were in residence on the banks of the Pedernales, the business of the day was ranching. Yolanda Boozer, one of LBJ's retirement secretaries, recalled, "Usually Mrs. Johnson was having coffee with him in the morning when I would arrive and he would be in his bed reading the newspapers. Then, in a matter of thirty minutes, he would be in the office ready to go on his rounds and see about his irrigation and his cattle. By then he would have talked to Dale [Malechek, his ranch manager] a number of times." [78] For the first year, "he became one of us," Malechek said. He rode the fence line and helped haul irrigation pipes. If he saw a cow where it should not be or showing signs of illness, he was instantly on the walkie-talkie with Malechek.[79] Initially, he brought the same intensity to his new role as rancher as he had to the presidency. A guest at the ranch recalled an early morning meeting with the hands. "Now, I want each of you to make a solemn pledge that you will not go to bed tonight until you're sure that every steer has everything it needs," LBJ said. "We've got a chance of producing some of the finest beef in this country if we work at it, if we dedicate ourselves to the job . . . But it'll mean working every minute of every day." [80]

But the spring and summer of 1969 were particularly dry in Texas, and Johnson did not have a farmer-rancher's patience or stoicism. After touring his sunblasted pasture, he summoned a guest to have a glass of iced tea. "It's all been determined, you know," he whined. "Once more I am going to fail. I know it. I simply know it. All my life I've wanted to enjoy this land. I bought it. I paid it off. I watched it improve. It's all I have left now. And then this rotten spring comes along as dry as any we've had in fifty years." [81] Johnson spent endless hours talking over every bull purchase and cow sale with Dale Malechek. "Gee, I hope he runs again for president," the foreman remarked to Jim Jones.[82] Malechek may have had more than one reason for wanting the boss out of his hair. The rumor among the Secret Service delegation was that the boss was sleeping with Jewell Malechek. John Richards, a member of the detail, recalled that LBJ and Dale each had their own bull and herd of cows. Johnson's stud proved barren while Malechek's produced prize calf after prize calf; the Secret Service boys observed that it was only fair.[83] The affair was probably nothing more than a flirtation. Given the state of Johnson's health, especially beginning in 1970, it could hardly have been otherwise. At the same time, observers noticed how comfortable Lyndon and Lady Bird seemed with each other after he got over his depression—the fond glances, the hand touches, the obvious pleasure when they were reunited after even the briefest separation.[84]

Jewell Malecheck was not the only new woman in LBJ's retirement life. During the last days of the presidency Arthur Krim had arranged a lucrative deal with Holt, Rinehart, and Winston for LBJ to publish his memoirs.[85] Sitting in solitude for long hours struggling with memory and prose was not Johnson's cup of tea. It was decided that he would dictate. Jim Jones, Walt Rostow, Harry Middleton, who would become the first director of the LBJ Library, and twenty-seven-year-old Tom Johnson, the White House aide who had agreed to become LBJ's Texas secretary, would do the research. To help with the writing, LBJ summoned Doris Kearns, a Harvard doctoral student in political science who had once been a White House intern. They talked for hours, she sitting at the foot of his bed as he, reclining on his pillows, reminisced. There were boat rides on the lake, picnics, and horseback rides.

Kearns recalled that when confronted with microphone and tape recorder, LBJ became rigid, his prose stilted and colorless. He was obsessed with producing a memoir that looked like a presidential memoir, that portrayed him and his administration as he would want history textbooks to portray them. Off the record, he was animated, funny, coarse, and insightful. But he allowed none of this to go on the record. When Kearns showed him a draft chapter including some pithy comments on Wilbur Mills, LBJ exploded: "God damn it, I can't say this—get it out right now, why he may be the speaker of the House someday. And for Christ's sake, get that vulgar language of mine out of here. What do you think this is, the tale of an uneducated cowboy? It's a presidential memoir, damn it, and I've got to come out looking like a statesman, not some backwoods politician." [86] The result, *Vantage Point,* contained information but no personality. Kearns made notes of their off-the-record conversations, however, and they became the basis for her influential *LBJ and the American Dream.*

There were those who bade Johnson to speak out on public affairs, to use the considerable influence traditionally available to ex-presidents. Roger Wilkins, who had served for a time as a White House aide, remembered running into his former boss at a party in New York.

His back was to us, and he was standing there telling a story, and his hair had turned white, but he was still huge . . . All of a sudden his face goes into a kind of puzzle and he says, "I know, I know you . . . Little Roger!" I was smoking a cigarette, and at that point he gives me a bear hug . . . So then he and I moved to the side, and I found myself saying, "Mr. President, when you were president you said that you wanted to finish the job that Lincoln had begun, and I'm puzzled. Just because Richard Nixon is president doesn't mean that you don't have one of the two most powerful voices in this country. That's a voice we desperately need now and I don't see why you're not speaking up . . ." And he said, "Do you really think so?" I said, "Oh, yes sir, I surely do . . ." So then I was off talking to another group later in the party and I looked across the room . . . and he was off by himself, leaning against the piano, just all by himself, looking at me, and I smiled at him and he smiled at me, a very gentle, sweet smile. He just waved at me and smiled. [87]

LBJ really did not believe Wilkins, and he was right. Most people wanted to forget Lyndon Johnson. Columnist Charles Roberts described his exile best: "The most militant civil-rights advocate ever to occupy the White House, reviled by Negro militants; a Southerner scorned by Southerners as a turn-coat; a liberal despised by liberals despite the fact he achieved most of what they had sought for thirty years; a friend of education, rejected by intellectuals; a compromiser who could not compromise a war ten thousand miles away." [88] Johnson now found nearly all public venues excruciating. He had attended the launching of *Apollo 11* in July 1969. The moon shot should have been a crowning moment for him, but instead he found it deeply humiliating. Waiting for Vice President Agnew to arrive, he was forced to sit in the bleachers in the blis-

tering sun with other VIPs, most of whom did not even acknowledge his existence. "I remember that moment," Johnson later confided to an interviewer.
"My trousers stuck like cement to the back of my legs, the sweat from my hair
kept dripping down my neck, and my stomach was upset. I knew right then I
shouldn't have come." [89]

At the end of the first year of retirement, LBJ looked fairly well. "His craggy
face was kind of mellow in those days," Warren Woodward recalled. "His hair
was long; it was swept back and curled on the ends like that of an elder statesman in the Andy Jackson vein. The lines in his face were deep, but . . . outside
the gaze of the public eye, he aged gracefully." [90] Johnson's heart condition
would not leave him alone, however. Severe chest pains sent him to Brooke
Army Medical Center in San Antonio in March 1970. [91] In the middle of 1971 he
was hospitalized again, this time for viral pneumonia. In the spring of 1972, he
flew to Tennessee for Buford Ellington's funeral and then on to Charlottesville,
Virginia, to visit Lynda and Chuck Robb and their children. There he suffered
another major heart attack, which put him into intensive care for three days. He
survived the trip back to Texas but had to be hospitalized again for an extended
period. From that day forward, Johnson could not go a day without a nitroglycerin tablet and oxygen; even then he was racked by severe angina. [92] "The chest
pains hit him nearly every afternoon," a friend recalled, "a series of sharp, jolting
pains that left him scared and breathless." [93]

Occasionally, LBJ did speak out on history and public affairs, but only in a
very controlled environment. He agreed to a series of television interviews with
Walter Cronkite that aired on CBS, but for the most part he kept his counsel.
There were private attempts at reconciliation which seemed always to revolve
around those associated with Vietnam. One such occasion was in New York at a
dinner hosted by the Krims. Bob McNamara and Mac Bundy were among the
guests. "After dinner he was in a very reflective mood," Arthur Krim recalled,
"and I remember him saying to those two something which I thought was over-
generous. That was, he said, 'You know, I want you fellows to know everything
that went wrong in Vietnam that's being criticized, it was my decision, not
yours' . . . He was more depressed later in the evening than I've ever seen
him." [94] Johnson agreed to participate in a five-hour off-the record seminar with
editors and columnists from the *Washington Post* on Vietnam. It came not long
after his hospitalization in 1970. Dick Harwood, one of the participants, recalled
the encounter: "His illness showed in his face, I thought, and from the side his
skin had the yellowish-gray look you find on dead men." At one point he was
asked about the events leading up to the October 31, 1968, bombing halt. "As he
talked," Harwood recorded, "he seemed to take on another appearance; the pal-
lor and signs of sickness went away and all of a sudden you were sitting with a
vigorous, commanding, strong man whose mind was so clear, so well-
organized, so quick that you suddenly became aware of the power of that personality . . . What came through above all was not his 'complexity' but the
simplicity of his passions and loves and hates and the singleness of his mind and

mental processes, a singleness that let him lay out so coherently and with calculated meanderings his case on the bombing halt."[95] Haynes Johnson, who was also present, remembered his saying in conclusion, "I want you to know, no matter how we differ about things, I feel I am at the table of friends, and I want to thank you for letting me come and visit with you.' " The journalists stood and applauded.[96]

Johnson wanted to go to the 1972 Democratic Convention, but his health would not allow it. Instead, he agreed to receive George McGovern, the Democratic nominee, at the ranch. McGovern recalled that he arrived at midmorning and immediately sat down to visit with LBJ and Lady Bird on the front lawn under a big oak tree. LBJ assured McGovern that he had his support—active support, not passive. It would probably be best if they avoided discussing Vietnam. "Now on the war," LBJ said, "I think you're crazy as hell, and you think I'm crazy as hell; so let's not talk about it." They were both old populists. Johnson believed in tranquilizing big business and finance while he pushed his social programs. McGovern was more confrontational, but on the goals to be achieved, they were of a mind.[97] "As we were finishing lunch," McGovern later recalled, "I could tell he was in some physical pain. So I asked him how he was feeling and he said, 'Well, every day I start out pretty well, but then by afternoon these damn pains start bothering me, and at four o'clock, I'm pretty well through. I go lay down.' "[98] After the election, LBJ confided to Tommy Corcoran that McGovern was the worst presidential candidate in American history. How in that day and time against Richard Nixon could a Democratic candidate carry only one state?

By the time he met with McGovern, LBJ realized he was dying. "He struck me as a man who really knew he had something terribly wrong with him," McGovern said, "although he didn't seem to be distressed about it."[99] His doctors had ordered him not to make any more speeches, but he could not resist an invitation to deliver the keynote address at a civil rights symposium at the Library scheduled for December 11 and 12, 1972. The affair was to begin with a reception at the ranch, but the day before the festivities were scheduled to start, Texas was engulfed by one of the worst ice storms in living memory. Earl Warren, the Humphreys, and other guests had to be bused into Austin from San Antonio. Against the urging of his doctors and Lady Bird, LBJ traversed the fifty miles from the ranch to Austin by car.

All the major figures of the Second Reconstruction were there, conservatives, moderates, and radicals. LBJ's opening remarks proved to be rather perfunctory, but he was to have another chance. On the last day of the conference a group of activists who wanted to attack the Nixon administration demanded to be heard. The organizers were reluctant, but Johnson insisted that the "redhots" be given their chance. When they finished their indictment, he mounted the steps to the podium, slowly, painfully. What followed was a recapitulation of his famous Howard speech that talked about a level playing field and the continuing need for affirmative action. "I'm kind of ashamed of myself that I had six years and couldn't do more," he declared. "So let no one delude himself that his work is done . . . To be black, I believe, to one who is black or brown, is to be proud, is to be worthy, is to be honorable. But to be black in a white society is not to stand on level and equal ground. While the races may stand side by side, whites stand on history's mountain and blacks stand in history's hollow. We must overcome unequal history before we overcome unequal opportunity."[100] He was forced to stop and pop a nitroglycerin pill in the middle of his speech, yet Johnson was his old animated, compelling self. The crowd rose to its feet, applauded, and then gathered around.[101]

LYNDON JOHNSON BREATHED HIS LAST at 3:50 in the afternoon on January 22, 1973. Fulfilling his worst nightmare, he was alone in his bedroom at the ranch. He called the switchboard and reported that he was in distress. Secret Service agents Ed Newland and Harry Harris rushed to his room with a portable oxygen unit. They found Johnson lying on the floor, not breathing. Newland attempted mouth-to-mouth resuscitation, but it was too late. Lady Bird, who was contacted while driving in her car in Austin, rushed back. At 4:19 Johnson was flown to Brooke Army Medical Center, where shortly after he was pronounced dead.

For the next twenty-four hours, LBJ's body lay in state at the Library, where some twenty thousand people filed by to pay their respects. During the first night of Lyndon's death, while the body was at the Library waiting for the doors to open the next morning, a coterie of old friends watched over the casket. Lady Bird had organized them. "I do not want him to be alone," she said. "Stand with him."[102]

From Austin the body was flown to Washington and transported by the traditional horse-drawn caisson to lie in state in the Capitol Rotunda. Sixty percent of the crowd that lined the route was black. The next morning a memorial service was held at the National City Christian Church. Leontyne Price sang "Take My Hand, Precious Lord." Marvin Watson, oddly enough, delivered the eulogy. He was ours, Watson said, "and we loved him beyond all telling."[103]

Burial day in Texas was bitterly cold but sunny. LBJ was entombed in the family plot on the banks of the Pedernales beneath a canopy of live oak trees. Lady Bird was dignified, composed, vulnerable. Father Schneider and John Connally spoke. "I remember a black man hobbled up," Luci later said. "He was ninety-two years old. I tried to comfort him by telling him my father loved him and his people. 'Ma'am, you don't have to tell me he loved me; he showed he loved me.' "[104] Ralph Ellison, the distinguished black intellectual, spoke for the inarticulate. Spurned by conservatives and cosmopolitan liberals, LBJ, he predicted, would "have to settle for being recognized as the greatest American President for the poor and for the Negroes, but that, as I see it, is a very great honor indeed."[105]

NOTES

ABBREVIATIONS

DDEL—Dwight David Eisenhower Library
DIRNSA—Director, National Security Agency
DSDUF—Declassified and Sanitized Documents from Unprocessed Files
FRUS—*Foreign Relations of the United States*
HSTL—Harry S. Truman Library
JFKL—John F. Kennedy Library
LBJA—Lyndon B. Johnson Archive
LBJL—Lyndon B. Johnson Library
LC—Library of Congress
NA—National Archives
NSC—National Security Council
NSF—National Security Files
NPS—National Park Service, Johnson City, Texas
OF—Office Files
PP—Personal Papers
RBJ—Rebekah Baines Johnson Papers
RG—Record Group
SFRC—Senate Foreign Relations Committee
SOF—Senate Office Files
VP—Vice Presidential
WH—White House
WHCF—White House Central File

Chapter 1: Roots

1. J. O. Tanner Interview, Jan. 15, 1976, National Park Service (hereafter) Oral Histories, Johnson City, Texas.
2. William C. Pool et al., *Lyndon Baines Johnson: The Formative Years* (San Marcos, TX, 1965), 3–5, 8–12.
3. "Johnson Homeplace Constructed in 1800s," *Daily News* (Athens, Georgia), Aug. 3, 1978.
4. Robert Dallek, *Lone Star Rising: Lyndon Johnson and His Times, 1908–1960* (New York, 1991), 14.
5. Ava Cox Interview, Sept. 11, 1975, NPS Oral Histories.
6. Second Interview with Otto Lindig, Mar. 1965, NPS Oral Histories.
7. Ronnie Dugger, *The Politician: From Frontier to Master of the Senate* (New York, 1982), 45.
8. Interview with Ida Felstead, May 7 and May 13, 1976, NPS Oral Histories.
9. Dallek, *Lone Star,* 17.
10. J. Marvin Hunter, *Trail Drivers of Texas* (Bandera, 1924), 362–363.
11. See "The Trail Driver Breed" in Dobie, *Flavor of Texas,* 145–159.

12. Joseph S. Hall, ed., "Horace M. Hall's Letters from Gilespie County, Texas, 1871–1873," *Southwestern Historical Quarterly* 62 (January 1959): 336–337.
13. Rebekah Baines Johnson, *A Family Album* (New York, 1965), 90.
14. Dallek, *Lone Star,* 18.
15. Ida Felsted Interview.
16. Edwin C. Bearss, "Historic Resource Study: Lyndon B. Johnson and the Hill Country 1937–1963" (Santa Fe, NM, 1984), 34–39.
17. Pool et al, *Formative Years,* 17–18.
18. Dallek, *Lone Star,* 16.
19. Otto Lindig Interview; Dallek, *Lone Star,* 18–19; R. Johnson, *Family Album,* 73–74.
20. Bryan R. Wilson, *Sects and Society: A Sociological Study of the Ilim Tabernacle, Christian Science, and Christadelphians* (Berkeley, 1961), 281.
21. Ibid., 286.
22. J. O. Tanner Interview.
23. Dugger, *Politician,* 54, 411; Dallek, *Lone Star,* 20; Bearss, "Hill Country," 51–52.
24. Allen Crider to LBJ, Feb. 10, 1955, Family Correspondence, Johnson, Sam E., Box 1, Johnson Papers, LBJL.
25. Pool et al., *Formative Years,* 22–23; R. Johnson, *Family Album,* 22–23; Dugger, *Politician,* 55.
26. R. Johnson, *Family Album,* 23; Pool, *Formative Years,* 23; Dallek, *Lone Star,* 22.
27. Ida Felton Interview.
28. R. Johnson, *Family Album,* 24.
29. Otto Lindig Interview.
30. Mark E. Young, "Myth versus Reality: The Creation of Lyndon Johnson," unpublished ms. in possession of author, 20–21. Dallek, *Lone Star,* 24.
31. Rebekah Johnson Bobbitt Interview, Mar. 13, 1973, NPS Oral Histories.
32. Dugger, *Politician,* 56.
33. Caro, *Path to Power,* 46–48; Pool et al., *Formative Years,* 25–28; R. Johnson, *Family Album,* 24.
34. Quoted in Dallek, *Lone Star,* 27.
35. "Sam Houston," Apr. 28, 1965, OF/Horace Busby, Box 51, LBJL.
36. R. Johnson, *Family Album,* 91–95; "Rev. George W. Baines, Jr.," *Texas Historical and Biographical Magazine,* Feb. 1965, OF/Horace Busby, Box 52, LBJL.
37. R. Johnson, *Family Album,* 67–68, 75–76.
38. Sam Houston to Lyndon, June 2, 1968, Family Correspondence, Box 2, Johnson Papers, LBJL
39. Ibid.
40. Josepha Baines Saunders Oral History 7, Mar. 4, 1976, NPS Oral Histories.
41. Sam Houston to Lyndon, June 2, 1968, Family Correspondence, Box 2, Johnson Papers, LBJL.
42. Woods Oral History.
43. Josepha Saunders Interview.
44. Woods Oral History.
45. Sam Houston to Lyndon, June 2, 1968, Family Correspondence, Box 2, Johnson Papers, LBJL.
46. Merle Miller, *Lyndon: An Oral Biography* (New York, 1980) 6–7; Dugger, *Politician,* 63.
47. Sam Houston to Lyndon, June 2, 1968, Family Correspondence, Box 2, Johnson Papers, LBJL.
48. Young, "Myth versus Reality," 7–12.
49. Miller, *Lyndon,* 7.
50. Pool et al, *Formative Years,* 25.
51. Press release, n.d., Johnson Birthplace, Reference File, Johnson Papers; Jesse Hatcher Oral History, Mar. 28, 1968, LBJL.
52. Dugger, *Politician,* 64.
53. Dallek, *Lone Star,* 29.
54. Doris Kearns Goodwin, *Lyndon Johnson and the American Dream* (New York, 1976), 24.
55. Otto Lindig Interview.
56. Sherman Birdwell Oral History, Oct. 21, 1970, LBJL.
57. Dugger, *Politician,* 57–59.
58. Pool et al., *Formative Years,* 29.
59. Dallek, *Lone Star,* 25.

Chapter 2: Growing Up

1. Jesse Hatcher Oral History, Mar. 28, 1968, LBJL; Ida Felsted Interview, May 13, 1976, NPS Oral Histories.
2. R. Johnson, *Family Album,* 17.
3. Birth certificate, Aug. 27, 1908, and Amendment to birth certificate, Feb. 2, 1961, Reference File, LBJL; Dallek, *Lone Star,* 30; R. Johnson, *Family Album,* 18.
4. Sam Houston Johnson Oral History, June 23, 1976, LBJL.
5. Ava Cox Interview, Mar. 2, 1978, NPS Oral Histories.
6. Miller, *Lyndon,* 6.
7. Kearns Goodwin, *American Dream,* 27.
8. Dugger, *Politician,* 66.
9. Ava Cox Interview, Jan. 22, 1976, NPS Oral Histories.
10. Ava Johnson Cox and Ohlen Cox Interview, Jan. 22, 1976, NPS Oral Histories.

11. Ava Cox Interview; Rebekah Johnson Bobbitt Interview, Mar. 13, 1973, NPS Oral Histories.
12. Byron Crider Interview, Jan. 16, 1976, NPS Oral Histories.
13. Ava Cox Interview.
14. LBJ–Ronnie Dugger Interview, Dec. 13, 1967, Diary Backup, Box 84, Johnson Papers, LBJL.
15. Miller, *Lyndon,* 10.
16. Kearns Goodwin, *American Dream,* 26–27.
17. Ibid., 27.
18. Woods Oral History.
19. Miller, *Lyndon,* 11.
20. Dallek, *Lone Star,* 34. See also Beulah Johnson Interview, Mar. 21, 1978, NPS Oral Histories.
21. Ava Cox Interview.
22. Kathryn Deadrich Loney Oral History, Jan. 21, 1965, LBJL. See also Stella Johnson Luxcon Leaman Interview, July 20, 1977, NPS Oral Histories.
23. Beulah Johnson Interview.
24. Miller, *Lyndon,* 11.
25. Dallek, *Lone Star,* 35.
26. Ibid.
27. Miller, *Lyndon,* 11.
28. Mamie Klett Interview, Apr. 1, 1976, NPS Oral Histories.
29. Dugger, *Politician,* 71.
30. Ibid.
31. Kitty Clyde Ross Leonard Interview, July 1, 1976, NPS Oral Histories.
32. Mamie Klett Interview.
33. Fritz Koeniger Oral History, Nov. 12, 1981; John Brooks Casparis Oral History, Jan. 7, 1982, LBJL.
34. Larry L. King, "Bringing Up Lyndon," *Texas Monthly,* Jan. 1976.
35. Sam Houston Johnson Oral History, June 23, 1976, LBJL.
36. Sam Houston to Lyndon, June 2, 1968, Family Correspondence, Box 2, Johnson Papers, LBJL.
37. George Reedy Oral History, III, June 7, 1975, LBJL.
38. Fritz Koeniger Oral History.
39. Sam Houston Johnson Interview, July 19, 1978, NPS Oral Histories.
40. Rebekah Bobbitt Interview.
41. Kitty Leonard Interview.
42. Ava and Ohlin Cox Interview.
43. Truman Fawcett Interview, May 1, 1978, NPS Oral Histories.
44. Charles Boatner Oral History, II, May 21, 1969, LBJL.
45. President and Isabelle Shelton Conversation, Mar. 21, 1964, Telephone Transcripts, White House Tapes, LBJL.
46. Ava and Ohlin Cox Interview.
47. Stella Johnson Luxcon Leaman Interview.
48. Pool et al., *Formative Years,* 57.
49. President and Isabelle Shelton Conversation.
50. See G. B. Rosborough to S. P. Brooks, Feb. 9, 1923, Rebekah Baines Johnson (hereafter RBJ) Papers, Box 6, LBJL.
51. Ruth Hunnicut Goddard Interview, April 6, 1976, NPS Oral Histories.
52. Rebekah Bobbitt Interview.
53. Miller, *Lyndon,* 35.
54. Cynthia Brandimarte, "Historic Resources Survey of Johnson City, Texas" (Spring, 1999), NPS.
55. Rebekah Bobbitt Interview.
56. Goddard Interview.
57. Kearns Goodwin, *American Dream,* 25.
58. Roy and Marie Byers Interview, May 24, 1979, NPS Oral Histories.
59. Fritz Koeniger Interview.
60. Ava and Ohlin Cox Interview.
61. Boatner Oral History.
62. Kearns Goodwin, *American Dream,* 24–25.
63. Ibid., 26.
64. Ava and Ohlin Cox Interview.
65. Dugger, *Politician,* 75.
66. President and Isabelle Shelton Conversation, Mar. 24, 1964, Telephone Transcripts, White House Tapes, LBJL.
67. Rebekah Bobbitt Interview.
68. Fawcett Oral History.
69. President and Isabelle Shelton Conversation, Mar. 21, 1964.
70. Boatner Oral History.
71. Sam Houston Johnson Oral History.
72. Dugger, *Politician,* 73; Sam Houston Johnson, *My Brother Lyndon* (New York, 1969), 10.
73. Gerrard Casparis Interview, Feb. 1, 4, and 5, 1976, NPS Oral Histories.
74. Truman Fawcett Interview.
75. Ibid.
76. Ava and Ohlin Cox Interview.

77. Ibid.
78. Dallek, *Lone Star,* 42.
79. Ibid., 43.
80. Ibid.
81. Ibid., 42–43.
82. J. O. Tanner Interview.
83. Louise Edwards Interview, July 22, 1976, Kitty Leonard Interview.
84. Truman Fawcett Interview.
85. Kitty Leonard Interview.
86. Dugger, *Politician,* 75.
87. S. Johnson, *Brother Lyndon,* 6–7.
88. Kearns Goodwin, *American Dream,* 34.
89. Dugger, *Politician,* 77.
90. Ben Crider Oral History, Aug. 1, 1968, LBJL.
91. Dallek, *Lone Star,* 51.
92. Bill and Mabel Stribling Interview, Jan. 30, 1976, NPS Oral Histories.
93. Dugger, *Politician,* 79.
94. Ibid., 78.
95. Pool et al., *Formative Years,* 45.
96. Dorothy Hallman to Otto Lindig, Dec. 8, 1965, Family Correspondence, Box 1, Johnson Papers, LBJL.
97. Dallek, *Lone Star,* 49.
98. Kearns Goodwin, *American Dream,* 39.
99. Pool et al., *Formative Years,* 37; Dugger, *Politician,* 85.
100. Pool et al., *Formative Years,* 37; Kearns Goodwin, *American Dream,* 38–39.
101. Pool et al., *Formative Years,* 37.
102. Dallek, *Lone Star,* 50.
103. Joe B. Frantz, *The Driskill Hotel* (Austin, TX, 1973), 18–19.
104. Mrs. Hugo (Elvira) Klein Interview, July 9, 1976, NPS Oral Histories, Lyndon to Grandmama, Dec. 3, 1920, RBJ Papers, Box 8, LBJL.
105. Rebekah Bobbitt Interview.
106. Dallek, *Lone Star,* 55, President and Ronnie Dugger Conversation, Dec. 13, 1967, Diary Backup, Box 84, LBJL.
107. Norman D. Brown, *Hood, Bonnet, and Little Brown Jug: Texas Politics, 1921–1928* (College Station, TX, 1984), 49–50.
108. Ibid., 50–57.
109. "Patman Cites Klan Fight by President's Father," *Washington Post,* Apr. 1, 1965.
110. S. Johnson, *Brother Lyndon,* 30.
111. Ibid.
112. Brown, *Hood, Bonnett,* 60–61. See also Welly Hopkins Oral History, I, May 11, 1965, LBJL.
113. Dugger, *Politician,* 91.
114. "Patman Cites Klan Fight by President's Father."
115. Roy and Marie Byers Interview.
116. Dugger, *Politician,* 105.
117. S. Johnson, *Brother Lyndon,* 34.
118. Dugger, *Politician,* 91.
119. Sam Johnson to Huffman Baines, Jan. 21, 1923, RBJ Papers, Box 8, LBJL.
120. Dugger, *Politician,* 91.
121. Miller, *Lyndon,* 21.
122. Louise Edwards Interview.
123. Miller, *Lyndon,* 23.
124. Dallek, *Lone Star,* 54.
125. Fawcett Oral History.
126. Louise Edwards Interview.
127. Dugger, *Politician,* 98–99.
128. John Brooks Casparis Oral History, Jan. 7, 1982, LBJL.
129. Louise Edwards Interview.
130. Mamie Klett Interview; Truman Fawcett Interview.
131. Louise Edwards Interview.
132. Ibid.
133. Ruth Crider Interview, Sept. 18, 1975, NPS Oral Histories.
134. Stribling Interview.
135. Louise Edwards Interview.
136. Ibid.
137. Dugger, *Politician,* 76.
138. Marie Fehmer to Horace Busby, Feb. 22, 1965, OF/ Horace Busby, Box 52, LBJL.
139. Ibid.
140. John Casparis Oral History.
141. S. Johnson, *Brother Lyndon,* 11.
142. Kearns Goodwin, *American Dream,* 40–41.

143. Dallek, *Lone Star,* 56.
144. Ibid., 53.
145. Georgia Cammock Edgeworth Oral History, Dec. 17, 1981, LBJL.
146. Louise Edwards Interview.
147. Dugger, *Politician,* 99.

Chapter 3: College

1. Rebekah Baines Johnson to Flora Eckert, July 11, 1922, Family Correspondence, Box 2, LBJL.
2. Woods Oral History.
3. Kearns Goodwin, *American Dream,* 43.
4. J. F. Koeniger Oral History, I, Nov. 12, 1981, LBJL.
5. S. Johnson, *Brother Lyndon,* 21.
6. Ibid., 21–22.
7. Dugger, *Politician,* 101.
8. Ibid.
9. Jesse Hatcher Oral History, May 15, 1975, LBJL.
10. J. F. Koeniger Oral History.
11. Ibid.
12. Lyndon B. Johnson, "I Grew Up Here, I Feel Comfortable Here," *New York Times,* May 8, 1966.
13. J. F. Koeniger Interview.
14. Dugger, *Politician,* 103.
15. S. Johnson, *Brother Lyndon,* 24.
16. Miller, *Lyndon,* 26.
17. Dallek, *Lone Star,* 60.
18. Vernon Whiteside Oral History, Aug. 1, 1985, LBJL.
19. Dugger, *Politician,* 104.
20. Dallek, *Lone Star,* 60.
21. Hatcher Oral History.
22. Dugger, *Politician,* 105.
23. Louise Edwards Interview.
24. Dallek, *Lone Star,* 57.
25. Dugger, *Politician,* 105.
26. Miller, *Lyndon,* 26.
27. Whiteside Oral History.
28. Alfred T. "Boody" Johnson Oral History, Nov. 27, 1979, LBJL.
29. Douglas Cater to Juanita Roberts, Jan. 15, 1965, Diary Backup, Box 12, Johnson Papers, LBJL.
30. Dugger, *Politician,* 106–107; Dallek, *Lone Star,* 60–61; Miller, *Lyndon,* 26–27; Alfred Johnson Oral History.
31. Jesse Hatcher Oral History, May 15, 1975, LBJL.
32. Whiteside Oral History.
33. Pool et al., *Formative Years* 70–71, 79.
34. Vernon Whiteside Oral History, II, Aug. 6, 1985, LBJL.
35. Clayton Stribling Interview, Mar. 20, 1976, NPS Oral Histories.
36. Pool et al., *Formative Years,* 86.
37. Ibid. 84–85.
38. Ibid. 84.
39. Horace Richards Oral History, Dec. 19, 1985, LBJL.
40. Miller, *Lyndon,* 27.
41. Dallek, *Lone Star,* 63.
42. Dugger, *Politician,* 109.
43. Whiteside Oral History, I.
44. Stribling Interview.
45. Stribling Interview, Whiteside Oral History, II.
46. Whiteside Oral History, II.
47. Richards Oral History.
48. Whiteside Oral History II.
49. President and Isabelle Shelton Conversation, Mar. 21, 1964.
50. Dugger, *Politician,* 110.
51. Ibid.
52. Ibid.
53. Stribling Interview.
54. Dallek, *Lone Star,* 71.
55. Pool et al., *Formative Years,* 91.
56. Dugger, *Politician,* 112.
57. Levette J. "Joe" Berry Oral History, Dec. 10, 1985, LBJL.
58. Pool et al., *Formative Years,* 95. See also Willard Deason Oral History, May 7, 1965; Woods Oral History; Whiteside Oral History, II, LBJL.
59. Dugger, *Politician,* 113.
60. Pool et al., *Formative Years,* 101–102; Miller, *Lyndon,* 29.

61. Dugger, *Politician,* 112.
62. Whiteside Oral History, II.
63. Whiteside Oral History, II; Dugger, *Politician,* 112–113; Deason Oral History; Miller, *Lyndon,* 28.
64. Stribling Interview; Mylton "Babe" Kennedy Oral History, May 9, 1980, LBJL; Pool et al., *Formative Years,* 103–105.
65. Richards Oral History.
66. Ibid.; Woods Oral History; Pool et al., *Formative Years,* 105.
67. Whiteside Oral History, II; Alfred Johnson, Woods Oral History.
68. Richards Oral History.
69. Pool et al., *Formative Years,* 108.
70. Richards Oral History.
71. Whiteside Oral History, II; Pool et al., *Formative Years,* 109.
72. Alfred Johnson Oral History.
73. Deason Oral History.
74. Pool et al., *Formative Years,* 109–110.
75. Whiteside Oral History, II.
76. Berry Oral History.
77. Miller, *Lyndon,* 27.
78. Berry Oral History.
79. Richards Oral History.
80. Ibid.
81. Kennedy Oral History.
82. Deason Oral History.
83. Pool et al., *Formative Years,* 97–98.
84. Kearns Goodwin, *American Dream,* 59.
85. Ibid.
86. Alfred Johnson Oral History, I.
87. Dallek, *Lone Star,* 71.
88. "President Started Out as Journalist," *Austin American Statesman,* Feb. 18, 1964.
89. Whiteside Oral History, I.
90. Michael E. Parrish, *Anxious Decades: America in Prosperity and Depression, 1920–1941* (New York, 1992), 208–209.
91. "LBJ at Cotulla," *Houston Post,* Jan. 27, 1964.
92. Dugger, *Politician,* 124.
93. Ibid.
94. Dallek, *Lone Star,* 81; Dugger, *Politician,* 124; S. Johnson, *Brother Lyndon,* 28–29.
95. Alfred Johnson Oral History, I.
96. Ibid., 7–8.
97. Julie Leininger Pycior, *LBJ and Mexican-Americans: The Paradox of Power* (Austin, TX, 1997), 8.
98. Ibid., 7–8.
99. Ibid., 18.
100. Ibid., 18–20; Dugger, *Politician,* 116; Dallek, *Lone Star,* 78–79.
101. Dugger, *Politician,* 116.
102. Miller, *Lyndon,* 33.
103. "LBJ at Cotulla."
104. Miller, *Lyndon,* 33–34.
105. Pycior, *LBJ and Mexican-Americans,* 21.
106. Ibid., 21.
107. Miller, *Lyndon,* 34.
108. Pycior, *LBJ and Mexican-Americans,* 22. See also Donoho to Hays Session, Feb. 19, 1929, LBJA Subj. File, Teacher, Box 73, LBJL.
109. Miller, *Lyndon,* 34.
110. Alfred Johnson Oral History, I.
111. Whiteside Oral History, II.
112. Ibid.
113. Rebekah to Mrs. Biggers, June 15, 1931, LBJA Subject File, Teacher, Box 73, LBJL.
114. Whiteside Oral History, I.
115. Dallek, *Lone Star,* 82.
116. *Ibid.*
117. Kennedy Oral History.
118. Woods Oral History.
119. "The Greatest of Vocations," *College Star* (SWT, San Marcos, Texas), Apr. 18, 1928.
120. Pool et al., *Formative Years,* 123.
121. Ibid., 126.
122. "Vision," *College Star* (SWT, San Marcos, Texas), Feb. 1, 1928.
123. "The Cynic," Collection of LBJ's Editorials, Diary Backup, Box 84, LBJL.
124. Ibid.
125. Ibid.
126. Kennedy Oral History.
127. Welly K. Hopkins Oral History, May 11, 1965, LBJL; Woods Oral History.

128. Mark E. Young, "Myth versus Reality: The Creation of Lyndon Johnson," unpublished ms., 30–31.
129. Hopkins Oral History.

Chapter 4: The Secretary

1. Dugger, *Politician,* 124–125.
2. Rebekah to Mrs. Biggers, June 15, 1931, LBJA Subject File, Teacher, Box 73, LBJL.
3. Lyndon to Uncle George, May 19, 1930, LBJA Subj. File, Teaching Certificates, Box 13, LBJL.
4. Dugger, *Politician,* 125.
5. Ibid.
6. Brown, *Hood, Bonnet,* 428–429.
7. Joseph A. Pratt and Christopher J. Casteneda, *Builders: Herman and George R. Brown* (College Station, TX, 1999), 37.
8. "His Slogan Was: 'Get the Job Done' . . . ," *Houston Press,* Dec. 13, 1963.
9. Miller, *Lyndon,* 36.
10. Pool et al., *Formative Years,* 152–153.
11. Miller, *Lyndon,* 35–36.
12. "Johnson Coached Teams Learned to Work to Win," *Interscholastic League* (Austin, TX), Feb. 1964.
13. Dallek, *Lone Star,* 90.
14. Gene Latimer Oral History, Dec. 12, 1981, LBJL.
15. Luther Jones Oral History, June 13, 1969, LBJL.
16. Miller, *Lyndon,* 36.
17. Pool et al., *Formative Years,* 156–157; Dugger, *Politician,* 126.
18. Latimer Oral History.
19. Willard Deason Oral History, II, Apr. 11, 1969, LBJL; Pool et al., *Formative Years,* 146–148.
20. President and Isabelle Shelton Conversation, Mar. 21, 1965.
21. Miller, *Lyndon,* 38–39.
22. Pool et al., *Formative Years,* 149. See also "Lyndon Quit Teaching for Political Path Up," *Houston Post,* Nov. 26, 1963.
23. Mark E. Young, *"The Political Education of LBJ"* (Ph.D. dissertation, University of Texas 1998), 32.
24. Sam Houston Johnson Oral History, June 15, 1976, LBJL.
25. T. Harry Williams, "Lyndon Johnson and the Art of Biography," *Among Friends of LBJ* (LBJ Library, Austin, TX), July 15, 1978.
26. Miller, *Lyndon,* 37.
27. Felix McKnight Oral History, Oct. 4, 1979; Welly Hopkins Oral History, May 11, 1965, LBJL.
28. Deason Oral History.
29. Kearns Goodwin, *American Dream,* 74.
30. Luther Jones to Eric Goldman, Apr. 6, 1965, (hereafter PP) Luther Jones, Box 1, LBJL.
31. Lyndon to Luther E. Jones, n.d., PP/Luther Jones, Box 1, LBJL.
32. Dallek, *Lone Star* 93.
33. Dugger, *Politician,* 165.
34. Miller, *Lyndon,* 38.
35. Dallek, *Lone Star,* 94; Dugger, *Politician,* 165.
36. Russell M. Brown Oral History, I, Jan. 10, 1978, LBJL.
37. Kearns Goodwin, *American Dream,* 76–77.
38. R. Brown Oral History, I; Sam Houston Johnson Oral History, June 15, 1976; Alfred Johnson Oral History.
39. Lyndon to Luther, Dec. 6, 1931, PP/Luther Jones, Box 1, LBJL.
40. Dallek, *Lone Star,* 97.
41. Lyndon to Rebekah, Dec. 9, 1931, Family Correspondence, Box 1, LBJL.
42. Latimer Oral History.
43. Lyndon to L.E., Apr. 18, 1932, PP/Luther Jones, Box 1, LBJL.
44. Brown Oral History, I; Luther E. Jones to Eric Goldman, Apr. 6, 1965, PP/L. Jones, Box 1, LBJL; Dallek, *Lone Star,* 100–101.
45. Kearns Goodwin, *American Dream,* 79–80; Miller, *Lyndon,* 40.
46. Jones Oral History.
47. Robert M. Jackson Oral History, April 5, 1965, LBJL.
48. Dallek, *Lone Star,* 98.
49. Dallek, *Lone Star,* 101.
50. Brown Oral History.
51. Lyndon to Mr. and Mrs. Latimer, June 21, 1933, PP/Gene Latimer, Box 1, LBJ.
52. Jones Oral History; Latimer Oral History.
53. Miller, *Lyndon,* 40.
54. Sam Houston Johnson Oral History; Dallek, *Lone Star,* 102.
55. Brown Oral History.
56. Russell M. Brown Oral History, Jan. 10, 1978, LBJL.
57. Mamie to Lyndon, Tuesday and Wednesday, 1932, Pre-Presidential Confidential File, Box 2, Johnson Papers, LBJL.
58. Ibid.; Sam Houston Johnson Oral History.
59. Sam Houston Johnson Oral History.

60. Brown Oral History.
61. Jackson Oral History.
62. L. E. Jones Oral History, II.
63. Dugger, *Politician,* 168, Brown Oral History, I.
64. Dugger, *Politician,* 168.
65. Ibid.
66. "Remarks at the Dedication of the Morgantown, W.Va., Airport," Sept. 20, 1964, in *Public Papers of the Presidents, Lyndon B. Johnson, 1964,* Vol. 1 (Washington, D.C., 1965), 586.
67. Brown Oral History, I.
68. Dallek, *Lone Star,* 105.
69. Miller, *Lyndon,* 41.
70. Dugger, *Politician,* 168–169.
71. Brown Oral History, I.
72. Dallek, *Lone Star,* 111.
73. Paul Conkin, *Big Daddy from the Pedernales: Lyndon B. Johnson* (Boston, 1986), 69–70; Young, "Political Education of LBJ," 38.
74. Dallek, *Lone Star,* 104.
75. Brown Oral History, I.
76. Dugger, *Politician,* 169.
77. Miller, *Lyndon,* 42.
78. Dugger, *Politician,* 172; Dallek, *Lone Star,* 107.
79. Brown Oral History, I.
80. Dugger, *Politician,* 173.
81. Brown Oral History, I.
82. Dallek, *Lone Star,* 108–109.
83. Alfred Steinberg, *Sam Johnson's Boy: A Close-up of the President from Texas* (New York, 1968), 76.
84. Horace Busby Oral History, I, Apr. 23, 1981, LBJL.
85. Steinberg, *Sam Johnson's Boy,* 76.
86. Ibid., 78.
87. Miller, *Lyndon,* 48.
88. Ibid.; Dugger, *Politician,* 73; Dallek, *Lone Star,* 112.
89. L. E. Jones Oral History, II.
90. Brown Oral History, I.
91. Ibid.
92. Al Philip Kane to Russell Morton Brown, Mar. 27, 1980, Brown Oral History, LBJL.

Chapter 5: Lady Bird and the NYA

1. Steinberg, *Sam Johnson's Boy,* 83.
2. Cameron and Lucille McElroy Oral History, Mar. 11, 1981, LBJL.
3. Kearns Goodwin, *American Dream,* 85.
4. Jan Jarboe Russell, *Lady Bird: A Biography of Mrs. Johnson* (New York, 1999), 29.
5. McElroy Oral History.
6. Ibid.
7. Jarboe Russell, *Lady Bird,* 49.
8. Ibid. 48.
9. Ibid., 51. Lady Bird claimed that she received the nickname from her black nurse, Alice T. Hie. Ibid.
10. Lewis L. Gould, *Lady Bird Johnson and the Environment* (Lawrence, KS, 1988) 8.
11. See *T. J. Taylor* vs *Minnie L. Taylor,* July 1909–Feb. 1911, Records of Calhoun and Harrison Counties, Texas, Furnished to author by Lewis Gould.
12. Steinberg, *Sam Johnson's Boy,* 85; Jarboe Russell, *Lady Bird,* 54–55.
13. Jarboe Russell, *Lady Bird,* 42.
14. Steinberg, *Sam Johnson's Boy,* 87.
15. Jarboe Russell, *Lady Bird,* 63.
16. Ibid., 60.
17. Ibid., 68.
18. Gould, *Lady Bird and Environment,* 9.
19. Ibid., 10.
20. Jarboe Russell, *Lady Bird,* 82.
21. Ibid.
22. Ibid., 90.
23. Gould, *Lady Bird and Environment,* 21.
24. Steinberg, *Sam Johnson's Boy,* 82.
25. Lady Bird Johnson Interview, Mar. 29–Apr. 2, 1993, NPS Oral Histories; Dugger, *Politician,* 176–177.
26. Jarboe Russell, *Lady Bird,* 93.
27. Ibid., 102.
28. Lady Bird Johnson Interview; Jarboe Russell, *Lady Bird,* 93–94; Dugger, *Politician,* 177.
29. Dugger, *Politician,* 178.
30. Lady Bird Johnson Interview; Gould, *Lady Bird and Environment,* 12.

31. Jarboe Russell, *Lady Bird,* 105.
32. Ibid.
33. LBJ to Bird, Sept. 18, 1934, "Love Letters," Reference File, LBJL.
34. Lady Bird to Lyndon, Sept. 17, 1934, "Love Letters," Reference File, LBJ.
35. LBJ to Bird, Sept. 18, 1934, "Love Letters," Reference File, LBJL.
36. Dugger, *Politician,* 179.
37. Bird to LBJ, Oct. 1, 1934, "Love Letters," Reference File, LBJL.
38. Jarboe Russell, *Lady Bird,* 108.
39. Ibid.
40. Ibid.
41. Bird to LBJ, Sept. 24, 1934, "Love Letters," Reference File, LBJL.
42. Jarboe Russell, *Lady Bird,* 110.
43. Luther E. Jones Oral History, II, Oct. 14, 1977, LBJL.
44. Bird to LBJ, Oct. 22, 1934, "Love Letters," Reference File, LBJL.
45. Jarboe Russell, *Lady Bird,* 111–112.
46. T. J. Taylor to Ida McKay, Nov. 23, 1934; *U.S. News and World Report,* Feb. 15, 1965.
47. Jarboe Russell, *Lady Bird,* 19.
48. Miller, *Lyndon,* 44–45.
49. Steinberg, *Sam Johnson's Boy,* 89.
50. Dugger, *Politician,* 181.
51. Jarboe Russell, *Lady Bird,* 20.
52. Ibid., 25.
53. Clifford and Virginia Durr Oral History, I, Mar. 1, 1975, LBJL.
54. Jarboe Russell, *Lady Bird,* 20.
55. Lady Bird Johnson Interview.
56. John Chancellor Oral History, I, Apr. 25, 1969, LBJL.
57. Gould, *Lady Bird and Environment,* 12.
58. Jarboe Russell, *Lady Bird,* 113–115.
59. Lyndon to Rebekah, 1935, Family Correspondence, Box 1, Johnson Papers, LBJL.
60. Rebekah to Children, Nov. 30, 1934, Family Correspondence, Box 1, Johnson Papers, LBJL.
61. Miller, *Lyndon,* 45.
62. Jarboe Russell, *Lady Bird,* 120.
63. Ibid., 124.
64. Ibid., 126.
65. Richard B. Henderson, *Maury Maverick: A Political Biography* (Austin, TX, 1970), 43.
66. Ibid., 62.
67. Ibid., 66.
68. Ibid., 65.
69. W. Ervin "Red" James Oral History, Feb. 17, 1978, LBJL.
70. D. B. Hardeman Oral History, IV, Jan. 19, 1977, LBJL.
71. Durr Oral History, II; W. E. James Oral History; Miller, *Lyndon,* 53.
72. Dallek, *Lone Star,* 125–127.
73. Dugger, *Politician,* 185.
74. Ibid.
75. Christie Lynn Bourgeois, "Lyndon Johnson's Years with the National Youth Administration" (M.A. thesis, University of Texas, 1984), 30–31.
76. Deason Oral History.
77. Ibid.; Bourgeois, "Johnson's Years with the NYA," 22–23.
78. Sherman Birdwell Oral History, III, Feb. 9, 1979, LBJL.
79. Dugger, *Politician,* 185.
80. Charles P. Little Oral History, II, July 24, 1978, LBJL.
81. Birdwell Oral History.
82. Ibid.
83. Deason Oral History.
84. Dallek, *Lone Star,* 131.
85. Sam Houston Johnson Oral History, Apr. 14, 1974, LBJL.
86. Deason Oral History. See also Deborah Lynn Self, "The National Youth Administration in Texas, 1935–39" (M.A. thesis, Texas Tech University, 1974), 54–60.
87. Deason Oral History, II.
88. Birdwell Oral History.
89. Ibid.
90. Dallek, *Lone Star,* 134.
91. Deason Oral History.
92. Birdwell Oral History.
93. Dallek, *Lone Star,* 135; Deason Oral History, V.
94. Jones Oral History; Deason Oral History.
95. Dallek, *Lone Star,* 136; Parrish, *Anxious Decades,* 395–397.
96. Parrish, *Anxious Decades,* 395–397.
97. Busby Oral History, V.
98. LBJ to John Corson, Sept. 22, 1935, LBJA, NYA, Box 73, LBJL, Miller, *Lyndon,* 56.

99. Quoted in Dallek, *Lone Star,* 135–136.
100. Miller, *Lyndon,* 56.
101. Ibid.
102. LBJ to John Corson, Sept. 22, 1935, LBJA, NYA, Box 73, LBJL.
103. Birdwell Oral History.
104. Ibid.
105. Deason Oral History, IV.
106. LBJ to W. K. Hopkins, Apr. 6, 1936, PP/Welly Hopkins, Box 1, LBJL.
107. Dugger, *Politician,* 189.
108. Rebekah to Lyndon, June 2, 1938, Family Correspondence, Box 1, LBJL.
109. Jarboe Russell, *Lady Bird,* 118–119.
110. Quoted in Dallek, *Lone Star,* 142.

Chapter 6: Congress

1. Steinberg, *Sam Johnson's Boy,* 105; Dugger, *Politician,* 190.
2. Kearns Goodwin, *American Dream,* 90.
3. Miller, *Lyndon,* 58; Dallek, *Lone Star,* 144; Deason Oral History, I, May 7, 1965, LBJL.
4. "Many Enriched by Wirtz Dream," *Houston Post,* Nov. 11, 1951; Steinberg, *Sam Johnson's Boy,* 104–105; Welly Hopkins Oral History, III, June 9, 1977, LBJL.
5. LBJ to Wirtz, Dec. 22, 1939, LBJA Selected Name File, Wirtz, Box 36, LBJL.
6. Mary Rather Oral History, II, Nov. 13, 1975, LBJL.
7. Hopkins Oral History.
8. Clifford and Virginia Durr Oral History, Mar. 1, 1975, LBJL.
9. Hopkins Oral History.
10. Steinberg, *Sam Johnson's Boy,* 102.
11. Durr Oral History.
12. Deason Oral History.
13. Steinberg, *Sam Johnson's Boy,* 106.
14. Dugger, *Politician,* 191.
15. Ibid., 192–193.
16. L. E. Jones Oral History, I, June 13, 1969, LBJL.
17. Dallek, *Lone Star,* 146–147.
18. Jones Oral History, I.
19. Dallek, *Lone Star,* 147.
20. Kari A. Frederickson, *The Dixiecrat Revolt and the End of the Solid South, 1932–1968* (Chapel Hill, NC, 2001), 16.
21. Jane S. Smallwood, *The Great Recovery: The New Deal in Texas* (Boston, 1983), 6,11.
22. Quoted in Brown, *Hood, Bonnet,* 429.
23. Frederickson, *Dixiecrat Revolt,* 17.
24. Young, "The Political Education of LBJ," 42.
25. Young, "Political Education of LBJ," 46–47.
26. Paul Bolton Oral History, I, April 6, 1981, LBJL.
27. Miller, *Lyndon,* 59.
28. Kearns Goodwin, *American Dream,* 91.
29. John B. Connally with Mickey Hershowitz, *In History's Shadow: An American Odyssey* (New York, 1993), 68–69.
30. L. E. Jones Oral History, I, June 13, 1969, LBJL.
31. Welly Hopkins to Charles West, Mar. 10, 1937, PP/Welly Hopkins, Box 1, LBJL.
32. Steinberg, *Sam Johnson's Boy,* 111.
33. Dugger, *Politician,* 196.
34. Wilton Woods Oral History, II, Apr. 20, 1982, LBJL.
35. Sherman Birdwell Oral History, I, Apr. 1965, LBJL.
36. Miller, *Lyndon,* 60.
37. Bolton Oral History, Apr. 6, 1981, LBJL.
38. *Austin American,* Mar. 1, 1937; *Austin Statesman,* Mar. 12, 1937.
39. Dugger, *Politician,* 197.
40. Ibid., 195.
41. Dallek, *Lone Star,* 153.
42. Dugger, *Politician,* 195–196.
43. J. F. Koeniger Oral History, I, Nov. 12, 1981, LBJL.
44. *Austin American,* April 6, 1937.
45. Dugger, *Politician,* 197.
46. Birdwell Oral History.
47. Sam Fore Jr. Oral History, Jan. 20, 1965, LBJL.
48. Dallek, *Lone Star,* 155.
49. Willard Deason Oral History, May 7, 1965, LBJL; Steinberg, *Sam Johnson's Boy,* 117–119; Dugger, *Politician,* 202–203.
50. Dallek, *Lone Star,* 161.
51. Charles P. Little Oral History, II, July 24, 1978, LBJL.

52. Dugger, *Politician,* 202; Steinberg, *Sam Johnson's Boy,* 120.
53. Miller, *Lyndon,* 63.
54. "Johnson Sworn In," *Dallas Morning News,* May 14, 1937.
55. Birdwell Oral History, I.
56. Rowland Evans and Robert Novak, *Lyndon B. Johnson: The Exercise of Power* (New York, 1966), 18.
57. Durr Oral History.
58. Miller, *Lyndon,* 64.
59. Michael Janeway, *The Fall of the House of Roosevelt: Brokers of Ideas and Power from FDR to LBJ* (New York, 2004), x–xii.
60. Stella Johnson Luxcon Leaman Interview, July 20, 1977, NPS Oral Histories; Gene to Bunny, Sept. 24, 1937, Pre-Presidential Confidential File, Box 2, LBJL.
61. Dugger, *Politician,* 204; Miller, *Lyndon,* 22.
62. Dugger, *Politician,* 204–205.
63. Ibid., 205.
64. Russell M. Brown Oral History, I, Jan. 10, 1978, LBJL.
65. Parrish, *Anxious Decades,* 305.
66. Durr Oral History.
67. D. B. Hardeman Oral History, IV, Jan. 19, 1977, LBJL.
68. "Johnson and Rayburn: The 1950s. An Era of Congressional Government," in *The Presidency and the Congress,* ed. William S. Livingston et al. (Austin, 1979), 227–251.
69. Hardeman Oral History.
70. Steinberg, *Sam Johnson's Boy,* 135.
71. Gene to Chief, May 31, 1938, Pre-Presidential Confidential File, Box 2, LBJL.
72. J. F. Koeniger Oral History; "In the beginning . . ." n.d. PP/Dorothy Nichols, Box 1, LBJL.
73. Dallek, *Lone Star,* 186.
74. Walter Jenkins Oral History, IV, May 13, 1982, LBJL.
75. W. E. James Oral History, I, Feb. 17, 1978, LBJL.
76. Dallek, *Lone Star,* 187.
77. Ibid.
78. James Reston Jr., *The Lone Star: The Life of John Connally* (New York, 1989), 40–45.
79. Miller, *Lyndon,* 69–70.
80. Ibid.
81. Connally, *History's Shadow,* 52–54.
82. Miller, *Lyndon,* 70–71. See also Herbert Henderson to Gordon Fulcher, Apr. 29, 1939, LBJA Selected Names File, Gordon Fulcher, Box 18, LBJL.
83. See LBJ to Gordon Fulcher, Feb. 7, 1938, LBJA Selected Names File, Gordon Fulcher, Box 18, LBJL.
84. Dugger, *Politician,* 209.
85. Miller, *Lyndon,* 69. See also Arthur Goldschmidt and Everett Looney Conversation, Sept. 15, 1939, PP/Arthur Goldschmidt, Lower Colorado River Authority (hereafter LCRA), Box 1, LBJL.
86. LBJ to Mr. President, July 29, 1939, Papers of Rebekah Johnson, Box 8, LBJL.
87. Arthur Goldschmidt and Elizabeth Wickenden Oral History I, June 3, 1969, LBJL.
88. LBJ to A. J. Wirtz, Aug. 13, 1937, LBJA Selected Names, Wirtz, Box 36, LBJL.
89. Dallek, *Lone Star,* 176.
90. Joseph A. Pratt and Christopher J. Castaneda, *Builders: Herman and George R. Brown* (College Station, TX, 1999), 62.
91. "Mirrors of Austin," (Austin, TX) *State Observer,* June 10, 1940.
92. Walter Jenkins Oral History.
93. Connally, *History's Shadow,* 69.
94. Jarboe Russell, *Lady Bird,* 127–128.
95. Ibid.
96. Connally, *History's Shadow,* 69.
97. Jarboe Russell, *Lady Bird,* 131.
98. Ibid.
99. Jarboe Russell, *Lady Bird,* 129.
100. James Rowe Oral History, Sept. 9, 1969, LBJL.
101. Jarboe Russell, *Lady Bird,* 131.

Chapter 7: Pappy

1. Dallek, *Lone Star,* 164–165.
2. Steinberg, *Sam Johnson's Boy,* 138.
3. Ibid.
4. Dugger, *Politician,* 221.
5. J. F. Koeniger Oral History, II, Nov. 17, 1981, LBJL.
6. Dallek, *Lone Star,* 169–170.
7. Ibid, 170.
8. Chandler Davidson, *Race and Class in Texas Politics* (Princeton, NJ, 1990), 64–111.
9. Jerry Flemons, *Amon: The Life of Amon Carter, Sr. of Texas* (Austin, Tx, 1978), 225–226.
10. Davidson, *Race and Class in Texas Politics,* 111–115.

11. Quoted in Janeway, *House of Roosevelt,* 146.
12. Davidson, *Race and Class in Texas Politics,* 27.
13. Ibid, 34.
14. Ibid, 35.
15. E. Parrish, *Anxious Decades,* 330.
16. Dallek, *Lone Star,* 192.
17. Steinberg, *Sam Johnson's Boy,* 145.
18. Ibid, 140.
19. Dallek, *Lone Star,* 193.
20. Ibid., 195.
21. Steinberg, *Sam Johnson's Boy,* 149.
22. Dallek, *Lone Star,* 199.
23. Ibid., 199.
24. Dugger, *Politician,* 224; Young, "Political Education of LBJ," 60.
25. "Rep. Lyndon Johnson Stepped in and Prevented G.O.P. Landslide," *Dallas Morning News,* Nov. 11, 1941.
26. Dugger, *Politician,* 34.
27. Dallek, *Lone Star,* 201.
28. Miller, *Lyndon,* 76.
29. Dallek, *Lone Star,* 205.
30. Ibid. 205.
31. D. B. Hardeman Oral History, Feb. 26, 1969, LBJL.
32. Steinberg, *Sam Johnson's Boy,* 155.
33. Miller, *Lyndon,* 81.
34. Willard Deason Oral History, III, Apr. 11, 1969, LBJL.
35. On the genuineness of Johnson's misgivings, see Alvin Wirtz to Carl White, Apr. 12, 1941, LBJA Selected Names File, Wirtz, Box 37, LBJL.
36. Dugger, *Politician,* 226.
37. Dallek, *Lone Star,* 309.
38. "F.D.R. Picks Johnson to Defeat Dies," *Dallas Morning News,* Mar. 23, 1941.
39. Steinberg, *Sam Johnson's Boy,* 161.
40. Ibid., 160–161; Dallek, *Lone Star,* 210–211.
41. J. J. "Jake" Pickle Oral History, May 3, 1970, LBJL.
42. James Reston Jr., *The Lone Star: The Life of John Connally* (New York, 1989), 59.
43. " 'Strikes Real Danger Here,' Johnson Says," *Dallas Morning News,* May 4, 1941.
44. Jake Pickle Oral History, I, May 31, 1970, LBJL; "Johnson for Starting Full Pension at 60," *Johnson City Record-Courier,* June 2, 1941.
45. Dallek, *Lone Star,* 212.
46. Steinberg, *Sam Johnson's Boy,* 164.
47. Ibid., 157.
48. Dallek, *Lone Star,* 1.
49. Miller, *Lyndon,* 83.
50. Connally, *History's Shadow,* 108.
51. Ibid.
52. Ibid.
53. Dallek, *Lone Star,* 214.
54. Marsh to Fulcher, PP/C. Marsh, Box 2, LBJL.
55. Marsh to Fentress, Feb. 13, 1941, PP/C. Marsh, Box 20, LBJL.
56. Memo to L.B.J., Jan. 8, 1941, PP/C. Marsh, LBJL.
57. This is a note on the letter on manic-depressives, n.d., 1941, PP/C. Marsh, Box 2, LBJL.
58. J. Willis Hurst Oral History II, Oct. 31, 1970, LBJL.
59. D. B. Hardeman Oral History, I, Feb. 26, 1969; Notes on telephone call; Wirtz, Young, Marsh, Apr. 11, 1941, PP/C. Marsh, Box 2, LBJL.
60. Dugger, *Politician,* 228.
61. Dallek, *Lone Star,* 216.
62. Dugger, *Politician,* 229.
63. Dallek, *Lone Star,* 216.
64. "Johnson Leads in Campaign Contributions," *Dallas Morning News,* June 27, 1941.
65. George Brown Oral History, I, LBJL.
66. Marsh to Fentress, Feb. 13, 1941, PP/C. Marsh, Box 20, LBJL.
67. Ibid.
68. Marsh to Fentress, Feb. 14, 1941, PP/C. Marsh, Box 20, LBJL.
69. Steinberg, *Sam Johnson's Boy,* 164.
70. Dallek, *Lone Star,* 214.
71. Miller, *Lyndon,* 88.
72. Dugger, *Politician,* 230.
73. Dallek, *Lone Star,* 219.
74. Dugger, *Politician,* 230.
75. Ibid.
76. Ibid., 232.

77. See. Welly K. Hopkins to Lyndon, Apr. 29, 1949; C. W. Dickinson to David J. McDonald, Steel Workers Organizing Committee, June 11, 1941, Papers and Welly Hopkins Box 6, LBJA.
78. Miller, *Lyndon,* 83–84; Dallek, *Lone Star,* 217–218.
79. Dallek, *Lone Star,* 220.
80. "Lyndon Johnson Elected Senator," *Dallas Morning News,* July 2, 1941.
81. John Connally, "In Search of LBJ," in Robert L. Hardesty ed., *The Johnson Years: The Difference He Made* (Austin, TX. 1993) 138; James Blundell Oral History, I, Oct. 29, 1974, LBJL.
82. Joe Frantz Oral History, I, Sept. 7, 1972, LBJL.
83. Dallek, *Lone Star,* 222.
84. Horace Busby Oral History, IV, July 29, 1988, LBJL.
85. John Singleton Oral History, I, July 5, 1983, LBJL.
86. Dallek, *Lone Star,* 223.
87. Marsh to Fentress, July 2, 1941, PP/C. Marsh, Box 20, LBJL.
88. Walter Jenkins Oral History, I, August 14, 1970, LBJL.
89. Dallek, *Lone Star,* 260.
90. Steinberg, *Sam Johnson's Boy,* 181–182; Dugger, *Politician,* 235.
91. Miller, *Lyndon,* 88.
92. Ibid.
93. Dugger, *Politician,* 235.
94. Ibid.
95. Brown, *Hood, Bonnet,* 430.
96. See, for example, Southern Political Situations, Feb. 2, 1948, PP of Charles E. Marsh, Box 22. LBJL.
97. "That American Spirit . . . ," *Austin American Statesman,* April 2, 1941.
98. Speech draft, n.d., 1941, PP/C. Marsh, Box 2, LBJL.

Chapter 8: War

1. Jarboe Russell, *Lady Bird,* 135.
2. Ibid., 134.
3. Quoted in Howard Jones, *The Course of American Diplomacy* (New York, 1985), 363.
4. Dallek, *Lone Star,* 220.
5. Steinberg, *Sam Johnson's Boy,* 186.
6. Miller, *Lyndon,* 89.
7. Steinberg, *Sam Johnson's Boy,* 188.
8. Marsh to Lyndon, Oct. 13, 1941, PP/C. Marsh, Box 2, LBJL; LBJ to Connally, Nov. 7, 1941, LBJA Selected Names File, Connally, Box 15, LBJL.
9. Connally to Johnson, Nov. 25, 1941, and LBJ to Connally, Nov. 27, 1941, LBJA Selected Names File, Connally, Box 15, LBJL.
10. LBJ to Sam Houston, Nov. 19, 1941, Family Correspondence Box 2, LBJL.
11. Lyndon to Albertine, Nov. 5, 1941, Family Correspondence, Box 2, LBJL.
12. Mother to Lyndon, Nov. 17, 1941, and Lyndon to Mother, Nov. 5, 1941, Family Correspondence, Box 1, LBJL.
13. Charles K. Boatner Oral History, Dec. 17, 1968, LBJL.
14. LBJ to President, Dec. 8, 1941, LBJA Subject File, Naval Career, Box 73, LBJL.
15. Connally to Johnson, Jan. 9, 1942, LBJA Selected Names File, Connally, Box 15, LBJL.
16. Lady Bird to Uncle Sterling and Aunt Lucy, Feb. 27, 1942, Papers of Rebekah Johnson, Box 8, LBJL.
17. LBJ to Under Secretary of the Navy, Apr. 30, 1942, LBJA Subject File, Naval Career, Box 73, LBJL.
18. Dallek, *Lone Star,* 232.
19. Ibid.
20. Ibid.
21. Marsh to Hofheinz, Mar. 13, 1942, PP/C. Marsh, Box 2, LBJL.
22. "Johnson Due to Enter Senate Race," *Dallas Morning News,* May 13, 1942.
23. A. J. Wirtz to Lady Bird, May 16, 1942, LBJA Name File, Wirtz, Box 37, LBJL.
24. Marsh to Lyndon, May 20, 1942, PP/C. Marsh, Box 2, LBJL.
25. Marsh to Lyndon, May 21, 1942, PP/C. Marsh, Box 2, LBJL.
26. Lady Bird to Uncle Sterling and Aunt Lucy, Feb. 27, 1942, Papers of Rebekah B. Johnson, Box 8, LBJL.
27. Lady Bird to Ella Powell, Apr. 13, 1942, LBJA Subj. File, Mrs. Johnson, Box 74, LBJL.
28. Lady Bird Johnson Interview.
29. Marsh letter of Dec. 17, 1941, PP/C. Marsh, Box 2, LBJL.
30. Marsh to Lyndon, Apr. 21, 1942, PP/C. Marsh, Box 2, LBJL.
31. LBJ Chronologies, 1937–1954, LBJL.
32. Dugger, *Politician,* 241–242.
33. Dallek, *Lone Star,* 235.
34. LBJ Chronologies, 1937–1954, LBJL.
35. Marsh to Lyndon, n.d., 1941, PP/C. Marsh, Box 2, LBJL.
36. LBJ Chronologies, 1937–1954, LBJL.
37. Dallek, *Lone Star,* 237.
38. Ibid., 217–218.
39. War Diary, June 5–26, 1942, LBJA Subject File, Naval Career, Box 73, LBJL.

40. Miller, *Lyndon,* 96.
41. Martin Caidin and Edward Hymoff, *The Mission* (Philadelphia, 1964), 124–125.
42. Ibid., 133.
43. Ibid., 146–147.
44. Ibid., 161.
45. Walter Gayle to LBJ, July 10, 1964, LBJA Subject File, Award of Silver Star, Box 74, LBJL.
46. War Diary, June 5–26, 1942, LBJA Subject File, Box 73, LBJL.
47. Caidin and Hymoff, Mission, 128.
48. LBJ to W. L. White, Feb. 8, 1943, LBJA Subject File, Naval Career, Box 73, LBJL.
49. War Diary, June 5–26, 1942, LBJA Subject File, Naval Career, Box 73, LBJL.
50. Lady Bird to Mrs. Johnson, June 14, 1942, Family Correspondence, Box 1, LBJL.
51. Quoted in Dallek, *Lone Star,* 240.
52. War Diary, June 5–26, LBJA Subject File, Naval Career, LBJL.
53. Award of the Silver Star, June 18, 1942, LBJA Subject File, Naval Career, Box 73, LBJL.
54. LBJ to Adjutant General, July 15, 1942, LBJA Subject File, Award of Silver Star, Box 74, LBJL.
55. Dallek, *Lone Star,* 241.
56. Ibid., 240.
57. Ibid., 242.
58. "I did not find . . . ," n.d., 1942, LBJA Subject File, Naval Career, Box 73, LBJL.
59. Dallek, *Lone Star,* 244.
60. John Morton Blum, *V was for Victory: Politics and American Culture During World War II* (New York, 1976), 5–6, 12–13, 117–121.
61. Dallek, *Lone Star,* 245–246, 252–253.
62. James H. Rowe Jr. Oral History, May 10, 1983, LBJL.
63. R. M. Brown Oral History, I, Jan. 10, 1978, LBJL.
64. Reston, *Lone Star,* 85.
65. Jarboe Russell, *Lady Bird,* 145.
66. Steinberg, *Sam Johnson's Boy,* 201–202; "The Johnson Wealth," *Wall Street Journal,* Mar. 23, 1964.
67. Clifford and Virginia Durr Oral History, II, Mar. 1, 1975, LBJL.
68. Paul Bolton Oral History, I, Apr. 6, 1981, LBJL; Miller, *Lyndon,* 107.
69. George Reedy Oral History, VIII, Aug. 16, 1983, LBJL.
70. Miller, *Lyndon,* 108.
71. LBJ to Weedin, Nov. 5, 1945, LBJA Selected Names File, Harfield Weedin, Box 22, LBJL; Dallek, *Lone Star,* 230.
72. Miller, *Lyndon,* 108.
73. Ibid.; Dallek, *Lone Star,* 230; LBJ to Rebekah, Apr. 16, 1943, Family Correspondence, Box 1, LBJL.
74. Dugger, *Politician,* 271.
75. Dallek, *Lone Star,* 251.
76. Rowe Oral History.
77. Jarboe Russell, *Lady Bird,* 152.
78. Ibid., 147.
79. Ibid., 148.
80. LBJ to Gene, Dec. 16, 1943, Pre-Presidential Confidential File, Box 2, LBJL.
81. Miller, *Lyndon,* 103.
82. Jarboe Russell, *Lady Bird,* 151.
83. Dallek, *Lone Star,* 256.
84. Dugger, *Politician,* 259–260.
85. Davidson, *Race and Class in Texas,* 139.
86. Ibid., 160–161.
87. Mr. and Mrs. C. W. Webb to LBJ, June 8, 1943, PP/Emma Webb, Box 1, LBJL.
88. Miller, *Lyndon,* 102.
89. Dallek, *Lone Star,* 260.
90. Wirtz to Watson, May 29, 1944, PP/James C. Cain, Box 1, LBJL.
91. Steinberg, *Sam Johnson's Boy,* 212.
92. Ibid., 212–213.
93. Ibid., 213.
94. Wirtz to Watson, May 29, 1944, PP/James C. Cain, Box 1, LBJL.
95. Steinberg, *Sam Johnson's Boy,* 217–218; John Connally in Hardesty, *The Johnson Years,* 142–143.

Chapter 9: Truman and the Coming of the Cold War

1. *New York Times,* Apr. 13, 1945.
2. Dugger, *Politician,* 263.
3. Quoted in Janeway, *House of Roosevelt,* 38.
4. Miller, *Lyndon,* 105.
5. Ibid.
6. Virginia "Jerry" Wilkie English Oral History, Mar. 3, 1982, LBJL.
7. Donald C. Cook Oral History, June 30, 1969, LBJL.
8. Ibid.
9. Dallek, *Lone Star,* 274.

10. Donald C. Cook Oral History, June 30, 1969, LBJL.
11. Quoted in Janeway, *House of Roosevelt,* 77.
12. Janeway, *House of Roosevelt,* 61.
13. Quoted in Jones, *American Diplomacy,* 42.
14. *Congressional Record,* 1946, 79th Congress, 2nd sess., A877-28; Dallek, *Lone Star,* 275.
15. Dallek, *Lone Star,* 291–292.
16. "Cong. Johnson Pledges Marshall Plan Support," *Austin American,* Sept. 30, 1947.
17. Dallek, *Lone Star,* 295.
18. Johnson to Wirtz, Apr. 29, 1947, LBJA Selected Names File, Wirtz, Box 37, LBJL.
19. LBJ to A. J. Reinhard, Aug. 27, 1942, LBJA Selected Names File, Connally, Box 15, LBJL.
20. Pratt and Casteneda, *Builders,* 142–143.
21. Wirtz to Johnson, Feb. 6, 1948, LBJA Selected Names File, Wirtz, Box 37, LBJL.
22. Janeway, *House of Roosevelt,* 150.
23. Dallek, *Lone Star,* 276–277.
24. Quoted in Randall B. Woods, *Quest for Identity: America since 1945* (New York, 2005), 17.
25. Lady Bird Johnson Interview.
26. For Marsh's views on race and politics in the South, see Marsh to LBJ, Feb. 2, 1948, PP/Charles E. Marsh, Box 22, LBJL.
27. Wirtz to Johnson, Feb. 6, 1948, LBJA Selected Names File, Wirtz, Box 37, LBJL.
28. Ibid.
29. Lady Bird Johnson Interview.
30. See LBJ to Paul Bolton, July 21, 1949, LBJA Selected Names File, Bolton, Box 12, LBJL.
31. Randall B. Woods, *Fulbright: A Biography* (New York, 1995), 116–117.
32. Charles Boatner Interview, June 5, 1979, NPS Oral Histories.
33. Horace Busby Oral History, IV, July 29, 1988, LBJL.
34. Horace Busby Oral History, V, Aug. 16, 1988, LBJL.
35. John L. Bullion, *In the Boat with LBJ* (Plano, TX, 2001), 19–20.
36. Albert D'Errico to G. W. Wentz, July 9, 1946, Family Correspondence, Box 2, LBJL.
37. G. M. Vincent to LBJ, Jan. 10, 1945, Family Correspondence, Box 2, LBJL.
38. LBJ to Albertine, Mar. 13, 1946, Family Correspondence, Box 2, LBJL.
39. Dallek, *Lone Star,* 278–279.
40. LBJ to Wirtz, Mar. 12, 1946, LBJA Selected Names File, Wirtz, Box 37, LBJL.
41. Busby Oral History, I, Apr. 23, 1981, LBJ.
42. Jake Pickle Oral History, I, May 31, 1970, LBJL; Dallek, *Lone Star,* 282–284.
43. Margaret Mayer Ward Oral History, Mar. 10, 1977, LBJL.
44. Ibid.
45. Pickle Oral History.
46. LBJ to Rowe, May 31, 1946, LBJA Selected Names File, Rowe, Box 32, LBJL.
47. Dallek, *Lone Star,* 285.
48. Pickle Oral History.
49. Ibid.
50. Marshall, *Walking the Tightrope,* 20; Dallek, *Lone Star,* 287.
51. Jarboe Russell, *Lady Bird,* 154.
52. Ibid.
53. Ibid., 153.
54. Ibid., 153–154.
55. Joe Phipps, *Summer Stock: Behind the Scenes with LBJ in '48* (Fort Worth, TX, 1992), 37.
56. Ibid., 41.
57. Kearns Goodwin, *American Dream,* 105.
58. Frederickson, *Dixiecrat Revolt,* 4.

Chapter 10: Coke

1. Jake Pickle Oral History, II, June 17, 1970, LBJL.
2. Miller, *Lyndon,* 117.
3. Connally to Congressman, Mar. 12, 1948, LBJA Selected Names File, Connally, Box 16, LBJL.
4. Sam Houston Johnson Oral History, Apr. 14, 1976, LBJL.
5. Pickle Oral History, II.
6. Connally, *In History's Shadow,* 114.
7. Horace Busby Oral History, II, Mar. 4, 1982, LBJL.
8. Connally, *History's Shadow,* 113.
9. Steinberg, *Sam Johnson's Boy,* 242.
10. Busby Oral History, II.
11. Ibid.
12. "Two Philosophies Involved In Race, Johnson Charges," *Austin American,* Aug. 11, 1948.
13. Busby Oral History, II; Pickle Oral History, II.
14. Phipps, *Summer Stock,* 86.
15. Ibid., 85–86.
16. Mary to Mr. Johnson, Pre-Presidential Memo File, Box 1, LBJL; Pickle Oral History, II; Clifton C. Carter Oral History, I, Oct. 1, 1968, LBJL.

17. Phipps, *Summer Stock,* 3.
18. Willard Deason Oral History, I, Apr. 11, 1969, LBJL.
19. Phipps, *Summer Stock,* 100.
20. "Johnson Fires Issues to Senate Race," *Austin American,* May 23, 1948.
21. Warren Woodward Oral History, I, June 3, 1968, LBJL.
22. Ibid.
23. Ibid., Connally, *History's Shadow,* 114–115.
24. Marsh to Lyndon, Oct. 22, 1947, PP/Charles Marsh, Box 5, LBJL.
25. "Johnson Accepts Dallas Helicopter," *Austin American-Statesman,* May 23, 1948.
26. Woodward Oral History, I.
27. Ibid.; Margaret Mayer Ward Oral History, I, Mar. 10, 1977, LBJL; Miller, *Lyndon,* 120.
28. Woodward Oral History, I.
29. Miller, *Lyndon,* 120.
30. Pickle Oral History.
31. Horace Busby, "Reflections on a Leader," in *The Johnson Presidency: Twenty Intimate Perspectives of Lyndon B. Johnson,* ed. Kenneth W. Thompson (Lanham, MD, 1986), 258, Miller, *Lyndon,* 120–121.
32. Phipps, *Summer Stock,* 21.
33. Ibid., 114–115.
34. Ibid., 142.
35. Ibid.
36. Ibid., 142–144.
37. Ibid., 144.
38. Ibid., 21.
39. Ibid., 120–121.
40. Ibid., 122–123.
41. Dallek, *Lone Star,* 306–307.
42. Phipps, *Summer Stock,* 172–173.
43. Dugger, *Politician,* 12–15.
44. Ibid., 315.
45. Dallek, *Lone Star,* 310–311.
46. Woodward Oral History, I.
47. Ibid.
48. "Marble Falls Dam Program Going Ahead, Johnson Says," *Austin American,* July 9, 1946.
49. Busby Oral History, V.
50. Ibid.
51. Steinberg, *Sam Johnson's Boy,* 248; Miller, *Lyndon,* 121.
52. Statement of Lyndon B. Johnson, Aug. 5, 1948, Press Release, n.d., 1948, PP/Charles Marsh, Box 1, LBJL.
53. Busby Oral History, I.
54. "Johnson Sees Threat of Isolationism Returning," *Austin American,* July 3, 1948.
55. Quoted in Dallek, *Lone Star,* 316.
56. Quoted in ibid., 319.
57. Busby Oral History II; Elizabeth Carpenter Oral History, Feb. 6, 1969, LBJL.
58. Drew Pearson Oral History, Apr. 10, 1969, LBJL.
59. Busby Oral History, III, LBJL.
60. Quoted in Dugger, *Politician,* 319–320.
61. Phipps, *Summer Stock,* 146.
62. Ibid.
63. T. Harry Williams, "Huey, Lyndon, and Southern Radicalism," *Journal of American History* (Sept. 1973), 60, 72.
64. Steinberg, *Sam Johnson's Boy,* 253.
65. Ibid.
66. Jarboe Russell, *Lady Bird,* 158–159.
67. Dugger, *Politician,* 320–321.
68. Charles Boatner Oral History, I, Dec. 17, 1968, LBJL.
69. *Austin American,* Aug. 28, 31, and Sept. 2.
70. Steinberg, *Sam Johnson's Boy,* 258–259.
71. Connally, *History's Shadow,* 117.
72. Miller, *Lyndon,* 124–125.
73. S. H. Johnson Oral History, Apr. 14, 1976, LBJL.
74. Dallek, *Lone Star,* 328.
75. S. H. Johnson Oral History.
76. Miller, *Lyndon,* 125.
77. Todd Copeland, "The County Attorney's Tale," *Baylor Line* (summer 2002): 23–29.
78. J. M. Rowe Oral History, I, Jan. 13, 1984, LBJL.
79. Ibid.
80. Dugger, *Politician,* 322–323; Steinberg, *Sam Johnson's Boy,* 259–260; Dallek, *Lone Star,* 328–329.
81. Miller, *Lyndon,* 125.
82. Dallek, *Lone Star,* 330.
83. J. M. Rowe Oral History, I.

84. "Witness Tells How LBJ 'Stole' Senate Election," *Austin American-Statesman,* July 31, 1977.
85. " 'Didn't Buy Votes,' Johnson Declares," *Dallas Morning News,* Sept. 7, 1948.
86. Miller, *Lyndon,* 128–129.
87. Rowe Oral History; "48 Senate Election 'Was Stolen' for LBJ, ex-Vote Judge Claims," *Houston Post,* July 31, 1977, Copeland, "The County Attorney's Tale," 23–29.
88. J. Pickle Oral History II, June 17, 1970, LBJL.
89. Dallek, *Lone Star,* 335.
90. W. Jenkins Oral History, VIII, July 22, 1983, LBJL; John D. Cofer to Edward Johnson, Oct. 23, 1948, PP/John D. Cofer, Box 1, LBJL.
91. H. Busby Oral History, IV, July 29, 1988, LBJL.
92. "Johnson Wins Party Nod as Senate Nominee, 29 to 28," *Dallas Morning News,* Sept. 14, 1948; Miller, *Lyndon,* 128–129.
93. "Roaring Convention Certifies Johnson and Ousts Dixiecrats," *Austin American-Statesman,* Sept. 15, 1948; Miller *Lyndon,* 130; Steinberg, *Sam Johnson's Boy,* 266; Dallek, *Lone Star,* 335–336.
94. Vernon Whiteside Oral History, I, Aug. 1, 1985, LBJL.
95. Dale Baum and James L. Hailey, "Johnson's Victory: A Reappraisal," *Political Science Quarterly,* 109, no. 4 (Fall, 1994): 610.
96. Ibid. See also "Possible Election Irregularities Which Benefited Coke Stevenson, 1948," Pre-Presidential Confidential File, Box 6, LBJL.
97. Baum and Hailey, "Johnson's Victory," 609.
98. Ibid., 599.
99. Phipps, *Summer Stock,* 117–118.

Chapter 11: A Populist Gentlemen's Club

1. Wayne Fields, *Union of Words: A History of Presidential Eloquence* (New York, 1996), 4–6.
2. Ibid., 5.
3. Frederickson, *The Dixiecrat Revolt,* 189.
4. Ibid., 4–7.
5. Dugger, *Politician,* 342–343.
6. Miller, *Lyndon,* 142.
7. Dugger, *Politician,* 342–343.
8. Dallek, *Lone Star,* 360; H. Busby Oral History V, Aug. 16, 1988, LBJL.
9. L. Carpenter Oral History, I, Feb. 6, 1969, LBJL.
10. "The fundament point is . . . ," n.d., 1956, senate office files of George Reedy (hereafter SOF/G. Reedy) Box 419.
11. D. B. Hardeman Oral History, II, Mar. 12, 1969, LBJL.
12. C. and V. Durr Oral History, II, Mar. 1, 1975, LBJL.
13. Connally to Congressman, Aug. 3, 1942, LBJA Selected Names File, Connally, Box 15, LBJL.
14. Dallek, *Lone Star,* 362.
15. Ibid., 361.
16. H. McPherson Oral History, III, LBJL.
17. Steinberg, *Sam Johnson's Boy,* 277.
18. W. E. James Oral History, Feb. 17, 1978, I, LBJL.
19. Ibid.
20. Dallek, *Lone Star,* 352.
21. Ibid., 353.
22. McPherson Oral History, III.
23. Dallek, *Lone Star,* 354.
24. See G. Reedy Oral History, I, Dec. 12, 1968, LBJL.
25. See Gilbert Fite, *Richard B. Russell Jr., Senator from Georgia* (Chapel Hill, NC, 1991).
26. Steinberg, *Sam Johnson's Boy,* 289.
27. Dugger, *Politician,* 343.
28. B. Baker Oral History, III, Feb. 9, 1983, LBJL; C. Albert Oral History, II, June 10, 1969, LBJL.
29. B. Baker Oral History, III. See also Earl Clements Oral History, I, Nov. 24, 1974, LBJL.
30. McPherson Oral History, III. See also B. Baker Oral History, III, Dec. 9, 1983, LBJL.
31. Young, "The Political Education of LBJ," 154.
32. Hubert H. Humphrey, *The Education of a Public Man* (New York, 1976), 124.
33. Ibid., 137.
34. McPherson Oral History, III.
35. Dallek, *Lone Star,* 379.
36. Ibid., 365.
37. H. Busby Oral History, V, Aug. 16, 1988, LBJL.
38. Ibid.
39. Ibid.
40. Dallek, *Lone Star,* 367.
41. Felton West, "Always Before, LBJ Had Opposed Cloture," *Houston Post,* June 14, 1964.
42. Dallek, *Lone Star,* 368.
43. Ibid.
44. Ibid., 369.

45. Ibid., 371.
46. Ibid., 372.
47. McPherson Oral History, III.
48. G. Reedy Oral History, VI, May 21, 1982, LBJL.
49. Ibid.
50. Ibid.
51. "Johnson Blasts Tidelands Talk," *Dallas Morning News,* May 20, 1952. See also "Kerr KO's Gas Consumer," *Dallas Morning News,* Mar. 31, 1950.
52. G. Reedy Oral History, VIII, Aug. 16, 1983, LBJL.
53. J. L. Rauh Oral History, July 30, 1969, LBJL.
54. Dallek, *Lone Star,* 376.
55. Dugger, *Politician,* 354–355; Dallek, *Lone Star,* 372–377; Young, "Political Education of LBJ," 1160–1161.
56. Rauh Oral History.
57. Dallek, *Lone Star,* 376–377.
58. Miller, *Lyndon,* 145.
59. Young, "Political Education of LBJ," 164–165.
60. Dallek, *Lone Star,* 365.
61. Booth Mooney, *LBJ: An Irreverent Chronicle* (New York, 1976), 24–25.
62. Hubert H. Humphrey Oral History, Aug. 17, 1971, LBJL.
63. Dallek, *Lone Star,* 353.
64. Young, "Political Education of LBJ," 154–155.
65. Miller, *Lyndon,* 148.
66. Dallek, *Lone Star,* 355.
67. Miller, *Lyndon,* 149.
68. See Clark Clifford with Richard Holbrooke, *Counsel to the President: A Memoir* (New York, 1991), 229.
69. Clark Clifford Oral History, I, Mar. 17, 1969, LBJL.
70. H. Busby Oral History, II, Mar. 4, 1982, LBJL.
71. G. Reedy Oral History, VIII, Aug. 16, 1983, LBJL.
72. Booth Mooney, "As Floor Leader, LBJ Improvised," *Dallas Morning News,* Dec. 4, 1963.
73. Dallek, *Lone Star,* 383–384.
74. Richard A. Baker and Roger H. Davidson, eds., *First among Equals: Outstanding Senate Leaders of the Twentieth Century* (Washington, D.C., 1991), 204; Dallek, *Lone Star,* 384.
75. Mooney, "As Floor Leader, LBJ Improvised."
76. Dallek, *Lone Star,* 388–389.
77. Ibid., 389.
78. See Reed to Sen. Johnson, Jan. 22, 1952, SOF/G. Reedy, Box 413, LBJL.
79. Rostow to LBJ, n.d. (NSF) Memos to Pres, Box 24, LBJL.
80. R. G. Baker Oral History, Dec. 9, 1983, LBJL.
81. Dallek, *Lone Star,* 389.
82. R.G. Baker Oral History.
83. Young, "Political Education of LBJ," 188–189; Reedy Oral History, IV, May 21, 1982, LBJL; Carl Albert Oral History, II, June 10, 1969, LBJL.
84. "Johnson Urges West-South Tie," *Dallas Morning News,* Oct. 12, 1951.
85. Quoted in Woods, *Quest for Identity,* 58.
86. Quoted in Ibid.
87. Reedy Oral History IV.
88. Ibid.
89. Quoted in Woods, *Quest for Identity,* 59.
90. Young, "Political Education of LBJ," 183–184.
91. Dallek, *Lone Star,* 399.
92. Reedy Oral History, IV.
93. Ibid.
94. Ibid.
95. B. Baker Oral History, III, Dec. 9, 1983, LBJL.
96. Quoted in Woods, *Quest for Identity,* 59.
97. Don Thomas Oral History, June 3, 1991, LBJL.
98. Ibid.
99. Ibid.
100. Jarboe Russell, *Lady Bird,* 160.
101. Leonard Marks Oral History, June 15, 1970, LBJL.
102. Don Cook Oral History, June 3, 1991, LBJL.
103. Jarboe Russell, *Lady Bird,* 163–164.
104. Ibid., 164.
105. Louis W. Kohlmeier et. al., "Lyndon's Pals: His Hometown Coterie Wheels and Deals in Land and Broadcasting," *Wall Street Journal,* Aug. 11, 1964.
106. Ibid.
107. Ibid.
108. Dallek, *Lone Star,* 415.

109. Ibid. 410–411.
110. Reed to Sen. Johnson, Aug. 14, 1952, SOF/G. Reedy, Box 413, LBJL.
111. Hal K. Rothman, *LBJ's Texas White House: "Our Heart's Home"* (College Station, TX, 2001), 40–43.
112. Jarboe Russell, *Lady Bird,* 161.
113. Rothman, *Texas White House,* 45.
114. Ibid., 46.
115. Lady Bird Johnson Interview.
116. Ibid.
117. Jarboe Russell, *Lady Bird,* 162.
118. Rothman, *Texas White House,* 57–58.
119. Dallek, *Lone Star,* 409.
120. Phipps, *Summer Stock,* 74.
121. Jarboe Russell, *Lady Bird,* 154–155.
122. Ibid.
123. Dallek, *Lone Star,* 407–408.
124. Jarboe Russell, *Lady Bird,* 165–167.

Chapter 12: Leader

1. Quoted in Dallek, *Lone Star,* 406.
2. Steinberg, *Sam Johnson's Boy,* 323.
3. D. B. Hardeman Oral History, Feb. 26, 1969, LBJL.
4. Steinberg, *Sam Johnson's Boy,* 324.
5. Young, "Political Education of LBJ," 194–195.
6. Ibid., 198.
7. Johnson and Hart Conversation, Apr. 22, 1952, Notes and Transcripts of LBJ Conversations, Box 1, LBJ Papers, LBJL.
8. Johnson and Shivers Conversation, June 11, 1952, Notes and Transcripts of Johnson Conversations, Box 1, LBJL.
9. Dugger, *Politician,* 340.
10. Johnson and Shivers Conversation, June 11, 1952.
11. Dugger, *Politician,* 340. See also LBJ to Mother, Family Correspondence, June 10, 1952, Box 1, LBJL.
12. Dugger, *Politician,* 341.
13. Steinberg, *Sam Johnson's Boy,* 325.
14. Ibid., 325–326.
15. Davidson, *Race and Class in Texas Politics,* 162.
16. Steinberg, *Sam Johnson's Boy,* 327.
17. Ibid.
18. Dallek, *Lone Star,* 418–419; Dugger, *Politician,* 374–375; Steinberg, *Sam Johnson's Boy,* 326–327.
19. D. B. Hardeman and Donald C. Bacon, *Rayburn: A Biography* (Austin, TX, 1987), 364–365. See also Reedy Oral History, VIII, Aug. 16, 1983, LBJL.
20. Dallek, *Lone Star,* 419.
21. Booth Mooney Oral History, Apr. 8, 1969, LBJL.
22. S. H. Johnson Oral History, IV, June 15, 1976, LBJL.
23. Charles K. Boatner Oral History, Dec. 17, 1968, B. Baker Oral History, IV, Feb. 29, 1984, LBJL.
24. "Johnson Holds Popular Edge with Texas Voters," *Austin American-Statesman,* Dec. 12, 1952.
25. "Shivers to Challenge Johnson?" *Dallas Times-Herald,* Nov. 12, 1952.
26. Mooney, *Irreverent Chronicle,* 13.
27. Dugger, *Politician,* 379.
28. S. H. Johnson Oral History, Apr. 13, 1976, LBJL.
29. Dugger, *Politician,* 379–380.
30. Joe Rauh Oral History, July 30, 1969, LBJL; Drew Pearson, "Democratic Friction," *Austin American-Statesman,* Nov. 20, 1952.
31. Walter Jenkins to Sen. Johnson, Nov. 13, 1952, LBJA Names File, Jenkins, Box 32, LBJL.
32. Johnson and Stevenson Conversation, Nov. 20, 1952, Notes and Transcripts of Johnson Conversations, Box 1, LBJL.
33. Humphrey, *Public Man,* 163.
34. Ibid., 163–164; S. H. Johnson Oral History.
35. Quoted in Dallek, *Lone Star,* 425.
36. Humphrey, *Public Man,* 164–165.
37. Nadine Eckhardt Oral History, Feb. 22, 1984, LBJL.
38. Reedy Oral History, VIII.
39. Kearns Goodwin, *American Dream,* 139.
40. *Time,* June 22, 1953.
41. Reedy Oral History, VIII.
42. Ibid.
43. Reedy to Senator Johnson, n.d., 1953, SOF/G. Reedy, Box 413, LBJL.
44. Quoted in Dallek, *Lone Star,* 437.
45. Mooney, *Irreverent Chronicle,* 12–13.

46. Reedy to Senator Johnson, Nov. 6, 1952, SOF/G. Reedy, Box 413, LBJL.
47. Reedy to Sen. Johnson, SOF/G. Reedy, Box 420, LBJL.
48. Reedy Memo to Senator Johnson, Nov. 7, 1958, SOF/G. Reedy, Box 427, LBJL.
49. McPherson Oral History, III.
50. Ibid.
51. Reedy to Sen. Johnson, May 21, 1953, Pre-Presidential Memo File, Box 2, LBJL.
52. S. H. Johnson Oral History, III.
53. Baker and Davidson, *First among Equals,* 207.
54. B. Baker Oral History, II.
55. Reedy Oral History, VII.
56. Miller, *Lyndon,* 157.
57. Baker and Davidson, *First among Equals,* 213.
58. Dallek, *Lone Star,* 429.
59. Reedy to Sen. Johnson, 1954, n.d., SOF/G. Reedy, Box 413, LBJL.
60. Reedy Oral History, I.
61. Kearns Goodwin, *American Dream,* 121.
62. Ibid., 124.
63. Reedy Oral History I.
64. Harry McPherson Oral History, IX, Feb. 7, 1986, LBJL.
65. Evans and Novak, *Exercise of Power,* 104.
66. Baker and Davidson, *First among Equals,* 215.
67. Kearns Goodwin, *American Dream,* 128.
68. Ibid.
69. Luci Baines Johnson, interview with author, Aug. 17, 2000, Austin, Texas.
70. Kearns Goodwin, *American Dream,* 130.
71. McPherson Oral History, III.
72. Gerald Siegel Oral History, I, May 26, 1969.
73. Steele to Williamson, Mar. 4, 1958, Steele Papers, Box 1, LBJL.
74. Steinberg, *Sam Johnson's Boy,* 349.
75. Ibid.
76. Ibid., 349–350.
77. Gerald Siegel Oral History, III, Feb. 11, 1977, LBJL.
78. Reedy Oral History, V.
79. Walter Jenkins Oral History, III, Sept. 23, 1976, LBJL.
80. Reedy Oral History, V.
81. Stephen Ambrose, *Eisenhower: The President* (New York, 1983), 164.
82. Quoted in Woods, *Quest for Identity,* 90.
83. Quoted in ibid.
84. Miller, *Lyndon,* 166–167.
85. Reedy to Senator Johnson, n.d., 1953, SOF/G. Reedy, Box 413, LBJL.
86. Quoted in Dallek, *Lone Star,* 452.
87. Miller, *Lyndon,* 173.
88. Ibid., 163.
89. Hubert H. Humphrey Oral History, II, June 20, 1977, LBJL.
90. Reedy to Sen. Johnson, n.d., 1953, SOF/G. Reedy, Box 413, LBJL.
91. Eisenhower and Clay Conversation, Feb. 25, 1954, Dwight D. Eisenhower Diary, Box 5, Eisenhower Library.
92. Reedy Oral History, III.
93. Miller, *Lyndon,* 170.
94. LBJ and Friendly Conversation, Jan. 19, 1953, Notes and Transcripts of Telephone Conversations, Box 1, LBJL.
95. Reedy to Sen. Johnson, n.d., 1954, SOF/G. Reedy, Box 413, LBJL.
96. Quoted in Woods, *Quest for Identity,* 69.
97. Reedy to Sen. Johnson, Jan.–Nov. 1954, SOF/G. Reedy, Box 413, LBJL, Dallek, *Lone Star,* 455–456.
98. John Steele to Williamson, Dec. 2, 1954, Steele Papers, Box 1, LBJL, Reedy to Johnson, Nov. 29, 1954, Pre-Presidential Memo File, Box 2, LBJL.
99. Miller, *Lyndon,* 173.
100. J. Rauh Oral History, July 30, 1969, LBJL.
101. B. Baker Oral History, I, Oct. 23, 1974.
102. Reedy to Sen Johnson, n.d., 1953, SOF/G. Reedy, Box 413, LBJL.

Chapter 13: Passing the Lord's Prayer

1. Ralph Huitt to G. Reedy, Mar. 29, 1954, SOF/G. Reedy, Box 412, LBJL.
2. Charles K. Boatner Oral History, Dec. 17, 1968, LBJL.
3. James H. Rowe Oral History, Sept. 16, 1969, II, LBJL.
4. Harry McPherson Oral History, VII, May 16, 1985, LBJL.
5. Mary to Sen. Johnson, Apr. 14, 1953, LBJA, Selected Names File, Box 32, LBJL.
6. George Reedy Oral History, Dec. 12, 1968, LBJL.
7. Young, "Political Education of LBJ," 240–241.

8. "Lyndon Says He Will Run Again in 1954," *Austin American-Statesman,* Oct. 2, 1953.
9. John Singleton Oral History, II, July 15, 1983, II, LBJL.
10. George Reedy Oral History, Dec. 12, 1968, LBJL.
11. "Sen. Johnson's Popularity with Both Factions Grows," *Austin American-Statesman,* Sept. 6, 1953.
12. Young, "Political Education of LBJ," 214.
13. Ann Feans Crawford, *Frankie: Mrs. R. D. Randolph and Texas Liberal Politics* (Austin, 1999), 33–37.
14. Dallek, *Lone Star,* 441.
15. Davidson, *Race and Class in Texas Politics,* 162.
16. Crawford, *Frankie,* 24.
17. D. B. Hardeman Oral History, I, Feb. 26, 1969, LBJL.
18. Warren Woodward Oral History, II, May 26, 1969, LBJL.
19. Ibid.
20. Davidson, *Race and Class in Texas Politics,* 163.
21. Looney to LBJ, Feb. 5, 1954, LBJA Selected Names File Everett Looney, Box 25, LBJL.
22. Reedy to Sen. Johnson, May 27, 1954, Pre-Presidential Memo File, Box 2, LBJL; Reedy to Lloyd Croslin, July 7, 1954, SOF/G. Reedy, Box 412, LBJL.
23. Dallek, *Lone Star,* 449.
24. Young, "Political Education of LBJ," 249.
25. Ibid., 250.
26. Dallek, *Lone Star,* 451.
27. Reston, *Lone Star,* 171.
28. Robert A. Calvert and Arnoldo De Leon, *The History of Texas* (Wheeling, Ill., 1996), 387–388; Jake Pickle Oral History, III, Mar. 1, 1971, LBJL.
29. LBJ and Shivers Conversation, Nov. 15, 1954, Notes and Transcripts of Johnson Conversations, Box 1, LBJL.
30. Reedy Oral History, VII, May 24, 1983, LBJL.
31. Dallek, *Lone Star,* 463.
32. Reedy Oral History, I, Dec. 12, 1968, LBJL.
33. Dallek, *Lone Star,* 470.
34. Kearns Goodwin, *American Dream,* 133–134.
35. Steinberg, *Sam Johnson's Boy,* 397.
36. Reedy to LBJ, July 2, 1953, SOF/G. Reedy, Box 413, LBJL.
37. Robert G. Baker Oral History, VI, July 24, 1984, LBJL.
38. B. Baker Oral History, Oct. 23, 1974, LBJL.
39. Dallek, *Lone Star,* 477.
40. Gerald Siegel Oral History, IV, June 17, 1977, LBJL.
41. Miller, *Lyndon,* 179.
42. LBJ and Kefauver Conversation, Jan. 11, 1955, Notes and Transcripts of LBJ Conversations, Box 1, LBJL.
43. Reedy, Oral History, VIII.
44. Kearns Goodwin, *American Dream,* 143.
45. Political Labels, Horace Busby, Feb. 9, 1959, SOF/G. Reedy, Box 462, LBJL.
46. Steinberg, *Sam Johnson's Boy,* 393.
47. Ibid.
48. Ibid., 395.
49. Siegel Oral History, III, Feb. 11, 1977, LBJL.
50. G. Reedy to Sen. Johnson, n.d., 1955, SOF/G. Reedy, Box 413, LBJL.; B. Baker Oral History, VI, July 24, 1984, LBJL.; Steinberg, *Sam Johnson's Boy,* 395–396; Dallek, *Lone Star,* 468–469.
51. Dallek, *Lone Star,* 481–482.
52. Reedy, Oral History, VIII. Aug. 16, 1983, LBJL.
53. Dallek, *Lone Star,* 482.
54. Reedy Oral History, I, Dec. 12, 1968, LBJL.
55. Steele to Williamson, June 9, 1955, Steele Papers, Box 1, LBJL.
56. Miller, *Lyndon,* 178.
57. Reedy to Sen. Johnson, Nov. 5, 1954, SOF/G. Reedy, Box 413, LBJL.
58. Miller, *Lyndon,* 177.
59. Ibid.
60. Dallek, *Lone Star,* 483.
61. Jarboe Russell, *Lady Bird,* 170.
62. Ibid.
63. Mary Margaret Wiley Valenti, Oral History, III, May 2, 1984, LBJL.
64. Jarboe Russell, *Lady Bird,* 170.
65. Nadine Brammer Eckhardt, Oral History, I, Feb. 22, 1984 I, LBJL.
66. Jarboe Russell, *Lady Bird,* 170–171.
67. Ibid., 168.
68. Ibid., 169.
69. Ibid., 172.
70. Ibid., 174.
71. Ibid., 172.
72. Ibid., 174.

73. Margaret Mayer Ward Oral History, I, Mar. 10, 1977, LBJL.
74. Jarboe Russell, *Lady Bird,* 174.
75. Dallek, *Lone Star,* 355.
76. Ibid., 356.
77. Horace Busby Oral History, Apr. 23, 1981, LBJL.
78. Ibid.
79. Dallek, *Lone Star,* 356.
80. Jarboe Russell, *Lady Bird,* 172–173.

Chapter 14: Back from the Edge

1. Lyndon B. Johnson, "My Heart Attack Taught Me How to Live," *American Magazine,* July 1956.
2. Pratt and Casteneda, *Builders,* 176–177.
3. Elizabeth Carpenter Oral History, I, Feb. 6, 1969, LBJL; Dallek, *Lone Star,* 485.
4. Miller, *Lyndon,* 181.
5. George R. Brown Oral History, II, Aug. 6, 1969, LBJL.
6. Jarboe Russell, *Lady Bird,* 175.
7. Miller, *Lyndon,* 181.
8. Jarboe Russell, *Lady Bird,* 175. See also Heart Attack, Business, Family, 1955, LBJ Handwriting File, Box 8, LBJL.
9. Dallek, *Lone Star,* 486.
10. L. B. Johnson Oral Interview, March 29–April 2, 1993, NPS Oral Histories.
11. See Willis Hurst Oral History, VI, Oct. 3, 1995, LBJL.
12. George Reedy Oral History, VIII, Aug. 8, 1983, LBJL.
13. Miller, *Lyndon,* 182.
14. Booth Mooney, "Heart Attack Brings LBJ a New Way of Life," *Dallas Morning News,* Dec. 16, 1965.
15. Jarboe Russell, *Lady Bird,* 176.
16. Reedy Oral History, VIII, Aug. 16, 1983, LBJL.
17. Ibid.
18. Miller, *Lyndon,* 182–183.
19. Reedy Oral History, VIII, Aug. 16, 1883, LBJL.
20. Miller, *Lyndon,* 182.
21. Mary Rather Oral History, Dec. 10, 1974, LBJL.
22. Reedy Oral History, VIII, Aug. 16, 1983, LBJL.
23. *American Magazine,* July 1956.
24. Mooney, "Heart Attack Brings LBJ a New Way of Life"; Willard Deason, Oral History, III, LBJL.
25. Mary Rather Oral History, Dec. 10, 1974, LBJL.
26. Jarboe Russell, *Lady Bird,* 178.
27. Ibid.
28. B. Baker to Sen. Johnson, Oct. 4, 1955, Pre-Presidential Confidential File, Box 1, LBJ Papers, LBJL.
29. Steinberg, *Sam Johnson's Boy,* 422.
30. Reedy to Sen. Johnson, Sept. 30, 1955, Pre-Presidential Memo File, Box 3, LBJL.
31. Reedy to Sen. Johnson, n.d., 1955, SOF/G. Reedy Box 415, LBJL.
32. Dallek, *Lone Star,* 490–491.
33. Mary Rather Oral History, Dec. 10, 1974, LBJL.
34. Reedy Oral History, VIII, Aug. 16, 1983, LBJL.
35. LBJ to Bobby, Nov. 26, 1955, Pre-Presidential Confidential File, Box 1, LBJ Papers, LBJL.
36. Corcoran to LBJ, Nov. 22, 1955, LBJA, Selected Names File, Corcoran, Box 32, LBJL.
37. Rowe to LBJ, May 7, 1956, LBJA, Selected Names File, Box 32, LBJL.
38. Reedy Oral History, VIII, Aug. 16, 1983, LBJL.
39. Carl Albert Oral History, I, Apr. 28, 1969, LBJL.
40. Quoted in Sidney M. Milkis, *The President and the Parties: The Transformation of the American Party System Since the New Deal* (New York, 1993), 193.
41. Rowe to Bird, Nov. 8, 1955, LBJA Selected Names File, Rowe, Box 32, LBJL.
42. G. Reedy to Sen. Johnson, n.d., 1955, SOF/G. Reedy, Box 421, LBJL.
43. Rowe to Sen. Johnson, Apr. 4, 1956, LBJA Selected Names File, Box 32, LBJL.
44. B. Baker Oral History, VII.
45. B. Mooney Oral History, I, April 8, 1969, LBJL.
46. Harny McPherson Oral History, VII, May 16, 1985.
47. H. McPherson Oral History, III.
48. Quoted in Woods, *Quest for Identity,* 91.
49. Quoted in ibid.
50. Rowe Oral History, I.
51. Randall B. Woods, *Fulbright: A Biography* (New York, 1995), 208.
52. Ervin Draft, Southern Manifesto, Papers of Richard Russell, University of Georgia, 1956.
53. Holland-Fulbright-Daniel-Sparkman revision, 1956 Southern Manifesto, Russell Papers, U. of Georgia.
54. Quoted in Haynes Johnson and Bernard M. Gwertzman, *Fulbright: The Dissenter* (New York, 1968), 170, 171.
55. Dallek, *Lone Star,* 496.

56. G. Reedy to Sen. Johnson, n.d., 1955, Box 415, LBJL.
57. Miller, *Lyndon,* 187.
58. G. Reedy to Sen. Johnson, n.d., 1956, SOF/G. Reedy, Box 419, LBJL.
59. Dallek, *Lone Star,* 497.
60. Ibid., 497–498.
61. Reston, *Lone Star,* 171–172.
62. G. Reedy to Sen. Johnson, Aug. 23, 1956, Pre-Presidential Memo File, Box 4, LBJL.
63. Johnson to Rowe, Oct. 28, 1955, and Rowe to Johnson Oct. 26, 1955, LBJA Selected Names File, Box 32, LBJL.
64. Dallek, *Lone Star,* 500.
65. Willie Morris, *North Toward Home,* (Boston, 1967), 244–245.
66. G. Reedy Oral History, Dec. 12, 1968, LBJL.
67. Reston, *Lone Star,* 173–174.
68. Ibid., 178–179.
69. Ibid., 178.
70. Davidson, *Race and Class in Texas Politics,* 164; Cecil Burney Oral History, I, Nov. 26, 1968, LBJL.
71. John Singleton Oral History, II, July 15, 1983, LBJL.
72. Dallek, *Lone Star,* 501.
73. Ibid.
74. Miller, *Lyndon,* 195–196.
75. Dallek, *Lone Star,* 502.
76. G. Reedy to Sen. Johnson, n.d., 1956, Pre-Presidential Memos File, Box 4, LBJL.
77. G. Reedy to Sen. Johnson, Aug. 13, 1956, Pre-Presidential Memo File, Box 4, LBJL.
78. Elizabeth Carpenter Oral History, I, Feb. 6, 1969, LBJL.
79. Rowe to LBJ, Aug. 11, 1956, LBJA, Selected Names File, Rowe, Box 32, LBJL.
80. Rowe to Sen. Johnson, Apr. 12, 1956, LBJA, Selected Names File, Rowe, Box 32, LBJL.
81. J. Rowe Oral History, Sept. 9, 1969, LBJL.
82. Steinberg, *Sam Johnson's Boy,* 438.
83. Ibid.
84. Miller, *Lyndon,* 199.
85. Rowe Oral History, I, Sept. 9, 1969, LBJL.
86. Clifton C. Carter Oral History, I, Oct. 1, 1968, LBJL.
87. Dallek, *Lone Star,* 504.
88. LBJ and John Sparkman Conversation, Sept. 17, 1956, Notes and Transcripts of Pre-Presidential Conversations, LBJL.
89. G. Reedy to Sen. Johnson, Oct. 19, 1956, Pre-Presidential Memo File, Box 4, LBJL.
90. G. Reedy to Sen. Johnson, Oct. 15, 1956, Pre-Presidential Memo File, Box 4, LBJL.
91. Dallek, *Lone Star,* 511.
92. Miller, *Lyndon,* 200.
93. Ibid., 201.
94. Tree to Rowe, Feb. 15, 1957, SOF/G. Reedy, Box 423, LBJL.
95. G. Reedy to Sen. Johnson, SOF/G. Reedy, Box 419, LBJL.
96. G. Reedy to Sen. Johnson, n.d., 1956, SOF/G. Reedy, Box 419, LBJL; H. McPherson Oral History, VIII, Nov. 20, 1985, LBJL.

Chapter 15: Containing the Red-Hots:
From Dulles to the Dixie Association

1. Steinberg, *Sam Johnson's Boy,* 446.
2. Randall B. Woods, "Bipartisanship," in *Encyclopedia of American Foreign Policy,* eds. Alexander De-Conde et al., Vol. 1 (New York, 2002), 155.
3. G. Reedy to Sen. Johnson, n.d., 1957, SOF/G. Reedy, Box 421, LBJL.
4. G. Reedy to Sen. Johnson, Speech Text, n.d., 1953, SOF/G. Reedy, Box 413, LBJL.
5. Dallek, *Lone Star,* 433.
6. Legislative Leadership Meeting, Feb. 165, 1953, Whitman Files, Leg. Meeting Series, Box 1, DDE Papers, DDEL.
7. LBJ and Dulles Conversation, Mar. 3, 1953, Notes and Transcripts of Telephone Conversations, Box 1, LBJL.
8. George Reedy Oral History, V, Oct. 27, 1982, LBJL; Legislative Leadership Meetings, Feb. 16 and Mar. 2, 1953, Whitman Files, Leg. Meet. Series, Box 1, DDE Papers, DDEL.
9. Quoted in Woods, *Fulbright,* 191.
10. Miller, *Lyndon,* 158.
11. G. Reedy to Sen. Johnson, n.d., 1954, SOF/G. Reedy, Box 413, LBJL.
12. Memo of Bipartisan Briefing of Cong. Leaders on Foreign Policy, Nov. 17, 1954, Whitman Files, Leg. Meeting Series, Box 1, DDE Papers, DDEL.
13. Dulles and Adams Conversation, May 8, 1956, Telephone Call Series, Dulles Papers, Box 11, DDEL.
14. Dallek, *Lone Star,* 436.
15. B. Baker, Oral History, V, May 2, 1984, LBJL. See also Gerry Siegel Oral History, I, May 26, 1969, LBJL.

16. Memo of Bipartisan Briefing of Cong. Leaders on Foreign Policy, Nov. 17, 1954, Whitman Files, Leg. Meet. Series, Box 1, DDE Papers, DDEL.
17. G. Reedy to Sen. Johnson, May 10, 1954, SOF/G. Reedy, Box 413, LBJL.
18. Memorandum on Air Defense, May 21, 1953, Pre-Presidential Memo File, Box 2, LBJL.
19. G. Reedy to Sen. Johnson, n.d., 1953, SOF/G. Reedy, Box 413, LBJL.
20. Reedy to Sen. Johnson, Apr. 13, 1953, SOF/G. Reedy, Box 4132, LBJL; LBJ to Sec. of Defense Charles Wilson, Sept. 8, 1955, White House Central File (hereafter WHCF), Alpha File, Box 1599, DDE Papers, DDEL.
21. See DDE and Dulles Conversation, Apr. 5, 1954, DDE Diary, Box 5, DDE Papers, DDEL.
22. Eisenhower and Walter Beedle Smith Conversation, Apr. 24, 1954, DDE Diary, Box 5, DDE Papers, DDEL.
23. Rowe to Johnson, Apr. 29, 1954, LBJA, Selected Names File, Rowe, Box 32, LBJL.
24. G. Reedy to Sen. Johnson, May 11, 1954, SOF/G. Reedy, Box 413, LBJL.
25. G. Reedy OH, VI, May 23, 1983, LBJL.
26. See Memorandum for the Record, June 23, 1954, Whitman Files, Leg. Meeting Series, Box 1, DDE Papers, DDEL.
27. Dallek, *Lone Star,* 444.
28. Chester Bowles to LBJ, Dec. 1, 1955, Pre-Presidential Memo File, Box 3, LBJL; Woods, *Fulbright,* 220–221.
29. G. Reedy to Sen. Johnson, Dec. 5, 1955, Pre-Presidential Memo File, Box 3, LBJL.
30. Steinberg, *Sam Johnson's Boy,* 476.
31. Ibid., 476–477.
32. Eisenhower and Dulles Conversation, Sept. 23 and Nov. 29, 1955, Telephone Call Series, Box 11, Dulles Papers, DDEL.
33. Quoted in Woods, *Quest for Identity,* 114.
34. See Eisenhower and Dulles Conversation, Sept. 7, 1956, Box 18, DDE Diaries, DDEL.
35. Rayburn and Dulles Conversation, Aug. 8, 1956, Telephone Call Series, Box 5, Papers of John Foster Dulles, Dwight D. Eisenhower Library (hereafter DDEL).
36. Reedy to Sen. Johnson, n.d., 1956, SOF/G. Reedy, Box 419, LBJL.
37. "Dean Acheson on the Suez Crisis," Rowe to Johnson, n.d., LBJA, Selected Names File, Rowe, Box 32, LBJL; Acheson and LBJ Conversation, Feb. 19, 1957, SOF/G. Reedy, Box 421, LBJL.
38. Notes by Senator Johnson for meeting with the President, Aug. 12, 1956, LBJA, Selected Names File, Box 32, LBJL.
39. LBJ's Notes at Dulles's House, n.d., 1957, SOF/G. Reedy, Box 421, LBJL.
40. Woods, *Fulbright,* 221.
41. See G. Reedy to Sen. Johnson, n.d., 1957, SOF/G. Reedy, Box 420, LBJL.
42. LBJ and Dulles Conversation, Feb. 26, 1957, Telephone Call Series, Box 6, Dulles Papers, DDEL.
43. Dallek, *Lone Star,* 512; Knowland and Dulles Conversation, Jan. 28, 1957, Telephone Call Series, Box 6, Dulles Papers, DDEL.
44. Reedy to LBJ, Aug. 12, 1957, SOF/G. Reedy, Box 420, LBJL; Reedy to Sen. Johnson, n.d., 1956, SOF/G. Reedy, Box 421, LBJL.
45. Byron C. Hulsey, *Everett Dirksen and His Presidents* (Lawrence, KS, 2000), 19.
46. Miller, *Lyndon,* 205–207.
47. Rowe to Lyndon Johnson, July 3, 1957, LBJA, Selected Names File, Rowe, Box 32, LBJL.
48. Kearns Goodwin, *American Dream,* 153–154.
49. G. Reedy Oral History, VIII, LBJL.
50. H. McPherson Oral History, May 16, 1985, LBJL.
51. Dewey W, Grantham, *The South in Modern America: A Region at Odds* (New York, 1994), 214–215.
52. Ibid., 121.
53. Rowe to Sen. Johnson, July 1956, LBJA, Selected Names File, Rowe, Box 32, LBJL.
54. Rowe to Lyndon Johnson, July 3, 1957, LBJA, Selected Names File, Rowe, Box 32, LBJL.
55. G. Reedy Oral History, VIII, LBJL.
56. Clinton P. Anderson, with Milton Viorst, *Outsider in the Senate: Senator Clinton Anderson's Memoirs* (New York, 1970), 14–45; Nixon and Dulles Conversation, Jan. 2, 1957, and Hill and Dulles Conversation, Jan. 3, 1957, Telephone Call Series, Box 6, Dulles Papers, DDEL.
57. B. Baker Oral History, III, Dec. 9, 1983; McPherson Oral History, VII, LBJL; Nixon and Dulles Conversation, Jan. 2, 1957, Telephone Call Series, Dulles Papers, Box 6, DDEL; Reedy to Sen. Johnson, n.d., 1957, SOF/G. Reedy, Box 420, LBJL.
58. Dallek, *Lone Star,* 520–521.
59. Kearns Goodwin, *American Dream,* 156–157.
60. Dallek, *Lone Star,* 522.
61. Leg. Leadership Meeting, Aug. 13, 1957, Whitman Files, Leg. Meeting Series, Box 2, DDE Papers, DDEL.
62. Miller, *Lyndon,* 206.
63. See, for example, Fortas to Johnson, Aug. 20, 1957, LBJA, Selected Names File, Fortas, Box 18, LBJL.
64. Anderson, *Outsider in the Senate,* 146–147.
65. Dallek, *Lone Star,* 524.
66. Miller, *Lyndon,* 200.
67. G. Reedy Oral History, III, June 7, 1975, LBJL.

68. G. Reedy to Sen. Johnson, Aug. 1957, SOF/G. Reedy, Box 420, LBJL; Dallek, *Lone Star,* 524–525.
69. Dallek, *Lone Star,* 525.
70. Legislative Leadership Meeting, July 23 and July 30, 1957, Whitman Files, Leg. Meeting Series, Box 2, DDE Papers, DDEL.
71. Joe Rauh to Walter Reuther, Mar. 4, 1959, Box 36, Rauh Papers, Library of Congress.
72. Quoted in Dallek, *Lone Star,* 526.
73. Ibid.
74. Kearns Goodwin, *American Dream,* 158.
75. Ibid.
76. Harry McPherson, *A Political Education* (Boston, 1972), 97–98.
77. Kearns Goodwin, *American Dream,* 159.
78. McPherson Oral History, VII, May 16, 1985, LBJL.
79. Kearns Goodwin, *American Dream,* 159.
80. Corcoran to Reedy, Feb. 18, 1960, Box 427, OF/G. Reedy, LBJL.

Chapter 16: Lost in Space

1. Quoted in Woods, *Quest for Identity,* 117.
2. Goodwin, *American Dream,* 151.
3. Robert A. Divine, *The Sputnik Challenge* (New York, 1993), xvi.
4. Ibid., xv.
5. Ibid.
6. G. Reedy to Sen. Johnson, Oct. 17, 1957, SOF/G. Reedy, Box 420, LBJL.
7. Dallek, *Lone Star,* 530.
8. Divine, *Sputnik,* 21–22.
9. Ibid., 56–58; Legislative Leadership Meeting, May 14, 1957, Whitman Files, Leg. Meeting Series, Box 2, DDE Papers; DDE and McElroy Conversation, Nov. 21, 1957, DDE Diaries, Box 29, DDE Papers, DDEL.
10. Divine, *Sputnik,* 38, 41.
11. Legislative Leadership Meeting, June 24, 1958, Whitman File, Leg. Meeting Series, Box 3, DDE Papers, DDEL.
12. G. Reedy to Sen. Johnson, Oct. 17, 1957, SOF/G. Reedy, Box 420, LBJL.
13. G. Reedy to LBJ, n.d., 1957, SOF/G. Reedy, Box 421, LBJL.
14. Fortas to LBJ, Jan. 16, 1958, LBJA, Selected Names File, Fortas, Box 16, LBJL.
15. Divine, *Sputnik,* 65; Eisenhower and Strauss Conversation, Nov. 25, 1957, DDE Diaries, Box 29, DDEL.
16. Reedy to Sen. Johnson, Dec. 1, 1957, SOF/G. Reedy, Box 421, LBJL.
17. Divine, *Sputnik,* 71.
18. Miller, *Lyndon,* 216.
19. Robert A. Divine, ed., *The Johnson Years, Vol. II: Vietnam, the Environment, and Science* (Lawrence, KS., 1987), 222–225.
20. Ibid.
21. Ibid., 226–228.
22. Rowe to LBJ, Nov. 21, 1957, SOF/G. Reedy, Box 421, LBJL.
23. Legislative Leadership Meeting, Feb. 4, 1958, Whitman File, Leg. Meeting Series, Box 3, DDE Papers, DDEL.
24. Divine, *Johnson Years,* 228.
25. Reedy to Sen. Johnson, Jan. 1958, SOF/G. Reedy, Box 428, LBJL.
26. Dallek, *Lone Star,* 534–535.
27. Wilson to Weisl, Nov. 22, 1957, SOF/G. Reedy, Box 421, LBJL.
28. Wilson to Siegel, Dec. 7, 1957, SOF/G. Reedy, Box 421, LBJL.
29. Dulles and Johnson Conversation, Feb. 27, 1958, Telephone Call Series, Box 8, Dulles Papers; Legislative Leadership Meeting, June 17, 1958, Whitman File, Leg. Meeting Series, Box 3, DDE Papers, DDEL.
30. *Time,* Mar. 17, 1958, 15–18.
31. Ibid.
32. Reedy to Sen. Johnson, Apr. 14, 1958, SOF/G. Reedy, Box 428, LBJL.
33. Rowe to LBJ, Mar. 21, 1958, LBJA, Selected Names File, Rowe, Box 32, LBJL.
34. Mother to Lyndon, Mar. 22, 1958, Family Correspondence, Box 1, LBJL.
35. Lyndon to Mother, Jan. 29, 1958, Family Correspondence, Box 1, LBJL.
36. G. Reedy to Sen. Johnson, Jan. 16, 1958, SOF/G. Reedy, Box 427, LBJL.
37. Reedy to Sen. Johnson, Apr. 18, 1958, SOF/G. Reedy, Box 427, LBJL.
38. Reedy to LBJ, May 13, 1958, SOF/G. Reedy, Box 427, LBJL.
39. Miller, *Lyndon,* 15.
40. Sam Houston Johnson Oral History, June 9, 1976, III, LBJL; Lyndon to Mama, July 24, 1957, Family Correspondence, Box 1, LBJL.
41. Lyndon to Mother, Family Correspondence, Box 1, LBJL.
42. Dallek, *Lone Star,* 537.
43. Reedy to Sen. Johnson, Mar. 1957, SOF/G. Reedy, Box 420, LBJL.
44. Ibid.

45. Rowe to Sen. Johnson, Apr. 30, 1958, LBJA Selected Names File, Rowe, Box 32, LBJL.
46. George Reedy to Senator Johnson, Apr. 16, 1958, Pre-Presidential Memo File, Box 6, LBJL.
47. Joseph Rauh Oral History, July 30, 1969, LBJL.
48. "Lyndon's Effect on Liberalism," *Texas Observer,* May 30, 1959.
49. "Q and A for LBJ," *Texas Observer,* Aug. 9, 1957.
50. "Lyndon's Two Faces," *Texas Observer,* Dec. 13, 1957.
51. Wechsler to Rowe, May 14, 1958, LBJA, Selected Names File, Rowe, Box 32, LBJL.
52. Ibid.
53. Reedy to Sen. Johnson, June 5, 1958, SOF/G. Reedy, Box 428, LBJL.
54. See Jim Rowe to James A. Wechsler, June 20, 1958, LBJA Selected Names File, Rowe, Box 32, LBJL.
55. George Reedy to Sen. Johnson, Sept. 21, 1958, Pre-Presidential Memo File Box 6, LBJL.
56. Rothman, *Texas White House,* 80–81.
57. Steinberg, *Sam Johnson's Boy,* 489–490.
58. Ibid.
59. Earle Clements Oral History, Oct. 24, 1974, LBJL; Warren Woodward Oral History, II, May 26, 1969, LBJL.
60. Ambrose, *Eisenhower,* 488.
61. Quoted in Dallek, *Lone Star,* 539.
62. George Reedy to Sen. Johnson, Feb. 28, 1959, SOF/G. Reedy, Box 429, LBJL.
63. Steinberg, *Sam Johnson's Boy,* 495–497.
64. Horace Busby to Sen. Johnson, Jan. 1959, SOF/G. Reedy, Box 428, LBJL.
65. Steinberg, *Sam Johnson's Boy,* 486.
66. "Johnson's Power Rockets to New Summit," *Dallas Morning News,* Jan. 11, 1959.
67. Steinberg, *Sam Johnson's Boy,* 505.
68. Steele to Williamson, Nov. 12, 1958, Steele Papers, LBJL.
69. Donald Grant, "Senator Johnson Bedazzles 'Em," *St. Louis Post Dispatch,* Nov. 19, 1958.
70. Kearns Goodwin, *American Dream,* 163.
71. Political Labels, Horace Busby, Feb. 9, 1959, SOF/G. Reedy, Box 462, LBJL.
72. Kearns Goodwin, *American Dream,* 163.
73. Ibid., 162–163.
74. Political Labels, Horace Busby, Feb. 9, 1959, SOF/G. Reedy, Box 462, LBJL.
75. Kearns Goodwin, *American Dream,* 165.
76. B. Baker to Leader, Sept. 20, 1957 and Oct. 14, 1957, Pre-Presidential Confidential File, Box 1, LBJL.
77. Stewart Alsop, "Lyndon Johnson: How Does He Do It?," *Saturday Evening Post,* Jan. 24, 1959.
78. Walter Jenkins to Sen. Johnson, May 21, 1959, SOF/G. Reedy, Box 426, LBJL; Powell and LBJ Conversation Mar. 19, 1959, Notes and Transcripts of Telephone Conversations, Box 1, LBJL.
79. Rowe to Lyndon, Jan. 17, 1959, LBJA Selected Names File, Rowe, Box 32, LBJL.
80. Daniel K. Inouye Oral History, Apr. 18, 1969, LBJL.
81. Miller, *Lyndon,* 219–221.
82. See Reedy to Senator Johnson, 1954, SOF/G. Reedy, Box 413, LBJL.
83. Miller, *Lyndon,* 221.
84. Earl Clements Oral History, III, Dec. 6, 1977, LBJL.
85. Harry McPherson Oral History, VIII, Nov. 20, 1985, LBJL.
86. Carroll Kilpatrick Oral History, July 18, 1978, LBJL.
87. Ibid.
88. Reedy to Senator Johnson, 1954, SOF/G. Reedy, Box 413, LBJL.
89. Mooney to Jenkins, May 7, 1959, PP/ Booth Mooney, Box 1, LBJL.
90. "The Johnson Image," May 1959, *Belden Poll,* SOF/G. Reedy, Box 426, LBJL.
91. Buzz to Reedy, May 22, 1959, SOF/G. Reedy, Box 426, LBJL.
92. George to Sen. Johnson, Sept. 29, 1959, SOF/G. Reedy, Box 430, LBJL.

Chapter 17: 1960

1. Steinberg, *Sam Johnson's Boy,* 510.
2. Ibid.
3. Rothman, *Western White House,* 83–85.
4. Pratt and Casteneda, *Builders,* 184.
5. "LBJ Presidential Aim First Evident on Isle," *Houston Post,* Dec. 30, 1963.
6. Laura Kalman, *Abe Fortas: A Biography* (New Haven, CT, 1990), 209.
7. Steinberg, *Sam Johnson's Boy,* 511.
8. Ibid., 513.
9. Reedy to Sen. Johnson, Mar. 21, 1960, Pre-Presidential Memo File, Box 6, LBJL.
10. Steinberg, *Sam Johnson's Boy,* 512.
11. Joseph Rauh Oral History, II, Aug. 1, 1969, LBJL.
12. Humphrey, *Education of a Public Man,* 215–216.
13. James W. Hilty, *Robert F. Kennedy: Brother Protector* (Philadelphia, 1997), 144.
14. Rauh Oral History, II.
15. James H. Rowe Oral History, II, May 10, 1983, LBJL.

16. Miller, *Lyndon,* 242.
17. Gerald Siegel Oral History, I, June 9, LBJL.
18. Johnson and Arbogast Conversation, May 24, 1960, Notes and Transcripts of Telephone Conversations, Box 1, LBJL.
19. Quoted in Dallek, *Lone Star,* 570–571.
20. Miller, *Lyndon,* 242.
21. John Singleton Oral History, II, July 15, 1983, LBJL.
22. Miller, *Lyndon,* 242.
23. Steinberg, *Sam Johnson's Boy,* 243; Miller, *Lyndon,* 243–244. See also James Blundell Oral History, Oct. 29, 1974, LBJL.
24. Rowe Oral History, II.
25. Dallek, *Lone Star,* 559.
26. Jeff Shesol, *Mutual Contempt: Lyndon Johnson, Robert Kennedy, and the Feud That Defined a Decade* (New York, 1997), 38.
27. Ibid.
28. Miller, *Lyndon,* 231. See also Buford Ellington Oral History, Oct. 2, 1970, LBJL.
29. Quoted in Dallek, *Lone Star,* 572.
30. Shesol, *Mutual Contempt,* 35.
31. Ibid.
32. Miller, *Lyndon,* 246.
33. Shesol, *Mutual Contempt,* 38.
34. "RFK and LBJ" July 14, 1960, Box W59, Arthur Schlesinger Jr. Papers, John F. Kennedy Library (hereafter JFKL).
35. Hilty, *Brother Protector,* 29.
36. Shesol, *Mutual Contempt,* 44.
37. Miller, *Lyndon,* 249.
38. Steinberg, *Sam Johnson's Boy,* 526.
39. Miller, *Lyndon,* 245.
40. Steinberg, *Sam Johnson's Boy,* 527.
41. Miller, *Lyndon,* 252.
42. Booth Mooney Oral History, I, Apr. 8, 1969, LBJL.
43. Ibid.
44. Diaries, May 16, 1964, Vol. 3, PP/Orville Freeman, LBJL.
45. Miller, *Lyndon,* 254.
46. Connally, *In History's Shadow,* 162–163.
47. Diary Entry, July 23, 1964, Box W-59, Schlesinger Papers, JFKL.
48. Dallek, *Lone Star,* 576–577.
49. George Reedy to Senator, June 14, 1960, Box 427, SOF/G. Reedy, LBJL.
50. Ralph G. Martin, *Henry and Clare: An Intimate Portrait of the Luces* (New York, 1991), 362–363.
51. Theodore H. White, *The Making of the President 1964* (New York, 1965), 407–409.
52. Hilty, *Brother Protector,* 160.
53. Miller, *Lyndon,* 256.
54. Russell Morton Brown to Merle Miller, Sept. 28, 1979; R. M. Brown Oral History, Jan. 10, 1978, LBJL.
55. James H. Rowe Oral History, II, Sept. 16, 1969, LBJL.
56. Hilty, *Brother Protector,* 157.
57. Shesol, *Mutual Contempt,* 49.
58. "LBJ and the Kennedys," *Life,* Aug. 7, 1970.
59. Shesol, *Mutual Contempt,* 51.
60. Bobby Baker Oral History, II, Oct. 31, 1974, LBJL.
61. Adam Cohen and Elizabeth Taylor, *American Pharaoh: Mayor Richard J. Daley* (Boston, 2001), 260.
62. Miller, *Lyndon,* 258.
63. Harry McPherson Oral History, VII, May 16, 1985, LBJL.
64. Miller, *Lyndon,* 258.
65. Steinberg, *Sam Johnson's Boy,* 532.
66. Shesol, *Mutual Contempt,* 54.
67. Connally, *History's Shadow,* 164–165.
68. Miller, *Lyndon,* 258; Earl Clements Oral History, II, Oct. 24, 1974, LBJL.
69. Dallek, *Lone Star,* 582.
70. Steinberg, *Sam Johnson's Boy,* 53; B. Baker Oral History, Oct. 31, 1974, LBJL.
71. Steinberg, *Sam Johnson's Boy,* 537.
72. See also Booth Mooney to Sen. Johnson, Aug. 1, 1960, PP/Booth Mooney, Box 1, LBJL.
73. Rowe Oral History, II.
74. James Blundell Oral History, I, Oct. 29, 1974, LBJL.
75. Jarboe Russell, *Lady Bird,* 188.
76. Ibid., 189–190.
77. Dallek, *Lone Star,* 583; Steinberg, *Sam Johnson's Boy,* 535.
78. Arthur to Jack, Aug. 26, 1960, Pres. Office Files, Schlesinger, Box 32, JFKL.
79. Bill Moyers, "What a Real President Was Like," *Washington Post,* Nov. 13, 1988.
80. Jenkins to Sen. Johnson, Oct. 3, 1960, Pre-Presidential Memo File, Box 6, LBJL.

81. Kenny O'Donnell Oral History, I, July 23, 1969, LBJL.
82. Legislature Meeting Notes, Aug. 16 and 23, 1960, Whitman Files, Leg. Meeting Series, Box 3, DDEL.
83. Walter Jenkins to Sen. Johnson, Sept. 3, 1960, Pre-Presidential Memo File, Box 6, LBJL. See also John Singleton Oral History, II, July 15, 1983, LBJL.
84. Miller, *Lyndon,* 265.
85. O'Donnell Oral History, I.
86. Miller, *Lyndon,* 266.
87. Elizabeth Carpenter Oral History, IV, Aug. 27, 1969, LBJL.
88. Jarboe Russell, *Lady Bird,* 199–203.
89. Ibid., 204.
90. Miller, *Lyndon,* 266.
91. Reedy to Sen. Johnson, 1960, Box 426, SOF/G. Reedy, LBJL.
92. Miller, *Lyndon,* 267.
93. B. Baker Oral History, II.
94. Blundell Oral History, I.
95. Miller, *Lyndon,* 268.
96. B. Baker Oral History, II.
97. Blundell Oral History, I.
98. Rowe to Sen. Johnson, Aug. 25, 1960, Notes and Transcripts of Telephone Conversations, Box 1, LBJL.
99. Leonard Marks Oral History, II, Jan. 26, 1976, LBJL.
100. Hilty, *Brother Protector,* 166–167.
101. Singleton Oral History, II.
102. Philip Bobbitt Interview with author, Nov. 8, 2003, Austin, Texas.
103. Jarboe-Russell, *Lady Bird,* 205.
104. Miller, *Lyndon,* 264.
105. Quoted in Janeway, *House of Roosevelt,* 177.
106. D. B. Hardeman Oral History, II, Mar. 12, 1969, LBJL.
107. Dallek, *Lone Star,* 586.
108. Ibid., 587–588.
109. Lady Bird Johnson Interview.
110. Hardeman Oral History, II; Barefoot Sanders Oral History, I, n.d., LBJL; Miller, *Lyndon,* 270–271; Steinberg, *Sam Johnson's Boy,* 543.

Chapter 18: Camelot Meets Mr. Cornpone

1. Dallek, *Lone Star,* 589.
2. Jarboe-Russell, *Lady Bird,* 208; Robert Dallek, *An Unfinished Life: John F. Kennedy, 1917–1963* (Boston, 2003), 295.
3. Miller, *Lyndon,* 273.
4. Quoted in Janeway, *House of Roosevelt,* 175.
5. John L. Bullion, *In the Boat with LBJ* (Plano, TX, 2001), 117.
6. Ibid.
7. Steinberg, *Sam Johnson's Boy,* 546.
8. Ibid., 549; Dallek, *Lone Star,* 3; Cliff Carter Oral History, Oct. 15, 1968, III, LBJL.
9. Shesol, *Mutual Contempt,* 62.
10. Miller, *Lyndon,* 276.
11. Shesol, *Mutual Contempt,* 62.
12. Miller, *Lyndon,* 277.
13. Kearns Goodwin, *American Dream,* 174.
14. Judith Martin, "Off the Record Chat by President Johnson," Nov. 20, 1968, Oberdorfere Notes, Ref. File, "Vietnam," LBJL.
15. Hilty, *Brother Protector,* 271.
16. Quoted in Lloyd C. Gardner, *Pay Any Price: Lyndon Johnson and the Wars for Vietnam* (Chicago, 1990), 38.
17. Hilty, *Brother Protector,* 274.
18. Harry McPherson Oral History, LBJL.
19. J. Edward Day, "My Appointed Rounds," 1965, Schlesinger Papers, Box W-59, JFKL.
20. George Reedy to Senator Johnson, Dec. 30, 1960, VP Files of G. Reedy, Box 6, LBJL.
21. George Reedy to Vice President, July 19, 1961, VP Files of G. Reedy, Box 6, LBJL.
22. McNamara Interview with Walt Rostow, Jan. 8, 1975, LBJL.
23. McPherson Oral History, LBJL.
24. James H. Rowe Oral History, I, Sept. 9, 1969, LBJL.
25. Kenneth O'Donnell Oral History, I, July 23, 1969, LBJL.
26. Dallek, *Lone Star,* 10.
27. George Reedy to Vice President, Feb. 9, 1961, VP Files of G. Reedy, Box 6, LBJL. See also Shesol, *Mutual Contempt;* 64; Dallek, *Lone Star,* 8–9.
28. Hilty, *Brother Protector,* 307; Louis Martin Oral History, May 14, 1969, LBJL.
29. Jarboe Russell, *Lady Bird,* 209.

30. George Reedy to Vice President, Aug. 11, 1961, VP Files of G. Reedy, Box 6, LBJL.
31. Miller, Lyndon, 279.
32. Jarboe Russell, *Lady Bird,* 209–210.
33. Mark Hatfield, *Vice President of the United States,* Senate History Office, 459.
34. Quoted in Woods, *Quest for Identity,* 209.
35. Ibid.
36. Ibid., 210.
37. See George Reedy to Senator, May 19, 1958 SOF/G. Reedy, Box 427, LBJL; Rowe to Sen. Johnson Jan. 21, 1958, LBJA Selected Names File, Rowe, Box 32, LBJL.
38. George Reedy to Vice President, May 17, 1963, VP Papers of G. Reedy, Box 8, LBJL.
39. George Reedy to Sen. Johnson, Apr. 1959, SOF/G. Reedy, Box 429, LBJL.
40. "Remarks by Lyndon B. Johnson, The Vice President of the United States," The Advertising Council, June 6, 1961, VP Files of G. Reedy, Box 6, LBJL.
41. Miller, *Lyndon,* 282.
42. Dallek, *Lone Star,* 13.
43. Miller, *Lyndon,* 283.
44. Sarah McClendon Oral History, I, Feb. 16, 1972, LBJL.
45. Shesol, *Mutual Contempt,* 89.
46. Vice President to President, May 23, 1961, Pres. Office Files, Special Correspondence, Box 30, JFK Papers, JFKL.
47. Carl Thomas Rowan, *Breaking Barriers: A Memoir* (Boston, 1991), 188.
48. Carroll Kilpatrick Oral History, I, July 18, 1978, LBJL.
49. Rowan, *Breaking Barriers,* 183.
50. Ibid.
51. Ibid.
52. Dallek, *Lone Star,* 14.
53. Steinberg, *Sam Johnson's Boy,* 568–569; Walter Jenkins Oral History, II, Aug. 24, 1971, LBJL; George Reedy to Vice President, n.d., 1961, VP Files of G. Reedy, Box 6, LBJL.
54. LBJ to the President, May 23, 1961, Pres. Office Files, Special Correspondence, Box 30, Kennedy Papers, JFKL. See also George Reedy to Vice President, Sept. 25, 1961, VP Files of G. Reedy, Box 6, LBJL.
55. "LBJ Philosophy Revealed," *Dallas Herald* Dec. 15, 1963.
56. Carl Rowan, *Breaking Barriers: A Memoir* (Boston, 1991), 82.
57. Miller, *Lyndon,* 289.
58. Dallek, *Lone Star,* 19–20; Steinberg, *Sam Johnson's Boy,* 569–570; Shesol, *Mutual Contempt,* 90; George Reedy to Vice President, Aug. 17, 1961, VP Files of G. Reedy, Box 6, LBJL.
59. Miller, *Lyndon,* 290.
60. Ibid., 43.
61. D. B. Hardeman Oral History, IV, Jan. 19, 1977, LBJL.
62. Walter A. McDougall, *The Heavens and the Earth: A Political History of the Space Age* (New York, 1985), 319.
63. Ibid., 362.
64. Quoted in Robert Dallek, *Flawed Giant: Lyndon Johnson and His Times, 1960–1973* (New York, 1998), 21.
65. McDougall, *Heavens and Earth,* 373–374, 387.
66. See Steele to Luce, June 12, 1963, Steele Papers, Box 1, LBJL.
67. Hilty, *Brother Protector,* 299–300, 307–308.
68. Dallek, *Lone Star,* 25.
69. Shesol, *Mutual Contempt,* 79–80.
70. Dallek, *Lone Star,* 25.
71. Hilty, *Brother Protector,* 299.
72. Ibid, 301.
73. George Reedy to Vice President, Aug. 17, 1961, VP Files of G. Reedy, Box 6, LBJL.
74. George Reedy to Vice President, 1962, n.d., VP Papers of G. Reedy, Box 7, LBJL.
75. George Reedy to Vice President, Apr. 10, 1961, VP Files of G. Reedy, Box 6; Peter Braestrup, "U.S. Agency Split over Negro Jobs," *New York Times,* June 18, 1962.
76. George Reedy to Vice President, n.d., 1962, VP Files of G. Reedy, Box 7, LBJL.
77. Stone to Vice President, Mar. 9, 1962, Files of Willie Day Taylor, Box 426, LBJL.
78. George Reedy to Vice President, Apr. 6, 1962, VP Files of G. Reedy, Box 7, LBJL.
79. George Reedy to Vice President, Nov. 30, 1961, VP Files of G. Reedy, LBJL.
80. George Reedy to Vice President, Jan. 17, 1962, VP Papers of G. Reedy, Box 7, LBJL.
81. George Reedy to Vice President, Jan. 18, 1962, VP Files of G. Reedy, Box 7, LBJL.
82. George Reedy to Vice President, Jan. 8, 1962, VP Files of G. Reedy, Box 7, LBJL.
83. George Reedy to Vice President, Jan. 18, 1962, VP Files of G. Reedy, Box 7, LBJL.
84. George Reedy to Vice President, Feb. 5, 1962, VP Files of G. Reedy, Box 7, LBJL.
85. George Reedy to Vice President, Jan. 19, 1962, VP Files of G. Reedy, Box 7, LBJL.
86. Louis Martin Oral History, II, June 12, 1986, LBJL.
87. "Major Accomplishments of the Equal Employment Opportunity Program," n.d., 1963, Files of Willie Day Taylor, Box 434, LBJL.
88. George Reedy to Vice President, n.d., 1961, VP Files of G. Reedy, Box 6, LBJL.

89. George Reedy to Vice President, Feb. 8, 1961, VP Files of G. Reedy, Box 6, LBJL.
90. "Major Accomplishments of the Equal Employment Opportunity Program," n.d., 1963.
91. Shesol, *Mutual Contempt,* 79–80.
92. Hilty, *Brother Protector,* 301.
93. Dallek, *Lone Star,* 35.
94. Ibid., 36.
95. James Farmer Oral History, I, Oct. 1969, LBJL.
96. Roy Wilkins to Dr. L. M. Polan, June 17, 1960, Papers of Joseph Rauh, Box 36, Library of Congress.
97. Louis Martin Oral History, I, May 14, 1969, LBJL.
98. Charles Stone to LBJ, Mar. 9, 1962, Files of Willie Day Taylor, Box 426, LBJL.
99. Reedy to Vice President, Aug. 4, 1962, VP Files of G. Reedy, Box 8, LBJL.
100. Hobart Taylor to LBJ, Aug. 29, 1963, Files of Willie Day Taylor, Box 428, LBJL.
101. GER to Vice President May 24, 1963, Files of Willie Day Taylor, Box 434; G. Reedy to Vice President, June, 1963, VP Files of G. Reedy, Box 8, LBJL.
102. "Johnson Cheered in Poll Tax Attack," *Austin American-Statesman,* n.d., 1962.
103. "Remarks of Vice President," Wayne State University, Jan. 6, 1963, VP Files of G. Reedy, Box 8, LBJL.
104. "Remarks by Vice President," Tufts University, June 9, 1963, LBJ Handwriting File, Box 2, LBJL.
105. Ibid.
106. George Reedy to Vice President, Aug. 1, 1962, VP Files of G. Reedy, Box 8, LBJL.

Chapter 19: Hanging On

1. Kearns Goodwin, *American Dream,* 273.
2. Shesol, *Mutual Contempt,* 75.
3. Hatfield, *Vice Presidents of the United States,* 460.
4. Simon and Vicky McHugh Oral History, I, June 6, 1975, LBJL.
5. George Reedy to Vice President, Aug. 1, 1962, VP Files of G. Reedy, Box 8, LBJL.
6. Dallek, *Flawed Giant,* 21.
7. H. Busby to Vice President, July 13, 1961, VP Files of G. Reedy, Box 6, LBJL.
8. Dallek, *Lone Star,* 34. See also RFK and LBJ, Jan. 28, 1963, Box W59, Schlesinger Papers, JFKL.
9. Arthur M. Schlesinger Jr., *Robert Kennedy and His Times* (New York, 1978), 623.
10. RFK and LBJ, n.d., Box W-59, Schlesinger Papers, JFKL.
11. GER to Vice President, Feb. 19, 1962, VP Files of G. Reedy, Box 7, LBJL.
12. RFK–LBJ, n.d., Schlesinger Papers, Box W-59, JFKL.
13. George Reedy to Vice President, Jan. 12, 1963, VP Files of G. Reedy, Box 8, LBJL.
14. Harry McPherson Oral History, LBJL.
15. Kearns Goodwin, *American Dream,* 171.
16. Steinberg, *Sam Johnson's Boy,* 571–573.
17. Quoted in Woods, *Quest for Identity,* 217.
18. GER to President, Oct. 4, 1968, NSF Memos, Rostow, Box 40, LBJL.
19. Shesol, *Mutual Contempt,* 94.
20. Ibid., 93.
21. Ernest R. May and Philip D. Zelikow, *The Kennedy Tapes: Inside the White House During the Cuban Missile Crisis* (Cambridge, MA, 1997), 597.
22. Ibid., 589–591.
23. Shesol, *Mutual Contempt,* 96.
24. Ibid.
25. GER to Vice President, Nov. 1, 1962, VP Files of G. Reedy, Box 8, LBJL.
26. Mike Gillette Interview with author, Aug. 5, 2000, Washington, D.C.
27. There was a separate structure on the Texas ranch grounds called the Mary Margaret House. Arthur Krim Oral History, II, May 17, 1982, LBJL.
28. Simon and Vicky McHugh Oral History, I, June 6, 1975, LBJL.
29. Marie Fehmer Interview with author, Dec. 12, 2000, Washington, D.C.
30. Ibid.
31. Ibid.
32. Jarboe Russell, *Lady Bird,* 212–213.
33. Gammons Diary, Aug. 31, 1963, LBJL.
34. Ibid., Sept. 1, 1963.
35. Quoted in Woods, *Quest for Identity,* 175.
36. Quoted in ibid.
37. Quoted in ibid.
38. Dallek, *Lone Star,* 31.
39. Kenneth O'Reilly, *Nixon's Piano: Presidents and Racial Politics from Washington to Clinton* (New York, 1995), 237.
40. Hilty, *Brother Protector,* 384.
41. Shesol, *Mutual Contempt,* 99–100.
42. Ibid., 101.
43. Memorandum, "The Negro demonstrations . . . ," May 21, 1963, Files of Willie Day Taylor, Box 434, LBJL.
44. GER to Vice President, June 7, 1963, VP Files of G. Reedy, Box 8, LBJL.

45. Memorandum, "It is obvious . . . ," July 24, 1963, Files of Willie Day Taylor, Box 434; Memorandum, "The current series . . . ," June 1963; Memorandum, "The current tension . . . ," June 1963, VP Files of G. Reedy, Box 8, LBJL.
46. Memorandum, "The civil rights message . . . ," n.d., 1963, Files of Willie Day Taylor, Box 434, LBJL.
47. Dallek, *Lone Star,* 36.
48. Memorandum, "The civil rights message . . ."; Shesol, *Mutual Contempt,* 102.
49. Dallek, *Lone Star,* 37.
50. "LBJ Explodes in Senate after Called Figurehead," *Houston Post,* Jan. 31, 1963. See also "Lyndon Johnson 'Doing Us in on Rights' Say Dems," *Washington Afro-American,* Feb. 2, 1963; GER to Vice President, Jan. 5, 1963, and Feb. 6, 14, and 16, 1963, VP Files of G. Reedy, Box 8, LBJL.
51. McPherson Oral History, LBJL.
52. Steinberg, *Sam Johnson's Boy,* 593–594; "Marshall Probers Wait File," *Dallas Times Herald,* May 28, 1962.
53. Walter Jenkins Memoranda of Conversations with Deke DeLoche, May 31 and June 1, 1962, Pre-Presidential Confidential File, Box 1, LBJL. See also Telephone Conversation between LBJ and Orville Freeman, Apr. 17, 1962, Notes and Transcripts of LBJ Conversations, Box 1, LBJL.
54. George Reedy Oral History, III, June 7, 1975, LBJL.
55. Leslie Carpenter Oral History, Feb. 6, 1969, LBJL.
56. Steinberg, *Sam Johnson's Boy,* 598.
57. Ibid., 599.
58. Miller, *Lyndon,* 297.
59. Leslie Carpenter Oral History.
60. McPherson Oral History, II.
61. Reedy Oral History, III.
62. Dallek, *Lone Star,* 43.
63. "LBJ Gets Support of R. Kennedy," *Dallas Morning News,* Apr. 27, 1963.
64. Dallek, *Lone Star,* 42.
65. Leslie Carpenter Oral History.

Chapter 20: Interregnum: Death and Resurrection

1. "LBJ Ascension Bears on Texas Political Balance," *Dallas Herald,* Nov. 24, 1963.
2. Connally, *In History's Shadow,* 169.
3. Cliff Carter Oral History, III, LBJL; Kenny O'Donnell Oral History, I, July 23, 1969, LBJL; RFK Oral History, May 14, 1964, Box W59, Schlesinger Papers, JFKL.
4. Willie Morris, *North toward Home* (Boston, 1967), 250.
5. Woods, *Fulbright,* 321.
6. "Lady Bird Preparing Ranch for JFK Visit," Nov. 18, 1963, *Houston Post;* Jarboe Russell, *Lady Bird,* 214–216.
7. Reston, *Lone Star,* 264–266; Carter Oral History, III.
8. John Singleton Oral History, II, July 15, 1983, LBJL.
9. Schlesinger and Manchester Conversation, Jan. 6, 1965, Box P38, RFK Oral History May 14, 1964, Box W59, Schlesinger Papers, JFKL.
10. Busby, "Reflections on a Leader," 253.
11. Cliff Carter Oral History, III.
12. Reston, *Lone Star,* 276.
13. Michael Schaller et al., *Present Tense: The United States Since 1945* (Boston, 1992), 238.
14. Martin Agronsky Interview with John Connally, Nov. 1963, Box 10, Papers of John Connally, LBJL.
15. Miller, *Lyndon,* 312.
16. Jarboe Russell, *Lady Bird,* 220.
17. Charles Roberts Oral History, Jan. 14, 1970, I, LBJL.
18. "Johnson's Recollection Reported Different," *Dallas Morning News,* Dec. 26, 1966.
19. Kenny O'Donnell Oral History, I, July 23, 1969, LBJL.
20. Jack Valenti Oral History, II, Oct. 18, 1969, LBJL.
21. Steinberg, *Sam Johnson's Boy,* 608; O'Donnell Oral History; Michael Beschloss, ed., *Taking Charge: The Johnson White House Tapes, 1963–1964* (New York, 1997), 100.
22. Valenti Oral History, II.
23. Marie Fehmer Notes, Nov. 22, 1963, Diary Backup, Box 1, LBJL.
24. K. O'Donnell Oral History I.
25. Valenti Oral History II.
26. Reston, *Lone Star,* 269.
27. LBJ-Valenti-Hardesty Conversation, Mar. 8, 1969, "Kennedy Assassination," LBJ Reference File, LBJL.
28. Beschloss, *Taking Charge,* 18.
29. Miller, *Lyndon,* 321.
30. Steinberg, *Sam Johnson's Boy,* 609.
31. Charles Roberts Oral History, I, Jan. 14, 1970, LBJL.
32. Charles Roberts Oral History, I, Nov. 14, 1970; George Reedy Oral History, III, Dec. 19, 1968, LBJL.

33. Miller, *Lyndon,* 322.
34. George Ball Oral History, July 8, 1971, LBJL.
35. Carl Albert Oral History, I, Apr. 28, 1969, LBJL.
36. Miller, *Lyndon,* 324.
37. Lady Bird Johnson's Unpublished White House Diary, Nov. 24, 1963, LBJL.
38. Jarboe Russell, *Lady Bird,* 227.
39. Cliff Carter Oral History, IV, Oct. 15, 1968, LBJL.
40. Miller, *Lyndon,* 325.
41. Jarboe Russell, *Lady Bird,* 227.
42. Gerry Siegel Oral History, II, June 9, 1969, LBJL.
43. Busby, "Reflections on a Leader," 257.
44. Miller, *Lyndon,* 325.
45. Kearns Goodwin, *American Dream,* 177.
46. Steele to Williamson, Dec. 2, 1963, Steele Papers, Box 1, LBJL.
47. Beschloss, *Taking Charge,* 14–15.
48. Ibid., 12–13, 16–17.
49. Robert G. Baker Oral History, Oct. 31, 1974, LBJL.
50. Steinberg, *Sam Johnson's Boy,* 615; Miller, *Lyndon,* 601; RFK and LBJ, May 14, 1964, Box W59, Schlesinger Papers, JFKL.
51. Miller, *Lyndon,* 329.
52. Harry McPherson Oral History, LBJL.
53. Ibid.
54. Bundy to President, Nov. 23, 1963, Cabinet Papers, Box 1, LBJ Papers, LBJL.
55. Freeman Diary, Nov. 24, 1963, PP/Orville Freeman, Box 9, LBJL.
56. C. Clifford, *Counsel to the President,* 390.
57. Miller, *Lyndon,* 330.
58. Kearns Goodwin, *American Dream,* 185.
59. See David Halberstam, *The Best and the Brightest* (New York, 1972), 217–220, 49–54, 309–313; Kai Bird, *The Color of Truth. McGeorge Bundy and William Bundy: Brothers in Arms* (New York, 1998), 23–117; Deborah Shapley, *Promise and Power: The Life and Times of Robert McNamara* (Boston, 1993); Thomas J. Schoenbaum, *Waging War and Peace: Dean Rusk in the Truman, Kennedy, and Johnson Years* (New York, 1998); author's interviews with McNamara, Bundy, and Rusk.
60. Irving Bernstein, *Guns or Butter: The Presidency of Lyndon Johnson* (New York, 1996), 265–266.
61. Freeman Diary, Nov. 22, 1963, PP/Freeman, Box 9, LBJL.
62. Ibid.
63. Hilty, *Brother Protector,* 23.
64. Ibid., 6–23, 39–45, 82–84.
65. Ibid., 496.
66. Ibid, 486, 128–130.
67. Harris Wofford, *Of Kennedys and Kings: Making Sense of the Sixties* (New York, 1980), 418; Robert F. Kennedy Oral History, Apr. 13, 1964, Box W59, Schlesinger Papers, JFKL.
68. LBJ and Clifford Conversation, Dec. 5, 1963; Beschloss, *Taking Charge,* 91; Schlesinger to RFK, Mar. 20, 1964, Box W-59, Schlesinger Papers, JFKL.
69. LBJ to RFK, Jan. 1, 1964, Box W59, Schlesinger Papers, JFKL.
70. Dallek, *Lone Star,* 67. See. Eric F. Goldman, *The Tragedy of Lyndon Johnson* (New York, 1969), 119.
71. Ibid., 124–125.
72. Ibid., 106–107.
73. Ibid., 107.
74. Ibid., 108–111.
75. Goldman, *Tragedy,* 115–117.
76. Quoted in ibid., 109.
77. Ibid., 108–111.
78. Quoted in Woods, *Quest for Identity,* 185.
79. See Fields, *Union of Words,* 215–216.
80. Text of President's Off-the-Record Remarks to Governors, Nov. 25, 1963, Diary Backup, Box 1, LBJL.
81. McPherson Oral History, LBJL; James Rowe Oral History, II, Sept. 16, 1969, LBJL.
82. See Clark Clifford Oral History, July 2, 1969, LBJL.
83. Kalman, *Abe Fortas,* 28–29.
84. Ibid., 3, 15–16.
85. Diary Backup, Nov. 23, 1963, Johnson Papers, LBJL.
86. Abe Fortas, "Portrait of a Friend," in Thompson, *The Johnson Presidency,* 7.
87. "Address before a Joint Session of the Congress," Nov. 27, 1963, *Public Papers of the Presidents: Lyndon B. Johnson,* (Washington, 1965), Vol. I, 8–10.
88. *Ibid.*
89. Miller, *Lyndon,* 338–339.
90. "Address before a Joint Session of the Congress," Nov. 27, 1963, Vol. I, 9.
91. Ibid.

92. "Remarks at the State Capitol in Austin, Texas," Nov. 2, 1964, *Public Papers of the Presidents; LBJ,* Vol. II, 1579–1580.
93. "Remarks to Members of the Southern Baptist Christian Leadership Seminar," Mar. 25, 1964, *Public Papers of the Presidents: LBJ,* Vol. I, 420.
94. Moyers to President, May 15, 1964, OF/Bill Moyers, Box 10, LBJL.
95. Cartha DeLoach Oral History, Jan. 11, 1991, I, LBJL.
96. Dallek, *Flawed Giant,* 53.
97. Hoover and LBJ Conversation, Nov. 23, 1963 in Beschloss, *Taking Charge,* 22–23.
98. Quoted in Busby, "Reflections on a Leader," 266.
99. LBJ and J. Alsop Conversation, Nov. 25, 1963, K6311.02, WH Tapes, LBJL. See also LBJ and John McCone Meeting, Nov. 26, 1963, Box 1, Meetings with the President, John McCone Memoranda, LBJL.
100. Barefoot Sanders Oral History, I, LBJL.
101. Transcript of Telephone Conversation between Pres. and Speaker McCormack, Nov. 29, 1963, Box 1, LBJL.
102. "Reaction of Soviet and Communist Party Officials to the Assassination . . . ," FBI Report, Dec. 1, 1966, NSF-DSDUF, Box 4, Johnson Papers, LBJL.
103. Hoover and LBJ Conversation, Nov. 29, 1963 in Beschloss, *Taking Charge,* 52.
104. Katzenbach to Moyers, Nov. 25, 1963, OF/Bill Moyers, Box 55, LBJL.
105. LBJ and J. McCormack Conversation, Nov. 29, 1963, Transcripts of Telephone Conversations, LBJL.
106. Transcript of Telephone Conversation between Pres. and Sen. Russell, Nov. 29, 1963, Box 1, LBJL.
107. Miller, *Lyndon,* 348.
108. Deloach Oral History, I, Jan. 11, 1991, LBJL.

Chapter 21: "Kennedy Was Too Conservative for Me"

1. Kearns Goodwin, *American Dream,* 226.
2. Dallek, *Flawed Giant: Lyndon Johnson and His Times, 1961–1973* (New York, 1998), 65.
3. Kearns Goodwin, *American Dream,* 182.
4. S. and V. McHugh Oral History, I, June 6, 1975, LBJL.
5. LBJ and P. Salinger Conversation, Dec. 14, 1963, WH Tapes, K6312.08, LBJL.
6. See Walter Jenkins Oral History, II, Aug. 24, 1971, LBJL.
7. Jarboe Russell, *Lady Bird,* 233.
8. Steinberg, *Sam Johnson's Boy,* 629–630.
9. James Reston, *Deadline: A Memoir* (New York, 1991), 313–314.
10. LBJ and Senz Conversation, Dec. 23, 1963, in Beschloss, *Taking Charge,* 115–116.
11. Lyndon and Lady Bird Conversation, Dec. 23, 1963, in Beschloss, *Taking Charge,* 122.
12. LBJ and Salinger Conversation, Dec. 23, 1963, in Beschloss, *Taking Charge,* 124–125.
13. Jarboe Russell, *Lady Bird,* 236–237.
14. LBJ and Eisenhower Conversation, Dec. 25, 1963, WH Tapes, K6312.17, LBJL.
15. Randall B. Woods, *A Changing of the Guard: Anglo-American Relations, 1941–1946* (Chapel Hill, NC, 1990), 25–27.
16. See Ronald Heinemann, *Henry Byrd of Virginia* (Charlottesville, VA, 1996), 10.
17. Bernstein, *Guns or Butter,* 31.
18. Notes of Troika Meeting, n.d., Diary Backup, Box 1, LBJ Papers, LBJL.
19. Diary, Jan. 1, 1964, PP/Orville Freeman, Box 9, LBJL.
20. John McCone Memos, NSF, Meetings with President, Jan. 17, 1964, Box 1, LBJL.
21. John McCone Memos., NSF, Meetings with President, Jan. 4, 1964, Box 1, LBJL.
22. LBJ and Robert Anderson Conversation, Jan. 7, 1964, WH Tapes, Transcripts of Telephone Conversations, LBJL.
23. Bernstein, *Guns or Butter,* 33.
24. Jack Valenti Oral History, V, July 12, 1972, LBJL.
25. Dallek, *Flawed Giant,* 73; LBJ and Byrd Conversation, Jan. 8, 1964, WH Tapes, Transcripts of Telephone Conversations, LBJL.
26. LBJ and R. Russell Conversation, WH Tapes, WH6401.15, LBJL.
27. Kim McQuaid, *Big Business and Presidential Power: From FDR to Reagan* (New York, 1982), 224.
28. Ibid., 226.
29. Diary, Dec. 10, 1963, PP/Orville Freeman, Box 9, LBJL.
30. "Johnson Impresses the Nation," May 1, 1964, LBJ Handwriting File, Box 3, LBJL.
31. See Robert L. Heilbroner, "Capitalism without Tears," *New York Review of Books,* June 29, 1967.
32. Bill Moyers, "Forging the Great Society," in Hardesty, *The Johnson Years,* 66.
33. Frank Cormier, *LBJ: The Way He Was* (Garden City, NY, 1977), 4–5. See also Charles Roberts Oral History, Jan. 14, 1970, LBJL.
34. Kearns Goodwin, *American Dream,* 258.
35. "The President's News Conference of Dec. 18, 1963," *Public Papers of the Presidents, Lyndon Johnson, 1963–64,* Vol. I (Washington, 1964), 54.
36. Bernstein, *Guns or Butter,* 82–90; David Burner, *Making Peace with the '60s* (Princeton, NJ, 1996), 169–170; Douglas Cater, "The Politics of Poverty," *The Reporter,* Feb. 13, 1964.

37. R. Sargent Shriver, "The War on Poverty," in Jordan and Rostow, *The Great Society,* 40.
38. Miller, *Lyndon,* 362.
39. Ibid.
40. "Annual Message to the Congress on the State of the Union," Jan. 8, 1964, *Public Papers of the Presidents: LBJ,* Vol. I, 91–92.
41. Burner, *Making Peace with the '60s,* 166–170.
42. Carl Brauer, "Kennedy, Johnson, and the War on Poverty," *Journal of American History* 69 (June 1982): 101.
43. LBJ and Galbraith Conversation, Jan. 29, 1964, WH Tapes, Transcripts of Telephone Conversations, LBJL.
44. Bernstein, *Guns or Butter,* 99.
45. LBJ and Shriver Conversation, Feb. 1, 1964, WH Tapes, Transcripts of Telephone Conversations, LBJL.
46. Dallek, *Flawed Giant,* 79.
47. LBJ and Carl Albert Conversation, May 26, 1964, WH Tapes, WH6405.06, LBJL.
48. "Remarks upon Signing the Economic Opportunity Act," Aug. 20, 1964, *Public Papers of the Presidents: LBJ,* Vol. II, 989.
49. "Annual Message to the Congress on the State of the Union," Jan. 8, 1964, *Public Papers of the Presidents: LBJ,* Vol. I, 112.
50. Diary Backup, Nov. 29, 1963, Box 1, LBJL; Bill Moyers, "War on Poverty," in Jordan and Rostow, *The Great Society,* 36–37.
51. LBJ and Whittington Conversation, Dec. 23, 1963, in Beschloss, *Taking Charge,* 126.
52. Bernstein, *Guns or Butter,* 104
53. Goldman, *The Tragedy of Lyndon Johnson,* 187.
54. LBJ and Shriver Conversation, Mar. 26, 1964, WH Tapes, Transcripts of Telephone Conversations, Box 3, LBJL.
55. LBJ and Moyers Conversation, Aug. 8, 1964, WH Tapes, Transcripts of Telephone Conversations, Box 5, LBJL.
56. Diary, Feb. 22, 1964, PP/Orville Freeman, Box 9, LBJL.
57. Bernstein, *Guns or Butter,* 105.
58. Dallek, *Flawed Giant,* 108.
59. S. and V. McHugh Oral History; "Remarks in the City Hall, Rocky Mount, North Carolina," May 7, 1964, *Public Papers of the Presidents: LBJ,* Vol. II, 638–639.
60. "Remarks at the 20th Washington Conf. of the Advertising Council," May 6, 1964, *Public Papers of the Presidents: LBJ,* Vol. II, 611.
61. Diary, May 18, 1964, PP/Orville Freeman, Box 9, LBJL.
62. Moyers, "War on Poverty," 36.
63. LBJ and O'Brien Conversation, May 11, 1964, WH Tapes, WH6405.03, LBJL.
64. LBJ and McCormack Conversation, May 11, 1964, WH Tapes, Transcripts of Telephone Conversations, Box 4, LBJL.
65. LBJ and Shriver Conversation, May 13, 1964, in Beschloss, *Taking Charge,* 347.
66. LBJ and Shriver Conversation, May 13, 1964, WH Tapes, Transcripts of Telephone Conversations, Box 4, LBJL.
67. LBJ and O'Brien Conversation, Aug. 7, 1964, WH Tapes, Transcripts of Telephone Tapes, Box 5, LBJL.
68. LBJ and McCormack Conversation, Aug. 6, 1964, WH Tapes, Transcripts of Telephone Conversations, Box 5, LBJL.
69. Bernstein, *Guns or Butter,* 110–111.
70. LBJ-Jenkins-Moyers Conversation, Aug. 8, 1964, WH Tapes, WH6408.13, LBJL.
71. Dallek, *Flawed Giant,* 110.
72. Bernstein, *Guns or Butter,* 111.
73. John Chancellor Oral History, I, Apr. 25, 1969, LBJL.
74. Hugh Sidey, *A Very Personal Presidency: Lyndon Johnson in the White House* (New York, 1968), 163.
75. Beschloss, *Taking Charge,* 307.
76. *Houston Post,* Apr. 29, 1964.
77. LBJ and Reedy Conversation, Apr. 28, 1964, WH Tapes, Transcripts of Telephone Conversations, Box 4, LBJL.
78. Arthur Krim Oral History, III, June 29, 1982, LBJL.
79. Beschloss, *Taking Charge,* 57.
80. Busby to President, Sept. 1, 1965, OF/Horace Busby, Box 51, LBJL.
81. Ibid.
82. Miller, *Lyndon,* 375.
83. Steinberg, *Sam Johnson's Boy,* 637.
84. G. Reedy Oral History, III, June 7, 1975, LBJL.
85. LBJ and Graham Conversation, Dec. 2, 1963, in Beschloss, *Taking Charge,* 85.
86. Diary, Dec. 28, 1963, PP/Orville Freeman, Box 9, LBJL.
87. LBJ and Rowley Conversation, May 13, 1964, WH Tapes, Transcripts of Telephone Conversations, Box 4, LBJL.
88. LBJ and Rowley Conversation, Jan. 6, 1964, WH Tapes, Transcripts of Telephone Conversations, Box 1, LBJL.

89. LBJ and M. Mansfield Conversation, Sept. 28, 1964, WH Tapes, WH6409.09, LBJL.
90. See David H. McKay, *Domestic Policy and Ideology: Presidents and the American State* (New York, 1989), 33, 53.
91. A. E. Goldschmidt Oral History, June 3, 1969, LBJL.
92. "Special Message to the Congress on Consumer Interests," Feb. 5, 1964, *Public Papers of the Presidents, LBJ,* Vol. II, 263.
93. "Remarks in Pittsburgh to the League of Women Voters," Apr. 24, 1964, *Public Papers of the Presidents: LBJ,* Vol. I, 535.
94. Walter Lippmann, "The Principle for the Great Society," *Newsweek,* Jan. 18, 1965.
95. Quoted in Woods, *Quest for Identity,* 141.
96. "Remarks to a Group of Civil Rights Leaders," Apr. 29, 1964, *Public Papers of the Presidents: LBJ,* Vol. I, 588–589.
97. "Remarks at the 12th Annual Presidential Prayer Breakfast," Feb. 5, 1964, *Public Papers of the Presidents: LBJ,* Vol. I, 172.
98. Goldman, *Tragedy,* 112.
99. Quoted in Dallek, *Flawed Giant,*
100. Valenti Oral History, July 12, 1972, V, LBJL.
101. "Remarks at the University of Michigan," May 22, 1964, *Public Papers of the Presidents: LBJ,* Vol. II, 704–706.

Chapter 22: Free at Last

1. Leroy Collins Oral History, Nov. 15, 1972, LBJL.
2. Bernstein, *Guns or Butter,* 44. On the importance of a community relations service, see Ted Kheel to George Reedy, June 10, 1963, VP Papers of G. Reedy, Box 8, LBJL.
3. Quoted in Woods, *Quest for Identity,* 176.
4. Reedy to LBJ, May 21, 1963, Willie Day Taylor Files, Box 434, LBJL.
5. Dallek, *Flawed Giant,* 114.
6. Anthony Lewis, "Civil Rights Issue: Administration Will Be Judged to Large Degree by Fate of This Bill," *New York Times,* Dec. 8, 1963.
7. George Reedy to Vice President, June 10, 1963, Willie Day Taylor Files, Box 434, LBJL.
8. Louis Martin Oral History, May 14, 1969, LBJL.
9. Bernstein, *Guns or Butter,* 44.
10. Harry McPherson Oral History, VI, May 16, 1985, LBJL.
11. LBJ and Young Conversation, Nov. 24, 1963, WH Tapes, K6311.02, LBJL.
12. Roy Wilkins Appointment, Nov. 29, 1963, Diary Backup, Box 1, LBJL.
13. LBJ and Randolph Conversation, Nov. 29, 1963, WH Tapes, Transcripts of Telephone Conversations, Box 4, LBJL.
14. "Over 300 Attend SNCC Conference," SNCC *Student Voice,* Dec. 9, 1963; LBJ and King Conversation, Nov. 25, 1963, in Beschloss, *Taking Charge,* 37–38; James Farmer Oral History, Oct. 1969, LBJL.
15. LBJ and Robt. Anderson Conversation, Nov. 30, 1963, WH Tapes, Transcripts of Telephone Conversations, LBJL.
16. "Remarks to New Participants in 'Plans for Progress,' " Jan. 16, 1964, *Public Papers of the Presidents: Lyndon B. Johnson,* Vol. I, 140.
17. LBJ and Anderson Conversation, Nov. 30, 1963.
18. Bernstein, *Guns or Butter,* 44, 49.
19. Charles Whalen and Barbara Whalen; *The Longest Debate: A Legislative History of the 1964 Civil Rights Act* (New York, 1986), 65.
20. Bernstein, *Guns or Butter,* 53–55.
21. J. Pickle Oral History, Mar. 2, 1972, LBJL.
22. Bill Moyers, "Civil Rights," in Jordan and Rostow, *The Great Society,* 78.
23. E. Ernest "Tex" Goldstein Oral History, Dec. 9, 1968, LBJL; Miller, *Lyndon,* 366.
24. LBJ and Robert Byrd Conversation, Apr. 10, 1964, WH Tapes, Transcripts of Telephone Conversations, LBJL.
25. LBJ and Rauh Conversation, Jan. 7, 1964, WH Tapes, Transcripts of Telephone Conversations, Box 1, LBJL.
26. Jack Valenti Oral History, V, July 12, 1972, LBJL; Dallek, *Flawed Giant,* 112.
27. Whalen and Whalen, *The Longest Debate,* 68.
28. Nicholas B. Katzenbach, "The Bold Dream," in Hardesty, *The Johnson Years;* 80–81.
29. Whalen and Whalen, *The Longest Debate,* 70; Miller, *Lyndon,* 368. The leading works on the civil rights acts of 1964 and 1965 are Steven F. Lawson, *Black Ballots: Voting Rights in the South, 1994–1969* (New York, 1976) and *Running for Freedom: Civil Rights and Black Politics in America since 1941* (Philadelphia, 1991).
30. Bernstein, *Guns or Butter,* 67.
31. McPherson, *Political Education,* 72.
32. Hulsey, *Everett Dirksen,* 8.
33. Bernstein, *Guns or Butter,* 61.
34. Miller, *Lyndon,* 368–369. See also Humphrey, *The Education of a Public Man,* 274–283.
35. Whalen and Whalen, *The Largest Debate,* 70.

36. Fields, *Union of Words,* 291. Fields observes the difference between Jeffersonian and Lincolnesque language: "The former dedicated propositions, the latter cemeteries."
37. "Remarks to New Participants in 'Plans for Progress,' " Jan. 16, 1964, *Public Papers of the Presidents: LBJ,* Vol. I, 141–142.
38. "The President's Sermon," *Fort Worth Star-Telegram,* May 4, 1964.
39. Quoted in Kearns Goodwin, *American Dream,* 321.
40. Burner, *Making Peace with the '60s,* 17.
41. "Remarks in Atlanta at a Breakfast of the Georgia Legislature," May 8, 1964, *Public Papers of the Presidents: LBJ,* Vol. II, 648.
42. Beschloss, *Taking Charge,* 341.
43. "LBJ Given Tumultous Welcome," *Dallas Herald,* May 8, 1964.
44. *Ibid.*
45. Diary, Dec. 10, 1963, PP/Orville Freeman, Box 9, LBJL.
46. Miller, *Lyndon,* 369.
47. Beschloss, *Taking Charge,* 331.
48. LBJ and Dirksen Conversation, May 13, 1964, in WH Tapes, WH6405.06, LBJL. See also Hulsey, *Everett Dirksen,* 13–18.
49. Bernstein, *Guns or Butter,* 71, LBJ and HHH Conversation, Feb. 25, 1964, WH Tapes, Transcripts of Telephone Conversations, Box 1, LBJL.
50. LBJ and Russell Conversation, Apr. 9, 1964 WH Tapes, WH6404.06, LBJL.
51. LBJ and Kermit Gordon Conversation, Apr. 29, 1964, WH Tapes, Transcripts of Telephone Conversations, Box 1, LBJL.
52. Dallek, *Flawed Giant,* 119.
53. Humphrey, *Public Man,* 283.
54. Quoted in Woods, *Quest for Identity Since 1945,* 189–190.
55. Ibid.
56. LBJ and White Conversation, June 23, 1964, in Beschloss, *Taking Charge,* 425.
57. LBJ and Hoover Conversation, June 23, 1964, in Beschloss, *Taking Charge,* 433–434.
58. LBJ and Eastland Conversation, June 23, 1964, WH Tapes, WH6406.14, LBJL.
59. LBJ and Farmer Conversation, June 23, 1964, WH Tapes, Transcripts of Telephone Conversations, Box 4, LBJL. For the Schwerner-Goodman affair, see O'Reilly, *Nixon's Piano,* 163–169.
60. LBJ and Hodges Conversation, June 23, 1964, WH Tapes, Transcripts of Telephone Conversations, Box 4, LBJL.
61. Quoted in Sidney M. Milkis, *The President and the Parties: The Transformation of the American Party System Since the New Deal* (New York, 1993), 197.
62. Miller, *Lyndon,* 371.
63. LBJ and W. Young Conversation, June 19, 1964, WH Tapes, WH6406.11, LBJL; Lee White Memo, July 2, 1964, Diary Backup, Box 7, LBJL.
64. Dallek, *Flawed Giant,* 120.
65. Bullion, *In the Boat with LBJ,* 275–276.
66. Jarboe Russell, *Lady Bird,* 234–235.
67. Beschloss, *Taking Charge,* 268.
68. Jarboe Russell, *Lady Bird,* 235.
69. Beschloss, *Taking Charge,* 268.
70. Jarboe Russell, *Lady Bird,* 238–239.

Chapter 23: Containment at Home and Abroad

1. See Thomas Schwartz, *Lyndon Johnson and Europe: In the Shadow of Vietnam* (Cambridge, MA, 2003), 6.
2. Ibid., 18.
3. Quoted in Schwartz, *Shadow of Vietnam,* 22.
4. Woods, *Fulbright,* 279–281. See also Jeff Woods, *Black Struggle, Red Scare: Segregation and Anticommunism in the South, 1948–1968* (Baton Rouge, LA, 2004).
5. Quoted in George H. Nash, *The Conservative Intellectual Movement in America Since 1945* (New York, 1979), 261.
6. China Experts Meeting with President, Feb. 2, 1968, Meeting Notes File, NSC, Box 2, LBJL.
7. "Remarks in Baltimore at the Celebration of the Bicentennial of American Methodism," Apr. 22, 1966, *Public Papers of the Presidents, Lyndon Johnson, 1977,* Vol. I, 452.
8. Halberstam, *Best and the Brightest,* 218.
9. Shapley, *Promise and Power,* xi–xvi, Halberstam, *Best and Brightest,* 225–228.
10. Diary Backup, Nov. 29, 1963, Box 1, LBJL.
11. McNamara Interview with Rostow, Jan. 8, 1975, LBJL.
12. Shapley, *Promise and Power,* 325.
13. McNamara Interview with Rostow, Jan. 8, 1975.
14. Author Interview with Robert McNamara, Aug. 2, 1991, Washington, DC.
15. Freeman Diaries, June 10, 1964, PP/Orville Freeman, Box 9, LBJL.
16. Author Interview with Dean Rusk, Oct. 14, 1988, Athens, GA.
17. H. W. Brands, *The Wages of Globalism: Lyndon Johnson and the Limits of American Power* (New York, 1997), 6.

18. Halberstam, *Best and Brightest,* 308–323.
19. Ibid., 51.
20. Ibid., 53.
21. Author Interview with McGeorge Bundy, Aug. 1, 1991, New York.
22. Brands, *Wages of Globalism,* 10.
23. Dallek, *Flawed Giant,* 89.
24. Brands, *Wages of Globalism,* 6.
25. LBJ and Gilpatric Conversation, Dec. 21, 1963, WH Tapes, K6312.14, LBJL.
26. Brands, *Wages of Globalism,* 25.
27. LBJ and McCone Conversation, Dec. 9, 1963, John McCone Memoranda, Box 1, NSF, LBJL.
28. LBJ and McCone Conversation, Nov. 25, 1963, John McCone Memoranda, Box 1, NSF, LBJL.
29. LBJ and McCone Conversation, Nov. 29, 1963, John McCone Memoranda, Box 1, NSF, LBJL.
30. LBJ and McCone Conversation, Dec. 12, 1963, McCone Memoranda, Box 1, NSF, LBJL.
31. George C. Herring, *LBJ and Vietnam: A Different Kind of War* (Austin, TX, 1994), 6–7.
32. Brands, *Wages of Globalism,* 23.
33. Dallek, *Flawed Giant,* 84.
34. LBJ and M. Bundy Conversation, Jan. 2, 1964, WH Tapes, Transcripts of Telephone Conversations, Box 1, LBJL.
35. James N. Giglio, *The Presidency of John F. Kennedy* (Lawrence, KS, 1991), 234.
36. See Ruth Leacock, *Requiem for a Revolution: The United States and Brazil, 1961–1969* (Kent, OH: 1990), 34–60.
37. Quoted in Giglio, *Presidency of JFK,* 236.
38. Dallek, *Flawed Giant,* 92.
39. William O. Walker III, "The Struggle for the Americas: The Johnson Adm. and Cuba," paper presented to "Beyond Vietnam" Conference, LBJL, Mar. 1997, 14–17.
40. LBJ-McCone-Bundy Conversation, Dec. 2, 1963, John McCone Memoranda, NSF, Box 1, LBJL.
41. Reedy to LBJ, Nov. 14, 1961, VP Files of G. Reedy, Box 6, LBJL.
42. LBJ and B. Moyers Conversation, Feb. 8, 1964, WH Tapes, WH6402.11, LBJL.
43. Gordon Chase to Bundy, Dec. 3, 1963, *FRUS, 1961–1963, XI,* 899. See also Memorandum of Meeting with President Johnson, Dec. 19, 1963, *FRUS, 1961–63, XI,* 904–909.
44. Thomas Clifton Mann, "Be There Yesterday: The Adventures of a Career Foreign Service Officer, 1942–1966" (Unpublished memoir, Austin, TX 1982), 166.
45. Ibid., 148.
46. Ibid., 244.
47. Diary Backup, May 11, 1964, Box 4, LBJL; David Eli Lilienthal, *Creativity and Conflict: The Journals of David E. Lilienthal, VI* (New York, 1983), 20, 129.
48. Beschloss, *Taking Charge,* 101.
49. "Johnson-Mann Policies Face State Department Resistance," *Houston Post,* Jan. 5, 1964.
50. LBJ and Jerry Griffin Conversation, LBJ Tapes, Dec. 16, 1963, WH Tapes, K6312.09, LBJL.
51. Brands, *Wages of Globalism,* 33.
52. Ibid., 31–32; Mann, "Be There Yesterday," 215–220; White House Meeting on Panama, Jan. 10, 1964, J. McCone Memoranda, NSF, Box 1, LBJL.
53. LBJ and Chiari Conversation, Jan. 10, 1964, WH Tapes, WH6401.28, LBJL.
54. White House Meeting on Panamanian Crisis, Jan. 13, 1964, John McCone Memoranda, NSF, Box 1, LBJL, LBJ and R. Russell Conversation, Jan. 10, 1964, WH Tapes, Transcripts of Telephone Conversations, Box 1, LBJL.
55. LBJ and R. Russell Conversation, Jan. 10, 1964.
56. LBJ and R. Russell Conversation, Jan. 22, 1964, Transcripts of Telephone Conversations, Box 1, LBJL.
57. LBJ and R. Russell Conversation, Feb. 26, 1964, WH Tapes, Transcripts of Telephone Conversations, Box 2, LBJL, LBJ and Ball Conversation, Jan. 23, 1964, WH Tapes, WH6401.20, LBJL.
58. Mann, "Be There Yesterday," 216.
59. LBJ and Mann Conversation, Jan. 14, 1964, WH Tapes, Transcripts of Telephone Conversations, Box 1, LBJL; Brands, *Wages of Globalism,* 35.
60. White House Meeting on Panamanian Crisis, Jan. 13, 1964, John McCone Memoranda, NSF, Box 1, McNamara and O'Meara Conversation, Jan. 13, 1964, WH Tapes, Transcripts of Telephone Conversations, Box 1, LBJL.
61. LBJ and Stevenson Conversation, Feb. 20, 1964, WH Tapes, WH6402.19, LBJL; Brands, *Wages of Globalism,* 36–37.
62. White House Meeting on Panamanian Crisis, Jan. 13, 1964, John McCone Memoranda, NSF, Box 1, LBJL.
63. LBJ and Mann Conversation, Mar. 10, 1964, WH Tapes, Transcripts of Telephone Conversations, Box 3, LBJL.
64. Brands, *Wages of Globalism,* 40.
65. LBJ and M. Bundy Conversations, Mar. 12 and 25, 1964, Box 3, LBJ and Chiari Conversation, Apr. 3, 1964, Box 4, Transcripts of Telephone Conversations, LBJL.
66. James Rowe Oral History, II, Sept. 16, 1969, LBJL.
67. Robert W. Komer Oral History, Aug. 18, 1970, LBJL.
68. LBJ and M. Bundy Conversation, April 5, 1964, WH Tapes, Transcripts of Telephone Conversations, Box 3, LBJL.

Chapter 24: "The Countryside of the World"

1. Seth Jacobs, "Our System Demands the Supreme Being," *Diplomatic History,* no. 4 (fall 2001): 600.
2. Quoted in Richard J. Ellis, *American Political Cultures* (New York, 1993), 24.
3. "Remarks at a Reception for Members of the American Society of Newspaper Editors," Apr. 17, 1964, *Public Papers of the Presidents: LBJ,* Vol. I, 485.
4. Ibid.
5. "This Is the Third World War," *The Economist,* Aug. 20, 1966; McPherson to President, Aug. 26, 1966, OF/H. McPherson, Box 52, LBJL.
6. Harry McPherson, "Johnson and Civil Rights," in Thompson, *The Johnson Presidency,* 57.
7. Lloyd Gardner argues that Johnson himself was imprisoned by the logic of universal social justice: "Certainly Johnson's leadership in the civil rights struggle was a manifestation of his belief that he was the Southerner who had to stand up to the heritage that had imprisoned his region in backwardness and a semicolonial status. It probably made him more prone as the president, however, to arguments that world events in 1964 required him to stand firm in Vietnam." *Pay Any Price,* 148–149.
8. A poll taken by Elmo Roper in Nov. 1963 indicated that when asked which peoples were America's most reliable allies, 65 percent said Western Europe, 29 percent South America, 18 percent Africa, and 17 percent Asia. Roper to Fulbright, Nov. 8, 1963, Box 5, Series 48.1, J. William Fulbright Papers, University of Arkansas.
9. Ibid.
10. Westmoreland on "the Taylor-McNamara Report": "The major task was to be completed by the end of 1965! Could begin withdrawing some advisors by the end of 1964! This was the beginning of the credibility problem. They bought a bill of goods from Harkins. I found this irreconcilable with the true situation." "Strategy," Mar. 13, 1973, W. Westmoreland Papers, Box 30, LBJL. See Howard Jones, *Death of a Generation: How the Deaths of Diem and JFK Prolonged the Vietnam War* (New York, 2003).
11. Jones, *Death of a Generation.*
12. See Douglas Kinnard, *Certain Trumpet: Maxwell Taylor and the American Experience in Vietnam* (Washington, DC, 1991), 41; H. R. McMaster, *Dereliction of Duty: Lyndon Johnson, Robert McNamara, the Joint Chiefs of Staff, and the Lies That Led to Vietnam* (New York, 1997), 326.
13. C. and V. Durr Oral History, Mar. 1, 1975, LBJL.
14. "Tactical nuclear weapons if Chicoms come in force," LBJ Handwriting File, Mar. 13, 1965, Box 6, LBJL.
15. "Congressional Briefing," Mar. 4, 1965, Congressional Briefings on Vietnam, Box 1, LBJL.
16. Quang Zhai, *China and the Vietnam Wars, 1950–1975* (Chapel Hill, NC, 2000), 138–139.
17. LBJ and McCone Conversation, Nov. 29, 1963, John McCone Memoranda, NSF, Box 1, LBJL. See also LBJ and Dirksen Conversation, June 22, 1964, in Beschloss, *Taking Charge,* 423.
18. Meeting on South Vietnam Situation, Nov. 25, 1963, John McCone Memoranda, Box 1, NSF, LBJL; Breckon to Miller, Dec. 2, 1963, *FRUS, 1961–63, IV,* 651–652.
19. Quoted in Woods, *Quest for Identity,* 226.
20. LBJ to Minh, Dec. 31, 1963, *FRUS, 1961–63, IV,* 745.
21. McNamara to LBJ, Dec. 21, 1963, *FRUS, 1961–63, IV,* 732–733; Memorandum of a Conversation, Saigon, Dec. 20, 1963, *FRUS, 1961–63, IV,* 716–717; Highlights of Discussions in Saigon 18–20 Dec., 1963, John McCone Memoranda, Dec. 21, 1963, NSF, Box 1, LBJL.
22. McCone and LBJ Conversation, Feb. 4, 1964, John McCone Memoranda, Box 1, NSF, LBJL; Bohlen to President, Apr. 2, 1964, *FRUS, 1964–68, I,* 216–219.
23. Ball to Rusk, May 31, 1964, *FRUS, 1964–68, I,* 400.
24. JCS to McNamara, Jan. 22, 1964, *FRUS, 1964–68, I,* 35.
25. M. D. Taylor Oral History, Sept. 14, 1981, III, LBJL. See also Forrestal to Bundy, Mar. 18, 1964, *FRUS, 1964–68, I.*
26. Ibid.; Presidential Meeting on Vietnam, May 6, 1964, John McCone Memoranda, NSF, Box 1, LBJL.
27. Beschloss, *Taking Charge,* 213.
28. *New York Times,* Feb. 19, 1962.
29. John Roche Oral History, I, July 16, 1970, LBJL.
30. Beschloss, *Taking Charge,* 410.
31. See, for example, LBJ and Rusk Conversation, Feb. 1, 1964, WH Tapes, Transcripts of Telephone Conversations, Box 2, LBJL, LBJ and M. Bundy Conversation, Feb. 6, 1964, WH Tapes, WH6402.07, LBJL; Bundy to LBJ, Feb. 10, 1964, NSF, Memos to President, Bundy, Box 1, LBJL; Presidential Meeting on Vietnam, Feb. 20, 1964, John McCone Memoranda, NSF, Box 1, LBJL.
32. Memorandum Prepared in the Department of Defense, Mar. 2, 1964, *FRUS, 1964–1968, I,* 119–120.
33. Bill Moyers, "Flashbacks, Nov. 24, 1963," *Newsweek,* Feb. 10, 1975.
34. LBJ to General Nguyen Khanh, Feb. 2, 1964, LBJ Handwriting File, Box 2, LBJL.
35. Presidential Meeting on Vietnam, Feb. 20, 1964, John McCone Memoranda, NSF, Box 1, LBJL.
36. See LBJ and McNamara Conversation, June 9, 1964, WH Tapes, Transcripts of Telephone Conversations, Box 4, LBJL; Moyers to LBJ, July 3, 1964, LBJ Handwriting File, Box 3, LBJL.
37. LBJ and Russell Conversation, June 11, 1964, in Beschloss, *Taking Charge,* 401.

38. "Bill Moyers Talks about LBJ, Power, Poverty, War, and the Young," *Atlantic,* 222, no. 1 (July 1968): 32.
39. LBJ and McNamara Conversation, Mar. 2, 1964, in Beschloss, *Taking Charge,* 257.
40. Minutes of National Security Council Meeting, Mar. 17, 1964, John McCone Memoranda, NSF, Box 1, LBJL.
41. Robert McNamara's Notes for Report to the President, May 14, 1964, *FRUS, 1964–68, I,* 323.
42. Kinnard, *Certain Trumpet,* 132.
43. Lodge to President, May 7, 1964, *FRUS, 1964–68, I,* 296.
44. Embassy to Department of State, July 25, 1964, *FRUS, 1964–68, I,* 566–567; Note 1, *FRUS, 1964–68, I,* 395.
45. Note 1, *FRUS, 1964–68, I,* 243.
46. LBJ and McNamara Conversation, Apr. 30, 1964, WH Tapes, Transcripts of Telephone Conversations, Box 4, LBJL.
47. LBJ and Russell Conversation, May 27, 1964, WH Tapes, Transcripts of Telephone Conversations, Box 4, LBJL.
48. Ibid.
49. See LBJ and McNamara Conversation, June 13, 1964, WH Tapes, Transcripts of Telephone Conversations, Box 4, LBJL.
50. LBJ and M. Bundy Conversation, June 17, 1964, in Beschloss, *Taking Charge,* 413.
51. Kinnard, *Certain Trumpet,* 56–60.
52. John McCone Memoranda, May 14 and 25, 1964, John McCone Memoranda, Box 1, NSF, LBJL. See also Kinnard, *Certain Trumpet,* 136–138.
53. LBJ and McNamara Conversation, June 18, 1964, WH Trapes, WH6406.10, LBJL.
54. Command Methods, Feb. 20, 1973, Diaries, Westmoreland Papers, Box 30, LBJL.
55. Quoted in Sidey, *A Very Personal Presidency,* 82.
56. "Strategy," July 27–Aug. 31, 1964, Mar. 19, 1973, Diaries, Westmoreland Papers, Box 30, LBJL.
57. Chairman, JCS to McNamara, June 5, 1964, *FRUS, 1964–68, I,* 457. See also McMaster, *Dereliction of Duty,* 327.
58. Manila to Department of State, Mar. 8, 1967, NSF Memos to President, Rostow, Box 14, LBJL.
59. Rostow to President, May 7, 1968, NSF Memos to President, Box 33, LBJL; Shapley, *Promise and Power,* 360–361; McMaster, *Dereliction of Duty,* 333.
60. M. Bundy to LBJ, May 22 and May 25, 1964, NSF, Memos to President, Box 1, LBJL.
61. Quoted in Dewey Grantham, *Recent America: The United States Since 1945* (Wheeling, IL, 1998), 257–258.
62. CINCPAC Communique, Aug. 3, 1964, Meeting Notes File, NSF, Box 2, LBJL.
63. Quoted in Stanley Karnow, *Vietnam: A History* (New York, 1984), 369.
64. LBJ and R. Anderson Conversation, Aug. 3, 1964, in Beschloss, *Taking Charge,* 493.
65. LBJ and Smathers Conversation, Aug. 3, 1964, WH Tapes, Transcripts of Telephone Conversations, Box 5, LBJL. See also LBJ and McNamara Conversation, Aug. 3, 1964, WH Tapes, Transcripts of Telephone Conversations, Box 5, LBJL.
66. Quoted in George Herring, *America's Longest War: The United States and Vietnam, 1950–1975* (New York, 1996), 120.
67. LBJ and McNamara Conversation, Aug. 4, 1964, in Beschloss, *Taking Charge,* 496–497.
68. Editorial Note, Aug. 4, 1964, *FRUS, 1964–1968, I,* 607–609.
69. Quoted in George McT. Kahin, *Intervention: How America Became Involved in Vietnam* (New York, 1986), 221.
70. Notes taken at Leadership Meeting, Aug. 4, 1964, Meeting Notes File, Box 1, LBJL.
71. Quoted in Karnow, *Vietnam,* 371.
72. LBJ and Bundy Conversation, Aug. 8, 1964, WH6408, LBJL.
73. LBJ and Johnston Conversation, Aug. 4, 1964, in Beschloss, *Taking Charge,* 501.
74. LBJ and McNamara Conversation, July 2, 1965, in Michael Beschloss, *Reaching for Glory: Lyndon Johnson's Secret White House Tapes, 1964–65* (New York, 2001), 382.
75. Lady Bird and LBJ Conversation, Aug. 4, 1964, in Beschloss, *Taking Charge,* 502.
76. Author Interview with William Bundy, July 5, 1990, Princeton, NJ.
77. Scott Share, "Doubts Cast on Vietnam Incident," *New York Times,* Oct. 31, 2005.
78. Quoted in Karnow, *Vietnam,* 372.
79. George Ball Oral History, July 9, 1971, LBJL.
80. Quoted in George C. Herring, *America's Longest War: The United States and Vietnam, 1950–1970* (New York, 1996) 122.
81. Ibid.
82. *Congressional Record,* Senate, Aug. 6, 1964, 18399–407; Author Interview with George McGovern, June 27, 1991, Washington, D.C.

Chapter 25: Bobby

1. Diary, May 4, 1964, PP/Orville Freeman, Box 9, LBJL.
2. Diary, May 16, 1964, Box 9, PP/Orville Freeman, LBJL.
3. Quoted in Dallek, *Flawed Giant,* 124.
4. Murray Kempton, "The People's Choice," *New York Review of Books,* Nov. 5, 1964.

5. Quoted in Dallek, *Flawed Giant,* 124.
6. LBJ and Lawrence Conversation, Dec. 9, 1963, in Beschloss, *Reaching for Glory,* 97.
7. Kearns Goodwin, *American Dream,* 211–212.
8. Undated note from Mrs. Johnson, Aug. 1964, "President's Decision to Run in 1964," Family Correspondence, Box 4, LBJL.
9. "The Democratic party and the Presidency in the Twentieth Century," Busby to LBJ, July 1964, OF/H. Busby, Box 52, LBJL.
10. Quoted in Milkis, *The President and the Parties,* 176.
11. Busby to LBJ, June 1964, OF/H. Busby, Box 52, LBJL.
12. "Image Assessment and Suggested Activities," Busby to LBJ, May 1964, OF/H. Busby, Box 52, LBJL.
13. Goldman to President, Sept. 24, 1964, OF/Bill Moyers, Box 53, LBJL.
14. Quoted in Gardner, *Pay Any Price,* 106.
15. Cater to LBJ, June 3, 1964, OF/Bill Moyers, Box 53, LBJL.
16. LBJ and Wirtz-Conversation, Feb. 27, 1964, WH Tapes, WH6402.22, LBJL.
17. LBJ and McNeil Conversation, Apr. 10, 1964, WH Tapes, Transcripts of Telephone Conversations, Box 4, LBJL.
18. Ibid.
19. Quoted in Goldman, *The Tragedy of Lyndon Johnson,* 88.
20. Ibid.
21. Unpublished Diary of Lady Bird Johnson, Apr. 21, 1964, LBJL.
22. LBJ and Wirtz Conversation, Apr. 17, 1964; LBJ and Kennedy Conversation, Apr. 22, 1964, WH Tapes, Transcripts of Telephone Conversations, Box 4, LBJL.
23. Quoted in *The Record* (South Bend, IN), May 1, 1964.
24. Dallek, *Reaching for Glory,* 128.
25. "LBJ Called Strong in the Deep South," *Houston Post,* Jan. 26, 1964.
26. LBJ and G. Smathers Conversation, Aug. 1, 1964, WH Tapes, WH6408.01; LBJ and L. Hodges Conversation, July 7, 1964, WH Tapes, WH6407.05, LBJL.
27. LBJ and Connally Conversation, Dec. 5, 1963, in Beschloss, *Taking Charge,* 91.
28. LBJ-Jenkins-Connally Conversation, Dec. 18, 1963, in Beschloss, *Taking Charge,* 106.
29. LBJ and Connally Conversation, Feb. 8, 1964, in Beschloss, *Taking Charge,* 230. See also "Air Chill between Governor and LBJ," *Houston Post,* Feb. 9, 1964.
30. LBJ and Valenti Conversation, Feb. 9, 1964, WH Tapes, Transcripts of Telephone Conversations, Box 2, LBJL.
31. LBJ and Hand Conversation, Feb. 9, 1964, Transcripts of Telephone Conversations, Box 2, LBJL.
32. Quoted in Reston, *Lone Star,* 297.
33. Ibid., 291–293.
34. Bobby Baker Oral History, Oct. 11, 1984, VII, LBJL. See also LBJ and B. Everett Jordan Conversation, Dec. 6, 1963, in Beschloss, *Taking Charge,* 92.
35. Reedy Oral History, VI, Feb. 14, 1972, LBJL.
36. Beschloss, *Taking Charge,* 220.
37. LBJ and Connally Conversation, July 3, 1964, WH Tapes, WH6407.03, LBJL.
38. Quoted in R. B. Woods, *Quest for Identity,* 187.
39. Quoted in Dallek, *Flawed Giant,* 132.
40. LBJ and Harte Conversation, June 4, 1964, in Beschloss, *Taking Charge,* 383.
41. Diary, July 22, 1964, PP/O. Freeman, Box 9, LBJL.
42. Dan T. Carter, *The Politics of Rage: George Wallace, the Origins of the New Conservatism, and the Transformation of American Politics* (New York, 1995), 163.
43. Ibid., 156.
44. Quoted in ibid., 135.
45. "FBI Agents Probe Riot in Harlem," *Houston Post,* July 23, 1964.
46. Valenti to President, Aug. 4, 1964, LBJ Handwriting File, Box 3, LBJL.
47. Cater to LBJ, June 3, 1964, OF/Bill Moyers, Box 53, LBJL. See also Busby to LBJ, June 1964, OF/H. Busby, Box 52, LBJL.
48. Stewart Alsop, "LBJ and RFK," *Saturday Evening Post,* Feb. 22, 1964.
49. Kenneth P. O'Donnell Oral History, I, July 23, 1969, LBJL.
50. Kearns Goodwin, *American Dream,* 208.
51. LBJ and E. Kennedy Conversation June 30, 1964, in Beschloss, *Taking Charge,* 445. See also LBJ-Gargan-R. Kennedy Conversation, Mar. 30, 1964, WH Tapes, Transcripts of Telephone Conversations, Box 3, LBJL.
52. Quoted in Dallek, *Flawed Giant,* 138.
53. RFK and LBJ, May 14, 1964, Box W59, Schlesinger Papers, JFKL.
54. LBJ and B. Bundy Conversation, July 29, 1964, in Beschloss, *Taking Charge,* 476. See also LBJ and RFK Conversation, June 9, 1964, in Beschloss, *Taking Charge* 388–390; Kenneth P. O'Donnell Oral History, I, July 23, 1969, LBJL.
55. LBJ and Clifford Conversation, July 29, 1964, WH Tapes, WH6407.18, LBJL.
56. O'Donnell Oral History, I.
57. Democratic National Committee to President, July 31, 1964, Box 3, LBJ Handwriting, LBJL.
58. Hugh Sidey, "In Search of LBJ: Washington Panel," in Hardesty, *The Johnson Years,* 201.
59. RFK and LBJ, July 1969, Box W59, Schlesinger Papers, JFKL.

60. See, for example, LBJ-Connally-McNamara Conversation, July 17, 1964, WH Tapes, Transcripts of Telephone Conversations, Box 5, LBJL.
61. Unpublished Diaries of Lady Bird Johnson, July 4, 1964, LBJL.
62. LBJ and B. Bundy Conversation, July 30, 1964, WH Tapes, WH6407.19, LBJL.
63. Carl Solberg, *Hubert Humphrey: A Biography* (New York, 1984), 240–241.
64. Ibid., Diaries, June 10, 1964, Box 9, PP/Orville Freeman, LBJL.
65. Humphrey, *Public Man,* 298.
66. Goldman, *Tragedy of Lyndon Johnson,* 202.
67. Diaries, Jan. 2, 1964, Box 9, PP/Orville Freeman, LBJL.
68. LBJ and Rowe Conversation, Aug. 6, 1964, Transcripts of Telephone Conversations, Box 5, LBJL.
69. J. Valenti Oral History, II, Oct. 18, 1969, LBJL.
70. Humphrey, *Public Man,* 300–301.
71. Dallek, *Flawed Giant,* 159.
72. "Memo Cites LBJ Order for Wiretaps," *Dallas Times Herald,* Jan. 26, 1975. See also O'Reilly, *Nixon's Piano,* 185–190.
73. Hilty, *Brother Protector,* 223–225; Richard Gid Powers, *Secrecy and Power: The Life of J. Edgar Hoover* (New York, 1987), 382–390.
74. Ibid.
75. See Anthony Summers, *Official and Confidential: The Secret Life of J. Edgar Hoover* (New York, 1993).
76. Cartha DeLoach Oral History, I, Jan. 11, 1991, LBJL.
77. Powers, *Secrecy and Power,* 393–399.
78. LBJ and Hoover Conversation, Feb. 28, 1964, WH Tapes, WH6402.22, LBJL.
79. Quoted in Ronald Radosh, *Divided They Fell: The Demise of the Democratic party, 1964–1996* (New York, 1996), 2.
80. John Dittmer, *Local People: The Struggle for Civil Rights in Mississippi* (Urbana, II, 1994), 239.
81. Ibid., 281; J. Rauh Oral History, III, Aug. 8, 1969, LBJL.
82. Quoted in Ditmer, *Local People,* 290.
83. LBJ and McCormack Conversation, July 14, 1964, WH Tapes, Transcripts of Telephone Conversations, Box 5, LBJL.
84. LBJ and Wilkins Conversation, Aug. 15, 1964, in Beschloss, *Taking Charge,* 517.
85. LBJ and HHH Conversation, Aug. 14, 1964, WH Tapes, WH6408.18, LBJL.
86. White to Spottswood, July 17, 1964, LBJ Handwriting File, Box 3, LBJL.
87. White to President, Aug. 19, 1964, Diary Backup, Box 8, LBJL.
88. Quoted in Cohen and Taylor, *American Pharaoh,* 321.
89. Quoted in Ditmer, *Local People,* 288.
90. Paul Johnson Oral History, Sept. 8, 1970, LBJL.
91. Ditmer, *Local People,* 296; J. Rauh Oral History, III, Aug. 8, 1969, LBJL.
92. Ditmer, *Local People,* 302.
93. See ibid., 287–302; J Rauh Oral History, III; Radosh, *Divided They Fell,* 1–15.
94. Quoted in Ditmer, *Local People,* 30.
95. Beschloss, *Taking Charge,* 527.
96. LBJ and Reedy Conversation, Aug. 25, 1964, in Beschloss, *Taking Charge,* 527.
97. *Time,* Aug. 28, 1964. See also "$3,484,098 Given as Johnson's Worth," *Dallas Morning News,* Aug. 15, 1964.
98. LBJ and Reedy Conversation, Aug. 25, 1964, in Beschloss, *Taking Charge,* 527–532.
99. LBJ and Jenkins Conversation, Aug. 25, 1964, in ibid.
100. LBJ and Reedy Conversation, Aug. 25, 1964, in ibid.
101. LBJ and Jenkins Conversation, Aug. 25, 1964, in ibid.
102. Lady Bird to the President, Personal, Aug. 1964, Family Correspondence, Box 5, LBJL. See also LBJ and Haynes Johnson Lunch, Oberdorfer Notes, Reference File, "Vietnam," LBJL.
103. LBJ-Humphrey-Reuther Conversation, Aug. 25, 1964, in Beschloss, *Taking Charge,* 533–534.
104. Diary, Aug. 27, 1964, PP/Orville Freeman, Box 9, LBJL.
105. Quoted in Miller, *Lyndon,* 392.
106. Quoted in ibid., 393.
107. Dallek, *Flawed Giant,* 166.

Chapter 26: Barry

1. Quoted in Richard Hofstadter, *The Paranoid Style in American Politics and Other Essays* (New York, 1964), 112.
2. LBJ and McNamara Conversation, July 24, 1964, in Beschloss, *Taking Charge,* 472.
3. Quoted in Dallek, *Flawed Giant,* 169, 170.
4. Dutton to Moyers, Sept. 26, 1964, OF/Bill Moyers, Box 53, LBJL.
5. Busby to the President, Sept. 28, 1964, OF/H. Busby, Box 52, LBJL.
6. Valenti to President, Sept. 7, 1964, OF/Bill Moyers, Box 53, LBJL.
7. Goldman to President, Sept. 24, 1964, OF/Bill Moyers, Box 53, LBJL, Dallek, *Flawed Giant,* 170.
8. LBJ and Reedy Conversation, July 20, 1964, WH Tapes, WH6407.10, LBJL.
9. Quoted in Dallek, *Flawed Giant,* 175.
10. Ibid., 180.
11. Ibid., 176.

12. LBJ and Drew Pearson Conversation, Sept. 5, 1964, in Beschloss, *Reaching for Glory,* 33.
13. LBJ and Steve Smith Conversation, May 11, 1964, WH Tapes, Transcripts of Telephone Conversations, Box 4, LBJL.
14. Bundy to LBJ, July 2, 1964, LBJ Handwriting File, Box 3; Horace Busby to President, July 20, 1964, OF/H. Busby, Box 52, LBJL.
15. LBJ and R. Anderson Conversation, Jan. 30, 1964, in Beschloss, *Taking Charge,* 195.
16. "Walter Mack Rallies GOP for Johnson," *Dallas Times Herald,* July 22, 1964.
17. Bundy to LBJ, Oct. 1, 1964, Diary Backup, Box 10, LBJL.
18. "Johnson Republicans," *Dallas Morning News,* July 30, 1964.
19. LBJ and R. Anderson Conversation, Jan. 30, 1964, in Beschloss, *Taking Charge,* 195.
20. "Remarks in Atlantic City before the Democratic National Committee," Aug. 28, 1964, *Public Papers of the Presidents: LBJ,* Vol. II, 1015.
21. LBJ and Sanders Conversation, Aug. 1, 1964, WH Tapes, Transcripts of Telephone Conversations, Box 5, LBJL.
22. LBJ and Connally Conversation, Aug. 9, 1964, WH Tapes, WH6408.15, LBJL.
23. LBJ and Sparkman Conversation, Sept. 21, 1964, WH Tapes, WH6409.13, LBJL.
24. Jarboe Russell, *Lady Bird,* 243.
25. Ibid., 242.
26. Ibid., 247–248.
27. Elizabeth Carpenter Oral History, Dec. 3, 1968, LBJL.
28. Jarboe Russell, *Lady Bird,* 253.
29. E. Carpenter Oral History.
30. Jarboe Russell, *Lady Bird,* 256.
31. Buford Ellington Oral History, I, Oct. 2, 1970, LBJL; E. Carpenter Oral History.
32. Lady Bird and Antonio Taylor Conversation, Oct. 10, 1964, WH Tapes, WH6410.07, LBJL.
33. Jarboe Russell, *Lady Bird,* 261.
34. Quoted in ibid., 263.
35. "Remarks at a Fund-Raising Dinner in New Orleans," Oct. 9, 1964, *Public Papers of the Presidents: LBJ,* Vol. II, 1283–1286.
36. "Remarks at City Hall, Macon, Georgia. October 26, 1964," *Public Papers of The Presidents: LBJ,* Vol. II, 1446.
37. LBJ and Rusk Conversation, Oct. 2, 1964, WH Tapes, WH6401.01, LBJL.
38. LBJ and Charles Guy Conversation, Oct. 11, 1964, WH Tapes, WH6410.08, LBJL.
39. Miller, *Lyndon,* 398. See also Kenneth P. O'Donnell Oral History, July 23, 1969, I, LBJL.
40. V. and S. McHugh Oral History, II, June 8, 1975, LBJL.
41. Ibid.
42. LBJ and Chester Clifton Conversation, June 25, 1964, WH Tapes, WH6406.17, LBJL.
43. "Remarks in Cadillac Square, Detroit," Sept. 7, 1964, *Public Papers of the Presidents: LBJ,* Vol. II, 1052.
44. Goldman to President, Sept. 24, 1964, OF/Bill Moyers, Box 53, LBJL.
45. "Remarks at a Luncheon for a Group of State University Presidents," Aug. 13, 1964, *Public Papers of the Presidents: LBJ,* Vol. II, 960.
46. J. Richard Piper, *Ideologies and Institutions: American Conservative and Liberal Governance Prescriptions Since 1933* (Lanham, MD, 1997), 14–15.
47. Larry Levinson to the President, Oct. 16, 1968, LBJ Handwriting File, Box 31, LBJL.
48. Ellis, *American Political Cultures,* 12–15.
49. See Moyers to the President, Oct. 3, 1964, OF/Bill Moyers, Box 10, LBJL.
50. Taylor to Rusk, Sept. 6, 1964, *FRUS, 1964–68, I,* 733–735.
51. Joint Chiefs to McNamara, Oct. 27, 1964, *FRUS, 1964–68, I,* 849.
52. LBJ and McNamara Conversation, Sept. 18, 1964, WH Tapes, WH6409.11, LBJL.
53. M. Bundy Memorandum for the Record, Sept. 20, 1964, *FRUS, 1964–68, I,* 778–779.
54. LBJ and McNamara Conversation, Sept. 18, 1964, WH Tapes, WH6409.11, LBJL.
55. LBJ and R. Russell Conversation, Sept. 18, 1964, WH Tapes, WH6409.11, LBJL.
56. M. Bundy to the President, Oct. 1, 1964, Diary Backup, Box 10, LBJL. See also Rostow to Bundy, Sept. 9, 1964, OF/Bill Moyers, Box 53, LBJL.
57. "Remarks in Manchester to the Members of the New Hampshire Weeky Newspaper Editors Association," Sept. 28, 1964, *Public Papers of the Presidents: LBJ,* Vol. I, 1161–1162.
58. "Excerpts from Remarks at a Meeting with the New Panel of Consultants on Peace and National Security," Sept. 23, 1964, *Public Papers of the Presidents: LBJ,* Vol. II, 1112–1113.
59. "Remarks in Manchester to the Members of the New Hampshire Weekly Newspaper Editors Association." Vol. II, 1165.
60. Cleveland to Moyers, Sept. 29, 1964, OF/Bill Moyers, Box 53, LBJL.
61. Vance Muse, "LBJ's Greatest Loss" *George* (May 1999): 94.
62. LBJ and Fortas Conversation, Oct. 14, 1964, WH Tapes, WH6410.08, LBJL.
63. Muse, "LBJ's Greatest Loss," 95.
64. Quoted in ibid., 96.
65. Cartha DeLoach Oral History, Jan. 11, 1991, LBJL.
66. Jack Valenti Oral History, III, Feb. 19, 1971, LBJL.
67. E. Carpenter Oral History.
68. Clark Clifford Oral History, July 2, 1969, LBJL.

69. Quoted in Muse, "LBJ's Greatest Loss," 103.
70. DeLoach Oral History.
71. LBJ and Fortas Conversation, Oct. 14, 1964.
72. DeLoach Oral History.
73. Muse, "LBJ's Greatest Loss," 103.
74. Ibid., Beschloss, *Reaching for Glory,* 76.
75. Dallek, *Flawed Giant,* 181.
76. LBJ and Lady Bird Conversation, Oct. 15, 1964, WH Tapes, WH6410.11, LBJL.
77. LBJ and Hoover Conversation, Oct. 23, 1964, in Beschloss, *Reaching for Glory,* 90–91.
78. LBJ and Hoover Conversation, Oct. 31, 1964, in Beschloss, *Reaching for Glory,* 101.
79. Carl Rowan to President, Oct. 19, 1964, Cabinet Papers, Box 1, LBJL.
80. *Houston Post,* Aug. 26, 1964.
81. Shesol, *Mutual Contempt,* 211–214, LBJ and RFK Conversation, Aug. 12, 1964, WH Tapes, Transcripts of Telephone Conversations, Box 5, LBJL.
82. LBJ and RFK Conversation, Sept. 3, 1964, WH Tapes, WH6409.05, LBJL.
83. LBJ and RFK Conversation, Oct. 26, 1964, in Beschloss, *Reaching for Glory,* 93.
84. LBJ and O. Johnston Conversation, Nov. 4, 1964, WH Tapes, WH6411.05, LBJL.
85. Dallek, *Flawed Giant,* 183–184; Miller, *Lyndon,* 402.
86. Quoted in Hulsey, *Everett Dirksen,* 38.
87. LBJ and Scotty Reston Conversation, Jan. 8, 1964, WH Tapes, WH6401.09, LBJL.
88. Beschloss, *Reaching for Glory,* 115.
89. LBJ and Wiesl, Conversation, Nov. 4, 1964, in ibid., 120.
90. LBJ and Joe Haggar Conversation, Aug. 9, 1964, Transcripts of Telephone Conversations, 4851, LBJL.
91. Humphrey, *Public Man,* 307–308.
92. Diary, Nov. 21, 1964, PP/Orville Freeman, Box 9, LBJL.
93. Ibid.
94. Diary, Dec. 10, 1964, PP/Orville Freeman, Box 9, LBJL.
95. LBJ and HHH Conversation, June 18, 1964, WH Tapes, WH6406.11, LBJL.
96. "Lyndon Johnson's Pledge," *Newsweek,* Feb. 1, 1965.
97. Ibid.
98. Liz [Carpenter] to the President, Jan. 20, 1965, Diary Backup, Box 12, LBJL.
99. Diaries, Jan. 22, 1965, PP/Orville Freeman, Box 10, LBJL.
100. "Lyndon Johnson's Pledge," *Newsweek,* Feb. 2, 1965, 12.
101. Ibid.
102. Edwin Weisl Oral History, Oct. 24, 1968, LBJL.

Chapter 27: A New Bill of Rights

1. "The State of the Union," *Newsweek,* Jan. 11, 1965, 18.
2. William E. Leuchtgenberg, "The Genesis of the Great Society," *The Reporter* 34 (April 21, 1966): 39.
3. "State of the Union," 17.
4. "Annual Message to the Congress on the State of the Union," Jan. 4, 1965, *Public Papers of the Presidents: LBJ,* Vol. I, 9.
5. Ellis, *American Political Cultures,* 74–76.
6. Henry Fairlie, "The Hidden Meaning of 'Consensus,' " *New Republic,* Jan. 1, 1966, 15–19.
7. Report to President on Economic Situation by CEA, Apr. 20, 1965, Cabinet Papers, Box 2, LBJL. See also Briefing Notes on the Outlook and Fiscal Policy for 1965, Dec. 1964, Diary Backup, Box 12, LBJL.
8. Statement of President at Cabinet Meeting, Nov. 19, 1964, Cabinet Papers, Box 1, LBJL.
9. McNamara Interview with Rostow, Jan. 8, 1975, Reference File, LBJL.
10. "The President's News Conference at the LBJ Ranch," December 27, 1963, *Public Papers of the Presidents: LBJ,* Vol. I, 89.
11. See Walter Heller, "The President and Economic Policy," in Thompson, *The Johnson Presidency,* 184–191.
12. Troika Staff Memorandum, Aug. 12, 1964, Diary Backup, Box 9, LBJL.
13. M. J. Rossant, "Johnson Follows Keynes," *Austin American,* Jan. 4, 1965.
14. Quoted in Woods, *Changing of the Guard,* 14.
15. Gardner Ackley to President, Jan. 22, 1965, Diary Backup, Box 12, LBJL.
16. See Robert L. Hardesty, *The LBJ the Nation Seldom Saw* (San Marcos, TX, 1983), 3.
17. Jordan A. Schwarz, *The New Dealers: Power Politics in the Age of Roosevelt* (New York, 1993), x–xi.
18. Moyers, "Forging the Great Society," 65.
19. Goldman, *The Tragedy of Lyndon Johnson,* 259.
20. Cater to President, Jan. 12, 1966, LBJ Handwriting File, Box 11, LBJL.
21. "Annual Message to the Congress on the State of the Union," Jan. 4, 1965, *Public Papers of the Presidents: LBJ,* Vol. I, 1.
22. "LBJ and His Congress: Made for Each Other," *Newsweek,* Jan. 18, 1965, 17.
23. Quoted in Dallek, *Flawed Giant,* 191.
24. Wilbur Cohen Oral History, I, Dec. 8, 1968, LBJL.
25. "Annual Message to the Congress on the State of the Union," Jan. 4, 1965, 1.

26. D. B. Hardeman Oral History, Feb. 15–28, 1965, LBJL.
27. Quoted in Kearns Goodwin, *American Dream,* 238.
28. LBJ and W. Reuther Conversation, Nov. 24, 1964, WH Tapes, WH6411.29, LBJL.
29. "Remarks before the National Conference on Educational Legislation," Mar. 1, 1965, *Public Papers of the Presidents LBJ,* Vol. I, 227.
30. Martin E. Marty, *The One and the Many: America's Struggle for the Common Good* (Cambridge, MA, 1997), 51, 56–57.
31. Goldman, *Tragedy of LBJ,* 304.
32. Bernstein, *Guns or Butter,* 187.
33. Goldman, *Tragedy of LBJ,* 36–37.
34. Bernstein, *Guns or Butter,* 184; Goldman, *Tragedy of LBJ,* 297.
35. Lawrence O'Brien Oral History, Sept. 18, 1985, LBJL.
36. Douglas Cater Oral History, I, Apr. 29, 1969, LBJL; Goldman, *Tragedy of LBJ,* 300.
37. Cater Oral History, I; Bernstein, *Guns or Butter,* 191.
38. Quoted in Dallek, *Flawed Giant,* 196.
39. Goldman, *Tragedy of LBJ,* 300.
40. Louis Martin Oral History, II, June 12, 1986, LBJL.
41. L. O'Brien Oral History, I; Goldman, *Tragedy of LBJ,* 302.
42. LBJ and Ralph Dungan Conversation, Apr. 10, 1964, WH Tapes, Transcripts of Telephone Conversations, Box 4, LBJL.
43. Goldman, *Tragedy of LBJ,* 306.
44. Rothman, *Texas White House,* 186–187.
45. "Remarks in Johnson City, Texas, upon Signing the Elementary and Secondary Education Bill," Apr. 11, 1965, *Public Papers of the Presidents: LBJ,* Vol. I, 413.
46. "Remarks to Members of Congress at a Reception Marking the Enactment of the Education Bill," Apr. 13, 1965, *Public Papers of the Presidents: LBJ,* Vol. I, 416.
47. Ibid.
48. Bernstein, *Guns or Butter,* 204–210.
49. LBJ and HHH Conversation, Mar. 6, 1965, WH Tapes, WH6503.02, LBJL.
50. See Allen J. Matusow, *The Unravelling of America: A History of Liberalism in the 1960s* (New York, 1984).
51. Dallek, *Flawed Giant,* 201–202.
52. Bernstein, *Guns or Butter,* 157.
53. Reedy to Sen. Johnson, n.d., 1959, SOF/G. Reedy, Box 429, LBJL.
54. Notes of an interview with LBJ during preparation of exhibits for LBJ Library, n.d., OF/Harry Middleton, "Exhibits," Box 64, LBJL.
55. Edward D. Berkowitz, *Mr. Social Security: The Life of Wilbur J. Cohen* (Lawrence, KS, 1995), 222–223.
56. Julian E. Zelizer, *Taxing America: Wilbur D. Mills, Congress, and the State* (New York, 1998), 28–31.
57. Ibid., 54
58. Wilbur Mills Oral History, Mar. 5, 1987, II, LBJL.
59. Zelizer, *Taxing America,* 221.
60. Wilbur J. Cohen, "Education and Health," in Jordan and Rostow, *The Great Society,* 103.
61. W. Mills OH, II, LBJL.
62. LBJ and C. Albert Conversation, Sept. 3, 1964, WH Tapes, WH6409.05, LBJL.
63. LBJ and W. Mills Conversation June 9, 1964, WH Tapes, WH6406.03, LBJL.
64. Zelizer, *Taxing America,* 231.
65. Bernstein, *Guns or Butter,* 171.
66. Quoted in Zelizer, *Taxing America,* 241.
67. Miller, *Lyndon,* 410–411.
68. Dallek, *Flawed Giant,* 209; Bernstein, *Guns or Butter,* 176.
69. "Biggest Change Since the New Deal," *Newsweek,* Apr. 12, 1965.
70. LBJ and L. O'Brien Conversation, Apr. 9, 1965, WH Tapes, WH6504.04, LBJL.
71. Dallek, *Flawed Giant,* 209–210.
72. Bernstein, *Guns or Butter,* 179.
73. Joseph A. Califano Jr., *The Triumph and Tragedy of Lyndon Johnson: The White House Years* (College Station, TX, 2000), 51–52.
74. Wilbur Cohen Oral History, Mar. 2, 1969, II, LBJL.
75. Bernstein, *Guns or Butter,* 180–181; Dallek, *Flawed Giant,* 211.
76. Miller, *Lyndon,* 412.
77. Ibid.

Chapter 28: The Crux of the Matter

1. Bernstein, *Guns or Butter,* 223.
2. See William H. Chafe, *Unfinished Journey: America Since World War II* (New York, 1991), 311.
3. LBJ and R. Wilkins Conversation, Nov. 4, 1965, WH Tapes, WH6511.01, LBJL.
4. LBJ and R. Wilkins Conversation, Oct. 30, 1965, WH Tapes, WH6510.03, LBJL.
5. Dallek, *Flawed Giant,* 212.
6. See Reedy to President, Nov. 29, 1963, Diary Backup, Box 1, LBJL.
7. Burner, *Making Peace with the '60s,* 18.

8. Hoover to Jenkins, April 14, 1964, Office Files of Mildred Stegall, Box 32, LBJL.
9. See David Chappell, *A Stone of Hope: Prophetic Religion and the Death of Jim Crow* (Chapel Hill, NC, 2004).
10. See Burner, *Making Peace with the '60s,* 5.
11. Taylor Branch, *Pillar of Fire: America in the King Years, 1963–65* (New York, 1998), 28.
12. Ibid., 150.
13. Hoover to Jenkins, March 9, 1964, Office Files of Mildred Stegall, Box 32, LBJL.
14. Ibid., 207.
15. When a friend urged King to be more circumspect, he replied, "I'm away from home twenty-five to twenty-seven days a month. Fucking's a form of anxiety reduction." Quoted in Bernstein, *Guns or Butter,* 216.
16. James Farmer Oral History, II, July 20, 1971, LBJL.
17. Lee White to President, Dec. 18, 1964, Diary Backup, Box 12, LBJL.
18. Quoted in Branch, *Pillar of Fire,* 555.
19. LBJ and Edward Clark Conversation, Nov. 7, 1964, WH Tapes, WH6411.12, LBJL.
20. Buford Ellington Oral History, I, Oct. 2, 1970, LBJL.
21. Bernstein, *Guns or Butter,* 215.
22. Ibid., 219–220.
23. Beschloss, *Reaching for Glory,* 171.
24. See LBJ and Katzenbach Conversation, Feb. 5, 1965, WH Tapes, WH6502.01, LBJL.
25. Lee White to President and Points that Dr. King Might Make upon Leaving the White House, Feb. 5, 1965, Diary Backup, Box 13, LBJL.
26. Carter, *Politics of Rage,* 125.
27. Author Interview with Roy Reed, Mar. 4, 2003, Fayetteville, AR.
28. "An American Tragedy," *Newsweek,* Mar. 22, 1965, 18–20.
29. LBJ and L. Hill Conversation, Mar. 8, 1965, WH Tapes, WH6503.04, LBJL.
30. LBJ and Katzenbach Conversation, Mar. 10, 1965, WH Tapes, WH6503.04, LBJL.
31. Wallace to President, Mar. 1965, Diary Backup, Box 15, LBJL.
32. Quoted in Carter, *Politics of Rage,* 252.
33. Dallek, *Flawed Giant,* 216–217; Bernstein, *Guns or Butter,* 230–231.
34. Roger Wilkins quoted in "LBJ," *The American Experience,* Public Broadcasting System, 1995.
35. Remarks Delivered to a Press Conference in the Rose Garden, Mar. 13, 1965, *Public Papers of the Presidents: LBJ,* Vol. I, 276.
36. McPherson to President, Mar. 12, 1965, Diary Backup, Box 15, LBJL.
37. L. B. Johnson, *Vantage Point,* 164.
38. Dallek, *Flawed Giant,* 218.
39. "Special Message to the Congress: The American Promise," March 15, 1965, *Public Papers of the Presidents: LBJ,* Vol. I, 281–287.
40. Ibid.
41. Ibid.
42. Quoted in Goldman, *Tragedy of Lyndon Johnson,* 322.
43. LBJ-Wallace-Ellington-Katzenbach Conversation, Mar. 18, 1965, WH Tapes, WH6503.09, LBJL.
44. LBJ and Ellington Conversation, Mar. 18, 1965, WH Tapes, WH6503.10, LBJL.
45. Statement by the President in Response to a Telegram from the Governor of Alabama, Mar. 18, 1965, *Public Papers of the Presidents: LBJ,* Vol. I, 296–297.
46. Valenti Notes on Meeting in President's Office, Mar. 18, 1965, Diary Backup, Box 15, LBJL. See also "Forces in Position," Mar. 1965, Diary Backup, Box 15, LBJL.
47. LeRoy Collins to President, Mar. 24, 1965, OF/Harry McPherson, Box 1, LBJL.
48. Cyrus Vance to President, Mar. 20–24, 1965, Diary Backup, Box 15, LBJL; Bernstein, *Guns or Butter,* 235–235. See also Ramsey Clark Oral History, Feb. 11, 1969, LBJL.
49. O'Reilly, *Nixon's Piano,* 255.
50. "Road from Selma: Hope—and Death," *Newsweek,* Apr. 5, 1965.
51. LBJ and Katzenbach Conversation, Aug. 17, 1965, WH Tapes, WH 6508.05, LBJL.
52. Ramsey Clark Oral History, II, Feb. 11, 1969, LBJL.
53. Bernstein, *Guns or Butter,* 236–237.
54. Busby to Moyers and White, Feb. 27, 1965, and Moyers and White to Katzenbach, Mar. 1, 1965, OF/Bill Moyers, Box 6, LBJL; Meeting in Cabinet Room of Bipartisan Congressional Leaders, Mar. 14, 1965, Diary Backup, Box 15, LBJL; LBJ and Vance Hartke Conversation, May 7, 1965, Transcripts of Telephone Conversations, Box 6, LBJL.
55. LBJ and Birch Bayh Conversation, May 7, 1965, WH Tapes, WH6505.06, LBJL.
56. Bernstein, *Guns or Butter,* 241.
57. LBJ and R. Wilkins Conversation, Nov. 4, 1965, WH Tapes, WH6511.01, LBJL. See also LBJ and Katzenbach Conversation, Aug. 17, 1965, WH Tapes, WH 6508.04., LBJL.
58. Bernstein, *Guns or Butter,* 241–242.
59. LBJ and Manatos Conversation, Feb. 4, 1966, WH Tapes, WH6602.02, LBJL.
60. Dallek, *Reaching for Glory,* 220–221.
61. "New Crisis: The Negro Family," *Newsweek,* Aug. 9, 1965, 32.
62. Ibid.
63. Moynihan to McPherson, Sept. 22, 1966, OF/H. McPherson, Box 22, LBJL.
64. Harry McPherson Oral History, III, LBJL.

65. George Reedy, "Affirmative Action Forgets Its Roots," *USA Today,* July 19, 1995, 11A.
66. Commencement Address at Howard University: "To Fulfill These Rights," June 4, 1965, *Public Papers of the Presidents: LBJ,* Vol. I, 635–640.
67. Moynihan to McPherson, Sept. 22, 1966, OF/H. McPherson, Box 22, LBJL.
68. Quoted in Dona C. Hamilton and Charles V. Hamilton, *The Dual Agenda: Race and Social Welfare Policies of Civil Rights Organizations* (New York, 1997), 132.
69. Ibid.
70. "South LA was a circumscribed realm of diminishing opportunity." Gerald Horne, *Fire This Time: The Watts Uprising and the 1960s* (Charlottesville, VA, 1995), 52.
71. "Los Angeles: The Fire This Time," *Newsweek,* Aug. 23, 1965, 15–16.
72. See, Terry H. Anderson, *Movement and the Sixties* (New York, 1996), 132.
73. Quoted in Woods, *Quest for Identity,* 250.
74. Stokeley Carmichael, "What We Want," *New York Review of Books,* Sept. 22, 1966, 5.
75. Quoted in Woods, *Quest for Identity,* 250–251.
76. See Fred Dutton to Attorney General, July 17, 1964, OF/Bill Moyers, Box 53, LBJL.
77. Ramsey Clark Oral History, Mar. 21, 1969, III, LBJL.
78. Ibid.
79. LBJ and M. L. King Conversation, Aug. 19, 1965, Diary Backup, Box 21, LBJL.
80. Attorney General to President, Aug. 6, 1964, OF/Horace Busby, Box 52, LBJL.
81. Califano, *Triumph and Tragedy,* 59–63.
82. Lady Bird Johnson, Diary, Aug. 15, 1965, in Beschloss, *Reaching for Glory,* 421.
83. LBJ and John McCone Conversation, Aug. 18, 1965, WH Tapes, WH6508.05, LBJL.
84. LBJ and J. McClellan Conversation, Mar. 23, 1965, WH Tapes, WH6503.11, LBJL.
85. Remarks at the White House Conference on Equal Employment Opportunities, Aug. 20, 1965, *Public Papers of the Presidents: LBJ,* Vol. II, 898.

Chapter 29: Daunted Courage

1. Robert K. Brigham, *Guerrilla Diplomacy: The NLF's Foreign Relations and the Vietnam War* (New York, 1998), 36–37.
2. Quoted in Beschloss, *Taking Charge,* 546.
3. See Halberstam, *Best and Brightest,* 157–160.
4. Rostow Interview with author, Nov. 11, 2001, Austin TX.
5. Rostow to President, May 21, 1968, NSF Memos to President, Box 34, LBJL.
6. Shapley, *Promise and Power,* 314.
7. Rostow to McNamara, Nov. 16, 1964, *FRUS, 1964–68, I,* 906–907.
8. Paper Prepared by the Ambassador in Vietnam, Nov. 1964, *FRUS, 1964–68, I,* 948–951.
9. Quoted in Herring, *Longest War,* 138.
10. Embassy to Department of State, Nov. 1, 1964, and Department of State to Embassy, Nov. 1, 1964, *FRUS, 1964–68, I,* 873, 878. See also Maxwell Taylor Oral History, June 1, 1981, II, LBJL; Kinnard, *Certain Trumpet,* 98–99.
11. Discussion with the President, Oct. 22, 1964, Box 1, John McCone Memoranda, LBJL.
12. George Ball Oral History, I, July 8, 1971, LBJL.
13. NcNaughton to McNamara, Mar. 10, 1965, *FRUS, 1964–68, II,* 431.
14. JCS to McNamara, Nov. 23, 1968, *FRUS, 1964–68, I,* 932–933; Memorandum of Meeting of the Executive Committee, Nov. 27, 1964, *FRUS, 1964–68, I,* 958–959.
15. LBJ and R. Russell Conversation, May 27, 1964, WH Tapes, Transcripts of Telephone Conversations, Box 4, LBJL.
16. T. R. Fehrenbach, *Lone Star: A History of Texas and the Texans* (New York, 1968), 197–198.
17. LBJ and Russell Conversation, Nov. 9, 1964, in Beschloss, *Reaching for Glory,* 137.
18. Quoted in Gardner, *Pay Any Price,* 158.
19. Notes on a Meeting, White, House, Washington, Dec. 1, 1964, *FRUS, 1964–68, I,* 965–967.
20. See Instructions from the President to Taylor, Dec. 3, 1964, *FRUS, 1964–68, I,* 974–977.
21. Quoted in Karnow, *Vietnam,* 383.
22. See G. Ball Oral History, I, July 8, 1971, LBJL; Author interview.
23. Memorandum for the Record of a Meeting, White House, Washington, Nov. 19, 1964, *FRUS, 1964–68, I,* 915; see also Ehrlich to Ball, Nov. 18, 1964, *FRUS, 1964–68, I,* 912–915.
24. Notes of the President's Meeting with Robert Manning, Oct. 19, 1967, Diary Backup, Box 79, LBJL.
25. George Ball Oral History, July 8–9, 1971, LBJL.
26. Shapley, *Promise and Power,* 332–333.
27. Bundy to Califano, Sept. 15, 1965, Diary Backup, Box 22, LBJL.
28. Embassy to Department of State, Jan. 2, 1965, *FRUS, 1964–68, II,* 1.
29. See Memo of Westmoreland Visits with Generals Mihn and Thieu, Mar. 24, 1965, P/W. Westmoreland, Box 5, LBJL; Taylor to Department of State and Memorandum to President Johnson, Feb. 19, 1965, *FRUS, 1964–68, II,* 328–329; "Khanh's Farewell," *Newsweek,* Mar. 8, 1965, 36.
30. See Karnow, *Vietnam,* 380–386; "Vietnam: Where Will It All End?," *Newsweek,* Jan. 4, 1965, 11–12; "Vietnam: A Monk and Two Generals," *Newsweek,* Feb. 8, 1965, 36–37; Westmoreland and Khanh Conversation, Jan. 28, 1965, P/W. Westmoreland, Box 5, LBJL; Taylor to President, Dec. 23, 1964, *FRUS, 1964–68, I,* 1031–1032.

31. Quoted in Karnow, *Vietnam*, 386.
32. Douglas Cater "In Search of LBJ," in Hardesty, *The Johnson Years*, 41.
33. President to Taylor, Dec. 30, 1964, *FRUS, 1964–68, I*, 1058.
34. "The Deadly and Perplexing War," *Newsweek,* Jan. 18, 1965, 28–29; Meeting on Course of Action in South Vietnam, Dec. 4, 1964, John McCone Memoranda, NSF, Box 1, LBJL. See also Personal Notes of a Meeting with President Johnson, Jan. 6, 1965, *FRUS, 1964–68, II*, 37–38.
35. Bundy to President Johnson, Jan. 27, 1965, *FRUS, 1964–68, II*, 95–96; Shapley, *Promise and Power,* 319.
36. Ibid.; Discussion with President re South Vietnam, Feb. 3, 1965, John McCone Memoranda, NSF, Box 1, LBJL.
37. "A Clear Test of Will," *Newsweek,* Feb. 15, 1963, 36–37.
38. Strategy and Policy, Feb. 5, 1973, Westmoreland Papers, Box 30, LBJL.
39. Chester Cooper Oral History, I, July 9, 1969, LBJL.
40. White House Meeting on Vietnam, Feb. 6, 1965, John McCone Memorandum, NSF, Box 1, LBJL. See also Meetings with General Khanh, Feb. 7, 1965, P/W. Westmoreland; President to Taylor, Feb. 8, 1965, Box 5, LBJL.
41. Lady Bird Johnson, unpublished diary, Feb. 7, 1965, in Beschloss, *Reaching for Glory,* 174.
42. Cooper Oral History.
43. Memorandum of Meeting, Feb. 8, 1965, *FRUS, 1964–68, II*, 187.
44. See Department of State to American Embassy, Vietnam, Feb. 13, 1965, *FRUS, 1964–68, II*, 263–264; Meeting at the White House, Feb. 10, 1965, John McCone Memoranda, NSF, Box 1, LBJL.
45. M. D. Taylor Oral History, I, Jan. 9, 1969, LBJL.
46. Lady Bird Johnson, unpublished diary, Feb. 11, 1965, in Beschloss, *Reaching for Glory,* 177.
47. Moyers to President, Feb., 1965, OF/Bill Moyers, Box 11, LBJL.
48. Quoted in Helen Thomas, *Dateline* (New York, 1975), 291. See also LBJ and McNamara Conversation, Mar. 1, 1965, in Beschloss, *Reaching for Glory,* 194.
49. See John P. McConnell Oral History, I, Aug. 14 and 28, 1969, LBJL.
50. See Taylor to Department of State, Mar. 2, 1965, *FRUS, 1964–68, II*, 394.
51. LBJ and McNamara Conversation, Feb. 26, 1965, in Beschloss, *Reaching for Glory,* 195.
52. LBJ and R. Russell Conversation, Mar. 6, 1965, in Beschloss, *Reaching for Glory,* 211–212.
53. Taylor to Department of State, Apr. 14, 1965, *FRUS, 1964–68, II*, 555. See also Summary of Views re Military Operations in Indochina, Apr. 19, 1965, P/W. Westmoreland, Box 5, LBJL.
54. LBJ and McNamara Conversation, Mar. 30, 1965, in Beschloss, *Reaching for Glory,* 258; Bundy to LBJ, Mar. 6, 1965, *FRUS, 1964–68, II*, 402–403. See also Taylor to Department of State, Mar. 18, 1965, and Wheeler to McNamara, Mar. 20, 1965, *FRUS, 1964–68, II*, 454–456, 465–467.
55. See National Security Action Memorandum No. 328, Apr. 6, 1965, *FRUS, 1964–68, II*, 537–539, Memorandum of Meeting in Rusk's Office, Apr. 3, 1965, P/W. Westmoreland, Box 5, LBJL.
56. LBJ and R. Russell Conversation, Mar. 6, 1965, in Beschloss, *Reaching for Glory,* 211–212.
57. Author interview with George McGovern, June 27, 1991, Washington, D.C.
58. "Vietnam and Beyond: Hard Decisions," *Newsweek,* Feb. 19, 1965. See also Press Release, Office of Sen. George McGovern, Feb. 17, 1965, P/G. McGovern, Box 1A, Seely Mudd Lib., Princeton.
59. Quoted in Beschloss, *Reaching for Glory,* 388.
60. LBJ and M. Bundy Conversation, Feb. 18, 1965, in Beschloss, *Reaching for Glory,* 185.
61. Quoted in Dallek, *Flawed Giant,* 258.
62. LBJ and G. McGee Conversation, Apr. 29, 1965, in Beschloss, *Reaching for Glory,* 295.
63. Quoted in Dallek, *Flawed Giant,* 259.
64. Ibid., 282.
65. Lady Bird Johnson, unpublished diary, Apr. 18, 1965, in Beschloss, *Reaching for Glory,* 280.
66. LBJ and Drew Pearson Conversation, Mar. 23, 1965, in Beschloss, *Reaching for Glory,* 238.
67. Lady Bird Johnson, unpublished diary, Mar. 13, 1965, in Beschloss, *Reaching for Glory,* 227.
68. Quoted in Dallek, *Flawed Giant,* 283.
69. Goldschmidt to President, May 4, 1961, LBJ Handwriting File, Box 6, LBJL.
70. Personal Notes of a Meeting with President Johnson, Apr. 1, 1965, *FRUS, 1964–68, II*, 511.
71. "Address at Johns Hopkins University: 'Peace without Conquest,' " Apr. 7, 1965, *Public Papers of the Presidents: LBJ*, Vol. I, 396.
72. See Gardner, *Pay Any Price,* 320; A. Goldschmidt and E. Wickenden Oral History, I, June 3, 1969, LBJL.
73. "A Path for Reasonable Men," *Newsweek,* Apr. 19, 1965, 25; "Address at Johns Hopkins University: 'Peace without Conquest,' " 394–398.
74. Denney to Rusk, Apr. 15, 1965, *FRUS, 1964–68, II*, 559; Memorandum of Conversation, July 29, 1965, *FRUS, 1964–68, II*, 275.
75. "Address at Johns Jopkins University: 'Peace without Conquest,' " 396.
76. Quoted in Gardner, *Pay Any Price,* 1965.
77. Brigham, *Guerilla Diplomacy,* 41.
78. Ibid., 54.
79. See Rusk to Department of State, May 15, 1965, *FRUS, 1964–68, II*, 664.
80. Editorial Note, May 31, 1965, *FRUS, 1964–68, II*, 700–701; Zhai, *China and the Vietnam Wars,* 134–135.
81. Zhai, *China and the Vietnam Wars,* 189.

82. Stategy and Policy, Apr. 2, 1973, Westmoreland Papers, Box 30, LBJL; Wheeler to Westmoreland, Mar. 11, 1965, Westmoreland Papers, Box 5, LBJL; See Meeting of the NSC Executive Committee, Apr. 11, 1965, John McCone Memoranda, Box 1, LBJL.
83. LBJ and McNamara Conversation, July 2, 1965, in Beschloss, *Reaching for Glory,* 381–382. See also Rusk to President, June 29, 1964, *FRUS, 1964–68, I,* 532.
84. LBJ and Birch Bayh Conversation, June 15, 1965, WH Tapes, Transcripts of Telephone Conversations, LBJL.
85. LBJ and Mansfield Conversation, June 8, 1965, WH Tapes 8107–09, LBJL.
86. Beschloss, *Reaching for Glory,* 309.
87. Quoted in ibid, 364.
88. JCS to McNamara, June 11, 1965, *FRUS, 1964–68, II,* 755.
89. LBJ and McNamara Conversation, June 4, 1965, WH Tapes, 8103–04, LBJL.
90. LBJ and McNamara Conversation, June 10, 1965, WH Tapes, 8116–8117, LBJL.
91. LBJ and McNamara Conversation, June 21, 1965, in Beschloss, *Reaching for Glory,* 365.
92. Bird, *Color of Truth,* 320–323; Goodwin, *Remembering America,* 400.
93. Stephen Young, "LBJ's Strategy for Disengagement," *Vietnam Magazine,* Feb. 1998.
94. LBJ to Lucy, July 2, 1964, LBJ Handwriting File, Box 3, LBL; Jarboe Russell, *Lady Bird,* 285; Beschloss, *Reaching for Glory,* 390.
95. Lady Bird Johnson, July 5 and July 11, 1965, in Beschloss, *Reaching for Glory,* 385, 391.
96. Quoted in Beschloss, *Reaching for Glory,* 392.
97. LBJ and R. Russell Conversation, July 19, 1965, WH Tapes, 8351–8352, LBJL. See also LBJ and Rusk Conversation, July 15, 1965, in Beschloss, 392.
98. Arthur J. Goldberg Oral History, LBJL.
99. "Worse Before It Gets Better," *Newsweek,* July 19, 1965, 17–18.
100. Karnow, *Vietnam,* 425.
101. Clifford Notes of Meeting, July 21, 1965, Papers of Clark Clifford, Box 1, LBJL; Notes of Meeting, July 21, 1965, *FRUS, 1964–68, III,* 193; Ball Oral History, II.
102. Connally, *In History's Shadow,* 179.
103. Sidey-Steele to Beshoar, July 30, 1965, John Steele Papers, Box 1, LBJL.
104. Lady Bird Johnson, July 22, 1965, in Beschloss, *Reaching for Glory,* 403.
105. "Certain Losses," *Newsweek,* Aug. 2, 1965, 16.
106. Lady Bird Johnson, unpublished diary, July 25, 1965, in Beschloss, *Reaching for Glory,* 406–407; Pencilled Notes—Vietnam, July 23, 1965, Box 1, Papers of Clark Clifford, LBJL.
107. Quoted in Sidey-Steele to Beshoar, July 30, 1965, John Steele Papers, Box 1, LBJL.
108. "New and Serious Decisions," *Newsweek,* July 26, 1965, 19–20.
109. Quoted in Karnow, *Vietnam,* 426.
110. Quoted in Sidey-Steele to Beshoar, July 30, 1965, John Steele Papers, Box 1, LBJL.
111. McNamara to Johnson, July 1, 1965, *FRUS, 1964–68, III,* 100–101.
112. LBJ and Birch Bayh Conversation, June 15, 1965, WH Tapes, Transcripts of Telephone Conversations, LBJL.
113. O'Connell Oral History, I.
114. See Memorandum of a Meeting with President Johnson, Feb. 17, 1965, *FRUS, 1964–68, II,* 303–304; LBJ and E. Dirksen Conversation, Feb. 17, 1965, in Beschloss, *Reaching for Glory,* 181–182.
115. Memorandum of a Meeting with President Johnson, Feb. 17, 1965, *FRUS, 1964–68, II,* 305.
116. See "Strategy," Mar. 12, 1973, Westmoreland Papers, Box 30, LBJL.
117. Bundy to President, Feb. 16, 1965, *FRUS, 1964–68, II,* 283.
118. Busby to President, June 1965, OF/Horace Busby, Box 51, LBJL.
119. "Congressional Briefing," Feb. 9, 1965, Cong. Briefings on Vietnam, Box 1, LBJL.
120. Congressional Reception, Feb. 11, 1965, Cong. Briefings on Vietnam, Box 1, LBJL. See also Diary, Feb. 11, 1965, PP/Orville Freeman, Box 10, LBJL.
121. "Statement by the President: 'Tragedy, Disappointment, and Progress in Viet-Nam,' " Apr. 17, 1965, *Public Papers of the Presidents: LBJ,* Vol. 1, 430.
122. "Statement by the President on Viet-Nam," Mar. 25, 1965, *Public Papers of the Presidents: LBJ,* 130
123. "Statement by the President: 'Tragedy, Disappointment, and Progress in Viet-Nam,' " 193.
124. Congressional Reception, Feb. 11, 1965, Cong. Briefings on Vietnam, Box 1, LBJL.
125. Congressional Briefing, Feb. 16, 1965, Cong. Briefings on Vietnam, Box 1, LBJL.
126. See Robert H. Wiebe, *Self-Rule: A Cultural History of American Democracy* (Chicago, 1995), 7.
127. Congressional Briefing, Feb. 16, 1965, Cong. Briefings on Vietnam, Box 1, LBJL.
128. LBJ and M. Bundy Conversation, Mar. 6, 1965, in Beschloss, *Reaching for Glory,* 205.
129. LBJ and McNamara Conversation, Mar. 6, 1965, in Beschloss, *Reaching for Glory,* 214–215.
130. Emmet John Hughes, "The High Cost of Fantasy," *Newsweek,* Dec. 13, 1965.

Chapter 30: Castro's and Kennedy's Shadows

1. Chronology of Pertinent Events in the Dominican Republic Situation, n.d., NSF, Box 8, LBJL.
2. Meeting with Congressional Leadership on Dominican Republic, Apr. 28, 1965, Meeting Notes File, NSF, LBJL.
3. Goodwin to LBJ, Apr. 29, 1965, NSF, Name File, Box 8, LBJL.
4. Quoted in H. Johnson and Gwertzman, *Fulbright,* 247.

5. Quoted in John Bartlow Martin, *Overtaken by Events: The Dominican Crisis from the Fall of Trujillo to the Civil War* (New York, 1966), 661.
6. Eric Thomas Chester, *Rag Tags, Scum, Riff-raff, and Commies: The U. S. Intervention in the Dominican Republic, 1965–1966* (New York, 2001), 17–18.
7. Ibid., 31–32.
8. Mann, "Be There Yesterday," 249.
9. LBJ and R. Russell Conversation, Feb. 15, 1964, WH Tapes, Transcripts of Telephone Conversations, Box 1, LBJL.
10. U.S. Senate, Committee on Foreign Relations, *Executive Sessions of the SFRC, Vol. 17, 1965* (Washington, DC, 1990), 491.
11. Chester, *Rag Tags,* 45–53.
12. Ibid., 59.
13. Ibid., 61–62.
14. See Discussion with the President, Feb. 27, 1964, John McCone Memoranda, Box 1, NSF, LBJL.
15. LBJ and R. Russell Conversation, Feb. 7, 1964, Transcripts of Telephone Conversations, 1932a WH Series, LBJL. See also Brands, *Wages of Globalism,* 41–42; LBJ and McNamara Conversation, Feb. 7, 1964; LBJ and R. Russell Conversation, Feb. 7, 1964, WH Tapes, Transcripts of Telephone Conversations, 1919a, LBJL; Meeting at the White House, Feb. 8, 1964, John McCone Memoranda, Box 1, LBJL.
16. See Robert D. Johnson, "Ernest Gruening and Vietnam," in R. B. Woods, *Vietnam,* 65–68.
17. Thomas J. Knock, "The Story of George McGovern," in R. B. Woods, *Vietnam,* 98–99.
18. LBJ and T. Mann Conversation, May 11, 1964, Transcripts of Telephone Conversations, 3375, LBJL.
19. Beschloss, *Reaching for Glory,* 289.
20. Mann, "Be There Yesterday," 250.
21. LBJ and T. Mann Conversation, Apr. 27, 1965, in Beschloss, *Reaching for Glory,* 286–287.
22. LBJ and M. Bundy Conversation, Apr. 29, 1965, Transcripts of Telephone Conversations, 736a, 737a, LBJL.
23. LBJ and Fortas Conversation, Apr. 28, 1965, in Beschloss, *Reaching for Glory,* 289.
24. Chester, *Rag Tags,* 81.
25. LBJ and Fortas Conversation, Apr. 29, 1965, in Beschloss, *Reaching for Glory,* 297–300.
26. LBJ and M. Mansfield Conversation, Apr. 30, 1965, in Beschloss, *Reaching for Glory,* 300.
27. LBJ-Rusk-McNamara Conversation, Apr. 29, 1965, WH Tapes, 7389a, LBJL.
28. LBJ and McNamara Conversation, Apr. 29, 1965, WH Tapes, Transcripts of Telephone Conversations, LBJL.
29. LBJ-McNamara-Moyers Conversation, Apr. 30, 1965, WH Tapes, Transcripts of Telephone Conversations, 7429, LBJL.
30. Pres. Johnson's Notes on Conversation with M. Bundy, Apr. 30, 1965, WH Tapes, Transcripts of Telephone Conversations, 7438, LBJL.
31. Ibid., 7432.
32. LBJ and Fortas Conversation, Apr. 30, 1965, in Beschloss, *Reaching for Glory,* 305.
33. "Statement by the President on the Situation in the Dominican Republic," Apr. 30, 1965, *Public Papers of the Presidents: LBJ,* Vol. I, 465–466.
34. "Radio and Television Report to the American People on the Situation in the Dominican Republic," May 2, 1965, *Public Papers of Presidents: LBJ,* Vol. I, 469–473.
35. Quoted in Dallek, *Flawed Giant,* 266. See also "President's News Conference of June 1, 1965," *Public Papers of the Presidents: LBJ,* Vol. I, 615–617.
36. Quoted in Dallek, *Flawed Giant,* 266.
37. Cyrus Vance Oral History, I, Nov. 13, 1969, LBJL.
38. George Ball Oral History, II, July 9, 1971, LBJL.
39. Chester, *Rag Tags,* 84, 90–92.
40. LBJ Conversation with Pentagon Situation Room, May 2, 1965, WH Tapes, Transcripts of Telephone Conversations, 7514, 7515, LBJL; LBJ Conversation with Amb. John Martin, May 2, 1965, WH Tapes, Transcripts of Telephone Conversations, LBJL.
41. LBJ and Amb. John Martin Conversation, May 2, 1965, 7519, 7520.
42. LBJ Notes, May 2, 1965, LBJ Handwriting File, Box 7, LBJL.
43. LBJ and M. Bundy Conversation, May 7, 1965, WH Tapes, Transcripts of Telephone Conversations, 7607, LBJL.
44. LBJ and John Chancellor Conversation, May 2, 1965, WH Tapes, Transcripts of Telephone Conversations, 7527, LBJL.
45. LBJ and Charles Mohr Conversation, May 6, 1965, WH Tapes, WH6505.29, LBJL.
46. President Notes on Conversation with Abe Fortas, May 5, 1965, WH Tapes, Transcripts of Telephone Conversations, 7581 LBJL.
47. Pres. Johnson's Notes on Conversation with John Martin, May 2, 1965, WH Tapes, Transcripts of Telephone Conversations, 7545 LBJL.
48. LBJ and John Martin Conversation, May 3, 1965, WH Tapes, Transcripts of Telephone Conversations, 7547, 7549 LBJL.
49. Memorandum of Schlesinger and Betancourt Meeting, May 2, 1965, Diary Backup, Box 16, LBJL; Chester, *Rag Tags,* 111.

50. Bennett to Secretary of State, May 17, 1965, WH Tapes, Record of Telephone Conversation Situation Room Series, May, 1965, LBJL; Chester, *Rag Tags,* 138.
51. Piero Gleijeses, *The Dominican Crisis: The 1965 Constitutionalist Revolt and American Intervention* (Baltimore, 1978), 64, 69, 259, 271–272.
52. LBJ and M. Bundy-Fortas-Mann-Palmer-Bennett-Martin Conversation, May 18, 1965, WH Tapes, Transcripts of Telephone Conversations, 7731a–7736a, LBJL.
53. Dean Rusk, *As I Saw It* (New York, 1990), 375.
54. LBJ and Fortas Conversation, May 19, 1965, WH Tapes, Transcripts of Telephone Conversations, 7776, LBJL.
55. Ibid.
56. LBJ and Moyers Conversation, May 19, 1965, WH Tapes, Transcripts of Telephone Conversations, 7779; LBJL.
57. Vance Palmer, Bundy, and Bennett to Sec. State, May 19, 1965, WH Tapes, Record of Telephone Conversation, Situation Room Series, May 1965, LBJL.
58. Lady Bird Johnson, May 20, 1965, in Beschloss, *Reaching for Glory,* 337.
59. LBJ and Fortas Conversation, May 23, 1965, in Beschloss, *Reaching for Glory,* 338.
60. LBJ and Fortas Conversation, May 19, 1965, WH Tapes, WH5505.7776, LBJL.
61. Quoted in Dallek, *Flawed Giant,* 280, LBJ and Hoover Conversation, June 4, 1965, WH Tapes, Transcripts of Telephone Conversations, 8102, LBJL.
62. LBJ and J. Edgar Hoover Conversation, Sept. 10, 1965, WH Tapes, WH6509.03, LBJL.
63. M. Bundy to Secretary of State, May 19, 1965, and Sec. State to Bundy, May 20, 1965, Records of Telephone Conversation, WH Series, Situation Room Series, May 1965, LBJL.
64. Chester, *Rag Tags,* 8–9; LBJ and Fortas Conversation, Aug. 16, 1965, WH Tapes, Transcripts of Telephone Conversations, 8542–43, LBJL.
65. LBJ and Fortas Conversation, May 23, 1965, in Beschloss, *Reaching for Glory,* 339.
66. M. Bundy to LBJ, Sept. 14, 1965, NSF, Memos to the President, Bundy, Box 4, Johnson Papers, LBJL.
67. *Congressional Record,* Senate, Sept. 15, 1965, 23855-63.
68. Reedy to Vice President, n.d., 1962, VP Papers of G. Reedy, Box 7, LBJL.
69. Fields, *Union of Words,* 12.
70. Joseph Alsop, "Matter of Fact Johnson's Achilles Heel," Feb. 17, 1965, PP/Orville Freeman, Box 10, LBJL.
71. LBJ and Reedy Conversation, Oct. 10, 1964, WH Tapes, WH6410.06, 5857, LBJL.
72. Leonard Marks, "Johnson and Leadership," in Thompson, *Johnson Presidency,* 293–294.
73. McPherson Oral History, VI.
74. Quoted in O'Reilly, *Nixon's Piano,* 270–271.
75. Cormier, *LBJ: The Way He Was,* 98.
76. Lewis, H. Lapham, "Who Is Lyndon Johnson?," *Saturday Evening Post,* Sept. 11, 1965, 65.
77. LBJ and Reedy Conversation, Mar. 28, 1964, WH Tapes, WH6403.17, PNO 3, LBJL.
78. "The President's News Conference at the LBJ Ranch," Jan. 16, 1965, *Public Papers of Presidents: LBJ,* Vol. I, 54–56; Diary, Jan. 14, 1965, PP/Orville Freeman, Box 10, LBJL.
79. Mann, "Be There Yesterday," 259–260.
80. E. Carpenter to President and Mrs. Johnson, July 31, 1965, LBJ Handwriting File, Box 9, LBJL.
81. See Busby to President, July 8, 1965, OF/Horace Busby, Box 51, LBJL.
82. Charles Roberts Oral History, I, Jan. 14, 1970, LBJ.
83. See Schlesingr to Moyers, Dec. 8, 1964, and Moyers to President, Dec. 10, 1964, OF/Bill Moyers, Box 10, LBJL.
84. David Lilienthal, *The Journals of David E. Lilienthal, VI* (New York, 1983), 126.
85. Roche to Moyers, May 28, 1964, OF/Bill Moyers, Box 53, LBJL.
86. David Reisman, Richard Hofstadter, and David Bazelon, "Kennedy and After," *New York Review of Books,* Nov. 29, 1963, 3–4, 9.
87. Quoted in Garry Wills, *The Kennedy Imprisonment: A Meditation on Power* (Boston, 1982), ix.
88. UPI AJO, Apr. 2, 1965, OF/Bill Moyers, Box 7, LBJL.
89. Kenneth O'Donnell Oral History, I, July 23, 1969, LBJL.
90. Harry McPherson, "Johnson and Civil Rights," in Thompson, *The Johnson Presidency,* 49.
91. Reed to Vice President, n.d., 1961, VP Papers of G. Reedy, Box 8, LBJL.
92. LBJ and N. Dickerson Conversation, Feb. 18, 1964, 2109, WH Tapes, Transcripts of Telephone Conversations, 2109, Box 2, LBJL.
93. LBJ and Moyers Conversation, May 26, 1965, in Beschloss, *Reaching for Glory,* 340.
94. Busby to President, Dec. 4, 1964, OF/Horace Busby, Box 52, LBJL.
95. See Busby, "Reflections on a Leader," 263.
96. See G. Reedy Oral History, III, June 7, 1975, LBJL.
97. John Chancellor Oral History, Apr. 25, 1969, LBJL.
98. George Reedy, "Johnson and the Press," in Thompson, *The Johnson Presidency,* 88.
99. Cormier, *LBJ,* 180.
100. "Foreign Policy: Drift or Design?" *Newsweek,* May 17, 1965, 27–28.
101. Steward Alsop, "The Inner-directed Mood," *Saturday Evening Post,* Feb. 27, 1965.
102. Lady Bird Johnson, unpublished diary, May 16, 1965, in Beschloss, *Reaching for Glory,* 328.
103. Steele to Beshoar, July 29, 1965, Papers of John Steele, Box 1, LBJL. See also Busby to President, Feb. 27, 1965, OF/Horace Busby, Box 52, LBJL.

104. M. Bundy to President, June 3, 1965, NSC File, Memos to President, Box 3, LBJL.
105. Walter Lippmann, "Can the Question of War Be Debated?," *Newseek,* Mar. 15, 1965, 23.
106. Emmet John Hughes, "Blood, Bridges, and Blarney," *Newsweek,* May 17, 1965.
107. Wilbur Cohen Oral History, III, Mar. 2, 1969, LBJL.
108. See Busby to President, Mar. 9, 1965, Box 15, Diary Backup, LBJL.
109. Reedy to Vice President, Feb. 16, 1962, VP Papers of G. Reedy, Box 7, LBJL.
110. Quoted in D. B. Hardeman Oral History, IV, Jan. 19, 1977, LBJL.
111. Jack Valenti Oral History, V, July 12, 1972, LBJL.
112. Goodwin to President, June 1, 1965, LBJ Handwriting File, Box 7, LBJL.
113. "Arts and the Man—and the State," *Newsweek,* June 28, 1965, 22–23.
114. Hans J. Morgenthau, "Vietnam: Shadow and Substance," *New York Review of Books,* Sept. 16, 1965, 3–4.
115. "Rinehold Niebuhr Discusses the War in Vietnam," *New Republic,* Jan. 29, 1966, 15–16.
116. M. Bundy to LBJ, June 3, 1965, NSF Memos to President, Bundy, Box 3, LBJL.
117. Moyers to President, June 5, 1965, OF/Bill Moyers, Box 11, LBJL.
118. "A Loyal Lieutenant Views LBJ," *Newsweek,* July 12, 1965, 16–17; Valenti Oral History, V, July 12, 1972, LBJL.
119. "Criticism of President's Style, Methods Mounts among Small but Important Group," *Wall Street Journal,* July 6, 1965.
120. James Reston, "Washington: A Just and Compassionate Society," *Washington Post,* Mar. 17, 1965.
121. Walter Lippman, "Key to LBJ: Inexhaustible Gift of Sympathy," *Washington Post,* May 28, 1964.
122. Jim Bishop, "Lyndon Johnson: A 'Can Do' Man," *Milwaukee Sentinal,* Apr. 3, 1965, LBJ Handwriting File, Box 6, LBJL.
123. Alistair Cooke, "The Democratic Candidate: A Four Part Profile," *Houston Chronicle,* Aug. 16, 1964.
124. *Newsweek,* Aug. 2, 1965, 19.
125. Reston, "Just and Compassionate Society."
126. Tom Wicker, "With Johnson on the Ranch," *New York Times,* Jan. 5, 1964.
127. "History and Presidents," *Miller Center Imprimature,* 2, no. 1 (August 1992): 2.
128. *New York Times,* Apr. 11, 1965.
129. Nicholas Lemann, "Mah Fell' Ummurrukuns," *Texas Monthly,* Jan. 1986.
130. "T.R.B. from Washington," *New Republic,* May 21, 1966.
131. Reedy, "Johnson and the Press," 157.
132. Jack Valenti, "The Compassionate President," in Robert L. Hardesty, ed., *The Johnson Years: The Difference He Made* (Austin, TX, 1993); 163.
133. L. F. Stone, "The Knack," *New York Review of Books,* Aug. 5, 1965, 4–5. See also Jack Bell, *The Johnson Treatment* (New York, 1965).
134. David Brinkley and Jack Valenti Conversation, May 20, 1965, WH Tapes, SR6505.03, 7961, LBJL.
135. LBJ and A. Ribicoff Conversation, Sept. 1, 1965, WH Tapes, WH6509.01, LBJL.
136. LBJ and Reedy Conversation, Apr. 8, 1964, WH Tapes, WH6404.08, PNO I, LBJL.
137. "An Interview with LBJ," *Newsweek,* Aug. 2, 1965, 19–20.
138. James Reston, *Sketches in the Sand* (New York, 1967), 390.
139. Reedy, "Johnson and the Press," 86.
140. Nancy Dickerson Oral History, Aug. 21, 1979, LBJL.
141. Quoted in David Halberstam, "Lyndon," *Esquire,* Aug. 1973.
142. Busby, "Reflections on a Leader," 263.
143. Lyndon to Mother, July 31, 1958, Family Correspondence, Box 1, LBJL.
144. Stewart Alsop, "What People Really Think," *Saturday Evening Post,* October 23, 1965, 27–31.

Chapter 31: A City on the Hill

1. See Dallek, *Flawed Giant,* 226–227.
2. LBJ and Ribicoff Conversation, Aug. 19, 1965, WH Tapes, Transcripts of Telephone Conversations, 8573, 8574, LBJL.
3. Valenti to President, Aug. 20, 1965, Diary Backup, Box 21, LBJL.
4. Quoted in Cohen and Taylor, *American Pharaoh,* 343.
5. LBJ and Ribicoff Conversation, Sept. 1, 1965, WH Tapes, WH6509.01, LBJL.
6. See Moyers to President, Aug. 12, 1964, Diary Backup, Box 8, LBJL; Moyers to President, Apr. 5, 1965, OF/Bill Moyers, Box 11, LBJL; "Poverty War: Birth Pains," *Newsweek,* Mar. 29, 1965; "War within a War," *Newsweek,* Dec. 20, 1965.
7. McPherson to Moyers, Mar. 16, 1965, OF/H. McPherson, Box 51, LBJL.
8. See also Cater to President, Mar. 30, 1965, LBJ Handwriting File, Box 6; McPherson to Moyers, Dec. 13, 1965, OF/H. McPherson, Box 51, LBJL; and *Newsweek,* Sept. 13, 1965, 26.
9. McPherson to President, Jan. 5, 1966, OF/H. McPherson, Box 52, LBJL.
10. McPherson to President, May 10, 1966, OF/H. McPherson, Box 52, LBJL.
11. LBJ and Fortas Conversation, July 29, 1965, in Beschloss, *Reaching for Glory,* 413.
12. Kalman, *Abe Fortas,* 240–245; LBJ and Katzenbach Conversation, July 29, 1965, in Beschloss, *Reaching for Glory,* 415–416.
13. Ibid.
14. See LBJ and Gov. Grant Sawyer Conversation, Aug. 17, 1965, WH Tapes, Transcripts of Telephone Conversations, 8547, LBJL

15. "Shriver and the War on Poverty," *Newsweek,* Sept. 13, 1965, 26.
16. "Statement by the President upon Announcing a Program of Assistance to Los Angeles," August 26, 1965, *Public Papers of the Presidents: LBJ,* Vol. II, 933–934.
17. LBJ and Ribicoff Conversation, Sept. 1, 1965, WH Tapes, WH 6509.01, LBJL.
18. Califano to President, Sept. 16, 1965, Diary Backup, Box 22, LBJL.
19. Quoted in Beschloss, *Reaching for Glory,* 224–225.
20. LBJ and Al Friendly Conversation, Aug. 28, 1965, WH Tapes, WH6508.13, LBJL.
21. Quoted in Beschloss, *Reaching for Glory,* 418.
22. LBJ and Wilkins Conversation, Sept. 13, 1965, WH Tapes, WH6509.03, LBJL.
23. LBJ and Katzenbach Conversation, Nov. 29, 1965, WH Tapes, WH6511.09, LBJL.
24. LBJ and Wilkins Conversation, Nov. 4, 1965, WH Tapes, Transcripts of Telephone Conversations, 9105–07, LBJL. See also LBJ and R. Wilkins Conversation, Oct. 30, 1965, WH Tapes, Transcripts of Telephone Conversations, 9048, 9049, LBJL.
25. LBJ and Wilkins Conversation, Nov. 4, 1965.
26. Joseph A. Califano Jr., *The Triumph & Tragedy of Lyndon Johnson* (College Station, TX, 2003), 130.
27. LBJ and Roy Wilkins Conversation, Jan. 5, 1966, WH Tapes, Transcripts of Telephone Conversations, LBJL.
28. LBJ and Heller Conversation, Feb. 9, 1966, WH Tapes, WH 6602.03, LBJL.
29. "Haynesville Justice," *Newsweek,* Oct. 11, 1965, 36.
30. Reedy to President, Oct. 2, 1965, LBJ Handwriting, Box 10, LBJL.
31. "Opening a Second Front," *Newsweek,* Nov. 8, 1965, 33.
32. What to Do Next?" *Newsweek,* Nov. 29, 1965, 27.
33. Harry McPherson Oral History, III, LBJL.
34. Carl Holman to Lee White, Dec. 16, 1965, OF/H. McPherson, Box 21, LBJL.
35. Lady Bird Johnson, Aug. 23, 1965, in Beschloss, *Reaching for Glory,* 422–423, 34.
36. Harry McPherson Oral History, May 6, 1985, VI, LBJL.
37. McQuaid, *Big Business,* 238–239.
38. Califano, *Triumph and Tragedy,* 86–87.
39. "Steel Answers—and Real Questions," *Newsweek,* Sept. 13, 1965, 19–20.
40. Quoted in Dallek, *Flawed Giant,* 305.
41. LBJ and Katzenbach Conversation, Sept. 2, 1965, WH Tapes, WH6509.01, LBJL.
42. Heller to President, Sept. 5, 1965, Diary Backup, Box 21, LBJL.
43. Milton Friedman, "Social Responsibility: A Subversive Doctrine," *National Review,* Aug. 24, 1965, 721–723.
44. "What Happens to Bargaining Now?," *Newsweek,* Sept. 20, 1965, 73–75.
45. LBJ and Wirtz Conversation, Jan. 10, 1966, WH Tapes, Transcripts of Telephone Conversations, January 1966, LBJL.
46. Quoted in Dallek, *Flawed Giant,* 307.
47. Bernstein, *Guns or Butter,* 443; McPherson to President, Dec. 1, 1965, OF/H. McPherson, Box 52, LBJL.
48. President Johnson's Notes on Conversation with Secretary McNamara, Aug. 11, 1965, WH Tapes, Transcripts of Telephone Conversations, 8530, LBJL.
49. "Dancing at the Dove," *Newsweek,* Oct. 4, 1965, 28–29.
50. LBJ and Liz Carpenter Conversation, Aug. 27, 1965, WH Tapes, WH6508.12, LBJL.
51. Quoted in Rogers M. Smith, *Civic Ideals: Conflicting Visions of Citizenship in U.S. History* (New Haven, CT, 1997), 14–15.
52. Quoted in ibid., 33.
53. Bernstein, *Guns or Butter,* 245–247.
54. Ibid., 248–249.
55. "Remarks at the Signing of the Immigration Bill, Liberty Island, New York," Oct. 3, 1965, *Public Papers of the Presidents: LBJ,* Vol. II, 1038.
56. Bernstein, *Guns or Butter,* 258–259.
57. Quoted in ibid., 257.
58. Quoted in ibid., 259.
59. LBJ and O. Freeman Conversation, July 7, 1964, WH Tapes, WH6407.05, LBJL.
60. "Remarks at the Signing of the Water Quality Act of 1965," Oct. 2, 1965, *Public Papers of the Presidents: LBJ,* Vol. II, 1035.
61. Lee White, "The Bold Dreamer," in Hardesty, *The Johnson Years,* 85.
62. "Remarks at a Meeting of the Water Emergency Conference," Aug. 11, 1965, *Public Papers of the Presidents: LBJ,* 1965, 868.
63. Jarboe Russell, *Lady Bird,* 279.
64. See Elizabeth Carpenter Oral History, II, Apr. 4, 1969 LBJL; Joe Frantz Oral History, Sept. 7, 1972, I, LBJL; James Rowe Oral History, Sept. 16, 1969, II, LBJL; Bobby Baker Oral History, VII, Oct. 11, 1984, LBJL: Goodwin to President, July 29, 1964, Diary Backup, Box 7, LBJL; LBJ to Udall, Jan. 21, 1965, LBJ Handwriting File, Box 5, LBJL; Paul Southwick to Mike Manatos, Sept. 7, 1965, Diary Backup, Box 232, LBJL;
65. Jarboe Russell, *Lady Bird,* 272–275.
66. Ibid., 281.
67. Ibid., 275.
68. Lady Bird Johnson, *A White House Diary* (New York, 1970), 247–248.

69. Ibid., 232.
70. Jarboe Russell, *Lady Bird,* 283–284.
71. "Statement by the President Announcing That He Would Undergo Surgery," Oct. 5, 1965, *Public Papers of the Presidents: LBJ,* Vol. II, 1043.
72. "The President Is Not a Usual Man," *Newsweek,* Oct. 18, 1965, 31.
73. "LBJ and the Fabulous 89th Go Home," *Newsweek,* Nov. 1, 1965, 21.
74. Ibid., 21–22.
75. Ibid.
76. See Emmet John Hughes, "The Two Presidents," *Newsweek,* Sept. 6, 1965, 13.
77. William E. Leuchtenburg, "A Visit with LBJ," *American Heritage* (May/June 1990), 47–64.
78. Diary, Sept. 30, 1965, PP/O. Freeman, Box 10, LBJL.
79. J. K. Galbraith to President, Oct. 19, 1965, LBJ Handwriting File, Box 10, LBJL.
80. Robert C. Wood, *Whatever Possessed the President? Academic Experts and Presidential Policy, 1960–1988* (Amherst, MA, 1993), 77–78.
81. Report to President and Cabinet on the Economic Situation by the CEA, Apr. 20, 1965, Cabinet Papers, Box 2, LBJL; Gardner Ackley to President, June 19, 1965, LBJ Handwriting File, Box 8, LBJL; Troika Staff Memorandum, Sept. 10, 1964, Diary Backup, Box 9, LBJL.
82. LBJ and McNamara Conversation, Dec. 2, 1965, WH Tapes, Transcripts of Telephone Conversations, 9305, LBJL.
83. Gardner Ackley to President, Dec. 17, 1965, LBJ Handwriting File, Box 11, LBJL.
84. LBJ and M. Bundy Conversation, Dec. 3, 1965, WH Tapes, WH6512.01, LBJL.
85. John L. Sweeny to President, Dec. 13, 1965, OF/H. McPherson, Box 50, LBJL.
86. Shapley, *Promise and Power,* 384.
87. Moynihan to McPherson, July 16, 1965, OF/H. McPherson, Box 21, LBJL; McNamara Interview with Rostow, Jan. 8, 1975, Reference File, LBJL.
88. Shapley, *Promise and Power,* 385; David Sanford, "McNamara's Salvation Army," *New Republic,* Sept. 10, 1966, 14.
89. Minutes of Cabinet Meeting, Nov. 1, 1967, LBJ Handwriting File, Box 11, LBJL.
90. McNamara Interview with Rostow, Jan. 8, 1975.
91. Minutes of Cabinet Meeting, Nov. 1, 1967.
92. Moynihan to McPherson, July 16, 1965.
93. LBJ and McNamara Conversation, Dec. 22, 1967, WH Tapes, WH6512.04, LBJL.
94. LBJ and Moyers Conversation, Dec. 31, 1965, WH Tapes, Transcripts of Telephone Conversations, 9349, LBJL.
95. Notes of Staff Meeting, 1968, Papers of Clark Clifford, Box 1, LBJL.

Chapter 32: Balancing Act

1. Draft Memorandum from Secretary of Defense McNamara to President Johnson, Nov. 3, 1965, *FRUS, 1964–68, III,* 514–515.
2. See Congressional Briefing, Mar. 4, 1965, Congressional Briefings on Vietnam, Container 1, LBJL; Notes on Meeting on Vietnam, Mar. 3, 1965, LBJ Handwriting File, Box 6, LBJL.
3. See "GI's Pour In—And the War Looks Up," *Newsweek,* Oct. 4, 1965, 38–39.
4. "Fury at Ia Drang: Now the Regulars," *Newsweek,* Nov. 29, 1965, 21–23.
5. "Profile of the Viet Cong," *Newsweek,* Apr. 12, 19565, 40–43.
6. Ibid.
7. "Strategy's Byproducts," *Newsweek,* Aug. 16, 1965, 30–31.
8. McPherson to Moyers, Aug. 6, 1965, OF/H. McPherson, Box 5, LBJL.
9. Moyers to LBJ, Aug. 3, 1965, LBJ Handswriting, Box 9, LBJL.
10. Marvin Watson to President, Sept. 2, 1965, Diary Backup, Box 22, LBJL.
11. Moyers to Stanton, Feb. 12, 1966, PP/Adam Yarmolinsky, Box 66, JFKL.
12. Cater to President, Aug. 14, 1965, LBJ Handwriting File, Box 9, LBJL.
13. LBJ and Mansfield Conversation, June 26, 1965, WH Tapes, Transcripts of Telephone Conversations, 8196–8197, LBJL.
14. Shapley, *Promise and Power,* 386.
15. Charles De Benedetti, *An American Ordeal: The Antiwar Movement of the Vietnam Era* (Syracuse, NY, 1990), 131–132; Chester Cooper to McGeorge Bundy, Oct. 26, 1965, OF/H. McPherson, Box 28, LBJL.
16. Quoted in Robert L. Beisner, "1898 and 1968: The Anti-Imperialists and the Doves," *Political Science Quarterly* 85 (June 1970), 197.
17. De Benedetti, *American Ordeal,* 128–129.
18. Cater to the President, Dec. 16, 1965, LBJ Handwriting File, Box 11, LBJL.
19. Reedy to President, Dec. 17, 1965, LBJ Handwriting File, Box 11, LBJL.
20. Arthur Krim Oral History, May 17, 1982, II, LBJL.
21. Hayes Redmon to Bill Moyers, Nov. 27, 1965, OF/Bill Moyers, Box 11, LBJL.
22. LBJ and McNamara Conversation, June 21, 1965, WH Tapes, Transcripts of Telephone Conversations, LBJL.
23. Hayes Redmon, Nov. 27, 1965, OF/Bill Moyers, Box 11, LBJL. See also McPherson to President, Sept. 22, 1965, OF/H. McPherson, Box 52, LBJL.
24. Lodge to President, Oct. 20, 1965, *FRUS, 1964–68, III,* 458–459.

25. See Maxwell Taylor to President, Feb. 26, 1965, and William Bundy to President, Apr. 26, 1965, LBJ Handwriting File, Box 6, LBJL; Cooper to President, Sept. 24, 1965, *FRUS, 1964–68, III,* 416.
26. LBJ and McNamara Conversation, June 21, 1965.
27. Edward Rice to William Bundy, Nov. 19, 1965, *FRUS, 1964–68, III,* 556–557.
28. Personal Notes of Meeting with President Johnson, Dec. 7, 1965, *FRUS, 1964–68, III,* 620.
29. Notes of Meeting, Dec. 18, 1965, *FRUS, 1964–68, III,* 662.
30. "E Pluribus Unum," *Newsweek,* Aug. 30, 1965, 21; LBJ and Eisenhower Conversation, Aug. 18, 1965, WH Tapes, Transcripts of Telephone Conversations, 8555a, 8555b, LBJL.
31. Rusk to President Johnson, Sept. 30, 1965, *FRUS, 1964–68, III,* 427.
32. Valenti to the President, Nov. 30, 1965, Diary Backup, Box 25, LBJL.
33. LBJ Handwritten Notes, n.d., 1965, LBJ Handwriting File, Box 11, LBJL.
34. Lodge to President, Aug. 31, 1965, *FRUS, 1964–68, III,* 363–364.
35. Notes of Meeting, Dec. 18, 1965, *FRUS, 1964–68, III,* 661; George Ball Oral History, July 9, 1971, LBJL.
36. Notes of Meeting, Dec. 17, 1965, *FRUS, 1964–68, III,* 647.
37. Hayes Redmon to Bill Moyers, Dec. 14, Box 11, OF/Bill Moyers, LBJL.
38. Rusk to Lodge, Dec. 28, 1965, *FRUS, 1964–68, III,* 717.
39. Moyers to Rostow, May 8, 1982, Reference File, "Walt Rostow," LBJL.
40. LBJ and Stennis Conversation, Aug. 18, 1965, WH Tapes, WH6508.05, LBJL.
41. Jack Valenti Oral History, July 12, 1972, LBJL.
42. "Sorry, Wrong Number," *Newsweek,* Jan. 31, 1966.
43. Harry McPherson Oral History, May 16, 1985, LBJL.
44. Ibid.
45. McPherson Oral History.
46. "Revolving Door at 1600," *Newsweek,* May 9, 1966, 26.
47. Valenti Oral History.
48. McPherson Oral History, LBJL; Jake Jacobsen Oral History, May 27, 1969, LBJL.
49. Lady Bird Johnson, Aug. 27, 1965, in Beschloss, *Reaching for Glory,* 424.
50. See Joseph A. Califano Jr., *Inside: A Public and Private Life* (New York, 2004), 3–45.
51. McPherson Oral History.
52. Bird, *The Color of Truth,* 342–420.
53. LBJ and Rusk Conversation, Nov. 29, 1965, WH Tapes, WH6511.09, LBJL.
54. Quoted in "Idea Man," *Newsweek,* Aug. 8, 1966, 19–20.
55. Nicholas B. Katzenbach, July 5, 1990, and George Ball Interviews with Author, July 6, 1990, Princeton, NJ.
56. Quoted in Califano, *Triumph and Tragedy,* 114–115.
57. Dallek, *Flawed Giant,* 299.
58. Schultz to President, Nov. 7, 1966, Diary Backup, Box 49, LBJL.
59. Califano, *Triumph and Tragedy,* 51.
60. From the President's Pocket, Mar. 8, 1966, LBJ Handwriting File, Box 13, LBJL.
61. "Remarks in Baltimore at the Celebration of the Bicentennial of American Methodism," Apr. 22, 1966, *Public Papers of the Presidents: LBJ,* Vol. I, 447.
62. Califano, *Triumph and Tragedy,* 115.
63. Dallek, *Flawed Giant,* 302.
64. "Annual Message to the Congress on the State of the Union," Jan. 12, 1966, *Public Papers of the Presidents: LBJ,* Vol. I, 3–6.
65. See Minutes of the Meeting between the President and the Bi-Partisan Leaders of the House and Senate, July 18, 1966, Diary Backup, Box 39, LBJL.
66. Diary, Apr. 4, 1966, PP/Orville Freeman, Box 10, LBJL.
67. Califano to President, Feb. 9, 1966, LBJ Handwriting File, Box 12, LBJL.
68. Bernstein, *Guns or Butter,* 430.
69. LBJ and Meany Conversation, Feb. 22, 1966, WH Tapes, Transcripts of Telephone Conversations, Feb. 1966, LBJL.
70. "Rising Prices: How Long, How High?," *Newsweek,* Sept. 5, 1966, 69.
71. Redmon to Moyers, Aug. 31, 1966, OF/Bill Moyers, Box 12, LBJL.
72. Congressional Briefing, Sept. 6, 1966, Congressional Briefings, Box 1, LBJL.
73. mjdr to President, Sept. 12, 1966, LBJ Handwriting File, Box 31, LBJL.
74. Special Message to the Congress on Transportation, Mar. 2, 1966, *Public Papers of the Presidents: LBJ,* Vol. I, 250–258.
75. Quoted in Califano, *Triumph and Tragedy,* 125.
76. Quoted in ibid., 126.
77. Ibid. 131.
78. Bernstein, *Guns or Butter,* 462–463.
79. See Milton P. Semer to President, June 10, 1966, LBJ Handwriting File, Box 15, LBJL.
80. Califano, *Triumph and Tragedy,* 132.
81. Bernstein, *Guns or Butter,* 465.
82. Gareth Davies, *From Opportunity to Entitlement: The Transformation and Decline of Great Society Liberalism* (Lawrence, KS, 1996), 137–138.
83. Ibid.
84. Califano, *Triumph and Tragedy,* 135.

85. L. B. Johnson, *Vantage Point,* 330.
86. Bernstein, *Guns or Butter,* 469.
87. Davies, *Opportunity to Entitlement,* 137.

Chapter 33: Divisions

1. "Remarks to the Delegates to the White House Conference To Fulfill These Rights," June 1, 1966, *Public Papers of the Presidents: LBJ,* Vol. I, 573.
2. "Crisis of Color '66," *Newsweek,* Aug. 22, 1966, 20–26, Dallek, *Flawed Giant,* 323.
3. Fortas to Valenti, Jan. 17, 1966, LBJ Handwriting File, Box 11, LBJL.
4. Ibid.
5. Notes on Meredith March, June 25, 1966, OF/H. McPherson, Box 22, LBJL.
6. Dittmer, *Local People,* 396. See also, Carmichael, "What We Want," 5–6.
7. Grantham, *The South in Modern America,* 255.
8. Quoted in Kearns Goodwin, *American Dream,* 320.
9. "Remarks to Members of the Bishops' Council, African Methodist Episcopal Church," Sept. 27, 1966, *Public Papers of the Presidents: LBJ,* Vol. II, 1072–1073.
10. Stephen C. Halpern, *On the Limits of the Law: The Ironic Legacy of Title VI of the 1964 Civil Rights Act* (Baltimore, MD, 1995), 45–52. See also McPherson to President, May 12, 1966, OF/H. McPherson, Box 52, LBJL.
11. "What Grenadans Are Like," *Newsweek,* Sept. 26, 1966, 33–34.
12. Cohen and Taylor, *American Pharaoh,* 351–353; Cater to President, Oct. 4, 1965, Box 23, LBJL; W. Wilbur Cohen Oral History, Dec. 8, 1968, I, LBJL; "Leaning on HEW," *Newsweek,* Oct. 18, 1966, 98.
13. Henry Wilson to President, Mar. 11, 1966, and Katzenbach to President, Mar. 15, 1966, LBJ Handwriting File, Box 13, LBJL.
14. Dallek, *Flawed Giant,* 324.
15. McPherson to President, Sept. 12, 1966, Papers of Nicholas B. Katzenbach, Box 15, JFKL.
16. "Special Message to the Congress Proposing Further Legislation to Strengthen Civil Rights," Apr. 28, 1966, *Public Papers of the Presidents: LBJ,* Vol. I, 461–468.
17. Katzenbach to Wilson, Mar. 15, 1966, LBJ Handwriting File, Box 13, LBJL, Katzenbach to President, Mar. 17, 196, Diary Backup, Box 37, LBJL.
18. LBJ and Moyers Conversation, Apr. 5, 1966, WH Tapes, WH6604.02, LBJL.
19. "Remarks of the President at the Olive Medal of Honor Ceremony," Mar. 21, 1966, Diary Backup, Box 33, LBJL. See also Sparks and Hardesty to Valenti, Apr. 1, 1966, Diary Backup, Box 33, LBJL.
20. See McPherson to President, Aug. 5, 1966, OF/H. McPherson, Box 52, LBJL.
21. "The Touchiest Target," *Newsweek,* Aug. 15, 1966, 29.
22. "Colorful Campaign," *Newsweek,* Oct. 17, 1966, 29.
23. McPherson to Katzenbach, Sept. 20, 1966, Katzenbach Papers, Box 15, JFKL.
24. Moynihan to McPherson, Sept. 22, 1966, OF/H. McPherson, Box 22, LBJL.
25. Andrew Kopkind, "Soul Power," *New York Review of Books,* Aug. 24, 1967, 3.
26. Roche to President, Feb. 16, 1967, LBJ Handwriting File, Box 20, LBJL.
27. McPherson to President, Dec. 19, 1966, and Moynihan to McPherson, Sept. 22, 1966, OF/H. McPherson, Box 22, LBJL.
28. Brands, *Wages of Globalism,* 105.
29. Quoted in Schwartz, *Shadow of Vietnam* 31.
30. John Chancellor Oral History, Apr. 25, 1969, LBJL.
31. "The Johnson Image," Apr. 20, 1965, OF/H. Busby, Box 52, LBJL.
32. Hugh Sidey, "More At Home with the Have-Nots," *Life,* May 12, 1967, 45a.
33. See Germany in Perspective, May 22, 1968, Diary Backup, Box 26, LBJL.
34. Quoted in Brands, *Wages of Globalism,* 89.
35. Schwartz, *Shadow of Vietnam,* 152. See also Breakfast Meeting at the White House, Apr. 22, 1964, and Briefing of President Johnson at Johnson City, Texas, Jan. 4, 1965, John McCone Memoranda, Box 1, LBJL; "Text of Interview with the President Published in 'America Illustrated' for Distribution in the Soviet Union," Sept. 27, 1966, *Public Papers of the Presidents: LBJ,* Vol. II, 1066–1070.
36. McNamara Interview with Rostow, Jan. 8, 1975, Reference File, "Rostow," LBJL.
37. "The Gold Drain: 'Playing for Keeps,' " *Newsweek,* Feb. 15, 1965, 67.
38. B. Johnson, *Vantage Point,* 306.
39. Reedy to Senator Johnson, Mar. 20, 1957, SOF of G. Reedy, Box 420, LBJL.
40. Schwartz, *Shadow of Vietnam,* 44–46. See also LBJ and McNamara Conversation, Nov. 30, 1965, WH Tapes, Transcripts of Telephone Conversations, 9200, LBJL; Meeting in President's Office, Dec. 16, 1965, Diary Backup, Box 26, LBJL.
41. Brands, *Wages of Globalism,* 102. See also Frank Ninkovich, *Modernity and Power: A History of the Domino Theory in the Twentieth Century* (Chicago, 1994), 259.
42. LBJ and R. Russell Conversation, Jan. 8, 1964, WH Tapes, WH6401.09, LBJL.
43. Ball Oral History.
44. Quoted in Schwartz, *Shadow of Vietnam,* 34–35.
45. LBJ and Robert Anderson Conversation, Mar. 27, 1964, WH Tapes, WH5403.16; LBJ and M. Bundy Conversation, June 1, 1964, WH Tapes, Transcripts of Telephone Conversations, Box 4, 5601, LBJL.

46. Francis Bator to President, Mar. 7, 1966, OF/Bill Moyers, Box 7, LBJL.
47. Schwartz, *Shadow of Vietnam,* 123.
48. Freeman Memorandum for Files, July 25, 1966, PP/Orville Freeman, Box 11, LBJL.
49. Freeman Memorandum for Files, Jan. 21, 1966, PP/Orville Freeman, Box 10, LBJL. See also Komer to President, Feb. 2, 1966, Diary Backup, Box 28, LBJL.
50. LBJ, *Vantage Point,* 226–227.
51. Diary, Feb. 3, 1966, PP/Orville Freeman Box 10, LBJL.
52. New Delhi had consistently denounced the United States for intervening in Vietnam. In 1967 Indira Gandhi cabled her and her country's best wishes to Ho Chi Minh on his birthday, expressing the wish that Vietnam would continue to benefit from his wise and dedicated leadership for a long time to come. Rusk to American embassy, New Delhi, May 18, 1967, NSF Memos to President, Rostow, Box 16, LBJL; LBJ and Freeman Conversation, Feb. 2, 1966, WH Tapes, WH6602.01, 9607, LBJL.
53. Diary, Feb. 3, 1966, PP/Orville Freeman, Box 10, LBJL.
54. Bowles to President, Mar. 26, 1966, Diary Backup, Box 37, LBJL.
55. Komer to President, Mar. 22 and 23, 1966, Diary Backup, Box 37, LBJL.
56. Diary, Mar. 30, 1966, PP/Orville Freeman, Box 10, LBJL.
57. LBJ, *Vantage Point,* 227. See also Komer to McPherson, Mar. 24, 1966, OF/H. McPherson, Box 52, LBJL.
58. McPherson to President, Feb. 23 and Mar. 28, 1966, OF/H. McPherson, Box 52, LBJL.
59. Henry Wilson to President, and Freeman to President, Sept. 16, 1966, LBJ Handwriting File, Box 18, LBJL.
60. LBJ, *Vantage Point,* 228–229; Diary, Sept. 3, 1966, PP/O. Freeman, Box 11, LBJL.
61. Bernstein, *Guns or Butter,* 439.
62. Harry McPherson Oral History, May 16, 1985, VI, LBJL.
63. McPherson to President, Apr. 14, 1966, OF/H. McPherson, Box 52, LBJL.
64. "Statement by the President upon Signing Bill Providing for the Joseph H. Hirshhorn Museum and Sculpture Garden," Nov. 7, 1966, *Public Papers of the Presidents: LBJ,* Vol. II, 1345; Bernstein, *Guns or Butter,* 440–41, 444–457.
65. Quoted in Bernstein, *Guns or Butter,* 273.
66. "Remarks to Members of the National Recreation and Park Association," Oct. 13, 1966, *Public Papers of the Presidents: LBJ,* Vol. II, 1174.
67. Ibid., 1176; Bernstein, *Guns or Butter,* 278–279.
68. Quoted in Jim Wright, *Balance of Power: Presidents and Congress from the Era of McCarthy to the Age of Gingrich* (Atlanta, GA, 1996), 41.
69. Califano Commencement Address at Mercy College, Califano to LBJ, June 4, 1968, OF/Joe Califano, Box 17, LBJL.
70. Ibid.
71. Ibid.; Dallek, *Flawed Giant,* 330.
72. See Gareth Davies, *From Opportunity to Entitlemen: the Transformation and Decline of Great Society Liberalism* (Lawrence, KS, 1996), 89.
73. Ellis, *American Political Cultures,* 71.
74. Burner, *Making Peace with the '60s,* 162.
75. Ellis, *American Political Cultures,* 57.
76. "Bill Moyers Talks about LBJ, Power, Poverty, War and the Young," *The Atlantic* 22, no. 1 (July 1968): 22.
77. Davies, *Opportunity to Entitlement,* 91.
78. Dallek, *Flawed Giant,* 331.
79. See Davies, *Opportunity to Entitlement,* 115–118.
80. Edward D. Berkowitz and Kim McQuaid, *Creating the Welfare State: The Political Economy of Twentieth Century Reform* (New York, 1980), 117–119.
81. John Roche Oral History, I, July 16, 1970, LBJL.
82. Quoted in Shesol, *Mutual Contempt,* 172.
83. McPherson to LBJ, June 24, 1965, OF/H. McPherson, Box 21, LBJL.
84. "The Bobby Phenomenon," *Newsweek,* Oct. 24, 1966, 30–31.
85. LBJ and Daley Conversation, July 19, 1966, WH Tapes, WH660702, LBJL.
86. Shesol, *Mutual Contempt,* 167–168; A. Goldschmidt and E. Wickenden Oral History I, June 3, 1969, LBJL; Wilbur Cohen Oral History, Dec. 8, 1968, LBJL.
87. McPherson to President, June 24, 1965, OF/H. McPherson, Box 21, LBJL.
88. Califano to LBJ, June 4, 1968, OF/Joe Califano, Box 17, LBJL.

Chapter 34: Civil War

1. Quoted in Shapley, *Promise and Power,* 361.
2. Notes of Meeting, Jan. 3, 1966, *FRUS, 1964–68, IV,* 11.
3. See also JCS to McNamara, Jan. 18, 1966, *FRUS, 1964–68, IV,* 80–81.
4. Diary, Jan. 29, 1966, Westmoreland Papers, Box 7, LBJL.
5. James to President, Jan. 6, 1966, LBJ Handwriting File, Box 11, LBJL.
6. See Notes of Meeting, Jan. 24, 1966, and Meeker to Rusk, Jan. 20, 1966, *FRUS, 1964–68, IV,* 126, 95.

7. See Sharp to Joint Chiefs, Jan. 12, 1966, *FRUS, 1964–68, IV,* 47–48.
8. "Vietnam: The Pause Comes to an End," *Newsweek,* Jan. 12, 1966, 16.
9. Notes of Meeting in the Cabinet Room, Jan. 27, 1966, Diary Backup, Box 28, LBJL.
10. See M. Bundy to President, Jan. 27, 1966, Diary Backup, Box 28, LBJL; M. Bundy to President, Jan. 26, 1966, *FRUS, 1964–68, IV,* 158–159.
11. Points, Jan. 28, 1966, Clifford Papers, Box 1, LBJL.
12. McNamara and LBJ Conversation, Jan. 17, 1966, *FRUS, 1964–68, IV,* 78.
13. "Statement by the President Announcing Resumption of Air Strikes on North Vietnam," Jan. 31, 1966, *Public Papers of the Presidents: LBJ,* Vol. I, 114.
14. Chester Cooper Oral History, July 17, 1969, LBJL.
15. "LBJ in Hawaii: A Look and a Promise," *Newsweek,* Feb. 21, 1966, 24.
16. Cooper Oral History, II.
17. "Strategy and Policy, 30 Jan–13 Mar 66," May 8, 1973, Box 30, Westmoreland Papers, LBJL.
18. Editorial Note, *FRUS, 1964–68, IV,* 215.
19. "LBJ in Hawaii: A Look and a Promise," 24.
20. Diary, Feb. 7, 1966, PP/Orville Freeman, Box 11, LBJL.
21. Presidential Notes, Feb. 7, 1966, LBJ Handwriting File, Box 12, LBJL.
22. "Strategy and Policy, 30 Jan–13 Mar 66," May 8, 1973.
23. Diary, Feb. 7, 1966, PP/Orville Freeman, Box 11, LBJL.
24. President and Nehru Conversation, Feb. 10, 1966, *FRUS, 1964–68, IV,* 218.
25. "LBJ in Hawaii: A Look and a Promise," 25.
26. Westmoreland to CINCPAC, Feb. 7, 1966, PP/W. Westmoreland, Box 7, LBJL.
27. Note (anonymous), 1966, NSF, NSC History, Box 44, LBJL.
28. "Fulbright Fears U.S. Eliminating Chance for Peace," *Arkansas Gazette,* Feb. 11, 1966.
29. "Hearings Coverage Draw Heavy Fire," *Washington Star,* Apr. 4, 1966; Melvin Small, *Johnson, Nixon, and the Doves* (New Brunswick, NJ, 1988), 78.
30. Marcy to J. Williams Fulbright, Feb. 22, 1966, Box 6, Folder Feb. 66, Papers of J. William Fulbright, SFRC, Record Group 46, National Archives.
31. J. William Fulbright to M. S. Craig, Feb. 11, 1966, Series 48:18, Box 47:5, PP/J. William Fulbright, University of Arkansas.
32. Moyers to White, Mar. 7, 1966, Box 219, White House Central File (hereafter WHCF), Nat'l Sec./Def., LBJL. Meeting in Cabinet Room, Feb. 26, 1966, Meeting Notes File, Box 2, LBJL.
33. Meeting in Cabinet Room, Feb. 26, 1966, Meeting Notes File, Box 2, LBJL.
34. Marvin Watson to LBJ, Feb. 21, 1966, WHCF, Box 342, LBJL.
35. Notes of Meeting in the Cabinet Room, Jan. 27, 1966, Diary Backup, Box 28, LBJL.
36. "Annual Message to Congress on the State of the Union," Jan. 12, 1966, *Public Papers of the Presidents: LBJ,* Vol. I, 7–11.
37. "Political Instability," 23 Apr–29 May 66, May 20, 1973, PP/W. Westmoreland, Box 30, LBJL.
38. Ton That Thien, "Back to the 1950s?," *Far Eastern Economic Review,* Dec. 23, 1965.
39. Memo for Record, May 6, 1966, NSF, PP/R. Komer, Box 4, LBJL.
40. See Jopseph Kraft, "Politics in Vietnam," *New York Review of Books,* June 23, 1966, 5.
41. See, for example, Lodge to Department of State, Mar. 23, 1966, *FRUS, 1964–68, IV,* 295.
42. Westmoreland and Ky Conversation, Mar. 9, 1966, PP/W. Westmoreland, Box 7, LBJL.
43. Embassy to Department of State, Mar. 13, 1966, *FRUS, 1964–68, IV,* 284.
44. Department of State to Embassy, Mar. 16, 1966, *FRUS, 1964–68, IV,* 286.
45. Rusk to President Johnson, Apr. 2, 1966, *FRUS, 1964–68, IV,* 314.
46. LBJ and McNamara Conversation, Apr. 7, 1966, 10021, WH Tapes, WH6604.02, LBJL.
47. Meeting at Chu Lai, Mar. 24, 1966, Box 8, PP/W. Westmoreland, LBJL.
48. Wheeler to Westmoreland, May 20, 1966, Box 8, PP/W. Westmoreland, LBJL.
49. LBJ and Rusk Conversation, Apr. 9, 1966, 10029, WH Tapes, WH6604.02, LBJL.
50. Notes of Meeting, Apr. 2, 1966, and Draft Scenario Prepared in Department of Defense, Apr. 5, 1966, *FRUS, 1964–68, IV,* 317, 327–328.
51. Karnow, *Vietnam,* 451.
52. Rusk to Lodge, May 22, 1966, PP/W. Westmoreland, Box 8, LBJL.
53. Quoted in Editorial Note, *FRUS, 1964–68, IV,* 397.
54. Department of State to Certain Posts, Apr. 14, 1966, *FRUS, 1964–68, IV,* 349.
55. Taylor to President, Apr. 12, 1966, *FRUS, 1964–68, IV,* 341.
56. Rostow to President, Apr. 18, 1966, *FRUS, 1964–68, IV,* 355.
57. Editorial Note, *FRUS, 1964–68, IV,* 194.
58. Note 2, *FRUS, 1964–68, IV,* 240.
59. Ibid.
60. LBJ and Rusk Conversation, Feb. 22, 1966, *FRUS, 1964–68, IV,* 241–242.
61. McPherson to Moyers and Valenti, Feb. 28, 1966, OF/H. McPherson, Box 51, LBJL.
62. LBJ and Larry O'Brien Conversation, Feb. 28, 1966, WH Tapes, WH 6602.10, LBJL.
63. Political Tactics, n.d., 1966, NSF, Komer Files, Box 2, LBJL.
64. Moyers to U. Alexis Johnson, Feb. 15, 1966, *FRUS, 1964–68, IV,* 227.
65. LBJ and Katzenbach Conversation, Mar. 17, 1966, WH Tapes, Transcripts of Telephone Conversations, March 1966, LBJ.
66. "Remarks at a Congressional Dinner Held in the National Guard Armory," May 12, 1966, *Public Papers of the Presidents: LBJ,* Vol. I, 502–504.

67. Harry McPherson Oral History, III, May 14, 1985, LBJL.
68. Diary, Aug. 10, 1967, PP/Orville Freeman, Box 11, LBJL. Johnson also recalled that in 1965 he had proposed the name of Robert W. Kitchens Jr., an African American, to be assistant secretary of state for cultural affairs. Fulbright expressed strong reservations, arguing that the programs were not comparable and that some host countries would not cooperate with a black. LBJ and Fulbright Conversation, July 9, 1965, WH Tapes, Transcripts of Telephone Conversations, 8324–25, LBJL.
69. LBJ and Talmadge Conversation, Mar. 17, 1966, WH Tapes, Transcripts of Telephone Conversations, LBJL.
70. LBJ and Long Conversation, Feb. 17, 1966, WH Tapes, WH6602.05, LBJL.
71. Quoted in William C. Berman, *William Fulbright and the Vietnam War: The Dissent of a Political Realist* (Kent, OH, 1988), 70.
72. LBJ and R. Wilkins Conversation, Jan. 5, 1966, WH Tapes, Transcripts of Telephone Conversations, Jan. 1966, LBJL.
73. See Rostow to Califano, May 16, 1968, NSF Name File, Rostow, Box 7, LBJL.
74. Komer to President Johnson, Apr. 13, 1966, *FRUS, 1964–68, IV,* 345.
75. NSC Memorandum, Mar. 28, 1966, *FRUS, 1964–68, IV,* 302. See also Komer to President, Apr. 19 and June 14, 1966, NSF, Komer Files, Box 2, LBJL; Herring, *Longest War,* 175.
76. Komer to President, Apr. 16, 1966, NSF, Komer Files, Box 2, LBJL.
77. Komer to Porter, May 11, 1966, NSF, Komer Files, Box 4, LBJL.
78. Maxwell Taylor Oral History, Sept. 14, 1981, II, LBJL.
79. Komer to President, Mar. 26, 1966, NSF, Komer Files, Box 2, LBJL.
80. Herring, *Longest War,* 176.
81. Hudson to Lansdale, Sept. 27, 1966, PP/W. Westmoreland, Box 9, LBJL.
82. See Lilienthall, *Journals, VI,* 282–283.
83. Komer to President, Oct. 14, 1966, NSF, Komer Files, Box 3, LBJL.
84. See Taylor to President, Aug. 30, 1966, NSF Memos to President Box 10, LBJL; Carver to Helms, Sept. 28, 1966, and Oct. 6, 1966, *FRUS, 1964–68, IV,* 668–669, 712–713.
85. McPherson to Moyers, Aug. 4, 1966, OF/H. McPherson, Box 51, LBJL.
86. Redmon to Moyers, May 13 and June 9, 1966, OF/Bill Moyers Box 12, LBJL.
87. Congressional Briefing, Feb. 24, 1966, Congressional Briefings on Vietnam, Box 1, LBJL.
88. Rusk to President, Apr. 24, 1966, *FRUS, 1964–68, IV,* 365.
89. Notes of President's Meeting with NSC, June 22, 1966, *FRUS, 1964–68, IV,* 448–452. See also McNamara to President, Jan. 24, 1966, and Taylor to President, Mar. 29, 1966, *FRUS, 1964–68, IV,* 113, 305.
90. LBJ and McNamara Conversation, June 28, 1966, *FRUS, 1964–68, IV,* 459.
91. Goldberg to President, May 14, 1966, Diary Backup, Box 38, LBJL.
92. LBJ and Mansfield Conversation, June 10, 1966, *FRUS, 1964–68, IV,* 418.
93. LBJ and Mcnamara Conversation, June 28, 1966, WH Tapes, WH6606.06, LBJL.
94. LBJ and Cy Vance Conversation, June 24, 1966, WH Tapes, WH6606.05, LBJL.
95. LBJ and Rostow, and LBJ and Vance Conversations, June 29, 1966, WH Tapes, WH6606.07, LBJL.
96. Ronald Steel, "A Visit to Washington" *The New York Review of Books,* Oct. 6, 1966, 5–6.
97. "Heresy at Omaha," *Newsweek,* July 18, 1966, 17.
98. LBJ and George Borwn Conversation, June 13, 1966, WH Tapes, WH6605.04, LBJL.
99. Hans J. Morgenthau, "Truth and Power," *New Republic,* Nov. 26, 1966, 8–11.
100. Hans J. Morgenthau, "The Colossus of Johnson City," *New York Review of Books,* Mar. 31, 1966.
101. Emmet Jon Hughes, "A Remembered Reckoning," *Newsweek,* July 11, 1966, 17.
102. "The War President," *New Republic,* July 16, 1966, 6.
103. See Redmon to Moyers, July 27, 1966, OF/Bill Moyers, Box 12, LBJL.
104. See Hans J. Morgenthau, "Monuments to Kennedy," *New York Review of Books,* Jan. 6, 1966.
105. Larry L. King, "Lyndon Johnson as Literary Critic," *New Republic,* Nov. 12, 1966, 36.
106. See Macy to President, Sept. 17, 1966, LBJ Handwriting File, Box 18, LBJL.
107. Diary, Sept. 20, 1966, PP/Orville. Freeman, Box 11, LBJL.
108. Valenti to President, Sept. 27, 1966, ExFg, Box 110, LBJL.
109. Vicky to Juanita, Apr. 29, 1966, LBJA Subj. File, Box 73, LBJL.
110. Valenti to President, Jan. 6, 1966, LBJ Handwriting File, Box 11, LBJL.
111. "Remarks in Vincennes, Indiana, upon Signing Bill Establishing the George Rogers Clark National Historical Park," July 23, 1966, *Public Papers of the Presidents: LBJ,* Vol. II, 775.
112. Alsop to Moyers, Jan. 11, 1966, OF/Bill Moyers, Box 7, LBJL.
113. Tom Wicker, "Many Americans Seem to Dislike, Distrust President," *New York Times,* July 20, 1966. See also Kinter to President, July 25, 1966, Diary Backup, Box 40, LBJL.
114. LBJ and E. McCarthy Conversation, WH Tapes, WH6602.01, LBJL.
115. LBJ and Luce Conversation, Feb. 21, 1966, WH Tapes, Transcripts of Telephone Conversations, Feb. 1966, LBJL.
116. LBJ and M. Bundy Conversation, Feb. 22, 1966, WH Tapes, WH6502.12, LBJL.
117. McNamara to President, Oct. 14, 1966, NSF, Meeting Notes, Box 2, LBJL.
118. Congressional Briefing, Sept. 6, 1966, Congressional Briefings on Vietnam, Box 1, LBJL.
119. Redmon to Moyers, Sept. 21 and 27, 1966, OF/Bill Moyers, Box 12; Fran Conniff to Moyers, July 26, 1966, Diary Backup, Box 40, LBJL.
120. Quoted in Margot Henriksen, *Dr. Strangelove's America: Society and Culture in the Atomic Age* (Berkeley, CA, 1997), 2.

121. "LBJ Hits the Trail—to the Pacific," *Newsweek,* Oct. 24, 1966.
122. Yolanda Boozer Notes, Oct. 19, 1966, Diary Backup, Box 48, LBJL.
123. "700,000 Jam Melbourne's Streets to Greet Johnson," *Dallas Times Herald,* Oct. 21, 1966.
124. Marie Femer Notes, Oct. 20, 1966, Diary Backup, Box 48, LBJL.
125. Farris Bryant Notes, Oct. 21, 1966, Diary Backup, Box 48, LBJL.
126. Meeting of President with President Park of Korea, Oct. 23, 1966, Diary Backup, Box 48, LBJL.
127. President's Meeting with Thieu, Ky, Co, Bui Dem, and Westmoreland, Oct. 23, 1966, Diary Backup, Box 48, LBJL.
128. Diary, Nov. 6, 1966, P/W. Westmoreland, Box 9, LBJL.
129. "Remarks to Members of the Armed Forces at Cam Ranh Bay, Vietnam," Oct. 26, 1966, *Public Papers of the Presidents: LBJ,* Vol. II, 1269–1270.
130. Impression of Gov. Farris Bryant, President Johnson's trip to Cam Ranh Bay, Oct. 26, 1966, Diary Backup, Box 48, LBJL. See also Rostow to Mrs. Johnson, Oct. 26, 1966, WHCF, Subj.: Field Trips, Box 28, LBJL.
131. Humphrey, *Public Man,* 340.

Chapter 35: Battling Dr. Strangelove

1. Jarboe Russell, *Lady Bird,* 224.
2. Quoted in ibid., 222.
3. Marie Fehmer Chiarado Interview with Author, Dec. 12, 2000, Washington, D.C.
4. "How to Deal with Daddy," *Newsweek,* Jan. 19, 1966, 21.
5. See "The Wonderful, Terrible Life," *Newsweek,* May 23, 1966, 37.
6. Jarboe Russell, *Lady Bird,* 287.
7. Quoted in ibid.
8. "The Wonderful, Terrible Life," 36–37.
9. "A White House Visit," Aug. 8, 1966, PP/J. Steele, Box 1, LBJL.
10. "The Wedding in Washington," *Newsweek,* Aug. 15, 1966, 17–18.
11. Quoted in Jarboe Russell, *Lady Bird,* 288–289.
12. Ibid.
13. Diary, Sept. 21, 1966, PP/Orville Freeman, Box 11, LBJL.
14. Quoted in Milkis, *Presidents and the Parties,* 189.
15. Quoted in ibid., 188–189.
16. James Rowe Oral History, II, Sept. 16, 1969, LBJL.
17. Humphrey, *Public Man,* 366. See also Edwin Weisl Oral History, II, Oct. 30, 1968, LBJL.
18. "Nixon and the GOP Comeback," *Newsweek,* Oct. 10, 1966, 30–33.
19. "Making of the President, 1972?," *Newsweek,* Sept. 5, 1966, 17.
20. See Hayes Redmon to Moyers, Sept. 1 and 27, 1966, OF/Bill Moyers, Box 12, LBJL.
21. Sherwin Markman to President, Sept. 4, 1966, LBJ Handwriting File, Box 17, LBJL; "Hitting the Trail," *Newsweek,* Aug. 29, 1966.
22. Moyers to President, Oct. 4, 1966, LBJ Handwriting File, Box 18, LBJL.
23. Wayne Aspinal Oral History, June 14, 1974, LBJL.
24. "The President's News Conference at the LBJ Ranch," Aug. 27, 1966, *Public Papers of the Presidents: LBJ,* Vol. II, 924.
25. See Redmon to Roche, July 26, 1966, OF/Bill Moyers, Box 12, LBJL; Diary, Nov. 27, 1966, PP/Orville Freeman, Box 11, LBJL.
26. "The [Republican] resurgence is a welcome antidote to the flagrant abuses of unchallenged power which we have suffered since January 1965." Walter Lippmann, "The War and the Election," *Newsweek,* Dec. 5, 1966, 23.
27. Quoted in Shesol, *Mutual Contempt,* 347. See also "T.R.B. from Washington," *New Republic,* June 27, 1966.
28. UPI 10, Dec. 1, 1966, Diary Backup, Box 49, LBJL.
29. See LBJ to Nelson Rockefeller, Nov. 18, 1966, LBJ Handwriting File, Box 18, LBJL.
30. Quoted in Dallek, *Flawed Giant,* 294.
31. Moyers to Rostow, July 15, 1966, and Moyers to President, Sept. 13, 1966, OF/B. Moyers, Box 12, LBJL.
32. LBJ and Moyers Conversation, Jan. 13, 1966, WH Tapes, WH6601.07, LBJL.
33. Miller, *Lyndon,* 457.
34. "LBJ Makes the Scene," *Dallas News,* Jan. 6, 1967.
35. Ackley to President, Feb. 27, 1967, LBJ Handwriting File, Box 20, LBJL.
36. Quoted in Califano, *Triumph and Tragedy,* 178–179.
37. Ibid., 179–180.
38. Quoted in ibid., 186.
39. McPherson to Rostow, Apr. 27, 1982, Reference File, Walt Rostow, LBJL.
40. See Marvin to President, and Cohen to Watson, May 28, 1966, Diary Backup, Box 36, LBJL.
41. Califano and White to President, Feb. 9, 1966, LBJ Handwriting File, Box 12, LBJL.
42. James Jones Oral History, June 28, 1969, LBJL.
43. McPherson to Rostow, Apr. 27, 1982, Reference File, "Walt Rostow," LBJL.
44. Temple to President, Jan. 13, 1968, LBJ Handwriting File, Box 27, LBJL.
45. Beschloss, *Reaching for Glory,* 261, n. 1.

46. Quoted in Califano, *Triumph and Tragedy,* 182–183.
47. Lady Bird Johnson, *White House Diary,* 471. A House investigation had found Powell guilty of misusing public funds.
48. See Robert Kintner to President, Jan. 11 and 13, 1967, LBJ Handwriting File, Box 19, LBJL.
49. James Reston, "Washington: Johnson and the Age of Reform," *New York Times,* Jan. 15, 1967.
50. Annual Message to the Congress on the State of the Union, Jan. 10, 1967, *Public Papers of the Presidents: LBJ,* Vol. I, 2–14.
51. "Remarks in Des Moines at a Democratic Dinner," June 30, 1966, *Public Papers of the Presidents: LBJ,* Vol. I, 690.
52. "LBJ, Wife, Attend Final Rites for 3 Astronauts," *Houston Post,* Feb. 1, 1967.
53. Lady Bird Johnson, unpublished diaries, 484, LBJL.
54. James Reston, "The Tragedy of Skepticism," *New York Times,* Oct. 2, 1966.
55. Lady Bird Johnson, *White House Diary,* 436.
56. Starbird to McNamara, Sept. 15, 1966, *FRUS, 1964–68, IV,* 636.
57. "The Battle for Hill 400," *Newsweek,* Oct. 10, 1966, 46.
58. "Americans at War," *Newsweek,* Aug. 1, 1966, 28.
59. Komer to Moyers, Nov. 22, 1966, NSF, Komer Files, Box 3, LBJL.
60. William Bundy to Rusk, Dec. 21, 1966, *FRUS, 1964–68, IV,* 962–966.
61. Editorial Note, *FRUS, 1964–68, IV,* 816–817.
62. Harry McPHerson Oral History, VI, May 16, 1985, LBJL.
63. LBJ and O'Brien Conversation, Mar. 30, 1967, *FRUS, 1964–68, V,* 297.
64. Rostow to Johnson, Jan. 3, 1967, *FRUS, 1964–68, V,* 14.
65. Johnson to Mansfield, Jan. 9, 1967, LBJ Handwriting File, Box 19, LBJL.
66. Department of State to Embassy in Soviet Union, Feb. 7, 1967, *FRUS, 1964–68, V,* 91–92; Harriman to President and Secretary of State, Feb. 2, 1967, NSF, Rostow Memos to President, Box 13, LBJL.
67. SUNFLOWER, Rostow to President, Feb. 7, 1967, and Cooper to Rusk and Harriman, Feb. 9, 1967 NSF Memos to President, Box 13, LBJL.
68. Johnson and McNamara Conversation, Feb. 12, 1967, *FRUS, 1964–68, V,* 150; Rostow to President, Feb. 11, 1967, NSF Memos to President, Box 13, LBJL.
69. Wilson to Johnson, Feb. 12, 1967, and Johnson to Wilson, Feb. 12, 1967, *FRUS, 1964–68, V,* 139, 143–144; Rostow to President and Rusk, Feb. 25, 1967, NSF Memos to President, Rostow, Box 14, LBJL.
70. Text of CIA Report, Aug. 28, 1967, Diary Backup, Box 75, LBJL.
71. Zhai, *China and the Vietnam Wars,* 166; Rostow to President, May 1, 1967, NSF Memos to President, Box 16, LBJL.
72. "My evaluation is that the Chinese are trying to break relations with Russia and then blame a failure of Hanoi to win the war on the Russians' connivance with the U.S.," Rostow confided to LBJ. Rostow and LBJ Conversation, Feb. 11, 1967, *FRUS, 1964–68, V,* 123.
73. Humphrey to President and Rusk, Apr. 4, 1967, NSF Memos to President, Rostow, Box 15, LBJL.
74. See North Vietnamese Official's Comments on Peace Negotiations, CIA Intelligence Cable, Sept. 15, 1967, NSF Memos to President, Box 22, LBJL.
75. Ho Chi Minh to LBJ, Feb. 15, 1967, *FRUS, 1964–68, V,* 174.
76. Johnson and McNamara Conversation, Feb. 12, 1967, *FRUS, 1964–68, V,* 151–152.
77. McNamara and Johnson Conversations, Feb. 13, 1967, *FRUS, 1964–68, V,* 165, 167.
78. Rostow to President, Jan. 19, 1967, *FRUS, 1964–68, V,* 50.
79. Sharp to JCS, Oct. 26, 1966, *FRUS, 1964–68, IV,* 780.
80. Editorial Note, Aug. 13, 1966, *FRUS, 1964–68, IV,* 579.
81. Diary, Dec. 14, 1966, PP/Orville Freeman, Box 11, LBJL.
82. Moyers to President, Sept. 13, 1966, OF/Bill Moyers, Box 12, LBJL. On Goldberg, see Rusk to President, Mar. 8, 1967, NSF Memos to President, Rostow, Box 14, LBJL.
83. The Situation in North Vietnam, Oct. 10, 1966, PP/W. Westmoreland, Box 9, LBJL.
84. *New York Times,* Dec. 25, 1966, Jan. 11–18, 1967.
85. Sharp to Wheeler, Dec. 24, 1966, *FRUS, 1964–68, IV,* 969.
86. Notes of President's Meeting with Clifford and Taylor, Aug. 5, 1967, Box 3, Tom Johnson Meeting Notes, NSF, LBJL. See also Goodpaster Meeting with General Eisenhower, Aug. 9, 1967, NSF Memos to President, Rostow, Box 20, LBJL.
87. North Vietnam, CIA Intelligence Cable, Sept. 1, 1967, NSF Memos to President, Rostow, Box 22, LBJL.
88. Transport Problems in Soviet Bloc Aid Shipments to North Vietnam, CIA IIC, Oct. 14, 1967, NSF Memos to President, Rostow, Box 23, LBJL.
89. See Zhai, *China and the Vietnamese Wars,* 156–157; Rostow to President, May 6, 1967, NSF Memos to President, Rostow, Box 16, LBJL.
90. "China: A Vast and Ominous Tumult," *Newsweek,* Jan. 23, 1967.
91. "Mao and the Struggle for China," *Newsweek,* Jan. 30, 1967, 32–33.
92. Rostow to President, May 1, 1967, NSF Memos to President, Rostow, Box 16, LBJL.
93. Rostow to President, May 6, 1967, NSF Memos to President, Box 16, LBJL.
94. Congressional Briefing, Feb. 15, 1967, Cong. Briefings on Vietnam, Box 1, LBJL.

Chapter 36: The Holy Land

1. Lodge to President, Mar. 1, 1967, NSF Memos to President, Rostow, Box 14, LBJL; Katzenbach to President, Feb. 11, 1967, NSF Memos to President, Rostow, Box 13, LBJL; Note 3, *FRUS, 1964–68, V,* 227; "Mr. Johnson Goes to Guam," *Newsweek,* Mar. 27, 1967, 27–28; Rostow to President, Mar. 10, 1967, Diary Backup, Box 57, LBJL; Komer to President, Mar. 18, 1967, Diary Backup, Box 58, LBJL.
2. Diary, Apr. 13, 1967, PP/W. Westmoreland, Box 11, LBJL.
3. Rostow to President, Mar. 17, 1967, NSF Memos to President, Box 14, LBJL.
4. Ellsworth Bunker Oral History, I, Dec. 9, 1980, LBJL; Rostow to President, Mar. 20, 1967, Diary Backup, Box 58, LBJL.
5. De Benedetti, *American Ordeal,* 181.
6. Johnson and Rusk Conversation, Mar. 18, 1967, *FRUS, 1964–68, V,* 256–257.
7. Ibid. See also George Denny to Rusk, Mar. 22, 1967, NSF Memos to President, Rostow, Box 14, LBJL.
8. "A Trip to Guam and a No from Ho," *Newsweek,* Apr. 3, 1967, 28.
9. Schlesinger to RFK, May 15, 1967, RFK Senate Papers, Personal Correspondence, Box 11, JFKL.
10. Rusk to President, Feb. 6, 1967, NSF Memos to President, Box 13, LBJL, Note 2, *FRUS, 1964–68, V,* 88.
11. Pearson Notes on Conversation with LBJ and Chief Justice Warren, Mar. 13, 1967, Papers of Drew Pearson, Box G 246, LBJL; "RFK's Denial Reported Sparked by LBJ Rebuke," *Houston Post,* Feb. 14, 1967. See also Jorden to Rostow, Mar. 3, 1967, NSF Memos, Box 14, LBJL; Rostow and Alsop Conversation, Rostow to President, Feb. 8, 1967, NSF memos to President, Box 13, LBJL.
12. "Men at War: RFK vs. LBJ," *Newsweek,* Mar. 13, 1967, 33–34.
13. Alsop and Greene Interview, n.d., PP/A. Schlesinger, Box W59, JFKL.
14. "That Man and 'That Boy,' " *Newsweek,* Mar. 20, 1967, 25.
15. Rostow to President, Sept. 15, 1967, NSF Memos to President, Rostow, Box 22, LBJL.
16. Diaries, Mar. 3, 1967, PP/Orville Freeman, Box 11, LBJL.
17. "Jacqueline Kennedy's 'Victory,' " *Newsweek,* Jan. 2, 1967, 16–17; "The Book," *Newsweek,* Feb. 7, 1967, 34; Christian to President, Feb. 9, 1967, LBJ Handwriting File, Box 20, LBJL.
18. "Thickening the Plot," *Newsweek,* Mar. 27, 1967, 37.
19. Roche to President, Jan. 13, 1967, LBJ Handwriting File, Box 19, 1967, LBJL.
20. "Much Adoo about Mac," *Newsweek,* Feb. 27, 1967, 99.
21. Pearson Notes on Meeting with LBJ and Chief Justice Warren, Mar. 13, 1967, PP/Drew Pearson, Box G 246, LBJL.
22. "The Home Front War," *Newsweek,* May 8, 1967, 31.
23. Wheeler to Westmoreland, Mar. 9, 1967, NSF-DSDUF, Box 3, LBJL.
24. Woods, *Quest for Identity,* 236–37.
25. Ibid.
26. Editorial Note, *FRUS, 1964–68, V,* 366–367; McNaughton to McNamara, May 6, 1967, *FRUS, 1964–68, V,* 381–382.
27. Editorial Note, *FRUS, 1964–68, V,* 649.
28. Harriman and McNamara Conversation, July 1, 1967, PP/Averell Harriman, Special Files, Subject File, McNamara, Library of Congress; Diary, Feb. 1, 1967, Box, PP/Orville Freeman, LBJL.
29. Diary, Apr. 27, 1967, PP/W. Westmoreland, Box 11, LBJL; Rostow to President, Apr. 27, 1967, NSF Memos to President, Rostow, Box 15, LBJL; Notes on Discussions with President Johnson, Apr. 27, 1967, *FRUS, 1964–68, V,* 349–351.
30. "The Home Front War," 31; Dallek, *Flawed Giant,* 473.
31. Wheeler to Sharp, May 28, 1967, NSF-DSDUF, Box 3, LBJL.
32. " 'Help Party, Don't Run,' Dissenters Tell Johnson," *Washington Evening Star,* July 31, 1967.
33. Quoted in Gilbert C. Fite, *Richard B. Russell, Jr., Senator from Georgia* (Chapel Hill, NC, 1991), 451.
34. Ibid.
35. J. William Fulbright to Richard Russell, July 14, 1967, Series 48:3, Box 16:4, PP/J. William Fulbright, UA.
36. Meeting of the President with Senate Committee Chairman, July 25, 1967, Tom Johnson Notes, Box 1, Johnson Papers, LBJL.
37. Walter Lippmann, "The Temptation of Lyndon Johnson," *Newsweek,* Feb. 27, 1967, 21.
38. Lady Bird Johnson Diary, July 16, 1965, in Beschloss, *Reaching for Glory,* 394.
39. Ibid., 518–519.
40. Jarboe Russell, *Lady Bird,* 290–291.
41. Michael Oren, *Six Days of War: June 1967 and the Making of the Modern Middle East* (New York, 2002), 15.
42. Diary, Mar. 23, 1968, PP/Orville Freeman, Box 11, LBJL.
43. McPherson Oral History, Sept. 19, 1985, LBJL.
44. "It Happened in November," *Washington Report on Middle East Affairs* (Nov/Dec. 1996); 96.
45. See, for example, Reedy to Carpenter, Mar. 14, 1962, VP Papers of G. Reedy, Box 7, LBJL.
46. Reedy to Sen. Johnson, Aug. 1958, SOF/G. Reedy, Box 427, LBJL.
47. Israel's drive to develop atomic weapons capability was allegedly in response to Egypt's decision to develop its own missile system. American intelligence was extremely dubious. "We think Israeli estimate of UAR missile capability grotesque (like USAF estimates of Soviet bombers in mid-50s),"

McGeorge Bundy memoed the president in 1964. "Nasser simply couldn't build an effective missile force (let him waste the money)." Bundy to President, Mar. 5, 1964, NSF Memos to President, Bundy, Box 14, LBJL.

48. Brands, *Wages of Globalism,* 187–188.
49. Oren, *Six Days,* 17.
50. Barnes to Secretary of State, July 24, 1964, NSF Country File, Middle East, Box 146, LBJL; Oren, *Six Days,* 19–20.
51. Quoted in Oren, *Six Days,* 20.
52. Ibid., 21–22.
53. Ibid., 35.
54. Stevenson to Rusk, Apr. 21, 1964, and General Comments of King Hussain on Arab Summit Conference, CIA IIC, NSF Country File, Middle East, Box 146, LBJL, Oren, *Six Days,* 25.
55. Komer to Wiesl, Feb. 19, 1966, NSF, Komer Files, Box 3, LBJL.
56. Komer to President, Jan. 26, 1965, NSF Country File, Middle East, Box 46, LBJL.
57. Quoted in Brands, *Wages of Globalism,* 190; Komer to President, Feb. 3, 1965, NSF Country File, Middle East, Box 146, LBJL.
58. Komer to President, Feb. 6, 1965, NSF Country File, Middle East, Box 146, LBJL.
59. In 1965 the United States delivered to Israel 210 tanks worth $34 million and forty-eight A4s worth $72.1 million. Brands, *Wages of Globalism,* 191. See also Talbot to Secretary of State, Feb. 10, 1965, NSF Memos to President, Middle East, Box 146, LBJL.
60. Quoted in Brands, *Wages of Globalism,* 192.
61. Komer Memo for the Record, Feb. 9, 1966, and Rusk to Humphrey, Mar. 31, 1966, NSF, Komer Files, Box 3, LBJL; McPherson to President, Mar. 3, Aug. 16, and Sept. 13, 1966, OF/H. McPherson, Box 52, LBJL.
62. Saunders to Rostow, June 24, 1966, NSF Subj. File, Foreign Policy, Box 18, LBJL.
63. Komer Memo for the Record, Mar. 21, 1966, NSF Komer Files, Box 3, LBJL.
64. Oren, *Six Days,* 27–28.
65. Ibid.
66. Rostow to President, May 17, 1967, NSF Memos to President, Rostow, Box 16, LBJL; S.M. to M., May 21, 1967, Diary Backup, Box 67, LBJL.
67. Eshkol to President, May 18, 1967, *FRUS, 1964–68, XIX,* 20.
68. Ibid.
69. Burns to Sec. State, May 18, 1967, *FRUS, 1964–68, XIX,* 16–17.
70. McPherson to Vice President, May 15, 1968, OF/H. McPherson, Box 51, LBJL.
71. Memorandum by the CIA, May 23, 1967, *FRUS, 1964–68, XIX,* 73–74.
72. Editorial Note, *FRUS, 1964–68, XIX,* 80.
73. Memorandum for the Record, May 26, 1967, *FRUS, 1964–68, XIX,* 127–136.
74. Memorandum of Conversation, May 26, 1967, Diary Backup, Box 66, LBJL.
75. Rostow to President, May 28, 1967, *FRUS, 1964–68, XIX,* 168.
76. McNamara to President, May 30, 1967, NSF, Memos to President, Rostow, Box 16, LBJL; Memorandum for the Record, NSC Meeting, May 24, 1967, NSC Meeting Notes, Box 2, LBJL; Hoopes to McNamara, May 19, 1967, *FRUS, 1964–68, XIX,* 33; Kosygin to President, May 27, 1967, *FRUS, 1964–68, XIX,* 159–160; Department of State to American embassy, May 27, 1967, *FRUS, 1964–68, XIX,* 162–163.
77. Rostow to President, May 26, 1967, NSF Memos to President, Rostow, Box 16, LBJL.
78. Rostow to President, May 30, 1967, NSF Memos to President, Rostow, Box 16, LBJL.
79. Rostow to President, May 31, 1967, *FRUS, 1964–68, XIX,* 202.
80. Memorandum for the Record, Note 2, *FRUS, 1964–68, XIX,* 223.
81. "Middle East: The Scent of War," *Newsweek,* June 5, 1967, 40.
82. "How the War Was Won," *Newsweek,* June 19, 1967, 27–28.
83. H. McPHerson Oral History, III.
84. McNamara Interview with Rostow, Jan. 8, 1975, LBJL; Dallek Interview with McNamara, Special Interviews, Mar. 26, 1993, LBJL.
85. White House to Kosygin, June 5, 1967, *FRUS, 1964–68, XIX,* 301; Johnson to Kosygin, June 6, 1967, *FRUS, 1964–68, XIX,* 325; President's Daily Brief, June 6, 1967, *FRUS, 1964–68, XIX,* 322.
86. Battle Memorandum for the Record, Note 1, *FRUS, 1964–68, XIX,* 310.
87. Memorandum for the Record, Nov. 17, 1968, *FRUS, 1964–68, XIX,* 287–292.
88. Paul Glynn Note, June 5, 1967, Diary Backup, Box 63, LBJL.
89. Rostow to President, June 4, 1967, NSF Memos to President, Box 17, LBJL; Wriggins to Rostow, June 12, 1967, *FRUS, 1964–68, XIX,* 442–443; Brands, *Wages of Globalism,* 208.
90. Diary June 6, 1967, PP/Orville Freeman, Box 11, LBJL.
91. CIA to White House Situation Room, June 7, 1967, NSF Memos to President, Rostow, Box 17, LBJL. See also Johnson to Kosygin, June 6, 1967, *FRUS, 1964–68, XIX,* 334; Davis to Rostow, June 6, 1967, NSF Memos to President, Rostow, Box 17, LBJL.
92. Levinson and Wattenberg to White House Staff, June 7, 1967, *FRUS, 1964–68, XIX,* 354–355; Rostow to President, June 7, 1967, NSF Memos to President, Rostow, Box 17, LBJL. See also Memorandum for the Record, June 7, 1967, *FRUS, 1964–68, XIX,* 346.
93. Quoted in Califano, *Tragedy and Triumph,* 205.
94. McPherson to President, June 11, 1967, OF/H. McPherson, Box 53, LBJL.
95. Rostow to President, June 1, 1967, *FRUS, 1964–68, XIX,* 219.

96. Brands, *Wages of Globalism,* 209, 211.
97. CIA Intelligence Memorandum, June 13, 1967, *FRUS, 1964–68, XIX,* 469–470.
98. Commander Sixth Fleet to *America* and *Saratoga,* June 8, 1967, *FRUS, 1964–68, XIX,* 363–364.
99. Eban to LBJ, NSF Memos to President, Rostow, Box 17, LBJL.
100. Rostow to President, June 13, 1967, NSF Memos to President, Rostow, Box 17, LBJL.
101. Brands, *Wages of Globalism,* 212.
102. Rusk to Harman, June 10, 1967, *FRUS, 1964–68, XIX,* 424–425.
103. Memorandum for the Record, Oct. 22, 1968, *FRUS, 1964–68, XIX,* 410.
104. McPherson to President, July 19, 1967, OF/H. McPherson, Box 53, LBJL.
105. Arab-Israeli Situation Report, CIA, June 14, 1967, LBJ Handwriting File, Box 22, LBJL; Burns to Secretary of State, July 19, 1967, NSF Memos to President, Rostow, Box 19, LBJL.
106. M. Bundy to President, July 10, 1967, Diary Backup, Box 70, LBJL.
107. Roche to President, May 22, 1967, LBJ Handwriting File, Box 22, LBJL.
108. Thomas Fenton, "U.S. Ignored Crisis Signs in Mideast," *Baltimore Sun,* June 11, 1967.

Chapter 37: Backlash

1. See George Kennan Statement on "The Communist World in 1967," Jan. 30, 1967, Box 16.4, PP/J. William Fulbright, University of Arkansas; Katzenbach to President, Jan. 27, 1967, Diary Backup, Box 34, and Rostow to President, Feb. 7, 1967, Diary Backup, Box 55, LBJL; Emmet John Hughes, "The Righteous Wreckers," *Newsweek,* Feb. 20, 1967, 21.
2. Rostow to President, Apr. 15, 1967, NSF Memos to President, Box 15, LBJL.
3. T. Johnson to President, Mar. 9, 1967, Diary Backup, Box 57, LBJL; Sherwin Markman Notes on Summit Conference Preparations, June 22–25, 1967, Diary Backup, Box 69, LBJL.
4. Ibid.
5. President's handwritten notes made in his meeting w/Chairman Kosygin, June 25, 1967, Diary Backup, Box 69, LBJL, Editorial Note, *FRUS, 1964–68, XIX,* 556.
6. Ibid.
7. "The Glassboro Summit," *Newsweek,* July 3, 1967, 116.
8. Brands, *Wages of Globalism,* 217.
9. Notes on President's Meeting with Bob Thompson, July 18, 1967, WH Aides, G. Christian, Box 1, LBJL.
10. Notes of Meeting, Oct. 3, 1967, *FRUS, 1964–68, V,* 838.
11. Jarboe Russell, *Lady Bird,* 291.
12. McPherson to President, Feb. 2, 1967 OF/H. McPherson, Box 53, LBJL.
13. "Remarks at a Ceremony at the Lincoln Memorial," Feb. 12, 1967, *Public Papers of the Presidents: LBJ,* Vol. I, 176–178.
14. See James E. Booker to Clifford L. Alexander, May 3, 1966, OF/H. McPherson, Box 22, LBJL.
15. De Benedetti, *American Ordeal,* 172–173.
16. McPherson to President, Apr. 4, 1967, OF/H. McPherson, Box 53, LBJL.
17. James Farmer Oral History, II, July 20, 1971, LBJL.
18. Califano to President, July 25, 1966, and Lodge to M. Bundy, July 26, 1966, Diary Backup, Box 40, LBJL.
19. Clifford Alexander to President, Apr. 18, 1967, Diary Backup, Box 62, LBJL.
20. Califano to President, June 28, 1967, LBJ Handwriting File, Box 23, LBJL, Negro Casualties in Vietnam, 1961–65, n.d., OF/H. J. McPherson, Box 22, LBJL.
21. Redmon to Moyers, Sept. 2, 1966, OF/Bill Moyers, Box 12, LBJL.
22. Wilson to LBJ, Feb. 4, 1966, WHCF, Box 322, LBJL.
23. C. Alexander Oral History, Nov. 1, 1971, LBJL.
24. Dallek, *Flawed Giant,* 439.
25. Califano, *Triumph and Tragedy,* 208.
26. Louis Martin Oral History, I, May 14, 1969, LBJL.
27. Dallek, *Flawed Giant,* 441–442.
28. See Robert V. Spike, "Fissures in the Civil Rights Movement," *Christianity and Crisis,* Feb. 21, 1967, 18–20. See also Moynihan to McPherson, Apr. 15, 1966, OF/H. McPherson, Box 21, LBJL.
29. McPherson to President, Jan. 19, 1967, OF/H. McPherson, Box 53, LBJL.
30. "Special Message to the Congress on Equal Justice," Feb. 15, 1967, *Public Papers of the Presidents: LBJ,* Vol. I, 188–189. See also Califano to President, Feb. 10, 1967, LBJ Handwriting File, Box 20, LBJL.
31. "Something Borrowed," *Newsweek,* Feb. 27, 1967, 28.
32. See "Newark Boils Over," *Newsweek,* July 24, 1967, 21–22.
33. Quoted in Califano, *Triumph and Tragedy,* 210.
34. "You Can't Run Away," *Newsweek,* July 31, 1967, 17.
35. Califano, *Triumph and Tragedy,* 212–213.
36. Ibid.
37. "An American Tragedy, 1967," *Newsweek,* Aug. 7, 1967, 19.
38. Ramsey Clark Oral History, IV, Apr. 16, 1969, LBJL.
39. Quoted in Califano, *Triumph and Tragedy,* 214.
40. Notes of the President's Activities During the Detroit Crisis, July 24, 1967, Diary Backup, Box 71, LBJL.
41. Ibid.

42. Quoted in Califano, *Triumph and Tragedy,* 217.
43. See the Detroit Riots Chronology, July 23–25, 1967, and AP208 ff, July 24, 1967, Diary Backup, Box 71, LBJL.
44. "An American Tragedy, 1967," 18.
45. "Havana: Fanning the Guerrilla Flames," *Newsweek,* Aug. 14, 1967.
46. "SNCC and the Jews," *Newsweek,* Aug. 28, 1967, 22; "What Has Become of the Treason Laws?," *Congressional Record,* Apr. 12, 1967, LBJ Handwriting File, Box 21, LBJL.
47. Cuba/Red China Involvement in Promoting Violence in the United States, CIA Report, July 26, 1967, NSF Memos, Box 20, Rostow, LBJL.
48. See Larry Levinson, Memo for the Record, July 31, 1967, Diary Backup, Box 72, LBJL; Emmet John Hughes, "The Great Disgrace," *Newsweek,* Aug. 7, 1967.
49. McPherson to President, July 26, 1967, and Alexander to President, July 22, 1967, LBJ Handwriting File, Box 23, LBJL.
50. See Summary of the President's Meeting with HUD's Urban Development Advisory Committee, July 31, 1967, Diary Backup, Box 72, LBJL.
51. Emmet John Hughes, "A Curse of Confusion," *Newsweek,* May 1, 1967, 17.
52. Quoted in Califano, *Triumph and Tragedy,* 220. See also the President's Meeting with the National Advisory Commission on Civil Disorders, July 29, 1967, Diary Backup, Box 72, LBJL.
53. McPherson to Johnson, July 29, 1967, Diary Backup, Box 72, LBJL.
54. "After the Riots: A Survey," *Newsweek,* Aug. 27, 1967, 18.
55. Diary, May 6, 1967, PP/Orville Freeman, Box 11, LBJL.
56. "LBJ at a Low Ebb," *Newsweek,* Aug. 21, 1967, 15.
57. "LBJ's War Budget—and Its New Math," *Newsweek,* Feb. 6, 1967, 30–31.
58. Califano, *Triumph and Tragedy,* 242.
59. Diary, June 10, 1967, PP/Orville Freeman, Box 11, LBJL.
60. Califano, *Triumph and Tragedy,* 244.
61. Meeting with Secretaries Rusk and McNamara, Leonard Unger and Walt Rostow, Jim Jones to President, Sept. 15, 1967, Diary Backup, Box 76, LBJL.
62. Notes on Meeting of the President with Joseph Kraft, Sept. 27, 1967, White House Aides, George Christian, Box 1, LBJL.
63. Quoted in Califano, *Triumph and Tragedy,* 245.
64. Ibid., 245–246.

Chapter 38: Of Hawks and Doves, Vultures and Chickens

1. McPherson to President, June 13, 1967, OF/H. McPherson, Box 29, LBJL.
2. Marie Fehmer Chiarado Interview with Author, Dec. 12, 2000, Washington D.C.
3. George Reedy, *Lyndon B. Johnson: A Memoir* (New York, 1982), 149.
4. See, for example, Father T. G. Mullaney to President, Aug. 16, 1967, LBJ Handwriting File, Box 24, LBJL; Lady Bird Johnson, *White House Diary,* 391.
5. LBJ to Lucey, June 26, 1967, LBJ Handwriting File, Box 23, LBJL.
6. Rostow to President, Nov. 15, 1967, Diary Backup, Box 82, LBJL.
7. "Prickly Sermon for LBJ," *Newsweek,* Nov. 27, 1967, LBJL.
8. Draft Memorandum from McNamara to President, May 19, 1967, *FRUS, 1964–68, V,* 423–424.
9. See Notes on Vietnam, July 24, 1967, PP/Clark Clifford, Box 1, LBJL.
10. See Stephen Young, "LBJ's Vietnam Strategy for Disengagement," *Vietnam Magazine* (Feb. 1998); De Benedetti, *American Ordeal,* 191.
11. "Ambush at Con Thien," *Newsweek,* July 17, 1967, 45.
12. Westmoreland to Harold Johnson, Sept. 1967, NSF Memos to President, Rostow, Box 23, LBJL.
13. Rostow to President, May 6, 1967, NSF Memos to President, Rostow, Box 16, LBJL.
14. Editorial Note, *FRUS, 1964–68, V,* 459–460.
15. Notes of the President's Meeting with Labor Leaders, Aug. 9, 1967, Diary Backup, Box 73, LBJL.
16. Depuy to JCS, Sept. 8, 1967, NSF Memos to President, Rostow, Box 23, LBJL.
17. "War over the War," *Newsweek,* Sept. 11, 1967.
18. Jones to President, Sept. 12, 1967, *FRUS, 1964–68, V,* 777–780.
19. Notes of Meeting, Oct. 17, 1967, *FRUS, 1964–68, V,* 889.
20. Military Assistance Command, Vietnam (hereafter MACV) Commander's Conference, May 13, 1967, PP/W. Westmoreland, Box 12, LBJL.
21. McNamara to President, Oct. 14, 1966, NSF, Meeting Notes, Box 2, LBJL.
22. Vice President to President, Feb. 13, 1967, LBJ Handwriting File, Box 20, LBJL.
23. Notes of the President's Meeting with Harry Reasoner, CBS, Aug. 14, 1967, Diary Backup, Box 73, LBJL.
24. Rostow to Califano, May 16, 1968, NSF Name File, Rostow, Box 7, LBJL.
25. Editorial Note, *FRUS, 1964–68, V,* 694–695; Note 5, *FRUS, 1964–68, V,* 47. See also Rostow to President, Feb. 4, 1967, NSF Memos to President, Rostow, Box 13, LBJL.
26. Carver Memo, Apr. 19, 1967, *FRUS, 1964–68, V,* 327.
27. Lodge to President, Apr. 21, 1967, NSF Memos to President, Box 15; Diary, May 7, 1967, PP/W. Westmoreland, Box 12; Bunker to Department of State, May 10, 1967, NSF Memos to President, Rostow, Box 16, LBJL.
28. Westmoreland to Wheeler and Sharp, July 1, 1967, PP/W. Westmoreland, Box 18, LBJL.

29. De Benedetti, *American Ordeal,* 180–183.
30. "The Draft: The Unjust vs. the Unwilling," *Newsweek,* Apr. 11, 1966, 30.
31. "Protest, Debate, Renewal," *Newsweek,* May 22, 1967.
32. McPherson to President, May 18, 1966, OF/H. McPherson, Box 52, LBJL.
33. "Special Message to the Congress on Selective Service," Mar. 6, 1967, *Public Papers of the Presidents: LBJ,* Vol. I, 277–285. See also Califano to President, June 12, 1967, LBJ Handwriting File, Box 22, LBJL.
34. Califano to President, Dec. 7, 1967, OF/Joe Califano, Box 16, LBJL.
35. See Meeting with president in his bedroom on Tuesday evening, Jan. 17, 1967, Diary Backup, Box 52; McPherson to President, Feb. 3, 1967, OF/H. McPherson, Box 52, LBJL.
36. Congressional Briefing, Feb. 23, 1967, Cong. Briefings on Vietnam, Box 1, LBJL.
37. Durga Das and Johnson Interview, June 21, 1967, Diary Backup, Box 52, LBJL.
38. LBJ and McAndrew Conversation, Feb. 27, 1967, Diary Backup, Box 56, LBJL.
39. Notes of Meeting, July 13, 1967, *FRUS, 1964–68, V,* 613.
40. McPherson to President, Nov. 4, 1967, OF/H. McPherson, Box 53, LBJL. See also Rostow to President, May 4, 1967, NSF Memos to President, Rostow, Box 16, LBJL.
41. Leslie Gelb Oral History, Apr. 30, 1984, I, LBJL.
42. Louis Harris, "How the U.S. Public Now Feels about Vietnam," *Newsweek,* Feb. 27, 1967.
43. Rostow to President, Oct. 19, 1967, NSF Memos to President, Rostow, Box 25, LBJL.
44. McPherson to President, Aug. 25, 1967, OF/H. McPherson, Box 29, LBJL.
45. Memorandum for Henry A. Kissinger, n.d., *FRUS, 1964–68, V,* 687.
46. Rostow to President Aug. 9, 1967, NSF Memos to President, Rostow, Box 20, LBJL; Memorandum of Meeting, Aug. 3, 1967, *FRUS, 1964–68, V,* 664–665.
47. Dallek, *Flawed Giant,* 481.
48. Ibid.
49. Katzenbach to President, Sept. 26, 1967, NSF Memos to President, Rostow, Box 23, LBJL.
50. Editorial Note, *FRUS, 1964–68, V,* 837; Rostow to President, Oct. 21, 1967, *FRUS, 1964–68, V,* 911; Herring, *America's Longest War,* 196–197.
51. Jones to President, Nov. 2, 1967, *FRUS, 1968–68, V,* 956.
52. Roche to President, Oct. 2, 1967, LBJ Handwriting File, Box 25, LBJL.
53. Quoted in De Benedetti, *American Ordeal,* 192.
54. Ibid.
55. Diary, Aug. 10, 1967, PP/Orville Freeman, Box 11, LBJL.
56. Jones to President, Nov. 4, 1967, *FRUS, 1964–68, V,* 989.
57. R. B. Woods, *Fulbright,* 464.
58. Notes of Meeting, Oct. 23, 1967, *FRUS, 1964–68, V,* 917.
59. Note 5, *FRUS, 1964–68, V,* 1077.
60. Quoted in Dallek, *Flawed Giant,* 495.
61. Califano, *Triumph and Tragedy,* 264.
62. Memo of Conversation between McNamara and Harriman, *FRUS, 1964–68, V,* 810.
63. McNamara to President, Nov. 1, 1967, NSF Memos to President, Situation Room, Vol. 113, Box 44, LBJL.
64. Draft Memorandum from McNamara to President, Nov. 1, 1967, *FRUS, 1964–1968, V,* 943.
65. Stephen B. Young, "LBJ's Strategy for Disengagement," *Vietnam Magazine* (Feb. 1998).
66. Jones to President, Nov. 2, 1967, Diary Backup, Box 81, LBJL.
67. Fortas Comments, Nov. 5, 1967, NSF Memos to President, Box 28, LBJL.
68. Clifford to President, Nov. 7, 1967, NSF Memos to President, Box 28, LBJL. See also Rostow to President, Nov. 20, 1967, NSF Memos to President, Box 28, LBJL.
69. General Westmoreland's History Notes, Nov. 13–28, 1967, PP/W. Westmoreland, Box 14, LBJL.
70. Schlesinger to RFK, May 15, 1967, RFK Senate, Personal Correspondence, Box 11, JFKL.
71. O'Donnell to Kennedy, Oct. 24, 1967, Box 9, JFKL; Goodwin to RFK, Sept. 9, 1967, Box 4, RK Senate Papers, Personal Correspondence, JFKL; O. Freeman to RFK, Nov. 27, 1967, PP/Orville Freeman, Box 11, LBJL.
72. Markman to Sanders, Aug. 23, 1967, WHCF, Box 324, LBJL.
73. Diary, June 19, 1967, PP/Orville Freeman, Box 11, LBJL.
74. "Dump LBJ?," *Newsweek,* Oct. 9, 1967, 25.
75. "The Move to 'Dump' Johnson," *Newsweek,* Nov. 27, 1967, 25.
76. Roche to President, Mar. 15 and June 6, 1967, LBJ Handwriting File, Boxes 21 and 22, LBJL.
77. Democratic party in Farm Belt, May, 1967, PP/Orville Freeman, Box 11, LBJL. See also Pierson to President, May 12, 1967, Diary Backup, Box 68, LBJL.
78. "The Move to 'Dump' Johnson," 25.
79. McPherson to Moyers, Mar. 8, 1966, OF/H. McPherson, Box 451, LBJL.
80. How They See LBJ, Oct. 27, 1966, PP/J. Steele, Box 1, LBJL.
81. Frankel to Christian, May 26, 1967, LBJ Handwriting File, Box 22, LBJL.
82. Memo of Conversation between President, Helen Thomas, and Jack Horner, Aug. 25, 1967, Diary Backup, Box 74, LBJL.
83. Interview by Hugh Sidey with the President, May 16, 1967, Diary Backup, Box 68, LBJL.
84. Notes of President Meeting with Max Frankel, Sept. 15, 1967, Diary Backup, Box 76, LBJL.
85. Watson to President, Nov. 28, 1967, and Panzer to President, Sept. 25, 1967, Diary Backup, Box 78, LBJL.

86. "Meet Candidate Lyndon Johnson," *Newsweek,* Nov. 13, 1967, 31.
87. "Live and in Color—The Real LBJ," *Newsweek,* Nov. 27, 1967, 23.
88. Sidey to President, Nov. 17, 1967, and Johnson to Sidey, Nov. 21, 1967, LBJ Handwriting File, Box 26, LBJL.
89. Johnson to Roberts, Feb. 5, 1967, Diary Backup, Box 53, LBJL.
90. Sidey, *A Very Personal President,* 100.
91. George Reedy to President, Mar. 29, 1968, LBJ Handwriting File, Box 28, LBJL.
92. George Reedy Oral History, III, June 7, 1975, LBJL.
93. Lady Bird Johnson, *White House Diary,* 477.
94. Juanita to President, Apr. 28, 1967, Diary Backup, Box 63, LBJL.
95. Ted Gittinger Interview with Author, June 22, 2000, Austin, Texas; John Richards Interview with Author, Oct. 14, 2002, Taylor, Texas.
96. Lady Bird Johnson, *White House Diary,* 553.
97. MJC to Watson, Aug. 3, 1967, Diary Backup, Box 72, LBJL.
98. Jarboe Russell, *Lady Bird,* 292.
99. Ibid., 293.
100. "White House Wedding," *Newsweek,* Dec. 18, 1967, 29, 32.
101. Quoted in Jarboe Russell, *Lady Bird,* 294–295.

Chapter 39: Tet

1. James Reston, "Johnson's Theme of 'Little Time' Puzzles Friends," *New York Times,* Nov. 30, 1966.
2. Roche to President, July 6, 1967, LBJ Handwriting File, Box 23, LBJL.
3. Quoted in Califano, *Triumph and Tragedy,* 254.
4. "Annual Message to Congress on the State of the Union," Jan. 17, 1968, *Public Papers of the Presidents: LBJ,* Vol I, 31.
5. "Backlash in Boston—and across the U.S.," *Newsweek,* Nov. 6, 1967, 29.
6. Release of U.S. Prisoners, Nov. 3, 1967, NSF Memos, Rostow, Box 25, LBJL.
7. Diary, Aug. 26, 1967, PP/Orville Freeman, Box 11, LBJL.
8. Ibid.
9. Quoted in White, *Making of the President,* 259.
10. See Cater to President, Oct. 11, 1967, Cabinet Papers, Box 11, LBJL.
11. Califano, *Triumph and Tragedy,* 223.
12. Ibid., 225–26.
13. "Special Message to the Congress: 'To Earn a Living: The Right of Every American.'" Jan. 23, 1968, *Public Papers of the Presidents: LBJ,* Vol. I, 46–47.
14. Califano, *Triumph and Tragedy,* 225–226. See also Califano to President, Mar. 11, 1968, OF/J. Califano, Box 16, LBJL; "Remarks at a Meeting of the National Alliance of Businessmen," Mar. 16, 1968, *Public Papers of the Presidents: LBJ,* Vol. I, 402–405.
15. Temple to President, Jan. 19, 1968, LBJ Handwriting File, Box 27, LBJL.
16. Clark to President, Feb. 12, 1968, PP/Warren Christopher, Box 1, LBJL.
17. Ramsey Clark Oral History, V, June 3, 1968, LBJL.
18. "Guilty or Not?," *Newsweek,* Mar. 18, 1968, 46.
19. Notes on Meeting with Negro Editors and Publishers, Mar. 15, 1968, Diary Backup, Box 93, LBJL. See also Califano to President, Mar. 2, 1968, OF/Joe Califano, Box 16, LBJL.
20. Harry McPherson Oral History, IV, Mar. 24, 1969, LBJL.
21. "Special Message to the Congress: 'To Protect the Consumer Interest," Feb. 6, 1968, *Public Papers of the Presidents: LBJ,* Vol. I, 174; "Meet Ralph Nader," *Newsweek,* Jan. 22, 1968, 65.
22. "Special Message to the Congress on Education: 'The Fifth Freedom,' " Feb. 5, 1968, *Public Papers of the Presidents: LBJ,* Vol. I, 165–167.
23. Mitchell B. Lerner, *The Pueblo Incident: A Spy Ship and the Failure of American Foreign Policy* (Lawrence, KS, 2002), 2.
24. Notes of President's Meeting with NSC, Jan. 24, 1968, Tom Johnson Meeting Notes, Box 2, LBJL.
25. "Prometheus Bound," *Newsweek,* Feb. 9, 1968, 15.
26. Diary, Jan. 31, 1968, PP/Orville Freeman, Box 11, LBJL.
27. Lerner, *Pueblo Incident,* 126.
28. "The VC's Week of Terror," *Newsweek,* Feb. 12, 1968, 24–25.
29. Quoted in Herring, *Largest War,* 210.
30. President to Bunker, Note 5, Feb. 2, 1968, *FRUS, 1964–1968, VI,* 105.
31. Remarks at Presidential Prayer Breakfast, Feb. 1, 1968, *Public Papers of the Presidents: LBJ,* Vol. I, 121–122.
32. When questioned, the Pentagon denied that such weapons had been sent to the battlefront but admitted that they were "in the neighborhood." At a meeting on February 10, LBJ asked McNamara, "Is it true there are no nuclear weapons in Vietnam?" His reply: "It is true there are none there." Notes of Meeting, Feb. 10, 1968, *FRUS, 1964–68, VI,* 168; Fleming to President, Feb. 9, 1968, WHCF, Subj. File, Box 342, LBJL. See also Rusk to JWF, Feb. 10, 1968, Box 16, PP/J. William Fulbright, University of Arkansas.
33. Quoted in Words, *Quest for Identity,* 268.
34. Ibid.
35. Notes of Meeting, Feb. 6, 1968, *FRUS, 1964–68, VI,* 13.

36. Westmoreland, "Paper on Significance of the Tet Offensive," Nov. 9, 1970, NSF-DSDUF, Box 3, LBJL.
37. Westmoreland to Sharp and Wheeler, Feb. 12, 1968, *FRUS, 1964–68, VI,* 184. See also Westmoreland to Sharp, Feb. 10, 1968, NSF-DSDUF, Box 3, LBJL.
38. Note 9, Notes of Meeting, Feb. 12, 1968, *FRUS, 1964–68, VI,* 196.
39. Notes of Meeting, Feb. 12, 1968, *FRUS, 1964–68, VI,* 190.
40. "A Broadside by Bobby," *Newsweek,* Feb. 19, 1968, 24.
41. Gulf of Tonkin Hearing, Feb. 21, 1968, Executive Sessions, SFRC, Record Group 46, National Archives.
42. McPherson to President, Feb. 8, 1968, LBJ Handwriting File, Box 32, LBJL.
43. LBJ to Clifford, Feb. 8, 1968, PP/Clark Clifford, Box 1, LBJL.
44. Notes of Meeting, Feb. 20, 1968, Note 6, *FRUS, 1964–68, VI,* 223.
45. Notes of Meeting, Feb. 20, 1968, *FRUS, 1964–68, VI,* 223–224.
46. Summary of President's Breakfast with Boys on Carrier *Constellation,* Feb. 18, 1968, Diary Backup, Box 90, LBJL.
47. China Experts Meeting with President, Feb. 2, 1968, Meeting Notes File, Box 2, LBJL.
48. "Watching and Waiting," *Newsweek,* Feb. 26, 1968, 21.
49. Bill Gill Notes on Rusk Bombing Halt, Lunch with Joe Califano, 1970, Reference File, "Vietnam," LBJL.
50. Significance of the Tet Offensive, Nov. 9, 1970, NSF-DSDUF, Box 3, LBJL.
51. Relations with South Vietnamese, Westmoreland Interview, Jan. 28, 1973, PP/W. Westmoreland, Box 30, LBJL.
52. Tet, Westmoreland Interview, Feb. 20, 1973, PP/W. Westmoreland, Box 30, LBJL.
53. Significance of the Tet Offensive, Nov. 9, 1970.
54. See Interview with General Westmoreland, Apr. 2, 1970, PP/W. Westmoreland, Box 30, LBJL.
55. Wheeler to President, Feb. 27, 1968, PP/Clark Clifford, Box 2, LBJL.
56. Notes of Meeting, Feb. 28, 1968, *FRUS, 1964–68, VI,* 272.
57. Bill Gill Notes on Rusk Bombing Halt Recommendations, Lunch with Joe Califano, Oct. 4, 1970, File Notes, Reference File, "Vietnam," LBJL.
58. Editorial Note, *FRUS, 1964–68, VI,* 307–308, Clark Clifford Oral History, July 2, 1969, III, LBJL.
59. Notes of Meeting, Mar. 4, 1968, *FRUS, 1964–68, VI,* 316–323.
60. Orberdorfer Notes, n.d., Reference File, "Vietnam," LBJL.
61. Editorial Note, *FRUS, 1964–68, VI,* 341–342.
62. LBJ and Russell Conversation, Mar. 7, 1968, *FRUS, 1964–68, VI,* 344–349.
63. Record of Meeting, Feb. 21, 1968, *FRUS, 1964–68, VI,* 230–233.
64. Oberdorfer Notes, n.d.
65. Dallek, *Flawed Giant,* 24–25.
66. Ibid. 24–25.
67. John Gardner Oral History, II, Dec. 20, 1971, LBJL.
68. Roche to LBJ, Dec. 4, 1967, PP/A. Schlesinger, Box W59, JFKL.
69. Diary, Mar. 22, 1968, PP/Orville Freeman, LBJL.
70. See Weisl to President, Jan. 26, 1968, LBJ Handwriting File, Box 27, LBJL; Rostow to LBJ, Feb. 22, 1968, NSF Country File, Vietnam, Box 102, LBJL.
71. C. Clifford Oral History, III, July 14, 1969, LBJL. According to Richard Daley's biographers, the idea had come from him. "Rather than go through the divisiveness of a primary challenge to a sitting president, Kennedy should get Johnson to agree to submit the future of the Vietnam War to binding arbitration. It must have seemed odd to Kennedy that his presidential candidacy, viewed by his supporters as a moral crusade, was being reduced to the level of a truckers' strike." Cohen and Taylor, *American Pharaoh,* 450.
72. Notes Taken at Meeting, Mar. 14, 1968, PP/Clark Clifford, Box 1, LBJL.
73. Andrew Kopkind, "Waiting for Lefty," *New York Review of Books,* June 1, 1967.
74. "Remarks at a Dinner of the Veterans of Foreign Wars," Mar. 12, 1968, *Public Papers of the Presidents: LBJ,* Vol. I, 381. Johnson and his lieutenants had long held McCarthy in mild contempt. "Around 1960–61," Harry McPherson said, "I began to realize that he [McCarthy] was spending all of his time down in the Senate Restaurant making bon mots for the press and no time on the floor helping with legislation or in committee. He was a master of what Hermann Hesse called feuilleton, extraneous information." McPherson Oral History, III.
75. Diary, Mar. 22, 1968, PP/Orville Freeman, Box 11, LBJL.
76. Ibid.
77. Herring, *Longest War,* 225–226; Summary of Meeting, Mar. 26, 1968, Meeting Notes File, Box 2, LBJL.
78. Herring, *Longest War,* 225.
79. UPI 162, Jan. 19, 1968, OF/H. McPherson, Box 50, LBJL.
80. Diary, Mar. 23, 1986, PP/Orville Freeman, Box 11, LBJL.
81. Quoted in Califano, *Triumph and Tragedy,* 268. See also Joe Califano, Memo of Conversation, July 25, 1971, PP/A. Schlesinger, Box W59, JFKL.
82. Ibid.
83. Lincoln's Second Inaugural Address, Mar. 4, 1865, Works of Abraham Lincoln, Liberty Online, libertyonline.hypermail.com.
84. Buzz to President, Mar. 29, 1968, LBJ Handwriting File, Box 29, LBJL.

85. Jarboe Russell, *Lady Bird,* 300.
86. James Jones, "LBJ's Decision Not to Run in '68," *New York Times,* Apr. 16, 1988.
87. George Gallup, "Johnson's War and Job Ratings Sink," *Washington Post,* Mar. 31, 1968.
88. Christian to President, Mar. 31, 1968, Diary Backup, Box 94, LBJL.
89. Rostow Memorandum for the Record, Mar. 31, 1968, NSF Memos, Box 31, LBJL.
90. Arthur Krim Oral History, IV, Nov. 9, 1982, LBJL; Marie Fehmer Notes, July 30, 1968, Diary Backup, Box 94, LBJL. See also Clark Clifford Oral History, Aug. 7, 1969, LBJL.
91. "The President's Address to the Nation Announcing Steps to Limit the War in Vietnam and Reporting His Decision Not to Seek Reelection," Mar. 31, 1968, *Public Papers of the Presidents: LBJ,* 469–476.
92. Ibid.
93. Simon and Vickie McHugh Oral History, June 9, 1975, LBJL.
94. Marie Fehmer to Dorothy, July 30, 1968, Diary Backup, Box 94, LBJL.
95. Sam Houston to President, Apr. 1, 1968, Family Correspondence, Box 2, LBJL.

Chapter 40: A Midsummer Nightmare

1. Quoted in Woods, *Quest for Identity,* 273.
2. Califano, *Triumph and Tragedy,* 274.
3. McPherson and Califano to President, Apr. 5, 1968, Diary Backup, Box 95, LBJL.
4. Califano to President, Apr. 5, 1968, Diary Backup, Box 95, LBJL. See also James Farmer Oral History, II, July 20, 1971, LBJL.
5. Talking Points Civil Rights Meeting, Apr. 5, 1968, OF/Joe Califano, Box 17, LBJL.
6. Quoted in Califano, *Triumph and Tragedy,* 275.
7. LBJ to Mrs. King, Apr. 5, 1968, OF/J. Califano, Box 17, LBJL.
8. Situation Room Information Memorandum, Apr. 5, 1968, Diary Backup, Box 95, LBJL.
9. Visits to Washington, Jan. 28, 1973, Box 30, PP/W. Westmoreland, LBJL.
10. Situation Room Information Memorandum, April 6, 1968, Diary Backup, Box 95, LBJL.
11. Quoted in Califano, *Triumph and Tragedy,* 279.
12. Adm. S. D. Cramer Memo for the Record, Apr. 5, 1968, Diary Backup, Box 95, LBJL. See also Califano, *Triumph and Tragedy,* 279–280.
13. Situation Room Information Memorandum, Apr. 6, 1968, Diary Backup, Box 95, LBJL; Califano, *Triumph and Tragedy,* 281–282.
14. Jim Jones to President, Apr. 5, 1968, Diary Backup, Box 96, LBJL.
15. Califano, *Triumph and Tragedy,* 282; UPI 030A, Apr. 7, 1968, Diary Backup, Box 95, LBJL.
16. Califano, *Triumph and Tragedy,* 276.
17. Califano to President, Apr. 10, 1968, LBJ Handwriting File, Box 29, LBJL; Barefoot Sanders to President, Apr. 5, 1968, Diary Backup, Box 95, LBJL; Harold "Barefoot" Sanders Oral History, Nov. 3, 1969, LBJL.
18. Harry McPherson, Oral History, VI, Apr. 9, 1969.
19. Barefoot Sanders to President, Apr. 5, 1968, Diary Backup, Box 95, LBJL.
20. Califano to President, May 2, 1968, OF/Joe Califano, Box 17, LBJL.
21. Notes of meeting, Apr. 11, 1968, *FRUS, 1964–68, VI,* 568.
22. Califano to President May 2, 1968, OF/Joe Califano, Box 17, LBJL.
23. "The President's News Conference of May 3, 1968," *Public Papers of the Presidents: LBJ,* Vol. I, 561.
24. Quoted in Califano, *Triumph and Tragedy,* 286.
25. See L. B. Johnson, *Vantage Point,* 453–456. See also Okun to President, Apr. 27 and May 13, 1968, Diary Backup, Box 97, LBJL.
26. On-camera Interview with President Johnson, Apr. 27, 1968, Diary Backup, Box 97, LBJL.
27. James Jones Oral History, II, June 28, 1969, LBJL.
28. Quoted in "Do or Die," *Newsweek,* May 6, 1968, 30.
29. Warren Christopher to Califano, Apr. 27, 1968, LBJ Handwriting File, Box 29, LBJL.
30. Minutes of the Meeting, May 1, 1968, Cabinet Papers, Box 13, LBJL.
31. Cater to President, May 2, 1968, LBJ Handwriting File, Box 29, LBJL.
32. Diary, May 21, 1968, PP/Orville Freeman, Box 12, LBJL.
33. Califano to President, May 17, 1968, OF/Joe Califano, Box 17, LBJL.
34. Christian Notes on President's Meeting with Ken Crawford, May 23, 1968, WH Aides, George Christian, Box 1, LBJL.
35. Diary, May 21, 1968, PP/Orville Freeman, Box 12, LBJL.
36. Green and Gwirtzman Conversation, Apr. 4, 1972, and Hackman and Edelman Conversation, July 29, 1965, Box F59, PP/A. Schlesinger, JFKL.
37. B. Woods, *Quest for Identity,* 274–75.
38. Diary, May 2, 1968, PP/Orville Freeman, Box 12, LBJL.
39. Califano, *Triumph and Tragedy,* 288.
40. Congressional Leadership Breakfast, Apr. 2, 1968, Meeting Notes File, Box 2, LBJL.
41. Diary, Apr. 24 and 26, 1968, PP/Orville Freemen, Box 12, LBJL.
42. Quoted in Califano, *Triumph and Tragedy,* 289.
43. MR to Marie, Apr. 23, 1968, Diary Backup, Box 97, LBJL.
44. Diary, May 26, 1968, P/Orville Freeman, Box 11, LBJL.
45. Quoted in Woods, *Quest for Identity,* 274.

46. "Bobby's Last, Longest Day," *Newsweek,* June 17, 1968, 22.
47. See Larry Temple Memo for Record and Pearson Memo for Record, June 5, 1968, Diary Backup, Box 102, LBJL; Lady Bird and Lyndon Johnson to Kennedy, June 6, 1968, Diary Backup, Box 102, LBJL.
48. Quoted in Califano, *Triumph and Tragedy,* 298.
49. Rostow to President, June 5, 1968, NSF Memos to President, Rostow, Box 35, LBJL; Christopher to Temple, June 8, 1968, PP/W. Christopher, Box 2, LBJL.
50. Clinton J. Hill to President, June 5, 1968, Diary Backup, Box 102, LBJL.
51. "Address to the Nation Following the Attack on Senator Kennedy," June 5, 1968, *Public Papers of the Presidents: LBJ,* Vol. I, 692.
52. Diary, June 5, 1968, PP/Orville Freeman, Box 12, LBJL.
53. Califano to President, June 6, 1968, OF/Joe Califano, Box 17, LBJL; Temple to President, June 5, 1968, LBJ Handwriting File, Box 30, LBJL; Califano, *Triumph and Tragedy,* 300–301. See also Diary, June 8, 1968, PP/Orville Freeman, Box 12, LBJL.
54. Califano, *Triumph and Tragedy,* 304. See also Christian to President, June 10, 1968, LBJ Handwriting File, Box 30, LBJL.
55. Ramsey Clark to President, June 14, 1968, PP/W. Christopher, Box 1, LBJL.
56. See "LBJ Picks a New Chief Justice," *Newsweek,* July 8, 1968.
57. Califano, *Tragedy and Triumph,* 308.
58. "LBJ Picks a New Chief Justice," 18.
59. Quoted in Dallek, *Flawed Giant,* 557.
60. Christopher to Temple, Dec. 20, 1968, PP/W. Christopher, Box 3, LBJL.
61. See George Christian Oral History, IV, June 30, 1970, LBJL.
62. Christopher to Temple, Dec. 20, 1968, PP/W. Christopher, Box 3, LBJL.
63. McPherson to Manatos, OF/H. McPherson, Box 51, LBJL.
64. Quoted in Califano, *Triumph and Tragedy,* 310.
65. Quoted in ibid.
66. Reese Cleghorn, "For Judge: A Man Who Baited the Courts," *Atlanta Journal,* Mar. 29, 1968.
67. Arthur Krim Oral History, IV, Nov. 9, 1982, LBJL.
68. Quoted in Califano, *Triumph and Tragedy,* 312.
69. Ibid., 313.
70. S. and V. McHugh Oral History, IV.
71. Supreme Court Justices as Presidential Advisors, July 16, 1968, OF/Joe Califano, Box 22, LBJL.
72. Christopher to Temple, Dec. 20, 1968, P/W. Christopher, Box 3, LBJL.
73. Eugene Rostow to Walt Rostow, Oct. 29, 1968, NSF Memos to President, Rostow, Box 41, LBJL.
74. Quoted in Califano, *Triumph and Tragedy,* 311.
75. Ibid.
76. Diary, Sept. 20, 1968, PP/Orville Freeman, Box 12, LBJL; "The Real T.R.B.," *Newsweek,* July 29, 1968, 66.
77. Christopher to Temple, Dec. 20, 1968, PP/W. Christopher, Box 3, LBJL.
78. Lady Bird Johnson, *White House Diary,* 712–713.
79. Quoted in Radosh, *Divided They Fell,* 83–84.
80. Diary, Apr. 21, 1968, PP/Orville Freeman, Vol. 9, Box 12, LBJL.
81. As of March 30, 159,000 individuals had registered to vote in Alabama, Georgia, Louisiana, Mississippi, and South Carolina. Of these, 152,046 were nonwhites. McPherson to President, Apr. 26, 1968, OF/H. McPherson, Box 53, LBJL.
82. See Chronology, Apr. 4, 1968, Diary Backup, Box 95, LBJL; American Embassy to Secretary of State, May 1, 1968, NSF Memos to President, Rostow, Box 33, LBJL.
83. Dobrynin and Harriman Conversation, Apr. 1, 1968, NSF Memos to President, Rostow, Box 32, LBJL.
84. Rostow to Rusk, Apr. 29, 1968, NSF Memos to President, Rostow, Box 33, LBJL.
85. Notes of the President's Meeting with Foreign Policy Advisers, May 6, 1968, Meeting Notes File, Box 3, LBJL.
86. Elsey's Notes of Clifford's Morning Staff Conferences, May 6, 1968, PP/George Elsey, Box 1, LBJL.
87. Goodpaster Memo for Record, May 8, 1968, NSF Name File, Eisenhower, Box 2, LBJL.
88. Notes of Meeting, Apr. 25, 1968, *FRUS, 1964–68, VI,* 599–560.
89. CIA Information Cable, South Vietnam, Mar. 18, 1968, NSF Memos to President, Rostow, Box 31, LBJL.
90. McPherson to President, Apr. 12, 1968, OF/H. McPherson, Box 53, LBJL. See also Bunker to Rusk, Apr. 6, 1968, NSF Memos to President, Rostow, Box 32, LBJL.
91. Rostow to President, Apr. 10, 1968, NSF Memos to President, Box 32, LBJL; Bunker to President, May 16, 1968, Ginsburgh to President, May 24, 1968, Rostow to President, May 22, 1968, and Taylor to President, May 23, 1968, NSF Memos to President, Box 34, LBJL; Elsey's Notes of Clifford's Morning Staff Conference, May 25, 1968, PP/George Elsey, Box 1, LBJL; Notes of Meeting, May 21, 1968, *FRUS, 1964–68, VI,* 695–696.
92. Rostow to President, June 3, 1968, NSF Memos to President, Rostow, Box 35, LBJL.
93. Bunker to Rusk, June 4, 1968, NSF Memos to President, Rostow, Box 35, LBJL. For more on Thieu's rivals and the network of corruption that supported them, see Lansdale to Bunker, June 7, 1968, NSF Memos to President, Box 35, LBJL.

94. CIA Intelligence Cable, June 9, 1968, NSF Memos to President, Box 35, LBJL.
95. Kosygin to Johnson, June 5, 1968, *FRUS, 1964–68, VI,* 754.
96. Notes of Meeting, June 9, 1968, *FRUS, 1964–68, VI,* 770, 776.
97. Editorial Note, *FRUS, 1964–68, VI,* 778.
98. Johnson to Kosygin, June 10, 1968, NSF Memos to President, Rostow, Box 35, LBJL.
99. Notes of Meeting, July 26, 1968, *FRUS, 1964–68, VI,* 895.
100. McPherson to President, July 3, 1968, *FRUS, 1964–68, VI,* 835–836.
101. Both men pointed out that their political and personal safety depended on such contacts being kept absolutely secret. They also observed that the government would be in a much stronger position to conduct such talks "two or three months from now." Bunker to Rusk, June 27, 1968, NSF Memos to President, Box 36, LBJL.
102. Rostow to President, June 25, 1968, NSF Memos to President, Rostow, Box 36, LBJL; Jenkins to Rostow, July 2, 1968, NSF Memos to President, Box 37, LBJL.
103. Rostow to President, June 20, 1968, NSF Memos to President, Box 36, LBJL.
104. Clark M. Clifford on his return from Vietnam and Hawaii, July 22, 1968, PP/G. Elsey Box 1, LBJL.
105. American Embassy to Secretary of State, July 3, 1968, NSF Memos to President, Rostow, Box 37, LBJL; Editorial Note, *FRUS, 1964–68, VI,* 883.
106. Andrew L. Johns, "Hawks, Doves and Elephants," Paper Presented to Annual Meeting of Pacific Historical Association, June 1, 2001, Maui, Hawaii, 18.
107. According to Wheeler, 28,400 in March, 37,700 in April, 30,600 in May, 16,900 in June, and 44,000 in July. Notes of Meeting, July 30, 1968, *FRUS, 1964–68, VI,* 920.
108. Announcement by Senator George McGovern, Aug. 10, 1968, PP/George McGovern, Box 1A, Mudd Library, Princeton.
109. Johnson and Rusk, Conversation, 2, July 30, 1968, *FRUS, 1964–68,* 919.
110. Diary, Aug. 20, 1968, PP/Orville Freeman, Box 12, LBJL.
111. LBJ and Kosygin, Clifford Handwritten Notes, July 29, 1968, PP/Clark Clifford, Box 1, LBJL; American Embassy, Moscow to Secretary of State, Apr. 3, 1968, NSF Memos to President, Box 33, LBJL.
112. Brands, *Wages of Globalism,* 119–120.
113. Minutes of Cabinet Meeting, Aug. 22, 1968, Cabinet Papers, Box 14, LBJL.
114. Bunker to President, Aug. 22, 1968, NSF Memos to President, Box 39, LBJL.
115. Quoted in Woods, *Quest for Identity,* 27.
116. Ibid., 276.
117. "Mule Teams at Work," *Newsweek,* Sept. 9, 1968.
118. See Humphrey, *Public Man,* 396.
119. "Drafting Lyndon Johnson: The President's Secret Role in the 1968 Democratic Convention," unpublished ms., LBJL.
120. Ibid.
121. Lady Bird Johnson, *White House Diary,* 701.
122. Diary, Aug. 22, 1968, PP/Orville Freeman, Box 12, LBJL.
123. Humphrey, *Public Man,* 389.
124. Connally, *History's Shadow,* 203.
125. Arthur Krim Oral History, Nov. 9, 1982, LBJL.
126. Quoted in Radosh, *Divided They Fell,* 121.
127. Ibid.
128. Quoted in Woods, *Quest for Identity,* 276.
129. Quoted in Howard K. Smith, *Events Leading Up to My Death: The Life of a Twentieth-Century Reporter* (New York, 1996), 342–343.
130. Lady Bird Johnson, *White House Diary,* 706.

Chapter 41: Touching the Void

1. Quoted in Dallek, *Flawed Giant,* 578.
2. Diary, Sept. 11, 1968, PP/Orville Freeman, Box 12, LBJL.
3. George S. McGovern, *Grassroots: The Autobiography of George McGovern* (New York, 1977), 105.
4. Freeman to Humphrey, Sept. 9, 1968, Diary Backup, Box 110, LBJL.
5. McPherson to Vice President, Sept. 12, 1968, OF/H. McPherson, Box 51, LBJL.
6. James Rowe Oral History, IV, Nov. 10, 1982, LBJL; Diary, Sept. 11, 1968, PP/Orville Freeman, Box 12, LBJL.
7. Freeman to Humphrey, Sept. 9, 1968, Diary Backup, Box 110, LBJL.
8. Wheeler to President, Box 17, 1968, NSF Memos to President, Box 41, LBJL.
9. Johnson and Clifford Conversation, Sept. 2, 1968, *FRUS, 1964–68, VII,* 5.
10. Notes of Meeting, Sept. 6, 1968, *FRUS, 1964–68, VII,* 15.
11. Diary, Sept. 11, 1968, PP/Orville Freeman, Box 12, LBJL.
12. Johnson and Dirksen Conversation, Box 1, 1968, *FRUS, 1964–68, VII,* 111.
13. Diary, Sept. 11, 1968, PP/Orville Freeman, Box 12, LBJL.
14. James Jones Oral History, III, June 11, 1972, LBJL.
15. Harriman and Rusk Conversation, Sept. 17, 1968, PP/W. A. Harriman, Box 500, Library of Congress.

16. Summary of Meeting, Sept. 24, 1968, *FRUS, 1964–68, VII,* 77–78. See also Notes on Pentagon Briefing, Sept. 24, 1968, PP/George Elsey, Box 1, LBJL.
17. Meeting Notes, Sept. 25, 1968, NSC Meeting Notes, Box 2, LBJL.
18. See Rostow to President, Sept. 21, 1968, NSF Memos to President, Box 39, LBJL.
19. Notes of Meeting, Sept. 25, 1968, *FRUS, 1964–68, VII,* 92.
20. Editorial Note, *FRUS, 1964–68, VII,* 106.
21. Humphrey, *Public Man,* 403.
22. Johnson and Humphrey Conversation, Sept. 30, 1968, *FRUS, 1964–68, VII,* 106.
23. Califano, *Triumph and Tragedy,* 325.
24. Intelligence Report Prepared in the CIA, Sept. 16, 1968, *FRUS, 1964–68, VII,* 43.
25. Diary, Oct. 19, 1968, PP/Orville Freeman, Box 12, LBJL.
26. Jones Oral History, III.
27. Lady Bird Johnson, *White House Diary,* 718.
28. Rostow to President, Oct. 8, 1968, NSF Memos to President, Box 40, LBJL.
29. See Notes of Meeting, Oct. 17, 1968, *FRUS, 1964–68, VII,* 230.
30. Summary Notes of President's Meeting with the Joint Chiefs on Vietnam, Oct. 14, 1968, Meeting Notes File, Box 3, LBJL.
31. Johnson and Rusk, Conversation, Oct. 17, 1968, *FRUS, 1964–68, VII,* 239.
32. Johnson and Mansfield Conversation, Oct. 16, 1968, *FRUS, 1964–68, VII,* 213.
33. Clifford Staff Meeting, Oct. 16, 1968, P/George Elsey, Box 1, LBJL.
34. Department of State to Embassies in Vietnam and France, note 6, October 20, 1968, *FRUS, 1964–68,* 267.
35. LBJ to Chuck, Oct. 24, 1968, LBJ Handwriting File, Box 31, LBJL.
36. Meeting with the President, Oct. 23, 1968, NSF Memos to President, Box 41, LBJL.
37. Stephen E. Ambrose, *Nixon: The Triumph of a Politician, 1962–1972* (New York, 1989), 207–208.
38. McNamara would later claim that the Nixon camp was even in touch with the North Vietnamese Army. Dallek and McNamara Interview, Mar. 26, 1993, LBJL.
39. Cartha "Deke" DeLoach Oral History, I, Jan. 11, 1991, LBJL; Rostow to President, Oct. 30, 1968, NSF Memos to President, Box 41, LBJL.
40. Jones Oral History, III.
41. See, for example, Director, National Security Administration to White House, Oct. 28, 1968, NSF Memo to President, Box 41, LBJL.
42. James Rowe Oral History, IV, Nov. 10, 1982, LBJL. See also Arthur Krim Oral History, V, Apr. 7, 1983, LBJL.
43. Rostow to President, Oct. 29, 1968, NSF Memos to President, Rostow, Box 41, LBJL.
44. HarVan Harriman, Vance Double Plus, Oct. 29, 1968, NSF Memos to President, Rostow, Box 41, LBJL.
45. Meeting in Cabinet Room, Meeting Notes File, Box 3, LBJL.
46. Director, National Security Administration to White House, Oct. 29, 1968, NSF Memos to President, Box 41, LBJL.
47. Notes of Meeting, Oct. 29, 1968, *FRUS, 1964–68, VII,* 416.
48. Ibid., 439–440.
49. Bunker to Rusk, Oct. 30, 1968, NSF Memos to President, Rostow, Box 41, LBJL.
50. Rusk and Vance Conversation, Oct. 30, 1968, NSF Memos to President, Rostow, Box 41, LBJL.
51. Bunker to Rusk, Oct. 30, 1968, NSF Memos to President, Rostow, Box 41, LBJL.
52. Situation Report by Read, Oct. 30, 1968, *FRUS, 1964–68, VII,* 457–458, Meeting in Cabinet Room, Oct. 31, 1968, Meeting Notes File, Box 3, LBJL.
53. Johnson and Humphrey Conversation, Oct. 31, 1968, *FRUS, 1964–68, VII,* 485–493.
54. Editorial Note, *FRUS, 1964–68, VII,* 493.
55. Editorial Note, *FRUS, 1964–68, VII,* 523–524.
56. Bunker to Rostow, Nov. 3, 1968, and Rostow to President, Nov. 4, 1968, NSF Memos to President, Rostow, Box 41, LBJL.
57. Editorial Note, *FRUS, 1964–68, VII,* 537–539.
58. See Rostow to President, Nov. 3, 1968, NSF Memos to President, Rowtow, Box 41, LBJL.
59. Johnson-Clifford-Rusk-Rostow Conversation, Nov. 4, 1968, *FRUS, 1964–68, VII,* 556–557.
60. Kenneth Crawford, "Middle-Class Revolt," *Newsweek,* Nov. 18, 1968, 52.
61. Krim Oral History, V.
62. Quoted in Lady Bird Johnson, *White House Diary,* 734.
63. Quoted in "Hands across the Interum," *Newsweek,* Nov. 25, 1968, 31.
64. Jones Oral History, III.
65. Steward Alsop, "Well, Good-By, Lyndon," *Newsweek,* Sept. 2, 1968.
66. "At the Helm," *Washington Post,* Nov. 8, 1968.
67. On-camera Interview with President Johnson, Apr. 27, 1968, Diary Backup, Box 97, LBJL.
68. See, Califano, *Triumph and Tragedy,* 333–334.
69. Lady Bird Johnson, *White House Diary,* 773.
70. Quoted in Califano, *Triumph and Tragedy,* 337–338.
71. Quoted in Miller, *Lyndon,* 530.
72. Ibid.
73. Ibid., 544.

74. Charles Boatner Oral History, IV, June 2, 1976, LBJL.
75. Miller, *Lyndon,* 545.
76. Rothman, *Texas White House,* 235.
77. Miller, *Lyndon,* 548.
78. Quoted in ibid., 546.
79. See Buford Ellington Oral History, I, Oct. 2, 1970, LBJL; Rothman, *Texas White House,* 240–241.
80. Kearns Goodwin, *American Dream,* 376.
81. Ibid., 377
82. Miller, *Lyndon,* 546.
83. John Richards Interview with Author, Oct. 2003, Taylor, TX.
84. Kearns, *American Dream,* 372.
85. Krim Oral History, IV.
86. Quoted in Kearns Goodwin, *American Dream,* 371.
87. Miller, *Lyndon,* 558–559.
88. Charles Roberts, "Johnson and the Press," in Thompson, *The Johnson Presidency,* 106.
89. Quoted in Kearns Goodwin, *American Dream,* 374.
90. Quoted in Miller, *Lyndon,* 551.
91. ". . . assigned to cover LBJ heart attack," Mar. 4, 1970, Oberdorfer Notes, Reference File, "Vietnam," LBJL.
92. J. Willis Hurst Oral History, Oct. 3, 1995, LBJL; Rothman, *Texas White House,* 252; Miller, *Lyndon,* 551.
93. Miller, *Lyndon,* 551.
94. Krim Oral History, IV.
95. Dick Harwood Notes on Meeting with LBJ, Apr. 7, 1970, Oberdorfer Notes, Reference File, "Vietnam," LBJL.
96. Haynes Johnson Notes on Interview with LBJ, Apr. 7, 1970, Oberdorfer Notes, Reference File, "Vietnam," LBJL.
97. Notes for Milt Gwertzman, Aug. 17, 1972, Box 11, Papers of George McGovern, Mudd Library, Princeton.
98. Quoted in Miller, *Lyndon,* 552.
99. Quoted in ibid.
100. Quoted in ibid., 561.
101. Rothman, *Texas White House,* 255.
102. Quoted in Jarboe Russell, *Lady Bird,* 310.
103. Quoted in Dallek, *Flawed Giant,* 623.
104. Quoted in Miller, *Lyndon,* 558.
105. Quoted in David L. Chappell, "Civil Rights: Grass Roots, High Politics, on Both?" *Reviews in American History,* Vol. 32, no. 4 (sec. 2004), 566.

ACKNOWLEDGMENTS

THIS BOOK HAS BEEN TEN YEARS IN THE MAKING, A monumental, exhausting, and infinitely rewarding undertaking. The mass of documentation involved in presidential biographies is always imposing, but this was particularly true of Lyndon Johnson because of the scope and complexity of the person and of the many events and initiatives of his administration—civil rights, Vietnam, and the Great Society. Without the skillful and patient guidance of the staffs of the Johnson, Kennedy, Eisenhower, Truman, and Roosevelt Libraries, as well as of the National Archives, the Center for American History at the University of Texas, and the National Park Service in Johnson City, Texas, I could never have completed the task.

Obviously, I am most indebted to the staff of the Johnson Library. Michael Parrish, though a civil war historian by trade, knew the Vietnam records intimately and generously shared his knowledge. Our long conversations concerning LBJ and his impact proved invaluable. Claudia Anderson and Linda Seelke were tireless in helping me through the finding aids and in seeing that previously unrequested material was reviewed and opened expeditiously. We became and remain friends. Regina Greenwell and Shannon Jarett spent endless hours helping me get previously closed national security documents declassified. Bob Tissing, John Wilson, and Allen Fisher were superb in handling various specialty areas of Johnson's life and presidency. Phillip Scott and Margaret Harman guided me through the 300,000 photographs in the audio-visual archives. Thanks to Betty Sue Flowers, director of the LBJ Library, for assembling and supervising this marvelous team.

During their graduate school days, Jeff Woods and Charles Argo did a prodigious amount of research. My agent, Gerry McCauley, helped me conceive and market the project. Bruce Nichols, my editor at Free Press, and the distinguished historian Lewis Gould read every word and provided invaluable advice. Also helpful at Free Press were Kadzi Mutizwa and Phil Metcalf. Finally, without my wife, Rhoda, who served as editor, research assistant, and soul mate, this project could never have been finished. All errors of fact, judgment, and style are, of course, entirely my own.

INDEX

ABOUT THE AUTHOR

Randall B. Woods is the John A. Cooper Distinguished Professor of History at the University of Arkansas, where he has taught since 1971. Author of the award-winning *Fulbright: A Biography,* he lives in Fayetteville, Arkansas.